Contributing Authors

DIETER BRUNNSCHWEILER
MICHIGAN STATE UNIVERSITY

JOHN F. DAVIS
UNIVERSITY OF LONDON

W. GORDON EAST
UNIVERSITY OF LONDON

F. KENNETH HARE
UNIVERSITY OF BRITISH COLUMBIA

GEORGE W. HOFFMAN
UNIVERSITY OF TEXAS

VINCENT H. MALMSTRÖM
MIDDLEBURY COLLEGE

HOMER PRICE
HUNTER COLLEGE OF THE CITY
UNIVERSITY OF NEW YORK

THEODORE SHABAD
THE NEW YORK TIMES

GUIDO G. WEIGEND
RUTGERS—THE STATE UNIVERSITY

THIRD EDITION

A GEOGRAPHY
OF EUROPE

Including Asiatic U.S.S.R.

Edited by

GEORGE W. HOFFMAN
UNIVERSITY OF TEXAS

THE RONALD PRESS COMPANY · NEW YORK

Library of Congress Catalog Card Number: 69–14670
PRINTED IN THE UNITED STATES OF AMERICA

Preface

For the third time within two decades the authors of this book are presenting to students and the interested reading public an authoritative interpretation of the physical and cultural geography of each of Europe's major regions and the Soviet Union. The basic organization of the book has stood the test of time and has needed little change—an organization around seven major regions, with emphasis on economic and political geography within their physical and historical context. An introductory chapter and two background chapters stress the continent's complex physical, biogeographical, and historical and economic background, and a concluding chapter analyzes Europe's problems and prospects. The Third Edition, more than the earlier two, emphasizes "change" in nearly every aspect of Europe's human geography.

In introducing the First Edition, the editor started his preface with the observation: "Europe at mid-century is in the process of rebuilding its economy for the second time within one generation. Inherent in this struggle are many basic problems, all of which are rooted in the continent's long and tumultuous history and its divergent geographical environment." Near the end of the 1960's, when the authors again took stock of the progress in Europe, they found that the rebuilding of the economy had not only been successfully completed, but most parts of Europe had succeeded in providing for their people a standard of living beyond the dream of most. On the other hand, the impact of Europe's rich and tumultuous history casts a long and dark shadow on the future of this continent with its divergent geographical environment.

The presentation of an integrated picture of the European scene follows the well-tried method of regional analysis and employs the use of subdivisions derived from the boundaries of broad cultural areas. The order of the chapters follows the logic of beginning with the British Isles, in many ways peripheral to the rest of the continent, and of closing with the Soviet Union, which is no less peripheral. Turkey has been omitted from the discussions; this arbitrary decision was based on the fact that her core and most of the country is located in Asia. On the other hand, independent Cyprus and Malta, both members of the Commonwealth, have been included.

The Third Edition has been extensively revised. To insure the closest possible integration and to prevent this book from becoming a collection of individual essays, the complete manuscript has been critically reviewed, as in earlier editions, by all contributors. In addition, the editor and authors are grateful to the many users who have been kind enough to pass on specific suggestions.

The text of each chapter is closely integrated with the maps, many of which are original in this edition. Many new illustrations have been added, and the latest available data are included in the statistical tables in Appendix III. These tables have been reorganized to provide easier access to basic regional reference data. The climatic graphs and basic background information of geologic time and tectonic evolutions appear as Appendixes, thus providing a far more comprehensive picture than if distributed throughout the text. Basic atlas references, whenever considered useful, were added to the bibliographies at the end of each chapter. Suggested readings in other languages should provide a stimulus to those students with language proficiency and a specific area interest. Place names in the text and on the maps generally conform to the accepted usage which is found in English-language atlases and the National Geographic Society maps.

The editor's appreciation is expressed to each of his associates for his scholarly contribution, for critically reading his colleagues' chapters, and for patience and cooperation during the intensive work of preparation. With the exception of three, all associates who contributed to the initial organization of this unique regional geography have also worked on the Third Edition. Dr. Homer Price has now joined the group and has written the chapter on Southern Europe. The assistance received from various government agencies in the United States and Europe, various agencies of the United Nations, and the embassies and/or tourist agencies of nearly every European country was essential to the work. Grateful acknowledgment is made for the invaluable help received from Mrs. Jean Hannaford, my research assistant, especially in the checking and compilation of data for the statistical appendix. Last, but not least, the editor gratefully acknowledges the invaluable help of his wife, Viola, during the many months of manuscript preparation, and the encouragement and assistance other contributors received from their wives. Finally, the essential assistance of the numerous and unnamed secretaries should not go unrecorded.

GEORGE W. HOFFMAN

Austin, Texas
  February, 1969

Contents

A GEOGRAPHY OF EUROPE

Including Asiatic U.S.S.R.

Introduction

Europe—A Geographical Expression

It is by no means self-evident why Europe has so long been recognized as a continent in its own right, since in physical geography it might appear as merely a large peninsular extension of Asia, which is four times its size. The Greek historian Herodotus could not see why his contemporaries of the fifth century B.C. distinguished three continents —Europa, Asia, and Libya—in what was to him one continuous land area. The eminent German scientist Alexander von Humboldt regarded Europe as part of one land mass (*Erdteil*) which he called Eurasia. Hugo Hassinger in Germany and Sir Halford Mackinder in Britain both emphasized the idea of a single land mass, which the latter called the World-Island—this was Europe, together with Asia and Africa. It is thus of some interest to inquire how a small part of Eurasia came to be regarded as a separate continent. It is further desirable to consider just what are the limits of Europe. This is indeed necessary if confusion is to be avoided, since four or more Europes [1] are presently known and referred to in the writings of geographers, statesmen, journalists, and others.

THE IDEA OF EUROPE AS A CONTINENT

The concept of Europe as a separate continent derives from the ancient Greeks of the fifth century B.C., who viewed the world they knew as tripartite. Although the Pythagoreans, a century earlier, rightly imagined that the world was a sphere, the idea long persisted of the earth as a disk encircled by the ocean and divided into three continents. It was thus represented in the so-called T/O maps (Fig. 1) of the Middle Ages. In such maps, Europe and Libya each made up a quarter of the world and were marked off from the remaining half, Asia, by the Mediterranean Sea. The word "Europe" was long thought to derive from the Semitic

[1] Thus there are (1) the Europe which stretches eastward to include the Ural Mountains, (2) the Europe which lies west of the Communist countries, (3) the Europe made up of the 19 countries which are members of the Organization for European Economic Cooperation and Development, and (4) Little Europe—the six countries of the European Iron and Steel Community and of the Common Market. See Fig. 10–4, p. 621.

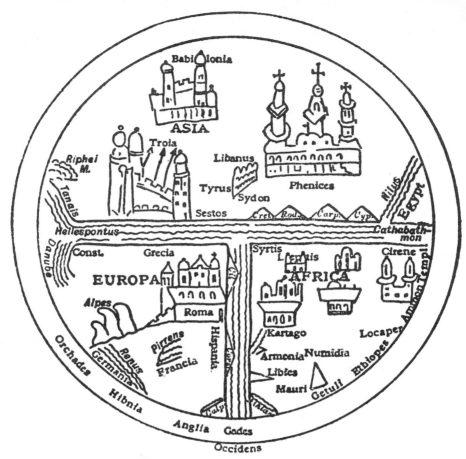

Fig. 1. A medieval T/O map of the world. The T-shaped Mediterranean Sea divides the world into one half, occupied by Asia, and two quarters, one of which is Europe and the other Africa. The representation of the three continents, the Mediterranean, and the encircling ocean is, of course, diagrammatic. Cadiz ("Gades") lies at the approach to the Mediterranean from the Atlantic. The Nile is shown entering the Mediterranean, and the Don ("Tanais") and the Danube are shown flowing into the Dardanelles ("Hellespontus").

word *erib* and thus to mean "the land of the sunset," or of the west. It was contrasted with "Asia," which lay beyond the Aegean and Mediterranean seas, and which meant "the land of the sunrise," or of the east. More recently a Greek derivation of Europe has been advanced.[2] This suggests that Europe means broad-faced. Such a term may fittingly have been applied by the classical Greeks to the territories of greater scale which lay to the north of their insular and peninsular homelands in and around the Aegean Sea.

Knowledge of the geography of Europe was inevitably very sketchy in the days of classical Greece. The Greeks were above all seamen, as Plato (fourth century B.C.) put it, "living round the sea like ants or frogs round a pool."[3] Herodotus, for ex-

[2] Denys Hay, *Europe: The Emergence of an Idea* (Edinburgh: The University Press, 1957): p. 1.

[3] E. H. Warmington, *Greek Geography* (London & Toronto: J. M. Dent & Sons, Ltd., 1934): p. 22. This work provides, with a commentary, numerous translated extracts from ancient Greek texts.

ample, who was well traveled and otherwise well informed, knew of the Black and Azov seas, of at least the lower courses of the great rivers Danube, Dnieper, and Don, something of the interior of the Southeastern Peninsula, and more of the Mediterranean coastlands. The interior of Europe was largely shut off from the Mediterranean lands by mountains and forests and by the extensive grass steppe of southern Russia, where already pastoralists roamed. The colder winters of Europe north of the Mediterranean Sea, which Greek writers exaggerated, were an added deterrent. Not much was known about the remote west and north of Europe—the British Isles and Scandinavia—before the remarkable voyages of Pytheas of Massilia (Marseille) around 300 B.C. It was the Romans, themselves primarily landsmen, who, in the course of their conquests, explored and opened up not only Britain but also large inner parts of the continent, up to and beyond the Rhine and Danube rivers. Even as late as the second century A.D. Ptolemy depicted on his famous world map the larger Scandinavian peninsula (i.e., Norway and Sweden) as an island (Fig. 2).

Thus vaguely conceived, Europe was only an idea for the learned few, philosophers, writers, and map makers. The Jews adopted the pagan Greek concept of the tripartite world, of which Europe was allegedly colonized by the descendants of Japheth, son of Noah. Roman trade penetrated beyond the imperial frontiers, as coin finds show, as far east as the river Neman and as far north as southern Sweden.[4] For the Roman, however, Europe had less significance than the sharply contrasted world around them which was either Roman and thus civilized, or extra-Roman and thus barbarian. During the medieval period which followed, Europe was conceived of not as part of the surface of a spherical world (as Ptolemy had shown) but as part of a disk-shaped surface surrounded by ocean. The special cartographic advance made in the later Middle Ages was the so-called portolan charts, which sketched the seas and coasts of Europe with some precision. Europeans were, however, more concerned by then with the concept of Christendom than with that of Europe which

[4] See Sir R. E. M. Wheeler, *Rome Beyond the Imperial Frontiers* (London: G. Bell & Sons, Ltd., 1954).

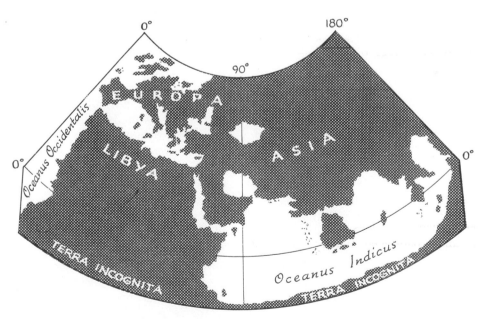

Fig. 2. The world according to Ptolemy.

formed only a part of this broader concept. The view of Europe as a distinct territorial unit was underlined, however, when Christian peoples there found themselves hemmed in to the east and to the south by non-Christian intruders. These were, in the south, Moors and others who had been won to Islam by the Arab conquests; in eastern Europe the Mongols of the Golden Horde, Shamans at first and Moslems only later (after *ca.* 1300); and in Asia Minor the Moslem Seljuk Turks. The crusading wars, to which went warriors from many countries of Europe to fight Moslems in the Holy Land, also lent some distinctness to the idea of Europe as a Christian citadel. It thus acquired a certain emotive significance in addition to its coldly territorial connotation.

There was a time, then, when the term Europe symbolized a loose cultural unit framed by more or less effective physical barriers. Before the great voyages of discovery which opened up the whole world in modern times, Europe was shut off by the Arctic and Atlantic oceans and by the deserts of northern Africa and Arabia. To the east where the continent broadens, forest and marsh, then more widespread than now, discouraged human settlement, while the steppe zone, which extends from eastern Hungary across the Ukraine and into Asia, invited continually the advance of enemies —nomadic horsemen.

It would be easy to exaggerate the degree of cultural unity achieved by medieval Christendom, for clearly race, language, religion, economy, and history divided it in many ways. Yet the Europe of today cannot claim the community of interest which was then fostered by a widely current language—Latin, known at least by the educated. As sundering forces emerged—the Reformation, nationalism, Fascism, and Communism—the political and ideological community of Europe disintegrated. The last hundred years or so, although they witnessed in Europe the political unification of both Italy and the German *Reich*, witnessed also the dissolution of old empires and a decline

in the concept of Europe's underlying unity (see Chapter 10). Europe has become, more than in the past, a geographical expression.

Viewed from the outside, however, Europe may appear to have more significance than when viewed from within. We are all aware that in world affairs Europe, and in particular western Europe, has played an outstanding part in the creation of Western civilization—by geographical discoveries, overseas colonization and economic development, and widely ranging achievements in the fields of science, technology, and the arts. In this sense Europe stands distinctly in the world, even though the contributions from the several parts of the continent are different and unequal. After all, Europe, like Asia, is an old continent. It has exploited its opportunities and, for a long time, largely dominated the world. But its status is changing as other lands, notably the United States and the Soviet Union, the latter in part European, have become settled, developed, and strong.

THE LIMITS OF EUROPE

Europe, then, is clearly not a simple homogeneous unit, either culturally or politically. However, it persists as a geographical reality and, this being so, we may well ask about its extent and its limits. Curiously perhaps, in view of its age-long settlement, Europe's limits appear always to have been, as they remain, partially uncertain. It has been wisely argued, for example, that Europe should include geographically those marginal lands of North Africa and the eastern Mediterranean Basin which share a common physical (including climatic) environment. These lands were for a long time politically as well as economically oriented toward Europe. Even the western limit of Europe raises problems. "Europe's domain," wrote the distinguished British Foreign Minister George Canning,[5] "extends to the shores

[5] H. W. V. Temperley, *The Foreign Policy of Canning* (London: G. Bell & Sons, Ltd., 1925): p. 471.

of the Atlantic, England's begins there." This view reminds us that, although the United Kingdom is geographically part of Europe, it is also the senior partner of a world-wide commonwealth. Iceland stands even further detached from continental Europe but, because of its long cultural links with Scandinavia, is rightly regarded as European. Greenland, in contrast, is now usually reckoned part of North America, with which it has increasing contacts, although historically and culturally it looks to Denmark, of which it is in fact a part.

To the southeast, Europe is now taken by west European geographers to include both Turkey and Cyprus which, though geologically parts of Asia, are oriented toward Europe politically and economically. Farther north, beyond the Black Sea, a variety of limits have been proposed at different times to divide what the Western world has chosen arbitrarily to distinguish as Europe and Asia. The limit given by Herodotus was the lower course of the river Phasis, now called the Rion, which descends from the Caucasus Mountains to enter the Black Sea north of Batumi. For this limit the classical Greeks later substituted that of the river Don and the Azov Sea, and this limit long persisted. The Don, in crossing first the wooded steppe and then the grass steppe in its southward course, bisects the Great Russian Lowland, so that this large physical unit lay both inside and outside Europe as it was first conceived. The Russian state, when it emerged, thus also lay astride the continental divide. It has always stood both inside and outside Europe. Dostoevski held the view that Russia should form a unit not in Europe but in face of Europe.[6]

Figure 3 shows some of the limits assigned to Europe in the east. In modern times the tendency has been to shift these to the east of the Don but not directly to the east of the Sea of Azov. Use has been made of visible geographic features—the Manych

Depression, the middle Volga, the Kama and Ural rivers, and, lastly, a line at the eastern foot of the Ural Mountains. Somewhat in contrast to these various proposed lines is another, well to the west and related to the obstacle (formerly very considerable) of the Pripet Marshes which now lie in the Belorussian S.S.R. (Fig. 2–1). The French geographer Jacques Ancel, in suggesting this as the eastern limit of the continent, argued that east of these marshes reigned the climate, broadly uniform landscapes, and immensities of Asia. For H. J. Mackinder,[7] writing in 1918, the "real" or "populous" Europe, before this century at least, extended eastward to a straight line drawn from Petrograd (now Leningrad) to Kazan, and then to the curved line from Kazan along the Volga and Don rivers to the Black Sea. Beyond these limits, he wrote, began "the vacancies of Central Asia." Geographers now draw Europe's eastern limit along the eastern foot of the Urals and thence along the Emba river to the Caspian Sea. This limit wholly ignores the internal boundaries of the U.S.S.R.

In this book no rigid and limiting definition of Europe has been assumed. Indeed, its scope has been enlarged to include the U.S.S.R. whose territory lies both within and outside Europe.

The question of limits apart—and such a discussion could well become profitless—the reality of Europe remains. While it is important that we should know what we mean when we read or talk about Europe, we should have no doubt that Europe's existence as a continent is a valid fact. It is a permanent regional division of the habitable world, which, together with the Far East, the Indian subcontinent, and northeastern North America, has proved to be one of the four outstandingly favored settlement areas of the world. Enclosed between the Arctic

[6] Cited by A. Mousset, *Le Monde Slave* (Paris: Société d'Éditions Françaises et Internationales, 1946): p. 42.

[7] H. J. Mackinder, *Democratic Ideals and Reality* (New York: Henry Holt & Co., 1919): 144–145. Since Mackinder wrote, much settlement and economic development have taken place east of this line, notably in the Ural area.

Ocean and the great North African deserts, between the Atlantic Ocean and the steppes and forests of the Great Russian Lowland, Europe presented a relatively small peninsular framework, accessible at many points from the Mediterranean Basin where civilized life developed by a process of diffusion from the riverine lands of Egypt and southwest Asia.

While the richly variegated physical background and historical development of Europe are themes of the two succeeding chapters of this book, it will help to allude here, in general terms, to two of Europe's special characteristics, namely, its geographical position and its main divisions.

THE GEOGRAPHICAL POSITION OF EUROPE

The geographical position of Europe can be conceived of in two distinct ways—as absolute and as relative. What is striking about the absolute position of Europe, as determined by the latitudes and longitudes within which it lies, is first its centrality in the

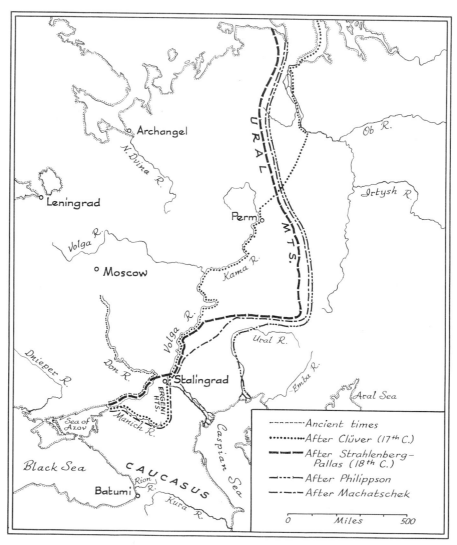

Fig. 3. Eastern limits of Europe. (Data from E. von Seydlitz.)

Northern Hemisphere and second the almost complete absence of hot and cold desert. Since the Northern Hemisphere contains the greater part of the earth's land surface and also those parts which have been longest developed, Europe's position is a strikingly good one for world-wide contacts by sea and by air. In the small proportion of its area which is economically useless because of extremes of cold or heat, it compares favorably with both North America and the Asiatic U.S.S.R., which include the same latitudes as Europe but extend farther both to the north and to the south.

Europe's relative position, in contrast, is not stable and has greatly improved in the course of world history. In prehistory Europe occupied a remote and terminal position in the world, aloof from the cradle areas of civilized life, yet accessible enough to receive civilizing currents from them, especially by sea. Although the Mediterranean Red Sea waterway, and other routes by land, gave Mediterranean Europe slender links with the populous and civilized lands of monsoon Asia from Greco-Roman times onward, the Atlantic—the "green sea of darkness," as the Arabs called it—was impassable, and western and northern Europe in particular occupied only marginal locations in the known world. This position changed radically when the Atlantic's sea routes to the Americas and to southern Asia were opened up in the late fifteenth century and improved still further as the newly discovered American lands and the later-discovered Australasian lands were colonized and developed. Thus Europe, especially those parts which had oceanic fronts, enjoyed greater opportunities, which it in fact exploited to conquer and settle overseas and to play the leading part in world commerce and the economic development of the other continents. In this last respect western Europe, and Britain in particular, took the lead in that expansion of manufactures associated with the Industrial Revolution. This was marked by the effective use of available resources of coal and other min-

erals, of capital, of transport facilities—especially by water, and not least of an inventive and skilled labor force. Thus as new lands grews in economic and demographic strength, Europe came to stand less and less on the edge of the oecumene but nearer its center: the term "Midland Ocean" for the North Atlantic in part expresses this idea. Moreover, in this age of air navigation, even the formerly forbidding Arctic flank of Europe is now crossed by convenient polar air routes to North America and monsoon Asia.

THE MAJOR GEOGRAPHICAL DIVISIONS OF EUROPE

Geographers are continually at pains to divide Europe into significant parts, the better to understand the diversity of its human environments, large and small. The task of dividing it into major regions, suited to discussion in this book, is a task of some difficulty. Various criteria may be employed, and each will produce a different set of regions. It is clear that, if divisions are made according to each of the environmental factors in turn, the continent will be divided into many different units which will little correspond. A map of Europe's major structural units or of its major climatic types will show little correspondence with those of either linguistic or political divisions. Accordingly, large-scale geographical units are selected for study in this book, broadly on ground of their relative positions (Fig. 4). We distinguish Western Europe,[8] Northern Europe, Southern Europe, Eastern Europe, and, beyond this, the U.S.S.R., which strides from the confines of Europe across Asia to the Pacific. To these is added Central Europe, the extent and implications of which have given rise to much discussion.[9] It must

[8] The British Isles, part of Western Europe, are separately discussed in Chapter 3.

[9] See, for example, K. A. Sinnhuber, "Central Europe—Mitteleuropa—Europe Centrale: An Analysis of a Geographical Term," *Transactions and Papers, The Institute of British Geographers* 20 (1954): 15–39.

Fig. 4. The major geographical divisions of Europe, as presented in this book.

suffice to note that Central Europe comprises here Germany, Austria, and Switzerland—countries which must find their place in any geographical interpretation of Central Europe. It will be noted that each of these major divisions is a group of states. This needs little justification in view of the importance of the political factor in the geography of Europe. Indeed, its political organization gives expression to the main national, linguistic, and other cultural aspects of the human geography. It will be evident that other schemes of division may be proposed and justified [10] and the division

[10] Thus in E. C. Marchant, ed. *Geography Teaching and The Revision of Geography Textbooks and Atlases,* published by the Council for Cultural Co-operation of the Council of Europe, Section II–General and Technical Education–No. 9 (Strasbourg, 1967): p. 140, West European geographers recommend a fivefold division of the Continent, only two of which are co-extensive with those of this book. These two are Western Europe and Northern Europe. As to the other three, Eastern Europe is taken to apply to European U.S.S.R., Southern Europe is enlarged to include Albania, Yugoslavia, and Bulgaria, and Central Europe includes, in addition to the countries allocated to it in Figure 4, Czechoslovakia, Hungary, Poland, and (possibly) Romania.

adopted here can be criticized in detail. While, for example, we have assigned Norway to Northern Europe and Portugal to Southern Europe, both occupy a western location and might be regarded also as parts of Western Europe. So also may Denmark be regarded geographically not only as part of Northern Europe but also as part of Central Europe. The attentive reader may consider such points as he reads. But divide Europe we must in our efforts to describe and account for the remarkable variety of its physical and human geography, mindful too of the outstanding role of this small but populous continent as the homeland of both Western civilization and Communism.

1

The Physical and Biogeographical Background

The main purpose of this chapter is to introduce the reader to the European landscape from the standpoint of physical geography. Even though it is recognized that the natural environment is not a set of factors which forces man into a particular type of occupancy in any particular area, its influence upon human pursuits has played and still plays a role hardly to be underestimated. It is, therefore, necessary to establish a solid framework of Europe's physical geography in order to evaluate the impact of these physical factors upon human activities. It is emphasized, however, that the approach in this chapter is strictly systematic in the sense that each physical and biogeographical element is discussed per se and not as a possible environmental factor in the human drama. This is left almost entirely to the discussions in the individual regional chapters, where more space is provided for analysis of the interplay between physical and cultural factors.

It should be stated clearly that the focus is always on Europe as a whole. We are here using a reducing glass to recognize the basic physical patterns of Europe, thereby intentionally refraining from going into details within individual areas. If regions of physical homogeneity, such as physiographic or climatic regions, are described and delimited, they are mainly intended to serve as a kind of physical framework for the ensuing regional discussions. This will enable the student to see the relationship of any region to its surroundings and to realize the magnitude of areal variations of the individual physical factors of Europe.

An attempt has been made to put equal weight on both descriptive and genetic analysis of the physical landscape. Although the genetic treatment of landforms and climate might handicap students with limited training in physical geography, it should lead all to an understanding, rather than just a superficial knowledge, of the European landscape.

THE RELIEF OF EUROPE

Horizontal Surface Configuration

General characteristics. One of the outstanding characteristics of the map of Europe is the interpenetration of land and

12

sea. Strabo [1] spoke quite aptly of the "very irregular shape" of Europe. We should not overlook, however, that this description applies only to the western half of Europe. East of the Finnish shore of the Baltic Sea and the Vistula-Prut line, the character of the land mass is quite different. We have to distinguish clearly between a peninsular and insular Europe west of the line mentioned, and a massive and compact one east of it. If we want to speak of a "European peninsula," as has frequently been done, it would begin at this line from which, in a westward direction, the width of the land mass decreases more or less continuously, the land opens toward the Atlantic, and the peninsular and insular coastal configuration becomes increasingly evident. The western Soviet Union, in contrast, forms an unarticulated body, decidedly different in its compactness, its landlockedness, and its openness toward the continental interior.

The degree of horizontal articulation of a continent can be expressed by several methods. If we compare the area of the main body of a land mass with that of its peninsular and insular members, a relatively good index of its compactness or brokenness can be obtained. Europe is easily the least compact of the earth's land masses. More than one-third of Europe consists of peninsulas and islands.

Another good measure is the mean distance from the coast.[2] In Europe the mean distance is 210 miles with 62 per cent of the land below and 38 per cent above this value. The small size of Europe would, of course, give a relatively small figure for mean coastal distance, but in comparison with Australia, the only continent smaller than Europe (by some 900,000 square miles), a considerably higher proportion of Europe can be considered as coastal fringe land.

[1] Loeb Classical Library, *The Geography of Strabo* (New York: Putnam's Sons, 1917): Vol. II, p. 467.
[2] The mean distance from the coast is obtained by drawing zones of equal distance from the sea, computing the sum of the products of area and coastal distance of each zone, and dividing it by the total area of all zones.

	Total Area (million square miles)	Area of Islands and Peninsulas (million square miles)	Area of Islands and Peninsulas (per cent of total area)
Europe	3.85	1.33	34.6
North America	8.92	2.33	25.5
Asia	17.06	4.11	24.0
Australia	2.97	0.66	22.0
Africa	11.51	0.24	2.1
South America	6.86	0.71	1.1

The coast of Europe. A closer examination of the coastal configuration reveals that the ground plan of Europe is determined to a great extent by the main structural units of the land mass. Size, shape, and relief of the coastal areas, the type of shore lines, and the submarine topography, all reflect the complex geological history of the land. A tripartition with respect to major coastal types clearly manifests itself. There are wide expanses of flatland along many coastal stretches, particularly along the Atlantic and Baltic shores of mainland northwestern Europe and north of the Black Sea. Offshore, the coastal lowland continues onto a broad submarine platform, the continental shelf (Fig. 1–4). Shallow seas, rarely more than 600 feet deep, and often less than 100 feet have inundated this presently invisible but inherent part of the continent. The continental slope, a marked declivity indicating the continental margin in a geological sense and the edge of the shelf, often lies several hundred miles offshore. Many islands rise from these submarine platforms. They are called shelf islands or continental islands, indicative of the fact that only a slight drop of sea level would join them to the continent with which they were very often connected through geological time.

The second coastal type is found in southern Europe. Most shore lines are characterized by steep ascent from the deep sea to the coastal hinterland. Coastal plains are narrow or missing except where the larger rivers have built deltas and alluvial plains into a sea little affected by tidal differences. The shelf is well expressed in a few areas only. Peninsulas and islands rise sharply from the sea bottom. We deal here with a coast line the major characteristics of which are determined by a complete reorganization of land and water in a major and not yet completed geological revolution. The formation of the Alpine mountain range made the Mediterranean and adjacent inland seas as by-products, so to say. In the south of Europe upheavals and breakdowns of the earth's crust, rather than fluctuations in sea level, were responsible for the coastal configuration. We speak of "ingressional" coasts, as compared to the "transgressional" character of the flatland coasts in the north.

Intermediate between the lowland and the steep coasts, a third littoral type can be differentiated. Cliffs are conspicuous along portions of the Atlantic coast, but they owe their origin to processes quite different from those mentioned in the case of the Mediterranean. The sharp break of the land in southern England and northwestern France is a result of incessant marine erosion, while the steep and strongly articulated (fjord) coasts of western Scandinavia, Scotland, and Iceland were produced mainly by glacial erosion and subsequent oceanic inundation. The land, in both the cliffed and the fjord coast stretches, was comparatively stable, but the forces of marine and terrestrial erosion were still able to carve deeply into the continental margin.

The individual sections of the European coast line will now be briefly discussed. The northern coast of European Russia is separated by the White Sea into two parts: the flat and ill-drained Timan coast in the east and the Murmansk coast in the west, with a much less extensive lowland fringing the block of the Kola Peninsula. The character of the coast changes abruptly west of Murmansk with the northern end of the Scandinavian mountain system abutting the Arctic Ocean with long and relatively wide fjords extending in a northerly (Porsanger) or easterly (Varanger) direction. The Barents Sea, extending from Novaya Zemlya to the longitude of the North Cape (26° E.),

is a typical shelf sea and most of the Arctic islands (Novaya Zemlya, Svalbard, Franz Josef Land—"Zemlya Frantsa Iosifa") are therefore geologically outlying parts of the mainland. The northernmost point of Europe lies on Mageröy (island) at latitude 71° N.[3] The shelf narrows into a submarine coastal platform of a few miles width around the northern end of Scandinavia.

In contrast to the Barents Sea, the Norwegian Sea overlies a deep basin with a maximum depth of over 10,000 feet. The Norwegian west coast is one of the most strongly articulated coasts of Europe, with a multitude of deep and long fjords (Fig. 1–1) separating peninsulas and promontories, and a great number of islands and island groups (e.g., Lofoten, Vesteralen) lying close to the mainland. The land rises sharply from the sea except where marine erosion, in combination with a subsequent upheaval of the land, has produced a conspicuous coastal platform ("strandflat" in Norwegian) slightly above present sea level. Scandinavia is set off from central and eastern Europe by a chain of straits (Skagerrak, Kattegat, Sund, Belts) and the Baltic Sea, all shallow transgressional water bodies, with the exception of the entrance to the Skagerrak, where a deep and old trench separates Norway from the shelf platform north of Jutland. The Baltic Sea, the "Mediterranean" of northern Europe, with its three extensions (gulfs of Bothnia, Finland, and Riga), divides the area into the Scandinavian, Finnish, and Baltic peninsulas. All islands rise from the shelf (the Danish group, Öland, Gotland, Dagö, and Ösel, and the Åland group). A lowering of the water level by 400 feet would leave the Baltic Sea almost completely dry.

The largest marginal sea of Europe is the North Sea, rarely exceeding a depth of 300 feet until the continental slope is reached west of the British Isles. In the areas of the "banks" (Dogger, Great Banks) and south

[3] This is exactly the same latitude as the northernmost point of Alaska.

Fig. 1–1. The innermost portion of a fjord near Tromsö, Norway, at latitude 70° N. Note the near-vertical wall (left) and the "*fjell*" plateau above the timber line here formed by stunted birch. (Courtesy Dept. of Geography, University of Zürich.)

into the Strait of Dover the depth of the North Sea averages less than 100 feet. Thus, the British Isles are shelf islands par excellence, structurally clearly a part of the European mainland. A submarine ridge (Wyville Thompson Ridge and Iceland Plateau) extends northwestward from the North Sea shelf, linking the Faeroe Islands and even Iceland to Europe. Iceland, however, even though showing affinities to northwestern Europe with its strongly fjorded shore line, had an entirely independent geologic evolution. It is mainly of volcanic origin, and, like the Azores Islands, was built on the submarine Atlantic Ridge. The British Isles, with Great Britain [4] and Ireland as the two dominating land bodies, rise in many places

quite abruptly from the shelf base. Marine erosion and tectonic readjustments during the formation of the Alps were mainly responsible for the separation of these islands from the continent. The affinities of the northern part of Great Britain and Ireland with the Scandinavian mountains and those of the southern portions of Great Britain with northwestern France are obvious if a map showing trends of mountain ranges, or age and type of rock material is consulted (Fig. 1–4). The coasts themselves are very similar on opposite sides of the North Sea and the English Channel—the fjords of the North Sea correspond to the "sea lochs" of western Scotland; the *falaises* of France to the cliffs of England (Fig. 3–3).

In contrast to these sharp breaks between land and sea, however, stand the "flat" coasts of the Netherlands, Denmark, northern Germany, Poland, and the Baltic provinces of the Soviet Union. Here, because of

---

[4] Great Britain with her 89,000 square miles is the eighth largest island of the world. Great Britain and Ireland together are 4,000 square miles smaller than Norway, but 4,000 square miles larger than Italy.

the postglacial rise of the sea level on one hand and the low relief of the coastal plains on the other, the marginal portions of the latter were inundated and the lower courses of the larger rivers became estuaries (Fig. 5–5). Extensive stretches of the shore line are occupied by belts of unstable sand dunes. Strings of offshore islands are separated from the mainland by tidal flats (the Dutch *Wadden* and the German *Watten*), flooded at high tide only. Curving sand spits (*Nehrungen* in German) with shallow lagoons (*Haffe*) on their landward side are conspicuous along the southeastern Baltic (Figs. 6–2, 6–3). All these features attest the recent formation and the unfixed position of the shore line. It needed the work of many generations to stabilize the land against marine inundations (Fig. 1–2).[5]

The North Channel, the Irish Sea, and St. George's Channel lie between Great Britain and Ireland, all of these water bodies being shelf seas containing numerous banks which, however, lie at greater depth than their counterparts in the North Sea. The westernmost point of Europe, shelf islands included, is located at Dunmore Head, a promontory in southwestern Ireland, at longitude 10° 30′ W. just one degree longitude farther west than the western extremity of the mainland (Cabo de Roca, 20 miles west of Lisbon).[6]

South of the latitude of Brittany, the largest peninsula, after Jutland, on the west coast of the mainland, the Atlantic re-enters toward the continent and forms the Bay of Biscay in the right angle between the southwest coast of France and the north coast of Spain. The straightness of the shore line is remarkable, but is of completely different origin on the two sides of the bay. The flat coast of France with long stretches of dunes and lagoons, *étangs* in French, especially south of the Gironde estuary, is fringed by a broad shelf, whereas the ocean bottom drops to a depth of over 10,000 feet within fifty miles in the Cantabrian Sea along the north coast of Spain. Here the shelf coast of western Europe, with its almost accidental location of the water-land boundary, comes to an abrupt end.

The coast of the massive Iberian Peninsula shows all evidences of being conditioned by comparatively recent geologic events. Its stable interior has withstood major deformations during the period of the formation of the Alpine mountain system, but its marginal areas were strongly affected by them. The straight shore lines are the result of foundering along faults, zones of vertical and horizontal shear within the earth's crust. The coast along the northwest corner of Spain has been recognized as one of recent submergence, with drowned valleys (*rias*) reminiscent of, but differing in their origin from, fjords. Seismic activity is strong (e.g., the catastrophic earthquake of Lisbon, 1755), and volcanic effusives are found along the fault cracks. All this is indicative of the fact that the shape of the land is conditioned by recent crustal instability.

At the Strait of Gibraltar, 10 miles wide at the constriction between Piedra Marroqui[7]

[5] The area of the Netherlands has been almost doubled since medieval times through the construction of many hundred miles of dikes. The catastrophic inundations of February, 1953, nevertheless, are a grim reminder of the never-ending battle against the sea.

[6] Land's End, the westernmost point of England but not of Great Britain, lies at longitude 5° 50′ W. 170 miles east of the Spanish "Land's End," Cape Finisterre. It is often overlooked that most of Spain lies in the Western Hemisphere and that all of Portugal is west of Great Britain. If we consider outlying islands in the Atlantic as part of Europe the westernmost extremities of Europe are northwestern Iceland (latitude 65° 30′ N. and longitude 24° 30′ W., i.e., some five degrees longitude farther west than the northeast coast of Greenland) and the island of Flores in the Azores archipelago (latitude 40° N., longitude 31° W.).

[7] Piedra Marroqui, latitude 36° N., is the southernmost point of the European mainland. Note that the 36th parallel crosses the United States from Cape Hatteras to Oklahoma and between Los Angeles and San Francisco, leaving the southern tier of the United States south of the southernmost point of Europe. Tokyo also has the same latitude as Piedra Marroqui.

Fig. 1–2. Portion of the North Sea coast northwest of Hamburg (Friedrichskoog). The artificial shore line follows the main dike behind which the former sea floor has been converted into agricultural land (*Marschen*). On the seaward-side of the dike further land reclamation is in progress on the tidal flats (*Watten*). (Photo: Plan & Karte, Münster.)

and the Moroccan coast, we enter the Mediterranean Basin. Coastal configuration and submarine topography bear ample evidence of the intensive geologic activity which has occurred in connection with the formation of the mountain systems of southern Europe (see also the discussion on tectonic evolution, pp. 20–30). In spite of its relatively small size the Mediterranean is a deep sea, or rather a series of deep sea basins separated by islands, peninsulas, and submarine swells. Shelf flats are restricted to narrow sills; only offshore from the conspicuous deltas of the major rivers are they more extensive. A typical Mediterranean shore is characterized by steep slopes and cliffs rising sharply from the sea (Figs. 1–18, 7–6). Small nichelike indentations are frequent, but deep embayments which would offer sheltered harbor sites are rare. Widespread, however, are coastal terraces, sometimes several miles in width, created by higher interglacial sea levels, somewhat alleviating the generally adverse character of the coast.

The western Mediterranean consists of two major basins separated from each other by the bastions of Corsica and Sardinia. The Balearic Islands rise from the western basin as remnants of a once unbroken mountain chain connecting the Pyrenees with the Sierra Nevada. The eastern basin (Tyrrhenian Sea) represents a typical kettle-like ingression (downwarp of the sea floor), which reaches to a depth of well over 12,000 feet in spite of its small size. Instability is further indicated by the many volcanic structures in its southern portion and adjacent land stretches (e.g., Vulcano and Stromboli islands in the Lipari group, Vesuvius, and Etna).

The eastern Mediterranean, east of the Apennine peninsula, Sicily, Malta, and Pantelleria, all of which are parts of a formerly uninterrupted mountain chain connecting the Atlas Range of North Africa with the Alps, exhibits a most pronounced coastal articulation in its northern part. In the Ionian and Aegean seas a former land bridge has foundered, leaving Crete and Cyprus as its largest remnants above sea level and a great number of closely spaced islands in the Aegean Sea as further evidence of a once continuous land mass (Cyclades, Sporades). Volcanic eruptions [8] and the most devastating earthquakes of recent times attest to the instability of the land. Deep troughs and basins are found close to the land. The Ionian Sea exceeds a depth of 15,000 feet fifty miles south of Cape Matapan, the southernmost point of the Peloponnesos, which with its three peninsulas represents the southern end of the Dinaric branch of the Alpine mountain system.[9] North of the Strait of Otranto extends the shallowest of all Mediterranean water bodies, the Adriatic Sea. Its Dalmatian shore is much more articulated than the Italian. Longitudinal islands and bays, both parallel to the coastal trend, are typical.

The straits of the Dardanelles, the Sea of Marmara, and the Bosporus (all three together called the Turkish Straits) form a geologically recent connection between the Aegean Sea and the Black Sea. The latter is deep in its southern part only, whereas the Bay of Odessa and the Sea of Azov are shelf seas. Lagoons and sand bars mark their shore line, and marshy tracts are widely distributed, particularly in the lowest portions of the large river valleys. West of Odessa there are peculiar long, narrow, and stagnant water bodies (locally called *limans*) representing former embayments, now separated from the sea by sand bars.

Vertical Surface Configuration

General characteristics. The great variety of landforms is obvious from a quick glance at any map showing all or part of

Europe. We might even speak of a "physiographic chaos" which it undoubtedly is if looked at one section after another without recognition of the relationship between the individual units. Once the continuance of the plains, the mountains, and the valleys is established on the basis of the geologic evolution, the confusion resolves into a still complex, but intelligible, pattern.

From a strictly topographical point of view Europe may be divided into four physiographic units (Fig. 1–3):

1. *Coastal Lowlands and Interior Plains.* The low-lying terrain of Europe forms an almost continuous belt along the Atlantic and Baltic coasts and widens into the vast Russian plains. Elevations rarely exceed 500 feet above sea level. Local differences in elevation lie within 100 feet.

2. *The Central Uplands and Plateaus.* The northwestern lowlands end rather abruptly along a continuous highland of hilly, plateau-like, or mountainous character, which stretches from south central France to northern Czechoslovakia. Altitudes are between 500 and 2,000 feet with isolated areas protruding well above 4,000 feet. The terrain in the lower portions of the upland is not exceedingly rough, but the higher lands are steep and heavily forested.[10]

3. *The Northwestern Highlands.* The mountainous terrain of Scandinavia, the north of the British Isles, and Iceland constitutes a special type of highlands. Even though often higher than the central uplands (above 8,000 feet in southern Norway), the surface configuration is more plateau-like than truly mountainous. Only in the steep descent to the shore do we find considerable differences in elevation within short distances. Really flat land, however, occurs only along larger rivers. All these highland areas were affected by pronounced glacial erosion.

4. *The Southern Mountain Ranges.* This heading is a broad generalization for a vari-

---

[8] The central lava cone in the sea-filled crater of the island of Santorin (Thera) appeared above sea level in 1925. Recent archeological evidence suggests that Santorin may have been the site of the island civilization referred to by Plato as that of Atlantis.

[9] The Peloponnesos was never, as the name implies, an island (*nesos*, Greek for island), but it is now a man-made island owing to the Canal of Corinth, connecting the Gulf of Corinth with the Gulf of Aegina, not quite 4 miles apart.

[10] Note that the forested nature of the mountains is reflected in mountain names, such as Black Forest, Bohemian Forest, etc.

1. Coastal Lowlands & Plains
2. Central uplands & Plateaus
3. Northern western Highlands
4. The Southern Mt. Range.

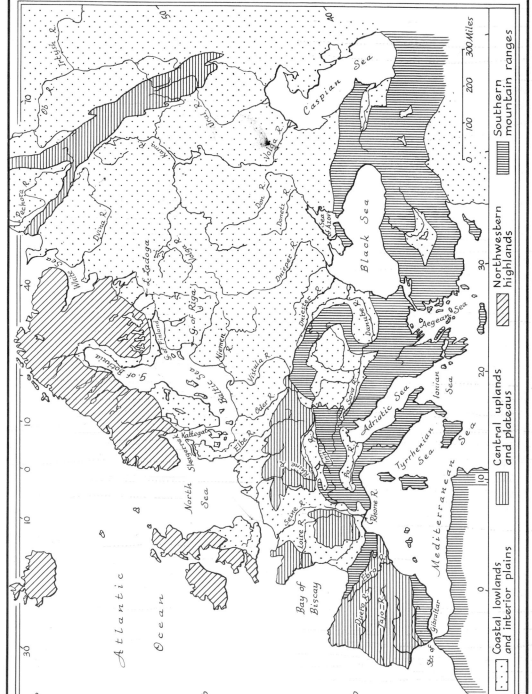

Fig. 1–3. Major physiographic divisions of Europe.

ety of landform units all of which have in common genuinely mountainous aspects. We will later refer to them as the Alpine system of mountains. It is here that we find the highest mountain ranges and peaks of Europe attaining crest altitudes well above 10,000 feet. The mountain ranges often are continuous over long stretches separating deeply incised valleys or extensive basins (e.g., Po, Danube basins) and plateaus (Spanish tableland, Anatolian plateau). The complexity of the relief in southern Europe will receive special attention in the following section in which the origin and evolution of the European landforms are explained.

Tectonic evolution and structural units. Both the horizontal and vertical surface configuration of Europe owe their complexity to a geologic evolution which time and again furnishes evidence that the greater part of the continent lies in an unstable zone of the earth's crust. The contrasts in present-day relief characteristics are strong—stronger than in most other parts of the world of comparable size.

The fact that northern Europe has a subdued relief as compared to southern Europe does not mean that in the north mountain-building processes were absent. They only lie further back in geological time than those which built the Alps. The mountain systems which evolved in earlier geological periods in the northern and central parts of Europe once probably rose to as majestic heights as do the present Alps. Through the subsequent periods, however, they were worn down by the uninterruptedly working forces of weathering and erosion, and today only roots or stumps of the original structure remain. In great contrast, the young mountain system in southern Europe shows all evidence of geologically recent folding, thrusting, and faulting of rock layers. In addition to these tectonic forces subsequent fluvial and glacial erosion and accumulation had a decisive influence upon the complex internal topography of the Alpine mountain system.

As far as the tectonic events are concerned

which led to the original orographic pattern of the continent, four major mountain-building periods can be differentiated. They are referred to, in order of antiquity, as the (1) Fenno-Scandian, (2) Caledonian, (3) Hercynian, and (4) Alpine orogenies.[11]

1. THE FENNO-SCANDIAN OROGENY. This orogeny, also called the Pre-Cambrian, affected the northwestern portion of the continent, but it lies so far back (an estimated one billion years) that the trends of the original mountains are no longer recognizable, at least not topographically. For all practical purposes, the outstanding geologic feature in the area around the Baltic Sea today is the predominance of granitic rocks, dated with the world's oldest, and composing an extensive, worn-down platform to which the descriptive term Fenno-Scandian, or Baltic, Shield has been applied.[12] Together with the Central Siberian (Angara) Shield, the Canadian Shield, and large parts of Greenland, the Baltic Shield probably represents a remnant of an old northern continent (Laurasia). It is truly the core of the European land mass, acting as a rigid block along and around which younger mountain systems were thrust up. Once the primeval European orogeny had ended, the Shield experienced only isostatic movements such as upheavals and subsidences en bloc. Periods of erosion alternated with transgressions of the sea. During the latter the crystalline foundation became covered with sediments, increasing in thickness toward the east. With the land mass finally rising above sea level in late Tertiary time the sedimentary plateaus of western Russia emerged and now form the Great Russian Lowland—plains and table-

[11] Fenno-Scandian after Finland and Scandinavia, Caledonian after the Latin *Caledonia* for Scotland, Hercynian after the Latinized word for the Harz Mountains in central Germany, Alpine after Alps. The orogenies are represented graphically in the geologic time sequence table in Appendix I.

[12] The term "shield" is used in reference to the shieldlike shape of the Fenno-Scandian terrain, with the Baltic Sea filling the concavity of the inverted side of the shield. Note the similarity with the Canadian Shield, with Hudson Bay in the center.

lands. In some parts of the covered section of the Shield late uplifts have exposed the crystalline bedrock or its oldest sedimentary cover (Azov-Podolian Massif, Voronezh Block, Timan Swell).

2. THE CALEDONIAN OROGENY. The beginning of the Paleozoic era was characterized by widespread marine transgressions over most of Europe, but in the Silurian period the Caledonian orogeny began to affect large sections of northwestern Europe. Structure, trend, and rock material of the Irish, Scottish, and Norwegian mountains are very similar and mainly due to the Caledonian orogenic period, during which early Paleozoic marine sediments were folded and overthrust, and at the same time highly metamorphosed. The thrust was directed northwestward in the British Isles against a then still existing portion of the "old north continent," the gneisses of the Hebrides and the Lofoten being interpreted as the easternmost edge of it (Fig. 1–4). On the other hand, the rock layers are overthrown toward the east against the Fenno-Scandian Shield in the Scandinavian mountains. The Caledonian system [13] can be followed northward into Svalbard and northern Greenland. It has since been under continuous erosion, and, during later orogenies, large sections of it have either foundered or were uplifted, arched, or tilted. One of the most conspicuous geologic formations of northwestern Europe, the Old Red Sandstone of Devonian age, represents the continental waste products of the Caledonian mountains.

3. THE HERCYNIAN OROGENY. Subsequent to the existence of this "Great Northern Red Land" the sea again began to cover much of Europe. For the Baltic Shield and the greater part of the Caledonian system this was the ultimate marine transgression, whereas the west Russian crystalline shield experienced further inundations by the sea.

The Carboniferous period began with a widespread submergence. The floor of the early Carboniferous sea, however, was already affected by the first spasms of the Hercynian revolution in so far as the "coal measures" must have been forming in slowly emergent swells with widespread coastal lowlands and marshes. The main axes of the Hercynian uplift were developing farther south, with the coal deposits being retained in large structural depressions or smaller basins along the northern flank of, or within, the Hercynian mountains (Wales, Namur, Ruhr, Upper Silesia, Donets basins).

To a remarkable extent, the remains of the Hercynian system dominate the relief of western and central Europe north of the Alps. Some of them are still topographically, and all of them are structurally, reminiscent of their original grandeur. The trend of the Hercynian mountains is clearly recognizable in many parts of Europe, in others only a detailed analysis of the structure will give clues as to their original direction. In some sections these folded mountains stand out sharply. Selective erosion has produced parallel ridges which give a strongly linear grain to the landscape.[14] This is particularly true in the central section of the system, where the mountain chains sharply separate the lowlands. These highlands are definitely mountainous with rock outcrops frequently visible through the dense forest.[15] The Ardennes in Belgium, the chains across the Rhine between Mainz and Bonn (Rhenish Slate Mountains, Hunsrueck, and Taunus), the ridges of the Harz in central Germany, the Rhoen, the Thuringian and the Frankish Forests all are distinct seg-

[13] There are no Caledonian mountains on any map of Europe, but structually one can refer to Caledonian mountains, Caledonian trend, Caledonian overthrust, etc.

[14] This landform pattern is comparable to the Ridge and Valley Zone in the Appalachians of eastern North America. The Appalachians also owe their original folding to the late Paleozoic revolution, called the Appalachian orogeny in North America. In central Asia the Altai orogeny corresponds to the Hercynian.

[15] In German the term *Mittelgebirge* is used for the central uplands. The *Mittel* or "middle" refers to their intermediate character, topographically speaking, between hill lands and mountains.

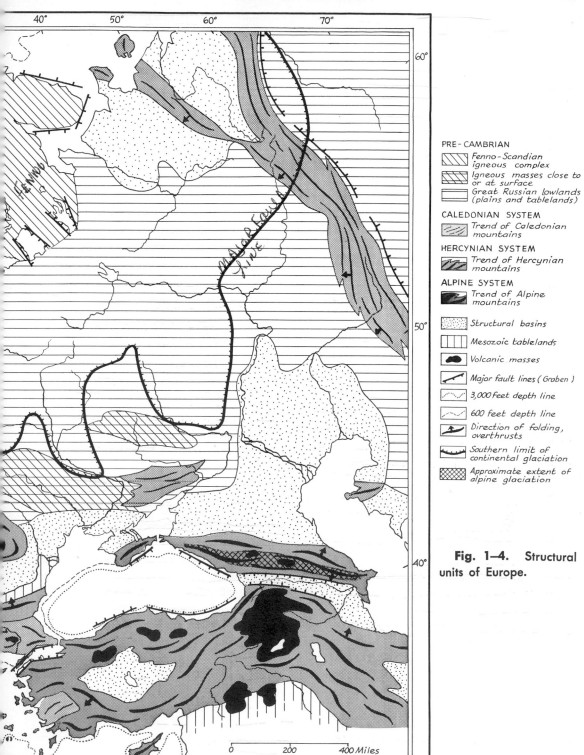

Fig. 1–4. Structural units of Europe.

PRE-CAMBRIAN

Fenno-Scandian igneous complex

Igneous masses close to or at surface

Great Russian lowlands (plains and tablelands)

CALEDONIAN SYSTEM

Trend of Caledonian mountains

HERCYNIAN SYSTEM

Trend of Hercynian mountains

ALPINE SYSTEM

Trend of Alpine mountains

Structural basins

Mesozoic tablelands

Volcanic masses

Major fault lines (Graben)

3,000 feet depth line

600 feet depth line

Direction of folding, overthrusts

Southern limit of continental glaciation

Approximate extent of alpine glaciation

ments of the Hercynian system (see Chapter 6, pp. 279–83). At the Fichtelgebirge the chain splits into a northern (Ore Mountains, Sudeten Mountains) and a southern branch (Bohemian Forest), enclosing the Bohemian Basin. Other topographically outstanding Hercynian remnants are the backbones of the Brittany and Normandy peninsulas (geologically referred to as the Armorican Massif [16]), Cornwall, and the Kerry Mountains in south Ireland, as well as the Urals in the extreme east of Europe, at the edge of the buried part of the Baltic Shield. The western and eastern branches of the Hercynian system converge in the Central Massif in southern France. There are other massifs,[17] particularly in the southern portions of the Hercynian belt: the Vosges and the Black Forest, two granitic blocks (*horste*) separated by the fault trough (*graben*) of the Upper Rhine Plain, further the Bohemian Massif, and the Rhodope Massif, to mention only the largest ones.

Hercynian structures are found within the Alpine body, where they now represent the granitic massifs of the Alps. The Iberian Peninsula—with the exception of the Pyrenees, the Cantabrian Mountains, and the Sierra Nevada—is also of Hercynian structure. Here, some of the Hercynian chains stand out sharply above the Spanish tableland, owing to their igneous cores (Sierra de Guadarrama) or to "horst and graben" tectonics (Sierra Morena).

The discontinuity of the Hercynian mountains as we see them today is attributable to three major post-Hercynian developments. First, the mountains were exposed to long periods of erosion. Second, marine trans-

gressions repeatedly inundated the European continent during the Mesozoic era; their sediments, lying unconformably over the eroded Hercynian structures, are proof that intensive planation had taken place before the transgressions. Finally, the Hercynian mountains were profoundly affected during the Alpine orogeny, which produced most drastic results in southern Europe but has influenced all of Europe in a more or less intense manner.

4. THE ALPINE OROGENY. When we direct our attention to southern Europe, it becomes immediately obvious how the previous geological events on the Eurasian continent bear upon the Alpine orogeny. The great arch of the Alps projects northward between the two largest resistant old blocks of the Hercynian foreland, the French Massif Central in the west and the Bohemian Massif in the east. In eastern Europe the crescent of the Carpathians bulges northeastward between the Bohemian Massif and a buried spur of the Russian Shield in Romania. The bend of the Jura Mountains is hemmed in on one end at the Central Massif, on the other at the Vosges and the Black Forest. The Mediterranean mountain chains are squeezed in between the Iberian, Tyrrhenian (exposed in Corsica and Sardinia), and Rhodope massifs. This complex, garland-like pattern of mountain chains (Fig. 1–4) has led students of tectonics to assume that the earth's crust has a high degree of mobility, and that its upper layers must have experienced vertical and horizontal dislocations of great magnitude. Whoever has seen the structure in the rock walls of Alpine valleys, with the layers of sedimentary rock crenulated in miniature meanders, or lying in sweeping folds several miles long, must be convinced that the present rigidity of rocks has only been reached after a long series of plastic deformations (Fig. 1–5).

The evolution of the Alpine mountain system may be briefly summarized as follows: Through most of the Mesozoic era southern Europe was covered by a primeval "Mediter-

[16] Armorica was the Roman name for Brittany, Latinized after a Celtic word for the peninsula.

[17] A massif is a large core of igneous rocks whose age is much older than that of the surrounding formations. In spite of having been subjected to repeated cycles of erosion, a massif still stands out topographically, especially if it has been raised en bloc as a *horst* (German for rock bastion), while the adjacent land foundered along slippage planes (faults) forming a sharply defined valley (*graben*, German for trench).

Fig. 1–5. The folded limestone mountains of the "Grande Chartreuse," between Grenoble and Chambéry, looking northward. In the extreme upper left the first anticlines of the Jura Mountains are visible, which here branch off from the Alps. Note the dense cover of coniferous forest, which contrasts with the vegetation of the dry southern portions of the French Alps. (Photo: Swissair.)

ranean Sea" (Tethys) [18] into which a very great amount of sedimentary material of mostly calcareous nature was deposited. An ancient sea lay between two large land masses, the Laurasian continent with all its Pre-Cambrian, Caledonian, and Hercynian elements in the north, and Gondwana Land, a southern continent, remnants of which can be discovered in the present land masses of Africa, India, and Australia. The accumulation of thousands of feet of sediments in the Tethys can be explained only if a continuous subsidence of its floor through most of the Mesozoic era is assumed. To a basin of such long persistence and of such large areal extent the name "geosyncline" has been applied. This "Alpine geosyncline," however,

lying in a weak zone between the stable masses of two continents, could not retain its subsidence indefinitely. According to the theory of continental drift,[19] the African land mass began to push northward, steadily encroaching upon the vast sedimentary trough. Since the Hercynian massifs acted as rigid blocks against the movement from the south, the weaker sedimentary layers had to yield to the tremendous tangential pressure exerted upon them. Already in mid-Mesozoic

[18] Named after the wife of Oceanos in Greek mythology.

[19] Even though the concept of a one-sided thrust due to a large latitudinal displacement of the Gondwana block is still adhered to by many European geologists, others have postulated a more or less *in situ* development of the Alps with the geosyncline being underthrust from both the north and the south. Cf. Leopold Kober, *Bau und Entstehung der Alpen* (Structure and Origin of the Alps) (Berlin: Borntraeger, 1923).

times ridges began to form in them which soon appeared as island arcs above sea level. All through the Cretaceous period the deformation continued and reached its peak in mid-Tertiary (Oligocene and Miocene). By this time the sedimentary layers and even the crystalline substructures were lifted miles above sea level and thrown into gigantic folds (anticlines and synclines), many of them overturned toward the north. In the late phases of the orogeny, higher portions of the folds overrode lower ones or were dragged along by thrust sheets gliding above the previously built mountain structures.

The movement came to an end along what is now the impressive "Alpine front" in the French, Swiss, and Austrian Alps, often forming sheer cliffs several thousand feet in height above the Alpine foreland (Fig. 1–6). Intrusions, volcanic eruptions, upheavals, and subsidences on a large scale accompanied and followed the orogeny. Even though the Alps are of geologically recent origin, they still are but a torso, the original continuity being retained merely in downfolded areas, while the upper thrust sheets and the vertices of the anticlines have been partially or completely destroyed by erosional forces affecting the mountain mass from the very moment it rose out of the sea.

As can be best seen on the structural map (Fig. 1–4), the Alpine orogeny involved the greater portion of the southern half of Europe. The major branches of the Alpine mountain system [20] in the Mediterranean

[20] The Tertiary orogeny affected all continents of the earth simultaneously, geologically speaking. The continuous mountain chains along the southern rim of Asia and along the west coast of the Americas are all part of the Tertiary orogeny.

Fig. 1–6. The north front of the Alps seen over the Alpine foreland (Swiss Midland, with Lake Zürich). Note the sharp topographic contrast between the folded limestone ranges and the smoother landforms of the foreland, composed of soft Tertiary sediments (*molasse*) and glacial deposits. (Photo: Swissair.)

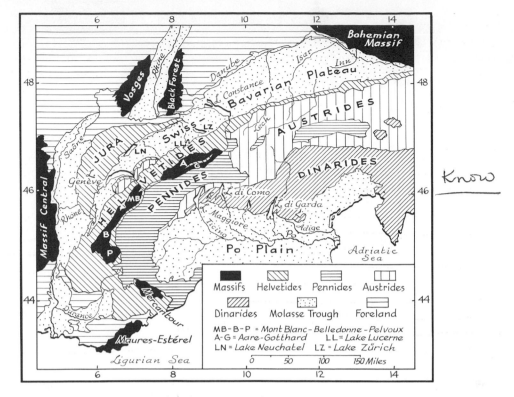

Fig. 1–7. Tectonic map of the Alpine system.

Know

realm are the Pyrenees, Sierra Nevada, Atlas, Apennines, Dinarides (collective name for the mountain chains in Yugoslavia and Greece), Taurus, and Anatolian chains. The Alps proper extend from Genoa to Vienna, with an outlier in the Jura Mountains and an eastern European extension in the Carpathians, the Transylvanian Alps, and the Balkan Range. Six major structural units are commonly differentiated:

1. *The crystalline cores, or massifs*. They occur along the axis of the western and central Alps, but are buried beneath the sedimentary folds in the eastern Alps. Owing to the absence of stratified rocks, some of the most rugged mountains and peaks are found within this unit [21] (Fig. 1–8).

2. *The northern limestone Alps* (Helvetides, after the Latin name for Switzerland, Helvetia). They form the frontal ranges

throughout the system, including the Jura Mountains. In a most complicated structure, several folds lie above one another, plunging northward immediately beyond the massifs and ascending toward the Alpine front. The "roots" of the Helvetides lie within or south of the massifs, often separated from the northern fold sheets (*nappes*) by erosion. The mountains are much more massive than those in the igneous zone, the banked sedimentary layers being conducive to the formation of summit plateaus, ledges, and step-like valley profiles. Again, local designations are illustrative: *Kasten* (chest), *dos* (back), etc.

3. *The eastern Alps* (Austrides, after Austria). Along the Swiss-Austrian boundary the nature of the rock material and the tectonic character of folds and thrust sheets change. The Austrides, in the process of folding, were pushed over all other tectonic units and formerly covered a much larger area than today. Evidence for this lies in

[21] The concentration of names indicative of jagged peak forms in this area is striking: *aiguille* (needle), *dent* (tooth), Horn, *fuorcla* (fork), etc.

Fig. 1—8. View of the Aare Massif, one of the granite cores of the Alps, from above the Grimsel Pass, Canton of Berne, Switzerland. At their highest stage during the Ice Age, glaciers covered all but the jagged crests along the divides. Finsteraarhorn (left center) reaches above 14,000 feet. The lakes are artificial and part of the impressive hydroelectric development of the Aare River headwaters. (Photo: Swissair.)

the remains of east-Alpine rocks on top of the Helvetian and Penninic folds (the so-called *Klippen,* i.e., isolated outliers of the Austrides in Switzerland and Savoy),[22] and the "windows" of west-Alpine formations within the eastern Alps, exposed by erosion ("Engadine" valley in Switzerland, the "Hohe Tauern" in Austria). The Austrian Alps are characterized in their northern and southern portions by a series of structurally simple, east-west trending limestone ranges, while their central zone consists of complex igneous and metamorphic masses. Owing to an eastward divergence of the major mountain ranges, the Alpine body here has its greatest

width (170 miles, as compared to less than 100 miles across the southern French-Italian Alps).

4. *The western Alps* (Pennides after the Latin *Alpes Pennini*). The fronts of the Pennine *nappes* advanced against the massifs and were unable to override them, thus becoming involved in the most complex plications anywhere in the Alps. The rock material is highly metamorphosed, the gneisses of the fold cores enveloped by enormous schist series. The culmination of tectonic activity which included the already-mentioned Austride overthrust over the Pennides, the deep incisions cut into the mountain mass by the tributaries of the upper Rhone and Po, and persisting glaciation combine here to form some of the most grandiose Al-

[22] The most famous *Klippen* peaks in Switzerland are the Matterhorn in the Valais Alps and the Mythen above the town of Schwyz.

pine scenery (Valais Alps of Switzerland, Graian Alps of France and Italy).

5. *The southern Alps* (Dinarides, from the Latin *Dinaria,* for northwestern Yugoslavia). The separation of the southern Alps from the Austrides and Pennides is based mainly upon differences in rock material and the different lie of the folds: their fronts face southward, owing to underpushing of the sedimentary formations by the African land mass. Calcareous rock types are particularly well developed in the southern Austrian Alps (*Karawanken*), in northeastern Italy (dolomites), and in northern Yugoslavia. This section of the Alpine system is often referred to as the southern limestone Alps.

6. *The Molasse troughs.* The Swiss-Bavarian plateau (also called foreland, plains, or *Mittelland*), the Po Plain, and the Saône-Rhone depression contain the sediments which accumulated throughout the orogeny in the longitudinal troughs adjacent to the rising mountain mass. Close to the Alps, conglomerate and sandstone formations represent the layers of deltas built by the primeval Alpine rivers into a Tertiary sea. The Molasse was overridden and tilted southward by the last advances of the Alpine front. By tracing the origin of the rock materials in the Molasse (as the Tertiary sediments are collectively called in French and German from Latin "ground stone") and by analyzing their tectonic relationship to the individual thrust sheets much has been learned about the sequence of orogenic phases in the Alps. At greater distances from the Alps the Molasse, including marine shale and limestone layers, lies practically horizontal.

The mountains and the valleys of the Alps which we observe today are, of course, much younger than the tectonic events which brought them into position. However, the pattern and arrangement of the major ranges and valleys convincingly lead to the conclusion that the present drainage system had its birth in a period when the Alps were still growing in height and extent. The longitudinal valleys, that is, the valleys parallel to the trend of the system in any particular

section, often represent original depressions in, or separations between, the major thrust sheets (e.g., the upper courses of the Rhone and the Rhine following the seam between the Helvetides and the Pennides, or the continuous string of valleys from the Drau to the Ticino along the root zone of the Austrides). The much steeper, narrower, and shorter transverse valleys more often than not follow primary axial depressions or are located in re-entrants of the north fronts of the *nappes*. After the last en bloc upheaval of the Alpine body in a very late stage, however, the rivers tended to be increasingly less dependent upon structure and rock hardness. They often take the shortest routes to the foreland, regardless of obstacles in their way.

The formation of the Alpine system had far-reaching effects upon the areas of Europe (read) not directly involved in the orogeny. The Hercynian massifs seem to have translated the tectonic forces to the sedimentary basins between them. They, themselves, were affected in so far as the majority of them were strongly uplifted and faulted. These vertical displacements produced the sharply linear features along coasts (e.g., west and north coast of Iberia, fjord of Oslo), or inland along the margins of most massifs. The Rhone-Saône valley, the Upper Rhine Valley between Basel and Mainz, the depression between the Slate Mountains and the Harz all belong to one big fault (*graben*) system. Volcanic eruptions of various types were widespread throughout the period of tectonic unrest (Auvergne in the Central Massif, Kaiserstuhl in the Upper Rhine Plain, Eifel and Vogelsberg in the German Uplands, Colli Euganei in the Po Plain). Parts of the ancient shield also were affected. They adjusted themselves to the new conditions by tilting (Scandinavian peninsula), subsidence (Caspian depression), uplifts (blocks of Voronezh, Podolia, Donets), or even faulting (Kola Peninsula, Ladoga and Onega lakes shore lines, to mention but a few examples). If we take into consideration the changes brought about by the glaciations, to be discussed in the following section, it becomes obvious that the present surface configuration of Europe owes its characteristics mainly to the Alpine orogeny and the subsequent geomorphic evolution. Geologically old in many parts, Europe, in a morphological sense, is therefore not an old, but a new world.

Europe During the Ice Age

The last one million years, the time span usually allotted to the Quaternary period, in which we still live, affected the European land in quite a different, but locally no less drastic manner as compared to the transformations which occurred during the periods of tectonic action. The Pleistocene was characterized in the northern and Alpine areas by repeated advances of ice sheets which, during the maximum extension, covered about half of Europe (Fig. 1–4). There is evidence of four glaciation periods and three interglacial periods, not counting postglacial time (see Appendix I for subdivisions of the Pleistocene). In each of the glacial periods the ice began to accumulate during a period of depressed summer temperatures (probably not more than 5° F. in the beginning) in the Scandinavian mountains, the Alps, and various isolated areas even in southernmost Europe (Sierra Nevada). Ice streams began to form in the higher portions of those areas and flowed out into the adjacent lowlands, often coalescing in the foreland into a widespread piedmont glacier. The Scandinavian ice sheet advanced over the North Sea and joined the local ice-cap over the British Isles. It also extended as far south as the present mouth of the Rhine River and came to a halt along the northern front of the Hercynian chains in central Europe. In eastern Europe it overrode the shield and its sedimentary cover southeastward to the Volga River, projecting deeply southward into the Ukraine, following the preglacial valley trains of the Dnieper and the Don. The Alpine valleys were filled by glaciers which, in their northernmost advance, reached into southern Germany and into the Jura Moun-

tains, forming a continuous piedmont glacier in the northern foreland, while just reaching the margin of the Po Plain in the south.

In both the northern and Alpine realms as well as in the non-glaciated areas, the glacial regime had a most profound effect upon the preglacial terrain. Four basic changes brought about by the Pleistocene glaciations must be differentiated:

1. *Glacial erosion.* Close to the center of the glaciated areas, evidence of erosional activity prevails clearly in the present landform characteristics. The Alpine valleys received their typical U-shaped cross-sections (Fig. 6–10), sharp crest lines and peaks were sculptured, and the bedrock surfaces were widely exposed, polished, and grooved (Fig. 1–8). The wide expanses of barren rock surfaces in the Scandinavian mountains and northern Finland, and the fjords along the entire Norwegian shore line—formerly glaciated valleys now drowned due to the postglacial rise of sea level—bear ample evidence of glacial erosion.[23]

2. *Glacial accumulation.* While the formerly glaciated uplands are devoid of a contiguous soil mantle the terrain in the marginal reaches of the ice sheets is characterized by landforms constructed by direct glacial deposition (moraines) or by meltwater emanating from the shrinking ice masses (outwash, or fluvio-glacial deposits). The terminal moraines, built up during longer stagnations of the ice margin, form more or less continuous hill trains, some of which are the most outstanding topographic features in the North European plain. The hills of eastern Jutland, the conspicuous Salpausselkä Ridge in southern Finland, and the sharply defined crescentic ridges at the lower end of many Alpine lakes (e.g., Lake Garda, Lake Zürich)

[23] Recent investigations, however, have established that the deep troughs of the Alpine valleys and the fjords, commonly considered as exclusively the result of glacial excavation, had already existed in preglacial times and that only part of their U-shaped cross-section is directly due to glacial erosion. Cf. Hans Annaheim, "Studies on the Geomorphogenesis of the South Alps," *Geographica Helvetica* (Bern, 1946): 65–149.

are good examples of terminal moraines. The till plains of unsorted morainic material of a mixed lithological nature (sand, clay, boulders) are more extensive in area. Sheets of sand and gravel were deposited in valleys and basins beyond the moraines, often to a depth of several hundred feet, by the outwash streams forming in front of, and along, the ice margin during the melting phase of glaciation. Many streams in the plains of northern Germany and Poland today occupy the broad valley trains which served as meltwater discharge channels during the retreat of the ice (appropriately called "ancestral river valleys," *Urstromtäler,* in German, see detailed description Chapter 6, p. 277). The lower portions of most Alpine valleys and the plains in the immediate Alpine foreland (e.g., Swabian Plains, Fig. 6–7) contain fluvioglacial gravels of great thickness into which postglacial rivers have entrenched themselves, leaving a series of terraces above the present valley floors.

3. *Eolian deposits.* Closely related to the glacial regime is the deflation of silt from the outwash plains and its deposition as so-called loess.[24] In a band of considerable width south of, and partly within, the morainic territory, the virtual absence of vegetation close to the ice enabled the strong west winds to pick up the fine-grained material and to transport it over great distances. Southeastern Europe, particularly the Ukraine, the lower Danube Basin, and the non-glaciated zone between the Scandinavian and Alpine ice sheets, became the major areas of loess accumulation. In these regions, the loess cover often assumes the importance of a major landform element, in so far as its thickness is great enough to build up veritable plateaus in which sharp gullies or even gorges (*ovragi* of the Ukraine) have developed because of its unconsolidated structure. Loess is also found in many valleys of the Alps and the Alpine foreland (Rhone, Rhine, Danube). It is an excellent

parent material for soils, and its distribution shows a close relationship to the most intensively used agricultural land of Europe.

4. *Postglacial upwarping.* The fourth transformation brought about by the advance of the ice is of a tectonic nature. The tremendous weight of the northern ice mass depressed the earth's crust to such an extent that in the retreating phase of the ice marine conditions prevailed over wide areas of the formerly ice-covered terrain. This is evidenced by marine fossils and wave-cut beaches, now lying several hundred feet above the level of the Baltic Sea owing to the postglacial emergence of Scandinavia. There are indications that this upheaval of the land has not yet been completed. In the Alps, it is difficult to separate the movements which might have been caused by the weight of the ice from those which occurred in the latest phases of the Alpine orogeny.

The effects of the Ice Age upon the relief of Europe, then, are of great importance not only locally, but regionally as well. Most local surface features are either directly or indirectly influenced by the morphologic processes active during the Pleistocene. Europe obtained its present outline only in the very latest period of geological time, since sea level returned to present normal not more than 7000 years ago.

Drainage Pattern

As a result of the morphological complexity and the strong articulation of the western part of Europe, the drainage pattern consists of a great number of units.[25] Even the East European plains, in spite of their homogeneous relief, drain into four different seas. Europe, in contrast to all other continents, does not have great collecting rivers. The divide between the Atlantic-Baltic-North Sea drainage system and that of the Mediterranean and Black seas, both of about equal area, generally trends southwest-north-

---

[24] The term *loess* (pronounced "luss") is used in Alsace meaning fine, dusty soil. The word is etymologically related to the English "loose."

[25] Readers are advised to make use of a good physical or physical-political map of Europe and follow the courses of the various rivers mentioned in this section.

east, but rarely follows the highest Alpine ranges. The sources of the Rhine and Rhone rivers in Switzerland, for instance, lie only 15 miles apart. These two rivers are confined in longitudinal valleys in their upper courses only, while those of the eastern Alps follow the trend of the Alps much longer before breaking out into the piedmont. The Danube, by far the largest river of non-Russian Europe, marks the boundary between the older and younger mountain systems in its upper course and then finds its way to the Black Sea by twice breaching the Alpine system, first between the eastern Alps and the Carpathians at Vienna, and then between the Transylvanian Alps and the Balkan range at the "Iron Gate." The Danube has encroached deeply into the Atlantic drainage system. Its source is now in the Black Forest, and before the down-faulting of the Rhine *graben* it originated even farther west in the Jura Mountains. In its lower course its mouth followed the eastward shrinking of the Tertiary Black Sea, successively collecting rivers which were formerly independent drainage systems (Tisza, Sava, Morava, the rivers from the Transylvanian Alps, and finally even Seret and Prut).

The Rhine is the only river which managed to keep its course between the Alps and the Atlantic against all tectonic dislocations in the area traversed by it. Its lower course once extended over the floor of the North Sea as far as latitude 57° N., as is evident from a submarine channel beginning at the present Rhine mouth and ending northeast of the Firth of Forth. Most other rivers flowing into the Atlantic, the North Sea, and the Baltic rise in the Hercynian chains (Loire, Seine, Meuse, Weser, Elbe, Oder, Vistula). The rivers of the Iberian Peninsula either follow long-established courses over the less resistant parts of the Meseta tablelands (Duero, Tajo, and Guadiana) or their courses are determined by faults along the younger mountain systems (Ebro and Guadalquivir). The rivers of the Baltic slope of Scandinavia show a remarkably parallel pattern in their courses over the inclined shield surface. Along the boundary between the Caledonian ranges and the shield, as well as farther downstream, the rivers have developed a series of rapids caused by lithological differences, or by the unequal rate of uplift in different parts of Scandinavia during the postglacial emergence of the Scandinavian peninsula.

The divide between Atlantic or Arctic drainage on one side and Black Sea-Caspian on the other has been pushed far northward by the Russian rivers west of the Urals (Chapter 9, pp. 538–42). Here the separation between river systems is often indistinct, with large swamp tracts communicating between two opposite watersheds. Many artificial canals now connect adjacent rivers, replacing former portages. The Volga is by far the longest river of Europe. Its source lies in the moraines of the Valdai Hills at an altitude of only slightly above 800 feet. In its upper course the Volga follows an easterly direction over an extensive outwash plain marginal to the terminal moraines. The gradients of the southwest Russian rivers are extremely small, except where they are forced to cross swells of the crystalline fundament, forming rapids, often the sites of hydroelectric developments (e.g., Kuibyshev on the Volga, Dnepropetrovsk on the Dnieper). These resistant rocks also have an influence upon the direction of flow in so far as the generally southeastern trend of the middle courses of these rivers is reversed toward the southwest in the lower courses. The "elbows" of the Don, Donets, and Dnieper are especially noteworthy. The Ural range represents quite a sharp separation between the European and Asiatic river systems, with all the Siberian rivers draining into the Arctic Sea. (For details see Chapter 9, pp. 538–42.)

As far as standing water bodies are concerned, the distribution of European lakes mirrors, for all practical purposes, the extent of the formerly ice-covered areas. Of the total area of fresh-water lakes in Europe

(52,700 square miles),[26] well over 80 per cent lies within the realm of the northern glaciation.

Finland has close to one-fifth of its total area covered by lakes. The Alpine valleys are rich in small lakes, but their combined area amounts to only 1,300 square miles. Most of the Scandinavian and Alpine lakes owe their origin either to glacial excavation of weaker rock materials, to the fact that they were dammed up by moraines, or that they lie in tectonic depressions. Ice-scoured lake basins prevail in the Norwegian, Swedish, and Scottish highlands (in the latter area they are called "lochs") as well as in the high Alps (cirque lakes); moraine-dammed lakes are typical in the moraine districts of both the Scandinavian and Alpine ice sheets. Central Finland has been called a lake platform, and the same could be said for the lake-dotted moraine belts in northeastern Germany and northern Poland. Very typical are the long, finger-like lakes at the threshold of many Alpine valleys (Lake Geneva, Lake of the Four Cantons, Lake Zürich, Lake Maggiore, Lake Como, and Lake Garda). For the formation of some of the larger lakes such as Lake Ladoga and Lake Onega [27] in Karelia (U.S.S.R.), Venern and Vettern in southern Sweden, and Lake Constance between Germany and Switzerland, tectonic as well as glacial action were contributing factors. The largest lake of non-glaciated Europe is Lake Balaton in southeastern Hungary (240 square miles, greatest depth 36 feet), a remnant of a much larger Pleistocene lake. Small lakes in quite impressive numbers are found in volcanic terrain in the form of crater lakes (Auvergne, Eifel, Apennine peninsula), or in the solutional depressions (dolinas and *polja*) of the karst areas of Slovenia.

[26] This figure approximates the combined areas of Lake Superior and Lake Michigan.

[27] These are the two largest European lakes, with an area of 7,100 square miles and 3,850 square miles, respectively.

THE CLIMATES OF EUROPE

In order to understand the climate of any portion of the earth's surface two basic sets of influences have to be considered. First, there are the terrestrial factors, in particular the absolute location on the globe and the position relative to water and land masses, and the surface configuration. Second, one has to deal with the atmospheric influences themselves, which can be studied in terms of the individual climatic elements.

In the case of Europe the terrestrial factors can be summarized as follows:

1. Europe is the only continent lying almost completely within the so-called temperate latitudes. Its south coast is well north of the Tropic of Cancer (latitude 23½° N.), and only its extreme north extends beyond the Arctic Circle (latitude 66½° N). We may refer to the extreme northern and southern zones of Europe as subarctic and subtropical, respectively, but they are really much more closely related to the atmospheric circulation of the mid-latitudes than to that of either the arctic or the tropics.

2. Europe lies in the western portion of the largest land mass of the earth and along the eastern margin of a large oceanic water body.

3. There is no continuous mountain range across Europe which would interfere with the free movement of air in a longitudinal direction. This means that the land is open to both oceanic and continental air masses.

4. There is a practically unbroken chain of high mountains from northwestern Iberia through south-central Europe into southeastern Europe, which effectively prevents large-scale latitudinal interchange of tropical and polar air masses. The Alpine mountain system, therefore, represents, especially in its central and western portions, a very sharp divide of weather and climate.

5. Europe is surrounded on three sides by large water bodies, parts of which intrude deeply into the land. Of paramount impor-

tance is the fact that the water temperature off the European west coast in the cold season is considerably higher than that measured on the adjacent land. The northeastern Atlantic receives a steady supply of warm surface water through the North Atlantic Drift, driven toward the northeast by the prevailing southwest winds over the eastern Atlantic. The importance of this North Atlantic Drift as a climate factor, however, has been and will probably continue to be greatly exaggerated. It is true that it keeps the harbors of western and northern Scandinavia ice-free as far east as Murmansk, but there is no such thing as a "warming of Europe by the Gulf Stream." While the indirect effect of the relatively warm northeastern Atlantic upon the heat and water balance of Europe cannot be underestimated it should be made clear at the outset that the positive climatic anomaly, i.e., the favorable thermal situation of northwestern Europe in winter, is essentially the result of an atmospheric circulation which involves a massive transfer of warm air masses from the subtropical Atlantic northeastward to its subpolar European sector.

Atmospheric Circulation, Air Masses, and Fronts

The weather over Europe is controlled by five pressure centers which are not normally located over Europe itself, but which direct the flow of air masses into the continent according to the physical laws of circulation: clockwise and converging movement of air in low-pressure systems (lows, cyclones, depressions), counter-clockwise and diverging movement of air around high-pressure systems (highs, anticyclones).

These five pressure systems are:

1. The low-pressure system permanently lying over the North Atlantic between Scandinavia and Greenland, commonly called the Icelandic Low.
2. The high-pressure ridge constantly centered southwest of the Iberian Peninsula, usually called the Azores High.
3. The low-pressure system located over the Mediterranean in winter, or the Mediterranean Low.
4. The high-pressure center located over central Asia in winter, usually called the Russian High.
5. The low-pressure system over southwestern Asia in summer, or the "Monsoon" Low.

It may be deduced from the maps showing mean pressure distribution (Fig. 1–9) that there must exist a westwind drift throughout the year over entire northwestern Europe, whereas the south and east are only marginally touched by the westerlies, particularly so in winter, when the Russian High and the Mediterranean Low establish their own circulations. Due to the increased pressure gradient between the Azores High and the Icelandic Low the westerlies are much stronger in the cold season. It will also be noticed that the winter westerlies have a distinct southwesterly component and are transporting relatively warm air masses toward the continent, in contrast to summer when, as a consequence of the northward expansion of the Azores High and the development of low pressure over eastern Europe, the air masses are entering the continent from a more northwesterly direction so that their temperature is lower than that of the air over the continent. There are other significant changes in the pressure and wind field which will be discussed subsequently in the sections dealing with the seasonal weather conditions.

Brief mention should be made of the upper-air circulation over Europe which exerts a decisive influence upon the movement of surface air. At the 10,000 foot level already, the surface pressure centers are no longer clearly defined and the circulation above this level is characterized by an uninterrupted west–east flow of air, the European branch of an upper planetary wind belt usually referred to as the circum-polar westerlies. They are stronger and reach farther south in winter when they dominate the circulation over the Mediterranean while

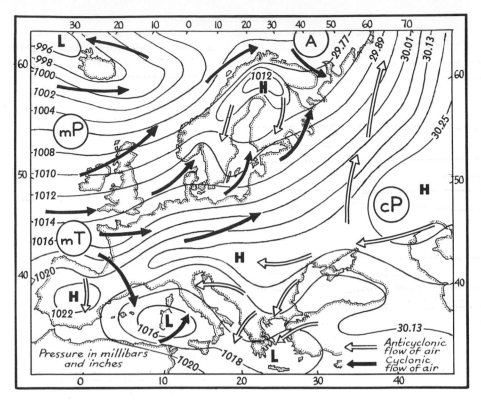

Fig. 1–9. Pressure distribution, prevailing circulation, and air masses. Top, in winter (January); bottom, in summer (July).

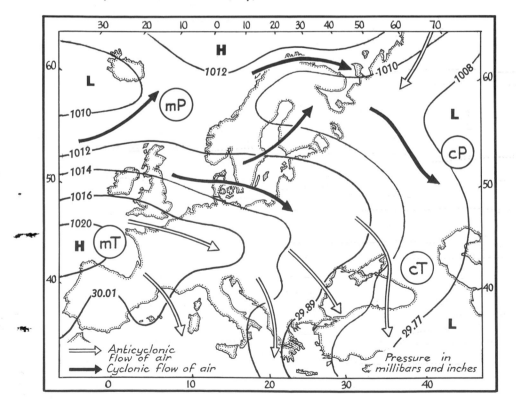

their axis lies over northern Europe in summer. Since the trajectories of surface storms are related to the direction of the upper winds, the charting of the latter plays a major role in daily forecasting procedures. The weather over Europe as a whole is to a large extent determined by the direction under which the upper westerlies approach the continent.[28]

One of the well-known facts about European weather is its changeability. The major reason for the short duration of any particular weather type lies in the high probability that even a slight change in the circulation pattern will bring about an air mass change. Five air masses are involved in shaping the weather over Europe—a larger number than in most other parts of the world of comparable size—and they differ markedly in their temperature and moisture conditions, which they acquired in their respective source regions (see table below, also Fig. 1–9).

Europe. It often lies diagonally (southwest–northeast) across northern Europe in summer and produces widespread rainfall. The winter rains of the Mediterranean, in turn, are connected with the penetration of a branch of the Polar Front south of the Alps. The significant role and interaction of circulation, air masses, and fronts will need further elaboration in the ensuing sections dealing with the seasonal aspects of European climate.

Weather conditions in winter. The two maps of Fig. 1–9 show the atmospheric conditions over Europe in the extreme seasons. The greater contrasts and complexity of the winter situation are at once obvious. The pressure difference between southeastern and northwestern Europe activates a strong southwesterly wind drift within which cyclonic storms travel toward and into the continent. The eastward progress of the maritime air masses, however, is blocked by

Air Mass	Source Region	Characteristics	Season of Occurrence
Arctic (A)	Arctic Sea	Very cold, dry	Winter
Maritime polar (mP)	North Atlantic	Cold, moist	Entire year
Continental polar (cP)	Eastern Europe and Asia	Cold and dry Warm and dry	Winter Summer
Maritime tropical (mT)	Southwestern Atlantic	Warm and moist	Entire year
Continental tropical (cT)	Southwest Asia	Hot and dry	Summer

The contact zone between air masses of tropical and polar origin is usually well defined on the weather map as a chain of cyclonic storms whose fronts interlock to form a continuous boundary between cold and warm air masses, called the Polar Front. The location of this frontal system determines to a major extent the daily as well as the seasonal pattern of precipitation over

the continental High on the south side of which cold air masses may reach the Mediterranean [29] and occasionally as far west as the Channel.[30] It is not unusual that in such situations central Europe may be 30–40° F.

[28] There are zones of particularly high wind speed embedded in the upper westerlies which are called jet streams. They are dynamically associated with surface cold fronts and, therefore, unstable weather conditions. The migration of the jet stream axis from Northern to Southern Europe is clearly related to the main rainy periods in the two regions.

[29] The years 1929 and 1957 are well remembered in Western Europe for their extremely cold winters which were both caused by an abnormal westward shift of the Russian anticyclone which prevented maritime air masses to reach the interior for several weeks.

[30] There are many local names for the feared cold northwinds breaking through the Alps into the Mediterranean Basin. The *mistral* of the Rhone valley, the *tramontana* of northern Italy, the *bora* of Yugoslavia, and the *vardarac* of northern Greece are best known.

colder than the shores of the North Sea which are under the continued influence of the southwesterly flow of mT–air. On the other hand, once a flow pattern dominated by a strong westerly drift has evolved over central Europe, unseasonably warm and rainy weather prevails, accompanied by extensive thaws, dreaded in the alpine resorts and flood-prone valleys alike.

The Mediterranean acts as a breeder of warm air masses in winter. Cyclogenesis is frequent in the Tyrrhenian and Adriatic Seas during polar–air invasions, and Atlantic cyclones, entering by way of Gibraltar, are intensified. The Lows then tend to migrate into the Levant, yielding heavy frontal precipitation along their paths.

The presence of the mountains makes itself felt in various respects. In addition to their effect upon local weather types in the Alps (see temperature inversion, *föhn*, below), they may influence the circulation pattern far beyond the alpine region itself, acting as a divide or obstacle in the wind field. With the entire Alps snow-covered, for instance, an Alpine High is likely to develop which may join with both the Azores and Russian Highs to form a powerful high-pressure ridge, diverting all cyclonic activity toward northwestern Europe. The Scandinavian mountains exert a similar, though areally less extensive influence upon the pressure pattern. A high-pressure cell, built up after incursions of arctic air from the north, forms an effective barrier against cyclonic intrusions from the Atlantic. While the Baltic side of the peninsula is under anticyclonic control with clear subzero weather, the coastal lowlands of Norway have stormy cyclonic weather with temperatures above freezing.

Under prolonged anticyclonic regime a peculiar weather type develops in the central and southern uplands of Europe. After cold continental air masses have penetrated into the valleys and basins in the wake of an easterly cold wave, they become stationary and have little chance to escape unless cyclonic conditions are re-established to draw the cold, heavy air out of these depressions. Owing to the inflow of warm upper air in combination with the accumulation of combustion products (condensation nuclei) in the calm air above the densely settled lowlands, a cloud layer soon begins to form along the boundary between the cold and warm air at elevation between 2000 and 3000 feet above sea level. The cloud deck, meteorologically referred to as stratocumulus, may attain a thickness of 1000 feet. Seen from above, it looks like a veritable sea of fog, with the mountains protruding like islands above the gleaming white cloud tops (Fig. 1–10). The strong insolation above the cloud layer raises daytime temperatures well above those in the cold air trapped below, creating a situation in which the normal decrease of temperature with increasing elevation no longer exists. This so-called temperature inversion occurs with great regularity in the Alpine region in fall and winter, and while it is a boon to the tourist industry in the mountains, the city dweller has to stick it out in the cold polluted air below a grey amorphous mass of clouds, without seeing the sun for days or even weeks.[31]

Another unique weather type in the Alpine region, is the *föhn*.[32] It arises when a well-developed Low approaches the Alps from southern France, but a High over the Balkans blocks its eastward advance. A strong southerly flow is then initiated between the two pressure centers which must cross the Alps at right-angles. Soon their southern slopes are enveloped in clouds and receive intense rains due to the forced uplift of the moist air masses, while at the same time the *föhn* regime is establishing itself north of the Alps, especially in the transverse (north–

---

[31] It is interesting to note in this connection that air traffic comes to a practical standstill if inversion fogs over Central Europe combine with advection fogs over Western Europe. On one memorable occasion British winter tourists headed for Switzerland landed safely on the frozen lake of St. Moritz—the only alternative was London!

[32] The German *"Föhn"* is derived from Latin *favonius,* meaning mild wind.

Fig. 1–10. View from above the **Jura Mountains** over the stratus-covered Swiss Plateau toward the central Swiss Alps. (Photo: Friedli, Swissair.)

Fig. 1–11. *Föhn* weather in the Alps. The broken lenticular clouds above the mountain crest and the excellent visibility are characteristic. Note, however, that the *föhn* does not reach the ground in the foggy foreland. (Photo: Swissair.)

south oriented) valleys, into which the de-hydrated air, heated in its descent, bursts down with gusty vehemence, often raising temperatures by as much as 20° F. within a few hours. From the northern foreland one may observe the characteristic stream-lined (lenticular) *föhn* clouds above the Alps (Fig. 1–11). Owing to the purity of the atmosphere, the latter seem to be at a touchable distance. The *föhn* is a fire hazard and also seems to affect human well-being, probably because of the rapid fall of pressure and low ozone content of the atmos-phere. It is most frequent in spring.

Winter climate. The most characteristic feature of the temperature map is the me-ridional trend of the isotherms over most of non-Mediterranean Europe (Fig. 1–12). Mean January temperatures decrease east-ward along any degree of latitude, while the temperature drop is very slight as one goes northward along a meridian. Bergen has almost the same average January tem-perature as Paris which lies 800 miles to the south (34° and 37° F., respectively), while Leningrad, at the same latitude as Bergen and not quite 1000 miles farther east, is 16° F. colder in January.[33] The tempera-ture gradient from coast to interior is par-ticularly strong between the west coast and the highlands of Scandinavia. Here winter temperatures drop by as much as 30° F. within a distance of 100 miles, an effect of both altitude and anticyclonic weather con-trol over the highlands.

The decrease of winter temperatures across central Europe is much more gradual, indica-tive of the transport of warm air masses into the inland areas.

The Mediterranean Basin is characterized by mean winter temperatures between 32° and 50° F., with daily maxima often in the seventies in its southern portion. However, it should be emphasized that the winter weather in this region is by no means warm. Periods of subfreezing weather occur each

[33] Consult representative climatic diagrams, Ap-pendix II.

winter whenever cold continental air is able to cross the Alps. Only isolated spots in the extreme southern portions of the penin-sulas and islands have not yet recorded tem-peratures below freezing at sea level.

The coldest area of Europe is the north-east, where the cold is rarely alleviated by invasions of maritime air. Normal daily means here are around 0° F. Temperatures below –40° F. have been measured in Mos-cow, and subzero temperatures occur regu-larly in all parts of eastern Europe. In severe winters, subfreezing weather may affect the continent as far west as the British Isles.

As far as the regional distribution of win-ter precipitation is concerned we observe, just as was the case with temperature, a decrease in the amount of precipitation east-ward over the lowland area, a sharp gradient across the Scandinavian peninsula. The pro-portion of precipitation falling in the form of snow increases in the same direction. However, most of the eastern-European low-lands, including the Great Russian Lowland, have a characteristically low snow accumula-tion in winter. Rarely does a station receive more than 10 inches of snow (recorded as 1 inch water-equivalent) in any of the winter months. Ample amounts of winter precipita-tion are recorded along the west coast of the British Isles, Scandinavia, and the Mediter-ranean peninsulas, and in the Alps. In the western and northern portions of the Medi-terranean, the winter rains usually begin rather abruptly in October with the first cyclonic storms appearing over the area. A majority of places along the northern shore of the Mediterranean have a fall and spring peak of rainfall and a noticeable lull in midwinter, the time when the rains are strongest farther south. This difference in the occurrence of the precipitation maximum between the southern and northern portion of the Mediterranean is closely related to the cyclonic weather along the Polar Front, which affects the northern Mediterranean twice (in fall and spring), the southern but once (during its southernmost position in midwinter). More than three-fourths of the

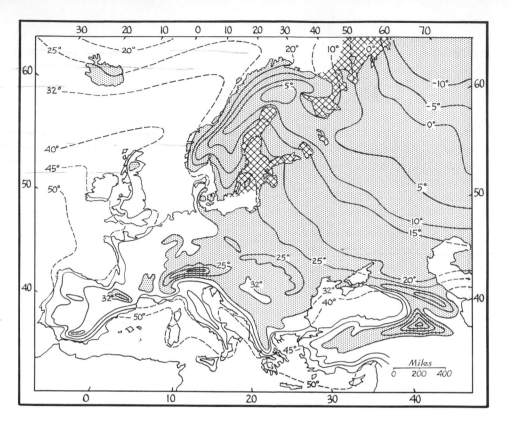

Fig. 1–12. Temperature distribution. Top, in winter; bottom, in summer.

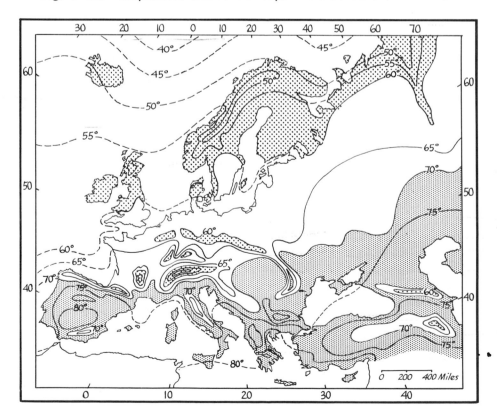

total annual rainfall is usually recorded between October and April at most Mediterranean localities. Both the duration of the wet season and the total amount of precipitation generally decrease from west to east. Precipitation is much more evenly distributed throughout the year in non-Mediterranean Europe. However, the winter months are still the rainiest in the Atlantic borderland. Only at a considerable distance inland can we recognize the shift to summer as the wettest time of the year.

Weather conditions in summer. The main pressure feature in summer is the Azores High, located some 5 to 10 degrees latitude farther north than in winter. It often forms an extension eastward far into the continent and prevents cyclonic storms from penetrating the Mediterranean. Pressure is also higher over the northeastern Atlantic with the Icelandic Low very much less in evidence than in winter. Thus, the north-south pressure gradient is smaller in summer, and as a consequence the westerlies are weakened. By early summer, however, the Russian anticyclone has been replaced by an extensive intracontinental low-pressure system which is attracting maritime air masses deep into the continent. The resulting rainy period over much of interior Europe is comparable in type, though not in intensity, to the summer monsoon rains of East Asia. Cyclonic weather prevails throughout the summer, and the great majority of places in the interior of the continent, therefore, record more precipitation during summer than during any other season.

The most drastic change from winter to summer is observed south of the Alps where anticyclonic pressure controls the weather practically uninterruptedly from May to September. While the winds over the western Mediterranean are variable, a conspicuous wind system with northerly components has established itself over the eastern half. These dry northerly or northwesterly winds are called *etesians* (Greek for "yearly returning winds"). They are particularly strong and persistent over the Aegean Sea

and the Adriatic. Cyclonic development in summer is rare and restricted to the extreme northern and western portions of the Mediterranean lands over which local heating produces convective showers and thunderstorms of high intensity and short duration. Air-mass differences over Europe in summer are not as sharp as in winter. The dominating air masses are still those from the Atlantic. Maritime tropical air is most frequently found over southwestern and central Europe. If it arrives in connection with an advance of the Azores High, a spell of fine weather results. If reaching the mainland in the warm sector of a Low, however, it will yield its moisture in prolonged warm-front rains which are usually terminated by the showers and thunderstorms along cold fronts formed by maritime polar air. In the transitional seasons waves of maritime polar air often bring snowy setbacks in spring or early snowfalls in fall in mountain locations. Along the northwest and north coast of Europe, maritime polar air with high cloudiness, fog, and drizzle rules the weather most of the summer. Continental polar air, covering western Russia, is much drier and often warmer than maritime air. It forms in relatively shallow summer anticyclones over central Asia or originates from altered maritime tropical air. The driest and hottest air mass is found over southeastern Europe. It is either altered maritime tropical air, desiccated and heated due to subsidence along the east flank of the subtropical high, or it arrives as true continental tropical air from the hot interior of Asia on the north side of the southwest-Asiatic Monsoon Low.

Summer climate. The arrangement of the summer isotherms (Fig. 1–12) shows a rather regular increase of summer heat from the shores of the Atlantic and the Arctic Sea southeastward into the continent. The dominance of cool maritime air over the entire northwestern sector of Europe is indicated by daily averages below 60° F. throughout the British Isles and Scandinavia. In contrast the continuous flow of warm air masses into southern Europe, coupled with the greater insolation at these latitudes, results in very hot summers, in spite of the presence of the large water bodies. The latter are not very effective heat moderators because the water surface temperature is only slightly lower than that of the air.[34] The heat poles of Europe lie in the southeastern portions of Spain and Greece where mean July and August temperatures climb above 80° F. and daily maxima above 100° F. are not unusual.

For most of non-Mediterranean Europe, the summer months are not only the warmest, but also the wettest months, the major exception occurring along the Atlantic shore where more than half of the annual precipitation falls in the colder half of the year. The summer peak of rainfall is becoming more and more pronounced with increasing distance from the Atlantic, but the amounts recorded across the northern lowlands differ little from west to east (compare the rainfall graphs of London with those of Brussels, Leipzig, and Moscow, Appendix II). If we take the cross section farther south, there is less uniformity, especially of total amounts of summer rainfall. While summer rainfall is very low throughout western France, the entire Alpine region stands out with a high concentration as well as a high total of rain in summer (see Säntis, a mountain station in Switzerland, Appendix II). Farther east, in the basins of the Balkan and especially in the south-Russian lowlands, summer rainfall decreases sharply. Although most of the year's precipitation still falls in the warm season it is no longer sufficient to counteract the losses caused by the excessive evaporation in these hot areas. The change in the type of natural vegetation in a southeasterly direction across southern Russia from forest to steppe grass and xerophytic plants clearly reflects the increasing degree of aridity. The precarious water balance remains a major natural handicap for dry-farming operations

in the steppe zone between the lower Danube and the southern Urals.

Whereas the steppe farmer looks for the June rains to guarantee a good harvest, the Mediterranean peasant knows that they will never come and has long since adjusted himself to the summer drought which affects the entire Mediterranean Basin. The average number of days with rainfall is less than ten in all except the marginal mountain areas, and their combined rain yield is less than an inch in the long-term average.

The mean annual accumulation of precipitation in Europe is presented in Fig. 1–13. Although it is generally believed that most of the continent has a moist climate, the fact is that a generous supply of moisture is only available at higher elevations and in some low-lying areas in which a combination of factors is conducive to above-average rainfall. The remarkably even distribution and low amount of precipitation from the Atlantic coast deep into Russia has already been mentioned concerning summer rainfall, but the same holds true for the annual pattern. If we consider that the map is based on average values it is easily seen that dry years, which may yield only half or two thirds of the normal amount, must produce widespread water shortages. For agriculture based on natural rainfall, the precarious moisture situation as far west as the Atlantic shore, where only 30 inches normally fall annually, becomes immediately obvious. It is not surprising, therefore, that irrigation has become a necessity to secure reliable crop returns even in areas which we will subsequently classify as having a maritime type of climate.[35]

Climatic Types and Regions

Having discussed the characteristics of individual climatic elements, we have now the

---

[34] It is interesting to note that one of the highest temperatures ever observed on the earth (136°F. in the shade) was recorded within 30 miles of the shore of the Mediterranean Sea at Azizia, Libya.

[35] In the deeply entrenched upper Rhone Valley in Switzerland, within a few miles of mountains with 100 inches annual precipitation, irrigation is necessary. Even in some of the Norwegian fjords irrigation practices are followed because of rainfall deficiency in summer.

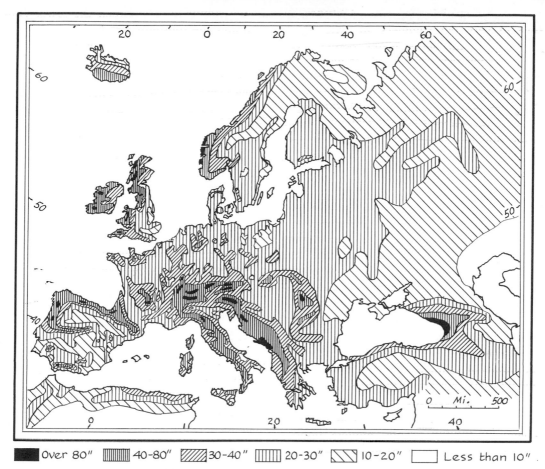

■ Over 80" ▥ 40-80" ▨ 30-40" ▥ 20-30" ⧄ 10-20" ☐ Less than 10"

Fig. 1—13. Annual precipitation.

task of integrating them into a climatic system. There are various ways of classifying climates. The one followed here is consistent with the approach chosen in the section on landforms. Emphasis is on the genesis rather than the description of climates, and the established types of climates should reflect the genetic factors responsible for them. As for the areal extent of individual types, it should be remembered that climatic regions are rarely separated by sharp boundaries. Only the higher mountain ranges, such as the Alps, the Pyrenees, or the Scandinavian mountains, are sharp climatic divides. In the extensive central and eastern lowland of Europe, changes from one climatic type to another are very gradual. Another problem connected with delimiting climatic boundaries is the effect of altitude. Increasing altitude produces much sharper climatic gradients than does either increasing latitude or increasing continentality. Genetically, however, mountain climates are affected by the same weather types as the surrounding lowlands, but they have an opposite effect upon individual climatic elements (lower temperature, higher precipitation).

Considering the major atmospheric controls of climate (pressure-wind systems, air masses, and fronts) four basic climatic types can be differentiated:

1. Maritime type (also called marine or oceanic type)
2. Transitional type
3. Continental type
4. Mediterranean (or subtropical) type

As can be seen from the map of climatic regions (Fig. 1–14), the first type occurs in westernmost Europe, the second in the eastern portions. Each of these two regions is characterized by the dominance of one air mass throughout the year: maritime air in the west, continental air in the east. The boundary between maritime and continental air masses is constantly fluctuating with the migrations of the Polar Front. Between the two extreme regimes in the west and the east, therefore, there exists a broad zone of transition from a maritime to a continental character of climate. Central and eastern Europe lie in this zone. Its changeable weather bears ample evidence of the conflict of air masses of different character.

The climate of the extreme western portions of Europe is typically maritime. Its basic characteristics are ample and evenly distributed rainfall, prevailing westerly winds, high humidity and cloudiness, a small annual range of temperature, and rarely subfreezing weather. The climate of the eastern

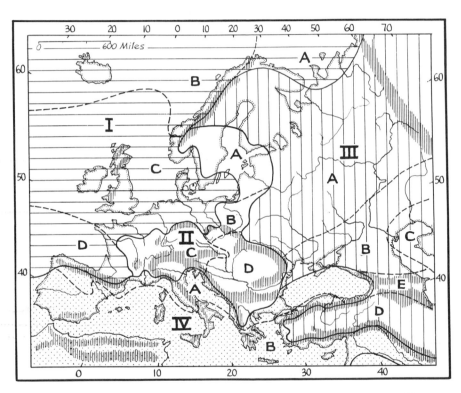

I. Atlantic Seaboard Region: Maritime Type
　　Provinces:
　　A. Arctic
　　B. Norwegian
　　C. North Sea
　　D. Biscay
II. Central Region: Transitional Type
　　Provinces:
　　A. Baltic
　　B. Polish
　　C. Alpine
　　D. Danubian

III. Eastern Region: Continental Type
　　Provinces:
　　A. Northern
　　B. Southern
　　C. Caspian
　　D. Anatolian
　　E. Caucasian
IV. Mediterranean Region: Subtropical Type
　　Provinces:
　　A. Northern
　　B. Southern

Fig. 1–14. Climatic types, regions, and provinces. Highland modifications within each region are indicated by shading.

region is a moderate form of the true continental type of climate. The annual range of temperature in the extreme east of the European U.S.S.R. is large, but still only less than 60° F. as compared to more than 120° F. in eastern Siberia. The corresponding values are around 40° F. for central Europe and some 20° F. along the west coast. We might say that the climate in eastern Europe (i.e., the European U.S.S.R.) is only half as continental as it could be, but three times more so than the maritime type. The type referred to as the "Mediterranean" is found over the peninsulas, islands, and waters of the Mediterranean and Black seas. Its dry summers make it distinctly different from the aforementioned types. In winter, the maritime influence is as great as in western and central Europe.

1. The maritime type. Each of the main types can be subdivided into subtypes (see summary, pp. 46–47), and the areas in which they occur may be called provinces. The maritime region contains four provinces: (1) the Arctic Sea coast, (2) the west coast of the Scandinavian peninsula, (3) the North Sea coastal lands, and (4) the extreme southwest of non-Mediterranean Europe. In addition, highland subtypes can be differentiated in all regions. The Arctic province lies north of the tree limit, and also extends above it, since it projects southward into the Scandinavian mountains. The province is characterized by very cold winters which, however, are still considerably warmer than those at intracontinental stations toward the southeast (compare type stations Kola and Vorkuta in Appendix II). The major difference between the other three maritime provinces lies in their thermal regime. Thorshavn (Faeroe Islands), one of the most typically maritime stations anywhere in the world, has the extremely small annual range of temperature of 13° F. (February 38° F., July 51° F.). Copenhagen is 10° F. colder in winter and 10° F. warmer in summer, and Biarritz in southwestern France (not shown in Appendix II) almost 20° F. warmer than Thorshavn in summer and winter. All these

maritime stations receive the highest amount of rainfall in the months of the cold season, with the maximum months delayed from autumn to early winter the farther south the station lies. The month with the highest rainfall is normally September in Bergen, October in London, and November in Bilbao, clearly revealing the southward migration of the rain belt along the Polar Fronts during the fall months.[36] On the west coast of the British Isles and on the outlying islands a midwinter maximum is recorded, a consequence of strongest air-mass contrasts and highest frequency of cyclonic storms at that time of the year (see diagrams of Thorshavn, Glasgow, Plymouth, Valentia, and Reykjavík).

2. The transitional type. The transition zone between the maritime and the continental climatic regions, called the central region in Fig. 1–14, can be divided into northern (Baltic), central (Polish), southern (Alpine), and southeastern (Danubian) provinces. In the Baltic and Polish provinces winters are much colder than in the southern provinces, while the boundary between the two is based upon the cooler and drier summers of the northern province. The Alpine province, especially its higher parts, receives a much higher amount of precipitation than any other transitional province. In total amount, but not in seasonal regime, precipitation in the higher Alps is comparable to that of the rainiest sections of the maritime region (annual total above 80 inches [Fig. 1–13]). The Appendix II diagrams of Stockholm, Kraków, and the three Swiss stations (Basel, Lucerne, and Säntis)[37] are representative of the temperature and precipitation regimes in the provinces of the central climatic region. All these stations

[36] A secondary maximum of rainfall is recorded at some stations along the Atlantic coast in spring at the time when the Polar Front returns to the north.

[37] Lying in the northeasternmost chain of the Swiss Alps, the Säntis observatory records an extremely high precipitation (110 inches). It is fully exposed to maritime air masses and has a high thunderstorm frequency. The station also shows the effect of altitude in thermal respects.

Type	Region and Provinces	Pressure and Winds	Air Masses and Fronts

Maritime	Atlantic seaboard region
	Provinces:
	Arctic
	Norwegian
	North Sea
	Biscay
	(Highlands)
		Stationary Icelandic Low in
		  winter.
		Stationary Azores High in
		  summer.
		Migrating lows.
		
		SW to W.
			mP, mT (A, cP)*
			Polar Front active all year (ex-
			  cept in Biscay province).
			Arctic Front in extreme north
			  in winter.

Transitional	Central Europe region
	Provinces:
	Baltic
	Polish
	Alpine
	Danubian
	(Highlands)
		Migrating lows throughout year.
		Extensions of Icelandic Low,
		Continental High in winter.
		Azores High often dominant
		  in summer.
		
		NW to SW.
			mT, mP, cP (cT)
			Polar Front activity throughout
			  the year.

Continental	Eastern Europe region
	Provinces:
	Northern
	Southern
	Caspian
	Anatolian
	Caucasian
	(Highlands)
		Stationary Continental High and
		  migrating lows in winter.
		Moderate cyclonic activity in
		  summer.
		
		SW in winter.
		NW in summer.
			cP, cT (mP, mT)
			Polar Front activity pronounced
			  in winter, weak in summer.

Subtropical	Mediterranean region
	Provinces:
	Northern
	Southern
	(Highlands)
		Stationary Mediterranean High
		  in summer. Migrating lows in
		  winter.
		
		Variable in winter.
		NW–NE in summer.
			mT, cT (cP, mP)
			Polar Front active in winter only.

* Less frequent or only locally significant.

show a marked summer maximum of precipitation. With the exception of Kraków, which already has a dry continental winter, they also receive at least 1 inch of precipitation in the driest month, usually January. The Danubian province is under the influence of continental air in summer (cT) and winter (cP), with maritime air intruding mainly in the transitional seasons. It generally receives less rainfall than the other four transitional provinces. Quite characteristic is the early summer maximum of precipitation at most of the interior stations (type stations Budapest, Dej, Prague), while those close to the Adriatic, Aegean, and Black seas have not only the convection rainfall peak of summer but also a secondary cyclonic maximum in early and late winter (see type station Kragujevac). Since they are at the same time located in highland areas, they are much wetter than the lowland stations.[38]

3. The continental type. The climatic characteristics common to all parts of the large eastern climatic region are the severe winter cold and the large annual range of temperature. The subdivision into five

[38] The combination of intensive winter and summer rains produces the largest total amount of precipitation of southern Europe in the Dinaric mountains close to the Gulf of Kotor (160 inches). The absolute maximum of precipitation in Europe occurs in southwestern Norway at the Jostedal Glacier (230 inches).

Types and Regions

Type	Precipitation	Temperature	Miscellaneous	Other Type Designations
Maritime	Even distribution through year, strongest in winter. Annual total above 30 inches. Snow rare at sea level.	Small annual range (20° F.). Rarely below 32° F. and above 86° F. Coldest month often February.	High cloudiness and humidity, and fog frequency. Arctic province much colder than other provinces.	Oceanic, marine west coast. Cf, ET (tundra) according to Koeppen system.
Transitional	Even distribution, but well-defined summer maximum, particularly in eastern provinces and highlands. Annual total increasing with altitude.	Moderate annual range (30°–50° F.). Absolute maxima $> 100°$ F., minima $< 0°$ F.	Mountain areas much colder and moister than lowlands, except during inversion weather in winter.	Humid continental, mesothermal. Cf, Df, ET according to Koeppen system.
Continental	Marked summer maximum, permanent snow cover in winter.	Large annual range (50°–70° F.). Minima $< 0°$, maxima $> 90°$.	Rapid change from winter to summer and vice versa.	Short-summer humid or semiarid continental, microthermal. Df, BS according to Koeppen system.
Subtropical	Marked winter rainy season. Summers dry, except in highlands and marginal areas.	Summers hot (means above 80° F.). Winters cool to cold, but above 32° F. Annual range 20°–40° F.	East coasts much drier than west coasts.	Mediterranean, Etesian, dry summer subtropical. Cs, BS according to Koeppen system.

provinces is based principally on variations in either the total amount or the seasonal distribution of precipitation. The northern province shows definite affinities to the neighboring provinces of the central climatic region (compare the similar total and regime of precipitation of type stations Moscow and Helsinki, Appendix II). Winter temperatures in the central Russian plains, however, are 10–20° F. lower than in the central region, the summers slightly warmer. With the increased influence of continental tropical air in summer, rainfall diminishes and the critical 20-inch isohyet is reached in the Ukraine. This is the semiarid southern province of the continental region, an area often afflicted by severe drought due to the unre-

liability of the summer rains and to the scorching winds (*sukhovei*) from the trans-Caspian source region of dry, hot continental air. The Caspian province is the westernmost extension of the Asiatic desert and the only large arid stretch of Europe. Annual precipitation is less than 10 inches (see type station Astrakhan). The interior of Anatolia is in a transitional area between the continental and Mediterranean types of climate. The thermal regime is similar to that in the aforementioned provinces, but the annual distribution of precipitation is entirely different, the pronounced summer dryness being the outstanding characteristic. The sources of moisture lie in the Mediterranean and Black seas, but due to the marginal mountain ranges little precipitation is received over the interior plateau. What there is comes in form of cyclonic rains before or after the anticyclonic control of midwinter. The Caucasian region forms a distinct climatic province characterized by ample precipitation throughout the year. In the coastal areas, influenced by Black Sea and Caspian cyclones, more rain falls in winter than in summer; in the interior, the reverse is true.

4. The Mediterranean type. The climatic region designated as the Mediterranean is unique in so far as dry, hot summers are coupled with rainy, cool winters. Rainfall generally decreases toward the south and the east, with a simultaneously growing number of dry months in these directions. The boundary between the two provinces delimited in the Mediterranean climatic region follows approximately the 1-inch isohyet of the driest summer month. North of this line, especially in the mountain areas, thunderstorm activity persists throughout the summer. Even though they are not treated as special provinces, reference should be made to certain areas which deviate from the normal type described above. The interior of Spain has a more "continental" version of the Mediterranean climate, with considerably colder winters and hotter summers than the coastal districts.[39] Several regions of Spain are extremely dry, such as the Ebro Basin in the rain shadow of the northern mountain ranges, and the coastal area between Múrcia and Almería where less than 10 inches annual rainfall is recorded. It also should be recalled that the Atlantic rimland of Spain has a distinctly maritime climate, with precipitation exceeding 50 inches throughout the Galician and Asturian mountains. Marked local contrasts, particularly between west and east coasts of islands and peninsulas, are typical, such as between the Adriatic and the Aegean side

[39] As the adage goes in Madrid, *"seis meses invierno, seis meses inferno"* (six months of winter, six months of hell).

of Greece (Corfu 49 inches annual rainfall, Athens 16 inches) or along the shores of the Black Sea (the lowest temperature ever observed at Samsun, on the Black Sea coast of Turkey, was 20° F.; at Taganrog, on the north coast of the Sea of Azov, −22° F.!). The Po Plain has been included with the Alpine province of the central climatic region, because cyclonic developments may occur at any time of the year. Thus, both the cyclonic winter rains of Mediterranean Europe and those of central Europe in summer contribute to the large total rainfall figures in this area. Milan, in the center of the Po Plain, is 11° F. colder in winter than Genoa. The two stations are only 80 miles apart, but the Gulf of Genoa is effectively protected by the Apennines from invasions of polar air.

By way of a summary the climatic regions and provinces are listed on pp. 46–47, with their corresponding meteorological and climatological characteristics.

BIOGEOGRAPHIC AND PEDOLOGIC ASPECTS OF EUROPE

Evolution of Biota and Soils

The present distribution of flora and fauna, as well as that of soils, is the result of three sets of influences: topographic, climatic, and anthropogenic. First, the evolution of the European land was not a regionally independent process which could have produced specifically European types of plants and animals. This is to say that Europe is as much a part of Eurasia biogeographically as it is structurally. The only boundary separating clearly different biotic areas in Europe follows the Alpine range and its western and eastern continuations. The zone north of the Alps is a part of the "Boreal" biotic realm, which also includes the higher latitudes of Asia and North America. South of the Alps, the Mediterranean biota are closely related to those of southwestern Asia and northern Africa.

Second, of paramount importance for the present floristic, faunistic, and pedologic associations were the climatic changes which affected Europe during and after the Ice Age. The ice sheets forced the biota into the unglaciated areas of central and southern Europe. The climatic zones shifted southward, and with them plants and animals. Most of Scandinavia was still covered by the ice some 10,000 years ago. Since then, with various interruptions during postglacial climatic fluctuations, flora and fauna, as well as soils and even landforms, have adjusted themselves to the present climatic conditions. The main biotic associations, therefore, have reached their present locations only recently, geologically speaking. Central Europe became an area of immigration of plants and animals from all sides, particularly from the east. It is questionable whether these migrations have really come to an end in the short span of postglacial time.

A third influence on biota and soils is man himself. "Natural vegetation" in Europe is only rarely natural in the sense of representing the original vegetation untouched by man. It has been established that well over 80 per cent of the European land was originally forested. Today only one-third of Europe is covered by trees, and much of this is either a cultivated second-growth woodland or, particularly in the Mediterranean area, degenerated scrub forest. The long use of the original forest as a lumber resource and the continuous process of clearing it for expansion of crop and pasture land has left only a few virgin timber stands, most of them in the boreal forest, some in the Alps. Even in the Russian steppes little of the natural grass cover remains after centuries of cultivation.

Plant Cover: Types and Distribution

Even though large stands of native vegetation are rare and widely scattered, over much of Europe it is possible to reconstruct the original plant cover by analyzing the species' composition of these refugial sites. We can assume that without the interference of man the European forests would have the same aspects as those which appear relatively undisturbed in the midst of the deforested land. Figure 1–15 attempts to take into consideration both the actual and potential distribution by showing the boundaries between the major plant formations as they would exist had man not interfered, as well as the actual location of larger tracts of native vegetation. Due to the small scale of the map the pattern is, of course, highly generalized, but it allows one to recognize the relationship of vegetation to climatic and topographic factors.

The predominance of forests (boreal, mixed-deciduous, and evergreen-hardleaf) over non-arboreal plant formations (tundra, steppe, desert) reflects the favorable thermal and moisture conditions over most of Europe. The latitudinal (west–east) rather than meridional (north–south) trend of the major vegetational boundaries shows that the decisive ecological control is thermal. This also applies to the vertical distribution of plant formations. The sequence: hardleaf forest, deciduous forest, coniferous forest, tundra from Southern to Northern Europe is repeated in the Alps, where the same formations lie above each other. The forest reaches its northern limit just short of the Arctic Sea, while in the Alps the upper timber limit lies between 5000 and 6000 feet. In both areas sufficient summer heat is the critical climatic factor. A mean temperature of 50° F. in the warmest month seems to be the minimum requirement for sufficient wood growth in trees in the northern and Alpine forests.

Other associations or individual species are limited in their distribution by excessive winter cold. This is particularly obvious with many Mediterranean plants which do not survive north of the Alps. In addition, lack of moisture, coupled with excessive summer heat, becomes critical for plant life in southern and southeastern Europe. The effect of aridity manifests itself in many ways in the Mediterranean flora and leads to a complete absence of arboreal vegetation in the grass steppes of southern Russia.

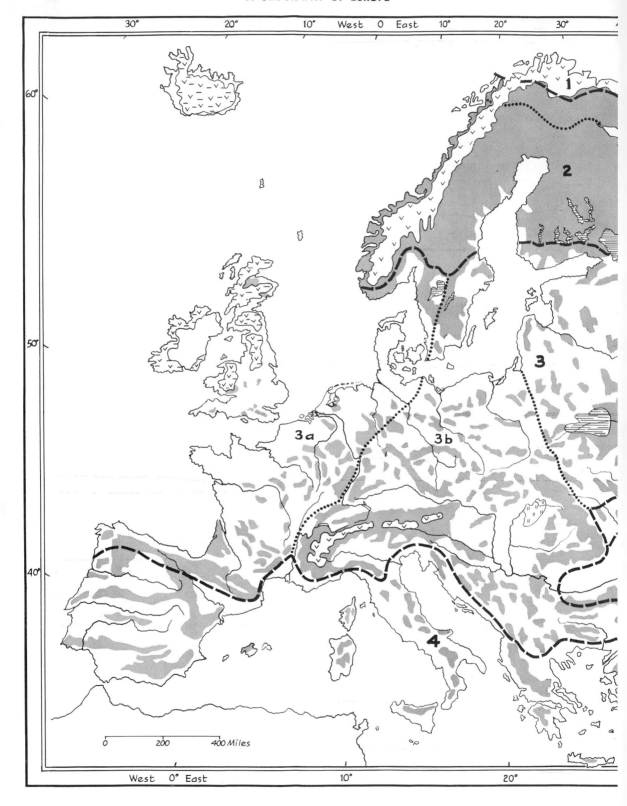

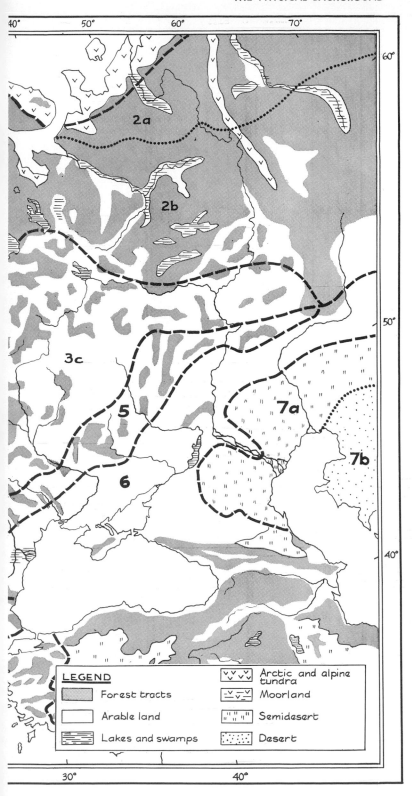

Fig. 1–15. Vegetation zones and actual distribution of forests. (1) tundra, *fjell,* Alpine meadows, heath and moorlands; (2) boreal forest: a, open; b, closed; (3) mixed forest: a, Atlantic association; b. central association; c, eastern association; (4) Mediterranean hardleaf forest, including large areas of secondary "maquis" associations; (5) forest steppe; (6) steppe; (7) desert: a, semidesert; b, desert.

LEGEND

Forest tracts
Arable land
Lakes and swamps
Arctic and alpine tundra
Moorland
Semidesert
Desert

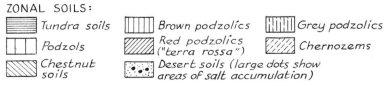

ZONAL SOILS:

Tundra soils	Brown podzolics	Grey podzolics
Podzols	Red podzolics ("terra rossa")	Chernozems
Chestnut soils	Desert soils (large dots show areas of salt accumulation)	

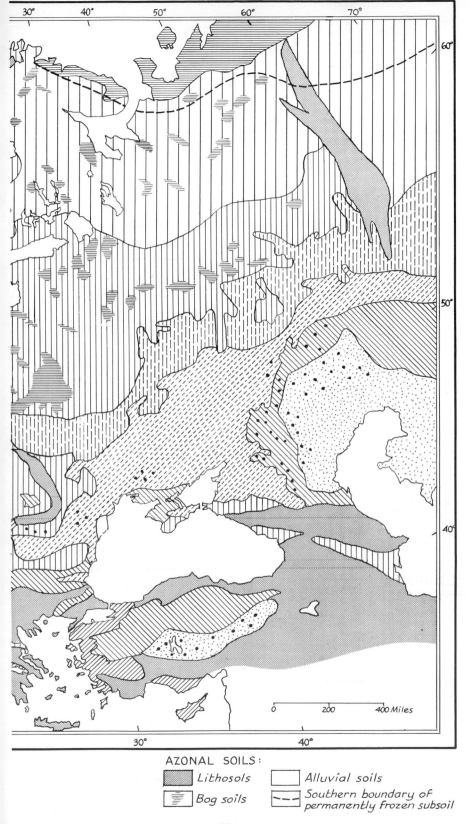

AZONAL SOILS:

Lithosols   Alluvial soils

Bog soils   - - - Southern boundary of permanently frozen subsoil

Fig. 1–16. Soil groups.

The combined effect of climatic and topographic factors upon the distribution of vegetation, then, is one of relatively simple zonation. The same is true for the distribution of the major soil groups to which we will briefly turn our attention.

Soil Groups

The map showing the major soil groups and their regional distribution in Europe (Fig. 1–16) is, of course, a greatly simplified rendition of the complex mosaic actually existing. The zonal soils (i.e., mature soils with well-developed profiles) show a marked correspondence to the vegetation zones. This is to be expected, since the soil classification still most widely used is based on the surface color of the soils, which is directly related to the kind of organic matter of the overlying plant cover and indirectly to the climatic conditions which controlled the type of vegetation in the first place. A strong genetic relationship between soils and climate is further indicated because the breakdown of the parent material and the differentiation of the entire soil profile by chemical processes depend greatly on the ambient temperature and moisture characteristics.

In spite of the great variety of parent materials—from the igneous rocks of Scandinavia to the predominantly sedimentary formations of central and southern Europe and to the widely dispersed glacial and alluvial deposits—the soil pattern of Europe is of remarkable homogeneity. This may be explained by the fact that most of the soils were developed under the original forests which were able to establish themselves solidly in the relatively short span of postglacial time (see p. 49). There is such a conspicuous similarity in structural and chemical characteristics of soils developed under either coniferous or deciduous tree cover that they may be grouped into one large family which is called the forest soils. They all have in common a layer of grey or grey-brown color immediately below the organic surface horizon to which the generic

name "podzol" (from Russian pod zola, "ash soil") has been applied. Podzolization has been recognized as the major soil-forming process in a humid-temperate forest environment, involving decalcification of surface layers and accumulation of clays in the subsoil. The whole soil profile is strongly acid in true podzols of the northern forest zone, whereas farther south, podzolization has been weaker but is still recognizable in the southern forest soils, including the red earths of the Mediterranean.

The steppe belt of Russia is underlaid by the "black earth" (*chernozem*), a highly fertile soil developed over calcareous loessial parent material (see p. 31), and enriched with up to 10 per cent organic matter. On both sides the black earth belt grades into pedologically less favorable zones (grey podzolics or degraded chernozems to the north, the salt-infested chestnut and desert soils to the south).

In a very generalized way the areally most extensive azonal soils, i.e., immature soils without a normally developed profile, are also shown on the map. The lithosols include all rocky and stony soils, exposed bedrock surfaces, and eroded mountain sides. Although they may not appear too prominently on the map they are indeed conspicuous in most mountain areas which, however, also contain many zonal soil sites too small to be shown at the scale of the map. Of the numerous poorly drained bog and swamp areas in Europe (hydromorphic soils) only some of the largest are indicated on the map. The same holds for the freshly deposited soils of flood plains and deltas (alluvial soils) which are, in great contrast to most other azonal soils, often of high agricultural value, as for instance the newly reclaimed marshland of the Netherlands.

Biogeographic Zones

In the following paragraphs the major biogeographic and pedologic aspects of each of the major natural landscape types of Europe are briefly discussed. The reader is referred to the regional chapters for further information on local climatic, biogeographic and edaphic characteristics in individual parts of the continent.

Tundra and Fjell. The Arctic zone, restricted in Europe to a narrow strip of "tundra"[40] along the Arctic Sea, is characterized by a rather luxuriant growth of low forms of vegetation. Lichen (symbiotic union of algae and fungi) prevail on drier sites, mosses and sedges in poorly drained areas. The tundra is not absolutely treeless: in the most favorable sites shrubs of birch and willow are found. Most of these wooden plants, however, creep along the ground. There is so little wood development in them that

[40] The word "tundra" is a derivation from the Finnish word *tunturi,* a mountain in Finland which projects above the timber line.

100-year-old specimens may have less than 1 inch stem diameter. The tundra is quite rich in flowering plants in midsummer, one of the pleasant surprises awaiting the traveler in the subarctic. The yellowish lichen carpet, formed by the reindeer "moss" (botanically a lichen), the silver green of the arctic willow, the darker green of the mosses and sedges, and the multicolored flowers (*Ranunculus, Saxifraga, Dryas, Silene, Erica*—to name some of the most abundant genera) give quite a vivid coloring to the tundra landscape (Fig. 1–17).

One can barely speak of tundra soils since a true soil development does not take place in the subarctic climate. In ill-drained depressions azonal "bog soils," actually slowly decomposing organic matter, black and extremely acid, are found to a considerable

Fig. 1–17. At the boundary between tundra and boreal forest in Swedish Lappland. The tundra with its moss, lichen, and sedge carpet is seen in the foreground; the coniferous forest occupies the lower levels in the center; and the Scandinavian mountains, with permanent ice fields, form the backdrop. (Courtesy Dept. of Geography, University of Zürich.)

depth. A conspicuous feature in the highest and northernmost portions of the tundra is the perennially frozen soil, called "permafrost."[41] It may be from a few feet to a few hundred feet thick, with only the uppermost feet or even inches thawing in summer. Seasonal thawing and freezing keep the surface layer in constant motion, making it very difficult for plants to gain a foothold. Permafrost action produces a peculiar sorting of the frost-shattered rock debris which is often arranged in circular, polygonal, or mounded fashion. Occupying only isolated tracts in the Scandinavian tundra (bogs, high mountains), permafrost becomes areally very extensive in the extreme north of European Russia, where it even penetrates the boreal forest (Fig. 1–16).

The tundra fauna is limited in species: the arctic hare, the snow fox, and various rodents, including the mass-migrating lemming, are the only year-round residential mammals. The semi-domesticated reindeer roams the tundra in summer only, retreating into the woodlands in winter. The polar bear, the seal, and the walrus (the latter close to extinction) inhabit the arctic seas. For uncounted numbers of migratory birds, the tundra and the shore cliffs are the summer breeding grounds. The same, unfortunately, is true for insects.

The type of vegetation in the Scandinavian highlands "fjell" (mountains) is closely related to that of the lowland tundra, and is often referred to as "vidda." Dwarf shrubs (particularly the dwarf birch, the stunted birch, and various willows and heather shrubs) are more numerous, however (Fig. 1–1). Above the tree limit, here mostly formed by birches, and below the lichen-moss tundra, there is often an extensive zone of meadows. Their herbs, grasses, sedges, and flowering plants are floristically and ecologically very similar to the association of the Alpine meadows. The tundra animals

Vidda

are also found in the northern portions of the fjell, supplemented by the elk (related to the American moose). Wolves and bears are occasionally found above the timber limit.

The boreal forest. The boundary between the tundra and the boreal forest has to be conceived of as a zone, several degrees of latitude in width (Fig. 1–15). It has been referred to as lichen woodland, with the open stands of conifers and the willow and birch thickets on the lichen carpet giving the landscape a parklike appearance. In places open tundra intermingles with the "closed" forest, forming a forest tundra.[42] The open boreal forest then grades into the closed boreal forest, a spruce-fir association with a solid undergrowth of mosses and herbs rather than lichens (the Russian *taiga*).[43] The closed boreal forest is the largest biotic unit of Europe, covering some one million square miles, much of it still in natural conditions (Fig. 1–13). In its western portions many of the stands are second growth, this area being one of the richest timber regions of Europe. Only a handful of species account for practically all coniferous trees (the Siberian-Uralian and European species of the spruce, the pine, the larch or tamarack, and the fir, listed in order of abundance). In the boreal forest the cleared areas, rather than the woodlots as in central and western Europe, are "islands" in the landscape (Fig. 1–15).

The fauna is much richer than in the tundra. The fur-bearing carnivores (bear, fox, wolf, lynx, weasel, skunks, badger) and herbivores (beavers, squirrel, hare, marmot, muskrat) are typical forest dwellers. In addition, a great variety of birds, attached to the conifers in their eating habits, and deer live in the boreal forest. Many of the animals

[41] This ground ice is called *tjaele* in Swedish, *merzlota* in Russian. Permafrost is much more widely distributed in Asiatic Russia than in European Russia.

[42] Extensive bogs and forest marshland are also typical in the transitional zone between tundra and boreal forest.

[43] *Taiga* is a Tannu-Tuvan word also used by northern Mongols. It means the bald summit of a forested mountain, but its original meaning has been corrupted in Russian and accepted by modern English to refer to the forest zone.

were formerly found farther west and south but have since retreated into the boreal forest with the disappearance of contiguous woodlands in the mixed-forest zone.

The relatively large amount of precipitation, little of which is lost by evaporation in the relatively cool summers, poor drainage conditions, and profusion of organic material decaying on the forest floor further the development of a specific soil profile under the boreal forest. Beneath the humus layer, excessive leaching takes place which removes all carbonates and other soluble substances except silicates and accumulates them in a clay-rich and often indurated lower soil layer. The leached horizon, left extremely acid, has a characteristically grey, bleached appearance. Podzols are inherently unproductive soils and at the same time often poorly drained either because of the hardpan or the thawing of snow and ground ice.

The mixed forest. South of approximately 60° N., the boreal forest becomes intermixed with broadleaf (deciduous) trees, the more so the farther west and south one goes. Only in the higher territory of central and southern Europe are conifers still found in pure stands. The zone of the mixed forest extends from the British Isles to the Urals; the Atlantic front of the zone stretches from southern Norway to northwestern Spain, while its eastern end comes to an apex in the Ural foreland. The triangular shape of the mixed-forest zone is indicative of the limiting climatic factors along its boundaries: excessive winter cold in the north, summer drought in the south; positively expressed, its range seems to be related to the area of year-round maritime influence. Within the mixed forest three subtypes can be distinguished (Fig. 1–15).

In the extreme west deciduous trees such as beech, elm, maple, and oak are more abundant than conifers, and there is an admixture of Mediterranean floral elements as far north as southern England. The chestnut advances to the Garonne, the grape to the Loire, and hardleaf evergreens are found in sheltered places of the British south coast.

In higher tracts of land or on sandy soils the pine is the characteristic conifer. In the central European section of the mixed forest the beech is the character tree, but it no longer forms pure stands except in a few isolated spots (e.g., island of Rügen, Carpathians). Most of the second-growth stands have a large proportion of softwoods (spruce and fir). In the lower stories of the mountain forests beech-spruce associations are typical. At altitudes above 2,000 feet there exists a zonation within coniferous associations, the pine and the larch climbing higher than the spruce, the first two forming the timber line in the Alps, the last arriving at its upper limits between 3,000 and 5,000 feet in the non-Alpine mountains. In the morainic terrain along the North Sea and the Baltic swamp, moor and heath associations are widespread.

As on its Atlantic side, the mixed forest of central Europe grades into an association of somewhat different composition toward the east. The beech no longer occurs, and the oak now often dominates the forest, intermixed with conifers toward the north, and with grassland toward the south. With the southern boundary of the boreal forest extending southward and the steppe reaching much farther north in the Volga lowland than in the Ukraine, these two formations form a common boundary near the Volga elbow at Kazan, thus preventing the deciduous forest from reaching the Urals.

The rich fauna originally inhabiting the mixed forest has been greatly reduced, particularly in the western and central sections, during the long occupancy of man in this most densely settled area of Europe. The wild horse and the European wild ox have long been exterminated, the bison more recently. The elk has retreated into the boreal forest, the bear northward and eastward, and into the southeast-European mountains. The fur animals are less numerous than in the boreal forest. Deer, fox, badger, and wild boar have the widest range. Restricted to mountain areas are the chamois, the wild goat, the marmot, and the Alpine eagle. The main domain of the wolf is eastern Europe, but sporadically he appears as far west as eastern France or even northern Spain.

Podzolization has taken place in most soils developed under the original mixed forest, but with decreasing intensity in a southward direction. Clay accumulation is still strong and the acidity is quite high, but leaching has been much less severe and hardpans have rarely developed. It is customary to call these soils "podzolics" and to classify them according to the color of the surface layer. Immediately south of the true podzols and in the higher terrain of southern Europe, the brown podzolic soil has developed, which grades into a grey-brown relative westward and into a grey podzolic southeastward, the latter being a transitional type to the black earth of the Russian steppes. Their satisfactory amount of organic and nutrient matter, loamy texture, and well-drained condition make the podzolics better than average soils. Many areas occupied by these soils have been under cultivation for centuries and are still highly productive. This is, of course, also a consequence of heavy fertilization and careful management of the soil by the European farmer.

Occurring in the area of the podzolics, but not shown on our map, are the so-called *braunerden* (German for brown earths) which lack the impoverished surface layer and excessive clay accumulation. Usually developed on limestone they have a higher content of organic and nutrient materials, but at the same time their shallow depth makes them more susceptible to erosion.

The steppe and the desert. South of the forest belt in Russia and in the basins of the lower Danube the surface cover was originally and still is in part characterized by wide expanses of grassland, or steppes (from the Russian word *step* for this grassland). There is a distinct transition zone between the forests and the steppe, extending diagonally across the southern European U.S.S.R., which is called the "forest steppe." This zone is characterized by an intermingling of oak forests and open grassland, the former dominating in the northern portions, the lat-

ter in the southern. The encroachment of the forest upon the steppe has had a distinct and negative influence on the soils of this zone in so far as the former grassland soils were subjected to podzolization. On the soil map these soils are designated as grey podzolics; they have also been called degraded black earths.

The absence of forests, except along rivers, and the almost continuous carpet of grasses, together with the black soils, or "chernozems" (Russian for black earths), are typical of the virgin steppe. Most of the steppe land in the south of the Soviet Union and in the southeast European basins represents today what might be called a "cultural steppe," since hybrid grains have long since replaced the native wheat grass. In the drier southeastern sections of the Russian steppes, however, where pasturage plays a greater role than grain cultivation, the original steppe aspect is retained.

The steppe is the result of climatic conditions which are intermediate between those responsible for the growth of forests toward the north and those which produce the desert toward the southeast. As far as the available moisture is concerned, the climate of the steppes is subhumid or semiarid. The combined effect of temperature, precipitation, and evaporation seems to allow a vigorous growth of herbaceous plants, but to preclude forest development. The fact that most of the steppe land is mantled by loess has undoubtedly had a bearing upon the evolution of the deep soil profile and, indirectly, upon the plant cover itself. The conspicuously black surface layer of the soils in the subhumid portions of the steppe is the result of the accumulation of plant material which became incorporated with the mineral matter of the subsoil. The upper layer of the chernozem has undergone little leaching so that the nutrient minerals are available to the plants. Of particular importance is the high content of calcium carbonate and humus. Additional assets of the black earths are their granular structure as well as their good drainage and aeration characteristics.

Chernozem

All this in conjunction with the often perfectly level surface of the land makes the chernozem one of the most productive soils of Europe. It must be said, however, that overcultivation of these soils has created serious problems of soil erosion and deflation in many areas. Natural enemies of soil productivity are podzolization in the north, already mentioned above, and the formation of lime hardpans (*caliche*) in the drier portions to the south. *CALICHE*

In the extreme southeast of the European U.S.S.R., with precipitation falling below 10 inches and with increasing summer heat, the steppe grades into a semidesert. The steppe grasses no longer completely cover the ground, and little organic matter can be taken up by the soils. Their color is now chestnut brown; they are extremely shallow and often contain lime or salt encrustations just below or at the surface. Due to the slowness of the soil-forming processes the type of surface material plays an increasingly greater role toward the Caspian and Transcaspian desert. Here, beyond the boundary of Europe as delimited in this text, soil development is at a minimum and is determined by surface deposits (clay flats, salt pans, sandy and stony desert).

The virgin steppe was the home of large herds of herbivores, but most of them have become extinct with hunting and the progressive cultivation of the steppe lands. Most of the wild horses (*tarpans*), antelopes, deer, roebucks, and wild boars did not survive the last century. The same is true for the many birds which originally inhabited the steppe. Only the bustard, the ptarmigan, and waterfowl are left in larger numbers. The typical steppe animals today are the rodents: hamster, ground squirrel, ground hare, and various species of mice and rats, and a few reptile species. Migratory locusts hatch in the delta thickets of the rivers and have occasionally devastated cropland in widely scattered steppe tracts.

The Mediterranean Zone. The Mediterranean lands are as unique from a biogeographical and pedological point of view as

they are climatically. Although little is left of the original plant cover in the area, there is enough evidence to be gathered from its remainders, and from secondary and cultural vegetation, to establish the existence of a unique type of Mediterranean vegetation to which the generic name "maquis" has been applied. The people of Corsica refer to the shrubby, thorny, and aromatic thickets of their island as *maki* from which the French *maquis* [44] and the Italian *macchie* are derived.

Most native Mediterranean plants have developed similar protective measures against the water deficiency and the high evaporation rate in summer. Their leaves are small, leathery, often spiny, and are glazed with a coating of waxy substances. The trees are evergreens and of small size; in a few places, such as the southern French Alps or along the east coast of the Adriatic, they still have the aspect of the original Mediterranean evergreen hardwood forest. Macchie or cultivated trees and crops have practically everywhere succeeded the former forest associations. The macchie can be best described as a dense scrub forest, the tree crowns rarely reaching higher than 20 feet (Fig. 1–18). Floristically, it consists mainly of oaks (live oak ubiquitous, cork oak in western part only), shrubs of the heather family (laurels, oleanders), legumes, and junipers. In sites of extreme dryness and over the lithosols of limestone outcrops, the shrubs are more widely spaced. Droughty grasses and thorny flowering plants, most of them bulb perennials, then form a "steppe maquis" [45] association.

Myrrh, myrtle, lavender, mint, and many other strongly aromatic species are typical representatives of the Mediterranean flora.

Macchie

---

[44] It will be recalled that the French resistance movement against German occupation forces during World War II used the name *le maquis,* with the implication that anybody going into the maquis thickets would be well hidden.

[45] There are a variety of local terms for this open type of maquis such as *garigue* in southern France, *phrygana* in Greece, *tomillares* and *monte* in southeastern Spain.

Fig. 1–18. View over the Gulf of Porto on the west coast of Corsica. The steeply sloping granitic mountainsides are covered by dense "maquis" vegetation. The remains of a Genoese watchtower stand above the harbor cove. (Photo: Miramont, Bastia.)

All these plants blossom profusely in spring, while in summer they are little more than desiccated, thorny stalks. The change in the appearance of the plant cover between the two seasons is most impressive indeed.

The altitudinal zonation of the Mediterranean plant formations was originally in the sequence: macchie—chestnut trees—beeches—conifers, the last establishing the timber line close to 6000 feet. It should be clearly stated, however, that one rarely sees a continuously forested mountain slope in the Mediterranean realm. Deforestation here has been much more thorough than in any other part of Europe. Overgrazing, clearing for cultivation, and the use of wood for charcoal burning have practically annihilated the forest, and a poor second-growth macchie has now replaced it. The long summer drought, the denuded nature of the soil, and the continuous use of potential forest sites as pasture land are making reforestation extremely difficult.

With the forest a good many animal species have disappeared. Still found are the wild goat, the mountain sheep (the muflon of Corsica and Sardinia), the wildcat, and the wild boar. The variety of reptiles (snakes, vipers, lizards, and turtles), insects, and mollusks is great. Birds are conspicuously few in number.

The soils of the Mediterranean lands are characterized by a distinct red color of the surface layer, particularly when developed on calcareous parent material. Genetically, these red earths are probably red podzolics, transitional in their characteristics between the midlatitude podzolics and the red tropical soils. The group name "terra rossa" (red earth in Italian) has often been used to include soils of the Mediterranean lands with red surface color, but these soils vary greatly in other characteristics such as calcium or silica content, texture, and drainage. If deeper profiles are developed, which is the exception, terra rossa is quite a productive soil. In their shallow and eroded phases they are difficult to manage. On steeply sloping terrain the only practical measure against erosion is the construction of terraces. In the alluvial lowlands and basins, however, the situation is entirely different. Deep and fertile soils are encountered the productive capacity of which, particularly under irrigation, is as high as that of any other European soil. The Po Plain, the *huertas* (gardens) in Spain, and the *conca d'oro* (the golden bowl) near Palermo in Sicily are but a few examples of intensively cropped Mediterranean lands.

It is this intensity of land use throughout the Mediterranean area which makes us wonder whether the people really have not made the best use of a not too favorable environment. Wherever there is a pocket of soil, a little piece of flat land, it has been transformed into a tiny garden. Many native plants have been cultivated into varieties which have much higher yields than their wild ancestors. The olive tree, above all, this sturdy and at the same time gracile senior of the Mediterranean plants, still grows wild throughout the area, but it is most conspicuous in the neatly set rows of the olive plantations. The bread grains, the grapevine, many stone fruits, and even the date palm are natives of the Mediterranean borderlands and have been hybridized over the centuries. Together with the citrus fruits, introduced from the Far East, they all make up the "fruits of the south," as the northerners fondly refer to the products of the Mediterranean garden.

CONCLUSION

The intention of the preceding pages has been to outline in brief the physical and biogeographic components of the European landscape. At the same time an attempt was made to give the reader an insight into the variety of factors responsible for the physical character of the European lands. The physical environment, then, has been sketched as the background to the human occupancy to be examined in the ensuing chapters. Only at the end of the book might one expect to find the answer to the question which could logically be posed at this point: To what ex-

tent did the natural setting determine what man did with this portion of the earth? But the answer to this question is not given; rather, it may be read between the lines throughout the text. It will become very obvious that the many contrasts of the European landscape are the result of an uninterrupted interplay between physical and human forces from the Stone Age to the present day. We only can say here that man found Europe offering both favorable and unfavorable environments and that he has learned to take advantage of friendly surroundings and to cope successfully with harsher environments. Both the fertile lowlands and the steep Alpine slopes are the homes of European people. What man did is visible in his works, what the environment did is concealed within them.

BIBLIOGRAPHY

(Major references are asterisked.)
Books in English

ANNAHEIM, HANS (ed.). *Across the Alps: Aerial Views Between Nice and Vienna.* Bern: Kümmerly & Frey, 1959.

*BRINKMANN, R. *Geologic Evolution of Europe.* Stuttgart: F. Enke Verlag, 1960.

COLLET, LEON WILLIAM. *The Structure of the Alps.* London: E. Arnold & Co., 1935.

*DE BEAUFORT, L. F. *Zoogeography of the Lands and Inland Waters.* London: Sidgwick & Jackson, Ltd., 1951.

GREAT BRITAIN, AIR MINISTRY, METEOROLOGICAL OFFICE. *Tables of Temperature, Relative Humidity and Precipitation for the World. Part III, Europe.* London: Her Majesty's Stationery Office, 1958.

FLINT, FOSTER R. *Glacial and Pleistocene Geology.* New York: John Wiley & Sons, Inc., 1957.

*KENDREW, WILFRID G. *The Climates of the Continents.* 6th ed. London: Clarendon Press, 1963.

*KUBIENA, W. L. *The Soils of Europe.* London: T. Murby, 1953.

LOBECK, A. K. *Physiographic Diagram of Europe* (with text). New York: Columbia University Press, 1951.

MOHRMANN, J. and KESSLER, J. *Water Deficiencies in European Agriculture: A Climatological Survey.* Wageningen: Veenman and Zonen, 1959.

TREWARTHA, G. T. *The Earth's Problem Climates.* Madison: University of Wisconsin Press, 1961.

Books in Foreign Languages

FIRBAS, FRANZ. *Spät-und nacheiszeitliche Waldgeschichte Mitteleuropas Nördlich der Alpen* (Late and Postglacial Forest History of Central Europe North of the Alps). 2 vols. Jena: O. Fischer, 1949–52.

°KOEPPEN, WLADIMIR, and GEIGER, RUDOLPH (eds.) *Handbuch der Klimatologie* (Handbook of Climatology). Vol. III. Berlin: Gebrüder Bornträger, 1932–36.

°MACHATSCHEK, FRITZ. *Das Relief der Erde* (The Relief of the Earth). 2 vols. Berlin: Gebrüder Bornträger, 1955.

PENCK, ALBRECHT, and BRÜCKNER, EDWARD. *Die Alpen im Eiszeitalter* (The Alps in the Ice Age). 3 vols. Leipzig: Tauchnitz, 1909.

RIKLI, MARTIN. *Das Pflanzenkleid der Mittelmeerländer* (The Vegetation Cover of the Mediterranean Countries). 3 vols. Bern: H. Huber, 1943–48.

STAUB, RUDOLF. *Der Bau der Alpen* (The Structure of the Alps). Bern: Beiträge zur geologischen Karte der Schweiz, No. 52, 1924.

Articles

BIEL, ERWIN. "Die Niederschlagsverhältnisse der Alpen" (The Precipitation Regime of the Alps), *Mitteilungen der Geographischen Gesellschaft* 73–74 (Vienna, 1931): 188–94.

CONRAD, VICTOR. "The Climate of the Mediterranean Region," *Bulletin of the American Meteorological Society* 24 (1943): 127–45.

°DAMMANN, W. "Klimatologie der atmosphärischen Störungen über Europa" (Climatology of Atmospheric Disturbances in Europe), *Erdkunde,* Vol. 14 (1960): 204–221.

DARBY, H. C. "The Clearing of the Woodland in Europe," *"Man's Role in Changing the Face of the Earth."* Chicago: University of Chicago Press (1956): 183–216.

FLEURE, H. J. "The Loess in European Life," *Geography,* Vol. 45 (1960): 200–204.

°FLOHN, HERMANN. "Witterung und Klima in Mitteleurope" (Weather and Climate in Central Europe), *Forschungen zur Deutschen Landeskunde* 78 (1953): 214 pages.

GREGORY, STANLEY. "Climatic Classification and Climatic Change in Europe," *Erdkunde* 8 (1954): 246–56.

GUILCHER, ANDRÉ. "La Formation de la mer du Nord, du Pas de Calais, et des plaines maritimes environantes" (The Formation of the North Sea, the English Channel, and the Surrounding Coastal Plains), *Revue de Géographie de Lyon* 3 (1951): 311–30.

°LOMBARD, AUGUSTIN. "Appalachian and Alpine Structures: A Comparative Study," *Bulletin of the American Association of Petroleum Geologists* 32 (1948): 709–44.

RÜBEL EDWARD. "Heath and Steppe, Macchia and Garigue," *Ecology* 2 (1914): 231–37.

SAURAMO, MATTI. "On the Nature of Quaternary Crustal Upwarping in Fennoscandia," *Acta Geografica* 14 (1955): 334–48.

SION, JULES. "Le role des articulations littorales en Méditerranée" (The Role of Coastal Articulation in the Mediterranean), *Annales de Géographie* 43 (Paris, 1934): 372–79.

VILLMOW, J. R. "Regional Pattern of Climates in Europe According to the Thornthwaite Classification," *Ohio Journal of Science* 62 (1962): 39–52.

ZOLLER, HANS. "Die natürliche Grossgliederung der fennoskandischen Vegetation und Flora (The Natural Division of Fenno-Scandian Vegetation and Flora), *Veröffentlichungen des Geobotanischen Institutes Rübel* (Zürich, 1955): 74–98.

2

The Historical
Background

Any attempt merely to glance at the many sharply distinguishable cultural landscapes of Europe, or to consider the many elements compounded in any one such landscape, emphasizes how clearly the handwriting of history appears on its map. Dissected plateaus of wooded and pastoral aspect have become populous regions of coal mining and of heavy industry. Wide areas of steppe, which linked like areas of Siberia and central Asia with south Russia and the Danube Basin, have passed from the control of the nomad horseman to that of the settled agriculturist and of the town-dwelling industrialist. The geographical values attaching to different parts of the continent show continual change throughout history: the Mediterranean lands, for example, no longer dominate in population numbers, in political energy, and in civilization generally. One-fifth of the world's population has found its home in Europe, and distributed itself there in a very unequal manner: here densely concentrated in specialized industrial or intensively developed agricultural areas, there thinly spread over a rural landscape of mountain valleys, widespread forests, heath, moor, or marsh.

The countryside of Europe reveals the many varieties of rural settlement and of urban forms. It contains some metropolitan giants which mask with their buildings and their transport lines the nature and form of the underlying rocks, yet which they dare not wholly ignore. The landscape of the "conurbation," a term used to describe those continuously urban areas which have arisen through the coalescence of two or more towns mainly during the last hundred years, must also engage attention. And away from the towns of whatsoever size and function, villages, hamlets, and single farms scatter all over the continent, their distribution posing intricate problems to the solution of which agrarian history, related as it is to the variety of physical environments, can contribute much.

Many other features of the human geography have also grown out of the past; for instance, the ports and resorts of the coastlands, and the patterns of inland transport by rail, road, and water. And, if attention is turned to the inhabitants of Europe themselves, these are still separable into ethnic, linguistic, national, and state groups, the locations of which were first sketched long ago.

Confronted by the wealth of Europe's history, the student of human geography may well wonder what is his precise task in turning back to the past for the light which it can throw on the present. In essence, he is concerned with the study of people and their settlements, of their forms of economy, and of their means of travel and of transport. Under each of these three main heads—settlement, economy, and "circulation"—a set of problems arises for separate discussion. Thus consideration of the peoples of Europe will refer to the growth and distribution of population, to rural and urban settlement, and to the ethnic types, languages, nations, and states as they are distributed over the continent. Similarly, attention will be turned to the variant patterns of agriculture, industry, and commerce, and to the patterns of transport on which they depend: all these will be noted in relation to their physical background and to their development through time.

THE PEOPLES OF EUROPE

Prehistoric settlement. Geography need concern itself little with the Paleolithic period,[1] which, despite its long duration of perhaps 500,000 years, has left virtually no mark on the landscape of the continent. Paleolithic man inhabited those parts of the continent which were not invaded by the Fenno-Scandian and Alpine glaciers,[2] where probably a tundra-like climate prevailed or, at best, humid oceanic conditions, as in the Mediterranean peninsulas. An archaeologist has estimated for the earlier or Lower Paleolithic period that the total energy at man's disposal in Europe—and all of it was human—did not exceed that of a four-engined plane: as an agent of geographical change, therefore, Paleolithic man can be ignored.

That transitional phase between the Upper Paleolithic and Neolithic cultures which has been termed "Mesolithic" deserves passing notice. When the north-German plain and the Baltic area had been abandoned by the glaciers and were being colonized by trees, some immigrants from the south, Mesolithic in culture, settled along its seacoasts and along the banks of its numerous lakes and rivers. From about 8000 B.C. until about 3000 B.C. these prehistoric tribes still lived by hunting, fishing, and food collecting, and were presumably ignorant of cultivation and of metals, and had no domesticated animals except the dog. Their tools and weapons were still fashioned of unpolished stone, flint, and bone; they had not yet learned to polish stone but only to flake and chip it; nor, with few exceptions, were they familiar with pot making. And this way of life lingered on, especially in northwest Europe, long after the Neolithic culture, based on agriculture and pastoral husbandry, had become established in Egypt, Mesopotamia, and northwest India.

The climatic and vegetational background to the Mesolithic period and the succeeding cultures of postglacial Europe is now being revealed in clear outline, thanks above all to the microscopic study of pollen grains preserved in datable layers of peat and other organic or semiorganic sediments.[3] It is now possible to envisage in relationship not only the main fluctuations of climate since the final retreat of the Fenno-Scandian and Alpine glaciers but also the various stages in the spread of forest-forming trees and the corresponding culture periods of the archaeologist. Four successive climatic phases have been distinguished: the Boreal, Atlantic, sub-Boreal, and sub-Atlantic, although the third of these is less clear. Compared with the cold pre-Boreal period which preceded it, the Boreal period was dry and increasingly warm; the Atlantic wet and warm; the

[1] The terms Paleolithic, Mesolithic, and Neolithic periods are used to describe settlement periods of prehistoric Europe.
[2] For geological terms, see Appendix I.

[3] On pollen analysis see H. Godwin, "Pollen Analysis: An Outline of the Problems and Potentialities of the Method," *New Phytologist* 33 (October, 1934): 278–305, and Stanley A. Cain, *Foundations of Plant Geography* (New York: Harper & Bros., 1944), especially Chapter X.

sub-Boreal was cool but perhaps not so dry as was formerly believed, while the sub-Atlantic, which lasted into the historical period of the Roman Empire, was marked by cold and moist conditions. Precise calendar dates for these periods are as yet difficult to determine. Nor is it clear that the specified climates apply farther afield than Northern, Western, and Central Europe. But the succession of climatic changes is by now broadly established, and so also is that of the corresponding changes of the vegetation cover.

In contrast to North America, Europe has relatively few indigenous tree species and even fewer today than it had during the Tertiary period. This scarcity is not the result of its present climate nor of the adverse conditions of the Great Ice Age. It is due to the two barriers aligned west-east: the middle mountain ranges and the Mediterranean Sea, which checked the retreat of tree species as climate worsened with the onset of the Great Ice Age. Fewer species were therefore able to immigrate into the continent from the southwest and southeast as the climate improved in the postglacial period. In the Boreal phase spruce, fir, pine, birch, and hazel established themselves as far north as central Sweden and Finland. In the succeeding Atlantic phase, these gave pride of place to mixed forests of oak, elm, linden, and common alder. The beech, especially sensitive to temperature and traveling fastest by way of river valleys, spread into Western and Central Europe from the Danube Basin during the sub-Boreal and sub-Atlantic periods. Both Mesolithic Europe, which may be dated to the late Boreal and Atlantic phases, and Neolithic Europe, which falls within the late Atlantic and the sub-Boreal phases, must be thought of as thickly clad with trees and undergrowth, excepting only those areas where tree growth was precluded by high altitude, bad drainage, or exposure to persistent gales. Even the considerable areas stretching from south Russia across the continent to the English Channel, where layer upon layer of loess had been deposited by wind during the Great Ice Age, are now known, thanks to pollen analysis, to have been covered, not with a steppe-heath flora, but with beech, hawthorn, juniper, yew, box, and ash. Also, the Mediterranean peninsulas had then an abundance of forest and scrub, rooted in an ample soil which, as a result of forest destruction by man and beast, has since been largely lost.

Attention can be paid here to only three particular aspects of the Neolithic and Bronze ages: the routeways (i.e., natural routes) used, the areas occupied, and the mineral sources exploited—since these are directly connected with the development of Europe as a home of man. It was by the diffusion of men and techniques from certain primary centers of progressive culture in Egypt and southwest Asia that Europe learned in turn, and adapted to its very different environment, the Neolithic and Bronze Age ways of life. The Neolithic culture, as it developed between 6000 and 3000 B.C. in its original homes, marked a major revolutionary change in man's use of his habitat. Its economic basis was food production by cultivation and stock rearing, and its social expression was, at first, the village and, later, the town. It brought technical inventions and new crafts: wheel-turned pottery, kiln-fired bricks, spinning and weaving, building, writing, trade, social organization, and the fashioning of works of art.

All these new triumphs of human ingenuity, to which the beginnings of metallurgy were later added, characterized the Neolithic culture or civilization. Given the original location of the homelands of the Neolithic culture, it is not surprising to find that the new culture was first to appear within the European realm in Crete and the other islands and coastlands of the Aegean Sea, whence it spread by sea and by overland routes. The area which, chiefly on climatic ground, Ellsworth Huntington found most favored for civilization in Europe—the Northwest, including the British Isles—was the last to receive it.

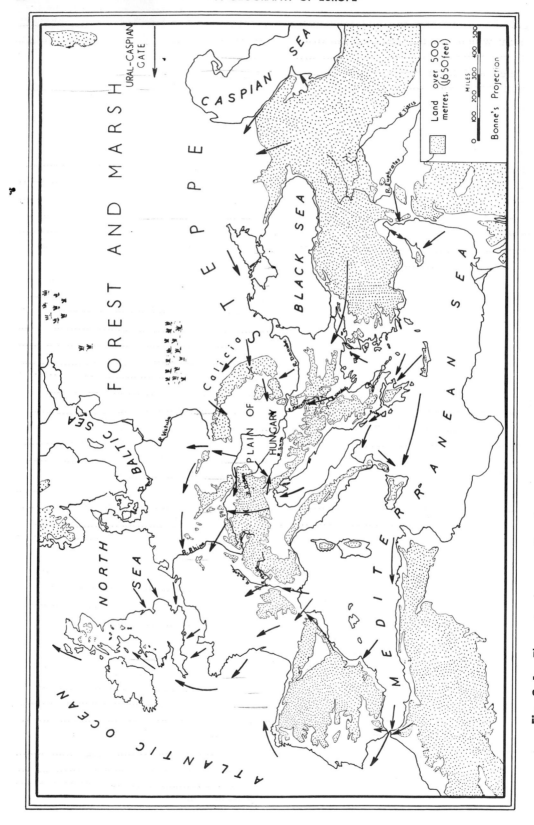

Fig. 2–1. The natural routes of prehistoric Europe. (The maps in this chapter were prepared by the author.)

Figure 2–1 illustrates the land and water routes by which, on the basis of the distribution of known prehistoric sites and artifacts, men and ideas seem to have spread into and throughout the continent. Prehistoric peoples were thus outlining the main areas of human settlement and linking them by sea and land channels of communication which have since then tended to remain in continual use.

It is doubtless highly dangerous to generalize about the areas occupied by European peoples in the various stages of the Neolithic and Bronze cultures, for several millennia are involved and the evidence cannot claim to be complete. There is, however, a striking correspondence between the areas settled by Neolithic peasants and certain areas of porous or pervious rocks. This applies particularly to the loess lands, but also to areas of sand, gravel, loam, limestone, and sandstone, all of which not only were well drained, but developed light-textured soils, easy to work with simple stone or wooden hoes.

The relative facility of cultivating such soils would seem to have been their main attraction; the absence of forest cover and its replacement by a steppe-heath type of flora under an allegedly dry sub-Boreal climate can no longer be offered as the explanation. Rather, it is now clear that the Neolithic peasants often settled in village groups at the wooded margin of the steppe, and made the first big clearance of forests by firing, in order to win land for agriculture and pasture. It is remarkable, too, that the lowlands and plateaus, once conquered in this way, have continued to be defended for the plow against a reinvasion of forests by a historical succession of colonists. Thus the Neolithic men of Europe and their livestock of the third millennium B.C. played a part in fashioning European downlands, steppes, and heaths from original woodlands. It is believed, for instance, that the great extent of heath in northwest Germany owes its origin to the agency of men and their grazing animals which, in the course of the sub-

Boreal period (i.e., during the later Neolithic and Bronze Age), entirely destroyed the former forests.

The Bronze Age in Europe, which may be dated from about 1800 B.C., called attention for the first time to the mineral wealth of the continent, principally in those places where rocks of Hercynian folding were exposed. Among the regions which were then important for their minerals were Transylvania with silver, gold, and salt; Bohemia with tin and copper from the Erz Gebirge (Ore Mountains); Spain with tin and copper; Ireland with copper and gold; and Brittany and Cornwall, the mineral resources of which included the scarce metal tin necessary, with copper, for bronze making. The knowledge of bronze first reached Bohemia and Hungary to be diffused therefrom by nomad intruders from south Russia. New trade routes by land and sea were then opened up, including those along which amber was brought overland to north Italy from the Baltic. Ireland, then remotely placed, assumed for a time a leading role in metallurgical industry and European commerce. The sea route from the Mediterranean through the Irish Sea to the Orkney Islands and Scandinavia, which is inferred from a study of tomb plans and vases to have been in use in the third millennium B.C., was clearly an established trade route by about 1500 B.C., as is shown by the finds of traded products of known origin. The development of agriculture continued during the Bronze Age with a few local changes, some of which are known with surprising accuracy. Thus, in Denmark, expert studies of the impressions of grain still detectable on the prehistoric pottery and of carbonized cereals found in peat reveal that barley was by far the most important crop there in the late Bronze Age, although several varieties of wheat were no less prominent in the later Neolithic period.

It was during the Bronze Age that immigrants from the steppe lands north of the Black and Caspian seas brought to the rest of Europe the domesticated horse, which was used for pulling war chariots and only later for riding. These immigrants spoke the Indo-European language, and it would seem that for a time, during the latter part of the second millennium B.C., a single speech prevailed in Europe. If for no other reason than this, the European Bronze Age is geographically memorable, as it is from the language introduced then that, by a process of regional differentiation, most of the present languages of Europe have developed.

Our sketch of the prehistoric settlement in Europe should conclude with a reference to the expansion of Iron Age peoples into western Europe during the last thousand years before the birth of Christ. The knowledge of the working of iron had penetrated into the Danube Basin from the East, and once again it was from a Danubian area that a new technique was rediffused. From the upper Danube Valley between Bavaria and the middle Rhine in Alsace, Iron Age culture was carried into France, Iberia, Scandinavia, and the British Isles. Several waves of migration ensued. In Britain, for example, three can be distinguished and broadly dated, and these appear to have consisted of Celtic-speaking peoples who were bringing with them successive Iron-Age cultures. These immigrant "Celts"—this term has only a linguistic meaning—were the ancestors of the many peoples established in north Italy, Iberia, Gaul, Bohemia, and Britain with whom the Romans later fought when, leaving peninsular Italy, they launched their career of conquest. Numerous Celtic river names in Europe, such as Rhine, Danube, and Thames, still attest their former presence.

As its climate improved and fluctuated with the retreat of the glaciers of the Great Ice Age, Europe, we have seen, became a "pioneer" or "colonial" field, occupied and exploited by a succession of immigrants of different cultural attainments. The temperate forested lands of Europe owed this initial development to the inflow of men and ideas from the precociously civilized countries situated in lower latitudes, above

all Mesopotamia, Egypt, and even Turkestan. In these movements we may note the important roles played by the island of Crete, the steppe of south Russia, and parts of the Danube Basin. In the course of the first millennium B.C., the prehistoric period in Europe gave place to the historical period, which is illuminated by literary records. They reveal, as is known also from archaeological evidence, that the Mediterranean lands of Europe reached the highest degree of social and political organization, of commercial activity, and of civilization in general: the Phoenicians, the Greeks, the Etruscans, and the Romans of classical antiquity focus the attention of the historian, while in Europe beyond the Mediterranean lakeland world more primitive conditions of life prevailed.

The nations and states. Even though present-day Europe still shows traces of its prehistoric past, the main features of its human geography are explained above all by processes operative during the historical period. The peculiar patterns of "nations" and "states" in Europe, to which we now turn our attention, are clearly the results of such processes. It is a remarkable fact that Europe, occupying only one-twelfth of the habitable earth, contains about a quarter of its independent states. No less does Europe house a high proportion of the self-conscious and articulate nations of the world. Time has served only to intensify the trend toward the creation of more and more so-called "nation states," and to produce what must appear to Americans, familiar with larger and simpler state-and-nation patterns, a parochially organized continent. This appears particularly true of Central and Eastern Europe since nations and states are much more simply arranged peripherally to these regions, in Western and Northern Europe.

As a glance through the pages of a historical atlas shows, state territories and the boundaries of states have changed continually. In contrast, the distribution of national groups shows marked stability. To define what constitutes a "nation" is not easy: like the concepts of "space" and "electricity" in physical science, it resists exact definition. But it is something more fundamental than the state, which, as twentieth-century history has shown, can be made and unmade. Social groups, bound together by common traditions and culture, have tended to become acutely conscious of their own individuality and have often, but not invariably, sought separate statehood, whether or not they possessed a single common language. But national self-consciousness and the idea of the "nation state" are relatively modern developments. Let us look back in time to see where and how the nationalities of Europe first appeared. It will be convenient to start this discussion by reference to the foundation and fortunes of the Roman Empire in the early centuries of the Christian era.

At its maximum extent in the second century A.D. (Fig. 2–2) the Roman Empire extended northward from the shores of the Mediterranean Basin to the Rhine and Danube and bestrode these rivers along parts of their courses—in the upper Rhine and in both the upper and lower Danube. Within this large part of the continent, Rome established centralized political organization and maintained the peace, security, and ordered life of her provinces by fortifying the imperial frontiers and by building a system of well-engineered roads. The Roman Empire

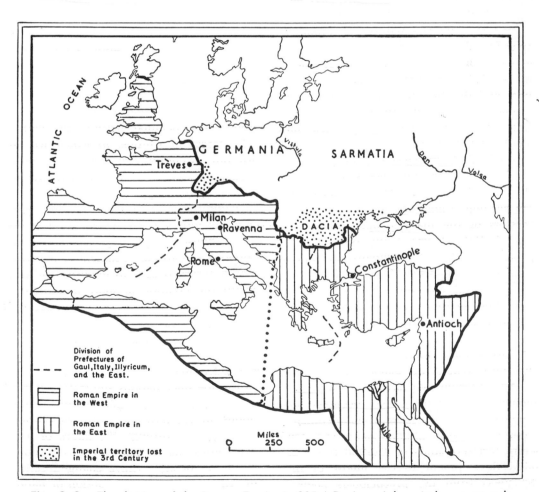

Fig. 2–2. The division of the Roman Empire in 395 A.D. Imperial capitals are named.

achieved remarkable success as a multinational state: its citizenship provided a common bond to many different peoples—Gauls, Iberians, Illyrians, Greeks, Britons, and others—and its language, the Latin of the hillmen of Latium, was widely adopted except in less accessible areas, and in the eastern basin of the Mediterranean where Greek speech maintained its cultural ascendancy. While there were many distinct peoples or nations and many forms of native speech, the several nation-groups had not, nor did they seek, separate statehood. Indeed, the political pattern of Europe in the second century was one of greater simplicity than any other of later time: there was the extensive, well-organized, and highly civilized Empire, and beyond it, in regions which were only loosely and lightly occupied, the "barbarian" world, so-called by the Greeks, not to express loathing or contempt, but because its inhabitants made in their speech "bar bar" noises unintelligible to them.

The cultural gradient between these two worlds was steep, yet they did not fail to react on each other. Finds of Roman coins as far east as the Vistula and as far north as central Sweden, point to trade relations. There were military engagements on both sides of the frontier. Barbarian peoples were, moreover, permitted at times to settle as colonists within the Empire, as were Germans, for example, in the plain of Alsace.

From the third century onward, the Empire weakened and for military and administrative convenience was divided in 395 A.D. into two parts, the eastern part being ruled by an emperor at Byzantium, renamed Constantinople (now called Istanbul), and the western by another emperor ruling from Rome or elsewhere as defense needs dictated (Fig. 2–2). The Eastern Empire, in which Greek or Hellenistic culture prevailed widely, succeeded in absorbing Slavic and other immigrants and in maintaining some semblance of imperial organization for another thousand years; known as the Byzantine Empire, it was overthrown only by the Ottoman Turks in 1453. The western half,

which included Italy, Iberia, Gaul, Britain, and North Africa, collapsed under barbarian pressure in the fifth century. It was then that the more vigorous peoples from the barbarian world took the future of Europe in their hands, and among them can be seen the forerunners of the principal nations of present Europe—notably those of the German (or Teutonic) and of the Slavic groups.

The collapse of Roman power in Western Europe opened wide the floodgates to conquering barbarian peoples who sought new homes within the Empire, in lands richer, because more effectively exploited, than their own. These movements, not just of armies but of whole peoples, are known as "the barbarian invasions of Europe" or the Völkerwanderung. Peoples of Germanic stock were the protagonists; in their wake pressed the Slavs, while there were also some intruding peoples from Asia and North Africa.

The earliest known homeland of the German people, where they had been established since the second millennium B.C., lay in the glaciated lowlands and hills between the lower Rhine and the lower Oder, the Danish peninsula and islands, and southern Sweden. For a long time stock-rearers and fishermen rather than tillers of the soil, they increased in numbers and pressed southward from their difficult environments of forest, marsh, and heath, and in the course of time comprised a number of distinct nations, more or less settled and attached to the soil by their practice of stock-rearing and shifting agriculture. One branch, the East Germans, migrated from the lower Oder across the basin of the Vistula to establish themselves on the steppe to the north of the Black Sea, whence some were allowed to settle in the lower Danubian lands of the Eastern Roman Empire and others moved westward to Italy, southern Gaul, and Spain. The other branch, the West Germans, more civilized through closer contact with the Western Roman Empire, included the Angles, Saxons, and Jutes, who colonized the English Lowlands, and the Franks, who, under

Charlemagne, re-created for a time the Roman Empire in the west and have left their name in the state of France.

The long-term effects of the barbarian invasions, conquests, and settlements were to replace the Western Roman Empire by a number of smaller states in Italy, Gaul, Iberia, Britain, and the Rhineland, while political patterns began to appear too in the broad area of Central Europe, between the Rhine and Vistula and the Baltic and Danube, which the Romans had labeled *Germania* on their maps. The history of the Franks from the fourth to the ninth century explains how, by no means inevitably, the kingdoms of the West Franks and the East Franks—to become respectively France and Germany—originated within particular territorial frames. Charlemagne's empire, formally created in 800 A.D., did not last long. In extent, it was both more and less comprehensive than the Western Roman Empire of earlier days; more because it included considerable areas beyond the Rhine, less because most of Spain and Britain, and part of Italy were not included. The partition of Charlemagne's empire among three of his grandsons, by the Treaty of Verdun in 843 A.D. (Fig. 2–3), was the most important of many such divisions of the period because it

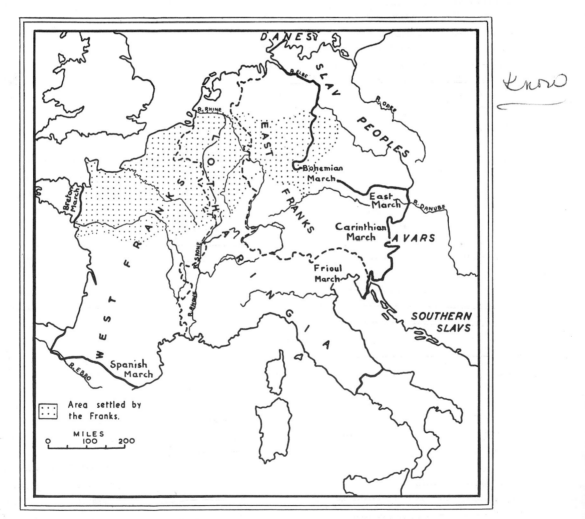

Fig. 2–3. The partition of the Carolingian Empire in 843 A.D.

had permanent effects. It outlined a kingdom, much smaller than Gaul, which was to
become France; another, east of the Rhine,
became Germany and grew greatly by eastward expansion. Between these two, a third,
elongated middle kingdom, based mainly on
the Rhine and extending from the North Sea
to the Apennines, lacked the possibilities of
political unity apart from surviving Roman
roads. It could not survive troubled times.
This territory proved indeed a bone of contention between its two neighbors right down
to the present century; it contained, too,
the "nuclear" or "core" areas for the states
now known as Switzerland, Luxembourg,
the Netherlands, and Belgium.

In the British Isles, the conquests and
settlement of the Germanic Anglo-Saxons,
Danes, and Norwegians brought political
subdivisions which, in west Britain and Ireland, included those of Celtic-speaking peoples. The newcomers established their
speech in the English Lowlands, thus effacing
the Latinized speech which developed and
persisted in most of the former imperial territories of the West. Only after yet another
conquest, by the Normans—French in speech
but Germanic in blood—was political unity
re-established at least in the most settled and
productive part of the British Isles, namely
England, the wealth of which William the
Conqueror astutely investigated by his famous Domesday Survey of 1086 A.D.

Italy suffered a succession of barbarian invaders. As in earlier and in later times, the
Alps proved defensively useless, a "splendid
traitor"; their passes served not to prevent
but only to canalize ingress into the land
which offered glittering prizes to the conqueror. Italy became a mosaic of states, including city-states, and so it still appeared
in the mid-nineteenth century, on the eve of
its unification as a kingdom under the House
of Savoy, with its base in Piedmont. In the
centuries which preceded this unification,
north Italy was largely bound politically to
trans-Alpine powers, notably the Holy Roman Empire and the Austro-Hungarian Empire; the Papal States stretched across penin-

sular Italy; south Italy and Sicily, caught in
the stream of Mediterranean sea power,
passed in part or as a whole first into Arab
and then in turn into Norman and Spanish
hands. But political disunity did not preclude the reflowering of city life—at Venice
(Venezia), Genoa (Genova), Siena, Milan
(Milano), Pisa, Florence (Firenze), Palermo,
and elsewhere—nor high attainment in the
industrial arts and in trade by land and by
sea.

The Iberian Peninsula, "Spain" as the Romans conceived it, was occupied also by
Germanic intruders: Suevi, Vandals, and
Visigoths from across the Pyrenees—and
Moslem Moors and Arabs, the former the
more numerous, from North Africa. In their
revival of classical learning, in their successful application of irrigation to agriculture,
and, above all, in their architectural legacy at
Cordoba, Granada, and Seville (Sevilla), the
Arabs have left memorials of their conquest.
But they never held permanently the northern provinces of Iberia, from which was
waged against them the Christian Crusade
which led to the establishment of the kingdom of Portugal in the thirteenth century
and that of united Spain in the fifteenth
century.

During the thousand years which followed
the fall of Rome (476 A.D.), new nations and
states emerged within the peninsular and
formerly Roman territories of Western Europe. Farther afield, in the broad lowlands
of Eastern Europe and European Russia, the
contemporaneous movements of the Slavs
have left their imprint on the map of the
nations and states of the continent. The Slav
peoples of Europe, who are conveniently
classified into eastern, western, and southern
groups, make up one-third of Europe's population and one-twelfth of mankind. The Slavs
in no sense constitute biologically a "race,"
nor indeed do they conform to a single
"ethnic type." They remain divided in religion, a result of geographical location and
orientation in medieval times. Russians,
Serbs, and Bulgarians belonged to the Greek
or Eastern Orthodox Church; Poles, Czechs,

Croats, Slovenes, and Dalmatian Slavs fell within the orbit of the Roman Catholic Church. Similarly, although it is language which provides the main bond between all the Slav peoples, the Russians, Serbs, and Bulgars have adopted the Greek Cyrillic alphabet, while others, notably the Poles, Czechs, Croats, Slovenes, and Dalmatian Slavs, use the Roman alphabet.

The original homeland of the Slavs cannot be precisely located. Tacitus, writing in 98 A.D., locates the Venedi (or certain Slavs) east of the Vistula and refers to their habit of wandering far and fast on foot, in the course of plundering forays, between East Prussia in the north and the Galician plateau in the south. As the Germans vacated Central Europe during the *Völkerwanderung* the Slavs pressed as far westward in their wake as the lower Elbe and its tributary the Saale. They also moved eastward into the mixed-forest region of the Great Russian Lowland, then lightly occupied by Finnic peoples, and southward into the Danubian and Balkan lands of the Byzantine Empire.

The economy of the early Slavs was primitive and their political organization weak. Swine rearers, hunters, and fishermen, they grew flax and hemp for clothing and for oil and gathered honey from the wild bees of the forest and made intoxicating mead from it. They had no horses or cattle, no heavy plow, no vines or grain fields. Already in the ninth century, however, they had a variety of musical instruments, including those made from marsh-grown reeds. Indeed the Slavs in their way of life clearly owed much to environmental influences; they suffered too from their geographical position in the eastern marches of Europe. Like a "soft anvil," they were exposed to the blows of two hammers which were as hard as steel: one the recurrent waves of mounted nomads from the east, and the other the German pioneers and colonists from the west.

We can only briefly indicate here the shape of the present patterns of Slavic Europe and how they were formed. The Slavs long remained an inland people, cut off from the seas by the Balts (Old Prussians), Lithuanians, Germans, and Swedes in the north; and by steppe nomads and the Byzantine Empire in the south. A broad wedge of non-Slav peoples remained within the Danube Basin: the Germans in Charlemagne's Ostmark (East March), which was to become Austria and the coreland of an empire; the Magyars, a mixed people, mounted horsemen from Asia, Finno-Ugrian in speech, who occupied the basin of Hungary toward the year 900 A.D.; and the Romanians, who developed their Latinized speech in the aloofness of their habitats in the Transylvanian Alps.

The eastward colonial movement of the Germans after the year 1000 A.D. into the lands between the Elbe and the Oder largely effaced or at least obscured the Slavs, but they have held their own in Bohemia and Moravia. Within the forested basin of the Vistula the Poles found and maintained their homeland, although the boundaries of Poland have fluctuated widely during the last thousand years. In the south, Slovenes, Serbs, and Croats have preserved their identity, now recognized in the federal structure of the Yugoslav state. Greece, although it was overrun more than once by the Slavs, resisted Slavic influences. Slavs, however, form the major element in the Bulgarian nationality, which takes its name from the Finno-Ugrian Bulgars, nomadic intruders from the steppe in the seventh century.

From the Russian forests, other Slavs—the Great Russians—ranged far afield to the White Sea, the Caspian, and, beyond the Ural Mountains, to the distant Pacific. But it was the invading Scandinavians (Varangians) of the ninth century who forged the earliest Russian states, and it was only in the fourteenth century that Muscovy, shaking off the Mongol tutelage, launched the expanding Russia which we know now as the federated Soviet Union or U.S.S.R.

Many of the patterns of the nations and states of Europe thus begin to emerge from the conquests and settlements which followed the fall of Rome. The student of particular nations and states will direct his attention to their original "nuclear" areas which are often geographically significant: the Elbe Plain of the Czechs in Bohemia, the Paris Basin of the French, and the upland plains (*polja*) of the Serbs, to cite three examples. Minor shifts of national groups and changes in the territorial content of states have been continual, and many European state patterns are of twentieth-century origin. We may note that the populations of these states are seldom strictly homogeneous; everywhere there were or are still "inliers" or "outliers" of other nationalities. These two geological terms can be usefully applied to such minority groups—the former to indicate that the groups were established before, and the latter after, the nationalities by which they are at present surrounded. Thus the Basques and Bretons form "inliers" in France, just as the Volga Germans formed an "outlier" in the U.S.S.R. In the so-called "Shatter Belt" of Eastern Europe (see Chapter 8), the distribution of nationalities is more complicated, and was much more so before World War II than now.

For many centuries before the French Revolution, when it was exceptional to believe or assert that each nation should seek separate statehood, imperial regimes attempted, not always with success, to subject different nations to a common rule. But this twentieth century, notably during World War I, witnessed the eclipse of several empires established on European soil: the Ottoman Turkish, which once reached west to include most of Hungary; the Russian; the Austro-Hungarian, which tried not ineffectively to hold together Austrians, Hungarians, Czechs, and other Slav groups of the Danube Basin; and the German, created only in 1871 by Prussian arms and statecraft. Out of the fallen empires and in pursuance of the principle of national self-determination, Poland, Czechoslovakia, Yugoslavia, Austria, Hungary, and Finland were either created or recreated. The Baltic states of Estonia, Latvia, and Lithuania won their independence for a short time but now find themselves constituent republics of the U.S.S.R. Romania, Bulgaria, and Greece have maintained the statehood which they won from the Turks with foreign aid in the nineteenth century, although there, as elsewhere in the politically unstable and ethnographically complex "Shatter Belt," boundaries have undergone much change. From one angle, the political pattern of Europe in 1969 shows a certain simplicity broadly similar to that of Roman times, with the Soviet Union and its satellites on the one hand and the "Western" states on the other.

Races and ethnic types. The European has yet to be born; European peoples abound. "A great multitude, which no man could number of all nations, and kindreds, and peoples and tongues. . . .": these words from the Book of Revelation may fittingly be applied to a continent whose human complexity is as great as its area is small. The peoples of Europe can be allocated to distinct groups on the basis of ethnic type, language, political allegiance, and in other ways. The findings of physical anthropology, archaeology, history, and linguistics help substantially to explain the present patterns, but part of the story of Europe's peoples, who during four or five millennia fashioned the habitat we now know, remains obscure.

Much has been lightly if feelingly written about the "races" of Europe, yet very little that is strictly scientific can as yet be said. "Race" implies biological relationships, especially genetic ones. If the existing peoples of Europe could be classified into clearly marked racial groups, could these groups be shown to be derived from early historical or prehistoric races? The idea of originally pure races from which present Europeans are descended has no authority in known fact. Since all the existing varieties of mankind belong to one species, and since man has always been the most adaptable and the most mobile of all animals, the quest for the geographical habitats of originally separate racial groups is a false trail. Certainly the anthropometric study of present Europeans has thrown no clear light on their genetic relationships, although physiological studies of blood groups may achieve more success.

~~It is wise therefore to turn to other aspects of the European peoples—to their ethnic types and their linguistic and national groupings—which can be discussed with more assurance and, indeed, are matters of everyday significance.~~ For it must be confessed that, while racial theories have been potent destructive agencies, the racial history of Europeans, were it ever fully revealed, would be a matter of purely academic interest. We have no grounds for believing that "race" divides the population of Europe into socially significant groups, as do languages and, above all, states.

Although the racial history and racial classification of Europeans remain obscure, it is possible to describe their ethnic characters and even to speak of specific ethnic types. The existing populations are studied as they appear, in respect to physical characteristics, such as head and nose forms, stature, hair texture and color, and eye color. Using such criteria, Deniker[4] postulated the existence and showed the broad geographical distribution of six principal ethnic groups and four subgroups. The six principal ones he called "Northern," "Eastern," "Ibero-insular," "Cevenole or Western," "Littoral," and "Adriatic or Dinaric." Later writers emphasized the prevalence of three distinct types called "Nordic," "Alpine," and "Mediterranean."

The following broad ethnic divisions have been recognized:

	Stature			
	Long Head		Broad Head	
	Tall	Short	Tall	Short
Brunette	Nordic	Mediterranean	Dinaric	Alpine
				Eastern European

[4] J. Deniker, *The Races of Man: An Outline of Anthropology and Ethnography* (New York: Charles Scribner's Sons, 1900): 325–34.

Such a classification is clearly too simple to cover the numerous varieties present even in small areas of the continent, although it points to some major contrasts of types and distributions. Indeed it is clear that the humble task of merely describing (let alone accounting for) the physical variety of Europeans has not yet been accomplished. Within any area, besides individuals of the main types, there are many others of variant subtypes, for the main types are determined in part by the personal judgment of the anthropologist and in part on the basis of average figures for the ethnic characters used as criteria; average figures in this context are no more significant than they are, for example, in climatology. The task of adequately describing the European peoples, to achieve precision, should involve estimates of the frequency with which the various types occur. Negatively, at least, it can be stated that no correlations appear between the distribution of ethnic groups and those of languages and nations.

The languages of Europe. Certainly today Europe is, for its size, the most polyglot area in the world. Although advances in the means of transportation have virtually erased physical obstacles to the intercourse of the peoples of Europe, very long periods in the past, when movement was difficult, witnessed the sharp differentiation of languages which presents today so formidable an obstacle to European unity. Philological study has established, as a generally accepted hypothesis, that most of the languages spoken from northern India to the extreme west of Europe derive from a single original language called Indo-European. Languages unrelated to this parent speech are spoken by only a small number of Europeans and have not always been established in written form. In ~~fact, these languages occur~~ rather as survivals or as intrusions within a land of Indo-European linguistic parentage. But the family relationship between the tongues has now no practical significance. All the languages of Europe differ to such an extent

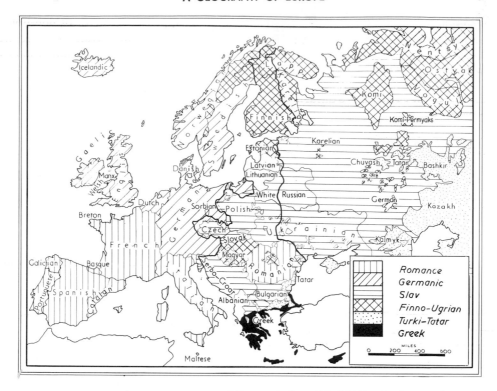

Fig. 2—4. Major linguistic patterns of Europe before World War II. Some subsequent adjustments of this pattern are referred to in the text. (After A. Meillet, modified.)

that it is rare for any two distinct languages to be mutually intelligible. This being so, and in default of any single common language—such as Latin provided for educated Europeans during the Middle Ages and the Renaissance—it is not surprising that language has served more than anything else to foster national consciousness and thus to play a great part in the political subdivision of the continent.

The languages of Europe, most of which fall within the two classifications Indo-European and Ural-Altaic, are listed below:

CLASSIFICATION OF THE LANGUAGES
OF EUROPE
(see Fig. 2–4)

A. *Indo-European*
1. Celtic (now confined to the Atlantic coastlands of the British Isles and Brittany): Irish and Scottish Gaelic, Welsh, and Breton. Also includes

Cornish (now dead) and Manx (almost dead).
2. Romance (descended from Latin): Italian, French, Walloon, Provençal, Spanish, Portuguese and Galician, Catalan, Romanian, and various Alpine languages, including Romansch and Ladin. Also the Sardinian and Dalmatian dialects of Italian.
3. Germanic (Teutonic north-European group): German (High and Low), Dutch-Flemish, Frisian, English, Danish, Norwegian, Swedish, Icelandic, and Faeroese.
4. Baltic: Latvian and Lithuanian.
5. Slavic: Great Russian, White Russian (Belorussian), Little Russian or Ukrainian (including Ruthenian), Bulgarian, Serbo-Croat, Macedonian, Slovene, Czech (including Moravian), Slovak, Polish, Sorbian (or Lusatian).
6. Hellenic: Greek.
7. Thraco-Illyrian (formerly widespread in the Balkans): Albanian.

B. *Ural-Altaic*
  1. Finno-Ugrian (which includes also many languages spoken in the Asiatic U.S.S.R.): Magyar, Finnish and Karelian, Estonian, Lapp, Mordvinian, Komi, Komi-Permyak, Udmurt, Mari, Vogul, Ostyak, Nentsy.
  2. Turkic or Turki-Tatar (mainly in Asia): Turkish (numerous outliers in the Balkan Peninsula), Kazan, Tatar, Crimean Tatar, Bashkir, Chuvash, Kalmyk, Kazakh.

C. *Semitic*
  Maltese (many Maltese also speak either English or Italian).

D. *Basque*

In Europe, as elsewhere, language is a mark of social contact and not of race. Peoples have either adopted the language of their conquerors or imposed their own language on their conquerors. The language that tended to prevail belonged to the higher material culture. The adopted tongue developed in turn regional characteristics which often became sharp enough to define a recognized language. Thus Latin, the speech of the first Romans of Latium, being the expression of the superior Roman civilization, was adopted in Western Europe, North Africa, and Danubian Europe. In the eastern Mediterranean countries, however, Greek held its own despite Roman conquests, by virtue of its high cultural tradition. In western Europe provincial Latin conditioned the growth during the Middle Ages of languages of the Romance group (Fig. 2-4): French, Provençal, Italian, Catalan, Spanish, and Portuguese. In the Swiss Alps there are still some small "islands" of Ladin and Romansch, while an "inlier" of Romance speech, containing though it does some Slavic elements, occurs in Romania, the territory of which once formed the Roman province of Dacia.

ROMANCE LANGUAGES. The distribution of Romance languages in Europe falls far short of the extent of Roman territories at their maximum. The areas from which Latin speech disappeared in favor of non-Romance languages were either frontier lands where Roman culture was less firmly established or lands where later invaders succeeded in imposing their language. Thus North Africa lost the Latin speech of its cities with the Arab conquest of the seventh to eleventh centuries, as Egypt lost its former Greek speech. Similarly, southern Britain, where Latin was widely spoken by the Romano-British population, assumed, except in Celtic-speaking Cornwall and Wales, the Germanic speech of its Anglo-Saxon conquerors. In the Balkan Peninsula, Slavic languages developed, except where Greek, Vlach, and Albanian maintained their hold. Finally, within the frontier regions of the Roman Empire, along or astride the Rhine and Danube as well as in Switzerland, the present limits of Romance speech lie well behind the former imperial limits.

GERMANIC LANGUAGES. The second large linguistic group, the Germanic, includes several distinct languages, together with others that are clearly akin. When Old German was first recorded (in some inscriptions of the third and fourth centuries A.D.), three distinct forms existed: Gothic, which has died out; Western German, which includes present-day German, Dutch, Flemish, and English; and Northern German, of which Danish, Swedish, Norwegian, and Icelandic are the chief subdivisions. The widely distributed High German dialect has become the basis of a literary language current throughout Germany, Austria, and the greater part of Switzerland, but locally there can be found variations in pronunciation and vocabulary.

English has moved far from the original Anglo-Saxon speech and has undergone much admixture, notably from Norman French, so that its relationship with modern German appears distant. More unity is apparent between the written and spoken languages of the Scandinavian world. There is still enough in common between the spoken languages of Denmark, Norway, and Sweden to permit the nationals of these countries to understand one another. Both Sweden and Denmark have written forms, different in grammar and pronunciation, which go back to the Middle Ages, while Norway employs two literary languages; one is based on Danish and the other derived from old rural Norwegian dialects (Old West Norse) very different in pronunciation from Danish. In Belgium and the Netherlands, Dutch and Flemish are two forms of Low German speech which have a common literary form: Netherlandish, more usually called Dutch.

SLAVIC LANGUAGES. The Slavic languages, which constitute the third group within the Indo-European family, still preserve more in common than do languages of the Romance and Germanic groups, since they developed slowly and retain archaic features. They began to diverge notably from the ninth century onward, and present today three major varieties. The eastern (or Russian) variety includes Great Russian, White Russian, and Little Russian. Each of these has a literary and a spoken form. Little Russian has a wide currency over an area now equated with the Ukrainian S.S.R. It has held the status of a literary language only since 1905 and is the official language of the second-most important republic of the Soviet Union. Whether spoken or written, Little Russian does not present much difficulty to compatriots of Great Russian speech. White Russian (Belorussian), spoken in the Soviet republic of that name, has little ground for separate status apart from Great Russian, which is by far the most widely used Slavic language in Europe and constitutes clearly the lingua franca of the whole U.S.S.R. The literary form of Great Russian was established in the eighteenth century, on the basis of the speech of the Moscow region.

The western Slavic languages, now represented by Polish, Czech, and Slovak, were once spoken as far west as the Elbe and its tributary the Saale. The so-called "Sorbian" or "Wendish" spoken, together with German, by over 100,000 people in Lusatia (the hill country southeast of Berlin) survives as a reminder of this former distribution. Polish

and Czech are surrounded by other Slavic languages and German, Magyar, and Lithuanian speech, but have resisted effacement; indeed, both have literatures dating back to the later Middle Ages. Czech and Slovak show spoken and written differences, although some claim they form only one language and not two.

The southern Slavic languages, separated from the western and eastern groups by peoples of German, Hungarian, and Romanian speech, are found in the broad northern part of the Balkan Peninsula between the Adriatic and the Black seas and north of the area in which Albanian, Greek, and even Turkish are spoken. Bulgarian and Serbo-Croat are the two chief languages of the southern group. Both had late medieval forms but were formalized as written languages only in the nineteenth century. In northwest Yugoslavia, Slovene is spoken by about two million people. Like Serbo-Croat, from which it does not differ greatly, it has been a written language since the later Middle Ages. In the Dalmatian coastlands, Slavic speech replaced a form of Romance speech related to Italian. So much variation occurs in Serbo-Croat and Bulgarian speech that in certain areas it is difficult to determine on any scientific principle which of these languages is being spoken; this is well illustrated in Macedonia, a frontier region of languages, where forms of Greek speech are also found.

To the Indo-European languages of the Romance, Germanic, and Slavic groups must be added Greek, Albanian, Celtic, and certain Baltic languages. The first has a limited range in the Aegean islands, the Peloponnesos, and the Greek peninsula as far north as Epirus and the coastlands of Macedonia and Thrace; modern Greek, be it noted, has changed so much since the days of ancient Greece that foreign students of classical Greek cannot take modern Greek in their stride!

Albanian, the literary form of which was established only in the second half of the nineteenth century, is the sole survivor of the Thraco-Illyrian languages once widely spoken in the Balkan Peninsula. It has borrowed much from neighboring languages in the past, especially from Latin. Two forms of Celtic survive in the west of Europe, where, at the dawn of history, this language was widely spoken. Gaelic survives in the lightly populated Scottish Highlands and Isles and provides the official language of Eire; (Brythonic) survives in Wales and Brittany. Welsh and Gaelic possess literatures and owe their survival not a little to national sentiment and stimulus. In the east-Baltic lowlands, Lithuanian and Lettish (in Latvia) are the two languages of the "Baltic" group, a third, Old Prussian, having been replaced by German in East Prussia by the sixteenth century. Lithuanian and Lettish are spoken by only a few million people. Although Lithuanian preserves the most archaic features of all the Indo-European languages of Europe, its literature dates only from the eighteenth century. Whereas Lithuanian has lost much ground over the centuries, Lettish has spread among Livonians who formerly spoke a Finnic language.

NON-INDO-EUROPEAN LANGUAGES. For the rest, the non-Indo-European languages of Europe can be noted briefly. Maltese represents a survival of Semitic speech from the days of the Arab conquest. Basque is believed, on the other hand, to have survived from the days before the settlement of peoples of Indo-European speech, for its relationship with other languages remains obscure. Before the Roman period, it was used widely in Iberia and in France south of the Garonne and west of the lower Rhone. Today it is confined to a small area athwart and west of the western Pyrenees, and even there educated people speak also either French or Spanish. Today, Basque is a factor in regional consciousness, as witnessed by the formation of a Basque republic during the Spanish civil war of 1936–38, and the provincial organization of Spain recognizes the distinctness of the Basques, the majority of whom occupy the province of Vizcaya.

VIZCAYA

FINNO-UGRIAN AND TURKIC LANGUAGES. There remain the numerous languages of the Finno-Ugrian and Turkic families, which are spoken by relatively small numbers in Europe, although over a considerable area. Finno-Ugrian is mainly represented by Magyar, which is spoken inside and outside the limits of the Hungarian republic, notably in the towns of eastern Transylvania, once a part of the Hungarian kingdom and now a part of Romania. The languages of the Finns, Karelians, and Lapps also fall within this group, as do several others still spoken in the northeast of the European U.S.S.R.: Nentsy, Ostyak, Komi, Vogul, and the rest. Indeed, as river names still testify, Finno-Ugrian speech once prevailed widely in the European area now dominated by Russian speech. Finally, the Estonian tongue, spoken by only about one million people, is Finno-Ugrian and closely related to Finnish.

The Turkic languages are spoken in European areas of the Soviet Union which are now organized as autonomous Soviet Socialist Republics, i.e., the Bashkir, Tatar (or Kazan), Chuvash, and Kalmyk. Turkic speech extends also to Eastern Thrace (European Turkey) and to the Crimean Peninsula but is spoken by only a minority of the population.

CONCLUSION. The language map of Europe thus depicts many frontiers or areas of transition through which it is possible to draw boundary lines, often only with much difficulty and rough accuracy. Although linguistic groups are often compactly located, they are seldom homogeneous, and in places appear widely scattered. In Northern, Western, Central and Mediterranean Europe they are relatively compact, but even there islands of other languages and marginal areas of mixed languages occur. In Eastern Europe, the distributions are much more complicated, although less so now than in 1938. Apart from "alien" minorities within the country and the mixture of language groups on the state margins, there are, or were until recently, many scattered "outliers." Moreover, areas of great complication occur where very many languages are spoken, and where, as a result, the mapping of the distribution of languages becomes well nigh impossible. Macedonia, now divided between Greece, Yugoslavia, and Bulgaria, represents the most striking illustration of this complexity, so that Gallic humor has coined the expression *Macédoine de fruits* to describe fruit salad.

The explanation of the language map of Europe cannot be found solely in the physical geography of the continent. It has been argued that "language areas . . . have been largely determined by the character of the surface and climate" and that "linguistic lines of cleavage . . . conform to a notable degree with physical features." [5] Only if men, like plants, had specific climatic and edaphic needs could one expect to find in physical geography a complete explanation of the language map.

Certain physical features or environments do, it is true, help to define the linguistic patterns in Europe. The lower Danube, flanked by a broad belt of marshes on its north bank, does divide Romanian from Bulgarian-speaking peoples. The boundary between French and German passes along the wooded summits of the high Vosges. The area of the Pripet Marshes separates Ukrainian and Belorussian speech. And the Pyrenees effectively separate French and Spanish. Areas of scantily settled steppe and rivers which are unnavigable upstream characterize the frontier region between Portuguese and Spanish. But, in the main, peoples and languages have negotiated physical obstacles such as mountains, rivers, highlands, and marshes. The watershed of the Alps does not neatly divide French and German from Italian; within the Alpine valleys, distinctive languages have developed in semi-isolation; neither do the eastern Pyrenees sharply divide the areas of Catalan and Provençal. As to the navigable rivers

of Europe, they commonly serve to unite rather than to divide, so that the Vistula Basin forms the homeland of Polish speech, while the Rhine Basin has become mainly Germanic, though invaded by French on its western flank. The Danube, in contrast, presents a succession of language areas astride its valley.

In lowlands and hilly country, the frontiers of language bear no obvious relationship to the relief and are clearly the expression of social forces operative long ago. Even so, former geographic features—now erased—may have been significant: thus the former Carbonnière Forest did in medieval times form a zone of separation between Flemish speech in the Scheldt Basin and French speech to the south.

In short, Europe's language map, like that of its nations and states, can be explained only in terms of historical geography, i.e., the movements of peoples, their initial settlements and subsequent colonization outward, and their mutual reactions when brought into contact with each other. By the end of the Middle Ages the language patterns were clearly outlined; one can point to specific linguistic frontiers, notably that of French and German in the Lorraine Plateau and that of Walloon and French on the Franco-Belgian border where the boundary has changed but little during the last thousand years. And, since the end of the Middle Ages, the many migrations, colonizing efforts, and compulsory and voluntary transfers of population, especially in the 1940's, have modified distributions fixed long ago.

DEMOGRAPHIC CONSIDERATIONS

Population growth, densities, and distribution. The population of Europe is estimated at nearly 600 million, that is, one-fifth of mankind, and is very unevenly distributed. The outstanding areas of high density occur in Italy and in a diagonal zone from the British lowlands and the Low Countries, in the northwest, to the Ukrainian steppe, in

[5] L. Dominian, *The Frontiers of Language and Nationality in Europe* (New York: Henry Holt & Co., Inc., 1917): 2–3.

the southeast. ~~The highest figure reached in a state area⁶ is 935 persons per square mile in the Netherlands (year 1964).~~ Notably low densities occur in northern Europe, including Fenno-Scandia and the northern lowlands of Germany, Poland, and the U.S.S.R.; in Iberia; and in the southeast-European peninsula. Apart from Iceland and the northeastern parts of the European U.S.S.R., Norway has the lowest density, 28 persons per square mile. Clearly the present densities and distribution of population, no less than the high degree of urbanization that characterizes Europe, are the result of historical changes, some of the last two centuries or less, and are the particular product of those changes connected with the increasingly effective exploitation of natural resources and opportunities.

From the dawn of history, Europe has always been one of the most densely populated areas of the world. Historians estimate the population of the Roman Empire, in its heyday, at 70 million when that of China, on the basis of its census of 156 A.D., reached an estimated 50 million. Europe contained only some of these 70 million, for some of the most populous areas of the Roman Empire lay outside its European boundaries—in Egypt, North Africa, the west coast of Asia Minor, Syria, and Palestine. Outside the Roman frontiers in Europe dwelt Celts, Germans, and Slavs, organized at first into tribes and later into nations. Their economy was so rudimentary as to support only relatively small numbers. Thus in the early Christian era, as today, Europe stood second only to Asia in population numbers, for to the numbers of Chinese must be added tens of millions of Indians and other Asians.

The distribution of population in the early centuries of the Christian era reflected the historical circumstance that progress in material culture, on which increasing numbers depended, spread from cultural centers in the east and southeast, i.e., Egypt, the

⁶ For England and Wales, part of the state territory of the United Kingdom, the 1961 census figure is approximately 815 per square mile.

Levant, Greece, and Rome. Italy was relatively populous in the Roman Empire, but it was the peninsula rather than the northern plain which then held the greater density of population. ~~Generally, southern Europe—Italy, Greece, southern Spain, and the Mediterranean islands—showed the highest~~ densities, while population grew scantier ~~farther away from the Mediterranean axis of the Empire.~~ Thus Britain, less populous than Gaul, had but an estimated one million people during its centuries as a Roman province (43 A.D. to about 400 A.D.), while Central and Eastern Europe—the so-called "barbarian" world beyond the Rhine-Danube frontiers—and still more Scandinavia, can scarcely have accounted for more than a few million.

It would appear that ~~the population of medieval Europe doubled between 1100 and 1300 A.D., fell sharply during the following century and a half, partly as a result of the Black Death, and rose to its former high~~ level by 1500. Central Italy appears to have had the densest population about the year 1300, when notable increases in density also occurred in France and the Low Countries, in northern Italy, in the English Lowlands, and, to a lesser degree, in the German-settled lands between the Rhine and the Neman (Niemen). In ~~other words, the pattern of well-populated lands had extended to the northwest since Roman times.~~ Farther east in Europe, in Bohemia, Moravia, the Vistula-Bug basin, and the forests of north and central Russia, colonization, principally by Slavs, must have led to greater though still scattered settlement and higher densities than those obtaining at the time of Rome. The Iberian Peninsula in the mid-fourteenth century appears not to have advanced in numbers since Roman times: warfare between Christian princes and Moslem conquerors, carried on in the south, may well have served to check the growth of population.

For the early eighteenth century, although official censuses were still lacking, it is possible to see rather more clearly the broad outlines of Europe's population map. For the whole continent the population is estimated to have been then about 100 or 110 million. France, the British Isles, the Low Countries, and Germany had still further increased their relative demographic standing. As compared with today, the continent was but sparsely settled, by populations for the most part rural, drawing their livelihood from agriculture but also in some areas from rural woolen industries. The highest densities reached, notably in the English Lowlands, central Lombardy, Westphalia, the Rhineland, and Saxony, were of the order of only 100 to 175 persons per square mile. Soil fertility was one important physical factor behind population densities, but not the only one. Urban concentrations were evidently related to industrial, commercial, and administrative activities, while some of the potentially best arable soils of Europe, notably the black earths of the Ukraine, the steppe soils of eastern Hungary, and those developed on the loess of Lower Silesia and Galicia, were as yet virtually unexploited.

A significant feature of the early-eighteenth-century map of population distribution is the semivacant tract which extended across the continent from the Baltic to the area between the Danube Delta and the Don. Of this sharp break in the settlement pattern between Western Christendom and Russia there are many complementary explanations: the extensive Pripet Marshes discouraged and diverted settlement; the Tatar (Mongol) invasions of the fourteenth century and many other wars had caused much destruction; the steppe lands were still subject to the mastery of the nomad; the material culture lagged far behind that of Western and Central Europe. It was in this zone that, from as early as the fourteenth century, Jews escaping from persecution in Germany and Western Europe increasingly sought refuge. They created what became known as "the Jewish Pale." The Baltic coastlands, covered widely with boulder clay and studded with small lakes, remained in 1720 very scantily populated, while in Northern Europe only the Swedish midlands (but not Scania and Småland) and the southern littoral of Finland were really populated. The upper Volga-Oka basin, where lay the old province of Moscow, and the area southward to Kiev were clearly the demographic core of Russia, although its density of population fell well below the highest figures of the time reached in Saxony, the Rhineland, the Low Countries, Italy, and England.

Attempts have been made to estimate roundly the populations of European countries in the early eighteenth century; some estimates for the years 1720, 1820, and 1930 are on page 83. Haliczer's figures[7] for the separate countries have been grouped here (1960 estimates have been added) to fit the major regions discussed later in this book. The areas of the named states, totaled for the several regions, are those of 1930. What do these round figures show? The British Isles, together with Western and Central Europe as defined in this book, although they occupy only one-seventh of the continent's area, accounted in 1720 for between two-fifths and one-half of its population. This proportion, however, fell to 36 per cent in 1968. In contrast, the European U.S.S.R. and Eastern Europe, which dominate in area (about 60 per cent), were so retarded in exploitation and settlement in 1720 as to contain less than one-third of Europe's population. This proportion markedly increased by 1968 to 46 per cent, thus exceeding that of the British Isles and Western and Central Europe, reflecting much higher fertility rates than those prevailing in the west. The least settled major division of the continent, Northern Europe maintained over the last three centuries its small proportion of the European population, namely 3-4 per cent. Southern Europe's share has decreased, from nearly one-quarter in 1720 to only about one-sixth in 1968.

[7] Josef Haliczer, "The Population of Europe, 1720, 1820, 1930," *Geography,* part 4 (December, 1934): 261–73. This article contains generalized distribution (dot) maps for the selected dates.

Estimated Populations of the Major Divisions of Europe in 1720, 1820, 1930, and 1968

Regions	Areas (thousand square miles)	Estimated Population (millions)			
		1720	1820	1930	1968
SOUTHERN EUROPE (Spain, Portugal, Italy, San Marino, Greece)	411	25	41	79	104
WESTERN EUROPE (France, Low Countries, Luxembourg)	239	22	36	59	73
BRITISH ISLES (United Kingdom, Republic of Ireland)	121	8	21	49	59
NORTHERN EUROPE (Denmark, Norway, Sweden, Iceland, Finland, Faeroes, Spitsbergen)	485	3.5	6	16	21
EUROPEAN U.S.S.R. (including Estonia, Latvia, Lithuania)	1,800	17	39	125	159[1]
EASTERN EUROPE (Poland, Czechoslovakia, Hungary, Romania, Bulgaria, Albania, Yugoslavia)	445	..	38	94	107
CENTRAL EUROPE (Germany, Switzerland, Austria, Liechtenstein)	176	18	28	75	91
EUROPE (estimates)	3,700	110	210	500	614

[1] 1966 figure.

In general, these estimates show the remarkable increase in Europe's numbers, notably during the period 1820–1968, even though net emigration was then very considerable. They also illustrate that, over the period 1720–1930, the rates of estimated increase were lowest in Western and Eastern Europe, higher in Central Europe, Northern Europe, and the "Shatter Belt," and highest in the British Isles and European U.S.S.R. Further, they draw attention to the tilting of the demographic balance toward Eastern Europe and the European U.S.S.R., where the long-delayed evaluation of natural resources has been and is still being increasingly achieved. The demographic race, it would seem, is being won—in Europe at least—by the late starters.

Emigration and migration. Some reference must be made to these dynamic aspects of Europe's population, notably during the last hundred and fifty years. There was an unparalleled exodus of population from Europe to lands overseas during this period; and there were also numerous smaller shifts of population, not always voluntary, within state territories and between states. The effects of the great outflow of Europeans

have, of course, been written indelibly into the geography of settlement and the economic development and nation-building in countries which not so long ago were either virtually empty or only scantily peopled, notably the Americas, Australia, southern Africa, and New Zealand. The internal redistributions of population within Europe after the end of the Middle Ages, although continual and numerous (and excepting those redistributions of the last 15 years), have produced only relatively minor changes in the distribution of population and of nationalities.

At least 60 million are estimated to have moved from Europe to North America and Australasia alone, during the hundred years preceding 1924. Others in smaller numbers migrated to South America, South Africa, and elsewhere.[8] Although probably more than one-third returned to Europe, the movements were clearly on a grand scale, stimulated as they were by the new steamship facilities and by the labor demands of agri-

[8] For a short account see J. S. Huxley and A. C. Haddon, *We Europeans* (London: Jonathan Cape, Ltd., 1935), Chap. 8, "Europe Overseas," by A. M. Carr-Saunders.

ture as it expanded overseas in response to growing demands for imported foodstuffs in the populous and industrial countries of Western Europe. It was the peoples of northwestern Europe,[9] with their established interest in the sea routes as avenues of commerce and/or of imperialism, who made the greatest contribution to emigration in the nineteenth century as in earlier centuries, while those of Southern and Eastern Europe and Russia dominated only during the first 15 years of this century.

Certain countries, especially Great Britain, Ireland, Italy, Germany, Spain, and Austria-Hungary, sent large numbers overseas; this fact bears on the interpretation of the differential rates of increase inferred from the summary on page 83. So also does the fact that there was a substantial outflow of Russians into their Asiatic territories (over 6 million persons moved there during the period 1901–14), where they found new lands for colonization and exploitation.

Despite Europe's long tradition of political division, no period in the continent's history has been without some movement of national groups, voluntary or enforced, from one state territory to another. While such movements were healthy in fostering economic developments, for instance, when German ironworkers, Flemish weavers, Dutch dikers, and Jewish traders applied their skill in new areas, they produced innumerable local political problems. With the growth of acute national consciousness particularly evident in this century, the presence of minorities of alien population was more and more resented in some national states.

The migration of the Germans, which was the most remarkable dispersion of people in Europe, continued long after their major colonial effort of the later Middle Ages. Between the sixteenth and the nineteenth centuries, they pressed east and southeast of Germany into the lands where less effec-

[9] The peoples of Northern and Western Europe contributed fully three-quarters to the ancestry of the population of the United States in 1920: *Ibid.,* pp. 245–46.

tively organized states either welcomed them or were unable to oppose their entry and settlement. Before World War II, German minority groups were to be found in Poland, the Baltic states, Hungary, Romania, Yugoslavia, Czechoslovakia, north Italy, south Ukraine, and the middle Volga region. The problem of the alien groups within would-be national states, characteristic particularly of the countries of Eastern Europe, was not restricted to Germans, for there were, for example, large Russian populations in Poland; Hungarian minorities in Romania, Yugoslavia, and Czechoslovakia; and Yugoslavs in the Istrian area of Italy. Wartime and postwar expedients have had marked success in effecting, either by forcible means or by voluntary action sometimes based on international engagements, many transfers of minority populations. These transfers were usually but not invariably to their national homelands. Thus, in response to national sentiment and in furtherance of the idea of the "nation state," Europe west of the Soviet Union shows closer concordance between its boundaries of states and of nationalities.

Internal migration of a different kind, leading to new patterns of population density, has been active in Britain during the last two centuries, and in much of continental Europe during the last hundred years. The Industrial Revolution and all that it entailed in industrial expansion and in new transport facilities was the major cause. The main effects were the great growth of town populations, the concentration of population in the coal fields and in other industrial districts, and the depopulation of many rural areas and of some highlands and mountain valleys, such as the Massif Central and Swiss Alpine valleys. This depopulation has been offset, in some areas, by the seasonal invasion of the holiday-maker.

THE SETTLEMENTS

The towns. The town, ranging between the extremes of the country market center and the outsize metropolitan city, characterizes as never before the settlement geography of Europe. The degree to which population is concentrated in towns shows marked regional differences. Europe contains, too, a large proportion of cities of the greatest scale: rather more than a quarter of the world's cities of more than one million inhabitants. While the traveler is impressed by the conspicuous antiquity of many European towns, he can scarcely fail to note many centers which have clearly arisen within the last hundred years as a result of the Industrial Revolution. The geographer's study of towns turns attention to many of their varied aspects: their sites, situations, and positions; their spatial growth and areal components; their population numbers; and not least their manifold functions: industrial, commercial, administrative, defensive, residential, and holiday-making—to cite only the chief ones. With these main topics in mind, let us glance at Europe's long urban history for what light it can throw on the geography of its towns today.

The town proper, in a form unambiguously urban, either as a specially organized community or as a built-up area, owed its firm establishment in Europe to ancient Greece and later to the Roman Empire. The town was indeed the hallmark of Romano-Greek culture. The Roman Empire took over many long-established towns—such as Athens (Athenai), Alexandria, and Marseille—situated around the shores of the Mediterranean; and to the Roman Empire is due the first spread of towns in Europe beyond the confines of the Mediterranean world.

Roman towns, although laid out in accordance with a plan, were very different in shape, this being largely determined by the local topography. They had a checkerboard road pattern, and were often but not invariably girdled by high walls. With only a few notable exceptions, these towns were by our standards very small. Londinium, which the Romans established as a port and bridging place at the head of the Thames estuary, occupied only half a square mile although

it was the largest town in Britain and the equivalent of large continental cities such as Cologne (Köln) and Mainz. Most towns were much smaller; only a few, notably the imperial capitals of Rome (Roma), Constantinople (Istanbul), and Lyons (Lyon), the capital of Gaul, stood well above the rest. Roman towns enjoyed amenities such as piped water and heated houses; their industries and trade were normally limited. Some urban settlements were roadside stations rather than producing centers, or watering places like Wiesbaden in Germany and Bath in England. Others were ports such as Ostia, the port for Rome, and Marseille, first founded by Greek colonists as early as the sixth century B.C. There were also the prototypes of the later Calais and Boulogne, controlling the passage of the English Channel.

A number of historic towns in Western and Mediterranean Europe occupy sites on or near former Roman towns: we may note here Milan (Milano), Naples (Napoli), Lyon, Bordeaux, Coblenz, St. Albans, Lincoln, Canterbury, Vienna (Wien), Belgrade (Beograd), Sofia (Sofiya), Niš, Dubrovnik, Split, and Thessaloniki (Salonika). The continuity of such towns as organized societies from Roman times onward cannot often be demonstrated, although this may fairly be claimed for some at least of the cities of the Eastern Roman Empire, Italy, and Gaul. Often, as in Britain, there was a marked hiatus in urban life, due to the destruction and disorganization which followed the collapse of Roman power in the west. Immigrant conquerors and settlers, either nomadic or essentially agricultural in their economy and unable for some time to establish peace and security over wide areas, had little use for towns, which were reborn later under more favorable conditions and in response to specific social needs. The newcomers were at first content to occupy but a small corner of a Roman town site, plundering its ruined buildings for stone and tiles with which to build their churches, as at Nîmes and Autun in Gaul. At some particular cities, such as Vienna, Belgrade, and Regensburg, it is of much interest to discover that Christian churches were built on the sites of Roman temples and that Roman street patterns survived into later times. In other cities, like London, the Roman street pattern did not survive and the Roman occupation level lies buried a few yards below the present surface.

As the Dark Ages passed into the later Middle Ages, and as growing populations won new areas for the plow, towns on new as well as old sites gradually have come clearly into view. Vigorous industrial and mercantile societies, striving to achieve legal privileges from the Crown or from lay or ecclesiastical lords, formed trade associations and established civic self-government. The distinguishing marks of these towns were a charter, a market, and a wall.

We can only hint here at the origin and rise of towns in the different parts of Europe and note that they greatly increased in economic stature, particularly in the thirteenth century. It was as places of industry and trade that they made their mark in an age when power was largely attached to the ownership of land. Site and positional factors help to explain why the urban settlement came into being and why it grew: towns commonly arose, for example, at bridging and navigable points on tidal rivers. An important social and economic factor in the siting and growth of cities was often provided by a royal residence, a monastic foundation, a bishop's palace, or a feudal castle.

A remarkable phase of town building is attested in Belgium and the Netherlands from the eleventh to the thirteenth century. Many towns, often laid out carefully to a plan, arose there for the first time under the protection of a seignorial castle or a religious foundation often, as at Brugge (Bruges), on a navigable river, or along a dike. In northern France a number of towns—Troyes on the Seine, Châlons-sur-Marne, Bar-sur-Aube —flourished during the twelfth and thirteenth centuries because their fairs drew foreign merchants by overland routes from as far

afield as Italy, Egypt, Syria, and Persia. With the opening (in 1317) of the sea route from Italy to the English Channel, such fairs as those of Brugge, Ghent, and Antwerp in Flanders took over the functions of these French fairs as entrepôts for a wide range of commodities of diverse origin.

The deliberate foundation of towns by royal or seignorial authorities, often for defensive purposes, accounts for other settlements, many of which failed to survive as such through lack of economic sinews. Winchelsea and Kingston-upon-Hull in England were thus founded by King Edward I (about 1300 A.D.), while in south France the so-called *bastide* towns (Villeneuve-sur-Lot is one) were laid out on a geometric plan in the thirteenth and fourteenth centuries. In south Germany the important regional capital of Munich (München) was a twelfth-century addition to a number of towns, such as Augsburg, which were originally of Roman foundation. Farther away, on the Great Russian Lowland, many of the fortified centers (*goroda*) of the Slavs grew into towns in the tenth century thanks to the political and mercantile energy of intruding Scandinavians.

Although certain periods stand out in the urban history of Europe, notably the later Middle Ages and the last two centuries, new towns were arising here and there at all times: one may note, as examples, the Channel port of Le Havre and the ducal capital of Mannheim in the Rhineland, respectively of seventeenth- and eighteenth-century origin. Madrid was a creation of the sixteenth century, succeeding as capital of a united Spain the old Castilian capital of Toledo.

To the colonizing efforts of the Germans, notably in the four centuries after 900 A.D., was due the basic distribution of towns in central and even east-central Europe. Sites already occupied by Slavs as local regional (or *gau*) centers or as fishing settlements were often selected, and some German place names with Slav suffixes such as *in* and *zig* (e.g., Berlin and Leipzig) recall this association. The new German towns east of the

Rhine were distributed differentially within the physically contrasted zones of north-central Europe. Some were established along the North Sea and Baltic coasts at estuary heads, as Hamburg and Bremen; at the heads of bays, as Lübeck and Danzig (Gdansk); or in the shelter of lagoons, as Königsberg (Kaliningrad). Inland there were relatively few towns within the desolate heaths, woods, and marshes of the Baltic heights, except where major rivers, such as the Elbe and Oder, cut gaps through the hills, on their way northward. In the depressed and ill-drained zone farther south, some towns grew up on west-east river routes —Brandenburg on the Havel, Berlin on the Spree, Poznań (Posen) on the Warta among them. It was within the loess-covered foothill belt where the northern plains approach the Hercynian mountains that town development (and settlement generally) was most marked in a zone of natural west-east communication: Dortmund, Magdeburg, Hanover (Hannover), Brunswick (Braunschweig), Leipzig, and Cracow (Kraków) were among the towns founded in this physically favored countryside.

Most of the towns of Central Europe in the later Middle Ages were in size comparable to the nucleated villages of today. Their function was to serve peasants making their way on foot, within a radius of 6–13 miles. But a small proportion of these towns, well placed on land and water routes, like some of the cities of the Hanseatic League, throve remarkably in the last centuries of the Middle Ages as ports and trading places with widespread relationships.

Early engraved plans of European towns have much to tell about the expansion of medieval towns as new areas were built up and enclosed by walls. Figures 2–5 to 2–8 show how four important towns of today appeared in the sixteenth century. They emphasize how small were even capital cities like Paris and Moscow (Moskva). And although the old town walls, elaborately strengthened in the sixteenth and seventeenth centuries to withstand cannon fire, have usually disappeared to provide space for boulevards and buildings, and few medieval buildings have survived, the old sites, as depicted in such plans, provided the nuclei around which European towns have

Fig. 2–5. Paris in the sixteenth century.

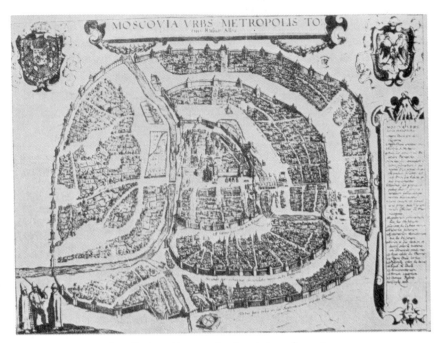

Fig. 2–6. Moscow in the sixteenth century.

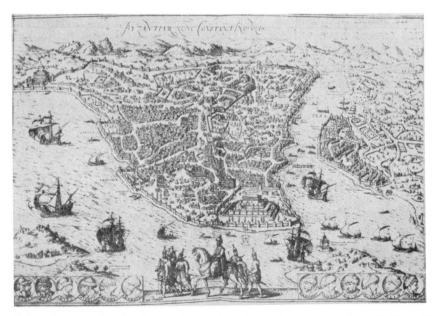

Fig. 2–7. Constantinople (Istanbul) in the sixteenth century. The Golden Horn, between the city and Pera, provided a sheltered harbor.

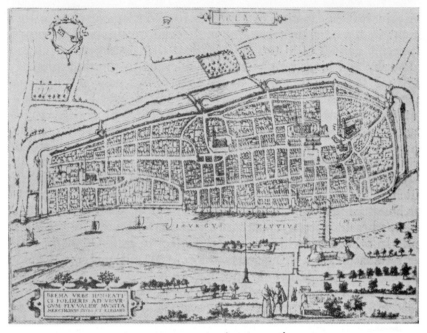

Fig. 2–8. Bremen in the sixteenth century.

so widely grown, especially during the last hundred years.

In present Europe the phenomenon of the "giant" city calls for explanation. This is essentially a modern development related to the increasing population numbers and transport facilities of the nineteenth and twentieth centuries. In 1700 Europe had only 13 or 14 large towns, nearly all capital cities. London, with a population of 959,-000, was the largest city in Europe in 1801, and only some 19 others, with about 100,000 or more, could then be accounted as of first magnitude. Chief of these were Paris and Constantinople (Istanbul) each with a population of about a half million. Some of the largest cities of today are merely those of 1800 grown in size; London, Berlin, Paris, Moscow, Leningrad, Vienna, Istanbul, and Marseille are well-known examples. Other large cities owe their stature to a development, often hand in hand with that of industry, only during the last hundred years or less. Some examples will clarify this point:

Population of Some Selected Towns of Europe—1800–1966

	1800	1850	1880	1920	1966
Essen	4,000	9,000	57,000	439,000	716,000
Duisburg	—	—	41,000	244,000	478,000
Düsseldorf	10,000	27,000	95,000	407,000	697,000
Munich	30,000	110,000	230,000	631,000	1,236,000
Rotterdam	53,000	90,000	148,000	511,000	723,000
Budapest [1]	54,000	178,000	371,000	926,000	1,969,000
Odessa	6,000	90,000 [2]	194,000	421,000 [3]	753,000
Belfast	40,000	87,000	208,000	387,000	399,000
Cardiff	2,000	20,000	83,000	200,000	289,000
Birmingham ..	71,000	242,000	437,000	919,000	1,102,000

[1] Until 1880 Buda and Pest were separately organized cities.   [2] 1858.   [3] 1926.

Clearly, behind the population figures for such towns lies an interesting chapter of civic history.

The rural settlements. Not the least striking of the marks which social groups have written on the European landscape throughout history are the varieties of rural settlement which visibly symbolize man's appropriation, adaptation, and use of the land. Not merely have these elements of the European countryside their own intrinsic interest but, in their varying forms and with their associated economies, they also help to create different landscape patterns. Basically different patterns of settlement are found in "champaign," or *champagne,* and "enclosed," or *bocage,* countryside, as they were traditionally described in England and France. One is characterized by large nucleated villages surrounded by unhedged arable fields in a largely treeless plain; the other by numerous small settlements—homesteads and hamlets—with small fields enclosed by quickset hedges or dikes, dispersed over a country generally wooded in aspect (see Fig. 8–9, page 452).

Rural settlements today are the outcome of many successive phases of colonial activity and of changes in agricultural practice. Some settlements were spontaneous and some were planned; some of the stages are old and relatively obscure, while others, notably those since the Agricultural Revolution of the eighteenth century, can be more clearly seen. The geographer's main task is to show the broad distribution of the settlement types and, looking behind the existing patterns, to attempt to explain their origin.

While it would seem that the principal explanation of Europe's rural-settlement map is to be sought in the agrarian technique and social organization of peoples at specific periods of history, it is evident that conditions of physical geography and biogeography are also relevant to the discussion.

Rural settlements appear in prehistory and may in some areas have fixed the sites of modern villages,[10] but it is to historical times that the student largely turns for the explanation of the contemporary map. Although the attribution of the communally organized open-field village with its surrounding unenclosed fields to Germanic influence cannot be accepted as generally and exclusively true, it is nevertheless clear that these features are revealed during the centuries which followed Germanic immigration and colonization in parts of northwestern Europe, notably in the English Lowlands, northern and northeastern France, southern Belgium, Lorraine, and the Rhineland. In other areas which were also subject to early Germanic settlement, such as Kent (England) and central and southern Gaul, as well as in countries not so affected, such as Wales and Brittany, settlements of the hamlet and homestead types, with early enclosed fields and *bocage* aspect, became prevalent. Indeed, in some places either Roman or pre-Roman Celtic settlements and agrarian systems survived as an element in shaping the countryside, despite German conquest and settlement. Certain settlement patterns and field systems also developed independently of influence from outside, for example, the communally organized villages and fields of Sardinia.

But if the photographic plate of Europe's rural-settlement map begins to "develop" during the Dark Ages, which followed the barbarian invasions of Europe, it clarifies and sharpens as further colonization of the later Middle Ages and of the last two centuries goes on. New branches are grafted onto the trunk of primary settlement as population grows and mastery is won over hitherto undeveloped areas of forest, marsh, moor, and steppe. Numerous marsh and forest villages are created by freeholding peasants and commonly set out in linear form along a

[10] A. Demangeon draws attention to the existence of Celtic villages in Roman Gaul and claims for these villages a Neolithic origin. See his *Géographie Économique et Humaine de la France* (Paris: Armand Colin, 1946), Vol. I, p. 187.

dike, a stream, or a road, with individual holdings running back at right angles to the village axis. At the same time colonization by single homesteads is also made, as in the drained polder lands of the Low Countries and in the woodlands of the English Weald. The increase in population in Western Europe, especially between the eleventh and thirteenth centuries, leads to the creation of many "daughter" settlements, i.e., homesteads or hamlets beyond the fields of the parent village. Some such settlements arise from "free lance" action, others—and this was the more usual reason—by the organized efforts of secular, ecclesiastical, and monastic landowners intent on the better exploitation of their lands. The new villages assumed many different forms.[11]

At a much later date, the Agricultural Revolution of the eighteenth century, which brought new possibilities of enhanced productivity from lands enclosed under individual ownership, became the cause of much new dispersed settlement, as tenants moved out from existing villages. The steppe lands of southeastern Europe, notably in the Ukraine and eastern Hungary, began in the second half of the eighteenth century to be transformed from an environment of seminomadic pastoral husbandry to one of settled villages, with cultivation as the basis of their mixed farming. As transportation facilities improved during the last two centuries, wealth won by urban dwellers in industry and commerce has also often been used to modify the rural landscape through building of large country houses and the creation of gardens and parks.

The student of rural settlement in Europe should thus be much concerned with the history behind geography. This is true whether he confines his attention to any one country or, indeed, to part of one country. France still shows striking contrasts, clearly observed by Arthur Young [12] during the years 1787–89, between the *champagne* of large hedgeless villages in the north, the *bocage* of smaller dispersed settlements of the west and center, and the mixed, once mainly nucleated, settlement of its Mediterranean south. Britain, too, shows such contrasts of landscape types and complicated patterns of settlement woven throughout history. The county of Pembroke in Wales, for example, as a result of Anglo-Norman colonization, contains old nucleated villages with fields now enclosed in its southern lowland, and the older dispersed Welsh settlements in its higher northern parts. Certainly many settlement types have established themselves without strict regard to physical geography. In the waterless limestone plateau of Causses as in neighboring well-watered parts of the Massif Central, dispersed settlements prevail alike; in the Pays de Caux, despite broadly uniform physical conditions, settlements are dispersed in the west and concentrated in the east. Yet in the more detailed study of the sites, distribution, and frequency of villages, correlations with physical conditions are often evident enough: for example, the alignment of villages along the scarp-foot and dip-slope edge of limestone plateaus, along the terraces of rivers, or on dry island sites in former fenland.

A workmanlike guide to the rural-settlement map of Europe is provided by Demangeon's genetic classification of settlement types.[13] This provides no easy key, since it assumes much knowledge of rural history. Settlements as they now appear may have changed drastically in form, even in recent times: witness how in Denmark, in the Channel Islands, and in many parts of Ireland [14] and Scotland present dispersed settlements

---

[11] See R. E. Dickinson, "Rural Settlements in the German Lands," *Annals of the Association of American Geographers* 39 (December, 1949), pp. 239–63, for a discussion and illustrations.

[12] Arthur Young, *Travels in France During the Years 1787, 1788, 1789* (2 vols.; Bury St. Edmunds, 1794).

[13] Albert Demangeon, *Problèmes de Géographie Humaine* (3d ed.; Paris: Armand Colin, 1947): 185–202.

[14] E. Estyn Evans, *Irish Heritage* (Dundalk, Eire: Dundalgan Press, 1942): p. 48.

replaced nucleated villages in the course of the nineteenth century.

Among nucleated villages Demangeon distinguishes three types on the basis of their origin. First, the communally organized "open-field village" which appears widely established in Western and Central Europe from the Dark Ages onward, although it is claimed that some originated in the clearings and settlements of Neolithic times. The dwellings of a nucleated village grew up around some or all of the following features: church, manor house, inn, bridge, spring or well, pond, and mill; only from this central area could the villagers have convenient access to their scattered holdings in the village fields. These lay open around the village and were cut into strips; its meadow and pastoral waste were communally used. The communal organization lasted on into the nineteenth century; the scattered strips have been by now mostly consolidated into compact units, but only exceptionally, as in England, have they been fully enclosed. This farming was proudly acclaimed in the eighteenth century as *la grande culture,* for the open-field system was operated on some of the richest soils of the continent, notably those which overlie the loess, although it included, too, some mountain valleys and heavy-clay lands.

The second type is the "village with contiguous fields." To this category belong the linear villages created in forest clearings and drained marshes in the later Middle Ages; from their origin, the lands adjacent to the village were divided into individually owned holdings. Such villages are found in the Low Countries and northwest Germany and in many forest clearings of the Hercynian highlands, for example, in the Black Forest and the Bohemian Forest.

The third type, the "village with dissociated fields," is best represented in Mediterranean Europe, where very large compact settlements perched on high sites, originally chosen in part at least for reasons of defense, stand aloof and distant from their fields, as indeed from their supplies of water. This settlement type is found in association with large estates in south Italy.

Similarly, four kinds of dispersed settlement can be distinguished. The first kind, the so-called "primary dispersion," was effected long ago. It is believed that much of the dispersed settlement of the Massif Central, Cornwall, and Wales is of this type, as well as that of Norway, the language of which has no word for "village." The second is "intercalated dispersion," which refers to dispersed settlement made subsequently to nucleated settlement, by a process of "filiation" from existing villages as organized clearance of the waste took place. The fifteenth century witnessed much settlement of this kind in France as feudal lords and monastic houses conceded to peasants parts of their demesne. The third kind of dispersed settlement, "secondary dispersion," takes place when, for reasons of agricultural convenience, peasants move out from their village and settle by their lands; the *tanyas* of Hungary and the *bastides* of Provence resulted from such secondary dispersion. Much of the settlement pattern of England is of this type, following the enclosure of the common fields, between the fifteenth and nineteenth centuries. Lastly, the "primary dispersion of recent date" can often be easily noted. From the nineteenth century onward, better transport facilities and superior water control and water supply permitted widespread dispersion of dwellings.

THE ECONOMY, INCLUDING CIRCULATION

The economy of Europe, in all its regional variations and in its diverse visible features has its roots in the distant past, although the effects of the last hundred years stand out with particular clarity. The student's interest in the economic geography of Europe is rightly directed to the maps of its agriculture, its forests, its mines, its industrial concentrations, its transport patterns, and its seaports, which together show the effects on the face of the land of a concerted effort to exploit what nature has provided.

The peculiar features of contemporary European economy—and notably its interregional and international trade relations—are discussed later in this book (Chapter 10). It is enough here to note its five broad characteristics. First, the industrial and commercial importance in the world of Western and Central Europe, based on the application of a large and skilled labor force to available natural resources in an area geographically well placed for, and historically conditioned to, oceanic commerce. Second, the continuing importance of agriculture throughout the whole continent and its higher relative importance in the broadening lowlands of Eastern Europe and the European U.S.S.R. Third, the well-developed railroad network, notably in Western and Central Europe, and the continent's many major seaports related to the routes of world trade. Fourth, the economic contrast between Western and Central Europe on one hand and the remaining greater part of the continent on the other, where industrialization in its modern forms came later and had a more restricted place. Lastly, the political dichotomy between East and West, which has sharpened since the end of World War II and clearly has its economic aspect. In the brief discussion which follows, the reader is invited to consider a little of the history which lies behind Europe's present economic map. For "what is" has sprung from "what was."

Agriculture. European agriculture was indeed, in Neolithic days, a very different thing from what it has now become. Long subordinate to stock raising, carried on in small temporary fields, on light shallow soils with the aid of a digging stick or hoe, and in a setting dominated by forest, the earliest agriculture lay technologically remote from modern forms with large permanent fields, tractors, selected seeds, fertilizers, and heavy farm machinery. Yet, technological progress

apart, and despite regional specializatic manufacturing industry and in mineral ploitation, Europe remains almost ever where an area of agricultural productivity. It absorbs in agriculture the greater part of its labor force. European agricultural economy shows little of that broad standardization which characterizes large areas of North America where terms like "cotton belt" and "corn belt" introduce the student gently into the complications of agricultural geography. On the contrary, Europe's agriculture presents great regional and local variety in response to physical conditions of climate, soil, slope, and other landform aspects, and to the differential energy and enterprise with which they have been used. In the size and organization of the farm unit, in the range and yield of crops, in the degree of "mixed farming," in the application of capital and mechanization, in the use of irrigation and of artificial fertilizers, in the emphasis on farming for subsistence or for "cash crops," in the manpower required per acre, and in the output per man-hour obtained—in all these and in other ways European agriculture is diversified. But thanks to this diversity and thanks, too, to much intensity of farming, especially in Western and Central Europe, the continent produces most of its food, leads the world in the production of wheat, and grows a wide range of other cereal crops including even rice. It also produces some specialized products like olive oil, wine, and essential oils; vegetable fibers like flax and hemp, though only a trifling amount of cotton; a wide range of fruits, including citrus; and much cattle fodder, sugar beet, and tobacco.

We may glance at two important background facts to the present-day agriculture in Europe. First, it represents the culmination of an age-long struggle to tame an environment little suited in its primitive state to large-scale agricultural development. The tillage of European soil results from prolonged and hard efforts which were devoted to forest clearance, marsh drainage, and soil improvement. Second, since it reflects the outcome of much scientific and technological progress, we should not ignore that outstanding phase of reorganization and improvement which is summed up as the Agricultural Revolution. This was effective at different times in different parts of the continent, between the seventeenth and the nineteenth centuries.

"The country . . . either bristles with woods or festers with swamps": this is how Tacitus described Central Europe in 98 A.D., through which, from the middle Rhine to the Carpathians, stretched the "Hercynian Forest," as Caesar named it. The German peoples at first had no inclination to destroy the forests which harbored their divinities and protected their settled islands of farmland. Nor were the Slav and Hungarian peoples to the east, and the Scandinavian peoples to the north, inclined to pit their strength against the vast permanent woods which encompassed them and were useful in providing them with game, timber, fuel, honey, wax, and some marginal rough grazing. When the Germanic peoples had possessed themselves of and settled in former imperial lands, their energies were turned first to the recovery of cultivated fields which had been wasted and abandoned. Only later was the pioneer clearing of forested land undertaken, although in England Anglo-Saxons and Danes were quick to launch fresh attacks on the woodlands.

The reign of Charlemagne (768–814 A.D.), however, witnessed the felling of great stretches of primeval woodland, notably on both sides of the middle and lower Rhine, in the Main Valley, and in Hesse. More land was needed for settlement, for stock raising, and for agriculture. In later centuries, as the Germans pushed eastward their conquests and colonization under the leadership of Church and State, forest clearance was made in scale and is recalled by many of the names of their settlements, notably those containing the elements *-rode, -reud, -ried, -rath, -rade, -brand, -hain, -schwend,* and *-grün.* The later centuries of the Middle Ages witnessed much forest clearance in France, and Germans and Flemings were called into Hungary to fell trees in Transylvania. Some woodlands disappeared by "assarting," i.e., by clearings made around existing settlements. But great stretches of hunting country, much of it wooded, were carefully preserved by law to gratify the hunting tastes of emperors, kings, and lords. Forest clearance was not wholly deliberate—witness the destructiveness of goats grazing the rugged hills of the Mediterranean countries; sometimes the first cutting led to soil erosion and further destruction of woods, as in the Dauphiné province of France in the western Alps. Nor was forest clearance wholly due to agriculture, a fact attested to by the inroads made by seafaring peoples of the Mediterranean Basin and by iron smelters, using charcoal for fuel, in such areas as the Harz, the Weald of England, and the Ural Mountains of Russia.

The clearance of the forests, together with the reclamation of marshland, heath, and bog land, the drainage of lakes, and the plowing up of the steppe—all contributed to the increase of the agricultural area. The increase of the arable area in response to the growth of population must have been continual. Figures available in the nineteenth century show the rapid increase, from 364 to 546 million acres between 1820 and 1880.

These changes markedly altered the face of the country. They produced too, notably in Western and Central Europe, a shortage of timber, which in turn led to efforts to reforest suitable unused areas. By the Railway Age there were only a few countries, notably Norway, Sweden, and Russia, which could offer timber for export. In Norway and Sweden, as in many other countries, forests are now "cropped," i.e., the annual cut is equated to annual replacement. Reforestation has meant much change in the character of such woodlands. Thus, in Germany, quickly growing conifers now dominate in forested areas where formerly deciduous species, useful for grazing as well as timber, held sway.

In addition to the clearing of woodlands, the reclamation of marshland and sea-invaded lowland, and the drainage of lakes have contributed to the agricultural area of Europe. Hollanders and Flemings, with the encouragement of their counts, lords, bishops, and monastic foundations, took the lead in the attempt to make profitable the lands lying near or just below the high-tide water level. In the late Roman period the sea invaded coastal Flanders (where a layer of marine silt covers the Roman occupation level) and submerged large parts of Roman-occupied Holland and Zeeland, where large artificial mounds—*terpen* or *werden*—had been built to provide dry points for settlements.

The drainage of parts of maritime Flanders, Zeeland, and Holland and their settlement by a free and independent peasantry began early and was going on vigorously in the eleventh century. Further invasions by the sea during periods of high tides or violent storms in the later Middle Ages only intensified the struggle of the Dutch against the sea. Hollanders and Flemings carried their skill into marshlands beyond their own countries—to the English Fenlands and to the estuarine lowlands of the Weser, Elbe, Oder, and Vistula. Cities and monastic houses in the north Italian plain similarly started in the twelfth century to drain the marshes which had formed largely through neglect of former Roman measures of water control. Nowadays, along the coasts and rivers of the Low Countries, the "polders," as the drained and diked lowlands are called, are held safe for dairy cattle and crops with the aid of steam and electric pumps, which have largely replaced the traditional windmills. In recent decades part of the Zuider Zee has been reclaimed, and its remainder, enclosed by a sea wall, has become the freshwater Ijsselmeer. The largest surviving ill-drained tract of the continent—a relic of the Great Ice Age—lies in the Pripet Marshes of the Belorussian S.S.R.; the Soviet government is by stages effecting their reclamation. Present-day European agriculture owes to the past the expansion of its area of field, pasture, and meadow; it owes to the past, also, the major changes in agrarian organization and the applications of modern science and technique. The Mediterranean lands of the Roman Empire were the first to lead in the art of agriculture, and, despite the shrinking of the agricultural area and the falling off in agricultural practice during the Dark Ages, Roman traditions largely survived, supplemented by Arab innovations—themselves in part based on Roman models—to inform the farming of Western and Central Europe. Within the Roman Empire the "two-course rotation," that is, the autumn sowing of either wheat or barley followed by fallowing, was developed to meet the need, under the Mediterranean climate, of "dry farming." Great care was taken by successive plowings of the topsoil of the fallow field to retain moisture for the following crop. To supplement the hoe, the farmers of the Empire used the *aratrum,* a light, wheel-less plow, with or without a colter, although the *caruca,* a wheeled plow which was better adapted to heavy soils, appears to have been invented then in north Italy. Roman agriculture knew, and in some measure grew, fodder crops such as vetch, lucerne, alfalfa, and chick-pea, so valuable for winter feed, while the value of enriching land by the application of stable manure, pigeon dung, wood ash, and vegetable compost was also well understood. The practice of transhumance, effected by the seasonal movement of sheep between high- and low-level pastures was well established in the Mediterranean lands of the Empire. Nor should we forget the remarkable success achieved by the Romans in irrigation and in the cultivation of the vine, the olive, and other fruit-bearing trees.

Western and Central Europe largely inherited these legacies but made their own modifications to suit the very different conditions of climate and landforms. It was a striking advance when tillage for crops superseded cattle raising as the dominant feature of the economy of the Germanic settlers in the west. It was not less striking when regular crop rotations, adapted to two or three fields, took the place of the former temporary cropping of burnt-over ground. The Roman *aratrum* long prevailed in use, although the *caruca*, much better suited to the northern lowlands and drawn by horses instead of oxen, was increasingly used at the end of the Middle Ages. Marling (i.e., liming) of arable fields was an important northern practice, although limited by transport deficiencies to areas with easy access to supplies of chalk. But with all its success in expanding the agricultural area and the supply of food and raw materials (wool, flax, etc.), agriculture in Western Europe became in many respects inefficient and resistant to progressive change. What has been called "the Agricultural Revolution of the eighteenth century" was necessary to provide the possibility and means of advance. And, even then, Eastern and parts of Mediterranean Europe were little affected: organization and practice there have only changed substantially during the last hundred years.

It is not surprising, geographically, that many of the ideas of the new husbandry were derived from north Italy and the Low Countries. That these areas, and in particular Lombardy and Flanders, led in agricultural efficiency was due not so much to physical advantages—although soil and climate were broadly favorable—as to the economic stimulus long exerted on the surrounding countryside by numerous rich and populous cities. The Agricultural Revolution was most marked in England and parts of northern France. It largely brought to an end the old communally organized fields and pastures of the open-field system, and it led to some consolidation of the strip holdings in the fields and, notably in England, to much new enclosure of fields by hedgerows, walls, and ditches. Individual ownership or holding of farmland brought new initiatives and techniques. It became possible to abolish the fallow field by scientific rotations and, at the same time, to grow winter fodder (roots and clover) for livestock. Especially in England, capital was increasingly applied

to agriculture for the production of more grain and meat. Transport by road, river, and canal was much improved. Poor soils were found to be not always useless: by heavy manuring, for example, the sands of central Belgium have become little distinguishable from the intrinsically richer marine clays farther north. By scientific stock breeding cattle doubled and sheep trebled in weight in the course of a century. The pressure of population, much of which was engaged in industry, was the economic stimulus behind the Agricultural Revolution.

The Americas made their contribution of plants which have now become long-established staples in Europe. Chief among these were the potato, corn (maize), and tobacco. The potato was first grown in gardens and later became a field crop. Although at first regarded by peasants as fodder rather than as human food, it became also a foodstuff of great importance, above all in Ireland, and was well adapted to the north-European lowlands. The sugar beet is a nineteenth-century innovation, the cultivation of which has been deliberately favored by European governments in order to secure their independence of seaborne supplies of cane sugar in time of war. By the middle of the last century it was being grown in northern France, Belgium, and throughout the loess belt of Germany, Bohemia, Moravia, Hungary, and the southern-European U.S.S.R.

We may conclude this brief sketch of the antecedents of present European agriculture by noting how agrarian changes, designed above all to break up large estates for peasant holdings, occurred in Eastern Europe (except in Hungary) after World War I. The establishment of "collective farming" in the U.S.S.R. brought radical changes, including mechanization, to the Soviet countryside. In some measure this system has been introduced into the Soviet satellite countries of Eastern Europe, following the breakup of surviving large estates.

Industry. The numerous industries of Europe may be distinguished into two groups: the extractive and the manufacturing. The extractive industries include mining and quarrying, fishing and whaling, and lumbering, the localization of all being determined by the facts of economic geology or geography. To this category of industries should doubtless be added industrial developments of this century, such as the generation of hydroelectric power and the extraction of nitrogen from the air. The manufacturing industries are legion, and, in so far as in most of them goods are made by machines rather than by hand, the term might appear literally misleading. On the one hand are a wide range of light industries, including luxury industries, where the skill of the craftsman is still all-important: French wines, Parisian gowns, Harris tweeds, Belgian lace, and German wooden toys, to name a few. On the other hand are those major industries on which modern industrialized states depend, where power-driven machinery is essential and large-scale plant usual—industries such as steel making, heavy chemicals, engineering, and shipbuilding.

Industry in Europe is no new phenomenon. In the Middle Ages there were already both urban and rural areas where industry played a dominant part in economy—for example, Flanders, with its many cities engaged in making woolen and linen textiles; the Harz; the Thuringian Forest and Siegerland, with their iron mines and smelters; and the English West Country, with its worsted manufacture based on the supply of water and of water power from its streams. The novelty resides in the fact that modern industry, using power-driven machinery, much capital, and a large labor force, is operated on a grand scale usually in and around towns and tends to group itself geographically within specific areas. In many parts of Europe today "industrial belts" must engage the interest of the student of geography.

The reasons for this localization spring from considerations of many kinds. The presence of local supplies of fuel and power —especially coal and hydroelectricity—is often the main explanation. The occurrence of either mineral ores or coal seams, in surface out-crops or at accessible levels below the surface, no less clearly explains the localization of mines and quarries and of related industries. The outsize towns like London, Berlin, Milan, Vienna, Paris, Moscow, and Leningrad are big industrial regions for quite different reasons. They provide ample labor, large markets, good transport facilities, and can with ease utilize electrical energy. Some industrial areas find their explanation in history, and their continued importance illustrates what can be best termed "historical momentum." Thus Lancashire, favored by the abundant soft water and supplies of wool from the Pennine moorlands, was traditionally engaged in the manufacture of linen and woolen textiles. But, following a start made in the seventeenth century, it has become a specialized area for cotton textiles, using American cotton imported via Liverpool, and steam-powered machinery. In contrast, other areas which were famous in the past for particular products failed to compete successfully when coal replaced water for motive power and charcoal for fuel. This happened, for example, to the English West Country, where the manufacture of Witney blankets survives to recall its more famous past, and to the English forests of Dean and the Weald, where iron was dug, smelted, and forged into implements and weapons of war down to the end of the eighteenth century.

We must allude here, also, to the Industrial Revolution, which, like that in agriculture, revitalized industry and gave it vastly enlarged scope. The Industrial Revolution had its home in Britain, where geographical, economic, political, and social conditions favored, indeed stimulated, industrial progress. In the eighteenth century Britain had built up overseas trade, based on sea power and imperial territories, and was amassing capital. The depletion of her forests focused attention on her resources of coal, of all the chief varieties, some of which were well located for shipment by sea and many of which contained seams of iron ore. Her labor sup-

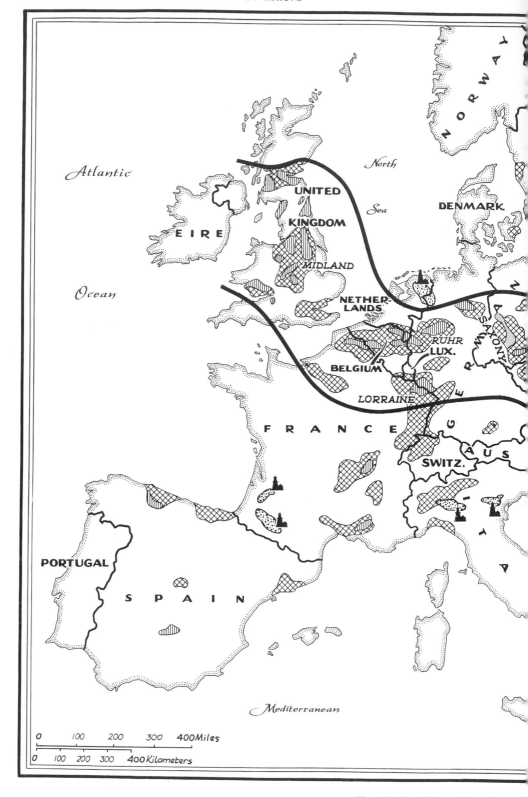

Fig. 2–9. The main industrial

THE MAIN INDUSTRIAL BELT OF EUROPE

Industrial region

Petroleum & natural gas

Bituminous coalfield

Lignite field

Baltic Sea

U. S. S. R.

POLAND

UPPER SILESIA

CZECHOSLOVAKIA

DONETS

RIA

HUNGARY

ROMANIA

YUGOSLAVIA

Black Sea

BULGARIA

ALBANIA

TURKEY

GREECE

Sea

belt of Europe.

ply was inadequate to keep pace with the growth of her trade in domestic staples, notably textiles, and this provided a stimulus to the invention of machines which could economize on labor. Certainly the application of the scientific ideas to industrial technique, together with the ingenuity of engineers and other craftsmen, was responsible for many remarkable inventions which transformed the organization, scale, and cost of industrial production. Among many triumphs of inventiveness were the steam engine, first used for pumping water from mines, the "spinning jenny" and new weaving looms, the use of coke for smelting iron ore, the Bessemer and Gilchrist-Thomas steel-making processes, which enormously increased the range of production and utilization of steel, and the more recent revolutionary developments in the chemical industries. On the basis of these and other technological innovations, notably in the field of transport, Britain became in the nineteenth century the "workshop of the world."

The geographical effects of this industrial activity are here relevant. First, it resulted in the rapid growth of Britain's industrial regions, marked by their high densities of population and high degree of urbanization, by their relation to coal fields—for, in the last century more so than today, coal was industrially king—and by their dependence on overseas trade. This overseas trade brought in essential raw materials, such as cotton, flax, silk, and wool and, increasingly after 1870, foodstuffs (above all, wheat and meat). The second geographical effect was the spread of the new ideas to the continent, where, after an appreciable time lag and in suitable areas, especially on coal fields, the present industrial regions began to take shape.

The industrial map of Europe shows a highly populated belt extending from the Pennines and South Wales in Britain to the Donets Basin in the U.S.S.R., where rocks of Hercynian folding are still exposed (Fig. 2–9). These rocks were originally rich in economic minerals, although some of the former lodes are now worked out. With them are associated considerable coal deposits of the Carboniferous period, which helps to explain the location and character of industrial regions engaged mainly in mining, smelting, steel making, heavy chemicals, and engineering. Within this diagonal belt across the continent lie the British industrial areas, some of which were just mentioned, the Franco-Belgian coal field, the Luxembourg and German Westphalian industrial regions, that of western Bohemia in Czechoslovakia, the Upper Silesian coal field of Poland, the Donets coal field and industrial region (mainly in the Ukrainian S.S.R.). Farther east is the industrial region which bestrides the central and southern Urals. In Iberia, too, where Hercynian structures also occur, a range of minerals—tungsten, copper, mercury, and iron, together with some coal in the north—testifies again to the link between geological history and economic geography, although these resources have not as yet become the basis of any considerable industrialization.

Other industrial regions of Europe are explained by considerations which differ from that of the Hercynian coal basins. For example, the extensive lignite and potash deposits of East Germany [15] have provided in recent decades an abundant low-grade fuel for many important industries, including chemicals, as in the middle Elbe region of Saxony. Another distinct category of industrial region includes large seaports such as Hamburg, Rotterdam, Marseille, and Glasgow, well placed for the economical import of raw materials and the distribution of their manufactured products. Shipbuilding and the many associated industries which it involves have established themselves at certain estuarine and seacoast sites near supplies of coal and steel: Clydeside below Glasgow in Scotland, Tyneside below Newcastle, and Hartlepool on the Wear in northeast England are outstanding centers. There remain, also, the newer industrial regions which draw their power resources from hydroelectricity.

[15] Officially known as The German Democratic Republic.

Hydroelectric power in Europe is derived —to an estimated 86 per cent—from its glaciated lands. Thus metallurgical, chemical, engineering, and other industries of the continent are not confined to areas with accessible supplies of solid fuel. Hydroelectrical undertakings, of course, call for a substantial capital investment and usually a considerable engineering effort. The relief features of a landscape eroded by ice, such as steep valley slopes and high-level lake basins, coupled with an abundant supply of running water from rainfall and snow melt, have provided the means for a number of countries deficient in coal to play their part, if modestly, in modern industry. Italy, Sweden, Norway, Finland, Switzerland, Austria, and Spain owe their industrial activity largely to "white coal." The Soviet Union, which produces much coal, continues to exploit the very considerable hydroelectric potentialities of its glaciated northern lands, of the Caucasus Mountains, and of its rivers. Nevertheless, only 20 per cent of its electric-energy consumption is derived from hydroelectric power.

While hydroelectricity, petroleum, and natural gas are now increasingly used as sources of energy throughout Europe, coal is still the principal source of power. Even so, the use of "white coal" explains the growth of some of the industrial areas which are aloof from coal fields. It explains, also, the dispersion of industrial undertakings, since electricity can be cheaply distributed over short distances, and the avoidance of the landscape features of the "black country" which disfigure so many industrial areas located on coal fields. Witness as illustrations the semirural location of industries in the Swedish midlands, the specialized clock- and watchmaking in the Swiss Jura, and the metallurgical industries at Zaporozhe and Dnepropetrovsk on the lower Dnieper in the Ukrainian S.S.R. While "white coal" is mainly used in light industries, it is particularly useful in a group of industries which make very heavy demands on electric power: electrochemicals, electric smelting and refining, nitrate making by extraction of nitro-

gen from the air, and synthetic rubber. Thus Norway has been able to develop the manufacture of nitrates, the refining of copper, and an aluminum industry based on imported bauxite.

While the industries of Europe depend primarily on its generous endowment of coal and lignite, which are widely distributed though often difficult to obtain, to these must be added its hydroelectric capacity, and its petroleum supplies, in large part imported. Outside the U.S.S.R., which has many important fields, notably that of the Volga-Urals ("Second Baku"), Europe's oil production accounts for only a small part of its consumption. However, domestic resources of natural gas now appear substantial.

Thanks to its wide command of mechanical energy and a long tradition of industrial skill, Europe has achieved, and has retained despite the destruction of World War II, a very high place in industrialization. It recovered rapidly from the damage and setbacks caused by World War II, and by 1955 Western Europe had raised its industrial production 70 per cent above its prewar (1938) level.

In the Soviet Union, where industrialization started some years later than in Western Europe, the rate of industrial growth has been higher. By 1955 the U.S.S.R. claimed to have trebled its prewar (1940) industrial output. At the end of the 1958–1965 seven-year plan the U.S.S.R. achieved a level of industrial output equal to about 60 per cent of that of the United States. Broadly, it is true to say that industrialization has spread eastward in Europe during the last hundred years and that the most recent developments in basic industries, those of the U.S.S.R. in its Asiatic territories, give the greatest promise of continued expansion. While the U.S.S.R. is largely self-sufficient in metallic and non-metallic minerals and in other raw materials—natural rubber, wool, jute, and tin appear to be its chief deficiencies —the rest of Europe is very dependent on seaborne supplies.

Iron-ore supplies are as a whole insufficient, although France (from her Lorraine mines), Sweden, Spain, and Britain are big producers. The European countries command large supplies of bauxite (in France and Hungary) and appreciable amounts of copper, zinc, mercury, sulfur, ferroalloys, and salt, but variously depend on imports for many metals and other industrial raw materials: aluminum, tin, nickel, chrome, lead, copper, manganese, wool, cotton, jute, and natural rubber. Most of the industrialized countries west of the U.S.S.R. and south of Fenno-Scandia need also to import timber. Scientific and technological progress, however, continues to provide new industrial products, of which artificial fibers and plastics are two striking illustrations.

Commerce. Leaving aside a discussion of trade within state territories, which of course vividly reveals the regional differences of climate, terrain, and economy, we shall glance here at the historical geography of the interregional trade within Europe, and at Europe's overseas commerce.

During many centuries—until the Columbian era—Europe's trading activities were confined largely within its own limits. The chief traders of Europe were first to be found in cities of the coastlands of the Mediterranean Basin; Phoenicians, Greeks, and Romans did not venture very much outside this virtually tideless sea. So, during the Middle Ages, the Mediterranean "lake" proved the main trade route of Europe, with cities like Constantinople, Venice, Pisa, and Genoa taking the lead through importing by overland and sea routes valuable goods from the monsoon lands of Asia and exporting the high-grade manufactures from their own workshops.

The rise of northwestern Europe in the centuries which followed the creation of Charlemagne's empire was reflected in the activities of industrial and commercial cities in that area. It made the interconnecting Baltic and North seas another highway for shipping their local produce, i.e., fish, salt, timber, flax, wool, and finished textiles. Between the two parallel maritime axes of trade—the southern and the northern—overland routes carried traders and goods. In 1317, the Venetians, having built sailing ships with oars (galleys) strong and mobile enough to face the troubled tidal waters beyond the Strait of Gibraltar, opened up direct trade by sea to the ports of Southampton, London, and Brugge.

As the limits of the known world expanded during the Age of Discovery, the positional values of the two inland seas of Europe—the Baltic and the Mediterranean—decreased, for in the sixteenth century geographical knowledge, advances in shipbuilding, new navigation aids, and commercial enterprise broadened the theater of trade by use of the ocean highways and created an all-sea route via the Cape to India and the East Indies. The riches of Central and South America and of the Indies were the chief lure. Trade followed the flag, for the power of the state was fundamental for the protection of shipping as well as for the securing of territory, trade depots, and privileges in distant lands. In this oceanic phase, it was the nations fronting the open sea which were the first to exploit the new opportunities, not only in trade but also in conquest, settlement, and proselytization of the Christian faith; in turn, Portuguese, Spaniards, Dutch, English, and French turned to overseas commerce. The first two have long lost the leading position which they earned by their early achievements in sea-borne exploration. The Dutch, as the "waggoners of Europe," had their commercial heyday in the seventeenth century. Britain, which had played during the Middle Ages a mainly passive role in overseas trade, achieved, thanks to its naval strength and empire building, a leading position among the commercial states of the world. Others, like Norway (with a large merchant tonnage), Germany, and Italy, joined much more recently in large-scale maritime commerce.

The interregional trade in Europe naturally arose from the variety of products which were available in different parts of the continent, partly because of climatic contrasts; now it is much reduced by the divergent politico-economic policies of the Soviet Union and the West. It is enough here to recall some of the distinctive products of particular countries and areas: the iron ore of Sweden, Lorraine, and Spain; the timber and timber products, especially of Sweden and Finland; the olive oil, tobacco, and citrus and dried fruits of Mediterranean countries; the early vegetables and flowers of Italy, Brittany, and Mediterranean France; the wines of France, Spain, Italy, Portugal, and Yugoslavia; Swiss watches and watch parts; Swedish electrical equipment; British machinery, transport equipment, tin plate, and textiles; French, Dutch, and Swiss cheeses and the high-class dairy produce of Denmark; and German capital goods and chemicals. On purely geographical grounds, it might have been expected that Eastern and Western Europe, since the former is relatively well-wooded and more agricultural in its economy and the latter is more emphatically industrial, would have engaged as in the past in a profitable trade in complementary products. But Soviet policy, which is now extended to cover its many satellite states in Europe, aims at diverting the trade of these areas from the West to itself and also at achieving, behind the "Iron Curtain," a high degree of economic self-sufficiency. This policy discourages interregional East-West trade in Europe. The attempt to link the trade of the U.S.S.R. and that of its satellites has achieved some success. The former commands many valuable commodities which it can make available to the latter, as it deems expedient: cotton, flax, hemp, manganese and chrome ores, apatites for phosphate fertilizers, petroleum, platinum, and gold. In exchange for these products it can obtain, for example, machinery and textiles from Czechoslovakia, coal from Poland, and bauxite from Hungary.

The overseas trade of Europe, which commands virtually one-half of the world's ocean-going merchant tonnage, is largely in the hands of the Western countries. One feature of this trade, which is world-wide, derived from the fact that many states, i.e., Britain, France, the Netherlands, Belgium, and Portugal, long had political dependencies overseas which afforded sheltered markets for their metropolitan products. Another feature, especially since 1945, has been the increasing volume of trade with the United States. Of the European exports to the United States, Britain supplies over one-quarter, and Germany more than one-fifth. The American market is valuable for countries with certain surplus raw materials, ores, and semiprocessed goods. Such are wood pulp and furs from the Baltic countries, Greek and Turkish tobacco, and Yugoslavia's copper ore. But the American market receives, too, some highly reputed and specialized products from the industrial countries of Western Europe. Central and South America also remain an important field for trade, but this particular trade has relatively decreased to the advantage of the United States.

Circulation. In this age of fast travel and speedy communication we are not likely to underrate the importance of routes of all kinds—by land, by sea, by inland waterways, and by air—"as a sustenance without which organized society would be impossible." [16] In the earliest days of human colonization in Europe, it is true, men used the routeways left open by nature: the inner seas, the river valleys, the unwooded or lightly wooded steppe. Travel by horse or horse-drawn coach and transport by pack horse, by sailing ship, and by river craft long provided the best means of movement, until the inventions of the last century brought the steamship and the locomotive. These were supplemented, in turn, through application of the internal combustion engine, by the motorcar and aircraft. Distinctive man-made elements of the countryside reflect social efforts to promote circulation and at the same time interpenetrate the region. The route patterns of European countries present

[16] J. H. Belloc, *The Road* (London: T. Fisher Unwin, 1924), Preface.

today features etched on the surface of the land in many past and sometimes remote periods of history. And although the railroads, highways, and navigable waters are now the paramount means of travel and of shipment of goods, prehistoric ridge-way and stretches of Roman road (in some areas still in use) survive to remind us of earlier geographies of circulation.

Trade and travel do not depend merely on routes; they are sensitive to political conditions. Roman roads, built by legionary and auxiliary troops, gave Europe, south of the Danube and west of the Rhine, its first system of engineered roads, which, thanks to the efficiency of Roman government, served the needs of soldiers, merchants, officials, and others. These highways, firm and cambered though of course narrow, were less useful after the collapse of centralized imperial government. Even though they suffered from neglect, they largely survived to serve the varied needs of governments and of the two Christian Churches—the one organized from Rome and the other (after 395 A.D.) from Constantinople.

The seaways—and this meant chiefly the Mediterranean—suffered no less from the fall of Rome and the subsequent advance (in the seventh century) of the Arabs into the Mediterranean Basin. Although the Eastern Roman Empire, centered on Constantinople, maintained some show of sea power, it was not until the rise of the Italian trading cities that the Mediterranean came to flourish as a commercial thoroughfare. In the same way it was the political and naval strength of the northern cities of the Hanseatic League which opened the Baltic and North seas to trade. Although Roman trade had spread into parts at least of the Baltic, Ptolemy (second century A.D.) had mapped Scandinavia as an island. The new importance of the Baltic Sea was marked when Adam of Bremen, in the eleventh century, described its maritime entries and the peninsular character of Scandinavia. A few centuries later, such was the stature of the Baltic in Euro-

pean commerce and politics, that it was carefully portrayed in a semipictorial map by Olaus Magnus.

Already in the later Middle Ages a system of roads, aligned roughly east-west and north-south, brought into relationship the various parts of the continent and its neighboring seas. Naturally, the contemporaneous distribution of population, cities, ports, and economic activities defined the starting points and goals of routes, the volume of traffic which they carried, and their relative importance. We may note how many Alpine passes carried well-frequented thoroughfares and linked the ports and industrial cities of northern Italy (and also Rome, the seat of the Pope) with France, Germany, and southeastern Europe. (For the present pattern of Alpine communications see Fig. 6–12.) In the western Alps, the Great St. Bernard and Mt. Cenis passes, approached via Turin, were preferred. The St. Gotthard Pass, its northern approach facilitated by the building of a bridge and valley road in the thirteenth century, joined Milan to the Rhine at Basel and to the Danube at Ulm. Farther east, the Brenner Pass became the principal link between the Italian and German lands of the Holy Roman Empire and for traders between northern Germany and northern Italy. In the eastern Alps, several passes carried roads from Venice toward the Drava and Sava rivers, along which passed roads leading to the Aegean Sea. The laden mule and ass afforded the means of transport. Thanks to modern engineering, the railroads, using long tunnels, can now ignore the passways, although they still must use the easiest gradients provided by the valleys.

Another interesting north-south route across the continent, which then served the needs of European commerce and now affords only internal circulation, was based on navigable rivers and portages. It was opened up in the ninth century across Russia from the Gulf of Finland to the Black and Caspian seas. In part, this route was an attempt to find an alternative to sea and land routes in the western basin of the Mediterranean which were obstructed by Moslem power. The importance of the new route lay in the fact that Constantinople was its chief southern terminal and that, as a result, Russia derived therefrom its Orthodox or Greek Christianity, its alphabet, some architectural influences, and perhaps some imperialistic notions too.

In some parts of the continent the medieval road system was largely that bequeathed by Rome, in others new routes were laid out in the course of conquest and colonization. Thus in the Balkan lands of the Byzantine Empire the major routes which made government possible were still those which linked Constantinople with Salonika and Durrës on the Adriatic coast and with Belgrade on the Danube via Sofia; another route led from Salonika to Belgrade via Niš. In each case the road was closely related to valley-ways and structural depressions. But in Central and Eastern Europe, largely as a result of German conquests, new roads were built to give access from the Rhine and Danube cities. Figure 2–10, based on an early topographic map made about the year 1570, shows that an effective route system existed in this part of the continent. Among the roads there shown, that which led eastward from Brugge, Antwerp, and Cologne to Leipzig, Breslau (Wrocław), and Cracow, the medieval capital of Poland, is of special interest. It follows one of the major lines of movement across the continent at all periods, and is aligned below the northern edge of the middle mountain zone.

The lack of west-east roads in the North German Plain, except for the Hamburg-Lübeck-Stettin-Danzig road, reflects the scantier settlement and lower value of these lands of glacial deposition. The route centers, too, arouse interest: Frankfurt and Würzburg (both on the Main), Nuremberg, Prague, Leipzig, Breslau, and Vienna. The principal rivers supplemented the land routes in no small measure: the Rhine, Elbe, Oder, Vistula, and Danube all played a part.

Figure 2–10 may be compared with Fig. 2–11, which depicts the principal highways of Europe in 1850, a time when the railroad network was at an early stage of its development. Paris was clearly *the* center of the French road system which had been recreated in the eighteenth century, although in the Roman period Lyon was the route center and Rheims, nearer the Rhine frontier, was the chief route focus of northern Gaul. London occupies a similar position as the chief focus of the routes of England. The closeness of the network of roads in Central Europe is very striking, testifying *inter alia* to its middle position and crossroad function within the continent. No less striking is the paucity and wide spacing of the roads in Southern, Eastern, and Northern Europe—which still obtain.

Waterways, too, contributed much to bulk transport within the continent. After the improvement of rivers by engineering works, the construction of canals, especially in the eighteenth century, was hailed as a triumph in man's control over nature. They provided water connections between navigable points on rivers and indeed could be built in watershed areas where no navigable rivers existed at all. Above all, they were designed to carry bulk cargoes—coal, stone, fertilizers, ore, timber—and, until the advent in turn of railroad and motor transport, proved indispensable, notably in the Netherlands and in Britain.

While the railroad and motor truck could and did efficiently usurp the functions of many canals, these have by no means lost importance. In countries like the Netherlands, canals serve more than one purpose. German canals provide not only routes (as in Westphalia) for ore and coal shipments to the Rhine and Ems, but also the means of internal distribution of goods (in north Germany). Moscow is known as "the Port of Five Seas" thanks to the waterways which link it to the Baltic, White, Black, Azov, and Caspian seas. In England, the Manchester Ship Canal makes inland Manchester a port for ocean-going shipping, while the commer-

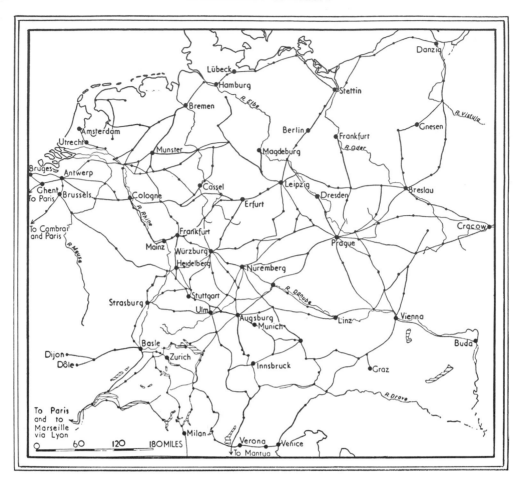

Fig. 2–10. The road system of Central Europe about 1570.

cial and strategical importance attached to the Kiel Canal needs no elaboration here.

Of the great rivers of the continent, the Rhine and Volga carry the largest tonnages of goods. The Rhine, which admits fleets of large barges far upstream, owes its importance primarily to its proximity to the Rhine-Westphalian industrial region and to the Dutch commercial cities near its outlets. The Volga, which lies wholly within one state territory, that of the U.S.S.R., carries upstream heavy cargoes of oil, salt, fish, and grain, which can reach as far as Moscow with the aid of the Moscow Canal. The Danube, "the king of rivers," as Napoleon called it, today plays a humble role and has lost the legal status of "an international

river" open to the navigation and trade of all nations.

Europe, owing to its central position in relation to the land areas of the earth, to its indented coastline, and to modern engineering works, boasts many of the great seaports of the world. One broad geographical contrast may be noted here—that between ports on navigable tidal rivers, such as London, Antwerp, and Hamburg, where docks must be provided with lock-gates because of the tidal range, and those of the almost tideless Mediterranean Sea, where modern docks offer access at all times and are not subject to the deltaic accretions of the rivers. Note, in particular, Marseille, Trieste, Genoa, Naples, Barcelona, and Salonika. The great

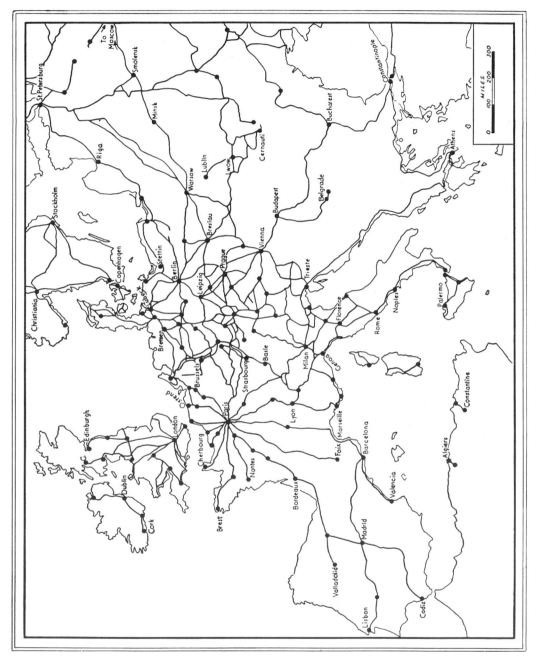

Fig. 2–11. The post roads of Europe in 1850.

international port of Rotterdam, related to the Rhine, improved access by canalization.

Finally, we may allude to the beginnings of railroad building born of the Industrial Revolution and the need for faster bulk shipment of heavy freight. Figure 2–12 shows that, by 1850, Great Britain already had a network of railroads, closest in the English Lowlands. Across the English Channel, the Low Countries and northern France had already built many connected lines, but to the north and east of Germany and in Mediterranean Europe railroad construction had scarcely begun. In Russia, only the line from

St. Petersburg (Leningrad) to the Tsar's summer palace at Tsarkoye Selo (opened in 1838) and the first stretch of the St. Petersburg-Moscow railroad had been constructed. Although many railroads must now be drawn on the blank spaces of this map, the network of lines remains relatively open outside Western and Central Europe.

CONCLUSION

The present is but the past flowing into the future. The geography of Europe has been fashioned during several millennia.

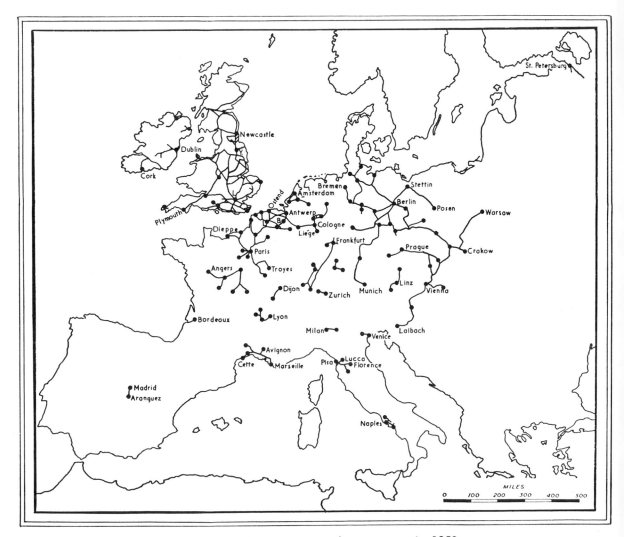

Fig. 2–12. The European railway pattern in 1850.

Changes are presently in operation and will continue. There is no finality in the human value which attaches to the areas of Europe. The value attaching to land changes, as ideas and technology change. While we note the high densities of population and the high degree of industrialization and commerce which characterize the more peninsular and more physically varied western part of the continent, we should not fail to recognize that the larger and physically more uniform eastern part of the continent has developed belatedly and will economically progress further. We should not fail to note, also, that, in the east, Europe merges with Asia and that in Siberia, Kazakhstan, and Central Asia it has projected its culture in the guise of Soviet communism and modern technology.

Above all, the study of the history behind geography underlines the many cleavages which divide Europe, despite the common cultural heritage which its peoples share. We have glanced at some of the past processes which explain the social and territorial divisions of the continent—its many tongues, nations, and states—which clearly reflect the earlier localism of human groups in days of slow and difficult travel and their close attachment to the soil. So far, political unity over large areas of Europe has been achieved only temporarily and by the coercive efforts of would-be master states. Soviet power and Soviet policy have produced, since 1945, some trend toward unity, if only within two opposed eastern and western segments of the continent. The unity of Europe is not yet.

BIBLIOGRAPHY

(*Introductory references are asterisked.*)

Books and Articles in English

BERESFORD, MAURICE W. *New Towns of the Middle Ages; Town Plantation in England, Wales and Gascony.* London: Lutterworth Press, 1967.

BURKE, G. L. *The Making of the Dutch Towns: A Study in Urban Development from the Tenth to the Seventeenth Centuries.* London: Cleaver-Hume Press, Ltd., 1956.

CHADWICK, HECTOR MUNRO. *The Nationalities of Europe and the Growth of National Ideologies.* London: Cambridge University Press, 1945.

CHILDE, VERE G. *Prehistoric Migrations in Europe.* Cambridge, Mass.: Harvard University Press, 1951.

CLAPHAM, JOHN H. *The Economic Development of France and Germany 1815–1914.* 4th ed. London: Cambridge University Press, 1945.

CLAPHAM, JOHN H., and POWER, EILEEN (eds.). *The Agrarian Life of the Middle Ages (The Cambridge Economic History,* Vol. I). London: Cambridge University Press, 1941.

CLARK, J. G. D. *The Mesolithic Settlement of Northern Europe.* London: Cambridge University Press, 1936.

COON, CARLETON S. *The Races of Europe.* New York: The Macmillan Co., 1939.

DARBY, HENRY C. "The Clearing of the Woodland of Europe" in *Man's Role in Changing the Face of the Earth,* William L. Thomas, Jr. (ed.). Chicago: University of Chicago Press, 1956.

———. "The Face of Europe on the Eve of the Great Discoveries," Vol. I, Chap. II of *The New Cambridge Modern History.* London: Cambridge University Press, 1957.

DICKINSON, ROBERT E. *The West European City.* 2nd ed. London: Routledge & Kegan Paul, Ltd., 1964.

DOMINIAN, L. *The Frontiers of Language and Nationality in Europe.* New York: American Geographical Society, 1917.

DOPSCH, ALFONS. *The Economic and Social Foundations of European Civilization.* Condensed by E. Patzelt and translated by M. G. Beard and N. Marshall. New York: Harcourt, Brace & Co., Inc., 1937.

DUGDALE, J. S. *The Linguistic Map of Europe.* London: Hutchinson University Library, 1969.

*EAST, W. GORDON. *A Historical Geography of Europe.* 5th ed. New York: E. P. Dutton & Co., Inc., 1966.

MORANT, G. M. *The Races of Central Europe: A Footnote to History.* New York: W. W. Norton & Co., Inc., 1940.

PIRENNE, H. *Economic and Social History of Medieval Europe.* Translated by I. E. Clegg. London: Routledge & Kegan Paul, Ltd., 1949.

POSTAN, MICHAEL M., and HABAKKUK, H. J. (eds). *Trade and Industry in the Middle Ages.* (*The Cambridge Economic History,* Vol. II, ed. by M. M. Postan and E. E. Rich.) London: Cambridge University Press, 1952.

POUNDS, NORMAN J. G., and SUE S. BALL. "Core-areas and the Development of the

European States System" in *Annals of the Assoc. of American Geographers* LIV (March, 1964): 24–40.

PROUDFOOT, MALCOLM J. *European Refugees: 1939–1952.* London: Faber & Faber, Ltd., 1957.

SMITH, CLIFFORD T. *An Historical Geography of Western Europe Before 1800.* London: Longmans, 1967.

WHEELER, SIR R. E. M. *Rome Beyond the Imperial Frontiers.* London: G. G. Bell & Sons, Ltd., 1954.

°WHITTLESEY, DERWENT. *Environmental Foundations of European History.* New York: Appleton-Century-Crofts, Inc., 1949.

°WRIGHT, JOHN K. *The Geographical Basis of European History.* New York: Henry Holt & Co., Inc., 1928.

ZEUNER, FRIEDRICH E. *Dating the Past: An Introduction to Geochronology.* 3rd ed. London: Methuen & Co., Ltd., 1952.

Books in Other Languages

ANCEL, J. *Manual Géographique de Politique Européenne* (Manual of the Political Geography of Europe). Paris: Librairie Delagrave, 1936–45.

BLOCH, M. *Les Caractères Originaux de l'Histoire Rurale Française* (The Original Character of French Rural History). Cambridge, Mass.: Harvard University Press, 1931.

BRAUDEL, FERNAND. *La Méditerranée et le Monde Méditerranéen à l'Epoque de Philippe II* (The Mediterranean and the Mediterranean World in the Epoch of Philippe II). Paris: Armand Colin, 1949.

DEMANGEON, ALBERT. *Problèmes de Géographie Humaine* (Problems of Human Geography). 3rd ed. Paris: Armand Colin, 1947.

DION, R. *Essai sur la Formation du Paysage Rural Français* (Essay on the Formation of the French Countryside). Tours: Arrault et Cie, 1934.

MEILLET, A. *Les Langues dans l'Europe Nouvelle* (The Languages of Modern Europe). 2nd ed. rev. Paris: Payot, 1928.

SCHMIDT, P. W. *Die Sprachenfamilien und Sprachenkreise der Erde* (Language Families and Language Regions of the World). Heidelberg: C. Winter's Universitätsbuchhandlung, 1926.

3

The British Isles

57,500,000 total pop. of U.S.

Two main islands—Great Britain and Ireland—make up the British Isles. Set between the ports of Northern Europe and the trade route to the Americas, these islands have for long exerted influence disproportionate to their small size. On their 121,000 square miles there live an estimated 57,500,000 people, a population density of about 470 to the square mile. A vast colonial empire once lay within the jurisdiction of the United Kingdom, and dominions many times her size owed allegiance to either the British Crown or the Commonwealth. The English language has become the most widely spoken lingua franca of the civilized world, as well as the mother tongue of millions non-British by birth.

Four peoples, three governments, and two states exist within the British Isles, and the succeeding account will be unintelligible to the student unless he has a clear notion of their political organization and mutual relations. Great Britain consists of the three national units of Scotland, Wales, and England, each conscious of its separate identity, but divided today by unmarked boundaries of very limited political significance. The United Kingdom includes these three units and the six counties of Northern Ireland— comprising most of the ancient province of Ulster. The Irish people is thus divided, for

the remainder of the island is the Irish Republic (Eire), created as the Irish Free State in 1921, and now independent of the British.

The United Kingdom is a parliamentary democracy (based on universal suffrage) with a limited constitutional monarchy. Paramount authority rests with Parliament, over which neither the Crown nor the Judiciary has any power; it has been well said of the British Queen that she reigns but does not rule. Parliament—seated in Westminster, on the bank of the Thames—governs England and Wales directly. In certain aspects of government: agriculture, health, planning, education, and home affairs, Scotland is governed through administrative departments responsible to the Secretary of State for Scotland; there is, however, no separate Scots parliament. Northern Ireland elects members to Westminster, but also has its own parliament in Belfast; this body legislates for most matters except foreign affairs, income tax, the post office, and the judiciary and fiscal policy, including customs and excise.

The Irish Republic is also a parliamentary democracy, with an elected President of limited constitutional powers not unlike those of the British monarchy. A long and harsh record of interference in Irish affairs earned for the Protestant English the bitter

111

anger of the Catholic population, a sentiment formerly fanned and exploited by most political groups. The partition of Ireland into two units is vociferously denounced by the southern Irish and as stoutly defended by the Protestant Ulstermen, who precipitated the Civil War by their refusal to accept government, as they put it, from Rome via Dublin.

English is the first tongue of most members of all four nations. Three of the old Celtic tongues survive, however: Gaelic (in the western Scottish Highlands), Welsh (spoken as the first tongue in parts of northern and western Wales), and Irish Gaelic, the tongue of the densely populated Atlantic shore of Ireland, the Gaeltacht. Manx (on the Isle of Man) is virtually extinct, as is Cornish. The Celtic tongues and the ancient traditions with which they are associated are jealously preserved by nationalist sentiment. In Wales, this nationalism takes the benevolent form—as a rule—of a widespread interest in a national literature and in song. In the Irish Republic, however, efforts are being made to revive Gaelic as the national tongue, and access to public office is confined to those who speak it.

In the seventeenth, eighteenth, and nineteenth centuries, through venturesome exploration, military conquest, and systematic emigration, the British created an enormous colonial empire. Since the Second World War the empire has all but vanished, and only a few tiny overseas territories remain under British rule. Most of the former colonies and self-governing dominions remain loosely associated in the Commonwealth, an organization still having some significance in world affairs, especially because certain trading preferences exist between its members. The dominions, as they were formerly called, have evolved into wholly independent states, joined together only by the Commonwealth, and in some cases (e.g., Canada, Australia, New Zealand) by the recognition of the Queen as titular head of state. The former African colonies, together with India and Pakistan, have generally adopted republican government, and have in some cases forsworn the Commonwealth links. Within Europe only Gibraltar remains of the former British colonies. Malta and Cyprus are independent within the Commonwealth.

The empire has thus vanished as a centralized political entity. But its effects will last for centuries. English often remains the practical language of affairs, even in countries with strong nationalist sentiments and official languages. Extensive cultural links persist, and the British continue to support technical-aid programs, even in former colonies that have become hostile. The British themselves show the marks of their former imperial role. Until recently they maintained costly world-wide defense commitments, and continue to feel involved in power politics to a far greater extent than their economic strength justifies. And London, once the imperial headquarters, continues to play a unique and important world role in financial matters, notably in banking, insurance, bullion and monetary exchange, shipping and financial entrepreneurship. This positive legacy of imperial greatness has survived two world wars, four devaluations of the pound and the eclipse of Britain's own position as the leading trading nation.

THE PHYSICAL LANDSCAPE

The land of the British Isles exhibits two strikingly contrasted aspects. The west and north, confronting the Atlantic, is hilly or mountainous, and has a wet, oceanic climate. The term "Highland Zone" is often applied to it. Southern and eastern England, by contrast, is the gently rolling "Lowland Zone," with a drier climate akin to that of the nearby European lowlands.[1]

The major divisions of the British landscape are structurally determined; each division has its characteristic types of rock and

[1] See, for example, H. J. Mackinder, *Britain and the British Seas* (London: Oxford University Press, 1902). Much of this geographical classic is written around the Highland-Lowland theme.

a distinct structural pattern (Fig. 3–1). The landscape also shows many traces of a complex erosional history, upon which we can barely touch in this chapter.[2] It falls readily into three provinces, each of which corresponds to one of the major divisions of the mainland of Europe:

1. *Caledonian Britain*, comprising a series of rugged uplands in the north and west, which continue the structural province of the Kjölen Range in Scandinavia.
2. *Hercynian Britain*, making up the rest of the Highland Zone, and including in addition the chief coal fields. As its name implies, this province corresponds to the Hercynian belt of the continental mainland.
3. *Lowland Britain*, consisting of the gently folded Mesozoic and Tertiary rocks of the English plain, and very comparable in structure, for example, with the Paris and Münster basins.

Caledonian and Hercynian Britain together make up the Highland Zone already mentioned. They have much in common, and might be considered together but for the vital difference that only the Hercynian structures affect the distribution of coal fields.[3]

The Three Major Provinces

Caledonian Britain. In this province, the surface structures largely date from a mid-Paleozoic disturbance. The belt consists of (a) the Scottish Highlands and the hills of Donegal and Mayo, a unit composed largely of gneisses and schists, with large granite intrusions; (b) the Scottish Southern Uplands and the mountains of southeast Ulster, where the bedrock is chiefly of greywackes, slates, and intrusive granites; and (c) the plateaus of North Wales and Wicklow-Wexford in

[2] For geological terms, see Appendix I.
[3] Valuable additional material is given in Great Britain, Geological Survey, *British Regional Geology* (London: H. M. Stationery Office, various dates), a series of short memoirs covering all parts of Great Britain.

Eire, where the rocks are similar but contain the giant Wicklow granite. In all these separate uplands, the physiographic trend follows the NE-SW run of the folding, as it does in Norway. All three consist of bleak, rain-swept highlands, broken into Irish and British segments by the Irish Sea and its channels. To them may be added the small, compact mountain region of the English Lake District, with its nucleus of early Paleozoic volcanics. To this upland the later mountain-building episodes have contributed much, but its affinities are Caledonian.

Though the rocks of Caledonian Britain range in age from Silurian to early Pre-Cambrian, and in lithology from fine-grained slates to massive, coarse-grained granites, differentiation between rock types is not of major geographical significance. Everywhere the land is rolling, considerable in elevation (usually 1500–3000 feet), and generally rather impervious. The Caledonian highlands are par excellence the scene of that characteristic British landscape, the moorland. Since they are nowhere heavily mineralized and nowhere present extensive lowland areas, they have remained unattractive lands for settlement since the Bronze Age.

Hercynian Britain. The continuation and structural contemporary of the Hercynian hill country of Central Europe and France, this second province presents a striking contrast to the bleak, thinly populated landscapes of the Caledonian belt. Coming as they did at the close of Carboniferous time, the Hercynian earth movements were able to involve in their structures the precious Coal Measures that were to be the basis of the British Industrial Revolution. The largest concentrations of population, London excepted, now occur in the coal fields along the margin of the Highland Zone.

This second component of Highland Britain is divisible into two broad parts. Southernmost Britain, from southwest Ireland to Kent, lies within the main belt of Hercynian folding (continued in Brittany to the south).

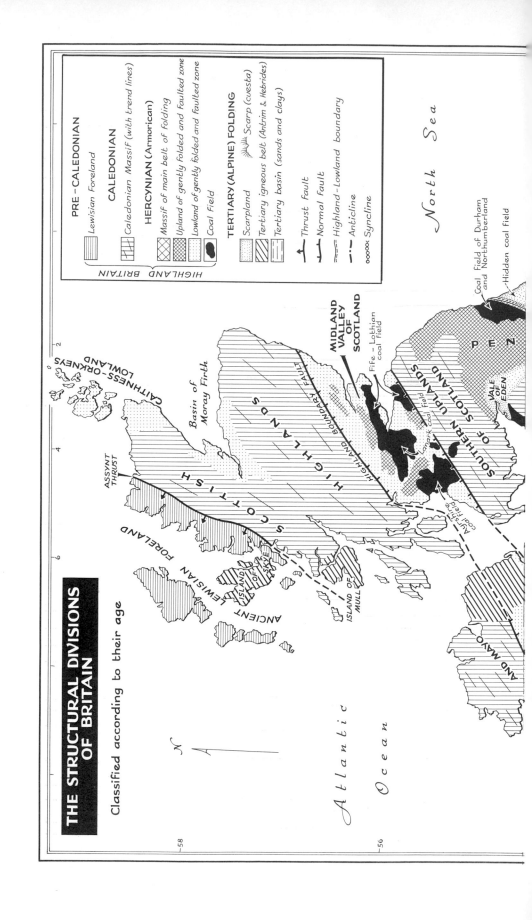

THE STRUCTURAL DIVISIONS OF BRITAIN

Classified according to their age

PRE-CALEDONIAN
Lewisian Foreland

CALEDONIAN
Caledonian Massif (with trend lines)

HERCYNIAN (Armorican)
Massif of main belt of folding

Upland of gently folded and faulted zone

Lowland of gently folded and faulted zone

Coal Field

TERTIARY (ALPINE) FOLDING
Scarpland   Scarp (cuesta)

Tertiary igneous belt (Antrim & Hebrides)

Tertiary basin (sands and clays)

Thrust Fault

Normal Fault

Highland–Lowland boundary

Anticline

Syncline

HIGHLAND BRITAIN

North Sea

Atlantic Ocean

CAITHNESS-ORKNEYS LOWLAND

Basin of Moray Firth

ASSYNT THRUST

SCOTTISH HIGHLANDS

ANCIENT LEWISIAN FORELAND

OUTER ISLANDS

SKYE

ISLAND OF MULL

AND MAYO

MIDLAND VALLEY OF SCOTLAND

HIGHLAND BOUNDARY FAULT

Fife–Lothian coal field

Lanark coal field

Ayrshire coal field

SOUTHERN UPLANDS OF SCOTLAND

VALE OF EDEN

P E N

Coal Field of Durham and Northumberland

Hidden coal field

58

56

2

0

4

6

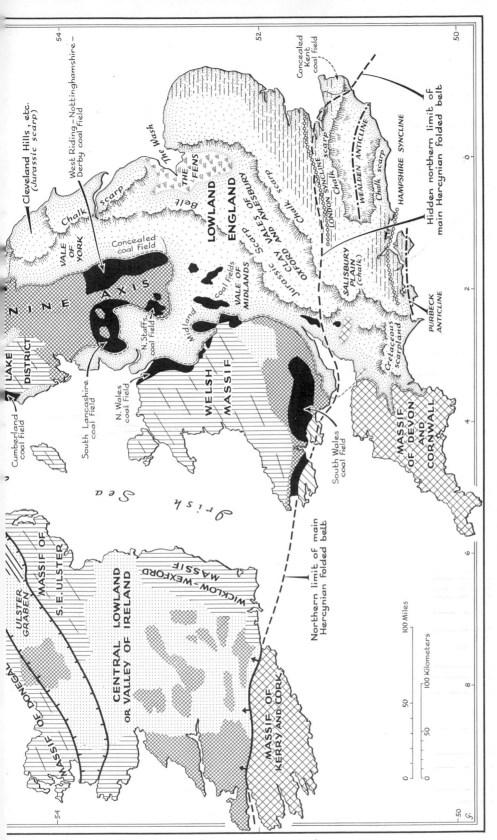

Fig. 3–1. The structural divisions of Britain.

The mountains of Kerry, Cork, and Waterford belong to this belt. Here the chief ranges trend roughly east-west, parallel to the folding. The valleys between the ranges have been partially drowned to form the celebrated "ria" coast. The peninsulas of Devon and Cornwall, Pembroke, Gower, and the Vale of Glamorgan in South Wales make up the rest. Most of the rocks of these areas are limestones, sandstones, shales, or slates, but large granite bosses occur in Devon and Cornwall, forming the high ground of Bodmin Moor, Dartmoor, and smaller uplands. This southern division of

ments, in Ayrshire, Lanarkshire, and Fife-Midlothian. The boundary faults are continued into northern Ireland, where a similar graben (unfortunately coalless) separates the Donegal-Mayo Caledonian massif from that of southeast Ulster.

The Pennine axis forms the backbone of northern England, extending from the Southern Uplands of Scotland to the Trent Valley in the Midlands. The upland consists chiefly of an upfaulted block, whose western rim is a high fault-line scarp looking across the lowlands of the Eden Valley and the Lancashire basins (Fig. 3–2). The eastern slope

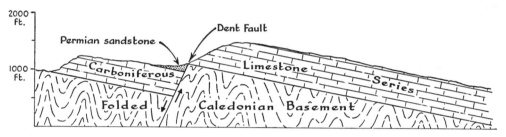

Fig. 3–2. Geological cross-section of the Northern Pennines, about latitude 54° 30′ N. The uplift is a tilted block of the Carboniferous Limestone Series (Mississippian period), bounded along its western margin by a fault scarp on the Dent Fault. Elsewhere in the Pennines, structure is more akin to a true upfold (anticline), but the western edge is usually faulted as above. (After D. A. Wray.)

Hercynian Britain resembles the Caledonian belt in landscapes. Coal-bearing rocks are rarely involved in the principal folded belt.

The second division lies north of the chief folded zone, and consists of an extensive series of gently folded and fractured basins or uplifts. The relief is varied, extensive lowlands alternating with some of the hilliest parts of Britain.

The Midland Valley of Scotland, the northernmost division, separates the Caledonian masses of the Highlands and Southern Uplands, from which it is divided by boundary faults, making it a true graben. Much of the floor of the Valley, the populous heart of Scotland, is underlain by sandstones, but certain areas of volcanic rocks have formed high hills, such as the Ochils and the Campsie Fells. There are three large basins containing coal-bearing sedi-

is less abrupt, the Carboniferous sediments that make up the entire upland dipping gently eastward beneath the younger rocks of Yorkshire and Lincolnshire. The upland is floored chiefly by the Millstone Grit, an estuarine deposit whose name suggests its connection with the metallurgical industries of Sheffield. In places, however, limestones form the upland surface, which is there dry and riddled with potholes, caverns, and dry gorges. Most of the Pennines are wet moorlands with summits averaging 1500 to 2000 feet.

On either flank of the Pennines are basins containing Coal Measures, some of which form major coal fields. On the west flank there are three such basins. The northernmost borders the north slope of the Lake District massif. The central basin, the largest, is the South Lancashire coal field, the home of the cotton textile industry. The third is the North Staffordshire coal field, around Stoke-on-Trent, forming the southwestern extremity of the Pennine upland. On the east flank there are two basins only, but both are large and important coal fields. In Durham and Northumberland the Coal Measures out-crop over a wide area of low moorland, and continue eastward beneath the sea and the younger rocks of the Lowland Zone. In West Riding, Nottinghamshire, and Derbyshire there is an even larger coal-bearing region, which is extended eastward as a "hidden" coal field beneath the younger rocks of the Trent Valley.

There is no Irish equivalent of the Pennine structures. The entire center of the island, the Central Valley, between the Caledonian and Hercynian massifs already discussed, is floored by gently folded sandstones, shales, and limestones, now largely obscured by glacial till and the great peat bogs. Though generally a lowland, central Ireland has several areas of considerable hills.

A large basin makes up much of South Wales and Herefordshire north of the main Hercynian folded belt. In Glamorganshire a large area of Coal Measures forms the South Wales coal field, a hilly country traversed by deep valleys in which the mining towns are clustered. In Herefordshire, by contrast, the Devonian Old Red Sandstone underlies a broad, fertile lowland famous for its brilliant red soils. Between the two contrasted landscapes is a line of formidable moorlands, the Brecon Beacons, Black Mountains, and other hills.

The remaining element in Hercynian Britain is the submerged floor of Lowland England, where the Paleozoic rocks are obscured by the younger cover. In many parts of the Midlands the buried landscape reemerges; the small South Staffordshire coal field and the basins of Leicestershire are of this type. The entirely concealed East Kent coal field was first deduced by geologists, and then proved (in 1890) by a trial boring put down in connection with the Channel tunnel project.

Lowland Britain. This third province is a rolling countryside whose highest cuestas (escarpments) barely exceed 1000 feet. Composed of Mesozoic and Cenozoic rocks much softer than those of Caledonian and Hercynian Britain, the Lowland Zone is essentially a cuestaform landscape with cuestas on the resistant limestones and sandstones, and broad lowlands ("vales" being the accepted local term) on the intervening clays and marls.[4]

In general, the beds dip gently southeastward toward the English Channel or southern North Sea. The oldest rocks outcrop in the Midlands, lapping like a sea against the limits of the Highland Zone, and the youngest occur in eastern East Anglia. But the simplicity of this picture is disturbed by the existence of four major east-west folds that dominate the outcrop pattern of southern England. These are (a) *the London basin* or *syncline,* roughly coincident with the lower and middle Thames basins; (b) *the Wealden anticline,* forming the peninsula of Kent, Surrey, and Sussex; (c) *the Hampshire basin* or *syncline;* and (d) *the Purbeck anticline,* delimiting that basin on the south. Much of the last system is drowned by the English Channel.

The two basins of London and Hampshire, respectively, form broad vales floored largely by Tertiary sands and clays (hence the common term "Tertiary basins"). The anticlines, however, bring to the surface the Mesozoic strata, and the cuesta-and-vale landscape of the east Midlands is renewed about their flanks.[5]

The Midlands of England are largely floored by bright red soils developed on the clays and sands of the Triassic outcrop. The Midland plain passes southeastward into a succession of cuestas and vales that makes up the whole of southeast England. Some of the cuestas are very significant in the life

---

[4] A very detailed account is given in S. W. Wooldridge and D. L. Linton, *Structure, Surface and Drainage in South-East England* (London: Institute of British Geographers, Publication 10, 1939).

[5] *Ibid.,* pp. 52–56, 80–97.

of the country. The Cotswolds, for example, developed on limestones of Jurassic age, have become a rich farming land famous for the beauty of its stone houses and rich villages. Elsewhere in the Jurassic outcrop are the iron-rich deposits of Northamptonshire, Lincolnshire, and East Riding. Scarcely less significant is the cuesta developed on the Chalk, an Upper Cretaceous limestone that provided the dry uplands on which early man preferred to live, as well as the flints from which he fashioned his tools (Fig. 3–3). None of these cuestas much exceeds 1000 feet (the highest being the Hambleton-Cleveland Hills in the East Riding of Yorkshire) and many are much less. The locations of the most significant are shown in Fig. 3–1.

The vales between the cuestas, being developed chiefly on heavy clays, remained for long under heavy forest. Today, however, they are mostly prosperous farmlands devoted to dairy farming.

The gentle folds that diversify the structure of the Lowland Zone were formed at the time when the great convulsion of the Alpine mountain-building period was in progress. The British Isles were in the groundswell of this disturbance. While the lowland of England was receiving the imprint of these movements, igneous activity broke out in the north of Ireland and in western Scotland. The islands of Mull and Skye, and the great basalt flows of Antrim were formed at this time.

The Effects of Glaciation

In common with most of Northern Europe, the British Isles succumbed to several glaciations during Pleistocene times, and the landscapes of both Highland and Lowland zones show many traces of this ordeal. The ultimate advance of the ice covered almost all of Britain north of a line from the Severn estuary to the coast of Essex. The ice sheets were local, deploying on to the plains from dispersal centers over the principal massifs of the Highland Zone. The main Scandinavian glacier did, however, reach eastern coastal districts during at least one of the glacial episodes.

Fig. 3–3. The Chalk Cliffs of Dover. Much of England's coastline is "cliffed" by the recent marine submergence. (Photo: UKIO.)

In the Highland Zone, the erosive effects of the glaciation were considerable. The uplands are typically thin-soiled, and there are many *roches moutonnées*, crag-and-tail phenomena, and the like to confirm the effects of the ice. These are conspicuously absent from the hills of Devon, where deep residual soils are widely developed. Ireland owes much of its present-day landscape to the glaciations. Its Central Lowland is plastered with drift, much of it yielding soils of high fertility. The drainage is badly disturbed, and there are numerous ponds and lakes. Large areas of peat bog—a characteristic Irish landscape—overlie the till and provide the inhabitants with much of their fuel.

Lowland England contains considerable areas of drift-covered terrain. Much of the east is covered by thin sheets of calcareous till, largely derived from the Chalk or Jurassic limestones over which the ice was forced to pass. The Midland tills are made up chiefly of Triassic debris. The rivers of southern and eastern England are flanked by numerous gravel terraces, associated with the frequent shifts of sea level in Pleistocene and recent times. The most recent movement of sea level has been upward, and most of the rivers reach the sea through drowned estuaries, with wide areas of marshes and saltings. The Wash, with the Fens that surround it, is the best-known example. Drainage and careful containment of the sea, the patient work of English and Dutch engineers for three centuries, has converted the Fens into the richest arable land of England.

Climate

Little need be written of the general character of the British climate beyond what has been said in Chapter 1.[6] The country exhibits in a marked degree the oceanic

characteristics typical of the whole northwest coast of Europe. Within Britain itself there are marked differences of climate, chiefly of rainfall and secondarily of temperature. The Highland Zone has in general a high rainfall and a small annual range of temperature, whereas the Lowland Zone is much drier and more extreme in its temperature cycle. Rainfall is lowest in the Thames estuary and in the Fenlands, but is nowhere so low as to create serious problems for the farmer except in drought years. The wettest parts of the Highland Zone—the Lake District and the Snowdon Massif—have stations with mean annual rainfall over 150 inches. At the opposite end of the scale are rainfalls of less than 20 inches in the Thames estuary.[7]

Winter is mild. Mildest conditions extend along the west coast, and even the Orkney Islands have mean temperatures of 40° F. in January (warmer than Paris). Coolest regions are the eastern coastal districts of Scotland and East Anglia and, of course, the high hills. Very heavy rainfall deluges the uplands, and severe gales are frequent along the south, west, and north coasts as Atlantic cyclones pass to the north of Scotland. Snowfall is uncommon, and rarely lies long on the west coast or the lowlands. The southwest coast is exceptionally mild, and may escape frost during many winters. Subtropical plants are open-grown in many places along the Cornish Riviera, which is also the place of origin for early vegetables and flowers for the London market.

The summer is warm enough for most of the common cereal and root crops, though corn (maize) cannot be attempted except for silage. Over the southern half of Ireland and Britain, July mean temperatures slightly exceed 60° F., whereas in the coolest parts of Highland Scotland they barely attain 55° F. Wheat can be grown over most of Ireland, Wales, and England; it ripens as far north as the Moray Firth. Oats and barley are at home throughout the country.

[6] The standard reference work is E. G. Bilham, *The Climate of the British Isles* (London: Macmillan & Co., Ltd., 1938). Note that temperature maps in this volume are reduced to sea level, a fact which deprives them of all value.

[7] See climatic graphs, Appendix II.

Vegetation

The landscape of Neolithic Britain was very densely forested, like that of eastern North America before white settlement. Today, after several millennia of assaults by man, the forests have all but vanished, and Britain has the poorest forest cover in Europe. The landscape of the lowlands shows few traces of the vanished forests, though hedgerow trees and farm woodlots or game coverts give the distant prospect a wooded look. Ireland has the least area of forest—if St. Patrick banished the snake from Ireland, his people have been almost as successful in ousting the tree. British forests have vanished under the combined needs of farmers for cleared land, the early navy for ships and their masts, ironsmiths for charcoal, and the general populace for firewood.[8]

The climax forest appears to be dominated by the pedunculate oak[9] and the durmast oak, both of which extend right across peninsular Europe. Oakwoods occur in every part of the British Isles. The durmast oak seems dominant in the woodlands on the thin, acid soils of the wet hill lands of the Highland Zone, whereas the pedunculate oak is dominant in the drier east. The two species hybridize freely. The common ash is often a codominant, and may form extensive pure stands, especially in limestone country. The beech is also common as an associate of the oaks. Like the ash, it may occur in pure stands, but it is largely confined to the south and southeast of England. Other hardwoods of common occurrence are the birches (discussed below), certain elms, willows, alder, poplar, lime, and the hornbeam.

This deciduous forest climax has been established in Britain since the climatic optimum some 7000 years ago. Since it now survives only in patches, it is impossible to sketch the constitution of the climax cover in any detail. In particular, one cannot say for sure whether the cover extended without essential thinning over the lower hills of the Highland Zone or over the dry chalk Downs of England, which may have been grassy.

The forests that covered Britain in the Boreal and pre-Boreal climatic periods (roughly 9000–5000 B.C.) were very different in composition. The birches were the most widespread trees, but their dominance was challenged by the Scots pine. Today the birches are common all over Britain, especially in open heaths and sandy soils. The pine forms considerable forests in Highland Scotland, but finds its ideal home on the sandy soils of southern England, where it forms a distinctive and handsome landscape. The Bagshot plateaus in the London Basin and the New Forest in the Hampshire Basin have the largest stands. There is also much ornamental woodland planted by park designers, usually of hybrids or of exotic conifers. Indeed, over many parishes in southern England the number of foreign species exceeds considerably the roster of native ones. There are probably more cedars of Lebanon in some English counties than in Lebanon itself.

The hills of the Highland Zone of Britain are characteristically treeless, and present the landscape known throughout the country as "moorland." Much of this vegetation is today established on land that would certainly sustain forest, but for the work of domesticated animals, rabbits, and other beasts. Moorlike vegetation also occurs on sandy common land in the Lowland Zone, often as an early stage in the succession leading to pine forest. Characteristic species are the lowland gorse and various brambles.

THE PEOPLING OF BRITAIN

Prehistory. The peopling of the British Isles began at so early a date that its detailed

---

[8] This section owes much to A. G. Tansley, *The British Islands and Their Vegetation* (Cambridge: Cambridge University Press, 1939). This monumental work also contains long treatments of soil, a topic little regarded in much-plowed England, where soil profiles of a mature sort are hard to come by.

[9] Recent opinion suggests that this oak may have been introduced by man.

story is forever lost. The earliest inhabitants have left us nothing but primitive flint tools and weapons with which to trace their homes and characteristics. Paleolithic man appears to have been scattered thinly around the coasts and in the hills of southern England, where he practiced in the second and third interglacial periods his crude economy of fruit gathering and hunting. The Riss-Würm glacial advances may have driven him from Britain, or perhaps into the sea caves and limestone caverns of southern England; we have no means of ascertaining his movements. In any event the early dawn of man's occupancy, though it was probably spread over a period a hundred times as long as that which has elapsed since Paleolithic times, has left no trace on the British landscape, and contributes nothing to present-day geography.[10]

It is all otherwise with the primitive societies that spread across Britain in Neolithic, Bronze Age, and Iron Age times (2500 B.C.–100 A.D.). The peopling of the islands proceeded in these years from both western and eastern sources. Within the Lowland Zone, pre-Roman settlement appears to have preferred the high limestone plateaus or sandy plains with loamy soils. Here the forest (of beech and ash) was thinner and may have yielded more readily to the primitive axe of the pioneer. Much of the lighter land was brought under the plow, or was used to pasture stock, and the settlements themselves tended to be grouped along spring lines. Salisbury Plain, on which several of the drier ridges converged, was the most thickly and continuously settled area; the fields of the farm on which the author of this chapter was born still bear the impress of this early agricultural civilization. The clay vales, by contrast, resisted for long the efforts of early man to occupy them; the dense oakwood and the abundant surface water were both unwelcome to a

people of limited technology. As Sir Cyril Fox put it,

This forest was in a sense unbroken, for without emerging from its canopy a squirrel could traverse the country from end to end. . . . [The forests were] haunted by lynx, wolf and boar, bear and fighting ox; and were hostile in themselves to Man, his flocks and herds.[11]

Thus in pre-Roman times both Highland and Lowland zones were thinly occupied by Celtic-speaking Britons. As later, more vigorous settlers invaded from the east, both the ways and the tongues of these primitive folk were banished into Ireland, Highland Scotland, Wales, and Cornubia. Vestiges of the old traditions linger in the ceremonial of the Welsh, the most tenaciously conservative of the Highland people. Such traditions find their expression in modern literature, as in the poetry of Dylan Thomas, and in local ritual (though not in the annual Eisteddfod, whose Druidic rites are charming but apocryphal). They also form the basis of resurgent Irish nationalism, whose disciples are striving doggedly to revive the moribund Gaelic tongue.

The Roman interlude. Upon this simple culture the Roman Empire imposed four centuries (A.D. 43–400) of Mediterranean civilization and law. The Roman conquerors entirely subjugated the Lowland Zone of Britain, but made little attempt to penetrate the Highlands. Civil administration was established over the Lowlands, and the Celtic peasantry was in considerable measure knit into the structure of a Romanized state. Towns of typical Mediterranean plan were constructed, and trade, already active in Bronze and Iron Age times, was substantially increased, both internally and externally. Wales, northern England, and southern Scotland were constituted military zones, whence the Roman legionaries watched the tribesmen of the hills beyond.

The most significant modern legacy of the Roman interlude was the military road system. As in other parts of conquered western

---

[10] A classic in the geographical literature of Britain is C. Fox, *The Personality of Britain: Its Influence on Inhabitant and Invader in Prehistoric and Early Historic Times* (Cardiff: National Museum of Wales, 1933).

[11] *Ibid.*, p. 82.

Europe, the Romans built straight, well-metalled highways which have in some areas survived into modern England as major routeways. Thus Watling Street, from Richborough (now defunct as a port, near modern Sandwich) to London (already the largest trading center) and across the Midlands to Wroxeter, today forms highways A2 and A5. Ermine Street (London-Lincoln-Humber) is still in several stretches a major north-south routeway. On the other hand Fosse Way, a route following roughly the belt of Jurassic scarps from Lincoln to Cirencester and Exeter, has for considerable distances lapsed to the status of a footpath (Fig. 3–4).

Of the cities that developed under Roman rule, some (like Silchester—*Calleva Atrebatum*) have vanished as such, others have flourished. Since the Roman interlude London, for example, has remained the largest commercial center of the kingdom. The root "-chester" is a corruption of the Latin *castra*, a camp, and its abundance in English place names is proof enough of the capacity of the Roman overlords to select sites that would stand the test of time.

The Anglo-Saxon, Norse, and Danish invasions. In the fifth century A.D. the Romanized Celtic civilization of Lowland England was eclipsed by renewed barbarian invasions from the east—the Angles, Jutes, and Saxons, whose Teutonic tongues and warlike philosophy swept the civilized culture of the Britons from the Lowlands into the Highland refuges of the west. In the Britain of the Dark Ages we lose sight of the progress of settlement and cannot regain our perspective until the Norman invasion. It is clear, however, that the Anglo-Saxons completely occupied the Lowland Zone and in several places penetrated deeply into the Highlands, as in southeast Scotland and

Fig. 3–4. The Fosse Way, near Tetbury, on the Cotswold backslope. The large arable fields and the abundance of hedgerow trees are typical of lowland Britain. (Photo: Aero Pictorial, Ltd.)

Devon. They showed a marked preference for well-drained, loamy soils, though they did not shun the oakwoods of the clay vales as thoroughly as did their Celtic predecessors.[12]

In the eighth and ninth centuries A.D. the young English kingdoms so established were themselves overrun by the second wave of "Nordic" invaders, the Danish and Norse Vikings. The Norwegians followed the outer-sea route round Cape Wrath and established scattered settlements all along the western seaboard; Caithness, Galloway, much of Ireland, the Isle of Man, the Lake District, and parts of South Wales were invaded. The Danes, in contrast, landed in great numbers in eastern England, establishing a broad belt of Danish settlement in the "Danelaw," essentially the Lowland Zone east of Watling Street. They also established a kingdom in Normandy, from which, two centuries later, the final invasion and conquest of Britain were to come.

Despite war and bloody rapine, ordinary events in pre-Norman Britain, it is clear that the Lowland Zone was fairly fully occupied at this time. Even the clay vales, with their damp oakwoods, had begun slowly to yield. We can attempt to reconstruct the process of settlement by the study of place names, a fascinating field of geographical research. Names ending in -ingas (now -ing) and -ingaham (now -ingham) are of early Anglo-Saxon origin, and -ton is of a later Saxon period. In the Danelaw, names ending in -by (Old Scandinavian -byr, i.e., village, town) and -thorp (Danish, hamlet) and those containing Danish proper names abound. Place-name research is an intricate and highly developed technique.[13]

[12] S. W. Wooldridge, "The Anglo-Saxon Settlement," chap. iii of H. C. Darby (ed.), *Historical Geography of England before 1800* (London: Cambridge University Press, 1936), p. 91. See also S. W. Wooldridge and D. L. Linton, "The Loam-Terrains of Southeast England in Their Relation to Its Early History," *Antiquity* 7 (September, 1933): 297–303.
[13] The method is explained in E. Ekwall, *The Oxford Dictionary of English Place-Names* (London: Clarendon Press, 1936), pp. vii-xxxiv.

The Norman Conquest. The Norman Conquest was the final episode in the peopling of Britain from outside her shores. The Normans were few in numbers, but they extended their autocratic rule over most of Britain and introduced a Latin element into the English language. The English feudal system was largely their creation, and the rural settlements of both England and Ireland bear many traces of their rule. Once again, it was in the English Lowlands that Norman feudalism was most readily established; beneath its heel the English peasantry and its manorial overlords occupied all but the most intractable soils. The Norman castle on its mound survives in many places to remind us of this vital phase in the taking up of the land. Over all England there spread the Norman conception of statehood, of authoritarian government, of codified and enforceable law. In the cities arose the great cathedrals, Romanesque at first, derived from France, but expressing later a rising English genius in Gothic architecture. Through the teaching of Norman, French, and Italian clergy the mainstream of European civilization resumed its flow into Britain.

The Highland Zone was less tractable. Wales was subjected to conquest, but could not be assimilated into the English kingdom until the Tudors—a Welsh family—ascended to the throne. Scotland, a poor, lightly settled land in which Saxons and Celtic clansmen intermingled, was nevertheless not united with the British crown until 1707, and separation still exists as a political aspiration. Ireland was conquered by part-Welsh earls who established Norman feudalism only to see it absorbed by Irish tribalism.

Nevertheless, the Norman period marked the final stage in the emergence of the English state and in the initial occupance of the soil. By the time the Normans themselves had been absorbed into the English people, and the English tongue was once again the language of power and government, England and Wales had become a consolidated kingdom that has never since bowed to invasion.

Scotland was as yet independent, but her days were numbered. Only Ireland stood beyond the pale, as she again stands. The peopling of Britain was thus complete, and the identity of her four subsidiary nations—Welsh, Scottish, Irish, and English—established.

Medieval Britain was a land of cities and trade on the one hand, and an entrenched, landed feudal aristocracy on the other; town and country were distinct in the landscape, at least to the Highland border.[14] They have remained distinct into modern Britain, whose geography can best be discussed in terms of the urban and rural landscapes.

The Rural Landscape

The British Isles as a whole are blessed with a climate that permits a varied and productive agriculture. Almost all the tillable land has been under the plow or improved grassland for generations and, in some areas, since Neolithic times. In the United Kingdom, 48,402,000 acres (about 81 per cent of the whole country) is in agricultural use, and about 1.8 per cent of the working population is employed upon it. In the Irish Republic, by contrast, one third of the labor force is engaged in agriculture. In highly industrialized Britain the gross agricultural product amounts to only about 3 per cent in value of the gross product of goods and services. In contrast, agricultural production and that of associated industries are the kernel of the national economy of the Irish Republic. Notwithstanding the apparently small contribution it makes to the national income, British agriculture is highly organized and productive.

The 11,136,000 acres of United Kingdom land not in agricultural production are largely inaccessible mountain or moorland, much of it peat bog, of which most is in the Scottish Highlands. The Land Utilisation Survey of Britain has reported that in Britain itself (excluding Northern Ireland) about

3,000,000 acres are occupied by houses with gardens, cities, industrial or mining sites, and for other agriculturally unproductive uses. In short, Britain's urban economy, which contributes almost all the national income, and which has made her one of the world's largest industrial powers, is based on only 6 per cent of her land, which remains overwhelmingly rural.

British farming is highly mechanized. The number of tractors (550,000) now exceeds the number of separate farms, a tenfold increase since 1939. Similar advances have occurred in the use of electric dairy equipment and combine harvesters. Agriculturally, Britain now ranks among the world's most mechanized countries.

The medieval landscape and its legacy. The modern British countryside is largely the creation of the past two centuries, when most of the enclosed fields, compact farms, and ornamental parklands that personify it were created. Until the seventeenth century most of the land was occupied under a husbandry derived from the medieval manorial system, or the more primitive organization of Celtic Britain. Though the Agricultural Revolution has effaced the older landscape effectively, it has not fundamentally changed the distribution of settlement. Certain villages have been abandoned, and much secondary dispersal of settlement has followed the enclosures; nevertheless, enough of the older pattern survives to make it necessary for us to glance at the husbandry of medieval times.

The Lowland Zone was cultivated under variants of the open-field system, in which the tenantry (largely in a condition of serfdom in earlier days) plowed intermingled strips of from a quarter to a whole acre in extent, within two or three arable fields. Each field was sown with a single crop—usually rye, wheat, oats, barley, peas, or some other "green" crop. One field was left under fallow. Beyond the arable fields was a common pasture on which a small head of cattle or sheep was tended. There was also much-treasured hay meadow along the

[14] H. C. Darby, "The Economic Geography of England, A.D. 1000–1250," chap. v of Darby, *op. cit.*, pp. 165–229.

stream courses. A woodlot for communal grazing, timber, and firewood made up the rest of the land. None of the fields was enclosed, though growing crops and hay were protected by hurdles. The village's inhabitants were thus communally concerned with the management of all the land; the individual farm was a thing of the future.[15],[16]

The two-field and three-field systems were widely distributed in the Midlands and the southwest. In East Anglia, the eastern London Basin, and Kent, however, the open-field system in its pure form never existed, and some measure of enclosure seems to have prevailed very early.

The Highland Zone was thinly settled, but was nevertheless agriculturally organized. The most widespread system of land use was the infield-outfield system. Here from two to fifteen tenant families operated (also communally) a looser form of husbandry. The infield was close to the settlement: it was plowed continuously, and upon it was spread all the available dung. The larger outfield was used for poor pasture, but strips of it were also plowed from time to time in a shifting fashion, so that in time all of it was cultivated and prevented from relapsing to rough grazing or moorland. This so-called "Celtic" system—a bad misnomer—was widespread in Scotland, the Pennines, Wales, and Cornwall, but also occurred on poor soils and uplands in Lowland Britain.[17]

The older husbandry all over Britain was close to a subsistence economy. Regional differentiation of farming practice was kept to a minimum because the necessities of life had to be produced locally. Nevertheless, upon the richer lands of the Lowland Zone and the outer fringe of the Highlands there arose a considerable surplus which was ul-

timately to color Britain's modern economy. The first and foremost was wool, for which medieval Britain was famous. It made her, first, a large exporter of raw wool and, later, the home of a prosperous woolen and worsted textile industry which remains one of her industrial staples.

All over the Lowland Zone, the old economy tended to create nucleated settlement: each village, a little world in itself (Fig. 3–5), was located at or near a source of drinking water, usually a spring. The dry tablelands of limestone or sandstone, and the wet, marshy clays, were avoided. Favorite sites were along the spring lines flanking the cuestas (Fig. 3–6).

The breakdown of the medieval system was slow. It was marked by enclosure of the old common pastures, as well as of the arable. At first the enclosure movement derived from the desire to create vast sheep runs, when wool was the most precious raw material in Europe. Later, however, enclosure became the preliminary to improvement in farming, for the new techniques of the eighteenth and nineteenth centuries could not be applied to open fields. The culmination of the movement came with the General Enclosure Act of 1845. Henceforward Britain was a land, not of communal manors, but of farms and farmers, each with his distinct plot of ground. The villages remained, but to them was added a disseminated farming population.[18] The enclosure movement also established a fourfold division of the rural population which persists to the present day in the Lowland Zone:

1. *Land-owners* deriving income chiefly from agricultural rents. This group includes corporations as well as individuals.
2. *Owner-farmers,* owning their own farms and land and living off the sale of produce, or off the produce itself.
3. *Tenant farmers,* renting their farms, and making up the largest group in modern Britain.

[15] *Ibid.,* pp. 189–207.

[16] A good summary of field systems is given in W. Smith, *An Economic Geography of Great Britain* (London: Methuen & Co., Ltd., 1949), pp. 3–23.

[17] The crofting system of modern Highland Scotland has certain affinities with the older Celtic husbandry. See I. F. Grant, "The Highland Openfield System," *Geographical Teacher* 13 (1926), 480–82.

[18] W. G. East, "England in the Eighteenth Century," chap. xiii of Darby, *op. cit.,* p. 471.

Fig. 3–5. Wherwell, Hampshire, which exemplifies the traditional village architecture of southernmost England. Note the thatched roofs, the half-timbered walls, and the carefully tended hedges. (Central Office of Information, London.)

Fig. 3–6. The cuesta of the South Downs (Chalk) at Poynings, Sussex. The beds dip toward the left, where the chalk forms a bold face about 600 feet high, largely supporting poor, dry pasture land. At the foot of the scarp is a wide shelf covered by fertile downwash; the shelf is under arable cultivation in large fields. Poynings is on the spring line and is a typical nucleated village clustered around its church. (Central Office of Information, London.)

4. *Laborers,* owning and renting no land but working for wages for the farmers. The farm laborer is the descendant of the villager displaced from his land by enclosure.

The tenant farmer is the characteristic countryman of Britain. Protected by legislation from arbitrary displacement, he no longer occupies a hazardous position.

The farm laborer is essentially an inhabitant of eastern and southern England. In Highland Britain, enclosure of the old "Celtic" townships did not displace so many landsmen, nor did it provide a market for agricultural hired labor. In Wales, Highland Scotland, the Pennines, and Ireland the typical unit is the family farm in which the farmer, his wife, and his family can work the land without assistance.[19]

The modern farming system. Present-day land use in Great Britain is well-known through the nationwide studies of the Land Utilisation Survey (directed by L. Dudley Stamp), whose maps of land use, on a scale of 1:63,360, cover the whole country, and whose nine-volume report, *The Land of Britain,* is unique in geographical literature.[20] Stamp's own *Land of Britain: Its Use and Misuse* is an appraisal of the results [21] and renders all other studies of the subject obsolete or incomplete. A similar survey exists for Northern Ireland (directed by D. A. Hills). A revised series for Britain only is now being published at the 1:25,000 scale under the direction of Miss Alice Coleman. These land-use studies have been supplemented by the publication of maps showing types of farming and land classification in terms of fertility. They show a complexity that makes nonsense of most attempts at a regional division of British rural life. It is more valid to think of broad agricultural types (Fig. 3–7).

England and Wales: farming types. In general it may be said that Anglo-Welsh farming tends toward two extremes:

1. An arable economy, in which most of the land is plowed regularly and sowed under crops. Such land is largely confined to the drier east and is most widespread in East Anglia, the Fenlands, and much of Yorkshire.
2. A pastoral economy, in which the land is left unplowed. There are two distinct subtypes, the rough hill grazing of the moorlands of the Highland Zone and the richer pastures widespread on the heavier soils of the Midlands of England.

Between these extremes there is a broad range of intermediate economies, in which arable and permanent improved grass intermingle. The three types are mapped in Fig. 3–8.

Hill sheep farming is typical of the higher moorlands of the Highland Zone, both in Wales, Devon, and Cornwall and in northern England. The farms are large, partially enclosed tracts of heather and grassy upland on which flocks of hardy mountain breeds are maintained. The flocks are of ewes, and the economy depends on the sale of the annual lamb crop.

Stock rearing is localized on the lower hill country of the three main parts of the Highland Zone: Devon-Cornwall (Fig. 3–9), Wales, and northern England. The land may either be improved pasture or arable. If the latter, however, it is usually under the specialized form of husbandry known as ley farming, in which the land is sown out to grass for two, three, or four years after each phase of cropping. The crops themselves are usually oats, barley, turnips, swedes, or other animal foodstuffs. The economy turns on the rearing of young cattle (or sheep in some cases) for sale to the rich fattening lands to the south and east. In most cases the cattle are of famous beef breeds like

[19] *Britain: An Official Handbook—1968* (London: H. M. Stationery Office, 1968): Chapter 12, pp. 314–315.

[20] L. Dudley Stamp (ed.), *The Land of Britain* (9 vols.; London: Geographical Publications, Ltd., 1943–46).

[21] L. Dudley Stamp, *The Land of Britain: Its Use and Misuse* (London: Geographical Publications, Ltd., and Longmans, Green & Co., Ltd., 1948).

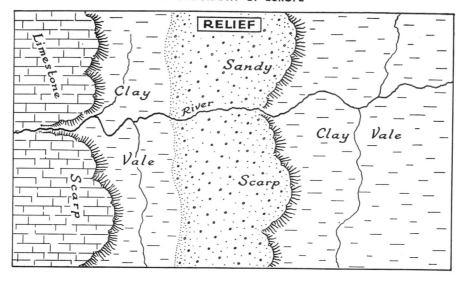

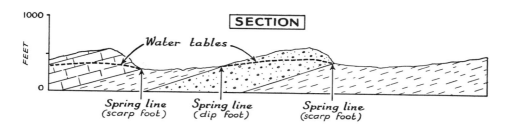

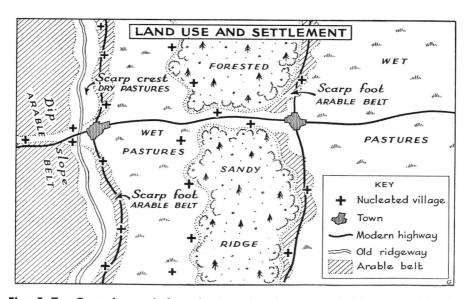

Fig. 3–7. Cuestaform relief, nucleation of settlement, and differentiated land use in Lowland England. The upper diagram shows a typical example of the relief, and the section diagram shows the location of spring lines. Upon these, many villages are sited. Large settlements tend to occur near the mouths of wind- or water-gaps at old bridging points.

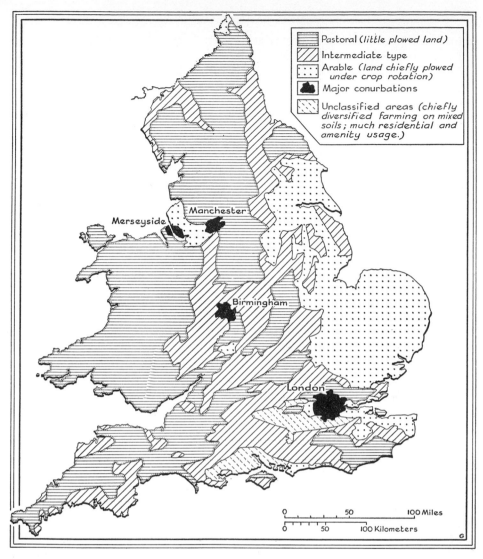

Legend:

Pastoral (little plowed land)
Intermediate type
Arable (land chiefly plowed under crop rotation)
Major conurbations
Unclassified areas (chiefly diversified farming on mixed soils; much residential and amenity usage.)

Merseyside

Manchester

Birmingham

London

0   50   100 Miles

0   50   100 Kilometers

Fig. 3–8. Dominant farming economies of England and Wales. Note the concentration of pastoral types on western moors, and on the clay vales of the Midlands; intermediate types are most widespread on limestone soils and in the Midland Vale.

Fig. 3–9. Stock-rearing country on a more tractable part of the Highland Zone, Vale of Widecombe, Devon. Note the small fields on the lower ground and the rough moors above the small village of St. Pancras. The farms are widely disseminated. (Photo: UKIO.)

the Hereford and Devon (which are now world-wide in distribution) or dual-purpose animals like the Shorthorn. The greater part of the world's beef production today comes from breeds fixed on these British hill farms.

Stock fattening, the complement of stock rearing, is widely dispersed among the Lowland pastoral and intermediate economies, but is especially noteworthy on the permanent grass of the clay plains of the English Midlands, particularly in Leicestershire.

Dairying is now the most widespread farming type of lowland Britain, where it attains its highest form in the clay vales of the south and east. Concentration upon dairying was determined originally by the nearness of great local markets. Nowadays, however, improved access by road, the marketing services of the Milk Marketing Board, and the increased demands of the large creameries have made dairying profitable in most areas where soils are not excessively light. The characteristic breeds are the Dairy Shorthorn and the Friesian, as well as the Jersey and Guernsey in the south.

Mixed farming is a collective term for the varied economies typical chiefly of the lighter soils of the Lowlands. Barley and wheat are common crops, and sheep are usually numerous, especially in the limestone belts. Much of this land now has extensive dairy herds and stock fattening. Here and in the still richer arable counties beef and pig production have risen sharply, to the point where nearly three-quarters of the country's meat supply can now be raised internally. Much of the beef now comes from dairy cows crossed with beef sires (usually by artificial insemination), and is fattened on barley.

Arable (crop) farming, in which the production of crops for sale off the farm is the preoccupation, is mainly an eastern type, being found on medium soils in the drier belts (Fig. 3–10). The till-covered plains of East Anglia, the rich, organic or silty soils of the Fens and the Vale of York are the largest areas.

Wheat and barley are the major cereals,

sugar beets and potatoes the chief root crops. Wheat yields have doubled, to over 4 million tons, since World War II, and barley (now used both for malting and for feeding to beef animals) has quadrupled, to over 8 million tons. Half the arable acreage of Britain is now under barley. In the Fens, crop farming is the only significant activity: the richest soils in England are here, farmed in drained areas reminiscent of the Dutch polders. Elsewhere, however, the crop economy is added to by extensive sheep flocks, by dairying, and by stock fattening. The plain of southwest Lancashire, the only western representative of this type, is a region concentrating largely on poultry, potatoes, and green vegetables.

Market gardening, in which arable specialization reaches its ultimate form, is not extensive but raises much of the needs of the large cities in small fruit, fresh vegetables, and flowers. The largest areas are: (a) the brick-earth belt of the Thames terraces east and west of London; (b) a part of the clay vale of Evesham; and (c) areas of sandy soil in Bedfordshire and Cambridgeshire. Regions (a) and (c) serve the London market.

Fruit farming is of limited significance in cool, cloudy England. Two areas, however, stand out—the west Midlands (Worcestershire, Herefordshire, Gloucestershire, Somersetshire) and Kent. The latter county has been aptly named the garden of England. The Kentish orchards, nurseries, and hop gardens occur in two principal belts, the loam-soil belt of north Kent, along the foot of the backslope of the North Downs, and the similar belt to the south along the backslope of a cuesta of calcareous sandstone. Apples, cherries, plums, and hops are the characteristic products.

Scotland: farming types. Scotland has less good land than England and has a shorter, cooler summer. Nevertheless its farming is technically advanced, and follows in several ways a distinctive tradition.

As in England, one can distinguish arable, pastoral, and intermediate economies, but

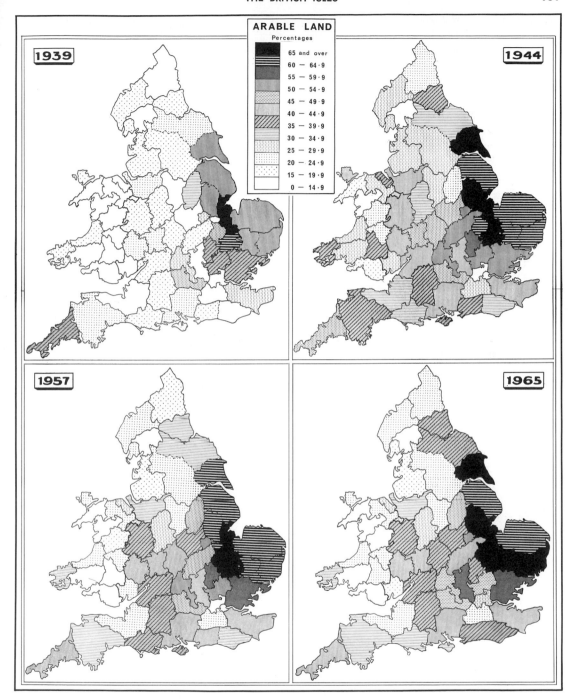

Fig. 3–10. The fraction of land in England and Wales under arable cultivation in four selected years. Note the effect of wartime plow-up campaigns, and the gradual postwar extension of plowed land, especially in Eastern England. (After H. C. K. Henderson.)

the distinction loses some of its significance. Much of the arable land is farmed on the ley principle—with several years of unplowed rotation grass following each period of cropping. On the other hand, purely pastoral economies are rare on the improved land; there is no Scottish equivalent for the great Lowland permanent pastures of England. Only the moorlands present large areas of unplowed but productive land. Four distinct farming types can be distinguished, and are outlined in Fig. 3–11.

Arable farming with livestock raising occurs on areas of level ground and loamy soils along the drier east coast. The chief crops in the arable rotation are barley, wheat (chiefly south of Aberdeen), potatoes, turnips, and other root crops designed for use as winter feed for livestock. There is also much rotation grass, the timothy-hay crop being especially valuable. A considerable volume of off-the-farm sales of crops is characteristic. Throughout the belt, however, there is a specialization in the feeding and

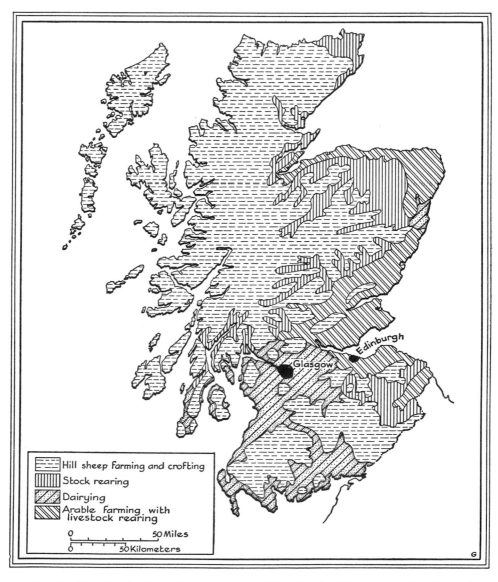

Fig. 3–11. Predominant farming types of Scotland. (After L. Dudley Stamp.)

fattening of livestock. In the Tweed Valley, sheep outnumber beef cattle; Cheviot, Border-Leicester, and their cross, the Half-bred, are the characteristic breeds of this spacious country. In the rest of the belt the fattening of store cattle from the nearby rearing lands is commoner than sheep farming. The eastern half of the Midland Valley has such an economy, and dairying is also considerable.

Stock rearing, as in England, is localized on the hilly margins of the main uplands, namely the Southern Uplands and the more accessible Highlands. Almost always the rearing is carried out on arable farms using long leys of rotation grass, and producing barley, oats, and turnips as the only significant crops. Famous beef breeds have characterized this country, the Aberdeen Angus in the northeast, the Highland in the west, and the Galloway in the western Southern Uplands. Sheep rearing, though common, is dominant only around the Tweed Valley.

Dairying is widespread, and is the dominant farming type in two principal regions, the western half of the Midland Valley (where it supplies the large markets of Clydeside) and around the western flanks of the Southern Uplands in Ayrshire, Wigtown, Kirkcudbright, and Dumfries, where the milk is sold wholesale to creameries or to the Scottish Milk Marketing Board. The Ayrshire cow is the typical dairy animal.

Hill sheep farming extends over the moorlands of the Southern Uplands and the Highlands; the Blackface ewes roam the bleak heather moors in thousands, with Cheviots on the grassy slopes. Crofting is a vanishing farming type, thinly scattered through the Highlands, and seen at its purest in the Hebrides and Shetland Islands. It involves the inherited tenure of tiny patches of cultivated land on the raised beaches and coastal platforms or valley floors, with limited grazing rights on the nearby hillsides.

Planning. One of the most striking developments since World War II in the United Kingdom has been the emergence of town and country planning as a national policy and interest. The acute pressure on land, the necessity of protecting the food supply, the problems of rebuilding war-damaged cities, and the widespread desire to protect Great Britain's lovely countryside have combined to awaken the nation to the need for land-use planning. All parties agree on the need, though there is some difference between them in the emphasis given specific problems. Space is lacking to recount here the immense body of work undertaken in this field. The most remarkable visible result of the planning movement is the construction of new towns, which are intended to rehouse the overcrowded population of the large cities and to achieve some measure of decentralization of light industry away from overcrowded areas.

The rural life of Ireland. The Irish landscape in no way resembles that of Britain to the east. Behind the apparent peace of the white farmhouses and the emerald-green pastures there lies a troubled history. It has already been said that a third of Ireland's working population lives off the land and that even her industry is largely concerned with agricultural produce. The mild climate, with its cool, cloudy summers and largely frost-free winters, has encouraged the development of a pastoral economy that allows a large-scale export of farm produce.[22]

In the early nineteenth century Ireland was a densely populated land of tenant farmers, occupying tiny farms rented, without security of tenure, from a land-owning class whose political and economic ambitions were best served by a minute subdivision of the land. Much of the land was arable, producing potatoes as the staple of the local diet and wheat for export to England. A

[22] The best reference on the geography of Ireland is T. W. Freeman, *Ireland* (London: Methuen & Co., Ltd., 1950). E. Estyn Evans, *Irish Heritage* (Dundalk: Dundalgen Press, 1942) and S. O'Faolain, *The Irish* (Harmondsworth: Penquin Books, Ltd., 1947) give excellent accounts of the cultural and traditional background of modern Irish life.

progressive increase in population taxed the resources of the land beyond its limit, and in 1845 there began a famine that caused 750,000 country folk to die of starvation before they could escape to the ports. There ensued a drastic revolution in population and land tenure, of which three elements can be distinguished here:

1. Large-scale emigration to Britain, the dominions, and America has reduced the population from 8,175,000 in 1841 to 4,283,000 in 1936–37, since when population has increased to about 4,350,000. Ireland is unique in Europe in showing a large decline in population since the early nineteenth century. There has also been—especially in Ulster—a migration from the country to the towns, notably to Londonderry, Belfast, Dublin, and Cork.[23]
2. The land has been transferred by governmental action from the landlord class to the farmers, who now own the land they farm, in both Northern Ireland and the Irish Republic. In the latter, especially, attention has been given to the congested lands of the western Gaeltacht.
3. The economy has become mainly pastoral, devoting the land to the rearing or fattening of cattle (largely for the British market), or to dairying and poultry farming.

Acute land hunger still exists, and farms remain remarkably small. Population pressure in some areas continues severe. Seventy-five per cent of the holdings of the Republic is in farms of 50 acres or less, and upon this minutely divided land dwells the greater part of the farming population: the smaller the farm size, the greater the rural population density.

The greatest concentration of small farms —and hence of high population density—extends up the west coast from the Shannon through the hilly Caledonian country of

[23] Cork is unique among the group in that its population has not markedly increased. Emigration from the town has offset the influx from rural districts.

Galway, Mayo, Sligo, and Donegal. This area contains a high proportion of those able to speak Gaelic.

Ulster is also a land of minute farms, but here there is a higher level of prosperity. The traditional crop is flax, grown for the production of linen, a famous specialization of the province. The acreage of flax sown fluctuates widely, and the remaining energies of the people are devoted to the raising (in the higher regions) or fattening of beef and young dairy cattle, of which there is some export to Britain. Dairying is also practiced, especially in Fermanagh.

The southern and eastern parts of the Republic present a happier picture than does the congested Gaeltacht. Farms are larger, and population densities lower. The land is mainly pastoral. Dairying predominates in the southwest, stock fattening in the eastern Central Plain. Sheep rearing and fattening is common in the Hercynian and Caledonian massifs. There is, however, a wide variety of local products, and specialization is nowhere excessive.

Ireland's agricultural surplus goes largely to Britain, on whom she is dependent for imports of many industrial products.

The Urban Landscape: Industrialization

Britain has been an industrialized nation since medieval times, when her woolen textiles began to figure largely in international and domestic trade. The Industrial Revolution began in Britain, a country rich in coal and mechanical skills. Well ahead of her nearest rivals, Britain became in the mid-nineteenth century the workshop of the world. She pioneered in the development of railways, the locomotive, textile machinery, the iron ship, and the Bessemer and open-hearth steel processes. In a brief century, Britain changed from the peaceful, agrarian aristocracy depicted in the pages of Addison and Steele into an arrogant industrial empire whose ships carried the world's commerce, whose capital city was the financial center of the earth, and whose exports of manufactured goods poured forth in a steady stream to all the world's markets.

She remains a modern, industrialized society. Her early start, however, has had unfortunate repercussions. The men who captained the nineteenth-century industrial expansion had little thought for the well-being of the vast new proletariat that flocked into the cities. These cities became squalid, overcrowded, and gloomy, and today still present abundant problems to the city planner in spite of huge rehousing programs. Britain's markets dwindled as manufacturing industries sprang up overseas. Two wars also disrupted her economy. Nevertheless, the United Kingdom remains a great industrial power, and still conducts about 13 per cent of world trade.

Industry in the Irish Republic contributes much less to her gross national product. Determined efforts have been made, nevertheless, to build up the lighter, more modern branches of industry, notably those arising directly from her large agricultural surpluses. Brewing, specialized textiles, confectioneries, and glassware are among the successful lines, and Dublin's reputation as a center of fashion has been shrewdly exploited.

Energy. Like all industrial states, Britain requires much energy. In 1966 she consumed the equivalent of about 325 million metric tons of coal. This was generated as follows:

	Per Cent
From domestically mined coal and coke..	59
From petroleum, almost all imported....	37
From nuclear reactors, and from natural gas	4

In the past decade there has been a very rapid rise in electricity, fuel oil, and gasoline consumption, and an equally drastic shift away from coal. The largest consumers of energy are industry (41 per cent), domestic heating and cooking (28 per cent), and road transport (8 per cent). Railways, for long a main consumer, in 1966 required less than 2 per cent. These are typical statistics for a modern industrial nation.

Coal lay at the root of Britain's industrial revolution, for long providing nearly all the power needed (through steam engines) for industrial plant, transportation, and domestic use. Her widely distributed coalfields (see Fig. 3–1) became magnets for the new manufacturing industries in the nineteenth century. The coke derived from the coal was the basis of iron smelting. From the coalfields there came enough high-quality bituminous coal to meet all these needs, and to supply the world's ships and hearths as well. In 1913 the mines yielded over 315 million metric tons, one-third of which was exported. After World War I, however, there began prolonged depression, and competition from petroleum products eroded the shrunken markets. By 1938, the yield was 231 million metric tons, of which 47 million were exported. During World War II, and until the 1950's, coal was again crucial to the national economy, but from 1956 onwards the swing to petroleum products (including natural gas) became overwhelming. The industry has been in public hands since 1947, when the National Coal Board was created. In 1966 the Board's mines produced 183 million metric tons, and a further rapid rundown is certain—to 100 million tons or less by 1980.

Nevertheless, the coalfields remain crucial to the economy. The exhaustion of thin, fragmented seams in the older mining areas has driven production increasingly towards large, modern pits employing modern mechanization. The largest fields are those of Yorkshire, Derbyshire, and Nottinghamshire, where much of the coal now comes from large pits in the Trent valley, where the coal is concealed beneath younger deposits. Other major producing areas include Northumberland and Durham, the Midland Valley of Scotland and South Wales. Ireland has no significant production, though peat is available in quantity and can be used to raise industrial steam.

The electricity-generating industry of Britain, also in public ownership, converted 75 million metric tons of this coal into electricity in 1966, also using 8 million tons of oil. Hydroelectric generation is negligible. Total electricity generated was no less than 184,835 million kilowatt hours. In 1962 nuclear power (in which Britain has pioneered) began to flow into the national distribution grid, and now contributes about 10 per cent of the production. For political reasons—essentially the fear of unemployment in mining areas—the industry is under pressure to continue the use of coal, but nuclear power is now competitive in price, and will continue its growth. The principal generating stations are shown in Fig. 3–12.

About 100,000 square miles of the floor of the North Sea are open to Britain for resource development, under international agreement. Intensive prospecting of the sea bed has revealed five large natural-gas fields, and pipelines are being or will be laid from these fields to the Norfolk, Yorkshire, and Lincolnshire coasts. Much of Britain's gas distribution system will be converted to use this gas, which may drastically lower fuel costs to industry and domestic users.

Ireland, too, has drastically altered her energy sources. Formerly dependent on British coal, she has converted to imported petroleum as effectively as the British, with the dieselisation of her railways and the spread of road transport. Hydroelectric development of the Shannon, and use of peat in thermal electric generation, have further diversified her sources.

Steel. Steel is the indispensable raw material of British industry. Iron manufacture has a long history in Britain; the local ores have been smelted since pre-Roman times, and the modern techniques of steel making had their origin here. Though she has since been eclipsed by the United States, Germany, and the Soviet Union, Britain has remained a major producer and is at present expanding her capacity rapidly. High-quality alloy steels and special finishes are a specialization. Until recently, production was largely in the hands of large, vertically integrated companies. Under the Iron and Steel Act of 1949 the industry passed into public ownership in 1951 and was administered by a public corporation. The Conservative Government elected in October, 1951, returned the industry to private hands, but in 1967 renationalisation began.

The raw materials of the industry—coal, ore, and limestone—are bulky, and their producing areas are highly localized. British ores are largely of low iron content, and of the bedded type. Most of them are extracted from the Jurassic cuestas of Yorkshire, Lincolnshire, and Northamptonshire. Much of the needed ore is imported, chiefly through Middlesbrough and South Wales ports. Most of the steel industry now carries on its operations with basic open-hearth, pneumatic, and electric converters. Total production of ingots and castings reached 29,-901,000 million metric tons in 1965 declining to 26,892,000 in 1966.

The producing areas are mostly on or near coal fields, the cost of coal transportation being the determining factor. In many instances, the smelting of pig iron was originally based on Coal Measure iron ores (as in South Wales, the Black Country, and Clydeside). These are largely worked out, and nearly all blast furnaces use Jurassic or imported ores. The largest producing centers are Clydeside (Glasgow, Coatbridge, Motherwell, etc.), supplying the local shipbuilding and engineering industries; Teeside (Middlesbrough); South Yorkshire and Derbyshire (Rotherham, Sheffield, and Chesterfield); and South Staffordshire and South Wales (the Swansea area, Cardiff, Newport and Ebbw Vale). The Scunthorpe (Lincolnshire) and Northamptonshire plants are unusual in being located on the ore body rather than on the coal field.

High cost, high quality, and local specialization characterize the industry. Thus the Swansea district is largely concerned with the needs of the local tin-plate industry, now undergoing expansion. Sheffield—a famous name among steelmen—is a steel-making town, having no blast furnaces. For centuries, it has specialized in quality work and has become the home of (among other

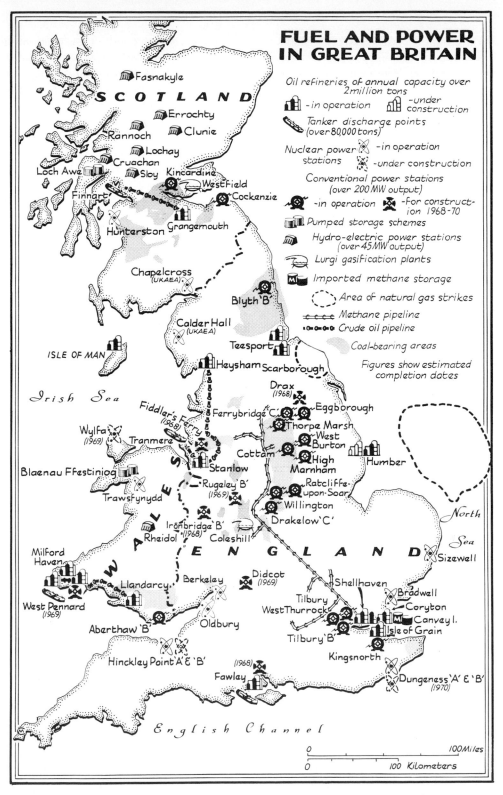

Fig. 3—12. Fuel and power in Great Britain (September, 1967). (*Source: Britain: An Official Handbook, 1968*. London: Her Majesty's Stationary Office, 1968, p. 268.)

types) high-grade alloy steels, Sheffield stainless being an example, based in part on imported pure iron. The nearby Coal Measure grit allowed a grinding industry, and the valleys behind Sheffield have long specialized in cutlery.

The non-ferrous metals.   The non-ferrous metals, though less bulky and less central to the economy, are essential to the steel and engineering industries. Aluminum, copper, lead, tin, zinc, nickel, and many less common metals are produced largely from imported semi-refined concentrates rather than the crude ore. Birmingham is the chief center, concentrating especially on alloy and aluminum ware; over 40 per cent of the labor engaged in these industries work in this city and the surrounding satellite towns. No one geographical factor can account for this specialization at Birmingham. Today the district has one of Britain's greatest concentrations of the engineering industries, and a ready market for semi-finished and finished non-ferrous articles is close at hand.

Other major centers of this complex group of industries are the London district (where again there is an immense local market and an accessible port), South Lancashire, the West Riding of Yorkshire, and South Wales.

The engineering industries.   The engineering industries represent the other end of the scale of heavy industry. Here again there is a long tradition of skill, and British engineers —especially the Scots—have penetrated every corner of the earth, as have their products. In recent years technical precedence and the greater part of the world's market have passed into American hands, but the British engineer was never busier than he is today. A very wide variety of finished metal goods is produced, and the industry is widely distributed. Nevertheless, certain marked concentrations are visible:

1. Shipbuilding and marine repairing are concentrated on the estuaries of the Clyde (home of the Cunard "Queens"), Tees, Wear, and Tyne, and at Belfast. From these yards more than half the world's shipping

was formerly launched. Heavy competition from Japan (especially for large tankers and bulk carriers), West Germany, and Sweden has reduced Britain's share of the world market to below 10 per cent. In 1966 she launched 1.3 million metric gross tons, well below her yards' capacity.

2. Textile machinery is a marked specialization of the South Lancashire and West Riding coal fields, where it feeds the large local textile industry. Machine tools, a growing trade, are widely disseminated.

3. The heavy constructional and automotive industries—bridges, locomotives, armaments, aircraft, automobiles, etc.—are typical of the Scottish lowlands (especially near the great firths), Manchester and South Lancashire, Birmingham and the Black Country, and the Yorks-Derby-Nottingham coal field. Britain is a large exporter of automobiles, most of which come from Birmingham, Coventry, and Oxford. Bicycles, popular in Europe, come chiefly from the Midland area.

4. Specialized light engineering, though widely disseminated, is increasingly concentrated in the London district, which is also the center of the new "luxury" industries; London is surrounded by hundreds of new plants producing a thousand-and-one small products which reach the country's largest market with ease.

Textiles.   These industries are among Britain's oldest skills. Using her traditional and home produced raw material, wool, her craftsmen had created for themselves a high reputation before the Industrial Revolution. It was in the textile industries that this Revolution really began, when successive inventions in the late eighteenth century made possible the use of power, first from water mills and then from James Watt's steam engine. The traditional industries were widely dispersed, in the southern Pennine valleys, in East Anglia (the early home of worsteds), in the Cotswolds, and in southwest England. With the advent of steam power and factory manufacture, however, the districts remote from coal either expired or specialized, and today production is concentrated overwhelmingly in South Lancashire (cottons) and the West Riding of Yorkshire (woolens and worsteds). Smaller areas of production are the Glasgow district (cottons) and Belfast (cottons, poplins, and linen). All the raw cotton and most of the wool and flax required are imported.

The specialization on cotton in South Lancashire dates from the early eighteenth century. Here there is soft water, a naturally high humidity, abundant coal for power (and, in earlier times, water-power), and chemical industries, on the salt deposits of nearby Cheshire. From this center British cottons grew to great significance in the national economy, and were the largest export (by value) from the late nineteenth century until World War II. In recent years, however, stiff competition in the Asiatic markets from cheaper Japanese and Indian cottons has severely restricted this trade, and the industry has been chronically depressed.

There are three distinct areas of specialization. Spinning of yarn from raw cotton is concentrated at the headwaters of the Mersey tributaries, north of Manchester, in and around the towns of Bolton and Oldham. Weaving of cloth takes place in the Colne and Ribble valleys, farther north, the largest centers being Burnley, Blackburn, Preston, Nelson, and Colne. Finishing—largely a chemical process—takes place in and around Manchester-Salford, the commercial and technological capital of the industry.

The concentration of woolen and worsted manufactures in the West Riding of Yorkshire is equally emphatic; the Aire and Calder valleys are the scenes of the largest production, which was originally based on local wool and an abundance of waterpower. More recently, soft water (from the outcrop of the Millstone Grit on the Pennines) and the local supply of coal have been the significant localizing influences; the inheritance of traditional skills and the absence of a competing metallurgical industry (which excludes the industry from the Sheffield-Rotherham district, equally suitable on most

other counts) have also assisted. The largest producing center is Bradford, in many ways the Manchester of the wool trade. Halifax, Huddersfield, Dewsbury, Keighley, and Wakefield are other large centers. Leeds is the commercial capital of the West Riding, but plays little role in the woolen and worsted trades at the weaving stage; the city concentrates, however, a large fraction of the clothing trade.[24]

Like cottons, woolen goods have long figured very large in the British export trade. Stiff overseas competition has been experienced in recent years, but the high quality of British cloth has maintained her position. Considerable modernization of plant is in progress, and efforts are being made to compete vigorously in the cheap-cloth field.

Linen (the raw material of which is the field crop flax) is another textile in which the United Kingdom has long dominated the world market. Spinning and weaving of linen were formerly widespread in Britain. The industry has become concentrated, however, in Ulster and especially in Belfast. Flax grown locally normally supplies about 10 per cent of the demand, and the rest is imported. Londonderry has a large production of finished linen and cotton goods, especially shirts.

Synthetic fibers now form the most vigorous part of the industry. In 1966 the country produced 400 million kilograms, an all-time record, production having doubled in the past thirteen years. About half the production consists of viscose rayon and acetate. The world's largest rayon plant is at Greenfield (North Wales), while other large plants are at Grimsy, Preston, and Wolverhampton. Most of the remaining output is nylon, although terylene polyester fiber is heavily produced to mix with wool, especially for tropical clothing. These industries have, in fact, largely replaced cotton in Britain's trade.

[24] The West Riding landscape in many ways exemplifies industrial Britain. See S. H. Beaver, "The West Riding," part 46 of L. D. Stamp (ed.), *The Land of Britain, op. cit.*

Communications

Overseas shipping and the ports. The British merchant fleet comprises almost a sixth of the world's shipping and is the largest active fleet afloat (the U.S. fleet being largely "mothballed"). The importance and heavy bulk of Britain's own overseas trade is a guarantee of her maritime activity. Her losses in shipping during World War II amounted to no less than 12,000,000 metric tons, yet her merchant fleet today exceeds 22.6 million gross registered metric tons, largely the result of rapid launching of new vessels. The trend is toward very large vessels. About 60 per cent of the fleet is less than ten years old. More than a third consists of oil tankers—14 per cent of the world fleet—and the latest additions are vessels for the new container traffic.

Britain has numerous ports, as befits a trading nation. Present volume of trade through her 300 harbors exceeds 170 million metric tons, more than half of which is petroleum or one of its refined products. Six ports—London, Liverpool, Hull, Manchester, Southampton, and Glasgow—now do 75 per cent of the total business in terms of value, 60 per cent of all foreign business in terms of tonnage.

London, discussed as a city below, is much the largest port, concentrating about a third of the overseas trade. The Thames estuary provides a deep, easy approach. The outer docks (for large shipping) are at Tilbury, in Essex, but most of the shipping comes right into the East End of the city. Though there are numerous wharves, much of the unloading is carried out by lighters and barges, which transfer the imported goods into warehouses that line the Thames for miles below (and even above) Tower Bridge. The commerce of the port is extremely varied, but especially noteworthy are the imports of perishable foodstuffs, for which London, with its warehouses and cold-storage facilities, is much the biggest port.

Liverpool, the second-largest port, handles over a fifth of the overseas trade in terms of value, ranks third in terms of tonnage, and is the principal transatlantic port. It is above all the Atlantic port of the industrialized north of England and the Midlands. The port is built at the mouth of the Mersey estuary (which has completely replaced Chester on the Dee as the main Irish Sea harbor); on the Lancashire shore is Liverpool itself, but there are also docks on the Cheshire shore in the large urban areas of Birkenhead and Wallasey.

Hull ranks eighth in terms of tonnage and fourth in terms of value. It stands on the north shore of the Humber estuary and has easy communications with the industrial north, especially the West Riding of Yorkshire. It has varied interests. Much of its connection has been with Northern Europe, but it also has a large coastwise trade and an immense trawling fleet. Grain, timber and oil are also landed here.

Manchester ranks seventh in terms of tonnage and third in terms of value. It is an inland city linked to the Mersey estuary by the 35-mile-long privately owned ship canal completed in 1894. The canal has 28 feet of water over the lock sills and allows ordinary cargo vessels to reach the port. Petroleum products are the main trade in both directions.

Southampton, fifth in the value of commerce and second in terms of tonnage, is the chief passenger port and the normal starting point of passenger ships to all western and southern destinations, including the important transatlantic traffic. Southampton Water is reached from the English Channel from either east or west by the Solent, a drowned river valley sheltered on the south by the Isle of Wight. The double entry is enhanced by a double high tide, a valuable adjunct in the handling of large ships, though even at low tide there is 35 feet of water. Much fruit is imported, as well as oil.

Glasgow, the remaining large port, is approached by the beautiful Firth of Clyde. It is the great port of lowland Scotland and has an active export trade in heavy engineering goods. Other chief ports are Bristol, Newcastle, and Harwich.

Inland communications. Road and rail penetrate every corner of inhabited Britain and Ireland and traffic densities are very high. The British railway system is nationally owned and is known as "British Railways." Nearly all the mainline trackage is two-, three-, or four-tracked, and both speeds and traffic densities are high. Most passenger movement is by rail for long hauls, and there is also an extraordinarily dense suburban traffic especially in the London area.

There is a large mileage of electric propulsion, chiefly in the south; London is linked to the coast at Bournemouth, Portsmouth, Brighton, and Eastbourne by frequent electric services that have brought many of the beach resorts within commuter range, though they are 50 to 80 miles from London.

The Irish railways present a less satisfactory picture. Northern Ireland was well served from Belfast and Londonderry by the old Northern Counties Committee lines, which were owned and operated by the L.M.S.R., a British company. Only the main line now remains. The former Great Northern links Belfast and Dublin. It is now publicly owned. Mainline services in the rest of the Republic are over the tracks of the *Coras Iompair Eireann;* there have been many abandonments of minor trackage.

The road systems of Britain and Ireland are the hard-surfaced end results of centuries of farm-track evolution and village-to-village lanes, modified in Ireland by considerable stretches of new roads built as relief projects after the famine. Exceedingly high traffic densities in Britain produce much congestion, and expressway construction is slow and expensive. Nevertheless most freight (except for heavy commodities) and passenger movement is now on the roads.

Civil air transport has grown greatly. London Airport is the world's busiest for intercontinental traffic, and Prestwick (for Glasgow), Manchester and Shannon also have transatlantic services. Much Anglo-Scottish and most Anglo-Irish passenger traffic is by air, and the routes to Europe—especially London to Paris—are heavily traveled.

The British canal systems (except for the Manchester Ship Canal) are old, narrow, and shallow. Though they carried over 9 million metric tons in 1965, most of them are little used, and many have been abandoned.

The Four Capitals

It is fitting that we should glance finally at the four capital cities of the British Isles: London, Edinburgh, Belfast, and Dublin. Wales is remarkable in having no true capital and no focal point in its communications system; it has been truly said that a future Welsh parliament, if one is ever convened, would have to meet in some border town like Wrexham or Shrewsbury if the legislators were to get there with a minimum of fatigue! The grain of the country renders any internal site difficult of access; good Welsh routeways lead to England.

London, home of the Crown, seat of the United Kingdom government, and center of the sterling bloc, the Commonwealth, and a host of other organizations, is still a great world city. It is vast, sprawling, but attractive, lacking any formal plan—unlike Paris and Berlin—but possessing an appeal that some others lack. Its status as a city arises not merely from its governmental functions, but from its role as the nation's leading port; from the commercial, financial, and legal power of the City's institutions; from the vast new industries that have sprung up on its outskirts; and from the intangible appeal of its cultural and intellectual eminence, to say nothing of the power to entertain in theaters, cinemas, restaurants, and bars. Its designers and retail tradesmen have indeed made London a major home of new fashion; Carnaby Street has become a legend.

The old core of the town, on a gravel terrace which provided the lowest feasible bridging point over the Thames, is still identifiable as the "City," in whose half a square mile are concentrated most of the banks, the insurance houses—including Lloyds—the Stock Exchange and St. Paul's Cathedral, as well as the headquarters of a large part of Britain's commercial and industrial empire. The shopping and entertainment districts lie two miles or more to the west, around Charing Cross, Trafalgar Square, Piccadilly Circus, and Oxford Street. Westminster, a half-mile upstream from Charing Cross, is the home of government. Around this differentiated center sprawls a densely populated ring of boroughs, residential and industrial, and still farther out a forest of new houses served by the electrified lines of London Transport and the southern lines of British Railways.

Edinburgh is the traditional capital of Scotland; today it houses many of the administrative branches of Scottish government, as well as the official seat of the Crown of Scotland. It is a handsome town on a striking site overlooking the Firth of Forth. The Castle and much of the old town lie on a steep, volcanic hill, whereas the chief shopping districts—of which Princes Street is renowned—lie on another ridge to the north. Between them is a deep valley unfortunately occupied by the partially concealed main line of the old London and North-Eastern Railway, and its Waverley Station. In spite of everything that the twentieth century has done to ruin it, the heart of Edinburgh remains one of the sights of Europe. In recent years, the town has been the site of an annual festival of music and drama that bids fair to outdo Salzburg.

Belfast is not so much a traditional capital as a modern industrial city. Nevertheless, it is the site of the Northern Ireland government and is closely identified with the Orange movement and the cause of Protestant Ireland. It is also the site of Queen's University.

Dublin dominates the life of the Irish Republic as Vienna does that of Austria. There are no competitors among the smaller towns of this rural country. Its harbor affords the natural gateway to the Central Lowland and was recognized as such by the Norsemen who established the town and by Normans who captured it in the twelfth century. Thenceforward it was the English capital of Ireland. They established its cathedrals, its old university (Trinity College), and the great castle that still dominates the city. In the eighteenth and nineteenth centuries the modern city was laid out by Georgian architects, whose broad streets, terraced houses, and formal squares gave the city an air of spacious dignity that it has never lost. Today it is the seat of the president and government of the Republic, and of the administrative machinery of both government and finance. The large industrialization it has undergone during the past century created behind the Georgian terraces a welter of slums, and overcrowding is still a problem. Nevertheless, the city retains a real beauty and fascination.

* * *

In common with other west-European nations, the United Kingdom and the Irish Republic saw a fairly steady recovery in the years following the end of World War II. Although there have been monetary difficulties, chiefly with the stability of the pound and anxiety about dollar resources, the British Isles are now enjoying the highest living standards in their history. The geographer can take some pride in this, since it has involved the rational and intelligent use of that most precious asset, the land, and in this process the professional geographer has played a considerable part.

There remains one uncertainty: the place of Britain in Europe. From most of the recent cooperative moves among European nations toward economic union, so vital to the maintenance of peace, Britain first stood aloof, and then, as her own position as a trading nation was progressively eroded, was kept out of the Common Market through the French government's unilateral veto. Today both her political parties are committed to Common Market membership, which since 1962 has twice eluded her. Instead she is allied to the ring of north European countries through the European Free Trade Association. Years of uncertainty have brought Britain to the point where she has replaced France as the sick man of post-war Europe. Late in 1967 a further devaluation of sterling was forced by her continued inability to balance her trading account. It is too early to say whether this at last will lead her—and by inference, Ireland—back to full prosperity and rapid growth. The British have at last recognized that their future lies with Europe. Now they must await the willingness to reopen a door from which they once, tragically, turned away.

BIBLIOGRAPHY

(Major references are asterisked.)

Books in English

*BILHAM, ERNEST G. *The Climate of the British Isles.* London: Macmillan & Co., Ltd., 1938.

BLAIR, HUNTER. *An Introduction to Anglo-Saxon England.* Cambridge: Cambridge University Press, 1956.

CLAPHAM, SIR JOHN HAROLD. *A Concise Economic History of Britain from the Earliest Time to 1750.* London: Cambridge University Press, 1949.

COURT, W. H. B. *A Concise Economic History of Britain from 1750 to Recent Times.* London: Cambridge University Press, 1955.

*DARBY, H. CLIFFORD (ed.). *Historical Geography of England Before 1800.* London: Cambridge University Press, 1936.

EKWALL, EILERT. *The Concise Oxford Dictionary of English Place-Names.* 3rd ed. New York: Oxford University Press, 1947.

FOX, C. *The Personality of Britain: Its Influence on Inhabitant and Invader in Prehistoric and Early Historic Times.* Cardiff: National Museum of Wales, 1933.

*FREEMAN, THOMAS W. *Ireland.* London: Methuen & Co., Ltd., 1950.

*GREAT BRITAIN. *Monthly Digest and Annual Abstracts of Statistics.* London: H. M. Stationery Office.

GREAT BRITAIN, DEPARTMENT OF ECONOMIC AFFAIRS. *The National Plan.* H. M. Stationery Office, 1965 (Cmnd. 2764).

GREAT BRITAIN, DEPARTMENT OF SCIENTIFIC AND INDUSTRIAL RESEARCH, GEOLOGICAL SURVEY. *British Regional Geology* 2nd ed. Eighteen regional monographs on British rocks and structure. London: H. M. Stationery Office, various dates.

HAWKES, JACQUETTA. *A Land.* London: The Cresset Press, 1951.

*HOSKINS, W. G. *The Making of the English Landscape.* London: Hodder and Stoughton Ltd., 1957.

JONES, LL., RODWELL. *The Geography of London River.* London: Methuen & Co., Ltd., 1931.

*MACKINDER, HALFORD J. *Britain and the British Seas.* New York: Appleton-Century-Crofts, Inc., 1902.

*MANLEY, GORDON. *Climate and the British Scene.* London: Collins, The Fontana Library, 1962.

SMITH, WILFRED. *An Economic Geography of Great Britain.* London: Methuen and Co. Ltd., 1949.

*STAMP, L. DUDLEY. *Britain's Structure and Scenery.* London: Collins, The Fontana Library, 1960.

———. *The Land of Britain: Its Use and Misuse.* London: Longmans, Green & Co., Ltd., 1948.

*———. *Man and the Land.* London: William Collins Sons & Co., Ltd., 1955.

——— (ed.). *The Land of Britain.* Report of the Land Utilisation Survey of Britain. London: Geographical Publications, Ltd., 1943–46.

*STAMP, L. DUDLEY, and BEAVER, S. H. *The British Isles.* 4th ed. London: Longmans, Green & Co., Ltd., 1954.

STEERS, J. A. *The English Coast.* London: Collins, The Fontana Library, 1966.

TANSLEY, ARTHUR G. *The British Islands and Their Vegetation.* 2 vols. London: Cambridge University Press, 1949.

TRUEMAN, A. E. *Geology and Scenery in England and Wales.* London: Pelican Books, 1949.

*WATSON, J. WREFORD and J. B. SISSONS (eds.). *The British Isles, A Systematic Geography.* London: Thomas Nelson and Sons, Ltd., 1964.

WOOLDRIDGE, S. W. and FREDERICK GOLDING. *The Weald.* London: Collins. 1953.

———, and D. L. LINTON. *Structure, Surface, and Drainage in South East England.* London: George Philip & Son, Ltd., The London Geographical Institute, 1955.

Atlas

The Atlas of Britain and Northern Ireland. Planned and directed by D. P. Bickmore and M. A. Shaw. Oxford: at the Clarendon Press, 1963. xii and 200 maps and 34 unnumbered gazetteer pages.

Articles

APPLETON, J. H., "Some Geographical Aspects of the Modernization of British Railways," *Geography* 52 (1967): 357–73.

COATES, B. E. and E. M. RAWSTRON, "Regional Incomes and Planning, 1964-1965," *Geography* 52 (1967): 393–402.

DARBY, H. CLIFFORD, "The Changing English Landscape," *Geographical Journal* 117 (1951): 377–98.

———, "Some Early Ideas on the Agricultural Regions of England," *Agricultural History Review* 2 (1954): 30–47.

EMBLETON, C., "Some Stages in the Drainage Evolution of Part of North-East Wales," *Transactions and Papers: Institute of British Geographers* 23 (1957): 19–35.

GRIGG, D. B., "The Changing Agricultural Geography of England: A Commentary on the Sources Available for the Reconstruction of the Agricultural Geography of England, 1770–1850." *Transactions and Papers: Institute of British Geographers* 41 (1967): 73–96.

HENDERSON, H. C. K., "Our Changing Agriculture," Inaugural Lecture, March 16, 1966, Birkbeck College, London, 20 pp.

KENT, P. E., "North Sea Exploration—A Case History," *Geographical Journal* 133 (1967): 289–301.

MAXWELL, I. S., "The Geographical Identification of Domesday Vills," *Transactions and Papers: Institute of British Geographers* 16 (1950): 97–121.

SIMPSON, E. S., "Milk Production in England and Wales," *Geographical Review* 49 (1959): 95–111.

SMITH, WILFRED, "The Location of Industry," *Transactions and Papers: Institute of British Geographers* 21 (1955): 1–18.

TARRANT, J. R., "Recent Industrial Development in Ireland," *Geography* 52 (1967): 403–08.

Northern Europe

4

If asked to define "Northern Europe" as a region, many persons would have only the haziest notion as to which countries should be included. Most of them would certainly begin by naming the Scandinavian countries, that is, Norway, Sweden, and Denmark, but which other nations to include (if any) would be a point of serious debate. In the following chapter, therefore, the author has chosen to define Northern Europe in terms of an areal concept which long has been an integral part of Scandinavian geographical thought: the so-called *Norden* concept.

The term itself means simply "the North," but in this connection is specifically intended to designate five nations in Northern Europe which are more closely related to one another than they are to any of the countries surrounding them. They are the three Scandinavian countries, together with Iceland and Finland. A sixth area, the Faeroes, while constituting an administrative part of Denmark, is usually regarded as a distinct geographic unit within the region.

The *Norden* concept derives its validity not so much from the facts of physical geography as it does from those of cultural and historical geography. To demonstrate this point one need only cite a few of the characteristics which distinguish the countries of Northern Europe as a regional group.

They are, for example, all nations of relatively small populations, the ethnic and linguistic compositions of which are both simple and uniform. In fact, the same ethnic and linguistic stock finds representation in all five countries, though in one of them it exists only as a minority. Moreover, the overwhelming majority of the peoples profess the same religious faith.

In each of these nations illiteracy has long since been abolished and the regional standards of education, health, and sanitation can scarcely be equaled elsewhere on the continent. Though their resources are neither varied nor abundant, the nations of Northern Europe have achieved a level of economic well-being which is among the highest in the world. Because there are no great discrepancies in the distribution of their national wealth, these countries are often regarded as working models of economic democracy. In the field of social legislation the nations of Northern Europe are outstanding pioneers, having long set the pace for the rest of the world. Though three of them retain a monarchial form of government, they all have well-established traditions of political freedom and democracy. Also, despite an earlier history marked by bloodshed and violence, the nations of Northern Europe have demonstrated such exemplary harmony and cooperation in the conduct of international affairs for the last century, that the region as a whole has come to be called "Europe's quiet corner." When seen in the light of such considerations, Northern Europe will be appreciated as a distinct geographic region with a character and qualities of its own.

THE PHYSICAL LANDSCAPE

Location, Size, and Configuration

The region of Northern Europe occupies a position in the Old World which is almost directly comparable to that of Alaska in the New World. Its southern border, the Danish-West German boundary, is situated in the same latitude as the southern tip of the Alaskan Panhandle (55° N.), while the North Cape of Norway, the northernmost point of continental Europe, is located on the same parallel as Point Barrow (71° N.). Longitudinally these two regions show a similar correspondence, for the distance is just as great from the eastern boundary of Finland to the western extremity of Iceland as it is from the Alaskan Panhandle to the outermost islands of the Aleutian chain. When the Norwegian islands of Spitsbergen (Svalbard) are included, however, the plane of reference must be altered, for the only regions in the New World which are located at a corresponding latitude (namely 74°–81° N.) are the northernmost islands of the Canadian archipelago and the northern quarter of Greenland.

In point of size, Northern Europe is about seven-eighths as large as Alaska. With an area of nearly 500,000 square miles, it constitutes just over one-eighth of the European land mass and has over 21 million people. Unlike Alaska, however, Northern Europe is not a single, relatively unbroken expanse of land (Fig. 4–1). Instead, it is a region of peninsulas and islands, each separated from the other by varying widths of open sea. By far the largest continuous land mass in Northern Europe is what we may call the Fenno-Scandinavian peninsula. Joined to

the subcontinent along a front extending from the Gulf of Finland to the White Sea, this compound neck of land stretches northward between the Gulf of Bothnia and the White Sea and then mushrooms out into the Scandinavian peninsula (which extends 1,200 miles to the southwest) and the Kola Peninsula (which extends some 300 miles to the east). The fact that this appendage is divided politically among Finland, the Soviet Union, Norway, and Sweden in no way detracts from either the physical continuity or the essentially peninsular character of the area as a whole. Northern Europe's only other land contact with the subcontinent is the peninsula of Jutland in Denmark. Owing to its location, this peninsula has been infinitely more important as a link between the northern countries and the remainder of Europe than the broader but less accessible Fenno-Scandinavian peninsula.

Apart from these two peninsulas, however, Northern Europe has no physical continuity, for its remaining areas are composed of islands. Among these are Iceland and the Faeroes in the Atlantic, Spitsbergen and Jan Mayen in the Arctic, the Danish archipelago and the Swedish islands of Gotland and Öland in the Baltic, and the Åland Archipelago at the entrance to the Gulf of Bothnia. As a consequence of this peninsular and insular configuration, Northern Europe stands somewhat apart from the rest of the subcontinent. This relative isolation has in turn played an important role in the historical and cultural development of the region and in large part explains the sense of community which exists between these nations today. A brief introductory description of the individual countries follows.

Norway. The Kingdom of Norway occupies the western and northern sides of the Scandinavian peninsula, extending through 13° of latitude and 26° of longitude. Lindesnes, its most southerly point, is located in the same latitude as Juneau, Alaska, while its northernmost extremity, North Cape, is situated on the same parallel as

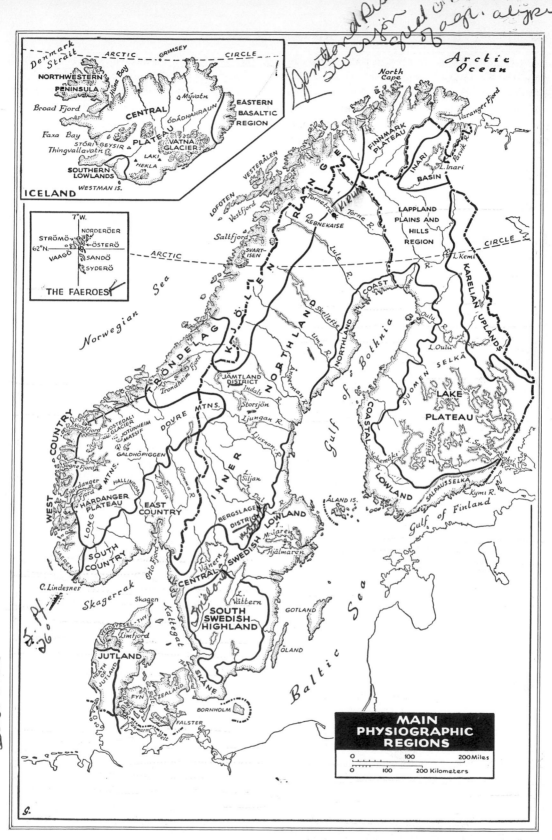

Fig. 4–1. Main physiographic regions.

Point Barrow. The country has an extremely attenuated shape, stretching some 1,100 miles from north to south. From a maximum width of 280 miles near 61° latitude, it constricts to less than 4 miles near 68° (measured from the Swedish border to the head of Tys Fjord) and then broadens out again to 160 miles in the Finnmark Plateau in the far north. If embayments are not included, its coastline measures about 2,100 miles, but if they are reckoned in, this figure rises to 12,500 miles, or roughly half the circumference of the earth. On its landward sides Norway is bounded by Sweden in the east (1,025 miles) and by Finland and the Soviet Union in the northeast (452 and 125 miles, respectively). Its total area is 124,556 square miles (slightly larger than the state of New Mexico), of which almost 10,000 square miles are made up by the 150,000 islands and skerries which line its coasts. In addition to its continental area, Norway has sovereignty over Spitsbergen and Jan Mayen in Arctic waters—and Peter I and Bouvet islands in the South Atlantic. Norway also claims a portion of the Antarctic continent under the name of Queen Maud Land.

Sweden. The Kingdom of Sweden is situated on the eastern side of the Scandinavian peninsula. Its shores face the Gulf of Bothnia in the north, the Baltic Sea in the southeast, the Skagerrak and Kattegat in the southwest, and the Sound (Öresund) separates it from Denmark. Like Norway, it has an elongated shape, extending 975 miles from north to south and 310 miles from west to east at its widest point. Its coastline measures about 1,600 miles in length, embayments excluded. On its landward sides it is bordered by Norway in the west (1,025 miles) and Finland in the northeast (332 miles). With a total area of 173,035 square miles, of which 158,450 are land, Sweden is the fourth largest country in Europe and is slightly larger than the state of California.

Finland. The Republic of Finland is situated east of the Gulf of Bothnia and north of the Gulf of Finland. The total length of its coastline along these bodies of water is about 680 miles, embayments not included. On its landward sides Finland is bounded by Sweden in the northwest (332 miles), Norway in the north (452 miles), and the Soviet Union in the east (787 miles).

Like both Norway and Sweden, Finland has an elongated shape, measuring over 700 miles between its northern and southern extremities. Except for the northernmost tip of Lappland and the Hangö (Hanko) Peninsula in the southwest, the entire country lies between 60° and 70° north latitude. With a total area of 130,125 square miles, of which 117,935 are land (somewhat larger than the combined areas of Michigan and Wisconsin), Finland is the sixth largest country in Europe (Fig. 4–1).

Denmark. The Kingdom of Denmark is located between the North and Baltic seas and is composed of the peninsula of Jutland (Jylland) and the islands lying to the east of it. At the same time it commands the sea approaches to the Baltic and the southern land approaches to the Scandinavian peninsula. In such a key position, Denmark can truly be called the "Crossroads of Northern Europe."

The largest continuous land area in the country is the peninsula of Jutland, which totals 9,186 square miles. Lying just north of it across the Lim Fjord is the island of Vendsyssel-Thy, which for all intents and purposes can be considered a part of the peninsula itself. Together, their combined areas total 11,410 square miles, or roughly two-thirds that of the entire country. On the west they face the North Sea, on the north the Skagerrak, and on the east the Kattegat. Near the base of the peninsula, Denmark shares a 42-mile land boundary with West Germany.

The Danish archipelago consists of some 480 islands, of which about 100 are inhabited. Most of them are very small, but together their areas come to 5,166 square miles. For the sake of convenience, we can consider them under three principal headings: (1) the Fyn group, (2) the Zealand group, and (3) Bornholm. The group centered on the island of Fyn is separated from the peninsula of Jutland by the Little Belt, a strait which is about a half mile wide at its narrowest point. On the east it is separated from the Zealand group by the Great Belt which averages 10 miles in width. This group in turn is separated from Sweden by the Sound, which constricts to a width of less than 4 miles near Helsingör. On the south both groups are separated from the German coast by the Fehmarn Belt. The most distant of the Danish home islands is Bornholm, about 90 miles east of Zealand and 25 miles off the coast of Sweden. Together the archipelago and the peninsula have an area of 16,576 square miles, or slightly less than the combined areas of Massachusetts and New Hampshire. The country's over-all coastline is 4,612 miles in length. Denmark also has sovereignty over the Faeroes and Greenland, in the North Atlantic.

Iceland. The most remote member of the European family of nations is the Republic of Iceland, lying just south of the Arctic Circle between 13° and 25° west longitude. Its nearest neighbor is Greenland, 200 miles to the west across the Denmark Strait, but it lies some 500 miles from the coast of Scotland and over 600 miles from the mainland of Norway. Despite this offside position with respect to the main currents of European life, Iceland served as a steppingstone to the West in the days of the Vikings and occupies a similar strategic position in the Air Age of today.

Roughly rectangular in shape, the island has a total area of 39,709 square miles (slightly less than the state of Virginia). Its coastline, about 3,600 miles long, is broken in the west by three large peninsulas and in the north and east by numerous fjords. Only the south coast is relatively unindented.

The Faeroes. Situated some 400 miles west of Norway and 250 miles southeast of Iceland are the Faeroes (Föroyar), located at 62° north latitude and 7° west longitude. Composed of 18 larger islands and numerous skerries, the archipelago has a total area of 540 square miles, or roughly half that of Rhode Island.

Geologic Structure

Within the limits of Northern Europe, rocks of both the most ancient and most recent geologic ages are found. Over most of Finland and Sweden, the eastern portions of Norway, and the northern coast of the Danish island of Bornholm one finds resistant granites, gneisses, and schists which date from the Pre-Cambrian period.[1] These outcrops are remnants of the so-called Fenno-Scandian Shield (Baltic Shield). Though the surface of this region was originally warped into several extensive mountain systems, by the beginning of the Cambrian period these had been all but eroded away and reduced to a peneplain. From Cambrian to Silurian times large sections of this plain were invaded by epeiric seas (shallow seas of temporary duration) and vast areas were covered with fossil-bearing sediments. By far the greatest accumulation of sediments took place in the west, where a geosyncline, or trough, had developed. About the end of the Silurian period, the sediments in this trough were compressed, folded, and faulted into a vast mountain range which extended from Scotland northward through Norway and Spitsbergen to the northeastern coast of Greenland. After this mountain-building process (the so-called Caledonian orogeny) had subsided, the entire shield area was once more subjected to a prolonged period of erosion. Only in Spitsbergen and the region of southernmost Sweden and Denmark did any noteworthy deposition take place. In Spitsbergen all geologic ages from the Cambrian to the Tertiary are represented, but of greatest importance are the coal-bearing deposits of the Carboniferous period. In southern Sweden and in Denmark,

---

[1] For geological terms, see Appendix I.

beginning in the Mesozoic Age and continuing into the Cenozoic, thick layers of limestone and chalk were laid down.

During the Tertiary period, the North Atlantic area was convulsed by a great diastrophic upheaval in which the relative land and sea levels were considerably altered. In the west, great outpourings of lava built up an island which embraced large parts of present-day Iceland and central Greenland and may have extended from Jan Mayen in the north to the Faeroes in the south. Concurrent with the appearance of "Greater Iceland," as this island is known, was the faulting and sinking of the western and northern portions of the Fenno-Scandian Shield. As the land west of the present Norwegian coast sank into the sea, the land to the east was elevated once more, with the greatest rise taking place along the newly formed coast. This caused a rejuvenation of all the watercourses in the vicinity and particularly intensified the erosion on the western slope, which then fell abruptly into the sea. Here the steep gradient and copious moisture allowed the streams to cut into the peneplained plateau with such vigor as to capture several drainage basins from the less active southeastward-flowing rivers.

Scarcely had Greater Iceland appeared and the Scandinavian peninsula been re-elevated when vast snow fields began to accumulate in the higher districts of both regions, eventually consolidating into great ice sheets. In Iceland the advancing ice met strong opposition in the flame and fury of the continuing vulcanism. Further tectonic disturbances had already reduced the island to more nearly its present proportions, however, for there is evidence that the ice sheet which covered the Faeroes was purely local in nature. Here, what was originally a single basaltic block that was slightly tilted to the south and east was progressively cut along old fault lines, by the combined forces of ice and sea, into a number of smaller islands.

Over the remainder of Northern Europe the ice sheets alternately expanded and contracted several times, rounding off the re-sistant uplands and broadening the existing valleys and depressions. In Finland, Sweden, and Norway most of the surface mantle was carried away, while Denmark became the resting place for much of this glacial material. During the final glaciation, the edge of the ice remained stationary over central and southern Jutland for some time, building up an extensive terminal moraine. In Finland too, one finds evidence of a stationary ice lobe in the two great recessional moraines which parallel the south coast—the so-called *Salpausselkä* (ridge). As the glaciers finally melted back for the last time, the lower-lying areas were inundated by postglacial seas (forerunners of the modern Baltic and its appendages), while numerous lakes formed in the ice-scoured fissures of the interior. At the same time the areas which had been depressed so long by the great weight of the ice began rising back into isostatic balance. This process is still in operation over much of Scandinavia and can be noted most effectively on the Bothnian coasts of Finland and Sweden. Here, near the cities of Vaasa and Umeå, respectively, the rise amounts to about one foot in thirty years. Though the Pleistocene ice sheets have long since disappeared from northern Europe, several plateau and valley glaciers of more recent origin are to be found in the highlands of Scandinavia and Iceland.

The Regions of the North

Using its geologic structure as a basis, we can distinguish five major subdivisions within Northern Europe, each of which embraces one or more physiographic regions. They are (1) the Scandinavian mountains, (2) the Fenno-Scandian Shield, (3) Sweden's Baltic islands, (4) Denmark and Skåne, and (5) the Faeroes and Iceland.

The Scandinavian mountains. Norway has fallen heir to most of Scandinavia's mountain backbone. Fully 72 per cent of its land area is composed of unproductive highland wastes of rock and swamp. In its various portions the mountain ridge is known by several local names. The southern part of the ridge is called the Long Mountains (Langfjellene) and separates the country into the East Country (Östlandet) on the east-facing slopes and the West Country (Vestlandet) on the western side. In the Jotunheim Massif, where the highest peaks are located (Galdhöpiggen—8,097 feet), the ridge turns in a more east-west direction and bears the name of Dovre Mountains (Dovrefjell), separating the East Country in the south from Tröndelag in the north. Here the main ridge is broken by the Tröndelag-Jämtland gap, but is resumed once again to the north as the Kjölen Range. Associated with this range is the mountain bulwark which makes up the Lofoten Islands and the coast of Finnmark. In its northern reaches, the main ridge of the Kjölen runs through Swedish territory, reaching its highest point in Kebnekaise, 6,965 feet. Finland's highest mountain, Haltiotunturi—4,344 feet, is likewise found in this section.

The Scandinavian mountains have a marked weather-divide effect, for they separate the distinctly maritime west coast from the more continental eastern interior. Thanks to the moderating influences of the North Atlantic Drift and the prevailing westerlies, winter temperatures average above freezing along the coast as far north as the Lofotens. Although the maximum precipitation in these coastal districts comes in winter, most of it falls as rain. Over the mountains and to the east, winter temperatures are considerably colder, so the moisture which falls at that season contributes to a deep and stable snow cover. Indeed, virtually all transmontane roads linking eastern and western Norway are blocked by snow from 6 to 7 months of the year. Everywhere on the western slopes the average annual precipitation exceeds 40 inches, and in the higher parts of the West Country it totals between two and three times that amount. In the area between Sognefjord and Nordfjord as much as 230 inches of moisure fall each year, helping to nourish the Jostedal Glacier, one of the largest ice sheets in continental

Europe. East of the mountains the average annual precipitation everywhere drops to under 40 inches and, in some sheltered valleys and in the far north, to less than 20 inches. Summers are warmer and sunnier than they are to the west, though this is also the season of maximum precipitation.

In the southern portions of the Scandinavian mountains, the coniferous tree line is reached at an elevation of less than 3,000 feet. In Tröndelag the limit falls to 2,000 feet and in the far north to 1,200 feet. Though scrub birches struggle upward an average of 800 feet higher, the greater part of the mountains lie well within the zone of alpine meadows. It is these open highland wastes that best typify the *fjell* of Scandinavia.

Although their height is not impressive when compared to such ranges as the Alps, the Scandinavian mountains have always constituted a distinct barrier to movement. Except near their northern and southern extremities, they are crossed by only one pass at less than 2,000 feet elevation. This is the strategically located Tröndelag-Jämtland gap which breaks across the range near the middle of the Scandinavian peninsula. With two exceptions (at either end of the Dovre Mountains), all of the passes within Norway itself are higher than 3,300 feet, and hence above the tree line. The Bergen Railway, which is the only all-land, year-round connection between Norway's two largest cities, makes its crossing at 4,271 feet, but only by burying 15 per cent of its total mileage in tunnels and snowsheds (Fig. 4–2).

Three similar but nevertheless distinct subdivisions make up the western slope of the mountains. They are, from south to north, the Norwegian West Country, Tröndelag, and the Kjölen Range province. The most distinctive feature of the Norwegian West Country is its narrow steep-sided valleys which in many instances have been scoured by the ice far below the level of the sea, producing deep fjords. The greatest of these is Sogne Fjord which measures some

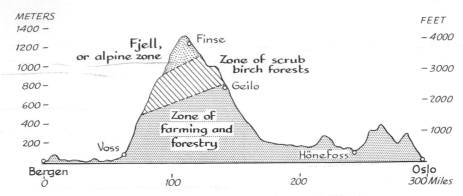

Fig. 4-2. Profile across the Scandinavian mountains, along the Oslo-Bergen railway. More than 30 miles of this railway, which links Norway's two largest cities, are above the timber line and another 30 miles are above the limit of permanent agricultural settlement. Due primarily to a difference in climate, the limits of the respective zones are lower on the west than they are on the east. (*Source: Rutebok for Norge.*)

125 miles in length and is over 4,000 feet deep near its outer end. Hardanger Fjord to the south is 105 miles long and over 2,900 feet in depth at its deepest point. Tributary streams have been left far up the fjord sides in hanging valleys; as a consequence, waterfalls are numerous. Places of habitation are limited to the more sheltered of the islands which line the coast, to the low strandflat which rims much of the shore, or to small patches of lowland at the heads of the fjords. The Jaeren district south of Stavanger affords a noteworthy exception, for here the coastal lowland is covered with rolling moraine deposits. Jaeren's early spring and long growing season help to make it one of Norway's best agricultural areas. Although the more sheltered parts of the West Country were once covered by a mixed forest, this region today possesses only a small fraction of Norway's productive woodland.

North of the Dovre Mountains, centered on the Trondheim Fjord, is the region of Tröndelag. Thanks to its easily eroded Cambro-Silurian deposits, this region is Norway's second most extensive lowland area and agricultural district. Though its clayey soils have been cultivated for centuries, the region is still largely clothed in a forest of spruce and pine.

Northward from Tröndelag, Norway is squeezed into the lower western slopes of the Kjölen Range. The varying geologic character of the range gives it a very broken relief, ranging from the sharp alpine peaks of the Lofotens to the relatively broad interior valleys which extend from Trondheim Fjord to Salt Fjord. In the more sheltered valleys good stands of conifers are found, while along the coasts a cover of scrub birch is characteristic.

The Arctic Circle, which bisects the Kjölen Range province, is scarcely evidenced by the relative mildness of the climate, though its presence is keenly felt in the marked seasonal variations in insolation which are experienced. In common with Lappland (the region where Norway, Sweden, and Finland meet in the north), this region at midsummer knows no darkness at all. In the latitude of the North Cape the sun remains constantly above the horizon from the middle of May until the end of July, and in Spitsbergen this period of continuous sunlight extends from mid-April until the end of August. In contrast, at the winter solstice (December 22), the regions north of the Arctic Circle receive no sunlight whatsoever, with the North Cape in continuous darkness from mid-November to the end of January. In Spitsbergen the sun does not rise from the end of October until the middle of February. Though the southern portions of Northern Europe likewise experience days and nights of very unequal duration, it is in these northerly areas that the most pronounced effects upon the activities of man are observed.

The Fenno-Scandian Shield. East of the Scandinavian mountains lies the vast Fenno-Scandian Shield. It may be likened somewhat to a broad, shallow saucer, for it is upturned not only on its western edge but also on the east where it culminates in the Karelian Uplands of eastern Finland. Its southernmost outliers, found in the South Swedish Highland, northeastern Skåne, and the northern part of Danish Bornholm, do not show this same east-west warping, but they do show evidence of the extensive faulting which has left its imprint on much of the rest of the region.

The eastern slope of the Scandinavian mountains (the highest and westernmost part of the Shield) is shared by both Norway and Sweden, though by far the larger part lies in the latter country. The long, gradual southeasterly slope is drained by Northern Europe's largest rivers, among them the Glomma (365 miles) in Norway and the Dal (323 miles) in Sweden. Many of the valleys are occupied by deep, fingerlike lakes, the east slope's counterpart of the western fjords. Typical examples are Mjösa, Norway's largest lake (140 square miles), and Siljan, Storsjön, and Torneträsk in Sweden.

The valleys of the Norwegian East Country and the Inner Northland of Sweden are relatively broad and open. Those of the East Country converge in the region of the Oslo Fjord, though in the southern portion of the area (the South Country) the valleys are narrower and their axes are more nearly north-south. There is also a tendency toward the convergence of several large valleys near the center of the Swedish Northland; there the mouths of the Ångerman, Indals, and Ljungan are located within a few miles of one another. In both of these areas the hilly terrain of the interior comes down to the edge of the sea without a bordering coastal plain.

Most of the Norwegian East Country and Sweden's Inner Northland lie well above the highest postglacial marine limit; hence their soils are almost entirely derived from coarse morainic materials. In the lower valleys of the East Country, however, easily eroded Cambro-Silurian deposits have contributed not only to the essentially lowland character of the region but also to its distinction as the most productive farming area of Norway. Apart from those in the Jämtland district, no similar deposits are found in Inner Northland. This fact, coupled with higher latitude and a more severe climate, make this vast region the least productive agricultural area of Sweden.

The irregular terrain of Sweden's Inner Northland merges imperceptibly into that of the Finnmark Plateau of northern Norway and the Lappland Plains and Hills region of northern Finland. Moraine deposits interspersed with resistant monadnocks and swampy plains characterize both regions. A major difference is in the orientation of their drainage. In Finnmark, which slopes toward the Arctic, the edge of the plateau meets the ocean in a series of bold and barren headlands, that of the North Cape rising nearly 1,000 feet out of the water. Most of Finnish Lappland, on the other hand, drains by way of the Kemi River system into the Gulf of Bothnia. Finland's only area of Arctic drainage, the Inari Basin, centers on the lake of that name, which is also the country's largest body of water. Its most important outlet is the Pasvik (Paats) River, which serves as the Norway-U.S.S.R. frontier through most of its length.

South of the Oulu River, the character of the Finnish countryside changes as the interdigitation of land and water becomes increasingly complex. This part of the Shield constitutes the Lake Plateau, Finland's most distinctive landscape. Delimited on the south by the Salpausselkä (two great moraines which run roughly parallel to the Gulf of Finland) and on the north by the Suomen Selkä (a secondary watershed), the Lake Plateau rises into the Karelian Uplands in the east and is even less well defined in the west. Its distinctive character, however, is its great profusion of lakes, interspersed with eskers, drumlins, and low crystalline hills. Its elevation averages between 300 and 500 feet, and its drainage is effected chiefly through the Vuoksi River in the east, the Kymi River in the south, and the Kokemäki River in the west.

The Karelian Uplands form the watershed between the Gulf of Bothnia and the White Sea. Compared to the Scandinavian mountains, they are merely a low ground swell, averaging between 500 and 700 feet in elevation. In the southern half of the region individual points top 1,000 to 1,200 feet, while in the north a number of summits range from 1,400 to 2,100 feet. The Soviet-Finnish boundary is drawn through this region but does not coincide with the watershed in all areas.

Those portions of the Shield which were downwarped sufficiently to be inundated by the postglacial antecedents of the Baltic Sea differ in several important respects from the remainder of the Shield. They became, first of all, areas of deposition for marine clays, a fact which distinguishes their soils very markedly from those above the highest marine limit. They are inherently more productive and hence have long been preferred in terms of agricultural settlement. Besides contributing to a difference in soil, however, the marine deposits have largely tended to obliterate local variations in relief, producing in the process the most extensive and unbroken plains areas within the Shield region. For example, the plains which form the Coastal Lowland of western and southern Finland average from 20 to 80 miles in width, and their continuation, the Northland Coast of Sweden, is from 20 to 30 miles wide. Although the Northland Coast is pinched out by the hills of Inner Northland south of Umeå, it is resumed near Sundsvall and broadens out into the Central Swedish Lowland. Though not a coastal plain in the strict sense of the term, the Central Swedish Lowland served as a strait between the Baltic and the ocean for the postglacial seas. It is characterized by relatively extensive flat plains, broken at intervals by low crystalline fault-block hills and large lakes. In the eastern half of the Lowland the fault blocks are aligned principally east-west, and off the coast they continue as a chain of stepping-stone rocks and islets through the Stockholm skerry guard and the Åland Archipelago into southern Finland. In the western half of the Central Swedish Lowland, the fault lines trend more north-south. Vänern, the largest of Sweden's lakes, has an area of 2,140 square miles and owes its existence partly to faulting and partly to inundation of the low plain. Vättern to the east occupies an ancient fault valley and, with an area of 735 square miles, is Sweden's second-largest lake.

South of the Central Swedish Lowland is an upland region which, like most of the higher portions of the Shield, was not covered by the postglacial lakes. This is the South Swedish Highland, whose moraine-strewn crystalline hills culminate at an elevation of 1,237 feet about 20 miles south of Lake Vättern. Traversed by numerous fault lines running in a roughly north-south direction, the region's uneven surface is accounted for by an alternation of horsts and grabens. Small lakes and swamps are especially common in the southern half of the area. On either coast the region slopes down to a narrow coastal lowland. The southernmost outcrops of the Shield are to be found in the horsts which trend northwest-southeast through the northeastern parts of the province of Skåne, and in the granite cliffs that line the northern coast of the Danish island of Bornholm.

With the exception of the South Swedish Highland, most of the Shield region lies in the lee of the Scandinavian mountains. As a consequence, the greater part of eastern Norway, Sweden, and Finland receives between 20 and 30 inches of precipitation a year, with the maximum concentration coming in the summer. Along the more exposed western edge of the South Swedish Highland, the annual average is nearly twice as great. Cloudiness is less pronounced than west of the mountains, and summers are warmer. Winters are correspondingly more severe than along the Norwegian coast, with temperatures falling off progressively toward the northeast. The snow cover over most of the Shield region is deep and stable, ranging from 2 to 3 months duration in the south to more than 7 months in parts of Lappland. Ice normally interrupts navigation in the Baltic for about 2 months each year, in the southern reaches of the Gulf of Bothnia for 3, at the inner end of the Gulf of Finland for 5, and in northern Bothnian waters for as many as 7 months.

Apart from those areas of good soils where extensive clearings have been made, the Shield region is primarily a land of forest. In southern Sweden and along the south coasts of Norway and Finland one finds a mixed-forest type where both deciduous and coniferous species occur, but by far the greater part of these countries falls into the zone of northern coniferous forests where spruce and pine are dominant. In Norway the proportion of land in forest to total land area is almost a quarter, while in Sweden it is more than half and in Finland it is nearly two-thirds. In no other region of Europe are the per-capita ratios of productive woodland as high as they are in these countries of the north.

Sweden's Baltic islands. Sweden's two Baltic islands, Gotland (1,160 square miles) and Öland (519 square miles), afford a unique variety of landscape within the Northern European area. Both of them are composed of tabular limestones of Cambro-Silurian age which dip slightly to the south-southeast. On southern Gotland sandstones from the same period are found. Owing to their generally level surface, low rainfall, and porous bedrock, there are no true valleys anywhere on the islands. On the southern half of Öland—an area known as the Alvaret—the limestone is clothed by a short-grass vegetation reminiscent of the steppe. Elsewhere on the islands patches of mixed

forest are found in which both the drought-tolerant pine and the lime-loving ivy are common.

Denmark and Skåne. Thanks to their common geological background, the landscapes of Sweden's southernmost province, Skåne, and most of Denmark are very similar. Structurally the lowland of southwestern Skåne, the Danish islands, and eastern Jutland comprise a gently to moderately rolling plain separated only by shallow arms of the sea. This till plain, composed as it is of lime-rich moraine deposits and clays resting on a bedrock of limestone and chalk, is among the most productive farm land in all of Northern Europe. Only in a few scattered localities is the bedrock exposed at the surface, as for example on the eastern end of the island of Mön, where the chalk cliffs rise more than 400 feet out of the Baltic. Running through central and southern Jutland is a chain of hills which marks the terminal moraine of the last glaciation. It is in these hills that Denmark's highest point—Yding Skovhöj, 567 feet—is located. To the west of the moraine, glacial streams built up extensive outwash plains of sand and gravel, an area which today constitutes Denmark's least-productive region—the so-called Heath of Jutland. Sweeping sand beaches and shifting dunes characterize Jutland's low western coast.

Owing to their location on the extreme southern margin of Northern Europe, Denmark and Skåne enjoy the mildest climate of any part of the region. Temperatures average near or above freezing during most winters and in the mid-60's during the summer. Precipitation, the bulk of which falls as rain, totals between 20 and 30 inches a year. The native vegetation supported by this mild, moist climate was a dense deciduous forest in which the beech tree was particularly common. However, as the land was taken under cultivation the forests gradually disappeared until today less than ten per cent of Denmark and Skåne remain in woods. Owing to man's long exploitation even these remaining groves have a parklike character, and they can in no way be compared with the forests found over most of the rest of Northern Europe. But if man has left his mark on the forests of the region, so has he also altered the originally barren Heath of Jutland, for there numerous plantations of spruce and pine have been made and considerable cultivation taken place.

The Faeroes and Iceland. Having once comprised parts of the same tabular island (Greater Iceland), the Faeroes and large sections of Iceland demonstrate a striking similarity of landscape. Gently dipping layers of basalt form bold headlands over 2,000 feet in height along the northwestern edges of the Faeroes and in eastern and northwestern Iceland. In the Faeroes the inclination is toward the southeast, so nearly all of the habitations are located on this lower and more accessible side of the islands. In Iceland the layers dip chiefly toward the interior of the island, reflecting the presence there of a zone of subsidence. In all of the basalt areas, mountain glaciation has produced numerous U-shaped valleys, many of which are partially submerged as fjords, and other boldly etched features such as cirques, arêtes, and horn peaks.

In the subsidence zone which runs diagonally across Iceland from southwest to northeast, volcanism and diastrophism (movements of the earth's crust) continue as active agents of landscape formation. As a result, the features are jumbled and chaotic. Most of interior Iceland is a plateau which averages about 2,000 feet in elevation, though numerous isolated mountains rise above the general level to heights of 5,000 feet and more. Some of these are horsts, others are volcanic cones, and still others are old volcanic necks which remained after the volcano itself had been eroded away. Great fault-searps like that at Thingvellir and extensive lava flows (of which the largest is the Ódáðhahraun in the northeast) add to the broken nature of the terrain. In the higher parts of the island, particularly athwart the height of land that crosses the country from east to west, lie several plateau glaciers, of which Vatna Glacier (2,200 square miles) is the largest. Extensive lowlands are found only in the south and southwest, though even there large areas are uninhabitable due to lava flows and the continuing deposition of outwash from the great glaciers.

Iceland is one of the most intensively volcanic regions in the world. Best known of its volcanoes perhaps is Hekla which has had more than a dozen eruptions within historic times, the most recent occurring in 1947–48. Occasionally, volcanic activity takes place beneath one of the glaciers, resulting in a spectacular and destructive phenomenon known as a "glacier-burst." Hot springs are found in virtually every part of the island and total several thousands in all. Many of them boil over periodically, sending great columns of superheated water and steam into the air. The most famous of these springs is the Stóri Geysir in Haukadalur, from which our word "geyser" was derived.

Due to their insularity, both the Faeroes and Iceland have climates which are decidedly maritime in character. In the Faeroes winter temperatures rarely dip to the freezing point and summer temperatures seldom get much above 50° F. About 60 inches of precipitation are received each year, with the maximum coming in the winter season and almost all of it falling in the form of rain. There are long periods of overcast, and winds of gale force are not infrequent. As might be expected, such a climate has not been conducive to tree growth; hence, most of the Faeroes are covered with grass.

In Iceland, the very size of the island contributes several aspects of "continentality" to the climate. The south and west coasts, bathed by the Irminger Current, a branch of the North Atlantic Drift, have a milder and wetter climate than the north and east coasts, which come under the influence of the cold East Greenland Current. Winter temperatures in the southwest seldom average below freezing, but in the north and east they normally drop into the low 20's; snow is thus more common and longer lasting in the latter region. In summer, temperatures in the low 50's are common to the coastal districts in all parts of the island. Precipitation, which in the south and west averages between 30 and 60 inches a year, usually amounts to less than 20 inches a year over most of the northern half of the island.

The dominant vegetation in Iceland today is grass, though at the coming of the first settlers there were rather extensive wooded areas (composed chiefly of scrub birch) in the lowlands. Small birch groves are now found only in isolated or sheltered valleys where they are protected by law. The greater part of the island is covered by a sparse mountain vegetation consisting of mosses and lichens, together with grasses, heather, and dwarf birches. In recent years conifers have been successfully introduced from other subarctic regions, demonstrating that the climate is not hostile to their growth. The country's largest experimental forest is located at Hallormstadhur in the northeast.

THE CULTURAL AND HISTORICAL BACKGROUND

Prehistoric Settlement

Although Northern Europe was the last major region of the subcontinent to be inhabited by man, owing to its long immersion in ice, Germanic tribes established themselves on the peninsula and islands of Denmark at an early date and later spread northward into Sweden and Norway. The earliest settlements in Finland appear to have been made on the southwest coast, and these too may have been Germanic in origin. About the beginning of the Christian era, however, the second and last major ethnic group to settle in Northern Europe began moving into southern and central Finland—these were Finno-Ugrian tribes. Apart from these two peoples, however (i.e., the Germanics and the Finno-Ugrians), no other ethnic group of importance is today represented in Northern Europe.

For some time, the chief forms of economic activity in Northern Europe continued to be hunting and fishing, though in those areas where easily cleared deciduous forests coincided with patches of good, easily worked soil, hunting and fishing were gradually replaced by agriculture. The greater part of Denmark early became the home of a relatively dense agricultural settlement, though this was much less true in Sweden, Norway, and Finland. In these countries, deciduous forests were formerly much more widespread than they are today, and while this served as an inducement to the primitive farmer, the paucity of good soils served as a strong deterrent. Early cultivation in these countries was largely restricted to easily tilled soils derived from Cambro-Silurian and/or marine deposits, as it is even to this day. When iron came into more general use, it not only allowed agriculture to spread into the coniferous-forest areas but also made possible the construction of better boats, a factor which greatly improved the communications of the time, particularly in Norway. A simultaneous deterioration of the climate soon nullified the gains made in farming, however, and in some areas, notably Norwegian Tröndelag, it is probable that all previous cultivation had to be abandoned. In the regions remaining, animal husbandry became the dominant form of agriculture and shelters had to be provided for the animals, which up until then had been pastured out-of-doors the year around.

The major lineaments of the present-day settlement pattern of Northern Europe appear to have already been well established in prehistoric times. Both agglomerated villages and dispersed farmsteads, found in Denmark today, were common at an early date. The oldest of the villages tended to be located in plains regions, the rolling hill regions being still largely in forest. In the wooded areas a more dispersed settlement was the rule. Main roads ran along water divides, and villages were located on watercourses only where fords had to be made. A much more important determinant of village locations was access to ground water in the form of ponds where animals could be watered. The Danish villages tended to take two general forms—a round village comprised of farms situated roughly in a ring around some central nucleus such as a pond or common pasture, and a linear village, usually comprised of two rows of farms strung out along a roadway. Round-village types were common on Zealand and on Jutland south of Limfjord and east of the Heath; the linear type was more prevalent on Fyn and in southern Jutland. Danish farm holdings were commonly made of bricks which were plastered over and whitewashed, and the roofs were often of thatch.

Although much of Sweden was early characterized by a settlement pattern of dispersed farms, villages have also been common since prehistoric times. The farms themselves fall into a half-dozen separate types, each distinguished from the other by the varying location of the animal shelters with respect to the dwelling house. The villages fall into three main groups—the linear village, the round village, and the family village, the latter being created through the subdivision of the original farms into smaller units. The linear-village type is most prevalent in east-central and southeastern Sweden and on the island of Öland. The round-village type is limited to those regions of the country where the Danish influence was the strongest, namely, Skåne and the adjacent west and south coasts. The family village was most common in the South Swedish Highland, west-central Sweden, and the southern parts of Swedish Northland. Though most construction was of wood, the form in which it was used varied from planks in Skåne to notched logs in Swedish Northland.

In Norway the settlement pattern was conditioned by the country's physical relief almost as strongly as it was by access to good soil. Apart from the lowland regions near the coast, early agricultural settlements were made on the sides of the more open valleys in the southeast. Such locations combined the advantages of soil (in this case, lateral moraines) and exposure to the sun, advantages

which locations either higher up or lower down the valley sides did not possess. From these *midtligärder* (literally, "farms on the middle of the slope"), settlement spread up into the high mountain pastures where the women would usually spend the summer in small huts (*seter*) tending the animals. The farms themselves were widely scattered and true agricultural villages did not exist. Unlike Danish farms, which might be centralized in one or two large buildings, those in Norway were composed of often as many as 20 to 30 smaller buildings, each with its specific use. Along the coasts the location of fishing settlements were determined not only by proximity to good fishing banks but also by suitable harbors and access to small patches of land where subsidiary agriculture might be carried on. As early as the ninth century Norwegian fishermen from the western and northern coastal districts made annual expeditions to the Lofoten fisheries. Thus, with transhumance being practiced in the farming regions and seasonal migrations taking place along the coast to fish or into the mountains to hunt, the population of prehistoric Norway can hardly be thought of as permanently situated.

The rural settlement pattern of Finland was likewise characterized by small, dispersed farms, and agricultural villages in the Central European sense are quite unknown even today. In so far as possible, the farms were located on river terraces or on small knolls or eskers, so that they would not only have better exposure to the sun but also some degree of protection from the frost. Finnish farm buildings were then and are today customarily built of wood, and besides the dwelling house there may be from a dozen to 30 separate outbuildings, each with its own specific purposes. Almost invariably one of these will be a *sauna* (steam bathhouse), usually located somewhat apart from the rest of the buildings and in close proximity to a lake or stream. In the Åland Islands, small, protected harbors early gave rise to little fishing villages.

Of the five Northern European countries, only Denmark and Sweden can be said to have towns which date back to prehistoric times. These originally grew up around heathen centers of worship or at tribal meeting places, but somewhat later advantageous trading sites were also selected. Among the earliest Danish towns were Aarhus, Viborg, and Ribe on Jutland, Odense on Fyn, Ringsted and Roskilde on Zealand, and Lund in present-day Swedish Skåne. The earliest Swedish towns grew up in the vicinity of the Mälaren, among them Uppsala and Birka, though the latter has since become extinct.

Originally, all the Germanic tribes spoke the same language, though by the beginning of historic times this had already evolved into three principal dialectal variants. Two of these were spoken in Northern Europe, namely, Gothic (now extinct) in the Baltic area and Old Norse (or North German) in Denmark, Sweden, and Norway. Both dialects used the runic characters of the Gothic alphabet in their written language. Among the Finno-Ugrian tribes there also were several spoken dialects but no written language at this time.

The Viking Period
(800–1100 A.D.)

About the close of the eighth century the story of the Scandinavian peoples suddenly emerges from the realms of legend into the pages of written history. For the next three hundred years these northern peoples demonstrated such a tremendous surge of activity that scarcely any part of Europe escaped their impact. Norwegians ranged from Spitsbergen and the White Sea in the north to the Mediterranean in the south, and likewise pushed westward to Iceland, Greenland, and the coasts of North America. In the east the Swedes coursed up and down the river systems of European Russia and ultimately reached Byzantium and the lands of the Caspian. The Danes were no less active, for they turned their attention to the lands bordering the North Sea and most particularly concentrated on the British Isles. Begun as voyages of exploration and trade, in many areas these expeditions took on the character

of sporadic pirate raids and later developed into organized campaigns of conquest and settlement. Named for the audacious seamen who led these expeditions, this dynamic chapter of Scandinavian history has come to be called the "Viking period" (Fig. 4–3).

What the causes for this outburst of peoples may have been is not known with certainty, though they have variously been attributed to overpopulation with respect to the level of technology, to large-scale political dissatisfaction (particularly in Norway), to the attractive realization that the countries of Western Europe were too weak to defend the wealth they were accumulating, and to a sheer love of adventure. Indeed, all of these factors may have played a part, but far better known are the effects of this dispersal. In Northern Europe there was not only a northward movement of peoples in the Scandinavian peninsula itself but also the beginning of a large-scale Swedish movement into Finland. It was during this same period that the Faeroes and Iceland were permanently settled, though both of these areas had probably been visited somewhat earlier by the Irish. Norwegians landed in the Faeroes sometime during the eighth century, and the first permanent settlement was made in Iceland in 874, near present-day Reykjavík. Once begun, the tide of emigrants from Scandinavia (particularly Norway) and from the Viking possessions in the British Isles swelled rapidly, and by 930 there were some 60,000 to 70,000 people on the island. This original period of settlement in Iceland, the so-called *Landnám*, saw all of the coastal areas populated while the interior remained virtually uninhabited, a pattern of distribution which has continued unchanged to this day. The story of this settlement has been preserved in one of the most complete works of historical geography in existence, the so-called *Landnámabók*.[2]

---

2 Written during the twelfth and thirteenth centuries, the *Landnámabók* contains the names of 417 of the earliest colonists and describes in detail how the land was apportioned. About a third of the persons so mentioned appear to have come from the British Isles.

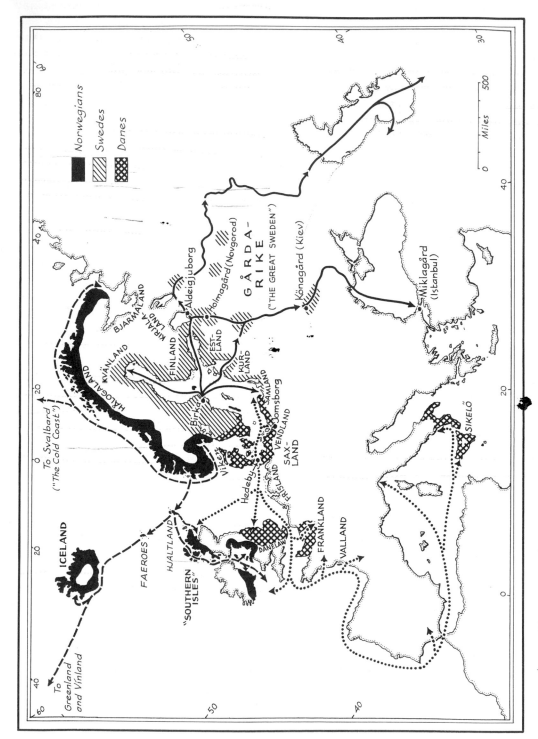

Fig. 4–3. Viking expeditions and settlements during the ninth, tenth, and eleventh centuries.

It did not take long for the settlers in Iceland to realize that their new environment offered them fewer opportunities (and greater obstacles) for making a living than had the lands they had left. As a consequence, various aspects of their culture had to be modified to conform to this more exacting milieu. The construction of wooden buildings, for example, was a virtual impossibility, for there was little suitable timber on the island. Instead the settlers were forced to build their homes of stone, earth, or peat. As the birch forests disappeared, the problem of fuel became more pressing and the people had to resort to burning driftwood and sheep dung. Furthermore, only the hardiest of the grains they had brought with them would ripen in the short, cool summers of Iceland, and during the fifteenth century, possibly because of the deterioration of the climate, even this cultivation had largely to be abandoned. With local exceptions, agriculture in Iceland came to mean harvesting hay during the summer to carry the livestock through the winter.

The Viking period saw the introduction of Christianity into Northern Europe and the respective unification of the three Scandinavian countries. In Sweden, both the Swedes and the Goths had been brought under one king and the country's borders had been pushed westward against the Norwegians and southward against the Danes. During this same period, the island of Gotland rose to prominence as a trading center, its chief town being Visby on the west coast. Though Christianity was introduced into the country early in the ninth century, its triumph was not complete until the middle of the thirteenth century, making Sweden the last great nation in Europe to bow to the authority of Rome.

In Norway the settlement pattern became more fixed as trade increased and as Christianity gained a foothold. The country's first trading center was founded near Larvik in the ninth century and shortly afterward Tonsberg became Norway's first town. In the next two centuries a number of other towns came into being—Bergen, Nidaros (present-day Trondheim), Oslo, Stavanger, Borg (now Sarpsborg), and Hamar. When Christianity came in about the year 1000, these embryonic trading towns were selected as sites for its churches, and from then on the growth of both church and town was reciprocal. In 1153 Norway became a separate ecclesiastical province, with an archbishopric established at Nidaros.

It was likewise during the Viking period that the Danish trading town of Hedeby (now the West German city of Schleswig) grew to importance. Also dating from this period are the *Dannevirke*, an extensive earthenwork defense line built across the narrows of Jutland just south of Hedeby, and several large, circular Viking encampments on Jutland and Zealand. As Christianity gained ground in Denmark during the tenth century, churches were established in the more important administrative and trading towns, and in 1104 a Danish archbishopric was created at Lund. First mention was made of Copenhagen (Köbenhavn) in about 1043 when it was referred to as a fishing and trading village, but after 1167, when a castle was established there, the town grew in importance. In Iceland the first *Althing*, or legislative assembly, convened at Thingvellir in 930, and it is from this date that the republic reckons its birth.

During the Viking period, a further step in the evolution of the language pattern of Northern Europe took place. Old Norse, which up until then had been the language common to all three Scandinavian countries, split into two parts—an East Norse spoken in Denmark and Sweden and a West Norse spoken in Norway, the Faeroes, and Iceland.

The Middle Ages

Soon after the close of the Viking period, the countries of Northern Europe began turning their energies to a more intensive development of their own resources and trade began to develop with Western and Central Europe. From Tönsberg in Norway timber was early exported to the Low Countries, and Bergen likewise became an early center for the marketing of fish. In fact, by the thirteenth century Bergen had managed to gain control of all Norwegian fish exports from the mouth of Hardanger Fjord to Finnmark, and in order to maintain this dominant position foreign merchants were forbidden to sail north of that city. In Sweden the mining of iron had probably begun during Viking times, and the production of so-called "osmund iron" in central Sweden (particularly the Bergslagen district at the southern edge of Swedish Northland) soon led to an appreciable export due to its relatively high quality for the period. Stockholm grew up as an important iron-shipping port, as did Göteborg sometime later, when iron exports from the Vänern district began. In the thirteenth century copper was also being mined in the Bergslagen, and together these two metals dominated Swedish exports for several centuries. Whereas Birka had been superseded by Stockholm, the ancient town of Visby was continuing to grow and prosper. In the south of Sweden the salting and marketing of Baltic herring was already a thriving business.

It was not long before the commercial league of the north-German cities (the so-called "Hansa") began casting covetous eyes on this growing trade of Northern Europe. Through a combination of shrewd business tactics, economic sanctions, and the threats or actual use of force, the Hanseatic merchants soon managed to gain control of the greater part of the region's commerce. When the Hansa established its factory in Bergen in 1343, it secured control of virtually the entire Norwegian coast, thanks to the dependence of this vast region upon imported bread grains which the Hanseatic League was in a position to monopolize. Though the exchange of dried fish and butter for grain, meal, and salt soon made Bergen the leading trading center of all Northern Europe, the general effect on the Norwegian economy was detrimental. When the Hansa's privileges were finally revoked in the sixteenth century, Bergen nevertheless continued its domination of northern Norway, and it was not until the middle of the nineteenth century that this region began to enjoy a measure of economic independence, thanks largely to improved communications.

In Sweden, the Hansa early monopolized the salting and marketing of fish in the south, and its influence was likewise strongly felt in mining and in the local government of the many new towns which came into existence at this time in the central portion of the country. Though a German settlement had been made in Visby as early as the twelfth century, that city gained its greatest prominence about the end of the thirteenth century, when it became the chief trading center of the Hanseatic League in the Baltic. Near the height of its power, however, it was sacked by the Danes (1361), and it never regained its former importance. In 1370, after long opposition, Denmark was likewise obliged to grant trade privileges to the Hansa.

During the Middle Ages several political changes took place in Northern Europe which have had a considerable influence on the subsequent development of the region. About the middle of the thirteenth century Norway reached the height of its power when all of its far-flung colonies recognized the Norwegian king as their sovereign. Within a century, however, the country's fortunes had been seriously reversed, for, with the extinction of her royal line in 1380, Norway and its possessions were joined to Denmark, first as an equal kingdom but then as a dependent area in 1536.

Throughout the medieval period Sweden continued to focus her attention on the east, turning her energies first to the Christianization and conquest of Finland, a task which she largely completed by the defeat of the Russians in 1323. This conquest was followed by such an influx of Swedes to East Bothnia that, from 1362 on, that region was recognized as an integral part of the Swedish realm. Though this political status was later altered by the course of events, the Swedish conquest of Finland had other consequences which were more enduring. In addition to bringing the country under the jurisdiction of the Western church, the Swedes considerably altered the Finnish settlement pattern. Not only were many Finns pushed north and eastward into the interior of the country, in turn dislodging the seminomadic Lapps, but the urban development of Finland was also initiated. The oldest Finnish town is Turku (in Swedish, Åbo), which was founded in 1229 and became the country's first capital. Rauma and Pori were founded in 1365, and Viipuri (in Swedish Viborg, in Russian Vyborg) was established in 1403. While the locations of these towns were largely determined by reason of their harbors and their opportunities for trade, the towns of the interior tended to grow up around fortresses. Savonlinna, Hämeenlinna, and Kajaani are examples of such towns. Helsinki was not founded until 1550. Furthermore, by introducing their own language, the Swedes had a profound influence on the linguistic character of the country. Not only is there a considerable Swedish-speaking minority in Finland today, but the Finnish language itself has incorporated many words of Swedish origin. It was during this period too, that the dialect of Turku became the national standard for the written language, having been used in the Finnish translation of the Bible.

After Norway was joined to Denmark in 1380, the Danes attempted to complete the union of the Scandinavian countries by attacking and conquering Sweden. In 1389 the Swedes were forced to join the Danish-sponsored Kalmar Union but, after a long series of bloody wars, broke out of this alliance in 1523. From then until the middle of the eighteenth century Denmark and Sweden were almost constantly at war with one another as they both struggled for mastery of the Baltic. By the middle of the seventeenth century it appeared that Sweden would ultimately be triumphant, for she had not only driven the Danes off the Swedish mainland in the south and annexed the Norwegian territories of Bohuslän (on the west coast of Sweden north of Göteborg) and Jämtland

but she had also turned the Baltic into virtually a Swedish lake by consolidating her hold on Finland and annexing Estonia, Latvia, the region around present-day Leningrad, and portions of the north-German coast at the mouths of the Oder and Weser rivers. Her dominance in the Baltic was short lived, however, for, with the rise of Russia under Peter the Great, Sweden was forced to yield or cede all of her overseas possessions except Finland. Thus, by 1750 the countries of Northern Europe had already passed the peak of their political greatness and were in a state of decline.

During the Middle Ages there was a further development of the urban settlement pattern of the Scandinavian countries as well as a further evolution of the language pattern. In Denmark there were 50 towns by the year 1300, most of which were situated on the coast at the shortest crossings between the islands, on fjords, or at river crossings. Several towns grew up at road junctions, near castles, and at the sites of monasteries. In 1416, when the Danish king chose Copenhagen as his capital, he further spurred the town's growth, and it became the country's leading center of learning when a university was established there in 1479. In Sweden, where there had been some 30 towns previous to 1600, a like number arose during its period of greatness. Among them was Eskilstuna, which has ever since been renowned for its fine-quality steel products. In Norway the seventeenth century saw the rise of several mining settlements, among them Kongsberg, Röros, and Lökken. The influence of King Christian IV of Denmark is witnessed in such place names as Kristiania (since renamed Oslo) and Kristiansand on the south coast. The Norwegian language also bears the imprint of the country's long association with Denmark, for throughout this period Danish was the official literary and commercial language of Norway and as such made its strongest inroads in the towns of the southeast. In the less accessible rural and mountain districts, however, old West Norse dialects continued to be spoken throughout the Danish period. In Sweden the strong influence of the Hansa is evidenced by the many German words which entered the Swedish language at that time.

No discussion of the Middle Ages in Northern Europe would be complete without some mention of the untold hardships which the people of Iceland were forced to bear during this period. In the centuries following the Landnám, it is reasonable to assume, the population grew gradually to something over 80,000 persons, but about the beginning of the fifteenth century a series of natural calamities struck the island, carrying away a great number of inhabitants. The Black Death is said to have wiped out nearly two-thirds of the population, while several volcanic eruptions and the deterioration of the climate, with its attendant starvation, also took a heavy toll. In 1602 the Danes imposed a trade monopoly on the island which only further aggravated the people's suffering. When the first census was taken in 1703, there were only about 50,000 inhabitants remaining. This number was further reduced by nearly one-fifth as a consequence of the catastrophic eruption of Laki Volcano in 1783. In the Faeroes, the Black Death is believed to have killed virtually everyone, with a resettlement of the islands taking place from western Norway somewhat later. This is believed to account for the fact that the present Faeroese population speaks a medieval Norwegian dialect rather than Old Norse as in Iceland.

The Modern Period

Since 1750, the countries of Northern Europe have abandoned all dreams of political expansion and greatness and instead have devoted their energies to the improvement of their economic and social conditions at home. Beginning about the end of the eighteenth century, land reforms were initiated in both Denmark and Sweden to correct the continually worsening situation which was created by repeatedly subdividing farm properties into ever-smaller units. In both countries a more scattered settlement pattern has resulted and new areas have been taken under cultivation. In Finland, land reforms were also begun after the country gained its independence and since that time an area as large as Swedish Skåne has been opened to new agricultural settlement. During the modern period, the strongest influence on the urban settlement pattern of Northern Europe has been the Industrial Revolution. Because it came rather late, in most instances after the middle of the nineteenth century, it was not attended by the over-crowding and congestion which have plagued much of industrialized Western and Central Europe. Instead, owing to the nature of its raw materials and sources of energy, industry in Northern Europe has tended to be rather evenly divided between rural and urban locations. Where towns already existed, it has spurred their growth, but where they did not exist, industry has given birth to them. Because many of its raw materials and most of its fuel must be imported, industry has found it of particular advantage to locate in port cities.

The past two centuries have seen a steady rise in the standard of living in Northern Europe and with it the transition from aristocratic monarchy to social democracy. During this same period, great numbers of Northern Europeans emigrated to North America, and the release of this population pressure on the land undoubtedly did much to promote the rapid economic advances which have since taken place. Throughout the modern period, the political destinies of the Northern European countries have rested largely in the hands of the Great Powers which surround them. In 1808–1809, Sweden was expelled from Finland by Russia, and Finland became a grand duchy of the Russian Empire. During the Napoleonic Wars Denmark reacted against British pressure by joining the French. As a result of this mistake, Norway was taken from her and joined to Sweden, though she still maintained sovereignty over Iceland, Greenland, and the Faeroes. The duchies of Schleswig and Holstein (on the southern frontier of Jutland) had always been a bone of contention between the Germans and Danes, and, when Denmark attempted to extend her constitution of 1849 to cover the Duchy of Schleswig, Prussia used this as an excuse to attack her in 1864 and take both territories from her. In 1905, Norway chose to end its union with Sweden and the two countries parted in peace. Throughout World War I the Scandinavian countries successfully maintained a policy of neutrality, though the war nevertheless had several important repercussions within the region. In 1917 Finland declared its independence from Russia, in 1919 she drew up a democratic constitution, and in 1920 she was recognized as an independent republic. In 1918 Iceland became a sovereign state in personal union with the king of Denmark, and in 1920, on the basis of a plebiscite, north Schleswig was returned to Denmark. In 1925, pursuant to a treaty signed in 1920, the Spitsbergen islands became a constitutional part of the Kingdom of Norway, followed by the annexation of Jan Mayen and the Antarctic islands of Bouvet, in 1930, and Peter I, in 1931. In 1939 Norway laid claim to a portion of the Antarctic Continent under the name of Queen Maud Land.

When World War II broke out, the countries of Northern Europe announced their intention to remain neutral, but this hope was shattered in November, 1939, when the Soviet Union launched the so-called "Winter War" against Finland. In the peace of March, 1940, Finland was forced to cede the city of Viipuri and the Karelian Isthmus, as well as a border region in the central Karelian Uplands. In addition, the Hangö Peninsula was to be leased to the Soviet Union for a thirty-year period. Then in April, 1940, Nazi Germany invaded and occupied both Denmark and Norway, and in order to forestall a similar move in the Faeroes and Iceland, these latter areas were occupied by the British. In 1941 the Americans took over the defense of Iceland. In June of the same year, three days after the Nazis attacked the So-

viet Union, the Finns entered the war on their side but were forced to sign a separate peace in September, 1944. Likewise in 1944, the people of Iceland voted to sever their ties with Denmark and become an independent republic. In May, 1945, with the end of the war in Europe, Denmark and Norway were liberated. In the peace treaty signed in September, 1947, Finland lost Viipuri and the Karelian Isthmus in the south once more, and the region in the central Karelian Uplands. In addition, the Petsamo (now Pechenga) region was taken from her, the Porkkala Peninsula was leased to the Soviet Union for 50 years, and $300 million in reparations were levied against her, payable over an eight-year period ending in 1952.[3] Of the Northern European countries, therefore, only Sweden escaped the direct effects of the war, though her neutrality was strained and precarious throughout. In the postwar period, Denmark, Norway, and Iceland joined the North Atlantic Treaty Organization, while Sweden elected to refrain from joining any alliance outside of the Scandinavian area which might precipitate an invasion of Finland.

Each of the Northern European countries is divided into several administrative subdivisions, and, though they have a different name in each country, they correspond most closely to the American county. In Norway, the unit is called a *fylke* and they number 20 in all, including one each for the cities of Oslo and Bergen. In Sweden the unit is a *län*, of which there are a total of 25 including one for the city of Stockholm. The Finnish unit is a *lääni*, of which there are 12, including the Åland Islands which enjoy a large measure of self-government. In Denmark the administrative subdivision is called an *amt*, and the country has 26 in all, including one for the Faeroes, which has the right to use its own language and flag and is to a

[3] As evidence of Soviet "good will," the reparations were scaled down to $227.5 million in 1948 and the Porkkala Peninsula was returned to Finland in 1955.

large extent self-governing, and three for Greenland. The Faeroes and Greenland each elect two members to the Danish Parliament. The Icelandic unit of local administration is the *sýsla*, of which there are a total of 23.

The modern language pattern of Northern Europe is a direct product of the region's historical development. In Iceland, the language is the direct descendant of the Old Norse which was introduced during the Viking period. Owing to Iceland's isolation, Icelandic has preserved its old grammatical system virtually unchanged since the days of the Sagas, in contrast to the more simplified Scandinavian languages. In a further effort to preserve this purity, original Icelandic terms have been coined to take the place of foreign words. This attempt to correlate a medieval language with modern technology and items of culture which are not native to Iceland has produced some rather imaginative compounds. Electricity, for example, is literally translated as "amber power," while a telephone is called a "talking wire." Many of the younger people speak English, and many of the older generation know Danish. The Faeroese language has likewise retained its medieval grammar and is accordingly very difficult for most Scandinavians to understand. Both Danish and Faeroese are recognized as official languages in the archipelago, however. In Denmark itself, Danish is the only official language, though there is a small German-speaking minority in Schleswig. Norway has two official languages, both of which are Norwegian but which differ in their historical development. They are *bokmål* (literally, "book language") and *nynorsk* ("new Norwegian"). *Bokmål* is a derivation of Dano-Norwegian, the official language of Norway during its long association with Denmark. *Nynorsk* is a composite of the rural dialects which continued to be spoken throughout the Danish period in the more isolated regions of the country, and was first given written expression about the middle of the nineteenth century. In Sweden there is only one official language, namely,

Swedish, though there are small Lapp and Finnish minorities in the northern part of the country. In north Norway the Lapps number about 20,000 and in north Finland about 3,000. In the latter country both Finnish and Swedish are recognized as official languages. In their written forms, the three Scandinavian languages are mutually intelligible in all three countries, although this is considerably less true of certain of the spoken languages, particularly Danish and Norwegian *nynorsk*.

In addition to their language ties, the countries of Northern Europe have several other cultural bonds of an enduring nature. In all of these countries the Evangelical Lutheran church has been the state church ever since the Reformation, though there is almost complete freedom of worship in the region today. In the fields of education, labor relations, customs, travel, and humanitarianism the nations of Northern Europe have demonstrated a strong sense of regional unity. Each year an inter-Nordic parliament with advisory powers is held in an attempt to correlate the economic and social policies of the region. Many of these advances in regional cooperation have come about as the result of efforts of an organization known as the "Nordic Union" which was founded in 1919. Of a less official nature, but no less important in strengthening the bonds of friendship between these northern countries, is the vast tide of tourists which flows between these nations every summer. With a uniformly high standard of living, a great variety of scenic and cultural attractions to visit, and travel restrictions reduced to a minimum, the peoples of Northern Europe are perhaps the most tourist-minded of any region on the continent. In all but a political sense, *Norden* is a symbol of the unity of Northern Europe.

NORWAY

Population

By 1967 the population of Norway had grown to more than 3.8 million, of whom

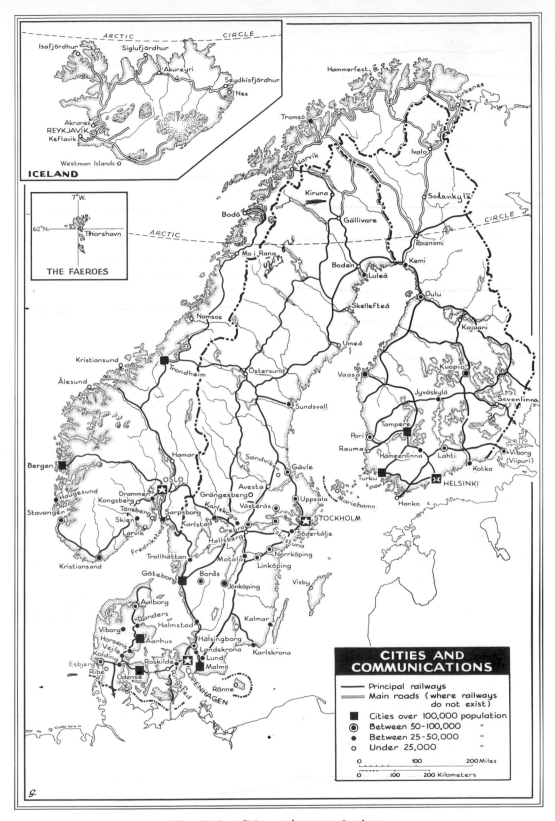

Fig. 4–4. Cities and communications.

about three-fifths lived in cities, suburbs, and rural agglomerations (Fig. 4–4). The largest city is Oslo, the capital, with 485,000 inhabitants (with suburbs, 600,000). Due to the redrawing of administrative boundaries, the size and rank of Norwegian cities changed dramatically during the 1960's.

One result of this change has been that Trondheim (Fig. 4–5), the historic capital and national religious center, now has 119,000 inhabitants, as compared to the west coast port of Bergen, with just under 118,000. Stavanger retains fourth rank with 80,000 inhabitants, while Kristiansand has climbed into fifth place with 52,000. The southeastern industrial cities of Drammen and Skien both have about 47,000 inhabitants and there are seven other cities with over 25,000 each. Many coastal and mountain districts

are losing population, but the districts bordering Oslofjord are growing rapidly. It is estimated that by 1990 they will contain over one million inhabitants, or more than one-fourth of the total Norwegian population.

Present Economic Life of Norway

Agriculture, forestry, and fishing. One of the most profound changes in the economic life of Norway since the end of World War II has been the marked shift in employment away from the primary occupations of farming, forestry, and fishing. Today less than 15 per cent of the Norwegians work in agriculture and forestry, while less than 4 per cent earn their livelihoods from such maritime activities as fishing, sealing, and whaling (Fig. 4–6). Because advanced education and professional training are eco-

Fig. 4–5. Situated near the mouth of the Nid River, from which its original name Nidaros was taken, Trondheim served as Norway's first capital and her principal religious center. In 1967, thanks to the annexation of its neighboring communes, Trondheim edged ahead of Bergen to become Norway's second most populous city. (Wideröe.)

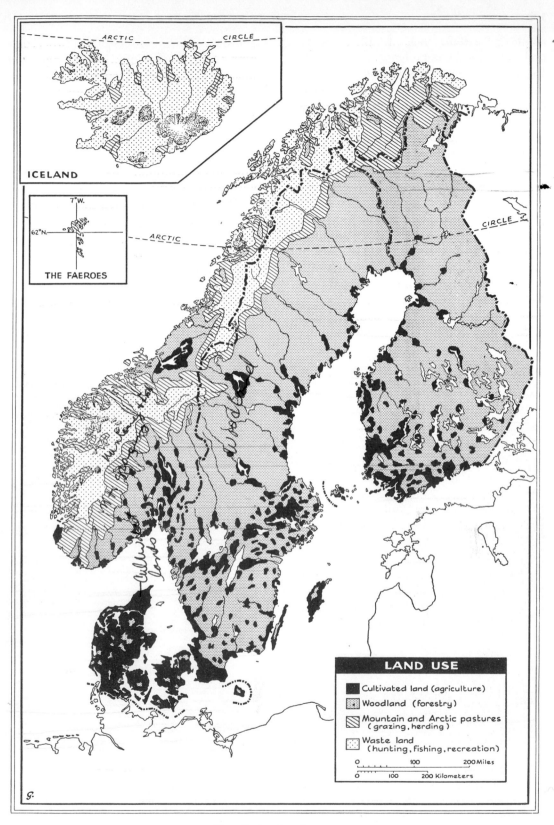

ARCTIC CIRCLE

ICELAND

7°W.

62°N.

ARCTIC CIRCLE

THE FAEROES

LAND USE

■ Cultivated land (agriculture)

▓ Woodland (forestry)

▨ Mountain and Arctic pastures
(grazing, herding)

▒ Waste land
(hunting, fishing, recreation)

0   100   200 Miles

0   100   200 Kilometers

G.

Fig. 4–6. Land use.

nomically within reach of all Norwegians, the attraction of higher-paid and more challenging jobs in industry and the service occupations, coupled with a rapid rise in national affluence, has accelerated the "flight from the land"; hence, it is becoming increasingly difficult to keep labor in the physically more arduous basic occupations.

For reasons of topography and climate, commercial agriculture has always been marginal in most of Norway. To this day, less than 3 per cent of the country's land area has been brought under cultivation. The most productive districts are those lowlands underlain by Cambro-Silurian deposits and/or covered by postglacial marine deposits. Of special importance are the plains in the lower valleys of the East Country, the rolling morainic lowland of Jaeren in the West Country, and the clay plains of central Tröndelag, which together comprise only 8 per cent of the country's total area but embrace almost half of its land under cultivation (Fig. 4–7).

More than half of all Norwegian farms have less than one acre of cultivated land each, and 98 per cent of them have less than 50 acres. In the light of recent studies, which indicate that only those farms having more than 25 acres of cultivated land are economically viable, it is scarcely surprising that only the larger farms in Jaeren and the more favored lowlands of the East Country operate with a net profit. About three-

Fig. 4–7. The farming district of Kvam in the upper part of Gudbrandsdal, in the Norwegian East Country. Most of the farmsteads are *midtligårder,* located on the middle of the slope where the soils and exposure are best. Hay meadows occupy much of the lower-lying land along the river, while forests clothe the higher, rockier slopes. (Normann.)

fourths of all Norwegian farm income is derived from livestock products, with milk alone constituting three-eighths of the total production.

As part of the modernization of agriculture which has taken place since the end of World War II, the consumption of artificial fertilizer and concentrated livestock feeds has risen sharply and mechanization has proceeded apace. The number of conventional tractors has increased tenfold, while two-wheeled tractors, which are especially useful in steep terrain, have gained widespread acceptance. The uneconomic production of bread grains has been de-emphasized until today two-thirds of all grain acreage is devoted to barley and most of the remainder to oats, both of which give fairly good yields in the cool, damp Norwegian climate. The specialized production of fruits (including apples, pears, plums, and cherries), berries, and flowers now provides a larger share to Norwegian farm income than does grain cultivation, with half of the total output coming from the inner districts of Hardanger and Sogne fjords. Jaeren is an important source of early vegetables, as well as of butter, cheese, poultry, eggs, and pork, while the interior valleys of the East Country rank among Norway's major producers of dairy products, potatoes, mutton, and wool. Fur farming also makes its largest contribution to agricultural income in these districts.

In the wooded regions of the East Country and Tröndelag, farming is often carried on as a joint occupation with forestry, while in the coastal districts of the West Country and north Norway it constitutes a seasonal combination with fishing. Some 80 per cent of the annual timber harvest comes from the East Country, with another 12 per cent coming from Tröndelag. The rapid shift to motorized transport during the 1960's is seen in the decline in the volume of timber floated down the major eastern rivers; whereas well over half of the commercial cut formerly moved to market in this way, the proportion is now nearer one-fourth.

As Norway's standard of living has risen in the post-war period, the country's traditional attachment to the sea has grown ever weaker. By the mid-1960's there were fewer than 50,000 full- and part-time fishermen in the country, and half of these lived in north Norway where alternative forms of employment are sharply restricted. That fishing in Norway remains essentially a small-scale family enterprise is witnessed by the fact that open wooden boats make up three-fourths of the entire fleet; more than two-fifths of the vessels are of prewar vintage. Catches have fluctuated so widely in recent years that participation in the traditional herring fisheries off of Ålesund and in the cod fisheries of the Lofoten area has steadily declined. Even so, when the catches are good, so much fish is caught in such a short time that well over half of it must be ground into meal or pressed into oil if it is to have any economic value at all. Thus, although Norwegian fishermen normally catch a larger volume of fish each year than do the fishermen of any other European nation, the average value per ton of the catch is lower than that of any country in Europe except Iceland. The failure of the Norwegian fishing industry to attract new labor and capital investment is evidenced in the steadily rising median age of both the fishermen and their vessels.

In like manner, Norwegian participation in sealing and whaling—the former carried on chiefly in Greenland waters and the latter in the Antarctic region—has declined markedly in recent years. Whereas Norway led the world in the production of whale oil until the late 1950's, it now ranks a poor third after the Soviet Union and Japan. An industry whose technology was largely developed by the Norwegians and whose heyday saw as many as thirty Norwegian floating factory ships in action off Antarctica in a given season is perpetuated today by the profusion of Norwegian place-names which dots the coast of the southernmost continent, the location of the International Whaling Commission's headquarters in Sandefjord (near the mouth of Oslofjord), and one lone expedition per year.

Mining and manufacturing. By the mid-1960's over 35 per cent of all Norwegians were earning their livelihood in industry. Of these only 2 per cent worked in mining and quarrying, while the remainder were employed in manufacturing. Although the bedrock of Norway contains a variety of metallic minerals, they are for the most part low-grade. The largest mining operation in the country is open-pit iron mining in the Syd-Varanger district near Kirkenes. The ore here contains about 33 per cent iron in a natural state, but it is beneficiated and shipped in briquettes of 65 per cent purity. Norway's next most important mineral resource is copper pyrite, from which both metallic copper and sulfur is extracted, the latter for use in the cellulose and chemical industries. Among the more important centers of pyrite production are Sulitjelma in the Kjölen Range and Lökken, southwest of Trondheim. Although nickel and silver were formerly mined in southern Norway, the principal minerals coming from this region today are molybdenum, titanium, columbium, and niobium (Fig. 4–8).

The industrialization of Norway began about the middle of the last century, when steam power was introduced into sawmilling and a number of small industries were begun using imported coal as fuel. The greatest industrial expansion has taken place since the turn of the century, however, thanks to the development of part of the country's vast hydroelectric resources. With the greatest waterpower reserves of any country in Europe, Norway has been generously compensated for its otherwise serious lack of energy sources. These reserves have been estimated to have a developable potential of nearly 15 million kilowatts when operated at 82 per cent efficiency, and although only one-third of this amount has been harnessed to date the country is already producing about 50 billion kilowatt-hours annually. This corresponds to an annual per capita consumption in excess of 12,000 kilowatts,

or more than double that of the United States. About 80 per cent of the reserves are advantageously located in the more densely populated southern half of the country, i.e., in the East and West Countries. The largest consumers of power are the basic metal industries (especially aluminum refineries), private households, and the electro-chemical industries.

Measured in terms of the value added by manufacture, Norway's leading industries are transport equipment (especially ships), basic metals, chemicals, processed foods, and paper. The building and repair of ships is primarily localized in the coastal districts of the East and West Countries, with major concentrations found in the Oslofjord, Stavanger, and Bergen areas. The basic metal industries, of which the non-ferrous branch is the more important, are mostly power-oriented. Because both the sources of the raw materials and the major consuming markets lie outside of Norway, the optimal location is one where a sheltered, deepwater anchorage coincides with cheap hydroelectricity. Thus, several communities have arisen in the fjords of western Norway centered on such industrial sites. Höyanger and Årdal typify settlements which have been created by aluminum refineries, while Mosjöen, an existing settlement in north Norway, has had its growth greatly spurred by the construction of such a plant there. Also, as part of its plan to promote the economic diversification of the northern counties, the Norwegian government built a large electric steel mill at Mo i Rana. Opened in 1955, this plant is the nucleus for an attractive, planned community which is already the second most populous municipality in north Norway.

Another Norwegian industry which is based on hydroelectric power is the electro-chemical industry. Foremost among such enterprises is the famous Norsk Hydro concern which produces saltpeter from air, water, and limestone. Initially its method was based on a Norwegian process requiring tremendous amounts of electric energy, so

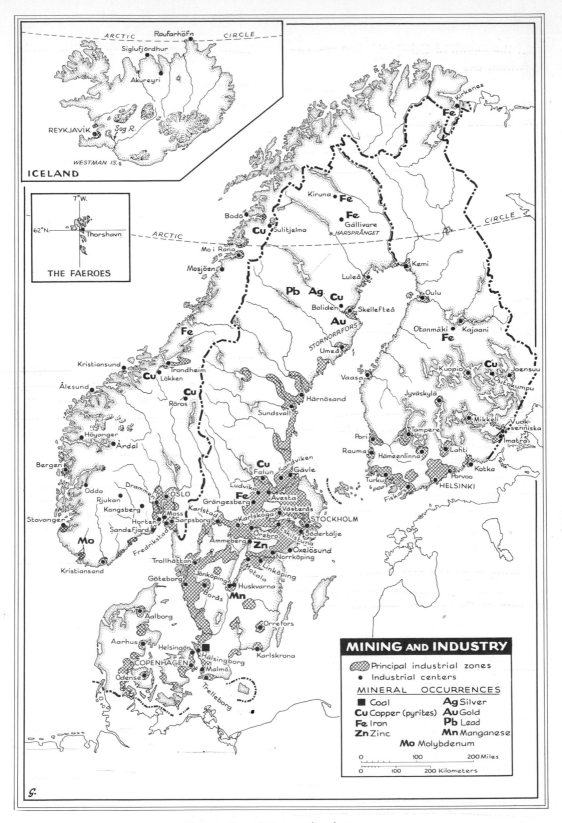

Fig. 4–8. Mining and industry.

it built three large power stations in the Rjukan district of Telemark, southwest of Oslo, and began production there. Switching later to an improved German process, the company transferred about half of its operations to the coast of Telemark, near Skien, although the Rjukan power stations still supply the energy for both installations. During World War II an attempt by the Nazis to use the Rjukan plant in the development of an atomic bomb was foiled by the heroic intervention of Norwegian saboteurs. Another branch of the electro-chemical industry is the production of carbide and cyanamide, the largest of such plants being located at Odda on Hardanger Fjord.

The food industries are dominated by the manufacture of dairy products, chocolate, and the processing of fish and meat. Large dairy plants are located in all the major Norwegian cities, though there are also sizable rural concentrations in the Jaeren district and in the interior valleys north of Oslo. The manufacture of chocolate—a highly remunerative way of utilizing surplus milk—is chiefly localized in Oslo and Trondheim. The largest concentrations of canneries are found in the areas of Stavanger, Bergen, and the South Country where fish, fruit, and vegetables all may be processed in season—an alternative which is not available to the many small canning and freezing plants which dot the coasts of north Norway.

The country's largest pulp and paper mills are situated near the mouths of the major rivers in the East Country, both for convenience of assembling their raw materials and shipping their finished products. The chief centers of the industry are Sarpsborg, Drammen, and Skien, but there is also some pulp production in Tröndelag.

Transportation and foreign trade. Transport in Norway has always been confronted with tremendous topographic and climatic obstacles, as well as by great distances between widely scattered settlements. It is not surprising, therefore, that the sea has been the dominant theme in Norwegian transportation all through the country's history,

particularly in the communications of western and northern Norway and in the country's trade relations with the rest of the world. A daily express service (*hurtigruten*) is maintained along the coast between Bergen and Kirkenes and the entire distance can be covered in about five and one-half days. Frequent local sailings are also maintained from Bergen and Stavanger to nearby island and fjord districts, while over 1,200 miles of ferry routes are operated to expedite road traffic, chiefly in western and northern Norway (Fig. 4–9).

The country's railway system was begun in 1854 and the most extensive network has been built in the valleys of the East Country. The last major line to be constructed was that to Bodö, north of the Arctic Circle, though in recent years several short tertiary lines have been shut down for lack of traffic. Despite valiant efforts to hold and regain traffic through modernization and electrification, Norway's railways are increasingly feeling the economic competition of road transport. Now that every second Norwegian family owns a car and two-thirds of all freight moves by truck, the annual operating deficit has become enormous. One line—that from the mines of Swedish Lappland to the north Norwegian port of Narvik—has the distinction of carrying the heaviest tonnages of any line in Northern Europe and accounting for one-third of all the rail ton-miles in Norway.

The automotive revolution has encouraged the Norwegians to accelerate the improvement of their highways, though to date only about one-eighth of the road mileage is hard-surfaced. Several large suspension bridges have been built in recent years, linking traditionally water-oriented areas of western and northern Norway with the national road net. Nevertheless, snow poses a major problem and most mountain roads between the East and West Countries are blocked from 6–7 months of the year. In winter the only dependable surface link between Oslo and Bergen is the railway, which has buried 15 per cent of its mileage in tunnels and snowsheds to effect the crossing.

Fig. 4–9. Nearly three-fourths of the area of Norway consists of rugged, wild, and unproductive land such as this, bordering Innfjord in the West Country. The warm waters of the North Atlantic Drift spill into the western and northern fjords, keeping them free of ice and giving Norway the highest temperature anomalies of any region in the world so near the pole. (Birkeland.)

During the 1960's there has been a rapid expansion of air services in Norway and it is now possible to reach all major cities within a few hours from Oslo. The Norwegian capital is the main air-traffic center of the country, handling about half of all international passenger arrivals and departures and one-third of all domestic traffic.

Norway's merchant marine has often been called her "floating empire," for without it the country could not maintain its high standard of living. Profits accruing from her overseas shipping make up the discrepancy in her foreign trade, allowing Norway consistently to import a greater value of goods than that which she herself is able to export. To meet the increasing challenge posed by the competition of "flag of convenience" fleets and discriminatory legislation, the Norwegians have energetically rebuilt and modernized their merchant fleet until today it ranks fourth in size and first in quality in the world. Over half of its vessels are less than 5 years old (compared to 7 per cent in the U.S., 27 per cent in the U.K., and 30 per cent in Liberia), and three-fourths are less than 9 years old. All told, the Norwegian merchant fleet comprises 10 per cent of the world's total shipping and 15 per cent of its tanker tonnage. The gross earnings of this great fleet have in recent years totaled the equivalent of some $1.1 billion, more than four-fifths of which has been earned in trade which never touched the home country.

Norway is dependent on many imported goods for maintaining her standard of living, and most of these must be in finished or semi-finished form, for with her small population and lack of capital Norway is unable to support a diversified industry of her own. Among her chief imports are transportation equipment (including ships and automobiles), machinery (both electrical and non-electrical), petroleum products, iron and steel, base metals for refining, and foodstuffs such as fruits, vegetables, and cereals. In return for these commodities, Norway exports non-ferrous metals (especially aluminum), fish products, ships, paper and pulp, and iron and steel. About three-fourths of all Norwegian trade is with other European countries, with just under half of the total being carried on with its EFTA partners and about one-fourth with the members of the EEC.

Norway's Arctic possessions. In the European Arctic, Norway has two territorial possessions—Jan Mayen and Svalbard. The former is a single volcanic island located at 71° N. latitude and 8° W. longitude. Earlier used as a base for whaling and sealing operations, its principal importance today is as a weather station. The territory of Svalbard is composed of the island of West Spitsbergen and the archipelago lying to the east of it, as well as Bear Island situated halfway between Spitsbergen and the north coast of Norway. With the exception of Bear Island the archipelago is largely covered by inland ice sheets. Formerly important as whaling and sealing bases, Svalbard has more recently served as a "jumping-off place" for Arctic expeditions and as the site of three Norwegian weather stations. Since 1900, coal mining has been carried on in West Spitsbergen, first by a United States firm but now by the Norwegians and Soviets. The Norwegian population numbers about 1,000, most of whom reside in the mining camps at Longyear City and New Ålesund. The Soviets number about 1,800 and are concentrated in the settlements of Barentsburg and Grumant City. The annual production of coal amounts to more than 800,000 tons, about equally divided between the Norwegian and Soviet mines. All export must take

place during the short summer season when the coasts are not blocked by ice.

SWEDEN

Population

In 1967 the population of Sweden totaled 7.8 million, of whom more than three-fourths lived in cities, towns, and rural agglomerations. Due to large-scale emigration in the late nineteenth and early twentieth centuries and to a consistently low birth rate in recent decades, the Swedish population has grown at a considerably slower rate than that of most European countries. Since the end of World War II, Sweden has opened its doors to numerous Baltic and Central European refugees and a growing number of immigrants has been attracted by the country's high level of economic prosperity, as well as having come for social and political reasons. Sweden's population is very unevenly distributed, with nearly four-fifths living in the southern two-fifths of the country. The greatest densities are found in the Central Swedish Lowland and in Skåne. The country's largest cities lie at opposite ends of the Central Lowland. In the east is Stockholm, the capital (Fig. 4–10), with 790,000 inhabitants (with suburbs, 1,250,000) and in the west is Göteborg, the country's principal seaport, with 425,000 residents (with suburbs, 540,000). Malmö, the regional center of the rich Skåne Lowland, ranks third with 250,000 inhabitants. In addition, Sweden has ten other cities each with a population of over 50,000.

Present Economic Life of Sweden

Agriculture, forestry, and fishing. By the late 1960's only one Swede in eight earned his living in the primary occupations of farming, forestry, and fishing. In the short span of roughly two generations, Sweden has been transformed from an essentially poor agrarian country with three-fourths of her people working in agriculture to an affluent industrial nation with almost three-eighths of her population earning their livelihood in manufacturing.

Fig. 4–10. The *Gamla Staden* or medieval center of Stockholm. Founded on the islands in the foreground, the Swedish capital city has gradually embraced a number of neighboring islands and spilled over onto the mainland on both sides of the Mälaren. Because of Stockholm's many waterways, it is often called "the Venice of the North."

This transformation has manifested itself in the agricultural sector of the Swedish economy not only by a decline in both the absolute and relative numbers of persons living and working on farms, but also by a steady decrease in the number of operating farm units, the total having fallen from more than 300,000 in the 1920's to about 200,000 today. At the same time, the average size of the Swedish farm has grown to about 35 acres and mechanization has proceeded to the point where agricultural economists feel that many Swedish farms are actually "overcapitalized" in equipment. Plant improvement and high fertilizer consumption has steadily boosted crop yields per acre and the productivity of labor is estimated to have increased by 5–6 per cent a year during the last decade.

Less than 9 per cent of Sweden's land area is under cultivation, though the percentage varies widely from one region to the next (Fig. 4–5). In the Skåne Lowland, for example, over 70 per cent of the land has been brought under the plow, in the Central Swedish Lowland from 40 to 50 per cent, and in the South Swedish Highland about 10–20 per cent. Inner Northland, on the other hand, has less than 0.5 per cent of its land under cultivation, while the Northland coast averages from 3 to 8 per cent and the Jämtland district, 3 per cent. As might be expected, the country's largest farms are located in the lowland regions of Skåne, central Sweden, and insular Sweden, while small farm units are the rule in the South Swedish Highland and in Northland (Fig. 4–11).

Fully four-fifths of Swedish farm income is derived from livestock products, with dairy products accounting for a slightly larger proportion of the total than meat. About 40 per cent of Sweden's arable land

Fig. 4–11. An isolated farmstead in Inner Northland. Though agriculture in this vast region is handicapped by poor soils and a short growing season, Inner Northland ranks as Sweden's chief source of timber, minerals, and hydroelectric power. (Svenska Turisttrafikförbundet.)

is devoted to the cultivation of hay and another 30 per cent is in oats, barley, and other fodder crops. Less than 20 per cent of Swedish crop land is used for the production of foodstuffs to be directly consumed by man, such as bread grains (wheat and rye), sugar beets, and potatoes.

Wheat finds its greatest acreage in the Skåne Lowland, the Central Swedish Lowland (particularly the Plain of Östergötland east of Lake Vättern), and insular Sweden. The cultivation of rye is rather evenly distributed over the country south of the Dal River, though in the better agricultural regions it has lost considerable ground to wheat. Oats take up a large part of the cultivated land in the western Central Swedish Lowland (especially around Lake Vänern) and in the South Swedish Highland. Barley is grown over most of the country, though in Skåne and insular Sweden it is the finer two-row variety used for malt and in Inner Northland it is the more tolerant six-row variety used for bread grain and fodder. The cultivation of potatoes is uniformly distributed over all of Sweden with the exception of the mountain districts, but sugar beets are limited to the Skåne Lowland and insular Sweden. Cattle are rather evenly distributed over the country, while swine are almost entirely confined to Skåne.

Over most of Sweden, farming is carried on jointly with forestry, for over half of the country's productive woodland is owned by individual farmers. This combination not only allows for regular employment all the year round—farming in summer and forest work in winter—but also makes for an increased measure of economic stability. To be sure, the resource value of Sweden's forests was not fully appreciated until about the middle of the nineteenth century, when the growing demand for timber in the industrializing countries of northwestern Europe was further accelerated by the discovery of paper-making from wood pulp.

Though the forest regions of southern Sweden have likewise benefited by this expansion of the wood-using industries, it has been of especial importance to Northland, where other means of economic livelihood are considerably more limited. Regrowth is slower there, but the quality of the wood is better. Moreover, the region is admirably suited for the transport of timber, for the heavy winter snow cover facilitates the movement of logs by sled during this season. In the spring the logs are floated down the larger rivers (among them the Ångerman, Indals, Ljungan, Ljusnan, and Dal) to the sawmills and pulp factories situated at their mouths. One disadvantage, however, is the long period during the winter when the ports are blocked by ice, making necessary the concentration of exports during the summer season. Company ownership of forests is concentrated in the more productive stands of central and southern Northland, while state ownership largely coincides with the more marginal stands of northern Northland.

Fishing plays a relatively minor role in the Swedish national economy, but is locally of great importance in the west coast province of Bohuslän, north of Göteborg. Most Swedish fishing takes place in the Kattegat and Skagerrak, with herring, cod, and mackerel representing the most important varieties caught (Fig. 4–12).

Mining and manufacturing. The subsoil of Sweden is the most richly endowed of any nation in Northern Europe. Metal-bearing ores are found in three principal districts of

Fig. 4–12. Ancient, ice-polished bedrock of the Fenno-Scandian Shield dominates the landscape of Bohuslän, north of Göteborg. Largely stripped of its postglacial marine sediments during its isostatic rebound, this region is the home of most of Sweden's commercial fishermen and a major center of granite quarrying. (Svenska Turisttrafikförbundet.)

the country, namely the Bergslagen district near the southern edge of Inner Northland, the Skellefte district centered on the river system of that name in northern Sweden, and the Lappland district in the far north of Northland.

In the early Middle Ages the mining of iron and copper was already important in the Bergslagen district, and by the middle of the fourteenth century these two metals made up almost 40 per cent of all Swedish exports by value. Two centuries later these metals constituted over three-fourths of the country's total exports. However, as Sweden's copper reserves gradually became exhausted, as the foreign competition of coke-smelted ores began to be felt, and as new domestic industries came into being, the relative importance of iron and copper in the country's economy declined. Without good coal reserves of her own, Sweden has met the challenge of foreign competition by continuing the production of high-quality charcoal-smelted pig iron, a commodity for which she has had a leading reputation ever since the production of "osmund iron" began about the close of Viking times. About 40 per cent of the total Swedish pig iron production is made up of such high-quality pig iron, its principal raw material being the relatively phosphorous-free iron ores of the Bergslagen. This production not only forms the basis of the Swedish domestic steel industry (discussed below) but also provides an important export of quality steel. Though methods for smelting ores which have a high phosphorus content were developed in the late 1800's, the bulk of these ores go into export (chief mining center: Grängesberg). Copper production at Falun has now all but ceased, though the mining of a number of other metals has become increasingly important in recent years. Among them are pyrites, lead, zinc, manganese, tungsten, and molybdenum.

The mineral resources of the Skellefte district are for the most part covered by a heavy overburden, and their discovery and exploration have depended largely on geophysical prospecting with special electric equipment. Composed chiefly of pyrites, the metal-bearing ores contain a great variety of minerals, among them gold, silver, copper, lead, zinc, and nickel. The chief center of operations in the Skellefte district is Boliden.

Sweden's greatest mineral deposits by far are the vast iron reserves in the Lappland district in the far north. Averaging between 60 and 70 per cent pure iron, these ores have a relatively high phosphorus content, and the greatest part of their production is exported. During the summer season, shipments go by electric railway to the port of Luleå at the head of the Gulf of Bothnia and to the Norwegian port of Narvik, but during the winter, when the Gulf is blocked by ice, all ore is shipped via ice-free Narvik. The two principal centers of production are Kiruna and Gällivare, with most of the mining now taking place below the surface, rather than in open pits as was formerly true. In late 1967 it was announced that huge new deposits of high-grade iron ore had been discovered in the Lappland district, more than doubling Sweden's known reserves.

Among the non-metallic mineral resources of Sweden the most important are limestone and oil shale. Each year more than 6 million tons of limestone are quarried in Skåne, insular Sweden, and the Central Swedish Lowland, chiefly for use in the cement industry. The oil shale deposit is located in the Central Lowland south of Örebro and is not only Sweden's principal source of fossil fuel, but also of uranium.

The Swedish manufacturing industries are the most diversified of any nation in Northern Europe. As measured by value added in manufacturing, the most important branches of Swedish industry are the manufacture of non-electrical machinery, transport equipment, food products, pulp and paper, iron and steel, and electrical machines. Taken together, the engineering industries account for about 40 per cent of all Swedish industrial employment.

There is little doubt but that easy access to high-quality iron and steel contributed greatly to the development of the Swedish engineering industries. In the middle of the seventeenth century, Sweden was the world's leading producer of iron, annually turning out an amount equal to one-third of the world's total consumption. She owed her foremost position not only to her rich iron ore deposits, but also to her extensive forests which supplied charcoal for fuel. As iron smelted with coke became increasingly important, however, she gradually lost ground to the coal-rich nations of the earth, and today Sweden accounts for only about one per cent of the world's total production of iron and steel. Though she is now far down the list in terms of quantity production, Sweden still remains one of the world's foremost producers of quality iron and steel. By specializing in the manufacture of stainless, alloy, and high-carbon steels, and by constant technological improvement (using electric furnaces and the oxygen process), the Swedish steel industry finds a ready market for its products both at home and abroad, though it cannot at present meet Sweden's own demand for ordinary commercial steels. Thus, by volume, Sweden is a net importer of iron and steel, though by value, the country has an export surplus of $75–80 million a year. Most of Sweden's steel mills are located in or near the Bergslagen, with the largest single plant being situated at Domnarvet near Sandviken. Two of the country's newest and largest mills have been built at tidewater, one at Oxelösund, built by private interests at the main shipping port for Bergslagen ores, and one at Luleå, built by the government, both to help diversify the economy of the Lappland region and also to help fill the nation's needs for structural steel.

The manufacture of iron and metal products is spread over a number of localities in the central and southern parts of the country, though the two largest concentrations of such industry are located in Eskilstuna and Stockholm. In the seventeenth century the groundwork for Eskilstuna's diversified production of high-quality goods had already been laid, and since then this Swedish city has become world famous for the matchless quality of its knives, scissors, carpenter tools, surgical instruments, locks, keys, machine tools, hardware, precision instruments, and silverware.

Numerous other products of the Swedish engineering industries have likewise earned acclaim for their quality and performance abroad. Swedish trade names in cream separators, refrigerators, vacuum cleaners, calculating machines, and various types of precision and electrical equipment are known the world over. The Swedish Ball-Bearing Company (SKF), with headquarters in Göteborg, is not only Sweden's largest corporation but also the world's largest exporter of ball bearings. The L. M. Ericsson Company, centered in Stockholm, supplies a large part of the world with its telephone equipment, and the name of Bofors is recognized as a world leader in armaments production. In the automotive field, Sweden is represented by Volvo, whose major assembly plant is in Göteborg, SAAB, centered in Linköping, and Scania-Vabis, which specializes in truck and bus production in its Södertälje plant. Although the export of Swedish motor vehicles did not really begin until the late 1950's, about half of the total production is destined for foreign markets today. Similarly, Sweden has emerged as one of the world's three or four largest shipbuilding nations, with her major yards located on the west coast near Göteborg and Malmö. About three-fourths of the tonnage built is under foreign contract, with Norway normally absorbing about one-half of the total export production. Sweden has managed to stay competitive in this field through the efficiency of its automated production techniques, while at the same time paying higher wages than any of its nearest challengers. Among the other centers of the engineering industry are Malmö (milling equipment), Trollhättan (aircraft engines, diesel motors, and turbines), Huskvarna (bicycles, sewing machines, and firearms), and Västerås (high-tension electrical equipment, including electric locomotives).

The wood-using industries of Sweden are even more strongly raw material oriented than the metal-working and engineering industries. The country's largest sawmills are found along the Northland coast, with particular concentrations near the mouths of the Indals, Ångerman, and Ume rivers. Located near the mouths of three major rivers, Sundsvall has become the largest single wood-processing center in Sweden and ranks with Arkhangelsk in the Soviet Union as one of the world's leading timber export ports. There are numerous smaller concentrations of sawmills in the southern portion of Inner Northland and in the eastern half of the South Swedish Highland. It is in this latter area that the greatest concentration of wood-working shops and furniture factories are also found. The distribution of pulp mills largely parallels that of the sawmills, though the two greatest concentrations are along the Northland coast (particularly between the mouths of the Dal and Ume rivers) and in the Lake Vänern area. Those along the Northland coast account for over half of the country's chemical pulp production as well as nearly all of Sweden's pulp exports. The production of the southern pulp mills goes largely into domestic paper-making, hence most of the country's paper factories are located in central and southern Sweden, especially around Lake Vänern and in the South Swedish Highland. Jönköping, in the heart of the latter region, is the center of the famous safety match industry.

Although a few specialty items are exported (such as hardtack, cheese, fish, preserves, and lingonberries), the Swedish food processing industry primarily produces for the domestic market. Skåne has the largest concentration of such plants, with flour mills, sugar refineries, dairies, distilleries, and canning factories all represented. The Swedish textile and clothing industry is also oriented to the home market, with the major production centers being Borås and Göteborg in

the west and Norrköping in the east. Stockholm is not only the country's leading fashion and design center in apparel, but also in home furnishings. Among the latter, Swedish crystal, produced principally in the South Swedish Highland in such places as Orrefors and Kosta, has attracted world attention.

In common with the rest of Northern Europe, Sweden is notably deficient in fossil fuels, but like Norway, is bountifully supplied with hydroelectric energy. Unlike Norway, however, Sweden has over 80 per cent of her total waterpower reserves in Inner Northland, where less than 10 per cent of her people live. As a result, Sweden has had to build a high-voltage transmission grid over 5,000 miles in length to link her great power dams in the north with her cities and factories in the south. Most of the newer lines carry 400,000 volts and some of them are over 600 miles long. Because of its key position, Sweden also provides a link between the Finnish and Norwegian grids on the one hand and the Danish and continental European grids on the other. Although Sweden imports power from Norway, it is a net exporter of electricity, the bulk of it going to Denmark by underwater cable. It is estimated that Sweden has a total developable potential of some 20,000,000 kilowatts, of which about half has been harnessed to date. The Swedes have also built auxiliary thermal-electric plants near their three largest cities and two nuclear-powered plants are scheduled for construction on the east coast between Stockholm and Kalmar, if and when such power becomes economically competitive. The country's largest power station at Harsprånget on the Lule river was superseded in size in 1959 by the Stornorrfors station on the Ume river, now the largest hydroelectric plant in Europe west of the Soviet Union.

Transportation and foreign trade. Until the early nineteenth century, most transport in Sweden was by lakes and streams during the summer and by "winter roads" during the winter. In the first half of the last century, however, Sweden, like most of the other nations in Europe, was seized with a canal-building fever, and the most important project of this period was the so-called Göta Canal joining Göteborg with the east coast of Sweden through lakes Vänern and Vättern. This canal still carries some commercial traffic between Lake Vänern and the west coast, but elsewhere it is used chiefly by tourist cruise ships and private pleasure craft.

In the 1860's railway construction began in earnest in Sweden, and today the country has some 8,450 miles of railroad, of which all but 560 miles are state owned (the major exception being the line linking the mines at Grängesberg with the export port at Oxelösund). Fifty-five per cent of the mileage is electrified, but 85 per cent of the traffic moves over these lines.

No country in Europe has reoriented its transport toward the automobile more than Sweden (today about one Swede in four has his own car) and few countries have done as much to meet the challenge of congestion. Although the country's conversion to right-hand traffic in 1967 was expensive (estimated to have cost about $200 million) and long overdue, Sweden has made rapid progress in improving its highway system, especially in the vicinity of the larger cities where traffic intensities are greatest. Stockholm, with its largely insular site, has posed an especially complex problem. However, a bold and comprehensive plan involving an ambitious bridge-building program, a subway system, the complete renovation of the city's commercial core, and the development of satellite towns such as Vällingby and Farsta, has helped Stockholm avoid the creeping strangulation which threatens so many of the older European cities.

Domestic air transport in Sweden expanded greatly during the 1960's, making all major provincial towns and even such outlying areas as Gotland and Lappland readily accessible from Stockholm and the other larger cities. To conduct international flying, Sweden has joined with Denmark and

Norway to form a corporation in which Sweden holds three-sevenths of the stock.

Like both Norway and Denmark, Sweden has built a merchant fleet far larger than is needed to conduct the country's own foreign trade. By 1967 the Swedish merchant marine totaled some 4.5 million gross tons, of which about three-fourths was exclusively engaged in traffic between foreign ports, and 70 per cent was less than 9 years old. In recent years the gross earnings of the Swedish merchant fleet have amounted to the equivalent of more than $300 million annually. The ports of Göteborg and Stockholm handle about an equal volume of traffic and together account for 30 per cent of Sweden's total foreign trade. West Germany ranks as the largest buyer of Swedish exports and the leading supplier of Swedish imports, with the United Kingdom in second place. Sweden's other major trading partners are Norway, Denmark, and the United States, the last enjoying a positive trade balance with Sweden as do both West Germany and the United Kingdom. Pulp, paper, iron and steel, ships, timber, and iron ore rank among Sweden's chief exports, while fossil fuels, iron and steel, automobiles, and foodstuffs constitute her most important imports.

FINLAND

Population

In 1967 Finland had some 4.7 million inhabitants, of whom about three-fifths lived in towns and cities. Some Finnish migration to the neighboring countries of Northern Europe took place before 1890, and in the ensuing half century almost 350,000 persons emigrated to the United States and Canada. Following the territorial cessions at the end of World War II, the country was obliged to absorb 480,000 Karelian refugees who chose to move rather than become Soviet citizens. The country's largest city is Helsinki, the capital, with 500,000 inhabitants (with suburbs, 650,000). The industrial city of Tampere has edged slightly ahead of the historic cultural and political center of Turku, though both cities today have about 140,000 inhabitants within their administrative boundaries and about 180,000 when suburbs are included. Three port cities (Pori, Vaasa, and Oulu), and two inland towns (Lahti and Kuopio) each numbered over 50,000 residents.

Though the tide of Finnish settlement has been advancing inexorably toward the northeast during the centuries, about half of the total population still resides in the coastal districts of the south and west. It is in these areas that the country's Swedish-speaking minority, amounting to just under 8 per cent of the total population, is concentrated. In the Åland Islands Swedish is the language of 96 per cent of the populace, though in no mainland province does the proportion exceed 24 per cent.

Present Economic Life of Finland

Agriculture, forestry, and fishing. Of all the countries of Northern Europe, none has a greater dependence upon the primary occupations than Finland. In the late 1960's about 30 per cent of the Finns earned their livelihood in farming and forestry, and usually in a seasonal combination with each other.

About 9 per cent of Finland's land area is under cultivation, the percentage varying from more than 30 per cent in sections of the coastal plain to less than 1 per cent in Lappland. Before World War II, the average Finnish farm consisted of 20 acres of tilled land, but, as a result of the emergency resettlement of nearly 40,000 Karelian farm families, agricultural holdings were further splintered until today the average Finnish farm has less than 17 acres of tilled land. Fully 90 per cent of the country's farms each have less than 40 acres of land that can be cultivated, though the farms larger than 40 acres comprise about two-fifths of the total land under the plow. These larger farms are concentrated in the southern and western portions of the country, especially on the Coastal Lowland, while small farm units are

the rule in the interior, to the north and east. Before Finland gained its independence, a very large proportion of Finnish farms were tenant operated, but a series of land reforms begun about 1920 has reduced this proportion to less than 5 per cent. That Finnish farming is overwhelmingly a family-type operation is revealed in the fact that only 3 per cent of the labor performed in agriculture is done by hired hands.

Like Norway and Swedish Northland, Finland has a climate which is best suited to the growing of fodder crops, and hence animal husbandry has become the dominant theme in Finnish farming. Over three-fourths of the country's cultivated land is in fodder crops, and, of the total, about half is in hay alone. In terms of acreage under cultivation, oats are second in importance, followed by barley, wheat, and rye. Hay is the principal crop in all regions of the country, but oats as a second crop give way to wheat in the more fertile soils of the Åland Islands and to barley in the far north. Though the Finnish yields per acre are the lowest of any country in Northern Europe, they seldom fell far short of those of countries, like France, whose climates are considerably more favorable for agriculture.

The aim of Finnish agriculture has been to make the country as self-sufficient as possible with respect to its food supply. Before World War II this goal had largely been achieved in such commodities as milk, butter, meat, eggs, and potatoes, but had not yet been reached in bread grains. Even in bread grains, however, a tremendous advance in this direction had been made, for whereas Finland produced only 40 per cent of its requirements of bread grains before World War I, it was almost 90 per cent self-sufficient in this commodity by 1938, thanks both to increased acreages under cultivation and higher yields per acre. Unfortunately, World War II and its subsequent cessions of territory largely nullified these remarkable gains, but by the mid-1960's Finland's import of wheat and rye had again been reduced to less than 15 per cent of her total consumption. To maintain even this level of self-sufficiency, however, Finland must continue to import considerable quantities of fodder concentrates and artificial fertilizers.

Nearly two-thirds of its land area is forest (Fig. 4–13); it is not surprising that most of Finland's farmers find remunerative winter employment in logging. About 60 per cent of the country's forest land is privately owned and accounts for 72 per cent of the total annual regrowth. Another 30 per cent of the forest area is held by the state, but inasmuch as this is largely localized in the Lappland region, it accounts for only about 16 per cent of the annual regrowth. Corporations hold only about 8 per cent of the country's forest land.

Fishing plays a smaller part in the economy of Finland than in that of any of the other countries of Northern Europe. This is due, of course, to the fact that Finland lacks access to the open sea, which the other nations possess. Of the annual catch, about three-fourths is Baltic herring and over half of these are taken in the skerries off the southwest coast. Sealing has also been carried on since ancient times off the west coast, and seals are likewise found in Lake Saimaa in eastern Finland. Altogether about 10,000 persons live from hunting and fishing in Finland, including the Lapps who tend their reindeer herds in the far north.

Mining and manufacturing. Finland's bedrock contains a great variety of minerals, but for the most part their metal contents are so low that mining makes only a minor contribution to the total Finnish economy. The country's largest mining operation is the extraction of copper and sulfur from the pyrite deposit located at Outokumpu in Karelia. This same ore body produces some iron residues which are used in the steel industry, but since 1953 the country's largest source

Fig. 4–13. Part of Lake Saimaa in eastern Finland. This landscape is characteristic of the Lake Plateau—Finland's most distinctive natural region. Settled within relatively recent historical time, the region is still sparsely populated and shows few evidences of human occupancy. (Finnish Tourist Association.)

of iron has been a vast titanium-iron deposit situated at Otanmäki in the north-central part of Finland. Although the Petsamo (now Pechenga) nickel mines were lost to the Soviet Union in the peace treaty of 1947, Finland still ranks as Europe's largest producer of this metal, as well as of cobalt and vanadium.

Without coal, Finland's industry was originally very closely tied to her waterpower sources, as exemplified by the development of the city of Tampere. The introduction of steam changed this situation somewhat, but the advent of hydroelectric power once more shifted attention back to waterfalls. Because of the nature of her topography, Finland's waterfalls generally have low heads of water, averaging 20 to 30 feet. Of advantage, however, is the fact that almost half of her waterpower reserves are located in the southern half of the country, where the large lakes also serve as natural regulators of the water level. About one-third of Finland's developed waterpower was lost to the Soviet Union through the territorial cessions of 1947, though the country's largest hydroelectric plant, located at Imatra on the Vuoksi river, remained in Finnish hands. However, in order to meet the increasing demand for power Finland has been obliged to build a series of generating stations along the Oulu and Kemi rivers, linking them by long transmission lines to the market area in the south. By 1967 almost all of Finland's developable waterpower resources had been harnessed and about one-third of the country's electricity was being produced by thermal plants operating on imported fossil fuels.

Today about one-fourth of the Finnish population derives its living from manufacturing, of which the wood industries constitute the most important branch, both in terms of value added and number of persons employed. Well over half of Finland's export earnings continue to be derived from forest products, though Finnish industry has become more diversified since World War II, due in part to the reparations demands of the Soviets.

Sawmilling in Finland began in the sixteenth century, with the eastern districts of the country around Viipuri taking an initial lead. The greatest impetus to growth, however, came about the middle of the nineteenth century, when Great Britain adopted a free-trade policy and steam power was introduced. Though the earliest mills were located at waterpower sites, since the advent of steam the newer mills have grown up at the mouths of the larger rivers. Using their own waste for fuel, these plants are ideally located with respect both to floating and shipping possibilities. Since the loss of Viipuri, Kotka has become the country's largest timber port, handling over one-fourth of the export trade. Among the other large timber ports are Pori, Oulu, Kemi, and Rauma. The post-war cessions not only cost Finland about one-eighth of her sawmill capacity but also the outlet of the Saimaa canal, which seriously complicated the movement of timber from eastern Finland. However, in 1962 Finland and the Soviet Union signed a 50-year treaty giving Finland the right to use the canal in return for bearing the cost of its rehabilitation and the payment of an annual toll.

In addition to sawn timber, box wood, and planed timber, the Finnish wood industry also produces plywood and prefabricated houses for export. Measured by the total volume of its saw timber production, Finland ranks third in Europe after Sweden and West Germany. It is, however, in the production of pulp and paper that the Finnish wood industries have particularly concentrated, for today the country ranks first in Europe in the production of newsprint and mechanical pulp and second only to Sweden in the output of the higher-grade chemical pulp. Many of the country's pulp and paper mills have grown up side by side with her sawmills, using the sawmill waste both for fuel and raw materials. In addition to the production of cellulose, the Finnish pulp and paper industry has a number of by-products which have given rise to further branches of industrial activity. Among them are rayon, fodder cellulose, turpentine, pine oil for soap and varnish and distilled spirits, most of which are destined for the home market. In the postwar cessions to the Soviet Union, Finland lost about one-fifth of the productive capacity of her cellulose industry and one-tenth that of her paper industry, but the country already regained its pre-war levels of production by the early 1950's and today is producing at more than two and one-half times the prewar rate.

Most of Finland's remaining industries produce chiefly for the home market, though Soviet reparations prompted the expansion of such branches as shipbuilding and the manufacture of electrical cables and machinery, and some export of their output is still maintained. The production of machinery and transport equipment now follow the wood and food processing industries in importance, in terms of value added. Although Finland produces both pig iron and steel, chiefly in coastal locations in the southwest near where the imported fuel is unloaded, she must continue to import most of the metal she uses in semifinished form. Helsinki and Turku rank as the major metal-fabricating centers, though Tampere also produces such things as railway locomotives, boilers, and turbines. The latter city is better known, however, as Finland's largest textile and clothing manufacturing center, the industry having grown up around a major waterpower site in the 1820's. Because the production of the Finnish textile industry is neither adequate nor sufficiently diversified to meet domestic requirements, textile goods still constitute a considerable item of import.

Like Sweden's industry, that of Finland is rather evenly divided between rural and urban locations. Though its principal concentration is in the more densely settled Coastal Lowland of the south, access to forest resources and relatively good water and rail transport have encouraged an increasing industrialization of the Lake Plateau and the northern Coastal Lowland. The Åland Islands, owing to their "offside" position, are the least industrialized province of the entire

country. A particular feature of Finnish industry as a whole is its large proportion of women employees, amounting to more than 36 per cent of the total. Indeed, an important factor in the growth of Finland's home-market industries has been her supply of cheap labor.

Transportation and foreign trade. Finland's earliest communications were by her lakes and rivers during the summer and by winter roads over the snow and ice through the rest of the year. As early as 1500, discussions began about the feasibility of joining Lake Saimaa and the eastern lake district with the Gulf of Finland by a canal, but nothing was done until the first half of the nineteenth century. Once completed, the Saimaa Canal became Finland's busiest inland waterway and its reactivation since 1962 has been of great importance, especially to the Finnish timber industry.

The construction of railways in Finland was commenced in 1862, at a time when the country was a part of Czarist Russia. As a result, its rail net uses the broad, Russian gauge, and, despite the railway bridge across the Tornio River to Sweden, Finland has direct rail traffic only with the Soviet Union. Finland's railways have played an important role in the economic development of the country by opening up new forest and farm lands, expanding the hinterlands of several timber ports, and by providing a trade link with its eastern neighbor. Although wood-burning locomotives were quite common until recently, Finland's railways have chosen to modernize through dieselization rather than electrification.

Most of the country's roads have been built since the coming of the automobile, though only those in the vicinity of the larger cities, particularly in the southwest, are hard-surfaced. The automotive revolution had not progressed as far or as fast in Finland as elsewhere in Northern Europe, for in 1967 there was one passenger car for every 12 persons.

Two airlines carry on the country's air

traffic, one primarily in international traffic and the other in domestic traffic. Helsinki is the main traffic center for both of them, as it is for the several foreign companies which provide connections to other west and east European capitals.

Sea transport is the decisive factor in Finland's foreign trade, for only her rail connections with the Soviet Union permit through-shipments by land. Because of the nature of her exports, Finland's foreign trade experiences wide seasonal fluctuations compared to that of Denmark, for instance. The export of wood products, which comprise some 70 per cent of the total, is concentrated in the summer and early autumn, with the result that efficient year-around use of domestic shipping in home waters is impossible. Moreover, because her exports are more bulky on the whole than her imports, almost half of the freighters arriving in Finnish ports are in ballast, while only 10 per cent of the ships depart in ballast. Winter ice conditions likewise mean a decrease in traffic, since only specially constructed ships or limited ports (Hanko and Turku) can be used. Helsinki is the country's largest import port, followed by Turku, Hanko, and Kotka. Kotka leads in export, with Helsinki second and Turku third. Although the Finnish merchant marine had totaled nearly 650,000 tons before World War II, by the end of the conflict it had been reduced to less than half that size. By 1965, however, it surpassed 1 million tons for the first time, of which three-eighths was less than 9 years old.

Until she won her independence in 1917, about 40 per cent of Finland's trade was with Russia. Germany was her second-best customer and Great Britain had third place. After Finland's independence, however, Great Britain climbed into first place, where-with the exception of a few years, she has remained ever since. Germany held second place until the close of World War II, when trade with the Soviet Union became important once more. Today, with nearly one-fifth of her total trade being conducted with her eastern neighbor, Finland is especially sensitive to whatever politico-economic pressures Moscow chooses to apply. Finland's principal exports are paper pulp, newsprint, and timber products, while chief among her imports are fuels, iron and steel, bread grains, and textiles.

DENMARK

Population

In 1967 the population of Denmark totaled 4.8 million, having increased more than six-fold since the country's first census was taken in 1769. From 1820 to 1940 about 300,000 Danes emigrated to the United States, though this is considerably less in proportion to the emigration from the other Scandinavian countries during the same period. Of the present population, 44 per cent reside in Jutland and 56 per cent on the islands to the east. In terms of its rural-urban distribution, the Danish population may be divided roughly into quarters: Copenhagen and its environs, the outlying provincial towns, suburbs and rural agglomerations of over 500 persons, and scattered rural habitations each giving residence to about a fourth of the total. Copenhagen reached the peak of its growth in 1950, though its subsequent decline has been offset by continued growth in the suburbs. Today the metropolitan area of the Danish capital has 1.4 million inhabitants and forms the nucleus of a Scandinavian "super-city" which, as projected, will straddle both shores of the Sound and contain over one-fourth of the combined populations of Denmark and Sweden by the year 2000. Copenhagen so dominates the country as a whole that no other city even remotely approaches it in size. Aarhus, the regional capital of Jutland, ranks second with about 190,000, suburbs included, and is followed by Odense on Fyn with 135,000, Aalborg with 86,000, and the North Sea port of Esbjerg with 56,000. Eleven other Danish towns have more than 25,000 inhabitants each.

Present Economic Life of Denmark

Agriculture, forestry, and fishing. Although agriculture has always played an important role in the economic life of Denmark, the specialized export nature which characterizes this occupation today dates back only to the latter part of the nineteenth century. When it became clear to Denmark that she could no longer compete with America and Russia in growing cheap bread grains for the industrial nations of Western Europe, the little nation turned to a concentrated production of livestock products, placing chief emphasis on the growing of fodder crops. Thanks largely to the high level of scientific instruction given to the farmers, to the adoption of the cooperative principle of organization, to a self-imposed regulation of quality, and more recently, to the widespread mechanization which has taken place, Danish agriculture has become a model of rational management, whose products can command the highest prices in the world markets.

In proportion to its area Denmark has more land in agricultural use than any other country in Europe—70 per cent. Even on the relatively infertile western plains of Jutland over half of the land is under cultivation. In general, the percentage of land devoted to the various crops is relatively uniform from one section of the country to the next, though this is least true in the Heath of Jutland. The greatest proportions of land in wheat are found on Bornholm, Zealand, and Fyn, where about 10 per cent of the cultivated area is devoted to this crop. Malt barley, likewise, finds its greatest concentrations east of the terminal moraine, and on the islands of Laaland and Falster it constitutes over one-third of the acreage. Sugar beets are also confined to the better soils and particularly to Laaland and Falster, where they make up another 20 per cent of the cultivated area. Oats, hay, green fodder, and root crops are quite uniformly distributed over the entire country, and in the sandy districts of western and northern Jutland crops of rye, potatoes, and mixed seed (barley and rye) reach their greatest extent.

The fact that only about 14 per cent of the Danish population is employed in agriculture today belies its tremendous importance to the life of the nation. Since the war the number of Danish farm units has been steadily decreasing, while their average size has been increasing. Today there are about 175,000 farms in the country, with the typical farm being just under 40 acres in area. In the same period the agricultural labor force has declined by about half, while total farm output has risen markedly. Although hired labor is much more common on Danish farms than it is elsewhere in Northern Europe, annually constituting about one-fifth of the work done, it has dropped sharply in recent years due to mechanization. Today more than three-fourths of all Danish farms either own or have access to tractors and over 90 per cent of them are equipped with milking machines. Evidence of the intensive and careful use the Danish farmer makes of his soil is seen in the fact that an average of 590 pounds of artificial fertilizer is applied annually to each acre under cultivation (Fig. 4–14).

In sheer volume, the Danish production of livestock products dwarfs that of the rest of Northern Europe. Each year the farms of Denmark produce more milk and butter than Norway and Sweden put together, and more meat and cheese than is produced in all four of the other North European states. The particular Danish specialization in eggs and bacon may be judged from the fact that Denmark has as much poultry and more than twice as many swine as all the other Nordic countries combined.

Denmark's specialized production of livestock products has had a number of interesting, and occasionally serious, consequences. Although she has become one of the world's foremost exporters of butter, bacon, and eggs because she cannot produce all of her own fodder requirements, Denmark has also be-

Fig. 4–14. View looking eastward from the lighthouse near the southeastern tip of Bornholm. In the foreground is a typical Danish farmstead. Built around three sides of a central courtyard are white-washed, half-timbered barns and implement sheds, with a brick dwelling house occupying the fourth side. (V. H. Malmström.)

come one of the world's leading importers of fodder concentrates. To fatten her swine she has had to maintain a considerable import of maize, and to maintain the fertility of her soils she has become a leading importer of artificial fertilizers. Despite her foremost position as an agricultural nation, Denmark has to import about one-third of the bread grains used for domestic consumption, and, in order to release as much butter for export as possible, vegetable oils are imported in large quantities to make margarine. Hence we have the apparent inconsistency that, in a nation which is one of the world's largest producers of dairy products, the domestic consumption of margarine per capita is two to three times that of butter. With her economy so utterly dependent on such exports and imports it is easily understood why Denmark's per capita foreign trade is among the highest in Europe.

Though Denmark's revolution in agriculture has been largely responsible for the high standard of living which the Danes now enjoy, it has also made the country's economy extremely vulnerable to international factors such as war, depression, and preferential trade agreements. Thus, when the United Kingdom, the largest importer of Danish commodities (with whom Denmark is linked in the European Free Trade Association), devalued its currency in 1967, the Danes were obliged to follow suit in order to remain competitive in British markets. At the same time, because Denmark's second-best customer and the largest supplier of her imports is West Germany, it has become increasingly difficult for Denmark to maintain its competitive position there, due to the latter's membership in the European Economic Community.

About 10 per cent of Denmark's land area is in forest, though the sporadic groves one sees today are a far cry from the dense beech and oak woods that once covered most of the countryside. Scientific forest management was begun as early as 1805, not only to preserve the remaining stands of hardwood but also to introduce the economically more useful softwoods. Thanks to the effectiveness of this conservation program, Denmark annually harvests sufficient beech and oak for its flooring, shipbuilding, and furniture industries and meets about half of its domestic requirements for spruce and pine.

The Danish fishing industry, like farming and forestry, also has an importance out of proportion to the numbers it employs. By the late 1960's, Denmark's 17,000 fishermen were landing more than 800,000 tons of fish annually. Seen in comparison to Norway, for example, this meant that one-third as many fishermen were catching about two-fifths as much fish; yet the total value of the Danish catch was more than two-thirds that of its northern neighbor. This is due, first of all, to a greater abundance of more valuable species in Danish waters, particularly the plaice and the eel. Secondly, Denmark's proximity to the consuming markets allows a greater proportion of the fish to be sold fresh rather than dried or salted. The chief ports of the fishing fleet are Esbjerg on the west coast of Jutland and Skagen on its northern tip.

Mining and manufacturing. The subsoil of Denmark produces a variety of non-metallic minerals. Some lignite is mined on Jutland and granite is quarried in northern Bornholm, chiefly for use as paving blocks in Danish streets and roads. Kaolin is also associated with the Bornholm granite and forms the principal raw material of the Danish porcelain industry. Clay and lime are extensively dug for use in the tile and cement industries. Some of the country's largest cement plants are located in the Aalborg area where both clay and lime occur together, and there is easy access to imported coal. Altogether the mineral industries employ less than 1 per cent of the labor force in Danish industry.

The industrialization of Denmark has paralleled the shift of Danish agriculture to specialized production for export, and food processing has quite naturally become one of the most important branches of industry. Its gross value of production is greater than that of any other industry, though in value added by manufacture and in number of workers employed, it has been surpassed by the engineering industry. With the exception of the more than 1,400 dairies scattered over the country which handle fluid milk, the food-processing industry has tended to locate in advantageous shipping ports rather than in rural districts near the source of sup-

ply. Despite the fact that Denmark has no resources of coal, iron, petroleum, or water-power, a number of other industries have grown up within the country, most of them designed to produce for the home market but some of them also producing for export. Among the latter are the engineering and shipbuilding industries. In 1898 a Danish firm acquired the patent of the diesel engine from its inventor, and in 1912 the first diesel-powered ocean-going ship sailed from Denmark. Since that time, the country has been a foremost builder of motor ships and marine engines. Among the other Danish industries which have acquired markets abroad are the manufacture of electrical machinery and equipment, chemicals and pharmaceuticals, and home furnishings. The fact that all Danish industries are dependent on imported fuel for power and most are likewise dependent on imported raw materials has led to the concentration of manufacturing in port cities. Nearly one-third of the Danish population makes its living in manufacturing today and more than two-fifths of all industrial workers are concentrated in the Copenhagen area.

Transportation and foreign trade. Transport in Denmark is encumbered by the country's lack of physical continuity. In 1967 Denmark had some 2,400 miles of railway, of which about three-eighths were privately owned. However, the disproportionately small role that the private railways play in the country's transportation scheme is seen in the fact that the state railways annually carry about 20 times as much passenger traffic and more than 50 times as much freight traffic as the private lines. Joining the various islands and linking Denmark's rail net to those of Sweden and West Germany are 135 miles of ferry routes.

Denmark is crisscrossed by a network of excellent paved highways, but the rapid growth in automobile traffic has accelerated the planning and construction of new super-highways and bridges. Under construction in the late 1960's was a new high-level highway bridge between Jutland and the island of Fyn, while at the same time planning was well underway on a series of bridges and tunnels spanning both the Great Belt and the Sound. In addition to the rapidly swelling volume of domestic road traffic—with one passenger car for every six Danes in 1967—a sizable transit traffic between the Scandinavian peninsula and the continent has developed. By the late 1960's, the total annual movement of persons between the Nordic Passport Region and the rest of Europe was equivalent to the entire population of Northern Europe, i.e., some 21 millions, and of these fully 95 per cent entered or exited by way of Denmark.

With 31 of its 40 cities having over 10,000 population and being located on navigable water bodies, it is not surprising that a considerable part of the domestic freight traffic of Denmark goes by sea. More than half of such movement is accounted for by mineral fuels, with other bulk cargoes including sand, gravel, stone, fodder, and grain. In terms of the volume of traffic handled, Denmark's busiest ports are Copenhagen, Kalundborg (due to a major oil refinery), Aalborg, and Aarhus.

In 1967 Denmark had a merchant marine which totaled more than 2.8 million gross tons. Of this tonnage, more than five-sixths consisted of motor ships, nearly seven-tenths were less than 9 years old, and over three-eighths was made up of tankers. The gross freight earnings of Danish ships in foreign trade annually contribute the equivalent of about $240 million to the Danish national economy.

Lacking great internal distances and possessing well-developed forms of surface transport, Denmark has experienced a rather modest growth in its domestic air services. However, regular flights are maintained between Copenhagen and eastern Jutland and between the Danish capital and Bornholm. Denmark has joined with Norway and Sweden to form the Scandinavian Airlines System, an international consortium in which Denmark holds two-sevenths of the stock.

Kastrup Airport at Copenhagen is its main traffic center, and from it emanate many intercontinental flights, including transpolar services to both western North America and eastern Asia.

Owing to the specialized nature of its economy, Denmark's foreign trade is not only large, but also relatively unbalanced. In most years, more than four times as many tons of goods are discharged at Danish ports as are loaded for shipment. This is because her imports, of which mineral fuels, iron and steel, fertilizers, feedstuffs, and timber lead the list, are much bulkier than her exports, among which meat, dairy products, and machinery rank highest. Denmark's chief sources of imports are West Germany, the United Kingdom, Sweden, and the United States. These same countries provide the best markets for her exports, though the United Kingdom consistently buys more from Denmark than do the others.

THE FAEROES

The present population of the Faeroes numbers about 37,000, of whom some 7,500 live in the capital, Thorshavn. Fishing and whaling support about one-third of the islands' inhabitants and account for fully 98 per cent of their exports. The annual catch runs to more than 130,000 tons, with cod constituting about five-sixths of the total and herring most of the remainder. About three-fourths of the catch is marketed after being salted, smoked, or marinated. The Faeroes' best customers are Italy, Brazil, the United Kingdom, and Spain. Though Faeroese fishermen range as far afield as Iceland, Greenland, and Svalbard, all whaling activities take place in the vicinity of the islands, themselves, particularly during the summer, when the small ca'ing, or grind, whales swarm along the coast. As recently as 1890 about half of the Faeroese population lived by agriculture, but today this proportion has fallen to 4 per cent. Sheep raising is the chief form of agricultural activity, and the islands' flocks total about 70,000 animals. Less than 4 per cent of the islands' area is under cultivation, and there is a small annual harvest of hay, potatoes, and root crops. Most foodstuffs and other commodities must be imported, with Denmark normally supplying about two-thirds of the total. In some localities, fowling along the cliffs and on the skerries provides an important adjunct to the food supply, though on the whole this activity is declining owing to the attraction of other less dangerous and more remunerative occupations. Coal of fair quality is mined on Syderö, though peat remains the islanders' chief source of fuel (Fig. 4–15). Larger settlements have communal generating plants for electricity, but most outlying districts still depend on wind-operated generators for their power. Industry, including such marine-oriented activities as ship repair, and fish processing, together with handicrafts, especially home knitting, gives support to about one-fifth of the islands' inhabitants. In recent years as many as 1,400 Faeroese have

been enticed by high wages into service in the Icelandic fishing fleet.

Inter-island communications are maintained by ships operating between Thorshavn and the other main towns, though at a considerable deficit. There are about 120 miles of motorable roads and several hundred motor vehicles on the islands, but a large part of the goods which are moved overland still goes by horseback or on the backs of men. During the summer, steamship connections between the Faeroes and Copenhagen are maintained on a schedule of once each week and during the winter, once every three weeks.

ICELAND

In 1967 the population of Iceland totaled 195,000 persons, of whom about four-fifths lived in towns and villages of 300 or more inhabitants. Reykjavík, the capital, had nearly 80,000 (with suburbs, 90,000), while Akureyri, the regional center of the north,

Fig. 4–15. View overlooking the town of Vaag on Syderö, most southerly island of the Faeroes. Note the broad U-shape of the valley and how the fjord has almost cut through to the ocean, seen in the background. Also, note the complete absence of trees. (V. H. Malmström.)

Fig. 4–16. Icelandic ponies grazing near Lake Myvatn, in the northeastern interior. Until rather recently the sturdy Icelandic pony served both as the primary means of overland transport and as a valuable adjunct to the food supply. Part of a lava flow and a table mountain (horst) may be seen in the background. (V. H. Malmström.)

was second in size with a population of about 9,500. Because it has the highest birth rate and the lowest death rate of any country in Europe, except Albania, Iceland is presently undergoing something of a "population explosion." Concurrently, the migration from the rural districts into Reykjavík has swelled to such proportions that today 46 per cent of all Icelanders live in the one city and its suburbs.

As recently as 1880 almost three-fourths of the people of Iceland gained their living through agriculture, but since that time a great expansion has taken place in both fishing and industry. Today only about 20 per cent of the population is engaged in the primary occupations of farming and fishing, with the balance definitely tipped away from the former and toward the latter. Less than 1 per cent of the island is under cultivation and the chief crops are hay, potatoes, and turnips. Marked fluctuations in yield from year to year testify to Iceland's location near a climatic frontier. Another 22 per cent of the island is covered with grass which affords pasturage for numerous sheep, cattle, and horses (Fig. 4–16). In the Southern Lowlands and the western half of the north coast, where local transport is best developed, fluid milk forms the chief source of agricultural income. Elsewhere, mutton constitutes the principal farm commodity entering commerce. In recent years, water from hot springs has been used to heat greenhouses and forcing-gardens, and Reykjavík now derives much of its fruit, vegetables, and cut flowers from such sources.

The backbone of Iceland's modern economic life is fishing, for although there are only about 6,000 persons employed in this occupation, over 90 per cent of the country's exports are derived from it. Cod and herring constitute the principal species caught, cod being taken off all coasts, and herring especially along the north coast. Because about half of the country's trawlers are based in

Reykjavík, the Icelandic capital has the distinction of being the largest fishing port. During and since World War II the movements of herring off the north coast have been extremely erratic, and in recent years most fishing activity has shifted toward the east between Husavík and Raufarhöfn. Landings at Siglufjördhur, the "herring capital of Iceland," have fallen off sharply, and many processing plants located farther west have lain idle for several seasons. In order to protect the spawning grounds of the fish on which the country's livelihood is so overwhelmingly dependent, Iceland extended its fisheries limit to 4 nautical miles in 1952 and then to 12 in 1958. The refusal of some other countries, notably the United Kingdom, to recognize these claims engendered considerable friction and ill will, but the matter was amicably settled in 1961. Icelandic fishermen have increasingly sought permission from their government to operate within the 12 mile limit, due to the growing age of their fleet.

Industry now supports over 25 per cent of the population, and, because most of its raw materials come from fishing and agriculture, its most important branch is food processing. Formerly the bulk of the fish catch was marketed after being dried and salted, but now a large part of the catch is sold iced or frozen. A considerably smaller proportion of fish is canned for export, as well as some mutton, shrimp, and lobster. A growing amount of butter and cheese is also finding its way into export, as are woolen knit goods. Two major additions to Iceland's industrial structure during the 1950's were a large electro-chemical plant built on the outskirts of Reykjavík to produce nitrate fertilizers for agriculture and a cement factory at Akranes to reduce the country's dependence on imported building materials. Lime for the latter plant is obtained by dredging sea-shells from the bottom of Faxa Bay.

Save for a poor-quality peat, Iceland largely lacks fossil fuel resources. It is, however, bountifully supplied with hydroelectric power, the reserves being estimated at more than 4.7 million kilowatts, of which half might feasibly be utilized. To date only about 130,000 kilowatts have been developed, but even this rather limited development has largely been responsible for the country's recent strikes in industrialization. During World War II another economic advance of great importance was made when an installation was completed for heating most of the city of Reykjavík by water piped from hot springs 11 miles to the northeast. Investigations into possible utilization of earth heat as a source of power are currently under way.

Until relatively recent times, all transport in Iceland was either by ship along the coasts or by overland horse caravan. While shipping still is of great significance, the automobile has completely revolutionized the country's land transport. Today Iceland has about 7,200 miles of motorable roads (only 30 of which are hard-surfaced) and one motor vehicle for every seven persons. Air transport is also of great importance, as evidenced by the fact that every second Icelander makes at least one plane trip each year. One company maintains frequent services between Reykjavík and the other main towns of the island, and this and another Icelandic airline engage in international traffic, the latter flying between New York and the major cities of northwestern Europe. Keflavík Airport, about 30 miles west of the capital, was reactivated as an American military base during the Korean War, and, although a U.S. naval contingent is still stationed there, it also serves as the country's main commercial airport for international flights.

With its small population dependent on imports for most of the essentials of life, Iceland has the highest per capita trade of any nation in the world. To pay for its required imports, Iceland exports fish and fish products (including oil and meal) and some mutton, wool, hides, and skins. In order of their value, the chief imports are machinery and transport equipment, manufactured goods, foodstuffs, and mineral fuels. Iceland's major trading partners are the United Kingdom, the United States, West Germany, Denmark, and the Soviet Union. Since the end of the Second World War, Iceland's overall trade balance has been unfavorable, though American military disbursements and the earnings of her international airline make significant contributions to closing the gap between imports and exports. The port of Reykjavík normally handles seven-eighths of the country's imports and two-thirds of its exports.

❊   ❊   ❊

To each of the countries of Northern Europe, diverse as they are, the challenge remains the same: how to make a living in an environment which offers many obstacles and provides few resources. That these countries have largely succeeded in meeting this challenge in the past is witnessed by their high standard of living today. How well they will succeed in meeting this challenge in the future will in large part depend on their ability to work together in ever closer and more harmonious cooperation and on their ability to avoid involvement in the intrigues of the Great Powers which surround them. Northern Europe, like all other regions of the world, can prosper only in an atmosphere of peace.

BIBLIOGRAPHY

Books in English

ANDRÉN, NILS B. E. *Government and Politics in the Nordic Countries.* Stockholm: Almqvist and Wiksell, 1964.

DE BIASI, MARIO. *Finlandia: Profile of a Country.* London: H. Evelyn, 1967.

FLEISCHER, FREDERIC. *The New Sweden: The Challenge of a Disciplined Democracy.* New York: David McKay Co., Inc., 1967.

GUTHMUNDSSON, BARTHI. *The Origin of the Icelanders.* Lincoln, Nebr.: Univ. of Nebraska Press, 1967.

JENSEN, BARTELL C. *The Impact of Reparations on the Post-War Finnish Economy.* Homewood, Ill.: Richard D. Irwin, Inc., 1966.

MALMSTRÖM, VINCENT H. *A Regional Geography of Iceland.* Washington: National Academy of Sciences–National Research Council, 1958.

————. *Norden: Crossroads of Destiny.* Searchlight Book No. 22. Princeton: Van Nostrand, 1965.

MEAD, WILLIAM R. *An Economic Geography of the Scandinavian States and Finland.* London: Univ. of London Press, 1964.

———— and SMEDS, HELMER. *Winter in Finland: A Study in Human Geography.* New York: Frederick A. Praeger, Inc., 1967.

MILLWARD, ROY. *Scandinavian Lands.* New York: St. Martin's Press, 1964.

NUECHTERLEIN, DONALD E. *Iceland: Reluctant Ally.* Ithaca, N.Y.: Cornell Univ. Press, 1961.

O'DELL, ANDREW C. *The Scandinavian World.* London: Longmans, Green and Co., 1957.

SOMME, AXEL (ed.). *A Geography of Norden.* Oslo: J. W. Cappelens Forlag, 1960.

WESTERLIND, ERIK A. *Sweden's Economy: Structure and Trends.* Stockholm: Bokförlaget Prisma, 1965.

Yearbook of Nordic Statistics. Stockholm: Nordic Council, 1962.

Books and Atlases in Other Languages

AARIO, LEO (ed.). *Suomen Kartasto* (Atlas of Finland). Helsinki: Kustannus-osake-yhtiö Otava, 1960.

MYKLEBOST, HALLSTEIN (ed.). *Norge: Land og Folk* (Norway: Land and People). 4 vols. Oslo: J. W. Cappelens Forlag, 1965.

NIELSEN, NIELS (ed.). *Atlas över Danmark* (Atlas of Denmark). 2 vols. København: H. Hagerup, 1949.

SÄLLSKAPET, SVENSKA, för Antropologi och Geografi. *Atlas över Sverige* (Atlas of Sweden). Stockholm: Generalstabens Litografiska Anstalts Förlaget, 1953.

5

Western Europe

France, Belgium, the Netherlands, and Luxembourg together constitute the western gateway to the Eurasian continent. A maritime outlook has come readily to these countries which have an extensive coastline stretching from the Ems River mouth to the western reaches of the Pyrenees. Their eastern borders join Central Europe without serious land barriers. The Iberian Peninsula to the south is accessible at either end of the Pyrenees, and Italy along the Riviera coast. The British Isles lie only 21 miles across the English Channel at the narrowest part of the Strait of Dover.

The Western European countries can be regarded as both maritime and continental in character. France, for example, has a coast line 1,925 miles long, and no part of the country is more than 300 miles from the sea. At the same time, Strasbourg is located only 400 miles from Vienna and 360 miles from Berlin. At their nearest points, the French and Dutch borders are only some 140 miles from the German Democratic Republic. Belgium and the Netherlands share only a short coastline, but they occupy the delta area of three of Europe's most important rivers for trade and transport. Thus, while France borders on four seas and extends

from southern to northern Europe, the Low Countries have a bridge location providing direct connections between the heart of Central Europe and the sea.

Western Europe includes the largest state in Europe outside the Soviet Union, as well as one of the smallest. France has more than twice the area of The German Federal Republic (West Germany) or the United Kingdom, but it has a smaller total population than either of them. Luxembourg, on the other hand, is one of the smallest states of Europe, having an area of only 998 square miles. Western Europe, also, can take pride in the successful formation of the first economic union of several states—the Benelux union—and in active participation of all four states in other regional organizations of the mid-twentieth century, such as the European Coal and Steel Community, the European Economic Community, and others.

The surface configuration of Western Europe is extremely diversified, ranging in elevation from the highest peaks in Europe, in the Alps, to below sea level, in the polders of the Netherlands. Yet, the alignment of the terrain is such that maritime air masses penetrate easily, providing much of Western Europe with a temperate marine climate.

197

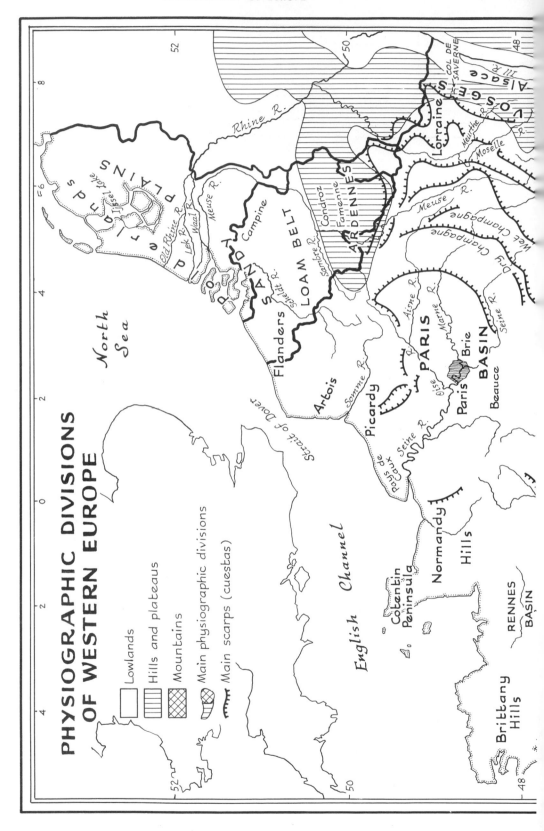

PHYSIOGRAPHIC DIVISIONS
OF WESTERN EUROPE

Lowlands

Hills and plateaus

Mountains

Main physiographic divisions

Main scarps (cuestas)

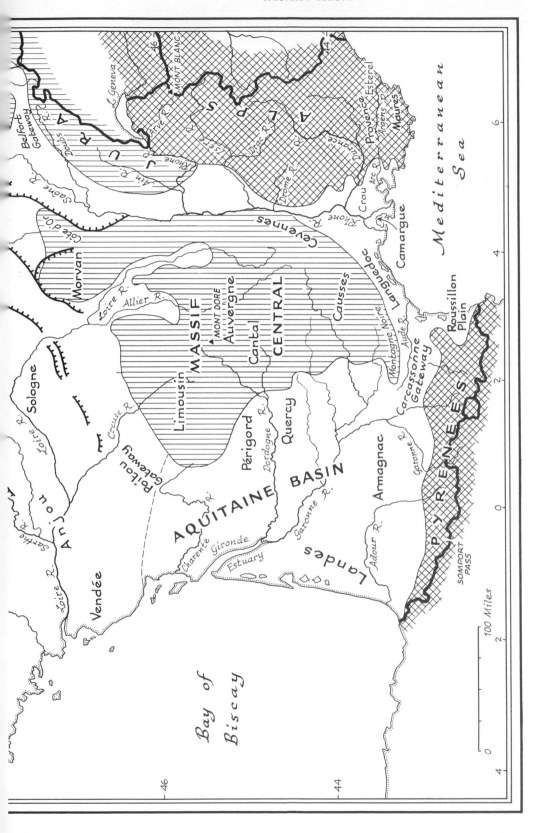

Fig. 5–1. Main physiographic divisions.

THE PHYSICAL LANDSCAPE

Upon general observation the physical landscape of Western Europe appears to be simple (Fig. 5–1). The grain of the terrain is arcuate, with the convex side toward the Atlantic Ocean, English Channel, and North Sea. There are three principal concentric bands of landforms: (1) Bordering the coast is the European Lowland which extends from the western Pyrenees into northern Germany and eastern Europe; (2) adjoining the lowland arc in the interior is an irregular area of hills and plateaus, stretching from the Carcassonne gateway to the Vosges and Ardennes; (3) framing Western Europe on the south and southeast are the high and rugged mountains of the Alps and Pyrenees.

A closer examination of the physical landscape reveals, however, that uniformity is only superficial and that there is great diversity within each of these belts. Hills appear in the lowland, and river valleys and wide corridors break up the continuity of hills, plateaus, and mountains.

The European Lowland

The southwestern section of the European Lowland is the Aquitaine Basin covering about 15 per cent of the area of France. It is a basin in which sediments have accumulated from the adjacent higher lands since late Tertiary times. The sedimentary layers are horizontal, so that the countryside is level or gently rolling and without scarplands.

The southern and southeastern part of the basin is a large piedmont alluvial fan deposited by the ancestral streams issuing forth from the last Pleistocene glaciers of the Pyrenees. The present Garonne River, its southern tributaries, and the streams of the Adour watershed have carved the fan in recent times into an undulating to rolling foothill area.

Between this fan and the Gironde estuary lies the Landes region—a low, flat, sandy plain behind the coastal dunes. These sands are of recent marine origin. Until only a century ago, the landscape presented a picture of desolation—shifting sand dunes and intervening marshlands and swamps—for a subsurface hardpan formation interfered with normal drainage processes. In the latter half of the nineteenth century, land was reclaimed, dunes stabilized, and extensive forests of maritime pine planted. Thus, the Landes became and remains a principal producer of lumber and naval stores (Fig. 5–2).

North of the Garonne-Gironde estuary, limestone bedrock is at or near the surface. Near the coast it is covered with unconsolidated sediments. However, eastward toward the Massif Central the surface rises gradually and culminates in the Périgord and Quercy limestone plateaus, which have karstic features at higher elevations but contain wide, fertile valleys.

There are three gateways leading out of the Aquitaine Basin into other physiographic provinces. The gateway of Carcassonne, a wide, sweeping corridor between the Pyrenees and the Massif Central, connects the Basin with the Mediterranean coastal plain. In the north, the low, featureless coast continues to the Loire estuary. Inland, the gateway of Poitou between low Hercynian massifs provides a connection between the Aquitaine and Paris basins.

The Paris Basin, occupying roughly one-fifth of the area of France, is a structural basin composed of a series of alternating strata of Jurassic and Tertiary limestones, sandstones, and clays of marine origin. During the Alpine mountain-building period, a gentle uplift and downward arching of the rock strata set the stage for subsequent erosion and the present landscape. Toward the east, these layers outcrop as far as Lorraine, southern Luxembourg, and southernmost Belgium. Differential erosion has produced the scarplands, with more resistant steep forested limestone scarps facing eastward toward Central Europe. Famous examples are the Île de France escarpment east of Reims and Épernay which bears the vineyards of the Champagne, the Côtes de Meuse of the western Meuse Valley, and the Côte de Moselle—the western slopes of the Moselle

Fig. 5–2. The Landes forest between Bordeaux and Bayonne. The sandy plain has been drained and planted with maritime pine. Note the movable sawmill on the edge of the forest. Pines are valuable as a source of naval stores and timber. (G. G. Weigend.)

Valley where the iron-ore-bearing strata are exposed. The prevailing bedrock in the Paris Basin is limestone, but over wide areas in the north and west it is covered with deep, fertile loam called *limon* [1] (Fig. 5–3). Variations in slope, the irregular distribution of loam, and the deeply incised rivers, often with wide floodplains and terraces, give considerable regional diversity to the landscape. The flat, featureless Beauce, south and southwest of Paris, contrasts with the undulating to hilly Artois between Picardy and Flanders.

Within the Paris Basin the portions not covered by loam either have a dry, almost karstic landscape in spite of an abundance of precipitation or they are poorly drained where residual clays are at the surface or where clay beds emerge. Conspicuous examples are the Dry Champagne and Wet Champagne. The former is dry chalk country, partly forested, partly used for grazing and some crop cultivation; the latter, adjoining the Dry Champagne on the east, was

[1] *Limon* is loess that has been redeposited by running water.

originally wooded, waterlogged clay country but is now in the main a drained and reclaimed prosperous agricultural area.

Two large river systems drain the Paris Basin. In the south, the Loire and its tributaries have a general east-to-west orientation and empty into the Bay of Biscay; the greater part of the Basin is drained by the Seine River system which extends from interior highlands northeastward through the center of the Basin to the Seine estuary on the English Channel. A few other streams outside these two systems are important, notably the Meuse and Moselle rivers in the east and the Somme River in the north. Generally, streams meander and are deeply incised. Where erosion has reached softer layers of sand and clay beneath the limestones, the floodplains are wide and soils on the lower slopes vary in composition and fertility, depending on the nature of the parent material.

West and southwest of the Paris Basin are the old worn-down Hercynian massifs of Normandy and Brittany, also known as the Armorican Massif. Although a few rounded

Fig. 5–3. Undulating landscape in the Picardy near Amiens. Fertile loam soils give rise to a prosperous agriculture. (Standard Oil Company of New Jersey.)

Fig. 5–4. The *bocage* landscape of Brittany. Undulating to rolling countryside, with fields and pastures enclosed by hedgerows. Some of the farmsteads are isolated, others are clustered in hamlets and villages. (French Embassy Press and Information Division, New York.)

hilltops reach elevations of over 1,000 feet, local relief is not pronounced.

In the Brittany peninsula there are two parallel east-west rows of granitic hills, of which the northern one has the greater height and continuity. The general elevation gradually increases from east to west until the highest peak is reached not far from the drowned valleys of the western end of the peninsula. For the most part, the landscape is not forbidding but a well-dissected, continuously rolling hedgerow country, known as *bocage* (Fig. 5–4), with deeply weathered granite yielding residual soils of low fertility. The coastal plain to the north and south slopes gently from the interior upland to the cliffy irregular and indented coast.

Between the Brittany peninsula and the Normandy hills is the Rennes Basin, a former lake bottom and now an extensive undulating lowland. Loose sediments largely have been eroded away and old Hercynian rocks are exposed at the surface.

Granitic rocks again come to the surface to form hills in Normandy east and northeast of the Rennes Basin and near the northern end of the Cotentin Peninsula. The slopes rise fairly rapidly from surrounding lowlands. At close range, however, these hills, as those in Brittany, present a rounded, well-dissected *bocage* landscape. The low sections of the Cotentin Peninsula as well as the coastal plains are marshy, and in part reclaimed like the polders of Belgium and the Netherlands.

Northeast of the Paris Basin is the Belgian Gate, a narrow section of the European Lowland, between the English Channel and the Ardennes. Here and in the adjoining Netherlands the bedrock is composed of Cretaceous and Tertiary sedimentary rocks dipping gently toward the northwest. However, it is covered with masses of unconsolidated sediments of fluvial, marine, and glacial origin. This part of the lowland has distinctive belts, each paralleling the coast.

A strip of sand dunes, sometimes 2 miles wide and 30 to 60 feet high or higher, borders the coast itself. In Belgium the northeastern section of the shore line near the Dutch border has recently been attacked by the sea and has retreated, resulting in destruction of even some older dune formations, whereas in the Netherlands sediments have been deposited by currents. Such deposition, combined with works of man, has resulted in a seaward shift of the Dutch shore line, creating several parallel dune belts.

Immediately behind the dunes, stretching from western Flanders to northern Groningen, are the "polder lands." These are generally below sea level in the Netherlands—amounting to between one-fourth and one-third of the Dutch land area—and just barely above sea level in Belgium. Formerly these lands were peat bogs, wet clay areas, and lakes, but now they have largely been drained and reclaimed for agricultural use. In Belgium, the polder region attains a maximum width of some 12 miles inside the dunes, but in the Netherlands the belt is much wider, with a maximum of some 30 miles south of the IJssel Lake (IJsselmeer) and in the low delta lands. Man's creation of the polder landscape has been a continuing process since the tenth century A.D.

Adjoining the polders are the sandy plains stretching from eastern Flanders and the Campine northeastward to southern Groningen. These range in elevation from at or near sea level on the polder side to 150 to 300 feet in the interior. They are interrupted by extensive river clay deposits in the delta lands of the Rhine and Meuse, and, further north, glaciation has altered the landscape considerably. In Belgium, the sandy plains are of recent fluvial origin and the sandy soils have been used for agriculture in Flanders ever since the Middle Ages. In the Campine, on the other hand, an impermeable subsoil delayed effective exploitation by man; some sections have remained heath land, others have been afforested with coniferous vegetation. With increased demand for food, large tracts have been improved and, together with stream valleys, are being utilized for pasture and crops. The discovery of coal there in the present century has created mining and manufacturing communities and transformed the original physical landscape even more.

In the delta lands, river beds can be recognized which at one time held glacial streams but which are now abandoned. Valleys, now occupied by the arms of the Rhine and Meuse rivers, are separated from one another by wide strips of low, flat clay land, protected from floods by dikes.

North of a line connecting Nijmegen, Wageningen, and Utrecht, or roughly north of the Meuse River, continental glaciation has been the agent chiefly responsible for shaping the landscape. The outwash sands were covered by ground moraines which subsequently were eroded away again in many places. Where they have remained, the ground moraines have a depth ranging from 3 to 15 feet and, in some localities, as much as 50 feet. The glaciers, moreover, have left a series of north-south ridges of morainic hills, most of them east and southeast of the IJssel Lake. The higher, sandy morainic and, in part, poorly drained areas of the eastern and northeastern Netherlands have provided a meager habitat for man, and, understandably, these were the last sections of the country to be settled. Some high moors still exist in the far northeast, but most of the area has been put to agricultural use, and recent planning calls for a vitalization through introduction of industries there.

The fourth belt of the European Lowland in Belgium and the Netherlands is a band of low plateaus between the sandy plains and the Ardennes. This region includes what has been called the heart of Belgium, as well as a small section in southern Limburg in the Netherlands. The undulating surface rises gradually in elevation to about 600 to 650 feet in the interior. Like parts of the Paris Basin, this section is covered with thick loam (*limon*) which has yielded rich soils and, therefore, is agriculturally one of the most productive areas of the Low Countries. The southern limit is the Sambre-Meuse corridor which marks the beginning of the Ardennes.

Only southern Limburg is northeast of the corridor and adjoins the Ardennes directly.

The drainage in the lowlands of Belgium and the Netherlands is dominated by the three great rivers which have contributed so much to the formation of this particular landscape—the Rhine, Meuse, and Scheldt. The Rhine at present has three distributaries which are, from north to south: (1) the Old Rhine, flowing through Utrecht and Leiden; (2) the Lek, which leads to Rotterdam; and (3) the Waal, which is interlaced with the Meuse just above Dordrecht (Fig. 5–5). The Scheldt, with its main course in Belgium and its mouth in the Netherlands, is the principal gateway of Belgium for maritime traffic. The three rivers have formed a series of long estuaries along the coast. The western Scheldt estuary must remain open for free access to Antwerp, but the Dutch are in the process of closing off the eastern Scheldt estuary and those of the Meuse and Waal in order to shorten the coastline, reduce dangerous salt infiltration from the sea, and create fresh-water lakes for irrigation.

Hills and Plateaus

The hill and plateau areas of Western Europe, such as the hills of Normandy and Brittany within the lowland, are of Hercynian origin. Only the Jura is an exception, because it was formed during the Alpine orogeny. Four principal massifs can be distinguished.

In the northeast, extending into southeastern Belgium, northeastern France, and northern Luxembourg, are the Ardennes, which have three distinct subdivisions. The Condroz adjoins the Sambre-Meuse corridor on the south. Formerly a plateau, it is now a dissected ridge-and-valley region also referred to as the Lower Ardennes. The wooded northeast-southwest trending ridges are of resistant sandstones, while the intervening valleys developed in softer, more easily eroded limestones and shales. General elevation increases from 650 feet near the corridor to about 1,150 feet in the south. On the south, and separating the Condroz

Fig. 5–5. The Rhine-Meuse estuary. The Hollandsch Diep (foreground) is the principal outlet of the Rhine-Meuse system. (KLM Aerocarto NV)

from the Higher Ardennes, is the Famenne depression, a poorly drained clay lowland lying at approximately the same elevation as the Sambre-Meuse corridor. The main massif is the Higher Ardennes south of the Famenne—a deeply dissected, largely wooded plateau surface noted for being flat and poorly drained and having both the highest annual precipitation in Benelux and the lowest density of population. The rocks are old and metamorphosed and yield a thin, infertile soil cover. The elevation of the plateau in Belgium and Luxembourg averages between 1,200 and 1,500 feet. It is highest in the east near the German border, where it rises to more than 2,200 feet, and lowest (about 900 feet) in the west in France. In Luxembourg the Ardennes cover roughly the northern third of the country, a region known as Oesling, as opposed to the Gutland farther south, which is structurally a part of the Paris Basin.

The second principal Hercynian massif is represented by the Vosges Mountains between Lorraine and Alsace. This massif is divided into two sections by the low Col de Saverne, located northwest of Strasbourg at an elevation of 1,086 feet. Through it pass the major transport routes connecting the Paris Basin with the southern Rhine graben. To the north of the Col de Saverne are the densely forested Lower Vosges which adjoin the Hardt Mountains in Germany. Hercynian rocks are covered by younger sandstones, the terrain is strongly dissected, and the general elevation of hilltops is between 1,200 and 1,500 feet. Elevation increases south of the Col de Saverne, and old metamorphosed rocks are exposed at the surface. Slopes are smooth and hilltops rounded even where the highest elevations are reached, close to 5,000 feet. The western slopes toward Lorraine are gentler than those in the east, where strong faulting delimits them against the Rhine graben. As in the Lower Vosges, this section has dense coniferous forests, but here the timber line is reached at about 3,500 feet. Above that level are grasslands utilized for summer grazing. On the rainier slopes originate some of the most

Fig. 5–6. Volcanic plugs in the Le Puy Basin. The Rocher de l'Aigville dominates the town of Le Puy in the foreground, and the town of Polignac lies at the foot of the basalt plug in the background. (French Government Tourist Office, New York.)

important streams of eastern France, such as the Moselle and Meurthe. In the east, however, streams are shorter and have steep gradients down into the Rhine Plain.

The Rhine graben is a rift valley filled in with hundreds of feet of alluvial sediments and loess deposits. Parts of the plain are poorly drained, especially the southern flood-plain between the Rhine and Ill rivers; in general, however, the graben is one of France's most fertile and prosperous areas. Farther south, between the Vosges and the Jura Mountains, lies the Belfort Gateway, also called the Burgundy Gate. This low rolling corridor, about 15 miles wide, makes a major break in the landscape of hills and plateaus, and has been of great economic and strategic importance. The significance of the gateway for transport and communication has not diminished, but strategically it is no longer of consequence.

The Jura Mountains, beyond the Belfort Gateway to the south, form a 180-mile arc around the Swiss lake country, attaining their greatest width in France—approximately 45 miles—south of Besançon. The massif is composed largely of folded and horizontal limestone which does not give the appearance of mountainous country even though the highest elevation is more than 5,000 feet. The higher parts of the Jura rise along the Franco-Swiss border on the inside arc, where the strata have been folded into many anticlines and synclines. This section often has been compared with the Ridge and Valley Province of the Appalachian Mountains, and indeed it has many similar characteristics, except that anticlinal valleys are rare. The trellis drainage pattern prevails, and stream capture has reduced the number of main streams to two—the Doubs and Ain rivers. The slopes are steep and carry a dense coniferous vegetation; settlements are located chiefly on lower slopes, in valleys, or at water gaps. Adjoining the folds on the west is the wider plateau section of the Jura. Here the limestone strata are horizontal and underground drainage prevails. Three plateau levels can be distinguished, descending in a

steplike manner westward toward the Saône Valley.

The fourth major section of hills and plateaus is the Massif Central, by far the largest of the four and the most diversified. This is one of the Hercynian massifs uplifted last during the Alpine orogeny and, in part, subsequently modified through extensive lava flows. Moreover, a tilting of the Massif Central in Tertiary times resulted in higher elevations along the southern margin and a general downward slope toward north and west.

The heart of the Massif Central is the Auvergne, a region where past volcanic activity is very much in evidence. Old volcanic cones in the western Auvergne provide the highest elevations in the Massif Central —Mont Dore and Plomb du Cantal, 6,186 feet and 6,094 feet, respectively. Their slopes have been dissected by running water and by Pleistocene ice. To the southeast of these domes are extensive basaltic lava flows, while to the north more recent volcanic activity has created a rugged, little-eroded landscape dotted with many volcanic cones (*puys*). The older basalts to the south are well weathered and have yielded fertile soils, but the choice of crops is limited by climatic conditions. In the eastern Auvergne, lava flows have been largely eroded away and have left rolling granitic surfaces and occasional volcanic plugs standing in the landscape like monuments (Fig. 5–6).

Elsewhere, the old crystalline rocks are exposed at the surface in the Limousin Plateau northwest of the Auvergne and in the highlands of the eastern rim, from the Morvan in the north to the Cévennes and Montagne Noire in the south. The Limousin Plateau is a flat to undulating old erosion surface at an elevation of close to 3,000 feet in the east with a gentle downward slope toward the west. The entire eastern rim, on the other hand, has been affected by faulting along the Rhone-Saône corridor and the Languedoc. Slopes rise steeply from adjacent lowlands to form a crest line which is high, forbidding, and continuous in the south but becomes lower, more dissected, and less of a barrier in the north. Northwest of Nîmes the continuity of the Hercynian rocks is broken by the Causses, a rugged karstic area of limestone having an average elevation of 2,500 to 3,000 feet. Here underground drainage is pronounced, leaving the surface dry and with little soil cover except for residual clay pockets.

The Massif Central, particularly the higher ranges, has heavy precipitation, and all of France's major river systems receive contributions of its surface runoff. The continental divide is located near the eastern and southeastern rim of the Massif, so that streams flowing toward the Rhone and Saône rivers and the Mediterranean Sea are short and swift and have steep gradients. In other directions, however, rivers descend gradually, cutting narrow gorges into the hard basement rocks and widening occasionally in sedimentary or structural basins.

Corsica can perhaps be considered transitional between hill lands and mountains. A longitudinal depression separates the young folded mountains, occupying the eastern third of the island, from the granitic Hercynian block to the west. Mountains and hills are well dissected and almost everywhere they reach to or near the coast where they descend precipitously (see Fig. 1–18). While the east coast is straight and runs approximately north-south, the west coast bulges westward and displays a ria shore line.

Mountains

The Pyrenees. France and Spain partake of the Pyrenees, the mountain ranges extending some 260 miles from the Mediterranean to the Bay of Biscay. Although the Pyrenees represent an almost continuous barrier for man as well as for climate, their structure and appearance differ greatly from one part to another.

In the west, from the ocean to the Somport Pass, the mountains are composed mostly of limestone and their average elevation is below 6,000 feet. Precipitation is heavy, and stream erosion has dissected and lowered the terrain sufficiently to create several fairly easy passes between France and Spain. From Somport eastward to the headwaters of the Garonne River are the Central Pyrenees—the most rugged and highest section of the mountain system. Hard crystalline rocks produce peaks of more than 9,000 feet, and the landscape has been much modified by glaciation. The mountain façade, however, is broken up by a series of transverse valleys, whose streams flow from glacial cirques northward across the ranges through a succession of gorges and basins filled with glacial debris.

The Pyrenees of the Ariège, between the headwaters of the Garonne and Aude rivers, east of the Central Pyrenees, present a strong contrast by their longitudinal rather than transverse orientation of landforms and drainage. The innermost section is the axial zone where, as in the Central Pyrenees, large areas are above the timber line and where meadows are used for summer pasture. In fact, here as elsewhere in the Pyrenees, as also in the Alps, forests have suffered and the timber line has been lowered because of the destructive custom of burning woodlands to gain additional pastures. The axial zone is flanked on the north by the "North Pyrenean Massif" or the "Middle Mountain," as it has been called, lying almost entirely below the timber line. This is a land of forests where relief has been produced in large measure by running water on resistant granites and schists and strips of infolded younger sedimentary rocks. The Pre-Pyrenees, or "Little Pyrenees," still farther north, are situated in juxtaposition to the Aquitaine Basin. The gently folded sedimentary rocks are for the most part densely forested and assume the character of a foothill country. Longitudinal drainage is typical of the Pyrenees of the Ariège, with streams flowing between ranges and cutting through them in steep, narrow, short defiles.

Finally, east of the Aude River are the Mediterranean Pyrenees—massive crystalline forms with high, isolated intermontane basins. Slopes descend steeply into the Roussillon Plain and to the Mediterranean, but only some 30 miles from the coast a pass of less than 1,000-foot elevation provides an easy route between France and Spain. The Mediterranean climate and vegetation extend from the coast to the lower slopes; at higher elevations, however, above 2,000 feet, rainfall becomes more abundant and the slopes are forested to the timber line, with alpine meadows at still higher elevations. Thus, the combined influence of altitude and distance from the sea has produced several zones of vegetation.

The Alps. The French Alps occupy the southeastern corner of the country. Bordered by the Mediterranean coast and Lake Geneva in the south and north, respectively, they extend toward the Rhone corridor in the west, and in the east and northeast they continue into Italy and Switzerland. In the northern French Alps four longitudinal divisions manifest themselves. The central core is composed of high crystalline massifs whose granites and schists are of Hercynian origin. The northernmost of these and also the most notable is Mont Blanc, which, at 15,781 feet, is the highest peak in Europe. Mont Blanc, like some peaks in the other massifs, is still extensively glaciated, the snow line reaching down to about 9,000 feet. Pleistocene glaciers have left a majestic and beautiful landscape of cirques, U-shaped valleys, hanging valleys, and other erosive features. Moraines are visible as far away as the Rhone corridor. Outliers of the Hercynian massifs farther south can be found along the border of France and Italy, not far north of the Riviera, in the form of the Maures-Estérel Massif, which parallels the coast between Cannes and Toulon, and in the high, rugged mountains of Corsica.

To the east of these massifs rise the folded internal Alps, composed of massive sandstones and limestones, much distorted by big overthrusts. Bordering the central core on the west and separating it from the Pre-Alps is the Alpine furrow (*Sillon Alpine*), a structural depression extending from Chamonix to south of Grenoble. It is followed by some important Alpine streams such as the Drac, middle Isère, and upper Arve rivers, which have deepened it through erosion. The Pre-Alps, west and south of this depression, are composed chiefly of Mesozoic limestones and form a wide arc from Lake Geneva to the Riviera coast. The Drôme River Valley, however, marks a notable change in orientation and dissection of the ranges. North of that valley the Pre-Alpine zone is quite narrow, and its continuity is broken up by transverse valleys eroded by streams descending from the internal ranges and forming gaps (*cluses*) as they pass through north-south ridges.

South of the Drôme Valley, the Pre-Alps widen to some 60 miles or more and the alignment veers to east-west, very much like that of the Pyrenees. This southern region, the Provence, has the semblance of a jumble of broken blocks 1,500 to 2,500 feet in elevation, with occasional higher peaks, and there is only one major valley—that of the Durance River. Moreover, a depression lies along the zone of contact between the Maures-Estérel Massif and the limestone ranges, providing an important routeway between Toulon and Fréjus; and the valleys of the Arc and Argens rivers form a corridor between the Rhone Delta region and the Riviera coast. The Mediterranean climate becomes increasingly pronounced southward, the periods of summer droughts lengthen, and forests give way to slopes that are either barren or covered with drought-resistant shrubs. All major streams draining the French Alps find their way into the Rhone River which, together with the Saône, follows a structural trench. This is the Rhone-Saône corridor, the southern gateway which has been of great significance in the historical development of Western Europe.

THE CULTURAL AND HISTORICAL BACKGROUND

The significance of location of the Western European states for human occupancy has been borne out by their function as gateways for movement of goods, people, and ideas to, from, and within the continent of Europe. Nevertheless, at some periods in history they have been on the periphery of activity and movement and have experienced slowdown or stagnation. By virtue of their maritime and land position, however, these states have contributed greatly to the political, economic, and social development of Europe as a whole and of many land areas across the seas, where they gained temporary colonial control or settled permanently.

The Maritime Position

Of the countries in Western Europe, all but Luxembourg border on the sea. It should not be assumed, however, that France, by virtue of the longest coastline, necessarily occupies the most important maritime position now. In the past, France was actively participating in overseas colonization, in direct competition with Belgium and the Netherlands, as well as with Britain and Germany. Thus, the sea position of France between the British and Germanic areas has encouraged rivalry with these other European maritime states both in medieval and modern times.

Mediterranean traders provided the early cultural contacts from across the seas, in the south and southwest of France. In the sixth and seventh centuries A.D., some Celts, fleeing from the Angles and Saxons, crossed the English Channel to France, invaded the old Armorica, and created a new Brittany there which has persisted to this day. The Celtic imprint was a lasting one, as people in western Brittany still speak a variety of Celtic. In the ninth century the Vikings, or Norsemen (later called Normans), after moving in and plundering the French shores, settled in the Bay of Normandy, between the Cotentin Peninsula and the Pays de Caux. The Normans, in turn, invaded England in the eleventh century and enriched English culture and, eventually, American culture with their Romance heritage.

In the Middle Ages the rudiments of a manufacturing complex developed in the North Sea area, through the zeal of the Hanseatic merchants and shippers. Wool weaving was the most strongly established industry. It was centered in Flanders and thrived there for many centuries. With mercantile and industrial growth tied closely to the area's seaward relations, a greater agricultural production was needed to sustain the increasing urban population. New lands were put into crops and agricultural methods improved. Gradually, land reclamation and crop rotation became widely accepted.

England moved across the English Channel into Western Europe as a continental power in the middle of the twelfth century when Eleanor, Duchess of Aquitaine, married Henry Plantagenet, who shortly afterward became Henry II of England. Three hundred years later British power on the continent declined. In the middle of the fifteenth century France's sea boundary on the English Channel as well as on the Atlantic Ocean became secure, and it has been accepted without question ever since. The only remnants from this period are the Channel Islands, a cluster of small islands off the coasts of Brittany and Normandy, which Britain has owned since 1259.

In the age of discovery and colonization, global aspects of maritime relations began to develop—first of France, then of the Netherlands, and lastly of Belgium. Antwerp had been one of Europe's most important ports since 1315 when the city joined the Hanseatic League. Traffic stagnated, however, beginning with the pillaging of the city by Spaniards in 1567 and with the closing of the Scheldt estuary by the Dutch until Napoleonic times. On the other hand, French and Dutch ports, particularly Bordeaux and Amsterdam, became gateways to the continent, especially during the eighteenth century. Since the emergence of Germany as a modern political and industrial power on the European continent the center of gravity in the ocean transport pattern has shifted from France to the Low Countries and the German North Sea coast, so that the maritime position of France has been weakened accordingly and has become peripheral in relation to the rest of Europe.

On the Mediterranean Sea also, maritime relations began in ancient times, with Marseille becoming France's gateway there. The port's role was vastly strengthened in the nineteenth century, when France began to colonize North Africa and when, after the opening of the Suez Canal in 1869, Marseille assumed the main function of colonial port, not only for North Africa but also for French possessions and commercial interests in Asia beyond Suez.

The Land Position

Traveling overland from where they had settled earlier in the south of Germany, the Gallic Celts arrived in Western Europe about 500 B.C. The incumbent population, an already rather numerous Neolithic people largely devoted to farming, amalgamated with them. The Roman conquest brought the influence of Mediterranean culture, especially the Latin language, over the greater part of the conquered territory, as far as the *limes* along the river Rhine, where the threatening Germans were held back. The Vandals, Alamanns, Burgundians, and Visigoths from northeastern and central Europe eventually moved sporadically into the West in varying numbers. They were followed by another Germanic people, the Franks, who created a number of kingdoms in Western Europe. Thus the Franks were imposing their rule over much of Gaul contemporaneously with the Celtic invasion of Brittany. The prevailing language remained Low Latin except in Brittany and in the peripheral Low Countries, Alsace, and eastern Lorraine, where a Germanic tongue evolved. The enduring power of the Franks in the old Gaul finally provided France with her name.

The division of Charlemagne's large empire into three north-south parts under the Verdun Treaty of 843 set up a long border zone, Lotharingia, later perverted to Lorraine, between the western and eastern Frankish kingdoms. It is especially noteworthy that the western kingdom returned to its Celto-Latin tradition and eventually became France, while the eastern kingdom, where both land and people were German, later developed into Germany. The intermediate zone, extending from the marshes of Friesland to the olive groves of Italy, was fought over and shifted one way and another up to the present century. Boundaries, whether linguistic, political, or religious, developed slowly and spasmodically.

France has enjoyed a longer continuous period as an independent state than her three neighbors to the north. Most of the present area of France has been effectively integrated since the fifteenth century. Some later expansion did take place toward the east into central Europe, as well as in the Mediterranean realm.

Alsace and Lorraine had been associated with tribal kingdoms and other medieval-type units until they were incorporated into France in the seventeenth century. On two occasions since then, Alsace and parts of Lorraine have been taken over by the Germans, but there is no longer any doubt that these areas are now integral parts of France. In the southeast, the Alpine zone of Savoy-Nice was a wide area of sparse population and an effective barrier to communication and transportation. It was joined to France permanently in 1860. Following World War II, a few changes on the Franco-Italian border extended French control still further eastward. In the south, land boundaries with Spain were stabilized in the Treaty of the Pyrenees of 1659.

The formation of France as a modern state took place by early unification in the Paris Basin, the core area, by expansion to include the greater part of France by the end of the fifteenth century, and by final border adjustments on the east and south in later centuries.

The significance of the land position of France in relation to German, English, Spanish, and Italian areas has shifted in the past according to the political and economic developments which have taken place in these neighboring states.

In the Middle Ages, France and Flanders were bound closely to the Apennine peninsula. Trade routes led from Italy by way of the Rhone Valley to the fairs of Champagne and thence to the free cities of Flanders. During the Renaissance, Italy held supreme mastery in all arts and crafts, and new ideas and techniques were brought home by French soldiers during the fifteenth and sixteenth centuries. The luxury silk industry of Lyon is, in fact, of Italian origin.

In the sixteenth century Spain had driven out the Moors and was looked upon as a strong colonial power. Spain, France, and England were all integrated states, functioning effectively, while Italy, although culturally pre-eminent, remained disorganized politically. France occupied a central land position between England and Spain. With the subsequent decline of Spain as a continental power, France emerged as the strongest state on the continent in the seventeenth and eighteenth centuries. This strength was accompanied by a shifting of mercantile interests away from the Mediterranean states to Western Europe. With industrialization in northwestern Europe and with the unification of Germany in 1871, Europe's balance of power shifted again and France's land position between Britain and the unified Germany assumed an importance which has persisted to this day.

After World War II, the combined land and maritime position of France took on new significance with respect to strategy in the East-West power struggle. France became an essential unit in the NATO alliance, because of her location between the United States and the Soviet Union.

For the Benelux countries the land position has been, and is, of paramount significance. The emergence of these three states can, at least in part, be ascribed to the ineffectiveness and eventual failure and breakup of the Holy Roman Empire. The Netherlands fought for and gained its freedom at the time of the Reformation; in 1648 it was recognized as an independent state. Already exploitation of its land and sea position had made the Netherlands a major power in European trade and overseas colonization. The right to control the Scheldt estuary, obtained in the Peace of Westphalia, eliminated competition from Antwerp in the Spanish Netherlands by closing that port off from the sea. Moreover, the immigration of Portuguese and Spanish Jews and French Huguenots brought new talent and resources to the recently founded country. Although the Scheldt estuary was reopened by Napoleon in 1803, the supremacy of the Dutch, astride the Rhine estuary, has not been challenged successfully in continental European trade and transport.

Belgium represents that portion of the former Spanish Netherlands which was unable to throw off the foreign yoke in the wars of independence. After a futile attempt to reunite Belgium and the Netherlands in 1815, Belgium finally was created in 1830–31 as an independent kingdom. Too many differences and animosities had evolved between the two countries in the two centuries of separation.

Having only land frontiers, Luxembourg has been by far the most land-oriented of the states of Western Europe. A remnant of larger feudal units, it gained political independence in 1839 and was declared neutral territory in 1867. Since joining a customs union with Belgium in 1922, an orientation toward the sea has become increasingly pronounced. With the creation of Benelux, the European Coal and Steel Community, and the European Economic Community, the land and sea positions have both assumed great significance in the economic life of the country.

It is of particular interest to note that none of the three Benelux countries first emerged as a buffer state, but that in the power struggles of the nineteenth century they all assumed that role.

Evolution of the Human Landscapes

Man has had a hand in shaping most landscapes in Western Europe. It may be difficult or impossible to determine the beginnings of some cultural landscapes, for their origins lie in prehistoric time and have never been recorded. During the Middle Ages the landscape was changed by the barbarian invaders or colonists, as the case may have been. The agricultural plots which had been cultivated in prehistoric times could be found here and there, but generally forests, marshes, and heath prevailed. Feudal rulers or missionaries of the Church led the drive to clear the forests in unsettled areas. It was in this period that the organization of the agricultural systems began and the settlement patterns were finally crystallized. However, neither physical factors nor human circumstances in themselves are sufficient for a penetrating analysis of these patterns. Wherever possible, an explanation of the many forms of rural and urban landscapes must be found in terms of total relationships among which one factor, physical or human, may or may not have predominated.

The rural landscapes. A glimpse of an aerial photograph of almost any part of Western Europe will reveal a maximal utilization of land and its division into many small fields and meadows. The plots appear to be extremely intricate, by virtue of both field pattern and colors of crops. They are larger than rice paddies in the Far East but far smaller than farm plots in the United States.

Four main rural landscapes stand out:

1. Open-field country is found in nearly all of France north of a line drawn from Geneva to Besançon, Dijon, Orléans, Blois, Chartres, and Rouen, and in Belgium south of a line leading from Tournai, Ath, Nivelles, Brussels, Vilvoorde, Louvain, Tongeren, and Maaseik, and in all of Luxembourg (Fig. 5–7). The landscape stretches without interruption, open and unadorned, without trees except in forests, without hedges, earth banks, isolated or scattered farm houses. The farmers live clustered in villages with a church at the center and surrounded by their fields.

Until the end of the eighteenth century, open-field cultivation was a community enterprise. A three-way division was made of the cultivated parish land, known as the three-field system: one for winter cereals (wheat, rye), one for spring cereals (barley, oats), and the third was left fallow. This sequence was first made compulsory by Charlemagne probably in the latter part of the eighth century. Rotation took place every year, and every year, in the absence of chemical fertilizers, one-third of the land was left fallow in order to reduce the ill effects from overworking the soil and to permit collective grazing of livestock. Following the harvest, animals could graze in the fields of stubble as well. While the individual farmers owned their tiny plots, the land had to be worked at the same time and under identical conditions as that of their neighbors. Announcements of prescribed times for plowing, sowing, and harvesting were made in church on certain Sundays. In deference to the rotation system and to allow livestock free movement on the common pastures, all plots of land were required to remain unenclosed. By the same token, each family head had to hold land in each of the three parts to secure for himself and his family a supply of all crops grown in the community.

The community system was closely tied in with the evolution of communal tenure practices during feudal times. Under this system, citizens of the community had certain property rights in communal lands, among which were rights in arable land, in forests, and in alpine pastures. In fact, one of the compelling reasons for the long endurance of the community system was the right to graze on fallow and harvested land. Farmers needed a large area for pasturing their herds, so open fields were essential. The number of animals that each family head could graze was determined by the extent of his holding, but a minimum of one cow and six sheep could be pastured even if no land was owned.

During the nineteenth century the practice of compulsory crop rotation gradually became outmoded. A decree early in the

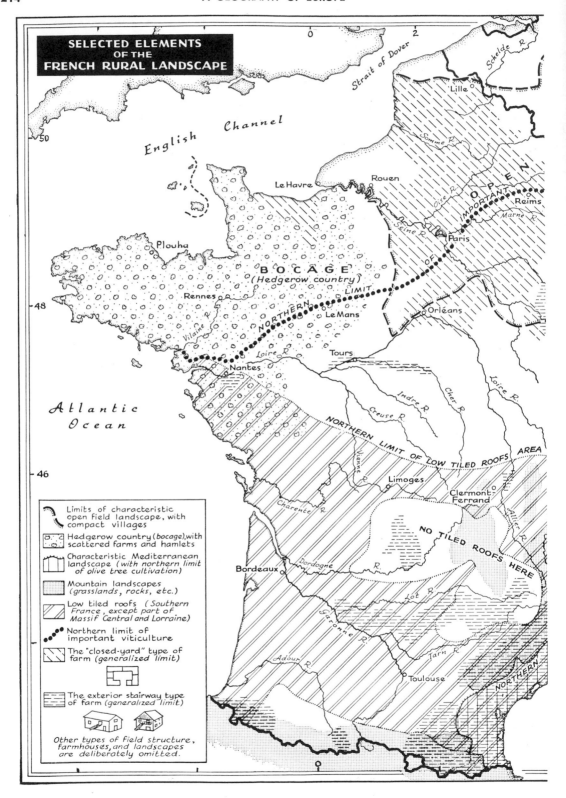

Fig. 5–7. Selected elements of the French rural landscape.

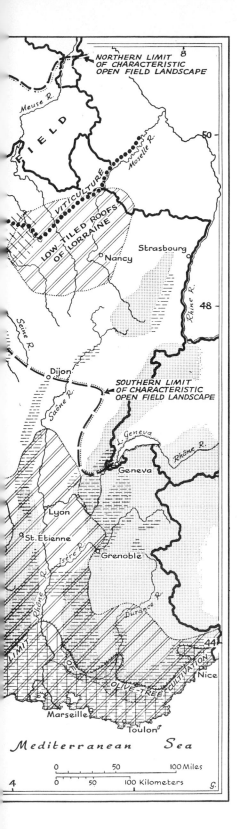

French Revolution had established freedom of cultivation and exploitation, which made possible individual improvement in rotation without community action. Nevertheless, the peasants resisted stiffly any changes in the time-honored practices. The introduction of previously unknown or little-known plants, especially clover, fodder turnips, Indian corn, potatoes, and sugar beets brought about the development of different crop successions. Besides, the widespread raising of fodder and the use of fertilizers and modern farm machinery all combined to bring about the abandonment of the traditional system.

2. The second chief type of rural landscape is the *bocage* of western France (Fig. 5–4). It is an enclosed, confining landscape, characterized by small, elongated fields and meadows encircled by high hedgerows or trees growing from ground level or from earthen dikes, deep-rutted twisting wagon lanes, scattered isolated farms, or occasional hamlets or villages. From aloft, the countryside appears like an immense compartmented forest riddled by thousands of clearings, yet actual forests and woods are rare. The Armorican Massif and the southwestern part of the Paris Basin are landscapes of this sort, as are many parts of the Massif Central.

The massive uniformity of the *bocage*, in part, might be related to the extremely individualistic character of the people and their desire to maintain overt evidence of ownership of their land. But what was the origin of the *bocage?* Several hundred years ago the landscape was more open heath than today. In the eighteenth century the semi-wooded heath or the *lande,* as it is called, covered between half and one-third of Brittany. Today it still persists on as much as 14 to 18 per cent of all land on the peninsula. Over the years, many open *landes* have become cultivated fields, enclosed by hedges in order to protect the cropland against livestock grazing in open areas beyond. In that way, the *bocage* landscape was created in an area where agricultural practices go back to Neolithic times.

One wonders whether the hedgerows and farm plots were laid out haphazardly or with some intent. A study of aerial photographs has revealed that Neolithic farmers had small enclosed fields similar to the *bocage* country of western France today. Furthermore, it was shown that most of the fields, still rectangular rather than square, point in certain directions and that these directions appear to be the same as those of the main alignments of the Megalithic monuments along the southern coast of Brittany at Carnac. In this area the directions correspond to the position of the sun at sunrise and sunset on certain days of the year, such as the solstices. This startling disclosure gives strong support to the supposition that the field patterns were laid out in Neolithic times by a sun-worshipping people. The tradition, once established, has been followed to our day when woods and heaths were cleared and returned to cultivation.

3. One might call the remaining portion of France, loosely speaking, the southern landscape, while pointing out the regional variations among southwestern, central, and Mediterranean sectors. Historically, the southern landscape developed an agriculture characterized by the relatively less productive two-field system, in which half the cultivable land was left fallow for one or more years, depending on local conditions of soil and slope. Enclosure was more common in the south, though no definite system prevailed, with individual buildings in hedged fields and compact hilltop villages built during the Middle Ages for defense. A predominantly hilly terrain doubtless contributed to the variety of field patterns. Often, size and dimensions of the plots were extremely irregular as a result of the necessity of finding the best location and soil for each crop. Except for the Mediterranean area, long specialized in horticulture, the farming was mainly unspecialized, and a great diversity of crops could be found throughout the countryside.

The land use of today reflects to a large extent these historical patterns. In the Medi-

terranean area the meadow is noticeably absent and wheat, olives, and vineyards fill the landscape, together with certain intensive truck-farming regions. Grazing lands are almost ubiquitous in the Massif Central and the other highlands, while a mixed livestock-and-crop economy has evolved in the Aquitaine and the Saône Valley. Nearly everywhere are vines used for the production of quality or ordinary wines in large amounts or only for the domestic needs of the farmer.

4. The rural landscape of Flanders and the western Netherlands represents a fourth main type. Reclaimed farmlands wrested from the sea or from lakes and poorly drained valley floors are known as polders—landscapes made up of canals, rows of poplars, green wet meadows, rectangular plots, and large, isolated or loosely grouped farmhouses. The appearance of the land changes toward the east. It becomes higher, plots are more irregular, and small woods are interspersed with fields and pasture land. The polder landscape is spectacular and its origin is well understood. Its evolution can be traced through the centuries and consists of four principal stages.

The sea polders were the earliest to be developed, beginning in the tenth and eleventh centuries.[2] Sea walls were built out from shore on sections of the coast where dunes were absent. The resulting slowdown in the ocean currents would create an area of sand and silt accretions which then could be diked off from the sea. In such a way, a complex of adjoining sea polders came into existence and to the present day some 940,000 acres of land have been reclaimed from the sea.

The second stage—the creation of inland polders—began in the fourteenth century in Holland, earlier in Flanders. Much of maritime Flanders was drained by the thirteenth century, because of the great demand for food in the flourishing Flemish textile towns. The windmill, which was first used for pumping water out of bogs early in the fifteenth

2 W. W. Reys, "The Dutch Polder Country," *Geografisch tijdschrift* 7 (August, 1954): 146–58.

century, accelerated land-reclamation processes so that, by the end of the sixteenth century, most of the mainland of Holland behind the dunes was settled. Moreover, it had become clear that joint efforts were necessary to coordinate drainage work and dike maintenance. For this purpose, the Dutch *waterschappen* and the Flemish *wateringues* were formed—autonomous syndicates which became drainage authorities.

Although reclamation and drainage were well organized, the settlement of the land was not. A peasant would obtain the right to a parcel of land extending from the dike into the polder; the strip of land could be extended on both sides of the dike to the boundaries of the village, so that a narrow elongated field pattern, possibly several miles long, came into existence. This type of land use was as uneconomical to operate as the fragmented properties in other parts of Western Europe.

In the third stage of land reclamation, beginning in the seventeenth century, land division was based on more rational considerations of land use and hydraulic conditions. This stage consisted of the drainage of inland lakes which, in turn, created the lowest polders in the Netherlands, reaching depths of nearly 22 feet below mean sea level. The largest of these, Haarlem Lake, could not be drained until the middle of the nineteenth century, when steam power was available for pumping. Even as late as this, water control was defective and general land-use planning was inadequate. The growth of rural settlement was spontaneous and unplanned, and transportation facilities were poor, making public services and administration extremely difficult.

In the twentieth century attention returned to the sea. With modern technology it was possible to isolate the Zuider Zee from the North Sea by means of a dike 19 miles long (Fig. 5–15) and to carve out five large polders with a total area of some 885 square miles (when completed). Even here, the distribution of centers of population was not adequately planned in the Wieringermeer

polder, the first to be settled, and administrative problems were encountered in connection with the Northeast Polder because of its large area.[3] For the remaining polders, economic and social planning is proceeding in the greatest detail in the hope that all major problems can be anticipated. Moreover, the even more ambitious Delta Plan for the diking of all but two Scheldt-Meuse-Rhine distributaries has been begun.

The open-field country, the *bocage*, the landscapes of southern France, and the polder landscape of the Low Countries are the four main types of rural landscapes. Transitional forms are numerous, and occasionally islands of *bocage* are found in the open-field area, and open fields in the hedge-row country.

The appearance and arrangement of the farmhouse complex vary greatly from one region to another. Many regional types have evolved according to local resources, traditions, and economies.

The high mountains of the Alps are practically the only area of Western Europe where there are frame houses or where houses have been built entirely of wood, often on a stone foundation. The use of wooden beams, moreover, on the walls and ceilings is not uncommon, and numerous picturesque half-timbered farmhouses can be seen in Normandy, the Basque country, and Alsace. Brick farmhouses are the custom in northern France and in the plains of Belgium and the Netherlands (Fig. 5–8). The use of brick has been increasing, gradually replacing stone, the traditional building material since Roman days. Brick is now used widely in new construction, particularly in the Benelux countries. The great diversity of local stones, so often of warm colors, contribute to the artistic aspect of many farms. The farm buildings of Brittany and Limousin have granite walls; those of the Loire coun-

[3] C. A. P. Takes, *Physical Planning in Connection with Land Reclamation and Improvement* (Wageningen, Netherlands: H. Veenman & Zonen, 1958).

Fig. 5–8. Typical Saxon farm building in the eastern Netherlands, near the Schoonebeek oil field. The thatched roof covers both the living quarters and the barn. (Standard Oil Company of New Jersey.)

try are of white, soft, and easily carved chalk; in the Auvergne the black volcanic blocks blend with the landscape. Some places have little stone available and houses are built with walls of pressed dried mud often strengthened with straw.

Roofing materials and roof styles are also a matter of utility and local tradition. The Roman half-cylindrical tiles can be seen throughout most of southern France, as in neighboring Italy and Spain; they require little slant of the roof. There are islands of such tile in Lorraine, and of small flat tiles arranged in a scalelike fashion in some rural areas of the Paris Basin. In southern France, on the other hand, there are islands of slate roofs in some Pyrenean valleys, such as the upper watershed of the Gave de Mauléon (the *Pays de Soule* in the Basque country) and adjacent valleys farther east in the Béarn, where slate is readily available locally. In Alsace and some other regions shingles are used. Steep roofs thatched with straw or reed are still seen in Normandy, Brittany, the Beauce, and the Low Coun-

tries, but, because they represent safety and sanitation hazards, they are gradually disappearing. Stone roofs occur in the Auvergne and in sections of the Jura and the Alps. In general, however, local color and artistry are slowly giving way to more utilitarian tiles.

Three traditional layouts of rural farmsteads can be recognized in the Western European countries, and all three reflect directly the economic requirements of rural life.[4] First, the *maison-bloc* plan, as it is called by French geographers, combines several farming functions under one and the same roof. There are two subtypes of this layout. In one, all parts of the building are on the ground floor, with the actual layout of functional space varying from one region to another (*maison-bloc en terre*). This type is widespread. It occurs everywhere in France —except in the Mediterranean region and in

[4] Albert Demangeon, *La France*, Vol. 6 of Vidal de la Blache, ed., *Géographie Universelle* (Paris: Librairie Armand Colin, 1946).

the Paris Basin—as well as in the Belgian Campine and Ardennes, the Luxembourg Oesling, and the Dutch Brabant. Occasionally, in the Basque country, the roof over this assembly is centered on the living quarters, so that it appears asymmetrical, with the longer side of the roof extending over part of the building housing the livestock, fodder, equipment, etc. However, this asymmetrical feature does not occur as frequently as one is led to believe from the literature. The other subtype is a two-story house (*maison-bloc en hauteur*) where living quarters are on one floor above or below stable and barn. In vine-growing areas, the latter are generally on the ground floor, together with the wine cellar.

The second layout is the farmstead with an enclosed yard. Farmhouse, stable, barn, carriage house, and outbuildings are laid out in a quadrangle within which the well or possibly a pond may be found, as well as the manure pile. The buildings are contiguous, or nearly so. This type of farmstead predominates in areas of intensive grain cultivation in northern France, central Belgium, and Dutch Limburg.

The third plan is the open-yard farmstead which is favored in the cattle-raising areas of western and central France—Normandy, Brittany, and parts of the Massif Central—of the Flanders Plain in northernmost France and western Belgium, and of the western Netherlands. The open-yard farm has gained popularity, since expansion of farm facilities is made easier with more space.

Everywhere in Western Europe farmsteads can be observed which do not adhere strictly to any one of these major types of layout. There are many transitions, none of which, however, appears to be localized in any one area.

The urban landscapes. France was the first of the Western European countries to evolve an urban landscape. Many French cities and towns can look back to the pre-Roman era. Analysis of place names of innumerable French towns points to the en-during influence of the Gallic tribes in whose domain the chief present-day French cities were already capitals. Cities like Le Havre, built on the commission of King Francis I, or Lorient, which was the port of the French East India Company, are some of the few towns that were established within the last few centuries.

Of the ancient towns no visible traces remain. In the south of France many of the old sites as well as newly selected ones became foci of Roman settlements. The core of the colony was called the "castrum" (*cité*), which was a stronghold surrounded by walls.[5] The cathedral, generally built within the castrum in late Roman or early medieval times, became the principal landmark. Later, in the Middle Ages, when crafts and trade developed, these cores of urban growth expanded and the market place, the *ville*, with its surrounding residences and shops, emerged contiguous with the *cité* and replaced it as the real focus of medieval urban life. In northern France and Flanders during the early Middle Ages, merchants developed small market colonies along main transport routes, frequently next to strongholds called *bourgs* or *burgs*, but often independently without walled protection. The original functions of these towns were manufacturing by artisans and trade and transport, linked with marketing the goods. By 1000 A.D., copper and iron work became the specialty of the Meuse Valley, while Brugge, Ghent, Ieper (Ypres), and others flowered into prosperous commercial and industrial towns famed for textile manufacture.

From the outset the market place was the pivot of regional economic activity and the core of future urban growth. The cathedral, the high ornate guildhall, the town hall, and the belfry usually flanked this central square, and the houses extended along roads leading out from it in various directions. Most of these towns enjoyed virtual independence

---

[5] Robert E. Dickinson, *The West European City,* 2nd ed. (London: Routledge & Kegan Paul, Ltd., 1964).

from the ruling lords, and were granted self-government sooner or later.

In certain parts of France and Belgium during the Middle Ages the cores for future town life appeared in such forms as the medieval castles and manor houses, which had in their immediate vicinity the settlement of vassals (as Chateauroux and Niort), and monasteries and ecclesiastical seats around which urban settlements clustered (Chartres and Limoges, for example). Occasionally the town core might merge with another core already existent nearby, to add to its size, but more often the core remained separate, evolving into a town on its own. Today the central core of an old city is easily identified by the narrow twisting streets, the presence of a cathedral, some medieval houses, possibly a castle, and remnants of old ramparts. In France an outer core has a good number of seventeenth and eighteenth century houses, as in Bordeaux and Nantes, whose ports brought them prosperity at a time when new ideas on city planning were afoot from both the aesthetic and the functional standpoints. Recent industrial developments generally have grown up on the urban fringes. Belgium, however, experienced stagnation of urban activities from the end of the Middle Ages until the nineteenth century, because of foreign domination and the closing of the Scheldt estuary by the Dutch. In the nineteenth century, first industrialization and then the emergence of Belgium as an independent kingdom brought a long-delayed but very vigorous growth of urban areas and activities, with principal concentrations in the Sambre-Meuse corridor, at Antwerp and Brussels.

In Holland, the founding of towns and general urban development took place at a later time. The low, marshy terrain of what is now the most densely settled part of the Netherlands was uninviting to colonists and, in fact, hazardous. The Romans penetrated only to the old Rhine River and founded such towns or garrisons as Utrecht and Nijmegen. The barbarians who migrated into Gaul bypassed the area or moved through it, destroying existing settlements. Higher ground to the east had soils of low fertility, and sparse population. It was not until Carolingian times that urban settlements were founded again. However, the majority of towns did not appear on the map until the twelfth and thirteenth centuries, which have been called the golden age of medieval new-town planning in the Netherlands.[6]

Once the Dutch realized their advantageous position with respect to currents of European trade, new centers grew rapidly and became prosperous. These centers were established primarily for the crafts, trade, transport, and local administration, as had been the Flemish towns two or three centuries earlier. Sites were selected in accordance with requirements of trade and transport—at road junctions (Groningen), ferry or fording points (Utrecht, Zwolle), or transshipment points (Arnhem, Rotterdam, Amsterdam). Little or no regard was given to site conditions. The central feature of many of these towns was a bridge across a river or canal in the case of dike towns, or a dam in the case of so-called dike-dam towns. In either case the bridge or dam assumed the function of market place. Around this center were grouped the other buildings and facilities necessary for the town's function. Some towns, such as Delft, were founded in the middle of a polder reclamation project to serve at first as a rural market. Later, however, the town was replanned in order to take on various urban functions. In fact, most Dutch towns have grown by continuous replanning and by effective integration of new surrounding areas into the urban patterns. Thus, urban growth, which has been continuous to the present day, has occurred chiefly by extension of existing towns rather than by establishment of new ones.

Regionalism. There appears to be a marked correlation between the long and relatively stable history of settlement in

6 Gerald L. Burke, *The Making of Dutch Towns* (London: Cleaver-Hume Press Ltd., 1956).

Western Europe and the development of regionalism. Long before the surrender of Vercingetorix to Julius Caesar in 52 B.C., settlement had taken place in much of France and the Low Countries outside the poorly drained lowlands. In contrast, Germany and other parts of Central Europe were inhabited by tribes that were more transient. With time, distinct characteristics became indelibly imprinted on the landscape as well as on the people living in it, resulting in pronounced regional differentiations of speech, customs, land use, and other visible features. The operative factors involved in this regionalism were many and varied. In some cases, natural barriers or physical uniformity contributed to a certain amount of homogeneity and kinship within a region. Or it may have been land use, form of settlement, or a combination of human and physical factors which formed the traditional *pays* in France and Belgium. A number of regions are known to have grown out of *pagi*, which had been small Gallo-Roman territorial divisions.

In France the old provinces were political units until they were abolished during the Revolution and replaced by the smaller *départements*. The area of each of these *départements*, of which there are now 95, was sufficiently small for citizens to reach the administrative center from any point in less than a day's ride on a horse. The ancient provinces, however, have retained their identity, and people are more prone to think and talk of "Brittany" or "Normandy" than of "Finistère" or "Manche." In fact, regions which lend themselves better to economic planning and statistical compilation, and bearing traditional names, have been evolved since World War II. Now France has 21 such regional divisions, in each of which are grouped several *départements*, ranging in number from two to eight. The ancient provinces in the Netherlands and Belgium still represent the official administrative divisions of these countries.

At an international level, the European Coal and Steel Community, the European Economic Community, and others, are all indications of the increasingly great role of economic relationships in the regionalism of Western Europe.

FRANCE

The People

Although France is by area the largest state of Western Europe, it is today among the less densely populated. France ranks seventeenth in Europe with 233 inhabitants per square mile in 1967, lower than any of her neighbors except Spain and Andorra. In September of that year it was estimated that the population of France had passed the 50 million mark. For Western Europe as a whole, the rural density of France is low (Fig. 5–9). Although the rural population is fairly evenly distributed throughout much of the country, some differentiation can be indicated. There are areas of very sparse population in the Causses—the dry limestone plateaus in the southwestern Massif Central—and the high sections of the southern Alps. An almost continuous belt having a population density ranging from 50 to 124 per square mile extends from the chalk plateaus of the eastern Paris Basin, through parts of the limestone plateaus in the southern Paris Basin not covered by loess deposits, to the Massif Central, the Pyrenees, the sandy Landes in the southwest, and Corsica in the Mediterranean. On the other hand, areas of relatively dense rural population include the coasts of Brittany, the rich loess-covered plateaus of Picardy, the fertile alluvial Rhine Valley of Alsace between Strasbourg and Mulhouse, and the valleys of the Loire and Garonne rivers.

Agriculture is still a very important component in the French economy, but manufacturing in the last decade has assumed an ever-increasing importance. One evidence of that trend was the increase in number of cities of more than 100,000 people from 24 to 32 between the two census years, 1954 and 1962, and the number of urban agglomerations of more than 100,000 from 33

Fig. 5–9. Population density of France, 1967.

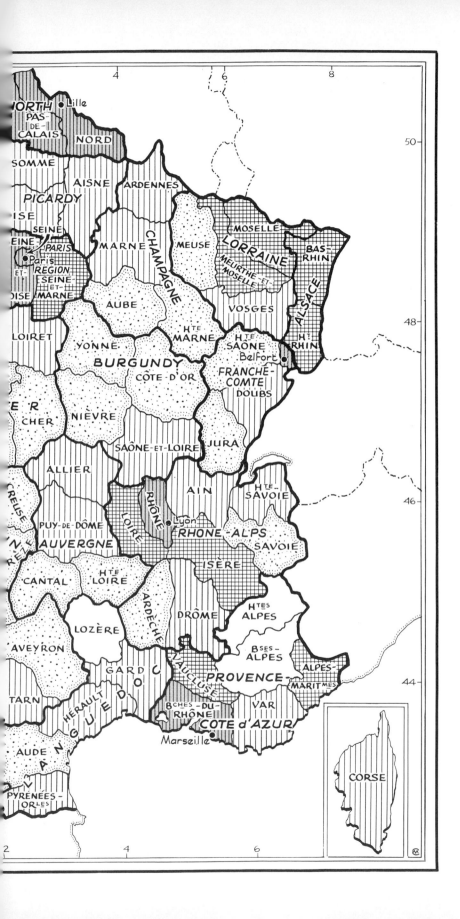

to 40. However, the population gap between Paris and other agglomerations is still astonishingly large. Greater Paris in accordance with the 1962 census contained 7.5 million inhabitants, about 16 per cent of the total population, or as many people as in the next 25 conurbations combined.[7] This has been of great concern to the French government, which is attempting to develop plans for decentralization of population and industry. Other regions of high urban concentration are the northern industrial region—a cluster of cities on and near the principal coal fields of France—and the metropolitan areas of Marseille and Lyon.

Demographically, France has attained a unique position in relatively recent times. Until the middle of the nineteenth century, France had the largest population in Western and Central Europe, having reached 20 million by the end of the sixteenth century and 26 million by the time of the French Revolution. In 1801, with more than 27 million, she surpassed Great Britain with only 11 million, Germany with 22 million, and Italy with 17 million. France's population continued to increase until the middle of the nineteenth century, when it numbered nearly 36 million inhabitants. In the second half of the nineteenth century, however, population increase as a whole fell off with continued industrialization and urbanization, and with the agricultural depression which began in the 1880's. Germany exceeded France in total population in the 1850's, Great Britain toward the end of the nineteenth century, and Italy in the 1930's. Between 1851 and 1938 France's population increased by only a little over 6 million, while in the same period the population of the United Kingdom increased by some 25 million, and even that of the Netherlands by some 5.5 million. Germany, between 1870 and 1938, gained about 28 million people. At the same time, urban areas, especially Paris and the north, increased their population at the expense of

rural areas—a gradual population shift which is still continuing.

While the low birth rate created a population problem in the century before World War II, the situation has been reversed since that war. The birth rate reached the highest level in the present century in 1950; since then it declined somewhat but has been fairly steady since 1958 at about 18 births per 1000 population. This, plus immigration from Algeria as well as from within the European Economic Community, has resulted in a rate of population growth which is greater than that of most European countries. Simultaneously, life expectancy has increased because of a declining death rate. By 1951, France had regained the 1938 population level.

The French population-density pattern had changed very little until the 1950's. Areas in both the north and south of France, which had a high density of population in the 1930's, continued to increase their density after World War II. They include Greater Paris, Lorraine, the Rhone Basin, and the Riviera coast, as well as some cities such as Lyon, Grenoble, Marseille, Toulouse, and Bordeaux. They are still the major centers of economic growth and poles of attraction for in-migration. The industrial north, however, has experienced only a modest increase in population density because the region has become economically stagnant. Sections which in the 1930's had manifested a decreasing population for the most part continued to decline after the war, at the same time facing a more impoverished local economy. Such areas include Brittany and the Massif Central. The major exception is the Haute-Savoie where population has increased in the wake of hydroelectric power and manufacturing developments.

The Nation

Language, one of the vital forces of French national consciousness, has been instrumental in unifying the somewhat diverse parts of France into a cohesive whole. The fact that the language of Île de France, a

[7] République Française, Institut National de la Statistique et des Études Économiques, *Annuaire Statistique de la France*, 1966.

Romance dialect, has been accepted as the official language throughout France is an indication of the early political control and cultural dominance of the Paris Basin—the core area of the French state. Provincial dialects still remain, and other languages are spoken in some areas, but these areas are nonetheless integral parts of the French nation.

The Breton language, a tongue derived from Celtic, is spoken in the Brittany peninsula west of a line extending from Plouha in the north to the mouth of the Vilaine River in the south. At the Atlantic end of the Pyrenees some 100,000 people speak Basque, a language the origin of which has never been determined; and at the eastern end of the Pyrenees live 185,000 people who speak Catalan, a Romance language. In Corsica an Italian dialect known as Corsican has its roots in the Pisan period (1077–1312) and probably earlier. Flemish is spoken in the area around Dunkerque, and German dialects are used throughout Alsace and parts of Lorraine. Practically all these people, however, are bilingual.

Minority problems are virtually non-existent in France. Despite an autonomist Breton movement and a separatist Alsatian party, in the past little actual support has been rallied around these causes. There are regional movements whose aims do not conflict with French unity itself. They exert pressures on the central government for protection and preservation of regional languages, dialects, customs, and traditions. The cohesion of the French nation was amply demonstrated during World War II when the Germans were unable to split France effectively. The Bretons as a whole remained loyal to the Free French; in fact, the population of Brittany was a large contributor to the French underground movement.

What factors, other than language, contributed to this common bond? Certainly not race. There is no such thing as a French race, for the French have absorbed many races and peoples who have invaded the country throughout history from all directions. Religion is another factor which has not been involved, at least not in recent times. The struggle between the Catholic Church and the state had been a divisive factor, but one which could not be traced to any regional distribution. During the French Revolution, however, religious equality was initiated, and since then the Church has not been officially recognized by the state. Although most French people are Roman Catholic, religious tolerance is extended to all sects.

It was the French Revolution that provided new national consciousness and strengthened regional homogeneity throughout the land. The Revolution spread common ideas of "liberty, equality, and fraternity" over the entire country and, indeed, over many parts of the modern world. General adherence to these ideas, as well as the long historical association of the various parts of France through wars, the Reformation, revolutions, overseas colonization, etc., all strengthened the common bond.

Finally, there has been the close tie of all parts of the country in its social and economic life. The social structure has evolved since the days of the Revolution. The most significant aspect is that there is no regional concentration of any one class or group. The only distinction that can and should be made is that between Paris and the rest of France. The Parisian considers people from outside Paris provincial, and, at the same time, all of France looks to Paris for political, economic, social, and intellectual leadership. Moreover, outlanders from the provinces have always been lured to the capital, seeking its cultural and economic advantages and, in the process, contributing to the total character of the city themselves. Indeed, the leadership of Paris is undisputed.

From the economic standpoint, a considerable integration of the various parts of France has been favored by the fact that a great variety of natural resources has promoted internal trade. A heretofore adequate and efficient network of highways and railroads has facilitated this trade and has tied the regions closely together.

Present Economic Life

France is a rich country from the standpoint of basic resources, yet, until recently, the average income of the French people was relatively low. The reasons were manifold. As was pointed out earlier, the population of France had been stagnant until recent years. Moreover, a considerable immobility had existed between various occupations. Industrialization was very slow in the first half of the present century and was concentrated in few nuclei, especially around Paris. This heavy concentration of industrial growth had left most of the country in an underdeveloped state which created patterns of social life inimical to economic progress. In 1959, however, President de Gaulle stabilized France politically and financially, and since then, the nation has experienced rapid economic progress.

Agriculture in France has also been backward, a condition which could be attributed partly to the fact that industry had not given agriculture tools or machinery at prices which the farmers would or could pay. There were too many persons on the farms who produced, at high cost, too little. Such circumstances had created a deterioration of the farmers' economic position in relation to the rest of the working population. Moreover, farmers have had a deep-seated reluctance to leave their land, and a scarcity of housing impeded movement from rural to urban and industrial areas. In the last decade, however, cooperative management has multiplied, the quantity of fertilizer used has doubled, and the manufacture of farm machinery has become one of France's major industries.

In general, France still remains a land of shopkeepers, small proprietors, and craftsmen, dedicated to the rights of the individual over those of the group. This structure has forestalled full conversion to mechanized industry, with the result that France's industrial production has not progressed as rapidly as it has in many other states of Europe.

In the middle 1960's France had a total labor force of about 20 million people, or 41 per cent of the total population, including some 6.5 million women. Nearly one-fifth of the women worked on farms, another one-fifth in hotel and restaurant businesses, and one-fourth was engaged in industry. About 18 per cent of the total labor force worked in agriculture, forestry, and fishing, and close to 30 per cent in manufacturing industries. These percentages represent a sharp decline in the labor force engaged in primary activities since World War II, and a relative increase in the labor force engaged in manufacturing.

In spite of the decline of the agricultural labor force, the number of French workers engaged in purely agricultural work is still high, compared with the Benelux countries. However, productivity and living standards of French farmers have risen sharply—real income increased by 35 per cent between 1959 and 1966.

Agriculture. Some 63 per cent of the total area of France is utilized for various agricultural pursuits. Of this, more than one-half is cultivated land, while another one-quarter is permanent grassland. France is normally self-sufficient in food except, of course, for tropical products, and even has some exportable surplus.

In general, France is a country of small farms. Some 29 per cent of all farms are smaller than 12 acres and another 45 per cent are between 12 and 50 acres. There are, of course, regional variations. Smaller farms are more numerous along the Mediterranean coast, where there is also a scarcity of cattle, and in Alsace-Lorraine. Larger farms, on the other hand, are concentrated in the eastern half of the Paris Basin. More than two-thirds of the farms were owned and operated by the farmers themselves; some 25 per cent of the French farms were operated by tenants, and about 2 per cent by sharecroppers. Although tenant farmers are scattered throughout the country, there are notable concentrations in the Breton peninsula and in the northern regions, especially the *départements* Seine-Maritime, Nord, Côtes-du-Nord, Pas-de-Calais, and Oise. The sharecropping system is practiced chiefly in the Aquitaine Basin, where the Landes *Département* alone had some 40 per cent of all sharecroppers in France.

In the past, various factors have hindered an increase in French agricultural production, as already discussed, but perhaps the greatest single factor underlying most of the difficulties was and still is land fragmentation, which has been proceeding throughout the centuries. Most plots are too irregular in shape and too small to be worked efficiently. A farmer may own many small plots located in different directions from the village, sometimes long distances away. The waste of time is enormous in terms of travel; crop rotation, irrigation, soil-erosion control, and other general aspects of farm operation are made difficult.

There are four principal reasons for this excess of fragmentation. Firstly, compulsory crop rotation, which began in medieval times and which no longer exists, has nevertheless left its imprint upon the French agricultural landscape. As was already pointed out, this system resulted in every peasant family obtaining holdings in each of the three basic sections of arable land belonging to the village. Subsequently, rights to individual pieces of land were divided again and again, resulting in the splintering of the arable land. Secondly, the basic law of France, the *Code Civil*, since its adoption in 1803 has required that land be divided up evenly among heirs upon the death of the head of household. The law was aimed at breaking up large feudal estates and at asserting and strengthening property rights of individual peasants. A third important reason for land fragmentation is what has been called "the narrowness of the land market." [8] The eagerness of peasants to buy more land but their inability to pay for large pieces, the piecemeal sale of domains when cash was needed, plus land speculation, all contributed to fragmenta-

tion. Finally, the village type of rural settlement in many parts of France facilitated, indeed perpetuated, the holding of many individual lots.

The seriousness of this situation was recognized as early as the seventeenth century, but all attempts to consolidate property holdings had been in vain until a sensible and flexible law was passed in 1941. This law represents a combined effort of the national and local governments and groups of resident farmers of each area where a consolidation project has been decided upon. The law became operative in 1943, and by early 1965 projects involving nearly 11 million acres of land in 84 *départements* had been completed.[9] However, there were still 35.6 million acres to be consolidated.

A recurrence of fragmentation will be avoided because, once a project has been completed, subdivision will no longer be permitted. Although in the majority of these projects complete consolidation cannot be effected at once, the reduction in the number of parcels of individual properties, and, thereby, the increase in the size of lots, makes possible the more rational planning and utilization of farms. This, in turn, is releasing several million people now on the land, for employment in manufacturing, professions, and services—all activities which advance the standard of living. Furthermore, the speed of penetration of modern ideas, machines, and methods has been increased, ingrained routine is gradually changing, productivity per agricultural worker is rising, and there is an accumulation of capital so urgently needed for continued progress.

Agricultural regions. In general, eight types of agricultural landscapes can be distinguished in France (Fig. 5–10).

1. THE LOAM-COVERED PARIS BASIN. A thick layer of loam (*limon*) covers most of this area which stretches from Belgium to the Loire River and from the Seine estuary

[8] Frederic O. Sargent, "Fragmentation of French Land: Its Nature, Extent and Causes," *Land Economics* 28 (1952): 218–29.

[9] République Française, Institut National de la Statistique et des Études Économiques, *Annuaire Statistique de la France,* 1965.

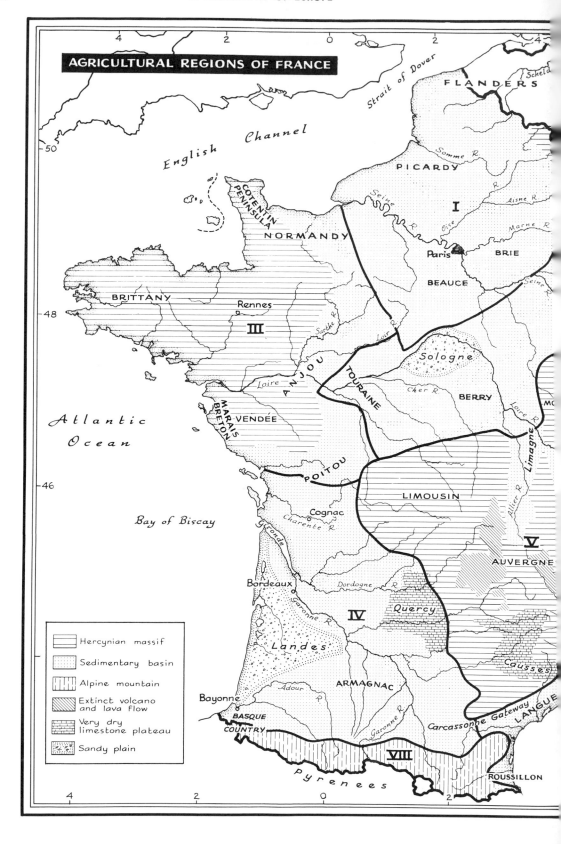

AGRICULTURAL REGIONS OF FRANCE

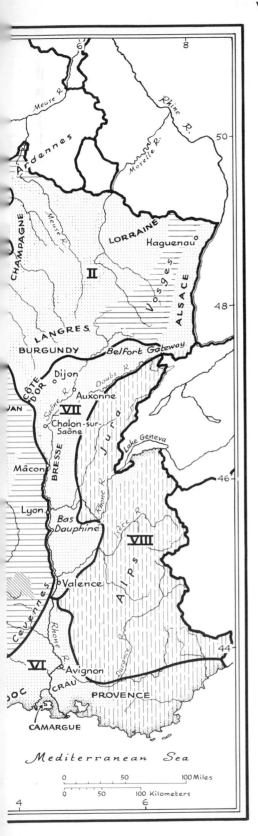

I. Loam-covered Paris Basin
II. Forest Belt
III. *Bocage* Areas of Western France
IV. Basin of Aquitaine
V. Massif Central
VI. Mediterranean Area
VII. Rhone-Saône Corridor
VIII. The High Mountains

Fig. 5–10. Agricultural regions of France. (After J. M. Sourdillat, *Géographie Agricole de la France*. Paris: Presses Universitaires, 1950.)

to the Champagne. Open, undulating to rolling plains and plateaus such as interior Flanders, Picardy, Brie, Beauce, and the Paris area fall within this section. It contains some of the most fertile soils and is among the technically most advanced agricultural areas of France, characterized by high yields and large farms with good equipment and permanent or temporary hired workers. This area covers about 15 per cent of the surface of France but grows close to 90 per cent of the sugar beets and more than 40 per cent of France's wheat and oats. The beets are harvested every year with the help of numerous migrant workers from Belgium. Beet pulp and molasses are used as cattle feed, and leaves are fed to the sheep or are plowed under. Associated with primary crops are many secondary crops included in complex rotations, and the raising of cattle and sheep.

The wide valley bottoms are used for truck and dairy farming, particularly the production of cheese. Dairying and poultry farming are also widespread on the Brie Plateau. The slopes of the Île de France escarpment, which delimit the Brie against the Dry Champagne to the east, carry the carefully tended vineyards of Champagne. The Paris region itself is an area of intensive horticulture. In the sandy and alluvial plains of maritime Flanders in the far north, extensive pasturing prevails.

This agricultural region is located in proximity to the industrial north. It has easy access to urban and industrial areas where employment is available and where the rural surplus population can be absorbed. Thus, favorable human and physical factors have combined to produce the most prosperous rural area in France.

2. THE FOREST BELT. This area includes the southern and eastern Paris Basin, as well as the Vosges, the Ardennes, and, for the sake of convenience, also the Rhine Valley. This section of the Paris Basin is composed of calcareous plateaus and plains which are not covered with loam. Precipitation, therefore, sinks readily into the ground, leaving the surface dry. Over wide areas the soils are thin residual clays, and much fertilizer is required for the growing of crops. Large sections of the plateaus are forested or fallow and open pasture. For example, in Berry, the southern Dry Champagne, and the plateau of Langres, sheep raising assumes considerable importance. Where crops are grown, cereals predominate. Crop yields are low, as are income and living standards of the farmers. Therefore, rural depopulation has been striking in this region, especially in the plateau of Langres (Burgundy), which has a very low population density.

Where the clays are thick, such as in the Wet Champagne and in parts of the Sologne, soils have been drained and used to advantage for crops. The most intensive rural land use and relatively high population densities can be found in the river valleys, such as those of the Loire, Meuse, and Moselle. There, a great variety of crops are grown in rotation and vines and deciduous fruit abound. Cattle are associated with agriculture everywhere.

The Hercynian massifs of the Ardennes and the Vosges Mountains also have extensive forests, with livestock and crop farming on the lower slopes and the valley floors. The eastern slopes of the Vosges descend steeply to the broad valley of the Rhine River in Alsace. On the lower hillsides are terraced vineyards growing grapes for quality wines. Between the Rhine and the Ill rivers lies a marshy floodplain. However, between this floodplain and the Vosges foothills is a terrace with rich loam soils, where both livestock and crop densities are high and where the major settlements are located. The soils are deeper and more fertile in northern Alsace. Tobacco, asparagus, and other vegetables are grown; the Haguenau region is one of France's outstanding hops-producing areas.

3. THE BOCAGE AREAS OF WESTERN FRANCE. This part of France has been called "the green lands," because, throughout most of it, fields are surrounded by hedges or trees on the same level as the fields or on earth

Fig. 5–11. Salt-evaporation ponds in the Marais Breton, a section of the coastal plain, south of the Loire estuary, which is barely above sea level. (French Embassy Press and Information Service, New York.)

mounds. Only in the *Marais Breton* along the Atlantic coast of the Vendée are there wide expanses of open, low-lying, poorly drained land given over either to pasture or to the production of salt from sea water (Fig. 5–11).

In general, farms of the *bocage* areas are scattered, small, and have an oversupply of labor. Wheat, dairy products, meat, apples, and vegetables are the leading agricultural products, but there is considerable regional variation. Cider competes with wine as the favorite beverage.

In Normandy, meadowland is three or four times more extensive than cropland. In the western part of the Cotentin Peninsula, up to 95 per cent of the land may be pasture and meadow. Crops are grown primarily for the feeding of livestock, and the entire economy is dominated by dairy farming—the production of butter, cheese, and milk for the Paris metropolitan area. Apple orchards dot the landscape, and one of the provinces, Calvados, has given its name to brandy distilled from apples.

Toward the west, Brittany presents very interesting contrasts. On the coast there is truck farming in several small areas,[10] but, on the whole, Brittany is primarily a producer of cereals, potatoes, and animal products. Since World War II, meadows and pastures have been gaining at the expense of cultivated land. On the other hand, the French government has encouraged the removal of apple trees, for the dual purpose of reducing the production of alcohol and increasing that of cereals. Since 1953, some wheat has been exported to the Netherlands and Germany directly from small Breton ports by means of Dutch and German vessels.

In the rolling Rennes Basin the landscape is somewhat more open, the fields are larger, and the production of cereals, particularly

[10] There are six principal areas: on the north coast in the vicinity of St.-Malo, St.-Brieuc, and north of Morlaix; on the west coast on the Plougastel peninsula opposite Brest; and on the southwest coast in the Concarneau area and southwest of Quimper.

wheat, is emphasized more than in other parts of Brittany. On the wide, gentle banks of the Loire Valley are the famous vineyards of Anjou, while in the floodplain the thick alluvial soils are used for truck farming and the growing of flowers. South of the Loire, livestock becomes more important again, particularly the fattening of beef, but a generally successful balance is maintained between livestock and crop farming.

4. THE BASIN OF AQUITAINE. Southwestern France also presents a great many contrasts in land use. Its intensity ranges from that of the very sparsely populated areas of the Landes between Bordeaux and Bayonne to that of the densely populated Bordeaux vineyard and truck-farming areas.

To the south of the Vendée and Poitou a landscape begins which is composed largely of open fields, nucleated settlements, and some scattered vineyard areas. This is the northern Charente which was one of the earliest viticultural areas of France, but where few vineyards have remained since the destruction of the European vines by the phylloxera in the late nineteenth century. Instead, the area has specialized in dairy farming. Milk and butter cooperatives have been formed throughout to improve purchasing and marketing procedures.

Farther south in the Charente, the percentage of land in vineyards increases, although even in the Cognac region vineyards take up less than 20 per cent of the land. The highest vine-growing densities there are south and southeast of Cognac, where up to 30 per cent of the land has been planted into vineyards. The entire region is known as the Cognac appellation area, where white grapes are grown for distillation and the manufacture of wine brandy named after the town of Cognac.

Southeast of Bordeaux, largely in the *département* of Gers, is the Armagnac area where the growing of white grapes for distillation into wine brandy is also significant. Here, also, vineyards do not cover more than 30 per cent of any one commune.

The highest vineyard densities are in the valleys of the lower Garonne and Dordogne and their tributaries, together with the slopes along the Gironde estuary. Grapes are grown here for the production of quality wines (Bordeaux wines) rather than brandies. The region includes many appellation areas, such as the famous *Sauternes, Médoc,* and *Graves.*

In the Basque areas south of the Landes forest (Fig. 5–12) as well as in the eastern part of the Aquitaine Basin, drained by the middle Garonne and Dordogne and their tributaries, corn has taken an important place, together with wheat, in crop rotation. In general, this is a prosperous agricultural region and, in some sections, farmers have formed efficiently run cooperative organizations. Thus, mechanization is more apparent there than in any other part of western and southern France. Cattle are part of the economy everywhere, and sheep are numerous in the foothills of the Pyrenees.

5. THE MASSIF CENTRAL. In the Limousin and other crystalline massifs farther east, such as part of the Auvergne and Morvan, the soils developed from the old hard Hercynian rocks. They are thin, of low fertility, and often poorly drained. Climatic conditions at higher elevations are severe and limit the choice of crops somewhat. On the high plateau surfaces, pasture land predominates and cattle are raised for beef and veal. At lower elevations and in a number of fertile alluvial basins, rye, oats, potatoes, forage crops, vegetables, and fruit are of considerable importance. Although rye is the basic cereal, wheat has been gaining ground where soil and climatic conditions are favorable.

In the volcanic portion of the Auvergne, agriculture consists of a livestock and crop combination. Soils are fertile and permeable, the cattle density is high, and farms are relatively large. Dairying is a specialty of this area, particularly the production of milk and cheese.

Sheep are raised throughout the southern portion of the Massif Central, especially in the dry limestone plateaus of the Causses.

Fig. 5–12. Basque village in the foothills of the Pyrenees. Corn, wheat, forage crops, and pasture are the principal uses of the land. Farmers live in such hamlets and villages, or on isolated farmsteads. (G. G. Weigend.)

This is the home of the world-renowned Roquefort cheese for which ewe milk and partially processed cheese are collected, not only locally but from an area extending from Corsica to the Basque country.

6. THE MEDITERRANEAN AREA (MIDI). The Mediterranean slopes represent a blend of traditional Mediterranean agriculture and modern commercialized farming under irrigation. The traditional combination of wheat on the narrow plains, vineyards and olive trees on the hillsides, and sheep on the denuded mountains can be found in much of the Provence and in Corsica. Transhumance is the custom, and each summer the sheep and goats are driven to high alpine pastures. Actually, pasture land is scarce and the practice of transhumance has declined with an increase of fodder grown under irrigation. In the Languedoc, commercial viticulture has become the principal activity. In the *département* Hérault, close to 66 per cent of the cultivated land is in vineyards, and

more wine is produced there than in any other *département* of France. This specialization has been of great concern to the French government. Extensive irrigation is being developed to diversify agriculture by enlarging the fruit and vegetable acreages.

Vineyards can be seen as far as the small fertile Roussillon Plain and the lower slopes of the Pyrenees. The former, however, also produces a great variety of vegetables, with the aid of irrigation, as well as peaches and apricots.

Perhaps the greatest specialization can be found along the lower Rhone River. In the vicinity of Avignon year-round agriculture is practiced; vegetables and grapes are grown in small fields, surrounded by high cypress hedges which serve as a protection against the mistral winds. All fields are irrigated in the dry summer half year, with water from the Durance River. Farther southeast, the Crau—a large, deltaic rocky plain—serves as winter pasture for sheep, and in the poorly drained delta area proper, the Camargue, a large reclamation project has been under way since 1947, for the production of sufficient rice for the home market (Fig. 5–13). In this area there are also some large land holdings on which fighting bulls are raised.

7. THE RHONE-SAÔNE CORRIDOR. Diversity is the key word for the Rhone-Saône Corridor. The Mediterranean crop combination extends up the Rhone Valley from the coastal plain into the interior. Slopes are covered with vineyards, and in the alluvial basins wide valley floors one finds the wheat and sugar beet combination and planted, irrigated meadows interspersed with pastures for dairy cattle. On the lower slopes deciduous fruit abound. In fact, the hill area, together with this section of the Rhone Valley, is the heart of the fruit belt where apples, apricots, peaches, and cherries are grown, mostly for table use. In the Lyon Basin is a high density of dairy cows, providing milk and other dairy products for the large urban area.

Fig. 5–13. Rice fields in the Rhone River Delta. This is a state farm, employing Spanish migrant labor. (G. G. Weigend.)

and on river terraces is an intensive cultivation of wheat, sugar beets, forage crops, some tobacco, and a great variety of fruit. The mulberry tree, which used to be significant for sericulture, has been on the decline.

Between Valence and Lyon the Rhone River clings to the slopes of the Massif Central, while from the left bank a hill land, the Bas Dauphiné, extends eastward. There, coarse gravels are covered with fertile, more recent alluvial and morainic deposits. In the

North of Lyon, where the recent alluvium of the Saône Valley is very fertile but in places poorly drained, meadows are used as common pasture after the grass has been cut; on the better-drained soils, wheat, sugar beets, and legumes are grown. Of great fame are some localized agricultural pursuits such as the Burgundy vineyards on the slopes of the Côte d'Or between Dijon and Chalon-sur-Saône as well as those farther south around Mâcon, the raising of poultry on the plain of Bresse, and truck farming in the Auxonne region.

8. THE HIGH MOUNTAINS. In the high mountains the agricultural economy is primarily pastoral. Nearly everywhere, depopulation of the higher areas has been accompanied by an extension and intensification of agriculture on lower slopes and valleys as well as in the forelands. Where the growing of rye, oats, and potatoes has been continued at high elevations, the yields are meager and not sufficient for subsistence. Thus, cropland gradually is giving way to meadow and pasture land where grass is cut for hay, and sheep and cattle graze in summer.

In the northern Alps and in the Jura, cow's milk is used for the production of many kinds of cheese, particularly the well-known Gruyère, or Swiss cheese, which is marketed everywhere in France. Throughout the Pyrenees, except in the westernmost section, sheep milk goes through the first stage in the cheese-production process, to be collected periodically for further processing in the Causses into Roquefort cheese. Adjacent to the Bay of Biscay, in the Basque areas, cattle, for milk and meat, and fruit and vegetable growing are emphasized to satisfy the demand for these products in summer when tourist trade is most active. On the Pyrenean slopes in the east, olives, vineyards, and chestnuts become important. Chestnut trees, however, have been on the decline everywhere because of a blight for which no control has yet been found. Experimentation with some foreign species not subject to the disease is in progress.

In both the Pyrenees and the Alps, valley floors and basins contain thick alluvial and glacial deposits whose fertile soils support a profitable livestock-and-crop-combination type of agriculture. Forests have maintained their traditional importance on the slopes all through the mountains except in the southern Alps where deforestation and depopulation have been particularly severe.

Agricultural production. Wheat remains the leading single crop of France in terms of

number of acres dedicated to it, in spite of the fact that the total wheat acreage has declined in the last few decades, especially since World War II. Gradually here, as in other parts of Western Europe, marginal lands have been converted to grassland or abandoned. This decline in acreage, however, was more than compensated for by an increased yield, so that the total production of wheat and other cereals rose significantly. The yield of wheat, for example, has risen from 23 bushels per acre in the years before World War II to 47 bushels in 1964, that of barley from 26½ bushels to 39, and that of corn from 27 bushels per acre to 38 bushels in 1964. These increases reflect the general improvement in French agricultural techniques, such as better seed selection and a considerable increase in the use of commercial fertilizers and lime. Total production of wheat and other cereals varies from year to year with climatic conditions. In 1965 wheat production reached an all-time high of nearly 14½ million metric tons, which was surpassed only by the United States, Canada, China, and the Soviet Union.[11]

Another characteristic of French agriculture has been the increasing importance of fodder crops which in their totality cover an area exceeding that devoted to wheat. Moreover, of all the cereals grown about one-half represents cattle feed. It has been estimated, in fact, that the total area used for the production of feed for animals is double the area used to grow products for human consumption, so animal husbandry has become the main focus of attention. In 1964, France was third in world production of meat, after the United States and the U.S.S.R.

France and Italy are the two leading world producers of wine.[12] A government-sponsored program to convert some of the vineyard areas to other crops has not been very successful. While the total acreage devoted to vineyards decreased somewhat since 1955, wine production has been lower only in

[11] For statistical data, see Appendix III.
[12] In 1965 France and Italy combined produced nearly one-half of the world's wine.

some years and there has been no evidence of a declining trend.

A line can be drawn roughly from the Loire estuary through Paris, the Reims area, and toward southern Luxembourg, to demarcate the northern limit of viticulture. The distinguished quality-wine production areas are those of the Garonne-Dordogne valleys in southwestern France, the Loire Valley in the west, the Champagne and Alsace regions in the north and northeast, and the Rhone-Saône corridor from Dijon to Avignon. The abundant vineyards of the Languedoc produce the largest quantities of ordinary table wine.

An interesting development has been the production of rice on the reclaimed lands of the Rhone River Delta and in the Languedoc. This crop has been so successful that since 1957 France has been producing between 100,000 and 135,000 tons annually. This has been sufficient for domestic use and even has permitted some export (Fig. 5–13).

Specialized horticulture has been on the increase in the Mediterranean region, the Rhone Valley, the valleys of the Garonne and the Loire rivers, the coast of the Breton peninsula, and the Paris area. However, in addition, large quantities of fresh vegetables and fruit are imported from North Africa, especially in winter and early spring. Efficient distribution systems radiating from the major ports have been developed so as to enable rapid delivery of the perishable products to all parts of France, mainly by truck.

Fisheries. In summer, the number of fishermen reaches 60,000. This figure is notably lower in the off-season, during the winter, when many fishermen seek employment in other occupations. In addition, some 20,000 to 25,000 people are employed in industries associated with fishing, such as canning, shipbuilding and ship repairing, refrigeration, and transport.

French fisheries are characterized by family-type ownership. About half the number of fishermen and vessels have home ports on the Atlantic coast between the western tip of Brittany and the Spanish border. The largest catch, however, is brought into ports on the Channel and North Sea. Boulogne, alone, by far the most important fishing port in France, accounts for more than one-third of the fresh fish catch. Of least importance in terms of number of fishermen and boats, as well as catch, is the Mediterranean coast. Most of the fishing vessels are small. With the number of sailing ships diminishing rapidly, the fishing fleet is becoming more and more motorized.

Fishing activities fall into three categories: The first, deep-sea fishing, involves a small number of trawlers—about twenty-five in all of France—covering long distances to fish for cod in North Atlantic fishing grounds, especially the Grand Banks of Newfoundland, including waters around the French islands of St. Pierre and Miquelon and around Greenland and Spitsbergen. Two ports, Bordeaux and Fécamp, account for about 80 per cent of the cod catch unloaded in France, and St.-Malo for another 10–12 per cent. Much of the catch is marketed dried or salted, but consumption of fresh cod has been increasing. Because the total catch exceeds home consumption, export of cod has been significant, the major markets being in Mediterranean Europe, Brazil, and the Caribbean. The second type, classified as "sea fishing," occurs in the open ocean and the Mediterranean, mostly beyond 50 miles from shore. Three-fourths of the fresh fish marketed in France are caught by vessels belonging to this category. The third type is called in France *pêche artisanale,* which includes fishing in coastal waters as well as from the shore line without fishing boats.

During World War II, the fishing fleet suffered very heavily. Some 60 per cent of the deep-sea fleet and 70 per cent of the sea-fishing fleet tonnage was destroyed. Postwar recovery was very slow, but the fleet is younger and much better equipped than it was before the war. Fish consumption per person in France is considerably below that of other maritime countries in northwestern Europe, such as Great Britain, Norway, and Sweden. This has been interpreted to mean that the national market is far from being saturated and that an expansion of fisheries can take place.

Industrial raw materials.

ENERGY RESOURCES. Consumption of energy in France did not change appreciably in the twenty-year period between 1929 and 1949; since then, however, total energy requirements have risen rapidly so that by 1966 consumption of energy had increased by more than 50 per cent over 1955. Consumption has exceeded energy production by far, and, therefore, France has been the biggest net importer of energy in Western Europe. Assurance of an adequate power supply has been a major problem in France's economic development.

In order to increase home production of various forms of energy, elaborate plans have been made and are being executed for more effective exploitation of domestic coal, gas, and waterpower, for discovery of more crude oil and gas, and for development of nuclear energy. A main handicap has been the peripheral location of the fuel reserves—coal in the north and northeast, crude oil and gas in the south and southwest, and waterpower in the south and southeast of France (Fig. 5–14).

COAL. Coal as a source of energy has been declining constantly. In 1966 only 38 per cent of all energy consumed in France was derived from coal. This amounted to 57 million metric tons, while French collieries in that year produced only 50.3 million metric tons. The deficit was made up by imports which have been costly in terms of foreign exchange. Before World War II the principal foreign suppliers of coal were Great Britain and Germany with smaller quantities coming from Belgium, the Netherlands, and Poland; in 1966, on the other hand, the chief suppliers were Germany, by far the most important, the United States, and the Soviet Union.

In spite of the need for more fuel, the French coal industry has not displayed much vitality. Thousands of miners have left the pits to seek jobs with better salaries under better working conditions; hence, a serious labor shortage exists. New miners are difficult to recruit, even through immigration, and it takes time to develop the necessary skills. On the other hand, many technical improvements have been made in existing mines, and in spite of the fact that coal is difficult to mine, except in Lorraine, output per man-shift underground in 1966 was 4,629 pounds, the second highest in Europe, after West Germany. If productivity is calculated by individual fields, the Lorraine coal field has reached an all-time high in Europe with 7,597 pounds per man-shift underground. New coal seams have been discovered, but the development of new pits is costly and time-consuming. It takes nearly ten years before maximum production can be reached. All in all, the coal industry has little flexibility, and increases in demand have been met, in the main, by increased use of petroleum products and hydroelectric power.

Unfortunately, much of the French coal is not good coking coal, making it necessary to import considerable amounts of coking coal and coke. France has tried to evolve new coking processes through which coke can be produced with types of coal available locally. For example, a new method of blending and coking Lorraine and Saar coal yields a soft, friable metallurgical coke, so Lorraine coal is increasing considerably its relative importance in the French economy.

The two principal coal fields are located in northern and northeastern France. About one-half of French coal production in 1966, 25.3 million metric tons—came from the *Bassin du Nord et du Pas-de-Calais*, located in a deep syncline along the northern slope of the Artois Ridge. The coal seams, an extension of the southern-Belgium field, are thin, displaced, and broken up by faulting into several basins. Thus, mining is difficult, especially by mechanical processes. The other field, contributing 31 per cent of total French coal production—15.5 million metric tons in 1966—is a continuation of the Saar coal field and is located in Lorraine east of

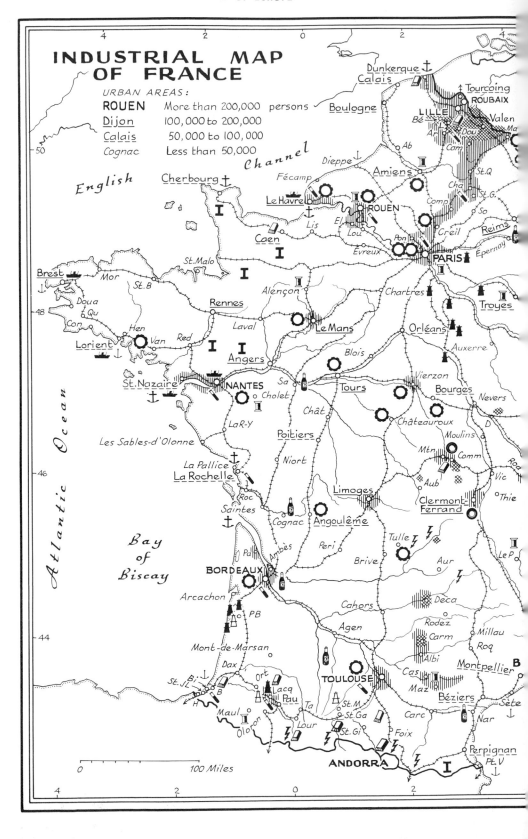

INDUSTRIAL MAP OF FRANCE

URBAN AREAS:

ROUEN More than 200,000 persons
Dijon 100,000 to 200,000
<u>Calais</u> 50,000 to 100,000
Cognac Less than 50,000

0   100 Miles

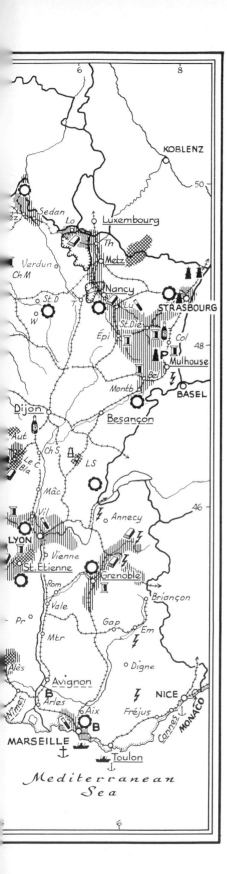

Fig. 5–14. Industrial map of France.

Legend:

- Main industrial area
- Main railroad line
- **P** Potash   **B** Bauxite
- Coal   Natural gas   Oil   Iron
- Primary metallurgy
- Shipbuilding
- Mechanical industries, engineering
- Textiles   Rubber
- Chemicals   Wine or brandy
- Port   Very important port
- Hydroelectric power

Metz, only 40 miles from the iron-ore fields. It is much easier to work than other French coal fields because the thickness of the coal seams facilitates the use of modern equipment. Although production from this field is smaller than from that of the north, the Lorraine contains more than half of the known coal reserves of France.

All other coal fields are secondary by comparison. Coal in the Massif Central was the earliest to be developed and to attract industries in the first half of the nineteenth century. For example, the St. Étienne field, at one time thought to be the best in France, attracted various metallurgical and mechanical industries, while the Blanzy-Le Creusot coal field was and still is utilized for high-quality-steel production by the great Schneider armament works. Only three of these fields are significant today, all situated along the eastern edge of the Massif near Blanzy-Le Creusot, St. Étienne, and Alès. The other smaller fields lie along a north-south line farther west in the Massif, a fault line extending from Décize and Commentry in the north to Décazeville and Carmaux in the south.

In recent years, new discoveries have been made. Of these, the most noteworthy is a small deep field at Lons-le-Saunier at the foot of the Jura Mountains. There may be several seams, and the probable reserves have been estimated at 260 million metric tons. Although it is anticipated that some coal will be sent to Lorraine, much of it, as that of other small fields, will be used locally for the generation of thermal electricity, the production of gas, etc.

Lignite has been only little used. Several deposits occur in the Provence, in southeastern France, and in the Landes south of Bordeaux. In 1966, total production in these areas amounted to 2.6 million metric tons.

France's coal reserves are not very great. The total proved and probable reserves amount to about 5.7 billion metric tons, which will be exhausted in 115 years at the 1966 rate of production. Even if possible reserves are included, this resource will be depleted in 150 years at most. Thus, development of alternative energy sources has been uppermost in the minds of French planners.

PETROLEUM AND NATURAL GAS. In 1966, some 50 per cent of the energy consumed in France was produced from petroleum and natural gas. Petroleum has claimed an ever-increasing share in France's energy balance; however, in 1966 more than 95 per cent of the required crude-oil tonnage had to be imported, chiefly from the Middle East and North Africa.

Prior to 1937, France made no concerted efforts to explore the home territory for petroleum and natural-gas resources. All crude oil and oil products were imported, except for about 60,000 metric tons produced at a small oil field at Péchelbronn in northern Alsace. Since 1937, however, organized exploration for oil and gas has been proceeding. In 1938, the Saint-Marcet gas field was discovered near St. Gaudens some 45 miles southwest of Toulouse, and in 1949 oil was struck at Lacq near Pau at the southern margin of the Aquitaine Basin. Since then, several productive oil fields have been discovered in the Landes, southwest of Bordeaux, in the southeastern quadrant of the Paris Basin, and in central and northern Alsace. A small gas field was found near Lons-le-Saunier in the Jura, and large fields of sulfurous gas at Lacq below the oil-bearing strata, at Pau, and in the Landes north of Parentis. Prospecting in the Bay of Biscay and the Gulf of Lion has been authorized.

The oil fields at Lacq and in Alsace are not significant in terms of quantity or quality. Annual production from these fields has been roughly 100,000 metric tons, and reserves are small. The first oil strike in the Landes was made in 1954 at Parentis-Lugos, and others followed. Estimates of total reserves were so encouraging that the Esso Standard Oil Company constructed a pipeline from Parentis to Bec d'Ambès at the confluence of the Garonne and Dordogne rivers, where a refinery was built in addition to the one already there. Discoveries in the

Paris Basin began in 1958 and were continuing in the middle 1960's. As a result of all these developments, crude oil production in France rose to about 3 million metric tons in 1966.

The possible gas reserves in the fields of southern France have been estimated to be as high as 800 billion cubic meters. A pipeline distribution network has been constructed, connecting the principal consumption centers of the southwest, Brittany, the Paris Basin, the northern and northeastern Massif Central, and the Lyon-Besançon region. The output of natural gas has risen from less than 100 million cubic meters in 1945 to some 8 billion cubic meters in 1966, and through recovery of sulfur from the Lacq gas, France has become the world's second largest producer of that mineral (1.4 million tons annually). Moreover, the Lacq region has attracted industry, such as a thermoelectric power plant using gas as fuel, an aluminum refinery, and chemical works. The new residential town of Mourenx was founded in 1957, and by the middle 1960's it had a population of some 15,000.

Another problem directly connected with production of crude oil and petroleum products had been the development of a large national refining capacity. Before 1930, there was no modern petroleum refinery in France. Since then, refineries have been put into operation in or near the major seaports, the largest ones in the environs of Le Havre and Marseille. A pipeline for refined products leads from the Le Havre region to Paris, and others are planned to connect the Marseille region with Lyon and Dijon in the Rhone-Saône corridor, St. Étienne, Grenoble and Geneva, as well as Strasbourg with the major cities in Lorraine. Moreover, the South European Pipeline carries crude oil from the Rhone estuary into Germany by way of the Belfort gateway, and two short pipelines for crude oil connect refineries in the interior with Nantes and Le Havre, respectively. In 1966 some 67 million metric tons of crude oil were refined in France, up from 25 million a decade earlier, and the refining capacity had increased in that period to more than 70 million metric tons.

HYDROELECTRIC POWER. Of the total electric power produced in France in 1966 (111 billion kwh) 47 per cent was generated by hydroelectric stations, representing some 12 per cent of all energy consumed. By 1966 France had 1,640 hydroelectric power plants with an installed capacity of 12.7 million KW, which was actually somewhat higher than the installed capacity of all the thermal power plants.

The great hydroelectric power sites are in the hilly and mountainous regions of the Alps, the Pyrenees, and the Massif Central, and in the valleys of the Rhone and Rhine rivers. By far the largest and most spectacular power plants are located in the Alps and in the Rhone Valley. The construction of the Génissiat Dam across the Rhone River, 30 miles from Lake Geneva, began in 1937 and was carried on even during World War II. In 1948 work was completed on the dam and power plant with a total installed capacity of 325,000 KW, and generation of power began in that year. Provisions were made for a bypass for inland shipping, which can be built should a Rhone-Rhine waterway connection through Switzerland materialize.

Along the middle Rhone, the Donzère-Mondragon project north of Avignon was begun after World War II, and power production was initiated in 1952. By the middle 1960's a series of dams had been completed which, together with the Génissiat installation, provided a total installed capacity of 2.5 million KW.

In the French Alps proper, streams have been utilized for power for electrochemical and electrometallurgical industries since the early part of this century. Planning for large-scale developments in this region has been proceeding since World War II and has revolved chiefly around the Isère and Durance watersheds. The development of the Durance River was nearing completion in the middle 1960's, with an annual production of 6.5 billion kwh as a target.

The major developments in the Pyrenees have taken place in the central section where they are highest. Hydroelectric power, natural gas, ready access to railroad transportation, plus an available labor supply from rural areas, have attracted electrochemical and electrometallurgical industries, such as those at Pierrefitte south of Lourdes and Lannemezan southeast of Tarbes.

Elsewhere, the most notable undertakings have been in the valleys of the Dordogne and Rhine Rivers. In the upper course of the Dordogne, seven dams are in operation having a total annual output of 2.2 billion kwh. The total developments in the Massif Central, however, amount to an annual production of 8 billion kwh. In the Rhine Valley the Grand Canal d'Alsace has been constructed, paralleling the Rhine River from Basel to Strasbourg. Seven power plants have an installed capacity of 1.2 million KW, producing annually some 7.2 billion kwh.

France has been developing the best sites first. By 1965 dam and power-plant construction at less suitable sites had begun, and, by 1975, 96 per cent of the waterpower resources will have been exploited.

ENERGY FROM NUCLEUS, TIDES, AND SUN. Uranium was first discovered in 1948 near Limoges. Subsequently other deposits were found in and near the Massif Central, and France increased its production from less than 100 metric tons of concentrated uranium in 1954 to some 1,600 tons in the middle 1960's, making the country the fourth most important producer in the western world.

The first generation of nuclear power began in 1956, and by the middle 1960's six reactors were in operation—three in Chinon near the confluence of the Loire and Vienne rivers, and three at Marcoule in the central Rhone valley. The net capacity of the former was 55,000 KW and of the latter 605,000 KW. France also has participated in the construction of a nuclear power plant at Chooz in the Ardennes, which is one of three generating plants being built under the Euratom program. The capacity of this reactor is 242,000 KW, which is divided equally between French and Belgian power grids. Finally, a reactor with an 80,000 KW generating capacity was to be completed and in operation by the middle 1960's in the Monts d'Arrée region of western Brittany.

For the first time in history the tides are being effectively utilized for the generation of electric power. A dam and power plant have been constructed in the Rance River, 2.5 miles upstream from St.-Malo and Dinard on the northern coast of Brittany. The Rance is a short stream, but the maximum difference between high and low tides can reach 44 feet, and the maximum flow 635,000 cubic feet per second. Power production began in 1966, and at capacity 540 million kwh are generated annually.

Larger projects contemplated for the utilization of strong tidal flows in the Bay of Mont-St.-Michel will probably not be carried out because of excessive cost and competition with other sources of energy, including nuclear energy.

Another experimental undertaking in progress involves several solar furnaces which have been constructed in the Pyrenees to determine whether direct energy from the sun can be harnessed successfully.

FERROUS AND NON-FERROUS MINERALS. France is fortunate in having been endowed with an abundance of iron ore, bauxite, and potash. She is less fortunate with other minerals, and much must be imported.

Exclusive of the Soviet Union, France has the largest iron-ore reserves of Europe, some 35 per cent of the total. This means some 6.56 billion metric tons of measured, indicated, and inferred ore, containing approximately 2.309 billion metric tons of iron. The bulk of it is minette ore, located in the Lorraine region roughly between Nancy in the south and Longwy in the north. Iron-bearing seams outcrop all along the west slopes of the Moselle Valley, where they have been exposed to fluvial erosion. The seams dip gently toward the west and south beneath the Brie Plateau. They are relatively undisturbed over large areas, in spite of faulting which has taken place in the geologic past. Thus, modern mechanized methods can be employed with ease at the surface as well as underground. The ore varies in iron content between 32 and 40 per cent, and may be either predominantly calcareous or silicious. Until the latter part of the nineteenth century, the high phosphorus content had precluded its exploitation in the modern iron and steel industry. In 1878, however, the Thomas-Gilchrist process was introduced for the removal of phosphorus from the metal. Mills in Lorraine began to employ the process only one year later, and early in the twentieth century the minette region had become one of the principal suppliers of pig iron and steel in Western Europe. More than 90 per cent of the total French iron-ore output of 55.7 million metric tons in 1966 was Lorraine ore. Mining methods are so efficient that in spite of the leanness of the ore it can be delivered at competitive prices in the industrial regions of northern France and western Belgium.

Other iron-ore deposits occur in Normandy south of Caen, in Anjou and southeastern Brittany, and in small scattered areas in the Massif Central and the Pyrenees. The Normandy ores are richer than those of Lorraine, having an iron content of 45–46 per cent. Reserves are considerable, nearly 1.4 billion metric tons, but only one bed is exploitable under present conditions. The Anjou-Brittany ores contain 48–52 per cent iron; they are chiefly magnetites, difficult to reduce.

There are ample bauxite reserves in southern and southeastern France, the extent of which has been estimated variously from 200 million metric tons in the mid-1940's to 68 million tons in recent years. Eighty per cent of the deposits are found in two *départements*—Var, in the Provence, and Hérault, in the Languedoc. The mines are located in western Var (northeast of Marseille) and west of the Rhone Delta. The remaining deposits are in Bouches-du-Rhône where

bauxite was first discovered; in the vicinity of the medieval, now nearly depopulated town of Les Baux, six miles northeast of Arles; and in the *département* Ariège in the Pyrenees southeast of Toulouse. Before World War II, France had been the leading world producer of bauxite, but in 1966 she occupied fourth place, with the lead taken over by Caribbean producers and the Soviet Union. Moreover, while world production during that period increased ninefold, France lagged behind with a fourfold increase.

France possesses the fourth-largest potash deposits in Europe, after the Soviet Union, Germany, and Spain—some 400 million metric tons. The mines are located in southern Alsace near Mulhouse. France ranks fourth in the world production of potash, following the United States, the Soviet Union, and West Germany, with a total of some 2 million metric tons of potash content in the latter 1960's. In view of the vital importance of potash in the manufacture of fertilizers for agriculture, special efforts have been made since World War II to modernize the mines and increase their production.

A few other mineral resources have some importance as, for example, the rock-salt deposits in the Luneville area in Lorraine, which form the basis for a local salt-refining and chemical industry. Also, there are widely scattered lead and zinc deposits in the Pyrenees, the Massif Central, Brittany, the Alps, and Corsica. The deposits are small, yielding only a fraction of the domestic requirements, but they are significant in times of crisis.

Manufacturing. About 30 per cent of France's active population in the middle 1960's was engaged in manufacturing. About 30 per cent of these were employed in the iron, steel, and metal-working industries. The Lorraine since before World War I has been a major contributor of iron and steel to the French economy: in 1966 some 62 per cent of total steel and more than 70 per cent of total pig-iron production. This region is, therefore, recognized as the single most important center for such manufacturing.

The Lorraine has not always held this dominant position. When charcoal was used as fuel, iron works were scattered widely on the basis of availability of ore and charcoal and of proximity to markets. After the introduction of coke as a fuel in about 1820, there occurred a gradual concentration of iron and steel manufacturing on coal fields, first in the Massif Central and then in the Nord-Pas-de-Calais region. When the Thomas-Gilchrist process made possible the use of minette iron ore in the Lorraine, that region gained momentum in spite of such drawbacks as its peripheral location in relation to its major markets, the absence of suitable low-cost water transport, and the lack of good coking coal.

The Lorraine iron and steel plants are grouped in three areas. Outstanding among these is the Metz-Thionville complex in the Moselle Valley. The mills there contribute about three-fifths of the Lorraine iron and steel output, and, in view of recent developments, chances for greater industrial expansion within this area have been enhanced considerably. It has already been pointed out that technological advances have made it possible to produce coke from Lorraine coal, only a short distance away. Moreover, the canalization of the Moselle River from Thionville (later extended toward Nancy) to Koblenz on the Rhine River was completed in 1964. As a result, transport costs have been lowered considerably for coking coal moving in, as well as for iron, steel, and metal products being marketed abroad.

The second area is the Longwy-Villerupt area near the Belgium-Luxembourg border, often referred to as the Northern District. This area produces a scant one-third of Lorraine's iron and steel. It is closest in land distance to the northern coal fields of west and central Europe, but there is no waterway system, a situation which has become crucial from the competitive standpoint since the completion of the Moselle Canal.

The remainder of the iron and steel output in Lorraine comes from the Nancy region, which finds itself at a disadvantage relative to the other two and is not likely to expand its basic industries. The region is farther from coking coal and good iron-ore deposits. The iron ore is not self-fluxing like that of the other areas, so limestone or calcareous ore has to be shipped in. Although the city of Nancy is a focal point for inland waterways, they are insufficient for present-day traffic.

The interdependence of Lorraine iron ore and Ruhr coal has been much overemphasized in past literature. Pounds pointed out [13] that in the past the Lorraine industrial region has obtained up to two-thirds of its fuel supply from the Ruhr, and that it could have absorbed even more. On the other hand, the Ruhr industrial region has been geared to higher-grade foreign ores, so that imports of minette ore have never exceeded 20 per cent of the total needed—and, in fact, imports from Lorraine have been much less than that for over a half century.

It is further significant that the French Industrial North and the Paris region are the best markets for Lorraine steel products. The Lorraine itself, and industries between the Lorraine and the North, also consume a considerable share. This again emphasizes the imbalance which exists in France between the high concentration of manufacturing in a few areas and the relative underdevelopment of the rest.

As production centers of iron and steel, the Industrial North and the Massif Central are relegated to second and third place, although industries there were founded earlier than in Lorraine. Contributions of the North have been increasing in the last decade. In 1966 this region produced some 22 per cent of France's pig iron and 27 per cent of her steel. It benefits from a good supply of scrap from the numerous local engineering indus-

[13] Norman J. G. Pounds, "Lorraine and the Ruhr," *Economic Geography* 33 (April, 1957): 149–62.

tries, so the steel produced here is of higher quality than Lorraine steel. Iron, steel, and engineering industries are centered in the Valenciennes and Douai regions, and the Sambre Valley southeast of Valenciennes. Production in the Massif Central, on the other hand, is quite specialized. High-grade alloy steels are produced primarily for the manufacture of armaments. Industries cluster around coal fields, notably at St. Étienne and Le Creusot. A more recent trend in France, as in Europe, has been the creation of large integrated steel works in coastal locations. One such complex in Dunkerque began operation in 1963 and was to have a steel production potential of 1.5 million metric tons by the middle of the 1960's. Additional coastal installations are planned at Marseille and possibly at other locations. In 1966, France ranked sixth as a world steel producer, with 19.6 million metric tons.

In the category of light engineering industries, the manufacture of automobiles has been one of the most active and rapidly growing enterprises. In the 1960's France's production lines have been turning out 1.5–1.7 million units annually, 82–86 per cent of them passenger cars. Export of cars has become a vital factor in the French economy. Production is centered largely in the Paris region, where labor is abundant, cars are most easily marketed, and excellent land and inland-waterway transport is at hand.

Among other metallurgical industries the production of alumina and aluminum stands out significantly. The original process for the manufacture of aluminum was developed in France in the middle of the nineteenth century. Production first began in northern centers, including Paris, and later moved to Salindres near Alès in the Languedoc. The introduction of the electrolytic process in 1889 relocated the primary industry toward hydroelectric-power sites in the Alps and the central Pyrenees. There are now two companies which obtain bauxite from their own mines, produce alumina and aluminum, and have their own marketing outlets. In the

middle 1960's, France produced 340,000 metric tons of aluminum, the highest output in Europe and the third largest in the world. Refineries for other metals, such as lead and zinc, are located either in the major ports, because nearly all the ores are imported, or in the vicinity of coal fields, chiefly in the Industrial North.

The chemical industry in France is relatively young but has made great strides, especially since World War II. Between the two world wars, chemical production was associated almost exclusively with coal, hydroelectric power, and imported phosphates and pyrites. Plants had grown up chiefly around coal fields, for the manufacture of coal distillates, or in ports, for the production of chemical fertilizers from imported raw materials. Electrochemical works were located in the Alps and Pyrenees where hydroelectric power is available.

Although the same basic distribution exists today, new types of chemical industries have been added. As already stated, sulfur is being produced from natural gas at Lacq. Other chemical plants, primarily for plastics, have been added to the array of chemical industries at coal fields, and have also been located near petroleum refineries to utilize their by-products.

The textile industry has a long tradition in France and, at one time, was widely scattered in many small regional centers of production. Since the conversion to modern factory-type manufacturing, however, the textile industry has concentrated more and more in four principal regions. The industry, which employs some 530,000 workers, produced about 1.3 million tons of textiles of all kinds in the middle 1960's.

The largest concentration of textile manufacturing is in the Industrial North, which has the heritage of Flanders. The character of the textiles made in this area is diverse— wool, linen, cotton, jute, and synthetic fibers —although a certain amount of specialization exists within the area. Lille, for example, has the bulk of French linen manufacturing, while cotton and wool processing focus on Roubaix and Tourcoing. Family ownership prevails. This means that the majority of enterprises are small in size, specializing in one type of operation and, since World War II, unable to withstand national and international competition without far-reaching governmental protective measures. Textile raw materials are imported from all parts of the world through Antwerp, Dunkerque, and Le Havre. Although the proximity of coal facilitated the factory-type development, it was not a major factor, inasmuch as the regional concentration had already taken place before coal was used. More significant were the presence of initiative, skilled labor, and well-established merchant houses which had commercial connections throughout the world.

In Normandy, the textile industry centers around Rouen, and consists primarily of cotton spinning and weaving. Practically all cotton used in France is imported through Le Havre, which operates a cotton exchange. Another cotton-processing area is in eastern France, particularly in the valleys of the Vosges Mountains and in the Alsatian Plain. Availability of soft water and rural labor were prime factors in establishing the industry there, as were proximity of Swiss capital and technical knowledge. Moreover, southern Alsace is well located with respect to transport and communication through the Belfort gateway, into Switzerland and Germany. The earliest industry was fabric printing, a specialization which is still prominent. Cotton processing developed in the nineteenth century, and between 1871 and World War I, while Alsace was part of Germany, it spread to the eastern and southern slopes of the Vosges, the Épinal and Belfort regions, respectively.

The fourth major region is the Lyon area where most of the manufacturing of silk, artificial, and synthetic fibers is pursued. The rearing of silkworms, which had been introduced into Mediterranean France in the fifteenth century and spread north into the Rhone Valley, has all but disappeared; most of the silk is imported from China and Japan. Capital and initiative of Lyon merchants, available rural labor, nearby water and waterpower, were factors in the concentration of the industry in this particular area. The cycles of fashion have meant long periods of alternating depression and prosperity in the silk industry, and the invention of artificial and synthetic fibers has presented a serious challenge. Some existing textile mills have been converted and new plants built, designed especially for the manufacture of the new fibers and their fabrication.

Closely linked with the textile industry is the production of many specialized items which have brought renown to certain cities and towns, such as the manufacture of lace in Le Puy, Alençon, and Valenciennes, of velvet in Amiens, and of ribbons in St. Étienne. Of far-reaching effect, however, has been the garment industry in general, which provides employment for some 600,000 to 700,000 persons, many more women than men. This industry is scattered widely throughout France, but the focus, of course, is on Paris, which provides world leadership in fashion design.

A myriad of other manufacturing industries could be named, too numerous for analysis here, ranging from shipbuilding in the chief ports to the manufacture of china in Limoges and watches in the Jura Mountains.

To recapitulate, it might be helpful to outline briefly the main industrial regions.

1. THE INDUSTRIAL NORTH encompasses a great variety of manufacturing, including iron and steel, chemicals, textiles, glass, and products of the engineering and food industries. This area is contiguous to Belgium and is part of the European industrial belt which extends discontinuously from the British Isles to the Soviet Union. There are local coal supplies and good communications with the sea and with the rest of France and Western Europe, as well as with Central Europe. Accompanying these advantages are a large skilled-labor pool, the old Flemish tradition,

and a vigorous group of industrialists and merchants.

2. ALSACE-LORRAINE's industrial structure is less balanced than that of the Industrial North. The iron and steel industry of Lorraine, the textile industry, particularly cotton processing, of the Vosges and Alsace, dominate the industrial scene. Local resources which aided industrial development have been Lorraine iron ore and coal, plentiful water and waterpower, good transport connections within France as well as with neighbors to the south and east, and an available supply of rural labor. In progress are improvements of inland waterways, more intensive development of hydroelectric power, and a greater diversification of industry than now exists, which, if they materialize, will provide a great degree of economic stability.

3. THE CENTRAL INDUSTRIAL REGION has Lyon as its principal focus. From there, industries extend in all directions—along the Rhone-Saône corridor into valleys of the Alps, to St. Étienne and valleys of the northern Massif Central. Here metallurgical, chemical, and textile industries are the prominent ones, utilizing local coal supplies, water, and waterpower, and drawing labor from rural areas.

4. THE PARIS AREA has no raw materials and no local power resources, yet it has become France's paramount manufacturing region. Paris—the hub of transport; the seat of government and administration; the center of commerce, finance, and culture; and the site of a large number of small handicraft factories—has become a large labor pool and market area as well. The *département* of Seine alone contains more than one-fourth of France's working population. Nearly all types of manufacturing are represented here in numerous workshops and small factories, as well as in some large plants. Outstanding are the engineering industries, including the manufacture of automobiles. Of greatest renown, however, is the function of the city as a fashion center, with all its associated luxury industries.

All raw materials must be imported from within or outside of France. This is facilitated by easy land and water transport routes which converge upon the city from all directions. Moreover, in addition to thermoelectric power produced locally, Paris obtains hydroelectric power from generating stations in the Massif Central.

5. There are many secondary industrial centers in and near ocean ports, in other major cities, and near sources of energy not included in the industrial areas above.

Communication and trade. France has developed a dense network of railroads and highways. Paris is the principal focus of both networks to such an extent that it may be difficult to travel from one peripheral area to another without passing through the capital.

In the last decade the total tonnage of freight hauled by railroads has not changed substantially. However, the relative status of the railroads has deteriorated since most of the increase in freight movements has been absorbed by highways and inland waterways. While a decade ago French railroads carried about 70 per cent of all freight hauled in France for distances of more than 30 miles, in the middle 1960's they carried only some 45 per cent.

The major project since World War II has been electrification. Some lines had been electrified between the two world wars, as, for example, the lines Toulouse-Dax-Bayonne and Bordeaux-Hendaye on the Spanish border, completed in the late 1920's. Power was available from nearby generating stations, and passage through the Landes forest of coal-burning engines, which were fire hazards, could be eliminated. With renewed efforts after World War II, the lines carrying the heaviest traffic have had priority and, by 1965, nearly 22 per cent of the track mileage had been electrified.

Freight tonnage carried on the highways has doubled in the last decade, and pas-

senger car traffic increased enormously, yet
construction of new highways more suitable
for mass transportation has made comparatively slow progress. Although the French
highway network is the densest in the world,
it is outdated and not suited to the rapidly
growing vehicular traffic. A program to
widen existing highways and to construct
new express highways has been begun. One
of the most notable projects was the construction of a 7½ mile long tunnel through
Mont Blanc which provides an all-weather
route through the Alps between Italy and
France. The entrance in France is at an elevation of 3,947 feet and that in Italy at 4,528
feet, both sufficiently low for keeping roads
passable at all times.

France has some 4,800 miles of navigable
inland waterways and canals. The network
is densest in the northeastern part of the
country. Nearly all inland navigation takes
place within an area delineated by a line
from Le Havre to Dunkerque, Strasbourg,
Lyon, and back to Le Havre. About 80–90
million metric tons of cargo are carried annually, which is more than one-third of the
tonnage carried by railroads. Nearly all
cargo is bulk, such as coal, petroleum products, and construction materials. The Seine
River is the most used waterway and the
Paris region, with some 23 million tons of
cargo in the middle 1960's, had the greatest
traffic concentration. Strasbourg, however,
was the largest inland shipping port, handling more than 9.5 million metric tons.
Strasbourg's position was achieved by virtue
of its location on the Rhine River and not because of inland-waterway connections with
the rest of France. Such products as potash
from southern Alsace and manufactured
goods from Lorraine arrive by railroad which
gives the port the best service with its hinterland. The main drawback of the inland-
waterway system has been that most of it was
constructed in the nineteenth century, which
means that for modern barge traffic the
canals are too narrow and have too many
locks. Moreover, the canals are operated on
an inadequate budget and are poorly main-

tained. An important agreement made between France and Germany in 1956 in conjunction with the Saar treaty provided for
canalization of the Moselle River between Thionville and Koblenz. In a separate
treaty with Luxembourg, France agreed to
aid that country in the building of certain
port installations on the new canal and in
electrification of the Luxembourg railroad
system. The canal was completed in 1964
and can accommodate 1,500-ton barges.
Canalization has been achieved by construction of 14 dams, including one at Koblenz
built by Germany during World War II.
For France, and specifically for the Lorraine
manufacturing area, realization of the canal
has meant greatly reduced transport charges
to and from Germany and ocean ports. The
canal has been extended to Metz and construction farther south toward Nancy is in
progress. Germany, on the other hand, has
gained hydroelectric power because nine of
the ten power houses built are located in
Germany between Trier and Koblenz, and
the tenth one on the border of Germany and
Luxembourg.

The development of the Rhone River has
so far been mainly for generation of hydroelectric power and for irrigation. A scheme
has been proposed for improvement of existing inland navigation and for an extension of
the waterway to Geneva, from whence a connection with the Rhine River could be made.
As yet, this project is visionary. Other more
realistic plans call for the construction of an
effective linkage between the Saône and
Rhine Rivers by way of the Gate of Belfort,
and between the Saône and Moselle Rivers.
All these plans would enlarge the hinterland
of Marseille and put that port in direct competition with Dutch and German seaports.

French airlines service nearly all parts of
the world. Air France is the largest airline
on the continent. Again, Paris is the undisputed leader, with some 58 per cent of all
passenger departures and arrivals in French
airports in the middle 1960's.

The French merchant marine in 1966
ranked tenth in the world; 46 per cent of its

ships were tankers. War destruction had been heavy, so France's fleet is one of the most modern in the world. French ships carried about one-half of France's total overseas exports and imports. Marseille and its associated ports handled by far the largest tonnage, 62.4 million metric tons in 1966. Le Havre was second, with 29.4 million tons, but, in combination with Rouen, a total of more than 41 million tons of sea cargo were handled on the lower Seine River. Other important seaports are, in order: Dunkerque, Nantes-St. Nazaire, Bordeaux, and Sète.

France's foreign trade has been imbalanced for decades. Imports by value exceeded exports by an average of 20 per cent from 1878 to the late 1950's, but since then a distinct improvement has taken place. In fact, for three years (1959–1961) exports exceeded imports in value, but since 1961 another reversal has occurred and imports have been from one to six per cent above the value of exports. The deficit has been covered by invisible imports of foreign exchange through tourist trade, offshore purchases, transport services, insurance, etc., as well as by direct financial aid. France must import industrial raw materials, including ores, metals, and textile fibers, as well as crude oil, coal, and tropical and subtropical foods. The upswing in French manufacturing has resulted in a precipitous increase of these imports.

In recent years, nearly half of France's exports by value have been bulk goods and semi-manufactured products, chiefly of the iron and steel industry. For example, Lorraine iron ores have been shipped to Belgium and semi-finished materials to Germany, Benelux, and the United Kingdom. Only some 45 per cent of the exports have been finished products which, from the standpoint of economic well-being, should be at the top of the list. Included are machines and machine parts, textiles and clothing, chemical products, and automobiles. The marketing of automobiles (especially Renaults) in the United States and other countries has been of particular importance. Among other ex-

ports, food products, and especially cereals, have assumed an ever-increasing importance, indicating again the great improvements which are being achieved in the agricultural sector of the economy.

As a result of the creation of the European Economic Community, France's foreign trade has undergone a re-orientation. While trade with the Franc Zone remained at about the same level throughout the 1960's, trade with Europe, and especially European Economic Community partners, intensified. Algeria has remained the principal partner in the Franc Zone, the Federal Republic of Germany, Belgium-Luxembourg, and Italy in Europe.

The French Community

In order to grasp the full significance of France as a world power, brief mention must be made of her areas of influence outside Europe. Many changes have taken place since World War II in parts of the world where France at one time was the colonial ruler. Nations in southeast Asia, formerly under French political control, have gained complete independence and statehood and, in 1958, an entirely new system was evolved regarding the relationship to France of all remaining overseas territories. Under the new constitution confirmed by all territories except Guinea, a French Community was created—a federal system of autonomous states, nearly all of them in Africa. At that time, the cumulative areas of the Community, except for France proper, was about 3.8 million square miles, nearly 18 times the area of France and about the same total area as the 50 states of the United States. The total population occupying this area was about 41 million, nearly as high as the population of France.

Since then, some members of the Community have formed economic unions and others have become independent states. In contrast to the British Commonwealth, many parts of which were settled by English-speaking people, the population in the French Community is composed almost entirely of natives.

THE BENELUX COUNTRIES

Belgium, the Netherlands, and Luxembourg—the Benelux countries—occupy an area of about 25,300 square miles, equivalent to 12 per cent of the area of France or half the area of North Carolina. The Netherlands accounts for about 50 per cent of the total area, and Belgium 45 per cent. Commerce, the *raison d'être* since the time of the Middle Ages in the Low Countries, has provided a mutual if competitive interest over the centuries. Thriving trade relations have grown from the unique location of Belgium and the Netherlands astride the deltas of the Rhine, Meuse, and Scheldt rivers. The Rhine River provides easy access to Central Europe, and the North European Lowland makes these two countries corridor lands between Central Europe and France, and thence to Mediterranean lands. The United Kingdom lies only 21 miles away at the narrowest part of the English Channel. Altogether, site and situation of the Low Countries is such that circulation of goods and people developed freely and effectively, making trade the basis of all economic activity. Only in periods when man interfered with this process did temporary economic stagnation result. Even Luxembourg has had the same *raison d'être* since the end of the nineteenth century, when, through utilization of its iron-ore reserves, it became a manufacturing state dependent on foreign trade for a higher standard of living.

The People

In 1966, the Benelux countries had reached a total population figure of about 22.2 million, of whom a little more than half were Dutch and some 9.5 million were Belgians. Thus there is a fairly close correlation between percentage of area and population among these three countries. Beyond that, however, an examination of population structure and growth since World War I brings to light very important differences.

In the eighteenth century and before World War I, population growth in the Netherlands and Belgium proceeded at approximately the same rate, so the population of the Netherlands, on the average, was consistently about 1.5 million below that of Belgium.[14] Luxembourg's population, in contrast, grew more slowly than that of the other two countries. By World War I it had increased by only 50 per cent since 1840, while that of the Netherlands and Belgium had doubled.

Population Growth of Benelux Countries * (thousand)

Country	1840	Pre-World War I	1966
Belgium	4,300	7,450	9,528
Netherlands	2,900	6,000	12,455
Luxembourg	172	261	335

* Estimates from statistical yearbooks.

World War I marks an important turning point. Population growth in the Netherlands accelerated, while that in Belgium began to slow down to such a degree that by 1933 the total population in each of the two countries was the same—about 8,200,000. Since then, the Netherlands has continued to outdistance Belgium, despite the facts that until 1960 emigration from the Netherlands has exceeded immigration (except in 1958 when 23,000 persons emigrated but 35,000 were repatriated from Indonesia) and that to Belgium in the first 6½ decades of this century more than 500,000 people were added as a result of an excess of immigration over emigration.

The principal reason behind the shift in population growth has been the differing birth rate–death rate balance in the two countries. While between 1900 and 1966 the Netherlands had a surplus of 7.5 million births over deaths, Belgium's surplus was only 2.5 million. In the 1960's, the Netherlands has had the highest birth rate in northwestern Europe, except for Ireland and Ice-

[14] T. Van den Brink, "Structure et Évolution Démographique dans les Pays de Benelux," *Benelux Kwartaalbericht,* Bull. Trimestriel 2 (1958): 1–11.

land, and one of the lowest death rates. In Luxembourg the birth rate has been somewhat below and the death rate about the same as that of Belgium, so the net increase in population there was the slowest among the three Benelux countries.

A rapid population growth has given the Netherlands some of the highest population densities in Europe and in the world. In South Holland, which includes The Hague and Rotterdam, the density is 2,600 per square mile, and in North Holland, where Amsterdam and Haarlem are located, it is more than 2,100. In Belgium, only three provinces reach densities of more than 1,000 per square mile—Brabant (including Brussels), Antwerp, and East Flanders (including Ghent)—but none approaches the high Dutch densities. Combining the density pattern in both countries, one nearly continuous belt of dense population emerges. It extends from North Holland between the North Sea and the IJssel Lake, southward, skirting the delta area toward Brussels, and thence northwestward into East Flanders. The only gap appears in the Campine in Antwerp province. A second belt of dense population extends from the southern section of Dutch Limburg southwestward along the Sambre-Meuse-Vesdre corridor to the French border.

The transition from high to low population densities is sharp in some areas, such as south of the Sambre-Meuse corridor. The sparsest populated sections of Benelux are in the Ardennes of Belgium and Luxembourg. Other areas of relatively low population density are Zeeland—the province occupying the Rhine-Meuse-Scheldt delta region—and the poorly drained sections of the northeastern Netherlands.

The Netherlands and Belgium are highly urbanized. While Belgium has the most populous city—Brussels and suburbs, with more than 1 million people—the Netherlands has many more large urban agglomerations. There are ten cities in Belgium with a total population of more than 50,000 each, while in the Netherlands there are 38. In Luxembourg the capital city, with a population of

80,000, is the only one falling into that category. It is difficult, in fact, to differentiate between urban and rural population in Belgium. The two are interwoven to a considerable degree, and commuting between places of residence and work is very common. Many workers, especially among the Flemish, are also part-time farmers who have been reluctant to leave their inherited property, for reasons of security as well as family tradition. The combination of housing shortages near the places of work and excellent transportation facilities has encouraged commuting to such a degree that, according to estimates, as much as 40 per cent of Belgium's active population may work outside their places of residence.

The Benelux nations. In Benelux, sharp cultural divides can be found. The most significant is the Walloon-Flemish language divide in Belgium which follows an approximate east-west line through a point just south of Brussels. The capital itself, and the province of Brabant in which it is located, are considered bilingual. To the north and east of the divide the languages are Germanic— Flemish and German in Belgium; Dutch, Frisian, and German in the Netherlands. To the south, Walloon is spoken—a French dialect which has never become a literary language.

The Walloons, occupying interior southern Belgium, did not share in the maritime activity of the Flemish and Dutch. They were not so much affected by the Reformation and Counter Reformation, and came under closer cultural influence from adjacent French-speaking areas. Historically, the Walloons have been the controlling ethnic group in Belgium, through their economic and political predominance, particularly in the early development of modern industry. Although French or Flemish was spoken locally, French had become the official language under Spanish rule, and its continued use as such produced a profound cleavage between those people speaking one or the other language. Only after long and often bitter struggles were both French and Flemish recognized as the official languages of Belgium.

Uneasiness persists and the cleavage is as yet unresolved. The maintenance of an equilibrium between the Flemish and Walloon populations has been one of the motivations in Belgian economic and political thinking. Of concern to the Walloons has been the rapid growth of Flemish population and a corresponding decline in Walloon areas. While in 1896 only some 30 per cent of Belgium's population was Flemish, and 60 per cent Walloon, by the middle 1960's some 55 per cent of the population was Flemish and only 33 per cent was Walloon. The number of people speaking both languages was 11 per cent of the population, most residing in Brabant province. Thus, by the middle of the twentieth century the Flemish-speaking population had gained numerical superiority.

A further difficulty has been the gradual loss of economic superiority of the Walloon sector. While Belgian industry at first was located in the southern coal fields, the newer industrial and mining developments have been in the Flemish sections—in the Campine and in Antwerp—as well as in bilingual Brussels. In general, however, the world wars have done much to reconcile the two factions and to promote a Belgian national feeling and a spirit of partnership.

The religious wars of the Reformation forced the separation of the Netherlands from the territory which was to become Belgium much later. The Calvinist section known as the Netherlands was able to throw off the foreign yoke and to establish an independent state, while the south remained Roman Catholic and under the rule of the Hapsburgs. As a result of this separation, a sharp divide soon manifested itself, which deepened and became formidable when the Dutch throttled Antwerp by closing the Scheldt estuary from 1648 until 1795. The political separation, therefore, originally resulting from religious differences, was an important factor in the creation of two different nations. The boundary between the two states no longer represents a religious one. While Belgium remains almost solidly Catholic, less than half of the Dutch are Protestant and close to 40 per cent are Roman Catholic. Thus, religion as a factor of national consciousness has waned.

With respect to the degree of integration of the various factors contributing to a feeling of "nationality," Belgium faces problems, chiefly of ethnic origin, with which neither of the other two Benelux countries has had to contend. In the Netherlands, such ties as the traditional importance of religion and the religious wars, one principal language, the long common memories of struggles against the sea, centuries of commercial wealth, and a political association of 300 years have all welded a nation corresponding closely with the territorial area of the state. Luxembourg, a remnant of a larger duchy, has never been united politically with any other state. It is a solidly Catholic country. The language spoken has been chiefly Luxembourgeois—a Germanic dialect which has been evolving into a literary language—since the French-speaking sections were incorporated into Belgium in 1839. However, many people are bilingual, and both Luxembourgeois and French are official languages. Culturally, the people of Luxembourg have been oriented toward France, despite the country's long economic association with Germany as a member of the *Zollverein*. Thus, in the middle of the 1960's the Luxembourgers are a nation speaking a Germanic language and having strong cultural ties with France, while at the same time linked to a customs union with Belgium, the Netherlands, and to the European Economic Community, as well as to other international organizations.

The Present Economic Life of Benelux

The idea of an economic union among the three Benelux countries was conceived in London during World War II by the three governments-in-exile. Steps toward effective union were begun on January 1, 1948, with the adoption of a common tariff. A series of further steps culminated in a treaty which was signed by the three countries in 1958, by which a full economic union was established for a period of 50 years.

This union was achieved in spite of economic competition and in the face of grave initial differences between the Netherlands and the other two states over money, wages, trade balance, etc. The great desire for an increasing economic security outweighed all other considerations, and seemingly insurmountable difficulties had been overcome by the 1960's.

Economic pursuits in all three countries are parallel and, to some extent, competitive. However, Belgium has the lowest percentage of its active population in manufacturing, 34 per cent as against 42 per cent in the Netherlands and 46 per cent in Luxembourg. In agriculture, too, Belgium has the lowest percentage of its active population, having declined from nearly one-third of the working population in 1920 to only 5 per cent in 1966. The principal reason for this decline has been an exodus from rural areas in the Ardennes into the mining and industrial regions of the Belgian gate. In comparison, 8½ per cent of the Dutch and 13 per cent of the Luxembourg working populations are engaged in agriculture.

Agriculture. Agriculture is still of great significance in all three Benelux countries. For home consumption, they all produce sufficient amounts of meat, dairy products, and vegetables. In addition, the Netherlands is geared to export agricultural goods, especially vegetables and dairy and horticultural products.

The size of farms differs considerably. They are smallest in Belgium, where there are 269,000 holdings, of which more than one-fourth are smaller than 2½ acres, and one-half less than 7½ acres. Thus, while Belgium has about 28 per cent less farm land than the Netherlands it has 53 per cent more farm enterprises. If all farms are included in the calculation, the average-size farm in

Belgium is only 6 acres as against 13 acres in the Netherlands.

Luxembourg has the largest farms. Only 18 per cent of the total number have an area of less than 5 acres; among the other 82 per cent, the average-size farm is 36 acres, with at least half of them having an area between 12½ and 50 acres.

Of the three Benelux countries, the Netherlands uses more of its total area as farm land than Belgium or Luxembourg—some 68 per cent. However, only 40 per cent of the Dutch farm land is actually used for crops, with the remainder utilized chiefly as permanent meadow and pasture. Belgium and Luxembourg both have considerable areas in the forested Ardennes, so only 55 per cent of the total area is farm land in Belgium and 53 per cent in Luxembourg. About half of the farm land in these two countries is given over to crops. However, in all three Benelux countries a considerable proportion of the crops harvested is consumed by livestock, so that, as in France, animal husbandry emerges as the mainstay of the agricultural economy. Cattle are raised for the production of both dairy products and meat, except in the Netherlands, where meat production assumes a secondary role.

In terms of area devoted to individual crops and of total production of each, wheat and barley are the chief small grains in Belgium and the Netherlands, wheat and oats in Luxembourg. In general, oats and rye have declined in importance in the last decade, but they still occupy significant acreages, especially in the Netherlands. This indicates a heavier emphasis on crops for livestock in the Netherlands than in the other two countries, mainly because of the importance of export of dairy products in the Dutch economy. The acreage in sugar beets has been increasing since World War II, so as to meet the home demand for sugar. Yields in the Low Countries are the highest in the world for the principal grains, yet needs are so great that large quantities must be imported to complement domestic production. Wheat yields are 64 and 56 bushels per acre, respectively, in the Netherlands and Belgium, as against 15 to 20 bushels in the United States. Oats yields are more than 90 bushels and rye close to 50 bushels per acre, compared with 40 and 14 bushels, respectively, in the United States.

The cooperative movement has been developed most strongly in the Netherlands. It began in the latter part of the nineteenth century, when grain imports from the New World impoverished farmers and forced them to reorient their agricultural economy as well as their social attitudes. Dairy farming gradually supplanted the growing of grain, and cooperatives replaced the strong individualism which had formerly prevailed.

The movement toward cooperatives began in 1877 when a group of farmers in Zeeland made a joint purchase of fertilizers. The first cooperative dairy plant was founded in 1886 at Warga in Friesland. Now there are some 5,000 cooperatives, specialized in practically every field of agricultural pursuit. Eighty-four per cent of all milk, 88 per cent of the butter production, and approximately 89 per cent of the total cheese production are now processed in cooperatives. Many buying cooperatives have been formed, also, for the purchase of fertilizer, fodder, seeds, etc., as well as sales cooperatives for the sale of agricultural products.

Especially noteworthy are the cooperative auctions for the sale of vegetables, fruits, and flowers. Farmers who belong to cooperatives of this type are obliged to sell through these auctions; nearly all marketed vegetables are sold in this way.

In recent decades the cooperative movement has expanded into sales and slaughtering of cattle, and has strengthened successfully the social and economic position of those farmers who have specialized in that branch of activity.

Agricultural regions. In Benelux seven agricultural landscapes can be distinguished:

1. THE POLDER LANDS. Along the inner fringe of the sand dunes are the polder lands, the development of which has been noted.

The surface is flat, and the soils are heavy marine or river clays of widely ranging fertility. Meadows and pasture land predominate, although grains, sugar beets, and potatoes are important as well, especially in Zeeland, the new IJssel Lake polders, the northern margin of Groningen and Friesland, and parts of maritime Flanders. Some areas have become quite specialized and are of world renown. For example, along the western margins of the Holland polders dune sand has mixed with heavier polder clay, resulting in a soil particularly favorable for intensive horticulture, including fruits, vegetables, tulips, hyacinths, and other flowers. The bulb area—some 32,000 acres—lies between Leyden and Haarlem. Between The Hague and the Hoek van Holland is the Westland, where 49,000 acres of land are used for the growing of fruits and vegetables, mostly under glass.

Drainage canals and ditches perform the function of fences, and gates are visible only at bridges across the waters. Farmsteads in the older polder lands of the Netherlands and Belgium form widely scattered clusters on dikes and along roads, while in recently developed Dutch polders modern regional planning has grouped them into villages and towns, spaced at regular intervals from one another in a calculated hierarchy.

In Belgium, West Flanders has only a small percentage of its area in polder lands, and those were reclaimed in the Middle Ages. In the Netherlands, land reclamation is a continuing process. The big project of this century thus far has been the draining of the Zuider Zee. This body of water became an inlet of the North Sea in the thirteenth century and has been a flood menace ever since. During World War I there were disastrous inundations and, simultaneously, wartime conditions created food shortages. The conviction grew that both problems could be solved by isolating the Zuider Zee from the North Sea and by draining sections of it so as to increase the agricultural acreage of the Netherlands and simultaneously to produce a fresh-water lake.

Fig. 5–15. The main dike separating the IJssel Lake (right) from the Wadden Zee (left), an arm of the North Sea. The tall building is the monument commemorating the closing of the dike in 1932. (KLM Aerocarto NV)

The project was begun in 1918, and the first polder—the Wieringermeerpolder, with an area of some 49,000 acres—was completed in 1930, two years before the main dike was closed (Fig. 5–15; for the locations of projects discussed here and in the following pages, see Fig. 5–19). With the completion of the 19-mile-long dike in 1932, the Zuider Zee became the IJsselmeer, named after the IJssel River, one of the distributaries of the Rhine.

The crown of the dike is 20 to 22 feet above sea level, and the width of the base is some 600 feet. It was constructed of material available locally, chiefly sand, and on the seaward flanks a thick layer of resistant, impregnable boulder clay taken from the floor of the Zuider Zee. In order to prevent scouring of the flanks of the new dike by wave action, they were covered with large willow and brushwood mattresses weighted down with boulders.

Fig. 5–16. Farmsteads in the newly settled Northeast Polder reclaimed from the former Zuider Zee. (KLM Aerocarto NV)

The completion of the dike had two immediate benefits. It shortened the coastline of the Netherlands from 1,150 miles to 840 miles, thereby reducing the area in danger of attack by the sea; the shores of the IJsselmeer were no longer exposed to the open ocean. Secondly, the dike provided direct communication with the northern provinces of the Netherlands.

The new lake has become a fresh-water reservoir which, at the completion of the entire project later this century, will have an area of about 300,000 acres. It is a reservoir for inland drainage as well as a source of fresh water for agriculture and industry.

Since the construction of the dike in 1932, the Northeast Polder, with an area of about 120,000 acres, was completed and has been settled (Fig. 5–16) and the East Flevoland Polder, some 135,000 acres, has been pumped dry and is in the process of settlement. There are two more polders to be drained, South Flevoland and Markerwaard, which will form a single large homogeneous area enclosed on three sides by existing lands. After completion of the entire project, about 885 square miles will have been added to the surface area of the Netherlands—approximately 7 per cent of the total present area, or 10 per cent of the total farm land—and roughly 300,000 people will have been settled on these new lands.

The second major project of the twentieth century is the Delta Plan through which three principal distributary arms of the Scheldt-Meuse-Rhine delta will be closed by means of four main dams. The western Scheldt estuary and the New Waterway will be left open, however, so as not to impede maritime traffic to Antwerp and Rotterdam, respectively. This project received its immediate impetus in 1953 when high tides and strong onshore winds combined to produce higher flood waters than ever known before. Many dikes broke, and more than 350,000 acres of land were flooded in the delta area, resulting in a great loss of life and property.

The Delta Plan was designed and initiated as a multiple-purpose project. Its aims

are to protect the polder lands in Zeeland in the future, shorten the coastline still further, stop infiltration of sea water, and make available bodies of fresh water for irrigation. Moreover, a tideless inland water body will improve transport and communication, thereby contributing to the economic and social development of Zeeland and South Holland. Work began in 1958; when it is completed, two arms of the sea will have been sealed off against the North Sea while the northernmost arm, the Haringvliet, will have sluice gates for the escape of surplus waters of the Rhine and Meuse rivers. The technical difficulties encountered here are eclipsing those the Dutch have had to solve in the Zuider Zee project. The tidal range in the estuaries is 13 feet against 3 feet at the former Zuider Zee entrance, dams have to be built on shifting sands instead of boulder clay, and depths are much greater. However, new techniques and materials, combined with traditional Dutch determination and skill, will bring this project also to a successful conclusion.

It has been predicted that its completion later in the century will alter the landscape and its economy profoundly. With good transport links, the delta region is expected to become suburban to the large cities of South Holland. Agriculture will change from the growing of grains and dairying to truck farming, and lakes and beaches will become a tourist and vacation paradise.

Whatever the future may bring, one industry is certain to be eliminated. The eastern Scheldt has been the location of a highly successful and prosperous oyster and mussel industry, but, with the construction of the dam across the estuary, the water will become fresh and shellfish cultivation will cease. Unfortunately, no new suitable sites for this type of fishing have been found, so this industry will die out.

The third major project involves the separation of the Wadden Zee from the North Sea by linking the Frisian Islands with dams and by anchoring the two ends to the mainland. This will again shorten the coastline and add more land to the Dutch area. Still in the planning stage, this project is only a dream and hope, but some day it will become a reality.

2. THE EASTERN NETHERLANDS. East of the IJssel Lake the expanses of peat bogs, high moors, and unconsolidated sands remained essentially sparsely settled until the seventeenth century. Then, drainage was begun by means of ditches and canals, and peat and other organic material were mixed with sand and fertilizer, thereby producing fertile soils for the growing of various small grains for livestock and man, and potatoes suitable for the production of starch. Dairy farming is important here, also, and pigs are being raised on by-products of dairies as well as on imported feed. Oat and rye straw are used for the manufacture of mats and cardboard.

Since the time when agricultural expansion began in this area, population has increased rapidly, mostly nucleated in rural hamlets and villages. This, plus mechanization of agriculture, gradual exhaustion of peat reserves, and poor land and water transport, has created problem areas the economy of which the Dutch government is attempting to improve through a program of industrialization.

3. THE CAMPINE. In northern Belgium and the southern Netherlands lies an undulating to rolling sandy landscape where an impermeable subsoil created poor drainage conditions and delayed human occupancy. The Campine has been typified as a "forest-animal region." [15] Certainly this is true in the Dutch and Belgian border zones, the heart of this area. In either direction, however, toward large population centers more land has been reclaimed for the growing of crops, the percentage of land in forest declines, and that under grass cover increases. For the Campine as a whole, one can generalize that cropland, chiefly rye, oats, and

[15] Fritz Quicke, *Les Régions Agro-économiques de la Belgique* (Liége: Sciences et Lettres, S.A., 1950).

potatoes, is widely scattered on better-drained soils, while along stream courses and canals are permanent pastures and irrigated meadows. Settlement is primarily in clusters of farmhouses interspersed with individual farmsteads situated along roads. Younger rural settlements and coal-mining towns appear among older established villages.

4. INNER FLANDERS. This is yet another section of the sandy belt which extends through Belgium and the Netherlands. Inner Flanders adjoins the polder land of maritime Flanders and Zeeland on the south, and stretches from the Campine westward into France. Like the Campine, this area is undulating, and rye and other crops, chiefly for livestock, are abundant. This belt, however, has been developed agriculturally since the Middle Ages, when the growth of Flemish towns necessitated an increase in local food production. Rural population density is very high and farms are small. Farmhouses are strung out loosely along roads, giving the impression of considerable scattering of rural settlement. Dairy farms and market gardening prevail near Antwerp and Ghent. Toward France in the west and in areas adjoining the fertile loam region in the south, there is a specialized production of industrial crops, notably sugar beets, flax (Fig. 5–17), chicory, and tobacco.

5. THE LOAM BELT. South of the sands of East Flanders and the Campine, elevation increases and fine, permeable fertile loam gives rise to the most prosperous agricultural region of Benelux. The belt extends roughly between the Meuse and the upper Scheldt rivers from France across central Belgium into Dutch southern Limburg and Germany. It is a mixed zone of livestock and crop farming, where wheat and sugar beets are principal crops for man, and rye and oats for animals. An infinite variety of secondary crops has produced a variegated rural landscape. On the other hand, some localities are highly specialized in the growing of industrial crops, fruits, and vegetables (Fig. 5–18).

Fig. 5—17. Flax fields in Inner Flanders. Processing plants are scattered through-out the area. (Belgian Government Information Center, New York.)

Fig. 5—18. Hothouses at Hoeilaart, 8 miles south of Brussels. (Belgian Government Information Center, New York.)

In the west, in areas adjacent to France, flax, chicory, tobacco, and hops are grown, especially in the valleys of the Lys and Scheldt rivers. Truck farming predominates near urban concentrations, as in the Brussels, Liége, and Malines regions. In the latter, vegetables cover as much as 40 per cent of the cropland and, near Brussels, a considerable amount of vegetable growing is done under glass. In the truck-farming regions, farms are among the smallest in Benelux, land division is extreme, and exploitation is as intensive as in the vegetable- and bulb-growing areas of the polders.

In the northern section of this region the landscape is open, except for frequently fenced-in meadows, and settlement is loose, consisting of clusters of four-sided farmsteads or open villages at road junctions. In the south the loam belt, like the Ardennes and Lorraine, was under the three-field system until the end of the eighteenth century, so that fences become rare and hedges have been planted around orchards which, in turn, surround compact farm villages.

6. THE ARDENNES. South of the Sambre-Meuse line is another region where livestock and forests predominate. In the Ardennes proper in Belgium and Luxembourg, closed agricultural villages, meadows, and fields appear as islands of various sizes in the forest. The soils are thin and of low fertility, and much more of the cleared lands is in meadow than is in crops. Cattle raising predominates over all other agricultural pursuits. Wet, narrow, deeply incised valleys as well as higher elevations have been avoided for settlement.

Toward the north and south from the main plateau, the percentage of land in forest decreases and population density and cropland for human consumption increase, although livestock remains the mainstay of the economy. In the Herve, the northeasternmost section, forests almost disappear and meadows and orchards dominate the landscape.

7. LORRAINE. In southernmost Belgium and southern Luxembourg extends a rolling landscape of scattered small rural settlements, but there are also many individual farms on fertile soils cleared in medieval times. A mixed type of livestock and crop farming prevails; oats occupy the greatest area, but potatoes and winter wheat are also important. Here as elsewhere in Western Europe, the trend in the last 50 years has been toward a livestock economy and the percentage of meadow and pasture land has been increasing. On the slopes of the Moselle Valley, vineyards provide Luxembourg with domestic wines, including the sparkling variety.

Industrial raw materials.

ENERGY RESOURCES. Of the three Benelux countries, Luxembourg alone has practically no energy resources, with the exception of a small waterpower potential and her forests in the Oesling—the Ardennes plateau section. In conjunction with the Moselle canalization, a hydroelectric-power plant has been built where the river forms the Luxembourg-Germany boundary. Coke and coal are imported mostly from Germany, and petroleum products from Belgian and Dutch refineries.

Belgium and the Netherlands both have their own fuel—the former, coal, and the latter, a combination of coal, petroleum, and natural gas (Fig. 5–19). However, production is far short of domestic needs. The Netherlands, as yet, must import two-thirds of its gross energy requirements and Belgium some 60 per cent, much of it in the form of petroleum and petroleum products.

COAL. Both the Netherlands and Belgium have coal deposits at their disposal, which have been and will continue to be vital in the economy of the two countries. However, sources of energy have changed drastically in the last decade. In Belgium, while in the 1950's 90 per cent of all energy consumed was derived from coal, in 1966 it was only 50 per cent, with imported petroleum and petroleum products providing most of the rest. Belgium still ranks as the fourth-highest producer of coal in Europe west of the Iron Curtain. Additional amounts of

Fig. 5–19. Industrial map of Benelux.

coking coal and coke have had to be imported, chiefly from Germany. Although labor productivity has been slowly increasing ever since World War II, the output per man-shift underground, at 4,400 pounds, has been consistently the lowest among the coal-producing countries of free Europe.

The coal mines in Belgium are located in two general areas. The southern or Walloon fields have the oldest coal mines in Europe. Lying in the Sambre-Meuse corridor, they can be divided into four mining regions. The Borinage, centered on Mons, and the Tournai region, northwest of it, are economically depressed areas where mines are small, numerous, and poorly equipped, and where the better seams have been exhausted. The closing of the pits and various industrial enterprises has brought about a great deal of unemployment and unrest. Many Belgians from this area have sought better and more attractive employment in adjacent mining and manufacturing areas of France, to which they commute, while Italians have immigrated to go into the pits at low wages. A third mining region is that between Mons and Namur, centered on Charleroi. Here the heavy concentration of many industries provides a better regional balance and a relatively prosperous economy, in spite of the difficult mining conditions. Finally, coal is being mined in the Liége area where it also forms the basis of a great variety of industries.

The number of pits in these four mining regions declined from 265 in 1900 to only 37 in the middle 1960's, the latter operated by 53 companies. Total production in the Walloon fields also has declined sharply, until in 1966 only 9 million metric tons were mined there, a little more than one-half of Belgium's coal production.

Nearly half of Belgium's coal comes from the Campine region, where large-scale mining did not begin until 1917. There seven large companies each operate one mine, producing more than one million tons of coal annually apiece. The Carboniferous coal seams lie in an area extending some 50 miles east-west from Dutch Limburg toward Antwerp. Their depth at the Dutch border is about 1,400 feet and they dip westward, so that about one-half of the estimated reserves are below a depth of 3,000 feet. In spite of the great depth, however, mining operations are easier and output per man-shift underground larger than in the southern coal fields, because the seams are thick and regular. The mines are widely scattered in open heath land and no major industrial concentrations have been formed; rather, the coal is shipped out mostly by inland waterway to the leading industrial concentrations in the Sambre-Meuse corridor, Brussels, Antwerp, and Ghent. Total coal reserves in Belgium are estimated as being about 2.8 billion metric tons.

In the Netherlands the situation is more favorable. The coal seams in Southern Limburg are a section of the measures extending from Aachen in Germany into the Belgian Campine. Because of the westward dip already mentioned, the seams are at a depth of only 300 feet at the German border and 1,400 feet near the Belgian border.[16] However, the seams vary in thickness from 2 to 8 feet and have been disturbed by folding and faulting. Output per man-shift underground is 5,100 pounds, which is somewhat higher than the output in the adjacent Belgian Campine and about the same as that of the German Aachen mines. The principal mining areas are at Heerlen and Kerkrade.

In 1966, the Netherlands produced from this field 10.3 million metric tons of coal, of which about half was high-grade coking coal, sufficient for home demand of coke as well as for some export of high-grade metallurgical coke. The over-all coal production could not meet Dutch demand and an additional 6.7 million tons had to be imported in 1966, most of it from Germany.

In northern Limburg there is a second coal field, which has not yet been exploited because of its great depth. It lies in the Peel district, extending in a southeast-northwesterly direction into North Brabant, and is located at depths ranging from 2,500 to 3,000 feet. The total estimated exploitable reserves of all Dutch coal fields are about 5 billion metric tons, but with the recent discovery of abundant natural gas resources, the relative importance of coal as a source of energy will decline.

PETROLEUM AND NATURAL GAS. Only the Netherlands is so fortunate as to have petroleum and natural-gas resources. The 1966 crude-oil production represented about 6.5

[16] F. J. Monkhouse, "The South Limburg Coal Field," *Economic Geography* 31 (April, 1955): 126–37.

per cent of all energy consumed, or 7 per cent of crude oil refined in the Netherlands, the rest having been imported from the Middle East and the Western Hemisphere. About 60 per cent of the 1966 production total came from the oil fields at Schoonebeek, in eastern Drenthe near the German border. The remainder came from scattered small fields near The Hague, Delft, and Rotterdam, which have been producing since 1953. Proven reserves are only about 13 million metric tons.

Domestic natural gas is on the way to becoming the Netherlands' principal energy resource. In 1959 and in subsequent years, one of the world's largest gas fields was discovered in the northern province of Groningen near the town of Slochteren (containing approximately 18 trillion cubic meters of gas), and smaller deposits in Friesland, North Holland, and the Frisian Islands (Fig. 5–19.) Gas production has been increasing and, in 1966, domestic natural gas covered about 7 per cent of Dutch gross energy requirements and 69 per cent of total Dutch gas production. A fuller utilization of this resource will be realized, within the Netherlands as well as in Germany, Belgium, and France, as the gas distribution network is improved and expanded. Already main pipelines have been completed to the central and southern Netherlands, Liége, Paris, and Cologne.

FERROUS AND NON-FERROUS METALS. The minette ores of the Lorraine Basin extend into southern Luxembourg as well as into the southern margin of the Belgian province Luxembourg. The ore layers are near the surface, but there is no uniformity in thickness or in areal extent. In Luxembourg they occur in at least five layers ranging in thickness from 3 to 12 feet and having an average iron content of a little over 30 per cent. In the Belgian section only one bed—4½ to 7½ feet thick—is workable. The Luxembourg fields have a proven reserve of 200 million tons of ore containing 56 million tons of metal. An additional 300 million tons of ore reserves, having an iron content of 78 million tons, are possible.

There are also hematite deposits in the Sambre-Meuse corridor, which were worked until 1946 when further extraction became economically unfeasible. However, there still is a proven reserve of 30 million tons of ore containing 10 million tons of iron, with much greater possible reserves. The seams outcrop for some 40 miles and vary in iron content from 26 to 40 per cent, but locally it may be as high as 58 per cent. Finally, lenticular beds of ferruginous sands are found about 25 miles northeast of Brussels, containing limonite with varying iron content below 28 per cent. These beds, also not exploited currently, contain a proven reserve of 50 million tons and a possible reserve of 100 million tons, with 12 and 20 million tons of iron, respectively.

Iron-ore production in 1966 was more than 6.5 million metric tons annually in Luxembourg and was only about 124,000 metric tons in Belgium, both insufficient tonnages to cover the demand in either country. Luxembourg obtained additional supplies from the French Lorraine, and Belgium from France, Luxembourg, and Sweden.

Manufacturing. Our previous discussion has shown that the economy of all three Benelux countries is based almost entirely upon manufacturing and foreign trade.

LUXEMBOURG. Until late in the nineteenth century, Luxembourg was strictly an agricultural country with very little manufacturing. The standard of living was low, and its population was diminishing, in part because of heavy emigration. With the successful use of minette ores in the iron- and steel-making processes, beginning in 1878, the situation changed drastically. A series of industrial towns sprang up in southwestern Luxembourg along the French border, at the base of the ore-bearing cuesta; Esch-sur-Alzette became the most important town. Since World War II, iron and steel works have also been established in new suburbs north of Luxembourg City.

Before World War I, as a member of the *Zollverein* and then in customs union with Germany, Luxembourg's economy became closely integrated with that of Germany, including the Saar and Alsace-Lorraine. The customs union with Belgium in 1922, however, gave the country the added advantage of free access to the port of Antwerp. This, in turn, stimulated the further development of the iron and steel industry, the products of which now make up 80 per cent of Luxembourg's total exports. Only small quantities of coke are produced locally. Most coke is imported from Germany, and, as already stated, additional ore is brought in from adjacent French mines. In 1966 only a fraction of the iron and steel products manufactured in the country were used locally, more than 95 per cent having been exported, chiefly to other European countries.

BELGIUM. In Belgium, the bulk of the iron and steel industry is located in the Walloon mining and industrial belt, with particular concentrations at Liége and Charleroi. Outside this area, iron and steel are produced in the Athus-Musson-Halanzy area in Belgian Luxembourg near the international border, based on minette iron ore, and at Clabecq on the Brussels-Charleroi canal. The industry is oriented predominantly toward the phosphoric minette ore of the Lorraine. All large plants have their own coke ovens, but coke production is not enough to cover home demand and some additional supplies must be obtained from Germany.

Steel production in Belgium has increased steadily from World War II. In 1966 it was some 9 million metric tons, nearly four times as great as in 1938; it has been consistently the highest among the three Benelux countries.

In conjunction with these industrial and mining complexes, other important industries have grown up, such as chemical plants, gas works, thermoelectric-power plants, the textile, china, and glass industries, and refineries of various metals. As has already been pointed out, the industrial concentra-

tions that have evolved in the Liége and Charleroi sections have given these areas considerable prosperity and economic security. The Namur area has no coal, but manufacturing began on the basis of local iron-ore deposits and waterpower. Excellent transport connections by water on the Meuse and Sambre rivers gave the city an advantage for further development, and today there are metallurgical and chemical industries, glass manufacture, zinc refining, and others.

The oldest industry in Belgium is the textile industry. It emerged in Flanders beginning in the eleventh century, with the processing of local and, later, English wool and the manufacturing of cloth, especially in Ghent, Brugge, and Ieper. Later, the linen industry developed, mainly localized in the valley of the Lys River whose lime-free waters proved particularly suitable for the retting of flax, and cotton spinning and weaving entered the textile complex in the seventeenth century. The most recent addition is the manufacture of artificial and synthetic fibers.

Today, the textile-manufacturing areas can be classified in two groups. There are the old specialized centers in Flanders where manufacturing of all types is widely scattered. Some Flemish cities are of world renown, such as Ghent, Kortrijk, and Roeselare in the linen industry, and Ghent in the manufacture of linen, cotton, and jute. Malines is known for the production of flannel, and Brussels for its shawls and tartans. Many other examples could be cited. Although wool gave the original impetus to the development of the Flanders textile centers, its manufacture is not concentrated there now to any degree.

Verviers in the Vesdre River Valley and its satellite towns represent the second group of textile mills, producing a great variety of wool and woolen goods. The woolens industry has been flourishing ever since the fifteenth century, when it moved there from Flanders to get away from local competition, guild restrictions, and high labor costs. The

Vesdre River has pure, soft water suitable for washing and fulling, cheap rural labor was available, and Walloon industrial activity had extended into the valley from Liége. Later, coal from the Liége basin became an additional advantage. Since World War II there has been some shifting of large companies to towns in Flanders, such as Malines and Diest, where they have begun operation with new and modern plants.

Two manufacturing centers outside the Walloon industrial belt—Brussels and Antwerp—deserve special mention. Brussels is located at the head of inland navigation on the Senne River. Its industrial area extends southwestward along the Senne River and the canal to Charleroi. More than half the population of Belgium lives within a 30-mile radius of the capital city, pursuing a great variety of urban, industrial, and agricultural activities. Antwerp, at the head of ocean-going navigation on the Scheldt River, some 55 miles from the sea, also has a rich industrial hinterland, thanks to the city's function as a seaport. Among the more important industries are shipbuilding, petroleum refining, and the processing of colonial goods.

The port has been a prosperous center of trade and transport since the city received its rights in 1291 and since it joined the Hanseatic League in 1315, with the exception of a period extending from the Spanish Inquisition and the closing of the estuary by the Dutch until the reopening by Napoleon in 1795. The population of Antwerp increased from 74,000 in 1830 to 130,000 in 1845 and 295,000 in 1900. In the middle 1960's, the Antwerp urban agglomeration amounted to a population of nearly 660,000.

THE NETHERLANDS. Traditionally, Dutch industry like that of Flanders has produced luxury goods since the end of the Middle Ages, such as Utrecht velvet and Delft earthenware. To these were added, beginning in the seventeenth century, shipbuilding and the colonial industries, which evolved chiefly in the large port cities of Amsterdam and Rotterdam. The colonial industries consisted of preparation and conversion of raw materials from overseas, such as the manufacture of cocoa and chocolate, the production of vegetable oils, the distillation of gin, diamond cutting, and the re-export of the finished products. The Industrial Revolution virtually bypassed the Netherlands on account of the nature of her existing industries and particularly because no coal or other mineral resources were known, on which to base heavy industry.

Industrialization began in the latter half of the nineteenth century, first with the development of manufacturing of agricultural products. The economic plight of Dutch farmers, because of cheap foreign grain imports, and the resulting changes in the basic agricultural structure of the country, have already been discussed. The production of high-quality agricultural products and their export have been of great importance in the Dutch economy ever since. Moreover, the discovery of coal in Dutch Limburg in the twentieth century, the development of new scientific methods, and the ever-increasing population problem, particularly since World War II, have intensified the efforts of the Dutch to create a modern industrial nation.

Coal has given rise to a concentrated industrial complex in southern Limburg. The production of high-grade metallurgical coke is linked with a diversified chemical industry and the production of gas. A high-pressure pipeline system extends through Limburg and North Brabant. In addition, there are several thermoelectric-power plants which are essential links in the Dutch power grid. The Dutch iron- and steel-manufacturing center, however, is not located here but in Velsen on the North Sea Canal, two miles east of IJmuiden. It uses imported iron ores in conjunction with coal and coke from the Limburg fields. Annual production of crude steel has been increasing steadily. In 1966 it amounted to 3.3 million metric tons, which covered 82 per cent of the home consumption for that year.

The pending rapid increase in the use of natural gas from the Groningen fields will facilitate the expansion of existing industries and the development of new ones in locations where availability of energy heretofore had been a limiting factor. Moreover, it is anticipated that with time, natural gas will replace other fuels insofar as is economically and technically feasible.

New scientific methods and modern technical developments have given rise to some very specialized varieties of manufacturing, some as port industries and others located inland. Rotterdam is one of Europe's chief oil-refining centers, and Rotterdam and Amsterdam have shipbuilding and its ancillary engineering industries. The production of chemicals and pharmaceuticals, flour milling, and the assembly of automobiles—all are based on imported raw materials and semi-manufactured products, as are some of the older, traditional industries discussed above. Some large, outstanding plants are located in the interior, such as the tin smelters at Arnhem and the famous Philips factory at Eindhoven, producing radio sets, phonographs, and electrical equipment.

The Dutch textile industry is concerned chiefly with the processing of cotton. Spinning is concentrated largely in the Rotterdam area, while cotton weaving and further manufacturing is scattered in the eastern and southern Netherlands. Outstanding is the Twente, an area in southeastern Overijssel, where Enschede and Hengelo have become cotton-textile centers. Since 1936 the production of high-quality rayon has taken on importance in association with cotton-textile industries, particularly in the Twente.

To alleviate population pressure and to aid rural problem areas in the far northern and northeastern sections of the country and in parts of North Brabant (southwestern and northeastern) and northern Limburg, the Dutch government has been encouraging and giving state aid to industries which wished to establish themselves and expand in those areas. Such industrialization has absorbed surplus rural population, improved road and water transport and the levels of regional economies, at the same time as it has aided the over-all industrialization policy pursued by the Dutch government.

Communication and trade. By virtue of their location on the Channel and North Sea, in the Belgian corridor of the North European Lowland, and astride the Rhine-Meuse-Scheldt deltas, both Belgium and the Netherlands are of paramount importance in terms of the European transportation pattern, and both have exploited their position to the fullest extent. But in the matter of highways modernization has, in general, been unable to keep up with the demands of present-day road traffic.

HIGHWAYS. Benelux, like France, is confronted with the problem of rapidly increasing traffic on the highways. In Belgium and Luxembourg the number of private cars doubled between 1959 and 1965, and in the Netherlands the increase was nearly threefold. In general, the network of highways and secondary roads serves all sections of Benelux, but the ever-growing automobile and truck traffic cannot be handled adequately on these roads. A modernization program is under way to improve and widen the more important existing roads, and connect the principal ports, cities, and industrial centers with a network of superhighways which will also tie in with the international road network.

RAILROADS. Belgium has the densest railroad network in the world, a total of 2,800 miles of rail, the greatest track densities lying within the two Flanders provinces, in Hainaut and around Brussels. Belgium has been called the turntable of European railroad traffic because nine international lines traverse the country, among them those of the Orient Express, Nord Express, Tauern Express, and others.

Belgian railroads carry about 64 million tons of merchandise annually, 15 per cent of which represents transit and 47 per cent derived from the country's import and export trade. Thus, internal cargo transport by railroad accounts only for 38 per cent of the total traffic, a fact which emphasizes the international position of Belgium.

A government program to modernize the railroads and thereby reduce the costs and increase the speed of transport has high priority and is proceeding through electrification and the use of diesel engines. By the middle 1960's, 24 per cent of the total rail net was electrified, including the main lines from Brussels to other major Belgian cities, and to Luxembourg.

In the Netherlands, railroads do not assume so vital a function as in Belgium. The railroad network was completed essentially by 1890, and by the turn of the century it was well integrated with the Belgian and German railroads. Only local additions made since then have increased the length of track which now amounts to 2,000 miles. Here, as in Belgium, modernization has been in progress; roadbeds have been improved, diesel engines put into service, and lines electrified. In the middle 1960's one-half the Dutch network was operated with electricity. Dutch railroads carried at that time 31 million tons of merchandise as against 180 million tons carried on Dutch inland waterways.

INLAND WATERWAYS. The density of the inland-waterway network in the Netherlands (miles per inhabitant) is the highest in the world. There are 4,000 miles of waterways, of which 76 per cent are canals. Small craft dominate the waterways, inasmuch as about 62 per cent of all waterways can accommodate only barges having a carrying capacity of less than 650 tons. However, 1,000 miles can be used by craft carrying more than 1,500 tons.

The principal rivers used for navigation are the Rhine River, unequaled with its direct connection to Central Europe, particularly the Rhine-Westphalian industrial region, and the Meuse, which, together with the Juliana Canal, opens the South Limburg industrial and mining area to 2,000-ton barges. Rotterdam is located on the Nieuwe Maas, the estuary of the Lek River, which is a distributary of the Rhine River.

The most vital canals are those connecting the large ports with the North Sea—the 16-mile-long New Waterway for Rotterdam and the 18-mile North Sea Canal for Amsterdam. The latter is served also by the 40-mile-long

Merwede Canal, which connects Amsterdam with the Waal River and thereby makes it a Rhine River port. The Juliana Canal was built to bypass an unnavigable section of the Meuse River. It parallels the Meuse along the right bank for some 21 miles from Maastricht to Maasbracht, where shipping returns to the river. Navigation is open for 2,000-ton barges which carry up to two-thirds of their total freight in coal and coke.

In Belgium the heavy emphasis on railroads noted above does not mean that inland waterways have been neglected or are not important. Belgium has 980 miles of navigable waterways, more than half of them canals, as compared to the Netherlands' 4,000 miles, and yet the density of its network (miles per inhabitant) is second highest in the world after the Netherlands.

Canals originated in Flanders during the Middle Ages, but the great effort in canal building, as elsewhere, came in the nineteenth century, and by 1880 most of the present network was in existence. The chief objective was to connect the interior industrial areas with Belgium's ports, particularly with Antwerp. This meant the connection of the basins of the Meuse and Scheldt rivers, which, in some instances, was achieved only with great difficulties—the construction of many locks and the excavation of deep cuts.

The latest canal construction in Belgium was that of the Albert Canal, 81 miles long, connecting Liége and Antwerp by way of the Campine coal fields. Completed in 1940 but damaged during World War II, it was not until 1957 that its entire length could be used to capacity by barges having a 2,000-ton capacity or less. In the middle 1960's the Albert Canal alone carried one-third of the total cargo handled by inland shipping, as calculated in ton-miles. The canal has stimulated traffic and created industries along its course. It also serves as aqueduct and reservoir for the Antwerp metropolitan area.

The pattern of Belgium's inland waterways can be seen as three axial north-south lines connecting two east-west canal systems, one in the north and one in the south. The axial lines are the Albert Canal, the canal from

Antwerp to Charleroi via Brussels, and the waterway connecting Antwerp with the Borinage (Mons) by way of Ghent. In the north the ports of Ostende and Zeebrugge are connected with Antwerp via Ghent, and in the south is the system of the Sambre and Meuse rivers. In 1947 a modernization program was undertaken which, when completed, will open all waterways to 1,350-ton barges. An outstanding project which is currently under construction is a ramp for ships on the Brussels-Charleroi canal at Ronquières, which will eliminate 20 existing locks and raise vessels 225 feet in one step.

More than 76 million metric tons of merchandise were carried in the middle 1960's on Belgian inland waterways, of which 60 per cent represented traffic generated by import and export, and only 7 per cent were transit cargo.

MARITIME TRANSPORT. The merchant shipping fleet of the Netherlands has not grown much in the last decade, while those of other European countries, such as Greece, West Germany and France, have surged ahead. Thus, with 5 million gross registered tons in 1966, the Netherlands stands only seventh in Europe and eleventh in the world. Belgium has been, and still is, one of the smallest shipping nations, having only some 900,000 gross tons. The reasons for this contrast in orientation toward the sea were analyzed previously. In terms of port services, Antwerp, Amsterdam, and Rotterdam compete with one another and have overlapping hinterlands which in both countries are rich, heavily industrialized, and very densely populated. The Dutch ports handle the greatest tonnage of any one country—145 million tons of in-going and out-going cargo in 1966; this is two times the tonnage moving in and out of Belgian seaports. About 130 million tons of cargo were handled by Rotterdam alone (Fig. 5–20).

Rotterdam's growth since its destruction in World War II has been phenomenal; by the middle 1960's it had become the world's number one port, handling more than 130 million tons of cargo, 85 per cent of it in bulk. Expansion of port facilities occupy the entire area between the old port and the North Sea. This is Rotterdam's new Europort, to be completed by 1980, where bulk facilities, most importantly crude oil, and port industries interlace to create a vast industrial area and port complex which may eventually even extend southward into the Delta region.

Rotterdam, as well as Antwerp, its closest competitor, can handle ships of 100,000 deadweight tons, but Rotterdam is creating a tanker harbor beyond the present limits of the shore line in the North Sea where 240,000 ton ships will be accommodated. Antwerp, on the other hand, was the first to develop facilities for container traffic, and Port Churchill, the new container port, is already in operation.

All three ports—Rotterdam, Amsterdam, and Antwerp—are well equipped and take pride in having rapid and efficient service as well as excellent inland and seaward transport connections. Both Dutch and Belgian load indexes [17] are very unfavorable, because of the ever-increasing need for raw materials in Western and Central Europe.

AIR TRANSPORT. Although air traffic of Belgian and Dutch lines has increased in the last decade, their relative standing in the European competitive picture has declined. In terms of total mileage and passenger miles flown in the middle 1960's, the Netherlands rank fifth after the United Kingdom, France, Italy, and West Germany, and Belgium ranks eighth. Sabena, the Belgian airline, and KLM, the Dutch airline, have worldwide connections. Both countries have a number of commercial airdromes, but the airports of Brussels, Amsterdam, and Rotterdam handle most of the international traffic. Helicopters are used widely for local services and on some continental flights.

[17] The load index, or load factor, is the percentage of space of a ship filled with cargo. It is to the advantage of a shipping line to have its ships sail with as high a load factor as possible.

Fig. 5–20. Rotterdam, on the Nieuwe Maas River, looking upstream. The head of ocean navigation is at the bridges in the left background; the Europort development is between here and the North Sea. (KLM Aerocarto NV)

FOREIGN TRADE. As stated earlier, foreign trade is the most vital aspect of the economy of each of the three countries. Unhindered international trade and freedom of the seas are fundamental to the high standard of living enjoyed in the Benelux countries, and even to their survival under their present economic system. All three countries rely heavily on imports of food, raw materials, and fuels. They export manufactured and semi-manufactured products. In the Netherlands the emphasis is on export of agricultural and horticultural goods, machinery, and chemical products, in Belgium on metallurgical products and textiles, and Luxembourg exports iron ore in addition to products of her iron and steel industry.

The most active trading partners are the Benelux countries themselves, other countries within the European Economic Community, especially West Germany, and, for trade of Belgium and Luxembourg, also France. Outside the Community, the United States and the United Kingdom are the most important partners.

The great dependence on foreign trade is indicated by the fact that about 38 per cent of the gross national product of Belgium and Luxembourg is derived from exports, in the Netherlands it is 31 per cent, while in France it is 11 per cent and only 4 per cent in the United States. In addition, Belgium and the Netherlands perform the important function of rendering services for the transit of goods to and from interior destinations, as well as for transshipment of cargoes in their various ports.

＊   ＊   ＊

Western Europe as defined in this book comprises four of the six members of the European Economic Community, or Common Market. Each state represents a great diversity of natural and human resources, and each is confronted with its own problems relating to the best use of these resources.

France has made the greatest strides toward an internal administrative reorganization and a greater economic capacity for production and foreign trade. The Dutch continue to progress in their battle against the sea and find themselves with a bountiful supply of energy which has already resulted in a re-evaluation of internal development schemes and still closer direct ties with EEC partners. The solutions of Belgium's internal problems are more complicated because of internal friction among the two major ethnic groups. Luxembourg, and in fact all of Western Europe, has benefited greatly from the ever closer relationships among the partners of the Community. There is much room for further growth of economic and political strength if all remaining plans for full economic union materialize.

BIBLIOGRAPHY

(Major references are asterisked.)

Books in English

BURKE, GERALD L. *Greenheart Metropolis: Planning in the Western Netherlands.* New York: St. Martin's Press, 1966.

EDELMAN, C. H. *Soils of the Netherlands.* Amsterdam: North-Holland Publishing Co., 1950.

EVANS, ESTYN E. *France.* New York: Frederick A. Praeger, 1966.

*MARTONNE, EMMANUEL DE. *The Geographical Regions of France.* Translated by H. C. Brentnall. London: William Heinemann, Ltd., 1933.

*MONKHOUSE, F. S. *A Regional Geography of Western Europe.* London and New York: Longmans, Green & Co., Inc., 2nd ed., 1964.

*NETHERLANDS. *Second Report on Physical Planning in the Netherlands.* Condensed edition, 2 parts. The Hague: Government Printing Office of the Netherlands, 1966.

PANNEKOEK, A. J. (ed.). *Geological History of the Netherlands.* The Hague: Staatsdrukkerijen Uitgeverijbedrijf, 1956.

ROYAL INSTITUTE OF ARCHITECTS. *Planning and Creation of an Environment: Experiences in the Ysselmeerpolders.* A report reproduced by the Government of the Netherlands, ca. 1965.

Books in Other Languages

BASTIÉ, JEAN. *La croissance de la banlieue parisienne.* (The Growth of the Paris Suburbs). Paris: Presses Universitaire de France, 1964.

*CHABOT, C. *Géographie Régionale de la France.* (Regional Geography of France). Paris: Masson, 1966.

*Géographie Universelle
　　Vol. II: DEMANGEON, ALBERT. *Belgique, Pays-Bas, Luxembourg.* (Belgium, the Netherlands, and Luxembourg). Paris: Librairie Armand Colin, 1927.
　　Vol. VI, Part 1: MARTONNE, EMMANUEL DE. *France Physique* (Physical Geography of France). Paris: Librairie Armand Colin, 1942. Part 2: DEMANGEON, ALBERT. *France Économique et Humaine* (Economic and Human Geography of France). 2 vols. Paris: Librairie Armand Colin, 1946, 1948.

*GEORGE, PIERRE and SEVRIN, ROBERT. *Belgique, Pays-Bas, Luxembourg.* (Belgium, Netherlands, Luxembourg). Paris: Presses Universitaires de France, 1967.

HABY, R. *Les houillères lorraines et leur région.* (The Lorraine Coal Mines and their Region). Paris: SABRI, 1965. Text and atlas.

*PINCHEMEL, PHILIPPE. *Géographie de la France.* (Geography of France). 2 vols. Paris: Armand Colin, 1964.

*SCHMITHÜSEN, JOSEF. *Das Luxemburger Land.* (Luxembourg). Leipzig: Hirzel, 1940.

Atlases

LUYKX, THEO. *Atlas Culturel et Historique de Belgique* (Cultural and Historical Atlas of Belgium). Brussels: Elsevier, S.A. 1954, 192 p.

Atlas de France (Métropole). Comité National de Géographie. Paris: Centre National de la Recherche Scientifique, 1951–1959. 80 plates.

TIMMERS, J. J. M. *Atlas van de Nederlandes Beschaving.* Amsterdam: Elsevier, S.A., 1957, 246 p.

Elsevier Atlas van Nederland, Belgie en Luxemburg. Samengesteld door De Winkler Prins Redactie. Amsterdam: Elsevier, S.A., 1960, 195 p.

Articles

AMERICAN GEOGRAPHICAL SOCIETY. *Readings in the Geography of France, Germany, and Netherlands.* Contributions by various authors. (Reprint Series No. 1.) New York: American Geographical Society, 1943.

BASTIDE, HENRI and GIRARD, ALAIN. "Les tendances démographiques en France et les attitudes de la population" (Demographic

Trends in France and Attitudes of the Population), *Population* 21 (January–February, 1966): 9–50.

BOICHARD, JEAN. "Perspectives de l'agriculture française" (Perspectives of French Agriculture), *Revue de géographie de Lyon* 41 (1966): 99–127.

DUSSART, FRANS. "Geographie der Ländlichen Siedlungsformen in Belgien und Luxemburg" (Geography of Rural Forms of Settlement in Belgium and Luxembourg), *Geographische Rundschau* 9 (January, 1957): 12–18.

DUSSART, FRANS. "Les Transports en Belgique" (The Transport Patterns of Belgium), *Zeitschrift für Verkehrssicherheit* 4 (1958): 1–16.

EDWARDS, K. C. "Historical Geography of the Luxembourg Iron and Steel Industry," Institute of British Geographers, *Transactions and Papers* 29 (1961): 1–16.

FLEMING, DOUGLAS K. "Coastal Steelworks in the Common Market Countries," *The Geographical Review* 57 (January, 1967): 48–72.

MARTIN, J. E. "Location Factors in the Lorraine Iron and Steel Industry," The Institute of British Geographers *Transactions and Papers* 23 (1957): 191–212.

MICHEL, ALOYS. "The Canalization of the Moselle and West European Integration," *The Geographical Review* 52 (October, 1962): 475–491.

POUNDS, NORMAN J. G. "Historical Geography of the Iron and Steel Industry of France," *Annals: Association of American Geographers* 47 (1957): 3–14.

ROIG, CHARLES. "Les aspects socio-politiques de la planification régionale en France" (Socio-Political Aspects of Regional Planning in France), *L'Actualité économique* 43 (April–June, 1967): 39–65.

ROZENTAL, ALEK A. "The Enclosure Movement in France," *The American Journal of Economics and Sociology* 16 (October, 1956): 55–71.

SARGENT, FREDERIC O. "The Persistence of Communal Tenure in French Agriculture," *Agricultural History* 32 (April, 1958): 100–08.

THIERNESSE, LOUIS and GILLAIN, PIERRE. "Aspects et problèmes de l'agriculture belge" (Aspects and Problems of Belgian Agriculture), *La Géographie* 18 (1966): 3–31.

THOMAS, TREVOR M. "The North Sea and its Environs: Future Reservoir of Fuel?" *The Geographical Review* 56 (January, 1966): 12–39.

THOMPSON, I. B. "A Review of Problems of Economic and Urban Development in the Northern Coalfield of France," *Southampton Research Series in Geography* 1 (March, 1965): 31–60.

VINCE, STANLEY W. E. "The Agricultural Regions of Belgium," *London Essays in Geography* (ed. L. Dudley Stamp and S. W. Wooldridge). Cambridge, Mass.: Harvard University Press (1951), 255–88.

WARREN, KENNETH. "The Changing Steel Industry of the European Common Market," *Economic Geography* 43 (October, 1967): 314–32.

WEIGEND, GUIDO G. "The Basis and Significance of Viticulture in Southwest France," *Annals: Association of American Geographers* 44 (March, 1954): 75–101.

WEIGEND, GUIDO G. "Bordeaux: An Example of Changing Port Functions," *The Geographical Review* 45 (April, 1955): 217–43.

6

Central Europe

The term "Central Europe" (Mittel-europa, *Zwischeneuropa*), so frequently mis-used, can hardly be mentioned without in-troducing political overtones. At best, it can be considered a flexible political-geograph-ical term describing an area whose borders shift in accordance with changes in national boundaries. In this chapter the term is used as a common denominator for the following countries: Germany within its post-World War II boundaries, Switzerland, Liechten-stein, and Austria.

It should be pointed out that, while con-cepts of Central Europe have differed, many writers and especially German geographers have stressed its geographical and cultural entity, and the fact that Germany constitutes its core. Furthermore, Central Europe has always been held to include that part of Europe in which at least a large portion of the population speaks a dialect of German. This region has at times included parts of France (Alsace and Lorraine) and the greater portions of Belgium and the Nether-lands, in the west; the territory of the former Austria-Hungary, Romania, most of Czecho-slovakia, sections of western Poland, and some of the southern Alpine valleys extend-ing into Italy, and Yugoslavia. Some geog-raphers have tried to base their delineation of Central Europe on its physical geography

and have seen a common denominator in the east-west alignment of the Alps, Central Up-lands, and Lowlands. Others have con-sidered Central Europe as a central transi-tional zone located between oceanic Europe in the west and essentially continental Eu-rope in the east. Most writers agree that Germany within its 1937 borders, Switzer-land, Austria, Bohemia, and Moravia should be included in its area; Karl Sinnhuber and Henry Meyer, among others, have discussed the different interpretations attached to the elusive concept of Central Europe.[1]

The central position of the three countries —Germany, Switzerland, and Austria—in re-lation to other sections of peninsular Europe is of great significance. Central Europe is bordered by France, Belgium, Luxembourg, and the Netherlands—all in Western Europe; by Denmark, Norway, and Sweden—all in Northern Europe; by Italy, in Southern Eu-rope; and by a great transitional region known by many names, but defined in this

[1] Karl A. Sinnhuber, "Central Europe—Mittel-europa—Europe Central: An Analysis of a Geo-graphical Term," *Transactions and Papers: The Institute of British Geographers* 20 (1954): 15–39; and Henry Cord Meyer, "Mitteleuropa in German Political Geography," *Annals of the Association of American Geographers* 36 (September, 1946): 178–94.

book as Eastern Europe. The borders of Germany have constantly shifted while those of the Alpine countries (*Alpenländer*) of Switzerland and Austria have remained relatively stable for many centuries. The North German Lowlands (plains), which form part of the great lowlands extending from western France deep into the Soviet Union (Fig. 1–3), have been used as a favorite invasion route from earliest historical times. The Vienna Basin has played an important role since the first century A.D., when the Romans used it as an outpost for offensive and as a base for defensive action. He who controls Vienna and its basin commands the narrows of the Danube, and gains access to the wide open spaces of the Carpathian (Pannonian) Basin. Vienna also lies astride the lowland route between the Adriatic Sea and the headwaters of the Oder (Odra) and Vistula rivers, and guards the southeastern entrance to Bohemia and Bavaria. Farther south, the several low passes across the Alps have facilitated the free interchange of peoples between Central and Southern Europe.

Most of the peoples of Central Europe, including those of the greater part of Switzerland, are German speaking. Their countries have a long and rich cultural tradition. Austria, with a glorious past and great power in the years of the Austro-Hungarian Monarchy, remained independent after 1919; Switzerland with its 25 cantons developed slowly from a nucleus (Urschweiz) formed in 1291 by a defensive alliance of the Forest Cantons (Waldstätten) Uri, Schwyz, and Unterwalden. Germany was politically unified in 1871. As a result of the outcome of World War II, it was divided into four occupational zones. While the western zones have united, and in September 1949 became The Federal Republic of Germany (West Germany), the eastern zone, occupied by the Soviet Union, in October of the same year became The German Democratic Republic (East Germany). In 1955, following a western agreement with The Federal Republic, the Soviet Union also recognized full sovereignty of The German Democratic Re-

public. In addition Berlin also was divided into four occupational zones. In the meantime, East Berlin has been absorbed into East Germany and is now the capital of The German Democratic Republic. West Berlin still has a special status. For example, it is represented in the West German parliament by non-voting observers only. It is a *Land* of the Federal Republic, but owing to the four power agreement of 1945 it cannot belong *de jure* to The Federal Republic, and is an enclave of West Germany within East Germany with very precarious lines of communications with The Federal Republic.

This chapter presents, first, an over-all view of Germany with the Oder-Neisse rivers as its eastern boundary. Over the years, the division of Germany, first laid out as an uneasy zonal compromise in the Allied protocol of September 12, 1944 and later confirmed at the Potsdam Conference of June-August, 1945, has taken on the status of a permanent international boundary. It has left its impact, especially on the political and economic division of the two Germanys during the postwar years. For this reason, in discussions later in this chapter there is always a differentiation concerning happenings since the Second World War between developments in the two halves of Germany, at times giving East and West Germany separate headings, especially emphasizing the different economic development in the two Germanys.[2]

However defined, Central Europe remains an area of transition. Structurally it ranges from sedimentary lowlands in north Germany, covered by thick continental glacial deposits, to crystalline highlands (Alps) with cirques and valleys carved out by Alpine glaciers; climatically, from the maritime

[2] Wherever a distinction between the two Germanys is needed, specific mention is made of West Germany (The German Federal Republic) and East Germany (The German Democratic Republic). When speaking of the territory east of the Oder-Neisse rivers, now part of Poland and/or the Soviet Union, Germans refer to these lands as "administered by Poland and/or the Soviet Union." This chapter refers to them as "lost territories."

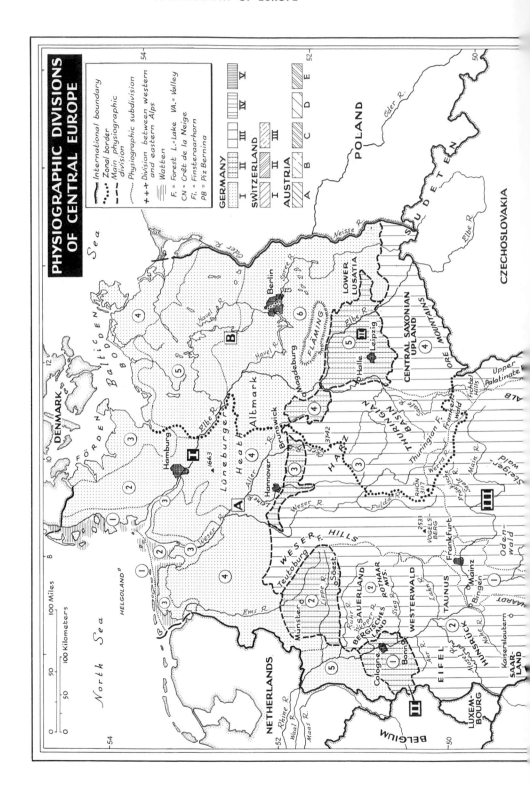

PHYSIOGRAPHIC DIVISIONS
OF CENTRAL EUROPE

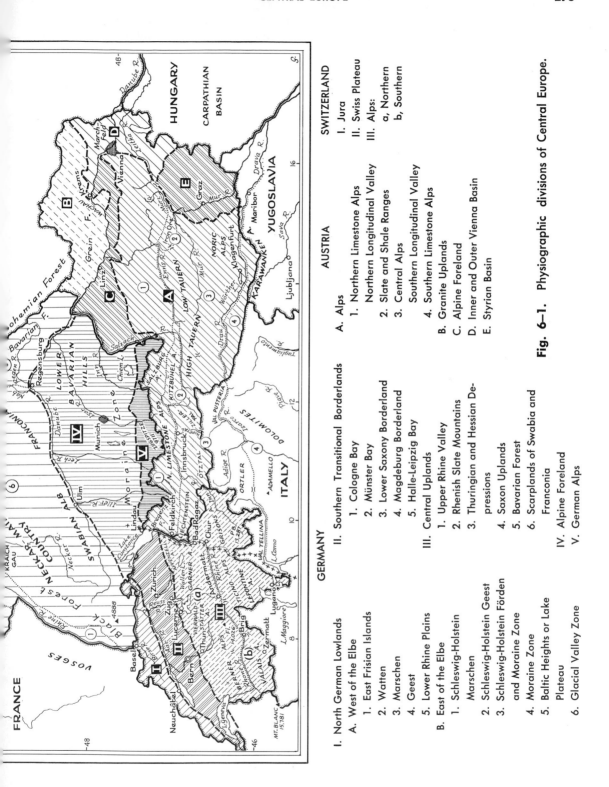

Fig. 6–1. Physiographic divisions of Central Europe.

GERMANY

I. North German Lowlands
  A. West of the Elbe
    1. East Frisian Islands
    2. Watten
    3. Marschen
    4. Geest
    5. Lower Rhine Plains
  B. East of the Elbe
    1. Schleswig-Holstein Marschen
    2. Schleswig-Holstein Geest
    3. Schleswig-Holstein Förden and Moraine Zone
    4. Moraine Zone
    5. Baltic Heights or Lake Plateau
    6. Glacial Valley Zone

II. Southern Transitional Borderlands
    1. Cologne Bay
    2. Münster Bay
    3. Lower Saxony Borderland
    4. Magdeburg Borderland
    5. Halle-Leipzig Bay

III. Central Uplands
    1. Upper Rhine Valley
    2. Rhenish Slate Mountains
    3. Thuringian and Hessian Depressions
    4. Saxon Uplands
    5. Bavarian Forest
    6. Scarplands of Swabia and Franconia

IV. Alpine Foreland

V. German Alps

AUSTRIA

A. Alps
    1. Northern Limestone Alps
       Northern Longitudinal Valley
    2. Slate and Shale Ranges
    3. Central Alps
       Southern Longitudinal Valley
    4. Southern Limestone Alps
B. Granite Uplands
C. Alpine Foreland
D. Inner and Outer Vienna Basin
E. Styrian Basin

SWITZERLAND

I. Jura
II. Swiss Plateau
III. Alps:
    a, Northern
    b, Southern

climates of Western Europe to the transitional climates in the east, or from the subtropical type prevailing in some of the valleys along the southern flank of the Alps to the more variable climates of the Alpine region proper.

Central Europe has considerable mineral wealth: coal in the Ruhr, the Saar, Lower Saxony, and the southern part of The German Democratic Republic; petroleum in eastern Austria and Lower Saxony; iron ore in central Austria (Erzberg). Austria and Switzerland have ample hydroelectric power, and Austria and Germany have valuable deposits of various metallic minerals and rare salts. The industries of the whole region are highly developed.

THE PHYSICAL LANDSCAPE

Central Europe is characterized by a great diversity in its physical landscape. In addition, every part of the structural and tectonic elements is closely tied to surrounding regions (Fig. 1–3), e.g., the Alps in Western Europe, the North German Lowlands as part of the western and eastern European coastal lowlands, and the Alpine Foreland as a continuation of the Swiss Mittelland and the Austrian Alpine Foreland. To provide a clear picture of the physical landscape of Central Europe the discussions are presented under two regional headings, those of Germany and those of the Alps, including the Alpine countries of Switzerland, Liechtenstein, and Austria.

Germany

Location and size.　No matter how one defines Central Europe, Germany forms part of it. In 1871, it covered an area of 208,189 square miles. At that time it was third in size among European powers. Since then it has undergone four territorial changes. By the Treaty of Versailles, Germany lost 27,200 square miles with a population of 6.5 million. It expanded again under Hitler, who incorporated the Sudetenland, Austria, and many other parts of Europe into the Third Reich between 1938 and 1944. But after the military defeat of 1945 it was reduced to 138,000 square miles (approximately the combined areas of Minnesota and Michigan). In the east, the former Prussian provinces of Pomerania, Brandenburg, and Upper and Lower Silesia have passed under Polish administration; East Prussia has been split up between the U.S.S.R. and Poland. Thus, present-day Germany is bounded by latitudes 47° and 55° N. and longitudes 6° and 15° E. Its greatest north-south extension is approximately 590 miles, and its maximum east-west extension 385 miles (Fig. 6–19), but it is divided into two sovereign States, each recognized by a number of countries; The Federal Republic of Germany, including West Berlin, with a mid-1968 population of 60,300,000; and The German Democratic Republic with a 1968 estimated population of 17,100,000.

Physiographic divisions.　Germany may be divided into five broad regions which resemble the main structural divisions (Fig. 6–1): (I) The North German Lowlands, a glaciated plain; (II) the Southern Transitional Borderlands, a belt of morainic material and highly fertile soil; (III) the worn-down fragments of the Hercynian system, collectively called the Central Uplands (*Mittelgebirge*); and (IV and V) the Alpine Foreland, once covered by the Alpine ice cap, together with the Alps, a young folded mountain system of which only a small fraction lies within Germany's boundaries. Each of these five main regions can be further subdivided according to structure, relief, climate, and soil characteristics.

Before discussing the regions and their subdivisions, it should be pointed out that in Germany the chief contrasts, both physiographic and cultural, appear between north and south. In the north, the glaciated lowlands include the transitional fertile borderlands. The south includes the diversified uplands of Central Germany, the Alpine Foreland, and the Alps. A dividing line, clearly marked on any physical map, may be drawn eastward from Aachen, along the southern margin of the Ruhr industrial area, along the

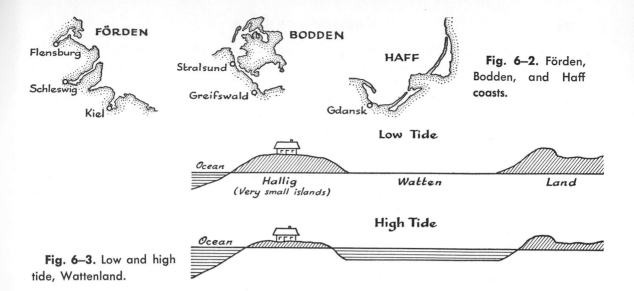

FÖRDEN

Flensburg
Schleswig
Kiel

BODDEN

Stralsund
Greifswald

HAFF

Gdansk

Fig. 6-2. Förden, Bodden, and Haff coasts.

Low Tide

Ocean

Hallig
(Very small islands)

Watten

Land

High Tide

Ocean

Fig. 6-3. Low and high tide, Wattenland.

edge of the Weser hills through Osnabrück and Hanover, along the northern edge of the Harz Mountains, and around the Leipzig Bay to Görlitz on the Neisse River (Fig. 6-1).

I. THE NORTH GERMAN LOWLANDS. The Lowlands escaped the uplift which has affected most of Southern and Western Europe since the Middle Tertiary. Unconsolidated deposits were laid down by the ice sheets which spread southward from Scandinavia in Quaternary times. Boulder clay, gravel, sand, and deposits of wind-blown loess vary in thickness between 40 feet and 500 feet.

In its successive advances the ice sheet encountered no obstacles short of the Central Uplands, where it was halted by the Ore Mountains (Erzgebirge), Harz Mountains, Weser hills, and other highlands. Subsequently, the ice movements across the Lowlands weakened. The various stages of glacial retreat are evidenced by moraines which give the region a hilly character. In its slow retreat northward, the ice sheet left two east-west-oriented depressions east of the Elbe River. These abandoned glacial-stream channels or spillways are called *Urstromtäler* by the Germans. Total yearly precipitation in the North German Lowlands decreases toward the east, except where influenced by relief. This is the only region where the full effect of maritime character-

istics is felt (Fig. 1-14). Toward the east, seasonal contrasts become sharper.

The North German Lowlands are generally divided into two subregions, one west and one east of the Elbe River:

West of the Elbe. Between the North Sea coast and the East Frisian Islands, which at one time formed a continuous dune wall, there are tidal flats, or *Watten*, which are flooded at high tide. Reclaimed areas, called *Marschen*, border the seashore and the estuaries of the Elbe, Weser, and Ems rivers. This land, like the polders in the Netherlands, has been reclaimed by diking and draining. The soil is rich and very suitable for grazing. Some sugar beets and vegetables are also grown profitably. Between the *Marschen* and the adjacent zone of Pleistocene sandy soils known as *geest* there are usually extensive meadow moors (bogs), level, treeless, and covered with grasses. The *geest* is located between the Elbe and the Ems. Within it, a somewhat higher area extending from the Elbe to the Weser-Aller rivers is known as the Lüneburger Heath. Its highest point, the Wilseder Berg (1,663 feet), lies east of Bremen and has been made into a national park. The *geest* is of limited agricultural value. Grazing is only of local importance. The climate is maritime, with cool summers and mild winters, considerable precipitation especially in winter, and strong winds (Figs. 6-2 and 6-3).

The *geest*, particularly the part west of the Aller, is often interspersed with bogs. These bogs still cover a large area despite the application of modern, Dutch-inspired methods of cutting and draining. Thanks to these methods, which in Germany are known as *Fehn* or *Behn* cultivation, it is now possible to raise vegetables and cattle here. New agricultural settlements in former bog country are called fen colonies (*Fehnkolonie*). Papenburg, on the lower Ems, is such a settlement. More recent methods have shown that cutting is unnecessary and that, with proper drainage and the addition of sand and clay, bog soils can be made into valuable arable land. Peat is burned in nearby power plants or used for domestic purposes. Since 1941, petroleum has been found west of the Ems, in the southern part of the Bourtanger Bog, and the wells of the so-called Emsland fields are bringing a further change to the cultural landscape of this once unproductive land.

East of the Elbe. The country east of the Elbe River has a history of more recent glaciation; morainic ridges extend in several

the Baltic coastline is usually further subdivided into a *Bodden* coast (irregularly shaped inlets behind irregular islands) between the Oder and Lübeck Bay in Mecklenburg, and a *Förden* coast (long, steep-sided drowned valleys formed by rivers underneath an ice sheet, similar to a fjord coast) so typical of the Baltic coast of Schleswig-Holstein (Fig. 6–4 and Fig. 6–1). Climatic conditions along the Baltic are more continental than to the west; low salinity and a very small tidal range allow the water to freeze over more readily. Most other ports are closed for two to four weeks.

South of this zone, extending 10 to 50 miles inland, is a strip of fertile lowlands covered with boulder clay. Crops such as sugar beets, rye, some wheat, and potatoes are grown here, and there are pastures for livestock.

Farther south, a zone of irregular hills marks a halt in the ice cap's last major retreat. This zone, commonly known as Baltic Heights or Baltic Lake Plateau (Fig. 6–1), is characterized by many lakes and undrained hollows, gravel, sand, boulder clay, and coniferous trees.

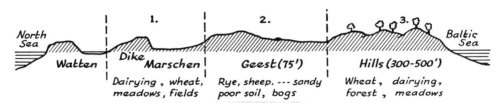

Fig. 6–4. Profile across Schleswig-Holstein.

parallel bands along the southern shore of the Baltic Sea. Going from north to south the following subdivisions may be distinguished.

A ground moraine zone, consisting of glacial loams and forming a fertile, rolling lowland belt. The many lakes in this zone are proof of its recent glaciation. The coast is clearly divided into a western and an eastern section, with the Oder River a distinctive boundary. The whole coastline is drowned, and the German section has many bays, gulfs, and islands. The western part of

Parallel to the main ridge of the Baltic Heights, a series of lower, more irregular, and less continuous terminal moraines marks the interruption of the slow retreat of the ice sheets.

Glacial Valley Zone. Between the morainal heights and the Central Uplands there is an extended plain of broad valleys (Fig. 6–1) alternating with somewhat higher ground consisting mainly of sandy soils. Here are the previously mentioned glacial spillways extending in an east-west direction and interconnected by diagonal valleys. These glacial spillways form broad and flat depressions now occupied in whole or in part by various rivers, such as the Havel and Spree near Berlin. Originally, the main drainage paralleled the front of the continental ice mass, but during the retreat of the ice many streams adopted a north-south course. The glacial spillways, however, are of great value in the construction of canals; the need for locks is almost obviated by the slight gradient from east to west. The southern boundary of the area of the glacial spillways is formed roughly by the upland zones of the Fläming and Lower Lusatia. It is here that the last ice sheet was halted by higher ground.

Originally the whole Glacial Valley was forested. German settlers after the twelfth century drained the swampy valleys, consisting largely of peat swamps and wooded or heath-covered sand dunes. Once drained, the alluvium itself offered more productive soil than that found in the sandy regions between the valleys.

II. SOUTHERN TRANSITIONAL BORDERLANDS. North of the Central Uplands and south of the glaciated lowlands lies a belt of thinly layered morainic material and highly fertile soil.

The width of this zone varies, but it broadens to include several bays (lowland embayments): (1) the Cologne Bay, which includes the Lower German Rhineland; (2) the Münster Bay; (3) the Lower Saxon Borderland; (4) the Magdeburg Borderland; and (5) the Halle-Leipzig bay.

This fertile belt consists of glacial soil covered by alluvial deposits which in turn are partially covered by loess. The whole belt has fertile brown forest and chernozem soils. Münster Bay has but a small area of loess near Soest. Situated between the dissected Central Uplands and the glaciated, moraine-covered lowlands, and cultivated since Neolithic times, this transitional belt is of outstanding importance to Germany and to the world.

Thanks to the natural quality of the land, to efficient crop rotation, and to the heavy application of fertilizer in less productive areas, this region has become a rich farm district in which wheat, sugar beets, barley, and vegetables predominate. The Transitional Borderlands also possess great mineral wealth, mainly bituminous-coal and lignite deposits in the Ruhr and the Rhineland, lignite in the Leipzig Bay, low-grade iron ore and petroleum in the Peine-Salzgitter area between Hanover (Hannover) and Brunswick, and potassium and common-salt deposits along the foothills of the Harz Mountains near Stassfurt and Halle.

This combination of great mineral wealth and valuable farm land supports a dense rural and urban population (500 to 600 per square mile). All the towns are old and have grown considerably in importance since the early Middle Ages. Situated for the most part at nodal points, where routes from the uplands fan out into the plain, these towns are also crossed by important east-west transportation arteries. The Midland Canal from the Ems to the Elbe is the most recent addition to the transport net; it provides a direct water connection between the Rhine, the Ruhr, Berlin, and the Oder.

III. CENTRAL UPLANDS. Between the North German Lowlands, the narrow belt of Transitional Borderlands, and the Alpine Foreland south of the Danube, there is a region of great diversity: rolling, dissected, and forested hills, granite massifs reduced by glacial action, old volcanoes, basins, plateaus, scarped limestone ridges, etc., all belonging to the Hercynian zone—the Central Uplands. The hilly and diversified character of this zone is the result of block movements, uplifts and subsidences, upwarpings and recessions, resulting from fractures and horizontal dislocations. Numerous horsts are characteristic of this block landscape. Volcanic intrusions, which are especially noticeable in the western part of the Uplands, are closely connected with these movements. The heights near the center of the Uplands escaped the ice cover for the most part, but the peripheral valleys, particularly those in the north, were broadened by ice action. Only the highest portions of the Uplands were covered by mountain glaciers, as shown by the ridges and cirques of the Black Forest (Schwarzwald), Bavarian Forest, and Ore Mountains.

The Central Uplands are not a climatic barrier. Rainfall increases very rapidly with increasing altitude. This is well illustrated in the Alb areas bordering the Alpine Foreland. Only during the winter, when cloud banks are much lower than in summertime, do the summits show above the zone of maximum precipitation. The snow cover in the Central Uplands is abundant and snowfalls continue as late as March.

The Central Uplands may be divided into numerous topographical units (Fig. 6–1).

Upper Rhine Valley. The Upper Rhine Valley, extending from Basel to Frankfurt, has a length of more than 180 miles, but a width of only about 25 miles. Flanked by mountains, it was formed by the sinking of land between two roughly parallel faults in Late Tertiary times. This is called a Graben. The Rhine enters the valley above Basel, at an elevation of 800 feet above sea level, and leaves it near Bingen, 253 feet above sea level. The length of the regulated section of the river is 224 miles. The surface of the valley consists of drained alluvial land, dry gravels, and some loess deposits which have made it into a very rich agricultural region (Fig. 6–5).

The valley clearly forms a physical unit with its surrounding mountains. The Jura lies toward the south, the Rhenish Slate Mountains to the north, the Vosges and the Hardt to the west, and the Black Forest and Odenwald to the east. The mountains flanking the valley in the east and in the west are part of a massif whose central section was downfaulted. They are dissected by valleys and are heavily forested. The Odenwald is separated from the Black Forest by a depression, the Kraichgau or Neckar Bergland. North of the Odenwald is the Frankfurt Basin, drained by the lower Main River. The highest summit in this mountain complex is the Feldberg (4,888 feet), located in the Black Forest. West of the Rhine, and linked to its upper valley by the depression of Kaiserslautern, lies the coal-rich Saar Basin.

The Upper Rhine Valley's equable climate permits a highly diversified agriculture including the cultivation of wheat, sugar beets, tobacco, hops, fruits, and grapes; vineyards occupy the foothills of the bordering mountains, especially between Karlsruhe and Darmstadt. Winters are very mild and July temperatures average about 70° F. The mountains have long winters and abundant precipitation.

Rhenish Slate Mountains. The Rhenish Slate Mountains form part of the Central Uplands, but in terms of regional geography they belong to the Rhine Valley.

The mountains (sometimes called the Rhine Plateau) are cut in two by the Middle Rhine River, which flows in a narrow, approximately 80-mile-long gorge from Bingen to Bonn. The surrounding heights rise to an average of 1,500 feet above the gorge. From Mainz the Rhine flows westward for some 15 miles, skirts the Taunus as far as Bingen, and then continues northwestward through the gorge to Bonn and to the Lower Rhine

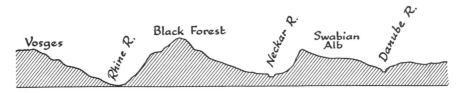

Fig. 6–5. Profile, Vosges to the Danube River.

Fig. 6–6. The Rhine at St. Goarshausen with the castle of Katz. Vineyards line the terraced slopes. Ships of many nations must carefully wind their way through the narrow and still dangerous stretch of the Rhine. (German Tourist Information Office.)

Plains beyond. The course of the Rhine in this section is antecedent, the river having cut its channel at the same rate that the underlying peneplain was being uplifted (Fig. 6–6). The Rhine gorge is often very narrow, and rapids had to be eliminated in order to make the river more navigable. Vineyards cover the terraced lower slopes of the steep-sided Rhine gorge; they are also found in terraces along the tributary valleys, notably along the Moselle, Lahn, and Aare rivers. Today, the Rhine is not only a busy waterway for a great variety of craft but its gorge is also an important tourist attraction.

The upland areas of the Rhenish Slate Mountains extend from the Main to the Ruhr and from the Ardennes to the Thuringian and Hessian Depressions. The boundaries of the several subdivisions coincide with the courses of the Rhine's various tributaries. Severely weathered young volcanic

deposits give the Westerwald better soils than are found in almost any other plateau region. In the Siegerland, whose mines and forests supplied Germany's first industries with iron ore and charcoal, some iron is still mined. North of the Sieg River, the plateau drops off to the Sauerland, beyond which the well-known industrial region of the Ruhr is located.

Thuringian and Hessian Depressions. This region is bounded by the Rhenish Slate Mountains in the west, the Saxon Uplands in the east, and the fertile Transitional Borderlands in the north. The Main River forms the southern boundary. The region is a mass of basins, broad forested uplands, and narrow but fertile plains, disturbed by volcanic activity, faulting, and to the north by much folding. Two subdivisions are commonly recognized: the Hessian Depression toward the west and the Thuringian Basin and Forest. Hesse is characterized by many individual forested mountain sections, the broad fertile river valleys (depressions) of the Weser and the Fulda, with the important crossroad town of Kassel, and the dissected volcanic Vogelsberg (2,533 feet) and Rhön (3,117 feet) mountains north of the Main River. In the north, two low wooded ranges, the Teutoburg Forest and the Weser Hills, protrude toward the plains between Münster and Hanover.

Thuringia is composed of three distinct parts: The Harz Mountains, the Thuringian Forest, and the Thuringian Basin. These areas offer great contrasts. The Thuringian Forest is a densely populated, wooded mountain range, whose highly skilled inhabitants are engaged mainly in manufacture demanding great skill; there is only limited agriculture. In contrast, the Basin, which is drained by the Saale River and its tributaries, contains rich agricultural land, mainly degraded chernozem. The Harz Mountains are located between the Leine and the Saale and trend in a southeast-northwest direction. Their upper parts are still covered with forests, while elsewhere such crops as hay and potatoes are grown. The Brocken (3,742 feet) is the highest summit. Even today, the Harz Mountains remain a transportation bottleneck in an area of heavy traffic.

Saxon Uplands. South of the Halle-Leipzig bay, the forested Ore Mountains reach an altitude of over 4,000 feet. These mountains drop off abruptly on the Bohemian side and slope gradually toward the bay. Their slopes, known as the Saxon Foothills support some agriculture, but the real value of this area lies in its mineral wealth, which includes uranium and lignite. The Ore Mountains, which run in a southwest-northeast direction, are separated from the Sudeten, which trend in a northwest-southeast direction, by the Elbsandsteingebirge, an area of great scenic beauty. The Elbe River cuts through this sandstone range in a deep canyon formed by downfaulting and later filled by clays and sandstones.

Bavarian Forest. Between the German-Czechoslovak frontier and the Danube and Nab rivers lies a sparsely populated forested region. This region, which is underlaid by granite and gneiss, is known as the Bavarian Forest. The forest reaches deep into Bavaria; within Germany it is subdivided into a southern and a northern part, the depression drained by the upper Regen River serving as a dividing line. The southern part consists of long, high ridges with wide basins, while the northern part has an irregular knob-and-valley topography and is generally lower than the former. Precipitation is abundant, ranging from 47 to 55 inches at an elevation of 2,400 feet, and fogs are very frequent. Most of the region is occupied by forest, with beech, fir, and spruce dominant.

Scarplands of Swabia and Franconia. East of the Black Forest and the Odenwald, there is a region variously identified as scarplands, plateaus, and basins. Most of it is drained by the Neckar and Main rivers. The scarps of the region face mostly toward the northwest, and the older formations are usually clearly visible.

As we proceed northeastward from the Black Forest and the Odenwald, we encounter various geologic formations, each of which leaves a distinct mark on the landscape. The scarplands of the Swabian and the Franconian Alb are cut out of limestone which forms a plateau up to 1,200 feet high. The scarps extend in a southwest-northeast direction from the upper Rhine to the depression of the Ries, which divides the Swabian from the Franconian Alb; thence they trend from west to east until they veer northward toward the Main River.

Climatic conditions are influenced by elevation which varies from escarpment to escarpment. The Swabian and the Franconian Alb have considerably less precipitation (27 to 39 inches) than the escarpments farther west, while the leeward side facing the Danube receives less than 20 inches. Thanks to the latitude (48° N. to 50° N.) and to the protection afforded by the forested mountains on the west, the climate is well suited to the growing of cereals, tobacco, hops, and some hard fruits; even corn and vines do well on the plains. Except for deposits of lithographic stone found in the Franconian Alb, the region is almost lacking in economic minerals.

IV, V. THE ALPINE FORELAND AND THE GERMAN ALPS. The German part of the Alpine Foreland lies between the Swabian and the Franconian Alb in the north, the Bavarian Forest in the northeast, and the Alps in the south. It forms a northward-sloping plateau in continuation of the Swiss Plateau. Relief differences are between 1,000 and 3,000 feet, but the Foreland has the appearance of a broad plain, with its lowest point (915 feet above sea level) at the confluence of the Danube and Inn rivers. The Foreland's geologic structure is closely related to that of the Alps. There also exist similarities in fauna and flora, and the Alpine climate influences that of the Foreland.

Morainic deposits—gravels, sands, and huge boulders—cover wide areas of the Foreland, in testimony of the extent of Alpine glaciers (Fig. 6–7).

The northern part of the Foreland is covered by glacial outwash material, and therefore it is hillier and better suited for agriculture. There are numerous bogs in the higher southern parts of the Foreland. Finger lakes, at right angles to the trend of the moraines, are especially numerous east of the Lech River. All the rivers rise in the Alps and cross the Foreland in broad, marshy valleys. They are not navigable, because of the irregularity of their flow. The Danube Valley occupies a depression 15 to 30 miles wide. Although it has a moderate gradient, the Danube carries sufficient water for navigation to begin at Ulm.

The climate of the Foreland, noted for its cold winters, becomes more continental as one proceeds eastward. A comparison between Regensburg (1,125 feet) and Lindau on Lake Constance (1,329 feet) is of interest. The January temperature in Lindau averages 30° F., the July temperature 64.4° F., while the yearly mean is 48° F. In Regensburg, January temperature is 26.6° F., July 64° F., and the yearly mean 45.3° F. It should be added that the area has a milder climate, in part because of the influence of a large water body. Precipitation increases with elevation. The quantity of summer rainfall and of melting snow determines the rivers' summer volume.

Mixed forests, predominantly coniferous, are at higher altitudes; forests occur mostly in small patches in the Foreland (Fig. 6–8). Soils are generally poor, so barley, oats, and

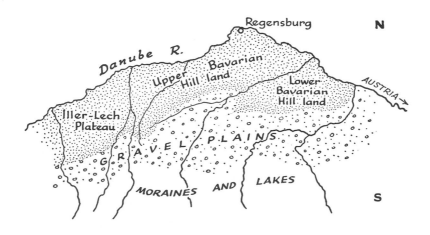

Fig. 6–7. Sketch of the Alpine Foreland.

Fig. 6–8. Bavarian Alpine Foreland. Flight direction northwest-southeast between rivers Lech and Isar toward Munich. Dispersed agricultural settlements with patches of forests and small agricultural holdings (photo taken from about 20,000 feet). (G. W. Hoffman.)

rye are the chief cereal crops, and dairy grazing is widespread. A few special crops are grown on better soils along several streams.

Only a small part of the Alps falls within Germany. The international boundary runs through the outer zones of the Northern Limestone Alps, from which rises Germany's highest mountain peak, the Zugspitze (9,711 feet).

German rivers. The even distribution of precipitation and ample snow cover provide German rivers with sufficient water for navigation. Most of these rivers, for example, the Ems, Weser, Elbe, and Oder, flow from the Central Uplands (and from their extension into Poland and Czechoslovakia) toward the North and Baltic seas. As a result of structural differences, the Rhine and the Danube have a different drainage pattern and direction of flow. As late as the Middle Tertiary, the Upper Rhine Plains and the Alpine Foreland were still covered by vast seas. When the waters receded, the Foreland was drained eastward by the Danube and northward by the Rhine. However, the lower altitude of the Upper Rhine Plains and the very short distance to the North Sea enabled the Rhine to erode headward and to capture the drainage of the western Foreland and of the

area around today's Lake Constance, which formerly fed into the Danube. This peculiar structural history also becomes apparent upon examination of the Rhine's course. The usual threefold division of rivers into upper, middle, and lower course is replaced in the case of the Rhine by a breakdown into five sections: Alpine Rhine (from its source to Lake Constance), high Rhine (to Basel), upper Rhine (to Bingen), middle Rhine (to Bonn), and lower Rhine.

Brief mention should also be made of the regimes of streams, i.e., the changes in the amount of flow and in the water level. The rivers which rise in the Central Uplands—the Ems, Weser, Elbe, Oder, the right tributaries of the Rhine, and the left tributaries of the Danube—reach high-water stage shortly after the melting of the snow, usually during the early spring; their low-water stage comes in July and August, largely because of increased evaporation. Typical mountain streams as well as parts of the Rhine and of the Danube reach their crest in the summer because of the late melting of snows in the high mountains and the heavy summer rains; their low-water stage occurs during the winter. On the other hand, the upper and middle Rhine receives a considerable volume of water from numerous tributaries rising in the Central Uplands, so the range between high and low water is reduced. The lower Rhine is characterized by an even regime, a factor of considerable importance for the river's economic usefulness.

Compared with their windward side, the leeward side of the Central Uplands has an abundance of rain. The waters of many mountain rivers are dammed and stored in reservoirs which provide protection against floods, storage for low-water periods, and water for industry and the generation of hydroelectric power. Most of these artificial lakes are within the Eifel, Sauerland, and the Bergischesland (south of the Ruhr).

The amount of ice cover on German rivers increases from west to east as expected, and impedes navigation. Great variations in the length of the winter freeze are characteristic. The Rhine at Cologne (Köln) is frozen over for an average of 20 days per year, the Ems for 27, the lower Weser for 37, the Elbe near Magdeburg for 45, and the Danube at Regensburg for an average of 37 days.

The Alps

Location and size. The Alps are Europe's greatest folded mountain system in terms of both elevation and extent. The length of the Alps along the inner edge of the arc is approximately 470 miles, and about 810 miles along the outer edge. The chord of the arc is approximately 340 miles long. Their width ranges from 80 miles near the highest peak (Mont Blanc, 15,781 feet) to 150 miles north of Verona. They cover about 85,000 square miles, or an area somewhat larger than Kansas.[3]

The Alps extend in an arc from the Altare Pass on the Gulf of Genoa to a line which approximates the railroad line Vienna-Graz-

[3] As far as possible the Alps are discussed as a whole in this chapter, since they form a physiographic unit. Their southern slopes are also briefly discussed in the chapter on Southern Europe, and the French Alps in the chapter on Western Europe. The tectonic evolution and structural units of the Alpine orogeny are discussed in Chapter 1, pp. 20–30. For geological terms, see Appendix I.

Maribor-Ljubljana. Southeast of the Altare Pass they connect with the Apennines. In France, near Lake Bourget (Lac du Bourget), the Jura Mountains detach themselves from the main body of the Alps, forming a separate spur. Lying between them and the Alps proper, the plateau extends from Lake Geneva to southern Germany.

The interior of the arc is occupied by the Po-Adriatic depression, toward which the Alps slope rather abruptly. Along the outer edge of the arc there are a number of old massifs against which the Alps had been pushed during the folding process. This Alpine arc has scores of peaks reaching above 10,000 feet, and several peaks in the Valais (Wallis) chain of Switzerland attain an elevation of 15,000 feet. Despite their relatively low latitude (43° N. to 48° N.), the Alps carry the most extensive glaciers found on the mainland of Europe.

Politically, the Alps extend into seven countries: Italy, France, Switzerland, Liechtenstein, Germany, Austria, and Yugoslavia. Of these, Switzerland, Liechtenstein, and Austria are referred to as "Alpine countries" in a true sense. This section of the chapter concerns itself chiefly with the Alpine countries.

Major divisions. A line running south from Lake Constance, up the Rhine Valley, and across Splügen Pass (6,923 feet) to Lake Como divides the Alps into two parts of very different topographic characteristics. West of this line, the western Alps are narrower, more compact, and higher, with more and longer glaciers and more incised valleys. East of this line, the eastern Alps are broader and lower; their longitudinal valleys are wider and interconnected across low watersheds. The highest peak in the western Alps is Mont Blanc. Local relief, often exceeding 9,000 feet over a short horizontal distance, greatly contributes to the impressive picture confronting the visitor. The eastern Alps, with their highest elevation at Piz Bernina (13,287 feet) in Grisons (Graubünden) canton of Switzerland, have several levels of summits (*Gipfelfluren*), and only near the previously mentioned line of division do they reach heights comparable to those in the western Alps.[4]

Most of Switzerland falls within the western Alps. Only the mountains of the eastern part of Grisons canton are included among the eastern Alps. All of Austria lies in the eastern Alps.

The western Alps are further broken down into two divisions: the Franco-Italian Alps, which lie south and west of a line extending from the eastern end of Lake Geneva through the upper Rhone Valley, the Great St. Bernard Pass (8,110 feet), and the Dora Baltea Valley to the Piedmont lowlands and the upper Po River; and the Swiss Alps, which lie between the Great St. Bernard Pass and a line through Lake Constance-Rhine-Lake Como.

Germany's share of the Alps is limited to a narrow outer strip of the Northern Limestone Alps, between Lake Constance and Salzburg.

In addition to the transverse division described above, there are several parallel longitudinal zones separated by deep valleys and distinguished by differences in rock types. Thus the Alpine chains are broken up into several distinct groups.

Physiographic Divisions. As was pointed out in the introduction, the structure of the Alps is largely the result of the folding of sediments between the Eurasian forelands and the African land mass (see Chapter 1, pp. 24–27). Before this folding occurred, rivers had worn down the mountains of more ancient origin and carried the sediments into the adjacent seas. The mature surface thus created was very low and had little local relief, but during the later stages of the erosion cycle it was again uplifted and warped. Denudation and weathering have sculptured the mountains into the youthful forms we see

today. These processes are much less evident in the eastern Alps than in the western Alps. During the Ice Age, the whole mountain system was repeatedly covered by ice and only certain regions in the southeast and the southwest, such as Styria, Carinthia, and Provence, escaped the effects of glaciation. Ice sheets cut and dug away large portions of mountains, and, as warmer temperatures returned, moraines, U-shaped valleys, Alpine cirques, and pyramidal peaks were left as evidence of glacial action. Denudation by glaciers and streams is also responsible for such features as the broad, steep-walled hanging valleys (Fig. 6–9), polished and striated boulders, and the many tongue basins blocked by morainic deposits at their outward ends. Glacial action has been especially important in widening and deepening what had once been a small longitudinal hollow into the present important central depression between Martigny on the Rhone and Chur on the Rhine. This same depression can be traced southwestward from Martigny into the high Alps and the Pre-Alps of France.

The transverse subdivision of the Alps into a western and an eastern part has already been described; more significant, however, is a division into several distinct longitudinal sectors along the deep valleys mentioned earlier. In many ways the lithological zones which we shall briefly describe here correspond to these longitudinal sectors. It should also be pointed out, however, that only in the eastern Alps can the following division into longitudinal zones be clearly recognized. (See also the description of the six major structural units, in Chapter 1, pp. 27–29.)

The central Alps consist of resistant crystalline rocks (granite, gneiss, and schist), which form the principal chain of the Alps. These formations extend from the edge of the Carpathian Basin to the Pennine Alps just northwest of the Po Basin (Fig. 6–1). In the eastern Alps the zone of resistant rocks is interspersed with bands of shale and slate, which are more easily eroded and thus account for the gentler slopes.

---

[4] The division of the Alps into two parts is widely accepted. The Italians, however, prefer a threefold division: (1) the *Alpi Occidentali,* with the Col du Ferret forming the boundary between it and (2) the *Alpi Centrali,* which in turn is separated by the furrow of the Brenner Pass from (3) the *Alpi Orientali.*

Fig. 6–9. Wengen, overlooking the U-shaped Lauterbrunnen Valley, Switzerland. Some of the waterfalls have a vertical descent of close to 1,000 feet. The view is toward the Bernese Alps. (Swiss Tourist Office.)

North of the central Alps lies a belt of generally lower ranges consisting of sedimentary rocks, especially limestone, and characterized by a very jagged sky line and deeply incised valleys (Fig. 6–1). This belt is known as the Northern Limestone Alps. A southern limestone zone, which is not found in the western Alps, begins east of Lake Maggiore, increases in width, and extends clear across the Dinaric Ranges. It contains volcanic extrusions such as the reddish-black rocks of the peripheral plateau of Bolzano (Bozen) see Chapter 7, pp. 370–72).

North of the Northern Limestone Alps are the rolling Foreland hills, a narrow and discontinuous zone (called Flysch zone), consisting mostly of slate, clay, and sandstone. This zone widens in Austria, where it forms an outer zone of the Northern Limestone Alps. In front of the Flysch zone, in the Alpine Foreland, there are stream-deposited beds of Molasse, which consist mostly of sandstone and conglomerates.

To clarify these differences and divisions, we shall list the main physiographic divisions and point out some of their distinctive features. For the sake of better identification, this presentation will follow existing political divisions which, with the exception of a slight overlap in Grisons canton of Switzerland, follow the widely recognized dividing line between eastern and western Alps.

Switzerland

Switzerland is normally divided into three distinct regions—the Jura, the Swiss Plateau,[5] and the Swiss Alps.

THE JURA. The Jura trends southwest-northeast from the Rhone to the Rhine and consists of several parallel limestone folds. The folds are well developed along the southeastern rim but flatten out toward the northwest and gradually merge into the undisturbed strata of the Swiss Plateau. The eastern slopes facing Switzerland are steepest and highest. The ridges run in the same direction as the axis of the folds and are separated from each other by longitudinal valleys. They become lower and narrower toward Basel and the Rhine and are therefore easier to cross in this area. The highest point, Crêt de la Neige (5,653 feet), is located in the southwestern part of the Jura, just inside France. The Jura's most important rivers are the Doubs, flowing almost entirely in France, and the Birse, which enters the Rhine near Basel. These rivers flow alternately in broad valleys and narrow gorges.

Thanks to abundant rainfall, the Jura's inhabitants practice dairying and lumbering and some wine growing on the southeastern slopes facing the Plateau. Because of the karstlike topography and underground drainage characteristic of the Jura's limestone formations, relatively few streams and lakes appear at the surface.

The Jura occupies 10 per cent of the total area of Switzerland and has roughly 13 per cent of its population. Its real importance lies in the fact that it is the home of the watchmaking industry.

THE SWISS PLATEAU. The Swiss Plateau, an "uplifted depression" between the Alps and the Jura, extends for 180 miles in a southwest-northeast direction from Lake Geneva to Lake Constance; it is up to 30 miles wide. The Plateau was dissected by

---

[5] This region is also known as the Plains, the *Mittelland,* or the Alpine Foreland (*Alpenvorland*).

rivers and covered by ice. Its many small lakes attest to the former presence and movements of the ice sheet; their shape indicates the advance of various ice tongues. Other typical features of glaciation are terminal and ground moraines, huge boulders or erratics, drumlins, and deepened valley floors. The Plateau varies in elevation from 1,200 to 2,200 feet and has a mean altitude of 538 feet. It occupies 32 per cent of the total area of Switzerland but contains roughly 67 per cent of the Swiss population.

The Plateau's climate is rather uniform; the mean January and July temperatures of Bern and Zürich are shown as examples:

	Mean January Temperature	Mean July Temperature
Bern, 1,870 feet	29.7° F.	63.8° F.
Zurich, 1,617 feet	30.2° F.	63.0° F.

Mist often covers the whole Plateau like a sea of clouds. Some localities have an average of 120 days of mist per year (see Fig. 1–10 and Chapter 1, pp. 37–39).

Precipitation ranges from 32 inches at Basel, 900 feet above sea level, to 46 inches at Lucerne (Luzern), 1,480 feet high, and to over 100 inches at Säntis, 8,202 feet high. However, only a small part of Switzerland has more than 47 inches of precipitation.

The Plateau is most suitable for dairying; it has excellent meadows and ample acreage on which forage crops are grown. In the southwest, there are sugar beet and tobacco fields, vineyards, and orchards.

The Swiss Plateau may be divided into three natural subregions of varying economic significance (Fig. 6–1): (1) the northeast from Lake Constance to a line from Baden to Zug, with wine growing on sunny slopes and considerable industry; (2) the center as far as a line through Solothurn-Bern-Thun-Brienz, largely agricultural; and (3) the southwest down to Lake Geneva, with specialized crops such as tobacco and sugar beets (Figs. 6–30 and 6–31).

THE SWISS ALPS. The Swiss Alps occupy 58 per cent of Switzerland, but only roughly

18 per cent of its population resides there. The Alps have no clear-cut boundary either in the direction of the Swiss Plateau or the North Italian Plains. Toward the Plateau, they become gradually lower, are often called the Pre-Alps, and acquire a different land-use pattern; unproductive land is rare. The Rhone-Rhine longitudinal trough divides the Swiss Alps into the northern Alps and the southern Alps. The northern Alps may be divided as follows:

1. The Bernese Alps have the largest concentration of glaciers and reach their highest elevation (14,026 feet) in the Finsteraarhorn (Fig. 1–8), the principal chain, 68 miles long.
2. The Vierwaldstätter Alps, located between the Aare and the Reuss valleys.
3. The Garner Alps, located between the Reuss and the portion of the Rhine Valley below Chur.
4. The Appenzell Alps, situated between Wallensee and Lake Constance.

The southern Alps may also be divided into four main groups:

1. The Valais Alps, located between the Great St. Bernard and the Simplon passes, have many lateral valleys which give access to lofty peaks, notably the Matterhorn. The Simplon Tunnel (Fig. 6–12), which takes the Paris-Lausanne railroad line into Italy, is at the farthest end of the Valais Alps.
2. The Ticino Alps and the Lepontine Alps are pierced by the important St. Gotthard Tunnel on the Zurich-Milan railroad line. These mountains slope toward the Po Plain.
3. The Adula Alps, west of Splügen Pass, form the connecting link with the Grisons Alps.
4. The Grisons Alps, which cover most of the area of the canton of Grisons, are not as high as other Alpine summits, but the valleys are less accessible. Many important passes connect the Rhine and the Inn valleys with Austria and Italy.

Liechtenstein

The small, independent principality of Liechtenstein lies between Switzerland and Austria. Liechtenstein has been able to maintain its independence largely because of its favorable location controlling the Gap of Ragaz, which in turn controls the valleys and passes of Grisons and the easy Rhine crossing west of Vaduz.

Until 1719, it was ruled by the lords of Vaduz and Schellenberg, and since then it has been independent. Its customs and railroads are now controlled by Switzerland. Liechtenstein had a 1966 population of 19,916 and in spite of its size, 67 square miles, it has a healthy economic foundation. The valleys are fertile, pastures plentiful, and vineyards highly developed. Cotton spinning and embroidering are of exceptional quality. Tourist trade is increasing and numerous small factories dot the landscape, enabling its people to seek employment in the country rather than migrate. Over 31 per cent of its population are foreigners, the highest percentage for any European country, with 42 per cent employed in the country's industries and handicrafts. A high percentage of these foreigners have lived in Liechtenstein for many years, though citizenship can only be acquired after the *Bürgerrecht* (citizen rights granted by villages) has been obtained, which is extremely difficult to obtain because of the conservative village representatives.

Austria

Earlier in this chapter we discussed the more general aspects of the eastern Alps; both their geologic origin and lithologic divisions were described. Now we shall treat the various mountain groups and valley regions on the basis of their customary division into three longitudinal zones separated from each other by two longitudinal valley troughs. Following the standard works of Krebs, Sölch, and other geomorphologists, the country has been divided into regions, whose names describe their location and main characteristics (Fig. 6–1).

THE ALPS. The Northern Limestone Alps form a belt of varying width across the northern parts of the provinces of Vorarlberg, Tyrol, the central and southern part of Salzburg Province, and Upper Austria as far as the Vienna Woods. The outer zone, also called the Flysch zone, is characterized by rounded hills, gentle slopes, a very dense network of valleys, and many pastures. The limestone zone, which becomes wider toward the east, consists of many sharp peaks, barren high plateaus, fewer valleys, and much unproductive land.

The central Alps are separated from the limestone zone by the longitudinal valley depressions which run from Feldkirch and Vorarlberg over the Arlberg Pass, to the valleys of the Inn, Salzach, and Enns, then along the diagonal route of the Schober Saddle to the Mürz Valley, and finally over the Semmering Pass to the Vienna Basin. Important transverse valleys open into this important east-west highway, which is dotted with settlements and also contains the largest city of the interior Alps, Innsbruck. The longitudinal valley varies in width from a hundred feet to one mile (Fig. 6–10).

At two places, slate and shale ranges are interposed between the Northern Limestone Alps and the central Alps. These mountains are located between the longitudinal valley depression described above and a second, wider but discontinuous, depression which runs from the Ziller Valley in Tyrol to the

Fig. 6–10. The Inn Valley, in the Austrian Tyrol. The view is west and northwest to the Karwendel and Wetterstein ranges of the Northern Limestone Alps. Note the Innsbruck-Garmisch-Partenkirchen railroad line incised on the flanks of the Wetterstein Range (right). (Stempfle, Innsbruck.)

valleys of the Salzach and Enns rivers. Within these ranges are the Kitzbühel Alps and the rich ore mountains of the Eisenerz. The slate-shale mountains, whose rounded summits rise just over 6,500 feet, provide excellent pasture.

Between the Northern Longitudinal Valley, the southern edge of the slate-shale mountains, and the Southern Longitudinal Valley are the central Alps. They consist of many mountain chains of varying length. They run from the transverse line which divides the western and the eastern Alps, to the Noric Alps of eastern Austria. Included in the central Alps are the highest sections of the Austrian Alps, their numerous glaciated peaks rising over 10,000 feet. Routes across the central Alps are not numerous (See Fig. 6–12, pp. 296–97).

The Southern Longitudinal Valley runs from Lake Como, along the upper Adda River (Val Tellina), over Tonale Pass, to the Bolzano-Adige-Isarco valley, to the Puster Valley (Pustertal), and thence along the Drau River. The Klagenfurt Basin, a highly cultivated depression filled in Late Tertiary times, lies between the central Alps and the Southern Limestone Alps. Frequent changes in rock composition make this zone a most picturesque one. Most of the mountains in this zone are located within Italy. The valleys of the Adige, Tagliamento, and Sava rivers offer the only through routes of any importance. With the exception of the South Tyrol, this entire zone is sparsely populated.

THE GRANITE UPLANDS. The Austrian Granite Uplands occupy the area between the Bavarian and the Bohemian border and the Danube, and also extend several spurs across the Danube. The Danube skirts the southern edge of the Bohemian Plateau and flows through a succession of narrows and basins. The river is swift and is now being harnessed in an ever-increasing amount for power (Fig. 6–38). Valleys are incised below rolling uplands covered by scattered dense forests and generally poor soils. The

well-known Wachau is an example of such a valley. Water is abundant, and small farm patches are widely distributed. The eastern part of the Uplands has better farm land. The Uplands are situated between 1,300 and 2,400 feet above sea level.

THE ALPINE FORELAND. The Alpine Foreland is located between the Northern Limestone Alps and the Granite Uplands (Fig. 6–1). Both the southern and the northern boundary are sharp and distinct. Covered by sediments of the Great Ice Age, the Foreland consists of numerous low hills, steep scarps, and terraces. Numerous glacial lakes reach the Foreland and remind the visitor of similar lakes in the Pre-Alps in Switzerland and in the German Alpine Foreland. The Foreland has forests and excellent farm land; south of Linz and below Krems there is a cover of loess.

THE INNER AND THE OUTER VIENNA BASIN. Included in this area is the territory north of the Danube—the Marchfeld and its extension eastward to the international border—as well as the land south and west of the Danube to the first Alpine slopes. This region has a dry, warm climate, a long growing season which permits some grape cultivation, and sufficient rainfall for high agricultural yields. It is also Austria's main sugar-beet region.

Because of the open character of the country, this area has been of great economic and strategic value since ancient times, and strong fortifications were built to control it. Carnuntum (Petronell), built in 73 A.D., and, later, Vindobona (Vienna) were Roman legionary fortresses which guarded the many routes which converge here. It was protected in the northeast by the slopes of the Vienna Woods, and on all other sides by the Danube and its many arms and tributaries, prior to the regulation of the river. Throughout history, the Vienna Basin has retained its importance in the political geography of Central Europe. Both from an agricultural and from an industrial standpoint, it is the most important region of Austria.

THE STYRIAN BASIN. The Styrian Basin consists of important valleys and of rolling hills which flatten out toward the Carpathian Basin. The region also includes southern Burgenland. There are broad valleys with fertile meadows, cultivated fields on terraces and gentle slopes, orchards and vineyards on steeper slopes, and deciduous trees on shady slopes. Settlements are scattered in the hill lands, while the larger villages and the cities are located in the main valleys. The climate is very favorable, less extreme than that of the Vienna Basin and conducive to intensive land utilization. The Mur Valley, with the important city of Graz, is the center of this region.

Climate. The main trait of an Alpine climate is its great variability; it is influenced by the elevation, length, and width of the mountains. Typical of mountain regions in general are local differences in exposure to the sun and length of shade; in the Alps, these are especially noticeable in the east-west longitudinal valleys. This factor is of great importance for the distribution of settlements and croplands on slopes: on sunny slopes settlements extend higher, while the colder, usually forested shady slopes are avoided by settlers. This pattern is particularly evident in the eastern Alps. The temperature-lapse rate amounts to approximately 3° F. per 1,000 feet elevation; it is somewhat lower in midwinter and higher in early summer. It is also higher along the southern slopes and edges of mountain ranges. Wide valleys are warmer in summer, but suffer from temperature inversion in winter and are therefore colder than nearby slopes. This phenomenon is especially noticeable in the Engadine (Grisons, Switzerland), in the Pinzgau and Lungau (Salzburg, Austria), and the Klagenfurt Basin (Carinthia, Austria). Only at elevations above 3,500 feet are winter temperatures on slopes as low as those of adjacent basins. In fact, slopes and terraces enjoy many more sunny, bright, and dry days than the valleys or basins they overlook, which frequently are filled with cold, heavy air and thick mist.

For all these reasons, Alpine settlements are usually located on slopes, terraces, and alluvial cones, for protection against low winter and night temperatures as well as flood danger. Temperature differences decrease and annual extremes are modified at increased altitudes largely because of exposure to sun, heating by insolation during the day, and earth radiation during the night, resulting in diurnal ranges of temperature. As a result, snow remains longer on the ground, August is often the warmest month, and late March the coldest. The following table illustrates the foregoing statements:

Mean Temperatures (°F.)

Mountain Stations

	Rigi	Saentis	Zugspitze
Height in feet	5,863	8,202	9,719
January	24°	16°	12° (Feb.)
July	50°	41°	35° (Aug.)

Valley Stations

	Luzern	Lugano	Bevers	Innsbruck	Bolzano
Height in feet	1,634	906	5,610	1,970	950
January	29°	35°	15°	26°	32°
July	65°	73°	55°	64°	72°

SOURCE: W. G. Kendrew, *The Climates of the Continents*, 5th ed. Oxford: Clarendon Press, 1963, pp. 334, 339, 381, 383.

Precipitation increases with the altitude, but its measurement is extremely difficult due to wind interferences. Interior valleys are much drier, often receiving less than 30 inches of annual rainfall. Cases in point are the Valais (Switzerland) or the Inn Valley (Austria), and especially the Upper Adige Valley (South Tyrol, Italy), where irrigation is practiced. (The Vintschgau in the Upper Adige Valley is the driest area in the Alps receiving between 15 and 20 inches average annual precipitation.) Furthermore, along most mountain chains precipitation varies from the windward to the leeward side. In winter, precipitation occurs in the form of snow which covers most of the Alps for from three to five months, and areas above 6,000 feet for as long as six months. Snow depths of 30 feet have been recorded in places.

A whole series of local winds is characteristic of the Alps. In addition to being swept by the westerlies, most valleys have a regular alternation of up-slope and down-slope winds. These winds are especially strong in transverse valleys open toward the margin of the mountains. Between Geneva and Salzburg, those transverse valleys which open up toward the north or the northwest are under the influence of the warm, dry *föhn* (see Chapter 1, pp. 37–39, also Fig. 1–11). The *föhn* is responsible for the sudden melting of snow and for avalanches which endanger isolated mountain communities. It occurs both in midwinter and toward the end of the winter, when it usually heralds the coming of spring. It is accompanied by overcast skies, a sudden rise in temperature (40° F. within two hours is not unusual), and considerable dryness. High temperatures are due less to the wind's southern origin than to the small loss of temperature incurred in rising to the summits and to the great increase in temperature resulting from the descent. Innsbruck has an average of 43 days of *föhn*. The *föhn* also accounts for the extension of agriculture into some high Alpine valleys. In the southern valleys of the Alps, one encounters a type of *föhn* which comes from the northern slopes. Its effect, however, is not as strongly felt as in the northern valleys.

Vegetation and land use. Alpine vegetation varies according to the climate of the different bordering regions. It is also characterized by vertical zoning. The central position of the Alps in relation to the different climatic types was noted in Chapter 1. As a result, surrounding climatic types extend their influences into lower altitudes. On the eastern slopes of the Alps, the black pine is common. In the hills of Styria one encounters alders and some true steppe plants. The greatest local differences are found along the upper Italian lakes and the northern shore of Lake Geneva, as well as in the southern French Alps, where drought-resistant shrubs replace forests and grasslands. Here the chestnut occurs up to 8,850 feet, while on the north side of the Alps this tree is found only in the warmer valleys and on the sunnier slopes. Other trees characteristic of this section are the olive, mulberry, and cypress.

Three vertical vegetation and land-use zones may be discerned (Fig. 6–11): (1) an arable zone, (2) a zone of forests, and (3) a zone of pastures. Above these zones is an area of rock debris and eternal snow. The exact width and succession of these belts depend not only upon elevation but also upon latitude, exposure to the sun, degree of slope, temperature, precipitation, and the acts of man.

1. The arable zone reaches an elevation of approximately 4,200 feet, but considerable variations are found from place to place. Its upper limit is at lower elevations in the northern part of the Alps, and at 4,600 to 5,600 feet in the south. In the Northern Limestone Alps rye, oats, barley, potatoes, beets, and flax are limited to areas below 3,280 feet. In the interior these crops are found as high as 7,200 feet. In the eastern Alps the upper limit for cereals averages 5,100 feet, and it is somewhat higher in the western Alps. On low sunny slopes grapes are common.

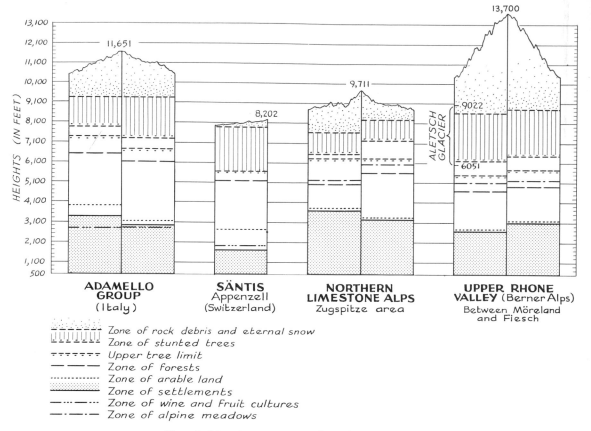

Fig. 6-11. Vegetation and land use in the Alps.

2. The forest zone is made up of coniferous trees at higher elevations and of deciduous trees at lower elevations. As one proceeds upward, the species change from the common beech, oak, and birch to spruce and fir, then to larch, and near the tree line to the stone pine. In the northern Alps (see pp. 290-91), the forests thin out at 5,200 to 5,900 feet; in the Valais, Engadine, and Ötztal Alps, they reach as high as 7,200 feet. In the eastern Alps, they seldom extend above 4,900 feet. The upper limit of trees is usually marked by a belt of stunted trees, such as the dwarf birch, dwarf pine, juniper, etc. In the limestone zone, the Grünerle and the rhododendron are especially numerous. The upper boundary of the forest zone is usually 2,600 to 2,900 feet below the snow line, which it parallels, but this distance is often increased by man in order to gain additional grazing land. This practice is rather common along the southern slopes of the Alps. Timber cutting and sawmilling are of great importance, especially in the more accessible parts of the Alps. Ancient conservation laws have played a vital role in the preservation of this "gold of the mountains."

3. Alpine meadows are of great economic significance. On them dairy cattle are grazed, and in some localities special breeds are raised for export. Transhumance, a typically Alpine form of cattle raising, is called *Sennenwirtschaft* or *Sennerei* here. Either the village or the individual farmers own pastures (each one provided with a hut) at different elevations; these are used in successive stages during the warm season. With the beginning of the colder season, the herdsman returns to the village. When the cattle are returned to their winter stables in

the valley, they feed on hay cut from meadows located at lower altitudes. Cattle pastures generally extend 900 to 1,600 feet above the forest zone, while sheep pastures extend close to the snow's edge.

Various colorful Alpine flowers with creeping and grasslike stems and woody roots are found in great numbers in the upper reaches of the Alpine meadows and among the rock debris during the very short growing season. They include primroses, buttercups, gentian, monkshood, and edelweiss.

Glaciation and hydrography. Precipitation, exposure to the sun, and latitude determine the extent of eternal snow in the Alps. The snow line ranges from 7,800 feet in the northern Swiss Alps to 10,500 feet in the central part of the Alps.

Precipitation in the mountains accumulates in the form of snow and ice, and is either quickly removed as dry or ground avalanches or more slowly as glaciers. Approximately 1,200 square miles, of which 500 are in the eastern Alps, are covered by glaciers. Alpine glaciers have been much reduced during the last 100 years, more in the eastern than the western parts. Because of its altitude, the central zone has most of the large glaciers, while the northern and southern limestone zones have small cirque glaciers for the most part. Compared with the extent of glaciation during the Great Ice Age, the area covered by present-day glaciers is small indeed. The longest Alpine glacier is the Aletsch Glacier (north of Brig, Switzerland) with a total length of 16 miles. The glacier which descends to the lowest elevation (3,500 feet above sea level) is the Lower Grindelwald Glacier in the Bernese Alps.

Alpine glaciers give rise to a great number of rivers. Many small torrents become mighty streams during the summer snowmelt season. Many Alpine rivers are regulated by lakes which they traverse and which keep their flow uniform. These lakes act as reservoirs, reduce the danger of floods, and contribute to the clearing of rivers by catching all the sediment carried in suspension.

Among the largest lakes are Geneva, Neuchâtel, Thun-Brienz, Lucerne, and Zürich, all in Switzerland; Constance, divided between Switzerland, Germany, and Austria; Maggiore and Lugano in Switzerland and Italy; Como and Garda in northern Italy; Chiemsee in Germany; and Wörthersee in the Klagenfurt Basin of Austria. Numerous smaller lakes, mostly cirque lakes and lakes impounded by landslides, are scattered throughout the western and the eastern Alps.

Mention should also be made of the Alps' importance as a central watershed for several river systems which empty into four different seas. The Rhine rises in the southern Alps and flows northward into the North Sea; en route it is joined by several northward-flowing tributaries of Alpine origin. All the right tributaries of the upper and middle Danube, notably the Inn, Salzach, Enns, Mur, and Drave (Drau), rise in the Alps and ultimately find their way to the Black Sea. The southern slopes of the Alps feed the Po and other rivers emptying into the Adriatic. And finally, the Rhone River, which rises in the Bernese Alps not far from the headwaters of the Rhine, flows west and south into the Mediterranean Sea.

Alpine communications. Despite the difficulties presented by the terrain, Alpine routes have been of great importance for transit traffic ever since prehistoric times. The few usable routes were first extensively traveled during the Roman period. Of the roads constructed at that time, some were not modernized until the late Middle Ages, and others not until the nineteenth century.

Three types of passageways, classified according to their orientation, may be distinguished in the Alps (Fig. 6–12):

1. Longitudinal furrows which run parallel to the main trend of the ranges and contribute so much to the accessibility of the Alps. Their continuity is preserved by the low, easily traversable divides which separate one longitudinal river valley from another. Examples of such furrows are the valleys of the Inn, Salzach, and Enns rivers, which form almost a straight line from west-

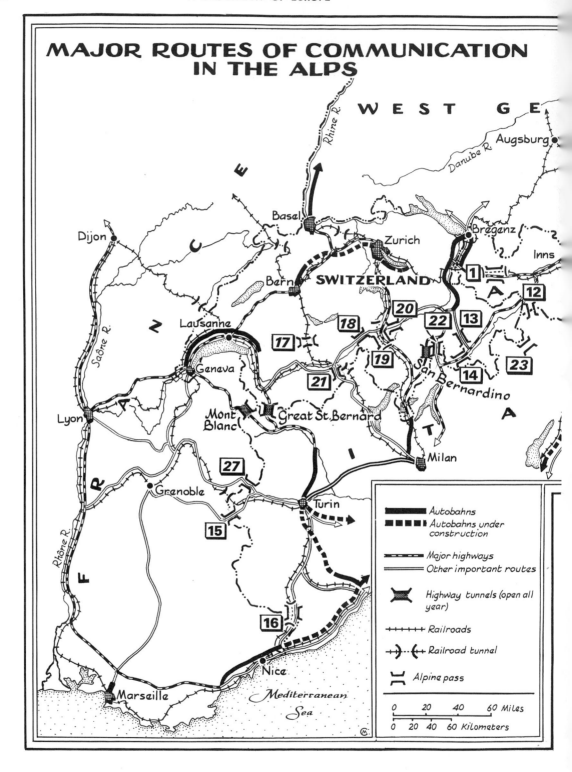

MAJOR ROUTES OF COMMUNICATION IN THE ALPS

Fig. 6–12. Major routes of

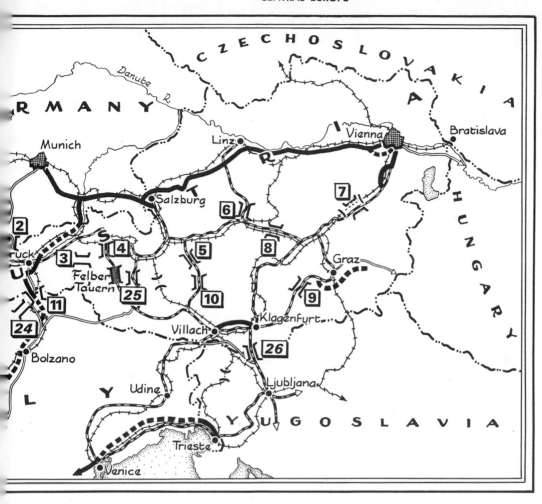

Alpine Passes (open all year)

1. Arlberg
2. Seefelder
3. Gerlos
4. Thurn
5. Radstädter Tauern
6. Phyrn
7. Semmering
8. Schober
9. Pack
10. Katschberg
11. Brenner
12. Reschen
13. Julier
14. Maloja
15. Montgenèvre
16. Tende

Alpine Passes (closed in winter)

17. Lotschen
18. Furka
19. St. Gotthard
20. Oberalp
21. Simplon
22. Splügen
23. Stilfser Joch
24. Jaufen
25. Glockner
26. Loibl
27. Mt. Cenis

communications in the Alps.

ern Austria to the Danube; the Rienza and Drau valleys in southern Austria, which connect Italian South Tyrol with Austria; and the Mur and Mürz valley chain in central and eastern Austria. In the Swiss Alps the most important of such furrows follows the upper Rhone and upper Rhine valleys from Lake Geneva to Lake Constance. Railroads follow most of these valleys and in many places use tunnels to penetrate the divides. The Arlberg Tunnel, which connects Tyrol and Vorarlberg in Austria, is a case in point.

2. Many transverse valleys, now of greatest importance in the transit traffic, were once obstructed by gorges which inhibited direct traffic until the Middle Ages. Along the Brenner Pass, the gorge between Chiusa (Klausen) and Bolzano (Bozen) in the Isarco (Eisack) defile route, for example, necessitated a traffic detour across the Renon Monte (Ritten Pass) northeast of Bolzano until the fourteenth century. Similarly, the St. Gotthard route was not opened until the thirteenth century, when a bridge was built across the Schöllenen gorge. Because the Alps are crossed by only a few direct north-south routes, these are of great significance. Several political units, notably Savoy, the Swiss Confederation, Graubünden (Grison), Tyrol, and to a lesser degree the church state of Salzburg, owe their existence to the establishment of pass routes. The Brenner Pass (4,495 feet) is the only Alpine crossing which a railroad can negotiate without the use of long tunnels. However, after it reaches the longitudinal valley of the Inn in Austria, one branch of the line uses several tunnels to pierce the ranges which bar access to southern Germany.

3. The diagonal routes are of lesser importance. One links the upper Inn Valley with Lake Como, via Maloja Pass; another, a proposed route, would lead from Chur on the Rhine over a series of passes to the upper Inn Valley and into the Val Venosta (Vintschgau) and Merano (Meran) in Italy. The diagonal line connecting the valleys of the Enns and Mur rivers via the Schober Pass in Styria and the Vienna Basin via the Semmering Pass with the Klagenfurt Basin are links

of great importance between Austrian cities and especially between northeast Austria and Italy.

Today, railroads follow all the important old trans-Alpine routes, using tunnels to avoid difficult mountain stretches. It is now possible to cross any part of the Alps in less than four hours. Among the more important tunnels are the Mount Cenis (completed in 1871), which connects Genoa and Turin with Lyon and Paris; the Simplon and Lötschberg tunnels, which link Milan (Milano) with Bern; the 9.5-mile-long St. Gotthard Tunnel (completed in 1882), which connects Milan and the Po Valley of Italy with northern France and western Germany via Zürich and the valleys of the Reuss and the Ticino; the Tauern Tunnel for traffic between the Alpine Forelands and the Klagenfurt Basin; the Karawanken Tunnel for communication between the Klagenfurt Basin, Yugoslavia, and Trieste; and the Semmering Tunnel, which constitutes the main connection between Vienna and the south.

Although the roads are snowbound for several months each winter, the Alps have never presented a serious obstacle to travel. Thanks to the modern roads and to the numerous railroads built since the beginning of this century, the Alps have become much more accessible to the peoples of the adjacent plains. Today, they attract an ever-increasing tourist traffic which provides new means of livelihood for their inhabitants, but at the same time raises serious problems of road congestion. New superhighways have been completed, are being built or planned, e.g., the St. Gotthard (Fig. 6–13), Salzburg-Vienna, Semmering-Vienna, and Brenner Pass roads. The latest engineering feat is the construction of tunnels under Mont Blanc; under the Great St. Bernard (Martigny-Aosta), providing a direct connection between Geneva, Alpine France, and the Po Valley of Italy; under the San Bernardino Pass (connecting Chur and Como); and under the Felber Tauern in Austria, connecting the Pinzgau Valley (Salzburg) with the Drau Valley (East Tyrol) and, therefore, Bavaria with Venezia (Venice).

Fig. 6–13. The recently improved section of the northern St. Gotthard Pass road in the gorge between Göschenen and Andermatt (canton of Uri), Switzerland. Above the road, which is kept open all year, the avalanche galleries of the cog railway are visible. A few hundred feet below the surface is the St. Gotthard Tunnel, 10 miles long. (Swiss Tourist Office.)

THE CULTURAL AND HISTORICAL BACKGROUND

The historical developments that are reflected in the changing political geography of Central Europe had in many areas certain broad trends in common. By following out these trends one may grasp the main characteristics of the historical geography of the region and gain as well a better understanding of its many present problems. The developments to be covered are: the migrations of the Germanic peoples following the decline of Rome; the establishment of the Marches [6] to defend the main routes through

[6] A territorial border or frontier. The word is from the Old French word *marche* and is of Teutonic origin.

the Danube Valley and the North German Lowlands from encroachments from the east; the growing independence of isolated regions, especially in the Alps, which resulted in the founding of the Swiss Confederation; the growth and decline of trade.

The Decline of the Roman Empire and the Age of Migration

Central Europe at the beginning of the Christian era was inhabited by various German-speaking peoples, such as the Saxons, Frisians, Goths, Vandals, Franks, and Alemanni. There were Celts in the mountainous regions of the south, and also Ligurians, Etruscans, and Illyrians. The Rhine became the frontier of the Roman Empire in the west after Caesar's conquest of Gaul (57–51 B.C.).

Thus, a corresponding advance farther east to the Danube was strategically desirable for Rome, to secure the eastern frontier and command important passes of the Alps. A Roman force advanced through the Adige (Etsch) Valley into Tyrol, and in 15 B.C. the province of Rhaetia was created. Shortly thereafter Noricum and Pannonia, both bounded by the Danube River and the crest of the southern Alps, were added. At one period the Romans tried to establish their frontier as far as the Elbe River, but were defeated by Germanic tribes. With Roman fortifications acting as a check to their westward and southward movement, Germanic tribes added an extensive agriculture to their primarily pastoral economy. This brought about increased population pressures, which contributed to the unification of various tribes into more powerful units, and to the natural desire for additional settlement space.

Much has been written and many reasons have been given for the decline of the Roman Empire. Certainly the constant drain on its resources for defense against the barbarians from the north was a major contributing factor. The breakdown of the Rhine-Limes [7]-Danube frontier zone during the fourth and fifth centuries allowed colonization by the various Germanic peoples, a process which had begun peacefully under sanctions of the emperors. The barbarian invasions brought new masters to Central Europe. The movement of the Germanic peoples toward the west and south also emptied wide stretches of land east of the Elbe, which soon were occupied by Slavic peoples from the east—an event of major historical importance in the relationship between Central and Eastern Europe.

The Germanic peoples were quick to follow the Roman withdrawal. Alemanni of Swabian stock proceeded from Brandenburg into central Germany. They crossed into southern and southwestern Germany, occu-

pied the Rhine Valley, the Neckar lowlands, and the Swiss Plateau, and also settled in parts of mountainous Switzerland and modern Austrian Vorarlberg. Saxons moved from the plains between the Ems and Weser rivers into Flanders and northern France; some even crossed to the southeast coast of England. Others moved in stages across the Thuringian Uplands and Plains to the Main and Danube rivers. Bavarians [8] occupied the Alpine Forelands of Germany and part of present Austria. Franks advanced from their original homes on the lower Rhine and in Westphalia across the Rhine into France and the southern part of the Low Countries. Other German tribes migrated beyond Central Europe. The Lombards traversed the Alps into the fertile Po Valley; the Vandals crossed into North Africa; the Goths settled in Iberia; and Burgundians in the valley of the Saône in France. Often these migrations were on a relatively small scale, with less than 25,000 people involved. One effect of this resettling of peoples was the establishment of many small political units. These were characteristic of medieval Central Europe and are still evident today in the political organizations of The German Federal Republic.

The Marches: Austria and Prussia

On the eastern frontier of the Holy Roman Empire, a system of Marches was established between the lands of sedentary peoples and those of nomads to the east (Fig. 6–14). At first these Marches served only for defense, protecting the Empire against attack by peoples from the east, such as the Avars, Slavs, and Magyars. But once the eastern frontier became stabilized, the Marches served as bases for expansion. Constant fighting necessitated a large standing army, and the rulers of the Marches used their special privileges to further their own interests. Out of these Marches grew independent kingdoms, two of which were later

---

[7] Outer defense wall from Danube near Castra Regina (Regensburg) to the Rhine near Confluentes (Coblenz).

[8] As the name of the Bavarians—Baioarii or Bajuvarii—indicates, they once inhabited "Boiiland" (Bohemia).

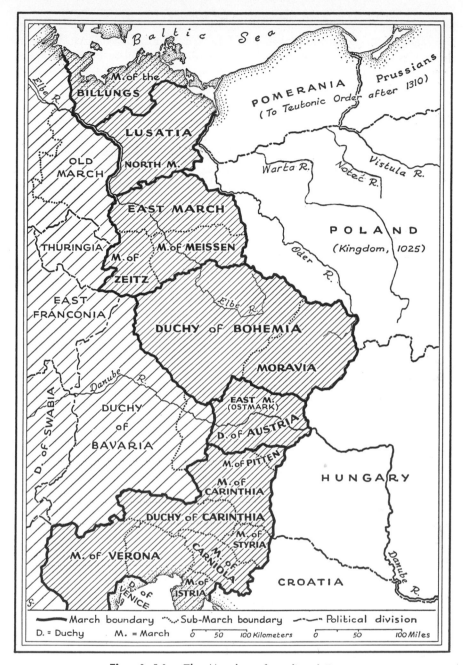

Fig. 6–14. The Marches of medieval Europe.

to play a decisive role in the fortunes of the Empire and of all Europe. In the south was the Eastern March (Ostmark), later to be known as Ostarichi (Österreich-Austria). Its boundaries were slowly extended to include the fertile Vienna Basin (1041), the approaches to it, and several Marches to the south. The margraves made their headquarters at Vienna which, due to its location, soon assumed a leading position as "a potential capital of the whole Middle Danube region." [9]

[9] Derwent Whittlesey, *The Earth and the State* (New York: Henry Holt & Co., Inc., 1944): 218.

After 200 years as the Eastern March of Bavaria, Austria became a duchy within the Holy Roman Empire. Its dukes were regularly elected as emperors and dominated the area roughly comprised by modern Germany, until Prussia, which included the Brandenburg March in the north, gained supremacy in 1871. Making use of the strategic location of the Vienna Basin and of the resources of its incorporated territories, the Hapsburg rulers of Austria, through superior military strength and astute foreign policies, expanded toward Bohemia and Galicia (Poland) in the north and toward Italy in the south, defeated the Turks, and incorporated Hungary and parts of present-day Yugoslavia into a loose federation.

In the north, between the forested Ore Mountains and the Baltic coast, and the Elbe and Oder rivers, a series of Marches similar in origin and function to the East March was set up. The Old March (Altmark), in the vicinity of Magdeburg on the Elbe, was soon followed by the Middle March (Mittelmark) and the New March (Neumark), until territory given up by westward-moving Germanic peoples before 600 A.D. was reoccupied. In this way the Wendish territory of Brannibor (Brandenburg) was acquired. This expansion to the east, greatly aided by military religious orders (Teutonic Knights and Knights of the Sword), culminated after 400 years of slow but steady advances, and of intermittent warfare, in the occupation of Prussia [10] and of Livonia farther north, and in the re-establishment of the Vistula frontier. Only in 1410, at the battle of Tannenberg, were the advancing Germans stopped by the growing strength of Poland, a check to further expansion never since overcome. Germans also advanced along the Baltic coast but left the hinter-

---

[10] Prussia at this time was a subdivision of Lithuania and its people spoke a language not unlike Lithuanian and Latvian. Their land was the former East Prussia, now divided between Poland and the U.S.S.R. See also Norman J. G. Pounds, *Poland Between East and West.* Searchlight book No. 22. (Princeton, N.J.: D. Van Nostrand Co., 1964).

land predominantly Slavic and under the control of the Polish crown, a factor of importance in the establishment of the Polish Corridor in 1919.

In their advances into the North German Lowlands and the Transitional Borderlands, the Germans occupied the area of Mecklenburg, Silesia, and present-day Saxony. The Slavs were absorbed, although some fled to the east, so with the exception of two small areas no vestige of Slavic culture remained. Names ending in old forms such as -ried (marsh), -hagen (fence), -schlag (fill), indicate the advances of the Teutonic pioneers. The March of Brandenburg, with its core area between the Elbe and Oder rivers, expanded in a series of acquisitions until in the seventeenth century it extended its influence across the North German Lowlands, from the Rhine to the Vistula. It is not possible in this brief summary to account in detail for the rise of Brandenburg from a March to the Kingdom of Prussia, but toward the end of the eighteenth century Prussia became the most powerful all-German state and was rivaled only by the former East March of the south, which was ruled by the Hapsburgs of Austria, heirs to the imperial title. All other former Marches were now incorporated into these two, whose rise and decline show many similarities.

The "Passlands": Switzerland and Tyrol

Regional units, individual valleys, and such small administrative districts as the gau, canton, or ecclesiastical division make up the basis for the major political groupings in the Alpine regions of Central Europe. These units are often quite isolated and separated from each other by such barriers as high mountains, deeply incised valleys, or gorges. At various times several of these units were united, and if grouped around a pass controlling important routes were known as "passlands." The Swiss Confederation around the St. Gotthard, and the Tyrol around the Brenner are typical passlands of the Alps. Their origin and importance are now to be briefly analyzed.

The Swiss Federation. The area under modern federated Switzerland was once part of the Roman Empire and was afterward integrated into the Holy Roman Empire. The passes of the Swiss Alps, for example, Splügen, St. Gotthard, Great St. Bernard, and important valley routes such as those along the Rhine, Inn, and Reuss rivers connect Germany and Italy and gave the emperors easy access to Rome (Figs. 6–15 and 6–16).

In 1291 the inhabitants of the mountain valleys controlling the most important of the north-south routes, the St. Gotthard, combined to fight the ambitions of the Hapsburg emperors. In that year the three valleys around Lake Lucerne which control the entrance to the St. Gotthard, comprising the cantons of Uri, Schwyz, and Unterwalden, solemnly formed the first federation (*Bund der Eidgenossen*). The Federation gained

allies and dependents in expanding from this core area along the St. Gotthard route to the North Italian Plain, and to the east and west. By hard fighting, the Federation asserted its independence within the Empire and soon received additional help from Lucerne and Bern in the west, Glarus in the east, and Zürich and Zug in the north. Swiss independence was acknowledged by the major European powers in 1648; its neutrality was guaranteed in 1815. Modern Switzerland consists of nineteen cantons and six half cantons. This complex organization is due to the complex relief of the country. And the fact that these units differ greatly from each other in area and size of population facilitated the addition of new cantons and also contributed to religious toleration. The constantly increasing trade across the Alps added to the economic well-being and the importance of the Swiss passlands. Over the

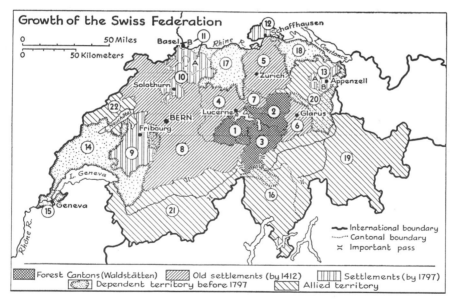

(1) Unterwalden, 1291	(9) Fribourg, 1481	(15) Geneva, 1815
(2) Schwyz, 1291	(10) Solothurn, 1481	(16) Ticino, 1813
(3) Uri, 1291	(11A) Basel (rural)	(17) Aargau, 1805
(4) Lucerne, 1332	(11B) Basel (urban), 1501	(18) Thurgau, 1803
(5) Zürich, 1351	(12) Schaffhausen, 1501	(19) Grisons, 1803
(6) Glarus, 1352	(13A) Appenzell–Outer Rhodes	(20) Saint Gallen, 1803
(7) Zug, 1352	(13B) Inner Rhodes, 1513	(21) Valais, 1815
(8) Bern, 1352	(14) Vaud, 1803	(22) Neuchâtel, 1815

Fig. 6–15. Growth of the Swiss Federation.

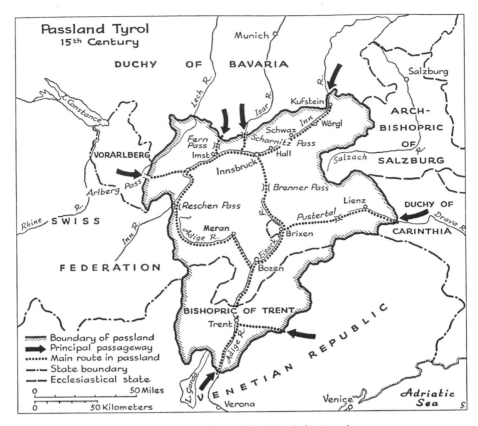

Fig. 6–16. The passlands of the Tyrol.

years cultural diffusion across passes, valleys, and gaps strengthened the unity of the Federation.

The Tyrol. The Tyrol, named for its first ruler, grew as a passland around the network of the Inn, Isarco, and Adige rivers, with the Brenner and Reschenscheideck passes serving as connecting links (Fig. 6–16). These routes were already extensively used by the Romans in their travel between the plains of Venetia and the Danube. The gorge of Finstermünz, on the Inn, and the Arlberg Pass are the exits to Switzerland and Vorarlberg. The two longitudinal valleys to Salzburg and along the Puster Valley to the Drau Valley are important routes toward the east, connecting with the rest of Austria. At the Inn ford, where the road from the Brenner meets the Inn River as well as the roads from Bavaria and Switzerland, a market place,

Innsbruck, was founded in 1180. Through its control of this important north-south route, Innsbruck became one of the leading cities of the Alps.

As the result of a series of successful wars and agreements, the borders of this triangular area were pushed out from its important roads; by the second half of the fourteenth century all borders of the Tyrol were located at the high mountain crests or at the constrictions of valleys. In this way the important passland was kept under one rule until the end of World War I, when its southern part (South Tyrol) became Italian and the Alpine passes for the first time in history formed the border. This division also cut the direct connection between southern Austria (Carinthia) and the Inn Valley.

The Swiss passland was able to obtain independence early in the modern era; but the Tyrol was too closely bound to the Hapsburgs. However, its inhabitants received limited freedom early. For example, a Tyrolese assembly with full representation of the peasants was founded in 1342, and a deed (*Freiheitsbrief*, comparable to the Magna Carta) for its citizens' assembly (peasants and burghers) was also drawn up.

The Brenner and the St. Gotthard routes were the main north-south links between the German and the Italian parts of the Holy Roman Empire, and commerce along them brought considerable wealth. These routes, with their passlands, still play a vital role in the European transportation pattern.

Settlement Forms

The beginnings of modern settlement forms may be traced back to the period shortly after the beginning of the Christian era, when various Germanic tribes occupied land with little or no woodland, such as in the fertile zone of the Transitional Borderlands between the Cologne Bay and Silesia, the fertile river valleys, and the drier, sandy heath lands of the North German Lowlands.

The Central European cultural landscape is characterized by certain types of rural settlements: a nucleated village with the farm houses all centered on the village lands and the isolated farmstead surrounded by its own fields. Besides these two extreme examples many successions result from geographical, social, or economic influences which have shaped rural communities. The relief of the land, the fertility of the soil, and the original nature of the settlement (whether established by squatters or by well-knit groups) are among the factors which have determined the type of settlement evident today. Also significant are the type and layout of houses and the system of field ownership.

One of the best-known types of habitation is the typical Alpine single-unit house (Fig. 6–17). It is a wooden or frame structure built on a stone foundation, with two stories, a balcony on the first floor, small windows often protected by green shutters, and an overhanging roof permitting dry storage of wood.

In the Alpine Foreland, the Black Forest, and the Central Uplands, one encounters a second type of structure, the so-called Franconian house. Several units, the living quarters, stable, barn, storage facilities, etc., are grouped around a court closed off by a heavy wooden gate.

A third group of structures, known as the Saxon or lower-German unit house, is found predominantly in the North German Lowlands. It is similar to the Alpine single-unit house in its interior make-up, but has only one story, while the Alpine house has two stories. This building is normally built of timber with some brickwork; the latter is especially characteristic of the Frisian farms of the northern coastlands.

The isolated farmsteads and hamlets are probably the oldest known forms of settlement.[11] These farmsteads or hamlets consisted of one or several farm houses, surrounded by woodland, meadows, common pastures, and arable land. Upon the breakup of a farm community, these farmstead lands were divided into small elongated strips and arranged in irregular furlongs or *Gewanne*.[12] Thus a hamlet was formed, a group of five to seven farmsteads, each with a number of such furlongs.

In the Southern Transitional Borderlands and in central and southern Germany, the hamlet has grown into a *Haufendorf*.[13] Here newly cleared land with better soils was added by additional clearings during the Middle Ages. This newly cleared land was divided into furlongs, and additional farms

[11] For a detailed discussion and illustrations of German settlements, see Robert E. Dickinson, "Rural Settlements in German Lands," *Annals of the Association of American Geographers* 39 (December, 1949):239–63.

[12] According to Eric Fischer and Francis E. Elliot, *A German and English Glossary of Geographical Terms*, Library Series No. 5 (New York: American Geographical Society, 1950), *Gewann* refers to the division of a village's communal lands into units of more or less uniform quality, enabling farmers to diversify their holdings by allowing each one to cultivate part of several *Gewanne*.

[13] *Ibid.*, a *Haufendorf* is a village in which the houses are irregularly clustered without any definite plan.

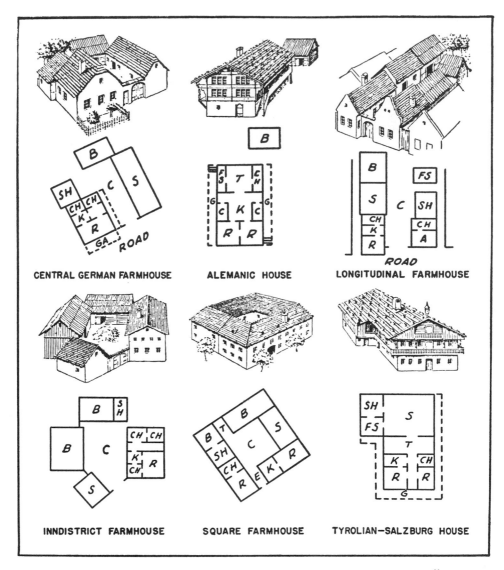

Fig. 6–17. Selected farmhouse types in Central Europe. (Hans Slanar, Österreichischer Mittelschul-Atlas.) B—barn, S—stable, C—court, SH—shed, CH—chamber, K—kitchen, R—room, FS—forage storage, T—threshing floor, G—gallery, A—separate house for retired farmer, E—entrance, GA—garden plot.

within the old hamlet were formed, so a village soon had 15 to 25 farms. Near the end of the Middle Ages many such settlements disappeared again and their holdings were incorporated into existing settlements. In these ways larger, clustered villages were gradually developed.

Two more regular forms of settlement, the shoestring village (*Strassendorf*) with the longitudinal farm house (*Streckhof*) (Fig. 6–18), and the closely related roadside village, date from the twelfth and thirteenth centuries. Land for settlement had been originally donated by the large landowner and was then divided evenly among the new owners so that each peasant received a single compact holding rather than a number of scattered strips.

Fig. 6–18. Wulkaprodersdorf, Burgenland, Austria. Main street with longitudinal farm houses. (G. W. Hoffman.)

Other regular types of settlements include a roadside village in which the road widens to enclose a centrally located common, large enough for a church, the so-called *Anger-dorf;* the *Runddorf,* or *Rundling,* in which a group of houses connected by a wall enclose a central courtyard with but one entrance; the *Marschhufendorf* in which a row of houses faces a dike in a tidal marsh and the strips of land run at right angles to the dike; and the *Waldhufendorf,* which extends along a wooded river bank, sometimes for several miles. It is similar to the street village, but less regularly spaced.

Relatively few new areas were brought under cultivation after the sixteenth century. East of the Elbe, marsh villages were founded in the glacial valleys and estates were organized by large landowners or *Junkers,* who concentrated on grain and dairy production. Earlier in this chapter, mention was made of the fen settlements which developed in the former peat bogs in the northwest. Some consolidation of hold-ings, particularly in mountainous areas, was accomplished, but has not progressed very far. Little alteration has taken place in the strip system of open fields. As Dickinson has pointed out, "The number of parcels was often reduced by the amalgamation of ad-jacent strips, but the strip system inside the arable land and the general grouping of the arable land, meadow, woodland and scrub invariably are the same today as they were hundreds of years ago." [14]

The Rise and Decline of Commerce in Central Europe

The importance of commerce in Europe and its main aspects are discussed in Chapter 10. The historical aspects of its development in the countries of Central Europe are briefly outlined here. As early as 1000 B.C. amber (a fossil resin), fur, leather, and other goods

[14] Dickinson, "Rural Settlements," *op. cit.,* p. 259.

from the Baltic Sea area were carried to the Italian plains along the valleys of the Elbe, Oder, Morava, and Danube, and through the Inn and other valleys of the Tyrol. During Roman times a variety of Mediterranean products, such as wine, parchment, and olive oil, were exchanged for hides, flax, timber, pelts, salt, etc. The barbarians beyond the Roman wall at times traded actively with the Romans. Obviously, during the barbarian invasions and during times of war, trade was considerably limited. But by the end of the medieval period, as governments became more effective and towns more numerous, the exchange of goods increased in an unprecedented way. Many towns, for example, Munich, were founded at important junctions of inland trade routes; at outlets of passes, as Innsbruck; and on the North German coast, especially at the heads of navigation, such as Bremen, Hamburg, or Lübeck. Trade in various local minerals was also active in Central Europe. Commerce in gold, silver, copper, and salt gave added importance to the passland of the Tyrol. The Harz Mountains contributed lead, zinc, and copper, as did the Ore Mountains. While the total mineral trade was relatively small, it did affect several local communities. For example, it is estimated that nearly 30,000 men mined silver at Schwaz, and another 20,000 in other communities of the Tyrol.

Various parts of Central Europe participated in the ever-growing exchange of goods. Cities increased in population and importance. A canal system was started in the North German Lowlands; rivers and coastal waters were used increasingly. Two major routes, both connecting the Alpine Forelands with the cities of the North German Lowlands and the Danubian lands, deserve special mention: (1) the Rhine, with its leading trading cities of Basel, Mainz, Cologne, etc., offered a direct route from the North Sea to the Alps; (2) the numerous navigable rivers of the North German Lowlands gave access to Vienna and the Danube by way of the Moravian Gate portage between the Oder and the Morava rivers.

Using the Baltic as its main route, the Hanseatic League was organized in 1256 as a loose association of about one hundred large trading towns of the North German Lowlands. The original aim of the League was to join forces in combating the pirates of the Baltic Sea, but it soon developed into a commercial and trade monopoly. Lübeck served as the League's headquarters, and during the three centuries of its hegemony trade flourished, roads and canals were built, and its trade spread westward and northward to British and Scandinavian ports and eastward as far as Novgorod in Russia. Its leading ports, many of which still retain the characteristic Hanseatic warehouses, are today among the ranking seaports and trade centers of Northern and Western Europe. The League declined and eventually broke up as a result of the discoveries in Africa and America which led to a reorientation of important trade routes, because of warfare with Denmark, the growth of British maritime power, and lastly because of internal dissension between strong-willed emperors and the League.

After the downfall of the Hanseatic League and a series of internal conflicts which culminated in the Wars of Religion, Germany played but a minor part in world trade for several centuries. Consequently, while Spain, Portugal, Holland, France, and England enriched themselves by trade with the newly won territories, the Holy Roman Empire was either torn by disunity or engaged in enlarging its southeastern holdings at the expense of the Turks. Not until the individual German states began to realize the importance of trade and undertook the formation of bilateral, then multilateral customs unions (Zollverein) after the Napoleonic Wars, did commerce once again play a more important role in Central Europe.

Disunity to Unity and Again to Disunity

The Holy Roman Empire was unable to control its constituent units, while they themselves were too small and powerless to make a decisive contribution to political or economic unity until late in the nineteenth century. Because of their location at Europe's invasion crossroads, and because of the dissected topography of the Central Uplands and the Alps, most political units remained small, often confining themselves to one small, narrow valley. The area occupied by these numerous powerless states stretched from the North German Lowlands to the Alps, and from the Rhineland to the Marches in the east.

While these small political units wrangled and fought each other, a number of strong leaders assigned to protect the Empire from newly organized borderlands (Marches) soon attained independence. Although the dukes of Austria had been the regularly elected emperors ever since 1273, the crown was meaningless and powerless in the face of opposition and the divergent aims of its many component states. Soon, therefore, disunity in Empire affairs was replaced by unity of purpose in the emperor's personal affairs, without regard to the welfare of the Empire as a whole. Religious disunity and foreign attachments by several political units added to the problems of the Empire. Meanwhile, the Marches of Austria and Prussia, both outgrowths of the Empire, began to fight for supremacy within it. They had expanded considerably from their original core, and each of them incorporated peoples of other language groups; in time each achieved some measure of national unity.

Only the threat of Napoleon brought the beginnings of unity to Central Europe. Almost two hundred minor political units disappeared, and for a time the Austrian Monarchy strove for greater centralization. Prussia incorporated many lesser German states, and the Swiss Federation received the promise of neutrality. By the end of the Napoleonic Wars, many rulers came to realize the need for greater unity, and various customs unions were established. This process was completed in 1844, when all German lands, with the exception of Austria and the free cities of Bremen, Hamburg, Lübeck, and Hanover, had joined the customs union.

Political unity, however, had to await the outcome of the contest for leadership between Austria and Prussia. The decision was reached in 1866, when Austria was defeated by Prussia on the battlefield. The cleavage between these two former Marches, ruled respectively by the Hapsburg and Hohenzollern dynasties, was too deep. Austria in general had nothing but contempt for Prussia, which in turn felt superior to Austria. When Prussia defeated France in 1871, all of the remaining German states joined it in proclaiming the modern German Empire (Deutsches Reich) with the king of Prussia as its emperor. Austria alone was not admitted.

Unity had finally been achieved in Germany, but not among Germans. During the centuries of disunity, political fragmentations, and conquests, many Germans had emigrated, especially to the frontier lands of Eastern Europe. Hand in hand with a revival of German nationalism, these Germans pledged their eternal loyalty to the fatherland and began to work for a Greater German Reich. World War I, 1914–18, followed. It ended in the defeat of Germany, in the loss of its recently acquired colonies, and in important territorial losses in Europe. Alsace, the Saar, a large part of the area between the Oder and the Vistula, and parts of Silesia were gone. And the Polish Corridor split East Prussia from the rest of Germany.

Austria, which had become a dual monarchy with Hungary in 1867,[15] entered World War I on the side of Germany and lost all of the territorial acquisitions it had made almost from the time of its organization as a Marchland. Various members of the Austro-Hungarian Empire became independent. Austria proper, with a population of 7 million of whom over 2 million lived in Vienna, began a new life of independence, largely within the area of her former Alpine holdings.

[15] See George W. Hoffman, "The Political-Geographic Bases of the Austrian Nationality Problem," *Austrian History Yearbook*, III (1967):120–46.

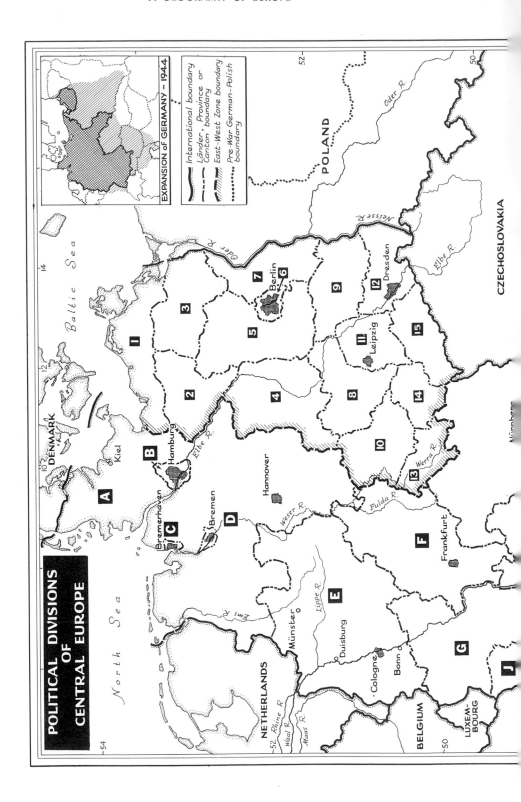

POLITICAL DIVISIONS
OF
CENTRAL EUROPE

EXPANSION OF GERMANY – 1944

International boundary
Länder, Province or
Canton boundary
East-West Zone boundary
Pre-War German-Polish
boundary

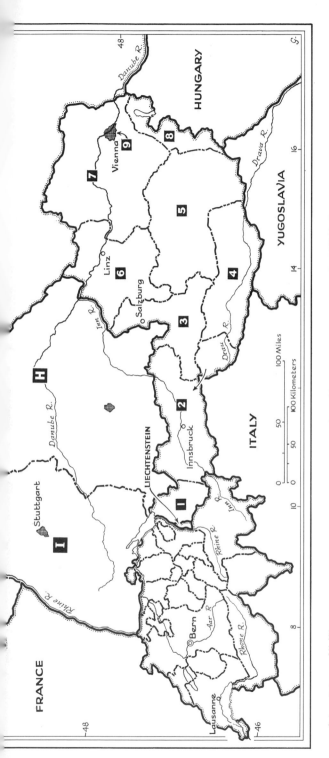

West Germany (*Länder*):
(A) Schleswig-Holstein
(B) Hamburg
(C) Bremen
(D) Lower Saxony
(E) North Rhine–Westphalia
(F) Hesse
(G) Rhineland–Palatinate
(H) Bavaria
(I) Baden-Württemberg
(J) Saar

East Germany (districts):
(1) Rostock
(2) Schwerin
(3) Neubrandenburg
(4) Magdeburg
(5) Potsdam
(6) Berlin
(7) Frankfurt
(8) Halle
(9) Cottbus
(10) Erfurt
(11) Leipzig
(12) Dresden
(13) Suhl
(14) Gera
(15) Karl-Marx Stadt

Switzerland: for canton names, see Fig. 6–32
and table on page 345.
Austria (provinces):
(1) Voralberg
(2) Tyrol
(3) Salzburg
(4) Carinthia
(5) Styria
(6) Upper Austria
(7) Lower Austria
(8) Burgenland
(9) Vienna

Fig. 6–19. Political divisions of Central Europe.

A defeated but united Germany soon recovered from the havoc of World War 1 and, turning to a strictly centralized nationalistic regime, was determined once more to attain leadership in the world. After occupying Austria (1938), the Sudetenland and various smaller border areas of Czechoslovakia, and then its states of Bohemia-Moravia (1939), the German leader, Hitler, concluded an agreement with the Soviet Union to partition Poland. The German invasion of Poland, a few days later, brought about World War II (1939–45). This conflict ended in disaster for Nazi Germany and the world as a whole. Germany lost over 5 million people, many of its cities were destroyed, and its economy was entirely disrupted. Some aftereffects of this collapse are still visible. Germany has lost most of the eastern territory it had acquired since the beginning of its eastward movement in the eighth century. All the lands east of the Oder, including the Baltic port of Stettin, have gone to Poland, and East Prussia has been partitioned between Poland and the U.S.S.R. The German population of the lost territories and other parts of Eastern Europe either fled or were forced to flee into the reduced area of postwar Germany.

Austria, once-more independent after years of postwar occupation but neutralizing itself by parliamentary action in 1955, considers itself a bridge between Western and Eastern Europe—others consider it a borderland against the latter. Thus her old function as a March is again being fulfilled.

We have now shown how Central Europe has gone through a full cycle from disunity to unity and again to disunity—from a conglomeration of numerous powerless states to a Germany split in two. Only Switzerland, which succeeded in keeping apart from the main stream of events, escaped the upheavals of the last century. Thanks to its location and to its spirit of defiance in the face of major threats, Switzerland progressed in peace, while the world around it was dislocated by wars.

GERMANY

Population

In discussing the population of Germany, the student should be aware of the profound changes which have taken place since 1939 through political developments. Millions of German refugees from the lost territories in the east, and Germans from Eastern Europe, are crowding every one of the German states and districts. The increasing ideological conflict and the slow economic recovery in East Germany during the 1950's, compared with the stabilized political as well as prosperous economic situation in West Germany, contributed to a sizeable drop in the population of East Germany. Though this movement was not entirely one way (23,000, for example, moved from West to East in 1961), it did affect, primarily, the more vigorous age-groups and for several years left a stagnating impact on the economic development of East Germany. Only after the erection of the Berlin Wall on August 13, 1961 did the movement slow down—234,000 in 1961 to 29,461 in 1964. The Wall, the barbed wire, and minefields had accomplished their primary purpose for the East German government. The population map of East Germany finally was stabilized. West Germany's annual rate of increase, including migration, averaged 1.1 per cent in 1956–1964; that of East Germany declined approximately 0.5 per cent per year for the period 1956–1961. This was the largest population change for the world.

On June 16, 1933 (last regular prewar census), the population of Germany, exclusive of the Saar, was 65,140,242, or approximately 355 people per square mile. On December 31, 1961 (last census June 6, 1961) the population of a much smaller Germany amounted to 73,254,000, of which 56,176,000 was the population of West and 17,079,000 of East Germany (population census 1964, 17,012,000) both including Berlin. Present-day Germany consists of The

German Federal Republic, divided into ten *Länder* (provinces) and West Berlin, with an area of 95,962 square miles, a population of 60,300,000 (mid-1968) and a population density of 628 per square mile; and The German Democratic Republic, divided into 15 *Bezirke* (districts) (Fig. 6–19), with an area of 41,648 square miles, a population of 17,100,000 (mid-1968), and a population density of 411 per square mile.[16]

Migration has had an important effect on the population structure for almost a century. Overpopulation, wars, and religious and political persecution have been the chief causes of emigration. Close to 6 million people left Germany between 1830 and 1937; 5.4 million of these entered the United States during this period. Some returned to Germany, especially in the years immediately preceding World War II. There was also some immigration from other parts of Europe, notably between 1891 and 1911. After Germany's catastrophic defeat in 1945, population movements took place on an almost unprecedented scale. Since 1945, in this connection, all of the territory east of the Oder-Neisse line, including East Prussia, has been incorporated into Poland and the U.S.S.R.—a loss of 24 per cent of Germany's 1937 territory and of 14 per cent of its population. While Germany's war losses amounted to more than 5 million people, and over 600,000 refugees emigrated overseas between 1945 and 1957 (200,000 to the United States), this deficit has been more than made up by postwar immigration into a smaller Germany. In 1952 there were about 12.1 million German-speaking refugees

in West Germany, 21.9 per cent of the total population at that time. They consisted of *Reichsdeutsche*, i.e., former citizens of German territories lost to the U.S.S.R. and Poland, and *Volksdeutsche*, ie.., ethnic Germans expelled from Czechoslovakia and from other countries of Eastern Europe.[17] While the relative population distribution has changed little during the last hundred years, the influx of the many refugees since 1945 has in many areas increased the population of what had been thinly settled areas (Fig. 6–20).

Certain regions of West and East Germany in the North German Lowlands, north of the zone of the Urstromtäler, are really the only remaining thinly settled areas of Germany. Hamburg and Berlin and their surrounding areas, and to a lesser extent, Bremen are the largest German cities in this region. The thinly peopled areas stretch in a northwest-southeast direction, south of Hamburg and Berlin. Growth before the war depended on workable resources and their associated industries. Due to the large-scale postwar migrations into West Germany, the areas of dense population saw a considerable expansion, especially from the Ruhr area to the borders of Switzerland, in the Rhine Valley, along the Southern Transitional Borderlands (this included East Germany, though for other reasons), the Neckar-Main valleys and several other prewar urban centers. In addition, many valleys of the Alpine Foreland, the Black Forest, and sections of the Thuringian and Hessian Depression increased their population densities as new industries spread to formerly completely rural settlements. West Germany's rural population (people in *Gemeinden* of less than 2,000 people) in the mid-1960's was 20 per cent of the total West German population.

Changes in the rural settlement pattern in East Germany since the early 1950's have

---

[16] Population figures used in this section have been taken from *Statistisches Jahrbuch für die Bundesrepublik Deutschland;* 1967, and the *Statistisches Jahrbuch der Deutschen Demokratischen Republik*, 1967, and where needed from previous years, as well as from other official publications.

It should be noted that West Germany lost territory after the war to Belgium (7 sq. mi.) and the Netherlands (26 sq. mi.), Luxembourg (2.3 sq. mi.) and France (2.7 sq. mi.). The first two territories were returned in 1956 and 1963, respectively.

[17] Gabriel Wülker, Friedrich Edding, Elisabeth Pfeil, Werner Essen, *et al., Europa und die Deutschen Flüchtlinge* (Frankfurt a.M.: Institut zur Forderung öffentlicher Angelegenheiten, 1952).

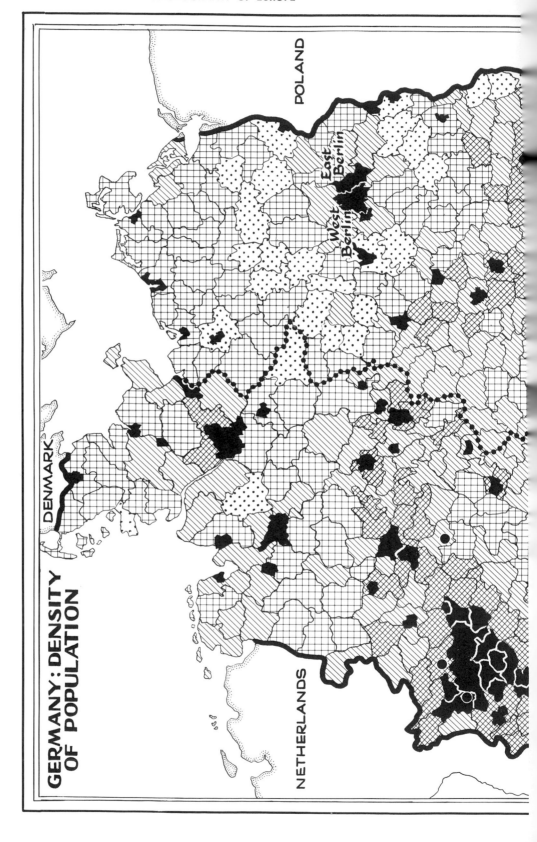

GERMANY: DENSITY
OF POPULATION

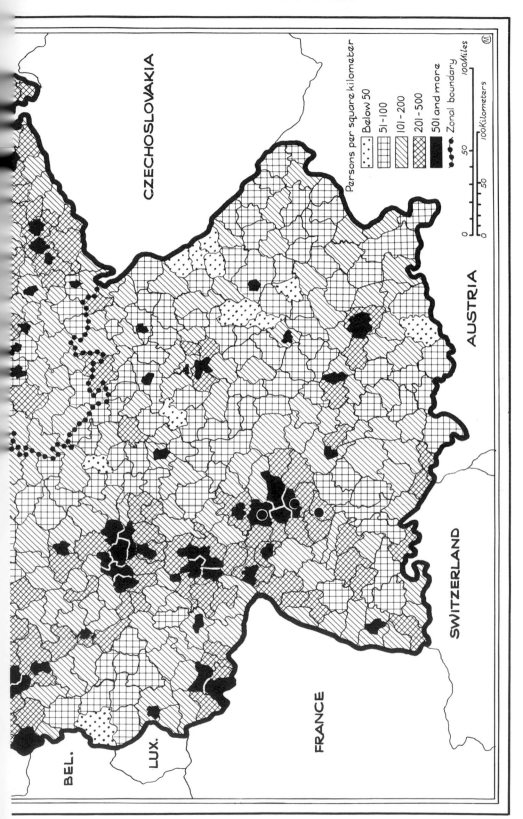

Persons per square kilometer

Below 50
51–100
101–200
201–500
501 and more
Zonal boundary

0   50   100 Kilometers
0   50   100 Miles

For West Germany, county seats with less than 60,000 population are part of the nearby county; those with a population over 60,000 are indicated by a circle.

Fig. 6–20. Population density of Germany, 1966. (Source: *Statistiches Jahrbuch fur die Bundesrepublik, 1967.*)

CZECHOSLOVAKIA

AUSTRIA

SWITZERLAND

FRANCE

BEL.

LUX.

been greatly accelerated. There is increased emphasis on industrialization and the use of local resources. For example, brown coal resources and the new industries closely associated with their use are located in the central parts of the Thuringian Basin, and the Central Saxonian Uplands, including the Ore Mountains. Small manufacturing and mining cities have expanded into former exclusively agricultural settlements in the southern borderlands. To this should be added the increased population of the cities of southeastern East Germany. In December, 1966, 27 per cent of East Germany's population still lived in *Gemeinden* with a population of less than 2,000. The whole pattern of rural settlements also has been much influenced by the collectivization of East Germany's farms. Individual farm buildings have lost their functions and a concentration of large farm buildings has become typical of the landscape. Agricultural workers of a number of collectives often live in blocks of apartments dotting the rural landscape. Still population densities are lower in East Germany than in West Germany, 411 per square mile as against 628 (1968 figures), and the traditional village of Germanic or Slavic origin can still be seen, scarcely changed over the years.

In 1939, 58 cities in Germany had a population of over 100,000 inhabitants each. In 1966 there were 56 cities in West Germany, excluding Berlin, and eleven in East Germany. Among the cities in West Germany with the largest residential population are the following: Hamburg (1,851,000), Munich (1,232,000), Cologne (861,000), Essen (721,000), Düsseldorf (698,000), Frankfurt-am-Main (685,000), Dortmund (657,000) and Stuttgart (631,000). West Berlin's population was 2,190,600. Those in East Germany are: East Berlin (1,080,700), Leipzig (594,100), Dresden (505,200), Karl-Marx Stadt, the former Chemnitz, (295,000), Halle (276,000), Magdeburg (267,800). Other cities of more than 100,000 are Erfurt, Rostock, Zwickau, Potsdam, and Gera. Thirty-three per cent of the population of West

Germany and 22 per cent of East Germany lived in cities with a population of over 100,000 in 1966.

It goes without saying that two world wars, a major depression, and a brief period of artificial prosperity during which a pronatal policy was being advocated—all within one generation—have left a deep mark on Germany's population structure. The natural increase (excess of births over deaths), which in 1910 stood at 13 per thousand, diminished steadily until in 1933 it reached a low of 3.5 per thousand. Recovery followed, and by the mid-1960's West Germany recorded a natural increase of 6.2 per thousand. East Germany at the same period had a natural increase of 3.0 per thousand. War losses have been made up both in East and West Germany, but the loss of employable males is being felt: in 1966 some 31 per cent of West Germany's and 47 per cent of East Germany's economically active population consisted of women. The over-all picture of the occupational distribution of the population in both West and East Germany followed a development characteristic of most industrialized countries—a slow but steady decrease in the agricultural employment over the last 50 years, while industry and services attracted most of the new recruits to the labor force. West Germany employed about 10 per cent of its labor force in agriculture in 1967, while the corresponding figure for East Germany was 16 per cent. These percentages indicate a reduction of four per cent for West and two per cent for East Germany since 1961. Industrial employment increased in West Germany from 32 per cent in 1961 to 37 per cent in 1967; it remained unchanged at 36 per cent in East Germany.

An important contributing factor to West Germany's economic progress and labor stability, especially since 1959, has been the many foreign workers. In spite of an economic recession in 1966 and 1967 (every indicator shows ascendancy again in 1968), there were 1,023,000 foreigners working on July 1, 1967, six per cent of the total labor force (the height was reached in June 1966 with 1,314,031). More than half of these are working in the two *Länder* of Baden-Württemberg and North Rhine-Westphalia, and one-quarter of them are women. Italians comprise the largest single national contingent followed by Greeks. The foreign workers are most numerous in the metal-working industries, the building trade and the various services, especially in German hotels and restaurants. A forecast published by the federal foreign workers central labor exchange in Nürnberg in mid-1967 estimates a need of two million foreigners in the 1970's.

German is spoken by the entire population, although in 1946 a small number of people reported their native language as Polish (those located near Cottbus), Wendish (these living between Spremberg and Bautzen), Danish, or Dutch. All these people are bilingual and their number has been rapidly diminishing; there were 141,000 Slavic people in 1900.[18] German may be divided into the following groups:

Low German (*Niederdeutsch*)	
Lower Frankish	Lower Saxon
│	
Lower Rhenish	

High German (*Hochdeutsch*)	
Middle German	Upper German
│	│
East Middle German	Bavarian
West Middle German	Franconian-Alemanic

The distribution of religions is extremely complex. North Germany before the last war was predominantly Protestant, south Germany Roman Catholic. In the rest of Germany the two religious groups are intermingled. For Germany as a whole, the 1933 census listed 60.8 per cent of the population Protestant and 33.2 per cent Catholic. With the loss of large territories in the east (where 66.6 per cent of the population had been Protestant and 30 per cent Catholic) and the postwar immigration of Germans,

[18] Roy Mellor, "A Minority Problem in Germany," *Scottish Geographical Magazine* 79 (1963):49–53.

the 1950 proportion had shifted in favor of the Catholics; 50.1 per cent Protestant, 43.8 per cent Catholic. West German census figures for 1961 list 51.1 per cent Protestant and 44.1 per cent Catholics.

While there are clear-cut differences of religion and of spoken dialects, there are no variations in the written language. Germans in Berlin, Cologne, Leipzig, and Munich, as well as those living in Zürich or Vienna, are united by the High German written language originated by Martin Luther. Illiteracy is negligible.

In politics, the German population reflects great geographical disunity and diversity. While it would be an exaggeration to speak of a political cleavage between north and south Germany, there are unmistakable differences in character between the people of the North German Lowlands and those of the Alpine Foreland, between the inhabitants of the Rhineland and those of Saxony. Throughout history, these differences were reinforced by protracted feuds between ruling houses and by religious cleavages which originally followed lines of political division.

Since the end of World War II, regional differentiation and decentralization have been advocated by the states *(Länder)* of The German Federal Republic, while The German Democratic Republic has been organized along strictly centralized lines into 15 districts. The impact of the political division of the country is difficult to forecast, but the establishment of different political organs, and especially the marked differences in orientation of the economic life in the two halves of Germany, will create immense problems once unification is possible.

Germans are proud of their past, they are extremely hard workers, and they have highly scientific minds which qualify them as competent chemists, engineers, and physicists. Because Germany suffers from overpopulation and is heavily dependent upon vital raw-material imports, the Germans have constantly looked for additional living-space, using various means to accomplish

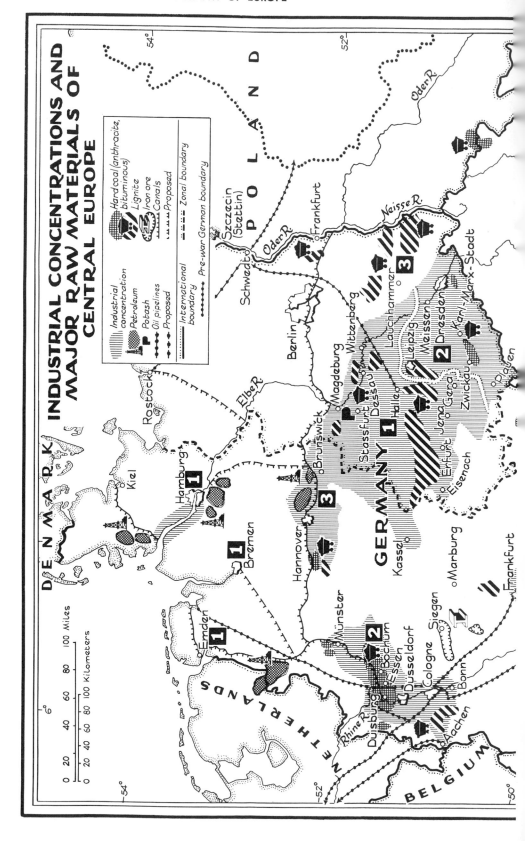

INDUSTRIAL CONCENTRATIONS AND MAJOR RAW MATERIALS OF CENTRAL EUROPE

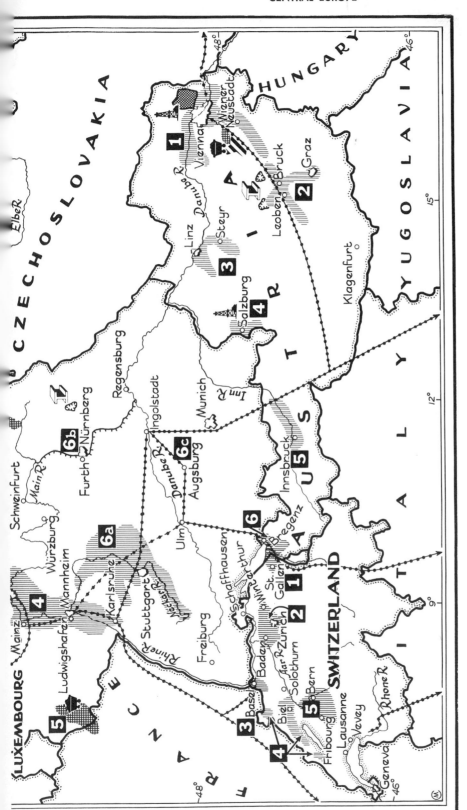

Fig. 6-21. Industrial concentrations in Central Europe.

West Germany:
(1) North Sea Ports
(2) Rhine–Ruhr
(3) Hanover–Brunswick
(4) Upper Part of Rhine Valley
(5) Saar
(6A) Neckar
(6B) Nürnberg
(6C) Munich

East Germany:
(1) Central Industrial Region
(2) Southern Saxony
(3) Lower Lausitz
(4) Greater Berlin

Switzerland:
(1) Saint Gallen
(2) Zürich–Winterthur–Baden
(3) Basel
(4) Jura
(5) Berne–Fribourg

Austria:
(1) Vienna Basin
(2) Styria–Mur Valley
(3) Linz–Steyr
(4) Salzburg
(5) Innsbruck–northeast Inn Valley
(6) Voralberg–Rhine Valley

their aim. It has often been said that the middle position in Europe has its dangers as well as its temptations.

Present Economic Life of Germany

Germany went through the Industrial Revolution following its political unification in 1871. Although other European countries had thus gained a head start, Germany, with its vast reservoir of human and material resources, its fertile soils capable of feeding a growing industrial population, and its central position, soon overtook its rivals in production and trade. Despite the defeat and the territorial losses of 1919, which for a time greatly slowed economic activity, Germany maintained its determination to achieve economic as well as political leadership. At the end of World War II, Germany's economic life was once more almost completely paralyzed. The countryside was scarred by bombed-out cities and destroyed industrial plants. It is astonishing, therefore, how rapidly new life developed amidst the burned-out ruins and dismantled plants,[19] only a few years after the cessation of hostilities.

An analysis of the basis of Germany's economic strength will go far to explain this recuperative power, as well as her renewed importance in world affairs. The growth of agriculture and manufacturing after 1871 was made possible above all by the presence of domestic resources. Thanks to her pioneer efforts in applying scientific methods to agriculture, Germany greatly increased her wheat yields and attained world leadership in the production of sugar beets and potatoes. She also became the world's largest rye producer. By 1937, Germany

produced close to 85 per cent of its food needs. This was an extraordinary accomplishment for one of Europe's most advanced industrialized countries. Industry, Germany's greatest asset, owed its rapid growth to the extensive coal deposits of the Ruhr, the Saar, and Upper Silesia. Plentiful coal and some iron ore was the basis of the iron and steel industry, which in turn supplied the basic materials for such vital industries as shipbuilding and the manufacture of rails, rolling stock, machines, tools, and armaments. Germany's other raw materials, including large potash and salt deposits for the fertilizer and chemical industry, also contributed to its leading position among Europe's principal manufacturing countries (Fig. 6–21).

Germany's present economic structure has undergone extensive changes from prewar days. Although the wartime loss of manpower has been largely offset by a great influx of immigrants, and German cities and industrial establishments have been rebuilt, the territorial losses and resultant loss of important raw materials constituted a serious impediment to the restoration of normal economic life. The results achieved are the more remarkable if it is realized that Germany is divided into two economic and political units and no peace treaty has yet been signed.

On the other hand, mention should be made of the considerable financial help which West Germany has derived from participation in the European Recovery Program (Marshall Plan). West Germany is also actively participating in many important European organizations (see Chapter 10), e.g., the European Coal and Steel Community (ECSC), the European Atomic Energy Community (EURATOM), and more recently in the European Economic Community (EEC). It is also a member of NATO, where its military contributions have been of major importance. East Germany is a member of the Soviet-sponsored Council for Mutual Economic Aid (COMECON), and the Warsaw Pact, the counterpart of NATO.

---

[19] According to the Potsdam Declaration of 1945, the four occupying powers—France, the United Kingdom, the United States, and the U.S.S.R.—were to dismantle many of Germany's industrial plants in order to reduce that country's war-making potential. By 1947, however, dismantling was discontinued in West Germany. In fact, the United States, through the European Recovery Program, restored some key plants in order to increase Germany's productive capacity. In East Germany dismantling was continued through the early 1950's.

In the following discussions we shall outline the major trends of Germany's present economic life, both West and East.

Agriculture and forestry. Two noteworthy features marked German agriculture before World War II: (1) the high percentage of land under cultivation—61 to 63 per cent in 1939—and (2) the remarkably high crop yields. Both these characteristics contributed to the country's high degree of agricultural self-sufficiency; in average years Germany was 75 per cent self-sufficient, and in good years as much as 85 per cent. Since 1945, however, considerable changes have taken place. Territorial losses in the east, traditionally an agricultural-surplus area, have had important repercussions on Germany's postwar output. Of total prewar production, the lost territories had supplied the following percentages: rye, 33; potatoes, 25; summer barley, 29; oats, 23; fodder, 25; sugar beets, 20; wheat, 15; horses, 25; pigs, 27; and cattle, 20. Furthermore, a Germany considerably reduced in area has to feed a much greater number of people. The normal flow of complementary interregional trade also has been hindered by various interzonal restrictions and by the fact that East Germany has 55 per cent of the arable land and 48 per cent of the total agricultural land (based on 1937 figures), with only 22.3 per cent of the population.

One conclusion is evident: more than ever before, Germany—East and West—needs a large crop output, with high yields and intensive land use. By using additional fertilizer, machinery, and every available spare bit of land, prewar food consumption of about 3,000 calories per inhabitant has been maintained in West Germany. It took 15 years after World War II, however, to reach this level in East Germany. This, obviously, has not been accomplished from domestic production alone. The amount of food West Germany must import averages 28 to 30 per cent of its total requirements, 30 per cent for East Germany. Wheat consumption, which greatly increased in importance, is reflected in greater imports by West Germany amounting to the equivalent of 25 per cent of total consumption; it is 40 per cent for East Germany (the pre-war level of wheat-harvest was only reached in 1965). Progress towards self-sufficiency in both West and East Germany has been rapid. On the whole West Germany is closer to self-sufficiency in cereals than prewar Germany; its deficit in sugar is the result of the severance of eastern lands (especially Saxony). Changes in diet from starch foods to meat and milk products are also reflected in the pattern of self-sufficiency both for West and East Germany.

A combination of factors is responsible for the high percentage of productive land and the high yields. Among them are the relief of the country, the climate, the nature of the soils, the distribution of population, and the location of human activities. There are considerable regional differences in rainfall and temperature. But the diversified type of farming that is practiced yields a variety of products.

In Germany as a whole, the proportion of poor soil to total arable land is high (Figs. 6–22 and 6–23). However, by the consistent application of manure, commercial fertilizers, and various soil-conservation measures over the last 150 years, a high crop yield has been achieved on these soils. A good part of Germany has grey-brown forest soils of various shades, mostly very light, leached, and acid, much like the soils found in New England. These soils can be used only for rye, oats, and potatoes, with oats cultivated only in the wetter areas. Loess soils (black and brown steppe soils) are found in patches, the largest of which is located between Brunswick and Leipzig (East Germany) in the zone of the Southern Transitional Borderlands. Although they have been in use since prehistoric times, these loess soils remain the most productive soils in Germany, thanks to careful cultivation, good conservation measures, and the regular application of fertilizers. The amount of land under agriculture has remained rather stable. It averages about 57 per cent of the total land area of West Germany and 60 per cent of the total land area of East Germany.

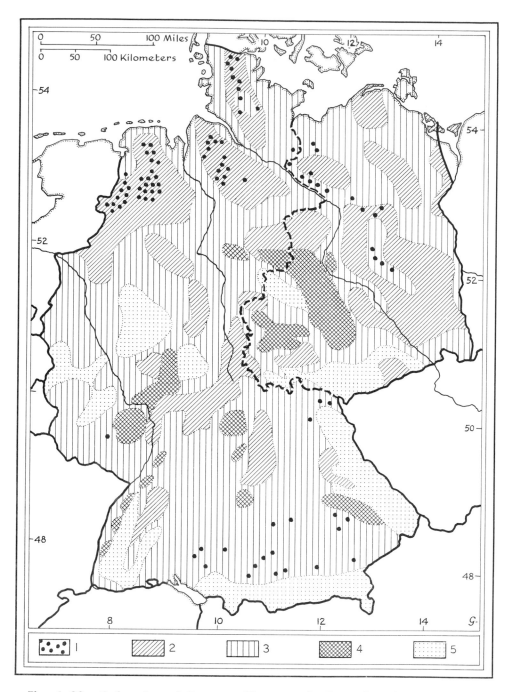

Fig. 6–22. Soil regions of Germany: (1) moor soils, (2) sandy soils, (3) mixed types ranging from sandy loams to clay, (4) black and brown steppe soils, (5) mountain soils. (After H. Niehaus, by permission of the American Geographical Society.)

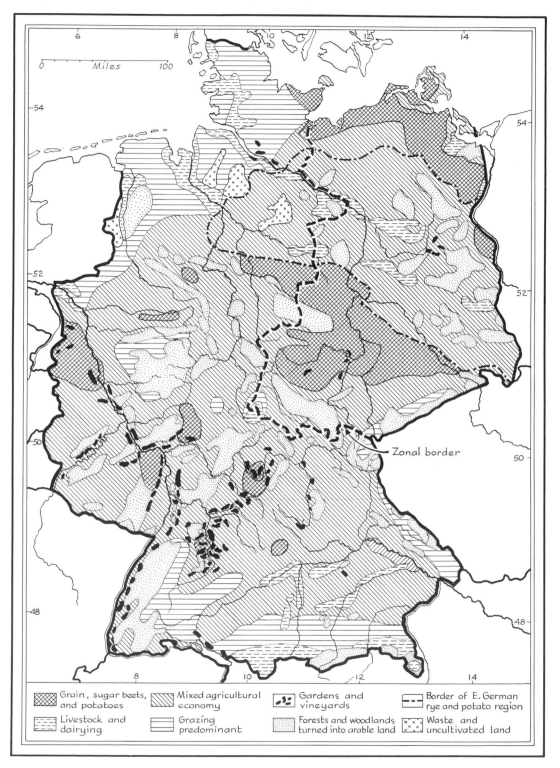

Fig. 6–23. The economic-production structure of German agriculture. (After E. Otremba, *Die Deutsche Agrarlandschaft.)*

Distribution of land patterns. Germany has always had a large number of small farms. This is due partly to predominantly poor soil and partly to historical reasons. Larger holdings, e.g., farms with over 250 acres, were found chiefly in eastern Germany, in territories lost after World War II.

WEST GERMANY. The average size farm in West Germany is approximately 20 acres. In some regions of West Germany, the farms are very much split up, because of traditional division among different heirs. Land consolidation, therefore, has top priority in West Germany, and it is hoped that this will increase productive capacity. In the mid-1960's large farms, 50 acres and larger, occupied 38 per cent of the cultivated area of West Germany and are located mostly in the loess regions west of the Elbe. If we compare the prewar (1937) percentage of all farms under 5 acres with the postwar figure, we find almost no change in the general distribution pattern in The Federal Republic. Medium-sized farms (5 to 50 acres) predominate in Bavaria and in the northwest, and in the mid-1960's comprised 58.5 per cent of the total cultivated area. Small holdings of less than 5 acres are common in the south, in central Germany, and in the west, especially the Rhineland; they comprise 3.5 per cent of the total cultivated area. The Rhineland, with its great urban concentrations, is West Germany's largest food-deficit area. In the mid-1960's about 14 per cent of the working population of West Germany was engaged in agriculture, though farming and forestry products contribute only about 6 per cent of the gross national production in West Germany.

EAST GERMANY. As a result of a series of drastic agricultural reforms in East Germany since the war, large farms (over 250 acres) which covered one-fifth of the total agricultural area in East Germany before the war were confiscated and broken up, as were many medium-sized and small farms. Voluntary agricultural societies became the forerunners of collectivization, and by the mid-1960's 7 per cent of all socialized land was in the hands of State-owned farms (*Volkseigene Güter*), with 90 per cent of the economically usable land and 93 per cent of all cropland collectivized. The average size of the collective farm is 890 acres. Generally, collectivized farming is characterized by poor performance. This can be ascribed to lack of motivation for the farm worker, mostly women; the movement of the younger people to the cities and, before 1961, to West Germany; insufficient investments and the inadequate supply of fertilizers available (the soils are very deficient in phosphates, which must be imported). Over-all decrease in the number of those employed in agriculture between 1950 and 1965 was estimated at 30 per cent. In 1965, 16 per cent of the labor force produced only 9 per cent of the Gross National Product. Today only 3 per cent of all farmers are outside collectives, but they contribute 9 per cent of all agricultural production.

Crops. The bread grains (oats, barley, rye, and wheat) and potatoes, of which Germany used to be the world's chief producer, constitute the base of Germany's diet. Rye, the most important cereal, is made into dark bread. Wheat is grown on heavier soils and in regions with warmer summer temperatures, predominantly in the Southern Transitional Borderlands; it must be imported both in West and East Germany. In addition to playing an important role in the human diet, potatoes are used as feed for pigs and as a source of alcohol and starch. They are Germany's most important crop. The distribution is similar to that of rye. Bread grains took approximately 64 per cent of the planted area in West Germany in the mid-1960's and 62 per cent in East Germany. Barley is in special demand for beer brewing. Oats is the typical crop of the moist regions along the Baltic coast and the North Sea. Grain crops are generally evenly divided between spring and autumn sowing, though both in West and East Germany the area is steadily diminishing in favor of industrial crops. The sugar beet, a source of sugar and fodder, is grown for the most part on loess soil at the foot of the Central Uplands; its distribution is similar to that of wheat. Various grasses, such as clover and alfalfa, are of special value for stock raising and dairying. Vegetable production is widespread. Industrial crops, such as hemp, flax, tobacco, hops, sunflower, and rapeseed, have increased in importance, but the area under cultivation is still relatively small (5 per cent in West Germany and 3 per cent in East Germany). Soybeans are a relatively new crop, and corn is grown in only a few areas. Vineyards are located in the Rhine gorge and in the Neckar, Main, Moselle, and Nahe valleys. German wines, e.g., the Rhine wines, are of good quality and the production is not sufficient to meet West Germany's demand. Some of the warmer regions of southern Germany have extensive orchards, and in addition, many roads throughout Germany are lined with fruit trees, especially apple trees.

Animal farming has greatly increased in importance. In East Germany close to 30 per cent of the cultivated area is under pasture and fodder crops. Dairy cattle are reared in the vicinity of large urban concentrations and in the Alpine Foreland. Draught animals generally have declined in importance.

To keep food imports down, considerable attention is given to coastal and deep-sea fisheries in both West and East Germany. In West Germany, more than 40 per cent of the fish landed consisted of cod and herring in the mid-1960's. The North Sea is the main fishing ground, where one-third of the catch is made. The rest is caught in the North Atlantic, mainly in Icelandic waters. Fishing grounds in the Baltic Sea are generally much poorer. Between 1950 and 1965 East Germany's ocean catch increased sixfold.

Forestry. In view of the importance of forests in Germany—28 per cent of the postwar area is covered with forests—a brief discussion is appropriate. During Roman times, large parts of present-day Germany were impassable, owing to the dense forest cover. The predominant forest types were distrib-

uted as follows: Scots pine and spruce in the northeast and in the glacial valleys, oak and beech in the Baltic hinterland, and beech, birch, and oak in northwestern Germany and in the middle Rhineland. Beech was dominant in the lower parts of the Central Uplands, and spruce at higher altitudes. Fir was commonly found in southern Germany.

Three main periods of forest clearing (*Rodung*) may be distinguished: sixth to ninth centuries (early German colonization period), ninth to fifteenth centuries (clearing due to population pressure), and eighteenth century (clearing due to industrialization and timber exports). Following the second period of clearings, oak was replaced by beech and spruce and forest conservation measures were initiated.

Thus German forests in existence today differ widely from the virgin forest of Roman times. The great changes in the forest cover evident throughout Germany have been brought about largely by man, through widespread extension of settlements and mining and smelting activities. Once predominantly broadleaved, Germany's forests are now chiefly coniferous, the latter type having been found especially suitable for reforestation. One may generalize by saying that conifers are dominant in the east and southeast, while broadleaf species are more common in the west.

Plains originally covered by deciduous trees now have spruce or Scots pine and some oak. Riverine forests are predominantly alder, poplar, ash, and elm. A zone of larch, spruce, and Swiss stone pine is commonly found in the Alps; one of silver fir, beech and some spruce in the Alpine Foreland. Scots pine has been found useful in the reforestation of sandy areas (dunes, heaths, and steppes). Certain tree types, such as the linden, poplar, willow, ash, and maple, which are commonly associated with German forests, occur only in small woods.

Thanks to effective conservation measures, large tracts of forest have been preserved, the ratio of coniferous to broadleaf species being 70 to 30. In general, the percentage of forest area increases from north to south. Bavaria, North Rhine-Westphalia, and Lower Saxony are the most heavily wooded areas. German forests suffered from over-cutting, especially during the war and immediately thereafter, but since 1949 large areas under timber have been replanted and carefully managed. Large tracts of forest lands located in West Germany since 1919 have been in State or community hands (*Gemeidewälder*). About 40 per cent are now in private hands. Forests in East Germany are all in State forests. Lumber is mostly used for construction purposes and as a raw material for paper and synthetic fiber manufacture.

Manufacturing. Germany is among the most important manufacturing countries of Europe, next in rank to the U.S.S.R. and the United Kingdom. Despite two defeats in the span of a quarter century and the destruction of a large part of its industrial facilities, Germany's industries have greatly increased production above prewar figures. New industries have been built and new production lines initiated with German production—both in the West and the East—have reached record levels. Industrial development received early German emphasis. Germany gained certain advantages in starting its industrial development relatively late, after the appearance of the first railroad in the 1830–40's. As a result of railroad expansion, industrial concentrations spread into many parts of the country and thus were not tied to the location of raw materials and waterways.

German industrial resurgence after World Wars I and II, and especially the devastations in West Germany after the Second World War, were in most cases made possible by large-scale capital investment, especially by Americans. It was the Marshall Plan which was largely responsible for the revitalization of West German industrial production, as well as for its expansion. The parting of ways between West and East German economic development can be dated precisely from the moment the Soviet Union

declined an opportunity to participate in the Marshall Plan. From that time on in 1948, the two halves of Germany followed different roads of economic development. The postwar plans put forth by the occupying powers, for a "pastoral German economy," and a "transfer of her manufacturing facilities to other countries," were soon abandoned for increased German participation in industrial output, and closer ties with other West European countries. The eastern part of Germany, whose industries were much less developed before the war than those of the West, in part due to its deficiencies of high-quality fuel, remained under strict Soviet supervision until the early 1950's. The industrial development in each zone followed its own needs and those of its Allies and as a result, the two German halves moved further and further apart over the years in their economic development. Many goods formerly produced in either zone, are now being produced in both halves, e.g., iron and steel works formerly concentrated in the Western half only, now have several plants in East Germany; chemical production formerly largely concentrated in the eastern half is now well represented in the West.

Besides the contributions of the Marshall Plan, the 12.5 million refugees from the East, many of them with industrial skills and experience, and the production of new industrial centers (often established by these refugees in West Germany) have made major contributions to the rebuilding and enlarging of West Germany's manufacturing, i.e., optical and precision instruments, printing, and high quality glass. The famous Zeiss works, for example, was evacuated from Jena at the close of the war and established near Stuttgart, Sudeten (Czechoslovakia) glaziers moved and established new production centers in nearby Bavaria.

The industries of East Germany have undergone many structural changes. New production lines were started, but they now depend heavily on the Soviet Union and several East European countries for many vital raw materials (Polish coal, Hungarian bauxite, Soviet iron ore) and are largely integrated into the production pattern of the Soviet bloc. With increased demands and specialization within the Soviet bloc East Germany's industries specialize in chemicals, optical equipment, steel mill equipment, passenger railway cars, trucks, and diesel engines.

Germany's industrial achievements are due to a number of factors which will be discussed in the following pages.

The raw-material factor. Coal is Germany's basic mineral resource and accounted for much of the early success in industrialization. Besides bituminous coal, sizeable amounts of lignite, called "brown coal" in Germany, are mined. However, it should be realized that the heating value of lignite is considerably inferior to that of coal: about four and one-half tons of lignite are needed to equal 1 ton of bituminous coal. Rich deposits of coking coal and other types of coal occur in the Ruhr (averaging above 80 per cent of West Germany's production) and in the Saar (12 per cent). Smaller fields of a wide range of all types of coal are in the Aachen region and near Zwickau, East Germany, on the edge of the Ore mountains (yielding less than three million tons a year).

Lignite is widely distributed over Germany. It occurs in thick deposits close to the surface and is extracted mainly by open-pit workings. Due to high transportation costs and low heating value it is compressed into briquettes which have a lower moisture content, are burned close to the pits, and are used to generate electric power. It is also used as a source of various chemical products. Through hydrogenation, lignite is converted into liquid hydrocarbons (gasoline and petroleum) and into the raw materials for synthetic rubber. With the postwar losses of the important bituminous coal mines in Upper Silesia (now in Poland), lignite has assumed an even more important position in the German industrial fuel picture. Germany's largest fields are west of Cologne in the lower Rhineland (producing 85 per cent of the total production of West

Germany) surrounding Leipzig, and at Nieder Lausitz (Bezirk Cottbus), the latter being East Germany's largest field.

West Germany in 1957 produced 153 million metric tons of anthracite and bituminous coal and 99 million metric tons of lignite. It is Europe's largest coal producer after the United Kingdom. In 1964, West Germany's mines produced 143 million metric tons of coal and 111 million tons of lignite, thus contributing 62 per cent of the total produced by the six countries associated in the Common Market. Its large supply of coal was thus an important reason for its key position in the European economy. But the production picture has radically changed since 1957, and especially since 1965. Of 162 anthracite and bituminous mines that were operated in 1957, only 75 were operating ten years later. This also meant a reduction in the working force of over 200,000. Actual output dropped to less than 126 million metric tons in 1966 and production may fall below 90 million tons after 1970 (plans call for the Saar mines to contribute 8 to 9 million tons as against an actual production of 15 million in 1966). Twenty-five million tons remained unsold in 1966. Lignite production dropped to 98 million tons in 1966. Oil, electricity, synthetic materials, and the rapid nationalization of the industry have combined to bring about these changes which leave their impact especially on the face of the Ruhr. Fig. 6–24 shows the changes graphically in West Germany's energy consumption.

Coal never played an important role in the economy of East Germany. It is largely dependent upon imports, for the most part coming from Poland. This deficiency in bituminous coal is made up by East Germany's extensive reserves and production of lignite which amounted to 257 million metric tons in 1964 (249 million tons by 1966). Its industrial usefulness, though, is limited. Over four-fifths of its needs are imported, though the picture is also rapidly changing here following those factors discussed earlier which left their impact on West Germany's industrial development.

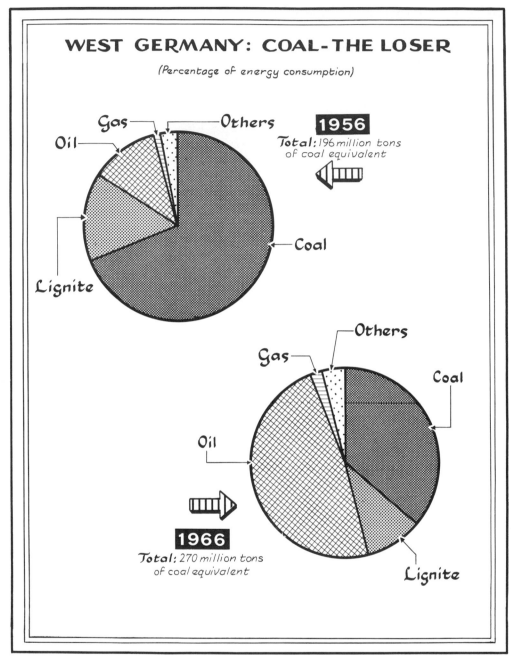

Coal mining employed 604,000 workers in 1956 and 295,000 in 1966.
Productivity amounted to 1.6 tons per man day in 1956 and 3.3 tons in 1966.
Estimated 1971 employment is 215,000.

Fig. 6–24. Percentage of energy consumption in The Federal Republic of Germany. (Source: *The Economist,* August, 1967.)

Despite the abundance of coal and the availability of potash, produced from large salt deposits around Stassfurt, northeast of the Harz Mountains (in East Germany), both Germanys suffer from considerable raw-material shortages. One such shortage is in iron ore, which has been mined since 1850 southeast of Cologne in the Siegerland and in the Lahn and Harz regions. The low-grade iron ore deposits of the Salzgitter district of Hanover and the small reserves of the middle Rhine cannot supply the needs of the Ruhr and other industries. Imports in the mid-1960's came from Sweden, Lorraine, Spain, and North Africa and provide over 65 per cent of its needs. The Klöckner tidewater plant at Bremen imports at highly advantageous economic rates both ore and coal. They are used locally and also shipped to plants throughout West Germany. East Germany's needs of iron ore (and most non-ferrous metals) are supplied largely by the Soviet Union. Other important minerals which must be imported include lead, zinc, copper, tin, sulfur, and pyrites; flax and silk must be imported for the textile industry. Germany became aware at an early date of the value of substitutes. Accordingly, many synthetic products and substitutes for essential natural resources were developed in Germany. East Germany mines uranium ore in the western Ore Mountains near Gera. The exact quantity is not known. It also mines copper ore in the eastern Harz where production is on the increase. Nevertheless, West and East Germany's dependence on key raw-material imports is an important economic handicap.

Waterpower is another important resource for German industries. It is concentrated in the Alps and in the valleys of the Central Uplands (dammed lakes). Even though much progress has been made in enlarging electric power generating facilities over the last 20 years, a great deal of electricity must be imported, some of it in exchange for Ruhr coal. In 1966, waterpower contributed 10 per cent of West Germany's electricity. Coal, lignite, petroleum and a small amount of natural gas made up the rest. Waterpower contributes only a little over one per cent of the total power needs of East Germany. Most of the electric power is produced from generators located at the lignite fields and this is constantly being expanded due to the greatly increased demands of the chemical industries and the electrification of the railways. Bituminous coal contributed less than three per cent of the generating power and some power is obtained by burning gas, either natural or gas from brown coal. Gas obtained from the latter is also transmitted by an expanding pipeline system for industrial use in the southwest; extensions to other parts of East Germany are planned. Diesel fuel is assuming increased importance.

West Germany's petroleum production has increased significantly, from 230,000 tons in 1933 to 7.9 million in 1966. The Hanover, Emsland, and Weser-Ems fields contribute over 80 per cent of the country's total output in crude oil. Smaller fields are located in Schleswig-Holstein, the Alpine Foreland, and the Upper Rhine area. There are a number of other minor producing fields. At the end of 1966 West Germany's production covered 14 per cent of its requirements. Most of it is refined in the Ruhr, Cologne, Wilhelmshaven, and Hamburg areas. This makes West Germany's industrial production as well as household uses increasingly dependent upon reliable overseas supplies. When it is considered that about 42 per cent of the imported oil in 1966 came from the politically unstable area of the Middle East, the serious impact on West Germany's economy can be easily understood. In spite of the large surplus coal, West Germany's industries and households follow the trend of rapid conversion from coal to oil. Consumption of oil has increased roughly 13 to 15 per cent annually. East Germany produces only a very small amount of oil.

Pipelines have been and still are being laid all over Central Europe (Fig. 6–21, also 10–1). They bring oil by giant tankers to the oil refineries and pipelines located in the

Rotterdam region, Europe's largest raw oil refinery and storage concentration (total capacity by 1970 estimated at 55 million tons annually as against 32 in 1960), to Wilhelmshaven and Hamburg, and other West and South European ports. Notwithstanding the great technical difficulties, especially in laying pipelines across or below the Alpine ranges and the crossing of rivers, the network is constantly expanding to satisfy increasing demands. Ingolstadt in Bavaria is the terminal point for the Transalpine (Trieste-Ingolstadt-TAL) pipeline and ultimately will have five refineries. It also is the terminal point for the Central European pipeline, 630 miles long, which brings supplies from Genoa and passes under the San Bernardino Pass and through Switzerland. The South European pipeline runs to Karlsruhe which has several large refineries and also has a connection with the refineries in Ingolstadt. Kelsterbach near Frankfurt is the terminal point for the Rhineland pipeline.

Schwedt in East Germany on the Oder is the main terminal point and center of important refineries for the Soviet-built "friendship" pipeline (coming from the Urals). A number of secondary pipelines distribute oil and other refinery products to important industrial and urban concentrations. A pipeline from Rostock to Schwedt distributes oil from tankers.

The locational factor. Among the more important factors of industrial location are: raw materials, transportation, manpower, and the proximity of agricultural land. German industrial concentrations are characterized by a combination of several of these factors. A belt of unequal width, extending from Aachen on the German-Belgian border to the Ore Mountains along the border of Czechoslovakia, includes the major West and East German concentrations. Major concentrations can be clearly established in ten regions. Six of these are located in West Germany and four in East Germany. In addition to those, much industrial production is centered in large cities. Berlin is handicapped by its division into West and East

Berlin and by being isolated within East Germany. West Berlin is in a much more difficult position than East Berlin. Still important mechanical and electrical industries (Siemens, Osram, Borsig), as well as printing, clothing, and food-processing industries employ over one-third of the total employed in manufacturing industries. Among the industrial territories lost since the war, Upper Silesia played an important role, though not comparable to that of the Ruhr. While Silesia contributed less than one-sixth of Germany's over-all production before World War II, its contribution to Poland's economy is of major importance (see Chapter 8, pp. 470–71).

The major concentrations located in West Germany include (see Fig. 6–21): (1) the North Sea ports of Hamburg and Bremen, (2) the Rhine-Ruhr region, (3) the Hanover-Brunswick region, (4) the Rhine-Main region, (5) the Saar, with Saarbrücken as its chief center, and (6) concentrations around (a) the Neckar valley with Stuttgart and Heilbronn as its chief centers, (b) Nürnberg which is located in the center of a ring of numerous small industrial cities, and (c) the Munich industrial region which stretches northwest to include Ulm and Augsburg. In addition, the important concentrations in West Berlin must be mentioned.

Most of the East German concentrations developed only after the war. They are grouped in the following industrial centers (Fig. 6–21): (1) the Central Industrial Region including the Thuringia-Harz concentrations, (2) Southern Saxony with concentrations in the northern part around Leipzig, Halle, Dessau, and in the southern part in Zwickau, Karl-Marx Stadt, and Dresden, (3) Nieder Lausitz, a newly developed region with Lauchhammer on its western margin and Hoyerswerda to the east, and (4) Greater Berlin, extending from East Berlin along its waterways which radiate from the city to Frankfurt on the Oder in the east.[20]

[20] See Norman J. G. Pounds, *The Economic Pattern of Modern Germany* (London: John Murray, 1963:70–84.

West Germany

1. THE NORTH SEA PORTS. Hamburg, the northernmost North Sea port on the lower Elbe, has been hard hit by the closeness of the zonal border, the loss of considerable Czech transit trade, and especially its unfavorable geographical location, the latter accelerated by political as well as technological developments. The advantageous geographical position of Rotterdam, especially its closeness to the industrial heart of western and southern Germany, together with the impact of the Common Market and Hamburg's inaccessibility to the ever-increasing size of tankers, puts the city in a disadvantageous position. Once a powerful member of the Hanseatic League, handling as late as World War II as much as 70 per cent of Germany's import and 57 per cent of its exports, the decline in its trading position forces the city to look for a greater diversification of its employment opportunities. By the mid-1960's only roughly one-third of the freight to and from West German ports, and only 16 per cent of German exports (Fig. 6–25) went through Hamburg.

There are extensive shipbuilding yards and machinery and tool plants in all German port cities, with the greatest concentrations in Hamburg, Bremen, and Kiel. Each seaport has its own trade pattern. Bremen is the major port for cotton imports destined for Central and Eastern Europe. It is also Europe's leading importer of various tropical produce. Bremerhaven, its outer harbor, car-

Fig. 6–25. Hamburg. St. Pauli Landing with Elbe tunnel. To the right the Stülcken dockyard, to the left background the free port area. (German Information Center, Houston.)

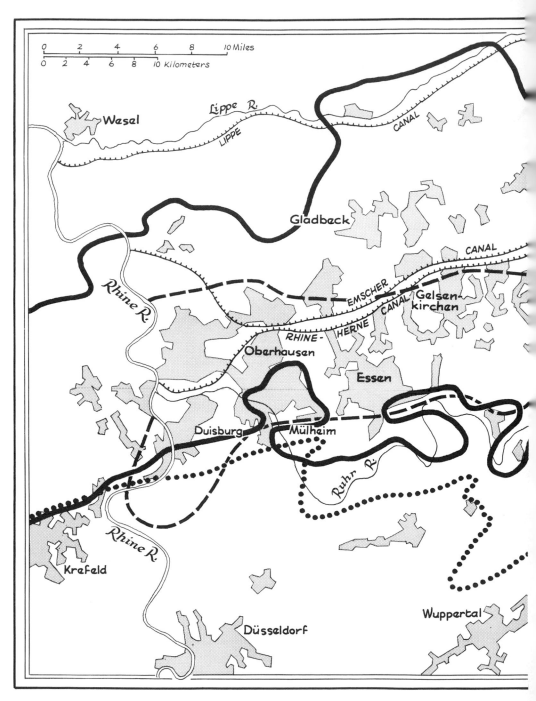

Fig. 6–26. Coal mining and

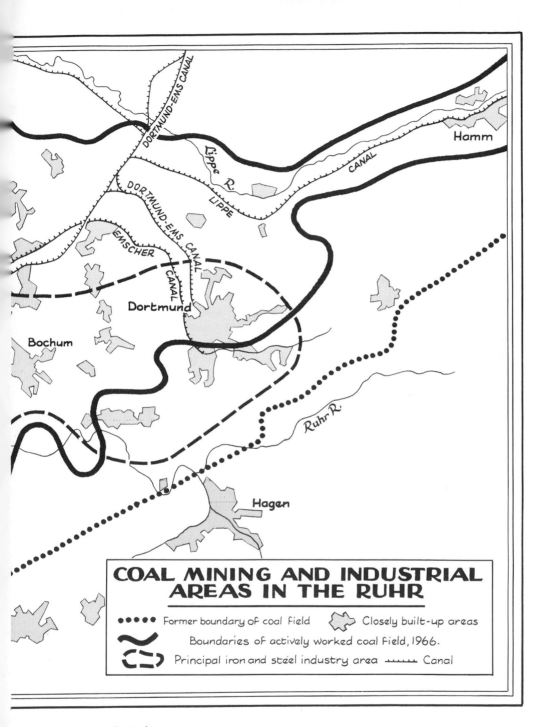

COAL MINING AND INDUSTRIAL AREAS IN THE RUHR

•••• Former boundary of coal field   Closely built-up areas

Boundaries of actively worked coal field, 1966.

Principal iron and steel industry area ⊷⊷⊷⊷ Canal

industrial areas in the Ruhr.

ries much of the traffic and has also important refineries. Emden, the third of Germany's North Sea ports, was originally built to capture some of the trade going to Rotterdam. Direct access to the Rhine-Ruhr industrial region, via the Dortmund-Ems canal, has been an important factor in Emden's growth, but comparatively few industries are located within its port area. The port of Kiel is located on the Kiel Canal, which connects the Baltic with the North Sea. It is the most important Baltic port of West Germany.

2. THE RHINE-RUHR REGION. This region is most important for its coal and iron-ore mines and for the production of coke, steel, chemicals, and heavy machinery. The core of the Ruhr area extends about 45 miles eastward from Duisburg on the Rhine in the west to Dortmund in the east and has a north-south extent of less than 15 miles. A more recent expansion has taken place north of the core area, near the Münster coal mines. The Ruhr has been important for some time. Production of coal and coke increased from 22,228 and 1,291 tons respectively in 1880 to 114,183 and 26,703 tons at the outbreak of World War I. It fluctuated during the interwar years depending on Germany's and Europe's economic needs and reached 130,500 tons of coal and 36,000 tons of coke in 1939. From a low of 33,380 and 5,338 tons in 1945 it steadily climbed to a height of 142,201 in 1964 for coal and 37,903 tons of coke in 1965. Since then the decline in production has been dramatic and stocks have increased. In mid-1967 unemployment in the Ruhr was six per cent.

In 1937, 70 per cent of the entire German output of steel originated in the Ruhr, a percentage which has barely changed despite altered postwar conditions. During the same year (1937), the Ruhr area produced over 25 per cent of Germany's electric power, 72 per cent of its coal tar, and 64 per cent of its crude benzene.

The importance of this region is due to its extensive, high-grade deposits of coking coal; its proximity to West Germany's only source of iron ore; the unrivaled natural artery of trade provided by the Rhine and its tributaries, the Lippe, and the Ruhr; and the dense network of canals which connects the Ruhr with most parts of Germany. Its location in the very heart of Europe's commerce and industry has consistently encouraged the expansion of its industries (Fig. 6–26).

This area is remarkable for its large concentration of cities, 20 of which have a population of over 100,000. Its chief city is Essen. Other large cities are Dortmund, Bochum, Duisburg (Duisburg-Hamborn), and Gelsenkirchen. Duisburg-Ruhrort, with a 1966 population of 484,000, is the leading Rhine port and the largest inland port of Europe (Fig. 6–27). The Ruhr is dotted with iron and steel works, locomotive and chemical plants, and factories manufacturing equipment for mines and steel mills.

The region surrounding the Ruhr also has a great variety of industries: textile and synthetic-fiber manufacturing along the banks of the Wupper River (Wuppertal as its center), the cotton textile center of Moenchengladbach on the west bank of the Rhine, the silk and steel center of Krefeld, the important chemical center of Leverkusen on the Rhine south of the Ruhr, as well as the great industrial center of Düsseldorf (the capital of North Rhine-Westphalia). West of Cologne, the rise of a number of industrial centers is closely linked to the coal basin extending from Belgium and the Netherlands into Germany, but especially the important brown coal deposits stretching northwest from Bonn to northwest of Cologne. Aachen is the center of a diversified industry, producing hardware, textiles, steel, etc. A number of oil refineries have been built near Cologne. All over this region are a great variety of industries and with its many concentrations and dense highway, river, and canal networks, it is easily Europe's most concentrated urban and industrial region. In addition, many of these industries are now closely integrated into the larger economic framework of the European Economic Community (Common Market). While

Fig. 6–27. Duisburg-Ruhrort, Europe's largest inland port. The city is located on the confluence of the Ruhr with the Rhine River (Ruhrort to the left of the photograph). Toward the right are the locks controlling the entrance to Herne Canal which traverses the Ruhr region. The city was founded in 1716 and with its modern port facilities, including 20 docks and over a hundred steam-power, diesel, and electric cranes, 111 silos for grain storage and over 500 oil tanks, is one of the most up-to-date and best equipped ports in the world. Total freight turnover in 1965 amounted to 32 million tons, mostly iron ore, petroleum, and coal. (Inter Nationes, Bad Godesberg.)

many of the cities of this region show considerable diversity in their economic structure between heavy metals and service industries, others, notably those located in the northern Ruhr, have a very unbalanced economic base. With coal mining declining during the last ten years and especially since the mid-1960's, and competition from oil and advanced technologies creating unemployment, these towns face a serious economic and social problem. Major efforts are now being made to attract new industries and thus contribute to a greater diversification of employment opportunities.

3. HANOVER-BRUNSWICK REGION. Northeast of the Ruhr is a more recently developed economic region. The cities of Hanover and Brunswick (Braunschweig) are at the center. Both were early centers of craft industries. In the 1930's, the low-grade iron ore deposits of the Peine-Salzgitter area near Brunswick attracted several heavy-manufacturing establishments which also used the dense river and canal transportation system for imports of coal and additional iron ore. Northwest of Brunswick is Wolfsburg, the center of the well-known Volkswagen works (Fig. 6–28). Chemical engineering and light industries are distributed in the smaller cities of this region.

4. THE UPPER PART OF THE RHINE VALLEY. This industrial region extends along the Rhine from Mainz and Frankfurt-am-Main southward to Karlsruhe. The region's chief drawback is the lack of raw materials. However, this disadvantage is overcome by its excellent location, transportation-wise. The canalized Rhine and Main rivers give easy access to the east and to the Rhine-Ruhr region to the north. The region's industries

Fig. 6–28. Volkswagen plant at Wolfsburg, workers settlement in foreground. Between the settlement and the plant the Midland Canal. (Bundesbildstelle, Bonn.)

manufacture precision instruments, tools, and typewriters. The twin cities of Ludwigshafen-Mannheim produce chemicals (dyes, fertilizer, nitrates, and pharmaceutical items). Mainz and Frankfurt are important centers for the manufacture of automobiles, railroad supplies, trucks, machines, and machine tools. Mannheim and Mainz are also active river ports, while Frankfurt was prewar Germany's leading commercial and financial center. It holds the same position in The Federal Republic of Germany.

5. THE SAAR. Situated along the German-French border, this region has changed hands several times in recent history. It owes its industrial development to the presence of coal deposits in proximity to the minette iron ores of Lorraine. Between 1871 and 1918, the region was part of Germany and the output of its newly established industries was shipped eastward on canals connecting it with the main Rhine Valley. By the Treaty of Versailles, eastern Lorraine was returned to France and the Saar was made an autonomous territory administered by France under League of Nations supervision, but it reverted to Germany in 1935 as a result of a plebiscite. After 1945, the Saar was made autonomous once more and its economy was closely tied to that of France. A semi-autonomous "European" status for the Saar was rejected by the people of the Saar in October, 1955, and in 1956 France and West Germany agreed on the Saar's political incorporation into The Federal Republic on January 1, 1957, and on its economic incorporation on January 1, 1960. The

overwhelming majority of the Saarländers are German by language and origin, and, obviously, this fact has always exerted a strong influence for the return to the German "motherland" of this 2,500-square-mile strategically located territory. The rich deposits of Saar coal which form the basis of a powerful iron and steel industry have made important contributions to the economy of West Germany.

6. THE NECKAR, NÜRNBERG, AND MUNICH INDUSTRIAL CONCENTRATIONS.

a. *The Neckar.* The region's chief centers are at Stuttgart and Heilbronn and the main transportation artery is the navigable Neckar River, which enters the Rhine at Mannheim. Cement works, numerous wood industries, textile plants, and precision-instrument and other metal industries dot the landscape. Automobile, machine, and shoe factories make important contributions. Stuttgart is one of West Germany's important industrial centers. A sizeable number of Zeiss factory workers (manufacturing cameras and various types of precision instruments) transferred at the end of World War II from Jena in East Germany, the original plant, to Oberkochen in this region where they established a new Zeiss factory.

b. *The Nürnberg Region.* Numerous smaller industrial cities are included in this region, e.g., Erlangen, Fürth, Schweinfurth, Würzburg. The latter two cities have important engineering works. Nürnberg is noted for its metallurgical products, foods, and toys. Once the Main-Danube canalization project is completed (in the 1980's), Nürnberg will be linked to West Germany's major river systems.

c. *The Munich Region.* The capital of Bavaria is a noted industrial center and has important electrical, optical, and food industries. Included in this region are the cities of Augsburg and Ulm to the northwest. Augsburg is the center of important engineering works. Because of the absence of good and dependable water transport, the region must concentrate on manufacturing which requires relatively little bulky raw materials.

In addition to the major manufacturing regions, numerous other industrial centers are scattered all over Germany. A certain distribution pattern is clearly visible: rolling stock and manufacture and repair shops are located near railroad yards; the principal agricultural market areas attract industries producing agricultural implements; the electrical, food, and apparel industries are represented in nearly all important cities; there is hardly a small village in West Germany which does not have some kind of factory.

East Germany

1. THE CENTRAL INDUSTRIAL REGION. This extends eastward from the middle Elbe River and south into the Central Uplands. Its various industries are largely based on lignite and rock and potash salts and this combination has made it the most important chemical-manufacturing region in all of Germany. Magdeburg and especially Halle are important centers, with five major chemical works located within 35 miles of the Halle district. The *Leuna Werke*, near Merseburg, are the largest works, manufacturing ammonia and common acids, as well as motor fuel which has been synthesized from brown coal. *Leuna II*, a second plant, is at present under construction and will include petrochemical products among its items produced. Other important chemical works in this area are the *Buna Werke* producing especially plastic materials, two electrochemical combines, the well-known factory for the production of photographic chemicals (*Agfa*), and a plant for the production of fertilizers. The Erfurt-Gera region is characterized by a large number of small industrial works, especially in the light, optical, precision, and chemical industries. The original optical-precision works of Zeiss (established in 1846) were rebuilt after the war and are still located at Jena. Lignite found in the region is the basic fuel for the production of electric power and for other energy uses. Two small but fully inte-

grated iron and steel works are located in this region; they are *Maxhütte* at Unterwellenborn on the northern edge of the Thüringerwald and a more recently built smelting plant at Calbe, *Eisenwerke West*, south of Magdeburg. This plant smelts the low-grade iron ores of the Harz region with the coke derived from brown coal at Lauchhammer (district Cottbus).

2. SOUTHERN SAXONY REGION. The industries which developed in southern Saxony, on the northern slopes of the Ore Mountains, are largely based on lignite and on a wide range of metallic ores, many of which are now exhausted. Some of the mining and industrial activity goes back to the Middle Ages. Lignite is still available and forms the basic source of power. A large number of skilled workers are employed in the numerous textile plants and in the woodworking and tanning industries which have grown up here. Important cities are Plauen (knitted goods, embroidery), Meissen and Dresden (porcelain), Karl-Marx Stadt (general textiles), and Leipzig, which is one of Europe's oldest trading centers. Before the war, Leipzig was a center of the fur trade and was also known for its publishing and printing houses of high repute. Its famous international fair, while handicapped by the postwar division of Germany, is still being held annually. The Leipzig Bay is linked with other parts of Germany by a network of canals, rivers (including the Elbe), and railroad lines.

3. LOWER LAUSITZ REGION. The industrial production of this most recently developed region is based on the sizeable brown coal deposits of Lausitz (East-Elbian field). Lauchhammer, located on the western margin of the region, has developed into an important center for engineering and chemical industries. Other industries developed in this region consist mainly of power-generation, manufacture of coke, fuel oil, and various related by-products from brown coal.

4. GREATER BERLIN REGION. This region includes the city of Berlin (East Berlin) and the industries along the various waterways radiating from the city as far east as the new iron and steel works, *Eisenhüttenkombinat Ost* on the Elbe River, 14 miles south of Frankfurt on the Oder and the new petrochemical works at Schwedt on the Oder (also the terminal point for the Soviet "friendship" pipeline). Its industrial structure is very diversified and based largely on electro-technical and mechanical industries in East Berlin, numerous light and consumer's industries, but also includes the old steel-finishing center at Eberswalde and Finow. Most raw materials must be imported, including all the iron ore (from Krivoy Rog in the Soviet Union and via Szczecin-Stettin) and coking coal which is shipped in by barge from Upper Silesia (Poland) on the Oder River. Important manufacturing centers in this region are the recently rebuilt and greatly expanded port city of Rostock on the Baltic Sea, various cities surrounding East Berlin, such as Potsdam, Brandenburg, and Fürstenwalde, with important engineering, electric, textile, and consumers' goods industries.

The transportation factor. Germany's industrial growth would not have been possible without the development of an efficient, highly integrated transportation system. Although considerably damaged by the war and divided by the zonal boundaries, the transportation system has made important contributions to postwar rehabilitation.

The physiography of Germany presented no major obstacles to the development of a dense rail network connecting all important cities and industrial areas. Rail densities are highest in the Rhine-Ruhr region, the Central Industrial Region, and the vicinity of Berlin, Leipzig, and Mainz-Frankfurt. An increasing part of Germany's rail mileage is being electrified. Two general patterns of freight movement may be distinguished: (1) raw-material imports and overseas exports move from and to the various ports and (2) raw materials and foodstuffs move from one region to another, including intrazonal traffic and overland to other European countries. The division of Germany left an important impact on a number of railway lines. The former dense east to west and northeast to southwest traffic flow has been changed due to the discontinuance of most direct traffic between West and East Germany. Only three direct routes are in operation. The present pattern is a north-south one connecting North Rhine-Westphalia and the North Sea ports with southern Germany. Two railway ferries connect East Germany with Denmark and southern Sweden.

Germany's principal waterways are the country's oldest transport arteries. Four large, navigable rivers flow from south to north across the North German Lowlands: the Rhine with Dortmund-Ems Canal extension to Emden, the Weser, the Elbe, and the Oder (now part of the German-Polish border). The three east-west arteries are the Danube and two canals, the Midland Canal and the Kiel Canal. The Midland Canal links the Ems with the Elbe and is extended eastward by various canals to the Oder. Completed in 1938, the 224-mile-long canal has a depth of 9 feet. Political controversies between the occupying powers have reduced its usefulness as a transit route, especially in and around Berlin. In order to prevent interference with shipping on the part of the Western powers, an additional canal has been built to bypass the Western zone of Berlin and thus afford a direct connection through the whole of the Soviet zone.

The Rhine carries more passengers and freight than any other German waterway. Since the mouth of the river is in foreign territory, Germany constructed the Dortmund-Ems Canal as a bypass through German territory to the North Sea. However, because the canal is too shallow and too narrow for modern barges, most of the Rhine shipping continues to travel down the river into Dutch territory. Increased traffic on the Rhine is in part due to the canalization of the Mosel River which was completed in early 1964. The canalization of the Mosel brought a direct connection between the drainage basin of the Meuse and rivers flowing to join the Seine and the Rhine. Barges loaded with coal can now travel to the ironworks near Thionville and Metz in northern France and return with iron ores from the Lorraine fields. This is saving shipping costs to French steelmen and German consumers who benefit from lower costs on such products as French wheat. Also, the additional 700 million kwh of electric power produced annually is much needed by both industrial and home users. Considerable opposition from German railways and Ruhr industrial interests held up the Mosel project. The former was afraid of competition for bulky raw materials, the latter of the retooling necessary for important Ruhr industries due to the different grade and quality of ores to be used. But the picture is rapidly changing, competition from pipelines starting at northern ports and road transport are threatening the huge investments made in the canalization of the Mosel river, though this competition is bringing much needed relief to the huge river traffic in the middle section of the Rhine river. Inasmuch as the Rhine flows through Europe's greatest industrial concentrations, upstream traffic is heaviest with coal, coke, and grain, while timber, potash, and iron ore are the main downstream cargoes.

The Elbe provides a natural link between the North Sea and landlocked Czechoslovakia, but due to the re-orientation of Czechoslovakia's foreign trade and the zonal boundaries, river traffic has much declined. The Oder River was always of lesser importance, but in spite of its now being a border river for a distance of 110 miles, traffic is on the increase, linking the important Silesian coal fields with the now Polish port city of Szczecin. In addition, most cargo for the earlier mentioned iron and steel works south of Frankfurt on the Oder comes by barge on the river.

The Danube has always been of minor importance as an east-west artery, largely because of its isolation from other German waterways, the absence of a major industrial region along its banks, and the fact that it flows in the wrong direction, eastward.

Many possibilities of connecting the Danube with Europe's other main rivers have been studied, but because of the high cost and technical difficulties, little has been done until recently. The idea of linking the Danube-Main and Rhine rivers is not a new one. A small canal was cut from near Nürnberg to the Danube above Regensburg in the nineteenth century. It is much too small for modern commercial traffic. A modern canal similar in capacity to the Main River is now under construction and will furnish an important link between the Rhine-Main and Danube river system sometimes during the 1980's.

Germany has excellent road communications. The density of the network is high, but even the superhighways (*Autobahnen*), most of them built before the war, are no longer able to carry the traffic. Although they were built primarily for strategic reasons—to facilitate troop movements—the superhighways are now used by an ever-increasing number of overland truck carriers and are constantly being expanded. Of the total transport volume of West Germany, the part played by trucks increased from 30.4 per cent to 35.6 per cent in the period 1959 to 1965; those by railroads decreased from 42 per cent to 34.7 per cent; domestic waterways from 26.2 per cent to 24.6 per cent, while the part played by oil pipelines in the overall transport volume increased from 1.4 per cent to 5.1 per cent. In East Germany railroads carried roughly half of the total freight, inland waterways three per cent, and trucks twelve per cent. Air freight plays for Germany only a minor role, though airlines serve all important West and East German cities. West Germany's *Lufthansa* has a dense flight network which includes many overseas areas, including North and South America.

Foreign and intrazonal trade. Since the early 1950's The German Federal Republic has participated increasingly in world trade. This expansion has made The Federal Republic one of the foremost trading nations in the world. She has enjoyed a net trade surplus and has assumed an important position in world business as financier. The structure of West Germany's trade, excluding intrazonal trade, has changed from prewar and early postwar years. Food imports play an important role—they now run on an average 22 to 25 per cent of total imports; industrial raw materials comprise 20–24 per cent of the value of her imports, and include large quantities of natural rubber, raw cotton, vegetable oil and fats, petroleum (two-thirds of her needs), important metalliferous ores, including iron ore, skins, hides, and wool. Imports also include a varied quantity of manufactured and semi-manufactured goods (45–50 per cent), such as instruments, machinery, and automobiles.

West Germany's exports also show a wide range of goods. Eighty-nine per cent of her exports, by value (mid-1960's), consist of industrial goods, chemical, electrotechnical goods, automobile, photographic equipment, ships and not inconsiderable foreign contracts for large steel constructions necessitating the export of considerable quantities of equipment. Of these, semi-finished goods contribute about 9 per cent. Raw materials contribute 4 per cent and food exports 2.4 per cent. The modernization of West Germany's industrial plants since the war has greatly raised the productivity of her workers and this has resulted in increased competitiveness on the world market. Coal and coke were major export items immediately after the war; they play only a minor role today.

The industrial countries of Western Europe, especially her Common Market trading partners, play a major role in West Germany's expanding foreign trade (36 per cent of her total exports and 38 per cent of her imports in 1966). While on balance she exports more to the industrialized countries of the west, she buys more from the primary producing countries (wool, cotton, coffee, etc.) than she exports. Her principal world trading partners, besides the countries of the Common Market, are the United States, Sweden, Switzerland, the United Kingdom, and Austria. West German trade with East European countries has been on the increase and as a result, she has resumed her traditional role as main western trading partner with most East European countries. Total trade averaged 5.5 per cent of her world trade.

Before World War II, trade between western and eastern Germany was extremely heavy, but because no formal lines of division existed, no exact records were kept. Since the unified-currency area was divided in 1948, lists of goods have been drawn up annually in intrazonal trade agreements. West Germany buys mostly lignite briquettes, clothing and footwear, wheat, barley, chemical products, meat, textiles and petroleum products. It exports mostly fertilizers, chemicals, and textiles. Intrazonal trade has been on the increase since the mid-1950's, but amounted only to 1.7 per cent of West Germany's total exports and 1.8 per cent of her total imports in 1965 (it amounted to 9.5 per cent of East Germany's foreign trade).

Foreign trade of East Germany plays a much smaller role than in the West German economy, though it has increased during the last fifteen years (Fig. 8–13). East Germany started out with a number of handicaps which influenced her economic development, especially during the 1950's. East Germany inherited only 36.6 per cent of the industrial capacity of the prewar Germany. Its population had been diminishing until 1961, and war reparation demanded considerable shipments of both goods produced and the dismantling of existing production units. Roughly 74 per cent of East Germany's foreign trade is with the Communist bloc countries, 85 per cent of its exports go to these countries. Of the rest, half is with West Germany and West Berlin. The Soviet Union, with its vital control of raw material and food imports, has a virtual monopoly on East German imports and exports. Fuel, industrial raw materials, and food products are the main imports. These include over six million tons of crude petroleum, 12 million tons of coal and coke (Poland, Czechoslovakia), over one million tons of iron ore (Soviet Union), besides considerable quantities of raw cotton, wool, leather, semi-manufactured items of iron and steel, tobacco, coffee, and cocoa. Detailed export figures by value are not published, but the major items are chemicals, machinery, optical and precision goods, textiles, and automobiles, especially trucks and electrotechnical goods.

SWITZERLAND

Population

The great diversity in the relief of Switzerland has been described earlier. A study of the origins of the Swiss state shows that it grew from an aggregation of autonomous units which combined to defend the important mountain passes against external attack. Siegfried wrote:

. . . the homogeneity resides in the principle of political resistance entrenched in a natural fortress, but the diversity is everywhere. . . . We find that each canton is different from its neighbor, whilst the various geographical areas are of such marked individuality that their inhabitants are fully conscious of the differences. In each neatly circumscribed valley, corresponding to the boundaries of a canton (I am thinking of Glarus, for example), each citizen knows instinctively why he belongs to his particular valley, to his particular canton. This is the solid basis of a democracy which has its roots both in the soil and in men's hearts.[21]

Switzerland had an estimated population of 6,200,000 in mid-1968, concentrated in an area of less than 16,000 square miles—somewhat smaller than the combined areas of Massachusetts and New Hampshire.[22] There are about 389 people to the square mile, but when it is realized that only 54 per cent of the total area is permanently inhabited (22

[21] André Siegfried, *Switzerland* (London: Johnathan Cape, Ltd., 1950):25.
[22] The last Swiss population census was in December, 1960. Most figures quoted are taken from the *Statistisches Jahrbuch der Schweiz: 1967.*

Fig. 6–29. Geneva, Switzerland on western end of Lake Geneva. View from European headquarters of United Nations in foreground across Lake toward France. Grand Salève on right (west) and Les Voirons with de Branta, 1457 m. in background center. Mountains in far background are part of the main Alpine chain toward Mont Blanc. (G. W. Hoffman.)

per cent unsettled and the rest inhabited only during the summer months), the density of 742 per square mile of productive land becomes the more significant figure.

The distribution of the population is very uneven, whether measured by its altitudinal distribution or by the size of populated centers. Some 61 per cent of Switzerland's inhabitants live below 1,500 feet, while only 3.6 per cent live above 3,000 feet. Forty-two per cent of the population is found in towns of 10,000 and over. Berne, Zürich, Basel, and Geneva are the four largest cities. Zürich with nearly half a million is the most populous city. Berne (population 168,000) is the capital and Geneva the seat of the European headquarters of the United Nations (Fig. 6–29). Appenzell-Inner Rhodes half canton is the smallest unit of the Federation, with 13,500 inhabitants. Roughly two-thirds of the people of Switzerland live on the Swiss Plateau, which comprises but one-third of the total area (Figs. 6–30 and 6–31).

The population is increasing rather rapidly, 15.1 per cent between 1950 and 1960 and 1.9 per cent annually between 1958 and 1965. In the mid-1960's the birth rate stood at 18.3 per thousand; the death rate dropped to 9.3 per thousand during the same period. In 1966, some 159,000 Swiss citizens lived abroad, the largest number in France, West Germany, and in the United States. Emigration has always played an important role in Swiss economic life, although the total has been far smaller on the average than that of most other European countries. Foreign workers have become essential to the Swiss economy. Between 1955 and 1967 their number increased from 271,149 to 788,000, including 153,500 seasonal and 58,600 border foreign workers. This large dependency of the Swiss economy on foreign workers (mainly Italians), e.g., 37 per cent of the total industrial employment, has forced the government to restrict foreign employment and steps have been taken to reduce the total number.

Fig. 6–30. A typical section of the densely settled, highly industrialized, and intensively farmed Swiss Plateau. Near the center, the Reuss and Limmat rivers join the Aare River, which flows 10 miles farther, through the Jura Mountains, to reach the Rhine River. (Photo: Swissair.)

Fig. 6–31. Emmental (canton of Bern) in the central part of the Swiss Plateau. Substantial farmsteads and hamlets, rather than rural agglomerations, characterize the landscape. In this valley the famous "Swiss" cheese (locally called "Emmentaler") was first made. Above the spruce forests in the background lie the pre-Alpine pastures and the first chains of the limestone Alps. (Photo: Swissair.)

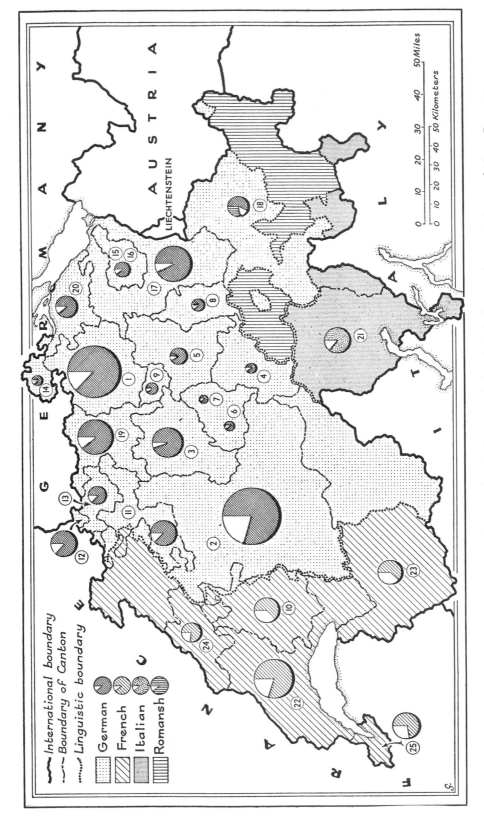

Fig. 6–32. The linguistic pattern of Switzerland. The size of the circle indicates the canton's population. For canton names, see the table on p. 345.

Switzerland's unity, unlike that of many other nations, is not imperiled by the fact that people of different religions and languages live within the confines of one small country. The numerical ratio of the various religious groups has not changed significantly over the centuries, though the number of Roman Catholics is steadily on the increase as the following figures show (total population, including aliens): in 1950, 56.3 per cent of the population was Protestant, in 1960, 52.7 per cent; 41.6 per cent in 1950 and 45.4 in 1960 was Roman Catholic. Long drawn-out religious controversies between several Swiss cities are recognized to have been extremely damaging to the country as a whole. Recognition of that fact, perhaps more than anything else, has convinced the Swiss people of the need for religious freedom.

The numerical language distribution is as follows (total population including aliens).

German dialects are spoken by 69 per cent of the population, French by 19, Italian by 9.5, and Romansh[23] by 0.9 per cent. The language boundary between the German- and the French-speaking parts of Switzerland runs in a north-south direction, diagonally from the Jura across the Plateau and the Alps. Italian is spoken in the canton of Ticino and to some extent in the adjacent areas of Grisons and in Glarus; Romansh is found predominantly in the valleys of Grisons. The linguistic line has changed only very little in the last century and does not follow cantonal boundaries. However, the dividing line is sharp. One village may be German-speaking, a nearby one French. Romansh was recognized as one of Switzerland's official languages in 1941, when 46,400 Swiss citizens were given permission to use

[23] A Rhaeto-Romanic language (Celto-Roman idiom) whose origin can be traced to the Romanization of Rhaetia.

Switzerland, Linguistic Distribution, by Cantons *
(see Fig. 6–32)

	Percentage Speaking				
	German	French	Italian	Romansh	Others
1. Zürich	88.1	1.9	8.0	0.4	1.6
2. Berne	80.5	14.4	4.3	0.1	0.7
3. Lucerne	94.3	0.9	4.0	0.2	0.6
4. Uri	94.5	0.3	4.7	0.4	0.1
5. Schwyz	94.3	0.4	4.7	0.3	0.3
6. Obwalden	96.2	0.4	2.9	0.1	0.4
7. Nidwalden	93.5	0.5	5.6	0.2	0.2
8. Glarus	86.9	0.4	11.7	0.4	0.6
9. Zug	90.4	1.1	7.0	0.4	1.1
10. Fribourg	34.0	63.4	1.7	–	0.9
11. Solothurn	90.3	2.0	6.9	0.2	0.6
12. Basel–Urban	89.4	4.2	4.7	0.3	1.4
13. Basel–Rural	88.1	2.4	8.3	0.2	1.0
14. Schaffhausen	91.1	0.9	7.1	0.2	0.7
15. Appenzell-Inner Rhodes	95.8	0.1	3.8	0.1	0.2
16. Appenzell-Outer Rhodes	93.0	0.4	5.5	0.2	0.9
17. St. Gallen	93.3	0.5	5.1	0.4	0.7
18. Grisons	56.6	0.5	16.1	26.1	0.7
19. Aargau	90.5	1.0	7.6	0.2	0.7
20. Thurgau	91.7	0.5	7.1	0.2	0.5
21. Ticino	9.4	1.5	88.2	0.2	0.7
22. Vaud	11.0	79.2	6.7	0.1	3.0
23. Valais	33.6	61.7	4.4	–	0.3
24. Neuchâtel	11.9	78.3	8.6	0.1	1.1
25. Geneva	13.3	70.0	9.6	0.1	7.0

* This compilation is based on the last Swiss population census, December, 1960.

it on a par with the other three languages. It is the consensus of many Swiss people that recognition of the Romansh language came just in time to save it from extinction. Official recognition includes the authorization to teach Romansh in public schools, a basic factor in the continuance of its life.

In the light of such great diversity of religion and language it is interesting to study the country's political unity over the last century. Since 1848, Switzerland has been a confederation (*Bundesstaat*) of 19 cantons and 6 half cantons. Of special significance, perhaps, is the active participation of the people in legislative matters. Frequent referenda give the Swiss citizen the feeling of direct responsibility for the actions of his government. The three highest authorities are the federal assembly, federal executive council, and federal court. In many ways there is similarity between Swiss democratic organizations and those of the United States. The number of representatives in the federal assembly is set at 200, and each canton, regardless of size, has two representatives in the Upper House. The two Houses in joint session elect the federal council which consists of seven members, the federal court, and, in case of war, the commanding general of the armed forces. At the head of the federal council is the president, elected from among its members for a term of one year. Berne is the seat of the federal assembly. The federal court, which acts on matters affecting the country as a whole, the cantons, or individuals, sits in Lausanne. Equality before the law, religious freedom, the right of assembly, of free speech, and the right to open a business are guaranteed in the constitution.

Limitations of space keep us from describing the great strength of this democracy in greater detail. A foreigner is surprised to see what great responsibilities are shouldered by the people. Cantonal governments are elected by direct popular vote. The famous outdoor plenary assemblies (*Landsgemeinden*) of Glarus are as old as the first settlements in this region. Education is compulsory. Swiss citizenship puts cantonal loyalty first and federal allegiance second. Perhaps the Swiss system of government is best epitomized by the expression "the Swiss Confederation administers; the canton governs."

Present Economic Life of Switzerland

General characteristics. Switzerland is poor in raw materials. Oil and coal are totally lacking, and hydroelectric power is the only important source of energy. Nevertheless, 40 per cent of the economically active population is engaged in manufacturing, which is widely dispersed over the countryside and often found in remote valleys. The casual visitor will understand that this pattern is the result of an ample supply of water and of local manpower. Still, most of the larger industrial plants are concentrated in the Swiss Plateau, where communications are least difficult. The northern part of the Plateau is more densely settled and industrialized, the central and southern parts have many farmsteads and hamlets rather than rural agglomerations. Figures 6–30 and 6–31 illustrate the strong contrast in the landscape of the Plateau.

In general, Swiss industry is noted not so much for its methods as for its high-quality precision products which require skilled craftsmanship based on a long tradition, but yet are easily adaptable to modern techniques.

Only 10 per cent of the economically active population is engaged in agriculture. As would be expected, agricultural methods vary from canton to canton in response to soil conditions and custom. Switzerland imports most of the cereals she needs and directs her efforts toward improving her livestock breeds and farming techniques. Whenever wars have cut off her imports, Switzerland has increased her cereal production, but only enough to feed her population. Farmers generally wield great power and are able to protect both their technical and political interests. Farmers' associations, unions and cooperatives, agricultural schools, etc. play an important role in the rural scene.

Agriculture and forestry. The 10 per cent (11.2 per cent if forestry is included) of the population still employed in agriculture continues to be a vital economic force. Agriculture is a flourishing part of Switzerland's economy, despite the severe handicap of poor soils and the large percentage of unproductive land.

The arable land is divided into medium- and small-size farms. Over 70 per cent of the farms occupy less than 25 acres each. The great pride the Swiss take in their homes and barns is reflected in the fact that farm buildings represent close to one-fourth of the entire capital investment of the farmer.

Relief, climate, and Swiss tradition combine to make the country outstanding in dairying. In a normal peacetime year dairying supplies about one-third of the total value of the country's agricultural products. A large part of the marketed milk is used in the manufacture of cheese, the rest in making butter, chocolate, etc. Such milk products as Emmentaler cheese (Fig. 6–31) and Suchard chocolate have acquired worldwide renown.

Stock feeding is normally second in importance to dairying. Cattle feeding and fattening is followed in terms of value by hog, goat, and sheep raising. The cattle economy is based on winter stall-feeding and summer grazing, the latter mostly in the mountains. Transhumance, moving animals from winter quarters in the valley to the high pastures, is still widely practiced. With the animals moved to the high pastures, valley meadows have several crops of hay, and winter feed is stored in the small barns distributed over the mountain pastures, which is characteristic in the Alpine countries. Orchard products include apples, pears, cherries, and prunes. Grapes are grown in several areas which have exceptionally mild climatic conditions, for example, along the shores of Lake Geneva in the upper Rhone Valley (Fig. 6–33), around the

lakes of the Plateau, and in the sunny valleys of the Ticino.

Cereal production, though normally less than 5 per cent of the total agricultural output, has fluctuated greatly during the last few years. Since it is cheaper for Switzerland to purchase cereals abroad than to produce them, emphasis has been placed on such agricultural export items as dairy products. During the two world wars, however, cereals could no longer be imported and great efforts were made to attain self-sufficiency in order to avoid a serious food shortage. During World War II much hay and pasture land was plowed up for the production of staple crops, and grains assumed major importance; the dairying industry was greatly reduced; the acreage of land in cereals was doubled between 1937 and 1944, and the acreage in potatoes more than doubled. The prewar pattern has again been re-established. Of the various grain crops, wheat takes up the largest area, followed by oats and rye. The potato crop is usually large enough to satisfy domestic needs but sugar, tobacco, fruits, and vegetables must be imported.

The forests of Switzerland are 70 per cent coniferous, mainly spruce, and 30 per cent broadleaved. As would be expected, 55 per cent of the area of the Swiss Alps is forested (70 per cent of the total forest growth) but only 20 per cent of the Jura (with 20 per cent of the forests) and 25 per cent of the Plateau (with 10 per cent of the forests mostly in small patches). While lumber production is considerable, the output is insufficient to meet demands.

Raw materials and industries. Switzerland's hydroelectric-power resources play a very important part in the country's economic development. In 1958, Switzerland produced over 16.7 billion kwh of electricity, 98 per cent in hydro power; by 1967, production increased to 30.5 billion kwh, with the same percentage of hydro power. "White coal" supplies an ever-increasing share of the country's energy requirements. In 1957,

Fig. 6–33. View of Rhone Valley (Canton Valais). In background, the village of Sierre and in foreground to the left, St. Leonard. The irrigated fruit and truck gardens occupy the floodplain. The terraces on the south-facing slopes to the left are covered with vineyards. Mountains to the left (north) are the Bernese Alps and right (south) the Valais Alps. (Swiss National Tourist Office, Zürich.)

coal, wood, and electricity provided 61 per cent of the energy consumed; by 1966 this proportion had fallen to 32 per cent, the difference being accounted for by constantly increased consumption of oil and gas. Refineries are at Collombey near Aigle (pipeline Genoa via Great St. Bernard tunnel) and at Cornauz in northwest Switzerland. The Cornauz refinery and one in the planning stage at Olten will be supplied with crude oil from the South European pipeline. A pipeline bringing natural gas from the Dutch fields at Slochteren is planned.

Mineral resources are an almost negligible industrial factor. Only 6,500 people were engaged in mining in the early 1960's. Coal deposits are insignificant. Peat is the most plentiful solid fuel. Annual imports of coal vary between 1.8 and 1.4 million metric tons, which represent more than 98 per cent of the country's needs. Iron ore was mined at one time, but today this activity is unprofitable.

The ore is of very inferior quality—a considerable drawback in view of Switzerland's need for high-grade steel. Approximately 228,000 tons of ore—more than 90 per cent of industrial requirement—are imported annually. Some rock salt is found in the Rhone Valley, and small amounts of asphalt are recovered in the Val de Travers of the Jura and gas in the Plateau.

Industry is an element of major importance in the prosperity of the country, even though Switzerland must import its raw materials and export its products in payment for its imports. Swiss industry is highly diversified and employed 49 per cent of the total labor force in 1960. Until the turn of the century the textile industry was in the lead. During the last half century, however, the engineering industries have risen to the dominant position. Today, the manufacture of machines, machine tools, and instruments outranks all other industries. Among the best-known Swiss-made products are electrical apparatus, textile machinery, engines of all types, locomotives, and agricultural machinery.

Watchmaking, which is centered in the Jura Mountains between Geneva and Schaffhausen, is the oldest branch of engineering. The cantons of Solothurn and Neuchâtel lead in the production of watches. In 1966, there were 441 factories. In addition, 775 factories manufactured watch parts. Swiss watch factories produce approximately 47 per cent of the world total and most of it is exported (14.3 per cent of Swiss exports). The industry is highly mechanized. Switzerland has almost a world monopoly because of the fame of its big-name watches. About 9.0 per cent of the country's industrial workers were employed in the mid-1960's in the watchmaking industry, 2.5 per cent of the total employed. The assembling of parts, which is the most important step in manufacturing, requires the great precision and technical skill characteristic of the Swiss workman.

Textiles, though a poor second in value to the output of the engineering industry, are nevertheless quite important. Many types of high-grade silks, ribbons, laces, knitted goods, and cottons are produced. The quality of the thread, the intricacy of the design, and the skill of the worker combine to give these textiles a highly competitive position in world markets. Eastern Switzerland, with St. Gallen, is the center of the textile industries.

The substantial chemical industry has developed largely since 1929. The production of aniline dyes laid the basis for the industry. Today, production is varied and includes items such as plastics, dyes, insecticides, pharmaceuticals, cosmetics, and perfumes. The industry is centered at Basel, a key transportation hub.

The production of grease, oils, and soap, the shoe and leather industry, and the manufacture of chocolate and other food industries are also important but do not rank as high in terms of value added by manufacturing. The lumber and woodworking industry, which employs roughly 8 per cent of the industrial labor force, in sawmills, paper mills, and woodworking establishments, deserves special mention. By rigid conservation measures and much scientific care this industry has operated on a sustained-yield basis for a long time.

In review, manufacturing in Switzerland is widely distributed. This is no handicap, in view of the country's size and its excellent transportation system. Highly trained workmen are found in nearly every Alpine valley, and the watchmakers of Le Locle and La Chaux-de-Fonds in the Jura, of Biel, Geneva, and Solothurn are world-famous.

In 1940, Switzerland began to build up her merchant marine; by 1967, the seagoing tonnage amounted to 282,000 tons, with 32 ocean-going ships. Thus Switzerland moves one step closer to the raw materials she must import. With these raw materials, with her financial resources, industrial know-how, and excellent system of technical education, Switzerland has all the ingredients for the high-value type of industrial output which has set a world-wide standard of perfection.

Tourism. Switzerland is one country which can legitimately classify its natural charm and beauty as a financial asset, because the tourist trade furnishes a considerable part of the national income. Tourists have the choice of staying in one of the ultramodern or one of the many small- or medium-size hotels, inns, or private homes.

Generally speaking, the Alpine regions of the Bernese Oberland, the Ticino, Zürich, Lucerne, and Interlaken are the most important centers of tourist trade. But it is not necessary to cite individual places. All of Switzerland offers scenic beauty, winter sports, and recreation to satisfy the tastes of any visitor. Today, Switzerland's hotel industry alone employs 114,000 people, but the economic benefits of the tourist industry are derived indirectly by a considerable part of the population. The tourist industry is well organized; there are a central tourist bureau, numerous travel agencies, many hotel-trade schools, and a school for restaurant personnel. The tourist industry in Switzerland is big business. The mid-1960 income was estimated at 750 million dollars.

Transportation. In the face of very obvious topographical difficulties, the Swiss have built an excellent transportation system. Tunnels and bridges of world renown have been constructed. The railroad mileage of nearly the entire Federal system is electrified, and most standard-gauge lines are state owned. Switzerland is famous for its many scenic mountain railways, some of which climb to heights exceeding 12,000 feet. The Swiss are world-famous as road builders. The recently improved St. Gotthard Pass road, the new all-weather road (with tunnel) of the Great St. Bernard and others (Fig. 6–13) are examples par excellence.

Basel is the major Rhine River port. It is located nearly 500 miles from the North Sea and in 1966 handled 8.5 million tons of freight. Coal and coke from the Ruhr, oil from Dutch refineries, and wheat from the United States are the chief commodities carried upstream; industrial products, wines, and cheese move downstream to the world markets, a much less important traffic. With Basel as their home port, 491 vessels of Swiss registry ply the Rhine below Basel.

Foreign trade. Switzerland's prospering economy and the high standard of living of its people are attributable to the large volume of foreign trade. The unfavorable trade balance—large import surpluses—is redressed by tourist income and international financial transactions. Switzerland's imports, in terms of value, consist of over 16 per cent food; 25 per cent fuels and raw materials for the chemical industries, cotton, and iron and steel goods; and roughly 59 per cent finished products. Her exports in terms of value are largely finished products (90 per cent), including chemicals. Watches and watch movements comprise 14 per cent of all exports. In 1967, 74 per cent of Switzerland's foreign trade was with European countries (80 per cent imports and 67 per cent exports). Germany, Italy, France, the United States, and the United Kingdom are Switzerland's most important trading partners. Because of its stable and prosperous economy, Switzerland for some time has been used as headquarters for international financial transactions (insurance, banking) which make important contributions to her trade balance. The Swiss currency is one of the world's most dependable international exchange media, and this has a favorable effect on her trade balance.

AUSTRIA

Population

Austria, with an area of 32,376 square miles, is somewhat smaller than the state of Maine. Its population totaled 7,400,000 in 1968, of which 1,636,600 lived in Vienna, the capital.[24] The country is divided into nine provinces, with an international border 1,646 miles long. Its greatest east-west extension is 360 miles, and the average width (from north to south) is 37 miles in the western and 170 miles in the eastern part of the country (Fig. 6–19).

The 1968 population density was 229 per square mile, a relatively low figure. How-

[24] The last census was taken in March, 1961. All statistical data are taken from *Statistisches Handbuch für die Republik Österreich* 1967, and other official publications.

ever, if we consider the mountainous character of Austria and the relative scarcity of fertile land, the density per square mile of agricultural land becomes substantially higher.

Three regional density groupings may be distinguished in Austria, Vienna excepted: (1) the agricultural and industrial areas of Lower and Upper Austria, Styria, and the Burgenland are the most densely populated; (2) the valleys and scattered lowlands of Carinthia, Salzburg, Tyrol, and Vorarlberg belong in an in-between group; and (3) the mountainous parts of the latter provinces are either uninhabited or often populated during the summertime only. Villages and towns are concentrated in the plains, valleys, basins, and hill lands, while isolated settlements predominate in the higher regions. In recent years the population of the western, more mountainous provinces of Austria has increased considerably. Industries were relocated here during World War II, in search of protection from Allied bombers, and after the war, in flight from Soviet occupation forces in the eastern part of the country. Furthermore, most of the postwar immigrants from Eastern Europe (those who did not emigrate) settled in the western part of the country.

One-third of Austria's population live in 5 cities of over 100,000 (including Vienna); one-third in villages of less than 2,000. It is interesting to record that 35 per cent of the population of the Tyrol and 20 per cent of that of Salzburg live at altitudes above 2,400 feet. The upper limit of wheat cultivation varies from 2,900 feet to 5,200 feet. Numerous small settlements may be found even at these upper elevations.

While the uneven geographical distribution of the population is a considerable handicap to the development of a balanced economy, the occupational distribution of the working population (according to the 1961 census) is a great asset to the country's economic strength: 46 per cent of the working population were engaged in industry and handicrafts, 17 per cent in commerce and

transportation, and 20 per cent in agriculture and forestry (a decline from 32 per cent since 1958).

One of the great difficulties of the Austro-Hungarian Monarchy was its nationality problem. In contrast, the population of postwar Austria is predominantly German in character. Most of the non-Germans live in the frontier districts of Burgenland, Styria, Carinthia, and in Vienna. On the whole, the present ethnic composition gives strength to the country because the Republic is not beset by any language difficulties such as those which troubled the Monarchy. Roman Catholicism is the predominant religion in Austria, claiming 90 per cent of the population.

Vienna is by far the largest city in Austria (Fig. 6–34); it is followed by Graz, the second city in size. Linz, Salzburg, and Innsbruck are the other three large cities. Vienna has lost much of the glamour and importance it had under the Austro-Hungarian Monarchy. Today, it is merely the oversized capital of a small country—a city only one hour's drive from foreign territory. Graz, a provincial capital, has always been a rather quiet city. Many of its citizens are retired people. The population of Linz has increased by more than 60 per cent over the prewar total. It is the center of important industries, many of which were established after 1940. Salzburg, site of the world-famous Salzburg Festival, has also greatly added to its population (Fig. 6–35). Innsbruck is the capital of the Tyrol and the largest city of the Austrian Alps; its university and beautiful surroundings are well known to the many tourists who visit the city every year (Fig. 6–36).

The historical geography and past function of Vienna and Innsbruck deserve brief discussion. Vienna is mentioned in a record as old as 935 A.D. and in 1137 was cited as a city (stadt). In 1221 its citizens received the privilege of self-government. During the twelfth century, Vienna occupied no more than the site of a former Roman camp, protected on the northeast by the

Fig. 6–34. Vienna, view toward the "Innere Stadt" with Danube Canal and Danube River in background. Note the two rings, broad boulevards (formerly protective walls). (Bilddienst der Stadt Wien.)

Fig. 6–35. Salzburg on the Salzach River with Mönchsberg and Hohensalzburg castle on the right and Kapuziner Berg to the left. The city grew on the site of an old Celtic settlement and the Roman city Juvavum; it controls important routes between the Alpine Foreland and the central part of the Austrian Alps leading south to Italy. Hohensalzburg was first built in 1077; its present layout was completed around 1500. The many churches indicate the city's importance as a Catholic center for all of south Germany. A bishopric was established here in 739. The two identical towers of the Dom, just below the castle, were built in Italian style (1652–57). Salzburg, the birthplace of the famous composer Mozart, is now the capital of the Austrian province of the same name. (G. W. Hoffman.)

Fig. 6–36. Innsbruck, capital of Tirol, 1600 feet, with Nordkette (Northern Limestone Alps). View from Maria Theresien street with Annasäule (erected in 1706) toward north. Serviten church toward the left and St. Jakob church in right background within old town. Innsbruck received city rights in 1239. (G. W. Hoffman.)

Danube and on the southeast and northwest by small rivers. There was no natural rampart to the southwest of the city. Situated near the crossing of important overland and river transportation routes, Vienna expanded rapidly through the years.

Beginning in 1438, the emperors of the Holy Roman Empire usually resided in Vienna. Thus, the function of imperial capital and permanent seat of the Hapsburg monarchy gave added impetus to Vienna's growth and importance (Fig. 6–34). Thousands of people moved to Vienna from all parts of the Empire, to participate in the city's political, economic, and cultural leadership. As recently as 1934, the census revealed that at least 24 per cent of the city's inhabitants had their birthplace beyond the borders of post-World War I Austria; the majority of these had come from what is now Czechoslovakia.

Innsbruck is located in the Northern Longitudinal Valley in western Austria. The Inn Valley had been first inhabited during the Neolithic and Bronze ages. The city was founded near an Inn River bridge which controlled a road leading to the west and northwest. Since the thirteenth century the city has expanded southward in the direction of the Brenner Pass, on the alluvial fan formed by the Sill River. In 1239, it received city status, and, as the route from Germany to Rome increased in importance, Innsbruck expanded rapidly. Situated at the natural focus of the whole North Tyrol, the city has always been a trading rather than an industrial center. Its population grew from 4,000 in 1600 to a 1967 population of more than 100,000.

Many of Austria's better-known towns of today owe their origin to a monastery. Examples are Melk, Klosterneuberg, and

Krems, all on the Danube. Other towns date back to strategically placed medieval castles, e.g., Graz, Kufstein, Steyr. Several others, such as Linz, Wels, and Salzburg, began as Roman settlements. In Lower Austria a number of fortified towns such as Tulln or Ybbs grew up along the Danube; their location may have been determined by the routes of the salt trade or by the existence of fords. The border fortifications *(Burgen)* established along the rolling wooded hills of Lower Austria and Styria (later Burgenland) became villages, but none of them assumed any real importance. Thus, as early as the fourteenth century, the pattern of the population distribution and the location of Austrian cities had been fixed.

Present Economic Life of Austria [25]

When, in 1918, Austria emerged as one of the "succession states" of the former Austria-Hungary, serious administrative and economic problems had to be solved in order to provide a livelihood for her 6.5 million people, nearly one-third of whom had lived in Vienna. The task of adjusting to a much smaller area was the major problem facing the government and the people of Austria between 1919 and 1938, when the country was incorporated into Germany. Thus, the newborn Republic of Austria had to struggle with problems of how to increase food production, reorganize the industrial structure, modernize and expand raw-material production, and establish a new basis for its foreign trade. It is generally agreed that Austria did succeed fairly well in re-establishing her economy, despite the serious economic and political crises of the interwar years.

In 1945, when Austria re-emerged as an independent country, after 7 years of occupation and complete absorption into the German war economy, it found itself in an entirely different situation, as compared with 1919. Although industrial capacity had increased, Austria's economy had been further unbalanced because most of the new facilities had been constructed to fit Germany's war needs. One favorable result was the fact that many new industries had been established in the western part of Austria and were thus beyond the reach of Soviet occupation forces after the war.

Starting once more from scratch, Austria's economy had to be completely rebuilt. The job in one respect was many times more difficult than after 1919; in another respect it was easier. Austria was occupied by four powers (the Soviet Union, the United States, the United Kingdom, and France), and this had an important effect on the rebuilding of the shattered economy. It made the future of Austria a direct concern of the United States. Austria became eligible for Marshall Plan aid in 1948 and received $1.3 million in United States aid, plus $386 million which it received before the start of the Marshall Plan, constituting a major contribution to the rebuilding of Austria's economy. Subsequent reconstruction of Western Europe revitalized its important foreign trade, transit, and tourist income. The conclusion of the State Treaty in 1955, while making heavy demands on the Austrian economy in terms of cash reparation payments and long-term deliveries of goods (6 years) and petroleum (8 years) to the Soviet Union, on the other hand did return important assets to the country. And most important, after 17 years, Austria again was master of its own house.

Unfortunately for Austria, it occupies one of Europe's most strategic areas. No great power can afford to have it dominated by another power. That is why postwar Austria was occupied, divided into four zones, and, since 1955, has been neutralized.[26]

Agriculture and forestry. When peace was restored in 1919, and an independent

---

[25] Material for this section is taken, by permission of the publishers, from various publications by the author, e.g., "The Survival of an Independent Austria," *Geographical Review* 41 (October, 1951): 606–21; "Austria," *Focus* (June 15, 1954).

[26] George W. Hoffman, "The Political Geography of a Neutral Austria," *Geographical Studies* 3 (London) (January, 1956): 12–32.

Austrian republic was organized, the new country found itself cut off from all its former sources of supply. Old trade channels within the Austro-Hungarian customs union and with the rest of Europe were severed, agricultural areas were cut in two by new international boundaries, and the new countries carved out of the former Empire were unwilling to export agricultural products except on a strict barter basis. Special attention was given to increased food production, but, in view of the climatic conditions and the generally poor soils in this mountainous country, there were sharp limitations to any plan for agricultural expansion. In the valleys, winter lasts three to four months; the higher parts of the Alps are covered by snow for six to nine months. The basins of the eastern and southern parts of the country are hot and dry during the summer. Forests cover about 38 per cent of the total area of Austria and about 46 per cent of its productive land. Nevertheless, agricultural production increased despite the lack of capital and the never-ending internal party strife. Before World War II, Austria had become about 75 per cent self-sufficient, an achievement which represented a new high in the country's agricultural economy.

World War II wiped out all the previous gains in Austria's food-producing capacity. Further shortages, loss of farm machinery, destruction wrought by moving armies, mass slaughter of livestock, and a shortage of manpower combined to bring about a situation similar to that experienced twenty-five years previously. Only the immediate postwar intervention of such international relief agencies as the United Nations Relief and Rehabilitation Administration and the aid given by private relief organizations and the occupation armies saved the Austrian population from malnutrition. Later, the Austrian government, in close cooperation with Marshall Plan aid, undertook to provide seeds and artificial fertilizer, initiated measures to control cattle tuberculosis, began a program of mechanization and electrification of farm equipment, and improved rural roads.

Furthermore, laboratories and farm educational institutions were established. By the mid-1960's, total agricultural production had risen to about 85 per cent of the 1937 level. This is indeed an important accomplishment when one realizes that only 20 per cent of the area is considered arable. Austria's chief crops are rye, wheat, oats, and barley, in that order of importance.

Austria is self-sufficient in potatoes, sugar, dairy products, and meat; corresponding percentages for other agricultural products in 1964–66 were: fresh fruit 85, wheat 87, rye 90, barley 62, oats 90, and maize 29. Nevertheless, with a population approximately 7.8 per cent larger than in 1937, Austria must constantly progress and solve the problem of how to increase acreage and agricultural output. Austria was made nearly self-supporting by improving existing acreage through reclamation and irrigation, and putting greater emphasis on regional planning and combining of the many small agricultural holdings,[27] as well as by placing much emphasis on mechanization. Only the corn acreage cannot be expanded substantially, for climatic reasons.

Land holdings are, for the most part, of small or medium size. Of a total of 396,000 land holdings (19.0 million acres) nearly 50 per cent were holdings under 12.5 acres, and even the majority of the 6,278 land holdings over 250 acres were under 500 acres.

Forests are of special importance and are one of Austria's most valuable natural resources. A comprehensive reforestation and conservation program has been under way during the last few years, protecting the forests against continuation of the overcutting of war and postwar years. The two most important timber-trade regions are the Alpine regions and the slopes of the Böhmer Wald in Lower Austria. Spruce is the most

27 George W. Hoffman, "Regional Planning in the Inn Valley of Austria," *Papers of the Michigan Academy of Science, Arts and Letters* 40 (1955): 181–89; "A Changing Cultural Landscape in the Middle Upper Inn Valley," *Southwestern Social Science Quarterly* 36 (June, 1955): 27–45.

Fig. 6–37. Erzberg (Ore Mountain) in Styria. Open-pit mining has been carried on here since Neolithic times. The mountain forms a peak of nearly 4,900 feet and is located in the Iron Ore Alps (Slate and Shale Ranges). See Fig. 6–1. Mining today is carried out in above-ground work on 30 graduated banks, each 80 feet high and 700 feet long. The total mining front has a length of 13 miles. The mountain is mined by the Austrian Alpine Montan Steel Corporation which also owns a metallurgical plant in Donauwitz and the United Austrian Iron and Steel Works (VOEST) in Linz. (Austrian Information Service.)

important tree, with Scots pine and beech of secondary importance. Her forests make it possible for Austria to be one of the few European countries which export timber, paper, prefabricated houses, and cardboard. During 1967 these exports were valued at 13 per cent of the total exports. Forest holdings, like agricultural ones, are small.

Minerals. With the exception of coal, Austria is fortunate in having considerable mineral deposits: lignite, iron ore, copper ore, manganese, lead, zinc, salt, talc, gypsum, magnesite, and oil (Fig. 6–21). The iron ore deposits of Styria are of excellent quality and suffice to meet domestic requirements (Fig. 6–37). Also mined in increasing quantities are antimony, bauxite, china clay, graphite, lead, and pyrite. Many of these minerals are exported, thereby contributing to Austria's growing foreign trade. The lack of adequate high-grade coal is a primary cause of many of the country's economic difficulties; more than 5 million tons of coal (bituminous coal, coke, and lignite briquettes) must be imported annually, about one-third coming from Poland.

Waterpower. Austria is one of the most important sources of hydroelectric power in Europe. Its potential is estimated at more than 30 billion kwh annually. In 1967 Austria produced a total of 24,439 million kwh of electricity. On an average, 11 to 23 per cent (1960–67) was exported, largely to West Germany. The present constant expansion of Austria's hydroelectric capacity assumes special importance in view of the country's coal shortage and increasing domestic demands.[28]

One of the most ambitious projects is the development of the Danube River for hydroelectric purposes. Along its 320-mile course

in Austria, a total of 14 hydroelectric plants are planned.[29] Jochenstein, on the German-Austrian border, was completed in 1956, Ybbs-Persenbeug in 1958, and Aschach in 1965 (Fig. 6–38). Wallsee-Mitterkirchen was initiated in 1965 and completion is expected by 1969. The even-water regime of the Danube, together with the gradual sloping of the topography toward the mouth of the Danube into the Black Sea, guarantees a steady supply of power, satisfying the growing demands of the Austrian population, as well as those of some neighboring countries. At the same time the work on the Danube has greatly benefited navigation.

Petroleum. Most of Austria's petroleum and refining facilities are near Vienna, on the left bank of the Danube and in Upper Austria. Production started in 1937 with 32,000 metric tons and reached after the war 3.4 million tons, but decreased again by 1967 to 2.7 million tons. The first major new discovery since the war was made in 1967, again in the same general area as the present production. Petroleum and petroleum products satisfy approximately one-half of the domestic demand. Austria's refineries also manufacture crude oil, produce 63 per cent of the needed gasoline and heating oils and a surplus in motor oil.

Output of natural gas has been greatly accelerated during the last few years. In 1966, gas contributed 8.0 per cent to Austria's energy production, oil 12 per cent, hydroelectric power 65 per cent, and coal 15 per cent. Pipelines carry the oil and gas to the main producing centers. A branch line of the Trieste-Ingolstadt oil pipeline (Fig. 6–21) is now under construction and will lead to the refineries near Vienna, which ultimately may also be connected with the

[28] George W. Hoffman, "Toward Greater Integration in Europe: Transfer of Electric Power Across International Boundaries," *Journal of Geography* 55 (April, 1956): 165–76; also annual reports by Ministry für Verkehr und Elektrizitätswirtschaft, reports by Verbundkonzern and Verbundgesellschaft —all in Vienna.

[29] United Nations, Economic Commission for Europe, *Development of Hydro Power Stations on the Danube: Existing, Under Construction or Projected,* E/ECE/360 (Geneva, 1959); Österreichische Kraftwerke A.G., *Die Donau als Wasserkraftsstrasse* (Vienna-Berlin: A. F. Koska, 1964); also annual reports of Österreichische Donaukraftwerke A.G., Vienna.

Fig. 6–38. Aschach power development on the Danube River, looking upstream. On the left bank the twin locks. Aschach was built by the Donaukraftwerke between 1959 and 1965. The drop of the river by 48 feet necessitates the damming of the river for 25 miles. The Danube power plants of Jochenstein, Aschach, Wallsee and Ybbs-Persenbeug greatly influence the water level of the river and contribute to better navigation on an important and difficult section of the river. Aschach has four turbines of 70.5 MW performance each, one of the largest in Europe. (Bundespressedienst, Vienna.)

southern extension of the Soviet "friendship line" now terminating at Bratislava, Czechoslovakia. A gas pipeline connection is now considered between Italy and Vienna with a connection to Bratislava, the terminal point of the Soviet line from the Ukraine, in this way opening up markets for Soviet gas in Central and Southern Europe. The whole project is part of a huge projected European undertaking involving Italy, Austria, France, and possibly other countries, acquiring gas from both Dutch and Soviet fields. As far as Austria is concerned, Soviet delivery of natural gas will in its initial stage

be in payment for the delivery of pipelines for the Soviet Siberian gas pipeline by the Austrian Iron and Steelworks in Linz (VOEST).

Industries. Austria's present and future industrial outlook is unquestionably more favorable than that of many other European countries. During World War II, the iron, steel, aluminum, and chemical industries were expanded. It is estimated that the equivalent of 12 per cent of Austria's prewar industrial capacity was removed by the Soviet Union during the period of occupation, 1945–1955. On the other hand, the Western powers restored all the plants in their zones to Austria in 1946, and (especially the United States) made major contributions to Austria's industrial rehabilitation.

Modernization since 1945 has made Austrian industries more competitive. The geographical pattern of industrial production underwent important changes during and following the war, with the Linz-Wels-Steyr triangle in Upper Austria and its important steel (Voest in Linz—Fig. 6–39) and chemi-

cal industries (Austrian Nitrogen Works in Linz) offering a completely new and modern addition to Austria's productive facilities. Also, many new medium-sized and specialized industries were built in the western half of Austria after 1939, a fact which is partially responsible for the population growth of Austria's western provinces. Vorarlberg in 1964 had the highest share of employed in industry, 42 per cent, closely followed by Lower Austria (41.8 per cent) and Upper Austria (41.6 per cent). Salzburg had the

Fig. 6–39. General view of United Austrian Iron and Steel Works (VOEST) in Linz on the Danube. Facilities were built between 1939 and 1944 and considerably enlarged since that time. Works are one of two major iron producing and processing concerns in Austria. The world famous LD-steelmaking process was developed jointly by VOEST in Linz and Austrian Alpine Montan Steel Corporation in Donauwitz. The VOEST plant covers an area of 2.6 square miles and employs close to 20,000 people. Production includes lathes, machinery of various description, machine tools, power station equipment, and plate-working machines, which are exported to 70 countries. Production of pig iron and crude steel amounts to more than 2 million tons. (Bundespressedienst, Vienna.)

lowest share with 22 per cent. It should also be noted that of the old industrial concentrations, those of middle Styria (steel and heavy machinery in the Eisenerz and middle Mur River Valley) were included in the modernization encouraged and financed with Marshall Plan funds. Those in the older industrial core, the Vienna Basin, were under Soviet control until 1955. They deteriorated and required much effort and investment following the departure of the Soviet troops. The importance of industry and manufacture in Austria is clearly shown by the facts that over 39 per cent of the labor force is engaged therein and that during 1966 manufacturing industries, including building and construction, accounted for 50 per cent of the gross national product.

Foreign workers in Austria play only a relatively small role, less than two per cent of the total employed (44,000 as of June, 1967). Nearly 80 per cent are from Yugoslavia. The war losses are now being felt and as a result the number of women among the labor force has been on the increase, 42 per cent. Austria has a mixed socialized-private economy and an average of 37 per cent of the labor force is employed in the nationalized industries.

Tourism. The tourist trade constitutes an important source of income for Austria. In this respect, Austria is in sharp competition with Switzerland. The provinces of Tyrol, Salzburg, Vorarlberg, and Carinthia are attracting annually thousands of foreign visitors. The total number of those visiting Austria is constantly increasing, making important contributions to her economy. The number of foreign overnight stays is largest in Tyrol and Vorarlberg (90 per cent of all tourists), followed by Vienna (80 per cent). In 1967, 69 per cent of Austria's recorded overnight stays by tourists (64 million) were foreigners with 75.4 per cent coming from West Germany, 5 per cent from the British Isles, and 2.8 per cent from the United States. Close to 600 million dollars in foreign exchange receipts benefited the Austrian economy.

Transportation. Austria's strategic location involves a special responsibility for the upkeep and modernization of its transportation system. Both domestic traffic serving the important tourist trade and transit traffic serving the rest of Europe must be considered. Several important international rail lines cross the country, and their modernization goes hand in hand with the further electrification of Austrian lines. Here again competition with Switzerland is keen. Electrification of the main east-west line from Vorarlberg to Vienna has been completed, and many other lines have also been electrified. The improvement of the highway network is of equal importance to a country so dependent upon transit traffic and tourist trade. Most parts of Austria are accessible by modern roads, and up-to-date highways criss-cross the country. Because of its mountainous character, the construction and maintenance of roads is not only difficult but costly. A new superhighway has been completed between Salzburg and Vienna and is being continued south of Vienna toward the Italian border. Additional ones are planned (Fig. 6–12).

The question of linking the Danube by canals with other European rivers has been discussed earlier in this chapter. It is clear that a link between the Danube and other trafficable waterways is as badly needed for Austria and for the rest of Europe today as it was in the seventeenth century, when Austrian and Bohemian merchants first proposed the Morava-Oder (Danube-Baltic) Canal.

With freedom of navigation again available on the full length of the Danube, Vienna is growing in importance as a port, both for Austria and as a transit station, but Linz is Austria's most modern and largest port. Since the completion of three Danube power stations an even regime of water has been assured on the river's most difficult section. Of the total goods shipped on

Austria's part of the Danube, 11 per cent is for domestic, 11 per cent for transit, and 78 per cent for non-Austrian international use. The main products shipped on the Danube are coal and coke, iron ore, crude iron, petroleum products, and grain. Austrian overseas traffic is one-third via Trieste (this share is on the decline), one-seventh via Rijeka, Yugoslavia, and one-fourth via Hamburg.

Foreign trade. Austria's foreign trade has greatly increased since the signing of the State Treaty, in 1955. The import deficit is largely redressed by the income from an increasing tourist trade. Exports have been increasing steadily, but, with the increased requirements of a constantly improving standard of living, imports have increased faster than exports. The import structure is as follows: food, fertilizers, and fodder (13 per cent); raw materials (18 per cent); semi-finished goods (17 per cent); and finished goods (52 per cent). Exports are divided among finished products (56 per cent), raw materials (15 per cent), semi-finished goods (24 per cent), and foods (5 per cent). Exports of finished goods have steadily increased. Among the imports chemical raw materials and products, special machinery, and optical products rank highest in terms of value. The main export items, in terms of value, include livestock, synthetic rubber, semi-finished products such as textile goods, products of non-metallic minerals, paper, wooden products, clothing, and products of the engineering and metallurgical industries, mostly of high quality.

Austria's foreign trade (1967) is chiefly with the countries of the EEC (47.3 per cent). Eastern Europe supplies about 13 per cent of Austria's trade, the United States contributes about 4 per cent. Austria's most important trading partners are West Germany and Italy.

Lately, increased emphasis has been put on expanding of trade with the underdeveloped countries of Asia and Africa, but the problem of credits for such an expanding trade has acted as a brake. Austria's overseas exports amounted to only one-eighth of its total trade in 1966, in contrast to Switzerland's one-third portion of trade.

❋   ❋   ❋

The problems of the individual countries of Central Europe vary greatly. Besides a common language and a common central position in Europe (excluding the territory of the Soviet Union), the four countries have little in common. Germany is still divided. East Germany is closely tied to the economic planning of the Soviet Union and its allies (68 per cent of its 1966 trade). West Germany has integrated her economy in a series of joint economic projects with the various organizations of the Common Market. The phenomenal growth of West Germany's economy during the late 1950's and first half of the 1960's resembles in many ways a similar growth during the late 1920's, though developments during 1966 and 1967 brought a considerable slow-down in its economic movements.

Traditionally neutral Switzerland and Austria, only neutral since 1955, have greatly differing economic bases. In Switzerland, the absence of raw materials for many years has forced that country to rely upon vital imports of raw materials and semi-finished products, and on exports of high-quality goods, including foodstuffs. Self-sufficiency in food supplies is neither desired nor possible. Still, Switzerland's neutral position during the two wars in this century made it an important financial center of the world and the headquarters of many international institutions. Switzerland's location dictated her joining OECD and the European Free Trade Area (EFTA). The Swiss economy is one of the most stable in the world though the growing economic power of the European Economic Community (EEC) is a matter of great concern to Switzerland, inasmuch as 38 per cent of Switzerland's exports goes to its members (20 per cent to EFTA).

Switzerland cannot join EEC due to its political implications on Swiss neutrality.

Austria, on the other hand, after tremendous war and postwar damages, including 10 years of occupation by Soviet troops, has greatly benefited from United States aid. This aid has enabled Austria to modernize and expand her raw-material and industrial capacity, modernize her agriculture, and lay the basis for a prospering economy. With Austria included in OECD and the Free Trade Area, its economy is closely tied to the fortunes of the West. At the same time, Austria benefits from closer economic ties with the Soviet Union and other Eastern European countries, which are important for her trade balance and for a continuing high production of her numerous manufactured goods. In many ways, Austria is a more viable state today than at any time since it became independent in 1919. On the other hand, her heavy reliance on trade with West Germany, the increased inward look of the countries of the Common Market and her inability to join it (the EEC) in view of her commitments as a neutral country, and the large investments needed to bring modern technology to its industries raise serious problems for continued prosperity and advance of Austria's economy.

BIBLIOGRAPHY

(Major references are asterisked.)

Books in English

BURGHARDT, ANDREW F. *Borderland, A Historical and Geographical Study of Burgenland, Austria.* Madison, Wis.: University of Wisconsin Press, 1962.

°CEPEDE, MICHEL, ABENSOUR, E. S., AND OTHERS. *Rural Problems in the Alpine Region: An International Study.* Rome: FAO, 1961.

°DICKINSON, ROBERT E. *Germany: A General and Regional Geography.* 2d ed. London: Methuen & Co., Ltd., 1961.

Manpower Policies and Problems in Austria. Reviews of Manpower and Social Policies No. 5. Paris: OECD, 1967.

MAYER, KURT B. *The Population of Switzerland.* New York: Columbia University Press, 1952.

°MUTTON, ALICE F. A. *Central Europe.* 2d ed. London: Longmans, Green & Co., 1967.

°POUNDS, NORMAN J. G. *Divided Germany and Berlin.* Searchlight Book No. 1. Princeton, N. J.: D. Van Nostrand Co., 1962.

———. *The Economic Pattern of Modern Germany.* London: John Murray, 1963.

———. *The Ruhr.* London: Faber & Faber, Ltd., 1952.

RUSSELL, FRANK M. *The Saar: Battleground and Pawn.* Stanford, Calif.: Stanford University Press, 1951.

°SIEGFRIED, ANDRÉ. *Switzerland: A Democratic Way of Life.* Trans. Edward Fitzgerald. London: Jonathan Cape, 1950.

°STOLPER, WOLFGANG F. *The Structure of the East German Economy.* Cambridge, Mass.: Harvard University Press, 1960.

WISKEMANN, ELIZABETH. *Germany's Eastern Neighbors.* London and New York: Oxford University Press, 1956.

Books in Other Languages

°BLANCHARD, RAOUL. *Les Alpes Occidentales (The Western Alps).* 7 vols. Grenoble: B. Arthaud, 1944–56.

BOBECK, HANS, AND LICHTENBERGER, ELISABETH. *Wien: Bauliche Gestalt und Entwicklung seit der Mitte des 19. Jahrhunderts (Vienna: Architectural Forms and Developments Since the Middle of the Nineteenth Century).* Graz-Cologne: Verlag Hermann Böhlaus Nachf., 1966.

°CASTELLAN, GEORGES. *La République Démocratique Allemande (The German Democratic Republic).* Paris: Presses Universitaires de France, 1961.

Die Donau als Wasserkraftstrasse (The Danube as a Source of Water Power). Vienna and Berlin: Alfred F. Koska, 1964.

°GABERT, PIERRE, AND GUICHONNET, PAUL. *Les Alpes et les États Alpins (The Alps and the Alpine States).* "Magellan" series No. 14. Paris: Presses Universitaires de France, 1965.

GEORGE, PIERRE, AND TRICART, JEAN. *Géographie de l'Europe Centrale (The Geography of Central Europe).* 2 vols. Paris: Presse Universitaires de France, 1954.

GUTERSOHN, HEINRICH. *Geographie der Schweiz in drei Bänden (The Geography of Switzerland in Three Volumes).* Berne: Kümmerly & Frey, 1958–64.

HAUSHOFER, ALBRECHT. *Pass-Staaten in den Alpen (Passlands in the Alps).* Berlin: K. Vowinckel, 1928.

KOBER, LEOPOLD. *Bau und Entstehung der*

Alpen (*Structure and Origin of the Alps*). Berlin: Gebrüder Bornträger, 1923.

KREBS, NORBERT. *Die Ostalpen und das heutige Österreich* (*The Eastern Alps and Today's Austria*). Stuttgart: J. Engelhorn's Nachfolger, 1928.

SCHEIDL, LEOPOLD, AND LECHLEITNER, HERWIG. *Österreich: Land, Volk, Wirtschaft* (*Austria: Land, People, Economy*). "Hirt's Stichwortbücher." Vienna: Verlag Ferdinand Hirt, 1967.

SELL, MANFRED. *Die Neutralen Alpen* (*The Neutral Alps*). Stuttgart: Seewald, 1965.

Atlases

Atlas der Republik Österreich (*Atlas of the Republic of Austria*). Vienna: Freytag-Berndt zu Artaria, 1961–.

GERMANY (FEDERAL REPUBLIC), INSTITUT FÜR LANDESKUNDE. *Die Bundesrepublik Deutschland in Karten* (*The German Federal Republic in Maps*). 93 sheets. Bonn: Statistisches Bundesamt, Institut für Landeskunde, und Institut für Raumforschung, 1965–.

IMHOF, ED., ed. *Atlas der Schweiz* (*Atlas of Switzerland*). Berne: Eidgen. Landestopographie, 1965–.

OTREMBA, ERICH, ed. *Atlas der Deutschen Agrarlandschaft* (*Atlas of the German Agrarian Landscape*). Wiesbaden: F. Steiner, 1965.

Articles

BOBEK, HANS. "*Schlüsselstellung in Europa*" (*"Key Position in Europe"*), *Spectrum Austria,* Otto Schulmeister, ed. (Vienna: Verlag Herder, 1957): 21–49.

DAMI, ALDO. "Les Rhétoromances" ("The Rheto-Romansh"), *Le Globe* (Bulletin de la Société de Géographie de Genève), 100 (1960): 25–68.

DICKINSON, ROBERT E. "The Morphology of the Medieval German Town," *Geographical Review* 35 (1945): 74–97.

GARNETT, ALICE. "The Loess Region in Central Europe in Prehistoric Times," *Geographical Journal* 106 (1945): 132–43.

*HARRIS, CHAUNCY D. "The Ruhr Coal Mining District," *Geographical Review* 36 (1946): 194–221.

*HASSINGER, HUGO. "Boden und Lage Wiens" ("Site and Situation of Vienna"), *Mitteilungen der Geographischen Gesellschaft in Wien* 84 (1941): 359–84.

HAUBRICH, HARTWIG. "Moselschiffahrt—Einst und Jetzt" ("Shipping on the River Mosel—Past and Present"), *Geographische Rundschau* 19 (August, 1967): 294–302.

*HELD, COLBERT C. "The New Saarland," *Geographical Review* 41 (1951): 590–605.

*HOFFMAN, GEORGE W. "The Political-Geographic Bases of the Austrian Nationality Problem," *Austrian History Yearbook* III (1967): 20–146.

*———. "The Political Geography of a Neutral Austria," *Geographical Studies* 3 (January, 1956): 12–32.

———. "The Survival of Independent Austria," *Geographical Review* 41 (1951): 605–21.

*KOHN, WALTER S. G. "The Sovereignty of Liechtenstein," *The American Journal of International Law* 61 (April, 1967): 547–57.

*MAYER, KURT B. "Migration, Cultural Tensions, and Foreign Relations: Switzerland," *Conflict Resolution* 11 (June, 1967): 139–52.

OTREMBA, ERICH. "Die Rhein-Main-Donau Linie im Rahmen des europäischen Wirtschaftsraumes" ("The Rhine-Main-Danube Lines in the Framework of European Economic Unity"), *Geographische Rundschau* 16 (1964): 56–63.

RANDALL, RICHARD R. "Political Geography of the Klagenfurt Basin," *Geographical Review* 47 (1957): 406–19.

*ROBINSON, G. W. S. "West Berlin: The Geography of an Exclave," *Geographical Review* 43 (1953): 540–57.

*SÖLCH, JOHANN. "The Brenner Region," *Sociological Review* 19 (1927): 318–34.

WINKLER, ERHART. "Österreich und die Schweiz" ("Austria and Switzerland"), *Festzeitschrift zur Hundertjahrfeier der Geographischen Gesellschaft in Wien: 1856–1956,* Konrad Winkler, ed. (Vienna: Geographische Gesellschaft, 1956): 209–35.

YATES, E. M. "Development of the Rhine," *Transactions and Papers,* Institute of British Geographers 32 (1963): 65–82.

7

Southern Europe

This chapter concerns itself with the countries of the Iberian peninsula (Spain and Portugal), Italy, and Greece, as well as a number of small political units: San Marino, Vatican City, the island states of Malta and Cyprus, Gibraltar, and Andorra. Southern Europe is roughly equivalent to Mediterranean Europe, and the two terms are used interchangeably here.

The countries of Southern Europe possess, in addition to their location, generally similar climate, vegetation, topography, hydrography, and economic structure and orientation. These and many other common physical and cultural features impart a striking unity to the area as a geographic region. There are, to be sure, many zones within countries included in this chapter which are very different from most of the region as a whole and could quite justifiably be excluded, e.g., rainy northwestern Spain, Alpine Italy, the Po Valley, and northern Greece. Similarly, a good case could be made for including in Southern Europe the Mediterranean coasts of France and Yugoslavia, Albania, and European Turkey. It is appropriate, however, to maintain the national state, for reasons already considered, as the unit for regionalizing in this book.

Certainly the over-all composite personality of the countries here included places each of them squarely in Mediterranean Europe.

THE PHYSICAL LANDSCAPE

Location and Size

Europe's mean location is considerably poleward of the United States. Even the southern tier of European nations we are concerned with here corresponds in latitude to the northern states of the conterminous United States. Madrid, Naples, and Thessaloniki are at New York's latitude, and the 49th parallel, which divides Canada from the western United States for more than 1,000 miles, is only about 140 miles farther north than Italy's northern confines.

Southern Europe extends much farther east-west than north-south. Greece's Dodecanese Islands lie 37 degrees of longitude, or two and one-half time belts and 2,100 miles, east of the Atlantic coast of Portugal. The maximum north-south extent is less than one-half that distance. Due to the peninsular and generally very irregular shape of the coastlines, land distances between places are very long, but water distances are often very short. Palermo, Sicily, is 2,300 miles by road from Gibraltar, but less than 1,100 miles away by sea.

Though distances tend to be great, with the vast expanse of the Mediterranean Sea and its many arms, the total size of Southern Europe is not impressive. It totals only about 397,000 square miles, or six times the size of New England. This land area is about one-tenth of Europe. The size of the individual political divisions varies greatly. Spain is by far the largest political entity in Southern Europe and is the second largest, after France, on the continent (excluding the U.S.S.R.). Its area of 194,000 square miles is slightly more than the combined size of the United Kingdom and West Germany. Italy, with 116,000 square miles, is one of Europe's medium-sized countries. Greece (51,000 sq. mi.) and Portugal (35,000 sq. mi.) rank among Europe's smaller nations, and the roster of minuscule political units includes Andorra, San Marino, Gibraltar, Vatican City, Malta, and Cyprus.

Land and Sea

Three widely separated peninsulas and many islands—this is Southern Europe, as delimited here. The presence of the Mediterranean Sea, the intricate interplay of land and water, and the overwhelmingly seaward orientation are the most striking and primary facets of this area's geography. This omnipresence of an easily trafficked inland sea has served since early historical times as a binding force for the inhabitants of its shores. Though politically united only during Roman times, and developing along quite different lines, the separate parts of Southern Europe have traditionally felt a common Mediterranean bond. This *esprit* has often translated itself into close ties, as seen in the exchanges among the colonies of the Phoenicians, Greeks, and Romans, which stretched from one end of the sea to the other, and again in the many contemporary cultural, technical, and research groups which embrace Mediterraneans of many nations, e.g., the Food and Agriculture Organization (FAO) Mediterranean Development Project.

The Mediterranean is a large sea, covering more than 1,100,000 square miles and stretching more than 2,300 miles from Gibraltar to the Syrian coast. Separating Europe from Africa and, in the east, from the beginnings of Asia, it is the southernmost and largest of the numerous intrusions of the ocean which give Europe its strongly maritime character. Europe has by far the longest coastline per square mile of area of any continent, and its shape has occasioned its being called a "peninsular extension" of the great Eurasian land mass. The Mediterranean is a warm and rather saline sea, and it is much deeper (mean depth is about 4,500 feet) than its counterparts in Northern Europe, the North and Baltic Seas. These latter bodies of water essentially overlie continental shelves, while the Mediterranean occupies what was at one time a much more extensive geosynclinal zone stretching to the Indo-Gangetic Plain and beyond. The western basin is separated from the larger eastern basin by the shallow waters (mostly less than 2,000 feet deep) of the Sicilian Straits, between Sicily and Tunisia.

The Mediterranean is connected with the Atlantic Ocean through the narrow Straits of Gibraltar (narrowest point: eight miles), where huge amounts of cooler Atlantic water pour across a sill which rises to within 1,300 feet of the surface. Some of the Mediterranean's more saline water flows out in the opposite direction into the Atlantic. In the east, there is an entrance to the Black Sea through the Dardanelles, the Sea of Marmara and the Bosporus. There is also an exchange through these narrow straits, and here, too, the receipt balance is heavily in the Mediterranean's favor. Only a third of the water lost through very heavy evaporation from the sunny, subtropical Mediterranean is replaced by precipitation and emptying rivers. The rest is restored by the Atlantic (about three-fifths) through the Straits of Gibraltar, and by the Black Sea (about one-twentieth). Its high salt content accounts for the deep blue color for which the Mediterranean is renowned. Very nearly cut off from the open ocean, the Mediterra-

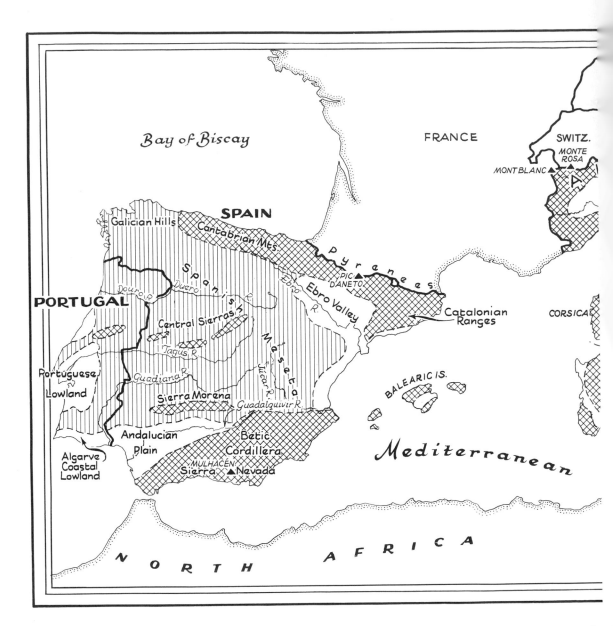

Fig. 7–1. Major physiographic

MAJOR PHYSIOGRAPHIC DIVISIONS OF SOUTHERN EUROPE

Lowlands   Plateaus and hills   Mountains
International boundaries   Physiographic division

0   100   200   300   400   500 Miles
0   100   200   300   400   500 Kilometers

WEST GERMANY

AUSTRIA

HUNGARY

ROMANIA

YUGOSLAVIA

BULGARIA

North Italian Plain

Adige R.

Apennines

Adriatic Sea

Tiber R.

ITALY

ALBANIA

Vardar

Rhodope Massif

GREECE

TURKEY

SARDINIA

IONIAN IS.

Pindus Mts.

PELOPONNESUS

Aegean Sea

CYCLADES IS.

DODECANESE IS.

SICILY

Sea

MALTA

CYPRUS

Same scale as main map

CRETE

divisions of Southern Europe.

nean is a nearly tideless water body. With few exceptions, among them the Provence and the northern Adriatic coasts, the diurnal tidal range averages no more than a foot. This characteristic was of considerable importance in primitive navigation. On the other hand, the lack of tidal scour has been a severe handicap to water transport in many places where rivers dump their deposits into the sea. Mediterranean rivers are abundantly supplied with sedimentary materials, characterized as they are by steep valley profiles and, in a subhumid climate, marked seasonality of flow.

Promontories and peninsulas alternating with coves and bays constitute the major part of the long, irregular Mediterranean coastline of Southern Europe. True, there are a few stretches of rather straight, unindented shore line, e.g., the Italian side of the shallow Adriatic, an emergent coast with many spits, and offshore bars and lagoons, but nowhere on the northern Mediterranean's edge can one find the enormously long stretch of unrelieved straightness that Egypt and Libya, and, for that matter, most of the Levant, present to the eastern basin. An even cursory look at the development of Mediterranean civilization reveals the tremendous benefits which plentiful, deep, and protected harbors offered and still offer the peoples along the northern shore of the large inland sea. The sinuous, almost incredibly complex outline of Greece, with the hundreds of islands dotting both its Ionian and Aegean sides, is rivaled in this respect by few places in the world.

There is another coast in Southern Europe —the Atlantic facade of western and northern Iberia. The drowned coast of Galicia, and the northern shore of Asturias and the Basque provinces have many excellent harbors. Intercourse with overseas areas and the development of fishing and maritime trade have always been outstanding. Southwestern Spain's Atlantic coast is much shorter, and it, as well as Portugal's southern coast, is much straighter and troubled with silting.

Geomorphology

The Mediterranean landscape. A phenomenon of absolutely fundamental importance in Southern Europe is the prominent occurrence of hills and mountains. In addition, there is the propinquity of a deep blue, rather calm sea; the dry and limpid atmosphere which accentuates already vivid colors; the stark features of widespread rocky outcrops and stony slopes of variegated hues everywhere surrounding the small, separated coastal plains and upland basins; and a nearly subtropical natural vegetation, green and lush in winter and spring and in irrigated oases, but otherwise generally sparse and lowly. These features combine to form what is called the Mediterranean landscape. If space permitted a great many variations and nuances in this landscape could be described; indeed, there are important zones within Southern Europe which do not fit this generalized image at all, e.g., the North Italian Plain and the Spanish Meseta, though the latter does incorporate extensive rugged features. The exceptions, however, do not invalidate the concept of the Mediterranean landscape and its application to Southern Europe.

It is a harsh landscape on the whole, for percentages of land in slopes (only marginally or extensively arable, if at all) are high, and plains are small and scattered. Also, the natural vegetation is of low productivity, except in the better watered northern and some of the higher, cooler zones. But the area is uniquely beautiful as well, and the qualities of the climate and the physical landscape, most of which are so unfortunate economically, contribute powerfully to the over-all attractiveness of Southern Europe. The region's cultural features, of course, enhance its appeal. Mediterranean Europe is superbly endowed from the point of view of sheer beauty and evocative human qualities, if not in ease of making a living. Interestingly enough, in this age of easy travel and greatly increased tourism, the former tends to promote the latter.

Iberia. The predominant structural feature of the Iberian Peninsula is the Meseta (Fig. 7–1), an old eroded massif of resistant rocks, folded and deformed during the Hercynian revolution. This wide plateau, which extends west to include sizeable parts of Portugal, was uplifted in later orogenetic activity, and the northern part was associated with the Tertiary folding of the Pyrenees-Cantabrian Mountains. Streams have deeply incised themselves in the high interior sections of the plateau. Steep-sided gorges are numerous, particularly in the west, along the middle courses of the Miño (Portuguese: Minho), Duero (Portugal: Douro), Tagus (Spain: Tajo; Portugal: Tejo) and Guadiana rivers. Faulting has broken the Meseta into several blocks (so that it may more properly be described as a series of plateaus rather than a single one) and given the region an outer fringe of rather steep and straight scarps. The largest of these blocks, divided by a series of more or less linear mountain ranges (the Central Sierras: the Gata, Gredos and Guadarrama mountains), and stretching from Central Portugal into Aragon, is roughly equivalent to Old (in the north) and New (in the south) Castile.

These are flat, largely treeless, and rather uniform plateaus (Fig. 7–2). The northern Meseta is somewhat higher than the southern, averaging about 2,500 feet. The southern part tilts gradually to the southwest. Along its southern margin the Sierra Morena drops down sharply to the Guadalquivir Lowland (Andalucian Plain). In the southwest, in Spanish Extremadura and Portuguese Alentejo, the Meseta merges less abruptly with the Portuguese Lowland. The Central Sierras and the other elongated mountain ranges of the Meseta, though now much worn down, still constitute significant barriers to transportation.

The northwest corner of Iberia comprises the old, but quite rough, Galician Hills, an area intricately dissected by streams whose slightly submerged coast forms a classic *ria* shore line. Farther east, the rugged Cantabrian Mountain country has also been much eroded by streams. South of the Spanish Meseta lies the broad triangular-shaped Andalucian Plain, once covered by the sea, but now the alluvial valley of the lower Guadalquivir River. Fringing coastal sand bars and the extensive marshy area of Las Marismas hamper use of the seaward part.

Fig. 7–2. Barren wheat land (already harvested in this late summer photo), in the western central Meseta, near the Portuguese border. The Sierra de Gata rises in the distance. (H. Price.)

The Portuguese Lowland is the largest of the coastal plains which dot Iberia's periphery at the base of the Meseta. A mountainous spur from the Meseta breaks up this plain north of Lisbon.

In eastern Iberia are three Tertiary mountain chains: the Betic Cordillera in the south; the Pyrenees in the north, forming the border with France; and the Catalonian Ranges. The Betic System includes the high Sierra Nevada ("snowy crest"). It has a very complex structure, with many separate longitudinal valleys, a number of which are fertile and very productive and have old and colorful cities, like Granada, overlooking them from protected slopes. Many of the overlapping ranges include promontories which dip into the sea, producing an irregular coastline. In the north, they reappear far out in the western Mediterranean basin as the Balearic Islands. This island chain, rising from an underwater platform, consists of four principal and many smaller islands. The largest by a considerable margin is Mallorca, whose beautiful, winding, precipitous western littoral rises in the rugged Sierra de Alfabia to 4,270 feet (Puig Mayor). The Pyrenees are a massive barrier, having no low passes and easily penetrable only near their western and eastern ends. Most transverse valleys are short and steep, abutting against a solid wall on the upland side. The central part of the Pyrenees is the most formidable. The French side is wetter, especially to the west, and more abrupt in slope than the Spanish side. Tucked away high on the south slope of the eastern Pyrenees, on the Franco-Spanish border, lies the tiny (191 square miles, 15,000 population) principality of Andorra.[1] The Catalonian ranges are much lower than the previous two and tend to parallel the coast, having the effect of

---

[1] Remote Andorra is a relic of the Middle Ages, having been independent since 1278, when the feuding Spanish Bishop of Urgel and the French Count of Foix agreed to recognize each other as co-princes of the Andorran valleys. It thrives today on sheep-raising, smuggling, some mining and lumbering, and, especially since World War II, tourism.

isolating the Ebro Basin, which broadens out around Zaragoza and Lérida, from the sea. North of Barcelona they meet the coast along the lovely, much indented Costa Brava (Fig. 7–3).

Italy. Remnants of a large old structural block are found in the western Mediterranean. Under the tremendous stresses and pressures of the Tertiary folding, the block was broken into many small pieces, and many of the fragments were submerged. Others, such as the high and rugged islands of Sardinia, Corsica, and Elba, and some of the hill country in western Tuscany, are characteristic areas of faulted structure. On the border between the Tuscan fault-block remnant and the Apennines is a structural line of extinct volcanoes which trends from northern Tuscany southward to quite-active Vesuvius, which was thought to be extinct until it erupted in 79 A.D. The ashes of this famous first explosion buried and preserved the city of Pompeii for posterity. Farther south is Stromboli, one of the few known constantly active volcanoes. Etna in Sicily erupts mostly through parasitic cones on its slopes. The lava flows have frequently destroyed orchards and towns but have also produced some good soils. Some cities, like Messina in 1908, have been victims of severe earthquakes connected with volcanic activity.

The Alps. Only parts of the Alps, primarily their southern slopes, belong to Southern Europe. During the glacial period they were completely buried by ice, and stream erosion since that time has not been able to obliterate the glacial features. Many valleys are lined by terraces where villages and fields have more security from floods than at the broad valley bottoms. Gradients are steep, offering many good sites for hydroelectrical installations.

The boundary of Italy encloses most of the drainage basin of the Po and its tributaries, following the divide more or less closely. The tributary valleys allow Mediterranean vegetation, climate, and crops, and Italian language and cultural habits, to pene-

Fig. 7–3. A view along Catalonia's beautiful and lucrative Costa Brava, showing the spectacular scenery and some of the results of a booming tourist industry. (Spanish Tourist Office.)

Fig. 7–4. The eastern shore of beautiful Lake Como, with its shimmering, snow-capped Alpine backdrop. The terraced slopes, with vine and floriculture, testify to the mild climate of this protected spot. Rail and road tunnels such as these are commonplace in the difficult Alpine topography. (H. Price.)

trate deep into the Alps. The same sort of penetration occurs in the French Alps to the west. These features are especially visible in the broad longitudinal valleys such as those of the Dora Baltea, Adda, Adige, and Rienza rivers. Unlike those of the Pyrenees, these valleys lead to easy passes, some used since prehistoric times. They have helped to minimize the barrier function of the Alps and have been the routes of numerous invasions in both directions.

Valleys and passes break up the Alps into numerous well-defined groups. In the west they are mostly bare, steep, jagged mountains with relatively small glaciers. Here they form two closely connected arcs, whose convex side faces France. They are highest at Mont Blanc (15,781 feet), the highest part of which is totally in France. A group of passes, of which Mont Cenis is the best known, provide the main connection between France and Italy. The Alps curve eastward from the Great St. Bernard Pass to the Simplon Pass.

East of the Simplon, glaciers have carved deep furrows which cup the blue waters of Lakes Maggiore, Lugano, Como, and Garda (Fig. 7–4). Eastward from Lake Garda a separate zone of limestone mountains constitutes the inner arc of the Alps. Among these, the Dolomites are the most widely known group because of their bizarre towers and crags, their white-and-pink walls standing above the green Alpine meadows, and the afterglow of their summits at sunset. Other limestone groups form bare, karstic plateaus with steep walls neighboring fertile valleys. In between are old volcanic extrusions such as the reddish-black rocks of the porphyry plateau of Bolzano. Farther in the interior, crystalline schists, similar to those of the western Alps, form dark, high, glaciated massifs. Their highest peaks, however, do not attain the elevations of the western Alps.

The Apennines. The Apennines are the southeastern continuation of the western

Alps, the two forming a semicircle around the western end of the North Italian Plain. The Apennines run through the entire Italian peninsula, in a bow-shaped chain. They first hug the shore of the Gulf of Genoa in Liguria, the famous Italian Riviera, and then cross the peninsula and sweep close to the shore of the Adriatic Sea. Continuing farther, they form the toe of the Italian boot, the peninsula of Calabria, and reappear in northern Sicily.

Throughout their length, the Apennines are a rather narrow and rugged mountain chain, though of moderate height. Limestone and sandstone formations are preva-

Alps and the Apennines filled in this upper part and created the North Italian Plain. This process is still going on at the combined delta of the Po, Brenta, and Adige, at the pace of almost 30 feet per year. The northern part of the North Italian Plain was later buried under the moraines and outwash plains of the great Alpine glaciers of the Ice Age. Rivers cut into this unconsolidated material, lowering thereby the groundwater table. It emerges in a line of springs (*fontanili*) at the border of the morainic, dry, unfertile zone and the alluvial materials (Fig. 7–5). The Po meanders in the floodplain, confined by natural and man-made levees.

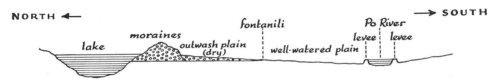

Fig. 7–5. The location of *fontanili* on the North Italian Plain.

lent, and this explains the lack of water in the higher parts. Where the Apennines recede from the Adriatic coast, extremely dry limestone plateaus of nearly horizontal strata form the spur of Mount Gargano and the plain of Apulia (Tavoliere Pugliese). They resemble the karst plateau of Yugoslavia, across the Adriatic Sea. Along the eastern Italian shore a straight, almost harborless coastline has developed.

The Apennines are the longest—though by far not the highest—of the south-European folded mountain chains, extending approximately 600 miles from the group of low passes north and northwest of Genoa, which mark the boundary between the Apennines and the Alps. Another 175 miles of mountain ranges stretch across Sicily and continue as the Atlas Mountains in northern Africa.

Different from the structures so far discussed is the northern third of the Adriatic Sea, which is a zone of downwarping between the uplifted folded zones of the Apennines and the Dinaric system of Yugoslavia. The Adriatic Sea once extended farther inland. Sediments brought by rivers from the

Greece. Greece, most of which is itself a peninsula, occupies the southern and most irregularly shaped part of the Southeast European Peninsula. Greece is the most mountainous of the Southern European countries, and sinuous coastal outlines with mountains plunging straight down into the sea—features typically associated with the Mediterranean landscape—reach their most prolific development here. Coastal plains are narrow and scattered, except in Thessaly and the northeast, and upland basins few and small. The country is made up almost entirely of two geomorphic divisions: the Pindus Mountain system and the Rhodope Massif.

The Pindus Mountains, a southern continuation of the Dinaric Alpine region, is a young, folded mountain range of extremely complex relief resulting from widespread faulting and subsidence. It presents a pattern of diverse individual, mostly very rugged, blocks separated by narrow depressions. The many arcuate, generally southeastward-trending extensions from the parent chain jut out finger-like into the Aegean, giving the eastern and southern coasts their extremely irregular configuration and their easy intercommunication via the sea. The islands of the southern Aegean, as can be seen by their frequently linear pattern, are the peaks of mostly submerged ranges, remnants of the now-drowned link between the Pindus ranges and the mountains of Asia Minor. The principal chain can be plotted in the south through the long islands of Ky-thera, Crete, Karpathos, and Rhodes, but there are others farther north. In the west, however, the grain of the rugged topography parallels the coast, whose hinterlands are therefore quite inaccessible and little developed. The Ionian Isles, of which Corfu (Kerkira) is the largest, lie off the west coast. In contrast to the Dinaric ranges, depressions in the Pindus Mountains form many transverse valleys, the largest of which is submerged and nearly severs the Peleponnesus from the rest of the mainland (the Gulfs of Patras and Corinth and the Saronic Gulf).

The western and central Pindus ranges, especially the former, contain many limestone formations, though this rock type is not so dominant as it is farther north in the Dinarides of Yugoslavia. In Epirus and Peloponnesus the prevalence of limestone mountains, with pervious rock soaking up scarce water, easily eroded soils, and no mineralization, makes a landscape which is hard to put to productive use and is in places quite barren and bleak. These parts of Greece abound in *dolinas* (sinkholes), *polja* (fields which formerly were karst lakes), and other karstic features. The central Pindus Mountains, lying between Epirus and Thessaly, present a massive, unyielding barrier of 6,800 to 8,600 feet, making up the Ionian-Aegean drainage divide. The Lower Vardar River plain, in northern Greek [2] Macedonia, is a wide valley whose life centers on the port of Thessaloniki.

The Rhodope Massif, the Greek part of which includes most of central and eastern Macedonia and Thrace, comprises an ancient crystalline block which was formed by Hercynian or even earlier orogeny and since has been greatly transformed by diastrophism. Its coastal plain, wider than those found in most of peninsular Greece, is prone to flooding in the late winter and spring, and some lower zones are permanent swampland. Rolling plains and hills commence northward, a prelude to the Rhodope Mountains proper. The northern Aegean islands and the elongated extremities of the Chalcidice (Khalkidhiki) Peninsula illustrate the alternating uplifting and subsidence that has taken place. The northern and central Aegean covers a large sunken area, structurally a part of the Rhodopes, as are the old block mountains (in which Mount Olympus is located) between Thessaly and Macedonia, the isle of Euboea (Evvoia), the southeastern tips of Boeotia and Attica, and the Cyclades Islands. The Cyclades end in the south at a fault line marked by active volcanoes and occasionally severe earthquakes. In historical times the volcanoes of Methana and Santorini (Thera) have erupted (Fig. 7–6).

Climate

We are concerned here primarily, of course, with the Mediterranean, or dry-summer subtropical, climate type (Koeppen's *Cs*).[3] The most restricted of all the dozen or so standard types, this climate is most extensively represented on the fringes of the Mediterranean Basin, and hence this area has lent its name to the climatic classification. It is often called "summer-dry, winter-wet." Accuracy is better served, however, by describing the concentration of precipitation as being in the "cooler seasons" or "in a season other than summer," since it very often turns out that fall, or fall and spring, are the rainiest seasons in Mediterranea. This refinement of the description in

---

[2] Greece controls only the southern part of the old historical region of Macedonia. The rest belongs to Yugoslavia and Bulgaria.

[3] See the section on climates in Chapter 1 for a recapitulation of the climatic features of Southern Europe, especially p. 48 on "The Mediterranean Type." For climographs, see Appendix II.

Fig. 7–6. Santorini (Thera), an island of volcanic origin. The precipitous slopes (note the severe grade of the zigzag road) are the inner walls of an old crater. (Greek government, Press Department.)

no way dilutes the overriding significance of the unfailingly characteristic dryness of the hot summer. Rainfall amounts are modest, this being sometimes classed as a "subhumid" climate. Spring is cooler than fall and is the most delightful time of year, when the days are warm and sunny and the countryside is verdant and fresh after winter's rains. Wild flowers abound, complementing the myriad greens of the rolling hills. The visitor is well advised to see Southern Europe in spring, when fine weather and the absence of summer hordes make the tourist's work and play most agreeable and the Mediterranean landscape is at its most fetching.

Two climatic features are especially instructive from the economic geographic point of view: (1) a long growing season, varying from about eight to virtually twelve months, and (2) a relatively high deviation from *average* climatic figures, particularly as regards rainfall dependability and length of growing season, i.e., the period between the last and first killing frosts. The Mediterranean climate is much like the tropical desert in summer, and quite similar in winter (though warmer and much sunnier) to maritime northwestern Europe.

There are, however, wide variations, quite apart from the non-Mediterranean zones, in the generalized climatic pattern of Southern Europe. As in any region of great topographic diversity, landforms and their directional orientation; location with regard to the sea, including distance from and openness to it; aspect of slope, e.g., north-facing vs. south-facing; and other factors strongly influence climate and produce a very complex pattern. A microclimatic approach is necessary to appreciate the extent of these nuances and their very practical meaning. Western Tuscany's 35 inches of rain a year, for instance, allow much greater agricultural productivity than northern Apulia's 20. And the protective Alpine backdrop of the western Ligurian coast (Riviera dei Fiori—"Riviera of Flowers") gives it freedom from severe frosts and winter temperature-averages ten to fifteen degrees Fahrenheit higher than in the Po Valley, only seventy miles north, an advantage which has encouraged the residents of the former region to develop it into a major floricultural zone. Upland areas are cooler, but the latitude of Southern Europe permits cultivation at considerable altitudes, especially where there is a southerly exposure. They are also usually much rainier, and the higher elevations receive considerable snowfall, e.g., the Italian Alps, the northern Apennines, and Spain's Sierra Nevada. The more humid uplands are an important source of irrigation water for the plains below, provide good summer pasturage, have the best and most extensively utilizable forests, and offer welcome relief from the summer heat to vacationers.

This perhaps most delightful of all "man-climates"—noted for its bright, sunny weather, blue skies, few rainy days, and rains of brief duration—is, however, less than ideal in other ways. The long, dry summer, unique among humid middle-latitude climate types, corresponds with a long part of the growing season. As such, it imposes certain stringent limitations on the natural vegetation and upon agricultural practices and choice of plant culture, just as does the topographic factor in Mediterranea.

The above discussion has dealt with the Mediterranean climate type to which, with important variations from place to place, most of Southern Europe belongs. The exceptions, that is, the non-dry-summer subtropical zones—mainly pluviose northwestern Iberia, the steppic parts of interior and east coastal Spain, and the humid North Italian Plain—are treated in the section in Chapter 1 to which the reader has already been directed.

Concerning the vegetative and soil characteristics of Southern Europe, little need be added to the summary given in Chapter 1 (see pages 59–61).

Hydrography and Water Resources

Rivers of Southern Europe are generally characterized by their shortness, their great seasonal fluctuation in flow, many being dry or nearly so during the latter part of the long dry Mediterranean summer, and their poor navigability. Most rivers also have a rather swift flow, especially those many short streams which descend abruptly from hill or mountain ranges to a nearby coast. Some rivers which flow through limestone areas, as in the eastern Italian Alps, parts of the Apennines, and western Greece, disappear in sinkholes, forming underground channels and caverns. Often these reappear as springs farther downstream in their courses. The general tendency toward a fall in the level of the Mediterranean Sea in recent geologic times and the elevated topography of the land areas have resulted in steep river profiles (the word cañon, meaning canyon, is Spanish) which, along with heavy convectional rains and deforested catchment basins, contribute to the propensity for flooding of the Mediterranean rivers. The Arno River flood of November, 1966, during which the city of Florence sustained enormous damage to its irreplaceable cultural and artistic treasures, is a good example. The above factors are also instrumental in maintaining the exceptionally heavy discharge of river-borne debris in streams' lower courses and at the coasts, forming in many places extensive floodplains and deltas. Even those streams which originate partly or wholly outside the Mediterranean climate realm, e.g., the Po, Ebro, Duero and Vardar, have erratic and seasonally very uneven regimes and carry great loads of sediment. Flood control has been an important consideration in water development programs on both a regional and local level. There are few stretches of navigable rivers in Southern Europe, and, unlike the more northern parts of the continent, river transport is unimportant.

Except in the restricted rainier areas mentioned, water is a scarce and much coveted resource in Southern Europe. The impact of this phenomenon can be seen clearly in the elaborate provisions for water rights in Roman law and their relative neglect in the body of Anglo-Saxon law. Irrigation, both riverine and from underground sources, is an ancient and highly important practice. Water availability (or lack of it) has had a strong influence on population distribution, the pattern of agglomerated settlement, and the location of industrial and urban areas in Southern Europe. Fortunately, on their rainier northern fringes, Spain, Italy, and Greece can harness considerable badly needed hydro power which their topography in general favors but their climate largely forestalls.

The provision of adequate water for foreseeable future needs is of high priority in present economic planning in most regions of Southern Europe. A great deal of attention is being given to implementing various water storage and hydraulic engineering schemes which will extend the irrigated area and help satisfy burgeoning urban and industrial water demands. Where water can be furnished in sufficient abundance the landscape, often latently very fertile and lacking only that one essential ingredient, can be made to bloom and produce bountifully. And enough water is also a *sine qua non* for fulfilling the expanding industrial potential which Mediterranean leaders are so eager to pursue. The Provençal saying, "eici l'aigo es d'or" (here water is gold), rings true.

THE CULTURAL AND HISTORICAL BACKGROUND

There are many common themes in the cultural and historical development of the various parts of Southern Europe. Nevertheless, it must be kept in mind that each country and the larger islands, too, have exhibited great individuality in their historical evolution, and a treatment of this subject is included under separate country headings.

The Development, Spread, and Eclipse of Mediterranean Civilization

The Mediterranean shores spawned our civilization. As the headline of a recent ad campaign of the Greek National Tourist Bureau proclaims, albeit with some paternalistic license, "You were born in Greece!" The long history of the spread of earliest civilization from Egypt and Mesopotamia gradually northward and then westward through the Mediterranean world is too well-known to recount here. To no other part of the world is so much credit owed for the development and dissemination of civilization, for advances in art and science, for the enlargement of the ecumene, and for the blossoming of commerce and cultural intercourse. Phoenicia, Minoan Crete, Greece, Rome, Byzantium, Moslem North Africa, Venice, Genoa, Spain and Portugal—all in their turn improved upon and passed along the torch of civilization. As successive centers of political dominance shifted westward, the older ones went into a relative decline. Still, as the continent emerged from the Middle Ages, most of Southern Europe stood out as a quite civilized, if somewhat torpid, area and one that had been so since long before the time of Christ. As such, the contrast to the backward rest of Europe was sharp.

In time, the fortunes of Southern Europe changed. For a century or two, starting in the mid-fourteenth century, Renaissance Italy revived the cultural supremacy and exemplar role of Mediterranea. Presently, this passed, and it was in any case unaccompanied by great political or economic influence. Even at the peak of its Renaissance flowering, the Italian peninsula was being ravaged by French armies. At about the same time, in the mid-fifteenth century, Turkish expansion removed Greece and Asia Minor from the sphere of European culture. By the late 1500's Iberian ascendency also faltered, and all Southern Europe fell into an unmistakable decline relative to its northern neighbors. In the past two centuries or more, with hegemony definitely established in the latter area, there has been a reversal of flow, one of those curious counter-movements of history, as cultural innovations and ideas have spread to the south and east from Frankish, Teutonic, Anglo-Saxon, and Nordic Europe. Greece, finally ousting the Turks, drew back into the Western cultural orbit in the 1820's.

The reasons for the relative cultural and economic retrogression of Southern Europe (the word relative must be emphasized, for in an absolute sense, continual progress has, over the long run, been registered) are many and more complex than first perusal would indicate, and they have been the subject of much inquiry and debate. In part it is due to the niggardly resource base, long exploited and in any case ill-suited to the demands of modern, or even pre-Industrial Revolution, manufacturing. Undoubtedly,

too, man's severe and chronic degradation of the vegetative cover and the soils has reduced the land's productive capacity to a point where even late twentieth-century man finds it difficult, too expensive, or, in many cases, impossible to revivify it (Fig. 7–7). Also, the impetus of cumulative scientific advances in the favored industrial nations of Northern Europe was self-perpetuating and inevitably widened the gap between them and the nearly stagnant southern lands. Finally, political and social factors made a major contribution. Other reasons seem more obscure, but scholars still debate the subject with much interest.

The Geographic Unity of Southern Europe

The three peninsulas and many islands of Southern Europe are widely separated and their longitudinal spread is considerable.

Fig. 7–7. A badlands landscape along the dry Ionian coast of Calabria. Once fertile grain land for the ancient Greeks, it is now so badly gullied and bared by rain that it is almost totally valueless for either crops or pasture. (H. Price.)

Each has its own very special historical evolution and distinctive contemporary traits. Even so, the essential unity of the area as a geographic region is remarkable.

Physical features. The omnipresence of the sea and its role in linking its borderlands together have already been amply stressed, as has been the character of the physical environment: the pervasive Mediterranean climate, topography, vegetation, soils, hydrography, and the poverty in mineral resources. These two aspects of Mediterranean Europe stand very high on the list of unifying features. Topography perhaps deserves some elaboration, since at first glance the landform pattern appears exceedingly complex and diverse. But this complexity, exemplified by the prevalence of rugged uplands and small coastal plains and upland basins rimmed by mountains and hills which often front directly on the sea, is not confined to any one zone or to a few zones. Instead it recurs in Southern Europe, and indeed one finds it to be a repetitive pattern from one end of the area to the other. Thus out of its very geomorphic diversity comes a striking element of similarity.

The human factor. In addition to unifying physical characteristics, there are observable throughout Southern Europe many common cultural and socio-economic features, as seen for instance in farming methods and types, livestock practices, the industrial structure, tertiary activities, trade patterns, and the tempo and quality of life.

Mediterranean farming patterns embrace one or more of three crop associations which are closely related to the climatic regime: (1) winter grains, particularly wheat, and some vegetables which grow unirrigated during the cool rainy season; (2) drought-resistant plants, especially trees (the olive, cork, almond, and other nut trees) and the grapevine, with deep and extensive roots and other natural equipment to withstand the parching hot season; and (3) a wide variety of irrigated crops: vegetables, deciduous and citrus fruits, flowers and ornamental plants, rice, and other specialized cash crops such as cotton and tobacco. Though representing, naturally, only a fraction of the acreage of non-irrigated farm land, these irrigated lands produce a major share of the total value of farm produce in Southern Europe (Fig. 7–8).

The human response to the landform arrangement is interesting in its duplication from one locale to another. The plains farmer, usually employing irrigation, where possible, in an intensive horticulture which renders impressively high per acre yields, is often quite advanced in the techniques he employs. He is keenly attuned to market conditions and studies what he can do to maximize his profits. This lowland dweller more often than not lives in a sizeable town and usually belongs to the mainstream of local and national life. The hill farmer, on the other hand, resides in a much more isolated and rural environment. He may cultivate cereals, pasture, and hay or he may be primarily a small-scale pastoralist. In either case, he usually employs centuries-old methods of farming. The conditions of his existence place him in an increasingly difficult competitive position in the modern world. This fundamental contrast in Mediterranean agriculture between the dynamic lowlands and the ever more anachronistic economy of the backcountry is growing and is a matter of social as well as economic concern as the depopulation of many of the highland regions rapidly proceeds. Thus, one sees that the tomato grower of the Salerno coast may not have much in common with his pastoralist neighbor in the nearby Apennines, but he will have a good deal in common with the viticulturalist of east coastal Peloponnesus or the carnation grower on the Gulf of Genoa coast near Savona. Similarly, that same pastoralist will find his counterpart in the Peloponnesian Mountains and the Ligurian Alps a few miles inland from the Gulf of Genoa.

The segment of the labor force employed in agriculture is larger in Southern Europe than in the more industrialized northwestern

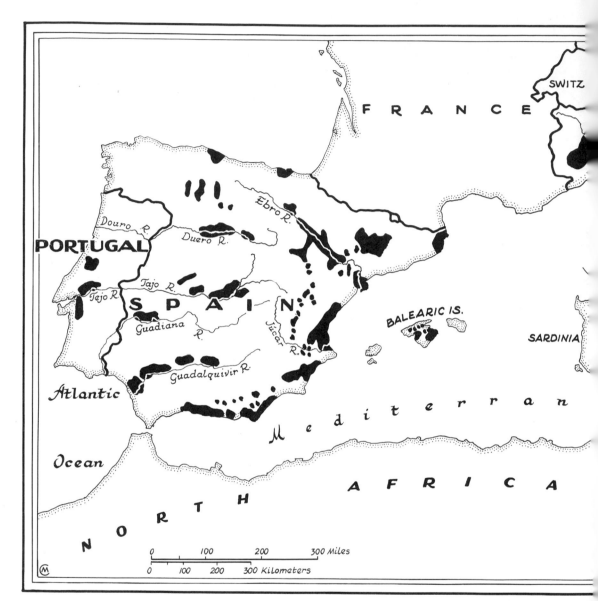

Fig. 7–8. Irrigated lands

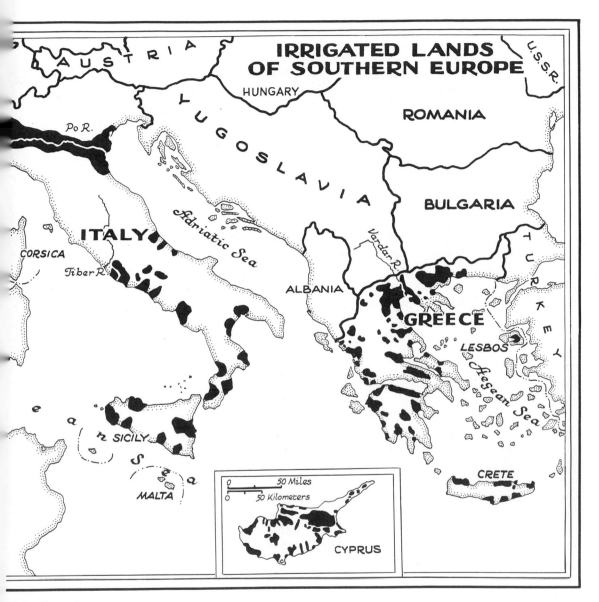

of Southern Europe.

part of the continent, despite the fact that the former is far from ideally suited to farming. Land fragmentation persists as a serious handicap, requiring farmers to tend tiny, widely separated plots—a wasteful practice. Moreover, there remains a large poor, landless peasant class. Many areas still use traditional methods, e.g., sowing, harvesting, and threshing of cereals by hand, and terracing. Fertilization, use of insecticides, selective breeding, farm mechanization and other aspects of modern farming have been until recently quite inadequately dispersed and still are in many less favored areas. The above conditions result in low yields per acre and/or per man-hour. Yet improvements in farming in the past two decades have been very substantial, due both to intensified government action and to advances in overall economic conditions. The northwestern European farmer continues to be more prosperous than his southern equivalent, but the exceptions to the rather negative features of agriculture in Southern Europe outlined above are numerous. The familiar generality depicting it as agriculturally substandard and backward throughout is certainly no longer accurate.

With the exception of northern Italy and a few enclaves elsewhere, Southern Europe is among Europe's least industrialized regions. As in most semi-industrial areas, manufacturing is less diversified, and the heavy and more sophisticated, research-dominated branches, e.g., steel, metal fabrication, and most engineering products, are poorly represented. Steel production in all Southern Europe is less than that of France.

Only Italy produces sizeable numbers of vehicles (two-thirds those of Britain) and some airplanes. The scale of industrial enterprises is small, too, in Southern Europe. The family-owned firm is still the norm, and the giant corporation which can employ vertical integration and enjoy great cost advantages through economies of scale is, again outside Italy, rare. Expansion and modernization of manufacturing is taking place in most countries, encouraged by strong government support and financial assistance. The prognosis is good, but there remain many problems, among which are a poor mineral and energy resource base, lack of skilled labor and management, scarce investment capital, and, in some areas, shortages of power or inadequate transportation facilities.

All of Southern Europe suffers from a chronic imbalance in foreign trade. Minerals, fuels, and a wide variety of other raw materials and foodstuffs, as well as a long roster of manufactured goods, must be imported, and imports have continually outpaced exports by a wide margin. From 1960 through 1966, for example, Spain's exports covered only 41 per cent of the cost of its imports! Furthermore, many traditional exports have tended to show inordinate fluctuations in earnings due to either production variations or demand and price changes, or both, and this constitutes a serious weakness.

Two items which help offset the trade deficit are income from tourism, one of Southern Europe's outstanding sources of revenue, and remittances from emigrants working in Northern and Western Europe or overseas. Mediterranean Europe offers much to attract tourists: reliable sunny weather, ample and very lovely beaches and lakes, colorful customs and dress, much improved accommodations, and moderate (though rising) prices. There are still many places of great charm and beauty, especially in Iberia and Greece, which are as yet unspoiled, and the future for tourism in Southern Europe is definitely very bright. Emigrant remittances reflect a phenomenon of vital economic and social significance to all of Western Europe, viz. the large-scale migration throughout the 1950's and 1960's of workers from Southern Europe to the countries of Northern and Western Europe, particularly West Germany. This arrangement has been of great benefit to both regions. The latter, suffering from chronic labor shortages, have acquired badly needed manpower, while Mediterranean lands gained welcome relief from population pressures and unemployment problems. At the same time, they net a major source of scarce foreign exchange. In 1968, it was estimated that 1,100,000 Spanish nationals were working in northwestern Europe, and the figure is higher for Italians. Whether or not this migration pattern has run its course is open to question. The economic slump of 1966–67, especially in West Germany, caused a very sharp drop of Southern Europeans emigrating and even a sizeable reverse flow of repatriates. With automation gaining rapidly in northwestern Europe, fewer foreign workers may be needed in the future, even in good times.

The pace of life is leisurely in Southern Europe. The hustle and bustle of the sprawling industrial centers like the Ruhr, metropolitan Paris, and the English Midlands are largely absent, outside of a few large urban agglomerations such as the western Po Valley, Barcelona, and Rome. The *siesta* during the early afternoon, a natural habit born of the desire to escape the hottest hours of the scorching summer months, the communal *passeggiata* (stroll) and buzzing cafes at dusk, the *al fresco* dining and lingering long hours over multi-course meals enhanced by local wines (the traditional entertainment of a Mediterranean evening), all testify to a way of life which the visitor finds quite different from anything else in Europe. In this mild and pleasant climate, life is more attuned to the outdoors than in rainier, colder climes. Beautiful parks and pleasure gardens with their flowers, fountains, and shade are a much appreciated aspect of the Mediterranean existence. With the proliferation of modern industry and the discipline it imposes, concessions have been made to a quickening tempo, especially in congested cities with hitherto unknown traffic jams. The long mid-day dinner break is no longer practical for many in Rome, Turin, and Athens, and the average Milanese can no longer indulge the siesta habit. But elsewhere, in the smaller cities and the rural areas, ingrained patterns hold firm, and the slower ways of Mediterranean folk continue to delight the throngs of tourists from richer lands.

SPAIN

Spain is Europe's second largest country in area, after France, and is fifth in population, with 32,400,000 people (1968). It occupies about five-sixths of the Iberian peninsula, the rest belonging to Portugal. The Balearic Islands, off Spain's Mediterranean coast, and the Canaries, southwest of the Spanish mainland, are considered as integral parts of the country, and they count among Spain's 50 provinces.

Propinquity and history have meant that the two Iberian nations share many features in common. In Europe's southwest corner, Spain and Portugal are truly transitional in location. Cut off from the rest of the continent by the massive barrier of the Pyrenees Mountains, they lie across the narrow Straits of Gibraltar from Africa and are subject to Mediterranean and Atlantic influences on the east and west. This has encouraged an intermingling of peoples that imparts great individuality to Iberian culture. Many geographers and writers have commented on the peculiar blend of traits that make Spain and Portugal in a sense "extra-European."

Spain is peninsular. It has a rather compact, massive shape. The plateau-like nature of much of the center, however, and the many fringing mountain ranges have made for a considerable degree of remoteness and isolation of the interior from the peripheral parts of the country. There is, on the whole, a surprisingly low orientation to the sea for a nation with such a long coastline. The capital, Madrid, near the geometric center of Spain, is about 190 miles from the sea at its closest point, a more interior location than any other capital in Southern Europe.

The intimate relationship between geography and history can be illustrated handsomely by Spain. Only scant attention can be focused here on the many strongly influential geographic factors, but they should be emphasized. First, there is the matter of sheer size. Long distances have combined with difficult access to the interior to make maintaining control over peripheral areas by the central government in Castile very trying and incomplete. Further, much of this intervening territory is sparsely populated, mountainous and/or arid. Relief itself is a contributing handicap. The average elevation of Spain is about 2,000 feet, second only to Switzerland in Europe. The hydrography, also, militates against easy communication, since there is only one river navigable for more than a few miles, the Guadalquivir. Silting at river mouths clogs harbors which might otherwise serve marine navigation. The geographical isolation from the rest of Europe, though undoubtedly partly self-imposed, is nonetheless based on the aforementioned Pyrenees barrier and the corner position of Iberia. The general aridity—the Meseta has Europe's only true steppe west of the U.S.S.R.—and the relatively poor standing in minerals have been other negative factors.

The social system which has developed and the outstanding national characteristics of the Spaniard are important elements, too, in explaining Spain. The small middle class, the poverty of the masses, and the stranglehold of the Church all have played a major role in the way things have developed in Spain. The individualism, occasional fanaticism, and preoccupation with tradition have long been parts of the Spanish character. The validity of "national characteristics" will always be in dispute, but some allusion to the general mores and ways of thinking is justified and even necessary. Take, furthermore, the concept of the "gentleman" (hidalgo) and the energy spent on maintaining his honor, the disdain for commerce and industry and the consequent refusal to invest, despite huge amounts of capital available from New World colonies, in permanent income-generating enterprises. Surely Spanish life has been strongly influenced by the ideas and ideals of her people.

Historical Background

Spain has seen the advent and absorption into its territory of numerous ethnic groups since the original Iberians were joined in the south by the Phoenicians around 1500 B.C. These great traders of the early Mediterranean world are thought to be the donors of Spain's modern name, deriving from the Phoenician word *span*, meaning "far away land." The Phoenicians established a number of trading colonies, including Cádiz (reputedly the oldest city in Europe), Seville, and Málaga. Later came the Greeks, bringing with them grapes and olives, which ever since have been staples in Iberian agriculture. They, too, founded trading posts. Celts arrived in the fifth century B.C. in Galicia and mixed with the local folk. The amalgam of early Iberia was further diversified by the Carthaginians from North Africa in the sixth and fifth centuries B.C. Their capital was Carthago Nova (today's Cartagena). The defeat of the Carthaginians in the Second Punic War late in the third century B.C. led to the systematic takeover of much of the Iberian peninsula by the victorious Roman legions and the beginning of a long and notably progressive era in Spanish history.

Roman Iberia. Rome was the first power successful in dominating effectively such a large chunk of this westernmost Mediterranean outpost (for outpost it was). With this consolidation of power came many of the advancements for which the *Pax Romana* is deservedly famous. With the exception, perhaps, of the Arabs (Moors), the influence of the Romans on Iberia's pre-modern development was the most lasting and profound. Rome supplied a religion and a code of law, and, most basic, a language. Roman engineers were responsible for the first real road system, and they built remarkable arched stone bridges and aqueducts, a few of which still remain and indeed are still used today. Many of Iberia's great historical cities date back to Roman times: the Roman provincial capital Tarraco (Tarragona), Emerita (Mérida), Caesarea Augusta (Zaragoza), Hispalis (Seville), and Olisipo (Lisbon) are but a few.

Moslem Spain and the *Reconquista*. The people of Northern Europe swept over Roman Spain early in the fifth century A.D. —the Goths first, and then the Visigoths and the Vandals. They acquiesced in the established order and more advanced culture, adding comparatively little to early Spain's growth. It was the Mohammedan, or Moorish, "infidels," moving north from Africa in 711 A.D. to commence a nearly eight-century-long residence, who infused a second great guiding spirit into Spanish life. The Moors rapidly asserted control over all of Iberia but the northwest and mountainous north. More highly civilized than the Spaniards they conquered, the Moors made important contributions toward advancing many branches of scientific learning, particularly astronomy, mathematics, botany, chemistry, and medicine. They spurred agriculture on tremendously through the introduction of marvelous irrigation systems, establishing vast *huertas* of cotton, sugar cane, citrus and other fruits, some of which they brought into Spain for the first time. There was also considerable Moorish influence on the language and on Iberia's place name geography, e.g., the Guadalquivir River *(wadi al kabir,* "the great river"), Algarve *(al gharb,* "the west"), and Gibraltar *(gebel al Tariq,* "Tariq's hill"). The Arab imprint on architecture has been strong and lasting and is particularly visible today in Andalucia (the South was always the stronghold of Moorish power and influence in Spain). The Giralda of Seville, the exquisite Alhambra at Granada, and Córdoba's Mesquita are among the most famous examples of Moorish architecture.

Christian Spain, retiring to the north, resisted further incursions by the Mohammedans, waging periodic war against its conquerors. Gradually, united by a common passion to drive the Arabs from their homeland, the Spaniards achieved their aim. The *Reconquista* (Reconquest) took seven centuries! Finally the power of the Moors in Iberia was broken with the fall of Granada in 1492, and Spain was united under the Catholic Monarchs, Ferdinand and Isabella.

The long struggle of the *Reconquista* left an indelible stamp on the Spanish character. The zeal, idealism, and intolerance which are often associated with it were forged through centuries of fighting and of an overriding preoccupation with a single, all-encompassing goal. The identification of Catholicism, or rather the peculiar Spanish brand of it, with the cause of national liberation was one of the Church's continuing sources of strength, promoting its firm entrenchment in Spanish authoritarianism for centuries to come. The pervasive twin traditions of militarism and ecclesiasticism, which have so often shackled Spanish initiative, grew out of this harsh period. The excesses of intolerance led to the expulsion of most Jews (those who refused conversion) in the fifteenth century, and of the *Moriscos* (descendants of the Moors) in 1610, thereby depriving Spain of a disastrously large proportion of its more enlightened and ambitious farmers and skilled artisans.

Empire and decline. The Catholic Monarchs launched Spain on an era of overseas exploration and conquest that brought glory and wealth. For many decades Spain was the greatest power in the world. The *conquistadores* won for Spain a vast empire in the New World. That restrictive and exploitative colonial policies led to the eventual disintegration of the Empire is no surprise, for the unwise political and economic programs pursued at home by Ferdinand and Isabella and their heirs made for chronic basic internal weakness. Even the vast mineral wealth flowing from the colonies could not save Spain from sure and steady decline, for most of it was squandered and precious little invested in improving the productive capacity of the nation. By engaging in recurrent and protracted wars in Europe and by their ineptness and corrupt rule, the Spanish kings of the sixteenth and seventeenth centuries dashed any chance the country might have had to move ahead on a par with other Western European countries. Spain, the mightiest nation in the world under Charles I (Charles V of the Holy Roman Empire), grandson of Ferdinand and Isabella, fell into a decline from which it never has recovered. By 1826 all its mainland Latin American colonies had broken away, and at the turn of the twentieth century only a few insignificant African possessions remained. Spain's present-day colonies consist of Ifni, Spanish Sahara, Cueta, and Melilla. Their combined population is slightly under one-quarter million.

Modern Spain. The fall of Alfonso XIII and the Spanish monarchy in 1931 ushered in a brief period during which an unsettled Spain was a republic. The republican period culminated in the exhausting and extremely destructive Spanish Civil War (1936–1939), out of which emerged the durable dictatorship of Generalissimo Francisco Franco (*El Caudillo*).

In rebuilding from the shambles left by war, Spain was severely handicapped by the almost immediate outbreak of World War II (1939–1945). Though Spain was neutral, that conflict threw the nation on its own resources by cutting off the usual sources of raw materials, industrial equipment and technical help, and by precluding almost all foreign investment. For at least an equal period after the War, too, while the European belligerents were themselves busy rebuilding, Spain was again denied much attention and assistance. She also failed to qualify for U.S. Marshall Plan aid because of her political isolation and unpalatability. Gradually, however, the economy has improved since the early 1950's. The regime has pursued of late a somewhat more enlightened policy of cautious and partial relaxation of its reins on political freedom and freedom of expression. Its posture in foreign political and economic affairs, too, has been liberalized and made much more internationalist.

The issue of Gibraltar remains a rather exasperating one for Spain. A tiny peninsula sticking out into the sea at the eastern end of the Strait of the same name, Gibraltar consists of little more than the "Rock" itself,

one of the Pillars of Hercules of the ancients (Fig. 7–9). The 2.3-square-mile territory, with about 28,000 inhabitants who are overwhelmingly non-Spanish, has been owned by the British since 1704 and has been a major military base for them. Spain seems determined to retrieve it, regarding it as *terra irredenta*, and she embarked on a drive to harass the British colony in 1965, ultimately sealing it off from the Spanish mainland. Britain appears just as adamant not to give it up, at least while under direct pressure. It is of little potential economic significance to Spain, but the matter threatens to poison Anglo-Spanish relations.

Population

Spain's large area gives it an over-all density of 166 per square mile, which is modest by European standards (average for Europe, excluding the U.S.S.R.: 242). It has, for instance, only one-third the density of Italy, and one-quarter that of West Germany. The general poverty of the masses in Spain then, despite many shortcomings of the physical geography, is perhaps more due to the failure to mobilize the country's resources than to overpopulation, though on this subject one encounters considerable dispute.

Spain's population growth has been rather more erratic than that of most of the rest of Europe. At present, Spain's annual birth rate of 21.3 per 1,000 population is one of Europe's highest; the death rate of 8.6 is somewhat lower than the European average. The natural rate of growth, then, of 1.27 per cent per year is well above the average for Europe. However, emigration, encouraged by the Spanish government, has been heavy during the last decade or more, so that the net rate of population growth has been well below 1 per cent per year, a rather reasonable figure for a nation struggling to raise its standard of living. Health standards are improving, and economically Spaniards are gaining rapidly. Illiteracy is much less common among young adults today than a generation ago, showing the effects of the

Fig. 7–9. Gibraltar. The town of Gibraltar and its harbor lie to the left (west) of "The Rock." The open Mediterranean is to the right, the Bay of Algeciras (Spain) to the left. (Gibraltar Tourist Committee.)

compulsory education system which has been implemented.

Population distribution is extremely varied in Spain. In Galicia and Asturias the rugged surface poses handicaps for farming that should dictate smaller population densities, and crowding does appear to underlie a rural poverty there which is only partially relieved by heavy emigration. In general, though, population density reflects (1) quality of agricultural resources, or carrying capacity of the land, and (2) suitability of local conditions for industry and commerce. There is a rather pronounced clustering around the coastal periphery. Over most of the arid and mountainous interior the population density is less than fifty per square mile, and there are only five cities of over 100,000 people in this region (1964): Madrid (2,558,000), Zaragoza (377,000), Valladolid (172,000), Badajoz (103,000), and Salamanca (101,000). There are a few favored spots (minerals, irrigation) in the interior upland which are moderately heavily populated, but these exceptions merely re-

inforce the inescapable feeling of emptiness which impresses the traveler in that generally sparsely populated landscape. Over the last 150 years, numbers have in fact declined appreciably in central Spain, due to traditionally heavy out-migration, especially from León, Aragón, and Old Castile. This is a region of nucleated settlement. A dispersed rural settlement pattern is mainly confined to pluviose northern and northwestern Spain and to densely settled irrigated zones.

Coastal Spain is far more favored for agriculture. It also has accessibility, the lack of which has always hampered the interior. That indispensable ingredient has led to the growth of commerce, industry, and urban agglomerations so noticeably wanting inland. Not that this belt of heavy population concentration is continuous, but the contrast to central Spain is sharp. In the irrigated *huertas* near Valencia there are densities of 1,200 people per square mile, and the *vega* of Murcia counts nearly that many. Furthermore, the coastal-interior contrast is clearly growing, as the peripheral industrial centers and ports continue to expand. Recent extension of irrigation and the booming tourist trade have swelled the population in coastal districts, some of which were virtually empty fifteen to twenty years ago. The provinces showing the fastest growth rate between 1960 and 1970 are almost all on the coastal periphery. This region counts twenty-four cities of over 100,000, nearly five times that of the interior. The largest are Barcelona, Valencia, Bilbao, Málaga, and Murcia.

Spain's unity is fostered by her religious homogeneity, more than 99 per cent of the populace subscribing to the Roman Catholic faith. The official language is Castilian Spanish, and this is understood throughout the country despite the existence of several dialects and even separate languages. Of these, Catalan, akin to French Provençal, and the wholly distinctive Basque tongue are the most important and coincide, not accidentally, with the strongest separatist feelings.

Interior Castile has always been the motive force behind the drive for Spanish national unity. In addition to the obstacle of difficult access to the outside, it has been bedeviled by strongly felt cultural differences among Andaluces, Gallegos (natives of Galicia), Catalans, Basques, and others who have continually pushed for greater autonomy or even, at times, separation. A further force in Spanish life that might well become disruptive in the future is an entrenched and growing anticlericism which the Church either does not admit or refuses to accommodate by accelerated reforms. Finally, there remain still latent rivalries and bitterness brought on by the brutal Civil War which have been forcibly suppressed but could surface under a more relaxed regime.

Present Economic Life

Spain has been in an economic decline or stagnation since her *siglo de oro* (golden century) ended nearly 400 years ago, and continues to be one of Europe's poorest, most backward countries. A most encouraging trend, however, has been manifested in the past two decades.

The 1940's were mostly years of hardships and isolation, during which the increase in gross national product barely paralleled the growth in population (only about 8 per cent). Throughout the period since the Civil War, however, the government has had a very major role in directing the economy, lately through formalized central and regional planning. It has channeled funds through an extensive system of subsidies, and price and wage controls. Also, it has imposed import restrictions, directed public works, and allocated scarce raw materials and power. Finally, the cumulative effects of, first, reconstruction, then of capital investment in industry, especially producer goods, and in improving transport facilities and other areas of the infrastructure began to tell. Spain showed signs in the early 1950's of a more rapid development of the economy. American aid, beginning in 1951 and increasing two years later with the formulation of a United States–Spanish Defense Aid Pact, has played an important role. Even more far-reaching has been the broad stabilization and economic reform plan of 1959, which, among other things, devalued the currency and further broke down Spain's aloofness by liberalizing trade and encouraging foreign aid and investment. Tourism has soared. Industry and, to a lesser extent, agriculture have responded to this new attitude and to other favorable growth factors. The gross national product rose by 65 per cent from 1960 to 1965, and per capita income in the latter year passed $500, a figure some economists feel is the take-off point for developing economies.

Agriculture. Spain is still primarily an agricultural nation. More than one-third of the labor force is in farming. About a third of the farmers barely eke out a subsistence from their small plots, and a large number of underemployed and unemployed landless farm workers poses a chronic problem. Farm methods, though improving, still remain relatively backward over much of the country. Fragmentation of farm plots is especially acute in the northwest, and in the south the poorly exploited *latifundia*, the large holdings of absentee landlords, abound.

About 40 per cent of Spain is classified as cropland, another 46 per cent as natural pasture and forests, and 14 per cent as non-agricultural land. Olives and vineyards occupy nearly one-tenth each of the cultivated area. Cereals also are important: one-fifth of the arable land is planted in wheat. A wide variety of Mediterranean crops—fruits and vegetables, nuts, and carobs among them—is produced in quantity, and sheep-raising is the major livestock activity. Productivity and yields per acre could be greatly improved, especially on unirrigated lands. In fact, the discernible potential for improvements in the agricultural sphere constitutes a bright hope in the economic future of Spain.

Spain is extremely diverse in its farming patterns (Fig. 7–10). Its northwestern corner, or "Atlantic" Spain, Galicia and Asturias, are hilly, wet, and cloudy. They specialize in crops and livestock not generally associated with Southern Europe: corn, potatoes, rye, and apples. Pigs and cattle are numerous, dairy products are shipped to the rest of Spain, and cider replaces wine as the regional beverage. The hillier zones are mostly in pastures and forests. Farther eastward, in the Cantabrian Mountains and throughout the Spanish Pyrenees, rugged topography severely limits cropland. Some wheat, rye, and apples are grown, but the most important agricultural activity is summer sheep-grazing. The Vascongadas (Basque Provinces) and Santander area, along the north coast east of Asturias, is an area of commercialized, prosperous mixed farming, favored by a nearby large market. Crop and livestock emphases are similar to those of Galicia-Asturias, with wheat as a main rotation crop and beans generally growing in the same fields with corn, using the cornstalks as trellis support.

The rest of Spain may be broadly divided into two zones: (1) the large, semiarid interior (the extensively farmed dry-cereal, sheep-grazing heart of Spain, with only a few pockets of irrigation); and (2) the coastal belt of Mediterranean agriculture (Fig. 7–10).

The Meseta plus the steppic middle and upper Ebro Valley correspond roughly to the grain-grazing interior, a region covering over one-half of Spain. Wheat is the most widely grown crop, extending over huge tracts of Old and New Castile. Yields are low, averaging a fraction of those in rainy northwestern Europe. Barley replaces wheat in the drier, hotter parts of New Castile and in La Mancha. The great bulk of Spain's large sheep population is here, and the fine Merino wool is a major commercial product. Goats become more important in the south, where the vine and esparto grass also are cultivated, and pigs scavenge for mast in the oak forests of Extremadura. The mountain ranges are principally used for summer pasture, with some barley and oats on the lower slopes. The restricted irrigated strips are mainly along the Tajo, Guadiana, Ebro, and Duero rivers. Strenuous hydraulic efforts are afoot on those and other streams to increase irrigated acreage, e.g., in the Badajoz region.

The coastal belt of Mediterranean agriculture could in reality better be called a series of agricultural zones, each quite distinctive in its individual characteristics. But they are all, nonetheless, geared to the limitations and advantages of the dry-summer subtropical climate, specializing in heat-loving, drought-resistant crops (mostly tree and vine), winter grains, and a vast variety of valuable irrigated crops. Per-acre yields in this region are often prodigious. Most of Spain's olives and olive oil, in which she leads the world, come from this region, as do all the oranges and other citrus fruit. Spain is the world's number one exporter of oranges, and it is a profitable endeavor in spite of the frost danger, which is more severe here than in any major citrus area. The principal citrus zone is the Levante (the

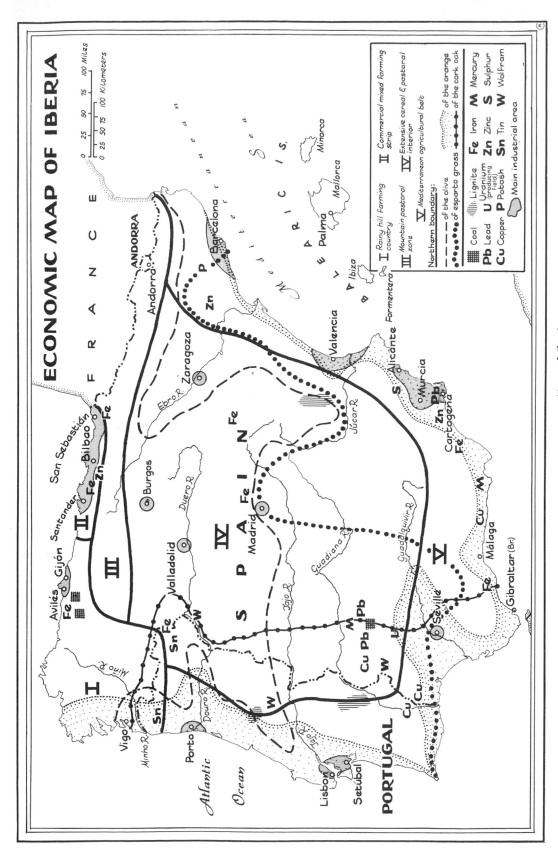

Fig. 7-10. Economic Map of Iberia.

coastal area around Valencia). Secondary areas of production are found all along the coast south and west of this main zone virtually up to the Portuguese border. Olives, though widespread, are principally concentrated in Andalucia. Vineyards too, are a ubiquitous feature of the Spanish Mediterranean landscape; the sections north of Almería are the biggest grape producers. Spain is the world's third-largest wine-producing nation, turning out about half as much as Italy or France. Málaga is famous for its export of fine table grapes. Tobacco and, especially, cotton are increasing.

The excellent systems of irrigation introduced by the Moors have been retained, with much expansion and improvement. Well over half of Spain's irrigated acreage lies in favored tracts of the coastal belt of Mediterranean agriculture. The *huertas* and *vegas* of eastern and southeastern Spain are proverbial for their intensive horticultural practices, which yield bountiful harvests of a wide variety of crops. Rice, an atypical crop in Mediterranea, is intensively cultivated in the lower Ebro Valley, the Guadalquivir Marismas, and in the Valencian Plain, with yields per acre registering the highest in the world.

Forestry and fishing. Much of the natural forest vegetation has been cut away over the centuries, so that less than one-tenth of Spain is now in woodland. Starting in the immediate post-Civil War period the government launched a reforestation program which has recently been intensified, with the cooperation and assistance of FAO. Spain, in fact, has a more vigorous forestry program than any other Mediterranean country and soon hopes to be self-sufficient in most forest products. Cork, of which Spain produces about one-quarter of the world's total, is an important export.

Fishing is underdeveloped for a country with such a long coastline. It is concentrated mainly along the northern and northwestern coasts. Though much shorter than the Mediterranean coast, Spain's Atlantic waters contribute about three-quarters of its fish catch. Most of the fishing is done near the coast. The fleet is old and in need of modernization, which, with increased efficiency and the possibilities offered by more deep-sea activities, could materially increase the catch. The principal varieties are sardines, tuna, and anchovies; much is canned and salted for export.

Mining and power production. Spain has a fairly extensive and varied mineral endowment, certainly the best in Southern Europe (Fig. 7–10). Nevertheless, the reserves of major metallurgical and power minerals are less than adequate for a country hoping to make rapid strides in industry. The iron ore and coal deposits near Bilbao-Santander and in Asturias have contributed to the location of the iron and steel industry there. Some other scattered deposits of these minerals are tapped in the east and south. Production of both is stagnant, however, and high-quality ores are imported to mix with lower domestic grades. Imported petroleum is steadily replacing coal as Spain's chief energizer. Spain's mercury deposits at Almadén and sulfur pyrites near Huelva are both very large. Other minerals include wolfram, zinc, copper, lead, and potash. Mineral production doubled between 1948 and 1962, but has been hampered by some of the same nagging problems that have nettled Britain, France, and other European countries in fairly recent times: depletion of some deposits, labor disputes, rising wages, and obsolete equipment and methods.

Hydroelectric output is modest. Power-short Spain is energetically harnessing this energy source, but the potential is limited and natural conditions frequently make it expensive. Unfortunately the Spanish side of the Pyrenees, Spain's major hydroelectric source, is much drier than the French side, and this combines with the marked seasonality of flow both there and throughout most of Spain to hinder hydroelectric development. Recognizing that the limited electrical capacity was a major bottleneck in economic expansion, Spain has increased it very rapidly in the past decade. Many of the newer plants are thermal. The output of electricity in 1968 was nearly double that of 1962.

Industry. Although Spain ranks among the least important industrial nations of Europe, the manufacturing sector, with encouragement and heavy investment by the government, has been vigorously expanding. Somewhat more than one-quarter of the labor force is in industry now.

Spain has three principal industrial zones: the Basque coast and Santander, Barcelona and its environs, and Madrid. The first, with Bilbao the outstanding center, is principally a heavy industrial region where iron and steel and shipbuilding are important. Barcelona is the country's most important and diversified manufacturing center and its major port and commercial city, with a long tradition in these activities. Its location has encouraged close ties with the rest of Europe. It has considerable water power nearby and some minerals, and the Catalans constitute a large market and a disciplined, skilled labor force. Metallurgical and engineering industries, chemicals, textiles, printing and publishing, and food processing are well represented in the industrial mix of the Barcelona region. Madrid's importance as an industrial center is recent, and it continues to expand rapidly.

The Murcia-Cartagena district, Valencia, Zaragoza, and, lately, Seville, Valladolid and Burgos qualify as secondary industrial zones (Fig. 7–10). A large state-built iron and steel complex at Avilés was opened a few years ago. The government has tried with some success to achieve a greater dispersal of industry in the last several years.

Spain still feels it must protect domestic industry, but it is struggling to become competitive in European and world markets for industrial goods. Much improvement in many directions has been made, but Spain was so far behind that the nation's manufacturers have not had sufficient time to overcome long standing multiple disadvantages.

Transportation and communications. The transportation system has proved a serious problem to economic growth. The traditional emphasis on regional self-sufficiency and the low standard of living have discouraged improvement of the rail and road networks, with the long distances and rough terrain they have to cover. More than one-fourth of the funds in the First Economic and Social Development Plan (1964–67) were devoted to modernizing roads and railroads, through dieselization, purchase of new rolling stock, track renewal, and highway construction and improvement. The rail system is state-owned.

Spain has some 300 ports, though the dozen largest account for well over three-fifths of the tonnage handled. Foreign seaborne trade is well developed, and Spain has a medium-sized merchant fleet (2,318,000 GRT in 1967). Though most vessels are old, the rate of replacement, largely through domestic shipbuilding, has quickened. Coastal shipping, too, is quite important, partly due to the inadequacy of land transport.

Considerable progress has been made in modernizing airport and air transport facilities, spurred on especially by demands of tourism. The two airlines–Aviaco and Iberia –are state-owned.

Foreign trade. Principal among Spain's exports are raw agricultural products and beverages, though processed foods and manufactured items are gaining, an indication of the advancing maturity and sophistication of the Spanish economy. Machinery and raw materials form a large share of the total imports, fuels alone amounting to a sixth. Fortunately, much of the steep rise in imports which has caused the worrisome trade imbalances in the past ten years is related to the large influx of capital goods required by the pronounced growth of Spanish industrial capacity. The long-range outlook therefore is brighter than current figures would seem to indicate. Tourism and remittances from Spanish nationals working abroad continue to offset much of the negative trade balance.

Tourism. The increase in foreign tourists in Spain has been remarkable. From a paltry intake from tourism of $246 million in 1960, the annual level rose to nearly one and a quarter billion dollars in 1967. The principal tourist centers are the Costa Brava, Barcelona, the Costa del Sol, Madrid, Toledo, San Sebastián, and the colorful Andalucian cities of Seville, Granada, and Córdoba. The Balearics, particularly Mallorca, also are popular tourist attractions. The millions of visitors who come to Spain each year already have had, aside from their economic contribution, a strong liberalizing effect on Spanish thinking and mores, especially among the young. The introduction to and identification with foreign ideas and customs has subtly but very definitely increased pressures for more rapid changes in traditionalist, conservative, and somewhat xenophobic Spain. These pressures may well cause combustible tensions if the government and church leaders fail to respond to them, but they will utimately serve a most useful catalytic purpose in drawing the country away from its introspective past.

*   *   *

Spain's relations with the European Community are a crucial question. Repeatedly it has applied for associate membership, and Spain's long-range aim seems clearly to focus on a closer meshing, in one form or another, of its economy into a European supranational structure. More than a third of the country's foreign trade is carried on with the Common Market countries, and exclusion limits expanded opportunities.

Spain finds itself in a period of great flux. This transitional nature of contemporary Spain extends to its government, after more than thirty years of strong-man rule by the Caudillo, to its economy, and to its relations with its European neighbors. Spain's future directions are uncertain, but signs point promisingly toward a progressive metamorphosis that will move the nation toward a new posture. The withdrawn, autocratic, and backward Spain of the past four centuries appears to be fading rapidly.

PORTUGAL

Portugal is a roughly rectangular-shaped country occupying the southern three-quarters of the west coast of Iberia, stretching through some 300 miles of latitude and extending on the average about 100 miles inland from the coast. It is about the size of Austria and slightly more than one-sixth the area of Spain. Its long Atlantic coastline has many natural harbors, including Lisbon, one of the world's finest. Portugal administers the Atlantic islands of Madeira and the Azores as a part of the metropole.

Historical Background

Maritime tradition. Portugal has an ancient and ingrained maritime tradition. No point in the interior is more than about 130 miles from the coast, and the sea has always been truly the focal feature in Portuguese history, as can be seen in its colonial and maritime activities and its extra-Iberian alliances. The early Phoenicians had ports on Portuguese coasts, and Portuguese fishermen and traders roamed far and wide long before the age of the conquistadores. It was Prince Henry the Navigator who launched a brilliant chapter in Portuguese exploration and conquest abroad. Vasco da Gama, Bartholomeu Dias, and Cabral are names now legendary in world history. The Treaty of Tordesillas assigned in 1494 vast New World land to Portugal. Brazil, its giant colony in the New World, broke away early in the nineteenth century, but Portugal still maintains large African holdings. It is ironic that perhaps the weakest of all the mother countries in the Age of Colonialism has almost single-handedly extended that age beyond its logical historical life. Portugal's African colonies are the last of the great European empires.

Relations with Spain. The Spanish-Portuguese border is one of the oldest and most stable in all Europe. Despite periodic ambitions of Spain—even as recent as in the early Franco days—to dominate the whole Iberian peninsula, Portugal has steadfastly maintained its independence since the *Reconquista*, except for a brief period. Only from 1580 to 1640 did Spain manage, due to Portugal's weakness at having expended so much energy overseas in acquiring territory, to exert nominal control over Portuguese soil. Credit for Portugal's persistent success in warding off the designs of a larger and more powerful neighbor is due partly to a long standing alliance with Britain, which, in her own interests, has consistently acted as protector. Britain went so far as to defend and occupy Lisbon during the Napoleonic Wars. The two Iberian countries have worked together on mutually beneficial projects and maintained cordial relations during the past two decades. Both countries seem to realize that they share much in common besides a long border and appear to want to preserve an atmosphere of harmony.

All things considered, Portugal's resources, square mile for square mile, are superior to those of Spain. The Portuguese on the whole are better favored climatically. Moderating Atlantic influences dominate almost two-thirds of the country, giving it a distinctly higher proportion of humid lands. Difficult topography is also less pervasive a problem in Portugal than in Spain. Furthermore, its more compact size, without the long, barren, sparsely populated stretches, and the proximity of the coast throughout have favored easier communications and, therefore, promoted national unity. The stronger orientation to and dependence on the sea surely counts as a fundamental contrast to its larger neighbor. Finally, Portugal, with its Atlantic facade, is, unlike Spain, actually only a peripheral Mediterranean nation. Historically its Atlantic ties and preoccupations have borne out this important locational difference.

Population

Portugal, with 9,500,000 people (1968), has a population density of about 270 per square mile, much greater than that of Spain. Including the Atlantic islands, it is administratively divided into 22 districts. A tri-angular section formed by the coast and a line drawn from the northernmost tip of Portugal, where the Miño (Portuguese: Minho) River leaves Spain and begins to separate Spain from Portugal, to the source of the Zêzere River, just southwest of Guarda, and thence to the sea down the Zêzere and Tagus rivers, would encompass almost all of the more densely settled parts of Portugal. Appended to this area should be the Setúbal peninsula, which includes Lisbon's across-river suburbs and the port city of Setúbal. The rest of the country—about two-thirds of its area—comprises the more rugged and interior parts of the northern half and the much drier area south and east of the Tagus. The population is sparse, almost everywhere less than 130 people per square mile, and in sizeable portions of Alentejo density dips below sixty. The principal exception is in the extreme south, where there is a rather heavy concentration of towns and dispersed rural settlements along the Algarve coast.

Though fundamentally of Mediterranean stock, the Portuguese are a blend, with a Celtic-Iberian infusion in the North and Moorish elements absorbed in the South. This admixture has been cited as one explanation for the liberal, racially unsegregated attitude in the Portuguese colonies. The Portuguese language—much akin to Galician—is universal, as is the Roman Catholic faith. It is rare indeed to find such complete nationwide uniformity of these two vital cultural features. There are no distinct regional or other minority groups of any consequence, and the absence of pressures from militant minorities has greatly abetted the achievement of national unity and consensus.

Portugal's birth rate (22.9) is the highest in Europe, except for Iceland and Albania. With a relatively low death rate (10.1), the country has thus a high rate of natural population increase. Fortunately, heavy emigration keeps the actual rate of increase to less than 1 per cent per annum. But the possible loss of the colonies, which absorb considerable numbers, and any reduction in demand for Portuguese workers abroad, could saddle the nation with a population problem of perhaps serious proportions, assuming the high birth rate continues.

The Regions of Portugal

The North (Fig. 7–11) is often called "Atlantic" Portugal, the South "Mediterranean," and the region in between is transitional in character. Though oversimplified and not entirely accurate, these labels are useful and appropriate. At the same time, Portugal is an extremely varied nation for its size, and the amplitude of even its intraregional contrasts, especially in the North, should be recognized.

The North. This region is set off from the others by the southern edge of the most pronounced physical boundary in this little country—the Serra da Estrela. Included in the North are the old historical regions of Minho, Trás-os-Montes, and Beira. The North is reminiscent of bordering Galicia, and hence has more similarities to northwestern than to Mediterranean Europe. Rainfall from moist Atlantic winds is much heavier than farther south, averaging more than thirty inches. About a third of the North gets more than sixty inches of precipitation annually. Thus, it has a predominantly green landscape, with fine year-round pastures and considerable forested tracts, much of which provides good quality timber. Snow covers the high mountain slopes in winter. This is by far the most rugged and hilly region of Portugal. About half of the North is above 1,600 feet. A bocage landscape prevails in the intensively cultivated lowlands. Plots are generally small. Porto, the country's second largest city, is the cultural and commercial hub of northern Portugal. Its urban agglomeration embraces a half million people and, with its port at Leixoes, controls most of the important wine export trade of Portugal, especially that of port wines. Historically prominent Braga, capital of Minho, and Aveiro, on the coast, are the only other towns of more than strictly local importance.

The Center. This transitional zone includes Estremadura, the lower Tajo Valley (Ribatejo), and Upper (Alto) Alentejo. Populous Estremadura (not to be confused with the Spanish region of the same name) occupies a rather broad coastal plain south of the Mondego River, where rainfull rapidly diminishes southward, and the extended drought of Mediterranean summers becomes marked. Vegetation, too, exhibits a very mixed character, with the olive, cork oak, and more drought-resistant vine strains appearing. Wheat, the principal cereal of the South and Center, overlaps with corn, a northern specialty. House types and farm structures change as well, and the dual occupation fishermen-farmers of the northern coast give way to non-farming fisherfolk at Peniche and other smaller centers along the central shore north of Lisbon. Estremadura's capital is also Portugal's, and it is by far the country's largest city. Lisbon, with well over a million people, counting its suburbs, dominates the life of the Center much as Porto does the North.

Ribatejo lies astride the structural trough of the lower Tajo River. The same transitional qualities prevail here, even population density. The population on the lands of the right bank is more than twice as dense as across the river. Ribatejo merges in the east with Lower Beira and Upper Alentejo, a sparsely populated area of higher elevation and more dissected mountain and plateau topography which includes the western extensions of the Spanish Meseta and the Serra de Mamade.

The South. Lower (Baixo) Alentejo and Algarve have a *bona fide* dry-summer subtropical climate, and its effects are clearly evident in the landscapes and agricultural types. Relief is much more subdued than in the North. Western Alentejo is essentially plainsland, including the Sado River Valley. Farther east are the low, rolling, and rather monotonous Alentejo plateaus, a region of mostly poor soils and inferior natural vegetation. Population density is low throughout,

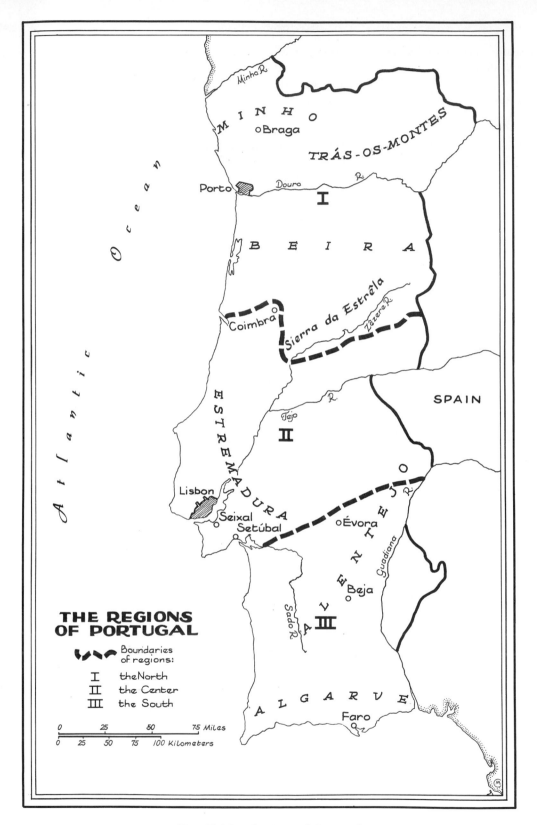

Fig. 7–11. Regions of Portugal.

being less than twenty per square mile on much of the poorer lands. The Alentejanos tend to be somewhat aloof and saturnine, and are a bit removed from the mainstream of Portuguese life. Coastal Alentejo is no more thriving than the interior and is in fact distinctive in maritime Portugal for being quite undeveloped. Of the towns, none of them large, Évora and Beja are the most important.

Algarve—the south coast of Portugal—is very different from Alentejo. Effectively cut off from the latter by the Monchique and Caldeirão Mountains, it is sheltered from northern influences and enjoys a subtropical climate similar to Spain's Costa del Sol. Rainfall is scant in this sun-drenched land, less than twenty inches. Irrigation, however, redeems some sizeable tracts. Algarve's south coast is fairly densely populated. It has a number of small but busy ports, of which the largest is Faro, the regional capital. The large population certainly cannot be ascribed to superior resources; water is scarce, harbors poor and troubled by silting, and minerals absent. It is instead no doubt related to the traditional careful management of what meager resources there are. Algarve is the most distinctive part of Portugal as well as the most isolated. It is also by far the most influenced by Arabic ways, as evidenced by its Moorish architecture, terraced slopes, the carefully tended and very old irrigation system, and the many place names derived from the Arabic (Algarve itself, for example). Algarvios speak a colorful dialect and maintain an individualistic way of life. Better and more direct road connections linking Portugal's South to Lisbon and the Center will soon be completed. This greatly improved access will no doubt result in major economic and other changes in Algarve.

Present Economic Life

Agriculture and forestry. Agriculture, the mainstay of the Portuguese economy, employs two-fifths of the working population. Unfortunately, this primary activity is quite inefficient. Efforts toward upgrading it have been timid and slow, and relatively backward techniques persist. Yields per acre are very low in most of the southern two-thirds of the country. Production was stagnant from 1954 through the early 1960's, and has increased very slowly since then. Many problems exist and most do not lend themselves to easy solutions. Land fragmentation and *minifundia* in the North and undercultivation and tenancy in the South prevail. A low level of mechanization, even for Southern Europe, is a handicap. Livestock production has risen only modestly, and irrigation has spread slowly. Fertilizers are scarce and expensive, and their use is consequently restricted.

In the North a very distinctive type of farming is practiced. The lowlands are very heavily populated, and farms are small, rarely exceeding ten acres. Cultivation is as intensive as almost anywhere in Europe. Careful soil management, admirably adapted livestock practices, ample rainfall, and widespread irrigation provide yields far above the national average. Corn, rye, cabbage, potatoes, beans, apples, and other vegetables and fruit are important crops. Trellised vines, many of them on terraced, south-facing slopes in the Douro Valley, produce large quantities of wine grapes. Portugal is the world's fourth-largest wine-producing country, and the North is its major region. Port wine and *vinho verde,* a light, bubbling wine, are important exports. Hills and mountains are used for pasturage. Cattle are numerous, and dairy products are produced in surplus.

Farther south the Mediterranean crops become dominant. Olives are important throughout the Center and South, especially in Ribatejo and eastern Alentejo. Wheat is widely grown, too, in "Mediterranean" Portugal. Fallowing is common, reducing production. Sheep graze the fallow lands and the poor slopes, and large numbers of pigs feed on the mast of oak forests which cover much of the Center and South. Irrigated areas, particularly in Ribatejo, produce many horticultural crops and cereals, including rice. The latter has also been introduced successfully along the lower courses of the Mondego, Tajo, and Sado rivers and around Aveiro. Market gardening flourishes near Lisbon and Setúbal. Algarve has its typical tree crops (figs, almonds, olives, and a great variety of fruits), beautifully cared-for terraced slopes, and green, garden-like, irrigated *hortas*.

Far less attention has been devoted to revitalizing Portugal's lagging agriculture than to other parts of the economy, though this oversight is being slowly corrected. The Portuguese import foodstuffs which they could themselves supply, e.g., cereals, dried fish, meat, and butter. There is a need for basic reforms in the agrarian structure which would enforce land regroupment in the North and destroy the privileged status of large property owners in the South. The Salazar government showed little inclination to pursue these goals, preferring to perpetuate the status quo. Without bold steps, however, many problems of agricultural advancement must remain intractable.

Forestry is rather important in Portugal, at least in two categories. It produces about one-half the world's cork, the raw bark and cork products constituting a leading export. Pines covering more than two million acres, largely of coastal dunes, make Portugal Europe's second producer, after France, of naval stores, which are also exported. About one-fourth of the country is forested; the vast bulk of the better quality timber is in the hilly parts of the rainer North. A modest reforestation program is operative.

Fishing. Portuguese fishermen roam widely and have a long history. The yearly catch is more than double that of Italy, in tonnage, and provides a vital part of the otherwise protein-poor Portuguese diet. Canned sardines, anchovies, and tuna are important exports. There are many fishing ports, among the principal ones being Lisbon, Setúbal, Peniche, Figuera da Foz, and Leixoes-Porto.

Mining and industry. Portugal is weak in the minerals basic to industry, and despite a variety of subsidiary ones, mining plays a small part in the economy. A small coal output is supplemented by large imports of coal and petroleum. Wolframite (tungsten) and tin from the northeast have a ready market; chromite also is mined there (Fig. 7–10). Manganese, sulfur, pyrites, and some copper are mined in Alentejo. High transportation costs from their isolated regions of occurrence hamper mineral exploitaton, as does the small size of most of the deposits.

Aware that a shortage of electricity was a foremost bottleneck in expanding the economy, the Portuguese government, starting in the early 1950's, has allocated large sums of money to increasing the electrical capacity and extending the grid, with great success. Most of this has been in the hydro sector, where the potential is considerable, though the seasonal flow complicates development. The Upper Douro and Zêzere rivers are the chief sites of hydroelectric installations. As by-products, considerable extensions of irrigated land are certain from these projects, and there is the possibility, with nearby power soon to be available, of tapping the large iron ore deposits near the Douro's Bemposta Dam. The country's kilowatt-hour production in 1970 is expected to be nearly double the 1963 figure.

Portugal is not a leading industrial nation. Nevertheless, strides in industrialization over the past twenty years are impressive, and there is no question that this sector of the economy is the most dynamic. Industry already contributes about one-half of the gross domestic product, and its share of exports has grown from one-third in the early 1950's to nearly two-thirds at present.

Lisbon and Porto are the two outstanding industrial centers. Profiting from its magnificent harbor on the deep Tagus estuary and its location near major shipping lanes passing Europe's southwest tip, Lisbon is an important port of call and entrepôt. Its primary commercial function has stimulated the growth of diversified manufacturing.

Chemicals, processing of a wide variety of domestic and colonial goods, and fertilizers are some of the best developed industrial categories. A new and very modern shipyard has been built on Lisbon's shore.

Porto and its suburbs concentrate on cotton textiles, now a major export, and processing of foodstuffs, especially fish, wine, fruits, and vegetables. A small metal-working industry may be the nucleus of much future expansion in that activity.

Many other smaller cities (the next-largest, Coimbra, is less than one-sixth the size of Porto) have small-scale light industry producing many consumer items and processing local farm and forest produce.

Heavy industry is not well developed, though the blast furnace and steel mill at Seixal, completed in 1961 and since expanded, supply about half of the country's iron and steel needs. The two petroleum refineries, at Lisbon and Porto, have a capacity of about 4 million tons annually (1969 estimate). With generous tariff concessions and material assistance from its European Free Trade Association (EFTA) partners, Portugal is gearing its industries away from traditional lines and toward those which are more demanding of capital, skilled labor, technology, and modern plant equipment, e.g., chemicals, petrochemicals, metal fabrication, vehicle assembly, and more complete processing of forest products.

Industry will no doubt continue to be the focus of attention in the Portuguese economy. The present Fourth Development Plan (1968–1973) envisages a rate of growth for the over-all economy of six and one-half per cent per year, with industry leading the way with a proposed 9 per cent yearly gain. Perhaps these high figures are not unrealistic, since some already have been exceeded.

Transportation. A sustained drive has been made in the past twenty-five years to modernize the transportation system. The road network, the outmoded railroads and major port facilities have been much improved. Transportation costs are high and continue to constitute a deterrent to economic progress both domestically and in the export field. Portuguese railroads use the broad gauge of the Spanish system, to which they are linked at several points. The recently opened (August, 1966) Salazar bridge, handling both rail and road traffic, is Europe's longest. It connects Lisbon with the south bank of the Tajo and its hinterland beyond and, though economically perhaps premature, will stand the South in good stead in the future. Furthermore, it symbolizes Portugal's determination to move ahead.

The Portuguese merchant marine is modest in size (about 650,000 GRT), roughly one-third the size of Spain's.

Foreign trade. Typical of Southern Europe, Portuguese imports exceed exports by a wide margin. Traditional export items of most importance are canned fish, wine, cork and other forest products, and a few minerals. Manufactured goods occupy an increasing share of the country's exports, though most are types which require relatively little transformation. Raw materials, fuels and lubricants account for two-fifths of the imports; food, beverages, and tobacco about one-tenth, and manufactured goods the other half.

Nearly two million tourists visited Portugal in 1966 and spent nearly one-quarter of a billion dollars worth of badly needed foreign currency. Emigrant remittances, well over half that figure, help further in offsetting the large trade deficit.

The Atlantic Islands. Madeira is an island group off the coast of Morocco and about 650 miles southwest of Lisbon. Only the two main islands, Madeira and Porto Santo, are inhabited. Many subtropical products, such as sugar and bananas and other fruits, are produced. Madeira exports the famous wine of that name. Tourism is well developed, as is fishing. The main island exports embroidered fabrics, wicker furniture, and baskets.

The Azores, about 900 miles out in the Atlantic west of Lisbon, include numerous very small and densely settled islands. They, too, produce a variety of frost-sensitive crops, with pineapples of particular importance. A spectacularly picturesque setting has encouraged the tourist trade. In addition they have served as an important stop for trans-Atlantic sea and air traffic.

The colonies. Angola and Mozambique are the chief overseas holdings, their total area dwarfing the mother country. Portugal vigorously defends its colonial policies and has persisted stubbornly in maintaining firm control, despite the militant pressures of world opinion and guerrilla fighting in Angola. The colonies have furnished a good market for products of the metropole and have contributed many raw materials. But the preoccupation of Portugal with them and the strain of holding on to them—in recent years nearly 40 per cent of the government budget has gone into defense—may easily produce telling political and economic effects which would turn Portugal's empire into a distinct liability.

The long, stable Salazar era (1928–1968) has ended too recently to predict future government policy on colonial and other matters, though swift or sweeping divergence from the predictable attitudes and actions of the immediate past seems unlikely. There is now certainly greater hope for more dynamic leadership in Portugal.

ITALY

Italy is about three-fifths the size of Spain and is seventh in size in Europe outside the Soviet Union. It ranks third in population, with 52,800,000 people (1968). Its long, familiar boot-like peninsula is washed by the Adriatic, Ionian, Tyrrhenian, and Ligurian seas, all, of course, branches of the Mediterranean. Italy's maximum latitudinal extent is roughly 750 miles, and the peninsula's average longitudinal spread is about 125 miles. The large islands of Sicily and Sardinia are Italian, as are many small islands offshore, only a few of which have more than a handful of people. Capri, Ischia, Giglio, Elba, and the Eolie (Lipari) Islands are the main

ones. Italy is divided into twenty *regioni* (regions), including the five autonomous regions, for administrative purposes.

The Italian mainland embraces two minuscule political units: Vatican City and the Republic of San Marino. The former is the smallest state in the world, comprising about one-fifth of a square mile. Wholly in the center of Rome, on the Tiber's right bank, Vatican City is the administrative and spiritual center of the Roman Catholic Church, the site of St. Peter's Basilica, and a major attraction for tourists and pilgrims. San Marino (23 sq. mi., population 17,000) lies nestled in the Apennine foothills of northeastern Italy, not far from the Adriatic Coast. A feudal remnant, it is the last survivor, largely due to its insignificance and isolation, of the many separate states that once made up what is today called Italy.

Development of the Italian Nation

The country's extremely long coastline and its central position have throughout history made it a pre-eminent Mediterranean land. The sea is an inescapable feature of Italian geography. True, there are long stretches of coastline both on the Adriatic and Tyrrhenian which are straight and nearly harborless, as well as numerous fertile interior basins which sustain a more or less self-contained life. Also, the densely settled Po Valley and the northern Alpine fringe are not markedly oriented to the sea. Nevertheless, Italy as a whole is strongly influenced by its peninsular and insular character. Maritime activities have always been important and still are today. Italy has Europe's fourth-largest merchant fleet; shipbuilding is an important industry; and fishing is widespread. The "Mare Nostrum" doctrine of the Fascist era, revived and reworked from Roman times, may have been politically warped and as a practical matter impossible, but geographically no country can better qualify as Mediterranean, except perhaps Cyprus or Malta.

Italy as a state is only a century old. During most of its history, what is today the

Italian nation was broken up into many and frequently fluctuating political units. This condition, in fact, persisted well into the last half of the nineteenth century and has had a profound effect on Italy's present-day cultural diversity. Certainly the long, narrow shape of the peninsula and its mountainous nature contributed to the political fragmentation. The ancient historical regions, many of them at one time petty kingdoms, duchies, or otherwise independent units, have a fascinating and chequered history. The drive for unifying the peninsula persisted after its break-up in post-Roman times, emanating first from one region, then another. Tuscany, Venetia, Liguria, and finally Piedmont rose to positions of great power and influence.

The Roman era. Despite the numerous geographical and political stumbling blocks to unification, a fair degree of historical, cultural, and linguistic cohesion came early. This was one of the major contributions of the Romans, who accomplished the first political unification of Italy (and, in fact, the only political unification of the entire Mediterranean region!). The remarkable Roman facility for assimilating culturally diverse peoples, for sharing the privileges of Romans with the vanquished, and for embracing the enemy on terms of equality, worked nowhere better than in the Italian homeland. Etruscans, Ligurians, Sards, Greeks, Gauls, Carthaginians—each with their own tongues— were all incorporated by early Rome. Within two centuries after 390 B.C., when Latium was weak and Rome was a puny, strife-torn town on the edge of hostile Etruria, Romans had progressively extended their control from the Po Valley through Sicily. H. G. Wells says of early Rome: "She understood the value of allies; she could assimilate; abroad as at home she could in those days at least 'give and take' with a certain fairness and sanity. There lay the peculiar power of Rome . . . she succeeded where Athens . . . had conspicuously failed." [4] This remark-

ably achieved basis for cultural and linguistic unification which Rome bequeathed to Italy survived the decay and vicissitudes of later centuries.

The Renaissance and *Risorgimento*. In the fourteenth century, the stirrings of revolt against ignorance and intolerance launched the Renaissance, that glorious age of transition from medieval to modern times when Italian enlightenment and influence spread throughout the rest of Europe. Italy, it is important to recall, went into the Renaissance with a common written language which had been perfected and popularized by Dante, Petrarch and Boccaccio. The political history of this and the post-Renaissance period in Italy is very complex. Generally, though, the medieval city-states evolved into somewhat larger units. Foreign powers took advantage of the peninsula's continued splintered state, and post-medieval times saw a continuing struggle there involving Spain, France, and Austria. Nevertheless, the sizeable States of the Church, headed by the Pope and separating the north from the south, proved the most consistent and formidable obstacle to unification.

The French Revolution made a profound impression on Italian thinking, and shortly thereafter Napoleon's armies succeeded in welding together a large part of northern and central Italy. This brief period (1805–1815), in spite of the Congress of Vienna's subsequent reestablishment of a much divided, foreign-dominated Italy, greatly strengthened the notion of unity and independence. The Italian *Risorgimento* was prepared and gradually gained strength. Unification, engineered by Piedmont under the brilliant Cavour, was achieved by 1870. From that time until the end of the Fascist era in 1943, Italy was a constitutional monarchy. Since 1946 it has been a republic.

Italy after unification. The Italian state occupied in 1870 essentially the same area it does today. Nonetheless, there persisted, after unification, a preoccupation with the northern boundary, a concern, it might be

[4] H. G. Wells, *The Outline of History* (Garden City, N.Y.: Garden City Books, 1956): 340.

stated, that has not always been rational and constructive. The problem is that the linguistic, historical, and physiographic boundaries there nowhere coincided. The result was the Irredentist movement, born of the desire to unite all Italian-speaking areas. In the northwest the physiographic boundary of high Alpine ridges against France was maintained, sacrificing Savoy, historically a part of Italy, and Nice, linguistically Italian (1860). Some tiny districts were ceded to France in 1947, and the French-speaking Val d'Aosta was given restricted autonomy. The main struggle developed in the northeast. World War I brought Italy a boundary which, for strategic and economic reasons, was largely drawn through German-, Slovene-, or Croat-speaking areas. Italianization was pushed into the German-speaking Alto Adige (southern Tyrol) region. The emigration of Germans, agreed upon with Hitler, was only partially carried out. The peace treaty of 1946 left the area with Italy and provided for a restricted autonomy. After World War II, Italy had to yield to Yugoslavia her Dalmatian and Istrian acquisitions of 1919, among them cities such as Pola. Trieste, after a transitional period, was annexed to Italy in 1954.

Italian irredentism has also claimed Corsica and Malta. The first is Italian-speaking and belonged to Pisa and Genoa for several centuries until it was annexed by France in 1768. Today it is closely integrated with France. Malta belonged to Sicily only from the end of the eleventh to the beginning of the sixteenth century. It is now independent and rather intensely nationalistic. The Ionian Islands, where Italian is something of a second language, were a Venetian colony from the fourteenth through the eighteenth centuries, but are today firmly a part of Greece. Italian irredentism seems largely a thing of the past.

Population

Though the approximately 455 people per square mile are fewer than in West Germany and the United Kingdom, Italy is nonethe-less densely settled, the more so since about three-quarters of the country is either too hilly or climatically unsuited to any but the poorest agriculture. The chronic problem of overpopulation has for the last century led to sustained and heavy emigration, both to the rest of Europe and to many other parts of the world. The Italian birth rate (19.2) is no longer among the very highest in Europe, and the rate of population increase, counting migration, which still records a substantial net outflow annually, is only about .7 per cent per annum, somewhat less than the rate for Europe as a whole. This modest increase (it would take 100 years to double at that rate) is manageable for the present-day prospering Italian economy.

Although historical events did conspire to retard the political unity and independence of Italy, they did not succeed in undermining such powerful unifying traits as a common language, culture, and religion. All of these the Italians possessed. In addition, there was the pride in the heritage of ancient Rome in which even the illiterate peasant of today still glories. Italy, then, has a relatively homogeneous population, and the identification of the average citizen with the Italian nation and way of life is unusually marked. Though there are no minority problems of great magnitude, a few areas do exist where local feeling has run strong. In two of these the predominant language is not Italian: the Aosta Valley, where a French patois is spoken, and northern Alto Adige (South Tyrol), where a sizeable German-speaking population has militantly demonstrated for absorption into Austria or at least greater local authority. The granting of autonomous status by the Italian central government has not placated this minority, since the inclusion of Trentino in the autonomous region insured an overall Italian-speaking majority. Alto Adige remains a recurrent and disturbing regional problem. The Aosta Valley, Sicily, Sardinia, and, since 1963, Friuli-Venezia Giulia are the four other Italian autonomous regions. There are a few tiny enclaves in Sardinia and along the Ionian coast where Catalan and Albanian, respectively, are spoken, and many dialects and subdialects persist throughout the country. An Italian is likely to prefer speaking in his own dialect when in his home district. But almost everyone speaks and understands Italian as well, and it is no exaggeration to say that it is the established and nearly universal tongue. Religious unity is also impressive. More than 99 per cent of the Italian population professes Roman Catholicism, although this figure should not veil feelings of strong antagonism or indifference toward the Church.

Most of Italy's over fifty million people live in the densely settled North Italian Plain and in the scattered coastal plains and small upland basins of the peninsula, shunning for the most part the rugged Alps and the mountainous interior parts of central and southern Italy and the islands. There is, indeed, a strong correlation between topography and population density.

Traditionally an urban society, Italy has today an even larger percentage (48 per cent) of its population living in towns and cities. There are fifteen with over 200,000 people. Rome has again become the largest city of Italy, largely because of its political and religious functions. The four "million" cities are, in order of size, Rome, Milan, Naples and Turin, with Genoa very close to the million mark.

Present Economic Life

Italy's economic status in Europe and the world has fluctuated widely throughout the last two millennia. At the beginning of the Christian era the Roman homeland, mistress of the civilized world, was omnipotent and enjoyed unprecedented wealth and luxury. The softness of life in fact has been cited by many historians as a predominant factor in the decline of ancient Rome. Every manner of product flowed to Latium from the very corners of the then-known world. In modern times, as the power center shifted away from Mediterranea, and especially in the post-Industrial Revolution age, Italy has in a relative sense become quite disadvantaged and has had to be considered among the poorer lands of Europe.

Italy's handicaps to achieving economic progress in twentieth century terms have been formidable. Politically fragmented until a century ago, Italy was forced to divert considerable energy toward accomplishing unification and then to consolidating her territory and welding her disparate regions into a national whole. This was at a time when Britain and France, for instance, were profiting from a strong national consensus of long standing and concentrating on empire building, which brought them as its natural concomitant an enormously vitalizing and lucrative colonial trade. The pressure in Italy of a large and rapidly growing population in a limited area poorly endowed with agricultural resources has already been alluded to. In addition, there is the paucity of minerals and energy sources. Modern Italy has seemed virtually condemned to a permanently bleak economic future. Indeed, it was largely the "have-not nation" rationale which inspired the debacle of the fortunately short-lived Fascist period, ending in 1943, which brought great suffering and privation to the Italian people.

At the end of World War II, Italy lay, as did much of Europe, in frightful economic shambles. In 1945, industrial production was barely a quarter of its prewar level, and agricultural output was only a half. The transportation system was shattered and inflation was rife. It is against this recent background that the present economic life of Italy should be considered. The post-World War II period has seen not only the recovery of the Italian economy but, beginning in the late 1950's, the emergence of a sustained and unprecedented prosperity which is so remarkable that it has been popularly tagged the "Italian miracle." The Italian GNP per capita is now nearly two-thirds that of Britain and has been growing in recent years at a rate much higher than that in the United States or Scandinavia. This economic boom is a tribute to the inventiveness, diligence, and ingenuity of the people of this sparsely favored land.

The economy used to be mainly agricultural and heavily dependent on tourism. Though these two areas of economic activity are still very important, and in fact their contribution has increased in value, their relative place in the total economy has declined in the wake of rapid industrialization since World War II. This has produced an economic structure much more balanced among agriculture and other primary endeavors, manufacturing, and tertiary or service activities. As seen in the following table, the number of farmers continues to dwindle, while those in industry and services increase, an indication of the nation's progress toward a more advanced economy.

Breakdown of the Italian Labor Force
(per cent of total)

	1954	1960	1967
Agriculture	39.3	34.0	23.8
Industry	32.4	38.0	40.7
Services	28.3	31.0	35.5

SOURCE: Commercial Office of the Italian Embassy, *Italy: An Economic Profile* (Washington: 1963 and 1968).

dant hydroelectricity and skilled labor, is much more industrialized, has the most modern agriculture to be found in Southern Europe, and is hence much more prosperous. The poorer South is overpopulated and suffers chronically from high unemployment. It has, in fact, one of Europe's lowest standards of living and by and large has not shared proportionately in the enormous forward strides the national economy has made.

Although there are important social and cultural differences, it is in the economic field that the gap that divides the "two Italies" is most demonstrable. The Italian North has many attributes that give it perhaps more in common with its northwestern and central European neighbors, with whom it has strong commercial ties, than with its own compatriots in the South. More than three-quarters of the nation's manufacturing is carried on in the North, where highly organized agriculture boasts the highest per-acre yields and output per worker as well. By virtually every social and economic index, e.g., literacy rates, annual per capita income, consumer durables consumption, and use of inanimate energy, the South comes off badly in comparison with the North. The following table illustrates this point:

Italy's North and South: Some Comparisons

	Area (%)	Population (%) 1966	Net National Product (%) 1951	Net National Product (%) 1966	Net National Product, per capita (Italy = 100) 1966	Gross National Product, by Sector, 1966 (%) Agriculture, Forestry, and Fishing	Industry	Services
North	60	64	74.6	75.5	124	60.0	82.8	73.2
South, including islands	40	36	25.4	24.5	68	40.0	17.2	26.8
ITALY	100	100	100.0	100.0	100	100.0	100.0	100.0

Note: The South includes the regions of Calabria, Basilicata, Puglia, Campania, Abruzzi, Molise, Sicily, and Sardinia.

SOURCE: *Moneta e Credito* (Banca Nazionale del Lavoro), December, 1967; *Review of Economic Conditions in Italy* (Banco di Roma), July, 1968.

The "two Italies." A primary fact of Italian life—distinguishable in almost every phase of the country's geography—is the contrast between the North and the South. The North is rainier, cooler, and possesses Southern Europe's largest lowlands. It has abun-

Economic pressures coupled with lack of understanding of the fundamental problem of regional disparity have often led to much hard feeling and acrimonious debate. The Northerners have felt that they "pay the taxes while the South manages the government and loafs." The Southerners have been envious of the more abundantly endowed North, have coveted their wealth, and have resented their derogatory and often condescending attitude.

The postwar government, recognizing the staggering problem which the long-neglected South presented, began in 1950 an ambitious program of land reform and reclamation, plus other agricultural improvements—the Fund for the South (*Cassa per il Mezzogiorno*). Through the *Cassa*, the state has attempted to promote industry as well, through both direct action and subsidization of private investment. Some very considerable results have taken place. Manufacturing, for instance, has caught hold in parts of Sicily and around Naples, Bari, and Taranto.

But despite notable successes, the North-South gap continues to burden Italy and still probably constitutes its most arresting economic and social problem. Without the *Cassa per il Mezzogiorno*, that gap might well have widened so hopelessly as to be by now nearly irremediable. Nevertheless, the all too evident disparity clearly has not been erased.[5]

Agriculture. With more than 4,000,000 workers in farming, Italy is one of Europe's greatest agricultural nations. Indeed, in certain major crop categories it is outstanding. Tree crops, including the vine, and cereals, especially wheat, are of primary importance, attesting to the country's credentials as a Mediterranean land. Somewhat more than half (53 per cent) of Italy's total area is cropped,[6] a remarkably high figure, considering that only about a quarter is classed as plainsland and that there are large areas with poor agricultural climate and/or soils. Another 17 per cent is in permanent pasture, most of it poor quality rough grazings,

though some lush meadows in the Po Valley are very productive.

Farm size varies in Italy from very small to quite large, having to do mainly with the quality of the land and the system of land tenure. Fragmentation of small plots (*minifundia*) and the *latifundia* system, with its attendant evils, have been attacked with considerable success by government land reform programs,[7] particularly in the South. These programs, while aiming directly at the creation of more viable-sized farms, have also had the salutary effect of raising productivity by increasing the number of family-owned and -operated farms.

Compared to northwestern Europe, Italy's agriculture is still somewhat backward, though notable improvements have been registered since the early 1950's. Mechanization has proliferated, fertilizer consumption has markedly increased, seed selection is now more universally practiced, better crop rotations have been popularized, livestock quality has been upgraded, animal husbandry practices improved, and poultry raising has made great gains. Quality standardization and modern packaging are common now, and there are much better marketing facilities and channels, especially for export items.

Italian agriculture varies greatly from one region to another, as a result of the country's diverse geography, physical and human alike. Three major agricultural regions may be noted (Fig. 7–12): the Alpine Pasture Zone, the North Italian Plain with adjacent foothills, and the Peninsula-Islands Region of Mediterranean Farming.

1. THE ALPINE PASTURE ZONE. This is the rugged, sparsely populated mountain zone which encloses the North Italian Plain on its northern and western sides. Relief and altitude impose severe limits on agriculture, and only a small area of valley floors and lower slopes support crop farming

[5] For a fuller discussion of the "two Italies," see Gustav Schachter, *The Italian South: Economic Development in Mediterranean Europe* (New York: Random House, Inc., 1965): Chapter 1.

[6] This figure includes cultivated grasses and other animal feed crops as well as areas devoted to tree crops, including the vine.

[7] G. Barbero, *Land Reform in Italy, Achievements and Perspectives,* FAO Agricultural Studies, no. 53 (Rome: FAO, 1961).

Fig. 7–12. Agricultural Map of Italy.

Fig. 7–13. Terraced farming on the steep, but sunny, south-facing slopes of the Sugana Valley, in the Dolomitic Alps. Tobacco is on the lower ground. The vine predominates higher up. (H. Price.)

(mostly apples and other fruit, some vine) and cultivated grasses (Fig. 7–13). Pastures, including some lush high summer meadows above the tree line, provide the basis for the dominant agricultural type—cattle grazing.

2. THE NORTH ITALIAN PLAIN. Sometimes called the Po Valley or the Lombardy Plain, this area comprises only about one-seventh of Italy. Though more famous as Southern Europe's leading industrial zone, the North Italian Plain is also Italy's most productive and progressive agricultural region. A fine climate for agriculture (by far Italy's best) with ample rainfall during the long, hot growing season; flat plains topography; and abundant fertile alluvial soils are prime ad-

vantages. One of Europe's most extensive irrigation systems and excellent farm practices ensure reliable yields which are high even by European standards. More than a third of Italy's wheat crop is produced here, as is all the rice (Italy grows more than two-fifths of Europe's total), three-quarters of the corn and most of the sugar beets. Wine grapes and large amounts of other fruits and vegetables are also grown. A major share of the country's beef, pork, dairy and other live-stock products is produced in this thriving lowland and its adjacent Alpine and Apennine foothills.

3. PENINSULA-ISLANDS REGION OF MEDITERRANEAN FARMING. This region is much larger. A great variety of crops and methods

Fig. 7–14. A "sea" of winter wheat cloaks the Tuscan hills mid-way between Siena and Arezzo. The cereal is beginning to mature under warm, sunny, late May skies. (H. Price.)

of farming exists, but fundamental contrasts with the other two more homogeneous agricultural regions—one a mountainous zone, the other mainly a plain—are striking. There is a recurring pattern of non-contiguous, usually quite small coastal plains and upland basins cut off from one another by intervening hills and mountains. There are numerous fertile, densely settled lowlands where intensive horticulture dominates, e.g., the Naples Plain and much of the narrow coastal stretches of Sicily. The dry-summer subtropical climate prevails, and generally farm land is poorer and farming techniques more backward. Winter wheat and barley, much of it grown on hilly land (Fig. 7–14), the vine, and tree crops (olives, deciduous and citrus fruits, carobs, almonds and other nuts) are outstanding in the crop mix. Many vegetables, both for local consumption and for trade, are grown. Cattle are numerous in the northern part, especially in Tuscany, where

there is a prosperous beef industry. Sheep and goats are more important in the drier south.

Other primary activities. In Italy, as in the Mediterranean Basin generally, forestry ranks as a minor activity. Even so, it is somewhat more important than in the rest of Southern Europe, since there are more upland regions which receive ample rainfall. In a land so intensively cultivated and grazed since antiquity, even marginally arable stretches do not remain wooded. Forested land, therefore, is mostly confined to hills and mountains which are rainy enough to support tree growth: the Alps, the Central and Western Apennines, and the Calabrian uplands. Conifers predominate in the Alps, and mixed deciduous and Mediterranean evergreen woods in the Peninsula. Man and the goat share the blame for the destruction of much formerly forested land, a substantial part of which should have remained wooded. A sizeable amount of reforestation has been carried out, assisted by the government, even in parts of the North Italian Plain. Round-wood production has been decreasing slightly in recent years, and Italy has to import most of its needs. Much wood is cut for fuel in rural areas. The Alpine area contributes nearly half of Italy's forest products, Trentino-Alto Adige being the leading zone.

Fishing is of surprisingly little importance, considering the extremely long coastline. The mediocre fish resources of the Mediterranean and the distance from better Atlantic grounds are the chief causes. Italy has made some attempt to modernize the fishing fleet and finance expeditions to non-Mediterranean waters. The annual fish catch, while a vital supplement to the protein-short Italian diet, is quite modest and ranks far below that of Spain and Portugal. Italy is a large net importer of fish.

canic steam, at Lardarello, in Tuscany. The mineral fuel shortage has prodded Italy to develop her large water power resources, which are situated mostly in the rainy high Alpine zone in the North (Fig. 7–15). As a result, Italy leads the nations of Europe in installed hydroelectric capacity, though the potential for further development of this valuable, yet still only supplementary, power source is limited now. The share of hydro power in Italy's source of energy breakdown dropped from one-third in 1950 to about one-eighth in the late 1960's. It will no doubt continue to diminish in the future. Italy is experiencing the same trend toward increased dependence on petroleum and natural gas, mostly imported, that Western Europe as a whole has shown in the past two decades. The following table illustrates the market shift in energy source, as well as the rapid increase in total energy consumption:

Italian Energy Consumption

	1950	1962	1964	1966	1967
Breakdown, by source (percent rounded):					
Firewood	11	4	3	2	2
Coal and lignite	34	16	12	11	11
Natural gas	2	10	9	9	9
Crude oil	21	52	60	72	73
Hydro, geothermal and nuclear	33	19	16	5	5
Total (million tons of coal equivalent)	31	78	92	109	118

SOURCE: Ente Nazionale Idrocarburi, *Energy and Petroleum, 1964;* Economic Studies Division, Ente Nazionale Idrocarburi (Rome).

Italy is poor in most mineral and energy resources. There are some 100,000 miners, a mere .5 per cent of the labor force, scattered throughout many regions. There are only very modest deposits of coal and lignite and negligible quantities of non-fuel minerals except for sulphur and mercury, which are mined in some abundance (Fig. 7–15). Despite rapid gains in the production of both petroleum (mainly in southeastern Sicily and near Ravenna) and natural gas (mainly in the North Italian Plain), domestic production meets only a small fraction of demand. An unusual but very minor source of power is geothermal, i.e., the tapping of vol-

Italy does possess enough sources of the more common non-metallic minerals, e.g., sand, clays, limestone, and gravel, to supply amply the glass, pottery, brick, cement, and other building materials industries. Also one very fine and plentiful resource is building stone; Italian marble, mainly quarried near Carrara, Massa, and Verona, is famous for its quality and beauty.

Evidence that Italy feels keenly its poverty in natural resources can be seen in its foreign trade pattern. Coal and petroleum comprise more than 15 per cent of all its imports, by value. An additional one-fifth is industrial raw materials other than fuels.

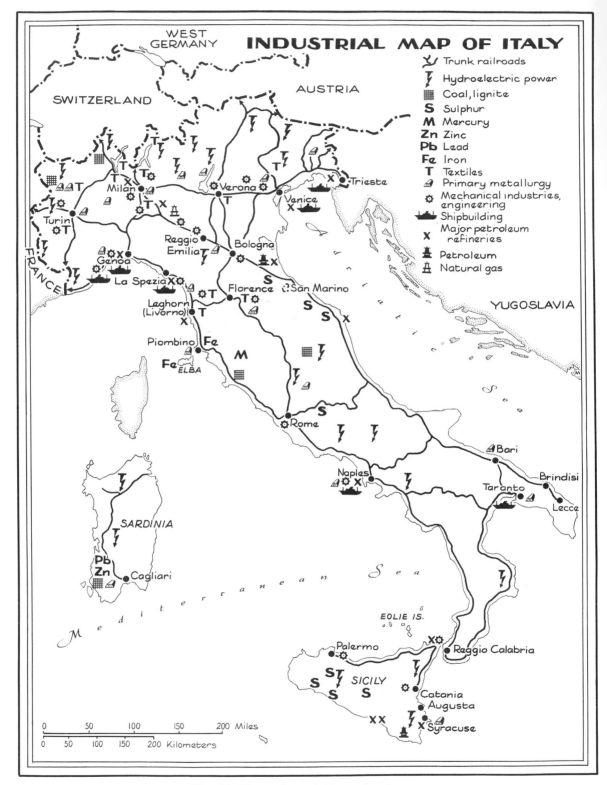

Fig. 7–15. Industrial Map of Italy.

Industry. Italy is Southern Europe's leading manufacturing nation by a wide margin and has, in fact, firmly entrenched itself as number four among Europe's industrial powers, after West Germany, Britain, and France. With two-fifths of the labor force in manufacturing, the industrial sector has paced the economy. Industrial production rose by a brisk eight and one-half per cent per annum in the 1950's and by nearly 9 per cent per annum from 1960–66. Especially important in assessing the role of industry in stimulating the general advance of the economy is the marked rise in the productivity of industrial workers. In the decade 1953–63, industrial production increased two and a half times, while the labor force employed in manufacturing grew by only one-third. By the late 1960's, manufactures accounted for nine-tenths of Italy's export earnings.

Manufacturing in Italy is markedly concentrated in the North Italian Plain (Fig. 7–15), especially the western part, using the port of Genoa. The Milan-Turin-Genoa triangle, including the many satellite cities of these three metropolises, is the focus of a preponderant share of the country's industrial might. Heavy industry, including iron and steel and shipbuilding, is centered mainly in and around Genoa, benefiting from cheap tidewater transportation. But manufacturing establishments are spread throughout the populous and prosperous western Po Valley, the largest manufacturing district in the entire Mediterranean Basin. Textiles, refined metals, metal fabrication, machinery of all sorts, vehicles, and electrical equipment are outstanding in what is a very diversified industrial complex. Nearly half of Italy's large oil refining capacity (first in Europe) is in the North Italian Plain. Milan, whose metropolitan area includes more than two million people, commands an excellent focal position with transport connections to both other Italian regions and Central and Western Europe. It employs more industrial workers than any other Italian city. Turin, historic Piedmont's proud capital, is the

home of FIAT, giant of the Italian automotive industry. Food processing industries, supplied by the rich and varied local harvests of Italy's largest plain, are also well established. The eastern Po Valley is serviced by the port of Venice-Porto Marghera, which, with nearby Mestre, comprises an important industrial zone. There is a string of smaller industrial cities near the southern edge of the eastern Val Padana (Po Valley): Reggio Emilia, Modena, Bologna, Ravenna, and Forlì, all of which are specialized to some degree in particular types of manufacturing.

There are a number of important industrial centers in peninsular Italy and the islands (Fig. 7–15). They include: La Spezia-Massa, Leghorn (Livorno), Spoleto-Rieti, Ancona, Rome's environs, Naples, Foggia, Bari, Taranto, and Syracuse-Augusta-Catania. Sicily's northeastern and southeastern coasts are the sites of major oil refineries.

Access to varied world raw material sources and markets is absolutely vital to Italian industry. There has been an increasingly strong trend, visible elsewhere in Europe, toward locating major new industrial centers at convenient seaport locations.[8] All of Italy's modern new integrated steel facilities are coastal: Cornigliano (Genoa), Piombino, Bagnoli (Naples), and Taranto. There has been in the past few years the introduction of much larger, faster, and fully automated tankers and dry cargo ships. These vessels significantly reduce costs for shipping bulky, low-value items like petroleum, coal, and iron ore, thus heightening the already unchallenged position of the world's merchant fleet as the cheapest form of transport. This situation, it seems clear, is in the process of diminishing the advantage that resource-rich nations have had over those forced to import, such as Italy. "The most promising steel industries in Europe are new ones in Holland and Italy, which, being big, modern and set up near seaports, can undersell the

[8] See, for instance, Douglas K. Fleming, "Coastal Steelworks in the Common Market Countries," *Geographical Review* 57 (January, 1967): 48–72.

old inland German mills, imprisoned atop their own uneconomic mines. With four new coastal plants opened by Italy's government-owned Finsider, Italian production increased 26 per cent from 1964 to 1965 . . ." [9]

Government initiative, both direct and indirect, in the country's economic life, is especially marked in industry. Its giant holding company, the Institute for Industrial Reconstruction (I.R.I.), controls fully one-third of the industrial capital of the nation, including a large share of the steel, machinery, shipping, shipbuilding, communications and transport equipment, and electric power industries. The Italian Fuel Corporation (E.N.I.), the vast state-owned petroleum and natural gas complex, is also very influential.

Transportation. Italy has an excellent rail (Fig. 7–13) and road network in the north and center, and a reasonably good one in the south. The whole system has been much improved since World War II, as the revamping of transport facilities was given high priority after the widespread destruction of that conflict. The state-owned and -operated railroads connect all the major cities with passenger and freight service. Sicily is joined with the mainland by a rail ferry across the narrow Strait of Messina. Many tunnels and winding roadbeds traverse the Apennines and the Alps, those through the latter giving northern Italy good rail and road connections with neighboring countries. The seven-mile long road tunnel under Mt. Blanc, opened in 1965, cuts many hours off the old, circuitous Paris-Rome route. Heavy trade between Germany and Italy flows through Switzerland, and Swiss foreign exchange earnings are significantly boosted by this transit traffic. Of the more than 13,000 miles of railroad trackage, nearly one-half is electrified. Major road construction and improvement programs, combined with diligent local maintenance, have made Italy's primary and secondary road system

much the best in Southern Europe. This is a sizeable achievement in a country with such difficult terrain (Figs. 7–4 and 7–7), and it represents a great economic asset. Expressways criss-cross the North Italian Plain, and the recently completed (1964) four-lane, 470-mile Autostrada del Sole (Highway of the Sun) connects Milan with Naples and major centers in between. It will soon be extended south to Reggio Calabria. The North Italian Plain has an elaborate oil and gas pipeline system.

The Italian merchant fleet ranks fourth in Europe. Italy is amply furnished with ports. Genoa is the leading one, supplying the wealthy North and a hinterland which extends beyond the border. Genoa, Venice, Naples, and Palermo are regular ports of call for large passenger liners of many flags. Brindisi is the gateway to Italian-Greek traffic. In addition to international sea lanes, there is considerable coastal shipping. The major world international airlines, including Italy's Alitalia, as well as domestic lines, service the main Italian cities.

Foreign trade. Italy, resource-poor and vitally dependent on a large volume of both imports and exports, has vigorously expanded its foreign trade since the middle 1950's. The following figures illustrate the essential make-up of Italian trade:

Italian Foreign Trade
1966–67 Annual Average
(percentages rounded)

	Imports	Exports
Food, beverages, and agricultural commodities	22	11
Energy (crude oil, petroleum products, etc.)	15	6
Raw materials	13	1
Semifinished goods	25	21
Finished goods for investment and production	14	28
Finished goods for consumption	10	33
Total	100	100
Total, millions of dollars	9,142.9	8,370.1

Source: Commercial Office of the Italian Embassy, *Italy: An Economic Profile* (Washington: 1968).

[9] *Time,* Atlantic Edition (August 12, 1966): p. 62.

The statistical picture of Italy's foreign trade mirrors the fundamental importance of exports and imports in the Italian economic structure. In 1966, the ratio between the value of foreign trade and GNP was 27 per cent. In the five-year period from 1962 to 1966 a cumulative growth of 52 per cent in the GNP, at current prices, was closely matched by the increase in foreign trade.

More than two-thirds of Italian export trade is conducted with industrialized countries (70 per cent in 1966, of which 41 per cent was with the EEC, 16 per cent with EFTA, and 9 per cent with the United States).

The greater part of Italy's imports originates from Western industrialized nations as well, their share being 63 per cent in 1966. The country's Common Market partners furnished 33 per cent in that year, EFTA 13 per cent, and the United States 12 per cent. Larger purchases of raw materials and crude oil, however, have increased greatly Italy's trade with developing countries. West Germany is by far Italy's major trading partner. France and the United States rank next in importance.

The trend in exports has been toward more highly fabricated, high-value items, incorporating special skills in engineering, design, and research innovation. Many traditional export groups such as textiles, clothing, and foodstuffs have declined relatively in favor of the "new" export categories, e.g., metallurgical and engineering products and chemicals.

Offsetting the usual trade gap are earnings from "invisibles," mainly tourism, emigrant remittances, foreign capital investments, and income from Italian international firms and capital investments abroad. It is remarkable that so poorly endowed a country, which is so densely populated by people who enjoy a reasonably high standard of living, has achieved the considerable balance of payments surpluses (and even close to actual trade surpluses in a few years) which Italy has managed to register regularly since the late 1950's.

Tourism. Italy is the tourist's delight *par excellence*, the world's number one tourist attraction. More than 27,000,000 foreigners visit this country each year, a number equal to half the population! Net receipts from tourism (adjusted for the spending of Italian vacationers abroad) total more than one billion dollars annually, a hefty contribution, indeed, to "invisible" earnings. Italy is blessed with a unique combination of attractive qualities, not the least of which is a populace famous for its sunny disposition and hospitable nature.

* * *

Italy's role as the leading power in Southern Europe is once more assured. A summary of the factors which have been important in the recent resurgence of the Italian nation would include: vast foreign aid from both public and private sources; strong governmental direction, encouragement, and action in making funds available when and where needed; the various stimuli stemming from membership in the European Economic Community; a much improved trade balance, spurred on by the growing prosperity of the Common Market and other trading partners in northwestern Europe; an ample labor supply, until recently considerably cheaper than most of the rest of industrial Europe; monetary stability; burgeoning tourism; important emigrant remittances; a reduced unemployment problem largely alleviated by increasing job opportunities in the North and by millions of Italians working abroad; and strong efforts toward redressing the imbalance between the North and South, e.g., the *Cassa per il Mezzogiorno*. Finally, there is the ingenuity and single-minded drive of the Italian people, stemming partly, undoubtedly, from a revulsion against the stagnation of the first three decades of this century and the vainglorious colonial and militaristic ventures of the Mussolini era. The will to achieve rapid economic and social progress is perhaps the key to the revitalized Italy of the late 1960's.[10]

GREECE

It is in Greece that the intimate interplay of land and sea so characteristic of the northern Mediterranean area reaches its maximum intensity. A glance at the map reveals the many prominent peninsulas sticking finger-like into the sea, and, on a smaller scale, the unending succession of promontories and coves and the myriad islands that is Greece. Nowhere is one far from the seashore. The mainland itself is very nearly cut in two by the Gulfs of Corinth and Patras; only a very narrow isthmus, cut by the Corinth Canal, connects the Peloponnesus with the rest of mainland Greece. There are numerous island groups, the main ones being the Ionians, the Sporades, the Cyclades, and the Dodecanese. In all, the islands number in the hundreds and constitute nearly one-fifth of the total area of the country. The largest islands are Crete, Euboea, Lesbos, Rhodes, Chios, Cephalonia, Corfu, and Samos. Several Greek isles lie off the coast of Turkey. Most are in the Aegean; a few are off the western mainland in the Ionian Sea.

Not only has the almost incredibly twisted outline of the coast and the many islands encouraged people to turn to the sea, but the nature of the topography, too, has been a factor. Generally, mountains and hills reach right down to the sea, isolating the small and scattered coastal plains from each other. Most of the more important plains front on the east coast, including those of Attica, Thessaly, and western and central Macedonia.

Historical Background

Ancient and pre-modern Greece. The glorious history of ancient Greece is too well

[10] See Shepard B. Clough, *The Economic History of Modern Italy* (New York: Columbia University Press, 1964): 290–91.

known to do more than cite a few of its pertinent features. Certainly the availability of water transport over a sea relatively easy to navigate stands out as a major geographical factor in the early development of Greece and a prerequisite of the extension of its power. Interior areas remained isolated and backward, a striking phenomenon which has persisted right up to the present. The earliest Hellenic civilization, in fact, was an insular one, flowering on Crete and some of the Cyclades isles. The city-states of the islands and mainland, each an individual nucleus of Greek civilization, remained distinctly separate, cut off from one another by forbidding terrain and water. True, the sea furnished easy means of transport and communication among the various centers, promoting the healthy intercourse that led to the remarkably cosmopolitan civilization of the early Greeks. But at the same time it afforded protection for the various entities that collectively made up ancient Greece and encouraged their independent political development. It is of great interest to note that the Greece we study in history books— birthplace of democracy and, indeed, of western civilization—was never unified until modern times. The old city-states were bound together in loose federations, their allegiances constantly shifting.

The Greeks were important early traders and colonizers, and, incidentally, counted among them are some of the outstanding early geographers. By 550 B.C. Greece had established colonies stretching from the northern and eastern shores of the Black Sea and Asia Minor through Mediterranean lands as far west as Spain, including Magna Graecia in southern Italy. The Hellenic world was extended far into western Asia by Alexander. Even when superseded politically by the Romans, Greek culture and influence did not wane, but actually gained strength. The Romans learned much from Greece; Greek was the language of the elite cultured class of Rome, and Greek literature and scholarship were highly prized. The phrase "playing Athens to someone's Rome" is still used to connote a culturally more advanced or mentor position vis-à-vis a less mature and sophisticated, but usually stronger, party.

Throughout the Middle Ages, the Greeks played a major role in the eastern Mediterranean within the Byzantine Empire, aided by an expatriate Greek element which has remained influential into the twentieth century. After Constantinople fell in 1453 to the Turks they swiftly overran Greece as well, and the Greeks formed part of the Ottoman Empire for nearly four centuries.

Modern Greece. Southern Greece united in revolting in the 1820's against the decaying Turkish regime and gained its independence in 1829, after a war of liberation in which it was aided by liberal factions throughout Europe (Fig. 7–16). Successive additions to the Greek state have taken place since: the Ionian Islands in 1864; Thessaly

and part of Epirus in 1881; Crete, the rest of Epirus, Macedonia, western Thrace, and many Aegean islands in 1912–1913, and eastern Thrace after World War I. Italy ceded the Dodecanese Islands after World War II.

Greece was thrown into turmoil in the immediate post-World War II period when civil war broke out between the Greek government and Communist guerrillas supplied by neighboring countries on the north. The country narrowly escaped slipping behind the Iron Curtain. After three years of difficult fighting and massive moral and economic assistance from the United States, acting under the newly formulated Truman Doctrine, peace was restored. Common fear of the U.S.S.R. has forged a friendship of convenience between Greece and a bitter and ancient foe, Turkey. Both are firm participants in western European defense pacts and have served as vital bulwarks of

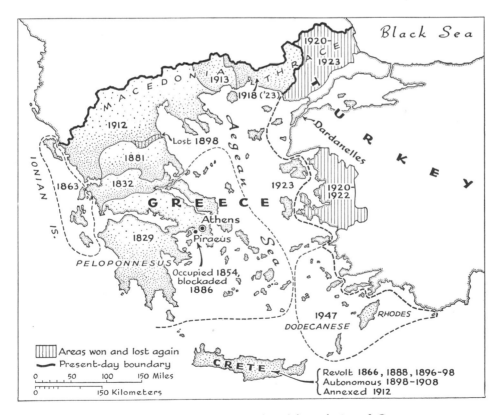

Fig. 7–16. The changing political boundaries of Greece.

the West in the eastern Mediterranean arena. Recently the Cyprus problem has cast an ominous shadow over Greek-Turkish relationships, though there are hopeful signs that both nations intend to work hard to settle this dispute amicably.

The seaward-oriented, insular, typically Mediterranean qualities of Greece should not be overemphasized. It is necessary to point out that the above-mentioned expansion of the modern Greek nation has meant the inclusion of a transitional or buffer-like zone in the north between the "heartland" Greece of the south and the Balkan interior beyond the frontiers. Northern Greece, i.e., north of about 39 degrees latitude, is distinctly different from more Mediterranean and maritime southern Greece. It is more continental, with a colder, rainier climate, and far less tied to the sea. Most of it was acquired more than three decades after the south achieved its independence, the bulk of it, in fact, not until the eve of the First World War (Fig. 7–16). Northern Greece has been much more colored by Turkish influences. Its ethnic make-up includes sizeable minorities, some of which have resisted Hellenization. It is here along the northern borders that are found some Mohammedan Albanians in the west, Macedo-Slavs in the center, and Bulgars and Turks in the east. There were large-scale exchanges of minority groups between Greece and Turkey and between Greece and Bulgaria shortly after World War I. Great hardships were suffered by these mostly penniless immigrants, and Greece was forced to accommodate a net gain in population of over one million. Nevertheless this event significantly reduced the country's problems of dealing with minorities.

Population

Greece is about one and one-half times the size of Portugal, or roughly the same size as New York state. With nearly nine million people (8.8 million in 1968), it has a population density of about 175 per square mile, well below the average for Southern Europe and about the same density as Spain's. The tendency to concentrate near the coasts that is true of other Mediterranean lands holds generally for Greece. The rugged interior is sparsely populated. Attica, the coastal plains of Macedonia and Thessaly, western Peloponnesus and many of the islands are moderately to very densely settled.

According to the 1961 census, 43 per cent of the Greek population is classified as urban, and nearly two million people—almost one Greek in four—live in Greater Athens, which includes Piraeus. Only two other cities have over 100,000 inhabitants: Thessaloniki (378,000) and Patras (102,000).[11]

Since early times there has been evidence of overpopulation in Greece. With poor agricultural resources and growing populaces, the city-states were propelled to look abroad for food and other resources. Fortunately, nature had provided excellent maritime possibilities, so the Greeks turned to trading and colonizing very early.[12] Ever since, they have imported foodstuffs and exported people, sometimes in very large numbers indeed. Temporary workers from Greece abound in northwestern Europe. Greek expatriates are found practically everywhere, and they have been historically and are today a powerful extension of Greek influence in the world, as well as a major source of monetary gain at home. Emigration has been unusually high in the 1960's, which has temporarily relieved population pressures. The birth rate is moderate and falls well below the average for Southern

[11] City proper, as opposed to urban agglomeration, figures for these cities are considerably less.

[12] Semple states that cereal shortages were a constant pressing concern for most of the early Greek mainland and island states, and that grain was brought to Piraeus from such varied sources as the Crimea, eastern Thrace, Syria, Egypt, Libya, Cyprus, and Sicily. See: Ellen C. Semple, *Geography of the Mediterranean Region* (New York: Henry Holt and Co., 1931), especially "Early Importance of the Mediterranean Grain Trade," 342 ff.

Europe. The death rate is quite low which reflects the important recent gains in health and living standards. Including migration, the rate of population increase has been fairly modest, averaging .7 per cent per year from 1958–1965. It is hoped that the combination of a decrease in the rate of natural population growth, continuing attractive outlets for emigration, and economic advances will serve to avoid any severe future problems of overpopulation.

There is considerable cultural homogeneity among Greeks. About 98 per cent of the population belongs to the Greek Orthodox Church, and modern Greek is the universal language. There are many dialects, to be sure, and fierce disagreements rage between those who favor a more formalized written and spoken language (Katharevusa) and those wishing to substitute entirely the popular spoken tongue (Demotic). Nevertheless, language is a strong unifying tie. A few other languages are spoken by the minorities mentioned earlier, but their influence and numbers have been declining. Literacy is rising rapidly, and by 1970 will be close to 90 per cent. In recent years the Greek government has paid much attention to encouraging technical and professional training schools to help fill the demand for skilled personnel already being felt in the wake of the modernization of the economy.

The average Greek is quick and open-minded. Politics is the burning interest even in the most remote village. Political strife has been bitter between the numerous parties. Newspapers and discussions in public places and inns play a great role in daily life. Coffee houses and inns have their tables and chairs outside the houses and are frequented mostly by men. Women have equal legal status, but custom makes the man predominant in all public places and affairs. In the villages women often do the hard work while men look on or direct. Work pauses during the noon hours, even the work in the fields. Shops and offices reopen at 3 or 4 o'clock and business and life go on far

into the night. Streets and squares in cities and villages are noisy and vivid, accentuating the natural vivacity of the landscape, its bright colors, and entrancing shapes. Everywhere the deep blue of sky and sea, the white of bare limestone, the silvery green of olives, the darker green of other trees, and the red hollow bricks of the roofs blend with the manifold forms of mountains and hills, the curving bays and beaches, and the sky-ward-pointing cypresses and pines. Man almost disappears in this landscape, except where he puts his monuments on dominating heights, such as the Acropolis of Athens, the St. George's chapel of Lycabettos, the temple to Poseidon on Cape Sounion, the Crusaders' castles of Mytilene, or the Venetian fortresses at the entrance of Corfu harbor. Towns are frequently built on slopes, but disappear into the landscape because the houses of native stone blend with the rocks. Villages are usually large, hamlets or dispersed settlements existing only in a few sections of northern Greece. The scarcity of water has forced people to live around the wells; centuries of insecurity have contributed to the habit of gathering on protected sites. Many of the war-ravaged villages have now been rebuilt, often more sanitary though less beautiful, and on less spectacular sites in the valleys near the fields and roads.

Present Economic Life

Greece has not been able to escape from one primary, unalterable fact: its physical environment is very harsh. Small, dry, hot, and rugged, more than one-half covered by bare rock and nearly useless sclerophyllous brush, with much of the tilled land worn out, poor in minerals, and yet moderately densely populated, it cannot be said to have been favored by nature. It must be remembered that the immense contributions for which Greece is justly famous were primarily in the cultural, not material, realm and in an age before industrial minerals figured so prominently in a country's prowess.

Of the three great peninsulas of Southern Europe, Greece is unquestionably the poorest from the point of view of physical geography. Neither the single large northern plain nor the extensive smaller coastal plains of Italy are duplicated in the Greek homeland. Nor is there the broad interior plateau and fairly large, in aggregate, coastal lowlands of Iberia. Greece, instead, consists of a profusion of rugged mountains, with steep-sided valleys usually restricted in extent and access, few interior basins and plains, and a narrow, interrupted coastal fringe of lowlands. Plains constitute only 16½ per cent of the total area. In light of these comparisons, it is remarkable that Greece enjoys an economic level higher than that of Spain or Portugal and in fact slightly above Southern Europe's average.

The Greek economy was badly disrupted by World War II and the civil war which followed. These conflicts subjected the country to severe material damage and manpower losses. A further negative result of great consequence was the demoralization which is always the natural concomitant of civil war. The latter exacerbated already virulent antagonisms and grudges which the fiercely independent Greek spirit and widespread poverty had long nurtured. Thus, rebuilding was delayed and greatly complicated, and in the early 1950's Greece found itself in a retarded state compared with other countries in a Europe recovering from the ravages of war. Probably only Spain, of the Mediterranean nations, has suffered more than Greece from war in the past generation. Fortunately, foreign aid, both military and economic, was forthcoming to buttress characteristic Greek perseverance. The economy has bounded ahead most satisfactorily on the whole in the last decade. The Greeks were the poorest people in Europe in the late 1940's. That this is no longer true is a tribute to Greek determination and acumen in the face of difficult circumstances.

Agriculture. Farming employs more Greeks than any other major activity (46 per cent in 1962), in spite of the less than ideal environmental conditions for agriculture. The relative importance of agriculture, however, is steadily shrinking, a trend common to all semi-developed economies which have long been overdependent on agriculture and notably weak in the secondary and tertiary sectors. Though yields are generally low and traditional farming techniques widespread, there have been consistent improvements in agriculture, spurred on by government subsidies and assistance in land reclamation, small community projects, and technical and educational research. Advances have also been made in the dissemination to farmers of information on modern agricultural methods and the means to employ them, including medium- and long-term loans. The United States has been of great help in assisting farm extension services which have upgraded crop and livestock farming in many rural zones. The American Farm School, a private institution in Thessaloniki, deserves special mention for its excellent work.

About twenty-nine and one-half per cent of the total area of Greece is cultivated [13] (note this is higher than the total percentage of plainsland!). Of this, about one-half (48 per cent) is in cereals, chiefly wheat, though important areas are in corn, rice, and barley. About one-quarter is in annuals such as cotton, tobacco, and pulses: 3 per cent is taken up in market gardening, and 21 per cent is devoted to arboriculture (vineyards, olives, fruit orchards). There have been strong efforts to reduce dry cereal acreages (contravened by popular but uneconomic wheat subsidies under the Papandreou government of 1964–65) and to promote heavier-yielding crops such as rice, tobacco, and cotton, the area of all of which has been multiplied rapidly. Many extensions of irrigation, mostly small scale, have been accomplished recently, and a major drive in that direction will probably raise the total

[13] This figure includes much poor-quality land and fallow that is cropped even as frequently as one in five years ("dry farming").

irrigated acreage by more than half in the decade 1965–1975. A great deal of attention has been and is still being given to eliminating overgrazing, especially by goats, on slopelands, where much destruction has taken place, and to up-grading the quality of livestock. There has been very substantial investment in mechanization in the past fifteen to twenty years.

In general the performance of Greek agriculture in the post-World War II period has been creditable, and the advances made compare very favorably to those of other northern Mediterranean lands, as indicated in the following compilation:

main cash crop and a very important export. It is of high quality and much sought after in world markets.

Most of the interior south and the coastal fringes south of Volos (around the Peloponnesus and up the west coast, as well as the islands) constitute the Mediterranean agricultural zones of Greece. Typical Mediterranean specialties dominate: vineyards, olives, wheat, and some irrigated vegetables, fruits, and cotton. Much of this area is slopeland, and the tree crops are an intelligent adjustment to the topographic pattern. Wine quality is improving and emphasis on the native *retsina*, little in demand outside

Some Agricultural Comparisons of Mediterranean Countries

	Area in Cereals	Production of Cereals	Cereal Yields, per Acre	Wheat Yields, per Acre	Irrigated Land, 1965	Irrigated Land, 1965	Total Agricultural Production	Per Capita Total Agricultural Production
					(000 hectares)	(1952–1956 = 100)	1965–1966 average (1952–1956 = 100)	
	1966–1967 average (1948–1952 = 100)							
Cyprus	107 [2]	177 [2]	165 [2]	167 [2]	94	118	150 [2]	132 [2]
Greece	102	207	203	189	576	152	171	157
Italy	84	133	158	151	*	*	127	118
Malta	75 [2]	75 [2]	100 [2]	111 [2]	*	*	*	*
Portugal	89	105	118	99	*	*	119	110
Spain	96	134	139	141	2169	122	133	121
Turkey	152 [1]	193	113 [1]	114 [1]	*	*	148	107
Yugoslavia	101 [1]	228	198 [1]	192 [1]	118	131	131	147

* Not available.
[1] 1965–1966 average.
[2] 1964–1965 average.
SOURCE: *F.A.O. Production Yearbooks* and (unpublished) F.A.O. statistics supplied January, 1968.

In increase of cereal yields in the recent past, as well as in percentage increase in total agricultural production, and in perhaps the most significant index—percentage increment in agricultural product per inhabitant— Greece leads the rest of northern Mediterranea. It also ranks high in increase in cereal production and increase in irrigated land.

There are very important regional variations in the pattern of Greek farming (Fig. 7–17). The northeastern and central portions of the country—Thrace, Macedonia, and northern Thessaly—concentrate on cereals, especially wheat. Tobacco is the

Greece, is being downgraded in order to spur exports.

The rest of Greece, a smaller area in the interior northwest, is extremely rugged and isolated and is best described as a hill-farming and pasture zone. The terrain imposes a severe limit to cultivation, and less than one-sixth of the land is tilled. With the much greater rainfall, corn replaces wheat as the chief crop. Pastures are plentiful, and grazing of sheep and goats is the principal farm activity of this region.

Other primary activities. Forestry is minor in Greece; only about one-sixth of its

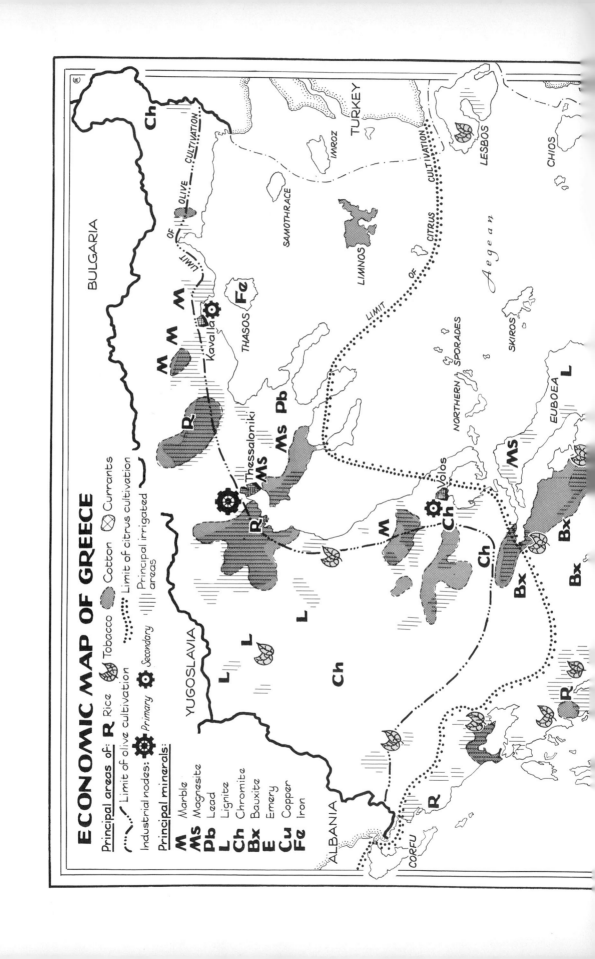

ECONOMIC MAP OF GREECE

Principal areas of: **R** Rice   🌿 Tobacco   🍇 Cotton   ⊗ Currants

〰️ Limit of olive cultivation   ⋯⋯ Limit of citrus cultivation

Industrial nodes: ⚙ Primary   ⚙ Secondary   ‖‖ Principal irrigated areas

Principal minerals:

M   Marble
Ms   Magnesite
Pb   Lead
L   Lignite
Ch   Chromite
Bx   Bauxite
E   Emery
Cu   Copper
Fe   Iron

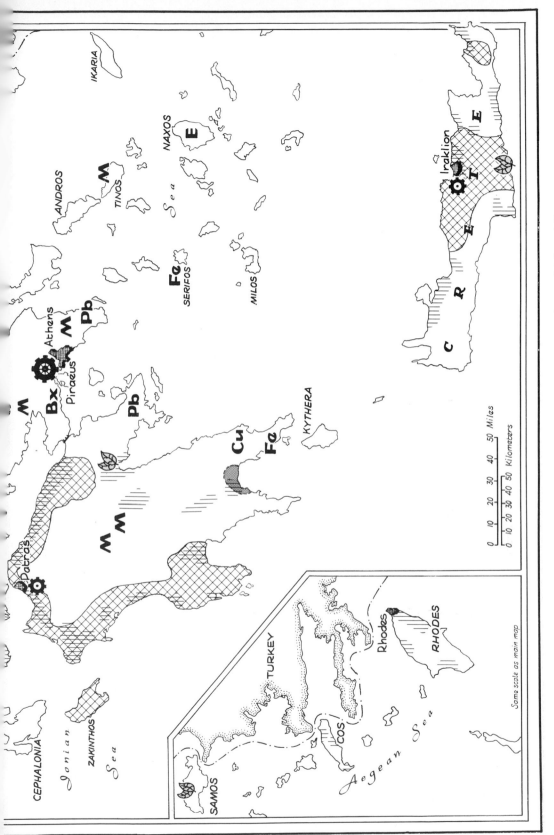

Fig. 7–17. Economic Map of Greece. (Source: *Economic and Social Atlas of Greece,* National Statistical Service of Greece, Center of Economic Research, 1964.)

area is forested. Though some naval stores and lumber are produced, two-thirds of the nation's forest product requirements must be imported. Some reforestation and construction of access roads have aided forestry, and a project recommended by a joint FAO–Greek government study in 1966 envisions a large saw mill and pulp mills complex near Missolonghi, across the gulf from Patras. Raw materials would be obtained from the Peloponnesus and from the coast and islands of western Greece.

The total fish catch is disappointingly small and, though steadily growing, much improvement is possible and anticipated. Tonnage is only one-tenth that of Spain, and domestic demand is not even met, thus requiring imports. Sponges are a minor export (Fig. 7–18). Government assistance has been helping to modernize the fleet,

proliferate fish hatcheries, and improve refrigeration and other facilities in the principal fishing ports.

Though a considerable variety and extent of minerals are known in Greece, mining and quarrying contribute less than 2 per cent to the gross domestic product. The main Greek minerals, judged both by reserves and production, are bauxite, lignite, and chromiferous iron ore (Fig. 7–17). Lignite, though now mined in fairly large quantities, is a poor substitute for coal and petroleum, and diminishes only minutely the necessarily large imports of those energizers. Bauxite has been exported, but will increasingly be used in the expanding domestic aluminum industry.

The electrical generating capacity of Greece has been vigorously augmented and is still being pushed. Only a fourth is hydro,

Fig. 7–18. Fishermen cleaning their sponge catch on the coast of Aigina, an island southwest of Athens. (Greek National Tourist Organization.)

despite the need to import the fossil fuels, demonstrating once more the difficulties and cost of developing water power in a Mediterranean land. By 1970 the electrical output is expected to be three to four times that of 1961.

Industry. Modern manufacturing is not favored in Greece either by mineral and power endowment or by tradition. Thus it is not an important industrial nation, and most of the manufacturing is small scale. In recent years, however, there has been important expansion in many categories of manufacturing, aided by foreign investment, which was in the 1960's many times the figure for the previous decade. Textiles (supplied with domestic cotton and some domestic wool) is the leading industry, and food and other agricultural raw material processing (grapes, wheat, olives, tobacco) are very widespread and important. Chemicals, cement, and many handicraft industries are well established. Some of the newer developments include a large aluminum plant at St. Nicolas, on the north shore of the Gulf of Corinth, using local bauxite; a $200 million industrial complex at Thessaloniki, including an oil refinery, a petrochemical plant, and a steel plant with a capacity expected to reach soon 1,000,000 tons a year; and modern shipbuilding and repair yards near Piraeus and Eleusis, west of Athens.

Athens-Piraeus and Thessaloniki, which are also Greece's leading ports, are by far the most important centers of industry (Fig. 7–17). Thessaloniki's strategic location at the end of a deep bay and commanding the entrance to the Vardar-Morava corridor has contributed to its growth and made it the natural maritime outlet for a large part of southeastern Europe. Northern Greece is the most promising area for development in the drive to counterbalance the inordinate importance that Greater Athens has in Greek life.

A considerable stimulus to the economy of the north could also be derived by closer collaboration between Greece and Yugoslavia on economic matters.[14]

An indication of Greece's rapid industrial progress can be seen in its trade. Until 1963 industrial products had never made up more than 5 per cent of total Greek exports. In 1967 they accounted for nearly a fifth, and included for the first time aluminum and refined petroleum products. By 1969 industrial production is likely to be double that of a decade earlier.

Foreign trade. With a large deficit in foreign trade to be made up each year, income from "invisibles" is vital to the Greek balance of payments. The three major sources are: tourism, shipping, and emigrant remittances. In 1966, when imports exceeded exports by $700 million, the intake from these three sources was $490 million, a great contribution toward closing the gap. Tourism has increased phenomenally in Greece and augers well for impressive future gains (Fig. 7–19). The merchant fleet is Southern Europe's largest, and, in fact, the sixth-largest in the world. (It would rank even higher if Greek-owned ships flying flags of convenience were counted.) Although much of this imposing total tonnage is fairly old, the fleet is being modernized, and port facilities, too, are being improved. A very large number of Greeks work abroad and send money home. Between 1958 and 1965, well over half a million Greeks emigrated. The future of this source of income, however, dependent as it is on external factors, now seems uncertain.

*　*　*

A stable, conservative government from 1955 through 1963 strongly directed the economy and encouraged agricultural and industrial growth. It was able to channel

[14] George W. Hoffman, "The Problem of the Underdeveloped Regions in Southeast Europe: A Comparative Analysis of Romania, Yugoslavia, and Greece," *Annals of the Association of American Geographers,* 57 (December, 1967): 659 ff.

Fig. 7–19. Ios, one of the Cyclades, is a typical Greek island. Its dry, mountainous landscape, sinuous coastline, fine sheltered harbor and small picturesque fishing village with whitewashed buildings offer the type of quiet beauty and charm that has made the Greek islands one of Europe's favorite tourist attractions. Note the carefully tended, garden-sized plots on the village outskirts. (Greek National Tourist Organization.)

funds into improvements in the infrastructure, shore up the currency, and make the investment climate more appealing, thus bringing Greece to a "take-off" stage where the fruits of hard work began to pay off. The GNP increased at an annual rate near 8 per cent throughout much of the 1960's, well above (nearly twice) the European average. Massive foreign economic aid has ceased, but now a major stimulus is bound to be the associate membership in the European Common Market which Greece gained in 1962. Other stimuli are the high rate of private investment in industry and tourism.

Unfortunately, the Greek political arena gives cause for worry. The uneasy political stability which democratic governments managed to maintain from 1949 on glossed over many deep fissures in the Greek body politic. After 1963 tensions and suspicions seemed to mount, and an undesirable polarization in the political spectrum toward well-drawn, ultra-conservative and ultra-liberal camps shattered the center and with it chances for compromise and reasonable dialogue. Then, in April, 1967, Europe's first successful military coup since the 1930's toppled the government and shook Greece. The bitterness engendered by this action may erode the benefits hoped for under a stable regime. It would be tragic if political rivalries and hostilities were allowed to erase the real gains that the Greeks, so deprived in modern history, have worked so diligently to achieve in the past generation and now seem to have within their grasp.

MALTA

The Maltese Islands, of which Malta, Gozo, and Comino are the largest, form collectively the state of Malta. These islands emerge as crests of a submarine ridge between southeastern Sicily and Africa. Roughly 60 miles from the former and 180 from the latter, Malta is in a highly strategic position, in the middle of and astride the narrowest section of the central Mediterranean Sea. It is, at the same time, remote. Its history reflects these seemingly paradoxical aspects of Malta's geography. It has been used for centuries as an important crossroads maritime base for commerce and military purposes. Yet its culture is quite distinct, and the Maltese pride themselves on their singular traditions and way of life. Malta gained independence from Britain in September, 1964, and is a member of the Commonwealth.

The population is almost entirely Roman Catholic. Maltese and English are the official languages, but Italian is widely spoken. The island of Malta, with the country's capital and main port of Valletta, has three-quarters of the tiny country's 122 square mile area and 90 per cent of its population. Its 319,000 (1967) people mean a population density of more than 2,600 per square mile. Despite heavy emigration (100,000 during the years 1949–1965, mostly to Australia, Canada, and Britain), this density, the highest in Europe, is a very great burden for so dry and hilly a land. Lithosols and very thin soils constitute a further disadvantage, and a predominantly limestone structure intensifies the aridity, though this rock type does provide underground aquifers which yield some water for municipal use and irrigation. (A desalinization plant, recently completed at Valletta, yields more than 1,000,000 gallons a day.) Its truly subtropical temperature regime is

an asset, and careful and continual efforts by Maltese farmers—as seen in the remarkable terracing which is a common feature of the landscape—have allowed two-fifths of the area to be put under cultivation. Pressure of population permits only a small place for livestock, though pork production has significantly increased, and Malta is now self-sufficient in milk. Potatoes, onions, and greenhouse products are large exports.

Lacking in natural resources and with a third of the population dependent in the recent past on activities connected with British military installations, Malta has been woefully dependent on foreign (i.e., British) military spending and other economic assistance. The country is assiduously seeking to broaden the base of its economy, especially through the expansion of tourism, horticulture, and light industry. One facet which has received concerted effort is the conversion of the naval dockyards to commercial ship repairing. Valletta, the capital and chief city, has an excellent harbor (Fig. 7–20), and plans are actively being explored to develop the protected, sixty-foot deep, Bay of Marsaxlokk, on Malta Island's southeast coast, as a free-port entrepôt for handling large bulk carriers and container ships, whose cargoes would be broken down and reshipped from there.

CYPRUS

Cyprus is, geographically and in statistical sources, regarded as a part of Southwest Asia. Its inclusion here is justified by its quite definitely European culture and orientation. Lying off the south coast of Turkey, this large Mediterranean isle is slightly larger than Corsica and about one-third the size of Sicily. With 600,000 people (1968), it has a density of 165 per square mile and a modest rate of population increase, 1.5 per cent per annum. Cyprus has an ethnic split (Greek Cypriots comprise 77 per cent of the population, Turkish Cypriots 18 per cent, others 5 per cent) which presents a serious problem. There has been

Fig. 7–20. Partial view of Valletta's busy Grand Harbor showing the old fortifications of St. Angelo and St. Michael. (Malta Tourist Bureau.)

no intermarriage, and the two groups view each other with suspicion and hostility. Turkish Cypriots hold three enclaves, including the main road from Nicosia to Kyrenia (Fig. 7–21), but there is a wide dispersal of the Turkish minority throughout the island.

Three structural divisions make up Cyprus (Fig. 7–21). Along the northern coast are the Kyrenia-Karpas Mountains, a narrow limestone range rising to over 3,000 feet. In the southwest, covering about one-half of the island, lies the Troodos Massif, reaching 6,400 feet, a large plutonic dome whose margins are covered by tertiary sedimentaries. In between, there is the long Mesaoria plain, open at either end to the sea.

Scarcity of water is a handicap, but agriculture occupies 38 per cent (1966) of the labor force. Rather typical Mediterranean crop emphases are found, citrus fruits and potatoes being especially important for export. Mining figures prominently in the export picture; the chief minerals are copper, iron pyrites, and asbestos (Fig. 7–21). Manufacturing is poorly developed, but expanding rapidly in food processing, cement, fertilizers, and some light consumer industries. Industrial production grew by 8 per cent per annum in the period from 1964 through 1966.

The island looks to an up-grading and expansion of its agriculture and to greater fulfillment of its poorly exploited, but considerable, potential for tourism to improve the economy and lessen the present dependence on foreign aid, military spending, and emigrant remittances.

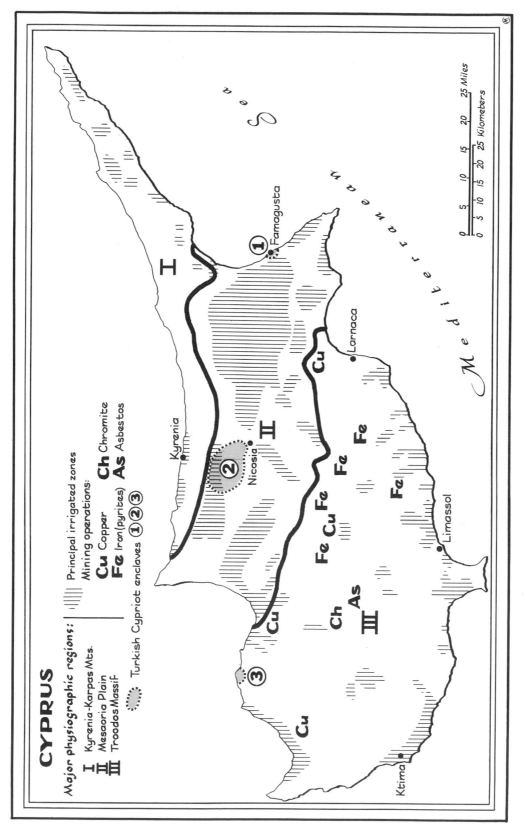

Fig. 7-21. Cyprus.

The future of the island nation of Cyprus is uncertain. Like so many Mediterranean islands, it has had a long history of domination by successive invaders, and it has always been within the sphere of influence of some major power, from the Mycenaeans and Phoenicians to the British annexation in 1914. Shortly after gaining independence from the United Kingdom in 1959, Cyprus embarked on another period of bitter civil war, reminiscent of the 1954–59 fighting, between the majority-Greek population, harangued by the ambitious archbishop-President Makarios, and the Turkish minority. An uneasy peace was finally restored, with the aid of a U.N. peace-keeping force, and it is hoped that reason has replaced the impassioned irrationality which more than once has brought Greece and Turkey to the brink of war. Some form of *enosis* (union with Greece) still may be worked out. A prerequisite for demonstrable economic progress in Cyprus and, in fact, probably for its survival as a viable independent entity, would appear to be the establishment of a permanent political *modus vivendi*. This alone can bring stability and some continuity in the massive economic efforts which must be undertaken.

*   *   *

There are discernible some general trends of basic importance in Southern Europe which apply to all of the individual countries to a greater or lesser extent. Above all, they have made in the past two decades very impressive economic progress. This fact is heartening and of major significance in itself. No less important, however, is the knowledge that this progress is based largely on long-range, fundamental and often structural revisions and improvements which should prove of lasting benefit and promote easier and more rapid advances in the future. Southern Europe is still Europe's poorest area, but the tempo of change has quickened in the 1960's, and there is an awareness of and pride in this transformation.

A second common thread of recent history is the implementation of formalized national and regional development plans and their nearly universal success. Goals have not always been met exactly on schedule, but they have led to more careful allocation of always scarce funds, more efficient removal of bottlenecks to economic and social improvements, and smoother dovetailing of mutually interdependent goals.

Finally, there has been a distinct movement toward greater contact and cooperation with other areas, particularly with the rest of Europe. Italy and Greece have committed themselves to the European Economic Community, and Spain has moved toward some form of association with it. Portugal has joined EFTA. All of the Southern European countries have an important role, formalized by treaties, in Western European defense plans. Greater participation in the activities of the United Nations and its agencies, especially the Economic Commission for Europe (ECE), Food and Agriculture Organization (FAO), and General Agreement on Tariffs and Trade (GATT), as well as those of other international organizations such as the World Bank, has very materially aided these countries. Devices such as economic studies and surveys, technical advice and assistance, loans and outright grants are having an important impact.

The human factor, as well—the mixing of people and cultures—has operated in accelerated fashion to broaden measurably the outlook of Southern Europeans. Tourists swarm to sunny Mediterranea, bringing more than just money. The young folk go abroad for work, returning in the majority of cases with new ideas and standards. Outside commercial ties have been strengthened, too. Southern Europe has begun to exploit in a major way another aspect of the natural advantages of its proximity to industrialized northwestern Europe: the demand there for valuable agricultural products, such as fruits, vegetables, wine, and certain other sub-tropical specialities which are prized because of their high quality and, in the case of some, their availablity early in the season. Southern Europe is very much a part of the spirit and substance of the trend toward unification that has been gathering force in post-World War II Europe.

BIBLIOGRAPHY

(Major references are asterisked.)

Books in English

AMERICAN GEOGRAPHICAL SOCIETY. *Readings in the Geography of the Mediterranean Region.* Reprint series 2. Contributions by various authors. New York: American Geographical Society, 1943.

CLOUGH, SHEPARD B. *The Economic History of Modern Italy.* New York: Columbia University Press, 1964.

°DICKINSON, ROBERT E. *The Population of Southern Italy.* Syracuse, N.Y.: Syracuse University Press, 1955.

FOOD AND AGRICULTURE ORGANIZATION, UNITED NATIONS. *FAO Mediterranean Development Project.* Rome: FAO, 1959.

°HOUSTON, J. M. *The Western Mediterranean World: An Introduction to Its Regional Landscapes.* London: Longmans, Green and Company, Ltd., 1964.

KAYSER, BERNARD, AND THOMPSON, KENNETH (with the collaboration of R. VATERNELLE and BASIL COUKIS). *Economic and Social Atlas of Greece.* Athens: National Statistical Service, the Center for Planning and Economic Research, and the Social Studies Center, 1964.

LANITIS, N. C. *Our Destiny—A Consideration of Some Crucial Problems Pertaining to Cyprus.* Nicosia: Proodos, 1963.

PAPANDREOU, A. G. *A Strategy for Greek Economic Development.* Athens: Center of Economic Research, 1962.

PINTADO, V. XAVIER. *Structure and Growth of the Portuguese Economy.* Geneva: EFTA, 1964.

SCHACHTER, GUSTAV. *The Italian South: Economic Development in Mediterranean Europe.* New York: Random House, 1965.

°SEMPLE, ELLEN CHURCHILL. *Geography of the Mediterranean Region.* New York: Henry Holt & Co., Inc., 1931.

STANISLAWSKI, DAN. *The Individuality of Portugal: A Study in Historical-Political Geography.* Austin: University of Texas Press, 1950.

THOMPSON, K. *Farm Fragmentation in Greece: The Problem and Its Setting.* Athens: Center of Economic Research, 1963.

UN SPECIAL FUND—FAO. *Economic Survey of the Western Peloponnesus, Greece.* 6 vols. Rome: FAO, 1965 and 1966.

WALKER, D. S. *A Geography of Italy,* 2d ed. London: Methuen, 1966.

°———. *The Mediterranean Lands,* 2d ed. London: Methuen, 1965.

WAY, RUTH. *A Geography of Spain and Portugal.* London: Methuen, 1962.

WRIGHT, JOHN K. *The Geographical Basis of European History.* New York: American Geographical Society, 1928. (Introduction and chap. 2, "The Alpine-Mediterranean Region.")

Books in Other Languages

BIROT, PIERRE, AND JEAN DRESCH. *La Méditerranée Occidentale (The Western Mediterranean).* Vol. 1. Paris: Presses Universitaires de France, 1956.

Informe Económico (Economic Report), latest (annual). Bilbao: Banco de Bilbao.

PARRILLO, F. *Lo sviluppo economico italiano (Italian Economic Development).* Milan: Giuffrè, 1963.

PASQUIER, ALBERT. *L'économie du Portugal (The Portuguese Economy).* Paris: Librairie Générale de Droit et de Jurisprudence, 1961.

°PHILIPPSON, ALFRED. *Das Mittelmeergebiet: seine geographische und kulturelle Eigenart (The Mediterranean: Its Geographic and Cultural Character),* 4th ed. Leipzig: B. G. Teubner, 1931.

°———. *Die Griechischen Landschaften (The Regions of Greece).* Vol. 1. Frankfurt am Main: V. Klostermann, 1952.

°SION, J., AND SORRE, M. *Méditerranée: Péninsules méditerranéennes (The Mediterranean: Mediterranean Peninsulas).* Vol. VII of *Géographie Universelle.* Paris: A. Colin, 1934.

°TOURING CLUB ITALIANO. *Attraverso l' Italia (Across Italy).* Milan: Touring Club of Italy, 1927–55.

Articles

BAYNE, E. A. "Non-Crisis in Italy," *Foreign Affairs* 45 (1967): 353–62.

DOZIER, CRAIG L. "Establishing a Framework for Development in Sardinia: The Campidano," *Geographical Review* 47 (1957): 490–506.

FLEMING, DOUGLAS K. "Coastal Steelworks in the Common Market Countries," *Geographical Review* 57 (1967): 48–72.

HOFFMAN, GEORGE W. "South Tyrol: Borderland Rights vs. World Politics," *Journal of Central European Affairs* 7 (1947): 285–306.

———. "The Problem of the Underdeveloped Regions in Southeast Europe: A Comparative Analysis of Romania, Yugoslavia, and Greece," *Annals of the Association of American Geographers* 57 (1967): 637–666.

———. "Thessaloniki, The Impact of a Changing Hinterland," *East European Quarterly* 2 (March, 1968): 1–27.

HOUSTON, J. M. "Irrigation as a Solution to Agrarian Problems in Modern Spain," *Geographical Journal* 116 (1950): 55–63.

Italy: Documents and Notes (bi-monthly). Information Service and Copyright Office, Presidency of the Council of Ministers of the Italian Republic, Rome.

KISH, GEORGE. "The *Marine* of Southern Italy," *Geographical Review* 43 (1953): 495–506.

°LAUTENSACH, HERMANN. "Portugal auf Grund eigener Reisen und der Literatur" ("Portugal: A Description Based on Personal Travel and Literature"), *Petermanns Mitteilungen* 46 (1932), 50 (1937).

McMANIS, DOUGLAS R. "The Core of Italy: The Case for Lombardy–Piedmont," *The Professional Geographer* 19 (1967): 251–57.

NAYLON, JOHN. "Land Consolidation in Spain," *Annals of the Association of American Geographers* 49 (December, 1959): 361–73.

PEPALASIS, A. A., AND THOMPSON, KENNETH. "Agriculture in a Restrictive Environment: The Case of Greece," *Economic Geographer* 36 (1960): 145–57.

WEIGEND, GUIDO G. "Effects of Boundary Changes in the South Tyrol," *Geographical Review* 40 (1950): 364–75.

8

Eastern Europe [1]

EAST CENTRAL AND SOUTHEAST EUROPE

Between Central Europe and the Soviet Union, bordered by three seas—the Baltic, Black, and Adriatic—are located seven countries: Poland, Czechoslovakia, Hungary, Romania, Bulgaria, Albania, and Yugoslavia. This group of countries is usually arbitrarily grouped, because of its general location in relation to other areas within Europe, as Eastern Europe, East Europe, Mid-Europe or East Central and Southeast Europe. It has been given specific names such as the "Shatter Belt" or the "Devil's Belt," which characterize its fragmentation into many political and cultural units, and the instability and resultant insecurity of its people. Lastly, the group of countries bears names which express its political function or position: the "Eastern March-lands," the "Cordon Sanitaire" of the interwar period, the "Iron Curtain" of the postwar period or simply "satellite" or "captive" countries (with Yugoslavia usually excluded from the last two expressions).[2] Eastern Europe as de-

fined here covers about 450,000 square miles, is roughly the size of Colorado, New Mexico, and Texas combined, and has a total population of about 106 million. The importance of this region has often been underlined. Sir Halford Mackinder[3] spoke of the importance of the "tier of independent states between Germany and Russia." Others mention its importance for Europe's balance of power.[4] Moodie[5] drew attention to "the reduction of the north-south extent of Europe between the Baltic and the Adriatic" and to the fact that this 500-mile-wide thoroughfare has been essential for the "movements of peoples, goods, and ideas between the Russian realm, on the one hand, and Central and Western Europe, on the other." Location is paramount in any ex-

author, which covers some of the problems of this area: "Eastern Europe: A Study in Political Geography," *Texas Quarterly* 2 (Autumn, 1959): 57–88.

[3] *Democratic Ideals and Reality* (New York: Henry Holt & Co., Inc., 1919, 1942): pp. 158 ff. He also refers to them as "middle states of East Europe."

[4] Henry L. Roberts, "Eastern Europe and the Balance of Power," in Norman J. G. Pounds and Nicolas Spulber (eds.), *Resources and Planning in Eastern Europe, Slavic and East European Series,* Vol. IV (Bloomington, Ind.: Indiana University Press, 1957): 1–11.

[5] W. G. East and A. E. Moodie, *The Changing World* (Yonkers, N.Y.: World Book Co., 1956): p. 111.

[1] Material on The German Democratic Republic (East Germany) is included in Chapter 6, Central Europe.

[2] Certain material presented in this chapter has been taken, by permission, from a study, by the

planation of the importance of this region with its seven political units. Eastern Europe is an area of transition, instability, and diversification, and this is clearly expressed in its physical as well as its cultural-political characteristics.

Physically, Eastern Europe consists of many well-defined and highly diversified regions. This variance of landforms is easily seen when comparing the many structural units analyzed later in this chapter (Fig. 8–1). Its mountains and other highlands never have been barriers to the movement of peoples. As a matter of fact, many easily accessible passes, gates, and river valleys, and most of all the Danube River, have acted as unifying factors. These important transportation links have played a significant role in the geography of Eastern Europe, inasmuch as they were often the reason for conflict over control of routes into the fertile basin areas. For example, the Polish Uplands served as an important routeway between Western Europe and northwestern and central Russia (Slavic and Germanic settlers had their first encounter here); the Morava-Vardar corridor assisted the Ottoman Turks in their easy penetration to the gates of Vienna; and control of important passes, gates, and basins facilitated the control of important lands to the western slopes of the Carpathian Mountains and beyond by the Hapsburg rulers of Austria.

The transitional character of Eastern Europe is also expressed by the great variety of climates, e.g., from the typical Mediterranean climates along the Adriatic littoral of Yugoslavia (with the bordering Karst Mountains precluding any inland penetration) to the semiarid steppe conditions along the lower Danube in the Dobruja. This variety of climatic conditions is shown in the great complexity of soils and the diversity of vegetation adding another variance to an already complex area.

The importance of the approximately 500-mile-long thoroughfare has been pointed out. Different peoples have used this thoroughfare since the dawn of European history, and

it is not surprising that for many the Danube corridor became their permanent home. The settlements nowhere coincided with the many complex and well-defined geographic regions. The peoples had to adapt themselves to the physical conditions they found. The major groups settling in this region were the Poles, Czechs, Slovaks, Magyars, Germans, Romanians, and the various south Slavic people of today's Yugoslavia (meaning Land of the Southern Slavs), Slovenes, Croats, Serbs, and Macedonians, and finally the Albanians. They brought with them different customs and beliefs. As a result of these movements, this area was occupied by people of many different cultures, and this fragmentation in turn contributed to the lack of a stable political-territorial framework.

Eastern Europe is rich in natural resources. Agricultural activities of a large rural population play an important role, but increased industrial activity in every one of the countries, often based on important local raw materials, is rapidly changing the economic structure of the area. With the exception of Albania, all the East European countries have close economic ties with the Soviet Union—and each other—anywhere from 34 per cent (Yugoslavia) to 70 per cent (Bulgaria) of their trade, although trade with Western countries has shown a slow but steady increase since the early 1960's.

THE PHYSICAL LANDSCAPE

Location, Size, and Configuration

Eastern Europe is somewhat larger than the combined areas of Central and Western Europe. Its east-west distance varies from 650 miles between the Adriatic and the Black Sea, to 240 miles between the Vienna Basin and the nearest border of the Soviet Union, and 400 miles between the western and eastern boundary of Poland. The longest north-south distance, i.e., from the Baltic to the Ionian Sea, is 1,000 miles. Its most northern point, near Gdynia (Gulf of

Gdansk, on the Baltic)—55° N.—has the same latitude as the southern tip of the Alaskan Panhandle, while its southern border along the Albania-Greece border, at roughly 39° N., is located on the same latitude as Cincinnati, Ohio.

The Soviet Union has a common border with every one of the Eastern European countries with the exception of Yugoslavia and Albania (it borders Bulgaria via the Black Sea). Germany, Austria, and Italy border Eastern Europe on the west, Turkey and Greece on the south. The countries of the region vary greatly in size and population: Poland, with 120,000 square miles and 32 million people, is the largest, and Albania, with 11,099 square miles and 2.0 million people is the smallest political unit. The region is centrally located on the European peninsula, and its transitional character is exemplified by its varied physiographic and cultural characteristics.

Main Physiographic Divisions

Diversity of structure is characteristic of the whole region. Owing to its location, the region participates in a great variety of structural and tectonic elements (Fig. 8–1), already mentioned in Chapter 1. The structural elements in the region can be divided into several units: those which form part of the Alpine mountain system, e.g., the Alps, the Carpathians, Balkan ranges, Dinaric ranges; Caledonian [6] structures which extend from the western Baltic to the Polish Uplands; and the Hercynian remains, including the Bohemian Massif, the Sudeten and Lysa Gora mountains and plateaus, the Dobruja, parts of the Rhodope Massif, and various structural islands in the Carpathian Basin. The Alpine mountain system also encloses several Tertiary and Quaternary depressions, of which the best known are the Hungarian and Transylvanian basins (joint name: Carpathian or Pannonian Basin).

In spite of the great structural diversity, it is possible to distinguish four major physi-

ographic regions in Eastern Europe: (1) the North Polish Lowlands; (2) the Polish and Bohemian Uplands, covering parts of Poland and Czechoslovakia; (3) the Carpathian Ranges and Basin, the Walachian Plain and Moldavian Tablelands, which cover parts or all of Czechoslovakia, Poland, Hungary, Romania, and Yugoslavia; and (4) the Southeast European Highlands, in Yugoslavia, Albania, and Bulgaria. In addition, mention should be made of two narrow transitional zones, the Southern Moraine Zone, which changes gradually to the south, leading into the Silesian Plain, and a rolling fertile zone of hills, the Carpathian Forelands.

North Polish Lowlands. The North Polish Lowlands, in geomorphological structure, are a continuation of the North German Lowlands discussed in Chapter 6 (pp. 277–79). Two clear-cut divisions can be made: the Baltic Coastal Zone and Heights (sometimes referred to as the Baltic Moraine Zone) and the Polish Lowlands.

Baltic Coastal Zone and Heights. Poland's coastline, since 1945, has increased from 85 miles to 431 miles and now extends from the estuary of the Odra (Oder) to the Bay of Gdansk. On the whole, the coastline is flat and sandy and long sand bars brought about strong sea currents enclose the depressions of the low coastal platform. This shore line has few good ports: Gdansk, the former Danzig; Gdynia, which was built after 1919 to give Poland an independent ocean outlet; and Szczecin, the former important German port of Stettin, on the mouth of the Odra. Szczecin today serves Poland as the outlet for the exports and imports of the Silesian industrial region—particularly coal exports and iron-ore imports.

South of the narrow coastline are high dune ridges which have been shifted inland by the onshore winds. Southward, a broad, undulating-ground moraine zone paralleling the shore line reaches an average height of 150 feet. These moraines indicate a stable stage of the last ice sheet and reach nearly

[6] For geological terms, see Appendix I.

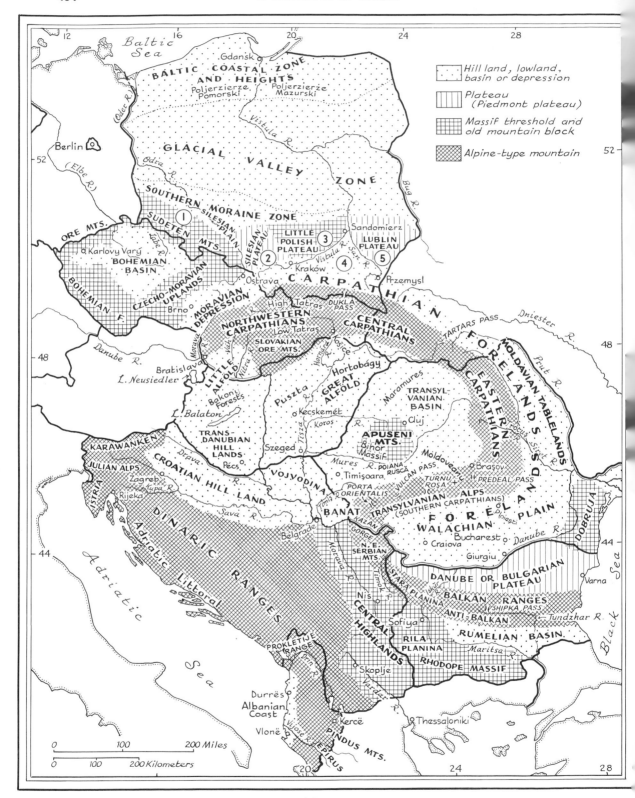

Fig. 8–1. Structural divisions.

1,100 feet southwest of Gdansk. The steeper slopes of the terminal moraines and sandy outwash plains are covered by coniferous forests. Cultivated land is found on the boulder clay of the gentler slopes. Lakes are plentiful in the valleys between the moraines and especially in the Masurian lake area of former East Prussia, in which they fill hollows thought to have been created by subglacial streams. These lakes and some marshes extend on both sides of the lower Vistula (Wisla). Large flat sections are absent in this irregular land surface, and gullies and creeks abound in the typical glacial till. The whole region is sparsely settled, with minerals lacking, agriculture poorly developed, an absence of good harbors, and only a few small and scattered urban concentrations.

GLACIAL VALLEY ZONE. Terminal moraines extending in an east-west direction form the southern boundary of the Baltic Heights. South of these moraines, extending all across Poland, are the Polish Lowlands, a belt of glacial valleys (*pradoliny*, comparable to the German *Urstromtäler*—primeval valleys of streams) which have a strong influence in the present drainage pattern of the Odra, Warta, and Vistula rivers. These rivers use part of the *pradoliny*, and their entries or departures are clearly indicated by the sharp bends of the rivers. Similar to the North German Lowlands, the glacial valleys offer excellent opportunities for connecting Poland's river systems. Two of the important ones are the Odra-Warta-Notec-Vistula-Bug and the Warta-Bzura-Vistula-Bug farther south. The first has a canal connecting the Notec with the Vistula at Bydgoszcz (Fig. 8–2). The Polish Lowlands, including the glacial valleys, present a generally flat and monotonous plain. The valleys, which are slightly below the level of the plain, have loamy soil scattered with moraines, rocks, dunes, and sand flats. Most of the lowlands were originally covered by forests, but only an area east of the Nisa (Neisse) River, stretching toward the middle Odra, is still heavily forested. The Vistula River, which occupies a dominant position in the lowlands, flows generally in a north-south direction through a broad valley. Originally the valley was marshy, and floods are still common. While the Vistula is navigable, it plays a much smaller role in transport than the Rhine River in Germany, or even the Odra River.

SOUTHERN MORAINE ZONE AND SILESIAN PLAIN. Transitional between the Polish Lowlands and Uplands, characterized by the dissected character of its surface, caused by postglacial erosion, lies the Southern Moraine Zone. In the valley of the Odra, the zone extends southward, known as the Silesian Plain. The Silesian Plain is limited on the southwest by the foothills of the Sudeten and on the east by the Hercynian Uplands of the Silesian Plateau.

Polish and Bohemian Uplands. Between the Southern Moraine Zone and the Carpathian Mountains stretches a zone of uplands, consisting of low plateaus and basins. The only exception is found in a brief extension of the lowlands along the valley of the upper Odra (the Silesian Plain). The upland zone is divided into two clearly defined sections, the Polish Uplands and the Bohemian Massif (also called Bohemian Plateau) and surrounding heights. South of the Polish Uplands and east of the Bohemian Massif are the rolling hills of the Carpathian Forelands and the valleys which lead to the Carpathian Ranges.

POLISH UPLANDS. The Polish Uplands consist of five clear-cut sub-regions (Fig. 8–1) which were intermittently covered with fertile loess deposited during the Ice Age by winds carrying loose surface material from areas that had been denuded of vegetation. (1) The Sudeten Mountains, largely composed of old rocks, are west of the Odra River, an area covered with loess, and an important cereal-growing region. (2) The Hercynian Uplands of the Silesian Plateau, east of the Odra River and overlooking the Silesian Plains, contain one of Europe's largest coal fields as well as other minerals. The

Fig. 8–2. Main railways and navigable waterways.

plateau's earlier role as an important frontier region is indicated by its many old castle ruins. (3) The incline eastward from the Silesian Plateau up to the Little Polish Plateau is slight. The high plateau consists of Cretaceous limestones, with some of the area covered by loess. The old rocks of this area contain some copper and iron ores. (4) Between the upper valleys of the Vistula and San rivers lies an important triangular depression: Crakow-Sandomierz-Przemysl. This depression is made up of alluvial deposits coming from the Carpathian slopes and on its southern margin is covered with fertile loess. (5) East of the Vistula and San rivers and south of Lublin is the Plateau of Lublin, consisting mainly of limestone covered with a heavy layer of loess. This is a treeless region, with wheat and sugar beets the main crops.

BOHEMIAN MASSIF AND SURROUNDING HEIGHTS. The very ancient structures of the Bohemian Massif consist of a series of wooded mountains with a few peaks over 4,000 feet, several longitudinal depressions in the southwest and east, some basaltic uplands in the northwest, and a very fertile loess-covered intermontane basin (Bohemian Basin). The Bohemian Forest forms the boundary in the southwest, the Czecho-Moravian Uplands toward the east; toward the northeast heavily eroded, horst-type mountains (crystalline nuclei, surrounded by gneiss, slates, and limestones) of the Sudeten with its highest elevation 5,200 feet in its northwestern part which also includes the headwaters of the Labe (Elbe) River. The lower eastern part of the Sudeten contains the headwaters of the Odra and Morava rivers and ends abruptly at the Moravian Gate (930 feet); toward the northwest are the crystalline Ore Mountains where important uranium ore (pitchblende) is found near Jáchymov. The Labe River divides the Ore Mountains from the Sudeten. In addition, the Massif contains a number of depressions which are often rich in Tertiary lignite, mineral springs, and other important raw materials, e.g., the springs and kaolin of

Marianske Lazne and Karlovy Varý, lignite of Replice, and iron ore in the Berounka Basin. These resources are the basis for an old and flourishing industry.

CARPATHIAN FORELANDS. South of the Polish Uplands and east of the Bohemian Massif is another transitional zone, a rolling zone of hills. This region is important agriculturally, and where loess is not present forests abound. The Moravian depression, between the Danube River (Vienna Basin) and the low gap of the Moravian Gate near Moravska Ostrava, forms part of the Carpathian Forelands. The Czecho-Moravian Uplands border the fertile longitudinal Moravian depression toward the west, and the Carpathian Mountains toward the east. The depression is one of Europe's important routes, connecting the North European plains with the Danube Valley, the Baltic, and the Black Sea drainage. Agriculture, encouraged by mild winters, warm summers, and sufficient rainfall, is dominant in the depression, with sugar beets, wheat, and maize most widely distributed.

Carpathian Ranges and Basin, Walachian Plain, and Moldavian Tablelands. The third of the major physiographic regions of Eastern Europe is characterized by its great uniformity. The Carpathians, together with their forelands, are usually subdivided into five separate physical regions based on characteristics of relief and general landscape. Extending from the east and south are the Moldavian Hill Lands and the Walachian Plain. Within the Carpathian arc is the Carpathian Basin, sometimes referred to as the Pannonian Basin. Through the whole length of this region flows the Danube River, cutting the Basin into unequal sections.

CARPATHIAN RANGES. The arc of the Carpathian Ranges and their forelands extends from the Vienna Basin to the Iron Gate for a distance of over 1,000 miles. This is about the length of the Alps, but the Carpathians reach only an elevation of 8,700 feet in the High Tatry located in the western Carpathians. The Ranges have a continuous outer sandstone belt of Tertiary rock and a discontinuous central zone of crystalline rocks and limestone. Toward the basin of the central zone there is a volcanic inner belt. Within the Carpathian Ranges various divisions are possible; for the purpose of our discussion four subdivisions are briefly analyzed: northwestern, central, eastern, and southern.

1. The northwestern Carpathians extend from the Danube and Morava rivers to Dukla Pass, at 1,640 feet elevation near the headwaters of the San and Hornárd rivers in eastern Czechoslovakia. The Carpathians are widest here and are penetrated by several longitudinal rivers which facilitate transportation and settlement. The most important is the Vah River, which separates the High from the Low Tatry and offers a most valuable connection between western and eastern Slovakia. The High Tatry is located south of the main chain of the western Carpathians. It is a zone composed of crystalline rocks which was glaciated during the Ice Age. Its many cirques, arêtes, waterfalls, and crest-shaped peaks are typical and similar to those of the high Alps. The mountains of the High Tatry average 6,000 to 8,000 feet, with Moldoveneanu (8,737 feet) the highest elevation in the Carpathian Range. South of the High Tatry are the Low Tatry, composed of gneiss and granite. South toward the Carpathian Basin are a series of young volcanic intrusions. The range is known as the Slovakian Ore Mountains. These stretch toward the Hornárd River and contain small deposits of iron ore, copper, gold, and silver. The area between the Tatry and the Dukla Pass has many deep valleys and small intermontane basins, and is heavily forested. Košiče on the Hornárd River is the most important town of eastern Slovakia, located on important north-south and east-west routes. The basins and valleys of the western Carpathians, on the whole, are well cultivated, with the greatest densities on the southern slopes of the Ranges.

2. The central Carpathians (also called Forest Carpathians) extend west from Dukla Pass, but their eastern border is poorly defined and is variously considered as between the sources of the Tisza River near Tartars Pass and as farther south. Here the mountain width is about 60 miles, with a number of low passes offering easy access between the Carpathian Basin and the upper Dniester. This is the former territory of Carpatho-Ukraine, which was part of Czechoslovakia and since 1945 has been part of the Ukrainian S.S.R.

3. The eastern Carpathians, located entirely within Romania, extend southward from Tartars Pass to the Prahova Valley south of Braşov. These mountains may also be divided into three zones: parallel ridges of the eastern sandstone belt, a central limestone and crystalline zone, and a western zone made up of young volcanic material. Rounded mountain tops, the result of weathering of the crystalline schists, is common. Peaks have a height of from 5,000 to 7,000 feet and glaciation has had only minor effects. The lower slopes are heavily forested with deciduous trees (beech predominant) and coniferous forests on the higher slopes, deep valleys, and gorgelike passes, and numerous pastures.

4. The Transylvanian Alps or southern Carpathians extend from the Prahova Valley to two tectonic corridors, Timiş-Cerna and Bistra-Strei, to the west and northwest. Porta Orientalis offers easy access, including a railroad line between the Carpathian Basin and the Walachian Plain. Numerous peaks of the Transylvanian Alps exceed 8,000 feet, and the various glacial features gave the name "Alps" to these ranges. Moldoveanu peak, 8,343 feet in the Fagaras Massif (located between the Prahova and Olt valleys), is the highest elevation. Only a central limestone crystalline zone and the foreland are represented. Typical features of this region are flat-topped plateaus and terraces, as well as numerous longitudinal depressions containing rivers. The present relief is largely the result of uplifting and warping and later stream erosion. Several important routes traverse the Transylvanian Alps at low altitudes, connecting the interior Basin with the Plains. All of these

routes are of long-standing historical importance: Predeal Pass (3,400 feet), Turnul Roşu (1,155 feet), and the Vulcan Pass (5,000 feet).

5. The Western Carpathians, a separate branch of the Carpathian ranges, stretch from the Danube River north to the Barcau Valley. Three main regions of different heights are distinguished: the Apuseni Mountains with the Bihor Massif (6,030 feet) is the highest part, the metal rich Poiana Rusca with a few peaks of 4,593 feet is south of it, and the Banat Mountains are located between the Danube and the Timiş corridor.

The sub-Carpathians (Forelands) form a continuous belt and contain important petroleum deposits in the flysch formations between Bîlteni-Ticleni, the Argeş, and Ploieşti regions to the area between the Trotuş and Tazlău rivers in the Bacău region. It is a densely settled region.

WALACHIAN PLAIN AND MOLDAVIAN TABLELANDS. The Walachian Plain, or "The Plains of the Lower Danube" as it is so often called, is a depression which in the Tertiary was a gulf of the Black Sea, but which by now has been entirely filled by river deposits from the Transylvanian Alps. The whole depression has been uplifted and is now about 150 feet above sea level. The Plain extends from the southern foothills of the Transylvanian Alps through the piedmont plateau of the Balkan Ranges to the Dobruja. The steppe plateau of the Dobruja blocks the straight course of the Danube and forces it into a northward direction. The Moldavian Tablelands form the northern boundary of the Walachian Plain. Navigation on the Danube, especially during floods, is extremely difficult because of the sluggish course of the river. Its many braided channels were formed by its alluvial deposits. These channels have cut broad valleys below the general level. Bordering the floodplains on both the Romanian and the Bulgarian side, cliffs rise as much as 300 feet above the marshes on the latter side.

The Moldavian Tablelands lie between the Siret and Prut rivers, with hills, especially in the central part, reaching an elevation of over 1,300 feet. The whole area consists of sedimentary rocks of the Tertiary age. With the exception of a central plateau, the entire region is a hilly steppe. The hills are loess covered with fertile chernozem soils. Recurrent and disastrous droughts do much damage.

CARPATHIAN BASIN. This depression is enclosed by the arc of the Carpathian Ranges, the Eastern Alps, and the Dinaric Ranges. The Basin itself, with an area of over 100,000 square miles with centripetal drainage, is not uniform in relief. It is divided into minor basins, hill lands, and mountains. Much of the Basin was covered by an inland sea until rivers from the surrounding mountains filled it with alluvial deposits. The division of the Carpathian Basin is as follows: the Little Alföld, the Transdanubian Hill Lands, the Croatian Hill Lands, the Great Alföld, the Apuseni Mountains, and the Transylvanian Basin. The Little Alföld [7] extends from the foothills of the Alps to the southeast slopes of the Bakony Mountains and north across the Danube to the foothills of the western Carpathians. The central portion of the Little Alföld is located southeast of Bratislava and consists of a large alluvial fan of gravel and silt. Neusiedler Lake, at the Austro-Hungarian border, is surrounded by swamps and mud flats and is one of the remnants of the inland sea.

South and west of the Little Alföld are the rolling hill lands of Transdanubia. They are covered by loess and have a general northeast-southwest alignment. Their greatest height is reached at about 3,300 feet. This subdivision is bordered on the east by the Danube and on the south by the Drava River. Lake Balaton, with a maximum depth of only 35 feet, is another of the shallow fresh-water lakes remaining from the inland sea. Between Lake Balaton and the Drava and Danube rivers is a low, dissected, very productive plateau covered with loess. The city of Pécs is in the center.

---

[7] *Al*—low, *föld*—land.

Between the Drava, the Danube, the Sava, and the foothills of the Slovenian Alps are the Croatian Hill Lands. These are very fertile loess-covered lowlands interspersed with limestone and crystalline hills. Patches of forest cover alternate with densely cultivated lands.

The Great Alföld stretches irregularly east and north of the Danube to the foothills and volcanic belts of the western and central Carpathians and the Banat and Bihor mountains. The Alföld is a perpetually settling block which has been covered by Tertiary and Quaternary strata and is dissected by the meandering Tisza River. The western part is an elongated, partly sand-covered region often referred to as "Mesopotamia." [8] Southeast of Kecskemét is the *puszta* (waste), a region of soil saturated with salt. Near Debrecen is Hortobágy, a steppe region covered with sand which has a high soda content. Most of the Banat between the Tisza and the Transylvanian Alps is covered with fertile black soil.

The Transylvanian Basin, east of the Great Alföld and the Apuseni Mountains, consists of Tertiary clay strata reaching an elevation of up to 2,000 feet. It also was once a sea basin which filled with river deposits, but it is now high and hilly, having been uplifted and dissected. The Basin also has quantities of natural gas and salt and is heavily forested at higher elevations.

The Carpathian Basin is transitional with regard to climatic conditions, which in this region are typical in many ways of the contrasts in parts of Eastern Europe. All four basic climatic types prevail, with the greatest transitions in the Hungarian part of the Basin. Rainfall declines from west to east, as, for example, between Bratislava and Szeged (total precipitation 28 inches in Bratislava and 22 inches in Szeged). Most of the rain falls in early summer, with smaller but still sufficient amounts in the latter part of the summer. October rains are important, especially for southwestern Hungary. Unfortunately, the summer rain occurs during a period of high temperatures and high evaporation which lessen the effectiveness of the precipitation. Temperature differences between summer and winter are considerable, but by no means extreme. Bratislava, for example, has an average January temperature of 30° F., Budapest of 28°, and Debrecen, in the eastern part of the Great Alföld, of 25°; the average July temperatures of these locations are 70°, 71°, and 71°, respectively. Temperatures are higher in the southern cities of the Great Alföld, e.g., Szeged has a January temperature of 30° and a July temperature of 75°. The nearby mountain ranges act as a climatic barrier and often limit oceanic influences. Certain changes indicate a progressive continental condition, e.g., the daily ranges vary from 30° in Bratislava to 40° in the eastern part of the Great Alföld.

Southeast European Highlands. Five physiographic regions can clearly be defined within the Highlands: the Alps; the Dinaric Ranges, including the Adriatic littoral; the Transitional and Basin Lands of the Morava and Vardar; the Rhodope Massif and depressions; and the Balkan Ranges. The structure and relief of these Highlands is extremely complicated and diverse, and the lithic composition varies from calcareous to the more resistant crystalline rocks. Volcanic intrusions indicate that the Highlands are an area of instability. Steep mountains and small intermontane basins and heavy erosion, especially in the southern Highlands, are typical. A large part of the Highlands is composed of karst, containing all characteristic karst features.

---

[8] As a result of Sumerian-Magyar affiliations in early historical time the Magyars, when occupying the Carpathian Basin in the ninth century, called it the Mesopotamian region between the Danube and Tisza rivers (Duna-Tisza Köze: Mid-Danube-Tisza, or Danube-Tisza-Mesopotamia) and, based on the old tradition, regarded this area as the center of their country. The region east of the Tisza was named Tiszántúl (Trans-Tisza, or Transtisia), while the area west of the Danube was called Dunántúl (Transdanubia). This explanation will clear up some of the errors and misunderstandings of these terms in various works. Hungarian (Magyar) verbiage, customs, and place names reflect, even at present, a strong Sumerian affinity.

Fig. 8–3. Primošten, on the central Dalmatian coast, south of Šibenik, founded during the sixteenth century is a small town with a population of 1200. The town is located on a peninsula between the bays of Raduča and Primošten and is connected with the mainland by a dam. The area is well protected from the north winds and therefore has a very mild climate. View is toward north with the small island of Smokvica and the larger island of Tmara toward the left, and the mainland with its promontories and the typical karst vegetation to the right. (Yugoslav Information Center.)

THE ALPS. The Karawanken chain of the Eastern Alps forms the northern boundary of the Southeast European Highlands. The limestone Julian Alps have their continuation in the Dinaric Ranges. The valleys are heavily forested, but the limestone rocks support only poor agriculture. The Ljubljana Basin is partly enclosed by the Julian Alps and the Karawanken chain. Between the Alps and the Dinaric Ranges an arm of the Pannonian Plain approaches the Adriatic to within a distance of 75 miles. This gap was important as an early route connecting the Baltic with the Mediterranean, and modern highways emphasize its importance as a routeway. The climate varies from extreme cold in the Alpine region, through somewhat higher annual average temperatures (53–56°) in the middle Drava and Sava valleys, to typical continental conditions farther east in the Croatian Hill Lands.

DINARIC RANGES. These parallel Ranges, folded in the mid-Tertiary period, trend southeast from the Ljubljana Basin and the Sava-Kupa Valley in the northeast to the Morava-Vardar passage. The width of the ranges varies from 60 to 100 miles, and the average elevation varies from 4,000 to 6,000 feet. Great diversity, ranging from the barren, dissected, and waterless High Karst in the west to a series of parallel forested mountains and hill lands in the north and northeast, characterizes this region. Commonly, the Dinaric Ranges are divided into three parts:

1. The narrow coastal zone, the Adriatic littoral, with its many islands and arms of the Adriatic Sea, presents a most picturesque landscape (Fig. 8–3). The coastal zone and the terraced hillsides have only a limited amount of soil, and Mediterranean crops such as olives, vines, and figs, and limited pasture land and cereal acreage, together with fishing, are important sources of income for the rural population.

2. Access to the interior is blocked by the High Karst, part of the Dinaric massif, a bar-

Fig. 8–4. View of the Dinaric massif, between Dalmatia and Bosnia. During Pleistocene times limestone detritus filled the karstic hollow, now the plain of Suho Polje. Sheep and goats have destroyed all but small areas of the forest cover (the black patches in the middle distance). Suho Polje is now a state plantation of almonds and other nut trees. (G. W. Hoffman.)

Fig. 8–5. Dolina under cultivation in Montenegro. Stone walls protect the terraces from erosion. The white (light) part of the lowest dolina is extremely sandy. (G. W. Hoffman.)

ren, mainly Mesozoic limestone zone which extends from northwest to southeast for 350 miles, and has a maximum width of 50 miles and an elevation averaging 8,000 feet. The relief gives this region its fortress-like characteristics (Fig. 8–4). The river valleys are very short and widely spaced because precipitation falling upon these limestone rocks sinks underground where it continues to flow. Rivers flow in deeply dissected valleys or through gorges which are difficult to traverse. They carry varying quantities of water and have considerable elevation differences between source and mouth. Their use for hydroelectric projects is now under way. The whole region consists of a series of barren, rocky plateaus with a series of flat ridges, the so-called *planina;* longitudinal troughs, *polja* (meaning fields), which were formed from subsiding hollows and subsequently enlarged when rain water and rivers dissolved the calcareous rocks; *dolinas,* small round depressions also formed by the solution of calcareous rocks; and *uvale* (larger *doline*—600 feet in diameter). The *polja, dolina,* and *uvale* are covered with alluvial deposits and/or red earth (terra rossa), a relatively fertile soil formed by the non-soluble material in the limestone (Fig. 8–5). Karst *polja* often are surrounded by peneplains (formed during the late Tertiary). Those of Lika and Livno are each about 45 miles in length. Mention should also be made of the important subterranean caves, typical for certain calcareous areas.

3. The inner part of the Dinaric Ranges, inner Bosnia and western Serbia, is less barren and rugged. Sandstone and limestone predominate in a few places and crystalline rocks of Pre-Cambrian origin are visible. Narrow and open valleys are interspersed and extensive mining and logging activities are carried on throughout the countryside. The slopes toward the Sava lowlands are the most densely settled areas of the region.

The Dinaric Ranges extend through all of Albania. One of them, the Prokletije Range, reaches over 7,000 feet astride the Albano-Yugoslav border. South of this range, a series of parallel ranges extends southward to merge with the Albanian Epirus Ranges. Between the coast and the Dinaric Ranges are hilly lowlands. The coastline does not have the characteristics of the Adriatic littoral of Yugoslavia, and it alternates between swampy depressions, marshy deltas, and sand bars, which enclose numerous shallow lagoons. The limestone hills are covered with *maqui* and offer few opportunities for agriculture. Grazing and mountain agriculture are the main occupations of the people of this region.

TRANSITIONAL AND BASIN LANDS OF THE MORAVA AND VARDAR. A region of great diversity is located south of the Danube, including the Morava-Vardar depression, with its many tectonic basins which originated in mid-Tertiary times. This depression affords a short route (about 300 miles) between the lowlands of the north and the Aegean Sea and its head port of Thessaloniki. West of the depression are the foothills of the southeastern Dinaric Ranges, which consist of detached mountain blocks and basins connected by narrow passages.

RHODOPE MASSIF. Crossing the Transitional and Basin Lands of the Morava and Vardar depression, in an easterly direction, is the relatively narrow Rhodope Massif also called Macedonian-Thracian Massif. It broadens southeastward and falls gradually toward the east into a series of uplands and dissected hills, which are broken by the Maritsa River northwest of Edirne. Toward the north, the Rhodope Massif and the Balkan Ranges enclose the Rumelian Basin (also called Maritsa Basin or Plain of Thrace), which is drained by the Maritsa River.

The highest part of the Rhodope Massif is in the Rila Planina, an area of volcanic origin, containing the headwaters of the Maritsa River. Mount Musala (9,596 feet), in the Rila Planina, is the highest mountain in Bulgaria. With the exception of some fertile basins and river valleys (e.g., Skopje, Stip, Struma), the whole Rhodope Massif is highly unproductive. Toward the central part, forested areas alternate with grasslands where grazing is prevalent.

BALKAN RANGES. Between the Walachian Plain in the north, the Rumelian Basin in the south, and the Rhodope Massif in the south and southwest, the arc of the Balkan Ranges forms a continuation of the Carpathian Ranges. The part south of the Danube to the Timok River is known as the Northeast Serbian Mountains and forms a link between the Carpathians and the Stara Planina (old mountains). This region reaches altitudes between 3,700 and 5,100 feet and is characterized by poor lines of communication, by karstic relief, and by valuable mineral resources.

The northern portions of the Balkan Ranges slope gradually to the Danube, where they fall off rather abruptly about 300 feet, in a wall of limestone and loess. This area is known as the Danube or Bulgarian Plateau. The plateau is extremely fertile, covered by loess, but dissected by deep and broad valleys. The contrast in relief and climate between the fertile valley plains and the plateau is great. The valleys have abundant water supply and are protected from the cold, dusty winter winds blowing across the plateau from the Walachian Plain. The Danube Plateau reaches the steppelike plateau of the Dobruja, with its eastern and northern border formed by the marshlands of the Danube. The Balkan Ranges are easily crossed by two north-south railways, via the Isker Valley to Sofiya and via the Shipka Pass, connecting the Danube port of Giurgiu (on the railroad to Bucharest) with the Maritsa Valley. The Ranges gradually become lower toward the east and, together with the Plateau on the north, enclose the small Varna Basin, which opens toward the Black Sea.

South of the main range of the Balkan Ranges are a number of significant depressions. The Tundzha depression, which results from a downfaulting of the land, is characterized by numerous hot springs and the widespread cultivation of roses. This specialization, which began many years ago, is responsible for the name "Valley of the Roses," by which this valley is known. The Anti-Balkan Range, with deeply cut valleys, extends south of this depression which in turn rather abuptly slopes to the depression of the Rumelian Basin. Another depression is that of Sofiya, the southern border of which is formed by a branch of the Balkan Ranges extending in a southeastern direction from the Pirot Basin in Yugoslavia toward the main range of the Rhodope Massif near Rila Planina. The basin has an elevation of 1,800 feet and is easily accessible through several river valleys. The largest depression is drained by the Maritsa River and opens toward the Aegean Sea. The fertile alluvial soil and abundance of water permit the growing of a great variety of crops, especially tobacco, cotton, rice, vines, and hardy fruits.

THE CULTURAL AND HISTORICAL BACKGROUND

In the Introduction, Eastern Europe was described as a zone of transition, a zone of clash and instability, a "Shatter Belt" for some and a cordon or curtain for others. The objective here is to describe in broad outlines the peopling of these lands, the settlements and social structure of the people, the political-territorial framework of the present countries, and finally the economic development of the post-World War I national states. At times the discussions include developments in the whole area, at times it will be necessary to refer to individual peoples or countries. At the same time, the close relationship between developments in this area and the main stream of European history must constantly be kept in mind. The location of the area between the main body of the Slavic people in Russia and the Germanic people in Central Europe; the settling of the numerically few Magyars and Romanians in the centrally located Pannonian Basin, thus dividing the Slavic people into a northern and a southern group; as well as the deep penetration of the Ottoman Turks over so many centuries have left important marks on the people and their institutions.

The Peopling of Eastern Europe

Before answering the question of who the people of Eastern Europe are, it is of interest to locate the main routes of the ancestors who established their present homes. People moved along certain well-defined routeways and easily penetrable passes, preferring grasslands and plateaus to forests and marshes. Inasmuch as these movements were not always the rapid invasion of raiders, it was important for the migrants with their herds constantly to seek fertile soils and pasture lands as they moved along. As a result of these limitations, the routes were few in number. On the basis of a reconstruction of the early vegetation and hydrographic pattern, and with the assistance of archaeological evidence, it is possible to trace in a general way the major routes by which these primitive people entered the area.

The lands of origin of many of these primitive people are still not exactly determined, but three source regions from which migrations came can definitely be established: the grasslands of western central Asia, the lowlands between the Odra and the Vistula, and the plateaus and basins of the Polish Uplands. Generally speaking, we can distinguish six routes or groups of routes leading to and within Eastern Europe:

1. The most northerly route led from the middle Vistula along the swamps and forests of the Baltic and made good use of the various river systems north of the Pripet Marshes. This was a part of the old Amber route.

2. A route led from the loess-covered plateau region (Lublin Plateau) south of the Pripet Marshes, southeastward along the loess belt into the Southern Russian Steppe.

3. Another route led from the Polish lowlands to the upper Odra, the Moravian Gate, using the easily crossed low watershed between the Odra and Morava [9] valleys, to the Danube and the Pannonian Basin.

4. Several routes cross the Carpathian arc from the northeast, e.g., Dukla Pass and Tartars Pass, affording an easy crossing from the Dniester Valley into the Pannonian Basin.

5. The important Vardar-Morava depression offered a relatively easy route both from the coastal plains of Thrace and from the Aegean Sea to the Danube Valley and the Pannonian Basin.

6. An important route led from the Adriatic Sea, through the valleys of the Kupa and Sava, to the Pannonian Basin.

Overpopulation and the search for new and better lands probably were the main reasons for the movements of so many people in the first millennium. Before the period of large-scale folk-wanderings got under way in the fifth century A.D., small groups had already established themselves within Eastern Europe. For example, the Romans, ancestors of the present Romanians, in their conquest of the lower Danube made contact with the Dacians in the lower Danube Basin; the Illyrians, first reported by Herodotus as living in the western half of the Balkan Peninsula, north of present-day Greece, are today represented by the Albanians, the name of an Illyric tribe. Throughout the third and fourth centuries A.D., people from the central-Asian steppes, known as Huns and Avars, crossed the Carpathian passes into the Carpathian Basin. Various Nordic people, also, appeared at diverse times.

Various Slavic people began to leave their original homelands during the second and third centuries and owing to their greater numbers easily slavicized the few settlers they found. The Slavs first settled west of the Pripet Marshes, then settled the broad river valleys and fertile rolling plains of the Vistula (Wisla), Morava, Danube, and Morava-Vardar rivers, but, as more and more moved through and settled along the well-established routes, some settled on land well beyond these easily accessible routes (Fig. 8–6). The Poles, whose original homeland

---

[9] Note that there are two Morava rivers in Eastern Europe, one in Moravia (Czechoslovakia) and another in Serbia (Yugoslavia). The name Morava means "frontier," and both rivers have played a great role in the history of migration in two key transitional lands of Eastern Europe.

Fig. 8–6. Ethnographic patterns of Eastern Europe. Majorities over 50 per cent are represented, on the basis of censuses taken since 1945 and unofficial data concerning German resettlement.

is believed to have been in the Vistula Basin,[10] spread to the Odra and perhaps beyond. The first Polish state emerged early in the Middle Ages on the plain between the

Warta and the Vistula rivers. The Czechs settled the valley of the Morava (Moravian depression) and in the Bohemian Basin; the Slovaks moved into the southern valleys of the western Carpathians; the Ruthenians settled most of the central Carpathians; and Slavic settlements in the territory of today's Yugoslavia commenced during the sixth century A.D. and occupied three geographically well-defined regions. In the north, the Slavs

[10] There is ample proof that the Poles were not the first occupants of the Vistula Basin. Being one of Europe's important migratory regions, it is obvious that these lands were the home of a succession of people with different racial history. But the fact remains that, in spite of Germanic pressures, the rural areas of the lower Vistula remained Polish.

settled the southern part of the Old Roman province of Pannonia, especially the valleys extending north and south of the Sava River; in the south, they occupied the watershed region of Raška, and the basins of the Drin River, in Albania. The Slavic settlements remained permanently in the first two regions only. Raška played a very important historical role inasmuch as it became the ancient center of the first Serbian state.[11] The various South Slavs, Serbs, Macedonians, Croats, and Slovenes, slowly spread over most of the area of today's Yugoslavia. The Bulgars (today's Bulgarians), of Asiatic origin with Finno-Ugric and Turkic affinities of race and language, first settled in Bessarabia, later in the Danube delta and in the seventh century moved across the Danube to the Danube Plateau which for some time was the core of the Bulgar state. They quickly became slavicized and lost their Finno-Ugric language. The origin of the Romanians is still controversial.[12] They made their homes mainly in the foothills of the Carpathians and later moved into the Walachian Plain, Moldavian Tablelands and the Carpathian Basin. The settlers were under Slavic and Magyar pressure, but they retained the language of Imperial Rome. This is one of the remarkable incidents in history, especially so since the Roman occupation of Dacia lasted only for 163 years.

[11] According to Jovan Cvijić, *La Péninsule Balkanique* (Paris: Librairie Armand Colin, 1918), p. 278, differences in physical appearance and emotional characteristics among the various South Slavic people appeared because of the isolation and inaccessibility of their settlements. Cvijić believes that the main differences between the people of the Balkan Peninsula are to be found in their physical characteristics and not in their language and religion.

[12] The Romanians consider themselves descendants of Roman provincials. In addition they also "claim that they are the true descendants of Trajan's colonists, that Transylvania is the cradle of their race, and that historic continuity has never been lost." The latter claim is certainly most difficult to document. R. W. Seton-Watson, "Romanian Origins," *History*, VII (1922–23): p. 243. Some historians speak of them as invaders from south of the Danube perhaps during the ninth century, others as late as the thirteenth century.

Closely related to the Romanians are the few surviving Vlachs, also known as Wallachs, whose language is closely related to modern Romanian.

Another people of Asiatic origin, the Ural-Altaic-speaking Magyars or Hungarians crossed the passes of the eastern Carpathians during the ninth century. Retaining many nomadic traits, and after a series of deep penetrations into the west by the year 1000, they settled in the dry grasslands of the Great Alföld. Not until the rule of King Stephen (997–1038) were pastoralism and transhumance replaced with agriculture. The closely related Szekely people settled in the nearby Carpathians, but opinion differs as to how they happened to settle such a distance from the main concentration of the Magyar people. The settlement of the Magyars thus contributed to the permanently established wedge between the Slavic people, dividing them into a northern Slavic group: Poles, Czechs, and Slovaks; and a southern Slavic group: Slovenes, Croats, Serbs, Macedonians, and Bulgars. At the same time it must be pointed out that, without a dependable reinforcement, the Magyars probably could not have held out alone against the numerically stronger Slavic people. And that brings us to the third element in this transitional zone, the Germans. Inasmuch as the movements of the various Germanic tribes were traced in some detail in Chapter 6 (pp. 300–02), only those aspects of Germanic settlement having to do with extension into Eastern Europe are discussed here.

Germanic penetrations extended along the whole east front from the middle Elbe and the Saale, its tributary (its eastern boundary until about 1200), to the southern Marches of Styria and Carniola (Fig. 6–14). Generally speaking, Germanic eastward movements commenced after the general pattern of Slavic and Magyar settlements had been well established. These eastward movements were brought about, in part, as a reaction to Slavic and Magyar penetration into the west; in part, for simple military conquest and territorial increases; in part, by missionary and trading activities; and, in part, by the need of various Slavonic and Magyar rulers for craftsmen and skilled artisans. The Magyars' need, in the thirteenth century, for additional settlers to protect their eastern boundary in Transylvania against recurrent Mongol forays and conquests is connected with the well-known settlements of the Saxons.[13] These German settlements—most of them ceased to exist after the changes brought about during and following World War II—were distributed among nearly all of the Eastern European countries, extended as far east as the middle Volga River, and for centuries played an important role as a powerful cultural minority.

Germanic movements across the northern lowlands resulted in the acquisition of territory between the Elbe and Odra, the so-called *Mittelmark* (later Brandenburg), in the early thirteenth century. At the same time the Order of the Teutonic Knights moved along the Baltic coast, conquering lands northeast to the Nieman River, part of which became Prussia (later East Prussia). During the beginning of the fourteenth century, land east of and along the upper part of the Odra came under the authority of the Holy Roman Empire. But, with the growth of Polish power at the end of the fourteenth century, Germanic conquests were halted, and even reversed in the territory east of the Odra, which resulted in the destruction of the Teutonic Order and the incorporation of conquered territory into the Polish-Lithuanian state. German settlers were permitted to remain, but colonization was not renewed until the eighteenth century. It reached its greatest extent after the partition of Poland at the end of that century. The demand for German craftsmen continued all through the period of Polish strength, and many Polish cities in the Uplands were founded by Germans, substantial

numbers of whom remained until the end of World War II.

German settlements within the Bohemian Basin are all connected with the movements of craftsmen, artisans, woodsmen, peasants, and miners and started as early as the late twelfth century and the beginning of the thirteenth. They were largely confined to the towns and countryside along the inner rim of the Ore Mountains and were encouraged by the Czech nobility, but some German colonists settled as far east as the Spis region in today's Slovakia (Fig. 8–7). German penetration into the Pannonian Basin included both agricultural settlers and those interested in establishing cities. Again German craftsmen, artisans, and miners were called into the country, together with general settlers assisting the defense of the country, and the earlier-mentioned Saxons settled in parts of Transylvania. German penetrations south, among the Slovenes, were missionary and trading missions, but they brought to a halt and often reversed the northward movements of the Slovenes. Slovene settlements north of the southern Alps, in Carinthia (Austria), are a reminder of those times.

There were other movements into this transitional zone, both military and peaceful, e.g., Swedes into the Baltic areas and Italians, especially Venetian traders, along the Adriatic littoral, while Jews from Western Europe came as tradesmen, hoping for freedom from religious persecution. It is thought that nearly half of the world's Jews lived in the Kingdom of Poland at the end of the Middle Ages. But none of these later penetrations left as deep an impact as that of the Ottoman Turks. Turkish conquest and control between the fifteenth and eighteenth centuries extended as far as the gates of Vienna and included in its furthest expansion most of the Carpathian Basin and Southeast Europe, and the only South Slavic people who escaped this destructive control were the Slovenes and some of the Croats and mountain-dwelling Montenegrins. The Magyar homelands were controlled for a

---

[13] Saxon is the general name applied to German settlers. The numerical superiority of the Slavs surrounding Magyar territory, and possible intrusions from the east, were constant sources of fear for this country.

Fig. 8–7. Spišské Podhradie, population 3500 in Hornbad basin, Eastern Slovakia. The town extends below the ruins of Spiš castle which is the largest castle in Slovakia. In the twelfth century the town was founded and was burned in 1780. It is a small agricultural community on the road from Košice and Prešov to the western part of Czechoslovakia. (G. W. Hoffman.)

comparatively short period, about 150 years, but during that time their numbers were reduced by half from the original estimated population of five million. Among the South Slavs the Serbs, Macedonians, and earlier-slavicized Bulgars, Vlachs, and Albanians were completely suppressed under Turkish rule. With the slow retreat of the Turkish armies toward Serbia and the southern Dinaric Ranges, brought about by the victorious Austrian army comprised of soldiers from many lands, these devastated countries were resettled. The settlements along the so-called Austrian-Turkish military border north of the Danube and along the Sava and Kupa rivers became a mirror of all the lands under the Hapsburg control. This is one reason why the new state of Yugoslavia, and parts of Romania after their founding in 1918, had such large minorities of Germans, Slovaks, Magyars, Czechs, Italians, etc. The last time territory was freed from Turkish control was at the beginning of the twentieth century, following the first Balkan War in 1912.

These folk-wanderings, military conquests, pioneering efforts, forced settlings, missionary efforts, and trading ventures brought about a great instability, backwardness, and oppression in this whole region. This was further accentuated by divisions of a religious nature and of class structure inherent in the prevalent system of land ownership. Christianization came from two centers, Rome and Constantinople. Often these two centers worked at cross-purposes. The religious boundary between Roman Catholicism and Eastern Orthodoxy extends north and south through all of Eastern Europe,[14] sepa-

[14] It should, however, be pointed out here that the first Czech state, the Moravian Kingdom of the ninth century, was Byzantine, and not Roman in its religious orientation. Two missionaries from Constantinople, Cyril and Methodius, were responsible for the spread of Byzantine culture and creed. When the Magyars penetrated into this important transitional area, the Czech and Slovak people were forced to flee into the surrounding, better-protected territories of the western Carpathians and the Bohemian Basin. One of the consequences was their change in orientation to a Western European and Roman culture.

rating the Poles and the Lithuanians from the Russians, the Romanians from the Magyars, and the Slovenes and Croats from the Macedonians and Serbs. This religious boundary has its greatest import where it divides a single political unit such as Yugoslavia, where it results in deep differences between the Croats and the Serbs. The religious division also influenced the outlook of the individual countries, toward Western or Eastern European culture, and had a lasting impact on the social and political organizations of this area. An additional element of instability resulted from the occupation of Constantinople by the Moslem Turks and the conversion to Islamic faith of many people living within Turkish-controlled territory. The division of the Christian Church in Western and Central Europe, the growth of Protestantism, especially among the various Germanic peoples, and their struggle during the fifteenth and sixteenth centuries, left deep marks of further division among some of the people of Eastern Europe, e.g., in the northern lowlands, but also among the Czechs and Magyars. The Poles remained faithful to the authority of Rome, and the Church closely identified itself with the struggle for national survival, against German Protestantism and Eastern Russian Orthodoxy.

Social Structure and Settlements

The different people settling the lands of Eastern Europe had certain preferences and aptitudes which usually became the mark of their civilization. The Slavic people were land tillers, hunters, stockbreeders, and fishermen and at first preferred to settle in lowlands. They cut virgin forests and some of them practiced seasonal pasturage. They raised cattle, pigs, and horses, and traded in timber and later in minerals. The Rumans (Romanians) and Bulgars, too, were land tillers and preferred open grasslands or plateaus and hill lands. The Albanians and Montenegrins survived in the mountainous areas into which they had been pushed. The Magyars, finding a great similarity with their

original physical environment, found in the dry grasslands of the Great Alföld the ideal conditions for a nomadic way of life, emphasizing pastoralism and despising tillage.[15] Germans settled in uplands and along rivers. They liked to alter the surroundings and are also well known as tradesmen, skilled artisans, and city builders.

The shelters built by these people and the settlements developed through the ages depended on existing materials, on military pressures exerted against the people, on their occupations, and on their location. Tent dwellings, typical for a nomad society, were common for the Magyars; clay houses were typical for the plains; wooden houses for mountains; and stone houses for the karst lands and the Adriatic littoral, and combinations thereof could be found in most borderland regions. Long narrow houses as well as small flat-roofed ones are usually found in lowlands; mountainous regions have everything from one-story, one-room houses to the high quadrangular buildings typical for the South Slavs and the Mediterranean people. Many houses have fortress-like characteristics.

Typical for the North Slavs living in the upland areas is the one-story, so-called smoking-room house, with open fire in the living room, small, partially covered entrance hall, and stables, all under one roof. Only the more wealthy peasants could afford a second room. Variations of this type are common in the mountainous areas south of the Danube. A variation common among the Magyars and lowland Slovaks is a one- to two-story house with a partially covered pillared entrance hall along the full length of the house, opened toward the yard. Still another variation, common among the Croats, is the one-story house with a wide overhanging roof covered with straw. Two rooms are customary, a kitchen-living room and a bedroom. Considerable storage space for winter feeding of the animals is provided in the

15 Only in the nineteenth century was a wheat economy substituted for the horse and the sheep.

Fig. 8–8. Farm house in the Zagorje (Croatia). It consists of two rooms and is painted blue. (G. W. Hoffman.)

attic. Livestock have a place nearby (Fig. 8–8). Sometimes the outsides of the houses are painted in different colors (blue being very popular). Obviously, the great intermixture of people, especially in those areas resettled after the Turkish wars, makes it difficult to establish a definite pattern. Migrants adjusted their original forms of shelter to existing conditions.

Urbanization was slow in coming. In the Carpathian Basin, to protect the croplands against constant pillages, villages developed, the so-called "village towns" or "peasant villages" (Fig. 8–9), with outlying houses occupied only during harvest times. Scattered hamlets with stone houses on steep slopes are typical for some of the southern Dinaric regions of Montenegro and Albania. These hamlets, too, were defensive in character and purpose. The layout of settlements depended upon local relief. In agricultural regions, both the closely patterned nucleated village (Fig. 8–9, bottom) and the so-called

"shoestring" village were typical; in forested areas there were round-patterned villages permitting an easy expansion where timberland was brought under cultivation. Dispersed settlements, found in mountain areas all over Eastern Europe, were typical for people following pastoral or lumbering occupations or in regions of poor soil. Closely packed villages with narrow streets are common in the mining communities of Bohemia and the western Carpathians, and in the coastal towns along the Dalmatian littoral. German influence usually can be traced to many of the market centers in the Bohemian and Polish Uplands, and in the closely built towns of Transylvania—houses two and three stories high and decoratively ornamented, administrative buildings with the church in the center, and a well-laid-out market place with streets radiating to the town's edges. Many towns in the Carpathian Basin are relatively new. They had to be rebuilt after the region was reoccupied following the

Fig. 8–9. Two characteristic settlement types of the Carpathian Basin: (above) a circular rural town established in the Middle Ages, for defensive purposes; (below) a square modern village laid out by engineers.

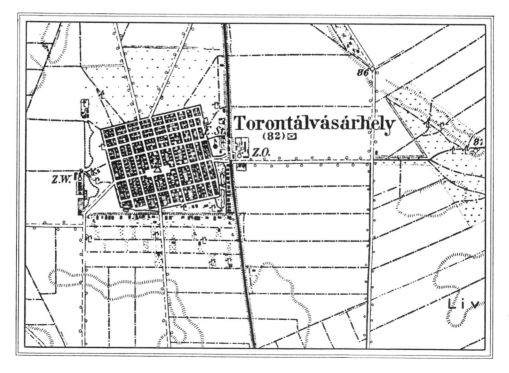

Turkish military defeats in the seventeenth and eighteenth centuries and therefore consist largely of one-story whitewashed stone buildings with tile roofs, with all of the wide tree-lined streets leading to a central square.

Turkish occupation, on the whole, did not result in new settlements, but rather in new sections of existing towns. Turkish settlements are characterized by houses which are closed toward the street and opened toward the interior. Sometimes a high wall with a heavy gate encloses a yard.

In the center of the Turkish part of the towns is the famous oriental bazaar, a place for trade and commerce which is the center of activities. The Turkish settlements usually were divided into a quiet living district and the business quarters. The houses of tradesmen, artisans—metal and armament industries, silk and gold embroidery—were usually concentrated in the center of the towns. On the whole, areas long under Turkish occupation developed fewer and smaller urban concentrations. Belgrade, at the northern end of the Morava-Vardar depression on the confluence of the Sava and Danube rivers, Skopje, located where the routes to Niš divide, and Sofiya, were the only larger settlements in the Slavic-settled regions under Turkish control. Towns within the Hapsburg Empire, the Prussian state, and Poland developed along important trade routes and/or near strategic sites. Good examples are Cracow on the upper Vistula River, one of Europe's leading trading cities for roughly 300 years; Prague, roughly in the center of the Bohemian Basin; Buda, on the high, western bank of the Danube River; and Pest, the commercial town on the low, eastern part, located where the Danube is easy to bridge, before it reaches the marshy course it takes through the plains to the south (Fig. 3–10). While the location of the city is extremely favorable geographically, it never was able to rival Vienna, its neighbor to the west, in terms of trade and strategic location.

During the nineteenth century railways were built to link important commercial and strategic centers. The Danube, at the Iron Gate, was made navigable. With transportation of goods over longer distances becoming easier and more abundant, thousands of agricultural workers moved into the rapidly expanding towns. By the end of the nineteenth century Bucharest, Prague, Lodz, Breslau (Wrocław), and Warsaw had become cities with a population of over 100,000, Budapest over half a million. Industrialization came later and much more slowly to the countries of Eastern Europe. Their first function was to supply raw materials to the newly expanding industries of Western and Central Europe, and only slowly did heavy industry move in. Industrialization was still slower in the former territory of the Turkish Empire and did not start until after World War II.

A brief reference has been made to the importance of and the implication of the class structure on the people of this region. Obviously, it would be too difficult to trace this structure back to the first settlers, but for a clear understanding of the tremendous changes in society during the last 20–25 years it is important to summarize briefly the basic structure as it existed at the onset of World War I.

Generally speaking, two structures existed in Eastern Europe: (1) that of the North Slavs, Magyars, and those areas of the South Slavs under control of the Austro-Hungarian Empire; and (2) that of those areas south of the Danube and Sava rivers formerly controlled by the Turkish Empire, especially the territory of the Serbs, Montenegrins, Albanians, and Bulgarians. The first group, the northern region, consisted of a number of feudal states—Prussia, Poland, Bohemia, Hungary, etc.—where the landed gentry was the leading class and the mass of the peasants were either serfs (in most regions until 1848, in the Russian part of Poland until 1867) or half free. This landed nobility, together with the high clergy, had a dominant influence on the central government. Often these central governments were weak and indecisive. Ever since the Middle Ages, and closely related to the growing importance of trade and com-

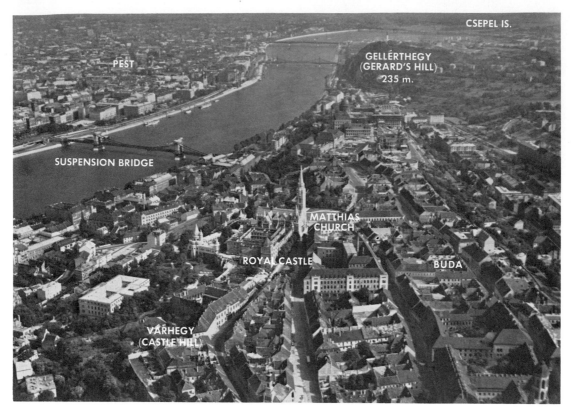

Fig. 8–10. Budapest, view from Várhegy (castle hill) south toward Gellérthegy (Gerard's hill). At the far south Csepel Island, the port of Budapest. Castle hill was the nucleus of New Buda. The municipality of Budapest was only organized in 1873 when Buda and Óbuda (old Buda) on the west bank were united with Pest on the east bank, though the settlements in this area have an old history. The Roman settlement Aquincum was located in present Óbuda. The limestone hills which overlook the west bank of the Danube are the farthest extension of the wooded Buda hills. (Interfoto MTI, Budapest.)

merce, a small but growing middle class living in towns and villages exerted an increasing influence.

The picture in the southern areas was quite different. Both the landed nobility and the middle class were largely non-existent in the Turkish-dominated lands. There the dominant class included Turkish officials, military leaders, and large landowners. Trade was in the hands of the Greeks and Jews. The original Serbian feudal state of the fourteenth century, with its landowners, high and low nobility, clergy, and dependent peasantry,[16] had been completely destroyed

by the Turkish conquerors. Peasant families lived in groups which were referred to as zadrugas or joint family units.[17] Their origin goes back to the tribal organizations of the southern Slavic peoples. Many of the people who could escape from the Turks fled into the impassable mountains, mainly Monte-

differs from the so-called "farmer," who produces primarily for the market.

[16] Eastern Europeans generally consider a "peasant" to be someone who is a self-sufficient farmer, who produces primarily for home consumption. He

[17] The zadruga was a consuming and producing collective on which several families lived and farmed in common. With the change from an autarchic to a competitive economy, the zadrugas became disorganized and large-scale emigration to towns and overseas led to their gradual dismemberment. See the authoritative discussions by Jozo Tomasevich, *Peasants, Politics and Economic Change in Yugoslavia* (Stanford, Calif.: Stanford University Press, 1955): 178–202.

negro, where their ancestors had incessantly carried on guerrilla warfare for generations. Among the people living in the mountains, especially the Montenegrins and Albanians, clan rivalry played an important role. The constant struggle for freedom from foreign oppressors became part of the daily life. These struggles were led by local leaders and were encouraged by the Orthodox Church, which during the national struggle for survival played an important role in preserving the Serbian state idea. The few intellectuals in the Eastern European countries came largely from the middle class and frequently had to fight to uphold their beliefs, and often were forced to emigrate. With the Industrial Revolution hardly affecting the masses, long-established modes of life remained unchanged in Eastern Europe for a longer time than in nearly any other part of Europe.

The Political-Territorial Framework

No discussion of the cultural and historical background would be complete without briefly analyzing the major origins and characteristics of the present political-territorial framework of the countries of Eastern Europe. It can be traced to four major nineteenth century developments which led to World War I: (1) the steadily growing power and imperialistic ambitions of a united Germany; (2) the declining position and power of the Austro-Hungarian Monarchy, brought about partially by the desire of its many national groups for independence; [18] (3) the disintegration of the Ottoman

[18] In connection with the one hundredth anniversary of the establishment of the Monarchy in 1867, a number of scholarly meetings were held during the last few years. The fiftieth anniversary of the collapse of the Dual Monarchy also was the occasion of scholarly analysis. The papers presented and comments prepared for an international conference on "The Nationality Problem in the Nineteenth Century Habsburg Monarchy: a Critical Reappraisal," which was held at Indiana University in April 1966, were published in Volume III, parts 1–3, *Austrian History Yearbook*, 1967–69. See also Hoffman, "The Political Geographic Bases of the Austrian Nationality Problem," *op. cit.*, Chapter 6, footnote 15, p. 309.

(Turkish) Empire, resulting in the emergence of a number of small, weak independent states in Southeastern Europe—Romania, Bulgaria, Serbia, Montenegro, and Albania; and (4) the growing antagonism between the Austro-Hungarian Monarchy and the Russian Empire, especially after 1878 when both openly competed for influence in the newly created independent states of Southeastern Europe.

World War I resulted in a complete redrawing of the map of Eastern Europe. Poland, Czechoslovakia, and Yugoslavia were each created from land formerly part of at least one of the three empires. Yugoslavia, since 1919, included the formerly independent states of Montenegro and Serbia. Romania's territorial expansion was at the expense of Austria, Hungary, and Russia, and its new boundaries penetrated deep into the Carpathian Basin. Bulgaria lost two areas to Greece and Yugoslavia. The effects of this changed map were far-reaching. The principle of "self-determination" which was applied to this fragmented region (both physically and culturally) was based on a concept which was too idealistic, and insufficient attention was paid to the creation of really viable states. The power vacuum caused by the almost simultaneous disappearance of the three empires was certainly not filled by the creation of these small, economically and politically weak new independent states. In addition, boundary disputes between nearly all of these new states; the early withdrawal of the United States, sponsor of the principle of "self-determination," from active participation in world affairs; and the unexpected early reemergence of a powerful Germany and later of the Soviet Union all contributed to a continued instability in this region. Eastern Europe, potentially rich in resources, but underdeveloped (except for a few areas), was suddenly left to itself, inexperienced in governing, a highly diverse population without a strong *raison d'être*. Discontent was obvious. This, naturally, was an open invitation to the powers of Europe to intervene.

Between the two wars, some efforts for regional cooperation, such as the Little Entente or the Balkan Entente, either faltered because of the absence of a common policy or were connected with motives of little value to the Eastern European countries themselves.

In addition, Germany's phenomenal reassertion of her power after 1936, and the appeasement policies of the West, left deep impressions of varying degrees on every one of the Eastern European countries. All through the 1930's, sound economic and social planning was replaced by economic self-sufficiency, the development of which would meet the needs of future wars. In other words, "economic nationalism" and "small-power imperialism" became the guiding motives of these countries. Anti-Semitic movements, often supported by Nazi Germany, and a constant round of changing governments, in certain countries semidictatorial governments for the most part strongly anti-Russian and in heavy German debt, usually lost contact with the broad mass of the people who seldom understood the intricacies of government. Czechoslovakia, generally considered the citadel of Western democracy, was undermined by a strong German minority, and the Czech majority in turn had difficulty with its Slovak brethren. After Austria's incorporation into Germany (March, 1938), the strategic position of Czechoslovakia became untenable, and shortly thereafter it, too, lost its independence after less than 20 years of precarious statehood. Disunity among the Allied Powers, and the emergence of the Soviet Union as a powerful factor in world affairs, influenced and lessened the importance of Eastern Europe as the so-called *Cordon Sanitaire* between the West and the East. The Soviet-German agreement of August, 1939, spelled the end of Poland and brought about her "fourth partition." The end of the independent states of Eastern Europe had arrived, and, within months after the Russian-German agreement and the beginning of World War II, the map of this region was again completely redrawn.

Pressures previously unknown in modern history forced over 20 million [19] people of Eastern Europe to leave their homes in the wake of German and Russian armies. Boundaries were completely redrawn between 1939 and the end of the war. Territories were exchanged like pieces of property by Germany, the Soviet Union, and Italy—and also by the countries of Eastern Europe themselves.

The collapse of Nazi Germany found the Soviet Union in control of most of Eastern Europe. American troops had advanced close to Prague and deep into what is now East Germany but, honoring an earlier agreement on occupation zones, had withdrawn, and their place was immediately taken by Soviet troops. Most of Yugoslavia was freed by local partisan soldiers under the leadership of Marshal Tito, a long-time Communist from Croatia, a feat which assumed great importance in the years that followed.

The defeat of Germany and Italy in World War II, disagreement between the Western Powers and the Soviet Union on a postwar policy with regard to the future of Eastern Europe, and, perhaps mainly, the geography of the region gave the victorious Soviet armies nearby a preponderance of power and a strong voice in the future of Eastern Europe.

Disagreement between the Allies and the Soviet Union made territorial settlements in Eastern Europe difficult, and in some instances impossible. The problem was further complicated inasmuch as Poland, Czechoslovakia, and Yugoslavia had been associated with the Allied Powers, while Hungary, Romania, and Bulgaria had been classed as enemy states, having been associated with Germany, even though under heavy pressure. The three Baltic states, Lithuania, Estonia, and Latvia, already had been incorporated into the Soviet Union during the war, a fact still not recognized by the United States. After considerable difficulty, peace treaties

[19] Malcolm J. Proudfoot, *European Refugees* (London: Faber & Faber, Ltd., 1957).

were signed with Hungary, Romania, and Bulgaria, all recognizing the *de facto* influence of the U.S.S.R., which gained 56,700 square miles of land from Poland, Czechoslovakia, and Romania.

A number of important territorial changes took place within the area. The most important affected Poland, even though this change has not yet legally been recognized. Poland's boundary was shifted westward from the 1939 location to the Odra and Nisa rivers, giving her the former German ports of Stettin and Danzig, the important rich Upper Silesian industrial area, and valuable farmlands. Over 7 million Germans from this region fled to Germany, mostly to the western part. The disputed area of western Tešín was returned to Czechoslovakia (it had been seized from Czechoslovakia in 1938). From its eastern territories, Poland lost to the Soviet Union farm and forest land and most of its oil reserves. About 4 million people lived in this area, but many returned later to Poland. This westward push of its borders forced Poland to rely on the Soviet Union, inasmuch as the security of Poland against a re-emergence of a strong Germany depends upon friendly relations with the Soviet Union. Despite resentment against Soviet domination, openly expressed in 1956, this basic political dependence certainly has an overriding influence.

Three other boundary changes have more than local importance: (1) the transfer of the Julian March (Istria) from Italy to Yugoslavia—the so-called statute of the Free Territory of Trieste never operated and, in October, 1954, the future of this area was amicably settled; (2) the forced cession of Czechoslovakia's Ruthenia (Carpatho-Ukraine) to the Soviet Union shortly after the war; and (3) the loss of three areas by Romania. With the acquisition of Bessarabia and northern Bucovina, the Soviet Union again gained a dominant position on the lower Danube. Also, the earlier transfer of southern Dobruja to Bulgaria (1941) was confirmed. Other minor territorial changes occurred between Czechoslovakia and Hungary.

With the exception of Yugoslavia and Albania, every one of the Eastern European countries now has a common border with the Soviet Union (Bulgaria with the Black Sea), permitting the Soviet Union easy entrance into these countries. In addition, all of them (again with the exception noted above) are militarily tied to the Soviet Union under the Warsaw Pact and cooperate economically within the Council of Mutual Economic Assistance (Comecon, CMEA, or CEMA). The boundaries drawn after World War II have by no means solved all the territorial problems of the countries involved. The situation is dormant for the moment and as long as Soviet authority is maintained no changes are to be expected. On the other hand, it must be stated that the mass transfer of minorities from nearly every country has solved a number of possible territorial disputes.

Economic Development

The economic foundation of the new national states. Most of the countries of Eastern Europe were economically backward before World War I. With the exceptions of some mineral exploitation and the establishment of a few industries, especially in Bohemia, Slovenia, and Upper Silesia, the area was predominantly agricultural. The exploited minerals for the most part were shipped to the industries located in the Vienna Basin or to some foreign countries in exchange for needed manufactured goods. Urban settlements, with few exceptions, were small in size and far between, and the rural population comprised between 70 and 90 per cent of the population in all regions except Bohemia, Upper Silesia, and parts of Hungary. Agriculture consisted mostly of large private and church estates, often owned by absentee landlords, and there was little opportunity for the land-hungry peasantry to obtain property. Communications tied regional centers with Vienna and to a lesser degree with Budapest, Berlin, and Leningrad, and usually were based on the strategic necessities of the Monarchy and the German and Russian empires. Generally speaking, the Russian and German interests in Eastern Europe were largely strategic.

An opportunity for basic economic and social changes was offered by the breakdown of the empires of Russia, Germany, and Austria in 1918, the incorporation of some of the small independent states of the southeast into newly organized larger units, and the emergence of seven independent states. Agriculture, the basis of the economy for every one of the newly independent countries, did increase in output between 1919 and 1938, but, in spite of various land reforms, the land hunger of the peasants could not be satisfied. Peasants, on the whole, were highly taxed, had to pay high interest rates, and were frequently caught in the price squeeze between industrial and agricultural prices. In addition, agriculture in Eastern Europe was influenced by the competition from overseas. All during the interwar period, a large percentage of the population was dependent upon agriculture for their income. The population was rapidly expanding, roughly three times as fast as in Western Europe, and agriculture was characterized by large surpluses and a low per capita per acre productivity.

With the exception of Czechoslovakia, the newly created states lacked a satisfactory basis for the development of industries, even though individual plants which later laid the foundation for a more concentrated industrialization did exist in Poland, Hungary, and Slovenia (Yugoslavia). Many of the new industries built were often operated on unsound principles. Often, local raw materials, which could have been the foundation for a prospering industry, were sold abroad and finished products were purchased at a high price. Foreign capital for fresh investments was scarce, and available funds usually found their way into extractive industries only. The exploitation of raw materials was largely in the hands of foreign investors. In Yugoslavia, for example, all of the capital in the copper mines at Bor (French concession), the lead mines at Trepča (English concession), and the manganese and bauxite mines was from foreign lands. Very little attention was given to the possibility of developing consumer goods from local raw materials such as agricultural products, timber, etc. Industries often produced goods for export only, without any thought of developing a domestic market. It was therefore not surprising that the world depression of 1929, the aftereffects of which were felt all through the 1930's, had a devastating impact on the whole economy of these countries. The few foreign investments which had ventured into this region for the most part dried up. Power competition encouraged a drive for autocracy, and what little economic reasoning was originally manifest in the development of the economy was clouded by divergent nationalistic aspirations.

Except in Czechoslovakia and, to a lesser degree, in Poland, the pattern of trade consisted of export of agricultural and raw materials (ores, oil) and import of manufactured goods. Eastern Europe served as the only European market from which to secure grain. The total trading volume during the interwar period was small, less than 7 per cent of Europe's imports and less than 10 per cent of its exports.

Looking back on the social and economic developments of the interwar years, it is rather surprising to see how much progress was made. Actually this region had only about ten years of peaceful, independent development, from 1919 to the outbreak of the world depression. This depression found the Eastern European countries still in the middle of making adjustments and major decisions based on their newly created independence. While the height of the depression was passed by 1934, its repercussions were felt to the beginning of World War II.

Postwar economic changes in Eastern Europe. Changes in the political geography of Eastern Europe have been manifested in the economic and social developments also. Efforts to modernize the economies of Eastern Europe by changing the direction and intensity of prewar plans in the early postwar years have varied from country to country, depending upon the degree of Communist control in the individual countries. Basically, each country copied to some extent the Soviet economy, stressing the need for investment both in human resources and capital goods. Major emphasis was given to developing industry, especially heavy industry, rather than agriculture and services. Great efforts were made to increase technical manpower and to absorb the large surplus agricultural manpower. Industrialization on this scale was impossible without key raw material shipments from the Soviet Union. It must be realized here that the natural endowment of Eastern Europe is simply insufficient for massive industrialization and, without the establishment of a Communist-Socialist framework and the political support of the Soviet Union, could not have been accomplished.

Three periods of economic development are clearly discernible in Eastern Europe thus far:

1. From the end of World War II to the late 1940's, emphasis was on reconstruction, re-equipping, and then expansion of already existing industries. During this period the state acquired considerable land through expulsion or voluntary withdrawal of foreign land owners, and various restrictions as to the size of private holdings.

2. The period from the late 1940's to the end of the 1950's is referred to as the "command economy phase" (Yugoslavia excepted after 1950), and emphasized centralized methods of planning and management. Simultaneously the area of state ownership was expanded and by increasing investments, especially in the heavy industries, a broad domestic base for further industrialization was established. The early part of this period was also characterized by emphasis on land reform in spite of considerable resistance by the peasantry, but after Stalin's death, land reform was slowed down. In Poland after 1956 and in Yugoslavia after 1953 most collectives were disbanded. Col-

lectivization was again emphasized (except in these two countries) late in the 1950's but generally concluded by the early 1960's.

3. Various attempts to reform, often called the phase of "new economic management," have characterized the development since the early 1960's. This process has gone furthest in Yugoslavia with the Economic Reform initiated in 1965 giving emphasis to decentralization of major economic and political decision-making processes. In the new system, also called "market socialism," the East European countries are slowly moving "toward decentralizing their economics by allowing prices to begin to reflect both costs and scarcities and by shifting power from the planners to the individual plant or enterprises."[20] While reforming their economics, citizens receive increased personal liberties. (The long-term impact of the Soviet occupation of Czechoslovakia cannot be estimated.)

The tight Soviet control of the East European socialist countries, diminished since the Polish and Hungarian uprisings of 1956, is being relaxed, permitting individual East European countries greater leeway in their planning priorities, including emphasis on increased western trade "both to gain access to western technology and management sophistication and to subject East European enterprises to the bracing discipline of western competition."[21] The reforms are, in effect, responsible for creating exchange between Eastern Europe and the West, though it must be remembered that the main goal of creating the institutional framework for a socialist society remains unchanged.

Economic changes in the various countries of Eastern Europe have led to great structural changes in the total economy, marked by an increase in industrial capacity (especially the relative shares of manufacturing in total output). Based on various economic compilations it is certain that industrial out-

[20] Gilbert Burck, "East Europe's Struggle for Economic Freedom," *Fortune* (May, 1967): 125.
[21] *Ibid.*, p. 125.

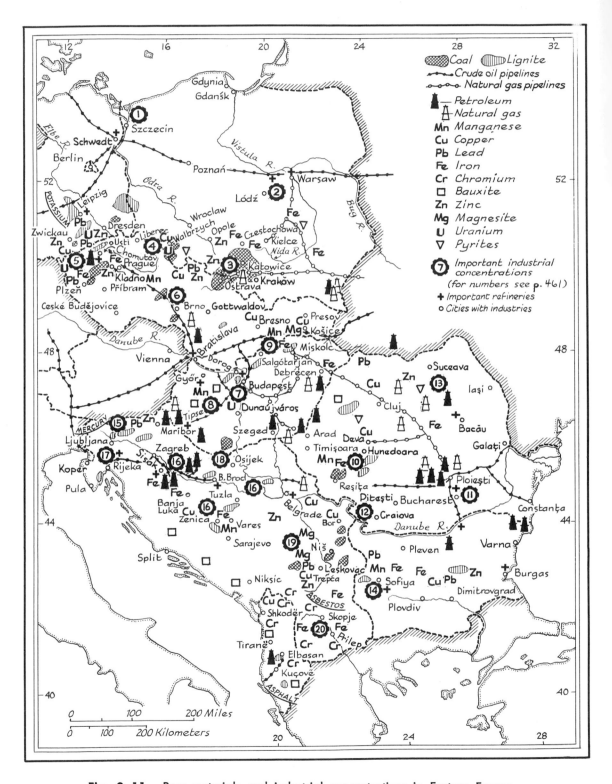

Fig. 8—11. Raw materials and industrial concentrations in Eastern Europe.

1. North Polish Port Cities (Szczecin, Gdynia, Gdańsk): shipbuilding, machinery
2. Warsaw–Lódź: textiles, machinery, chemicals, paper, food
3. Polish–Czech Upper Silesia (Katowice–Ostrava–Karvina): metallurgy, machinery, chemicals
4. Prague–Kladno–Podebrday: metallurgy, machinery, chemicals, electrical equipment, food
5. North Bohemian region (Plzeň–Chomutov–Liberec): metallurgy, chemical, ceramic, textile
6. Brno region: chemical, textiles; metallurgy
7. Budapest: metallurgy, machinery, food, textiles, leather, paper; electrical
8. Northeast Transdanubia: textiles, electrical equipment, glass, rolling stock
9. Northern Hungary (Salgótarján–Ózd–Miskolc): machinery, tools, armaments, metallurgy
10. Banat (Reşiţa–Hunedoara): metallurgy, machinery, textiles, food, chemicals
11. Bucharest–Ploieşti: chemical, electrical, food, machinery; petroleum extraction
12. Southern Romanian region (Craiova–Piteşti): petroleum extraction, petro-chemical, petroleum engineering
13. Eastern Romanian region (Galaţi–Iasi–Suceava–Bacau): chemical, electric power, antibiotics, food, metallurgical products
14. Pernik–Sofiya–Kremikovci: metallurgy, machinery, electrical, leather, textiles, food
15. Northwestern Yugoslavia (Ljubljana basin, Celje, Maribor): engineering, electric machinery
16. Sava Valley, including northern Bosnia (Zagreb–Sisak–Zenica–Tuzla–Belgrade): metallurgy, petro-chemical, machinery, textiles, food, electrical, chemical
17. Northern Adriatic Littoral (Koper–Pula–Rijeka): shipbuilding, engineering
18. Northern Yugoslavia, incl. Slavonia (Varaždin–Osijek Vojvodina, lower Morava valley): agricultural machinery, food processing, textiles, metallurgy, chemical
19. Serbia proper (Niš–Kraljevo–Leskovac): varied small-scale industries, engineering, food, textiles
20. Skopje basin (Kumanovo-Tetovo, Titov Veles): metallurgical, chemical, agricultural products, textiles.

put in the decade 1956–65 rose by approximately 150 per cent in Bulgaria, Romania and Yugoslavia (the less developed of the Socialist countries), by 80 to 100 per cent in Hungary and Poland (the middle group), and by 70 per cent in Czechoslovakia and East Germany (the most developed of the Socialist countries). Spulber estimates that "for the area as a whole, a rate of growth of roughly 8 per cent per annum throughout 1951–64 compared favorably to a rate of 6 to 7 per cent in Western Europe for the same period."[22] Only farm output shows little gain, livestock production having increased more rapidly than crop output. Compared with agricultural production in Western Europe (in West Germany 38 per cent over the prewar level, in France 30 per cent, in Denmark 65 per cent), the countries of Eastern Europe, according to Western estimates, show overall increases from 6.2 per cent in Albania, and 4.5 per cent in Bulgaria, to a range between 1.5 and 2.2 per annum in the other countries.

Some of the more fundamental changes that have evolved since World War II are:

1. Planned industrialization is the core of economic development in Eastern European countries. Main attention has been given to manufacturing industries, especially heavy or basic industries. Most spectacular has been the growth in steel and mechanical engineering, energy sources, chemicals and plastics. This growth was accomplished without the benefit of Western investment goods. While mining activities in various East European countries were greatly increased, the Soviet Union, by necessity, became the major source of raw material, especially of iron ore and petroleum (Fig. 8–11).

[22] Nicolas Spulber, "Economic Modernization," in *The United States and Eastern Europe,* edited by Robert F. Byrnes. The American Assembly, Columbia University (Englewood Cliffs, N.J.: Prentice-Hall, 1967):63. The reader should be reminded here of the very low starting base of industrial output which made possible some rather spectacular rises with relatively little absolute growth.

Perhaps most important has been the expansion of iron and steel production, the modernization of older plants, and the establishment of many new ones. Those in Nowa Huta (Poland), Košice (Eastern Slovakia), Dunaújváros (Hungary), Galati (Romania), and Zenica, Sisak, Nikšić and Skopje (Yugoslavia) are the major newer developments. But the rapid industrial expansion, especially of the iron and steel works, has increased reliance on outside fuels and various mineral resources. The large coal fields in Silesia and Moravia, Europe's largest oil fields of the sub-Carpathians, and the natural gas of Transylvania both in Romania, the hydroelectric power potential especially in Romania and Yugoslavia, and at numerous locations along the Danube, and the bauxite deposits in Hungary and Yugoslavia are important. The most serious deficiencies are undoubtedly iron ore (only about 20 per cent of the metal content needed is supplied by Eastern Europe) and petroleum. Production of heavy industry is confined, on the whole, to the modernized older industrial centers, but a few new large industrial clusters have been added. In spite of this industrial expansion, there exists still a wide difference between the older industrial countries (Czechoslovakia and East Germany) and the more advanced industrialized regions within individual countries and the other countries of Eastern Europe. The industrial level in Czechoslovakia and East Germany is close to that of Western Europe. The other countries represent in Spulber's words "an enormous dead weight left by the past on the shoulders of the present and the future." [23]

2. Agricultural resources of Eastern Europe are more generous (Fig. 8–12): the proportion of agricultural land to the total territory is relatively high, varying from 42 per cent in Albania to 65 per cent in Poland. Before World War II, Eastern Europe (exclusive of the U.S.S.R.) had 33 per cent of Europe's wheat area, 50 per cent of the rye

[23] Spulber, "Economic Modernization," *op. cit.*, p. 76.

area, and 65 per cent of its maize (corn) area. This produced roughly 25 per cent of Europe's wheat, 50 per cent of its rye, and 70 per cent of its corn. But the neglect of agriculture in Eastern Europe until the late 1950's, the increase in population, and the rise in the standard of living certainly have changed this picture. Over-all, the East European countries today are responsible for only a small net amount of exported food, and several of the East European countries must import considerable quantities of grain (two-thirds of the import requirements are met by the Soviet Union). Increased investments, greater application of modern technology, and often also a basic change in philosophy with regard to the peasant, are needed to increase both the quality and quantity of agricultural production. Industrialization, for example, has created an increased demand for a variety of industrial crops, e.g., cotton, flax, hemp, oil-seeds, and sugar beets (although the area where it can be grown is limited).

Land reform was needed in many of the East European countries, and by 1948 most of the land was actually in the hands of the peasantry. The land reform of the 1950's brought collectivization, often forcibly introduced, and this, in turn, brought basic structural changes. By the early 1960's the socialist sector (state and collective farms) totaled 85 to 95 per cent of the total agricultural land except in Poland (14 per cent) and Yugoslavia (12 per cent). Even in these countries, socialization of the countryside is still the ultimate goal of their governments. The whole attitude of most governments toward agriculture has followed closely that of the Soviet Union. State farms were established mainly for plant breeding and experimental purposes; collective farms of various types (often called cooperatives) with land and labor contributed by the peasant allow him to retain a small private household plot, usually for vegetables and fruit, a cow, a few pigs, and poultry. He is allowed to sell surplus on the nearby open market or to the collective. The pattern of

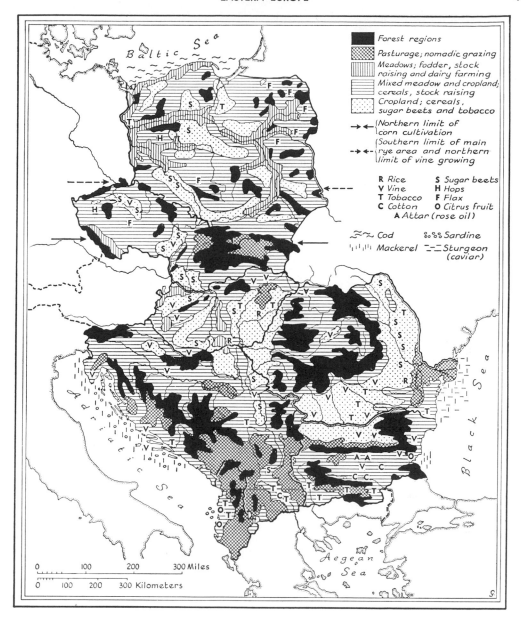

Fig. 8–12. Land utilization in Eastern Europe.

irregular and small farm strips has been replaced by large fields suitable for combines
and tractors. The many small colorful
clustered farm buildings have disappeared
and have been replaced by new solidly
built stables, and equipment and repair
buildings. The rural landscape is going
through a rapid change. Again Poland and
Yugoslavia are, for the most part, exceptions.

Collectivization also influenced the pattern
of rural employment. The displacement of
men by the machine resulted in intense
cultivation of his small plot, and urban unemployment in some cities, i.e., if the rural
surplus manpower moves to cities without
adequate employment opportunities. It
raises still further the question of whether
large scale mechanization is justified when

a large surplus of agricultural labor is available.[24]

3. The process of urbanization has been greatly accelerated. Urban population (ratio of urban to total population) by the mid-1960's had risen to about 33–40 per cent in Albania, Hungary, Romania, and Yugoslavia, and to 46–59 per cent in Bulgaria, Poland, and Czechoslovakia, although the great majority of the people still live in localities with less than 10,000 people (the percentages for Poland and Hungary are somewhat smaller). Small and medium-size towns grew proportionately at a much faster rate than cities of over 100,000.

Important changes have taken place in the distribution of manpower. The agricultural labor force has declined from well over half to about 40 per cent of the total, especially in the southern countries of Eastern Europe. Industrial manpower increased rapidly and reached roughly 25–35 per cent of the total employment by the late 1960's. Czechoslovakia has the highest percentage of industrial manpower among East European countries (47 per cent). The demand for industrial manpower necessitated the adoption of special measures for training managers and engineers. Great effort is made to modernize the educational system, reduce illiteracy, and produce technically trained manpower by systematically organizing vocational schools.

4. Interregional cooperation was accomplished largely through Comecon which was established in 1949 but which made little headway until 1956. Bilateral agreements between individual East European countries (including East Germany) and the Soviet Union and barter agreements between member states are the main media of trade. Multilateral trade, still of minor importance,

reflects on their industrial and commercial growth.[25]

Since 1956 numerous commissions in various areas of industrial specialization under Comecon have sponsored technical agreements and joint investments for cooperation, such as the "friendship pipeline" from the Urals to the refineries in East Europe, an electric-power grid, joint investments in manufacturing and mining, and a Comecon bank to act as clearing house for trade. As might have been expected, the setting of priorities for the development of individual production branches aroused fear and jealousy among some East European countries. Romania, especially, resented the low priority, or even absence of such, for the development of its heavy industries. Comecon's role is not comparable with that of the Common Market (EEC), and while economic integration has not materialized it has achieved modest success in interregional cooperation, especially in technical cooperation, and the economies of the East European countries are becoming increasingly interdependent. The Iron Gate project undertaken between Romania and Yugoslavia is a strictly bi-lateral undertaking.

5. Three clear trends in foreign trade policies and practices since World War II can be followed: (i) the period of reduced foreign trade between 1947 and 1953 and the strong division into Eastern and Western blocs. This period was characterized by East Europe's close ties with the Soviet Union, by Soviet domination of the intrabloc market, and a moderately well enforced western embargo on strategic goods; (ii) during 1954 and the early 1960's, trade between some of the East European countries and the West developed again. Yugoslavia's trade with the Soviet Union and other East European countries had reached zero after Stalin's break with Yugoslavia, and did not start again until after his death. In the meantime she established close trade links with many Western countries, including the

[24] There are approximately 20–24 workers per 100 acres of arable land in Romania and Yugoslavia compared with 4–6 in northwest Europe. According to a recent report published by the FAO in Rome, until farm manpower falls below 12 per 100 acres the question of whether agricultural mechanization can claim specific priority is a very dubious one.

[25] For a detailed account see Michael Kaser, *Comecon* (London: Oxford University Press, 1965).

United States, which assisted her with massive economic aid. Intra-bloc trade started to expand from its low level in 1956, but the Soviet Union's efforts to integrate foreign trade and production plans for the whole area on the whole remained unsuccessful; (iii) the period since the mid-1960's is characterized by greater diversification in the direction of trade, by growing east-west trade relations, by a lessening in East European economic ties with the Soviet Union, by increased emphasis on quality production and proper pricing policies, and by a general expansion of the volume of foreign trade see Fig. 8–13 and the following table.

has been affected by the impact of industrialization. Both intra-East European and East European-Soviet trade are heavy in machinery of all types and engineering equipment, both insignificant before the war. On the other hand, the structure of East European trade with the West has changed little since the prewar period—exporting food, fuels, and semi-manufactured products and importing industrial equipment and machinery.

Trade between Eastern Europe and the United States is small, though slowly on the increase. Most-favored-nation treaties exist between the United States and Poland and Yugoslavia. East Europe's trade relations

Eastern Europe's Pattern of Trade, by Area
(per cent)

	1937			1958			1966		
	U.S.S.R.	Peoples' Democracies	Rest of World	U.S.S.R.	Peoples' Democracies	Rest of World	U.S.S.R.	Peoples' Democracies	Rest of World
East Germany	—	—	—		73	27	41	27	32
Czechoslovakia	1	10	89		70	30	34	30	36
Poland	1	6	93		62	38	32	26	42
Hungary	—	13	87	30	37	33	33	30	37
Romania	1	17	82		75 (1957)	25	33	21	46
Bulgaria	—	12	88	52	25	23	49	19	32
Albania (1964)	—	—	—	—	—	—	—	35	65 *

* Western Europe 8 per cent.

Sources: 1937 data compiled by Nicolas Spulber and published in "Factors in Eastern Europe's Intratrade and Cooperation," *Journal of International Affairs*, XI, 1 (1957), p. 23. 1958 data in *Statesman's Yearbook: 1960* (London, 1960). 1966 data from *Yearbook of International Trade Statistics, 1966*. United Nations Statistical Office: New York, 1968.

Altogether 55–70 per cent of the total trade of the Comecon countries (which includes East Germany, but excludes Yugoslavia) is within the bloc. Only less than 40 per cent of Albania's trade is with the Comecon countries. The percentage of trade with West European countries has increased during the last few years averaging roughly 25–38 per cent. West Germany, France, Italy, and the United Kingdom are the foremost trading partners. In 1945 some 22 per cent of the exports of the bloc countries went outside the area; in 1966 this figure amounted to more than 40 per cent. The whole structure of foreign trade obviously

with the West are increasing, and this, in turn, may well bring reduced trade within the bloc (as percentage of the total), but no radical change can be expected.

POLAND

Population

At the end of World War II Poland was re-established as an independent nation after having been partitioned between Germany and the Soviet Union. Even though its western boundaries have not been permanently decided by treaty, it may be assumed that they will persist. Earlier, the western shift

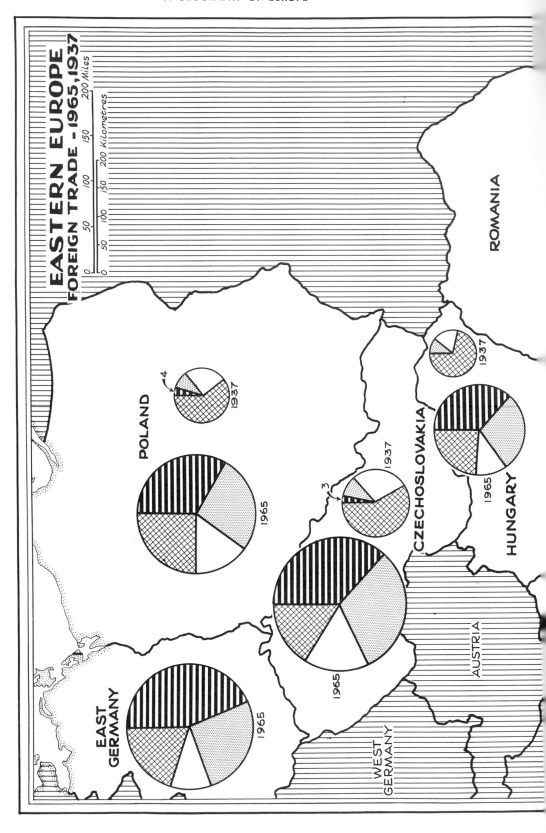

EASTERN EUROPE
FOREIGN TRADE - 1965, 1937

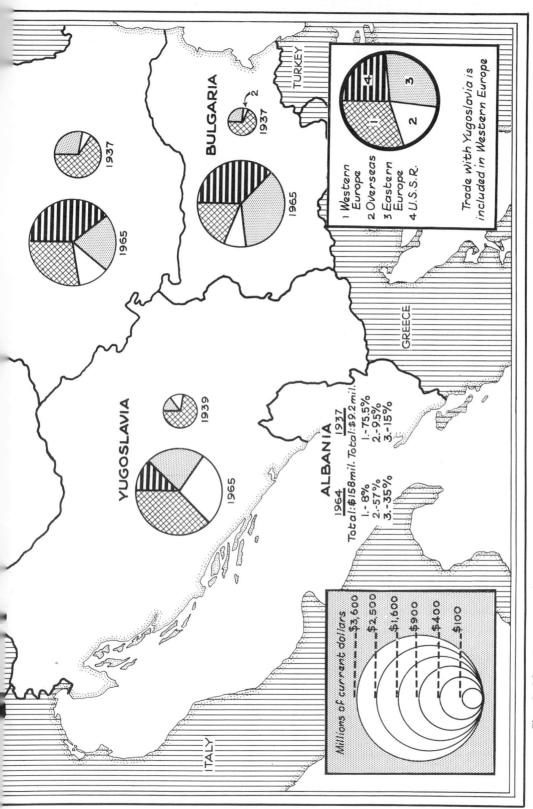

Fig. 8–13. Foreign trade in Eastern Europe, 1966, 1937. (Yearbook of International Trade Statistics. New York: United Nations Statistical Office, appropriate years.)

TURKEY

BULGARIA

1937

1965

1937

1965

YUGOSLAVIA

1965

1939

GREECE

ITALY

1 Western Europe
2 Overseas
3 Eastern Europe
4 U.S.S.R.

Trade with Yugoslavia is included in Western Europe

ALBANIA

1964	1937
Total: $158 mil.	Total: $9.2 mil.
1.- 8%	1.- 75.5%
2.- 57%	2.- 9.5%
3.- 35%	3.- 15%

Millions of current dollars

$3,600
$2,500
$1,600
$900
$400
$100

Fig. 8–14. Warsaw is located on the left (west) bank of the Vistula River on a high terrace about 100 feet above the river. The city is of recent origin (first mentioned in the fourteenth century) and was greatly damaged with large sections completely obliterated during World War II. The view is from the Palace of Culture and Science toward northwest, the Slaski bridge and Praga on the right (east) bank of the river. (G. W. Hoffman.)

of the whole Polish territory was briefly mentioned—loss of territory in the east to the U.S.S.R. and gain of former German territory in the west and north along the Baltic coast. It must be stressed that this westward push of its borders has, on the whole, created a more viable Poland. The mass exodus and exchange of population certainly settled for the time being the problem of her ethnic minorities.[26] Poland has

[26] One of the most amazing migrations in the history of mankind took place in the territory of Poland between 1939 and 1949. Close to 10 million people either fled, were expelled, or voluntarily changed their residence. Over 90 per cent of the Jewish population was killed. Statistics indicate that close to 8 million people who lived in Poland in 1939 are now living elsewhere and roughly 1.8 million people who are now living in Poland lived elsewhere in 1939. Of those 8 million people now living outside Poland, close to 7 million are ethnic Germans who either fled or were expelled after 1945. Of those, 5.9 million came from former German territory now administered by Poland (the "Western Territories"). Former Polish citizens now in Western countries are largely in the United States, Israel, and Canada. People now living in Poland who lived elsewhere before 1939 came largely from territories ceded to the U.S.S.R. War losses of the Polish population are estimated at 6 million people killed.

a total population of more than 32 million in an area of roughly 120,000 square miles (approximately the size of New Mexico), giving an average density of 268 per square mile. Administratively, Poland is divided into 23 provinces (voivodeships), including the cities of Warsaw, Łódz, Kraków, Poznań and Wrocław and those 23 are subdivided into rural and urban counties (powiaty) and rural district settlements (gromada). The capital, located on the Vistula River, is Warsaw (Warszawa), a city with over 1.26 million people (Fig. 8–14). Poland's most densely inhabited regions are in the Polish Uplands from the Silesian Plain, the industrial region of Upper Silesia, across the Carpathian Foreland, to the upper San Valley. In this region densities of between 800 and 1000 square mile are common, with average densities of 300 the norm. Twenty-three Polish cities now have populations of over 100,000 with Warsaw, Łódz, Wrocław, and Poznań the largest. The important industrial region of Upper Silesia (Katowice Voivodeship) has the largest concentration of cities with over 50,000 people. As a result of the many territorial and demographic changes, the urban percentage of the population has changed from 26 (in 1939) to 46 per cent (in 1966).[27] The former German territory now administered by Poland and called "Western Territories" is of great political and economic importance. The present population is no longer German but is ethnically almost entirely Polish.

Poland's population is ethnically unified, with only small, dispersed minorities of Czechs, Jews, Germans, and Ukrainians. A large majority of the people are Roman Catholic, but a religious census is not part of the official census. The population structure is typical for countries with heavy war losses. Forty-six per cent of the population in June, 1966 were 24 years of age or under, 32.4 per cent were in the age group of 25 to 49 years. Birth rates in Poland were among the highest in Europe, but have greatly decreased in the last few years, natural increase of 19.5 per thousand in 1956 was only 9.4 in 1966. Much emphasis has been given to raising the educational level of the population: 76 institutions of higher learning are distributed among twenty cities in Poland. Forty-two per cent of those enrolled during 1966–67 were in technical work, 11.5 per cent in medicine, and 8.9 per cent in agricultural sciences. The illiteracy rate for those 7 years old and older in 1960 was only 2.7 per cent.

The occupational distribution (total gainfully employed) has undergone many changes since the war. In 1960, industry, construction, and mining employed 29 per cent of the population and agriculture, forestry, and fishing 48 per cent, a drop from 65 per cent in 1937.

Present Economic Life

Poland's economic structure has undergone basic changes from the prewar period. With the addition of the German part of the highly industrialized Silesian area, together with the great emphasis on industrialization

[27] The last general census was in December, 1960; some data used are latest official estimates.

during the whole postwar period, and the loss of 46 per cent of her prewar area to the Soviet Union, an area which contained more than half of Poland's cultivated land, the prewar agricultural emphasis of the economy has basically changed. The addition of the two important Baltic ports of Stettin (Szczecin) and Danzig (Gdańsk) and full control of the Odra and Vistula rivers have greatly improved the country's river and ocean transport system.

Agriculture, fishing, and forestry. Sixty-four per cent of the total land area of Poland is classified as agricultural, with approximately half arable land (Fig. 8–12). Twenty-six per cent is in forests and 10 per cent is classified as waste and fallow land. A broad belt between Warsaw in the east and Poznan in the west has the largest per cent of cropland (over 50 per cent). Other intensively cultivated areas include the loess plains of Silesia, and the Lublin Uplands, with a narrow strip bordering the Beskidy. The least intensively cultivated areas are found at the end-moraine regions of Pomerania and Masuria, the outwash sands and hills, and the mountains of the south (Fig. 8–1).

The Polish Uplands and Foreland have the best pastures and meadows. Fifty-six per cent of the total area cultivated is in cereals, rye being by far the most important, followed by wheat, oats, and barley. Rye and oats are grown all over the country; the Silesian Plain, the Polish Uplands, and the lower Vistula Valley are the dominant wheat areas; and barley predominates in former German Silesia and the Polish Uplands. Potatoes occupy 18 per cent of the cultivated land and are well distributed throughout the country because they are a basic item in the people's diet. Sugar beets are the predominant industrial crop; others are flax, hemp, hops, and chicory. Other crops include fodder plants, legumes, vegetables, rapeseed, linseed, and hemp. Corn, wine grapes, and even tobacco acreages are restricted by climate. Yields of most crops have improved and mechanization and the use of fertilizers are increasing though yields are still low compared with West European standards. Earlier imports of grain have become unnecessary and certain items of high-quality food exports, such as eggs, bacon, and ham, are increasing. Considerable improvement of farmland by drainage or other means has been striking.

Pigs are the most numerous form of livestock, and the number of cattle is on the increase. The horse is still the main draft animal and horses are well distributed throughout the country, with the greatest densities in the central parts of Poland. Efforts are now under way to reduce the number of horses, inasmuch as they consume much fodder. The Bialystok and Poznań voivodeships account for more than 20 per cent of the sheep population, although sheep and goats are also widespread in the Carpathian mountain valleys. Milk production has greatly increased from prewar times, and the production of eggs increased by over one-third in the last ten years. Fishing has increased in importance, thanks to the greater length of the Baltic coastline of postwar Poland, with cod and mackerel the chief catches. The 316,400 tons of fish landed in 1966 play an important role in the proper food balance of the population. Polish trawlers are now also in offshore waters catching cod and herring in the North Sea.

Forests as a natural resource are of major importance to Poland, but great wartime damage and the loss of important reserves of hardwood (oak, beech, birch, and aspen) in the east have forced Poland completely to discontinue its former large exports. As a matter of fact, war damage to forests and to the lumber and wood industry was the single most important damage inflicted on any branch of Poland's economy. Coniferous forests occupy roughly 87 per cent of the present forest area of approximately 20 million acres over 80 per cent of which are state forests. Since the war, wood pulp, plywood, and lumber production has been encouraged, and various by-products, e.g., ship supplies and tanning extracts, are now produced within the country.

Land ownership, too, has undergone basic changes since the prewar period. Collectivization was introduced in the early 1950's, but discontinued after the 1956 upheavals. At the end of June, 1966, 60 per cent of the agricultural land was in private hands. State farms cover 12 per cent of the total arable land. A total of 10 per cent of the holdings are over 25 acres in size (1960 census) but they cover 32.5 per cent of the agricultural area. Agricultural production is increased mainly by means of the so-called voluntary cooperatives, "agricultural circles," whose origin goes back to the nineteenth century. Discontinued after the war, many thousands have been organized since the fall of 1956. Their main function is the renting of tractors and other machinery and the purchase of fertilizer and seed. The Polish government has made clear its opposition, in the long run, to peasant farming and its intention to replace it with state and collective farms. While the present peasant agriculture may be wasteful and produce insufficient yields, the only alternative, collectivization, has shown that it produces even less.

Mining and manufacturing. Poland's mineral balance, except with regard to bituminous coal, has not greatly changed from prewar years. Raw materials other than coal, lead, and zinc are insufficient for the increased industrial requirements and must be imported (Fig. 8–11). Among Poland's minerals, coal assumes the dominant position. The bituminous coalfields in the Upper Silesian basin (about one-fifth extends across to Czechoslovakia) are among the most important of Europe, after the Ruhr and the Midlands of the United Kingdom. Coal mining dates from the middle of the eighteenth century. Production of bituminous coal in 1966 was 122 million tons. Accessible reserves are estimated at over 95 billion tons at a depth of about 3300 feet and are only exceeded by the Ruhr coal fields in Europe. Coal is both the principal source of energy for industry and the most important raw material for the expanding chemical and metallurgical industries. The most important bituminous mines are located around Katowice and near the Czech border, the so-called Upper Silesian fields. These form part of the great though discontinuous coal belt extending from the British Isles across Germany. Seams with a maximum thickness of 555 feet are among the thickest in Europe, and the working depth (1,300 to 2,600 feet) is much more favorable for mining than in the Ruhr or British deposits. A smaller bituminous coal field with thin seams, but high proportion of coking coal is located in Lower Silesia (the Sudets). Poland's total coke production in 1966 was 14.7 million tons. In spite of these important producing fields, approximately 1.1 million tons of coking coal was imported in 1966. Lignite production comes chiefly from open-pits, reaching 24.5 million tons in 1966. The most important deposits are close to the southwest boundary and also between Łódz and Poznań at Konin. The lignite is used by the new thermal power stations and some of the power produced is exported to East Germany. Some lignite is also exported. The power produced in this region is the basis for intensive plans of industrialization.

Most of the iron-ore deposits are of low-grade quality. The main deposits are located in the Kielce-Radom district, and near Czestochowa, the bedded Jurassic ores producing 3.0 million tons in 1966. Poland's mills must import as much as 84 per cent of its iron ore, much of which comes from the Soviet Union, a smaller amount from Sweden (to which Poland exports coal), and from Brazil.

Poland is short of nearly all ferrous metals. It has a sufficient supply of non-ferrous metals such as zinc and lead, located near Kielce in central Poland and in Upper and Lower Silesia. Sulfur and sulfuric acid are valuable by-products of the processing of lead and zinc ores which occur along the Upper Vistula valley. Arsenite ores, mined south of Wrocław, are important. Low-grade pitchblende (uranium) deposits are located near Walbrzych and Jelina Gora. Deposits of salt, gypsum, and lime are plentiful and supply the growing chemical industry. Low-grade copper deposits from Silesia are now used to produce electrolytic copper, important for domestic requirements. New deposits have been brought into operation in the mid-1960's between Lublin and Glogow and should, in the near future, obliterate the need for imports. Some potash is located west of Lublin, but most of the important deposits are in territory ceded to the Soviet Union.

Poland's most important petroleum fields were also located in the Galician area ceded to the Soviet Union. Her present production comes from fields southeast of Sanok in the Carpathian Forelands, and newly discovered deposits at Ostrów and Wielkopolski but supplies only a small part of her domestic requirements. Natural gas production is equally important. Much of Poland's needs of petroleum and petroleum products come from the Soviet Union and an oil pipeline has been completed from the Urals to Plock on the Vistula with a refinery north of the city. The production of electric power is based largely on thermal (coal and lignite) production, and plans call for greatly expanded production.

Industrial production in Poland, in contrast to agricultural, has greatly increased since the end of the Second World War. All industry is state-owned. Following a pattern discussed earlier, large capital investment, especially in heavy industry, was provided with a much smaller expansion in consumers' goods industries. Heavy industries account for 38 per cent by value of total industrial production in 1966. With the exception of Nowa Huta (Leninworks) east of Kraków, no entirely new large center has been founded (Fig. 8–15). Older industries were expanded and modernized. New industries, especially chemical and mechanical, have been established in new locations at Tarnow and Rzeszów, but they are the exception rather than the rule. Fig. 8–11 shows the key industrial regions of Poland. The most important concentrations are the Warsaw-Łódz

Fig. 8–15. Nowa Huta, integrated iron and steel works located outside Kraków. General view. (G. W. Hoffman.)

and Katowice-Ostrava regions (Fig. 8–11, nos. 2–3). Other important concentrations are at Gdańsk-Gdynia, Bydgoszcs-Toruń, Kielce-Holy Cross Mountains, Silesia and Sudets, Wielkopolski and most of southeastern Poland. Each of these concentrations and regions has its own major specialization. The core of Polish manufacturing today is located in the 786 square-mile coal-rich area of Upper Silesia stretching between Katowice and Opole. If the newly built and expanded steel mills near Krakow and the mills at Czestochowa (Bierut works) are added, over 80 per cent of steel output and rolled products in Poland are accounted for.[28]

While the iron and steel industries have assumed great importance in Poland's economic growth, textile, clothing, and footwear manufacturing has an old and important tradition, and Łódz is often called the "Polish Manchester." Owing to its location, the city is also an important manufacturing center for chemical, metallurgical, electrotechnical,

food-processing, and other miscellaneous industries. Łódz and its district produces roughly 65 per cent of all Polish cotton goods and 60 per cent of all woolens. Important industries are also concentrated in Warsaw, Kraków, Kielce, Czestochowa, Wrocław, Szczecin, and other cities. Expansion in manufacturing has continued throughout the various three-, five-, and six-year plans. Shipbuilding facilities, which became Polish property with the acquisition of the most important Baltic ports of Szczecin and Gdańsk, have been modernized and expanded. Traditional glass production is carried on mostly in Silesia and has been greatly enlarged at Walbrzych. Chemical production is of recent origin and specializes largely in fertilizers, paint and varnish, and pharmaceuticals. In the area between Warsaw, Lublin, Radom, Łódz, Poznań, and Bydgoszcz are concentrated a scattering of small and medium-sized plants, e.g., sugar refineries, food canneries, breweries, and flour mills. Southward, in the uplands and the valleys of the Carpathians, are woodworking plants and paper mills.

[28] Norman J. G. Pounds, "The Industrial Geography of Modern Poland," *Economic Geography,* 36 (July, 1960):231–53.

Communications. Poland's transport network largely reflects the country's historical development. The part east of the Vistula has few rail connections, while rails are densest in the former German and Austrian territories. Inasmuch as both the old and newly built industries are located in these territories, as well as in the upland regions, the transport network satisfies most industrial needs. This network was in a deplorable condition following the end of World War II. Besides repairs, a few connecting lines and changes from narrow to standard gauge have been completed since 1945. Steam traction still predominates, but electrified track is rapidly increasing from 295 to 1380 miles in a ten-year period.

Poland's railroads can easily be identified as two separate systems, but most of the key cities are well interconnected (Fig. 8–2). The first system focuses on Warsaw with several lines radiating from the capital. The other system consists of two north-south lines: from Gdańsk to Katowice and from Szczecin via Poznań to Wrocław and the industrially important line in the south from Wrocław-Katowice-Kraków with extensions westwards to East Germany and eastwards to the U.S.S.R. Other lines are the Baltic coastline and the important line from Katowice via Ostrava, and the Morava Gate to Vienna. The Polish railroads carried 57 per cent of Poland's freight (in ton–km) in 1966, with roughly a third of it being coal, coke, and iron ore.

The highway network has been greatly enlarged in the postwar years. Good roads radiate from Warsaw, but the roads formerly under Russia are often less than adequate. Cross-country roads are narrow and few. Roads carry roughly a quarter of the passengers carried by rail, but only a very small percentage of the freight. With private automobiles still scarce, good bus routes interconnect most small towns. Generally, railroads and bus services are ample in the western part of the country, roads and bus services only are adequately developed in the east. Air traffic tripled between 1960 and 1966 when it reached 335 million passenger kilometer. The official Polish state airline is LOT—Polskie Linie Litnicze.

Poland's inland waterways include 2,750 miles of navigable rivers and canals. The importance of the Odra, navigable for more than 400 miles and connecting the Baltic Sea with the important industrial region of Upper Silesia via the Gliwice canal has greatly increased since the war. Once the locks are completed along its upper course, medium-sized and large barges will be able to use this important inland water route. Sixty-two per cent of all the Polish waterway traffic moves on this river and canal. Ore shipments and other bulky raw materials are its main freight. The southern Odra is canalized and offers a connection to Katowice. The Vistula is navigable for most of its length, but below Warsaw accommodates only very small vessels (less than 400 tons) largely due to its fluctuating water level. Its importance for the movement of freight is presently negligible. The lowlands have a number of important canals. The most important east-west connection follows the lower Bug River and a stretch of the Vistula to the city of Bydgoszca, continuing on the Notec Canal to the Notec River, which in turn flows into the Warta and it in turn into the Odra near Kostrzyn. A good part of this important east-west route is in need of modernization to make it navigable even for vessels up to 250 tons. Poznań also is well located and connected with the major river and canal systems of the Polish lowlands. Plans call for many additional canals, especially the canalization of the Bug to the Soviet border where plans have been drawn up to modernize present links connecting it with the Dnepr. Plans are also under way to improve navigation of the upper Vistula to Kraków. All this, it is hoped, will ultimately make it possible to ship iron ore directly from the Ukraine to the steel and iron works of Nowa Huta. The most ambitious of the future schemes is to join the waters of the upper Odra, Vistula, and Morava and link this system with the Danube. The total volume of freight carried on Poland's waterways, 1.1 per cent, is of minor importance considering all internal freight traffic.

The Polish deep-sea fleet has now reached more than 991,000 GRT tons. Additional cargo vessels, tankers, and small passenger vessels are scheduled to be added during the next few years. The freight turnover at the important ports is steadily increasing and has reached over 26 million tons annually. Besides Szczecin, Gdańsk, and Gdynia, several other ports have local importance. Exports of coal and coke and imports of ores are the largest items. Szczecin has the largest transit traffic.

Foreign trade. The structure of Poland's foreign trade has undergone basic changes from the prewar period, when trade was predominantly with the United Kingdom, Germany, and the United States. Today more than 60 per cent of Poland's total foreign trade is carried on with the Soviet Union and the other Socialist countries. The Soviet Union, Czechoslovakia, and East Germany are the largest bloc trading partners; the United Kingdom and West Germany the largest non-bloc partners, with trade with The United States on a slow increase. The volume of foreign trade is steadily rising in the postwar period, with a small excess of imports over exports. The structure of Poland's trade is typical for an agricultural country shifting to a mixed type of economy. Roughly a quarter of all imports and exports by value consist of machinery and equipment. Foodstuffs comprise nearly 13 per cent of the exports and 11.5 per cent of her imports (tropical goods, wheat and other bread crops). Fuel and raw materials comprise 47 per cent of the imports and 34 per cent of the exports (1966); coal (though diminishing), rolled products, machines and machine tools, ships, zinc and zinc sheets, chemicals, foodstuffs, and cotton and wool fabrics head the exports. Among the most important imports are iron ore, petroleum products, crude oil, zinc concentrates, rubber, cotton, wool and other textile raw materials, rawhide, oils and fats, tobacco, coffee, rice, wheat, and maize.

Tourism has received recent encouragement. Sopot on the Baltic and Zakopane in the Tatras are the best known. Total receipts are small.

CZECHOSLOVAKIA

Population

The prewar Republic of Czechoslovakia had a lifetime of less than twenty years. Between the organization of the country in October, 1918, and its breakup as a result of the Munich Agreement in September, 1938, it constantly had to cope with its multinational population. Between the annexation by Germany of the largely German-speaking Sudetenland and the Treaty of Moscow in July, 1945, when the country's easternmost province of Ruthenia was incorporated in the Soviet Union, Czechoslovakia underwent tremendous population and territorial changes.[29] Between Munich and the end of the war, a large strip of the country's territory in southern Slovakia and Ruthenia, with approximately one million people, was awarded to Hungary. Poland, in October, 1938, occupied and later annexed the small and controversial Tešin region. In March, 1939, Czechoslovakia itself was removed from the map as an independent country. With the occupation of the Czech territory by Germany (Bohemia and Moravia became a German protectorate), Slovakia became independent under German protection and Ruthenia was occupied by Hungary. After

[29] Approximately 2.4 million Sudeten Germans were transferred to Germany under the Potsdam Agreement, and an additional 800,000 Germans fled either with the retreating German army or after the war. More than 24,000 Hungarians who had moved to territory awarded them in Czechoslovakia in 1939, returned to Hungary. Roughly 140,000 Czechoslovak nationals could not be accounted for at the end of the war. Another 800,000, living in Ruthenia, were transferred to the U.S.S.R. About 55,000 Jews survived the war, but most of these have emigrated to Israel. Altogether, Czechoslovakia lost roughly 3.4 million people between 1939 and 1945. Another 50,000 political refugees left after the Communists came to power in mid-February, 1945. In 1966, 6 per cent of the total population were of non-Czech and Slovak nationalities.

Fig. 8–16. Prague (Czech Praha) is located on the Vltava River. View toward Prague castle (Hradčǎny). The main civil settlement Staré Město (Old Town) developed on the east bank in medieval times within a bend of the river and was overlooked by Letná and the higher Hradčǎny hills. St. Vitus cathedral can be seen in the back of the castle which is now the Presidential seat. (G. W. Hoffman.)

the war, however, territories annexed by Germany, Hungary, and Poland were restored to Czechoslovakia.

The estimated population of some 14.4 million people (1968) dwell in an area of 49,370 square miles, roughly the size of New York State, with an over-all population density of about 292 per square mile. Administratively, Czechoslovakia is divided into 10 regions, *kraje*, and 108 districts, *okresy*. The prewar provinces of Bohemia and Moravia are now comprised of 7 *kraje*, the remaining 3 *kraje* comprise the former province of Slovakia. Thirty-one per cent of the population live in these three Slovak *kraje*. The Slovaks contribute 29 per cent of the total population, 86 per cent of which live in Slovakia. Prague, the eleventh *kraje*, is the capital (Fig. 8–16), and has a population of one million (1966). Plans for the establishment of a federal State with autonomous regions for the Czech and Slovak parts of the country are now contemplated. Six cities have a population of over 100,000 inhabitants: Prague, Brno, Ostrava, Plzeń, Košice, and Bratislava, the last two located in Slovakia. In 1966, 2.2 million people lived in cities of over 100,000. The country has 12 cities in the population group 50,000 to 100,000, but basically it is a country of small towns and villages. Greatest population densities are found in the industrial regions of Ostrava, Prague, and Plzeń, where there are over 500 people per square mile.

Because of Czechoslovakia's increased industrialization and the greater mechanization of agriculture, many rural communities have lost people, and this is clearly reflected in the increase of those living in urban localities— 49 per cent in 1946 as against 59 per cent in 1960. In addition, the war had a different impact on the Czech and the Slovak region. In the Czech region, population increased much more slowly and population changes between 1938 and 1947 were more profoundly felt. Population dropped in the Czech region by 21 per cent, while it dropped by only 5 per cent in the Slovak region.

The various migrations and war losses naturally have affected the average annual growth as well as the whole population structure. In addition, the Czech reproduction rate is the lowest in Eastern Europe and close to the West European level. The birth rate of the Slovaks is high. The number of live births for all of Czechoslovakia fell from 23.4 per 1000 in 1948 to 15.6 in 1966. The high natural increase of the Slovaks contributes to the expanding labor force in the Czech lands (roughly 3.3 per cent of the population were Slovaks), and at the same time, acts as an important contributing factor for the establishment of industry in Slovakia.

Ethnographically the population is now much more homogeneous than in the prewar years. Minorities have greatly declined with the mass migration of the Germans (ethnic Germans made up 1.9 per cent of the population in 1966, as against 23.6 per cent in 1930). Hungarians occupy a narrow strip to the south, along the Hungarian boundary, and number about 550,000. There are also 70,000 Poles in northern Moravia and small groups of Ukrainians and Jews. Six per cent of the total Czech-Slovak population are minorities as compared with 35 per cent before the war. No religious census has been taken since 1930, at which time, 77 per cent of the Czechoslovakian people declared themselves Roman Catholics, and 13 per cent belonged to various Protestant denominations. Most of the Germans who have since left were listed as Roman Catholic.

Illiteracy has been of minor importance in Czechoslovakia since 1930. Public schools in Czechoslovakia had a high reputation before World War II. The whole system was reorganized in 1948 when a uniform educational system was established. Much emphasis has been placed on additional vocational training since that time, and the 1965 figures showed that 5 per cent of those in school were attending higher educational institutions. Czechoslovakia also has the highest number of foreign students of all Eastern European countries. The occupational distribution has undergone important changes during the last 20 years. About 95 per cent are employed in the socialized sector of the economy. Twenty per cent of the labor force was employed in agriculture and 47 per cent in industries and construction (1966). Approximately one-third of those employed in industry work in plants producing finished manufactured goods.

The basic population problem in Czechoslovakia is between the Czechs and Slovaks. Though related, they have not always worked well together. A Slovak State under German patronage was established during the Second World War, but the rift is still noticeable, though both people are fully aware of the need of the Czechoslovak State.

Present Economic Life

With the breakup of the Austro-Hungarian Monarchy, an independent Czechoslovakia retained nearly 60 per cent of all the industries of the Monarchy. Over 80 per cent of the Monarchy's coal production was located in Czech territory. The Ostrava-Karviná region, with important reserves of coking coal and iron ore from the Slovak Ore Mountains, which was developed as an important ferrous-metallurgy center for the Monarchy, now became available to the new state. These raw materials and industries, together with a highly developed agriculture, were a great asset. On the other hand, the old Monarchy's free markets were lost and much of the prewar period was consumed in adjusting Czechoslovakia's large industrial production to the needs of the reduced market area and in increasing the country's foreign trade. After the liberation of Czechoslovakia from Nazi rule, nationalization, and land reforms set the pattern typical for Communist countries. The economic development since the war has been closely integrated, with the goals of the various Soviet plans. Industrial expansion received top priority, especially for Slovakia (close to one-third of all investment capital). Investments in agriculture were small and progress lagged far behind. The large industries which had been in existence in pre-Communist times and the relatively little war damage gave Czechoslovakia a unique position among the Soviet bloc countries. From a purely economic point of view, Czechoslovakia's contribution of technical knowledge, and her export of machinery, tools, instruments, processed food, railroad rolling stock, and engines, are the most important contributions to the whole Soviet bloc. It is estimated that total industrial production increased twelvefold since the war.

Agriculture and forestry. Changes in the land-use pattern since before the Second World War have been small. Fifty-eight per cent of the total land area of Czechoslovakia is classified as agricultural, of which roughly 41 per cent is arable, 14 per cent is permanent meadows and pastures, 34 per cent is forested, and 9 per cent is classified as waste and unproductive (Fig. 8–12).

Agriculture is dominant in Bohemia but, measured by the number of those engaged in it, plays a greater role in Slovakia. The prevalence of agriculture, however, decreases toward the east; the Bohemian Basin, the Moravian depression, and the Slovakian part of the Little Alföld are the most intensively cultivated regions. The Carpathians are important for pasturage. Wheat, barley, oats, and rye are the most important cereals in the Czech lands; maize is cultivated, for the most part, in Southern Moravia and the Slovakian portion of the Little Alföld. Rye is the predominant cereal crop, followed by oats and potatoes in Slovakia. In 1966, 52 per cent of the sown area was planted in grains, 31 per cent in fodder, 9 per cent in potatoes and 8 per cent in industrial crops. A greatly decreased harvest of hops, important for the beer industry, comes from the Ohre Valley and the Moravian Basin. Tobacco, sugar beet, oil seed, and flax production have increased over the last few years, most tobacco being grown along the lower Morava and Danube rivers. Cattle are important mainly in Bohemia and Moravia, sheep rearing in Slovakia. Efforts have been made to increase the area under wheat, but imports of considerable quantities are still needed (1.0 million tons in 1966), as well as small quantities of other grains. Over-all production increases have been small, partly due to labor shortages, but also due to a

relatively high efficiency already existing. Czechoslovakia differs from the other East European countries inasmuch as output per unit of labor has achieved a considerable increase since the war, largely due to the large-scale mechanization and a decrease by nearly half of agricultural labor since 1939. Agriculture and forestry contributed only 14 per cent to the national income.

Although the forest lands in Ruthenia are lost to the Soviet Union, forests remain an important natural resource in Czechoslovakia. Close to half of the forests are coniferous, 30 per cent are deciduous, and the rest are mixed. The Administration of State Forests controls nearly all forest lands. Because of overcutting during the war and increased demands for industrial production, timber cutting has been curtailed. Coniferous woods supply most of the wood production, with roundwood, pulpwood, and pit props predominant. The importance of forestry is shown in the large number of those employed in it, over 103,000 in 1966.

Land reforms were first introduced in 1919. As a result three-fourths of the agricultural land held was in units of less than 50 acres. A second reform was introduced in 1945 as a result of the departure of the German-speaking population. Even after the distribution of close to 5 million acres to individual farmers between 1945 and 1948, the government held 41 per cent of all agricultural land (in part due to the shortage of labor). An upper limit of 124 acres was established for private farm holdings, but 97 per cent of the farm units were actually less than that amount. Collectivization of agriculture was introduced in 1949[30] and in spite of considerable relaxation in the mid-1950's, close to 90 per cent of the agricultural land is now socialized. The remainder is in small plots of the members of the collective. In 1967, state farms held 30 per cent of the

[30] The socialized sector included collectives, state farms, and state tractor farms. The latter were abolished in the late 1950's following the example of the Soviet Union.

Fig. 8–17. Karviná, an industrial city in Czech Silesia, near the Czech-Polish border. (Pictorial Service, Czechoslovakia.)

total agricultural land, cooperatives 60 per cent. Private farmers accounted for about 10 per cent.

Mining and manufacturing. Earlier it was stated that Czechoslovakia has a unique position among the East European countries. It is the most highly industrialized country of Eastern Europe. Historical reasons explain a good part of this development. Bohemia and Moravia were the preferred regions for industrial investments of the Austro-Hungarian Monarchy. On the other hand, this development certainly would not have assumed such proportions had it not been for large deposits of coal, various other minerals, and large quantities of lumber and pulpwood (Fig. 8–11). The main center for coal mining is the southern part of the Upper Silesian coal basin near Ostrava-Karviná (Fig. 8–17). Over 40 per cent of the coal is of coking coal quality and much is exported to other Socialist countries. Smaller fields are distributed throughout Bohemia. Total production amounted to 32 million tons in 1966. Lignite (74 million tons in 1966) is mined mainly in the Teplice-Sanov-Chomutov area and the

upper Nitra Valley in Slovakia. It is used for industrial fuel (including for power stations), domestic fuel, and as a raw material for the growing chemical industry. Some Soviet coal imports go to Eastern Slovakia's new thermal station. Iron ore in the Ore Mountains of Bohemia southwest of Prague and in the Slovakian Ore Mountains has been exploited on a large scale since the mid-nineteenth century, but today is insufficient for Czechoslovakia's domestic requirements and the quality has decreased rapidly. Close to 80 per cent of her industrial needs must be imported, mostly from the Soviet Union. Kaolin, of great importance to the world-famous china and glass industry, occurs in the Karlovy Vary and Plzeń regions of Bohemia. Graphite is mined near Brno and Plzeń and is of importance for pencil production. Mining of non-ferrous metal ores today is negligible. Small quantities of tin, uranium, manganese, and antimony are the chief products. The output of petroleum and natural gas was of minor importance. The bulk of her needs comes from the Soviet Union on the "friendship" oil pipeline and is refined at Slovnaft refinery near Bratislava.

Czechoslovakia has also invested $550 million (for the period 1966–1974) for the development of the West Siberian oil region in exchange for crude oil shipments to commence in 1970. Production of electric power has sharply risen since the war, it amounted to 36.5 billion kwh of electric power in 1966, 88 per cent was generated by steam. The well-known mineral springs and spas centering around Karlovy Vary serve as important health resorts.

The 11 *kraje* referred to on page 475 serve as important regions for economic planning and while variations obviously exist, internal regional connections between urban settlements and industries are supposed to take priority over links with regions. The aim of the planners was to build each important commercial and industrial concentration (central place) as an economic region. The major existing manufacturing concentrations, to some degree, are related to existing *kraje*.

Manufacturing industries are concentrated in three important regions in Bohemia (Fig. 8–11):

(1) the coal-mining, and iron and steel works of Ostrava-Karviná (north Moravia *kraje*). The Czech metallurgical industry is concentrated here producing 80 per cent of the pig iron and 70 per cent of the crude steel. The main contribution is semi-manufactured items (see 3 in Fig. 8–11).

(2) the Prague region, with extensions westward to Kladno (Rakovník, Beroun), east to Kolin and Podebrday, and north to the Elbe River. This is a varied industrial region, including coal-mining, iron-smelting, steel manufacturing, metal, chemical, food, and lumber industries. Clothing manufacture is concentrated in Prague (see 4 in Fig. 8–11).

(3) the North Bohemian region, with its varied industries, many located in small towns, extends roughly from Plzeń to Chomutov in the west and to Liberec in the east (see 5 in Fig. 8–11).

Raw materials more abundant in the nineteenth century than now laid the basis for many of the industries. Power and lignite are important today for a growing chemical industry. Included here are the metal, chemical, and ceramic industries of Plzeń and Karlovy Vary. Steel works are located at Chomutov and the Czech glass and ceramic industries are centered here. Textile industries are dominant to the east of the Labe. The industries of these regions were hardly touched by the war and contributed much to the early postwar industrial expansion in the Soviet-bloc countries. A dense railway network, most of which was built before World War I, helps to transport the great variety of products within the country and to various foreign countries.

Other important industrial cities often separated widely from a larger industrial cluster include the metal and chemical industries in Brno (see 6 in Fig. 8–11). The latter also has important textile plants. Bratislava has a variety of manufacturing and is also being developed into a major petrochemical center. The more important valleys of Slovakia (Va, Nitra, Hron) have in recent years received numerous industrial establishments. The Morava valley has many small industrial towns with Gottwaldov the largest. The new integrated East Slovakian iron and steel works in Košice is already playing a key role in the industrialization of this region. Iron ore will be shipped in from Krivoy Rog (Soviet broad-gauge rails lead directly to the plant). Other ores will go on to Ostrova and return with coking coal. This will cut the distance for the iron ore shipments by close to half (the ore now goes to Ostrava), which is especially important considering the long empty runs the ore cars had to make. Products of the metallurgical industries include rolling stock, power equipment, tools, precision instruments, and armaments.

Finally, some importance should be credited to the long-established home and small-scale industries for the production of leather goods, musical instruments, toys, jewelry, lace, and other consumer products. Industries producing flour and sugar, dairy products, malt, starch, glucose, and tobacco, and the well-known beer industries of Plzen and Ceske-Budejovice, play their role in the economy of the country. Based on a good foundation, Czechoslovakian industrial capacity has much expanded in the last 25 years and in per capita production of power, solid fuels and steel rank close to the industrial countries of western Europe.

Communications. The communications network is extremely dense in the Czech region, but the mountains of Slovakia form a barrier and have relatively few railroads and highways. The roads are of excellent quality and all important main railroad lines are double tracked. Prague is the chief railway center, with lines fanning out in all directions, and Bratislava, in Slovakia, is an important terminus. The main west-east line is electrified. Freight carried by railroads has shown a consistent increase during the last few years, with coal, coke, and iron-ore comprising close to 40 per cent of the tonnage. It is estimated that close to 90 per cent of all freight (in ton-miles) goes by rail. Czechoslovakia has the densest road network of all East European countries. Most roads are hard-surfaced and all parts of the country are well interconnected.

Navigable waterways, a total of roughly 300 miles, play a decidedly secondary role, with the Danube, the Labe, and the Vltava as far as Prague the only navigable rivers. The Danubian ports of Komarno and Bratislava are important transit ports. There has been much talk and planning for an Odra-Danube canal, economically of great importance in an integrated Eastern Europe. Iron ore could be shipped on the Odra to the iron and steel works of Ostrava and coal, including coking coal, could be exported to the iron works in Hungary, south of Budapest. Such a canal would go from Kozle on the Odra in Poland via the Ostrava-Karviná region, the Moravian Gate to the Morava and the Danube. Technical difficulties are by no means insurmountable. Plans for such a canal long predate World War I. Domestic

air traffic has greatly increased in the last ten years and something like 60 towns now have connections with larger population centers and many cities in the world. Czechoslovakia has developed since 1952 an ocean fleet (home port Szczecin, Poland), whose aggregate registered gross tonnage was close to 100,000 tons in 1965.

Foreign trade. Foreign trade is of great importance to Czechoslovakia's highly developed industrial complex, but because of shortages in fuels, minerals, foodstuffs, and other raw materials the country must import large quantities. In 1965 exports contributed 14 per cent of Czechoslovakia's gross national product, which on a per capita basis is higher than that of any other Eastern European country. Foreign trade has greatly expanded since World War II.

Industrial products are the main exports with machinery and related products contributing 50 per cent of the total value of exports (1966). Goods included in this category are metal-working machinery, engines, tractors, electric motors, automobiles, and textile machinery. Twenty-nine per cent of the exports comprise fuels, raw and other basic materials (coal, chemicals, and steel products). Consumer goods comprised 17 per cent of the exports and foodstuffs four per cent. Before the war, machinery and related products accounted for only 6 per cent of Czechoslovakian export.

Before World War II, trade with the Soviet Union was only 2 per cent of Czechoslovakia's total trade and that with the Eastern European countries amounted to 15 per cent. A drastic change has occurred here and in 1966 Czechoslovakia's trade with the Soviet Union amounted to 34 per cent of her total trade, that with the Eastern European countries, including East Germany, was 30 per cent. East Germany is Czechoslovakia's best bloc country customer after the Soviet Union. In the mid-1960's it was estimated that half of Czechoslovakia's total export to Communist countries consisted of machinery and related products, and 25 per cent of basic industrial raw materials and semi-processed goods, including 1.5 million tons of coal (mostly coking coal) to Poland and Hungary. In return Czechoslovakia obtained 55 per cent of her fuel and raw and semi-processed materials, and 19 per cent of her foodstuffs from these countries. The Soviet Union supplied Czechoslovakia with 78 per cent of her iron ore needs in 1964, 90 per cent of petroleum, over 50 per cent of the imported coal, and 34 per cent of machinery products (37 per cent came from East Germany).

West Germany is the best non-Communist trading partner of Czechoslovakia, followed by the United Kingdom, Austria, Italy and the Netherlands. Czechoslovakia's total trade with non-Communist countries between 1959–1964 averaged about 27 per cent. Main imports are foodstuffs, inedible raw materials, and manufactured products. Exports to non-Communist countries are primarily to finance supplementary needs for her economy. Czechoslovakia's trade with the United States is of minor importance (1.3 per cent of its total trade), but it has increased steadily since 1959. Among the main United States exports are agricultural products and raw materials. Imports include glass and glass products, footwear, machine tools, bicycles and light fixtures.

HUNGARY

Population

The only territorial change for Hungary after World War II was the loss of a small area, 24 square miles, opposite the Czech city of Bratislava. Otherwise, the area remained unchanged because territories gained during World War II were also lost. Hungary, with an estimated population of 10,-200,000 in mid-1968, an area of 35,919 square miles (roughly the size of Indiana), has a population density of 284 per square mile. The lowest densities are in the southern part of Transdanubia and the Hortobágy steppe, the least fertile lowland areas. Perhaps a word should be said here about the settle-ment pattern which has been greatly influenced by Hungary's long, difficult history. The Turkish invasions of the sixteenth century intensified an already existing picture of a thinly settled Great Alföld, the moderate densely settled northern hill lands, and Transdanubia, the densest area of the country. The plains were literally depopulated, the peripheral area serving as population refuge. When the lands were reconquered by Austrian armies late in the seventeenth century, they were immediately settled by two processes: (1) peasants from many nationalities were conscripted from all parts of the Austro-Hungarian Empire, and were settled, for the most part, along the southern boundaries of the Banat and Slavonia (for protection against new Turkish invasions) in well-planned, compact villages; (2) the central parts of the Alföld were distributed by Austria to a small Hungarian nobility which established cattle farms and these were ultimately replaced by agricultural settlements.

Administratively, Hungary is now divided into 19 counties (*megye*) and these are subdivided into districts (*járás*), cities or towns (*város*), and communes (*község*). Urban growth has been rapid, but uneven. Twelve cities have a population of over 50,000, 35 cities of 20–50,000. Typical for the urban settlements of the country is the fact that many of these are functionally just oversized villages. The changing rural-urban ratio of the population shows a decline in the rural population from 64 per cent in 1941 to 40 per cent in 1966.

Norman Pounds classifies the cities based on their morphology and function into three groups:

(1) Budapest, actually the twin cities of Buda and Pest on opposite banks of the Danube, is the most important administrative, commercial, and manufacturing center of the country with a population of 1.9 million (see Fig. 8–10);

(2) the cities west of the Danube and along the northern border, often re-

Fig. 8–18. Kiskunfél Gyháza, a typical Hungarian agricultural town with a population of 33,000. The town is located on the important road from Budapest to Szeged in the Danube-Tisza interstream region. The settlement was repopulated after the Turkish withdrawal in the middle of the eighteenth century. The most important industry in the town is a modern chemical and food industrial machinery plant employing over 3000 workers. Note the built-up town center with the Catholic and Protestant churches and the large area covered by its houses. (Interfoto MTI, Budapest.)

sembling those of Austria and frequently of medieval origin. These cities grew up as market towns and many today have important industries: Györ, the Danube river port; Veszprem, in the Bakony; the one-time capital of Hungary, Székesfehérvár; the important industrial city of Mosonmagyaróvár with an aluminum-smelting plant; the new steel making center of Dunaújváros, the largest city of the west, Pécs, which has important engineering industries; and in the northern hills the twin cities of Miskolc-Diósgyör with their iron-smelting and metal industries;

(3) the cities of the great plain, Great Alföld, whose functions are predominantly rural and their morphology still shows the strong agricultural emphasis. The largest city located in the eastern margin of the plain is Debrecen. Szeged is the largest city in southeastern Hungary. Typical for these cities is the impressive city center, but once this has faded the city rapidly assumes the character of a large village. Many of these cities are merely over-grown villages (Fig. 8–18).

Hungary, too, has had considerable population transfer since 1939.[31] The various migrations and war losses naturally have

[31] This includes people transferred because of the various territorial changes during the war, e.g., Czechs and Slovaks expelled during 1939; and the Hungarians moved from truncated Romania to the pre-1939 Hungary. A number of exchanges were arranged after World War II. By far the largest change involved the German ethnic group, of which about 260,000 were expelled or fled from Hungary. Mention should also be made of war losses and of the reduction in the Jewish population. Few survived the war, and most of those emigrated to Israel or the United States. Another mass movement of people occurred in connection with the 1956 revolt. A net migration loss of 186,000 resulted from the movements between October, 1956, and the end of 1958. More than 86,000 were permanently resettled in various European countries, 84,000 in overseas countries.

affected the average annual growth as well as the population structure. A slow rise in the birth rate and a decline in the death rate during the last decade have brought the natural increase to approximately 4 per thousand. On the whole, the nation's net population growth has been exceedingly small.

Ethnographically, the population of Hungary is extremely homogeneous (Fig. 8–6), in large part due to the population exchanges since 1920 and the drastically changed boundaries as a result of World War I. Ninety-seven per cent of the population speak Hungarian as their mother tongue; the language is Magyar. Germans are the largest minority group; others are Slovaks, Serbs, Croats, and Romanians. The people of Hungary are predominantly Roman Catholic (70 per cent), and about 27 per cent are members of various Protestant sects.

Illiteracy in Hungary is nearly non-existent; technical training and higher education receive much emphasis. Enrollment in technical fields of higher education has greatly increased and similar developments are noticeable in secondary schools. The shortage of skilled workers, which is typical for all Eastern European countries, has brought increased attention to specialized training, in both secondary and higher education. Hungary has 7 universities, but some of them consist of individual departments only. Finally, the occupational structure of the population shows that 31 per cent are active in agriculture (the percentage is declining), about 32 per cent in manufacturing and mining.

Present Economic Life

Hungary's economic structure underwent major changes after World War II. Communist influence in Hungary became complete after 1949, and plans to change the largely agricultural character to that of a mixed agrarian-industrial country started with the first five-year plan, 1949–54. Constantly changing goals, forced industrialization, stagnation of agriculture, and the after-effects of the 1956 upheavals (when industrial production remained inactive for more than three months) influenced the whole economic development of the country.[32]

In spite of the fact that Hungary's new iron and steel industries must import the key raw materials (coal, coke, and iron ore), the building of these industries in itself is certainly not to be blindly condemned. With economic collaboration among the Eastern European countries and the Soviet Union progressing, and with an excellent rail and river transport network available with the neighboring states, these needed raw materials can easily be shipped in. In addition, Hungary has ample labor and excellent technical schools. The problem is one of paying for these raw materials. Export of surplus bauxite and manganese ore, together with agricultural surplus, could easily pay for the needed minerals. This would be even easier if the new industries were better fitted for the needs of the country, e.g., tool making and food processing instead of strong emphasis on heavy machinery. Unfortunately, surplus cereals for export are a thing of the past. With one branch of the economy in poor health, the other part is unable to carry the total load. This is the real problem of Hungary's unbalanced economy.

Agriculture and forestry. Agriculture in Hungary has undergone many changes during the last twenty-five years. Not only was this a change in the basic structure of the land holdings, with collectivization of nearly all agricultural land completed in the 1960's, but the population dependent upon agriculture has dropped rapidly—52 per cent in 1939 to roughly 30 per cent in the late 1960's. This was largely the result of the impact of the collectivization, the elimination of small farms, and the massive introduction of modern agricultural technology of agricultural machines and artificial fertilizer. Seventy-

[32] The Soviet Union and its allies had to support the Hungarian government's purchase of raw materials with loans in excess of $250 million. See *The New York Times,* November 21, 1958.

six per cent of the total land area of Hungary is classified as agricultural, 17 per cent as forests and woodlands, and 7 per cent as unproductive; 60.4 per cent of the total area is under crops. Cereals (Fig. 8–12) have been traditionally the most important crops, but the picture has changed during the last ten years, the acreage under bread grains (wheat and rye) totals now 24 per cent and that of coarse grains (maize, barley, and oats) 36 per cent. Maize, needed for livestock, has increased at the expense of wheat and rye; the importance of wheat for export has also declined. Rye is now cultivated on the poorest soils. Maize, wheat, and barley are the main crops of the Little and Great Alföld; potatoes dominate on the sandy areas of eastern Hungary and near the Austrian border. Sugar beets, the cultivation of which has been expanded, are found in both the Little Alföld and Transdanubia. Many new industrial crops have now been planted, foremost among them being cotton which is planted in the southern part of the Transdanubian region; also sugar beets and leguminous plants such as peas, beans, and lentils are common. Irrigated vegetable acreage increased by more than 10 times since the war. Rice acreage has also increased in the last few years, especially in the semiarid alkaline soils of the Hortobágy Plain which now is crossed by an important canal, though the total area is still less than half of one per cent of the cropland. The production of paprika (eaten dried, as a spice, or green) is sufficient to permit export of large quantities. The marketing center is at Szeged. Mention also should be made of the important viticulture. The wines from the Lake Balaton and Tokaj regions are best known, and those grown on volcanic-based loess soils yield a quality high enough to be exported.

Animal husbandry provided close to 46 per cent of the total value of agricultural production before the war. It declined to 39 per cent by 1966. The number of pigs has increased considerably, the highest density in the trans-Tisza region. The number of horses has much declined, while the number of sheep has more than doubled since the war. Cattle are typical for the Little Alföld and for southern Transdanubia. The special Hungarian breed, white and long horned, is slowly being replaced by Austrian and Swiss breeds which are better milk producers. The Little Alföld and Transdanubia are the main cattle-breeding regions, but the seminomadic cattle and horse of the *puszta* and the Hortobágy are a thing of the past. Agricultural exports have undergone considerable change. Cereal exports have been discontinued, specialized products such as vegetables, eggs, poultry, canned fresh and frozen fruit, and quality wines predominate now. Agricultural products contribute close to 27 per cent of the total exports.

Forestry is of minor importance in Hungary, and imports are essential for nearly every type of lumber and wood product. Seventeen per cent of the country's area is under forest, with the oak predominating. Considerable effort has been made in forestation, e.g., for windbreaks and shelter belts, and to increase Hungary's slim forest reserves.

Collectivization [33] has had its ups and downs in Hungary since the war. It started in the latter part of 1948 and reached its height during 1952. Its low was reached after the 1956 revolution, and since that time it has slowly increased, accounting now for 97 per cent of the total arable land. Crop yields have been on the increase during the 1960's. Crop farming contributes about 35 per cent of the total value of agricultural production.

Mining and manufacturing. Hungary's increased industrial development must depend upon fuels and mineral supplies from abroad. Fuels available in quantities sufficient to be mined include the coal near Pécs and Komló on the southern slopes of the Mecsek hills, and a small field in the north. Bituminous coal accounts for approximately

[33] Includes both individual collectives and state farms.

14 per cent of the total coal production, and some coking coal has been produced from the coal in the Mecsek fields. All other coal-field yields are insufficient. At best they yield some low-grade lignite, production of which has greatly increased from 8.4 million tons in 1938 to 26 million in 1966. Tatabánya is the center for the lignite production. Lignite is used extensively for power production and as a household fuel. With few water power sites, this low-grade coal plays a key role in the economy.

Petroleum and natural-gas production was originally started by the Standard Oil Company of New Jersey in 1937. Petroluem production rose to 1.7 million metric tons by 1966. Fields are located in southwestern Hungary and southeast of Budapest. Pipelines connect these fields with refineries at Budapest. Needed imports come via the "friendship" pipeline which enters Hungary north of Budapest. In 1966–67 the largest oil field in Hungary was discovered in southern Hungary, in the Szeged basin. The increased production from 117,000 tons to 500,000 tons between 1966 and 1967 is already indicative of the wealth of this field. Natural gas production, too, has greatly increased during the last few years and is expected to increase by an additional 40 per cent by 1970. Plans for importing Soviet gas have been abandoned and important industries have been converted from coal to gas, but imports from Algeria via a new pipeline from Rijeka (Yugoslavia) to Zala (Western Hungary) are still contemplated. Hydroelectric power generation is very small, but future plans call for a large generating station on the Danube north of Budapest at Vac.

The only metalliferous mineral produced in Hungary is bauxite. Production of all other, including iron ore, is insignificant, and reserves are very small. The iron deposits are in the Sajo valley at Rudabánya (near the Czechoslovakian boundary) and production amounted to 747,000 tons in 1956. Manganese, copper, lead, zinc, and uranium are available in very small quantities, man-

ganese being perhaps the most important in total production. Bauxite, however, is Hungary's richest mineral resource, and reserves are estimated at close to 16 per cent of the world reserves. Bauxite is found in many places, but the center of production is in the Bakony-Vertes hills, close to existing lignite mines. Some of the bauxite includes important by-products such as aluminum oxide, iron, and sulfur.

Industrial production had already expanded between the two wars, but main emphasis was on light industries with only little scattered heavy industrial production. The new regime immediately introduced basic changes in line with Communist ideology. Manufacturing industries were emphasized. The number of employed has more than doubled since 1948, while those employed in light industries amount to only a quarter of all industrial employment. Three major industrial regions and a number of minor areas can be clearly defined (see 7, 8, 9 in Fig. 8–11).

1. Budapest with its suburban region has Hungary's largest industrial concentration in terms of manpower employed and value of output. There exists a great diversity: metallurgical plants, paper and textile mills, machine and tool factories, airplanes and armaments, tractors, diesel and electric locomotives, coaches, freight cars, trucks, sugar, tobacco, flour mills, food processing, and various pharmaceuticals.

2. The second major region includes all of northeast Transdanubia. This region combines mining and manufacture of such items as rolling stock, textiles, electric equipment, and glass. The factories make use of the coal at Ajka, and the power plants use local lignite. The Tatabánya lignite region includes cement plants and power production. Much of Hungary's bauxite and manganese production also originates in this region.

3. The third important region extends along Hungary's northern border from Salgótarján to Ózd and Miskolc. This region is one of Hungary's oldest industrial regions. Its machinery, tool, and armament industries

make important contributions to the whole economy. In this region there are also two integrated iron and steel works, at Diósgyör and Ózd respectively, which use imported ores from Slovakia, together with a small amount of local ores.

Newly developed industrial concentrations include the integrated iron and steel works at Dunaújváros, south of Budapest, on the Danube (Fig. 8–19). This plant originally was planned for Mohacs near the Yugoslav Frontier, to process Yugoslav ores, but after the Stalin-Tito break this site was abandoned even though much had been invested in it. Another industry greatly expanded since the war is the alumina-aluminum production. Alumina [34] plants are northwest of Györ (Mosonmagyaróvár, the

oldest works) near Komárom. Aluminum refineries are at Tatabánya and Inota, and there is also an alumina-aluminum complex at Ajka. Rolling mills are at Budapest and Székesfehérvár. While much processing of bauxite and alumina takes place, the high expense of electric power generation makes it advisable to ship considerable quantities of alumina and bauxite via the Danube to the Soviet Union for conversion into aluminum, while the metal ingots are returned to Hungary for manufacturing for export. Bauxite and alumina is also exported to other East European countries, as well as to Austria.

Another industry greatly expanded since the war is the chemical industry. Numerous small plants existed before the war, and most of them have been modernized and con-

[34] Three distinct processes comprise the aluminum production: preparation of alumina from the ore; smelting by an electrolytic process; and rolling of

ingots into sheets, the latter usually at a distance from the smelters.

Fig. 8–19. Over-all view of the Iron and Steel Works of Dunaújváros (old name: Sztalinváros), south of Budapest. Its favorable location on the Danube gives it easy access to raw materials and markets. View toward east with Danube in background. (Interfoto MTI, Budapest.)

verted to natural gas. The output of caustic soda, chlorine, oxygen, and other gases has been increased. With increased demands for fertilizers, organic dyes, drugs, rubber goods, etc., the expansion of the coal-chemical and petrochemical industry has been of great importance.

A large new chemical combine at Tisza-palkonya on the middle Tisza River is one of the first integrated industries built in close cooperation with other East European countries. Natural gas via pipeline from Romania has an important role; some coal is available locally. This plant manufactures nitrogen and plastics based on polyvinyl, and polystyrene and orlon.

Other manufacturing is scattered over the whole country, most of it in larger cities, e.g., Debrecen, Szeged, and Pécs. Plants include sugar refineries, food-processing plants, tobacco-processing plants, textile mills, flour mills, etc.

Communications. Budapest is the transportation hub of the country, with lines radiating in every direction. Highways, most of them asphalted, parallel the important rail lines. The whole transport network was originally built to serve a much larger region. The most important rail lines in terms of freight traffic are: (1) the line linking Vienna, Budapest, and Arad, in Romania; (2) the two lines between Budapest and the Soviet Union, one via Miskolc and the other via Debrecen; (3) the Budapest-Kecskemet-Szeged line to Timişoara in Romania; and (4) the direct line to Yugoslavia. The main lines are double tracked, the line from Budapest to Vienna electrically operated. The most important additions to the rail network have been in the direction of the Soviet Union. Mention should be made that several new tracks in northeastern Hungary use the wider Soviet gauge and run parallel to existing tracks. Hungary plays a most important role in the whole rail network of the East European states. Much use is made of roads in short hauls and more than half of the goods transported (1965) are carried by trucks.

About 1,000 miles of waterways are navigable, which mileage includes all of the Danube and the Tisza as far north as Dombrad. Most of the waterways are obstructed by ice for 60 to 90 days, and barges and boats must remain in winter ports. The Danube is navigable for boats up to 900 tons, most of the Tisza for craft up to 600 tons. Other but less dependable navigable waterways include the Körös and Drava rivers, and the Sio, Ferenc, and Hortobágy canals. The Hungarian section of the Danube across the Plain is very intensively used and much foreign trade (especially bulky goods) between Hungary and Yugoslavia, Bulgaria, and the Soviet Union is transported by river barges. Budapest has important docks, most of them located on Csepel Island. Once the project enlargement of the Hortobágy canal has been completed, navigation on the Tisza should increase and benefit the exchange of agricultural products.

Foreign trade. The pattern of Hungary's foreign trade has undergone many changes from the prewar period, when agricultural goods were the main products exported. Also, before 1939, trade with the Soviet Union was practically non-existent (largely cereals and bauxite). Today exports of agricultural products (27 per cent of the total) consist largely of highly specialized products. Other exports include machinery and equipment (31 per cent), manufactured consumer goods, and minerals, largely bauxite. Exports of manufactured goods have greatly increased in the last several years (18 per cent in 1949 to 33 per cent in 1966). Chief imports are coal, petroleum, and iron ore, raw materials for food industries and certain foodstuffs, machinery and equipment, and chemicals, fibers, etc. Hungary's foreign trade volume has sharply increased since the war, with exports to the Socialist countries amounting to about 64 per cent and 27 per cent to the developed Western countries in 1967. Trade with non-Socialist countries has been on the increase, West Germany holding first place.

ROMANIA

Population

As a result of the Second World War Romania was reduced by three regions: Bucovina and Bessarabia were annexed by the Soviet Union, and the loss of the southern Dobruja to Bulgaria in 1940 was made permanent. At the end of World War II the country was occupied by the Red Army, and Communist leadership was gradually introduced, not unlike the other Eastern European countries. Romania until early 1968 was administratively divided into 18 regions (*regiune*) and these were subdivided into *raions* and *communes*. The total population was 19.4 million, in mid-1968, occupying an area of 91,699 square miles (somewhat smaller than the state of Oregon). Over-all population density was 212 per square mile. Early in 1968 administrative-territorial changes were introduced to bring about closer political and economic coordination, dividing the country into 39 *judetul* (*judets*) —counties or districts, the capital of Bucharest (also a district), 46 municipalities (*municipiul*), towns (*oraşul*) and villages (*comuna*). The new regional divisions are based mainly on economic-social-cultural units which specialize in one or more branches of industry or agriculture.

Urbanization of the population in Romania has proceeded slower than in most other East European countries. Before the war only 21 per cent of the population lived in towns and cities. Rapid expansion since the Second World War, especially the industrialization of many smaller towns, has changed the urban-rural ratio to about 38 to 62 per cent. Bucharest with a population of 1.34 million in 1967 is the only large city. There are 12 additional cities with a population of over 100,000—Cluj, Ploieşti, Timişoara, Iaşi, Constanţa, Galaţi, Craiova, Arad, Brăila, Braşov, Oradea, and Sibiu—and eight over 50,000. The functions of the Romanian towns have undergone rapid changes because of increased industrialization and the incorporation of surrounding agricultural villages. A few new strictly industrial towns have been established. It is also important to point out that in territorial planning as practiced in Romania, new plant locations, whenever possible, were directed to rural areas, especially less developed regions, thus controlling the flow of surplus agrarian population. The most densely populated areas, aside from the urban concentrations, are in the Walachian Plain, the Siret Valley, and the central part of the Transylvanian Basin between Cluj and Tîrgu Mureş.

Romania, like all other Eastern European countries, has experienced great population changes. Tying its fortunes to a possible German victory, Romania's turnabout at the end of the war did not save her from losses to the Soviet Union and to Bulgaria, although Transylvania was recovered from Hungary. The losses clearly show in the latest census, which lists the population by nationalities and mother tongues. Those listed with Romanian as their mother tongue comprise 88 per cent of the population, and those with Hungarian over 8 per cent.[35]

The Magyars and the Szèkely (or Skeklers) are not separated in Romanian statistics (about 1.6 million). In 1952 an Autonomous Hungarian Region was organized (called Mureş-Autonomous Magyar Region) with nearly 80 per cent Szèkely, but in the 1968 administrative-territorial reorganization this region has been divided into three counties. The Hungarian population of Romania has well developed cultural centers and the University of Cluj is a joint Romanian-Hungarian institution.

The German population, the second largest minority, was reduced from 700,000 before

---

[35] Romania lost 6.18 million in the population transfers of 1940 and regained 2.6 million in 1945. War losses are estimated as slightly over half a million. So-called *Volksdeutsche* (in this case the earlier-mentioned Saxons) first joined the German Army and over 200,000 fled at the end of the war; close to 100,000 ethnic Germans were deported to the Soviet Union in 1945. The Jewish population was reduced almost 80 per cent by German and Hungarian deportations, and most of those who were left have emigrated to Israel since the war. Taking all this into consideration, the population had a net loss of close to 2.7 million people.

the war to 377,000. They live in the Braşov and Sibiu region of Transylvania (often called Saxons) and the Timişoara plain, known as the Banat (called Swabians). The Saxons are predominantly city dwellers and Lutherans and the ancestors of the earliest foreign settlers. The Swabians were originally concentrated in the Banat and settled by the Hapsburgs in the seventeenth century. They are largely farmers and Roman Catholics. There are other minorities, Czechs and Slovaks, Tartars, Bulgarians, Jews, Ukrainians, and Gypsies. Romanians live in the Moldavian SSR (part of Bessarabia) beyond the Prut River, but much Russian influence and settlement have occurred here since 1945 and also during the long period of Tsarist occupation between 1812 and 1918. There are also some Romanians living in the Ukraine, and a small number in Bulgaria, Hungary, and Yugoslavia. Nearly 80 per cent of the Romanians are members of the Romanian Orthodox Church; 9 per cent are Greek Orthodox.

The population structure is similar to that of the other East European countries. Annual natural growth has averaged 10 per thousand inhabitants (1955–1966). The population is relatively young, with over 25 per cent under the age of 15 and 46 per cent between 15 and 44 years of age. There is a certain structural similarity with Poland and Yugoslavia.

Total enrollment in all sorts of educational institutions increased greatly since the war. It is especially marked in the secondary technical schools and higher education. Education is compulsory for ten years. Illiteracy was high in the prewar purely Romanian regions and, while this has declined, exact up-to-date figures are not available.

To complete the picture of the population structure, the occupational distribution should be noted. The latest available figures show a slower impact of industrialization than in most other Eastern European countries. Those employed in industry constitute 19.7 per cent of the total employed population, those in agriculture 55.0 per cent (74.1

in 1950), in construction 6.7 per cent, in transportation and communication 2.5 per cent, in internal trade 4.1 per cent, and in various branches of administration 1.0 per cent.

Present Economic Life

Changes in Romania's economic life have been slower but just as insistent as in the other Eastern European countries. Industrial development was still in its infant shoes at the outbreak of the Second World War. Only those branches of industry attracting western capital, such as petroleum refining, were developed. Starting in the 1950's, a high rate of industrial expansion was achieved, in good part based on the resources of petroleum and natural gas. The industrial growth can be seen in the structural changes in the national income, with a rapid decline in percentage of agriculture (7 per cent between 1938 and 1966) and the share of industry increasing from 31 per cent to nearly 49 per cent between 1938 and 1966. In the mid-1960's it was claimed that gross industrial output was more than six times that of 1950. All means of production were nationalized in the early postwar years. The changes in the economy have been less erratic than in some of the other East European Socialist countries.

Agriculture, forestry, and fishing. Sixty-two per cent of the total land area of Romania is classified as agricultural. Forest land amounts to 27 per cent and the rest is classified as waste, water, and fallow. Forty-four per cent of the total land is arable. The highest percentage of arable land is found in the Walachian Plain and other Danube districts and the lowland areas bordering Hungary, including the Timişoara Plains (Banat). Cropland has tended to increase as marginal land (large-scale reclamation and irrigation in the Balta regions of the Danube) has been brought under cultivation. Maize followed by winter wheat are the main cereals. Close to 35 per cent of the cropland was under maize in the mid-1960's (Fig. 8–12). Highest yields come from the Banat region. Maize is still the main food of the people and is called *mamaliga* (*puliszka* in Transylvania). Barley is grown in close association with wheat, oats, and rye mountain crops. The total output is of minor importance. Rice is of local importance, especially in Walachia and the lower course of the Danube and parts of the western plains. Increased emphasis is given to its cultivation. Potato acreage has increased since the Second World War and is used both as food and industrial raw material. They are mainly grown in northern Romania and Transylvania. The sugar beets acreage has greatly increased, the beets being grown mainly in the western lowlands, northern Moldavia, Oltenia, and Transylvania. The acreage under sunflower, rape, cotton, and tobacco has increased, but these crops still play only a minor role in the total production. Other important products are beans and peas, but average yields are low; linseed and soybean (some of which is exported) are cultivated in the Walachian Plains and are important for vegetable oil. In addition, the cultivation of grapes is widespread and commercial vineyards are largest in Moldavia, especially around Iaşi and the Carpathian foothills. The apples and pears of Baia Mare and the plums of Bistrita are well known for their quality. In spite of greatly increased use of fertilizer and tractors, Romania's yields, in cereals as well as in industrial crops and potatoes, are generally unsatisfactory.

Livestock is equally important for food and as the main source of traction power. The total numbers of cattle and pigs have increased slowly. Sheep are very numerous. The sheep are similar to the Merino, with which they have been crossed, and are valued for wool, cheese, and milk, an important cash income for the farmer. Pigs are most numerous in the Transylvanian Basin, but are found in nearly every part of the country. The number of horses is rapidly diminishing, but they are still used on the fields. Generally the greatest amount of livestock is found in the southern Carpathian foothills.

Danube fish contribute close to 80 per cent of the catch. Great possibilities exist in the marshy lagoons of the Black Sea coast and the Danube Delta, with an annual catch of over a quarter of a million tons. Fishermen live in small hamlets on the many islands in the Delta. Carp, pike, perch, and, from the Black Sea, sturgeon (important for its caviar) are plentiful. Fishing in the Black Sea is only of minor importance.

Forestry is of great importance to the country's economy. Exports of a great variety of timber played a key role in the interwar period and have increased since the war. As was the case in Czechoslovakia, a realization of the danger of overcutting has finally set in and conservation measures, e.g., reforestation, and shelter belts in the plains, have received added attention. Coniferous forests, especially in the Carpathian Mountains, with the fir and spruce predominant, and deciduous forests, predominant in Transylvania, contain the most useful trees. The famous oak forests have been completely depleted.

Land ownership in agriculture has undergone many changes since 1918. As in other Eastern European countries, land reforms were initiated as soon as the Communist regimes came to power. Holdings in excess of 125 acres and those of churches were distributed to the landless and poorer peasants. Compulsory delivery quotas were initiated and much private equipment was confiscated. Socialization of agriculture was started in 1949 and most of the agricultural land was collectivized by 1962. Ninety-five per cent of the cropland was collectivized. In the mid-1960's there were over 4,600 collective farms averaging in size about 4,700 acres, together with 730 state farms with an average size of 7,400 acres. Collectivization was followed by long overdue technical improvements. The area under irrigation has been expanded, the use of artificial fertilizers greatly increased, trained agronomists are being used in an ever-increasing number, and acreage under industrial and fodder crops has greatly increased, especially in the last ten years.

Generally it can be said that farm production has increased since the war and certain products today are high on the list of exports.

Mining and manufacturing. The basis for industrial expansion in Romania is its wide range of mineral wealth. It was the shortage of capital which restricted growth of industrialization in the prewar years and not mineral shortages. Foreign capital was attracted only by those industries which gave dependable high returns, such as the petroleum and timber industries.

First place in the mineral wealth of Romania must be given to petroleum and natural gas. Romania is the largest oil and gas producer of Europe outside the Soviet Union. (It accounts for 88 per cent of the crude oil extraction in the Warsaw Treaty Organization and 80 per cent of the gas output, excluding the U.S.S.R.) Most of the petroleum fields are located in the Carpathian flysch formations and the sub-Carpathians. The Ploieşti region is one of the main oil bearing regions in the country (Fig. 8–11), and together with the oilfields in the Bacău region, has been in production since the third quarter of the nineteenth century. New oil deposits have been found since World War II. Crude oil extraction of the Argeş region (since 1951), with important fields south of Piteşti, now ranks second only to the Ploieşti fields. Other new fields recently opened are located at Berca, Boldeşti and Cîmpina. Production reached 13.05 million tons in 1967 and 11 per cent of Romania's total investments are earmarked for prospecting in the 1966-1970 plan. The natural gas fields distributed throughout the central part of the Transylvanian Tableland have a very high methane content and only few other hydrocarbons. Pipelines connect important industrial and urban centers, and an important line connects the fields with the integrated chemical combine at the middle Tisza River in Hungary (see p. 487). Natural gas is making an ever-increasing contribution to the growing chemical and steel industry, and for the production of thermal power. The Oltenia region ranks first as regards gross oil-well gases. About fifty per cent of the gas is marketed abroad.

Reserves of anthracite are small. Bituminous coal reserves are sufficient and it is mined largely in the upper Jiu Valley (north of Tirju-Jiu) and the Banat together with iron ores. Lignite is plentiful and it is also mined in the upper Jiu Valley. Iron ore output increased considerably in postwar years, but on the whole Romania is poorly supplied. The main mines are located at the Poiana Ruscǎi and the Banat Mountains, and iron ore content is between 25 and 35 per cent. More than one-half of its needs must be imported. The Soviet fields in Krivoy Rog are estimated to have supplied, in 1965 alone, close to 50 per cent of Romania's needs. Other minerals are much more plentiful; extensive low grade manganese ores in the Suceava region, with smaller deposits in the Banat, the important bauxites of the Bihor Mountains, phosphates, copper, lead, zinc, pyrites, manganese, and chrome. All have increased in output and are essential to Romania's growing industries. The Carpathian Mountains have small deposits of a great variety of ores and minerals; gold, silver, copper, lead, zinc, pyrites, some radioactive minerals, and others.

Every Romanian government during the last 50 years has put major emphasis on industrialization hoping to broaden the base of the economy. With complete control of all the means of production, transportation, and labor supply, the Communist government has systematically stressed heavy industry. An excellent base already was available. The emphasis after the war was on capital goods industries; consumer industries received very little or no investments, and only recently have these increased. Generally speaking, the major emphasis is still on the oil, steel, chemical, and timber industries.

The basis of industrial production has been considerably enlarged and broadened in terms of greater distribution. A taxonomic division of the concentration of industrial production in Romania was recently published in "Types de Concentration Terri-

Fig. 8–20. Iron and steel city of Hunedoara. View toward the south with the iron and steel works in the background. Modern two- and three-family housing in the foreground with large new apartment houses to the right. The Hunedoara iron and steel combine is now the biggest metallurgical enterprise in Romania. (Institute of Geology and Geography, Academy of Sciences, Bucharest.)

toriale de L'Industrie en Roumanie."[36] According to this analysis, it is possible to distinguish four large industrial districts—southern, southwestern, central, and eastern—and within each district, several clearly marked concentrations comprising several industrial branches. Each of the four industrial districts specializes in certain branches of production, based largely on available raw materials and with a nucleus established for the most part in prewar industries.[37] In addition to these major industrial concentrations, individual industrial units (referred to as industrial knots and complexes), with several centers gravitating towards one or two stronger centers and often interlinked by multilateral production links and industrial centers, primarily in big cities, are emerging, greatly influencing the country's industrial distribution.

Iron and steel works in operation before the Communist take-over are in Reşiţa in the Banat, where they have been in operation since 1771. They were mod-

ernized in the interwar period and again since 1950. In addition, new blast furnaces were added. In 1965 the Reşiţa works contributed roughly 25 per cent of the total iron and steel production. Another important plant, which started production in 1895, is at nearby Hunedoara (Fig. 8–20). In the mid-1960's it accounted for over 30 per cent of the over-all output. These two steel works supply mainly blooms and billets. Close by is the old Călan works which produces foundry iron. A new and fully integrated iron and steel plant is under construction at Galaţi with planned steel capacity of four million tons by 1970. The Soviet Union at first opposed the building of this plant as not needed in the general bloc economic plans, but now it is participating in its completion. Romanian oil and natural gas will make an important contribution to this plant, though imported iron ore and fuel will be essential. It is estimated that the old, modernized, integrated iron and steel works and the new plant together by 1970 will bring Romania's total steel production to over six million tons (1938: 284,000). There is also a small integrated plant at Otelul Roşu (between Reşita and Hunedoara) and at Cîmpia Turzii near Cluj, which produces various drawn steel goods. Rolling mills are found at Nadrag in the Banat, at Roman in Moldavia, at Brăila, Galaţi (being absorbed into the new plant), and Bucharest. The steel industry has provided an excellent basis for the engineering, armament, and electro-

[36] C. Herbst, I. Bacabaru, and N. Caloianu, "Types de Concentration Territoriale de L'Industrie en Roumanie," *Revue Roumaine de Géologie, Géophysique et Géographie. Série de Géographie*, Vol. 8 (1964):39–43.

[37] For details, see George W. Hoffman, "The Problem of the Underdeveloped Regions in Southeast Europe. A Comparative Analysis of Romania, Yugoslavia, and Greece," *Annals of the Association of American Geographers*, 57 (December, 1967): 637–66, especially the discussion on page 646 and Fig. 2. Material used in this article has also been used in these discussions.

technical industries, all expanded since the war. Among the goods produced are farm machinery, drilling equipment, trucks, diesel engines, machine tools, precision apparatus, turbines, generators, armaments, and seamless pipes.

The chemical industry is based on a large number of natural resources, such as petroleum, natural gas, salt, and pyrites. Before 1938 it was second only to the metallurgical industries in value of production. Its centers are in the Braşov-Ploieşti-Bucharest, and Cluj regions. Methane gas is used to produce carbon black, and four factories are now engaged in its production, permitting some export. Other products of the chemical industry are mineral fertilizer, caustic soda, sulfuric acid, synthetic rubber, and paper. Of special importance is the greatly increased production of pharmaceutical products, mainly of salicylic acid and its derivatives, saccharine, and antibiotics. Superphosphates, ammonium sulfates, and calcium cyanamide are produced in growing quantities. Sodium carbonate is produced in three factories, of which the Ocna Mureşului plant in Transylvania is the largest. The

sedge growing in the Danube Delta is an excellent base for the cellulose industry.

Romania has a variety of smaller, widely distributed agricultural industries and industries producing construction materials. Among the new industries is a big fiberboard and paper mill in the Danube Delta. The 150,000 acres of marsh reeds will be used as raw materials for this new industry. Moldavia, one of the least developed areas, which includes the regions of Bacău, Iaşi, Suceava and Galaţi (Fig. 8–11, no. 13), now has metallurgical industries, a large petrochemical plant, a synthetic fiber and thread plant, and factories for the production of plastics and antibiotics. Hand in hand with the expansion of the industrial network, production of power, both thermal and hydroelectric, is on the increase. A number of major developments in the Carpathian ranges have been completed (Argeş) or are under construction. Renault is now building an 80 million dollar plant in Piteşti which is scheduled to produce 50,000 cars annually by 1969. Also by 1971 the Iron Gate project, which is being jointly developed with Yugoslavia (Fig. 8–21) is expected to be com-

Fig. 8–21. Iron Gate dam and power plant building site, 1967. View from Romanian side near Turnu Severin across the Danube to Yugoslavia. (Institute of Geology and Geography, Romanian Academy of Sciences, Bucharest.)

pleted and Romania's share of the total power generated will amount to roughly five billion kwh. The main dam is scheduled for completion by 1969 and this will cause numerous villages to disappear and 14,500 people will be in need of new houses. With the raising of the river level behind the dam, navigation will be made fast and safe in a notoriously dangerous stretch of the river. The important power stations are interlinked by a grid system. Romania's use of electric power per unit of population is still among the lowest in Europe. Finally, the building of a proper infra-structure, both for regions considered underdeveloped and for those which are more developed, is of importance, having received often secondary priority to the building of industries.

The industrial regions of Reşiţa-Hunedoara, Bucharest-Ploieşti and Craiora-Piteşti (Fig. 8–11, nos. 10, 11, 12) are the more advanced regions and in 1965 accounted for 58 per cent of the total value of industrial production, though it is expected that their contributions will decrease to 37 per cent by 1970. Production of heavy industry accounted for 65 per cent of the gross industrial output in 1965 as compared with 45 per cent in 1938, machine building being the largest component in the heavy industry (25 per cent of the gross industrial output).

In the future territorial planning of Romania's economic expansion, the south and southwest areas are now the most economically attractive for concentrated investments due to the availability of key raw materials, excess of manpower, and excellent transport facilities. The five-year plan, 1966–70, favors the sub-Carpathian region at the expense of the rest of the country. Nearly 52 per cent of all investments in this period will go to the south and southwest, while the rest of the country will receive only 48 per cent. The south and southwest contain roughly two-thirds of the population of the country. The former regions of Dobruja, Iaşi, and Bucharest are to remain predominantly agrarian, but the rich subsoil should bring success to the planned diversification of the agricultural production of these lands. Constanţa city and port, which includes a stretch of the littoral along the Black Sea, has received considerable investments for building a tourist industry. The Mamaia area, for example, with its many modern hotels, today ranks as one of Romania's main tourist attractions (Fig. 8–22).

Communication. Romania's transportation network is underdeveloped, in part because it was originally oriented toward centers away from the present borders similar to the situation in most East European countries (the exceptions being Hungary and Albania). Due to historical reasons it also never developed a major railway node. Though Bucharest served as such a node for the old part of Romania (before 1918), Transylvania had no such nodal point, though perhaps Timişoara in the west and Braşov in the interior basin act as important central nodal points. The railroad and road pattern of Romania is clearly circumscribed by the Carpathian ranges. Attention since 1945 has largely been focused on connecting existing lines or adding short lines important to the economic growth of a particular industry (Fig. 8–2). There has been a shortage of rolling stock and engines, but the latter have slowly been modernized and increased in number.

The main west-east lines connect Bucharest with the western part of the country. Two lines cross Transylvania and cut across the Carpathians at Turnu Roşu Pass, and at Braşov there is an important crossing of two western lines and an eastern line. One line traverses the Walachian Plain and continues to Constanţa on the Black Sea. The Carpathians are skirted by a line running northeast from Ploieşti. Another line runs south from Bucharest to the Danube, crossing it over a two-kilometer long bridge to connect with an important Bulgarian line to the Maritsa Basin. Most of the rails are of standard gauge and only a few are double tracked. All together, six lines cross the Carpathian ranges, an insufficient number for present needs.

Fig. 8–22. Mamaia, Romania's largest seashore beach and resort, is located a few miles north of Constanța on a narrow strip of sand separating Lake Siutghiol from the Black Sea. The fine siliceous sand resulted from the longtime fragmentation of the sea shells. The many hotels, shopping centers, restaurants, sports grounds, and clubs now serve 100,000 tourists each summer. (Institute of Geology and Geography, Academy of Sciences, Bucharest.)

The Danube is the only navigable waterway and can be used from the Black Sea to Brăila by vessels up to 6,000 tons using the Sulina channel of the lower Danube. Vessels with a draft up to six feet are used for the rest of its course. But navigation is often seriously handicapped by low water level in summer and ice in winter. The Danube never played an important role as a major traffic artery. This can be seen in that no industry of importance (except two chemical works) or major towns are located along the river. The much talked about Danube-Black Sea Canal has never been completed and work was abandoned in 1953. Constanța is the most important port on the Black Sea, and Brăila and Galați are Danube ports. Romania's road system is insufficient for its present economic expansion and has one of the lowest ratios of any country in Eastern Europe. Considering Romania's opportunities to develop its tourist industry, the addition of all-weather roads and modern turnpikes is essential, but even more important is the building of a basic all-weather road network connecting all of the country's small towns and villages.

Foreign trade. The structure of Romania's foreign trade has undergone changes similar to those of other Eastern European countries, with regard not only to its geographic distribution but also to the types of goods involved. Germany as the major trading partner was replaced by the U.S.S.R., which, together with the other socialist countries, now absorbs some 58 per cent of Romania's foreign trade (1966), excluding Yugoslavia. Imports from the Soviet Union such as iron ore and fuels are essential for its industrial expansion program. Among non-Communist trade partners, West Germany ranks first. Romania is giving much effort to enlarging its trade with non-East European countries and has been in part successful, from 22 per cent in 1960 to 33 per cent in 1966. Chief exports before the war were wheat, flour, petroleum, timber, and livestock. These are still important and include, for example, exports of vegetable origin (averaging 15 per cent of the total value) including wheat and lumber, but increased emphasis is now placed on more sophisticated types of food products (refined sugar, sunflower, wines, oil, and meat), a greater variety of wood products, including furniture, a variety of manufactured items (about one-fifth of the total value) including electrical goods, oilfield equipment, tractors, and also cement, footwear, and textiles. Natural gas is exported to Hungary and manganese ores and some non-ferrous metals find easy customers. Major imports consist of machinery (41 per cent of the total value in 1966), iron ore, coking coal, and tropical foodstuffs. It is estimated that over one-third of its imports are needed for its expanding industrial effort.

BULGARIA

Population

World War II had relatively little effect on the population of Bulgaria. The southern Dobruja was regained from Romania in 1940, and was permanently assigned to Bulgaria after the war. Bulgarian troops, as allies of Germany, occupied portions of Greece and Yugoslavia (Macedonia), but had to retire to their prewar boundaries at the end of the war. The Soviet Union declared war on Bulgaria and occupied the country, and thus was able to place the Communist party in power. In Bulgaria, the country traditionally closest to Russia, with a strong Communist party, nationalization of industries and property, including collectivization, was accomplished much faster than in any of the socialist countries.

The population of Bulgaria was estimated at nearly 8.4 million in 1968, occupying an area of 42,822 square miles, roughly the size of Tennessee, with a population density of about 196 per square mile. Administratively, Bulgaria is divided into 28 districts (okruzi) including Sofiya, the capital, with a population of 817,972. Other important cities are

Plovdiv, 222,737; and Varna, 180,062. Districts are subdivided into counties (obstini). The over-all population-density figure is somewhat misleading because 15 per cent of the country's area is unproductive with a population density of less than 100 inhabitants per square mile in the mountainous regions, while in certain arable lands (41 per cent of the total area) population densities of over 400 per square miles are the norm (Danubian Plateau and Maritsa valley). The urban population is rapidly increasing and was figured as 46.5 per cent in 1965. Sofiya, which has nearly tripled its population since 1934, and Plovdiv are the traditionally industrial cities. Several newly developed or reoriented towns, with new industries or newly started or enlarged mining activities, have undergone rapid growth, e.g., Dimitrovgrad, a Soviet-style industrial boom town, is now one of Bulgaria's most important industrial centers, with a population of 41,787 in 1965, as compared with 3,600 in 1946. Pernik, an old coal and iron ore center, now has an important ferrous metallurgical industry (population 75,844 in 1965, in comparison with 16,000 in 1934). Apart from the few larger cities, including the new industrial and mining towns, most Bulgarian settlements are still essentially market and agricultural towns and villages (Fig. 8–23). Most of the small villages are still nucleated (Haufendorf) and the original hamlet grew into a very loosely agglomerated village. The mountainous settlements are scattered and isolated farmsteads are still dominant, especially in the Stara Planina.

Today 88 per cent of the people are Bulgarians, nearly 10 per cent Turks and the rest belong to several smaller minorities.[38] Most of the 50,000 Jews shown in the 1934 census emigrated to Israel. A majority of

[38] Population movements, such as the departure of 190,000 Turks after World War II, have been customary in the history of Bulgaria. Over 200,000 Turks and 40,000 Greeks left after World War I; 250,000 Bulgars came from the Thracian and Macedonian parts of Greece. With the incorporation of the southern Dobruja in 1940, about 62,000 Bulgarians were exchanged for 110,000 Rumanians.

Fig. 8–23. Village street in Melnik, southwestern Bulgaria, showing multi-storied houses with prop-supported overhanging rooms. (Committee on Cultural Relations, Sofiya.)

the 150,000 Gypsies,[39] who are Moslems, now have been integrated into the economy. The Pomaks, roughly 140,000 live in the Rhodope Mountains, are Bulgarian-speaking people of Moslem faith (similar to the Serbs and

[39] Gypsies, presumably coming from India, entered Bulgaria with the Turks in the fourteenth century. They have preserved their ancient language and customs. The nomadic way of life is traditional with them, and it is extremely difficult to persuade them to live in permanent settlements.

Croats of Moslem faith in Bosnia and Herzegovina). Ninety per cent of the population belongs to the Eastern (Bulgarian) Orthodox Church (Fig. 8–24). Moslems comprise about 9 per cent of the population, and there is a very small minority of Roman Catholics and Protestants. The language of the Bulgarians is Slavic, but shows dialect differences between East and West Bulgarian, and the Struma region with its

Fig. 8–24. Rila Monastery located less than 80 miles south of Sofiya in the Rila Mountains. Founded in the tenth century, it served as the intellectual center for most of Bulgaria and parts of Serbia throughout its history. The monastery was destroyed and rebuilt numerous times, and in its present form largely exists only since 1833. Only the 75 feet high Hrelyu Tower can be traced back as early as the fourteenth century. Today the monastery with its 173 rooms, monastic museum with its priceless printed books and manuscripts is a national museum. Among the valuable treasures is the first Bulgarian globe made by the monk Neofit Rilski. (G. W. Hoffman.)

Macedonian dialect. Approximately one million Bulgarians live outside their country, mainly in northern Greece, Yugoslav Macedonia, and Romania.

Because of relatively few war losses, Bulgaria is one of the few Eastern European countries which do not have a male deficit in their population. Sixty-six per cent of the population is of working age (15 to 64 years of age), 24 per cent are under 15 years of age. This indicates a relatively high percentage of labor potential now and in the future. The Bulgarian birth rate was originally the highest in Europe (39.6 births per thousand of population in 1920–24) but has dropped to an estimated natural increase of 6.6 per thousand (in late 1960's). Bulgaria ranks high in literacy. Since 1950, education has been compulsory from age 7 to 15 years, in either 4- or 7-year primary or

11-year general education schools. Technical training on the secondary level, such as vocational and professional education, has been greatly accelerated. Sofiya has the only university, but various higher institutes, including University institutes, have been established in a number of cities. The working population amounts to more than half of the total population, and almost half is occupied in agriculture. Thirty-five per cent of the workers are in industry, mining, and construction, and the rest in commerce, trade, and administration.

Present Economic Life

The economic policies established by the Communist regime in 1945 generally followed the pattern discussed in earlier sections. The Soviet example was followed and heavy industry received top priority.

Nationalization of all sectors of the economy proceeded rapidly and the various long-term plans have completely changed the economic structure. Despite emphasis on industrial growth, Bulgaria remains in many ways an agricultural country. A better economic balance has been established and the problem of the surplus agricultural population and unemployment, for the first time, has been successfully attacked. The changes can be seen in the composition of the national income. Agriculture's contribution decreased from 57 per cent in 1949 to 33 per cent in 1965. Manufacturing exceeds agriculture. Heavy manufacturing forged ahead of the contributions of the food industries (reduced from one-half to one-quarter).

Ninety-six per cent of the arable land now has been collectivized. It accounts for 86 per cent of the total agricultural output. The socialist sector of the national economy now accounts for 98 per cent of the total industrial output and more than 99 per cent of the retail trade. This is the highest percentage of any of the Eastern European countries and certainly is in line with their ultimate goal.

Agriculture, forestry, and fishing. Forty-one per cent of the total area is classified as arable, 11 per cent as pastures, 33 per cent as forests and 15 per cent as unproductive. The best arable land is in the Danubian part, southern Dobruja, and the central areas of the Maritsa Basin (Fig. 8–12). Meadows are common in some of the western districts, pastures in the coastal lands south of Burgas, in the central part of the Balkan Ranges, and in some western mountain areas. The chief areas for cereal production are the Danubian Plateau, southern Dobruja, and the Maritsa Basin. Wheat (27 per cent of all croplands) and maize (14 per cent) are the main agricultural crops, although rye, barley, and oats are well distributed. Production of wheat has been increasing in spite of a reduction in area sown, and a considerable amount now is available for export. Maize is grown primarily on the Danubian Plateau and while it is largely for fodder, a small amount is used for human food. Barley is the most widely distributed cereal crop and is used mainly for fodder. Rye, oats, millet, and rice occupy only small areas, rice mainly in the flooded lowland of the Maritsa, and lower Tundzha. In the mid-1960's, industrial crops contributed 16 per cent of the total agricultural output. In order of size of area planted, oil bearing plants take first place, followed by sunflower (on the Danubian Plateau and in the central lowlands), flaxseed, rapeseed, poppyseed, and ground nuts. The area under sugar beets increased fivefold between 1939 and 1966. Flax, hemp, and cotton were introduced by the Turks and production has increased since the Second World War with cotton grown mainly in the central lowlands between Plovdiv and the Tundzha valley. Bulgaria is well known for its vegetables, e.g., tomatoes, eggplants, pumpkins, beans, and peas. Olive trees are found in the southern coastal regions. An excellent quality of tobacco (Virginian) is grown, mostly in the Arda Basin and on the southern slopes of the Rhodope Massif. Yields are high. The so-called mountain variety (jebel), which is well suited for mixing, is exported.

Bulgaria also has a wide range of fruits and wine grapes. Apple orchards are concentrated in the Sofiya district, lemons on the Black Sea coast south of Burgas, plus widespread peach, apricot, pomegranate, almond, fig, and plum orchards. Of great importance—Bulgaria being the leading world producer—is rose oil (attar), derived from roses grown on the Tundzha depression. Much effort is made to grow those agricultural, fruit, and wine crops which are unique for Bulgaria, and the area under cereals has been decreased to make room for an expansion of those exportable crops. Large-scale irrigation projects have been undertaken to raise the yields and to add new agricultural lands. Agriculture is now highly mechanized, with thousands of small tractors. To avail themselves of greater export possibilities, structural changes of crops were initiated during the late 1960's. Production of vegetables is increasing (plans call for 50 per cent between 1965 and 1970), the production of canned fruit and vegetables by one-third in the same period. These are expected to be exported primarily to Great Britain and the Common Market countries.

Animal husbandry, too, characterizes Bulgarian farming. Sheep, a large number of cattle, pigs, and poultry indicate the rural wealth. The main grazing areas are in the central part of the Balkan Ranges, in the area between Sofiya and Plovdiv, and southeast of Burgas. The water buffalo is still common in the northern part of the country. Draught animals have been greatly reduced in number mainly due to the collectivization of the land; and the larger land holdings have brought about more intensive cultivation by the use of tractors.

Dense and largely virgin stands of coniferous forest are found in the Rila Planina of the Rhodope Massif. Deciduous and mixed forests are widely distributed. Scrub growth is found in the hill lands, and oak woods are common in the eastern part of the Balkan Ranges and south of Burgas. Overcutting during and following the war has been replaced by conservation and reforestation. Commercial fishing is poorly developed. Meager supplies of mackerel account for approximately two-thirds of the Black Sea fishing.

Bulgaria at the beginning of the collectivization drive in 1945 was already a land of small holdings. The estates of the largely Turkish land-owner class were already distributed among the peasants. Even in the prewar years the problem was one of insufficient land available and too small and fragmented land holdings (15 per cent of all land holdings were under 2.5 acres and 43 per cent under 7.5 acres). Collectivization met with little resistance. By 1950 more than half of the land had been collectivized and late in the 1950's the drive had been completed. The successful and voluntary peasant cooperatives of the prewar period had already prepared the peasants for the government takeover. In the mid-1960's, 920 cooperatives (collectives) averaged about 11,000 acres each, though in the steppe-like Dobruja a single collective may exceed 25,000 acres.

Agricultural yields have risen slowly due to the small increase of fertilizers (though their use ranks low in the European average), and a more intensive application of modern technologies, including increased irrigation. Bulgarian agricultural exports, especially of vegetables, fruits (both fresh and canned), tobacco, and wine are increasing and the new all-weather road via Yugoslavia to western Europe provides added opportunities.[40]

Mining and manufacturing. The newly built heavy industries are based only in part on fuels and minerals available in Bulgaria. Lignite is substantial but bituminous coal and anthracite occur only in small quantities. Lignite is found in the Pernik basin and in the central part of the Struma valley near Stanke Dimitrov and Brezani. One basin is close to the city of Burgas and is being used for the city's industries. Another deposit, a fairly large-sized one, of low-grade lignite worked in open-cast pits is near Dimitrovgrad. It supports important industrial concentrations. Finally, the fields in the lower Struma and Mesta valleys will supplant the Pernik field which nears exhaustion. In 1965, production from all fields reached 26.3 million tons. Discoveries of petroleum and natural gas have greatly aided Bulgaria's economy. Production of crude oil has jumped from 4,700 tons in 1954 to 285,000 tons in 1957, then declined to 160,000 in 1964 and increased to 229,000 by 1965. Production is expected to reach one million by 1970. Most of the wells have been drilled in northwest Bulgaria and near

[40] S. H. Couseus, "Changes in Bulgarian Agriculture," *Geography*, 52 (January, 1967): 12–22; also George W. Hoffman, "Transformation of Rural Settlement in Bulgaria," *Geographical Review*, 54 (1964): 45–64.

Varna. Recent discoveries were at Koshava and Vidin. Lignite contributes heavily to the production of the thermal power which in turn contributes more than three-fourths of the electric power consumed. Numerous small hydro-generating plants have been constructed on the rivers which flow from the Rhodope Massif and the Stara Planina. The largest stations are those on the Arda and Batak rivers, and on the upper Iskar, southeast of Sofiya. An atomic power station with an installed capacity of 800 mw is now under construction. It is based on Soviet designs. By 1970 the share of oil and gas in Bulgaria's energy consumption is expected to amount to 43 per cent, compared with 29 tons in 1966.

Iron ore reserves are adequate for present needs and are found in Kremikovci, northeast of Sofiya, and Krumovo in the lower Tundzha valley. The ores of Krumovo are of higher grade. The reserves of the first are considerably larger. Other ore deposits are of small size or of low quality and include lead-zinc ores, copper, and manganese, some of which are exported. The lead-zinc ore deposits are both in the western part of the Stara Planina and in the Eastern Rhodope Massif. Rudozem, Madan, and Istrem are new mining towns with floating plants. Copper mines are in the Burgas region and the western Stara Planina. The mines at Medet in the Sredna Gora are the largest now exploited. Manganese is exploited near Varna. Industrialization under the various long-term plans generally has been achieved, while consumer goods production until recently had been neglected. The main objectives of these plans were increases in the production of the electrical equipment, mining, and non-ferrous and ferrous metallurgical, chemical, building, and food-processing industries. The production increases brought about were largely exported to the Soviet Union and to the other bloc countries.

Earlier in this section, mention was made of the administrative divisions into 28 *okruzi* (see p. 496). These are expected to take the place of regional planning units and each of these *okruzi* has a significant industrial focus from which it gets its name. Sometimes Bulgaria is only divided into six regions for planning purposes, each with an economic specialization. The northern three regions and the southeastern region specialize in agriculture; the northwestern and northeastern regions, with the exception of Varna and Ruse, emphasize mostly industries. The north-central region has light industries and agriculture and the southwestern and south-central regions are the heaviest industrialized regions of Bulgaria, the first with over one-third of Bulgaria's total industrial production, the second with over one-fourth. Other important industrial concentrations coincide largely with the key cities: Sofiya, Plovdiv, Dimitrovgrad, and Varna. Most of them have a multitude of industries, though Plovdiv concentrates on food-processing, textiles, and non-ferrous metallurgical industries. Dimitrovgrad, a new city, specializes in chemicals, cement, and some light industries, and Varna in refineries, shipbuilding, and textiles. Included in this region is the chemical complex on nearby Reka Devnja. There are numerous other towns with few industries often serving as focus for a larger surrounding area.

Before the war there were no integrated iron and steel works in Bulgaria. The first such plant was started at Pernik in 1949 and later expanded to include 5 open-hearth furnaces, a rolling mill, and 2 blast furnaces. Both coal and iron ore are found close by as described earlier. The second integrated plant was built at great cost at Kremikovtsi, close to Sofiya and uses locally available iron ore (30 per cent). Total production of pig-iron and steel reached close to 1.6 million tons in 1966.

Most of the engineering industries have been built since 1950, and they will account for 30 per cent of the total industrial growth by 1970 and constitute 40 per cent of the total exports. Much agricultural machinery is being produced and some of the smaller items such as lathes, drilling and boring equipment, machine tools, and hoisting equipment are already being exported. Sofiya, Varna, Pernik, Plovdiv, and Burgas are the centers for this production.

Many industrial projects have been completed during the last few years, adding to the production capacity of Bulgaria. These include a chemical combine, at Dimitrovgrad, which produces nitrogenous fertilizer based on low-grade lignite. A new fertilizer plant recently was completed at Vraca, which will supply northwest Bulgaria, and synthetic fiber is manufactured at Vidin, Svistov, and Jambol. Refineries have been built at Burgas and Varna in connection with the discoveries of petroleum and natural gas, and others are planned. Inorganic acids and salts, organic compounds, explosives, dyes, soap, drugs, and cellulose are now being produced in small quantities. Soda ash and caustic soda are produced at Devnia, west of Varna, from local salts and brine. Carbide and sulfuric acid (a by-product of copper and lead-zinc smelters and from local pyrites) are produced at Dimitrovgrad. With the financial and technical aid from the Soviet Union, additional expansion of the chemical industry is under way. Various textile plants in a number of old manufacturing towns have been modernized and enlarged, and sugar refineries, flour mills, food-processing plants, and tobacco factories are widely scattered. The food and tobacco industries depend exclusively on domestic raw materials. To satisfy the heavy demand to own an automobile, Fiat has set up an assembly line in Torech and Renault is building one in Kazanluk to be completed by 1969 with an annual production of 10,000 cars. Generally speaking, Bulgaria's important larger industries are located in the Maritsa Basin, between Burgas and Sofiya, while craft and manufacturing towns are widely distributed in the Danubian Plateau, the Stara Planina, and the Thracian Plain.

Communications. The Maritsa Basin has the densest transportation network in Bulgaria. The important main thoroughfare since earliest times went from Yugoslavia through the Nišava valley and the Dragoman Pass to the Sofiya Basin and proceeded via the Ikhtiman Basin and the Momin Gorge to the Maritsa Basin through Plovdiv to Svilengrad on the Turkish border. This route has a number of important junction towns with connections both to the north and south. Highways follow the major railroads, but only about one-tenth are all-weather roads. A large improvement program is under way. The major rail pattern is west-east and a few north-south, with some branch lines (Fig. 8–2). The program of the last few years has been to complete and connect individual lines. Most of the lines are of standard gauge, but only the line from Sofiya to Plovdiv is double-tracked, as well as electrified. About five per cent of the rail net is still narrow gauge. While construction of rail lines has been rapid, improvements in the rolling stock have been slow. Most of the needed freight cars and locomotives must be imported. Both freight shipments and the number of passengers carried have greatly increased since the war. Sofiya, Plovdiv, and Stara Zagora are the most important railroad loading stations. The Danube is the only navigable waterway, but its main use to Bulgaria is for the distribution of goods between its eight river ports from Vidin to Silistra. Ruse is the most important port in terms of volume of goods handled. Domestic airlines do not play an important role and Sofiya has the only international airport of the country. Bulgaria's two ocean ports, Varna and Burgas, handle an increased volume of goods, both for transit traffic and Bulgaria's domestic needs.

Foreign trade. Before the war only 12 per cent of Bulgaria's trade was with the countries of Eastern Europe, while 88 per cent was with the rest of the world, and trade with the Soviet Union was non-existent. In the mid-1960's the Soviet Union was Bulgaria's most important trading partner (49 per cent) while the other socialist countries participated with 19 per cent. East

Germany, Czechoslovakia, and Poland are Bulgaria's main trading partners after the Soviet Union, and among the important non-Communist countries are West Germany, France, and Italy. Foreign trade is increasing both in terms of volume and the diversity of items traded. Agricultural products still hold first place (nearly 50 per cent by value) in exports, but emphasis is on higher-quality products, such as fruit, tomatoes, wine, livestock, and tobacco (the most important items). Refined minerals exported include lead, zinc, and copper. Machinery and mechanical equipment now account for one-fourth of all exports. Other goods include certain consumer goods of industrial origin. Imports of machinery and mechanical equipment account for 32 per cent of all imports by value, followed by essential raw materials, such as petroleum and coking coal, minerals and crude metals, foodstuffs, and raw cotton. The relatively new tourist industry (centered on the Black Sea coast) is taking an increasingly important place in Bulgarian foreign currency earnings.

Major exports today are fresh and canned fruits and vegetables, tobacco, and non-ferrous metals. A special effort has been made to export more fruits and vegetables, textile goods, and wood materials. Before the war, tobacco, vegetables, and fruit were nearly the only export items of importance. Imports include tractors and agricultural machinery, power and electrical equipment, petroleum and petroleum products, ferrous metals, and raw and semi-processed textiles. The total value of exports and imports is relatively small.

ALBANIA

Population

Albania is the smallest and least developed country in Eastern Europe. It is strategically located along the Adriatic shore, facing Italy at the entrance to the sea. Its population numbered about 2 million in mid-1968, occupying an area of 11,101 square

miles, roughly the size of Maryland, with a density of 180 per square mile. Administratively Albania is divided into 27 districts (*rethi*), and these are subdivided into localities (*lokaliteti*) and numerous villages (*shati*). The capital is Tiranë, with a population of over 161,000, and is the most industrialized city of Albania. Other large towns are Shkodër (48,140), Dürres (49,770), Korcë (46,600), and Vlorë (48,360). More than 66 per cent of the population is classified as rural, but densities are very uneven. About two-thirds of the people live in the coastal lowlands and the valleys leading from the mountains to the lowlands. This area contains three-fourths of all Albanian towns over 5,000 inhabitants, including all the important market and commercial settlements such as Tiranë, Shkodër, Elbasan, Berta, Dürres, and Korcë. Most of these towns have growing industrial activities.

The mountainous topography of most of Albania has often restricted the influence of invaders to coastal regions, giving the people a natural refuge from outside domination. The many small natural regions, at the same time, have isolated the people from each other and have retarded the growth of their national unity. Independence was proclaimed only in 1912, and it was one of the Balkan areas longest under foreign control. Because of World War I, which in part was fought on its territory, independence was not implemented until 1920. However, the freedom of Albania was short-lived, wedged as the country was between rival powers. Italy occupied Albania in April, 1939, and used it as a base for her attack on Greece. Under pressure from a new and stronger Yugoslavia at the end of World War II, Albania's leaders welcomed Stalin's break with Tito, but when the Soviet Union, in the latter part of the 1950's, again gave indication of reconciliation with Yugoslavia, the worried Albanian leaders, fearing neighboring Yugoslavia's influence, looked for an ally, albeit some distance away, but which at the same time provided security against occupation.

Again, Communist China suited that purpose.

The people of Albania are divided by the Shkumbi River into two major groups, the Gegs in the north and the Tosks in the south. These two groups comprise close to 98 per cent of the population.[41] In addition, scattered Vlach settlements occupy the highland pastures and Greeks (approximately 30,000) are found along the southern boundary. Some Gypsies, Bulgars, and Turks live in the rural areas. About 70 per cent of the people are Moslems, as a result of the long Turkish rule; 20 per cent are members of the Albanian Orthodox Church; and 10 per cent are Roman Catholics. Over 1.2 million Albanians live outside their country. The largest number live in Yugoslavia, where they are organized in an autonomous province within the Serbian Republic. About 50,000 Albanians live in the United States, and between 150,000 and 250,000 live in southern Sicily and Italy, to which their ancestors fled from the Turks in the fifteenth and sixteenth centuries. Smaller numbers live in Greece and Turkey. The Albanian language is classified as one of the Thraco-Illyrian sub-families of the Indo-European languages, and has certain similarities to Romanian (Vlach).

Constant wars against foreign invaders and tribal feuds have had their effect on the population structure. Albania has the highest birth and death rate of any Eastern European country. The natural increase is estimated at 22 people per thousand inhabitants. The working population (ages 15 to 65) comprises two-thirds of the people.

The illiteracy rate is among the highest in Europe, but a concerted effort has been made to reduce it. A law promulgated in 1946 made learning to write obligatory for all persons from 12 to 40 years of age. At the same time, it created a preschool system

[41] There are cultural differences between these two peoples, e.g., the traditional family system is still strongly developed among the Gegs. They are also considered the better fighters, while the Tosks are more industrious. Two-thirds of the Albanians are Gegs and most of the Albanians living in Yugoslavia are also Gegs.

for the whole country. Teacher's training schools, adult-education centers, and special professional schools have been organized since 1950. A university was organized in the 1950's.

Present Economic Life

Following World War II, Albania patterned its economic organization after those of the Communist countries, especially (in the first few years) after that of Yugoslavia. Planning received first priority. Between 1951 and 1955 (first five-year plan), 43 per cent of the total state budget was spent for industrialization. During this period the ratio between industrial and agricultural production was changed from 27.5 and 72.5 per cent to 43.5 and 56.5 per cent. The same trend continued during the following five-year plans, with the aim of changing Albania from a backward agrarian country to an agrarian-industrial country. The importance of manufacturing, for example, can be seen by the increase during the last few years in industrial employment, including mining, from 22,000 in 1950 to 85,000 in 1965.

It is estimated now that still about 18 per cent of the working population is engaged in agriculture and cattle raising, 33 per cent in mining and industry, 13 per cent in construction and the rest in various administrative services.

Agriculture and forestry. Of the total area, 43 per cent is agricultural, 43.5 per cent is forest, and 13.5 per cent is unproductive marsh, rocks, scrub woodland, or eroded mountain slopes. Only 41 per cent of the total agricultural land is arable—tilled or in orchards and vineyards (Fig. 8–12). Much effort has been put into reclamation measures and proper soil conservation, including re-afforestation. Between 1939 and 1965 the area under cultivation increased by more than two-thirds. The proportion of cultivated land under irrigation increased from 10 per cent to 42 per cent. The introduction of modern technology, especially mechanization of arable farming and the use of fertilizers, has increased greatly, especially since the collectivization of all agricultural land was completed in the 1960's.

Maize and wheat are the main crops. The wheat acreage, to some extent, is restricted by the excessive moisture of the soil in winter at low elevation. Rye and potatoes are cultivated in various mountain valleys. Sugar beets, especially in the Korcë basin, cane sugar, and various vegetables are grown for local use. Rice is cultivated around Tiranë, Vlonë, Berat, and Elbasan; and cotton acreage has increased. Fruit growing at Vlonë and Elbasan now receives greater attention. Walnuts, olives, and tobacco are exported in small quantities. As far as evaluating over-all increases in agricultural production and their effect on the standard of living of the people—considering the rapid increase of the population—it is extremely difficult to make a judgment. Production figures published show general increases, e.g., 1963 production of bread-grains (1963 was an exceptionally good harvest) shows a 40 per cent increase since 1950. Increased production was especially strong in the industrial crops: cotton, sugar beets, tobacco, sunflowers, flax, and hemp and some of these are being exported.

Animal husbandry is important and is the traditional occupation of the population but quality is still poor. Cattle are valued as both food and draught animals. The most important animals are the sheep and goats, raised for their wool, cheese, and milk. Pigs, because of the religious belief of a high percentage of Moslems, are limited to the Christian communities. Horses have been replaced by mules and donkeys. Poultry raising, especially of turkeys, is widely distributed.

Forests for many years have been "mined," not only by the different occupying powers but by the people themselves. Only recently have conservation measures been undertaken. Woodlands, richest in the northern part of the country, consist of different varieties of oak, with beech and coniferous species also represented. Walnut and chestnut trees are of special value. *Maquis* is widespread in the drier lowlands and hill lands. On the whole, second-growth forests of immature trees are widespread, especially in the southern part of the country. The effects of drought, erosion, and forest mining as well as of tree browsing by sheep and goats have almost completely destroyed the vegetation cover in the neighborhood of settlements.

The drive to collectivize was started as early as 1947 and peasants put up strong resistance. Confiscation of farm tools, land, and herds of over 50 heads of sheep or goats, together with high delivery quotas and low prices, did not succeed in forcing the peasants into collectives. The drive slackened between 1951 and 1957, but the pace increased again and by 1961 had been completed with 93 per cent of the cropland in the socialist sector.

Mining and manufacturing. Until the Second World War, industries were practically non-existent in Albania. Since 1947, economic planning has stressed industrialization, in part based on little-developed local metallic and non-metallic minerals (Fig. 8–11), some of which were exploited by the ancient Greeks and the Roman Empire. In the Albanian economy, mining employs the largest share of the industrial labor force and mining industries form a vital part of the country's industries. Lignite mining began after the First World War, but did not increase until the early 1950's. It now averages around 300,000 tons annually. It is used mostly for power generation. Bituminous coal is lacking in Albania. Petroleum, one of Albania's greatest economic assets, has been exploited since 1918. The petroleum-bearing region is in the southwest, the most important fields being located between Elbasan and Vlonë, between the Drin and Mat valleys. Production increased from 191,500 metric tons in 1952 to 990,000 metric tons in 1965, or 65 per cent between 1960 and 1965 according to official reports. Albanian crude oils have a great density and are valued for their great average weight. A number of refineries have been built and pipelines, some built by the Italians, bring the petroleum to Krionere, on the Vlonë Bay, or to Cerrik, near Elbasan. The Cerrik refinery, completed in 1955, can process 150,000 metric tons of crude oil annually. Natural gas from the oil field is now being exploited by the different industries and power stations of the country. Much exploration is going on.

Another important mineral is high-quality lignite, some of which resembles asphaltite. The main mines are between Tiranë, Elbasan, and Lushnje in the Krrabe Mountains, in the Vijosë River Valley, and in the Pogradec-Korcë area. Also important are the bitumen and asphalt deposits between the Kudhesi Mountains and the Vijosë River. Asphalt occurs in a semi-liquid state in the limestone. The output of both asphalt and bitumen has increased considerably since 1945, and the bitumen-processing plant at Vlonë provides a number of important by-products for paving, waterproofing, and the manufacture of insulators and roofing shingles. Of the principal metallic minerals, chromium was mined at Kukës, in the middle Drin valley, in the mountains southwest of Lake Ohrid, in the Murdita massif, south of the Drin. The production is largely exported. Production rose from about 36,000 tons under Italian management to 830,000 tons in 1965. Copper is mined in northern Albania, between the Drin and Mat valleys, but the ore content is reported to be very low. Production increased from 18,000 tons at the end of the war to 144,673 tons in 1964. An electric wire and cable factory has now been built at Shkodër using the copper. Copper products are an important source of foreign trade income. Iron ore averaging 25 per cent iron is found in widely scattered areas, but because of the high costs of transportation and the low grade of the ore, no real progress has been made in their utilization, though there are plans to use the ores found near Pogradec (southern part of Lake Ohrid), in a proposed ferrous metallurgical plant to be built near Elbasan. Magnetite ores are found in northern Albania. Minor deposits of pyrites, arsenic, mercury, lead, zinc, nickel, magnesite, and bauxite occur, but their commercial exploitation depends very much on an improved road network. Large deposits of clay in the Shkodër district and other scattered areas have always been important to the Albanian pottery industry.

Few of Albania's industries compare in size and output with those developed in other Communist countries. Considering the little progress made before 1945 and the absence of sufficient capital for investments, the increase in industrial production has been rather remarkable. Factories were built during the 1950's with the assistance of the Soviet Union, and this process is now continued with aid from Communist China. The new industries are all closely tied to existing raw materials and are generally of small-scale. They include manufacturing of cement, paper, glass, textiles, footwear, tobacco-curing, and food-processing. At Tiranë and Durrës, trucks and other machinery are assembled and repaired, and a small shipyard is located at Durrës. The capacity of the two smelters for chromite and copper has been expanded during the last few years, and production of basic chemicals has recently started, caustic soda at Vlonë and sulfuric acid and superphosphates at the Tiranë-Durrës area, a potential industrial region. The production of fertilizer now receives top priority. Future plans include a tractor factory.

Communications. Little effort has been made to build Albania's transportation network because of the large investment needed. It is obvious that the absence of a modern transport and communication network has retarded the growth of the economy, especially the opening up of the known mineral resources in the mountainous parts of the country. The standard-gauge lines built since the war brought the total railroad network to 96 miles in 1964. All connect newly developed mines with the larger cities or ports. Roads have received more attention than rails during the last few years. However, only those roads used for heavy traffic are asphalted and several important market centers of the interior are still without asphalted roads. Despite its shortcomings the road network is more important than the railroads in the transport of freight and passenger movements. Roads carry an estimate of 91 per cent of the volume of both. The Drin and Bojanë rivers are navigable, but only for a very short distance. Albania has three principal seaports, Durrës, Vlonë, and Sarandë, which form the main links with the outside world. They all possess warehouses and petroleum-storage tanks. Vlonë has a good natural harbor with a bay 9 miles long, protected by the strategically important island of Sazan (Saseno), controlling the Straits of Otranto at the narrowest part of the Adriatic between Italy and Albania. Air traffic is small and carries mainly passengers to Rome and Belgrade.

Foreign trade. Prewar trade was largely with Italy and Yugoslavia. Between 1945 and the late 1950's the Soviet Union and the East European countries (with the exception of Yugoslavia) were the main trading partners. Since that time Communist China has replaced the Soviet Union and is also assisting Albania's chronic foreign trade deficit with credits and other aid. Fifty-five per cent of all foreign trade in 1965 was with Communist China, while trade with the Soviet Union has practically ceased. The East European countries, especially Czechoslovakia, account for one-third of all foreign trade. Altogether 90 per cent of Albania's trade during the 1960's has been with the Socialist countries. Italy is the main trading partner of the non-Communist world.

Major exports consist of minerals (copper, chrome, bitumen), petroleum and petroleum products, and agricultural products, as well as some wool, leather, and cigarettes. Imports primarily consist of industrial plant equipment and machinery, industrial raw materials (e.g., iron ore, rubber, and chemicals) and certain foodstuffs, especially wheat and sugar. Albania is still a member of Comecon, but has not actively participated during the last few years.

YUGOSLAVIA

Population

The Federal People's Republic of Yugoslavia, with a 1968 population of 20.2 million, an area of 98,766 square miles (roughly equal in size to Wyoming), and a population density of 205 per square mile, is eighth in population in Europe and second among the countries of Eastern Europe. It occupies a transitional position between the Alps of Austria and the mountains of the Southeast European Highlands, between the Adriatic Sea and the Carpathian Basin. This location played a most important role throughout history and left distinct marks on the political, social, and economic development of the various regions of the country.[42] Yugoslavia has undergone many political and economic changes since its organization in 1918–19. None had more far-reaching results than those brought about by World War II. After being occupied and divided among its neighbors during the war, a new Yugoslavia was organized as a multinational Communist state. Territorial gains were small, but important: the former Italian cities of Zara (Zadar), on the Dalmatian littoral, and Fiume (Rijeka), together with Istria. But the city of Trieste remained within Italy by the agreement of 1954.

Administratively, Yugoslavia is a federation of six Socialist Republics: Serbia, Croatia, Slovenia, Bosnia and Herzegovina, Macedonia, and Montenegro. The Republic of Serbia includes Serbia proper, the Autonomous Province of Vojvodina, and the Socialist Autonomous Province of Kosovo.

Serbia is the largest republic, both in area and population (41 per cent of Yugoslavia's total population), followed by Croatia

[42] Some material contained in this section has been taken, by permission, from George W. Hoffman, "Yugoslavia: Changing Character of Rural Life and Rural Economy," *The American Slavic and East European Review* 17 (December, 1959): 555–78. See also George W. Hoffman, "Yugoslavia in Transition: Industrial Expansion and Resource Bases," *Economic Geography* 32 (October, 1956): 295–315.

(22 per cent) and Bosnia and Herzegovina (17.6 per cent). Each republic and autonomous province is divided into communes (*opstine*). These communes are peculiar to Yugoslavia, each consisting of a town and its surrounding area. The capital of Yugoslavia is Belgrade with approximately 700,-000 inhabitants in 1967; it is also the capital of the Republic of Serbia (Fig. 8–25). Zagreb is the capital of Croatia and is the second-largest city, with a population estimated at 503,000 in 1967. Sarajevo, Ljubljana, Rijeka, Novi Sad, Split, and Skopje are cities of over 100,000. As is the case in all underdeveloped countries, the urban increase has been rapid. It is now estimated to be close to 40 per cent of the total population. The largest concentration of settlements is found in the plains of the Sava, Drava, and Morava rivers and the autonomous province of Vojvodina. The Banat, Bǎcka, and Zagorje (near Zagreb) are among the densest urban regions of Eastern Europe. The interior mountainous regions of the Dinarics and most parts of Macedonia are among the least densely settled, but within each political unit there exists large differences which reflect also on degree of economic development.

The present population structure shows the effects not only of three wars within one generation but also of the large population migration during and following World War II. Altogether, Yugoslavia lost between 2 million and 2.6 million people between 1939 and 1959.[43] The impact of World War II is

[43] These losses are explained as follows: 1.7 million people died as a consequence of warlike actions; 100,000 of a total of 700,000 Yugoslav prisoners or workers in German war industries chose to remain abroad; and at least another 100,000 Yugoslavs fled abroad after hostilities ended (many of these emigrated to the United States). The ethnic German population was reduced by 90 per cent, roughly 445,000 (many of whom fled with the retreating German Army). Most of the Italians (150,000) living in Istria, which was transferred to Yugoslavia after the war, emigrated to Italy; most of the surviving Jews, roughly 8,000, emigrated to Israel; and 104,000 Turkish inhabitants, mostly from Macedonia, returned to Turkey between 1950 and 1959, a movement still continuing.

Fig. 8–25. Belgrade on the confluence of the Sava and Danube rivers. View from Kalmegdan fortress toward northwest with New Belgrade and Zemun in the background and the island of Veliko Ratno Ostrvo opposite the confluence of the two rivers. Belgrade, the Celtic Singidunum always played an important role as fortress in one of Europe's strategic areas, due to its geographic location. The fortress and the slowly growing town nearby was disputed between many people throughout history. (G. W. Hoffman.)

clearly visible in the smaller number of people, especially males between the ages of 25 and 39. The present structure indicates a rather young population, with more than three-fifths (63.5 per cent) in the economically important ages between 15 and 64 years. The population in the less developed regions increases at a much faster rate than in other parts of Yugoslavia—it comprised 30.5 per cent of the total Yugoslav population in 1940 and 33 per cent in 1961 and should increase to 36 per cent in 1971. According to a recent Yugoslav study, these higher natality and natural increase differentials resulted from the fact that one-third of the population in the less developed regions provided over one-half of the natural increases of Yugoslav population.

About 89 per cent of the people of Yugoslavia belong to the various groups of the South Slavs (Fig. 8–6). These include Serbs, Croats, Slovenes, Macedonians, and Montenegrins. National minorities include Albanians (called Shiptars), Magyars, Turks, Slovaks, Gypsies, Germans (0.4 per cent as against 3.6 per cent in 1931), Romanians, Bulgars, Vlachs, Czechs, and Italians. The Vojvodina has the largest number of non-Slavic people, more than a third of its total population. Generally speaking, the individual Slavic peoples form a large majority of their respective political units, e.g., in the Republic of Serbia Serbians account for three-fourths of the total population, but in the two autonomous provinces the Vojvodina and Kosmet, their percentage of the total population amounts to only 55 and 24 per cent, respectively. Bosnia and Herzegovina is a special case inasmuch as most of the original Slavic Serbs and Croats became Moslem and list themselves by religion and not by nationality. In the 1953 census, 87 per cent of Yugoslavia's population indicated adherence to one of the religions. Approximately 41 per cent were Orthodox, 32 per cent Roman Catholic, 12 per cent Moslem, and 1 per cent Protestant. The rest are listed as "others" and "undeclared." Religious differences are still of importance. There are close linguistic affinities between the various South Slavic languages. The present administrative boundaries follow generally ethnic divisions, but the intermixture of people does make this extremely difficult. In most places these boundaries follow historical precedent.

One of Yugoslavia's most pressing tasks is its drive for reduction of its still large illiteracy rate. While the Yugoslav average illiteracy rate for the ages of ten and above is 19.7 per cent, for example, in Bosnia and Herzegovina it is 32.5, in Kosmet 41 per cent, while in the advanced Republic of Slovenia it is only 2 per cent. The impact on the future economic development of the country is a serious one. The more than one-third of Yugoslavia's population having a generally lower educational level slackens the mean pace at which the educational level of all the people of the country would be raised. Most of Yugoslavia's illiterates live in the mountainous parts of the country, settlements which even mobile schools have difficulty in reaching. Another factor in the divergent cultural development is the long Turkish occupation of the southern and central parts of the country and the closer association of the Slovenian and Croatian areas with Western European cultural developments. Much effort has been made to increase educational opportunities and to raise the quality of instruction. Compulsory education has been extended from 4 to 8 years. New universities have been opened, so that now there is at least one in every republic except Montenegro (which has some departments).

The linguistic, cultural, and economic divisions posed a difficult problem for Yugoslavia when it was formed in December 1918. This is basically unchanged after 50 years of existence as a unified state. The rapprochement of the different South Slavic people is a slow process, fraught with the dangers of cultural, political, and economic nationalism. The organization of Yugoslavia as a federal state in 1945 under the leadership of Marshall Tito, was considered a necessity based on the disruptive experience of the inter-war years. It was hoped that socialism would offer the people of Yugoslavia a unifying bond which ultimately would replace the narrow nationalism. More than 20 years later the centrifugal forces of the state still exert their disruptive power, though their impact is now felt most of all in the economic field.

National Communism itself has been influenced by the ethnic forces at work. It is hoped by the government that large-scale decentralization of most government functions, centered thus far in Belgrade, will stress the issue of regional responsibilities in building the national traditions of a federal Yugoslav state.

Present Economic Life

The economic geography of Yugoslavia reflects the different historical-political developments and influences in the individual provinces. From earlier discussions it can be seen that basically the country can be divided into two large divisions: (1) the mountain core, with interspersed fertile valleys and forested hill lands, with isolated settlements, a great variety of mineral resources, and some localized industries, many of which were built after 1945; and (2) the peripheral lands, consisting of fertile plains, hill lands, and basins connected with isolated mountain blocks and interior valleys— a rich mixed-agricultural region with a large variety of industries which have greatly increased since the war. The critical over-population in the agricultural areas, indicated by the fact that there were 100 people to every 247 acres of agricultural area in 1953, one of the highest ratios in all of Europe, and the backwardness of agricultural production have been at the bottom of most difficulties during the last 40 years.

Broadening the basis of the economy by a greatly expanded program of industrialization was the cure prescribed by every government after 1919. Internal opposition and the huge task of building unifying economic and social conditions among the different

peoples slowed down progress before World War II. But, starting in 1946, industrialization became one of the basic principles of the new state. Increasing the amount of consumer goods and improvements in agriculture at first were given low priority and only in the last few years, a proper industrial base having been established, these two neglected branches of the economy have been given attention. The industries are supplied by an increased domestic raw-material output. Production has increased in the new heavy industries as well as in the consumer industries. Today in certain industries there exists an over-supply. Agricultural output (a record of 4.8 million tons of wheat in 1967) and the quality of yields responded well to increased investments and to more liberal governmental policies. Large-scale United States foreign aid ($1,986 million between 1946 and 1967 [44]), in addition to aid from France and the United Kingdom, contributed greatly to the success of these policies. Today the economic base of prewar Yugoslavia has completely changed. Industry now contributes 38 per cent of the national income, agriculture 27 per cent, and trade 13.6 per cent, as against 25, 50, and 3 per cent, respectively in 1938.

Fifty-three per cent of the economically active population depends upon agriculture for their principal income (49 per cent of the total population). The population depending on agriculture in 1946 was 76.5 per cent.

[44] *Special Report prepared for the House Foreign Affairs Committee on US Overseas Loans and Grants and Assistance from International Organizations July 1, 1945–June 30, 1966.* Total includes Yugoslav repayments of principal and payment of interest in connection with loans granted under the assistance programs. During 1966–67 total assistance increased by $11.8 million. No assistance was given to Yugoslavia in 1967–68. Generally, it can be said that roughly 61 per cent of the above figure was for agricultural commodities, 3 per cent for clothing, textiles and footwear (UNRRA) and 36 per cent for industrial and agricultural equipment and supplies and Technical Assistance. Of the total assistance in agricultural commodities, wheat deliveries are estimated to have represented more than half of the total, with cotton in the second place (15 per cent of the total).

This reduction indicates the tremendous changes in the rural life and economy since the war. Still considerable agrarian unemployment, estimated at 1.4 million people, is a fact and will remain so until the country has modernized its economy.

In spite of all the progress made, there exists one problem in Yugoslavia's economic development which makes it unique among the East European countries. Not only are there great differences in the level of economic development between the various republics and within the republics, but the multinational character of the country also greatly adds to the problems of finding a solution. The different cultural levels of the people are the result of many different cultural, economic, and political conditions coming from both West and East. The contrasts between the regions of present-day Yugoslavia are striking and every index reflects this dichotomy between north and south, between the developed and underdeveloped parts of the country. Questions are constantly being raised concerning how Yugoslavia should be developed and they point up the national-regional differences which are evident everywhere when determining economic policy. Even the best thought-out economic decisions cannot stand up to emotion. This, perhaps, is the main reason why the problem of underdeveloped areas cannot be treated exclusively with economic arguments. Advances in the position of the large underdeveloped areas are obvious and must be continued if a viable state is the ultimate goal of the multinational population (Fig. 8–26).

Agriculture, forestry, and fishing. Of the total land area, roughly 58 per cent is classified as agricultural land, 35 per cent as forests, and 7 per cent as unproductive. Of the agricultural land, 56 per cent is arable land and gardens (Fig. 8–12). The area of agricultural production is widely scattered with the main grain regions in the northern and northeastern sections, the watersheds of the Sava, Danube, and Morava rivers. There are great differences in the distribution of arable land in the country, e.g., 11 per cent in Montenegro, 87 per cent in the Vojvodina. The reverse is true of permanent pasture land, where percentages vary from 8 in the Vojvodina to 67 in Montenegro. Slovenia has the greatest percentage of meadows. The Vojvodina also shows the greatest percentage of and the most intensive use of arable land. The heavy concentration of arable land (21 per cent) in the relatively small area of the Vojvodina, which comprises 8.4 per cent of the total land area of the country, is one of the problems of agriculture. Climatic influences in this region also create great fluctuations in the production of maize (corn) and wheat, the most important grains for the country. The Vojvodina and its adjacent plains produce half the bread grains grown in the country, 80 per cent of the sugar beets, 80 per cent of the oils of vegetable origin, and 75 per cent of the vegetable fibers.

Market and consumer customs, as well as climatic conditions, influence the production of a large number of products. Besides maize and winter wheat, barley, rye, and rice production have some local importance. These, together, are cropped on roughly 67 per cent of all arable land, with maize grown on about one-third of the cropland, followed by a somewhat smaller area for wheat. Industrial crops likewise provide a variety of products, e.g., hemp, flax, cotton, sugar beets, tobacco, and hops. The Vojvodina and the Vardar Valley are the main regions for sugar beets and tobacco. Hemp production is among the highest in Europe. The area under cotton and flax has been greatly increased in the postwar years, but both products must also still be imported. The area and yield of tobacco have also greatly increased, and over two-thirds of the production is now exported. Among the oil-bearing fruits and seeds grown in Yugoslavia are sunflower seeds, olives, linseed, etc. The production of a greater variety of vegetables is encouraged, and, thanks to favorable climatic conditions, especially along the Adri-

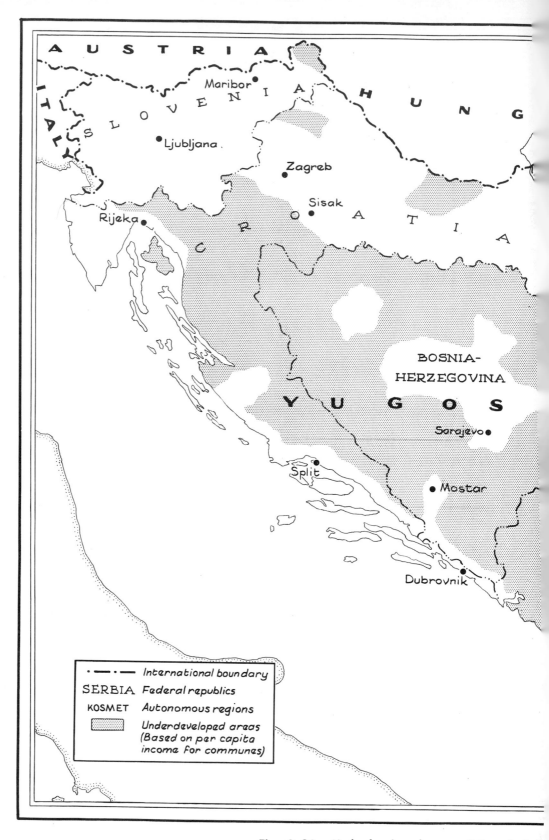

Fig. 8–26. Underdeveloped areas of Yugoslavia.

UNDERDEVELOPED AREAS OF YUGOSLAVIA

VOJVODINA

AUTON. REG.

Novi Sad

Belgrade

ROMANIA

HUNGARY

Niš

BULGARIA

MONTENEGRO

KOSMET AUTON. REG.

Titograd

Skopje

ALBANIA

MACEDONIA

GREECE

Based on per capita income for communes.

atic coast and in sections of Macedonia, many vegetables can be produced throughout the year. A small but important contribution is made by the fruit and vineyard production. A large variety of fruits is grown. Yugoslavia is best known for its plum orchards, which comprise 70 per cent of the total number of fruit trees. A portion of the plums is exported either fresh, dried, or processed; fresh prunes are used in making brandy, called *Sljivovica*. Other fruits include apples, olives, pears, cherries, apricots, and a large variety of grapes. Slovenia produces the most apples. On the whole, fruit growing is largely considered a secondary occupation for the peasant.

Following grains in importance is livestock breeding. The extensive pasture lands and meadows in Yugoslavia naturally encourage this branch of agriculture. But constantly recurrent droughts left their impact on livestock which fluctuated accordingly. Generally, the increase in the number of animals has been slight in part due to a slow increase in fodder crops. Sheep are dominant and found chiefly in the karstic Dinaric ranges and in Serbia and Macedonia. The quality of their wool clip is slowly improving. Cattle are widely distributed (except in the karst region), and pigs are concentrated in the northern lowlands and the oak and beech-wood of Serbia (Morava valley). Dairy farming has received much impetus and is of great importance in Slavonia, Bosnia, Serbia and the hills of northern Croatia and southern Slovenia. Transhumance is still practiced though it has declined in most parts of Yugoslavia.

Agricultural production is greatly fluctuating. The low priority given to agriculture for such a long time, serious droughts, various attempts to collectivize agriculture, and expropriation of all cultivable land of over 25 acres per person in 1953 resulted in stagnation of agricultural output. On the whole, production seems to have taken a turn for the better after 1959. The introduction of special wheat varieties, hybrid corn, greater mechanization, and more modern agrotech-

nical methods is slowly raising the rate of production. The government now is greatly aiding the private peasant, but reserves the right to take over all land which is not properly cultivated. Imports, especially of wheat and certain vegetable and animal oils, are still necessary.

Forests are of great importance for the national wealth. Large quantities of timber and firewood are supplied for domestic needs, and raw materials for the domestic production of cellulose, artificial fiber and paper, dry distillery products, etc., are of great importance. Most of the woods are coniferous forests (pine and juniper); the broadleaved trees are mainly beech and oak. Forest conservation and reforestation (51 per cent of the forests require constant artificial reforestation) are given much attention.

Fishing has some importance, especially among the rural population along the Dalmatian coast with its many deep channels and islands. Over 3,000 fishermen are engaged in this branch of the economy as a permanent occupation, while over 15,000 fish seasonally. Mackerel and sardines are the main catches. Most of the fishing is done by individuals, but cooperatives assist the fisherman in buying equipment and selling his catch. Several processing plants are located along the Adriatic coast.

Land ownership, too, has undergone important changes during the last 40 years. As a result of three land reforms, Yugoslavia has become a land of small family holdings (legal limit: 24–36 acres of agricultural land). Of the agricultural population, 96 per cent own their land and 94 per cent live in their own homes. Collectivization was discontinued in 1953 and the Peasant Work Cooperatives, the main organs for collective farming, were permitted to disband. In the mid-1960's about 12 per cent of the agricultural land was part of the socialized sector. But it must be noted that a considerable part of the agricultural land, which is in the socialist sector, is also the most suitable for large-scale agricultural operations on an intensive basis. General Agricultural Cooperatives now play an increasingly important role; they own tractors, supply the peasants with technical assistance, fertilizers, seeds, etc., and generally act as credit and market organizations. They are the main source of help for the peasant who wishes to raise his income by increased production on small landholdings.

Mining. Industrialization in Yugoslavia has always had available an important base: raw materials and a large labor supply; the real problem has always been their exploitation. The prewar development was characterized by large foreign capital investments in Yugoslavia's mineral resources and by the building of certain selected industries which concentrated on primary production of domestic products. The creation of employment opportunities by locating new industries or by expanding existing ones was not of primary interest to foreign investors.

With the exception of bituminous coal, Yugoslavia ranks high in reserves of a great variety of minerals (Fig. 8–11). Close to 82 per cent of the coal reserves are lignite and 17.8 per cent brown coal (low-grade fuels with a calorific value only a little higher than peat), while only 0.2 per cent is bituminous coal. The major deposits of the latter are in Raša (Istria) and Ibar (Serbia), but must be processed before they can be used for coking (coke plants are at Lukavac and Zenica). Total production of bituminous coal amounted to 1 million tons in 1966 and has shown a drop in recent years. One and two tenths million tons of coke was produced in the same year. Lignite deposits are numerous, largest are located in central Bosnia and Herzegovina. Others of importance are in northern Croatia and Slovenia. The expansion of production during the last years has been very rapid. Brown coal production has risen from 4.3 million in 1939 to 10 million tons in 1966. That of lignite from 13 million to 18 million tons. New methods to beneficiate the higher quality Tertiary coals for coke production have been per-

fected and those of the Zenica-Sarajevo basin are now important for metallurgical fuel for the iron-smelting works of Bosnia. The production of briquettes from lignite and brown coal also is increasing, and in addition, the modern practice of building steam-powered generators near lignite fields and using the energy produced by means of high-tension cables is becoming more widespread. The shortage of carboniferous coal is a considerable handicap in the development of a steel industry, and imports are essential. Yugoslavia in 1966 imported 1.8 million tons of coal and 171,000 tons of coke.

Since the Second World War, the production of petroleum and natural gas has considerably increased and estimates of reserves are constantly being revised upward. The production now covers roughly half of the needs of Yugoslavia. It is concentrated in the middle Sava Valley of Croatia, between Kutina, Bjelovar, and Durdevać in the Drava Basin, in smaller fields in the Vojvodina, and in northeastern Slovenia. Production of natural gas has also been greatly expanded and pipelines have started to send gas to industries and urban consumers. Crude petroleum production amounted to 2.2 million tons in 1966 with 1.55 million tons in Croatia. Domestic production is refined at Sisak, Bosanki Brod and Pancevo; imported petroleum near Rijeka. Capacity is about 8.8 million tons a year but is not fully used. Future prospecting will be concentrated along the Adriatic coast which is believed to rank high as to gas and oil prospects.

Mining has always played an important role in Yugoslavia. Ores are well distributed in the Dinaric mountain region, and increased discoveries have added to the reserves. Iron-ore deposits are more numerous than in any other country in Eastern Europe, but most of them are small. The center of iron-ore mining is near Ljubija (medium grade limonites) and Vareš (haematic) in Bosnia, from which ores are shipped directly to the nearby blast furnaces of Sisak and Ilijaš near Sarajevo. New mines have been opened west of Prilep, in Macedonia. Together with nearby coal fields, they form the basis for the new iron and steel works in Skopje, Macedonia.

Exploitation of non-ferrous metals has greatly expanded in the postwar years, most important of which are copper, lead, and zinc. The largest deposits of copper ores are in northeastern Serbia, in Bor and Majdanpek. They are located south of the Iron Gate. The Majdanpek mines were already worked in classical and medieval times. Those of Bor have the largest reserves of ore in Europe, an open-cast pit, and the low-grade ore is reduced to blister copper at the mine, and refined electrolytically before it is shipped to the factories. Four-fifths of Yugoslavia's lead production are at Trepča near Mitrovica (it also produces zinc ore) and much of it is exported, especially to the United States. Deposits are also at eastern Bosnia, southern Serbia, eastern Macedonia and Mežica in the upper Drava valley (Slovenia). Production now covers all domestic needs and Yugoslavia ranks first in the production for all of Europe. The lead-zinc ores contain valuable by-products, e.g., silver, bismuth, antimony, manganese, and sulfur. Zinc production, too, is important. It accounted for 12 per cent of the European and 2 per cent of the world's production in the mid-1960's. Extensive reserves of mercury are mined at Idrija, western Slovenia and are smelted nearby. Yugoslavia's bauxite is of excellent quality, and reserves are estimated at 5.5 per cent of the total world reserves. The largest deposits occur along the Adriatic coast.

Other important ores, though of small production, include chromium (second in Europe), manganese, the rare ore molybdenum, and antimony. Magnesite mining increased greatly (75 per cent in Serbia). Yugoslavia and Austria are the two largest producers in Europe. Graphite is mined principally in Slavonia (Croatia), gypsum in western Macedonia, and important deposits of rock salt are found near Tuzla, in Bosnia. There are also sizeable deposits of fine chalky marl near Split and Istria, very important for the manufacture of cement. Raw materials necessary for construction are widely distributed in the country with clay for brick-making, in the Pannonian Plain, and marble quarried in Istria, on the island of Brac, and in Venoac, Serbia.

Production of sufficient power plays a key role in Yugoslavia's plans for industrialization. Sufficient water power resources are available to place Yugoslavia among those countries with the largest unused reserves; [45] only 7 per cent of the hydroelectric potential, however, has been tapped, an amount which will greatly increase with the completion of the earlier mentioned joint Yugoslav-Romanian Iron Gate project for harnessing the waters of the Danube River.[46] Yugoslavia's share of this project will be over 5 billion kwh annually (see also p. 493). Precipitation is advantageously distributed in Yugoslavia. In the Alps and the Dinaric Mountains the maximum rainfall occurs in the spring and fall, as well as the beginning of winter. Southern Serbia and Macedonia have dry summers, but snow in the higher mountains supplies the rivers with abundant water during the early part of the dry season. Karst mountains dropping sharply toward the Adriatic Sea provide a great potential and several hydroelectric plants utilize this drop. Thermal power-stations mainly located near lignite and brown-coal fields have greatly increased Yugoslavia's electric power capacity, but shortages still plague from time to time both domestic and industrial production. Total 1966 production was 17.1 million kwh (58 per cent from hydro power).

Manufacturing. Before 1938, most industrial production was concentrated in and around the Ljubljana Basin, Maribor, Zagreb, and Belgrade, with a few smelters near important mines. Thirty years later, the base of industrial production has been greatly

[45] Milos Brelith, *Yugoslav Water Resources as a Power Reserve* (Belgrade: Yugoslavia, 1958).

[46] George W. Hoffman, "The Iron Gate Project on the Danube River," *Professional Geographer*, XVI (March, 1964): 45.

broadened. New industries are located in the older manufacturing centers and the more advantageously located regions as far as access is concerned, e.g., Slovenia, northern Croatia, the northern valleys of Bosnia, the Vojvodina and the cities of the Morava and Vardar valleys. Political considerations demanded that some plants be located in the underdeveloped, mostly southern Republics, where rural overpopulation had reached serious proportions. Strategic considerations demanded a greater dispersal of individual plants into the core of the country (this contributed heavily to the accelerated economic development of central Bosnia at the time of the Yugoslav-Soviet conflict in the early 1950's).

Important industrial regions and centers with diversified production, usually based on some important local raw materials or those available nearby, such as the iron and steel works, quickly expanded. Among the most important industrial regions are the following (Fig. 8–11, nos. 15–20).

1. The northwestern region including most of Slovenia with engineering, electric and mechanical equipment industries centered in the Ljubljana basin, Celje, Maribor, etc.

2. The concentration of industries in the Sava River valley, between Zagreb and Belgrade, including northern Bosnia. Industrial production located in this region has several advantages. A large number of key raw materials, e.g., coal, iron ore, timber, and oil, are nearby. The Sava is navigable from its confluence with the Danube at Belgrade to Sisak, and the railway network and road system have recently been modernized. Attention should be drawn to the fact that this is not a continuous concentration, but these industries are located in numerous towns, small and medium-sized, all through the Sava valley and its tributaries.

3. The northern part of the Adriatic littoral (Koper, Pula, Rijeka, and Bakar) where shipbuilding and engineering industries are concentrated.

4. The northeastern regions including Slavonia in northern Croatia with Varaždin and Osijek, important centers for agricultural machinery and food-processing and textiles, and the Vojvodina and the lower Morava valley focused on Belgrade, Yugoslavia's most industrialized city. Food and consumer industries, but also the iron and steel and chemical industries, are centered here.

5. The region of Serbia proper, extending from Titovo Užice to Niš and Leskovać, including also the industrial centers of Kragujevac, Valjevo, and Paraćin, has a varied and often highly concentrated industrial production, mostly of small-scale industries and many established in the nineteenth century or between the two wars. Engineering, food processing, and textiles are the main industries.

6. A relatively new and expanding industrial area in Macedonia, centered in the Skopje basin between Kumanovo-Tetovo and Titov Veles. Industries here, with the exception of the integrated iron and steel works in Skopje, and some newly developed metallurgical and chemical plants, concentrate largely on agricultural products and textiles. Prilep and Bitola in the south emphasize the production of local products, leather, textiles, and tobacco. Some industrial concentrations are also in the making in the Kosovo-Mitrovica-Priština area of eastern Kosmet consisting of small industries producing textiles, chemicals, and timber-based products. Also the Split-Sinj-Omis region of the central Adriatic Littoral and its hinterland is rapidly expanding and producing cement, textiles, and ships. Additional smaller centers should be added to these concentrations and they are numerous, but they mostly stand alone. The steel works in Nikšić are an example (Fig. 8–27).

The metallurgical industries are basic in the expanding industrial effort. They have greatly increased in numbers and in the variety of their products. Integrated iron and steel works are located in (1) Jesenice (upper Sava valley of Slovenia) which is the oldest integrated plant of present-day Yugoslavia, (2) Sisak (Croatia) at the confluence of the Sava with the Kupa rivers, (3) the

Fig. 8–27. Nikšić steel works in Montenegro. The steel works were developed in the early 1950's and are located in the Montenegrin karst some 140 to 200 miles from coal sources (Mostar) and Ilijaš and Zenica (pig iron). For economic reasons only a steel works was constructed thereby eliminating the long haulage of low-grade ore and coke. High-quality sheet steel is the main product of the works, but high costs still make federal government subsidy necessary. The location of the plant was determined by transport facilities, available labor from an area suffering from acute rural unemployment, the establishment of a basis for the growth of metal-working industries and the location in close proximity to large water-power supplies from stations on the Zeta River. (G. W. Hoffman.)

largest integrated center, at Zenica (northern Bosnia), producing close to 50 per cent of the total Yugoslav raw steel output and 60 per cent of the pig iron and coke. This is part of the Zenica-Ilijaš-Vares combine and related heavy industries in the valleys between Banja Luka-Zenica-Tuzla-Doboj of northern Bosnia, (4) Smederovo downstream on the Danube from Belgrade, and finally (5) the newest and still incomplete integrated works at Skopje in Macedonia. Other important iron and/or steel plants are at Store and Ravne near Maribor in Slovenia and at Nikšić (Montenegro).[47] The total goal of pig-iron and crude steel production for Yugoslavia by 1975 is 2.6 million and 3.2 million respectively as against 1.1 and 1.9

million in 1966. Experts generally assume that it is unlikely that this can be achieved, and recent technological changes make this probably unnecessary. Still the expansion is a remarkable one considering pig-iron and crude steel production in 1948 of 183,000 tons and 368,000 tons respectively.

Other production which has expanded or has been introduced during the last twenty years includes various engineering and electrical, chemical, textile, and food-processing industries. There is hardly any branch of industry which is not now producing or for which plans have not been made to start production in Yugoslavia. Both increased diversification and the purchase of licenses from foreign firms are part of this intensive drive to make Yugoslavia an industrial country. Self-sufficiency is not expected; rather, the intention is to integrate Yugoslavia's productive efforts with those of other advanced in-

[47] F. E. I. Ian Hamilton, "Location Factors in the Yugoslav Iron and Steel Industry," *Economic Geography*, 40 (January, 1964): 46–64.

dustrial countries, hoping in this way to raise the standard of production and increase the standard of living.

Communications. The basic problem of transportation in Yugoslavia reflects both economic and historical influences. Slovenia, large parts of Croatia, and the Vojvodina formed part of the Austro-Hungarian Monarchy and had excellent rail connections with each other as well as with the core, the Vienna and Budapest area. The rail network in these regions has been modernized and on the whole is sufficient to meet demands, even though the many single-track lines are a handicap.

Connections between the peripheral regions, the mountainous core, and the Adriatic littoral are inadequate and were little improved during the interwar years. In addition, the low transportation density, brought about in part by different rail gauges, is in itself a great handicap to the economic development of the country. Single-track lines made up 93 per cent of all railroads in 1967. Fundamentally, the problem in rail and road transportation is one of inter-connecting three physiographically and economically diverse regions: the northern lowlands, the mountainous core, and the Adriatic littoral. Important efforts during the last years, as to modernization, new construction, and changes from narrow to standard gauge, have been undertaken. The industrial region of northern Bosnia, between Banja Luka and Doboj and Sarajevo has now been linked both with the Serbian and Croatian railway system. Other work completed or under way includes the change from narrow to standard gauge of the Sarajevo-Adriatic (at Ploče) line and the building of the Bar-Belgrade railroad, a ten or more year venture. A section south of Belgrade and between Bar and Titograd has been completed.

From 1939 to 1966 total rail mileage increased from 6,520 miles to 7,195 miles. Freight carried increased in the same period by 50 million tons and passengers carried by 155 million passengers. Railroad rolling stock has increased more slowly than have the amount of freight and the number of passengers carried, but a few new crack trains, especially those for the international through traffic, are now in operation. A program of modernization, especially in the Vojvodina, has begun, and, when sufficient electric power becomes available, a number of key lines will be electrified.

The highway transportation network also was in a deplorable condition at the end of World War II. Voluntary youth brigades were used to provide modern roads for at least the main thoroughfares of the country. The superhighway from Belgrade to Zagreb was completed shortly after the war. A new superhighway between Ljubljana and Zagreb was completed in 1958, and the connection between Belgrade and the border of Greece and also Bulgaria, as well as the Adriatic Road from Rijeka to Kotor Bay has been completed. The Adriatic Road will eventually be extended to Skopje. Numerous secondary roads have been completed and the highway network has greatly improved in the twenty-five years since the Second World War. Automobile traffic has greatly increased and a network of gas stations is being completed. There also is an increase in goods being shipped by truck.

Yugoslavia has spent much effort on increasing its merchant marine since the war. The indented 460-mile-long Adriatic coastline has a number of good ports, but the mountainous hinterland has limited their effectiveness. Rijeka is the main port, but is already insufficient for the freight traffic. Nearby deep Bakar bay has been expanded to supplement Rijeka and is specializing in oil imports. A pipeline is now being laid from Bakar to Pancevo on the Danube. Split is Yugoslavia's second maritime port in terms of goods turnover. Pula, Koper in the north, and Sibenik, Ploče, Dubrovnik, Buda, and the new port of Bar in the south carry only a fraction of that of Rijeka. The merchant marine has been greatly modernized and expanded, but most of the building has been for foreign orders.

With the exception of traffic on the Danube, and to a lesser degree on the Tisza and the Sava, traffic on the waterways is of minor economic importance. The Sava is navigable to Sisak but this is now being expanded to Zagreb. The new Danube-Tisza-Danube Canal in the Vojvodina not only serves for the movement of freight but is also useful for irrigation purposes. The port of Belgrade with an annual freight turnover of over three million tons, 54 per cent Yugoslav and 46 per cent custom cargo, is being greatly expanded in close coordination with the work undertaken at the Iron Gate on the Danube River. Lastly, Yugoslavia's air network, JAT, has been greatly expanded.

Foreign trade. It is obvious from the foregoing discussions that Yugoslavia's whole foreign-trade structure has undergone basic changes from prewar times. Changes have been made not only with regard to the type of goods but also geographically. The break with the Soviet Union in 1948 caused Yugoslavia's trade to be reoriented. In prewar years Yugoslavia traded mainly with Austria, Italy, Czechoslovakia, and Germany. In the first postwar years trade was directed mainly toward the Soviet Union and other countries in Eastern Europe. In 1966 imports were divided with 31 per cent coming from the Soviet bloc (including 10 per cent from the Soviet Union), 39 per cent were from other European countries (26.1 from EEC), 13.5 per cent from the United States (there certainly will be some decline brought about by the cessation of PL480 agricultural products sales), and the rest from other overseas countries. Thirty-six and five tenths per cent of the exports went to the countries of the Soviet bloc (15.9 per cent to the Soviet Union), 42 per cent to other European countries (27.8 per cent to EEC), 6 per cent to the United States, and 15.5 per cent to other overseas countries. According to value, the United States has been the largest trader since 1950, but this was brought about largely by economic aid.[48]   Yugoslavia's

greatly increased exports went to a large number of countries, e.g., Italy, the Soviet Union, West Germany, the United States, the United Kingdom, and many newly opened markets, especially in the Asian and African areas. Before the war, Yugoslavia's main exports consisted of food products, minerals, and forest products. Today, this list has been greatly expanded. Among the important exports are: food (20 per cent—1966 figures), fuels, lubricants, and other raw materials (10 per cent), semi-manufactured and manufactured goods, such as furniture, footwear, and light industries (35 per cent), machinery and transport equipment (25 per cent), and chemical products (6 per cent). Imports are divided between food, mainly bread grains (15 per cent), raw materials, fuels, and lubricants (19 per cent), semi-manufactured and manufactured goods (27 per cent), transport equipment (29 per cent), and chemical products (10 per cent). The over-all volume of goods exchanged with foreign countries has risen constantly in the last eight years. Yugoslavia has made a special effort to reduce its large dependence on food imports, rice, cotton, and lard, and on chemical products, especially fertilizer. Special mention should also be made of the increased benefit to Yugoslavia's chronic balance of payment deficit of foreign tourists' spending, estimated at over $200 million in 1967. Finally, it should be mentioned that in September 1964, Yugoslavia became an associate of the Council for Mutual Economic Aid (Comecon), and was given observer status at the headquarters of EEC in Brussels. With over one-half of Yugoslavia's trade with the two big trading groups in Europe—Common Market and Comecon—and a chronic trade deficit, it is only natural that she is concerned about the influence and future development these organizations will have.

*   *   *

[48] Besides foreign aid, the United States exported to Yugoslavia powdered milk, wheat, raw cotton, soya oil, pit coal, etc. Yugoslavia exported to the United States fermented tobacco (22 per cent of the total exports to the United States), refined lead, hops, ferromanganese, etc.

The developments in Eastern Europe permit a number of important conclusions.

1. The instability of the area has been due to its location with regard to its powerful neighbors, first the empires of Austria, Prussia, Russia, and Turkey, and later Germany and the Soviet Union. When the four pre-World War I empires disappeared in 1917–19, the newly-created national states were too weak to uphold their independence against increased pressure, first from Germany and later from the Soviet Union. Yugoslavia alone has been able to reassert her independence since 1949, and Romania and especially Albania since the early 1960's have initiated a more independent economic and political line from the other East European countries.

2. The basic economic geography of the region has been changed since World War II, so much that a return to the pattern of prewar Europe is inconceivable. Eastern Europe (including Eastern Germany) today is the world's fourth largest industrial complex, with a total population of over 120 million people, an industrial labor force of over 14 million, a crude steel output of over 10 million tons, an electric power output of over 170 billion kwh, a large variety of modern machinery and production, and a foreign trade close to 25 billion dollars per year. In turn, Eastern Europe has become an important market for industrial and agricultural products in the ever-widening trade exchange. All this does not mean that the problems of the less developed East European countries and/or regions have been solved. The problem of Yugoslavia's underdeveloped regions, the backwardness of many villages in nearly every country, the growing differences in the standard of living between developed and underdeveloped regions of the same country, and the improved quality of production necessary to meet competition on international markets are only a few of the problems in need of constant attention.

3. Economic development in the region differs from that of the West. Economics are of planned character, though planning is less doctrinaire, and there exists an ever-growing possibility for local initiative. Total investments have been high, with as much as 40 to 50 per cent going to industry. Industrial production has reached the point where international trade has become essential. While the East European countries are anxious to increase their trade with the west, they are in the difficult position of possessing over-supply of many products, especially engineering products, for which the western market offers little or no outlet (due to poor quality or prices that are not right). Therefore, dependence on Comecon with its long-term guaranteed and therefore secure market often becomes the only way out of this vicious circle. Here it must also be pointed out that the Yugoslav example, with its rapidly changing institutional system, has left a deep impact on most other East European countries. Its economic reforms have been accompanied by some liberalization in the cultural and political sphere. A gradual change in important features of the economic systems of most East European countries— planning, management, and incentives—has taken place. Some of the Communist regimes have also relaxed their policies on private plots and have permitted an increase in the acreage allotted to the peasants and the use of small machinery.

4. It is clear that both the values and outlook of the East European countries have radically changed in the postwar period. In spite of many wasteful actions, and dogmatic approaches to the problems of development so clearly seen by the investment priorities, changes have been marked. Economic development has not been uniform in all countries, but the time has already come when a clear distinction must be made in the plans and goals of individual countries. A number of centrifugal tendencies work toward the loosening up of the once cohesive bloc with the ultimate result of bringing East and West Europe together into a closer economic partnership, thus reducing existing economic and even political barriers.

BIBLIOGRAPHY

(Major references are asterisked.)

Books in English

*BYRNES, ROBERT F. *The United States and Eastern Europe.* The American Assembly. Englewood Cliffs, N.J.: Prentice-Hall, Inc., 1967.

East-Central Europe Under the Communists. Albania, ed., Stravo Skendi; Bulgaria, ed., L. A. D. Dellin; Czechoslovakia, eds., Vratislav Busek and Nicolas Spulber; Hungary, ed., Ernst C. Helmreich; Poland, ed., Oscar Halecki; Romania, ed., Stephen Galati; Yugoslavia, Robert F. Byrnes. New York: Frederick A. Praeger, Inc., for the Mid-European Studies Center, 1956–67 (Seven books published separately).

FISHER, JACK C. *Yugoslavia—A Multinational State.* San Francisco: Chandler Publishing Co., 1966.

———, ED. *City and Regional Planning in Poland.* Ithaca, N.Y.: Cornell University, 1966.

HAMILTON, F. E. I. *Yugoslavia, Patterns of Economic Activity.* New York: Frederick A. Praeger, Inc., 1968.

HOFFMAN, GEORGE W. *Balkans in Transition.* Searchlight book No. 20. Princeton, N.J.: D. Van Nostrand Co., 1963.

*——— AND NEAL, FRED WARNER. *Yugoslavia and the New Communism.* New York: The Twentieth Century Fund, 1962.

MAY, JACQUES M. *The Ecology of Malnutrition in Central and Southeastern Europe.* Studies in Medical Geography vol. 6. New York and London: Hafner Publishing Co., 1966.

———. *The Ecology of Malnutrition in Five Countries of Eastern and Central Europe.* Studies in Medical Geography vol. 4. New York and London: Hafner Publishing Co., 1963.

MCNEILL, WILLIAM H. *Europe's Steppe Frontier 1500–1800.* Chicago and London: The University of Chicago Press, 1964.

*MONTIAS, JOHN M. *Economic Development of Communist Rumania.* Cambridge, Mass.: The M.I.T. Press, 1967.

*MORARIU, TIBERIU, VUCU, VASILE, AND VELCEA, ION. *The Geography of Romania.* Bucharest: Meridiane, 1966.

OSBORNE, R. H. *East-Central Europe: An Introductory Geography.* New York: Frederick A. Praeger, Inc., 1967.

*PÉCSI, MÁRTON, AND SÁRFALVI, BÉLA. *The Geography of Hungary.* London: Collet's in cooperation with Corvina Press, Budapest, 1964.

PENKOV, IGNAT, AND PENKOVA, MILKA. *Economic Geography of the People's Republic of Bulgaria.* New York: U. S. Joint Publications Research Service, 1958.

POUNDS, NORMAN J. G. *The Upper Silesian Industrial Regions.* Slavic and East European Series, vol. XI. Bloomington, Ind.: Indiana University Press, 1958.

———. *Poland Between East and West.* Searchlight book No. 22. Princeton, N.J.: D. Van Nostrand Co., 1964.

———, ED. *Geographical Essays on Eastern Europe.* Indiana, Indiana University Publications, Russian and East European Series, vol. 24. Bloomington, Ind.: Indiana University Press, 1961.

SÁRFALVI, BÉLA, ED. *Applied Geography in Hungary.* Studies in Geography of Geographical Research Institute of Hungarian Academy of Sciences, No. 2. Budapest: Akademiai Kiado, 1964.

SPULBER, NICOLAS. *The Economics of Communist Eastern Europe.* New York: John Wiley & Sons, Inc., 1957.

*TOMASEVICH, JOZO. *Peasants, Politics, and Economic Change in Yugoslavia.* Stanford, Cal.: Stanford University Press, 1955.

WANKLYN, HARRIET G. *Czechoslovakia: A Geographical and Historical Study.* London: George Philip & Son, Ltd., 1954.

WILKINSON, H. R. *Maps and Politics: A Review of the Ethnographic Cartography of Macedonia.* Liverpool: University of Liverpool Press, 1951.

Books in Other Languages

BESHKOV, ANASTAS. *Volksrepublik Bulgarien. Natur und Wirtschaft* ("People's Republic of Bulgaria. Landscape and Economy"). Berlin: Verlag Die Wirtschaft, 1960.

*BIROT, PIERRE, AND DRESCH, JEAN. *La Méditerranée et le Moyen-Orient* (Mediterranean and the Near Orient). Vol. 2, first part: Pierre Birot, *Les Balkans* (The Balkans). Paris: Presses Universitaires de France, 1956.

BLANC, ANDRÉ. *La Yougoslavie* (Yugoslavia). Paris: Librairie Armand Colin, 1967.

———. *Géographie des Balkans* (The Geography of the Balkans). Paris: Presses Universitaires de France, 1965.

*———, GEORGE, PIERRE, AND OTHERS. *Les Républiques Socialistes d'Europe Centrale* (The Socialist Republics of Central Europe). Collection Magellan No. 15, Paris: Presses Universitaires de France, 1967.

GUNTHER, HORST. *Die Verstädterung in Jugoslawien Darstellung und Probleme.* (The Urbanization of Yugoslavia: Presentation and Problems). Reihe I. Giessener Abhandlungen zur Agrar-und Wirtschaftsforschung des Europäischen Ostens, Band 35. Wiesbaden: Otto Harrassowitz, 1966.

Atlases

ROZEDOWSKI, JAN, ED. *Polska, Atlas Geograficzny.* Warsaw: Panstwowe Przedsiebiorstwo Wydawnictw Kartograficznych, 1967. 37 pages of maps.

Magyarország Nemzeti Atlasza (Hungarian National Atlas). Budapest: Kultura, 1967. English edition to be published during 1969. 100 pages of maps, text.

Atlas Geografie, Republica Socialistá România. Bucharest: Editura Didactica Si Pedagogicá, 1965. 111 pages of maps, photographs, text.

MARDEŽIĆ, PETAR, AND DUGAČKI, ZVONINIR. *Geografski Atlas Jugoslavije (Geographical Atlas of Yugoslavia).* Zagreb: Znanje, 1961. 256 pages and text.

Uceben Geografski Atlas (General Geographical Atlas). Sofiya: Upravlenie geodeziia i kartografiia, 1959. 95 pages of maps, statistics, index.

Czechoslovak Republic. *Ustredni sprava geodezie a kartografie. Atlas Ceskoslovenske socialisticke republiky ("Atlas of the Czechoslovak Socialist Republic.")* Prague, 1967. 58 sheets with 433 maps, diagrams, tables.

Articles

ANTAL, Z. "The Economical Geographical Questions of the United Electric Power System of the European Socialist Countries," *Annales Universitatis Scientiarum Budapestiensis de Rolando Eötös Nominatae.* Sector Geographica. Vol. 2–3 (1966–67): 145–168.

BEYNON, E. G. "Budapest: An Ecological Study," *Geographical Review* 33 (1943): 256–75.

°BICANIĆ, RUDOLF. "Economics of Socialism in a Developed Country," *Foreign Affairs* 44 (1966): 633–50.

BLANC, ANDRÉ. "L'évolution contemporaine de la vie pastorale en Albanie méridionale" ("Present Changes of the Pastoral Life in Southern Albania"), *Revue de géographie alpine* 51 (1963): 429–61.

———. "Problems de géographie urbaine en Roumanie" ("Problems of the Urban Geography of Romania"), *Revue géographique de l'Est* (Nancy), 3 (July–September, 1963): 307–31.

CVIJIĆ, JOVAN. "The Zones of Civilization of the Balkan Peninsula," *Geographical Review* 5 (1918): 470–82.

°ENYEDI, GYORGY. "The Changing Face of Agriculture in Eastern Europe," *Geographical Review* 57 (1967): 358–72.

FISHER, JACK C. "Planning the City of Socialist Man," *Journal of the American Institute of Planners* 28 (November, 1962): 251–65.

°HAMILTON, F. E. I. "Location Factors in the Yugoslav Iron and Steel Industry," *Economic Geography* 40 (1964): 46–64.

°HOFFMAN, GEORGE W. "Thessaloniki, the Impact of a Changing Hinterland," *East European Quarterly* 2 (March, 1968): 1–27.

°———. "The Problem of the Underdeveloped Regions in Southeast Europe: A Comparative Analysis of Romania, Yugoslavia, and Greece," *Annals of the Association of American Geographers* 57 (December, 1967): 637–66.

———. "Transformation of Rural Settlement in Bulgaria," *Geographical Review* 54 (1964): 45–64.

———. "Eastern Europe: A Study in Political Geography," *Texas Quarterly* 2 (1959): 57–88.

———. "Yugoslavia: Changing Character of Rural Life and Rural Economy," *The American Slavic and East European Review* 717 (1959): 555–78.

———. "Yugoslavia in Transition: Industrial Expansion and Resource Base," *Economic Geography* 32 (1956): 294–315.

IVANIČKA, KOLOMAN. "Process of Industrialization of Slovakia," *Geografický Casopis* 16 (1964): 215–24.

———, ZELENSKA, A., AND MLADEK, J. "Functional Types of Country Settlements in Slovakia," Aspects of the Study of Regional Geographical Structure. *Acta Geologica et Geographica Universitatis Comenianae Geographica* (Bratislava) 6 (1966): 51–92.

KLEMENIĆ, VLADIMIR. "Some Elements of Urbanization and Regional Development of Slovenia," Aspects of the Study of Regional Geographical Structure. *Acta Geologica et Geographica Universitatis Comenianae Geographica* (Bratislava) 6 (1966): 145–74.

KOSTANICK, HUEY LOUIS. "The Geopolitics of the Balkans," in *Balkans in Transition,* ed. Charles and Barbara Jelavich. San Francisco and Los Angeles, Cal.: University of California, Berkeley and Los Angeles, 1964.

KOSTROWICKI, JERZY, ED. "Land Utilization in East-Central Europe: Case Studies," *Geographia Polonia* 5 (1965): 7–498.

LESCZYNSKI, STANISLAW. "The Geographical Bases of Poland," *Journal of Central European Affairs* 7 (1948): 357–73.

MAGNER, THOMAS F. "Language and Nationalism in Yugoslavia," *Canadian Slavic Studies* I (Fall, 1967): 333–47.

MOODIE, ARTHUR E. "The Eastern Marchlands of Europe," in *The Changing World*, ed. W. Gordon East and Arthur E. Moodie. Yonkers, N.Y.: World Book Co., 1956: 110–37.

*POUNDS, NORMAN J. G. "The Spread of Mining in the Coal Basin of Upper Silesia and Northern Moravia," *Annals of the Association of American Geographers* 48 (1958): 149–63.

————. "The Industrial Geography of Modern Poland," *Economic Geography* 36 (July, 1960): 231–53.

*ROGLIĆ, JOSIP. "Yugoslav Littoral," in *The Western Mediterranean World*, James M. Houston. London: Longmans, Green and Co., 1964: 546–79.

RUSINOW, DENNISON I. "The Other Albanians: Some Notes on the Yugoslav Kosmet Today," *Southeast Europe Series, American Univer-* *sities Field Staff Report Service* 12, 2, Yugoslavia (November, 1965).

SANDRU, ION, AND CUCU, VASILE. "Some Considerations on the Development of Geography in the Socialist Republic of Romania," *Professional Geographer* 18 (July, 1966): 219–23.

*SPULBER, NICOLAS. "The Pace of Change in the Economic Structure of the Balkans," in *The State and Economic Development in Eastern Europe*. New York: Random House, 1966: 61–88.

VUCINICH, WAYNE S. "The Nature of Balkan Society under Ottoman Rule," *Slavic Review* 21 (December, 1962): 597–616.

WILKINSON, H. R. "Jugoslav Macedonia in Transition," *The Geographical Journal* 118 (1952): 389–405.

9

The Soviet Union

In contrast to the maritime and peninsular nature of Europe in the west, a broad continuity, massiveness, and continentality characterize the continent in the east. No longer is it dissected by long arms of the sea into great tongues of land. Instead one finds Europe, at its widest extent, forming a bridge to Asia. This entire transition area falls within the confines of the Union of Soviet Socialist Republics (U.S.S.R.), commonly known as the Soviet Union.

Although the U.S.S.R. covers large parts of both Europe and Asia, it is clearly one of the most strongly unified political units in the world and cannot rationally be divided for discussion. Since the general scope of the present volume is limited to Europe, the European part of the U.S.S.R., which also happens to be the core area of the entire Soviet Union, will receive most of our attention in this chapter. However, major facts of the geography of the Asian section will be discussed, especially where they are of exceptional magnitude in relation to the entire country or where they bear more or less directly on a particular aspect of the European U.S.S.R.

THE PHYSICAL LANDSCAPE

Size, Location, and Boundaries

With a total area of 8,500,000 square miles, the Soviet Union is the largest continuous political unit in the world (Fig. 9-1). It is about two and a half times as large as the United States (including Alaska and Hawaii).

The European U.S.S.R. (including Transcaucasia) occupies roughly the eastern half, or 2,000,000 square miles, of Europe. Vast as this area is—corresponding to two-thirds of the continental United States—it represents only one-fourth of the total area of the Soviet Union. The remainder of the country—Siberia, Kazakhstan, and Central Asia—covers the northern third of Asia.

To realize just how vast the Soviet Union is, let us recall that from the westernmost point of the country, at 20° E., near Kaliningrad in former East Prussia, it ranges over 170 degrees of longitude to Cape Dezhnev (170° W.) on the Bering Strait opposite Alaska, or almost halfway around the world. In terms of time zones, this means that when it is noon on the Soviet-Polish frontier it is 11 P.M. on the shores of the Bering Strait; by way of comparison, when it is noon in San Francisco it is only 3 P.M. in New York City.

This vast east-west span is matched by a spectacular north-south extent. From the northernmost continental point, at Cape Chelyuskin (77° 44′ N.) on the Arctic Ocean, a latitude corresponding to Spitsbergen (Svalbard), the Soviet Union extends nearly 3,000 miles south to Kushka (35° N.) on the Afganistan frontier, at the latitude of Crete.

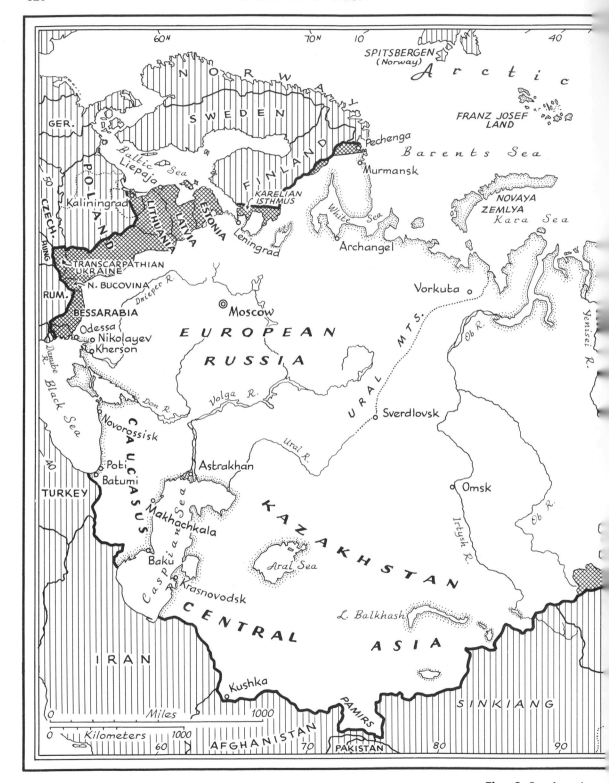

Fig. 9–1. Location

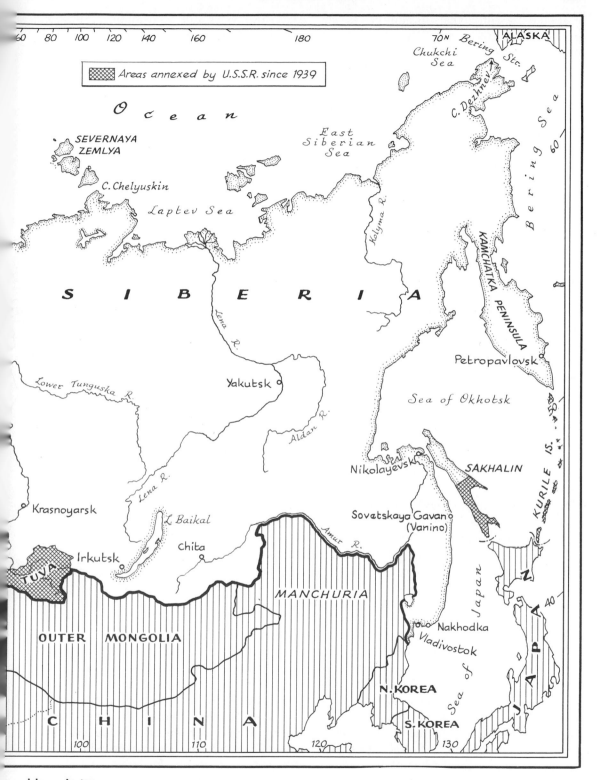

Areas annexed by U.S.S.R. since 1939

and boundaries.

It should be noted that, in addition to the arctic island groups of Franz Josef Land and Severnaya Zemlya (North Land), the U.S.S.R. lays claim to the entire polar sector between the meridians of Murmansk (32° E.) and of the Bering Strait (168° 45′ W.) and as far as the North Pole itself.

The size of the Soviet Union is also evident from the length of its land and sea boundaries, which total about 37,000 miles. In contrast, France, the largest country of western Europe, has frontiers with a total length of 3,300 miles. More than two-thirds (27,000 miles) of the Soviet boundaries are coastline.

Although the length of its coastline far exceeds the length of its land borders, the Soviet Union is far more a continental than a maritime nation. Most of its littoral is bordered by frozen seas and low, marshy shores. The greater part of the coasts lies in sparsely settled or totally uninhabited regions along the seas of the Arctic Ocean. Where the coastal density of population is somewhat higher, closed or nearly closed seas make access difficult. Only a few rocky shores provide the country with natural harbors, and year-round access to the open sea is offered only by one short stretch of shore line.

In terms of their significance for transportation, the seas bordering on the Soviet Union may be divided into four groups:

1. Seas that permit direct access to the oceans of the world—the Barents Sea, the White Sea, and the Sea of Japan. Of these, only the Barents Sea, warmed by the North Atlantic Drift, permits year-round navigation at its port of Murmansk. The White Sea, an appendage of the Barents Sea, with which it is connected by a 30-mile neck (*gorlo* in Russian), is frozen from November until May, bottling up its lumber port of Archangel. The Sea of Japan, in the Soviet Far East, provides access to the Pacific Ocean from the Soviet ports of Nakhodka and Vanino, which is the harbor of the city of Sovetskaya Gavan. However, a cold ice-carrying current along the Soviet Siberian coast also rules out year-round utilization except with the use of icebreakers.

2. Seas that permit access to the world oceans through straits controlled by other nations—the Baltic Sea and the Black Sea. These seas, which are the ones nearest to the main Soviet population and production centers, provide the most important maritime routes for Soviet foreign trade. The Baltic Sea, for example, offers the shortest route between the U.S.S.R. and the countries of western Europe and the Atlantic Ocean. Although its most important port, Leningrad, is icebound from November until April, the more westerly ports of Liepaja (in Latvia) and Kaliningrad are ice-free almost the year around. Similarly, the Black Sea offers the shortest route to the Mediterranean and southern Europe from the Soviet ports of Odessa, Nikolayev, and Kherson in the Ukraine, and Novorossisk, Poti, and Batumi in the Caucasus. Winter ice conditions are negligible in the Black Sea and its usefulness, from the Soviet point of view, is impaired only by the fact that Turkey controls the straits at the exit from the sea. However, the Black Sea–Danube route is now heavily used for bulk-goods traffic between the Soviet Union and its allies in Eastern Europe.

3. The Caspian Sea, which is actually a lake and is used almost entirely for Soviet domestic shipping, such as petroleum cargoes between Baku, Makhachkala, Astrakhan, and Krasnovodsk. Shipping links with Iran, the other Caspian nation, are negligible.

4. The Arctic and sub-Arctic seas, where ice conditions through the greater part of the year and the absence of economically developed coastlines reduce navigation to negligible proportions. The Arctic Sea Route serves the scattered coastal settlements of northern Siberia during the navigation season, which has been extended to 120 days (July–October) by icebreakers, including the atomic icebreaker, *Lenin*.

Arctic seas, which account for most of the Soviet short line, are the Kara, Laptev, East

Siberian, and Chukchi seas of the Arctic Ocean, and the Bering and Okhotsk seas of the Pacific.

On land, the Soviet Union borders on 12 countries. In the extreme northwest, in the Pechenga area, the U.S.S.R. has a short common frontier with Norway. Before World War II, the Pechenga area (then known as Petsamo) provided Finland with access to the Barents Sea. Since the war, the Pechenga area, with important nickel mines, has been part of the Soviet Union. Farther south, other Soviet-Finnish border changes resulted in the cession of the Karelian Isthmus and nearby areas to the Soviet Union.

The Baltic states of Estonia, Latvia, and Lithuania, which had been part of Russia before World War I and had been independent between the two world wars, were incorporated into the U.S.S.R. in 1940.

The Soviet frontier with Poland starts on the Baltic Sea and traverses former East Prussia, which has been divided between the two countries since the end of World War II. The rest of the Soviet-Polish border was also agreed to in 1945 along an ethnic partition line that shifted Belorussian and Ukrainian settlement areas formerly under Polish rule to the Soviet Union. A similar ethnic adjustment took place in 1945 between the Soviet Union and Czechoslovakia, when the latter ceded the Transcarpathian Ukraine (Ruthenia), an area inhabited by Ukrainians. The cession of this area also gave the Soviet Union a common border with Hungary. At the southern end of the Soviet Union's European frontier, Romania ceded northern Bucovina, with a predominantly Ukrainian population, and Bessarabia, with Ukrainians and Moldavians, to the U.S.S.R. in 1940.

South of the Caucasus, in Asia Minor, the Soviet Union borders on Turkey and Iran, the Iranian frontier being continued east of the Caspian Sea. Afghanistan, which follows as the next neighbor of the Soviet Union, forms a peculiar panhandle in the northeast, separating the Soviet Pamirs from Pakistan across an area only 10 miles wide. The Soviet frontier with China is interrupted by

Outer Mongolia, which intervenes between China's Sinkiang and Manchuria. Finally, the Soviet Union has a brief common border with North Korea, on the Sea of Japan. Territorial transfers along the Soviet Union's Asian frontier include Tuva (the former Tannu-Tuva), which passed to the Soviet Union in 1944, and southern Sakhalin (the former Karafuto) and the Kurile Islands, seized from Japan in 1945. It should also be noted that Soviet territory is close to America across the Bering Strait.

Landforms

The U.S.S.R. (Figs. 9–2 and 1–3) consists, essentially, of a vast lowland lying north of the high mountain and plateau belt that extends east and west across the heart of the Eurasian land mass. The major divisions of this lowland are the Great Russian Lowland (plains and tablelands) west of the Ural Mountains; the West Siberian Plain, east of the Urals; the Turan Lowland, east of the Caspian Sea; and the Central Siberian Plateau. These major lowlands are bounded in the south and east, roughly along the Soviet frontier, by the Carpathians, the Caucasus, the Kopet Dagh, the Tien Shan and Pamirs, the Altai and Sayans, and the East-Siberian highlands.

By far the dominant feature of the U.S.S.R. in Europe is the Great Russian Lowland. Representing an eastward broadening of the North European Plain, this lowland, interrupted occasionally by low hill lands, rises almost imperceptibly toward the Urals in the east. Geologically [1] it consists of a basement of Pre-Cambrian crystalline rocks, overlain by sedimentary deposits of marine and continental origin. At the northwestern and southwestern rims of the plain, the Pre-Cambrian formations appear as surface outcrops in the form of crystalline shields or blocks. In the northwest the Baltic Shield includes Karelia and the Kola Peninsula; in

---

[1] For geological terms, see Appendix I. For a more detailed discussion, see Chapter 1.

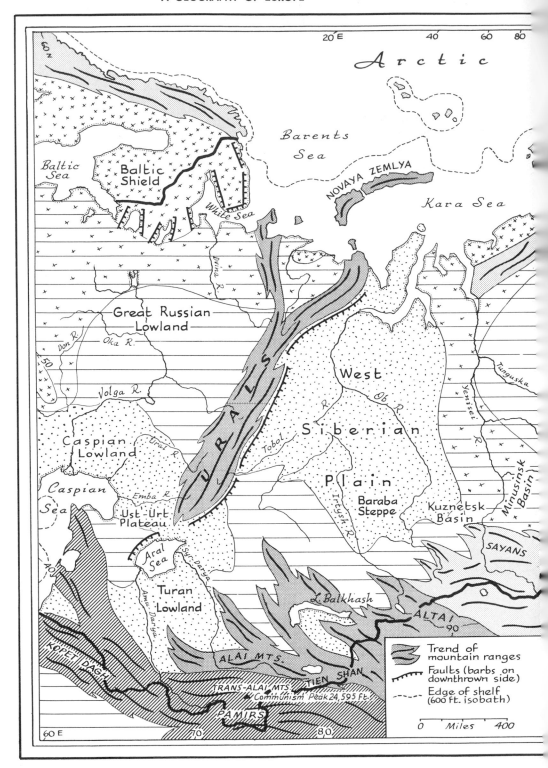

Fig. 9–2.   Structural units

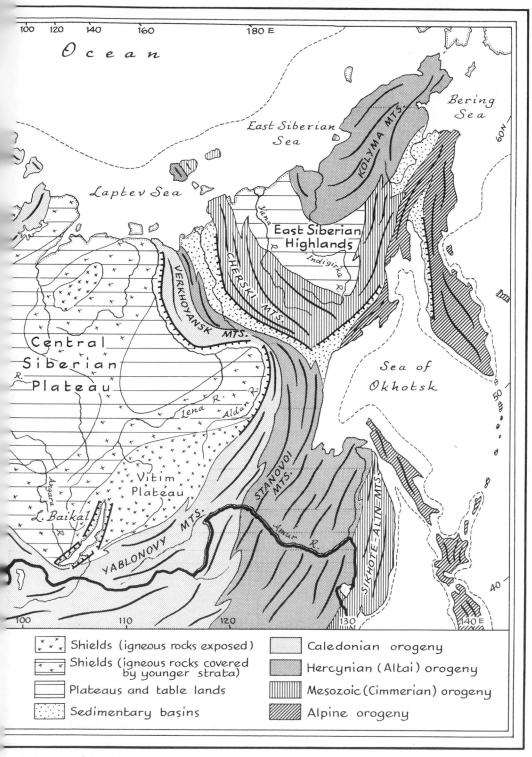

of the Asian U.S.S.R.

the southwest, the Azov-Podolian Massif extends through the Ukraine, forming an eroded upland.

In addition to these crystalline outcrops, further relief has been added to the plain by occasional downfaulting, as in the Donets Basin, where major coal deposits of the Carboniferous period have been preserved, and by upthrusting, as in the Voronezh Block. Other eroded remains of uplifts are the Volga uplands (with the Zhiguli Mountains) along the right bank of the middle Volga, the horst of the Ufa Plateau, west of the Urals, and the Stavropol Plateau north of the Caucasus. However, the rolling lowland topography of the Great Russian Lowland never rises above 1,300 feet.

While the main relief features of the Great Russian Lowland reflect past tectonic action, the detailed topography has resulted from the Pleistocene ice sheet that covered the northern part of the lowland and from recent marine transgressions in the extreme north and the southeast.

As in the rest of northern Europe, ice radiating from the Scandinavian highlands covered the northwestern and middle portions of the Great Russian Lowland. A subsidiary center of ice expansion was located on Novaya Zemlya. The ice sheet reached its maximum penetration during the Riss (Illinoian) period, when the southern boundary of glaciation extended to the edge of the Azov-Podolian hills and the Central-Russian hill lands, forming two tongues in the Dnieper and Oka-Don valleys. The Riss glacial boundary then followed the western edge of the Volga uplands and continued to the middle Urals at about 60° N. Although the ice sheet thus covered the greatest area in the Riss stage, it is the latest glacial period, the Würm (Wisconsin) stage, that left behind most of the effects of the Ice Age, having partly obliterated the marks of the Riss period.

The advancing and retreating ice scoured and denuded the ancient rocks of the Kola-Karelian Shield, leaving a topography of bare crystalline outcrops and glacial lake basins and virtually no soil mantle. Most of the deposition of morainic materials (boulders, pebbles, sand, clay) took place in the northern part of the Great Russian Lowland. Here terminal moraines, arrayed in festoons, are a conspicuous feature of the landscape. The most important morainic ridge remains as a continental watershed, separating the Baltic-Arctic drainage system in the north from the Black Sea and Caspian basins in the south. This major divide consists of the Lithuanian-Belorussian hill lands, the Valdai Hills, and a series of low ridges extending to the Urals.

Beyond the moraines, in southern European Russia, the plain is dominated by outwash valleys of sheets of sand and clay deposited by the great streams that formed along the ice margin during the melting phase. Finely ground silt from these outwash plains was later spread by the wind and deposited over the Ukraine in the form of loess. Erosion of this fine-grained dust-like material has produced the characteristic ravine and gully relief of the Ukraine. In the southeastern part of the Great Russian Lowland, any traces of glacial deposits have been obliterated by the action of the repeated transgressions of the Caspian Sea, which reached far up the Volga Valley during the Ice Age. In the north of European Russia, detailed surface relief dates from postglacial transgressions of the Baltic, Barents, and White seas.

Among the mineral resources of the Great Russian Lowland, metals are associated with the ancient magmatic and metamorphic rocks of the Kola Shield (apatite and nephelite) and of the Azov-Podolian hills (iron ore of Krivoi Rog). The sedimentary mantle of the plain contains rich fuel and other non-metallic resources such as coal of the Donets Basin, the Moscow Basin, and Vorkuta; petroleum and natural gas of the Volga-Urals area and the North-Caucasus foreland: potash, rock salt, oil shale, and phosphates.

The Urals extend almost 1,500 miles south and north, separating the Great

Russian Lowland from the West Siberian Plain. This narrow mountain range was formed in the Hercynian orogeny, and was repeatedly eroded and reuplifted in subsequent periods. The contemporary Urals reach an elevation of 6,000 feet in the undeveloped northern part and in the south, where they consist of several parallel ranges. However, in the heavily industrialized middle section, where the Trans-Siberian Railroad makes use of low passes, the Urals resemble a heavily eroded plateau rather than a mountain range. Prolonged denudation of surface rocks has given access to the older rock formations rich in minerals that have provided the basis for the highly developed mineral-extracting and -processing industry of the Urals. Among the main metals found there are iron ore, copper, bauxite, platinum, nickel, and chromium.

The Urals drop abruptly in the east to the West Siberian Plain, a low, level region that displays far less local relief than the Great Russian Lowland. The Siberian Plain is underlain at great depths by a crystalline basement, and even the younger Tertiary and Jurassic rocks outcrop only in a few isolated places through the thick mantle of unconsolidated sedimentary rocks. Like the Great Russian Lowland, the Siberian lowland has been shaped largely by glacial topography. The low-lying Arctic coast was subjected to postglacial marine transgressions. The plain displays moraine topography as far south as 60° N. Beyond the moraines the landscape is dominated by mighty outwash plains with broad, swampy interfluves. Still farther south we find perfectly level tableland studded with lakes, as in the Baraba Steppe, the Siberian dairy land.

East of the West Siberian Plain, beyond the broad Yenisei Valley, the terrain rises to the Central Siberian Plateau, a dissected upland. As late as the middle Tertiary period this region was a rolling lowland, and it was once again uplifted in the Quaternary period and deeply dissected by rejuvenated river systems. Most of the Central Siberian Plateau is below 3,000 feet.

South of the West Siberian Plain, the Turgai tableland leads to the large Turan Lowland of central Asia. This lowland consists of rolling plains and low plateaus rising to not more than 1,300 feet. Surface forms, especially in the plains, are made up largely of sand, believed to have been deposited by Ice Age streams whose old river channels still traverse the Turan Lowland.

The mountain ranges that skirt the great inland plains of the Soviet Union extend in an almost unbroken belt from the southwest, along the southern and eastern borders, to the northeast. The Great Russian Lowland and the western part of the Turan Lowland are bounded on the south by the Soviet examples of alpine mountain building. They are the Carpathians, the Crimean Mountains, the Caucasus, and the Kopet Dagh.

The Carpathians enter the Soviet Union over a short distance, separating the Transcarpathian Ukraine from the rest of the Ukraine. Made up of rocks such as sandstone and shale that are easily eroded in a humid climate, the Carpathians display rounded contours further subdued by their forest cover. The highest point in the Soviet Carpathians is Mount Goverla (6,800 feet).

The Crimean Mountains, in the southern part of the Crimea, consist of three parallel ranges, of which the highest and southernmost drops abruptly to the Black Sea coast around Yalta, the Soviet subtropical "Riviera." The highest point of the mountains, which are made up largely of Jurassic limestones, is the Roman-Kosh (5,000 feet).

By far the most impressive example of alpine structure in the Soviet Union is the Greater Caucasus system, extending 800 miles across the isthmus between the Black Sea and the Caspian. Several peaks exceed 15,000 feet, the highest being Elbrus (18,500 feet). The Caucasus rises far above the snow line, and valley glaciers are found on the slopes of the main peaks. Glacially eroded mountain features, such as U-shaped valleys, cirques, knife-edge divides, and comb ridges, are typical of the high middle reaches of the Caucasus.

The southern slopes of the Greater Caucasus drop sharply to the Transcaucasian lowland, made up of the valleys of the Kura and Rion rivers. These sediment-filled tectonic troughs separate the great range to the north from the so-called Lesser Caucasus, a system of folded and blockfaulted mountains adjoining the Armenian highlands. The Lesser Caucasus and the Armenian highlands consist both of sedimentary rocks and of volcanic formations such as tuffs, lavas, and volcanic breccia.

East of the Caspian Sea lies the 400-mile-long Kopet Dagh on the Soviet-Iranian frontier. Of considerably less elevation and complexity than the Caucasus, the Kopet Dagh rises to almost 10,000 feet.

Except for copper and other non-ferrous metals found in the Caucasus, these alpine mountain systems are poor in ores. However, foreland troughs filled with great thicknesses of recent sediments contain some of the main oil fields of the Soviet Union.

The highest mountain systems along the southern border of the U.S.S.R. are found in the southeastern part of Soviet Central Asia, in the Pamir-Alai and Tien Shan complexes. The Pamir-Alai system consists of the Alai and Trans-Alai ranges, rising to 24,595 feet at Communism Peak (known as Stalin Peak until 1961), and the adjoining Pamir high plateaus, with an average elevation of more than 15,000 feet. The Tien Shan rises to 24,400 feet at the Pobeda (Victory) Peak, which was discovered by Soviet mountain climbers during World War II. The Tien Shan and the Pamir-Alai are separated by the Fergana Valley, a deep tectonic depression which is one of the main economic and population centers of Soviet Central Asia.

Southern Siberia is bounded by the mountains of the Altai and Sayan systems, both of which were originally formed during the Caledonian orogeny of the early Paleozoic era. After a period of peneplanation, the rigid basement rocks were once again plicated in the Tertiary period into broad gentle folds that were also disrupted by faulting. The combination of downthrusting and uplifting gave rise to the present complex folded and blockfaulted character of the Altai and Sayan systems. The tectonic depressions between these mountains include the Minusinsk Basin, an agricultural and mining area, and the Kuznetsk Basin, an industrial district based on local coal deposits.

Eastern Siberia contains a complex array of mountain ranges with a predominant southwest-northeast trend. The most important systems are the Yablonovy, Stanovoi, and Sikhote-Alin ranges, in the south, and the Cherski, Verkhoyansk, and Kolyma mountains in the north.

Climates

Except for a small modified Mediterranean region in the southern Crimea and nearby parts of the Caucasus coast, the humid subtropical section of Transcaucasia, and the monsoon region of the Soviet Far East, the U.S.S.R. has a continental climate par excellence, with continentality increasing from west to east. This quality of the Soviet climate results from the weakness of moderating maritime influences; low precipitation, most of which occurs in summer; a great annual temperature range; long winters; and brief spring and autumn seasons.[2]

The Soviet Union is situated in latitudes where the Eurasian land mass reaches its greatest east-west extent, so most of the country is far from the moderating effects of the Atlantic and Pacific oceans. The efficiency of the humidity-laden westerly winds of Atlantic origin, which play such an important role in the climate of Europe north of the Alps, decreases noticeably eastward. Nevertheless, maritime air is responsible for most of the precipitation within European Russia. Being situated on the shores of the Arctic Ocean and lacking any major east-west mountain ranges except on its southern

[2] See climatic graphs, Appendix II. See also the discussion in Chapter 1 on climatic types and regions, pp. 42–48.

borders, the U.S.S.R. is exposed widely to invasions of arctic and polar air masses.

A key factor in determining the average climate conditions of the U.S.S.R. is the great continental high-pressure ridge, especially well defined in winter, which extends, as a continuation of the Azores High, along the line Kishinev-Kharkov-Saratov-Uralsk in southern European Russia. This high-pressure ridge can be traced eastward through Kazakhstan until it joins the Siberian High. This anticyclonic ridge governs the wind circulation of European Russia, particularly during the cold season. To the north, winds are predominantly westerlies and southwesterlies, relatively humid and warm, while to the south they are primarily dry, cold easterlies and northeasterlies. The effect is generally milder winters in the northwestern half of European Russia and drier and colder winters in the southeast.

During the summer, the Siberian High disappears and is replaced by a low-pressure system located over the heated interior of southwest Asia. At the same time, the permanent Azores High, shifting northward, has an even more pronounced effect on the climate of the Soviet Union by governing predominantly westerly and northwesterly winds over most of the country. Although the anticyclonic ridge extending through European Russia loses its eastern support in the Siberian High, it does not disappear in summer. It is maintained, though to a much weaker degree, by the intensified summer activity of the Azores High, from which high-pressure cells occasionally travel eastward into the continent. Being considerably weakened, the anticyclonic ridge loses its wind-dividing role in summer.

The year-round predominance of westerlies holds true for almost all of the Soviet Union except along the Arctic coast and on the Pacific. There we find a monsoonic circulation, with winds blowing outward from the frigid continent in winter, and inward from the cooler oceans in summer.

In terms of air masses, the Soviet Union is dominated by three types: arctic, polar con-tinental, and tropical continental. Arctic air, formed over the Arctic Ocean and distinguished by low temperature, low humidity, and high visibility, affects the northern half of the Soviet Union. Arctic air plays an especially important role in eastern Siberia, where the westerly drift from the Atlantic is greatly weakened or entirely absent. From time to time arctic air breaks through to the south, even reaching the mountain systems along the southern frontiers of the country. These invasions of arctic air into the middle and lower latitudes are especially significant in spring and autumn, when they cause either late May frosts or early fall frosts. As the arctic air moves south it is transformed into polar air, with higher temperatures and lower relative humidity. Frequent invasions of this desiccated arctic air are one of the basic causes of droughts in the newly cultivated virgin lands of southern Siberia and northern Kazakhstan. In southern European Russia, anticyclones traveling eastward from the Azores High are a contributing factor in droughts.

Maritime polar air from the Atlantic Ocean hardly ever reaches the territory of the Soviet Union in its pure form, having lost much of its moisture en route over Europe and having acquired the characteristics of continental polar air. Invasions of this modified maritime polar air in winter produce prolonged thaws in the Great Russian Lowland. Most of the polar air of the Soviet Union is of continental origin, being generally dry, as well as hot in summer and cool in winter.

Continental tropical air affects the climate of the southern U.S.S.R. mainly during the warm season. This air is formed over Central Asia, Kazakhstan, the North-Caucasus foreland, and the southern plain of European Russia through transformation of continental polar air and is distinguished by high temperatures, low humidity, and low visibility. Tropical air penetrates northward as far as the forest steppe zone and, in the peak of summer, even into the forest zone. In winter, however, even central Asia is

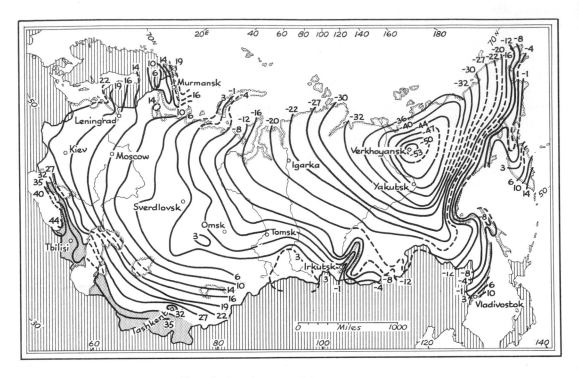

Fig. 9–4. Average July temperatures.

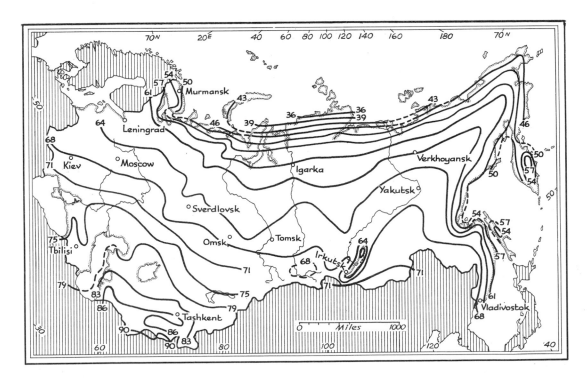

Fig. 9–3. Average January temperatures.

dominated by polar air, though of a warmer type than is found elsewhere in the country.

Average January temperatures are below freezing in almost the entire Soviet Union (Fig. 9–3). The only exceptions are the south coast of the Crimea, Transcaucasia, and the extreme south of Central Asia. The combined effect of the moderating Atlantic westerlies and the cooling of the Eurasian interior produces a roughly northwest-southeast alignment of January isotherms. The coldest area is northeastern Siberia with −50° F. or less. In July, on the other hand, only some Soviet arctic islands have temperatures close to freezing (Fig. 9–4). The hottest summers occur in southern Central Asia, where average July temperatures exceed 90° F. In contrast to the January isotherms, the July temperature lines run close to the parallels of latitude with downturned ends in the east and west being caused by the relatively cooler air near the Atlantic and Pacific oceans.

Precipitation ranges from 20 inches or more in the western-Russian plain to about 5 inches in eastern Siberia (Fig. 9–5). Except for the Pacific summer monsoon in the Soviet Far East, virtually all the precipitation in the Soviet Union is of Atlantic origin. In addition to decreasing from west to east, precipitation also drops noticeably toward the north and the south from a relatively moist middle zone centered at 60° N. This precipitation pattern is particularly well expressed in the eastern part of the Great Russian Lowland and in western Siberia, where the tracks of cyclonic storms generally move along the middle belt astride the 60th parallel. The lowest precipitation is recorded in the Turan Lowland of central Asia and southern Kazakhstan, where the annual total is less than 5 inches. Over almost the entire area of the U.S.S.R. there is a well-defined warm-season maximum of precipitation associated with more-active cyclonic activity during that part of the year. The maximum occurs in the second half of summer in the northern tundra and forest zone, in early summer in the steppe, and in spring in the arid regions. Winter precipitation maxima

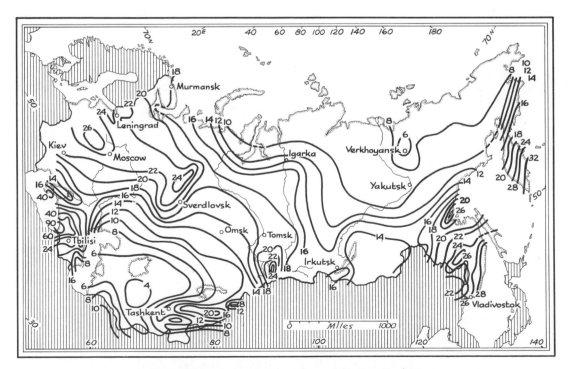

Fig. 9–5. Average annual precipitation (inches).

are typical of the Mediterranean-type climates on the shores of the Black Sea.

The duration of the snow cover ranges from 260 days in the northern tundra of Siberia to 40 days in the Ukrainian steppe and 20 days in central Asia. The thickness of the cover also varies widely, reaching a maximum of more than 30 inches northeast of the Great Russian Lowland, on the western slopes of the Urals, and northeast of the Siberian plain, where long frosts combine with relatively ample winter precipitation. In the northwestern part of the Great Russian Lowland, abundant snowfall is neutralized by frequent thaws, and in the colder southeast snowfall is relatively limited.

The special climatic province of the southern Crimea, sheltered against northern air masses by the Crimean Mountains, has its counterpart on the southern slopes of the Caucasus between Novorossisk and Tuapse. Yalta, a typical station in this Mediterranean-type climate, is the center of the Soviet "Riviera." It has hot, dry summers, with a July average of 76° F., and relatively mild, moist winters with a January temperature of 38° F. Of the annual precipitation of 24 inches, 11 inches fall in winter (November–February) and 6 inches in summer (May–August).

Another separate climatic province is the humid subtropics of western Transcaucasia, which combine a hot summer and mild winter with high precipitation and high relative humidity. Batumi, a typical station in this Soviet tea- and citrus-growing area, has an annual precipitation of 100 inches. The annual range of temperatures is one of the smallest in the Soviet Union, with averages of 75° F. in July and 40° F. in January. Occasional invasions of cold air from the northern steppes across the Caucasus can be disastrous for the local citrus crop, as in the winter 1949–50 when the temperature dropped to 8° F. The humid subtropical climate of the Lenkoran area on the Caspian, on the opposite side of the Transcaucasian isthmus, is a more continen-

tal variant of the coast climate, with hotter summers, cooler winters, and only half as much precipitation.

An important physical aspect of the Soviet Union is the widespread occurrence of permafrost. Permanently frozen subsoil characterizes 47 per cent of the entire territory, being found mainly in eastern Siberia. Its geographical distribution coincides with areas that have average annual temperatures below zero and cold, relatively snowless winters. Because of the great thickness of the permafrost layer, which exceeds 1,000 feet in many areas, and occurrences of well-preserved remains of the mammoth, a Pleistocene elephant, and beds of fossil ice, some geographers suggest that permafrost is a residual phenomenon of the Ice Age. Others maintain that permafrost is a currently active phenomenon, disturbing the soils and producing the waterlogged conditions in large parts of Siberia in summer. Because the top layers of soil thaw and become waterlogged under permafrost conditions, allowance must be made for the settling of buildings, roads and railroad track in construction projects of the far north and eastern Siberia.

Drainage Patterns

In spite of the long and cold winter, which freezes rivers up to 8 or 9 months a year, and the accident of relief, which orients over half the drainage area of the Soviet Union toward the Arctic Ocean, the river systems of the country have long played a vital role in its history and economy. From earliest times, they have served as routes across the steppes as well as the forests. Low, short portages, later partly replaced by canals, have welded the systems together, particularly in European Russia. Russia's early territorial expansion, especially the drive through Siberia in the sixteenth and seventeenth centuries, was effected by means of these interconnecting water routes. The railroad era of the late nineteenth century brought the waterways into partial decline. Recent developments, such as the use of hydroelectric power, the construction of new canals, and the renovation of old ones, have given the water ways of the U.S.S.R. a renewed role in the economy.

The rivers of the Great Russian Lowland are characterized by an insignificant gradient and a consequently slow, meandering course (Fig. 9–6a). This is a direct result of the low elevation of the main morainic divide, which forms the Lithuanian-Belorussian and Valdai hills and reaches its highest point in the Valdai section at 1,053 feet. The streams rising on the northern slope of the divide, which trend generally west-southwest–east-northeast, flow to the Baltic Sea and the Barents Sea. Drainage south of the main divide is into the Black and Caspian seas. Most of the rivers of the Great Russian Lowland have a well-defined spring maximum as a result of melting snows; a low water level in the summer, when high temperatures cause increased evaporation, canceling out the summer maximum of precipitation; and a secondary maximum in the fall, when reduced evaporation results in greater river flow. The duration of the ice cover in European Russia ranges from 2 months in the extreme southwest (Dniester River) to 7 months in the northeast (Pechora River). In winter, the water level is maintained only by ground-water supply and is once again at a low stage. The principal rivers of European Russia are the Pechora and the Northern Dvina, which flow, respectively, to the Barents Sea and the White Sea; the short but important Neva River and the Western Dvina and Niemen, which drain into the Baltic Sea; the Dniester, Dnieper, Don, and Kuban rivers, which enter the Black Sea and the Sea of Azov; and the Volga, Ural, and Terek rivers, which flow to the Caspian Sea.

Unlike the rivers of the Great Russian Lowland with their strong spring maximum, the streams associated with the mountains on the southern margins of European Russia (Carpathians, Crimea, Caucasus) are fed by fairly regular rainfall all through the year and lack a well-defined seasonal high-water stage. The uniform precipitation and the higher gradient of these mountain streams have made them suitable sites for harnessing waterpower. Most of the hydroelectric stations of the Great Russian Lowland rely on rapids, where rivers cross resistant crystalline outcrops (as in the Kola Peninsula, Karelia, and the Ukraine), or simply on the large volume of a great stream with low gradient (as the Volga River).

The rivers of the West Siberian Plain (Fig. 9–6b), all part of the Ob-Irtysh drainage system, have a longer spring maximum than the streams of European Russia. The longer duration of the Siberian high-water stage is caused by three major factors: the delayed melting of snow under the vast forest cover of the Ob-Irtysh basin, the slow runoff from the virtually flat watersheds typical of the Siberian plain, and the abundance of lakes and marshes, which tend to store water for a period of time. On the Central Siberian Plateau, on the other hand, the spring maximum is high and brief, the summer and fall levels are subject to sudden rises after rains, and the winter stage is quite low. In this category are rivers of the Yenisei and Lena systems. In this case, the sharp break between winter and summer, which is characteristic of the climate of this region, the deeply dissected relief and steepness of slopes, and the presence of permafrost greatly reduce penetration of water into the ground, speed the runoff, and thus neutralize the effect of the dense forest cover in slowing the melting of snows. The rivers of the Turan Lowland are characterized by an extremely short, high spring stage fed almost exclusively by the rapid melting of snow on the bare steppes and semideserts, followed by a long, low stage during which many rivers dry up under arid, hot summer conditions.

Rivers that descend from high-mountain systems, especially in Soviet Central Asia, have a high-water stage through the entire warm season, when they are fed by the increased melting of mountain glaciers. Under these conditions, the maximum level often

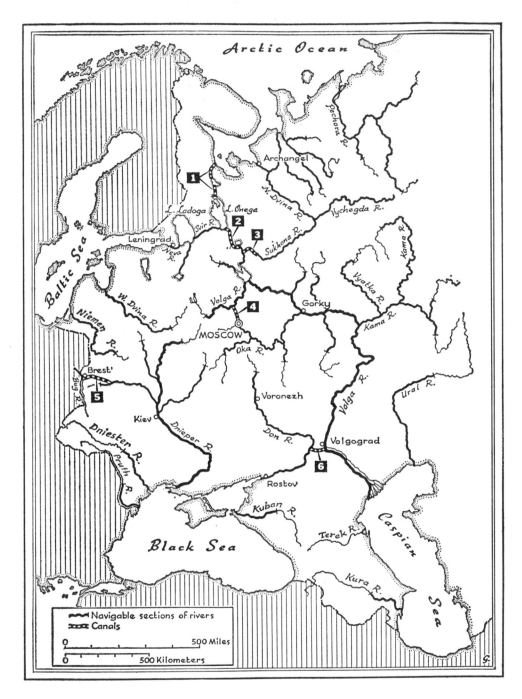

1. Baltic–White Sea Canal
2. Volga–Baltic Waterway
3. North Dvina Canal
4. Moscow Canal
5. Dnieper–Bug Canal
6. Volga–Don Canal

Fig. 9–6a. Chief waterways of the European U.S.S.R.

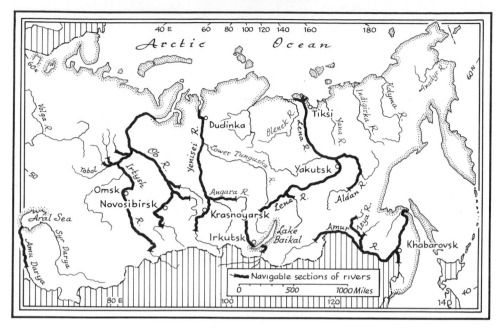

Fig. 9–6b. Chief waterways of the Asian U.S.S.R.

corresponds with the highest summer temperatures in July and August. These glacier-fed streams are extremely useful as the need for irrigation water in the arid piedmont plains is greatest during the height of the warm season. Examples of these rivers are the Ili, Chu, Syr Darya, and Amu Darya.

In the Soviet Far East, in the basin of the Amur River, the rainy summer monsoon produces a high summer stage in the rivers. The spring maximum is short-lived or entirely absent, in view of the thin snow cover left by the dry, cold winters of the monsoon region.

The Soviet Union is rich in lakes ranging in size from the huge Caspian Sea to small glacial lakes dammed by morainic hills. Most of the large lakes are of tectonic origin, including the Caspian Sea, the Aral Sea, and lakes Issyk Kul, Baikal, and Balkhash.

The Caspian Sea is a salt lake whose water level lies 94 feet below sea level, having dropped 8 feet between 1929 and 1956. The currently increasing deficit in the water balance of the Caspian Sea is attributed to reduced precipitation and increased evaporation due to great solar activity, and to the growing economic utilization of the water of tributary rivers, especially the Volga, for irrigation, industry, and hydroelectric power generation. Several plans for replenishing the water level of the Caspian have been proposed, including some that called for the diversion of the rivers of Siberia and northern European Russia or for a direct link with the Black Sea. However, none of these plans has reached the stage of implementation. The salinity of the Caspian Sea (13 per thousand) is lower than that of the world oceans (35 per thousand) and reaches its lowest value in the northern shallow portion of the sea near the inflow of the fresh water of the Volga and Ural rivers. The deep middle and southern sections of the Caspian Sea are connected through a narrow inlet with the shallow gulf Kara-Bogaz-Gol on the east coast, which acts as a natural evaporating basin for the Caspian. This basin, of very high salinity, deposits salt beds that can be used as sources of chemical raw materials.

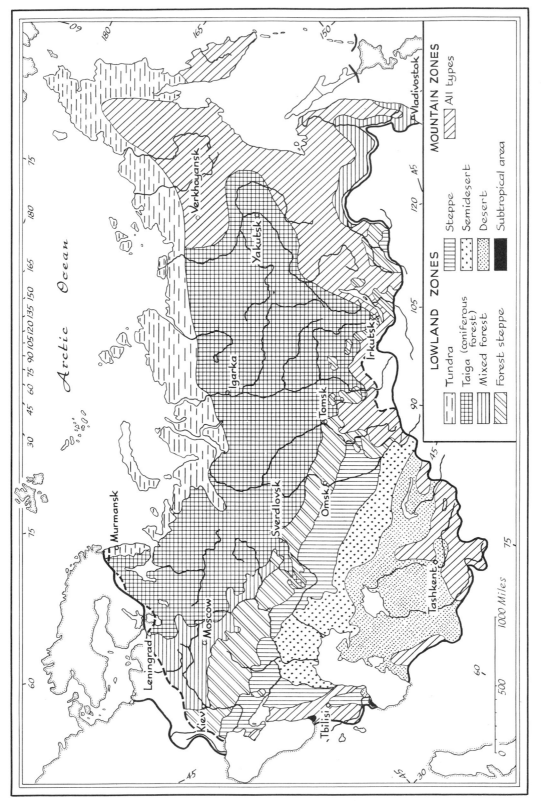

Fig. 9-7. Biotic zones.

Other tectonic lakes, if located in lowlands, tend to be relatively shallow, e.g., the Aral Sea and Lake Balkhash. Those situated in mountain country are deep, with steep shore lines and uneven bottom relief. Lake Baikal, which fills a graben with a maximum depth of nearly 6,000 feet, is the deepest inland body of water in the world. Despite its distance from the oceans, Lake Baikal contains animals of oceanic habitat, such as true seals.

Soils and Vegetation

Largely as a result of the predominantly lowland topography and climate, particularly the east-west trend of summer isotherms, the territory of the Soviet Union falls into a pattern of latitudinal soil and vegetation zones. The zones are the tundra, the forest, the steppe, and the desert.

These biotic zones (Fig. 9–7) developed after the retreat of the last Pleistocene ice sheet. While the tundra remained along the margins of the retreating ice, the rest of the freed territory was invaded by deciduous trees from western Europe and by conifers from Mongolia, as well as by steppe and desert associations from the foothills of the Altai and the Caucasus.

Tundra belt. The tundra belt lies along the coasts and on the islands of the Arctic Ocean; it is widest in northern Siberia on the Kara Sea and reaches as far south as 60° N., at the neck of the Kamchatka Peninsula. The tundra covers more than 10 per cent of the total area of the U.S.S.R. Its chief characteristic is the absence of forest vegetation. Low temperatures hinder the development of physical and chemical decay of the scanty plant cover, producing only a thin top layer of humus above the permanently frozen subsoil. The short growing season (2 to 2½ months, with no monthly mean above 50° F.), the low annual mean temperature (below 32° F.), the low precipitation (8 to 12 inches) and the thin, though widespread, snow cover make it difficult for plants to exist. Dwarf birches and willows

hug the ground where warmer temperatures prevail. Lichens are found in dry sandy areas, while moss and sedge occur in damper low-lying locations. On south-facing slopes, small flowers come to life during the short summer. Along the southern margin of the tundra, the wooded tundra forms a transition to the forest zone. Typical animals are the reindeer, the lemming, the hare, and the arctic fox and the ermine, which are of special value for their furs. The white partridge and the arctic owl are the most characteristic birds. During the summer, masses of waterfowl nest on the cliffs along the coast.

Forest zone. South of the tundra lies the vast forest zone which occupies more than one-half the U.S.S.R. The light-grey podsolized soils, typical for this zone, consist of a topsoil layer, 3 to 6 inches thick, of a white-to-grey color and contain about 2 per cent of humus. Below them is an ash-colored horizon, up to 12 inches thick, which contains a considerable amount of silica and has been leached of most of the plant food. The lowest layer, a brownish zone, colored by iron hydroxide, contains the material washed out from the upper horizon and lies on the unaltered parent material, which is usually clay or sand. The podzol-forming process is speeded by the abundance of moisture and the consequent leaching of the soil. These conditions are best met by a clay base and a correspondingly high water table, while on sandy parent material, where ground water lies deeper below the surface, the process is developed to a lesser extent.

The vast taiga or coniferous forest (see Chapter 1, p. 56), comprising about one-third of the forest lands of the world, extends through the northern part of the European U.S.S.R., across the Ural Mountains, and over most of Siberia. In the European U.S.S.R. pine and spruce are the most common species. Toward the Urals they merge with the Siberian larch, fir, and stone pine. The most widespread species in eastern Siberia is the larch, which penetrates farther north into the tundra than any other tree and provides an unbroken cover over the mountains. A subzone of mixed coniferous and deciduous forests extends in a wedge from the western frontier of the U.S.S.R. to the Ural Mountains. In Siberia its extent is negligible. In addition to coniferous types, the mixed forests include elm, oak, maple, and ash. The linden extends farthest north of all the deciduous types. A separate mixed-forest zone in the Amur-Ussuri region is characterized by a mixture of northern conifers (spruce, pine, larch, and fir) with Manchurian walnut, oak, and elm, as well as wild apricot and peach. Large sections of the forest zone are covered by marshes and peat bogs. This is especially true of western Siberia, where considerable precipitation and nearly level watersheds produce marshes extending over tens of thousands of square miles. Large mammals such as elk, reindeer, and other deer are common in the forest zone. The brown bear and the lynx are the principal carnivores, while rodents such as squirrels, rabbits, and beavers are also widespread. Typical birds are the woodpecker and the grouse.

Steppe zone. The steppe zone extends in an uninterrupted belt from the western border of the U.S.S.R. to the Altai Mountains. It is characterized by a natural grass cover and limited tree growth and covers about 12 per cent of the total area of the U.S.S.R. The transition between forest and steppe is gradual and gives rise to the so-called wooded steppe. The characteristic soil is black earth (Russian *chernozem*), which is one of the most productive of the world and accounts for two-thirds of the arable land of the U.S.S.R. It is generally developed on loess or loess-like loam; its color varies from black to chocolate brown, and its thickness from 3 to 5 feet. The highly developed root system of the steppe grasses is favorable to the formation of humus, which, in the prevailing dry climate, is not leached from the topsoil and accumulates on the loess base. The high humus content of the black earth, generally ranging from 5 to 10 per cent and reaching

even 20 per cent in some areas, renders this soil remarkably fertile. Along the edges of the black-earth belt, the humus content decreases gradually and the black earth changes into grey forest soil in the north and into chestnut and brown soils in the south. The principal causes for the limited tree growth are low precipitation, occasional droughts, and the deposition of mineral salts below the humus layer. In the wooded steppe the scattered tree clusters consist of oak in the European areas and birch in Siberia. Few large expanses of virgin steppe have been preserved. Most of the black earth has been put under cultivation. In the remnants, meadow grass occurs in the northern wooded portion of the steppe, while elsewhere fescue and feather grass are typical.

Desert zone. To the south and the southeast the steppe is succeeded by the desert zone, where vegetation is scattered or wholly absent. The scanty growth results from low rainfall and excessive summer temperatures. This zone, which includes the northern and the eastern shores of the Caspian Sea and the Turan Lowland, extends to about 51° N., where it meets the mountains of Central Asia. Covering about 18 per cent of the U.S.S.R., the desert belt is divided into the northern subzone of the semidesert and the southern subzone of the desert proper. The semidesert is a transition area, similar to the wooded tundra and the wooded steppe. The climate becomes progressively drier, rainfall averages 8 inches yearly, and bare areas appear amidst the patches of grass. The humus content of the brown soils decreases, while the salinity shows a definite increase. In many areas where the salt is washed to the surface, salt marshes (Russian, *solonets* and *solonchak*) are formed. Characteristic plant forms are wormwood and, in the saline soils, saltwort. In the desert proper, rainfall is sometimes less than 4 inches annually. Winters are short, though relatively cold, and summers become unbearably hot, the temperature reaching 120° F. in the shade. Stony and clayey desert flats are nearly devoid of vegetation. Sandy deserts have some wormwood and sage growth, and thickets of *saksaul* bushes are common. The grey desert soil contains considerable quantities of carbonate of lime and yields rich crops when properly irrigated.

Subtropical and mountain vegetation. Subtropical forest vegetation is confined to the western and eastern sections of Transcaucasia and to the slopes of the Crimea, the Caucasus, and some mountains of Central Asia. In these areas forests have continued to exist since the Tertiary period. They are usually a mixture of deciduous and coniferous types, accompanied by a luxuriant undergrowth. Except in Transcaucasia, where conditions of warmth and moisture continue to approach the climate of the Tertiary period, plants have undergone a selective process resulting in the dominance of a few types adapted to the changed climatic conditions. These are generally trees such as oak, hornbeam, and beech in the Crimea and the Caucasus, and maple, pistachio, almond, walnut, and apple in the mountains of Central Asia. The lateritic yellow and red soils in these regions have also remained from the Tertiary period. They contain no calcium, only a little silica, and a large proportion of clay and may be the remains of weathered volcanic rocks.

High mountain or alpine vegetation occurs below the snow line throughout the mountain regions of the U.S.S.R. The lower limits of the alpine-meadow belt vary from 1,000 feet in the northern Urals, where they tend to be replaced by tundra, to 8,000–9,000 feet in the Pamir-Alai mountain system in the south. The elevation of the snow line, which represents the upper limit of the alpine zone, varies with the precipitation and the location of the slopes. In the mountains of the Far East and eastern Siberia, alpine meadows are entirely absent. The forest cover extends virtually to the summits and leaves only the highest elevations covered with mountain tundra. Less than 0.5 per cent of the total area of the U.S.S.R. falls within the alpine-vegetation zone.

THE CULTURAL AND HISTORICAL BACKGROUND

Historical Geography

Early Russian history has been shaped to a very large extent by the nation's forests and rivers. It was in the forests that early Slav settlement took place, in relative seclusion from the nomadic or semi-nomadic Asian tribes that roamed the southern steppes. And it was the extensive river system of the Great Russian Lowland that was instrumental in the rise of the Muscovite state and ultimately brought about the unity of the Russian lands.

At the beginning of the Christian era, Slav tribes inhabited the west-central reaches of the vast Russian lowland, on both sides of the north-south river axis formed by the Volkhov, Lovat, and Dnieper rivers. This was the zone of the mixed forests, in which the primitive population engaged in rudimentary agriculture, beekeeping, and trapping.

Along the Black Sea coast, Greek colonies had been established at the river mouths and in the Crimea as early as the seventh and sixth centuries B.C. These settlements, some of which had probably been based on earlier Phoenician sites, were Tyras at the mouth of the Dniester, Olbia near the Dnieper estuary, and Tanais on the Don Delta. On the Crimean coast were the colonies of the Heraclean Chersonese (the modern Sevastopol), Theodosia (the modern Feodosiya), and Panticapaeum (the modern Kerch).

Between these two settled belts, the forests and the littoral, extended the steppe, dominated since earliest times by warlike horsemen from Asia. The earliest reference is to the Cimmerians, who are believed to have occupied the area between the Dniester and the Don from the tenth to the eighth century B.C. and are mentioned by Homer. They were followed by the Scythians who, according to Herodotus, occupied these open spaces until displaced in the third century B.C. by the Sarmatians. During the first millennium of the Christian era many peoples passed here in the great migration: the Goths, who split (about 200 A.D.) into west and east wings—the Visigoths and the Ostrogoths; the Huns under Attila, who swept through in the late fourth century; the Avars, on their way to the Balkans; the Bulgars, who also divided here (about 500 A.D.), one branch continuing to modern Bulgaria and the other moving into the middle reaches of the Volga River. Finally, following the passage of the Magyars (about 800 A.D.) a certain stability returned to the steppe with the formation of the Khazar domain in the Don-Volga area, with its headquarters at Itil, which was located on the site of modern Astrakhan.

In the meantime, intruders from Scandinavia had also appeared in the secluded forest, beginning in the early ninth century. These were the Varangians or Northmen who, in search of a trade route to Constantinople, had made their way south along the Volkhov-Dnieper river axis. They settled at trading sites that already had been occupied by the Slavs: Novgorod, Pskov, Smolensk, Chernigov, and Kiev. Moved by their common interest in trade and by their need for defense against the steppe peoples, the Slav tribes gradually consolidated under Varangian leadership into what became known as Rus (or Russia), a name of uncertain origin. Originally centered on Novgorod, this early Russian state moved its capital to Kiev in 882 and is therefore known today as Kievan Russia.

Kievan Russia, one of the leading states of early medieval Europe, was essentially a loose confederation of principalities, each centered on a trading town, united under the rule of a senior prince. The Varangian trade route along the Volkhov and Dnieper rivers was its life line, and as long as the perilous Dnieper rapids and the threat of the steppe peoples could be overcome Kiev prospered. Commerce was primarily with Constantinople. The Slavs sent furs, honey, and slaves, and imported silks, wine, fruit, and gold. It was also from Constantinople

that Eastern Orthodox Christianity penetrated into Kievan Russia. The conversion of the eastern Slavs to the Orthodox religion was an important factor in their subsequent isolation from the mainstream of Roman Catholic European culture. Trade also moved along the Volga, in whose upper reaches stood the remote Slav towns of Rostov, Suzdal, and Murom. The Volga was the direct link with Central Asia, serving en route the domains of the Volga Bulgars and of the Khazars.

The Kievan state was to be short-lived. In the tenth century, new warlike nomad tribes appeared in the steppe, ending the relatively stable rule of the Khazars and making the Dnieper route more and more difficult to use. Raids by these nomads began to threaten Kiev and led to its gradual decline in the twelfth century. A shift in the political center of gravity of the Slav domain followed. One new power nucleus formed in the southwestern principalities of Galicia and Volhynia, which were shortly to be absorbed by the expanding Polish and Lithuanian states.

The major movement from the Kievan area was, however, to the northeast, into the remote forests in the upper reaches of the Volga. A period of intensive colonization began in the watershed area between the upper Volga and Oka rivers. This mesopotamia, or *mezhdurechye* as the Russians knew it, had already been sparsely settled by Slavic and Finnic tribes. The influx of refugees from the southern forest margins resulted in a great increase in population and the consequent political rise of the principality of Suzdal-Rostov, later known as Vladimir-Suzdal, or simply Vladimir, as the ruling power shifted from city to city.

The central watershed in the midst of the Great Russian Lowland was the nucleus of the future Russian state. It was relatively less exposed to attack from the nomad horsemen of the southern steppe, and was also protected by the river lines of the Volga and Oka and by the surrounding forest clearings. Many of the population turned to handicraft industries as a livelihood. Linen, leather, woolen cloth, wood, and metal goods were produced. Trade was with Kiev by the Dnieper route, with the Caspian area via the Volga, and with western Europe through the trade centers of Pskov, Novgorod, and the Baltic Sea coast. Goods were also traded with the Genoese ports in the Crimea, notably Kaffa, the modern Feodosiya.

Novgorod had built an empire of its own, following the decline of Kiev. Situated on the direct route between the Volga Valley and the Baltic Sea, Novgorod became one of the chief trading depots of the Hanseatic League. Merchants extended Novgorod's power throughout northern European Russia to the arctic shores and across the northern Urals, levying fur tribute and founding colonies.

During the thirteenth century, the nascent Russian domain was threatened by foreign incursion. Tatars under Mongol leadership established the Golden Horde on the southeastern margins, following devastating raids through Russian towns in 1237–40. In the northeast, the Novgorod empire, under the leadership of Alexander Nevsky, defeated the Swedes (1240) and the Teutonic and Livonian Knights (1242), but the rising Lithuanian state annexed the southwestern Russian principalities in the fourteenth century.

Ringed by the Tatars in the east and the Lithuanians in the west, the Russian state proceeded to consolidate its holdings (Fig. 9–8). Political leadership had passed to the small principality of Moscow, or Muscovy. Spurred by the victory (1380) of Dmitri Donskoi over the Tatars, the Muscovite state expanded through the fifteenth century, absorbing the other Russian principalities and, in 1478, absorbed Novgorod with its vast northern holdings. Under Ivan III, who reigned from 1462 to 1505, Muscovy ceased to pay tribute to the Golden Horde (which had disintegrated into the Tatar khanates of Kazan, Astrakhan, Sibir, and the Crimea) and began to call itself the "Russian" state. Ivan IV (the Terrible), who reigned from

1533 to 1584, was the first to assume the title of tsar (in 1547).

With the consolidation of the Russian state completed, Ivan embarked upon the initial conquests of non-Russian territory. The weakened Tatar khanates of Kazan (1552) and Astrakhan (1556) fell and the Volga became for the first time an all-Russian river. Samara (the present Kuibyshev) in 1586, Tsaritsyn (the present Volgograd) in 1589, and Saratov in 1590 were founded in rapid succession as the first Russian outposts on the lower Volga.

On the western slopes of the Urals, the Stroganovs, a landed family of salt and fur merchants, eyed with envy the reputed riches beyond the Urals. On their initiative, the Cossack Yermak and his band crossed the Urals in 1581 and subdued the Tatar khanate of Sibir, on the lower Irtysh River. Other Cossacks followed and penetrated rapidly eastward by land and river, building a string of small fortified posts (*ostrogs*) and levying fur tribute from the sparse indigenous population. In less than 60 years, the vast reaches of what came to be known as Siberia were traversed and the Pacific shores reached by 1640.

Following a period of chaos, the "Time of Troubles," marked by the appearance of pretenders (the false Dmitris) and by Swedish and Polish-Lithuanian intervention, Russia rallied again in 1613 under Michael, the first of the Romanovs. In a series of wars against Poland during the seventeenth century, the Russians even succeeded in annexing the left-bank Ukraine and Kiev.

However, the country was still a semi-oriental state. Medieval in culture and outlook, it was not regarded as a member of the European community of nations. In its economic development Russia was far behind the European West, and its distrust of foreign ways and innovations kept it ignorant and isolated. Whatever industry had been developed was concentrated in the Moscow region. There were a number of ironworks based on Tula ore, linen, leather, and other handicrafts. Salt, obtained at Solikamsk on

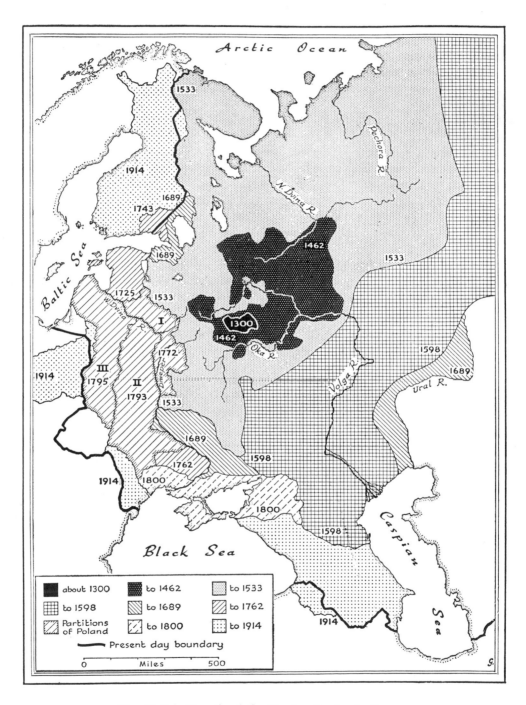

Fig. 9–8. Growth of the Russian Empire in Europe.

the Kama River and Solvychegodsk on the Vychegda River (*sol* is the Russian word for "salt"), was an important article of trade. Grain and flax were the leading agricultural products; fur-bearing animals were hunted in the northeast and in Siberia, while grazing was the main activity in the southeastern steppe adjoining the lower Volga. Except for Astrakhan, on the closed-in Caspian Sea, the only maritime outlet was Archangel, through which English merchants had established trade links in the late sixteenth century.

It remained for Peter I (the Great), who reigned from 1689 to 1725, to revolutionize Russia politically, economically, and culturally. Peter, who was the first to assume the title of emperor, westernized Russia by a series of reforms that were imposed on the people by the most stringent measures. He created a Russian navy, modernized the army, founded the first major industries, and recast the administrative organization of the country. Moved by the desire to make Russia a maritime European power, Peter directed his efforts at territorial expansion toward the Baltic Sea. In the Northern War, he wrested Estonia and Livonia from Sweden and shifted the Russian capital from Moscow to his newly founded St. Petersburg, a "window on Europe." He also began the push toward the Black Sea and succeeded in briefly winning (1696–1711) the fortress of Azov from the Crimean Tatars, but it remained for his successors to reach the Black Sea on a broad front. Peter the Great also temporarily gained hold (1723–32) of Baku from Persia.

It was particularly in the economic sphere that Peter's achievements were remarkable from the geographic point of view. He began the industrialization of the Urals, establishing a number of copper and iron smelters and arms factories to supply his troops. Yekaterinburg (the present Sverdlovsk) in 1723, Yegoshikha (the present Perm) in 1722, and Nizhni Tagil in 1725 were founded at this time. A Russian shipbuilding industry was developed, with yards at St. Peters-

burg and Archangel, as well as at Voronezh (on the Don) and Kazan (on the Volga), while the Vyshnevolotsk Canal, the first to link the upper Volga with the Baltic Sea, was built from 1709 to 1722. The reorientation of Western European trade, which began to flow predominantly through St. Petersburg, led to the gradual decline of Archangel in the north.

Following Peter's death, a number of inferior rulers kept Russian achievements static, but the country soon became a leading European power under Catherine II (the Great). Under her "enlightened despotism," Russia secured the lion's share in the successive partitions of Poland (1772, 1793, 1795), reaching approximately the present Soviet boundary, with the exception of Galicia, Bessarabia, and East Prussia. Catherine's wars against Turkey were equally successful, and, by the treaties of Kutchuk-Kainardji (1774), the surrender of the Crimean khanate (1783), and the treaty of Jassy (1791), Russia conquered the southern steppe and reached the Black Sea between the lower Kuban River and the Dniester. The Russian colonization of Alaska also dates from Catherine's reign.

Under Catherine's successors, Russia became involved in the French Revolutionary, later Napoleonic, wars which culminated in Napoleon's disastrous march on Moscow. Among the territorial acquisitions in the early nineteenth century were the greater part of the Caucasus (1801–13), Finland (1809), Bessarabia (1812), and, following the Congress of Vienna (1815), the Grand Duchy of Warsaw (Russian Poland). Except for minor changes, Russia's European frontiers were to remain unaltered until World War I.

Economically, Russia underwent a great transformation in the nineteenth century. The agricultural frontier was expanded with the settlement of the rich chernozem zone of the southern steppe, which began to yield hard-grained export wheat and sugar beets. With the construction of ports on the nearby Black Sea (Odessa, Nikolayev, Mariupol,

Novorossisk), an active export trade in grains began to develop during the nineteenth century. This flow was speeded after the building of railroads. The first long line linked St. Petersburg and Moscow in the 1850's, and a rail net developed in radial fashion around centrally located Moscow. In addition to those in the old industrial region of the Urals, manufacturing complexes developed at St. Petersburg (mainly metal fabricating, based on imported raw materials) and in the Moscow-Ivanovo belt, where textile mills were supplied first by foreign, later by Central-Asian, cotton. The development of the use of metallurgical coke led to the decline of the once-flourishing charcoal-based metallurgy in the Urals and to the rapid rise of the coking coal of the Donets Basin and the nearby iron-mining district at Krivoi Rog in the Ukraine. In addition to the Black Sea grain ports, Russian foreign trade was handled through the Baltic ports of Libau (Libava), Riga, and Reval (Tallinn), as well as St. Petersburg. The development of the northern lumber industry for export also gave new impetus to the port of Archangel.

These were, in very broad terms, the conditions that existed on the eve of World War I, which Russia entered on the side of the Allies. The territorial adjustments that followed the war and the Russian Revolution of 1917 were outlined at the beginning of this chapter. The considerable economic transformation that followed the establishment of the Soviet regime is described below in the section on Russia's present economic life.

Evolution of the Political-Administrative Structure

We have noted that Peter the Great was the first Russian ruler to introduce (in 1708) a modern administrative structure into the expanding Russian Empire, creating large internal divisions known as governments (*guberniyas*). The first such divisions were the governments of Moscow, Ingermanland (renamed St. Petersburg in 1710), Archangel, Kiev, Smolensk, Kazan, Azov, and Siberia. The number of units increased steadily through the eighteenth and nineteenth centuries, in part through the incorporation of new territories, but essentially as the result of the subdivision of originally larger units. The governments were divided into *uyezds,* and these in turn into volosts. In 1917, on the eve of the Revolution, the Russian Empire consisted of 101 governments, 812 *uyezds,* and 16,760 volosts.

Although the tsarist system of local government cannot be described as static, the changes in the structure seldom reflected reorganization for economic-geographic purposes. The creation of new units or the abolition of existing divisions was usually predicated on purely administrative or military criteria. This is especially obvious in view of the later Soviet reorientation of the administrative system on strictly economic grounds. To cite a typical example of the lack of economic dynamism in the tsarist system, let us consider the case of Ivanovo-Voznesensk (now called simply Ivanovo). This city, a major cotton-milling center northeast of Moscow, had a population of 54,208 according to the census of 1897. Although it was the largest city within the government of Vladimir, it remained relegated administratively to the rank of a minor provincial town within Shuya *uyezd* of the Vladimir government. One of the first administrative measures of the Soviet regime was to create a new government with Ivanovo-Voznesensk as its center.

The profound changes that occurred in Russia following the Bolshevik Revolution of 1917 were closely reflected in the political-administrative structure. The process of territorial change took place along two parallel lines: (1) creation of national autonomous units for non-Russian ethnic groups, and (2) reform of the administrative-territorial units along economic lines.

In the late nineteenth century about 100 distinct ethnic groups inhabited the territory of the Russian Empire. According to the 1897 census, out of a total population of 130 million, only 43 per cent were reported as

Great Russians. As a result of this circumstance, the young Soviet regime proclaimed in the very first days of the Revolution the "Declaration of Rights of the Peoples of Russia." This act guaranteed (1) the equality and sovereignty of the peoples of Russia; (2) their right to self-determination, even to the extent of secession and the formation of an independent state; (3) the abolition of all national and national-religious privileges and restrictions; and (4) the free development of national minorities and ethnic groups inhabiting Russian territory. Following this declaration and subsequent legislation, the formation of national autonomous units proceeded rapidly, though it now appears clear that these ideals have not been fully put into practice.

The Russian Soviet Federated Socialist Republic and the Ukrainian Soviet Socialist Republic were proclaimed in 1917. After an interval of civil war, the Belorussian S.S.R. and the German Volga and Bashkir autonomous republics were organized. In 1922, the Georgian, Armenian, and Azerbaidzhan republics were joined to form the Transcaucasian S.F.S.R. Finally, in December, 1922, the Russian, Transcaucasian, Ukrainian, and Belorussian republics were joined in the Union of Soviet Socialist Republics. By that time about twenty lesser autonomous units had also been created.

While the formation of autonomous national units was proceeding during the early years of the Soviet regime, plans were laid for the reform of administrative units within ethnically homogeneous areas. This reform was essentially a reorganization of the then-existing structure into integrated economic units. In 1922, at the start of the New Economic Policy of relaxed state control, there began the gradual transition from the former structure of government-*uyezd*-volost to a new territorial system of *oblast*-okrug-*rayon*. By 1930, the last government had been abolished. Originally only a few large economic regions of the *oblast* (or *krai*) type were to be constituted in the U.S.S.R. Large size was soon found to be an obstacle to efficient administration, however, and during the late 1920's smaller first-order divisions were formed, and the intermediate unit—the administrative okrug—was dropped in 1930. The *rayons* were subordinated directly to the first-order unit, whether *oblast, krai,* or republic.

The present administrative-territorial structure of the U.S.S.R. has thus evolved along two parallel, though closely integrated, patterns: the creation of national autonomous units and the reform of the administrative divisions for purposes of economic management.

It is the principle of national autonomy that governs the division of the U.S.S.R. into the so-called union republics, which are the country's primary units (Fig. 9–9). These republics are said to form a voluntary union of nations and to reserve the right of free secession, according to the Soviet constitutions of 1924 (Article 4) and 1936 (Article 17). Of course, in view of the purely nominal autonomy, no union republic has ever raised or is likely to raise the question of secession. From the original 6 union republics at the time of the formation of the U.S.S.R., their number increased to 11 at the time of the promulgation of the 1936 Constitution, and to 16 in 1940, with the formation of the Karelo-Finnish and Moldavian republics and the accession of the 3 Baltic states. The Karelo-Finnish republic was reincorporated into the Russian S.F.S.R. in 1956, and the present number of union republics is 15. All except the Russian S.F.S.R. are known as Soviet Socialist Republics, the form "Socialist Soviet Republic" being no longer in use. The Russian S.F.S.R., which is the leading and most important republic in every respect, is a federation of a number of major nationalities associated with the Russian nation and therefore continues to be known as a Soviet Federated Socialist Republic, or simply as the Russian Federation.

The principle of national autonomy determines also the formation of lesser units, below the rank of union republic. These are the autonomous republic, the autonomous

Fig. 9-9. Soviet union republics

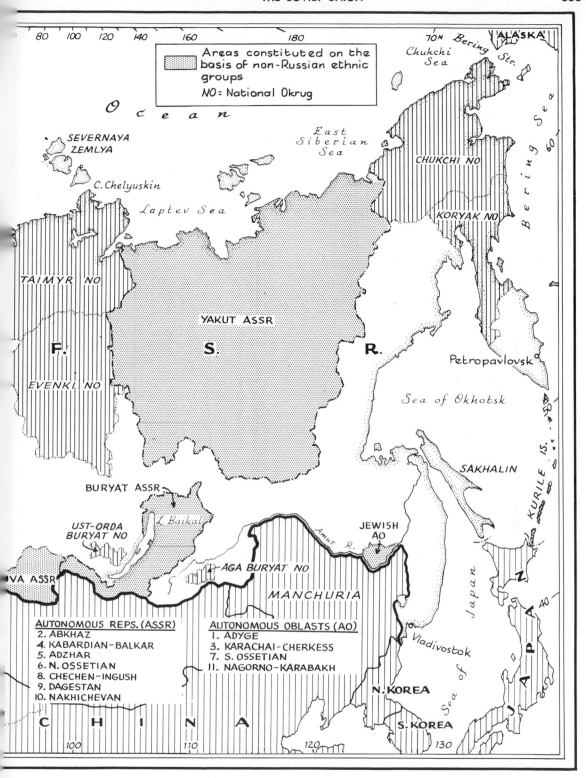

Areas constituted on the basis of non-Russian ethnic groups

NO = National Okrug

ALASKA

Bering Str.

Chukchi Sea

East Siberian Sea

Bering Sea

O c e a n

70N

60

CHUKCHI NO

SEVERNAYA ZEMLYA

KORYAK NO

C. Chelyuskin

Laptev Sea

TAIMYR NO

F.   S.   R.

YAKUT ASSR

Petropavlovsk

Sea of Okhotsk

EVENKI NO

SAKHALIN

KURILE IS.

BURYAT ASSR

L. Baikal

UST-ORDA BURYAT NO

JEWISH AO

Amur R.

AGA BURYAT NO

TUVA ASSR

Z

MANCHURIA

J A P A N

40

AUTONOMOUS REPS. (ASSR)
2. ABKHAZ
4. KABARDIAN-BALKAR
5. ADZHAR
6. N. OSSETIAN
8. CHECHEN-INGUSH
9. DAGESTAN
10. NAKHICHEVAN

AUTONOMOUS OBLASTS (AO)
1. ADYGE
3. KARACHAI-CHERKESS
7. S. OSSETIAN
11. NAGORNO-KARABAKH

Vladivostok

Sea of Japan

N. KOREA

C H I N A

100   110   120   130

S. KOREA

and other autonomous areas.

oblast, and the national okrug. The autonomous republic is subordinated directly to the union republic in which it is located and is formed by relatively important ethnic groups. The Russian S.F.S.R., as would be expected, contains the greatest number of autonomous republics—16 out of a total of 20. The autonomous *oblast,* formed by less important minorities than those in the preceding category, is subordinated to a *krai* within the Russian S.F.S.R. and directly to the union republic in the case of the lesser constituent units of the U.S.S.R. Out of a total of 8 autonomous *oblasts* 5 are contained within the Russian S.F.S.R. The national okrug is the lowest category of the major types of the autonomous units. It occurs only in the Russian S.F.S.R. and forms the basis of organization primarily of small Siberian ethnic groups.

The various categories of autonomous administrative units form what has been called the "nationalities ladder." Theoretically, in accordance with the Soviet nationalities policy, an ethnic group is assigned an autonomous category in accordance with its population and its degree of political and cultural advance. Then, depending on future growth and development, the group may ascend the rungs of the ladder to higher categories of autonomous units. Four autonomous republics—the Kazakh, Kirghiz, Karelian, and Moldavian units—have been raised to the status of full constituent republic during the three decades of Soviet rule. Of these, the Karelian unit was again demoted in 1956 because of its small size and population. In practice union republics have been created only on the periphery of the Russian S.F.S.R. —in order to enable them to secede if they so desired, according to the Soviet view—and only for groups having more than 1 million people (the Karelo-Finnish S.S.R., with about 600,000 inhabitants, was a notable exception, probably the result of temporary political expediency). As a result of this policy, important ethnic groups within the Russian Federation—such as the Tatar and Bashkir autonomous republics—have little chance of ever achieving the status of union republic, although they may number more than 3 million people.

The greatest number of promotions in autonomous categories has been from autonomous *oblast* to autonomous republic. About ten such transfers took place in the Russian S.F.S.R. during the 1930's. Only in one isolated case—the Kirghiz group—was an advance through two successive categories achieved: the Kirghiz Autonomous *Oblast,* formed in 1924, became an autonomous republic in 1926 and a full union republic in 1936. However, with the exception of the Karelian and Moldavian groups, no group has been promoted to the status of union republic since the promulgation of the 1936 Constitution, and it would appear that at least the autonomous aspect of the Soviet administrative structure has assumed a certain stability after the early dynamic period.

National autonomy in Soviet administration is reflected in the organization of the highest legislative body of the U.S.S.R.—the Supreme Soviet of the U.S.S.R. This body consists of two chambers, the Soviet of Nationalities and the Soviet of the Union. According to the Constitution, members of the Soviet of Nationalities are elected on the basis of the major autonomous divisions—32 (until 1966, 25) for a union republic, 11 for an autonomous republic, 5 for an autonomous *oblast,* and one for each national okrug. In the Soviet of the Union, on the other hand, the representation is based on the population at large, with one deputy for every 300,000 inhabitants. In the union republics and the autonomous republics, the Supreme Soviets are unicameral. There, election proceeds on a population basis only, with the size of an electoral constituency varying from 150,000 (Russian S.F.S.R.) to 2,000 (Nakhichevan A.S.S.R.).

Parallel to the autonomous aspect of the Soviet administrative system is the economic-administrative unit. Ethnically homogeneous territories are divided into units delimited so as to represent a well-integrated economic region. Ideally, such regions produce one or more commodities for export to other parts of the U.S.S.R., while remaining as self-sufficient as possible in basic consumer goods, construction materials, and similar items. The *oblast* is the largest type of economic unit and is found in most of the union republics. The Russian S.F.S.R. also contains the *krai*, which has essentially the same status as an *oblast*. The existence of a *krai* is determined by the fact that it contains an autonomous *oblast*.

Rural local government resides in the *rayons*, villages, and other local bodies, such as nomad headquarters. The *rayon*, first formed in 1924, is intended to be a miniature *oblast*. The same economic principles guide its creation, though on a much reduced scale. All major administrative units, such as *oblasts, krais,* autonomous divisions, and the lesser union republics, are divided directly into *rayons*. These vary tremendously in area, from nearly 150,000 square miles in the sparsely inhabited Siberian north to less than 100 square miles in the Ukrainian chernozem zone. The village Soviet, and other types of local council, are the smallest rural administrative units and comprise one or more villages, hamlets, or other populated places.

Urban local government resides in the cities and towns, the latter being called city-type settlements and workers' settlements in Soviet terminology. Just as in the case of the territorial units, economic considerations guide the creation of the urban centers. The establishment of an industry or the opening of a mine in a previously rural agricultural community generally leads to the establishment of a workers' settlement or a city-type settlement. In the Russian S.F.S.R., the criterion for the creation of such a town is a minimum population of 3,000 and 85 per cent non-farm employment. As the locality grows and its population and production increase, it may be converted into a city, which in turn may be subordinated successively to the *rayon*, the *oblast*, or *krai*, or even to the republic. The progressive rise of urban centers is thus an excellent clue to industrial development.

POPULATION

In discussing the national-autonomous aspect of the Soviet administrative structure we have already indicated one of the key features of the population of the U.S.S.R., that is, its multinational aspect. Other characteristics that distinguish the demographic development of the U.S.S.R. from that of other European countries are: (1) a relatively high rate of natural increase—10.9 per thousand in 1966; (2) the spectacular urbanization, which went hand in hand with the forced-draft industrialization starting in the early 1930's; and (3) the state-sponsored internal migration of large segments of the population.

With a population of 235.5 million in mid-1967, and increasing at a rate of 2 million a year, the Soviet Union ranks third in population among the world's nations, after China and India. Of the total, 179 million live in the European part of the U.S.S.R. (including the Urals) and 56.5 million in the Asian part.

From the long-range point of view the most important characteristic of the population has been its rapid natural increase. From 1913 to the first Soviet census of 1926, the population of the country (within its 1926 limits) increased from 139.3 million to 147 million. This increase was achieved through the difficult periods of World War I, the Russian Revolution, and the subsequent civil war. During the following 13 peacetime years until the census of 1939, about 23 million were added to the Soviet population, which thus reached 170.6 million.

During 1939 and 1940, the U.S.S.R. annexed large sections of Eastern Europe, including the Baltic states of Estonia, Latvia, and Lithuania, eastern Poland, northern Bucovina, and Bessarabia, with an estimated population of about 21.5 million as of 1939. This brought the total population of the U.S.S.R. to 192.1 million as of 1939 (including 1.4 million in areas which were returned to Poland in 1945). On the basis of natural rate of increase (13.2 per thousand in 1940), it can be estimated that the population of the Soviet Union was about 197 million in early 1941 and, if there had been no war, would have risen to about 212 million by early 1946. Actually the population of the Soviet Union at the end of World War II is now estimated to have been 170–175 million. In other words, the wartime effects, including military losses, excess civilian deaths, a deficit in births, and forced or voluntary emigration, set back the Soviet population by about 40 million. The Soviet Union again reached its 1941 population level by about 1955. In recent years, the population has been growing at the rate of 2 million a year. The Soviet birth rate has been about 18 per thousand annually, while the death rate has been about 7 per thousand.

The effect of wartime losses and emigration has been especially pronounced in the western areas of the Soviet Union which were occupied by the Germans in World War II.[3] In 1968 one of the western republics that was completely overrun by the Germans—the Belorussian S.S.R.—still had not recovered its prewar population level. Others, such as Estonia, Latvia, and Lithuania, just barely exceeded the 1939 level. The republics that escaped German occupation, by contrast, show larger population increases. This is especially true in the cases of Armenia, whose population was swelled by the return of several hundred thousand Armenians from abroad during the postwar period; Uzbekistan, which received many evacuated industries and their labor force during the war; and Kazakhstan, the site of large-scale industrialization and agricultural development in the postwar period.

A noteworthy characteristic of the Soviet population is the predominance of females over males. The percentage of females was 52 in the censuses of 1926 and 1939, and rose to 55 in the census of 1959. This male-female ratio reflects the huge male-population losses in wars, especially in World War II, and applies particularly to the older-age groups.

[3] For statistical data, see Appendix III, Tables 8a–8f, pp. 654–56.

According to the preliminary report of the 1959 census, the percentages of males and females are more or less identical in age groups below 32 years, which have not been affected by wartime losses.

Rural and urban settlement. The share of the urban population has steadily increased under the Soviet Union's industrialization program. Before the start of this program in 1928, the urban percentage had been relatively stable at 18 per cent. Subsequently it rose to 33 per cent in the 1939 census, and to 48 per cent in the 1959 census. It was 55 per cent in 1967. The geographical distribution of both the urban and rural population is extremely irregular, as one would expect from the diversity of climatic and other physical-geographic factors. These disparities in density, while particularly marked in the Asian part of the U.S.S.R., are evident also in Europe. A dense-population wedge with its base on the Leningrad-Odessa line penetrates eastward on the population map, coming to a point in the middle Urals and continuing in a narrow ribbon along the Trans-Siberian Railroad. The densely inhabited heartland of the European U.S.S.R. coincides roughly with the mixed deciduous-coniferous forest zone and the chernozem steppe. The density is generally more than 50 per square mile. Lower densities are found in the coniferous taiga of the European north and Siberia and in the semidesert and desert of southeast-European Russia and Central Asia.

In these sparsely populated areas, rural settlements lie along communication lines, notably rivers and, more recently, railroads. The gravitation of population to newly built railroads was dramatized during World War II by the construction of the North Pechora Railroad leading to the coal-mining center of Vorkuta in the European north. This rail line, which cut diagonally across the relatively dense population bands along river routes, in turn became an artery attracting settlement. In these northern forests, rural population centers tend to be small agglomerations. By contrast, in the southern steppe, villages are traditionally large, frequently reaching a population of 15,000 or more in the so-called *stanitsas* of the Kuban Cossacks.

Collectivization of agriculture in the 1930's produced a revolution in the rural settlement pattern. In general, the trend was toward concentration of the population of scattered villages and hamlets in centrally located collective farm settlements characterized by a rectilinear main street, orchards and gardens, and administration and recreation buildings of the collective. Hamlets and isolated farmsteads were gradually abolished. The collective-farm mergers in 1950, which were designed to combine the already substantial farms into even larger units, also presaged the creation of even more centralized farm settlements or "rural cities" (*agrogorod*). The creation of such urbanized farm centers met opposition and was not pressed, although collective farms were merged as planned. The *agrogorod* plan remains the ultimate goal of Soviet rural-settlement planners and may yet be realized as part of their agricultural reforms.

While the future of Soviet rural-settlement patterns is still in doubt, the trend in urban settlement can be assessed more precisely. The rapid rise of urban population under the Soviet regime can be ascribed to several factors. Foremost has been the rural-urban migration needed to fill the growing manpower need of Soviet industry. A large part of the urban increase was of course contributed by the natural increase of the urban population itself. Moreover, changes in the definition of urban centers led to the reclassification of hundreds of villages as urban communities, in accordance with the Soviet concept of the urban center. Moreover, new urban centers developed from virtually nothing, as a result of the construction of new industrial plants or mines. One of the most spectacular examples of such Soviet urban growth is Karaganda, an insignificant village as late as 1930 that became a city of 166,000 in 1939 and expanded further to 500,000 in 1967. Equally impressive is the rise of the steel center of Magnitogorsk in the Urals,

which was founded in 1931 and rose to a population of 146,000 in 1939 and 357,000 in 1967.

Industrial areas of the Soviet Union where the urban population accounts for 75 per cent or more of the total include the Moscow and Leningrad areas, the Urals, the Donets Basin, the Kuznetsk Basin, and the Karaganda area. Other urban centers are scattered throughout the country wherever mining or industrial activity has caused the formation of such agglomeration. In 1967, the Soviet Union had 199 cities with a population of 100,000 or more each, compared with 79 such cities in 1939. The 30 largest cities and their 1939 and 1968 populations are shown in Table 8b (page 654).

One of the factors in the rapid urbanization of the U.S.S.R. is the facility with which the Soviet regime has regulated internal migration in accordance with state policies. The transfer of large numbers of people has been in part compulsory, but has also been effected through higher incentives such as increased pay and better housing, in areas that had a shortage of industrial labor. Such regions include the European north and vast sections of Siberia and the Far East, where climatic and other physical conditions are inhospitable and do not attract settlement.

Another type of compulsory migration occurred during World War II, when a number of ethnic groups accused of collaboration with the Germans and of fifth-column activity were forcibly removed from their historic homelands and exiled to Siberia and Central Asia. These groups were the Volga Germans, the Crimean Tatars, the Kalmyks, and, in the northern Caucasus, the Karachai, Balkar, Chechen, and Ingush peoples. Under the current liberalized regime, these peoples regained their civil rights in 1956–57, and most of them returned to their homelands. Only the Volga Germans and the Crimean Tartars were not restored to their historical areas of settlement.

Another mass migration was the settling by Russians from densely inhabited regions of central European Russia in the annexed areas of northern East Prussia and southern

Sakhalin, from which the German and Japanese populations, respectively, had been expelled after the war.

Ethnic groups. Although the number of ethnic groups in the Soviet Union is generally put at 100 to 150, the so-called multinational character of the population has to be considered in proper perspective. In this connection two facts are of the greatest importance. These are the dominant position of the Russian people and the relatively small number of national groups with, say, more than 20,000 persons.

No exact figure on the number of nationalities is meaningful. The 1926 census recognized 188 individual groups, but in a few cases numbers were either not reported or only a few individuals were reported for a specific ethnic group. In the incomplete returns of the 1939 census, in which a number of important Siberian peoples were not reported, the total number of nationalities with more than 20,000 persons was 49. When the major missing Siberian groups (Yakuts, Buryats, Khanty or Ostyaks, and Evenki or Tungus) and the Tuvinians, who were incorporated into the U.S.S.R. in 1944, are taken into account, the number of ethnic groups with more than 20,000 persons was 54. The 1959 census listed 108 ethnic groups including 68 with more than 20,000 persons each. The most meaningful classification of the Soviet Union's ethnic groups is based on their languages. The major language families in the Soviet Union are tabulated on page 559 with the number of persons in each group according to the 1959 census.

The Russians constitute more than half the total population of the U.S.S.R., with the ratio somewhat higher (about 60 per cent) in Asia and somewhat lower in Europe. As would be expected, the percentage of Russians is greatest (83 per cent in 1959) within the territory of the Russian S.F.S.R., while in the other union republics and in some of the lesser autonomous units they constitute generally less than 25 per cent of the population. With the Ukrainians and the Belorussians, who form 18 per cent and 4.5 per cent, respectively, of the Soviet population, the Slavic element stands out clearly as the dominant group with nearly 75 per cent of the total number of people within the Soviet Union. Lesser Slavic peoples are the Poles, who are scattered among the Belorussians and the Ukrainians, and the Bulgarians, who live largely in southern Bessarabia.

Next in importance are the Turkic and Finnic language families. The more numerous Turkic peoples (about 8 per cent of the total) live largely in Asia, and the Finnic peoples (less than 3 per cent) primarily in Europe. The Finnic peoples occupy the tundra and forest, while the Turkic groups extend across steppe and desert.

The Tatars, the most important European branch of the Turkic family, are concentrated in the Volga region, where they have an autonomous republic, but are also widely dispersed through the rest of the country. The related Crimean Tatars, estimated at 200,000 on the eve of World War II, were ousted from the Crimea in 1944 because of collaboration with the Germans in World War II and were resettled in Soviet Central Asia. There they regained their civil rights in 1956. Adjoining the Volga Tatars are the Bashkirs, a Turkic steppe people that settled on the western slopes of the Urals in the tenth century. Like the Volga Tatars, who are descended from the fifteenth-century Kazan khanate, the Bashkirs are organized politically in an autonomous republic. The third major Turkic people in the European U.S.S.R. are the Azerbaidzhani Turks in Transcaucasia on the Caspian Sea. Although their language is closely related to that of the Osmanli Turks, the Azerbaidzhanis have acquired their culture and the Shiite Moslem religion from the Persians who dominated the present Soviet Azerbaidzhan until the early nineteenth century. The leading Turkic groups in the Asian U.S.S.R. are the Uzbeks, Kazakhs, Kirghiz, and Turkmen in Central Asia, and the Yakuts in Siberia.

Of the Finnic ethnic family, the Volga-Ural division (or the Eastern Finnic branch)

Languages of the USSR

Language Family	Language Subgroup	Major Languages	Number of Persons in the Corresponding Ethnic Group in Thousands (1959 census)
Indo-European	Slavic	Russian	114,114
		Ukrainian	37,253
		Belorussian	7,913
		Polish	1,380
		Bulgarian	324
	Baltic	Latvian	1,400
		Lithuanian	2,326
	Iranian	Tadzhik	1,397
		Ossetian	413
		Tat	11
		Kurdish	59
	Armenian	Armenian	2,787
	Germanic	German	1,620
		Yiddish	2,268 *
	Romance	Moldavian (Romanian)	2,214
Turkic		Tatar	4,968
		Bashkir	989
		Azerbaidzhani	2,940
		Uzbek	6,015
		Kazakh	3,622
		Kirghiz	969
		Turkmen	1,002
		Yakut	237
		Karakalpak	173
		Tuvinian	100
Finnic	Eastern branch	Komi	431
		Mordvinian	1,285
		Chuvash	1,470
		Mari	504
		Udmurt	625
		Nentsy (Samoyedes)	23
	Western branch	Estonian	989
		Karelian (Finnish)	260
		Lappish	2
Caucasian	Southern	Georgian	2,692
	Northern	Abkhaz	65
		Cherkess (Circassian)	30
		Kabardian	204
		Chechen-Ingush	527
		Dagestan languages	944
Mongolian		Buryat	253
		Kalmyk	106
Manchurian		Evenki (Tungus)	25
Paleoasiatic		Minor Siberian languages	

* Only 21.5 per cent of ethnic Jews declared in the 1959 census that their native language was Yiddish. In almost all other groups, 80–90 per cent or more of the members declared to be speakers of their native languages.

is the most numerous. These peoples live on the western slopes of the Urals and along the middle Volga River, in close contact with the Tatars and the Bashkirs. The leading representatives in numbers are concentrated along the Volga. They are the Mordvinians (or Mordvians) and the Chuvash (the latter with considerable Turkic linguistic influence) on the right bank, and the Mari (formerly called Cheremiss) and the Udmurt (formerly called Votyak) on the left bank. Finnic primarily from the linguistic point of view, these peoples have acquired a predominantly Russian culture through centuries of contact with the Slavs, with some survivals from their Finnic ancestors and the ancient Khazars and Volga Bulgars. To the north of this Finnic concentration, along the northern Urals, are the more primitive Komi (formerly Zyryan) and the closely related Komi-Permyaks (or Permian Komi). Along the shore of the Arctic Ocean, in the far north of the European U.S.S.R., are the Nentsy (formerly known as Samoyedes), who are distantly related to the Finnic family. With the exception of the Nentsy and the Komi-Permyaks, who are organized into national okrugs (the only such autonomous units in the European U.S.S.R.), the Eastern Finns form autonomous republics within the Soviet administrative scheme.

The Western Finns along the Baltic region are considerably fewer within the confines of the U.S.S.R. The main group are the Estonians, who came entirely under Soviet control in 1940 and constitute the northernmost of the three Baltic republics. They are traditionally Lutheran Protestants and have long been under the influence of Germanic culture. The next Finnic group, the Karelians, number only about one-fourth of the 1 million Estonians. They are very closely related to the true Finns, whose language they speak, but are of Russian culture and traditionally Russian Orthodox. In conjunction with the true Finns, who are few in number (93,000 in 1959) in the U.S.S.R., the Karelians constituted from 1940 to 1956 the Karelo-Finnish S.S.R. Since then they have

returned to their original status of autonomous republic. In the Kola Peninsula live the Soviet Lapps (known as *Saamy* in the Soviet terminology). Finally, the Western Finns include a number of small splinter groups in the vicinity of Lake Ladoga and Lake Onega. These are the Veps, the Vote, and the Izhora (Inger), numbering no more than 50,000 in 1959.

The two southern Baltic states, Latvia and Lithuania, are inhabited by peoples of the Baltic language subgroup. The Lutheran Latvians (or Letts) were influenced by a Germanic cultural veneer and are associated in their republic with the closely related Roman Catholic Latgalians of Polish culture. Polish cultural influence, typical also for the Lithuanians, dates from the long period of Polish rule in these regions after the sixteenth century.

Farther south along the relatively narrow European isthmus between the Baltic Sea and the Black Sea we find at its southern end another important non-Slavic minority, the Moldavians (Romance subgroup). Russia's century-long control over the Moldavians in Bessarabia after 1812 added some Russian strains to their essentially Latin and Romanian background. As a result the Moldavians use the Romanian language written in the Cyrillic script. After World War I only about 250,000 Moldavians remained within the U.S.S.R. and constituted the Moldavian Autonomous S.S.R. within the Ukraine, on the left bank of the Dniester River, then the Soviet-Romanian frontier. Following the acquisition of Bessarabia in 1940, the number of Moldavians under Soviet control rose to more than 2 million and their political organization was raised to that of a union republic.

By far the greatest ethnic diversity, exceeding even that of the middle-Volga region, exists in the Caucasus. Russians having settled predominantly in the steppes of the northern Caucasus, the largest minority groups are found on the southern slopes, in Transcaucasia. Here, in addition to the Azerbaidzhani Turks, are the Armenian and southern-Caucasian (Georgian) subgroups, each constituted as a union republic. The Armenians form a distinct linguistic group of the Indo-European family. Settled traditionally around Mount Ararat, within the territories of Russia, Turkey, and Persia (Iran), the Armenians were greatly decimated between 1894 and 1915 by systematic Turkish policies of extermination. As a result of these trials, the bulk of the population remained in Russian Armenia, a considerable minority in northwestern Iran, and the rest scattered through the lands of the Middle East and other parts of the world. Of the present estimated Armenian world population of 3.5 million, two-thirds live in the U.S.S.R. However, only 40 per cent of the Soviet Armenians live in the Armenian S.S.R. proper, with the remainder scattered through the rest of the Soviet Union. After World War II, the Soviet government invited Armenian émigrés to return to Soviet Armenia. About 200,000 émigré Armenians returned, chiefly from the Middle East. In addition to their own union republic, the Armenians also constitute the majority population (89 per cent in 1926) of an exclave—the Nagorno-Karabakh Autonomous *Oblast*—within the Azerbaidzhan S.S.R.

The Georgians in the U.S.S.R. numbered 2,692,000 persons in 1959. They are concentrated in their relatively homogeneous republic and constitute the leading member of the Caucasian language family. Within the Georgian S.S.R., the Mingrelian, Svanetian, and Adzhar groups are associated with Georgian in the south-Caucasian languages. The Adzhars, who are Georgians of Moslem religion and influenced by Turkish culture, form a separate autonomous republic within Georgia. Another Georgian dependent unit —the Abkhaz Autonomous S.S.R.—is the chief representative of the north-Caucasian languages on the southern slopes of the mountains. The other members, considerably dissected by areas of Russian settlement, are the Cherkess (Circassian) people, also known by their own native appellation of Adighe; the related Kabardians (or Kabar-

dinians); and the diverse mountain groups of Dagestan, including the Lesghians, Avars, Darghins, Laks, and Andi. The Chechen and Ingush peoples, who temporarily lost their ethnic identity after World War II, also are members of the north-Caucasian subgroup.

Several peoples of the Caucasus are members of the Iranian subgroup of the Indo-European language family. These are primarily the Ossetians, settled in the central part of the Caucasus, where they constitute the North Ossetian Autonomous S.S.R. of the Russian S.F.S.R. and the South Ossetian Autonomous *Oblast* of the Georgian S.S.R. The Ossetians are believed to be descendants of the ancient Alans, a steppe people of the northern Caucasus, last reported at the time of the Mongol-Tatar raids of the thirteenth century. Smaller Iranian splinter groups are the Talysh, in the Talysh (or Lenkoran) lowland adjoining the Caspian Sea; the Tats, at the eastern foot of the Caucasus, in Azerbaidzhan; and the Kurds, on the slopes of Mount Ararat, in Armenia.

Several ethnic groups of the Soviet Union are not associated with any political autonomous divisions commensurate with their numbers. The largest of these groups is the Jews, the Germans, and the Poles. The Jews, reported to number 3,020,141 in the 1939 census (then the seventh-largest group), were estimated to have increased to 5,000,000 on the eve of World War II as a result of the annexation by the U.S.S.R. of eastern Polish areas with a large Jewish population. Following the massacre of the Jews by the Germans during the war, the Jews numbered 2,268,000 at the 1959 census. A separate Jewish Autonomous *Oblast*, commonly known as Birobidzhan, for its capital, was established in 1930 on the Amur River in the Soviet Far East to encourage Jews to settle in an area of their own. However no mass migration developed from the traditional Jewish settlement areas of Belorussia and the western Ukraine or from the large urban Jewish population scattered through the major cities of the U.S.S.R. In 1959, there were only 14,000 Jews in the Jewish Autonomous *Oblast* out of a total population of 163,000. By contrast there were 240,000 Jews in Moscow and 170,000 in Leningrad. The Jews were deprived of their cultural privileges (newspapers, books, and schools and other Yiddish institutions) by Stalin in an anti-Jewish campaign in 1948. Some of these cultural rights (Yiddish publications, traveling performing groups) were restored after the middle 1950's, but the facilities are still inferior to those granted to many of the smaller ethnic groups.

The Soviet Union's ethnic Germans, who numbered 1,620,000 in 1959, were deprived of their autonomous republic on the Volga River after the Nazi German invasion in 1941 and did not regain territorial autonomy after the war. However they have again been granted cultural facilities, such as German-language classes, books, newspapers, and radio broadcasts in areas (Kazakhstan, southern Siberia) where they are now concentrated. The number of Poles rose as a result of annexation of former Polish territories in 1939, and amounted to 1,380,000 in 1959. The Poles live mainly along the western borders of the Soviet Union and have also been granted some cultural rights, such as Polish-language newspapers, books, and schools.

Religions. Before the Bolshevik Revolution of 1917, the Russian Orthodox Church was the state church of the Russian Empire, with the tsar as its head. Other religious denominations were tolerated. An abrupt change took place after the revolution, with the separation of church and state and the expropriation of all church property. Atheism, formerly a crime against the state, was welcomed by the new Soviet regime and supported by active antireligious propaganda.

Public places of worship had been a characteristic feature of the urban and rural settlements of Russia. This applied not only to the typical bulbous church towers of the Russian Orthodox Church but also both to the mosques and minarets of Central Asia and to the Lamaist monasteries of Buryat-Mongolia. After the revolution, this feature of the landscape remained in part, though many churches were demolished, and a great number of these places of worship became public buildings, clubs, theaters, libraries, or museums. Moreover, the house of worship has not been considered a necessary element in the planning of collective farm settlements or new industrial and mining towns and has remained in older centers only as a reminder of the past.

The intense antireligious propaganda that swept the Soviet scene during the 1930's was temporarily abandoned during World War II in order to remove any obstacle to the marshaling of all forces against the German invader. The Russian Orthodox Church resumed some of its former authority, but merely as a voice of the Soviet government, and is credited with a considerable share in the mobilization of the Soviet people during the war. After the war antireligious propaganda was resumed, but the major religious denominations of the U.S.S.R. have been maintained in the postwar period.

Thus, while religion has definitely been relegated to a minor position, the Church has not been abolished, and it may prove useful to survey briefly the religious affiliations of the major ethnic groups of the U.S.S.R.

By far the dominant Church is the Russian Orthodox Church, which embraces not only all the Slavs but also the Finnic peoples of the European U.S.S.R. that have been long exposed to Russian culture. Among the Belorussians and Ukrainians there is a considerable Roman Catholic minority, particularly among the people of western Belorussia and the western Ukraine, both annexed from Poland in 1939. Also among the Ukrainians, notably in Transcarpathia, there are adherents to the Uniate rite of the Roman Catholic Church. Roman Catholicism is the predominant denomination of the Lithuanians and the Latgalians, both peoples of Polish cultural background. Lutheran Protestantism is prevalent among the Latvians and Estonians, as well as among the few Finns in the U.S.S.R., whose religion is their chief distinction from their Russian Orthodox Karelian colinguists.

The Armenians and the Georgians each have their own independent Church. The Armenian, also known as Gregorian, is an independent Christian Church with Western and Eastern elements in its rites, while the Georgian is one of the oldest Orthodox Churches of Byzantine heritage. Islam is important in European U.S.S.R. among the Azerbaidzhani Turks, the Tatars, and the Bashkirs, while additional adherents may be found among the Turkic peoples of Central Asia. Mention should be made, finally, of the Buryats of southern Siberia, who are the only representatives of Lamaist Buddhism in the U.S.S.R.

PRESENT ECONOMIC LIFE

Before the Bolshevik Revolution, the Russian Empire had a primarily agrarian economy. Today the U.S.S.R. is an industrial power second only to the United States. While it would be profitless to discuss the question—one that is sometimes raised—of whether Russia would not have made the same progress under the old regime, it is pertinent to recall some of the major developments of Soviet economic history since the revolution.

Soviet Economic History

In the wake of the overthrow of tsarist power came a period (1917–21) of extremist and ruthless measures used by the young Soviet regime in the chaos of civil war and foreign intervention. State control spread rapidly over all phases of the economy; all land and mineral resources were nationalized; industries, means of transportation, and all buildings were declared state property; private banks were merged into the state bank; and a government monopoly over foreign trade was instituted. At the same time, arbitrary food requisitions, mounting inflation, and a confused economic administration created dissatisfaction among the peasants, which, coupled with a decline in industrial discipline among the workers, endangered the very existence of the struggling new state.

In order to appease the peasantry and revive the economy, Lenin initiated the New Economic Policy (NEP), which was in effect a temporary concession to capitalism. Domestic commerce and small- and medium-scale industry were partly returned to private hands, with the government retaining control over all key industries and means of transportation. Under this mixed economy the U.S.S.R. gradually raised its production and by 1928 had regained or exceeded the output of 1913. At the same time the state had expanded its share in the economy and gradually reduced the role of private enterprise through a variety of restrictive measures such as high profit taxes and discrimination in the supply of raw materials and in the use of transportation facilities.

In 1928 the Soviet regime initiated the first of its five-year plans aimed at a sharp increase in industrial output under strict government control and planning. Shortly thereafter began the process of agricultural collectivization. This forcible consolidation of individual farms into cooperatives reached its climax in the early 1930's, in one of the most tempestuous periods of Soviet history, marked by the deportation of rich peasants (kulaks), the slaughter of cattle, and a drop in agricultural production, with a resulting famine in 1931–32.

Nevertheless, under planned conditions, industrial output soared during the first (1928–32) and second (1933–37) five-year plans. Emphasis was placed on heavy industries at the cost of consumer goods. A gradual eastward shift of the industrial center of gravity of the U.S.S.R. resulted in a new geographical distribution of industry. At the same time, agricultural production began to increase, after the upheaval of collectivization, through the application of modern farming methods, mechanization, and similar measures facilitated by the creation of large collective farms.

The third five-year plan (1938–42) was interrupted by the German invasion in June, 1941. Although the principal economic regions of the U.S.S.R. fell to the invader in 1941 and 1942, the results of the industrial expansion of the 1930's bore fruit. Industrial production of the eastern part of the U.S.S.R., dating chiefly from the first two five-year plans, and the removal of some 1,300 plants from the path of the German forces played a key role in enabling the Russians to stem the German advance. This and the subsequent expulsion of the enemy from the U.S.S.R. were aided in no small measure by vital shipments of supplies by the Allies.

The early postwar period was dominated by the fourth five-year plan (1946–50), designed to rebuild the war-damaged economy and to foster the further development of eastern industries untouched by the war. The fifth five-year plan (1951–55) was marked by further increases of production. A sixth five-year plan (1956–60), adopted by the Twentieth Communist Party Congress, in 1956, was scrapped in September, 1957, after unrest in Eastern Europe had forced a review of priorities in economic development. The break in the five-year rhythm necessitated the adoption of a seven-year plan (1959–65) by the Twenty-first Communist Party Congress in 1959. With the promulgation of directives for a new five-year plan by the Twenty-third Party Congress in 1966, for the period 1966–70, Soviet planners once again reverted to the customary length of the planning period.

Agriculture

The present organization of Soviet agriculture is the result of revolution following a long process of evolution. Having been dominated by conditions of serfdom and feudalism until the partial emancipation of 1861, later modified by the reforms of 1906, agriculture in Russia before the revolution was mainly in the hands of more than 13 million peasant households owning 500 million acres and of 30,000 large-estate owners who aggregated 380 million acres. The estates were either in pasture land or tilled by tenant farmers. According to Soviet data, the peasant holdings included 1 million so-called rich farms that averaged 126 acres compared with the average poor farm of 19 acres.

After expropriation of estates in the 1917 revolution and redistribution of land among the peasants, there emerged 25 million small peasant holdings. About 35 per cent of these were classified as poor, 60 per cent as medium wealthy, and 4 to 5 per cent as rich. The so-called rich peasants (kulaks) employed outside labor. On the eve of collectivization in 1928, only 1.7 per cent of the farms were of the collective type. As a result of the mergers in the early 1930's, the 25 million small farms of the 1920's were welded into fewer than 250,000 collectives.

The Soviet agricultural revolution was repeated on a smaller scale in 1939–40 in areas annexed by the U.S.S.R. The redistribution of largely expropriated estates was begun soon after the assumption of Soviet control, was partly canceled under German occupation in World War II, and was resumed by the Russians after the war. Peasant farms in the annexed areas, which included the Baltic states, remained in private ownership until 1949 before being collectivized.

The completion of the collectivization process throughout the Soviet Union was followed in 1950 by a consolidation of collective farms. These mergers took place primarily in areas where the average acreage per collective farm was small; in the central, western, and northern sections of the European U.S.S.R.; in the Caucasus; and in the irrigated areas of Central Asia. The number of collective farms declined from more than 200,000 before 1950 to 37,000 in 1966, both as a result of mergers and because of transformation into state farms.

Unlike collective farms, which are cooperatives and distribute the net proceeds in proportion to the work performed by members, the state farms are government enterprises that pay salaries to their workers. Initially state farms served mainly as model and experimental farms in areas where climate or soils presented difficult agricultural conditions. Gradually the state farms gained in importance, especially after new agricultural lands in northern Kazakhstan and southern Siberia were cultivated in the middle 1950's and organized largely in the form of state farms. By the middle 1960's, about half the Soviet Union's cultivated land (500 million acres) was in state farms and half in collective farms. State farms generally differed from collective farms by a larger size (three times the cultivated acreage of a collective farm, on the average), larger animal holdings (about double that of the average collective farm) and more machinery and equipment. The number of state farms rose from 5,000 in 1950 to 6,500 in 1959, largely as a result of the cultivation of the new lands, but the trend continued in the 1960's, reaching 12,200 by 1966.

Collective and state farms, which employ about 25 million people in agriculture (two-thirds on collective farms and one-third on state farms), account for all the grain, cotton, sugar beets and most of the animal products sold to the state for distribution through government marketing agencies. However, an additional 6 million people cultivate only small private garden plots that provide a significant share of the nation's potatoes, vegetables, eggs, and other animal products both for their own consumption and for sale at farmer markets.

Of the Soviet Union's total area of 8.6 million square miles, 30 per cent is classified as land suitable for agricultural use. This sector includes 19 per cent pastures and hay meadows and 11 per cent arable land. The rest of the Soviet Union's area consists either of forest and brushland (38 per cent) or of other agriculturally unsuitable land such as swampy, saline, sandy, or mountainous land (32 per cent).

Although some agricultural land may be found in each of the natural vegetation zones of the U.S.S.R., ranging from the tundra in the north to the humid subtropics in the south, most of the sown acreage is concentrated in the wooded-steppe and steppe zones of the country. The fertile chernozems of that belt account for more than 60 per cent of the nation's sown acreage. To the north and south of the chernozem zone, there is a sharp drop in agricultural use. Only slightly more than 4 per cent of the forest zone is considered arable, and in the

drier chestnut-soil steppe to the south the share of arable lands is 25 per cent. The degree of agricultural use of Soviet territory decreases also from west to east. This may be explained not only by worse climatic and soil conditions in the Asian parts of the Soviet Union but also by the later settlement and development of these eastern areas compared with the European U.S.S.R.

New agricultural lands. In an effort to assure a more reliable supply of food from year to year, the Soviet government sponsored a major expansion of the sown acreage between 1954 and 1956. In these three years, 90 million acres of previously fallow or virgin land were plowed and sown almost entirely in wheat. About 45 per cent of the new land was in the eastern parts of the Russian republic, mainly in western Siberia; 55 per cent of the land was in the northern *oblasts* of Kazakhstan, where chernozems and darker chestnut soils are found. Most of the new land was organized as huge state farms employing much machinery and relatively little manpower. Migrants from European Russia who responded to the government's appeal for new settlers flocked eastward to the virgin lands. During harvest time these permanent residents must be supplemented by thousands of seasonal volunteers who travel from the western industrial cities to bring in the crop.

The new lands are situated in an area which is excellently adapted to mechanized farming but noted for certain serious natural handicaps. Precipitation is insufficient and unreliable, with an annual average of 10 to 15 inches. A relatively high degree of alkalinity in the soils also adds to the risks for dry farming. In view of these conditions, wheat growers in the area may expect at best an alternation of medium and low yields with an occasional good crop year. However, even with low yields, the total output on the millions of acres involved in the new-lands program represents a substantial addition to the Soviet wheat crop. In fact, droughts do not appear to occur simultaneously both in the European part of the

U.S.S.R. and in the new lands of Siberia and Kazakhstan, so each area represents a kind of safety cushion for crop failure in the other. The lower yields obtained in the new lands compared with grain production of the Ukraine, the northern Caucasus, and other parts of the more favored European U.S.S.R. are evident from the following figures: although the eastern regions account for half the total Soviet acreage sown to grains (before the new-lands program of the middle 1950's it was only one-fourth), they account for 44 per cent of the total grain crop in good years and less than 30 per cent in poor years. However, because of the sparse population of the eastern regions, these grain-growing areas retain a relatively small share of the crop for their own use and account for a substantial part of the deliveries to the state for distribution through the government's marketing channels. The share of the eastern regions in government grain procurements ranges from about 60 per cent in good years to 30 per cent in bad years.

In the deserts, semideserts, and dry steppes of central Asia and other arid parts of the country, irrigation is required for the raising of crops and, when successfully applied, provides high yields. The Soviet Union has the world's third-largest irrigated acreage, after China and India. It rose from 10 million acres before the Bolshevik Revolution to 15 million in 1940. The present Soviet irrigated area is 27 million acres out of a total sown area of nearly 500 million acres. Work is also proceeding on swamp drainage and the reclamation of marshy soils adjacent to major crop regions. Among areas where drainage work is being carried on are the Pripet Marshes of the western Ukraine and western Belorussia, parts of the Baltic republics, northwestern and central parts of the European U.S.S.R., and the Baraba Steppe of western Siberia. A major reclamation project is under way in the Colchis lowland of Georgia, along the Black Sea, where a formerly malarial swamp is gradually being transformed into tangerine groves and plantations for tea and other subtropical crops.

While these soil-conservation and land-reclamation measures may ultimately result in minor changes in the geographical distribution of Soviet agriculture, the wooded-steppe and true-steppe zones will undoubtedly remain the chief agricultural belt of the U.S.S.R. for a long time to come.

Production and yields. The expansion of acreage that has already taken place is reflected in Soviet statistics. The total sown area increased from nearly 300 million acres in 1913, the last year of peace before World War I, used by Soviet statisticians as a base year, to almost 500 million acres at the present time. The relatively short growing seasons permits only one crop a year to be grown on this acreage. Less than one-third is sown in winter crops, which are found in areas that do not have excessively cold winters or where a thick snow cover provides protection for the germinating seeds. Most of the Soviet acreage is planted in the spring. The increase in sown area under the Soviet regime was accompanied by changed proportions of the various crops: the share of grain crops has gradually been reduced with expansion of acreages devoted to industrial crops (cotton, flax, hemp, sunflowers, sugar beets), potatoes, vegetables, and especially fodder crops.

In spite of these changes of emphasis, grain still dominates Soviet agriculture, accounting for 60 per cent of the total sown acreage, having decreased from 88 per cent in 1913. The Soviet grain area remained fairly constant after the Bolshevik Revolution, fluctuating between 250 and 275 million acres. Since 1953, however, it has rapidly expanded as a result of the virgin-lands program, reaching 300 million acres in 1966. Grain yields in the Soviet Union are generally low because of poor soil and climatic conditions and inadequate fertilizer application. The Soviet Union long made a practice of estimating crops before the harvest and publishing these estimates as production figures. These inflated figures, which amounted to 120 to 130 million metric

Fig. 9–10. Wheat harvesting in the Kuban plain of the Northern Caucasus, a principal wheat-producing region of the U.S.S.R. (Novosti, from Sovfoto.)

tons of grain in the early 1950's, concealed losses incurred during the harvest. As it turned out, the actual barn crop was only 65 to 70 per cent of the published figures. In the middle 1950's, the Soviet government decided to publish barn-crop data (Table 8c, Appendix III). The production increase since 1954 reflects the sharp increase in acreage resulting from the virgin-lands program in western Siberia and Kazakhstan.

Grain-growing areas. The principal grain-growing areas in pre-revolutionary Russia were in the chernozem zone of the southern and southwestern European U.S.S.R. Since the eighteenth century, grain production in the northern non-chernozem areas had continued to decline under the impact of the cheaper grain of the newly settled chernozem zone. The country thus combined a grain-deficit region, consisting of the non-chernozem belt extending from Belorussia in the west to the upper Volga around Gorky in the east, and a grain-surplus region, coinciding essentially with the chernozem zone. Although efforts were made under the Soviet regime to achieve a more uniform distribution of grain production, the non-chernozem areas continued to require grain shipments from other parts of the country. At the same time, the grain-surplus regions shifted eastward. Western Siberia, the Urals, the middle Volga lands, and Kazakhstan—areas of recent expansion of grain acreage—became the principal producers of surplus grain in the Soviet Union. Lesser surpluses are expected from the more densely settled Ukraine, the northern Caucasus, and the chernozem *oblasts* of central European Russia, where industrial crops and animal husbandry increasingly compete for acreage with grain.

A significant characteristic of Soviet grain farming, reflecting the nature of the country's diet and level of nutrition, is the heavy dominance of food or bread grains. Wheat, rye, buckwheat, millet, and rice account for 70 per cent of the total grain acreage. Such heavy reliance on cereal grains is generally typical of relatively backward agricultural economies. More advanced farming countries show a crop pattern tending more toward feed grains as a basis for a meat-dairy diet. In the United States, for example, feed grains (corn, oats, barley, and sorghum) account for 80 per cent of the total grain harvest.

Wheat is by far the most important grain in the Soviet Union, accounting for 55 per cent of the grain acreage. The Soviet Union is the world's leading wheat producer, ahead of China and the United States. Most of the wheat acreage is concentrated in the chernozem belt, extending from the Ukraine in a generally northeasterly direction through the middle Volga Valley and the southern Urals to western Siberia and northern Kazakhstan (Fig. 9–10).

Winter wheat is grown at the southwestern end of the chernozem zone, while reduced snow cover and more extreme winter temperatures toward the east necessitate the sowing of lower-yielding spring wheat (Fig. 9–11). The recent eastward shift in grain

leading producer of rye (the only other important rye producers are Poland, West and East Germany, and Czechoslovakia). Rye has less exacting soil and moisture requirements than wheat and is grown in the poor, acid podzolic soils of the central regions of the European U.S.S.R. Under the Soviet regime rye sowings have been steadily losing ground, declining from 70 million acres (28 per cent of the grain acreage) in 1913 to 40 million (14 per cent) in the middle 1960's. Much of the rye has been replaced by winter wheat. Lesser food grains include millet and buckwheat, which are used to make kasha,

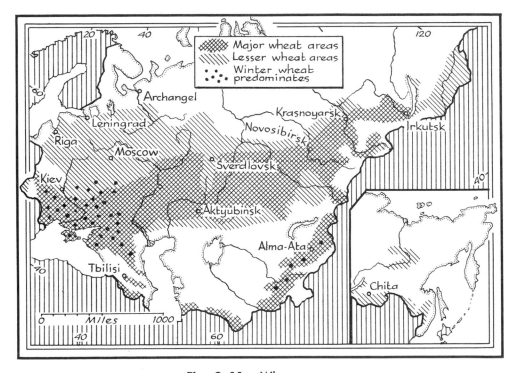

Fig. 9–11. Wheat areas.

growing has in fact resulted in a reduction of the winter-wheat share. Before the virgin-lands expansion, in 1953, the winter sowings accounted for 37 per cent of all wheat acreage. By the middle 1960's the winter-wheat share had dropped to 28 per cent.

Rye, the only grain except wheat commonly used to make bread, is the second-most-important Soviet grain, and, as of wheat, the Soviet Union is also the world's

a mush or porridge that is a traditional Russian dish. Rice, an unimportant crop in the Soviet Union, is grown on 350,000 acres, mainly in irrigated lands of the Uzbek and Kazakh republics of Central Asia, in the Kuban Delta of southern European Russia, and in the Soviet Far East.

Oats and barley are the traditional Soviet feed grains. Oats thrive in a moist, cool climate and have less demanding soil requirements than any other small grain except rye. Most of the Soviet oats acreage (5 per cent of the grain acreage in 1965) is in poor, acid soil unfit for either wheat or barley. Barley is a short-season crop and can be grown farther north and at higher elevations than any other grain. It accounted for 15 per cent of the total grain acreage in the middle 1960's.

Before 1955, corn production in the U.S.S.R. was largely limited to the southern-most parts of European Russia (southern Ukraine, northern Caucasus, Moldavia, Georgia), the only areas that combine sufficient heat and moisture for corn growing. The Soviet Union has no counterpart of the Corn Belt of the United States, which is unique in its ideal conditions for corn growing. In spite of the natural handicaps, the Soviet government launched a major corn-growing campaign in 1955, sponsored by Nikita Khrushchev and inspired by the example of the United States, to bolster the lagging forage supply. The Soviet authorities conceded that not much of the corn in the Soviet Union would mature as well as corn does in the United States, because of the short Russian growing season. A large part of the Soviet corn was therefore to be used for silage or green fodder rather than for grain. Under the new program corn acreage rose from 10 million acres in 1954 to 80 million in 1963. Of the total acreage, 20 per cent was harvested for grain and the rest for silage and green fodder. In an old corn district, such as Moldavia, where climatic conditions encourage corn growing, 85 per cent of the total corn area is harvested for grain. In a northern zone, such as Latvia, on the other hand, corn does not mature and is used entirely for silage or green forage. After Khrushchev's downfall in 1964, corn acreage returned to its old levels.

Industrial crops. Under the Soviet regime, increases in the sown acreage have been accompanied by a growth in the percentage of industrial-crop acreages. The area sown in industrial crops rose from 12 million acres in 1913 to 37 million in the middle 1960's. The principal crops are sugar beets, cotton, flax, hemp, and sunflowers.

Sugar beets, the Soviet Union's only source of sugar, require moisture and warmth and find these conditions in the wooded-steppe zone of the European U.S.S.R. About 70 per cent of the beet sowings are concentrated in the western Ukraine, with an additional 20 per cent coming from the adjoining chernozem areas of the Russian S.F.S.R. (Belgorod, Kursk, Voronezh). Under the Soviet regime, the sugar beet has been introduced into many other areas, including irrigated fields in Central Asia. The new areas account for 10 per cent of the national beet production. The Soviet Union is by far the world's leading sugar-beet producer, but its yields per unit area are relatively low.

The sunflower is the Soviet Union's principal source of edible oils. Its major production areas coincide with the wheat-surplus areas of the southern steppes. The largest sunflower sowings are found in the southeastern Ukraine, the Kuban plains of the northern Caucasus, the middle Volga Valley, western Siberia, and northern Kazakhstan. Nowhere else in the world are sunflowers planted on such a huge scale. In addition to sunflowers, which supply two-thirds of the Soviet Union's edible oils, oil-bearing crops include castor beans, soybeans, and sesame seeds.

Cotton, the Soviet Union's principal fiber crop, is now grown entirely on irrigated lands of Central Asia, southern Kazakhstan, and Transcaucasia. Attempts to expand cotton growing to the non-irrigated lands of the northern Caucasus and the southern Ukraine have been abandoned. At one time, these areas accounted for 25 per cent of the entire cotton plantings, but yields were so low that the non-irrigated lands contributed only 4 to 5 per cent of the cotton crop. Two-thirds of the Soviet cotton comes from the Uzbek S.S.R. of Central Asia, and 10 per cent from the Tadzhik S.S.R., which regularly achieves the highest yields per acre.

The northwestern part of the European U.S.S.R., in the forested podzolic belt, has conditions favorable to the growing of fiber flax, a plant that flourishes under cloudy, humid climate with a July mean below 70° F. Because of the plant's high demands on the soil, it is generally cultivated in rotation with alfalfa, which provides a basis for dairy farming. Almost half of all the flax area is in the Kalinin and Smolensk *oblasts* and in the Belorussian S.S.R. Soviet flax growing underwent a serious crisis in the early 1950's, when the planted acreage was sharply reduced because of a shortage of seed. The seed shortage, in turn, resulted from low yields and excessive losses during the harvest and threshing in previous years. Greater government concern for the flax crop resulted in a recovery. The Soviet Union is the world's only major fiber-flax producer.

Hemp, another important Soviet fiber, requires more warmth than flax and is grown farther south, between the flax and sugar-beet zones. Hemp grows best in low-lying floodplains and reclaimed marshlands, such as are found on the margins of the Pripet Marshes in southern Belorussia and the northwestern Ukraine.

While no tropical products such as coffee, cacao, and bananas are grown in the Soviet Union, its subtropical areas do produce tea, citrus fruit, wine, and tobacco. Most of these products are grown in Transcaucasia and on the southern coast of the Crimea. The cultivation of tea and citrus fruit, mainly tangerines and lemons, is concentrated along the Black Sea coast of the Georgian S.S.R., where humid subtropical conditions prevail. Wine is produced in the Moldavian S.S.R., the Crimea, the northern Caucasus, and elsewhere. As to tobacco, the Russian inferior *makhorka* type stems mainly from the chernozem belt. The better-grade Turkish tobacco is produced in the southern Crimea and the Caucasus.

Livestock. Just as the European U.S.S.R. contains the greater part of the sown acreage, it harbors the greater proportion of the Soviet Union's livestock, with emphasis on hogs in the west, dairy cattle in the north, and sheep in the southeast.

Dairy farming is promoted both in areas that furnish adequate pastures and in the suburbs of large cities, which constitute an important market for fresh milk. In the more remote areas, the emphasis is on butter and cheese making, as well as the production of condensed and powdered milk. The latter areas include the flax-growing zone, where alfalfa and other grasses are grown in rotation with flax, and the vast natural meadowlands of the northern European U.S.S.R., especially Vologda *Oblast,* and of southwestern Siberia.

Although most populated parts of the Soviet Union now combine the raising of dairy and beef cattle, the latter type is characteristic of the seminomadic grazing areas in the arid lands of the southeast, where the stock is grazed in the mountains during the summer and in the lowlands during the winter. In contrast to the former nomadic way of life, the stock is now accompanied only by its herders while the rest of the population, settled in permanent villages, raises crops.

Sheep raising is the principal type of animal husbandry in arid regions and mountainous areas. Before World War II, the Soviet regime sought to promote the production of finer grades of wool, the so-called merino and crossbred types, and their share in the wool clip rose from 9 per cent in 1913 to 64 per cent in 1940. The northern Caucasus, especially the Stavropol area, specializes in merino-type sheep. A special type of sheep is the karakul, which is raised chiefly in the Uzbek and Turkmen republics of Central Asia.

Hogs are raised mainly in the Ukraine, Belorussia, the Baltic republics, the Kuban, and the central chernozem areas, where potatoes, corn, and by-products of the food industry are used as feed.

The livestock sector was long a problem area of the Soviet economy, largely because of feed shortages. Since 1953, government policy has encouraged expansion of the feed base with a view to achieving an increase in livestock numbers and in various animal products.

If we discount India, whose cattle population is the world's largest but has low productivity, the Soviet Union is second only to the United States in its cattle holdings. In hog numbers, both the Soviet Union and the United States fluctuate around 50 million head, sharing second place behind Communist China. In its sheep population, the Soviet Union is second to Australia.

Among other non-industrial activities in the U.S.S.R., hunting and fishing play an important role in the economy. The hunting of fur-bearing animals has been a traditional source of riches in the history of Russian expansion. The Soviet Union continues to be the leading world supplier of furs, exporting about 50 million rubles ($55 million) worth each year, half of it to Britain. The principal Soviet fur-hunting regions are eastern Siberia, the Soviet Far East, and northern European Russia. Fox farming is also being fostered.

Fisheries. Most Soviet fisheries are located in the Barents Sea, the Baltic, the Caspian, and the Far East. The Caspian Sea, accessible by the Volga to the consumption centers of European Russia and to salt supplies (at Lake Baskunchak), accounted for 65 per cent of the total Russian catch before Soviet times. With the huge amounts of organic matter carried into the Caspian Sea by the Volga, the Ural, and other rivers and the shallowness of its coastal reaches, the Caspian has been regarded traditionally as a natural fish nursery. However, with the gradual development of modern deep-sea fisheries under the Soviet regime, the share of the Caspian dropped to 15 per cent by the 1960's. The Far Eastern waters of the Sea of Okhotsk and, more recently, the Barents Sea have moved to the foreground in fish production. The share of deep-sea fisheries in the total catch rose from 0.2 per cent in 1913 to 70 per cent in the 1960's, while inland and coastal fisheries

declined proportionately. The most recent development has been the sending of Soviet trawlers to the fishing banks of the North Sea, Newfoundland, and other parts of the North Atlantic, which now accounts for about 10 per cent of the total Soviet catch. Since World War II, Soviet whaling ships have also made their appearance in the Antarctic. The principal fishing ports are Murmansk on the Barents Sea and Astrakhan on the Caspian. Soviet whalers have their base at Odessa.

In terms of its total catch, the Soviet Union is one of the world's leading fishery nations, rivaling the United States and surpassed only by China and Japan.

Mining and Industry

Since the start of the first five-year plan, in 1928, the Soviet Union has experienced a remarkable growth in industrial production, set back temporarily by World War II. New factories, power stations, and mines have been put into operation and modern machinery and techniques have been introduced. In accordance with the aim of achieving a self-sufficient industrialized economy in the briefest possible time, emphasis was laid on the rapid growth of heavy industry, such as the production of machinery, industrial chemicals, and power-generating and transportation equipment, as well as the mining of fuels, metals, and other minerals. The production of consumer goods, though increasing, lagged proportionately behind the development of heavy industry.

Typical of this tendency was the emphasis on the production of trucks in the automotive industry. In the peak production year before World War II, 1938, the Soviet Union turned out 182,400 trucks and only 27,000 automobiles. In the postwar period, auto production increased more rapidly than that of trucks, but trucks still outnumbered cars. In 1966, for example, Soviet plants produced 230,000 cars out of a total motor-vehicle output of 675,000.

The rapid development of industry under the Soviet regime has been accompanied by a considerable shift in the geographical distribution of production from a few old industrialized areas to vast new under-developed regions. Before the Bolshevik Revolution and through the 1920's, there was a heavy concentration of industry and mining in five areas of the European U.S.S.R.: the Donets Basin, the Urals, Moscow, Leningrad, and Baku. Outlying European regions such as the Kola Penin-sula, the northeastern Pechora area, and the arid southeast were entirely undeveloped. Beyond the Urals, exploitation of natural resources was restricted to the narrow forest-steppe and steppe zone along the Trans-Siberian Railroad, and, in Kazakhstan and Central Asia, only the long-settled oases could be considered as playing any sub-stantial role in the economy.

The gradual shift of the industrial center of gravity toward the east first became apparent during the prewar five-year plans, particularly in the case of the Urals-Kuznetsk combine. This much-publicized Soviet in-dustrial experiment involved the exchange of Kuznetsk coking coal and Urals iron ore over a distance of 1,200 miles and resulted in the creation of two of the Soviet Union's leading new steel centers—Magnitogorsk in the Urals and Novokuznetsk in the Kuznetsk Basin. In more recent years, the Kuznetsk Basin has relied increasingly on local iron-ore resources, and the Magnitogorsk plant on coking coal from a less remote source at Karaganda.

The gradual eastward shift of industry received a sudden impetus during the emer-gency period of World War II, which led to both the removal of about 1,300 industrial plants from war-threatened areas west of the Leningrad-Moscow-Stalingrad line and the accelerated building of industries and mines in the east. During the war, industrial out-put in the Urals and Siberia, as well as the Volga Valley, rose by three to four times. A further indication of the industrial growth of the east is the increase of cities in the war period. Of the total number of 67 new cities created in the U.S.S.R. during the

years 1942–45, 53 were situated east of the Volga River. After the end of the war the eastern industries remained in their new location, while the destroyed areas of the west were rehabilitated, in part with the aid of machinery removed by the U.S.S.R. as war booty from East Germany and Man-churia.

The eastward shift of industry spurred by the wartime emergency was in keeping with a policy of industrial decentralization that motivated Soviet planners throughout the Stalin period, from the middle 1920's to the middle 1950's. This policy was based on several considerations. First, there was the national-security factor. At a time when military strategy was still based largely on ground armies, the Soviet authorities were concerned about removing some of their key industries away from exposed frontier re-gions into what they considered to be the safer interior. The ability of the Soviet Union to resist the German invasion in World War II, partly on the basis of defense industries located in the Urals and Siberia, demonstrated that decentralization on stra-tegic grounds had some validity during that period. Second, the Soviet authorities were interested in industrializing outlying areas inhabited by non-Russian ethnic minorities. It was felt that industrialization would give the indigenous population a sense of accom-plishment and strengthen their loyalty to the Soviet regime. Third, the industrialization program was predicated on the theory that it was efficient to move some industries close to sources of raw materials and to some of the outlying markets because this would re-duce long rail hauls and ease the strain on an overworked transport system.

Since the middle 1950's, that is, after the death of Stalin in 1953, strict cost accounting has gradually become the principal factor in Soviet industrial location, overshadowing the earlier strategic, ethnic, and political considerations. Soviet planners found that, on purely economic grounds, it was often cheaper to haul raw materials to developed manufacturing areas than to try to build industry from scratch in remote parts of the country. An important aspect in this policy change was the new attitude toward the use of manpower. Under Stalin, when a large pool of forced labor was available for development projects in remote areas, say, of Siberia, and manpower could be mobilized by other administrative means, Soviet planners rarely confronted the problem of assuring a supply of labor for industry in previously uninhabited regions. After Stalin, gradual relaxation of manpower controls made it increasingly difficult to attract labor resources to areas that were physically inhospitable, for example, because of a harsh climate. Moreover, the higher wages needed to attract labor to such areas and the living amenities required to induce newcomers to settle in such areas greatly increased development costs. Soviet planners came to the realization that industrial development of outlying areas, such as the northern forest of Siberia or the desert of Central Asia, should be limited to resource-oriented industries requiring little manpower, and that labor-oriented manufacturing was most economical in the heavily populated areas of European U.S.S.R. even if it meant transporting electric power, fuels, and raw materials over long distances.

Power and fuel resources. How the new development policy is based is illustrated in the case of power and fuel resources. While most of the population and manufacturing are concentrated in the European part of the Soviet Union, 90 per cent of both coal and water power resources lie in the Asian part. Recent discoveries of oil and natural gas in Western Siberia and Central Asia have accentuated the resource significance of the eastern regions of the U.S.S.R. Under the old location policy, the presence of these raw-material sources might have stimulated the development of industrial complexes nearby, far from the established economic centers of European Russia. While this is true to some extent, especially in Central Asia where manpower is available, the predominant trend under the new cost-oriented

policy is to make the newly discovered raw materials and energy available to the manufacturing centers in the European part of the country. In the case of oil and natural gas, this is being accomplished by long-distance pipelines; in the case of coal and water power, by the construction of high-voltage power transmission lines from big mine-head thermal power plants and hydro-electric stations.

Another trend in the power and fuel economy of the Soviet Union has been the growing role of oil and natural gas. For years the Soviet economy was largely dependent on coal for fuel while oil and gas played a secondary role. Through the 1940's and early 1950's, for example, coal accounted for more than 60 per cent of all fuels used compared with 15–20 per cent crude oil and 2 per cent gas. The heavy reliance on coal under Stalin was based on several factors. First, coal resources were generally known and widely distributed, thus enabling easy exploitation in keeping with the policy of decentralization. Second, coal was associated in the mind of Soviet planners with the foundations of an industrial economy. Third, even after it was realized that modern industry had advanced beyond the coal-steel stage to a more complex system relying to a greater degree on oil, gas, and chemicals, the rigidity of the Soviet planning system under Stalin made it difficult to reorient development priorities promptly. It was only after Stalin's death that the stress on cost factors, combined with more intensive and successful exploration of the nation's oil and gas resources, brought about an upsurge of the Soviet oil and gas industry, the construction of a system of pipelines, and the development of a related petrochemical industry. This shift was reflected in the structure of the fuel economy. In the late 1960's, coal accounted for less than 40 per cent of all fuels used, the share of oil rose to almost 40 per cent and that of natural gas to almost 20 per cent. The role of peat and firewood, once significant elements in the Soviet fuel picture, had dwindled.

COAL. Soviet coal reserves are sufficient to meet foreseeable needs of the country for many centuries to come. Of the major producing fields (Fig. 9–12), the Donets Basin, the Kuznetsk Basin, and the Karaganda Basin contain high-grade coals, in part suitable for conversion into metallurgical coke. The Donets Basin, in the Ukraine, and adjoining Rostov *Oblast* of European Russia have by far the best locations with respect to the Soviet Union's industrial centers. The Donets Basin (commonly abbreviated Donbas) has been the country's largest producer. Before World War II it mined considerably more coal than all the other fields together. Although the share of the Donbas has now dropped to about 36 per cent of the total, its actual production has steadily increased and reached 209 million metric tons in 1966. It is the Soviet Union's principal supplier of coking coal, accounting for about 60 per cent of the national output. The Donets Basin, whose reserves are estimated at 190 billion tons, serves industry and transportation in most of European Russia as far east as the Volga Valley.

Next in importance among Soviet coal fields is the Kuznetsk Basin (Kuzbas), of southern Siberia. This field, with reserves of more than 800 billion tons, provides easier mining conditions than the Donets Basin. The Kuznetsk Basin has thick seams of good bituminous coal which is mined at an average depth of 500 feet compared with almost 1,000 feet in the Donets Basin. An increasing share of Kuzbas coal is being obtained from open-cut mines. The cheap Kuzbas coal supplies mainly the industries of western Siberia and the Urals. However, because of the fuel deficit in European Russia, much of the output of the Kuznetsk Basin had to be shipped beyond the Urals in recent years.

The third major coal field of national importance is the Karaganda Basin of central Kazakhstan, whose development began in 1930. A large part of Karaganda's coal reserves of 60 billion tons is suitable for coking. Its output supplies chiefly the Urals,

Kazakhstan, and Central Asia, but, as in the case of Kuzbas coal, part has gone to European Russia in recent years.

Among the remaining coal basins in European Russia are those of Vorkuta, Moscow, and the Urals. The Vorkuta basin, whose development began during World War II, supplies steam coals and some coking coals to the northern part of European Russia, including Leningrad. The low-grade-lignite basin south of Moscow is important only because of its proximity to the Soviet capital. Its coal, high in ash and moisture content, has been used primarily in local power stations serving Moscow. Of the various coal fields of the Urals, the leading producers are the Kizel field of sub-bituminous coal, some of it suitable for coking, and the Chelyabinsk and Karpinsk lignite basins.

In view of the growing role of petroleum and natural gas, emphasis is placed on the expansion of coking-coal mines and on the mining of cheap steam coals from open cuts in the Nazarovo and Irsha-Borodino areas of southern Siberia and Ekibastuz in northern Kazakhstan.

Although Soviet coals range widely in rank, all types are lumped together in production statistics. In recent years, Soviet coal output has consisted of 15 per cent anthracite, 20 per cent coking coal, 35 per cent other bituminous coals, and 30 per cent lignite. Anthracite is mined almost entirely in the Donets Basin, coking coal mainly in the Donets, Kuznetsk, and Karaganda fields, and the other ranks in scattered deposits throughout the Soviet Union. Changes in the regional distribution of Soviet coal production are shown in Table 8d (page 655).

PETROLEUM. Before World War II, the old oil fields of Baku, Grozny, and Maikop, in the Caucasus, accounted for about 86 per cent of the Soviet Union's total crude-oil output. By the late 1960's, Soviet production had increased more than ten times the 1940 level and about 70 per cent of the total output came from a vast new petroliferous province between the Volga and the Urals. The rapid emergence of the Volga-Urals region since 1950, notably the fields in the Tatar, Bashkir, and Kuibyshev areas, is comparable to the dramatic discovery and exploitation of the world's other great oil fields in America and along the Persian Gulf. Intensive exploration led to the discovery of rich oil-bearing horizons of Devonian age in the Volga-Urals area, which is moreover situated more favorably with respect to industrial markets than the old Baku district. The Volga-Urals oil-producing district serves three great pipeline systems carrying crude oil to refineries. One runs eastward to Siberia where refineries have been constructed at Omsk and Angarsk, near Irkutsk. The second runs westward to Eastern Europe, supplying Soviet crude oil to refineries in Poland, East Germany, Czechoslovakia, and Hungary. The third pipeline system serves a number of refineries built in the 1950's and 1960's near consuming centers in European Russia (Fig. 9–12).

Continued exploration for oil has led to the discovery of two new petroleum-bearing provinces that are expected to rival the Volga-Urals district in the 1970's and 1980's. The new producing areas are situated in remote parts of the Soviet Union, with harsh physical conditions, slowing the development effort and requiring the construction of new railroads, pipelines, electric power stations, and towns. One lies in the Mangyshlak Peninsula, a desert area of Kazakhstan on the northeast shore of the Caspian Sea, south of the minor Emba oil district. Commercial production in Mangyshlak began in 1965, and is planned to reach 15 million metric tons by 1970. The other new petroleum province is the Ob-Irtysh river basin of western Siberia, with producing centers at Nefteyugansk and Uray. Commercial output began in 1964, when the first 200,000 tons of crude oil were transported by barge to the Omsk refinery during the brief Siberian shipping season. In 1967 a pipeline from Nefteyugansk to Omsk was completed. Production is planned to rise to 25 million tons by 1970.

Outside these three major oil-producing regions, the Soviet Union still obtains crude oil from Baku and the other old fields of the northern Caucasus (Grozny, Maikop), from the Nebit-Dag and Fergana areas of Central Asia, Okha in Sakhalin, Ukhta in northern European Russia and the Ukraine. However, none of these fields shows any promise similar to the Volga-Urals, Western Siberia and Mangyshlak.

Changes in the geographical distribution of Soviet crude-oil production are shown in Table 8d (page 655).

NATURAL GAS. The sudden upsurge of the Soviet petroleum industry has been paralleled by a similar development of the natural-gas industry. Before World War II, the Soviet Union recovered only 375 million cubic meters of dry natural gas, which, in the absence of long-distance pipelines, was used locally. Most of the country's gas output in 1940 was so-called casing-head gas, or wet gas, obtained in conjunction with petroleum and separated from the crude oil at the well head. The first major Soviet gas pipeline was built during the war, in 1943, in the Volga Valley, carrying natural gas from Buguruslan to Kuibyshev. This was followed after the war by the completion of the Saratov-Moscow pipeline, in 1946, and of the Dashava-Kiev line, in 1948, which was extended in 1951 to Moscow. Natural-gas output rose tenfold by 1950, compared with 1940 (Fig. 9–13).

Exploration of prospective natural-gas deposits was greatly intensified in the 1950's and 1960's, resulting in the discovery of important commercial reservoirs. Early discoveries were made in the southern part of the European U.S.S.R., at Shebelinka, south of Kharkov, in the Ukraine; in the Stavropol and Krasnodar areas of the northern Caucasus; and at Karadag, near Baku. A system of pipelines was laid northward from the northern Caucasus to Moscow and Lenin-

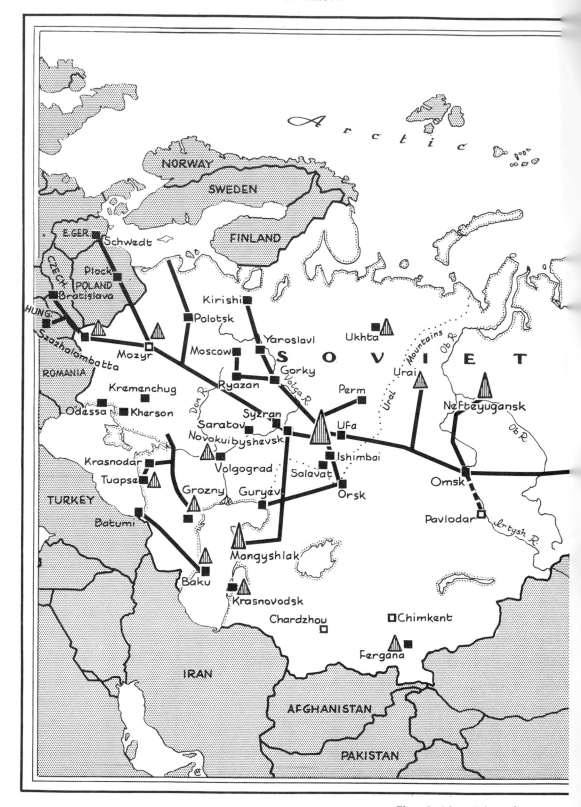

Fig. 9–12. Oil-producing

O c e a n

U N I O N

Lena R.

Lena R.

Yenisei R.

Angara R.

Angarsk

Okha

SAKHALIN

Komsomolsk

Khabarovsk

JAPAN

MONGOLIA

CHINA

◿ Oil fields	□ Oil refinery (Under const.)
■ Oil refineries	
━━ Oil pipelines	▬ ▬ Oil pipelines (Under const.)

```
0    200   400   600   800   1,000 MILES
0  200 400 600 800 1,000 KILOMETERS
```

areas and pipelines.

Fig. 9–13. Gas-producing

areas and pipelines.

grad. Later discoveries yielded even larger deposits of natural gas in the Central Asian deserts and in the northern forests and tundra of western Siberia. The first gas-transmission main from Central Asia was completed to the Urals in 1963, and the first of a series of pipelines from Central Asia to central European Russia opened in 1967. The west Siberian gas fields is to be linked by a system of transmission mains with European Russia after 1970. The need for transporting vast amounts of natural gas from producing fields to consuming centers thousands of miles distant has stimulated the use of large-diameter pipe in the Soviet Union. The laying of 40-inch gas mains, as well as 40-inch oil pipelines, has become commonplace, and plans call for the steady expansion of pipe diameters to 60 and even 80 inches as manufacturing facilities become available. Changes in regional distribution of natural gas production appear in Table 8d.

The availability of natural gas has eclipsed other sources of gas dating from the Soviet Union's solid-fuel era, when gas was obtained from the distillation of oil shale and, experimentally, through the underground burning of coal. The underground gasification of coal has been abandoned as uneconomical, and oil shale, produced mainly in Estonia and in Slantsy (Leningrad *Oblast*), is being used mainly as a power-station fuel.

PEAT. Another traditional fuel that has been holding its own in the face of oil and gas competition is peat. Although peat has little heating value, the location of peat bogs near the great industrial centers of central European Russia and Belorussia (Fig. 9–13) has enhanced the importance of peat as a power-station fuel. This is especially true of Belorussia, where other solid fuels are lacking. In the middle 1960's, Belorussia accounted for 20 per cent of Soviet peat production for use in local power plants.

WATER POWER. Although most of the potential water power resources of the Soviet Union lie in Siberia, hydroelectrical de-velopment was first concentrated in European Russia near the large consumption centers. Water development projects were concentrated on Caucasus mountain currents and on rapid-strewn rivers of the Baltic Shield between Leningrad and the Kola Peninsula as well as on the slow-moving but large streams of the middle reaches of the European U.S.S.R.—the Volga and the Dnieper. The first of a series of hydro-electric installations on the Dnieper River went into operation at Zaporozhe in 1932, reaching a capacity of 558,000 kilowatts. After destruction in World War II, it was rebuilt and expanded to 648,000 kilowatts. However the largest European hydro stations are situated on the Volga River. They are the Kuibyshev power plant (Fig. 9–14) with a generating capacity of 2.3 million kilowatts, opened in 1955, and the Volgograd station with 2.5 kilowatts, which went into operation in 1958. Surplus electric power from the Volga valley is transmitted by high-voltage lines of 500 kilovolts to Moscow and to the Urals. An 800-kilovolt transmission line between the Volgograd hydro station and the Donets Basin using direct current, which is a more economical form of electric power transmission over extra long distances than the conventional alternating current, went into operation in 1962 as a prototype for some of the great power transmission lines that will carry low-cost electricity to Euro-pean Russia from huge hydroelectric sta-tions and mine-head thermal power plants in southern Siberia and northeastern Kaza-khstan (Fig. 9–15).

In Siberia the first giant hydroelectric station went into operation at Bratsk on the Angara River in 1961 and reached a gen-erating capacity of 4.1 million kilowatts in 1967. Two more generators, bringing the capacity up to the original design of 4.5 million kilowatts, are to be installed at a later time when needed. The second great Siberian water power installation, near Kras-noyarsk on the Yenisei River, began pro-ducing electricity in 1967. Its generating units of 500,000 kilowatts each are more than

Fig. 9–14. The 2.3-million-kilowatt hydroelectric station near Kuibyshev, on the middle Volga River, opened in 1955. (Sovfoto.)

twice the capacity of the 225,000-kilowatt units at Bratsk. The ultimate capacity of the Krasnoyarsk station, planned to be reached in 1970, is 6 million kilowatts. Several additional giant stations are planned along both the Angara and the Yenisei rivers. The first, in order of priority, are the Ust-Ilimsk station, below Bratsk, which is to have a designed capacity of 4.3 million kilowatts, and the Sayan station, above Krasnoyarsk, planned at 6.4 million kilowatts. Both stations were under construction in the late 1960's. In addition to these great hydroelectric stations on Siberian streams, the power potential of the Asian part of the U.S.S.R. is being expanded through the construction of huge thermal electric stations at brown-coal strip mines of the Kansk-Achinsk

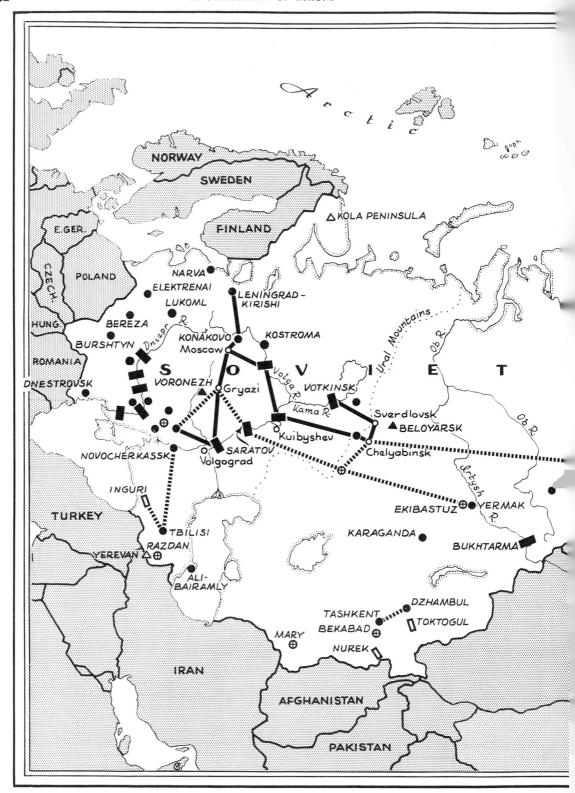

Fig. 9–15. Electric

power map.

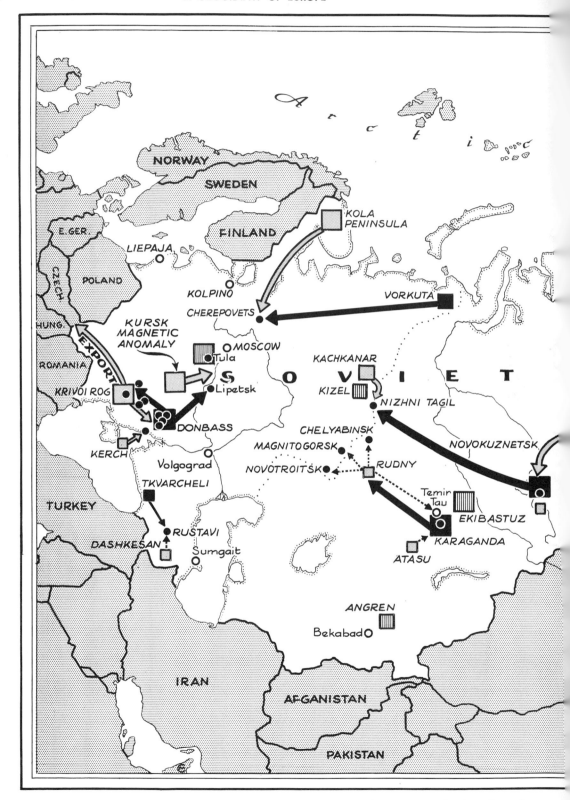

Fig. 9–16.   Coal and steel map

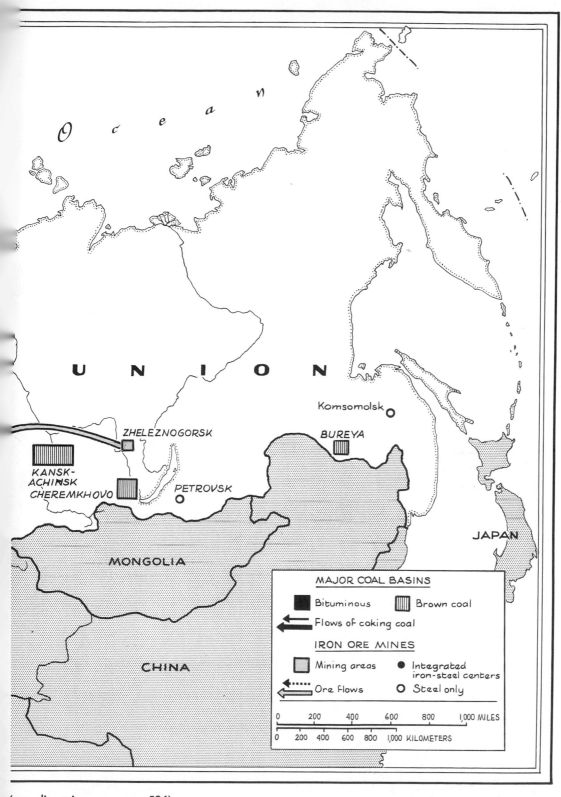

(see discussion on page 586).

basin in southern Siberia and the Ekibastuz basin of northeast Kazakhstan. The first such mine-head station, opened in Nazarovo in 1961, was designed to have a capacity of 2 million kilowatts. In 1968 the Yermak thermal plant, burning Ekibastuz brown coal, went into operation, and was to reach a capacity of 2.4 million kilowatts. In the late 1960's the first of a series of gigantic stations, with a capacity of 4 million kilowatts, was under construction at Ekibastuz. The Ekibastuz power complex will transmit its electricity to central European Russia over a 1,500-mile direct-current transmission line of 1.5 million volts. A similar line is planned between southern Siberia and the Urals.

In contrast to the early construction of small power stations, partly because of the desire for industrial decentralization and partly because of a technological lag in turbine design, the trend in the Soviet Union since the 1950's has been toward big power complexes and the construction of long-distance transmission lines enabling the shifting of large blocks of power from one time zone to another as needed. In 1940 about 60 per cent of the electric power in the Soviet Union was produced by small stations with a capacity of less than 100,000 kilowatts. By the late 1960's, with total power output 15 times greater than the 1940 level, the small stations account for 20 per per cent or less of the total.

About 80 per cent of the total electrical capacity is in thermal power stations, and 20 per cent in hydroelectric stations, a proportion that is expected to persist for the foreseeable future. Atomic power development has been lagging behind that of the United States and Western Europe, with only two large civilian plants in operation in the late 1960's, and two others under construction. Those in operation were the Voronezh atomic power plant in central European Russia, opened in 1964 and raised to a capacity of 600,000 kilowatts in 1968, and the Beloyarsk plant, east of Sverdlovsk in the Urals, which also went into operation in

1964 and was raised to a capacity of 300,000 kilowatts in 1968. The two plants under construction are in the Kola Peninsula, an energy-deficit area, and in the newly developed gold-mining district of Bilibino in northeast Siberia. A fifth major atomic power station, with a capacity of 600,000 kilowatts, functions as a production reactor for fissionable materials at an unidentified site in Siberia. The capacity and output of Soviet power stations are shown in Table 8d, Appendix III.

Iron and steel. The first ironworks appeared in Russia in the early seventeenth century in the region between Tula and Moscow, using local iron ore and charcoal. During the reign of Peter the Great, Russian ferrous metallurgy shifted to the Urals, where higher-quality iron ore and timber for charcoal were abundant. During the late nineteenth century, when Russia began smelting iron with coke instead of charcoal, the center of production shifted again—to southern European Russia, where the proximity of Krivoy Rog iron ore and Donbas coal furnished the basis of a new, expanded industry (Fig. 9–16).

This southern region, which lies essentially in the Ukraine, is the leading Soviet producer of iron and steel and has maintained its dominance despite the creation of additional iron and steel centers elsewhere. In 1913, the south accounted for 75 per cent of the country's iron ore, 69 per cent of the pig iron and 57 per cent of the steel. By the late 1960's the Ukraine's share in Soviet production was still substantial despite a slight decline: 60 per cent of the nation's iron ore, 50 per cent of the pig iron and 40 per cent of the steel. The old iron-ore district of Krivoy Rog continued to play the chief role in supplying the Soviet steel industry with raw material. However, in view of the gradual depletion of high-grade ore near the surface and the increasing costs of mining this ore at greater depths, the previously untapped low-grade ores began to be used in the middle 1950's. Within the next 10 years

Fig. 9–17. One of the blast furnaces at the Krivoy Rog iron and steel plant in the Ukraine. (Sovfoto.)

five large concentrators with associated open-pit iron-ore mines went into operation, converting the low-grade ore, with an iron content of 35 per cent, into a usable concentrate of 60–65 per cent iron. In the late 1960's, half of the output of the Krivoy Rog basin, which totaled 85–90 million tons, consisted of the so-called direct-shipping, or high-grade, ore and the other half of concentrate obtained from the low-grade material. The Krivoy Rog basin provided iron ore not only for the southern metallurgical plants, which were producing about 40 million tons of pig iron in the late 1960's, but also for export to Eastern Europe (about 25 million tons of ore).

The southern iron and steel plants are grouped in four clusters. One, situated near the coking coal of the Donets Basin, contains the integrated iron and steel centers of Donetsk, Makeyevka, Yenakiyevo, Kommunarsk, and others. The second, consisting of two seaboard plants at Zhdanov, on the Sea of Azov, uses iron ore from the Kerch Peninsula of the Crimea, shipped in barges

across the sea. Kerch ore is phosphoric, watery, and powdery, requiring extensive treatment before use. However, it yields basic slag, a phosphatic fertilizer, as a by-product at Zhdanov. The third cluster is situated halfway between the Donets Basin coking coal and Krivoy Rog iron ore, and consists of three iron and steel centers along the Dnieper River—Zaporozhe, Dnepropetrovsk, and Dneprodzerzhinsk. Finally, there is a plant at Krivoy Rog itself. Initially a relatively small producer, it was greatly expanded after the middle 1950's in conjunction with the use of low-grade ores and reached a pig-iron capacity of 7 million tons in the late 1960's, making it the Soviet Union's second largest producer, after Magnitogorsk in the Urals (Fig. 9–17).

The Urals is the second-largest iron and steel district of the Soviet Union, with integrated plants at Novotroitsk, Chelyabinsk, and Nizhni Tagil in addition to Magnitogorsk. Production was long based on local iron-ore resources and long-haul coking coal from the Kuznetsk Basin and Karaganda.

However, the limited iron-ore reserves of the Urals are gradually being exhausted and the district must depend increasingly on outside supplies. These have been found nearby in northwest Kazakhstan. There the iron-mining center of Rudny went into operation in 1957 and by the late 1960's accounted for one-half of all the iron ore used by the Urals blast furnaces. Two other new iron-mining centers for the Urals are under development in northwest Kazakhstan at Lisakovsk, southwest of Rudny, and Kachar, to the northwest. The iron ore from Rudny moves mainly to the three southern steel centers of the Urals —Magnitogorsk, Chelyabinsk, and Novotroitsk. The northern plant, at Nizhni Tagil, is supplied by a newly developed deposit of vanadium-bearing iron ore at Kachkanar, which began operations in 1963. The Urals' share in the country's pig-iron output rose from 18 per cent in 1940 to 36 per cent in 1956, but then declined to 28 per cent in 1966 as a result of the expansion of iron smelting in European Russia and the Ukraine. The Urals' share in steel production is somewhat greater (32 per cent in 1966) because of the availability of scrap metal.

Outside of the Ukraine and the Urals, there are several smaller iron and steel districts in the European part of the U.S.S.R. An integrated plant at Cherepovets, where the first blast furnace was completed in 1955 and the first steel furnace three years later, uses iron ore from the Kola Peninsula and coking coal from the Pechora coal basin. The long hauls of about 1,000 miles for ore and coal have raised the cost of pig iron above that of other Soviet centers situated more favorably with respect to raw-material sources. However, the production of steel at Cherepovets is more economical because of the availability of scrap metal from nearby Leningrad. In the Kursk Magnetic Anomaly, an iron-bearing district so-called for its effect on magnetic compasses, high-grade ore deposits went into exploitation in 1959 at Gubkin and the following year at Zheleznogorsk. In the late 1960's these two mining centers shipped about 15 million tons of rich ore a year to expanding iron and steel centers at Tula and Lipetsk. In addition construction was under way at Gubkin and Zheleznogorsk on concentrators with a capacity of 30 million tons of low-grade ore each, which would yield 13–15 million tons of usable concentrate with an iron content of 64 per cent. The development of the Kursk Magnetic Anomaly is being pressed despite difficult mining conditions (water-logged deposits) because of the favorable situation of the ore district in central European Russia. In Transcaucasia, a small-scale integrated iron and steel operation involves iron ore from Dashkesan, coking coal from Tkvarcheli and metallurgical furnaces at Rustavi, producing 800,000 tons of pig iron and about 1.5 million tons of steel.

In the Asian part of the U.S.S.R., integrated iron and steel production is found in the two coking-coal basins, the Kuznetsk Basin and Karaganda. In the Kuznetsk Basin an early iron and steel plant at Novokuznetsk (known as Stalinsk until 1961), in operation since 1932, was supplemented in the middle 1960's by a second integrated operation, the so-called West Siberian Plant. In addition to local coking coal and iron ore, the Kuznetsk Basin plants also use ore from a newly developed mining center at Zheleznogorsk east of Bratsk in the Lake Baikal region. At Karaganda, a plant has been in operation since 1960 on the basis of local coking coal and of iron ore shipped both from the Atasu deposit, to the southwest, and from Rudny, in northwest Kazakhstan. Before the opening of the integrated iron and steel center at Karaganda, a small steel plant (without pig-iron production) had been in operation since World War II at the suburb of Temir-Tau. Changes in the distribution of the Soviet iron and steel industry are shown in Table 8e (page 655).

Closely associated with the iron and steel industry is the production of ferroalloys. Manganese, the most important of these alloys because it is indispensable in the production of steel, is mined at Chiatura in Soviet Georgia and at Nikopol in the Ukraine. These two deposits alone account for about two-thirds of the world's manganese production. In 1965, out of the U.S.S.R.'s manganese production of 7.6 million metric tons, Chiatura produced 2.9 million metric tons and Nikopol 4.7 million metric tons, with lesser amounts mined in the Urals and Kazakhstan.

Non-ferrous metals. Intensive geological exploration throughout the vast territory of the U.S.S.R. has uncovered adequate reserves of virtually all non-ferrous metals needed by a modern industrial economy. Until World War II the chief centers of the copper industry were in the Urals, where production began in the early eighteenth century. As late as 1937, the Urals smelted 84.2 per cent of the Soviet Union's copper. Since then the development of the copper deposits of Kazakhstan, notably at Balkhash and Dzhezkazgan, has placed this Soviet Asian republic in the lead with about 45 per cent of the country's copper-smelter output, and more than 60 per cent of the nation's copper-ore production. Copper is also produced in Armenia (at Alaverdi) and in the Uzbek S.S.R. (at Almalyk).

Lead and zinc are commonly found together in so-called polymetallic ores, with which silver, gold, copper, and other metals may also be associated. The chief Soviet mining region of lead-zinc ores is the Altai region of eastern Kazakhstan. Lead is usually smelted near the mines because it requires a large degree of concentration and relatively little coal. The principal Soviet lead smelters are therefore located near the nation's lead-mining areas: Chimkent and Leninogorsk, in Kazakhstan; Ordzhonikidze, in the northern Caucasus; and Tetyukhe, in the Soviet Far East. Zinc, on the other hand, must be shipped to cheap power sources for electrolytic processing. The Soviet Union's zinc is refined in the Donets Basin (at Konstantinovka), in the Urals (at Chelyabinsk), in the Kuznetsk Basin (at Belovo), in the northern Caucasus (at Ordzhonikidze), and

at the large Ust-Kamenogorsk plant, completed in 1955.

The first Soviet aluminum was produced in 1932 at Volkhov, near Leningrad, on the basis of bauxite mined nearby at Boksitogorsk. A second aluminum plant was opened later in Zaporozhe, on the Dnieper. During World War II, when these two plants were partly dismantled and moved eastward, the Soviet aluminum industry was relocated in the Urals at Kamensk and Krasnoturinsk, on the basis of bauxite mined at Severouralsk, which turned out to be the most important high-grade bauxite source of the Soviet Union. In the postwar period the Urals has remained the country's principal producer of alumina (the intermediate product in the aluminum-refining process) while aluminum electrolysis capacity has been concentrated increasingly near the cheap water power sources of eastern Siberia (Irkutsk, Bratsk, Krasnoyarsk). Because of a shortage of high-grade bauxite outside the Urals, the Soviet industrial planners have turned to other types of aluminum ores. The aluminum industry of northwest European Russia, including alumina plants at Boksitogorsk and Pikalevo and aluminum reduction facilities at Volkhov, Nadvoitsy, and Kandalaksha, is based on the processing of nephelite (an aluminum silicate) from the Kola Peninsula. Similarly the aluminum industry of Transcaucasia, with plants at Yerevan (Armenia) and Sumgait (Azerbaidzhan), uses alunite, which is converted into alumina at Kirovabad.

Other aluminum reduction plants in the European part of the U.S.S.R. use imported raw materials. The Zaporozhe plant processes Greek bauxite shipped in by sea, and the Volgograd aluminum plant (adjoining the Volga hydro station) takes advantage of its low-cost power to reduce Hungarian alumina to aluminum and shipping the refined metal back to Hungary. In the Asian part of the U.S.S.R. additional raw-material sources have been developed in Kazakhstan, where low-grade bauxite from Arkalyk is transformed into alumina at Pavlodar, and in Siberia, where the Achinsk alumina plant uses nephelite.

Nickel production, often combined with cobalt, is centered in the southern Urals, around Orsk, and in the Arctic regions of the Soviet Union, in the Kola Peninsula and at Norilsk in northern Siberia. Most of the mining and processing of non-ferrous and rare metals, such as tin and tungsten, mercury, molybdenum, gold, as well as certain non-metals, such as diamonds and asbestos, is located in the Asian U.S.S.R. The only major exceptions are molybdenum from Armenia, molybdenum and tungsten at Tyrny-Auz in the northern Caucasus, and titanium-zirconium placers in the Ukraine. The Ukraine also contains one of the Soviet Union's principal uranium mines, at Zheltye Vody, at the northern end of the Krivoi Rog iron district. Most of the rest of Soviet uranium comes from Central Asia, except for one producing center in Estonia, at Sillimae on the Gulf of Finland.

Manufacturing. In the past, manufacturing (particularly metal fabricating) was concentrated in Leningrad, Moscow, Gorky, Kharkov, Riga, and other cities of central and western Russia. Although the old manufacturing centers still retain a dominant position in national production, metal fabricating is now distributed throughout the entire country. The European part of the Soviet Union accounts for three-fourths of the machinery output while the share of the Urals and the rest of the U.S.S.R. is one-eighth each.

The production of heavy machinery, such as mining and metallurgical equipment, is oriented toward sources of raw steel. The largest centers in this category are Sverdlovsk, in the Urals; Kramatorsk, in the Donets Basin; and Novosibirsk, near the Kuznetsk Basin. Since the building of railroad rolling stock requires large amounts of steel, the production of locomotives also gravitates toward steel-producing areas, with diesel engines being produced at Kharkov and Lugansk, and electric locomotives at Novocherkassk, all near the Donets Basin. Farm machinery, on the other hand, is manufactured near consumer areas, because of the great bulk of the finished product and the need for adapting it to local conditions. The largest producers of agricultural implements are at Rostov, in southern European Russia; at Saratov, in the Volga Valley; at Kurgan and Omsk, in western Siberia; and at Tashkent, in Central Asia. Other manufacturing plants working for specific industries also tend to be located near such industries. For example, much of the Soviet Union's petroleum equipment still originates in the old oil centers of Baku and Grozny, and textile machinery is manufactured predominantly in the Moscow-Ivanovo textile belt of central European Russia.

Automobile and tractor plants have been sited, in the Soviet Union, with respect to proximity to suppliers of steel products and to consumer areas and with respect to the availability of skilled labor. The first Soviet automobile plants were located in Moscow, Gorky, and Yaroslavl, all in central European Russia. Under the impetus of World War II and postwar expansion, further auto plants were built in the Urals (at Miass), in the Volga Valley (at Ulyanovsk), in Transcaucasia (at Kutaisi), at Minsk, and at Togliatti (the former Stavropol) on the Volga. The earliest Soviet tractor plants were Volgograd, Kharkov, and Chelyabinsk. New plants are located at Vladimir and Lipetsk, in central European Russia; at Rubtsovsk, in western Siberia; and at Minsk.

The Soviet chemical industry stresses the manufacture of fertilizers to insure higher agricultural yields. The apatite ore of the Kola Peninsula supplies about 80 per cent of all the raw material for the phosphate-fertilizer industry. The principal superphosphate plants are located at Leningrad, Odessa, Konstantinovka, Dzerzhinsk, Perm, and Alga (near Aktyubinsk). Other phosphate sources are the phosphorite deposits of Kara-Tau in southern Kazakhstan, supplying superphosphate plants at Dzhambul, Samarkand, Kokand, and Chardzhou in Central Asia, and high-phosphorus blast-furnace slag, produced at Zhdanov as a by-product of the smelting of Kerch iron ore. Low-grade phosphate rock found in several parts of European Russia is used to make simple ground fertilizer for application in the non-chernozem belt.

Nitrogen fertilizers have been obtained in the U.S.S.R. either as a by-product of coke-oven installations or by synthesis from the air. Most of the Soviet nitrogen-fertilizer plants are located near coal sources: Gorlovka, in the Donets Basin; Kemerovo, in the Kuznetsk Basin; Novomoskovsk (the former Stalinogorsk), in the Moscow basin; and Berezniki, in the Kizel Basin of the Urals. The Chirchik fertilizer plant in the Uzbek S.S.R. long used cheap hydroelectric power for the hydrolysis of water to obtain hydrogen needed for ammonia synthesis. However the increasing availability of natural gas and the construction of an expanding pipeline network has reoriented the production of hydrogen needed for ammonia synthesis from coal and water to the use of natural gas. Not only is this method used in new plants, for example, Grodno (Belorussia), Ionava (Lithuania), and Rovno (Ukraine), all of which are fed by gas from the Dashava fields in the Carpathian foothills, but many of the older coal-oriented plants, for example, Novomoskovsk, have been converted to the new methods.

Potash fertilizer has been produced in the Urals, at Berezniki and Solikamsk, and at Kalush, in the Ukraine. In the 1960's a third major potash deposit was developed at Soligorsk in Belorussia, accounting for one-third of the national output.

Other chemical raw materials found in the U.S.S.R. include rock salt (at Artemovsk, in the Donbas; in Lake Baskunchak, on the lower Volga; and elsewhere), mirabilite or Glauber salt (in the Kara-Bogaz-Gol inlet, of the Caspian), and native sulfur (in the Kara-Kum desert, of Turkmenia; at Alekseyevka, near Kuibyshev; and at the new Rozdol mine, of the western Ukraine). Most of the Soviet Union's sulfuric acid is derived from pyrites and from non-ferrous smelter gases, rather than from native sulfur.

In the absence of natural rubber sources, the U.S.S.R. placed early emphasis on the development of a synthetic-rubber industry. Starting in the early 1930's, it built synthetic-rubber plants in central European Russia (at Yaroslavl, Voronezh, Tambov, Yefremov, and Kazan), utilizing potato and grain alcohol to make general-purpose synthetic rubber by the butadiene process. Another method, based on limestone, was used by a plant at Yerevan (Armenia) to make a special-purpose synthetic rubber known as chloroprene or neoprene. In recent years, in an effort to save feed crops for greater livestock production, Soviet authorities have pressed for the substitution of petroleum gases as a raw material for synthetic-rubber production. The first Soviet synthetic-rubber plant utilizing oil-refinery gases went into operation in 1953 at Sumgait, near Baku. Since then, additional rubber plants based on petrochemicals have been built in the petroleum-bearing province of the Volga-Urals, as at Sterlitamak, Togliatti, and Nizhnekamsk, and in oil-refining centers, such as Omsk and the Volga town of Volzhsky (part of the Volgograd industrial complex).

The upsurge of the petrochemical and natural-gas industries has stimulated industrial chemical fields that were previously neglected, such as synthetic resins, plastics, synthetic fibers, and detergents. The production of chemical fibers, for example, began virtually from scratch in the middle 1950's, with most new producing centers situated in the European part of the country.

In view of the immense amount of new industrial construction in the U.S.S.R., emphasis is still being given to expansion of the building-materials industry. The policy has been to provide each major economic area with its local production, and, therefore, no concentration of the industry is evident. However, the production of cement has been traditionally associated with two major centers—Volsk, on the middle Volga, and Novorossisk, on the Black Sea. The recent conversion of kilns at these two centers from coal burning to cheaper natural gas illustrates the impact the new fuel is having on the Soviet economy. A new cement source has been added to traditional raw materials (cement rock or limestone). This is cement obtained as a by-product from the processing of nephelite to alumina in the new Siberian aluminum industry.

Timber is one of the Soviet Union's leading resources. About 30 per cent of the country is in forest, which accounts for more than one-fifth of the world's total wooded area. The Soviet Union's forests are especially valuable because 80 per cent of the stands consist of coniferous woods used for construction lumber and pulpwood. As with so many of the Soviet Union's resources, most of the timber is found east of the Urals, in Siberia, far from the main population centers. Because of the inaccessibility of most of the Siberian timber stands, the center of gravity of the industry remains in the European U.S.S.R. Sawmills are typically located at the mouths of northern rivers used for logging or at river-rail crossings. Some of the leading sawmilling centers in European Russia are Archangel, the Soviet Union's chief timber-export port, and Leningrad and Volgograd, where logging routes terminate. In Siberia, most of the timber is processed along the Trans-Siberian Railroad, except for the northern Siberian port of Igarka, which ships out sawn wood during the brief Arctic ice-free navigation season.

The plywood industry, which uses the deciduous birch and alder as raw material, is concentrated in the mixed-forest belt in the middle and western reaches of the European U.S.S.R. Paper mills, in contrast, use coniferous softwoods and are located predominantly as large integrated plants in the European north. Most of the Soviet pulp and paper mills lie north of the line Kiev-Moscow-Gorky-Perm, with older centers toward the west and newer plants toward the east.

Cotton milling is the most important branch of the Soviet textile industry. It continues to be concentrated in the old production centers of the Moscow-Ivanovo region and Leningrad, which still supply more than 80 per cent of the cotton cloth. However, new mills have been established in the cotton-growing areas of Central Asia and Transcaucasia, as well as in other textile-consuming areas, such as the Ukraine, the Volga Valley, the Urals, and Siberia.

The Soviet Union is one of the few remaining producers of linen. This industry was traditionally located in the Central Industrial Region of European Russia, with Vyazniki and Kostroma as the principal centers. Under Soviet rule, new mills have been established in flax-growing areas of western European Russia, notably at Smolensk and Pskov and in Belorussia.

The Soviet woolen industry has had its traditional textile centers in the Moscow and Leningrad areas, for fine cloths, and in the Central Chernozem Region and the middle Volga, for coarse cloths. In recent years, the industry has been further decentralized with the establishment of new woolen mills in sheep-raising areas (the Caucasus and Central Asia) and in other consumption centers, such as the Ukraine.

In the food-processing sphere, the U.S.S.R. occupies a leading place in the world in the production of wheat flour and beet sugar. The food industry is widely distributed with a view to local self-sufficiency. The largest food-processing centers are located both in consumption areas and in agricultural regions. Meat-packing plants, for example, are found in such large urban centers as Moscow, Leningrad, Gorky, and Sverdlovsk as well as in the stock-raising areas of the Volga Valley, Kazakhstan, and Siberia. Dairying has two favored locations for butter production—the Vologda region in the northern European U.S.S.R. and the Omsk-Novosibirsk belt of western Siberia. The canning of fruit and vegetables is markedly found in the northern Caucasus, the Ukraine, and Moldavia.

Transportation

In a country the size of the Soviet Union, where production and consumption centers are often thousands of miles apart, modern means of transportation are of vital importance. The U.S.S.R.'s transportation net has been shaped by a number of geographic factors. The predominance of lowland country has offered few obstacles to the building of railroads. Most of the rivers, in contrast, are frozen 3 to 9 months a year, the navigation season being longest in the southwest and shortest in the northeast. Moreover, the largest rivers flow through the virtually undeveloped forests of Siberia to an Arctic Ocean that is frozen most of the year, thus restricting economic utilization of the greatest natural waterways. Highways have played a negligible role because of the Soviet lag in the construction of roads and in the production of motor vehicles. Coastwise shipping, while of some importance, is beneficial only where raw materials and consumers are located near the seaboard. As a result of these factors, it easily becomes apparent that railroad transportation greatly outweighs all other means of transport in the Soviet Union. In the late 1960's, railroads accounted for 66 per cent of all freight traffic, followed by waterways (inland and coastal) with 22 per cent, trucking with 8 per cent, and pipelines with 9 per cent.

A glance at the railroad map of the U.S.S.R. (Fig. 9–18) shows a relatively dense net (approaching the density found in Western Europe) west of the line Kharkov-Moscow-Leningrad, a gradual thinning out toward the Urals, and east of the Urals only isolated strands, seemingly lost in the vast regions they traverse. In the European U.S.S.R., where Moscow is the natural center of the rail net, the greatest density of lines is found in the Central Industrial Region and in the Ukraine, notably the Donets Basin.

Since the Bolshevik Revolution in 1917, when the new Soviet state inherited 44,000 miles of lines, the length of the Soviet railroads has risen by 85 per cent. With a total system of 83,000 miles in the late 1960's, the Soviet Union was second only to the United States in the length of railroad lines. Tsarist railroad construction, which proceeded rapidly after the 1870's, was restricted almost entirely to European Russia, with only the Trans-Siberian and the Trans-Caspian railroads extending into the outlying regions of Siberia and central Asia. About 85 per cent of the tsarist-Russian railroad net was located in European Russia. Soviet rail construction, in contrast, was motivated largely by a desire to obtain access to raw materials and potential industrial sites in the outlying regions. As a consequence, the overwhelming majority of new lines were laid to reach these sites. Among the most important railroad projects of Soviet times are the Turkestan-Siberia Railroad, paralleling the Trans-Siberian between Magnitogorsk and Taishet; the north-south Trans-Kazakhstan Railroad, through Karaganda; and the Pechora line to the Vorkuta coal basin in the remote Arctic section of northern European Russia. The Trans-Siberian Railroad and other important lines have been double-tracked to increase their capacity.

Although the length of lines in operation is only about one-third of that in the United States, railroad freight volume has risen rapidly in recent years with increased production of major commodities. In the late 1960's Soviet railroads carried twice as much freight every year as United States railroads, which meant that Soviet freight-traffic density (ton-miles of freight per mile of road) was almost six times as high as it was in the United States. Modernization of equipment long lagged behind the heavy use made of the Soviet rail system, and as late as 1958 about three-fourths of all railroad traffic was by steam traction. However, within the following decade steam traction was virtually eliminated, with electric and diesel traction accounting for more than 90 per cent of all freight traffic. Major trunk lines that have been electrified include the Trans-Siberian as far east as Lake Baikal, Moscow-Gorky-Sverdlovsk, Leningrad-Moscow-Caucasus, and Moscow-Kiev-Prague.

In spite of the natural handicap imposed by the long winter season, the waterways of the Soviet Union, particularly of the European part, play a major role in carrying freight during the open season. The total

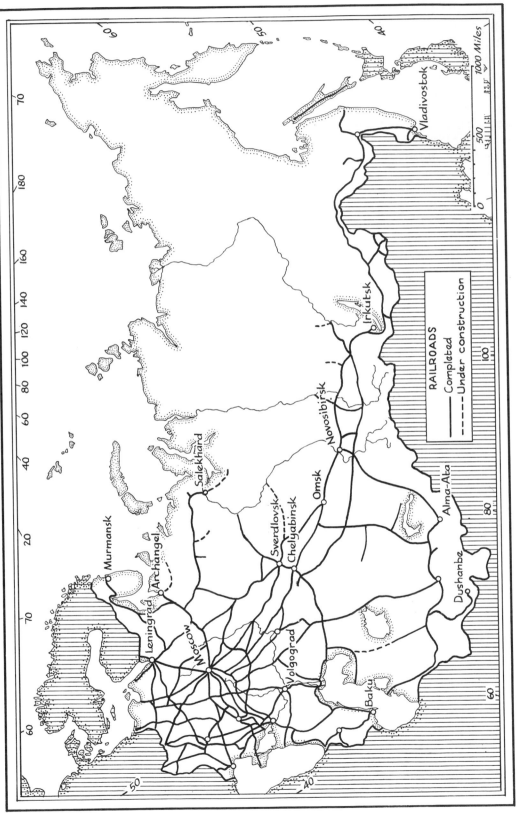

Fig. 9–18. Main railways.

Fig. 9–19. One of the locks on the Moscow Canal opened in 1937. The waterway links the Soviet capital with the upper Volga River. (Sovfoto. Photo by V. Savostyanov and M. Redkin.)

length of navigable waterways is about 80,000 miles. Although much of this mileage is accounted for by the great Siberian rivers, these play a relatively minor role in transportation. About half the waterway traffic is handled by the Volga River and its tributaries. If the northwestern rivers (including the Neva, at Leningrad) are included in the Volga system, we find that less than one-quarter of the navigable waterways of the U.S.S.R. carry 70 per cent of the river traffic.

The dominant position of the Volga system is explained by the fact that it serves the most populated and economically the most developed part of the country. The Volga system extends from the Baltic to the Caspian and from Moscow to the Urals, thus covering most of European Russia. The Volga's position has been further enhanced by the construction of canals linking it to other river systems of European Russia. The eighteenth-century Mariinsk canal system, enlarged and modernized during the early 1960's as the Volga-Baltic Waterway, links the upper Volga with Leningrad. This major Baltic port, in turn, is connected with the White Sea by the Baltic-White Sea Canal,

completed in the early 1930's. The upper Volga is linked with Moscow by a canal completed in 1937 (Fig. 9–19). The Volga River is also connected with the Don River, and thus with the Sea of Azov and the Black Sea, by the Volga-Don Canal, at Volgograd, completed in 1952. The Volga-Don Canal is navigable only for shallow river boats, thus limiting its usefulness as a transport route.

In view of the continental character of the Soviet Union, maritime shipping plays a distinctly subsidiary role. However, a large part of Soviet foreign trade is sea-borne, and from this point of view shipping is of some importance. The Black Sea handles more than half of Soviet overseas trade, particularly oil, grains, and coal. The leading Black Sea ports are Odessa, Nikolayev, Zhdanov (on the Sea of Azov), Novorossisk, and Batumi. On the Caspian Sea, the coastwise shipping of petroleum and petroleum products between the ports of Baku, Astrakhan, Makhachkala, and Krasnovodsk accounts for a substantial share of Soviet water freight. The Baltic Sea is the shortest route from the Soviet Union to the Atlantic Ocean. Some of the Baltic ports such as Leningrad, Tallinn, and Riga are frozen in during part of the winter, but others farther west (Liepaja, Kaliningrad) can be kept open. The Arctic seacoast of European Russia is accessible all year in the area of Murmansk, thanks to the North Atlantic Drift. Archangel, the White Sea port, is frozen in during the winter. Although the remainder of the Arctic coast in Siberia is frozen 9 months a year, some ships, aided by icebreakers, use the so-called Northern Sea Route during the brief navigation season, to carry goods from the European Arctic to the Soviet Pacific area. There the principal ports are Petropavlovsk, on the Kamchatka Peninsula, and Vladivostok, the eastern terminus of the Trans-Siberian Railroad. Because of the lack of other means of transport, shipping routes are the lifelines in the Soviet Far East, maintaining links between the mainland and the outlying Soviet settlements on Sakhalin, Kamchatka, and northeastern Siberia. A new port, Nakhodka, which has been developed in recent years, east of Vladivostok, because of its ice-free harbor handles most of the Soviet Union's foreign trade in the Pacific. Vladivostok, the former main Pacific port, is plagued by ice during the winter.

Trucking plays a minor role in the Soviet freight-forwarding scheme. Long-distance trucking such as the coast-to-coast services in the United States is virtually unknown. Trucks handle primarily short-distance hauls to and from railroads and river landings, as well as between nearby urban centers. The total length of hard-topped roads in the Soviet Union is 250,000 miles, of which only 50,000 miles are asphalt-covered or concrete highways. The highway net of European Russia has been improved somewhat in recent years with the construction of first-class highways between Moscow and Brest (on the Polish border), Simferopol (in the Crimea), Yaroslavl, Kazan, Kuibyshev, Leningrad, and other cities.

The Soviet Union has an active air transport system, with a total length of 290,000 miles of scheduled air lines. These are especially important in northern Siberia, where, except for sleds and ships in summer, they provide the only means of transport, although at infrequent intervals. Elsewhere, the most heavily traveled routes parallel the Trans-Siberian Railroad and other major rail lines.

Foreign Trade

The foreign trade of the U.S.S.R. has been increasing rapidly in recent years as a result of a government policy change promoting trade as a means of extending Soviet influence throughout the world and of obtaining industrial equipment needed for the country's economic expansion program. The volume of Soviet foreign trade rose from $1.4 billion in 1946 to $17 billion in 1966. About two-thirds of the trade was with other Communist countries, mainly East Germany, Czechoslovakia, Poland, and Bulgaria. Trade with China, which was the Soviet Union's leading trade partner in the late 1950's, has dropped sharply in view of the political rift between the two countries. Twenty per cent of the Soviet Union's trade is with industrially developed countries of the West, especially Finland, Britain, West Germany, Italy, and France as well as with Japan. Trade with developing countries accounts for 12 per cent of the total volume, the principal partners being India and the United Arab Republic.

Although traditional Russian exports, such as manganese, chrome, asbestos, timber, and furs, continue to account for a significant part of Soviet exports, the U.S.S.R. has also become a major exporter of machinery and industrial equipment, which goes mainly to some of its Communist trade partners and to developing countries. Soviet iron-ore exports support the iron and steel industries of Eastern Europe, and coking coal also moves to East Germany, Czechoslovakia, and Bulgaria. A rapidly expanding petroleum industry is leaving an increasing share available for export. In the late 1960's the Soviet Union was exporting about 30 per cent of its output, or 70–80 million metric tons, of which two-thirds was shipped as crude oil and one-third as refined products. Among chemical exports, apatite concentrate (a phosphatic raw material) and potash figure prominently, again mainly to Eastern Europe. The Soviet Union also exports its domestic short-staple cotton to Eastern Europe, while importing the long-staple grades from the United Arab Republic.

In general the Soviet Union prefers to keep imports of raw materials to a minimum, in order to have more foreign exchange available for purchases of industrial equipment and, lately, more food and consumer goods. Typical Soviet imports are tropical products, such as coffee, cocoa beans, tropical fruits, cane sugar (from Cuba), and natural rubber. In the late 1960's about one-third of all imports (by value) consisted of machinery and industrial equipment; however these imports constituted only 4 per cent of total Soviet consumption of machinery. Food and consumer goods indicated a rising trend, accounting by value for 35–40 per cent of all imports. Changes in Soviet foreign trade patterns are shown in Table 8f (page 656).

*   *   *

The increasing reliance on consumer goods imports reflects the growing attention being given in the Soviet Union to raising the standard of living. While the early period of industrialization, from the 1930's to the 1950's, interrupted by World War II, was concerned mainly with basic industries, such as coal, steel, industrial machinery, and heavy chemicals, Soviet planners now feel they have reached a stage of development that is adequate both to insure the nation's defense capabilities and heavy industrial growth and to provide more for the consumer. The increasing role of the consumer, for example, was a factor behind the economic reform of the middle 1960's, which relaxed the previous detailed planning procedures of central government agencies by giving greater attention to market demand, cost reduction, and profits. The increasing consumer orientation of the economy is also evident in a decision, adopted in 1965, to expand the nation's production of passenger cars. The new trend has been made possible in part by the development of cheap and flexible petroleum and natural-gas resources and the associated growth of a petrochemical industry capable of producing low-cost plastics and other synthetics for the consumer as well as for the rest of the economy. At the same time Soviet economic planners are seeking to revitalize the nation's agriculture, long a neglected sector compared with industry, by promoting greater mechanization, raising farm prices, and generally allocating a greater share of investment to the farm sector. A growing awareness of costs as a factor in economic development is expected to limit further settlement of inhospitable areas such as the Siberian forest and the Central Asian desert and to concentrate labor-oriented industries in the traditional population centers of the European part of the country. The Asian regions are likely to figure increasingly as suppliers of raw materials, fuels, and energy, through long-distance oil and gas pipelines and power-transmission systems, or as electrical workshops for European Russia. Within the European part of the U.S.S.R., an attempt will be made to halt the excessive growth of large industrial cities by locating new industries increasingly in small towns that were bypassed by earlier industrialization drives and suffer from underemployment.

BIBLIOGRAPHY

Books in English

BALZAC, S. S., VASYUTIN, V. F., and FEIGIN YA. G. *Economic Geography of the USSR.* American edition, ed. Chauncy D. Harris. New York: The Macmillan Co., 1949.

BERG, LEV S. *The Natural Regions of the USSR.* New York: The Macmillan Co., 1950.

COLE, J. P. *A Geography of the USSR.* Baltimore, Md.: Penguin Books, 1967.

EAST, W. GORDON. *The Soviet Union.* Searchlight book No. 15. Princeton, N.J.: D. Van Nostrand Co., 1963.

HOOSON, DAVID J. M. *The Soviet Union: People*

and Regions. Belmont, Cal.: Wadsworth, 1966.

———. *A New Soviet Heartland?* Searchlight book No. 21. Princeton, N.J.: D. Van Nostrand Co., 1964.

LYDOLPH, PAUL E. *Geography of the USSR.* New York: John Wiley & Sons, 1964.

MELLOR, R. E. H. *Geography of the USSR.* New York: St. Martin's Press, 1964.

SALISBURY, HARRISON E., ed. *The Soviet Union: The Fifty Years.* New York: Harcourt, Brace and World, 1967.

SHABAD, THEODORE. *Basic Industrial Resources of the USSR.* New York: Columbia University Press, 1969.

Soviet Geography: Review and Translation. A monthly translation journal published by the American Geographical Society, New York, since 1960.

Atlases

Atlas Selskogo Khozyaistva SSSR (Atlas of Agriculture of the USSR). Moscow, 1960.

Fiziko-Geografichesky Atlas Mira (Physical-Geographic Atlas of the World). Moscow, 1964. With translations of map legends and explanatory text in *Soviet Geography* (May–June, 1965). Of a total of 250 map plates, 60 are devoted to the USSR.

KISH, GEORGE. *Economic Atlas of the Soviet Union.* Ann Arbor: University of Michigan Press, 1960.

Oxford Economic Atlas—The USSR and Eastern Europe. Rev. ed. Oxford University Press, 1960.

Articles

DEMKO, GEORGE. "Trends in Soviet Geography," *Survey* 55 (April 1965): 163–70.

FRENCH, ROBERT A. "Contemporary Landscape Change in the U.S.S.R.," *Liverpool Essays in Geography,* eds., Robert W. Steel and Richard Lawton (Liverpool, 1968): 547–62.

GERASIMOV, I. P., and others. "Natural Resources of the Soviet Union, Their Study and Utilization," *Soviet Geography* V (October, 1964): 3–15.

HOOSON, DAVID J. M. "The Middle Volga, an Emerging Focal Region in the Soviet Union," *Geographical Journal* CXXVI (June 1960): 180–90.

LISTENGURT, F. M. "Prospects of Economic and Territorial Growth of Small and Middle-size Cities of the Central Economic Region," *Soviet Geography* VI (October, 1965): 51–59.

LYDOLPH, PAUL E., and SHABAD, THEODORE. "The Oil and Gas Industries in the USSR," *Annals of the Association of American Geographers* 50 (December, 1960): 461–86.

SHABAD, THEODORE. "Geography of the Soviet Synthetic Rubber Industry," *Rubber and Plastics Age* 41 (1960): 1161–64.

——— and LYDOLPH, PAUL E. "The Chemical Industries of the USSR," *Tijdschrift voor econ. en. soc. geografie* 53 (August–September, 1962): 169–79.

10

Europe's Place in the World

PROBLEMS AND PROSPECTS

The Introduction and first two chapters of this book reviewed the physical, historical, and economic backgrounds to Europe as a whole. Succeeding chapters turned attention to the five major regions of the Continent (see Fig. 4, p. 10). Each of these regions was seen to be made up of a number of independent states, the geography of which was discussed in turn. The well-tried method of regional analysis, applied in this book, has been adopted the better to comprehend the markedly complex geography of this old and populous, but also dynamic, continent. Certainly this method tends to emphasize Europe's spatial differences which are real enough, being the reflection of differences in the physical and human endowment. In particular, the human geography of Europe reveals very sharp changes from place to place contrasting in this respect with that of North America. In Europe are assembled so many countries and nations; so many languages, political systems, social attitudes, and levels of material well-being coexist there. The Bolshevik Revolution of 1917 and Soviet expansion westwards as a result of World War II served further to divide the Continent. It is not surprising that Europe is said to be a "fragmented" or "mosaic" continent—a geographical expression rather than a culturally homogeneous unit. And, although this has some truth, we should not forget that the European nations share a common historical tradition which may prove strong enough in the decades ahead to foster closer association between them (see below, pp. 615–27).

As a conclusion to this collaborative study it is clearly fitting to look again at Europe including the U.S.S.R. choosing as themes those which best help to explain their geographical individuality and standing in the world. Our themes will relate in the main to the demographic, economic, and political aspects of geography. We shall be concerned inevitably with some of the many divisions of the Continent but not exclusively, since trends may be discerned towards economic and political integration.

EUROPE'S INDUSTRIAL ADVANCE

The extent, degree, and speed with which the many sharp social and economic changes associated with the Industrial Revolution took place in the different countries of Europe varied considerably. This revolution was already in progress in the United Kingdom in the late eighteenth century, whereas it had little affected tsarist Russia before the early twentieth century, while many countries of southern and eastern Europe still remain largely agricultural in their economies.

The expansion of markets and of maritime trade, made possible by the overseas imperialism of Portugal, Spain, the Netherlands, France, and Britain, stimulated industrial expansion in western Europe during the last 150 years. Britain was first to be able to expand her markets in every continent, for trade followed the flag. Being internally united, Britain could focus its energy fully on economic expansion. Germany, in contrast, was divided until 1871 into a large number of petty states; thus its market was split into fragments. It was not until the latter half of the nineteenth century, with the creation of a large customs union (the Zollverein) and Bismarck's unification policy, that internal trade in Germany became easy and industrial development and expansion could take place rapidly.

The United Kingdom. In Britain the steam engine not only served to drive machines in factories and mines but also offered superior means of transport by railways and steamships. The transport revolution opened up the grasslands of the New World to immigrant farmers and thus enabled the United Kingdom to import increasing quantities of food at low prices, to feed the ever-expanding industrial population. By the mid-nineteenth century Britain had changed from a predominantly agricultural country to the leading industrial country, with a large overseas trade, which exchanged manufactures to pay for necessary food and raw materials. Much of the surplus income from this trade was used for overseas investment; railways, mines, ports, and other installations in many parts of the New World owed their existence to British capital. These investments brought their returns and Britain was soon able to

buy more than she sold, by using the interest from her overseas investments to make up the difference. This situation persisted until World War I, when Britain was forced to sell some of her overseas investments; during World War II most of the rest had to be sold to help finance the war effort.

France. This was the second major power to move toward industrialization. Shortage of good-quality, easily mined coal proved one of the chief drawbacks, especially as the coal fields were divorced from the chief ore fields. It was not until after the Thomas-Gilchrist invention of 1878, which made it possible to use the phosphoric iron ore of these fields, that they were fully exploited and the French iron and steel industry became well established. By then France was not far ahead of Germany in the industrial race, and the latter soon overtook her. Industrialization in France, compared with that in the United Kingdom, was slower and less complete, partly because of more modest natural endowment and partly because the policy of protecting agriculture reduced the flow of industrial workers from agriculture. Further, France had smaller overseas markets and a different social attitude toward large-scale industry, which starved it of adequate capital.

Germany. The political fragmentation of Germany—the so-called German Confederation—long remained a formidable obstacle to industrial progress. The cost of sending goods across so many frontiers was prohibitive, so trade and industry stagnated. The establishment by the Great Powers in 1815 of free navigation on the Rhine, following Napoleon's overthrow of a medley of feudal principalities there, marked one advance, while a yet greater advance was made by the Zollverein, which, from its beginning in the 1830's, gradually grew to include most of the major states. However, the real era of large-scale industrial development began under the leadership of Prince Bismarck, after the successful conclusion of the Franco-Prussian

War of 1870–71, which won eastern Lorraine and Alsace for the newly established German Empire. Germany, like Britain, possessed much good-quality coking coal (in the Ruhr and Upper Silesian fields) and some iron ore, while more of the latter could be obtained from Sweden and Lorraine. In the center of peninsular Europe, therefore, a large European trade area developed, especially east of and along the Rhine; canals were dug and railways were built to provide necessary transport facilities. As a late starter, Germany benefited by the mistakes, experience, and inventions of others. Thus, by 1900 she had become a powerful industrial country. Also entering late the competition for colonial territories, she joined in the final scramble for Africa and, not being satisfied there, looked for further politico-economic conquests in Europe—with disastrous results in two wars world-wide in extent.

Austria-Hungary. Until its collapse in 1918 at the close of World War I, this multi-national empire, ruled by the Hapsburg dynasty from its capitals at Vienna and Budapest, comprised a considerable area mainly within the Danube Basin and enjoyed outlets to the sea at the head of the Adriatic. Toward the end of the nineteenth century modern industries were established in its chief towns and in Bohemia, the Empire's "workshop." Bohemia provided the bulk of the Empire's coal and iron ore, while important consumer industries were developed in and around Prague and Pilsen. The Danube River, internationalized in 1856, together with railways, provided means of transport within the Empire, which, except for Dalmatia, became a single customs unit in 1866.

Russia. Industrial progress came late to Russia. Even so, before 1900 her production of petroleum was the highest in the world and by 1913 that of coal, pig iron, and steel was roughly at the level reached in France. The emancipation of the serfs in 1861, the adoption of the gold standard in 1897, and the resort to foreign capital (especially from France) marked stages toward modern in-

dustrialization. Railway building, late to start, was rapid after 1891, and before the outbreak of World War I Russia had a railway system in her European territory and links with her Pacific, central-Asian, and south-Caucasian provinces. Such industries as she had developed were then technologically advanced and were restricted to European Russia. Here was located the major center of the iron and steel industry based on the Donets coal field and the rich iron-ore deposits of Krivoi Rog, while in and around the capital (St. Petersburg) and Moscow were the two largest single industrial concentrations. The textile industry, established in factories at Moscow, Ivanovo, St. Petersburg, and Łódz (in the Polish part of Russia), was relatively large, was using Russian-grown flax, and was already drawing one-third of its supplies of raw cotton from Russian Central Asia. The sugar-beet industry in the Ukraine had also been built up. But Russia was still a land of peasant farming and of surpluses of primary products (grain, flax, hemp, timber), and her very considerable industrial resources, especially those which lay beyond the Volga, remained largely untapped before the planned development of the U.S.S.R. began a generation ago.

THE EFFECTS OF TWO WORLD WARS ON EUROPE

World War I had considerable economic effects upon both victors and losers. Large amounts of property, private and industrial, were destroyed, the economic life of the continent was disrupted, and millions of people were killed or died as a result of war. It was followed by a period of inflation and economic upheaval and, although some degree of economic stability was achieved in the late 1920's, this was soon disrupted in the 1930's. The economic depression was first evidenced by the Wall Street crash of 1929, which was followed by the failure of some European banks and a period of depression which lasted well into the 1930's. Although recovery began during the later 1930's, it was cut short by the outbreak of World War II.

An unforeseen result of World War I was the Bolshevik Revolution of 1917 and the creation, in place of the Russian Empire, of a territorially reduced and federated Soviet Union or U.S.S.R. The Soviet Union soon vigorously set about the planned development of its economy and its defense forces.

Tsarist Russia was not alone in being brought to ruin by the unbearable strains of World War I. This period also witnessed the collapse of the German, Austro-Hungarian, and Ottoman empires and, out of their ruins, the emergence of many new national states: Poland, Austria, Hungary, Czechoslovakia, Yugoslavia, Turkey, and the four Baltic republics. But the interwar period (1919–39) was marked also by the rise of dictators in several countries, notably, Hitler in Germany, Mussolini in Italy, and Franco in Spain. And dictatorships commonly lead to wars; in this case, World War II, which established beyond doubt the primacy of the United States in the Western world.

The Second World War, like the first, resulted in great loss of life and in destruction which, however, was even greater and more widespread. Once again trade and economic life generally were seriously disrupted, although recovery was remarkably rapid. To the economic rehabilitation of Europe the United States contributed generously and wisely, where its financial and/or technical aid were welcomed.

In the political field the results of World War II were decisive. To effect the defeat of Germany, Italy and Japan the industrial and military might of the United States, the manpower of the U.S.S.R., and the resources of the British Commonwealth were all committed. From the conflict the United States and the U.S.S.R. emerged as the only Great Powers. Much had changed geopolitically since 1914, when five of the seven acknowledged Great Powers were in Europe. Moreover, in Europe, as in the world, the legacy of World War II has been division along ideological lines. The division of Europe is typified by Germany which, reduced in area, now consists of The German Federal Republic oriented to the west, and The German Democratic Republic linked with the east; moreover, Berlin, the former German capital, belongs legally to neither, being divided into zones of military occupation. Yugoslavia under the Communist rule of Marshal Tito has close relations with the two main parts of the Continent, while a number of small neutral states are uneasily poised between them.

THE RESOURCES OF EUROPE AND THE U.S.S.R.

By any criterion Europe and the U.S.S.R. stand prominently in the world in respect to developed resources. Their chief resource resides in their manpower, derived from a numerous, vigorous, versatile, and highly skilled population. This explains the remarkable development of manufacturing industries, wide in scale and varied in type. The agricultural sector of the economy, notwithstanding sharp regional contrasts including levels of efficiency from the highest downwards, is also highly productive. Moreover, Europe occupies the dominant position in international trade, transport, and finance.

Manpower. With a population estimated for 1969 at 645 million, Europe clearly commands an abundant labor force. However, its population is now increasing very slowly in comparison with those of the other continents: it has no longer a quarter of the world's population as it had in 1800 but scarcely one fifth. Actually the yearly growth rate of the population of Europe, excluding the U.S.S.R., is only 0.8 per cent, and since 1959 the rate has fallen below this figure in European U.S.S.R. The Continent's yearly increment is thus only about 5 million. The growth rate varies only slightly in the major parts of the Continent west of the U.S.S.R.; the death rate is now generally low, and growth is somewhat reduced by net migration, i.e., more people emigrate from Europe than come to settle there. In European U.S.S.R. the small growth in numbers is due both to a declining birth rate and to internal redistribution, for there is a steady outflow of workers to Soviet territories beyond the Urals. Emigration has always characterized Europe and this was stimulated by the fact that it enjoyed a faster growth rate in the nineteenth and early twentieth centuries than did the rest of the world. Thus Europe provided the reservoir of men for the flow of settlers to the newly developing lands in the Americas, Australasia, southern Africa, and Siberia. The outflow from Europe since the year 1800 has been estimated at between 50 and 60 million.[1] Between 1846 and 1921 North America alone received yearly an average of over a million European immigrants, not all of whom remained there. Such emigration was very high during the years 1900 and 1910 and reached its peak in 1913. Each part of the Continent at different times yielded its quota of emigrants but, in proportion to its total population, Ireland yielded most.

This glance at the demographic position of Europe suggests that Europe's place in the world is declining and will continue to decline as its share of mankind decreases. It suggests, too, that, given the relatively low birth and death rates and continued emigration, its numbers are now unlikely to increase much. This is no matter for serious concern since the Continent is already densely if unevenly settled and since lightly settled lands are to be found only marginally—in Ireland, Iceland, and the northern regions of Norway, Sweden, Finland, and European U.S.S.R. Moreover, by comparative standards, the working population of Europe is well housed, well off, well fed and, thanks to its educational systems, has acquired (and continues increasingly to acquire) scientific, technological and organizational skills and the ability to adjust to ever-changing conditions. Emigration, however, is decreasing, and a shortage of manpower in the years

[1] J. Beaujeu-Garnier, *Geography of Population* (London: Longmans, 1966): p. 179.

ahead threatens to slow down the rate of industrial growth, the more so that, being often highly selective, it draws off younger workers with more expertise and initiative, thus increasing the proportion of elderly nonworkers who remain at home. Where such emigration occurs, as when citizens from the United Kingdom and other countries leave for Australia and Canada, some compensation is provided by immigrants whom the expanding economies of West European countries are able to absorb. Thus there are 2 million non-native citizens of the United Kingdom, made up of Irish, Australians, West Indians, Indians, Pakistanis, and others.

The internal redistribution of population within the Continent, rather than migrations to and from it, has merited even more interest since the end of World War II. There were massive forced migrations of Germans, Poles, and others, consequent on the defeat of Hitler's armies and on boundary changes, which brought 15.6 million refugees to The Federal German Republic, West Berlin, and Austria by 1956. Already in 1950, refugees made up 20 per cent of the population of the first-named country, and clearly they were a valuable addition to its manpower resources and thus helped substantially in its industrial recovery and growth. Although each country exerts some control over the entry of voluntary immigrants, immigration to some has been considerable, bringing with it certain strains in respect to housing and social services but also welcome increments to the labor force. France has resettled a million French citizens from Algeria, as earlier in this century it absorbed numerous Poles, Italians, and others.

Another form of population mobility relates to the seasonal migration of workers who make a very important contribution to the expanding economies of certain countries, notably to those of The Federal German Republic and France, while at the same time relieving unemployment in the countries from which they have come. Such labor transfers are markedly developed and successful within the Common Market (see below), the Commission of which has been at pains to organize and facilitate the internal migration of workers, both temporary and permanent. In general, certain regions within the Common Market, especially in the north, have been short of labor, while others, notably southern Italy, have an excess of labor. This situation extends beyond the limits of the Six, for Spain has also been providing seasonal (and permanent) migrants, and Switzerland has been a large importer. A few figures will indicate the large scale and the direction of these seasonal movements which supply workers especially for manual and less desirable jobs, not only in the factories and on construction sites of receiving countries but also for their holiday resorts and for their farms at harvest times. In 1963 Switzerland admitted 387,000 mainly temporary workers and The German Federal Republic 378,000. In the 1950's Italy supplied over half of such immigrant workers, although this share declined to 32 per cent in 1966. This decline, however, has been partially offset by an increasing number of immigrants from Spain, Portugal, Greece, Turkey, and Yugoslavia. The different national groups tend to go to specific countries: thus Turks and Greeks go mainly to West Germany and Belgium, Yugoslavs mainly to West Germany, Spaniards to France, and Italians to Switzerland (see Table below). It is estimated that between 1947 and 1963 nearly a million workers moved from Southern to Northern Europe, of whom about one-eighth were accompanied, or later joined, by their families.

However, the number of permanent foreign workers entering the Community countries is now declining. In the first nine months of 1966 the six Community countries issued 486,260 initial labor permits to permanent migrant workers, 180,000 of them from other Community countries; this compares with 562,816 in the first nine months of 1965—a decline of 14 per cent. These population movements, now carefully controlled by the issue of labor permits by the Community countries, clearly create serious social problems: exporting countries, like Greece, lose too many workers; receiving countries face problems of housing and of assimilation. However, the mingling and closer association of European nationals gives an element of reality to the idea that Europe, or at least Western Europe, has a unity of interest and purpose.

No brief review of the mobility of the European population today would be complete without reference to the scale and range of travel thanks to the paid holidays

The Pattern of
(temporary and permanent,

From	Italy	Spain	Portugal	Greece	Turkey
To					
Germany	134.9	51.7	0.2	58.0	27.9
France	21.1	144.9	27.1	—	—
Belgium	3.9	7.3	0.3	3.6	5.8
Netherlands	2.6	5.4	0.3	1.6	0.7
Switzerland	287.2	38.2	—	—	—
U.K.	6.6	9.3	1.1	0.6	—
Total	456.3**	256.8**	29.0	63.8	34.4
Per cent	42	23.8	2.7	5.9	3.2

* Including 208,000 Algerians.
† Excluding workers living close to inland boundaries and who work in a neighboring country.

of workers and to the commuting of workers into towns, especially the largest ones, from their homes on and beyond the urban periphery. This latter movement in north-western Europe even extends across international boundaries.

In short, the manpower of Europe, both in the West and the East, is almost fully employed and countries, where industrial expansion is strongest, have had the good fortune to be able to draw in surplus workers from outside. Another positive manpower factor is that women add measurably and increasingly to the labor force: in Western and Northern Europe between 25 and 33 per cent of women in the "active" years so contribute, while in the Socialist countries the proportion is higher, as high as 50 per cent in Romania and the U.S.S.R. In another demographic respect, too, the Socialist countries have the advantage of a larger proportion of the active age-groups; in the countries to the west, the proportion of elderly non-workers is higher and tends to rise, the result in part of emigration which applies more markedly to the working age-groups.

Agricultural resources. The land is Europe's chief inanimate resource. Although Europe is a highly industrialized continent, agriculture, directly or indirectly, provides a livelihood for the greater proportion of its inhabitants. The land yields a wide range of plants useful for foodstuffs and for industry. If the U.S.S.R. is included, this range includes not only food and fodder grains, temperate fruits, sugar beets, and various oil-bearing plants, but also the principal fibers—wool, flax, hemp, cotton, and raw silk—and forest products. Political obstacles limit the freedom of trade exchanges between Western Europe and the U.S.S.R., so, although the latter supplies its neighbors with cotton and other fibers, the Western countries look overseas for raw materials, especially wool and cotton, and also for some of their food. Much food has to be imported, in addition to that which Europe is climatically unable to grow. Some countries, especially the United Kingdom, West Germany, Norway, Switzerland, and Greece, have to import a large part of their needs. However, Europe (outside the U.S.S.R.) produces foodstuffs in very considerable quantities, which accounted in 1966 for the following percentages of world production: wheat 21, barley 35, oats 34, rye 50, maize 14, potatoes 47, and meat 22. Note also that Western Europe achieves the highest yields of many temperate crops, for example, wheat yields (in tons per acre) were as follows in

Labor Migration
in thousands, in 1963 †)

Yugoslavia	Others	Total	Per cent	Workers from Non-EEC Countries
19.4	85.4	377.5	35.1	203
2.0	21.7	216.8	20.1	295*
—	5.4	26.3	2.4	21
0.4	5.8	16.8	1.6	12
—	65.5	386.9	35.9	—
0.5	34.4	52.5	4.9	—
22.3	218.2	1076.8	100	531
2.1	20.3	100		

** In 1961 Italians were 54 per cent and Spaniards 19 per cent of total.
In 1963 Italians were 42 per cent and Spaniards 24 per cent of total.
Source: *European Community,* July–August, 1964.

1966: United Kingdom 1.4, Netherlands 1.6 (cf United States 0.7). Such high yields in Western Europe are the result of more intensive cultivation, and those of the Americas reflect a low man/land ratio. In Western Europe, too, farming is highly capitalized and mechanized. The same is true of the U.S.S.R., where, however, yields per acre are low. On the other hand, there is little mechanization in parts of the continent where labor is abundant and the holdings are very small. Often areas of the highest densities of agricultural population have the lowest agricultural yields, because capital for improvements is lacking. Labor, being plentiful, is often inefficiently employed; as a result there is under-employment or concealed unemployment. Land reforms to create larger holdings are being carried out here and there, while in Eastern Europe cooperative farming marks a new development of the postwar years. In some areas, too, drainage and irrigation schemes should extend the cultivated area and promote agricultural productivity.

Industrial resources. Europe's industrial equipment is considerable. A series of rich coal fields stretch from Britain, through Belgium and France, across the Rhine to Silesia, and on to the U.S.S.R. The iron ores contained in the Coal Measures, which supplied the coke-fueled blast furnaces of earlier days, have now been worked out, but several rich iron-ore fields occur, lying apart from the coal fields, notably, the low-grade minette ores of Lorraine and Luxembourg, and the high-grade hematites of both Arctic Sweden and Krivoi Rog in the Ukrainian S.S.R. These major resources are supplemented by large deposits of low-grade Jurassic ores (e.g., in Britain) and of hematite (e.g., in Spain and Norway). The current demand for iron ore by the European steel makers has far outgrown home supplies, and much is imported from Canada, North Africa, Venezuela, Brazil, India and elsewhere. Before charcoal was replaced by coke as a smelting agent, the forests of Europe provided ample fuel for the industry, and the

streams of this temperate area provided water power to maintain the blast. In this century the water power resources of Europe are being harnessed for another form of energy—hydroelectricity. These derive principally from Tertiary mountain systems and from the older glaciated highlands of Great Britain and Northern Europe, while on some of the large rivers, particularly in the U.S.S.R., Austria, and France, ambitious power projects have been, and still are being carried out. Even more ambitious are the tidal schemes, still mainly in the planning stage.

Recently, atomic energy has been commercially harnessed for electricity generation and atomic-power stations have been and are being constructed in the United Kingdom, France, U.S.S.R., and elsewhere in Europe. Although well supplied, as a whole, with coal and electric power, Europe, apart from the U.S.S.R., Austria, and Romania, largely lacks petroleum. There are many small fields in West Germany, France, Hungary, Yugoslavia, the Netherlands, and Great Britain, but these are quite insufficient for domestic needs. The United Kingdom and the Scandinavian countries import 99 per cent and West Germany 86 per cent of their requirements.

The recent discoveries of large deposits of natural gas in the northern part of the Netherlands and, more recently still, in the North Sea have much altered the fuel resource picture of Western Europe. Previously only small amounts of natural gas had been obtained from fields in Italy, southwest France and elsewhere, and liquid methane from Algeria, transported by special tankers to France and Britain. As yet the full potential of the North Sea gas fields is not known, nor is it known to what extent oil may also be found in commercial quantities there.

These new natural gas finds, together with the expanding nuclear power station program and other refinements taking place in electricity generation and fuel use, are resulting in a reappraisal of fuel consumption patterns in Western Europe.

Both oil and natural gas can be cheaply transported in bulk by pipelines and already the Dutch gas fields supply gas in this way to Belgium, France, and West Germany; while oil pipelines link the Ruhr and other parts of Western Europe to the major oil ports (see Fig. 10–1). In the United Kingdom, too, a new gas grid is being constructed and by 1975 natural gas will be supplying some 15 per cent of Britain's fuel needs.

The shares of the various fuels supplied to the Community countries as a whole can be seen in the following table.

Energy Requirements of European Community Countries

	million metric tons coal equivalent		per cent share	
	1965	1967	1965	1967
Coal	225	201	37.7	31.3
Lignite	34	35	5.7	5.4
Petroleum	271	328	45.3	50.9
Natural gas	23	34	3.8	5.2
Primary electricity	45	46	7.5	7.2
Total	599	644	100	100
Community sources of which	322	310	53.8	48.2
Coal	(202)	(178)	(33.8)	(27.7)
Imports	277	334	46.2	51.8

SOURCE: *European Community*, April 1967.

It is readily apparent that the EEC, as indeed Western Europe as a whole, is becoming increasingly dependent upon imported fuel. In common with the United Kingdom, the EEC countries foresee a considerable decline in coal production and consumption, partly as a result of increasing fuel efficiency in power stations and partly due to the changeover to other sources of power. This changing pattern of power sources will result in a continued weakening of the locational pull of the coalfields as centers of manufacturing.

At present the main manufacturing belt of Europe broadly coincides with the coalfields. From Britain the manufacturing belt continues through northern France and Lorraine and the Sambre-Meuse valley of Belgium, into the Saar and the Rhine-Westphalian industrial complex, then along the edge of the Harz Mountains and into Silesia, to reappear in the great industrial areas of the European U.S.S.R. Most of these industrial areas contain the chief centers of the iron and steel industry, alongside which have grown heavy engineering and heavy chemical industries. Already, however, modern developments in transport and communications, power production and power transmission have led to the diffusion of industry. Not only are considerable industrial regions established around capital cities, such as London, Paris, Berlin, and Moscow, and around the principal ports, such as Hamburg, Göteborg, Marseille, Leningrad, and especially Rotterdam-Europoort, but increasingly industry is seeking in Western Europe coastal locations in order to avail itself of the economies of sea transport for bulky imported raw materials, including cheap American coal. Examples include the iron and steel industry (Dunkirk, Europoort, and the new works at Port Talbot and Newport in South Wales), oil refining and petrochemicals, all of which are increasingly developing in coastal areas and especially along the lower parts of estuaries, for example, those of the Humber and Tees in Britain. There are also a number of important industrial regions depending largely on hydroelectric power in central Sweden, the Swiss Plateau, and others rather more scattered in parts of southern Norway and elsewhere.

The major industries of the countries of Europe, and in particular the iron and steel industry, have become largely interdependent. Thus, petroleum and textile fibers for certain Eastern European countries come from the U.S.S.R., West Germany imports much of its iron ore from Sweden, and France receives coking coal from the mines of Rhine-Westphalia. A similar interdependence characterizes the heavy engineering industry: steel sheets and billets, for example, are exported from one country to another where they are used for constructional

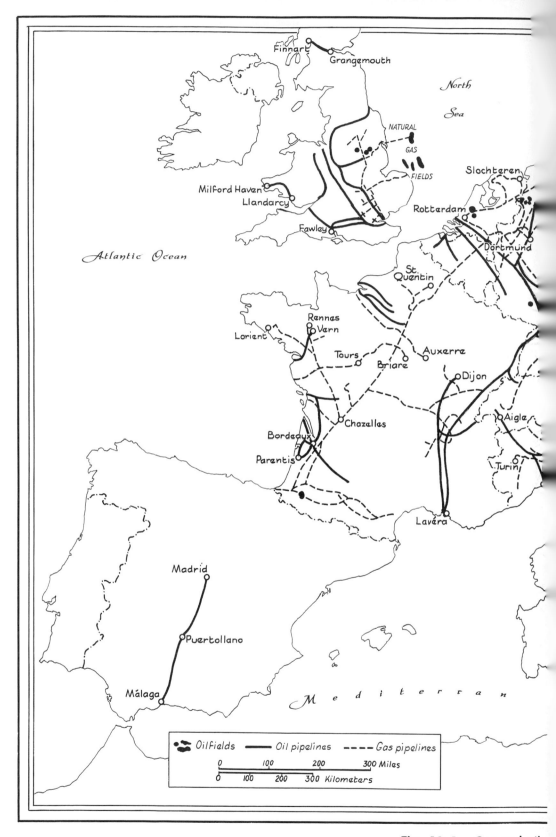

Fig. 10–1. Gas and oil

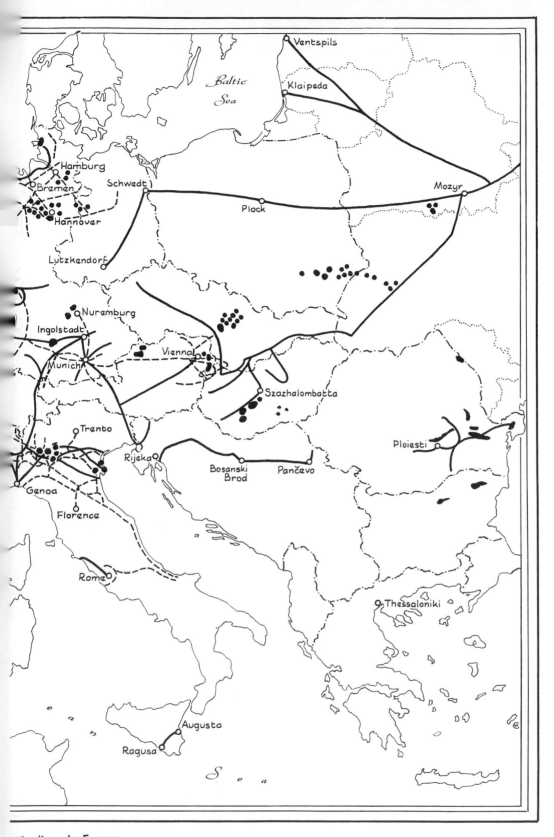

pipelines in Europe.

engineering and the manufacture of automobiles. A new industrial development of postwar years is oil refining. Whereas formerly much of this was done in the country of origin, the greater part is now done in the country of consumption. And in association with the refineries has grown a large, complex petrochemical industry in such centers as Fawley (England), Grangemouth (Scotland), Hamburg, Rotterdam, and Marseille. Indeed, the chemical industry, using the by-products of the coal, iron and steel, nonferrous metals, oil, and other industries, has become of very great importance, yielding products which range from explosives to toothpaste, from plastics to dyes, and from fertilizers to drugs.

The light industries make up another group of industries, of considerable scale measured by the numbers employed and by the value of their output. These industries, being market-oriented, are widely scattered, with concentrations in and around capital cities and other large towns. Among their products are radio and television equipment, electric appliances (telephones, washing machines, etc.), clothing, furniture, and food products. These light industries are more developed in countries where the standard of living is high enough to sustain a demand for varied consumer goods and semiluxuries. In such countries, too, the number of service industries multiplies and transport facilities increase. These service industries, notably, finance, banking, and insurance, like the light industries, are found in the more highly developed countries and particularly in London and to a lesser extent in Zurich, Amsterdam, and Copenhagen.

THE PLACE OF EUROPE AND THE U.S.S.R. IN WORLD COMMERCE

The economies of the countries of Western Europe recovered much more rapidly after the Second than after the First World War, and the expansion of their output and trade has continued steadily since the initial period of rehabilitation. This favorable course of events owed much to the stimulus of Marshall Plan aid and of other such help from the United States.

An acute and recurrent trade difficulty since the end of World War II has centered on the balance of payments. Before 1914, when sterling was accepted by most of the world as the principal means of payment, this problem did not arise. The position of sterling, however, weakened after World War I, when many countries, including the United Kingdom, abandoned the gold standard, while other currencies acquired greater strength. Thus, in the world after 1945, a sharp division arose between the dollar trade areas of North America and part of Latin America and the sterling area, which is smaller but more populous and more widely spread. The dollar area occupies about 12.6 million square miles and accounts for a population of over 300 million, while corresponding figures for the sterling area are 8.4 million square miles and over 720 million. The sterling area includes the United Kingdom, other members of the Commonwealth (except Canada), and the British colonies and trust territories, as well as the Republic of Ireland, Burma, Jordan, Libya, Iceland, Kuwait, and the sheikdoms of the Persian Gulf. In 1968, owing to the continuance of the adverse trade balances of the United Kingdom and the U.S.A., first sterling and then the dollar was subjected to great strain and vigorous co-operative efforts were applied to restoring world confidence in both, so as to ensure that there was a sufficiency of reserve currency to make possible the continued growth of world trade.

Despite all difficulties, Western Europe is still responsible for a remarkably high proportion of world trade. Western Europe, i.e., Europe excluding the U.S.S.R. and the East European countries, accounts for 42 per cent of the world's exports, compared with 19 per cent for North America. Similarly, Western Europe (so defined) absorbs the greatest share of the world's imports—

46 per cent, compared with North America's 16 per cent. In contrast, the share of the U.S.S.R. and European Communist neighbors in world trade is small. Since the last generation has witnessed the growth of the foreign trade of the United States at a rate faster than that of Western Europe, it may appear surprising that the latter still maintains the paramount position as buyer and supplier in many markets of the world. This does not include, however, Latin America, where for various reasons, and in particular because of its investments there, the United States holds the larger share of the trade.

About two-thirds of the imports of Western Europe consist of agricultural products and raw materials, but the relative importance of agricultural products has declined considerably, and continues to decline as the following figures suggest:

Agricultural Imports as Percentages of Total Imports

	1938	1959	1965
U.K.	58	37	30
Netherlands	47	27	20
West Germany	26	16	13

SOURCE: United Nations, *Economic Survey of Europe in 1957* (Geneva, 1958); and United Nations, *Economic Survey of Europe in 1965* (Geneva, 1966).

This decline reflects the results both of domestic drives for increased food production and the growing use of home-produced artificial fibers, which has reduced the demand for fibers other than wool, for which demand has actually increased. Among imported fuels petroleum bulks largest, while iron ore and non-ferrous metals make up a substantial share. Petroleum requirements have increased enormously and are reflected in the large volume of shipments from the Middle East, where several oil-producing countries are members of the sterling area. On the other hand, shipments from Venezuela, a dollar country, which was the chief prewar source, have greatly declined relatively in the postwar years. Changes in its ability to buy dollar goods, as well as

changes in demand, have altered the sources of Western Europe's imports as the following figures indicate:

Principal Sources of Western Europe's Imports by Value
(per cent)

	1928	1937/8	1952	1966
United States	31	22	22	27
Canada	9	8	9	5
Latin America	21	19	11	10
Overseas sterling areas and primary exporting countries *	38	49	58	47

* The term "primary countries" covers the greater number of the countries which depend on the export of primary products. It refers to all such countries outside Europe, North America, Japan, the U.S.S.R., and mainland China.

SOURCE: United Nations, *Economic Survey of Europe in 1957* (Geneva, 1958); and United Nations, United Nations *Statistical Yearbook* 1967, 1968. In 1966 the U.S.S.R. accounted for 5 per cent and Japan 4 per cent of Western Europe's imports.

About 60 per cent of Western Europe's imports come from countries within Western Europe. One-quarter of its exports go to primary overseas markets. While there has been a marked decline in Europe's exports of textiles to these markets, because the textile industry is one of the first to be developed in countries undergoing industrialization, the export of capital goods has markedly increased. The development of the Common Market and European Free Trade Association has led to increases in trade, especially of the former, where trade between members trebled during the ten years 1955–65, whereas that for Western Europe as a whole has only doubled in the same period.

Eastern Europe has always played a much less striking part in world trade than has Western Europe, and this was emphasized after World War II by political obstacles to East-West trade, one of which is the embargo placed by the Western powers on the export of strategic goods. Even so, the share of world trade of the U.S.S.R. and its European Communist neighbors increased since 1950 from 7 per cent to about 10 per cent (excluding Yugoslavia). The U.S.S.R. more than doubled the volume of its trade during these years, while its neighbors nearly doubled theirs. It is noteworthy that the trade of this bloc is, for the most part, politically oriented, i.e., directed to Communist countries within Europe, the Mongolian People's Republic, North Korea, North Viet-Nam, Cuba, and until 1960 to the Chinese People's Republic. Thus in 1966 the U.S.S.R.'s exports to, and imports from, the other countries of the Communist world amounted to two-thirds of her total trade, while the figures for her European Communist neighbors broadly correspond (Fig. 8–13).

The European Communist countries (excluding Yugoslavia), and above all the U.S.S.R., are increasingly concerned in supplying not only Mongolia, Cuba, and India but also the United Arab Republic, Syria, and Iraq, and are at pains to expand trade with South America, which can offer coffee, hides, and leather.

Within the East European countries (including East Germany), the trade pattern has changed as these countries, for currency and other reasons, became cut off from Western markets and as the U.S.S.R. set about coordinating their economies. The policy announced in 1957 of unified seven-year plans for the Comecon countries, which aimed to coordinate their production and to overtake that of the "capitalist world," revealed in its outcome local shortages of fuel and, indeed, of grain, whereas both coal and grain had been staple exports of Eastern Europe. It revealed also that the success of such plans depended on the supply by the U.S.S.R. not only of petroleum, iron ore, steel, and textile fibers but also of capital and equipment, especially mining equipment for the further exploitation of the Polish coal resources in Upper Silesia.

Faced by basic shortages, the U.S.S.R. and Eastern Europe have clearly welcomed some increase of trade with Western Europe. Of

the U.S.S.R.'s imports only 10 per cent came from Western Europe in 1950, but these exceeded 15 per cent in 1965, while of her exports only 10 per cent went to Western Europe in 1950, but 16 per cent in 1965. Finally, it is important not to underestimate the role which the U.S.S.R. can, and doubtless will, increasingly play in world commerce. In its avowed purpose of showing the world the alleged superiority of the "Socialist camp," it can trade virtually where, when, and how it pleases, as political expediency suggests. A notable example of its methods was its sudden launching on the world market in 1958 of supplies of tin at prices attractively low for consumers and embarrassingly low for Western tin suppliers. Yet, in respect to its gold and diamonds, it makes use of existing West European markets.

In sum, just as there are at least two Europes in world politics, so there are at least two Europes in world trade. Of the two, Western Europe holds the paramount trade position not only on its own continent but also in the world. The trade between the European Communist countries and the U.S.S.R., is dominant within the Communist world, which accounts for one-third of mankind; its share of other markets, although small, is growing, and any major reduction of its high expenditure on armaments and space research could release a large portion of its industrial capacity for the manufacture of capital goods for export and of domestic consumer goods. However, before the U.S.S.R. moved armed forces into Czechoslovakia in August, 1968, it almost seemed that the two Europes, in respect to trade as well as political relations, no longer stood so widely apart. Thanks to efforts of the East European countries themselves to reduce their dependence upon the Soviet Union and also to diplomatic initiatives originating in the West, especially in Bonn and Paris, East–West trade was growing at a fast rate. The U.S.S.R.'s trade with West Europe between 1960 and 1966 increased by 87 per cent, while that of the East European countries increased by

50 per cent. By the autumn of 1968 it was not clear whether the efforts, notably of Romania and Czechoslovakia, to add to their trade with the U.S.S.R. an expanding trade with West Europe, would wholly succeed.

In Western Europe, interest focuses on the development of the Common Market as a step toward economic (and political) integration, and on the possibility of creating, in addition, so-called free-trade areas. The broad purpose of these experiments is to substitute the strength of unity for the weakness of fragmentation in a world where economic progress imperatively calls for cooperative thought and action.

THE POLITICAL PATTERNS OF EUROPE AND ITS BORDERLANDS

Reference was made in the Introduction to the remarkable political fragmentation of Europe and in Chapter 2 an attempt was made briefly to explain it. To this special feature of the continent we now return because the state pattern of Europe is a background fact fundamental to the discussion of its current problems, whether these relate to economic affairs, military defense, or movements for political integration. "We are dealing, in the case of Europe," wrote Count Keyserling a generation ago, "with an astoundingly manifold, astoundingly riven structure: the Balkans constitute its truest prototype." [2] The political map of Europe, a map which has been changing throughout history, and markedly since World War I, epitomizes the disunity of Europe, the *genius loci* of which, until recently, has been political parochialism. In sharp contrast to many lands of more recent settlement and development, for example, North America and Australia, Europe presents an assemblage of independent states of every size and shape, ranging from the immensity of the U.S.S.R., which, with its Asian territories, controls 8.6 million square

miles of territory, to the minuteness of the Vatican City which controls only 108.7 *acres*. If a count is made of the European states which are sovereign and independent a total of 34 [3] is reached, equivalent to a quarter of the world total. This figure includes 2 states which are legally described as "international enclaves," namely, San Marino and the Vatican City, and 2 other microstates, Liechtenstein and Monaco. Ironically enough, the number of independent states in Europe has increased in this century which has witnessed such rapid progress in transportation and communication. Thus if the European states in 1914 are numbered, the total is only 23.

How can we explain this preference for many hedged states rather than for the broader territorial frameworks which exist in the Americas, Australia, and the U.S.S.R.? As was suggested in Chapter 2, the answer is to be sought in the long-operative processes by which Europe was settled by peoples who staked their claim to the land. In both geography and history Europe has been lavishly endowed. Notably west of the Vistula, as also in its southeastern peninsula, Europe's countryside expresses physical and human variety and diversity in contracted space. But everywhere throughout the continent separate languages and nationalities developed, as well as national consciousness and nationalism—a powerful force. Nations, proud of their cultural heritages, struck their roots in particular areas, although political boundaries at any particular time paid scant respect to their limits. At the Conference of Versailles after World War I nationalism was so strong and articulate a force that several new European nations arose out of the ruins of stricken empires, with boundaries which only in rough measure respected their claims. As a result, the length of boundaries

---

[2] Count Hermann Alexander von Keyserling, *Europe* (New York: Harcourt, Brace & Co., Inc., 1928): p. 343.

[3] Such a simple arithmetical exercise gives justifiably different results. The total of thirty-four includes the German Democratic Republic, but not the Ukraine S.S.R. and the Belorussian S.S.R., although these two are members of the United Nations. Nor does it include Andorra, which is not fully independent.

in Europe increased from 13,000 miles in 1914 to 17,000 miles in 1938,[4] but this change only increased the number of disputed areas of international friction, no less than 56 of which were reliably noted in the interwar period 1919–39.[5] Europe was then made up of nations each pulling its own way with growing determination, to the detriment of its own interests and those of the world.

World War II brought further territorial adjustments. Germany was truncated and partitioned; it remains divided into two very unequal parts, one of which, The German Federal Republic, has benefited economically from the mass movement of refugees from Eastern Europe,[6] notably from East Germany, which has been organized by the U.S.S.R. as The German Democratic Republic. The German capital, too, was divided into occupation zones and a Russian and three "Western" sectors remain, the three last forming unenviably an international exclave in The German Democratic Republic. Austria suffered military occupation and division into four zones, but its unity and independence were restored in 1955, with its neutrality solemnly affirmed by treaty. The three independent republics of Latvia, Lithuania, and Estonia, born after World War I, were incorporated into the Soviet Union, although this change has never received formal international sanction. Poland was drastically reshaped and its access to the Baltic improved by the gain of land from Germany and by losses to the U.S.S.R. The most notable territorial changes brought by World War II, which cast their shadow over the whole continent, are those which enlarged the Soviet Union on its western side. This expansion, which involved the annexation of territories from

Finland, Poland, Germany, Czechoslovakia, and Romania, projected the U.S.S.R. westward into Eastern Europe. Moreover, the shortened, more westerly boundaries of the U.S.S.R. do not mark the effective limit of its penetration, for with some success it has created a tier of politically dependent and, where possible, Communist states. These consist of former cobelligerents such as Poland, ex-enemy states such as Finland, and former enemies *and* cobelligerents such as Romania. While Finland, rendered militarily defenseless under postwar treaties, has preserved a Western democratic system of government, and while Yugoslavia under Marshal Tito remains a Communist but nationalistic state independent of Moscow, the other neighbors or near-neighbors of the U.S.S.R. are under Communist, one-party rule: Poland, Czechoslovakia, Hungary, Romania, and Bulgaria.

However, Albania broke its ties with Moscow by orienting itself on Peking. By adopting a neutral posture in the dispute between Moscow and Peking, Romania has tried to weaken its links with the U.S.S.R. and to pursue its own nationalistic policy. Czechoslovakia too was trying to follow the Yugoslavia model by devising its own national version of communist rule, but this policy was more than the Soviet Union would tolerate. Thus in September, 1968, while retaining transport rights under treaty across Poland, the U.S.S.R. has powerful armed forces stationed not only in East Germany but also on the Czechoslovak border with West Germany and Austria.

The wheel of history turns. Nazi Germany, from its vantage place in Central Europe, made its bid for the mastery of Europe and failed: Mitteleuropa, as the German power center of Europe, has gone. Into Mitteleuropa has intruded the Soviet Union, the greatest military power in Eurasia. It holds with its own armed forces an advanced position in East Germany and through its satellites, of Bohemia. It also has a strong position on the Baltic Sea, and, at the Danube Delta, controls a direct route to

[4] S. Whittemore Boggs, *International Boundaries* (New York: Columbia University Press, 1940): p. 13.

[5] Richard Hartshorne, "A Survey of Boundary Problems in Europe," *Geographic Aspects of International Relations,* C. C. Colby, ed. (Chicago: University of Chicago Press, 1938).

[6] Malcolm J. Proudfoot, *European Refugees: 1939–52* (London: Faber & Faber, Ltd., 1957).

the Turkish straits. World War II thus eliminated one major danger only to create another. Post-war Europe was divided along ideological lines into a Western and an Eastern Europe, separated by the so-called "Iron Curtain," a phrase of Nazi origin which Winston Churchill used and thus publicized, but this division has become somewhat less pronounced. The major problem for both Europes became economic and political survival and the preservation of the civilization for which each stands. The United States has intervened in Western Europe with military, financial, and political force in an effort to preserve the uneasy balance. On both sides of the theoretical divide, policies have been pursued toward closer association for economic purposes and for security, and it is becoming increasingly recognized that the age of the small independent state is passing and that only larger and stronger political units can face the hazards of the future. These have markedly reduced owing to the U.S.S.R.'s sharply changed relations with its former Chinese ally. Yet a number of countries are unaligned or less clearly aligned. There are neutral states—Switzerland, Austria, Sweden, and the Republic of Ireland; democratic Finland and Communist Yugoslavia, both nicely poised between East and West; and Spain, ruled by a dictatorship, its outlook clearly oriented toward the West.

THE TREND TOWARD ECONOMIC AND POLITICAL INTEGRATION

The "astoundingly riven structure" of Europe has deep roots in history, and it is only by stages that larger functional units and eventual federal union may be expected. Certainly, attempts to create unity by force have always failed: witness the attempts of Napoleon, Kaiser Wilhelm II, and Hitler to dominate the continent. Even powerful persuasion from outside may arouse reactions: although in 1947 the U.S. government offered substantial financial aid to "the entire continent west of Asia, including the

United Kingdom and the U.S.S.R.," this offer was accepted by only 17 of the European states (Fig. 10–2), and the emergence of the two Europes became at once apparent. Nevertheless, since the end of World War II, Europe is, at long last, beginning to shed some of its political and economic parochialism in recognition of the common heritage of culture which it shares. And even though the trend is toward the separate integration of two Europes, opposed and divergent, this may be considered a hopeful trend toward currently attainable ends. Indeed, but for the external danger from Soviet military power, coupled with encouragement from the United States, Western Europe would have hardly advanced toward economic and political partnership to the extent that it has. An earlier difficulty which no longer persists was that several of the leading countries of Western Europe, notably the United Kingdom and France, retained political commitments to overseas territories and peoples. However, the social, economic, and financial systems of the Western European countries are by no means uniform. We attempt in the table on page 617 to explain briefly the new organizations which have been created to reduce, if not to eliminate, the weaknesses and dangers of independent statehood in Western Europe.

The initiative of the United States, personified in General Marshall, took the form of imaginative and realistic help for the peoples of Europe, who were exhausted by their war effort. Marshall Plan aid made possible the rebuilding of war-oriented and war-stricken economies and the rapid recovery of production. It gave birth to new cooperative institutions—the Organization for European Economic Cooperation (OEEC) and later the European Payments Union (EPU). OEEC was a notable achievement which worked fruitfully and since 1961 has been replaced by the Organization for Economic Cooperation and Development (OECD), which is no longer a purely European body since its membership now embraces the United States, Canada, and

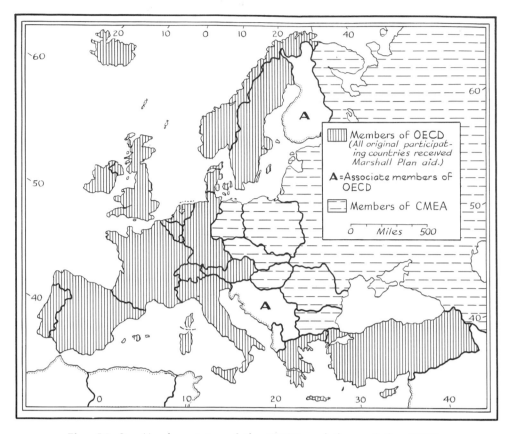

Fig. 10–2. Member states of the OECD and those of the CMEA.

Japan, with Australia, Finland, and Yugoslavia as associates in certain of its activities. In all, the membership of OECD, excluding associates, numbers 21.

On the economic front, too, the General Agreement on Tariffs and Trade (GATT), concluded in 1948 by many nations inside and outside Europe, did much to ease the flow of trade but at the same time called attention to the obstacles to the economic integration, in a full sense, even of Western Europe. GATT was instrumental in lowering tariff walls and in preventing tariff wars, but it was in no sense concerned with setting up a supranational authority which would entail a real divestment of the sovereignty of independent states. Herein lies the heart of the problem of economic and political union as distinct from economic and political association. Clarence K. Streit's *Union Now,*

which made its vigorous appeal to Europe in 1939 to abandon its time-dusty habits of independent nationalistic and thus parochial organization in favor of an Atlantic Federal Union better suited to an age of mechanized communication and transport, could and can have no effect unless the wide powers of national sovereignties are in some measure curtailed. And the idea of such curtailment has seemed hardest to accept by the greater Western European countries. Not surprisingly, although disappointingly to advocates of federalism seeking dramatic results, the first steps toward the abandonment of sovereignty with a view to the formation of larger, more viable economic units were taken by the smaller countries, and their difficulties on this road, by no means trivial, are a warning of the more serious difficulties that confront the greater European powers.

The States of Europe and the Alliances and Organizations to Which They Belonged in 1968

	Received Marshall Plan Aid	Council of Europe	NATO	OECD	WEU	ECSC	EEC (CM)	Euratom	EFTA	Warsaw Pact and Comecon (CMEA)
Albania										
Austria	x	x		x					x	
Belgium	x	x	x	x	x	x	x	x		
Bulgaria										x
Cyprus		x								
Czechoslovakia										x
Denmark	x	x	x	x					x	
Finland				Assoc.					Assoc.	
France	x	x	x	x	x	x	x	x		
East Germany										x
West Germany	x	x	x	x	x	x	x	x		
Greece	x	x	x	x			Assoc.			
Hungary										x
Iceland	x	x	x	x						
Ireland	x	x		x						
Italy	x	x	x	x	x	x	x	x		
Luxembourg	x	x	x	x	x	x	x	x		
Malta		x								
Netherlands	x	x	x	x	x	x	x	x		
Norway	x	x	x	x					x	
Poland										x
Portugal	x		x	x					x	
Romania										x
Spain				x						
Sweden	x	x		x					x	
Switzerland	x	x		x		Assoc.		x	x	
Turkey	x	x	x	x			Assoc.			
U.K.	x	x	x	x	x	Assoc.		Assoc.	x	
U.S.S.R.										x
Yugoslavia				Assoc.						
Non-European Members										
Australia				Assoc.						
Canada			x	x				Assoc.		
Japan				x						
Mongolia										x (Comecon only)
U.S.A.			x	x				Assoc.		

NOTE: 'Assoc.' indicates that the country has associate membership in the organization.
NATO   North Atlantic Treaty Organization
OECD   Organization for Economic Cooperation and Development
WEU   Western European Union
ECSC   European Coal and Steel Community
EEC   the European Economic Community, also known as the Common Market
EFTA   the European Free Trade Association, also known as the Outer Seven
CMEA   Council for Mutual Economic Aid (also known as *Comecon*)

Benelux. In 1921 the small landlocked state of Luxembourg formed a customs union with its neighbor Belgium, and the Netherlands, which borders Belgium, became a partner in 1947 (Fig. 10–3). Benelux has developed by stages, facing and overcoming difficulties and national fears. It has reduced tariffs between the three countries, thus increasing the flow of their trade, and has established a common tariff to the outside world. It has achieved success by hard effort, by give and take, and by willing the

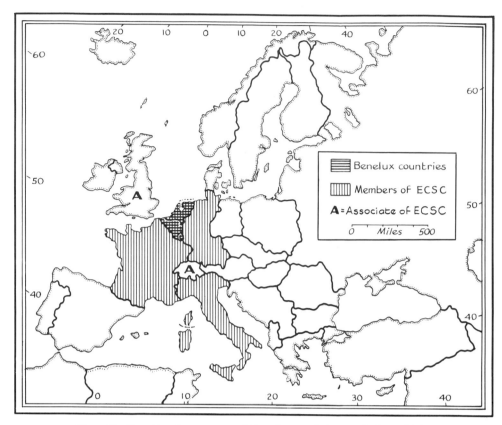

Fig. 10–3. Member states of Benelux and those of the ECSC.

success of its venture. It is significant, however, that the attempt to expand Benelux by the inclusion of France and Italy had to be abandoned because of the reluctance of France.

The North Atlantic Treaty Organization. The initiative of the United Kingdom in concluding the defensive Treaty of Brussels in 1948 with France and the Benelux countries, together with stimulus from the United States and Canada, made possible the achievement of the North Atlantic Treaty Organization (NATO) in 1949. While this is fundamentally a grand alliance for defense, it also seeks to strengthen free institutions and was thought to contain the seeds of a broadly based multinational community. In the interest of common defense, NATO combines resources of no less than 15 countries: the United States, Canada, the United Kingdom, France, Italy, West Germany, Portugal, Belgium, the Netherlands, Luxembourg, Denmark, Norway, Iceland, Greece, and Turkey; the last two joined the organization in 1952, and West Germany joined in 1955. NATO geared all these countries into cooperative activity for the maintenance of the peace in Europe necessary for economic progress. It recognizes the belief, shared by almost all of its members, in democratic institutions and thus an aversion from totalitarian forms of government. Geographically, NATO gives expression to the concept of the North Atlantic as the "Midland Ocean" and of the Mediterranean Sea as but an arm or tributary of this ocean. Yet, with all its international machinery for action, NATO remains little more than a grand defensive alliance, conceived in military terms. Its façade of unity has conspicuously failed to conceal the divergent foreign policies of its principal partners in extra-European theaters such as Southeast Asia and the Middle East. Moreover the idea that a North Atlantic community might be forged has never taken root; indeed the policy of President de Gaulle, which envisages the Common Market as a "third force," strong, independent and comparable politically with the U.S. and the U.S.S.R., runs wholly contrary to this. Even as a defense structure NATO appears to have weakened in recent years. France has withdrawn her armed forces from the joint military command, although she declared in 1967 that she had no intention of withdrawing from this organization, the headquarters of which has been removed from Paris to Brussels. There has been clearly, too, a conviction that, as the Iron Curtain has become less divisive and as the Soviet Union remains preoccupied with its internal development problems and with a hostile and neighboring China, the Soviet danger to Western Europe has measurably reduced.

The sudden jolt to the West European countries given by the military intervention of the U.S.S.R. and four of its Socialist allies in Czechoslovakia has served only to strengthen NATO and to reaffirm its usefulness in maintaining peace in Europe.

Western European Union (WEU). The breakdown of the attempt to establish a European Defense Community, when France rejected the concept in early 1954, finally resulted in a wider organization being established in October, 1954, which consisted of the Benelux countries, Italy, West Germany, France, and the United Kingdom. This became known as the Western European Union and its Council meets every three months. These regular meetings provide one of the main meeting places for government officials of the EEC countries and the United Kingdom, notably since the breakdown of talks on Britain's entry to the Common Market in January, 1963.

Council of Europe. This body was established in 1949 with its headquarters at Strasbourg, and its membership has gradually expanded until now there are 18 members. The Council works through a Council of Ministers and also a consultative assembly which meets each year and works, especially in the cultural field, toward closer cooperation between member countries with an ultimate aim of a more unified Europe.

The European Coal and Steel Community. Under the leadership and inspiration of M. Spaak, then prime minister of Belgium, "Little Europe" emerged and achieved a marked success when the Schuman Plan for the European Coal and Steel Community (ECSC) was launched on January 1, 1952. Member states are The German Federal Republic, France, Italy, and the three Benelux countries (Fig. 10–4). Economic interdependence cannot be better illustrated than by the coal, iron, and steel industries of Western Europe, where, on economic grounds, the flow of these commodities across international frontiers should be free and where, too, industrial locations should be chosen ideally on economic rather than purely political grounds. ECSC organizes the pooling of the fuel, ore, and scrap resources of "Little Europe" and has established a common market in coal, iron ore, and steel and, by capital loans and expert advice facilities, the re-equipping of existing plants and the locating of new plants. The initial success of ECSC owed a considerable amount to its timely inception when markets were expanding, but since then it has successfully weathered a number of difficulties, including temporary recessions and the need to adjust the coal industries of member countries to the changing pattern of demand and to the problem of uneconomic collieries in certain areas. A measure of the success of ECSC can be gathered from the table on page 620 which shows how much the production of steel has increased; after the U.S. and the U.S.S.R., the ECSC is the largest producer of steel in the world.

Comparative Production of ECSC (EEC), U.K., U.S.S.R., and U.S.
(million tons)

	1950			1966		
	Coal	*Iron Ore*	*Steel*	*Coal*	*Iron Ore*	*Steel*
ECSC (EEC)	217	44	31.6	200.8	70.8	73.8
U.K.	220	13	16.5	174.4	13.6	24.3
U.S.S.R.	185 (1951)	40	27.3	586.6	160.3	97 (1965)
U.S.A.	505	99	87.8	476.8	90.7	119.7

SOURCES: *British Iron and Steel Federation Statistical Yearbook 1967 et al. Stravna Sovetov za 50 let (Country of the Soviets during 50 years)* Moscow, 1967, pp. 58–59.

From the political point of view, ECSC has achieved much, above all by closely associating France and West Germany, to their mutual benefit. Britain became linked with ECSC as an associate in 1954, and Switzerland signed a form of association in 1957.

The European Economic Community (EEC): The Common Market.

The success in launching the European Coal and Steel Community encouraged the six members of ECSC to explore the possibility of creating a customs union (Fig. 10–4). After meetings at Messina in 1955 and at Venice in 1956 they agreed on the idea of a common market and declared their aim in the Treaty of Rome of March, 1957, as follows:

The Community's mission shall be, by establishing a common market and gradually removing difficulties between the economic policies of member states, to promote throughout the Community by the harmonious development of economic activities, continuous and balanced expansion, increased stability, a more rapid improvement in the standard of living and closer relations between its member states.

The treaty came into force on January 1, 1958, and the common market envisaged was to be achieved in stages spread over 12 to 15 years. The first steps to free trade within the Community were taken 1 year after this date.

The measures envisaged by the EEC, in pursuit of its declared objectives, are comprehensive, radical, and enlightened. Restrictions on trade and on the movement of capital and labor between the six states are being removed; a common policy on agriculture, transportation, and fisheries is being formulated; and a common trade policy is being established toward states outside the Community. A European Investment Bank and a European Social Fund have been set up, and measures to coordinate national economic policies and even to align national laws are contemplated. And the Community has made links with associate overseas countries, e.g., the colonial (or formerly colonial) dependencies of France, Belgium, Italy, and the Netherlands, so as to increase trade and promote economic and social progress.

To carry out this ambitious program the Community created administrative, legislative, judicial, and financial machinery. This consists of a Council of Ministers, drawn from member countries, which acts either unanimously or by majority decision (the voting powers of members are realistically weighted: France, West Germany, and Italy each have four votes, Belgium and the Netherlands have two each, and Luxembourg has one). The Council of Ministers is advised by a Common Market Commission of nine members who are chosen by the Council on the recommendation of the governments of member states. The Consultative Committee is composed of a number of parliamentarians chosen by the national parliaments. A Court of Justice exists, as also two committees with consultative powers, an Economic and Social Committee and a Monetary Committee. Further provisions cover national contribu-

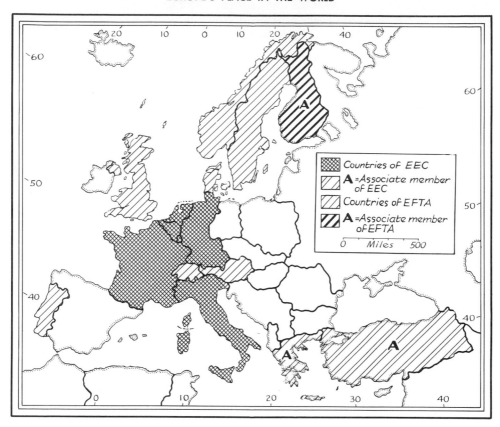

Fig. 10—4. Member states of the EEC and those of the EFTA.

tions to the European Investment Bank and to the Overseas Investment Fund.

What economic resources do the six states command and how far are these adequate to their set task? They command a total population of 186 million (providing thus a labor force only a little smaller than that of the United States) and a substantial industrial potential, as the comparative figures in the table below clearly show.

It is not yet clear that this promising blueprint will necessarily be translated into the envisaged fine edifice within the prescribed period of 12 to 15 years. Its first specific advance was made on January 1, 1959, when 10 per cent reductions of existing tariffs were made, bringing repercussions both within and without. There have since been a progressive series of tariff and quota reductions but the final adjustments which were to have been made by July 1, 1968 have not been achieved.

The Community has been faced with many problems, not only temporary economic ones associated, for example, with the adjustments required in some branches of agriculture and the difficulties over documentation and regulations for intra-community freedom of road, rail, and barge traffic, but also more fundamental problems of a political nature. Some of the difficulties are both political and economic: for example, the stability of the currencies of member countries is necessary before the free flow of capital funds can be achieved. As yet, the question of a unified currency has not been decided. Different levels and types of social services have led to variations in labor costs; and the need to achieve some comparability and interchange privileges, which is required for mobility of labor, raises serious political questions. Some of the Community's agricultural problems are also deeply rooted in politics, especially

Populations and Production (in Million Tons) of the European Economic Community in 1966 as compared with those of OECD, U.K., U.S., U.S.S.R., and Eastern Europe

	EEC	OECD [1]	U.K.	U.S.	U.S.S.R.	Eastern Europe [2]
Population (million)	181.6	311.2	54.7	194.6	230.6	100.1
Coal (hard)	200.8	388.2	174.4	476.8	585.6	159.1
Lignite	107.3	122.7	—	2.8	149.8	404.7
Petroleum (million metric tons)	18.3	55.9	0.1	429.9	265.1	15.0
Natural gas in billion cubic meters	21.5	48.3	0.2	487.2	143.0	21.0
Steel	73.8	110.5	24.3	119.7	97.0	28.9
Aluminium	1.0	1.8	0.2	3.1	1.3	0.2
Sulfuric acid	12.2	19.0	3.4	22.5	8.5	4.2
Cement	85.8	132.9	17.0	65.0	72.4	31.8
Motor vehicles (all types in million units)	5.8	8.4	2.2	11.1	0.8	0.3
Oil refining capacity	297.3	407.8	72.2	512.4	225.0	33.7

[1] Excluding Turkey but including United Kingdom. Also includes non-European members.
[2] Excluding Yugoslavia and Albania.
SOURCES: United Nations' and others.

since many member governments depend on considerable parliamentary support from the agrarian voter. Fortunately, in the early period after its inception, the conditions of trade were such that EEC was able to grow and to expand economically at the same time—one favorable factor was heavy American defense spending in Europe—and this gave it strength to withstand trade fluctuations and policy differences later on. However, it is in the political sphere that the strains are most evident and the divisions deepest. An initial political problem concerned agriculture and France's reluctance to agree to a formula for the integration of its agriculture with that of its fellow members.

It should be recalled that Britain could have joined the European Economic Community at its inception in 1958 but, for a variety of reasons, did not seek to do so. The original membership of six has since then increased only in respect to associate members. Greece was so admitted in 1962 and Turkey in 1963. On July 1, 1963, the scope of the Community was further broadened by the signing of the Yaoundé Convention which associates the Malagasy Republic and 18 other independent African states with the Community. All these were

formerly colonies of Community members. In 1966 Nigeria became the first English-speaking country to become an associate member. Trade agreements have been signed with Israel, Lebanon, and Iran and negotiations on associate membership with Kenya, Uganda, Tanzania, Morocco, Algeria, and Tunisia were in early 1968 at various stages of progress.

Thus the Six have re-established links with many countries outside Europe. However, such associations are much more limited than full membership and it is with regard to those European countries seeking full membership that problems are greatest, for as the Community gets larger so the difficulty of agreement increases, and one of the factors involved in Britain's wish to join is the knowledge that, should she be admitted, other countries, especially Denmark, Norway, and Ireland, would quickly submit applications. Such an enlarged Community would have a population of 250 million, a steel production of 110 million tons, and would become far and away the world's largest trading group.

The failure of the United Kingdom's application to join EEC as a full member is worth discussion for the light which it sheds on the nature and purpose of this organization which might appear as both a unifying and divisive force in Europe.

THE UNITED KINGDOM AND THE COMMON MARKET. The decline of the United Kingdom from a former position of financial, economic, and political ascendancy is one of the outstanding changes in Europe (and in the world) since the end of World War II. The problem has been one of adjustment to sharply changed circumstances characterized above all by the abandonment of empire and by the rise of two super-states and of other major industrial competitors, notably the Common Market and Japan. Britain has had to reduce what were once world-wide commitments, to face recurrent difficulties in maintaining the world's major reserve currency—sterling—and, at the same time, to try to preserve her relatively high living standards. The Commonwealth, which came into being as a loose organization of independent states which were once part of an empire controlled from London, confers no special advantages on the United Kingdom, although it constitutes an area within which it conducts more than one-quarter of its overseas trade. Clearly Britain needs new objectives and new alignments. The idea of joining the Common Market, although this has never been fully thought out and evaluated in respect to the benefits and costs involved, led to Britain's approach to the Six in 1961 to explore the possibility of membership and again in 1967 when formal membership of EEC was requested. Britain's failure to secure entry, and her failure in 1967–68 even to get negotiations started, was the direct result of the attitude and policy of France directed by President de Gaulle. The Low Countries, especially the Netherlands, have always been strong supporters of Britain's entry and other members have supported this view. When, however, in late 1967, the Six had to decide whether or not negotiations should begin, it became apparent that some countries, notably The Federal German Republic, wished to try to persuade France rather than invite a head-on confrontation, while others, including the Netherlands, favored non-cooperation with France.

It must be admitted that there was some substance to the French case. The trade balance of the United Kingdom was persistently adverse and sterling as a reserve currency was subject to strong pressure. The Six faced difficult, unresolved problems notably those relating to agriculture which, it could be argued, should be first settled before they were further complicated by the entry of a new member of major political and industrial weight. Further, Britain's entry would have facilitated that of Denmark, Norway and Ireland and, with Sweden, Switzerland, Austria, and Spain also seeking association, the Community would have become so enlarged as greatly to increase the difficulties of decision making. However, the rigidly obstructive position adopted by France is more easily explained in political terms: the admission of Britain would have jeopardized de Gaulle's position as leader of EEC and also his efforts to build up a "third force" which would be "a counterweight to the immense power of the United States." In the event de Gaulle's will prevailed and, although EEC was strained and shaken, it survived intact. Yet the whole episode in no way advanced the high purpose inscribed in the Treaty of Rome that the Six, by enlisting new adherents, should work towards the unification of Europe.

Other Options Open to Britain? It should be noted that, although Britain has ceased to be a world power in the political and military sense, it is sustained by world commerce. Of this about one-quarter is with the Commonwealth, excluding Canada, and almost as much is with the EEC. The share of Britain's trade with North America is nearly as large, and that with its EFTA partners not greatly less. Of the options which in theory lie open to Britain the attempt to create a common market within a strengthened EFTA or within the Commonwealth seems both impracticable and unpromising. The best option is to seek the creation of a North Atlantic Free Trade Area (NAFTA). This concept, to which President Kennedy called attention in 1961 as an Atlantic Partnership, has been carefully examined by groups of experts on both sides of the North Atlantic. It envisages the association of the

The nuclear power program has reached the following stage in Euratom (net power output in megawatts):

	Belgium	France	W. Germany	Italy	Netherlands	European Community	Britain
In service	—	833	317	607	—	1,757	3,494
Under construction	143	1,741	618	—	52	2,544	3,330
Total	143	2,574	935	607	52	4,301	6,824

SOURCE: *European Community*, November 1966.

U.S.A., Canada, and EFTA, which others might join, notably Japan, Australia, and New Zealand. Clearly a free trade area of this great size could produce economies of scale, large markets, great specialization and strong competitiveness. It is estimated that NAFTA would achieve a higher real rate of growth of national product than the EEC with Britain included. Here would seem to be a rational and highly attractive alternative policy for Britain, looking across the oceans rather than across the English Channel. However, NAFTA has not as yet been officially sponsored and if it came to exist, Britain might find herself uncomfortably placed in Europe between two hostile blocks —NAFTA and EEC.

European Atomic Energy Union (Euratom). This organization, established by the Treaty of Rome in 1957 and concerned with the peaceful and profitable use of nuclear energy, owes its origin to the initiative of the six member countries of the European Coal and Steel and the European Economic Communities. Euratom takes note of the increasing industrial demands for fuel and power, and of the eventual needs for supplies of nuclear energy at a reasonable cost. It is clearly alive to dangers of this new source of power. The Union provides funds for research and for the dissemination of knowledge about atomic energy and tries to insure that its uses will be peaceful only. Similar institutions to those set up by the ECSC are contemplated. The U.S. signed an association agreement with Euratom in 1958 and this agreement was broadened and made closer in 1964; Canada and the U.K. became associate members in 1959.

This power station construction program has already resulted in a big increase in actual electricity production:

	Production (in MkWh)	Per cent total electricity production
1960	130	—
1965	4,354	1.1
1970 (est.)	28,000	5
1975 (est.)	120,000	15

European Free Trade Association. The Common Market is an organization of only six of the eighteen countries of Western Europe which are already cooperating within the OECD (Fig. 10–4). The remaining countries were unwilling, after consideration, to align themselves with the policy agreed to by the Six. In particular, the United Kingdom, the chief industrial country outside the Common Market, refused to join, for various reasons.[7] Full membership for the United Kingdom would mean the relaxation of commonwealth preference, especially for foodstuffs other than wheat and for industrial raw materials. Its trade with its Commonwealth partners slightly exceeds that with the Six, although the former is shrinking and the latter is growing. The United Kingdom's position as banker for the whole sterling area presented another difficulty, and, more generally, the ultimate aims of the Common Market, involving a surrender of sovereignty, were too radical for

[7] André Siegfried has remarked that "England is as a ship moored off the coast of Europe, always prepared to weigh anchor." Cited by J. Goormaghtigh, "European Integration," *International Conciliation* 488 (February, 1953): p. 58.

its immediate acceptance. The United Kingdom and, indeed, most of the other members of OECD are necessarily concerned with their trade prospects now that the Common Market is launched. They are desirous, too, of continuing and strengthening their association, and are apprehensive lest the activities of the Six should rend the economic unity of Western Europe toward which they have been arduously striving. Indeed, "the European idea," the eventual need of joint institutions of a political character, is the important issue involved in the EFTA idea.

The idea of a "free trade area," of which the Common Market might provide the nucleus around which other countries of Western Europe could be grouped, was a United Kingdom proposal which appeared to find general approval. The United Kingdom estimated that its trade position in Western Europe would suffer under the Common Market and could improve within this free trade area if it attentively studied the needs of this important market. But the broader and more fundamental consideration was that Western Europe as a whole could consolidate and strengthen its economic position in the world only by some such positive and rational policy, which might effect a general rise in living standards and help towards the development of a community spirit.

The central idea of the proposal of a free trade area was the removal of tariffs, quotas, and similar restrictions within it, although the external tariffs of each member would remain. Further, it recognized that member countries would be unwilling to renounce agricultural subsidies and that its policies involved no opening of the doors to free movement of labor and no infringement of state sovereignty. While many critics have rated this a weak scheme, it seemed likely to prove acceptable to the Six, as well as to the United Kingdom, Austria, and the Scandinavian countries, but not to France, which has the weakest and most protected economy of the Common Market states.

The breakdown of the free trade area talks, and the rejection of the British plan for an interim arrangement which would have extended the quota enlargements inside the EEC to all OECD nations on a reciprocal basis, forced governments outside the EEC to consider the problem afresh. The chance of a free trade area on a limited scale arose in the summer of 1958, when the employers' organizations and industrial federations of the United Kingdom, Sweden, Norway, Denmark, Austria, and Switzerland agreed on the outlines of a free-trade area which they wished to see in operation for Europe. Discussions on this subject at government level took place in the summer of 1959 at Stockholm, between the representatives of these six countries and also of Portugal. The agreement reached by the Treaty of Stockholm in November was ratified in the spring of 1960. Thus was formed the European Free Trade Association (EFTA), popularly known as "The Outer Seven." It was so called because the seven countries lie around the EEC (Common Market) block (Fig. 10-4).

The EFTA is a loose organization of independent states with two distinct purposes. First, it seeks to create by 1970 a free-trade area by the removal of all the trade barriers between the Seven. Second, it hopes to create a good position from which to bargain with EEC. Unlike the six Common Market countries, the Seven have no interest in ultimate federal union: three of them are neutral states—Switzerland, Sweden, and Austria—while the United Kingdom has bonds with the Commonwealth, and Portugal with its overseas dependencies. Also unlike the Common Market, the Outer Seven is not establishing a common tariff against the outside world. Fortunately, the interests of the countries of both trade groups are closely interlocked. West Germany exports more to the Outer Seven than to her Common Market partners, and the Outer Seven as a group exports more to the Common Market than to one another. Various attempts have been made to bridge the gulf between EFTA and EEC but without real success. The possibility of some of the members becoming partners in EEC would lead to a break up of the existing EFTA. In that event, those members left might then either form an agreement of association with EEC or form a new EFTA which might embrace other countries, such as Finland and Iceland.

Council for Mutual Economic Aid. Under the pressure of Moscow, the Communist countries of Europe refused Marshall Plan aid, and also refused to join the Organization for European Economic Cooperation, which was set up to implement it. In reaction, they set up in 1949 the Council for Mutual Economic Aid (CMEA or COMECON), which, however, confined its activities largely to providing a market place where the Communist countries could coordinate their bilateral trade agreements. Stalin's idea was that the Soviet satellites should industrialize at all costs, whereas Khrushchev's was to link them to each other and to the Soviet Union by economic planning which would achieve regional specialization and division of labor in the interests of the whole bloc. After studies were made of the economic capacity of the member countries, Moscow announced in 1955 a unified five-year plan. It was hoped thus to start in 1956 on a plan which set as its eventual goal "overtaking the capitalist world." The proposed plans were grandiose, however, because they did not take full account of acute shortages of capital, fuel, and power, and industrial raw materials which the U.S.S.R. was either unwilling or unable to supply. The assertion by the Poles of some degree of independence of Moscow and the rise to power of Gomulka, coupled with the revolt of the Hungarians, reflected politically the difficulty of carrying out joint economic plans in the satellite countries. These plans had to be scaled down, while the U.S.S.R. was forced to provide emergency economic aid.

Actually, the original targets set for the 1956–60 plan period were replaced in June, 1957, by lower, more realistic ones to be reached during the seven-year period 1959–65. East Germany concentrated on the chemical industry related to its huge brown-coal deposits, and receives petroleum by pipeline from the U.S.S.R. On the other hand, the steel industries of East Germany received no further investment funds, which were turned to the more economic steel-producing centers of Czechoslovakia and of Poland. New Polish mines were opened, with Czech and East German equipment, but the Zwickaw mines of East Germany were to be eventually abandoned. Increased aluminum production in Hungary, using local bauxite, and cellulose production in Romania, using reeds from the Danube Delta were envisaged, with technical help and equipment from East Germany. Machine building of various types will be rationalized, so that the most efficiently located sites are to be developed and the uneconomic ones shut down. In short, it was hoped that a policy of economic integration in Eastern Europe could be rationally conceived, and as it is applied the Soviet satellites will be tied more firmly to each other and to the U.S.S.R. The pace of development depends largely on the extent to which the U.S.S.R. is willing and able to supply necessary capital, fuel, and raw materials, and on the extent of dependency on the U.S.S.R. each of the Communist countries is willing to accept. It already had to be modified to the extent that some members, notably Romania, prefer their own national objectives.

The Warsaw Pact. In reply to NATO, the U.S.S.R. reorganized its defense system by the Warsaw Pact of 1955. It thus associates itself militarily with Poland, East Germany, Czechoslovakia, Hungary, Romania, and Bulgaria. Note that the deviation of Yugoslavia from Moscow's line causes a territorial break in the pattern of the Warsaw Pact states, while that of Albania deprived the pact members of its only Mediterranean seaboard.

THE UNITY OF EUROPE

It may be argued that the method of regional analysis applied in this book has the disadvantage of emphasizing regional differences and thus obscuring aspects of unity. The reader will not need to be reminded that, as has been shown in this chapter as also in those which precede it, Europe presents the character of a patchwork quilt, so many and varied are the patterns which are revealed alike on its surface and in the fabric of its political, social, and economic life. The history of Europe, which began long before its inhabitants could make written records, clearly lies behind the regional variety and richness of its cultural geography. In this respect Europe compares only with Asia and is in contrast to the other continents where human societies have been agents of geographical change during a span of only centuries rather than of millennia. But one should ask whether social and cultural diversities, although they present evident divisions within the Continent, prevent its unity in important respects. There are so many states, more or less of the nation type; so many languages which restrict easy communication; so many organizations for primarily economic purposes; so many policies and attitudes; and so many Christian creeds and indeed religions that one may well wonder whether Europe has an identity and reality as a whole and, if it has, whether these are clear and explicable.

The answers to these questions are in the affirmative, although it is by no means easy to explain simply the nature and strength of European unity. Nor is it easy to assess how deep and divisive are current differences and cleavages, which have been much reduced since the first edition of this book was written, and how long they may last.

First, it seems clear that, viewed from outside, Europe is a unit which one can validly conceive. This was first recognized by thinkers and travelers of ancient Greece, to whom "Europa" signified a specific and distinctive quarter of their known world (see Introduction, pp. 3–5). So also it appears today, for example, to those who come from the United States for reasons of business, study, or pleasure or to serve in the armies of NATO. In a similar way European vis-

itors to the United States, whatever their nationality, are very conscious that they are European, as the authors of this chapter have always felt, even when their native language is English. All this is merely a reflection of the fact that the national cultures of the peoples of Europe are rooted in a common soil and that, as they have developed, they have been nourished—but not equally—by the selfsame sources of civilization. So it is that as he moves across the Continent from one end to another, the national of a European country feels, in a certain sense, at home, for he sees continually recurrent cultural features, alike in town and country, which have much in common. As a matter of history, the European peoples have all derived much alike from the civilizations of Greece, Rome, and Byzantium,[8] as also from the Christian religion. While these have been the major cultural influences on Europe, embracing as they do all sides of civilized life—literature and the other arts, law, religion, philosophy, science, and statecraft—there have been others, too, notably those associated with Judaism and Islam. Europe was fortunate in its early start, as in its cultural sponsors, but it is a mark of its peoples that they have always shown remarkable vitality, energy, originality, and inventiveness. Again, as a matter of history and in illustration of this, recall the cultural and political leadership achieved by France in the seventeenth century and the industrial revolution—a landmark in world history—which had its home in Britain in the succeeding centuries. Thus, looked at from inside, there is an underlying unity to Europe which springs from its history yet resides essentially also in regional diversity.

The vitality and energy of Europeans have taken many forms. One has been its fertility in men, noted above (pp. 602–03); another has been its addiction to war. Of these, some at least were fought against would-be dictators; some to defend European civilization against armed intruders of non-Christian

[8] This city was renamed in turn Constantinople and, as now, Istanbul.

faith; others were revolutionary wars fought to overthrow regimes that obstructed the freedom and betterment of life for the masses. In such wars at least Europeans fought for reasons of principle and may be thought to have advanced human progress, even though their results often fell short of expectation. And lastly, it has been a mark of Europeans that they have sought continually to liberate the individual for creative work, to advance knowledge, and to increase wealth, as the basis of welfare: in this last respect, it is clear that, despite the destructiveness of two wars of this century, they retain their former powers, even though in the decades ahead they will be outpaced by North America and the Soviet Union whose technological superiority and untapped resources should confirm their ascendancy.

If one considers now the major differences and cleavages of the Continent, it is well to remember that these have always existed. There were the Roman Empire in Europe and the Europe of the "barbarians" which lay beyond it. There were the Roman Empire in the West, and that in the East. There were the Christian Europe of the Catholic Church organized from Rome and the other Christian Europe which focused on Constantinople. Parts of Europe for centuries were under Moslem rule in Iberia, as in the lower Danubian lands and the Southwestern Peninsula. There have always been divisions and cultural differences and today, although they have taken an ideological form due to the rise of Soviet Communism, one is struck by the evidence of their erosion. The Soviet empire, built by Stalin to defend the U.S.S.R. and to prepare the way for a Communist Europe, is now challenged even if it is neither undermined nor falling in ruins. The pressures toward the liberalization and democratization of rigid governments controlled by the single Party and exerted by populations better educated, better-off, and more demanding than formerly are proving irresistible in one country after another, and strong nationalist policies have had more scope, as in Romania and Czechoslovakia,

thanks to the Sino-Soviet conflict which has toppled the monolith of Communism. Thus the East European allies of the U.S.S.R. are trying to lessen their dependence on their overlord and to trade more vigorously with West Europe, while retaining reformed Communist regimes and their vital links with Moscow. Thus also the U.S.S.R., with its long Asiatic flank now exposed to a hostile China, seeks stable and workable relations in Europe. COMECON remains but is subject to the stresses and strains imposed by member countries whose nationalistic interests persist. The Warsaw Pact remains, backed by the military power of the U.S.S.R. which stations forces still in Poland, East Germany, and, since August 1968, in Czechoslovakia. Certainly the two Germanies and the Berlin Wall remind us that an ideological (and national) division persists as a barrier to European unity, for no solution appears in sight. In West Europe the European Economic Community has become a strong and successful economic bloc, although it has probably passed through its period of supergrowth. It has not, however, succeeded in creating either a political union of the Six, still less a unified Western Europe. Even so, it has weathered many difficulties and crises and confirms that some wide measure of unity may be achieved for specified purposes. Moreover, given time, it may prove able to unify a great part of the Continent by admitting the countries, notably those grouped in EFTA, which have been knocking at the gate. And since trends toward such unity must grow from grass roots, interest attaches to the growing scale of labor migration, cultural exchanges, and tourism, as also to a variety of quietly informative, cooperative studies which have been sponsored by the Council of Europe.

Last, if one looks far into the future, it is worth asking what the limits of Europe are within which unity might ultimately be achieved. By common consent the U.S.S.R. is a single unit and the Urals have no meaning as a limit. At least in its national cast, Soviet Siberia has European characteristics;

so also has North America. On a long view, the valid unit is not Europe, however it is determined, but the Northern Hemisphere, "with its common origin of Christianity, Indo-European language, Roman heritage, and urban civilization." [9]

EUROPE'S ROLE IN THE WORLD

Europe's influence on the world has been unsurpassed. European discoverers ventured across the oceans to chart newly found lands in the Americas and in Oceania, and to penetrate Africa south of the Sahara. They forged, too, maritime routes to the lands of ancient civilization in the Asian Orient. These efforts established two kinds of political dependencies, those which served primarily as trading stations and those which served also as homes for European immigrants. Settlement overseas, particularly in North and South America, Australia and New Zealand, and parts of southern Africa, introduced European languages, techniques, economy, and ideas and initiated the development of the nations of the New World. In time, these nations successively shook off the political control exercised by the mother countries in Europe. Even so, many of these nations are still, if somewhat loosely, associated with their European "parent." The most extensive and powerful group, with territories in every continent, is the Commonwealth, of which the United Kingdom is senior partner. Extensive, too, and strategically important, are the territories, mainly in Africa, associated with France. Certain European nations, therefore, contributed much to the unrolling of the world map, and then to the evaluation of the resources of this expanded world. This is not the place to discuss Europe's no less striking contributions in the fields of science and technology, and of literature and the other arts.

The role of Europe in the world has, however, sharply changed. The works which it

[9] Hugh Seton-Watson, "How big is Europe? Is Russia European?" in *One Europe: Is It Possible?* (London, BBC Publications, 1966): p. 21.

initiated in so many parts of the world in establishing railroads, ports and towns, agriculture, industry, and trade have borne fruit, so much so that former economic and political dependencies have acquired enhanced stature both politically and economically. Economic nationalism and economic progress in oversea countries now give them a higher degree of self-sufficiency in manufactures formerly derived from European factories. The impact of two world wars, with all the sheer waste of manpower and wealth and all the dislocation which they entailed, brought to an end Europe's dominant position in the world's economy and politics, as it consolidated the primacy of the United States in the Western world. Europe's changing status is indeed relative, not absolute. It has rehabilitated and even expanded its economy since the end of World War II. Moreover, in Europe's eastern part, the Soviet Union and the Eastern European countries, starting late, and with forceful deliberation, to exploit their very considerable natural resources, are expanding industrially faster than any other country or group of countries and are now becoming increasingly capable of challenging the Western powers in the markets of the world. Also, further afield and making up, together with the U.S.S.R. and the other Communist countries, that third of humanity which is subject to Communist rule, the Chinese People's Republic, with its great reservoir of population, moves slowly forward toward a position which, before the end of this century, may be such as to embarrass or discomfort and compete with not only the Western world but its former Russian ally as well.

Europe west of the Communist countries has written the chapter of its history which was concerned with its leadership of the world. It now seeks, burdened as it is by defense costs, to maintain its still relatively high standard of living. No longer able to supplement its own food resources by the importation of cheap food from overseas, it concerns itself attentively with its own fields and farms, so as to increase their productivity. Aware that economic stability and progress are not a narrow local problem, it attempts, within its means, to promote economic developments in underdeveloped countries. Faced by changed demands for its manufactures in the world market, it strives, by specialization, to produce what is really wanted and, above all, to keep ahead in new productions (e.g., of nuclear-power plants) and in the provision of more elaborate manufactures, such as aircraft, automobiles, and ships. Clearly, to attain these ends, much depends on the maintenance of its high level of scientific and technological research and on the increasing skill of more and more workers.

A marked characteristic of Western Europe is its political fragmentation, the survival of many relatively small national states into an age of fast and easy transportation and communication. West of the East European countries, there are, excluding microstates, no less than 20 national states, which occupy only about a third of Europe as conventionally defined, an area equivalent to that of the United States, Australia, or Brazil. In this relatively small area, which coincides with the westerly peninsular protrusion of the continent, are concentrated 340 million people (one-tenth of mankind), the largest components being found in West Germany, the United Kingdom, Italy, and France. While it is being increasingly recognized that political fragmentation weakens the economy of Western Europe, as it also weakens its defensive strength, there are no short cuts either to effective political integration or to the creation of the community spirit which this necessitates. Only as education and thought bring the conviction that economic advantages and greater security can so accrue, and external political, economic, and military pressures, too, urge the relaxation of state sovereignties, can measures be taken, by stages, to produce larger functional units which make for a more rational economic use of available resources. The effects of these measures in creating new intergovernmental organizations are, we

have seen, in no sense dramatic, and they point to no sudden creation of a federal political structure for Western Europe such as the U.S.S.R. achieved in its vast Eurasian territories or such as characterize many nations of North and South America. But the reaction against political and economic separatism in Western Europe is in full swing, and so, in so far as specific multinational associations prove their value in specific fields of common interest, the ultimate goal of federation begins to loom on the horizon. For it should not be forgotten that, underlying its very evident divisions, Europe is rooted in a cultural past, distinctively its own.

BIBLIOGRAPHY

Books and Articles

BARACH, A. B. AND MODLEY, R. *The New Europe and its Economic Future.* New York: The Macmillan Co., 1964.

BENOITE, EMILE. *Europe at Sixes and Sevens.* New York, 1961.

Britain and Europe. London: Economist Intelligence Unit, 1957.

"The Common Market," *The East Lakes Geographer* I (1964).

The Commonwealth and Europe. London: Economist Intelligence Unit, 1960.

COPPOCK, JOHN O. *North Atlantic Policy—The Agricultural Gap.* New York: Twentieth Century Fund, 1963.

DEWAR, MARGARET. "Economic Cooperation in the Soviet Orbit," *The Yearbook of World Affairs.* London: Stevens & Sons, Ltd., 1939, 45–47.

DEWHURST, J. FREDERIC. *Europe's Needs and Resources.* New York: The Macmillan Company for the Twentieth Century Fund, 1961.

DIEBOLD, WILLIAM, JR. *The Schuman Plan: A Study in Economic Cooperation 1950–1959.* New York: Frederick A. Praeger, Inc., 1959.

The Economist (May 14, 1966), 723 (manpower map).

Europe + Energy. Luxembourg: The Spokesman of the ECSC's High Authority and European Community Information Service, 1967.

FAWCETT, CHARLES B. *The Bases of a World Commonwealth.* London: C. A. Watts & Co., Ltd., 1944.

HOFFMAN, GEORGE W. "The Role of Nuclear Power in Europe's Future Energy Balance,"

Annals Association of American Geographers XLVII (March, 1957): 15–40.

HOFFMAN, M. L. *The Problems of East-West Trade*. No. 511. New York: International Conciliation, 1957.

KASER, MICHAEL. *COMECON Integration Problems of the Planned Economies*. New York: Oxford University Press, 1965.

KINDLEBERGER, CHARLES P. *Europe's Postwar Growth*. Cambridge, Mass.: Harvard University Press, 1967.

KITZINGER, U. W. *The European Common Market and Community*. London: Routledge and Kegan Paul, 1967.

LICHTHEIM, GEORGE. *The New Europe—Today and Tomorrow*. New York: Frederick A. Praeger, 1963.

LISTER, LOUIS. *Europe's Coal and Steel Community*. New York: Twentieth Century Fund, 1960.

NYSTROM, J. WARREN, and MALOF, PETER. *The Common Market: The European Community in Action*. Searchlight book no. 5. Princeton, N.J.: D. Van Nostrand Co., 1962.

POLACH, JAROSLAV G. *EURATOM*. Dobbs Ferry, N.Y.: Oceana Publications Inc., 1964.

POSTAN, M. M. *An Economic History of Western Europe (1945–1964)*. London: Methuen, 1967.

QUIN, MARC. *The OEEC and the Common Market*. Paris: Organization for European Economic Cooperation, 1958.

Official Publications

(*Including statistics and statistical compilations*)

Basic Statistics of the Community (annual). Brussels: Statistical Office of the European Communities, 1965.

COMMUNAUTÉ EUROPÉENE DU CHARBON ET DE L'ACIER. *Bulletin Statistique* (bimonthly).

———. *Informations Statistiques* (quarterly).

ECONOMIC COMMISSION FOR EUROPE. *Economic Survey for Europe* (annual).

———. *Economic Bulletin for Europe* (three times a year).

Efta Bulletin and *Efta Reporter* (both monthly).

JOURNAL OF COMMON MARKET STUDIES (quarterly).

OECD OBSERVER (monthly).

ORGANIZATION FOR EUROPEAN ECONOMIC CO-OPERATION. *Statistical Bulletin* (bimonthly).

———. *Economic Growth 1960–1970*, 1966.

"Planned Nuclear Power Production in the EEC," *European Community* 80 (April, 1965).

UNITED NATIONS. *Statistical Yearbook* (annual).

———. *Demographic Yearbook* (annual).

Appendixes

DURATION (millions of years) ERA		TIME PERIODS (Geologic Formations)		AREAS AFFECTED BY	
				Fenno-Scandia	Northwest Europe
CENOZOIC	1	QUATERNARY	RECENT	⇒ ⇒ ⇒ ⇒ Vistula Warthe Saale Elster	⇒ ⇒ ⇒ "Newer Drift" "Older Drift"
			PLEISTO-CENE		
	70	TERTIARY	PLIOCENE MIOCENE OLIGOCENE EOCENE PALEOCENE	(A)	(A)
MESO-ZOIC	160	CRETACEOUS			
		JURASSIC			
		TRIASSIC			
PALEOZOIC	370	PERMIAN			
		CARBONIFEROUS		(H)	(H)
		DEVONIAN			
		SILURIAN		(C)	CALEDONIAN
		ORDOVICIAN			
		CAMBRIAN			
PROTEROZOIC	1,000	PRE-CAMBRIAN		BALTIC	⇒

OROGENIES (▇), MARINE CONDITIONS (〰), GLACIERS (⇒)

Central Europe	Alpine Europe	European Russia	Asiatic Russia
⇒ ⇒ ?	⇒ ⇒ ⇒ ⇒ Würm Riss Mindel Günz	⇒ ⇒ ⇒ Valdai Dnieper Oka	⇒ ? ⇒
(A)	**ALPINE**	(A)	(A)
			CIMMERIAN
HERCYNIAN	(H)	**URALIAN**	**ALTAI**
(C)			(C)
			⇒
			ANGARA

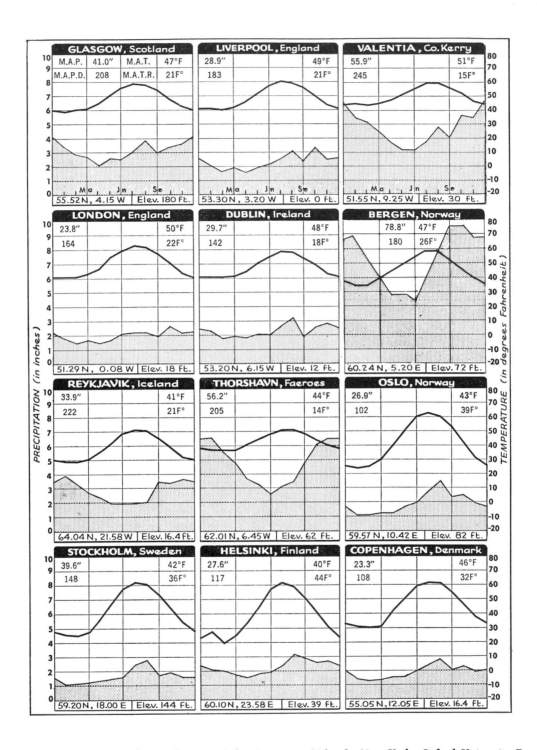

* Data from W. G. Kendrew, *Climates of the Continents* (4th ed.; New York: Oxford University Press, 1953); Great Britain, Air Ministry, Meteorological Office, *Tables of Temperature, Relative Humidity and Precipitation for the World. Part III, Europe* (London, 1958). Explanation of data given below

Selected Stations in Europe

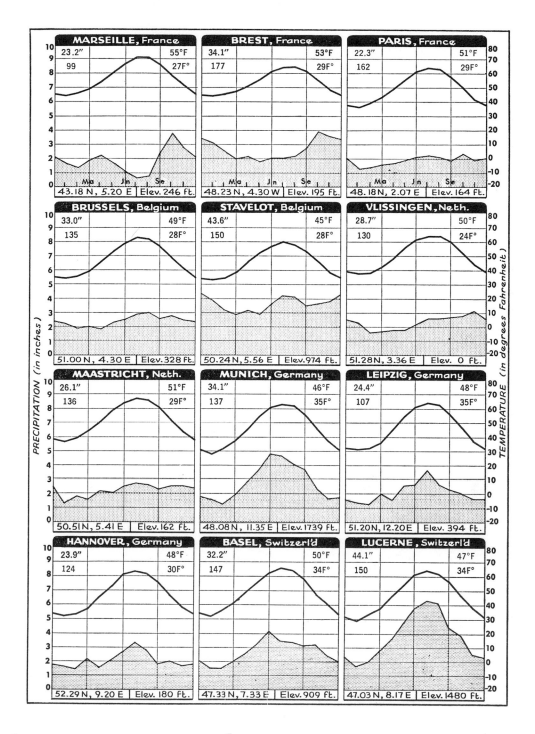

Station	M.A.P.	M.A.T.	M.A.P.D.	M.A.T.R.	Location	Elevation
MARSEILLE, France	23.2″	55°F	99	27F°	43.18 N, 5.20 E	Elev. 246 ft.
BREST, France	34.1″	53°F	177	29F°	48.23 N, 4.30 W	Elev. 195 ft.
PARIS, France	22.3″	51°F	162	29F°	48.18 N, 2.07 E	Elev. 164 ft.
BRUSSELS, Belgium	33.0″	49°F	135	28F°	51.00 N, 4.30 E	Elev. 328 ft.
STAVELOT, Belgium	43.6″	45°F	150	28F°	50.24 N, 5.56 E	Elev. 974 ft.
VLISSINGEN, Neth.	28.7″	50°F	130	24F°	51.28 N, 3.36 E	Elev. 0 ft.
MAASTRICHT, Neth.	26.1″	51°F	136	29F°	50.51 N, 5.41 E	Elev. 162 ft.
MUNICH, Germany	34.1″	46°F	137	35F°	48.08 N, 11.35 E	Elev. 1739 ft.
LEIPZIG, Germany	24.4″	48°F	107	35F°	51.20 N, 12.20 E	Elev. 394 ft.
HANNOVER, Germany	23.9″	48°F	124	30F°	52.29 N, 9.20 E	Elev. 180 ft.
BASEL, Switzerl'd	32.2″	50°F	147	34F°	47.33 N, 7.33 E	Elev. 909 ft.
LUCERNE, Switzerl'd	44.1″	47°F	150	34F°	47.03 N, 8.17 E	Elev. 1480 ft.

PRECIPITATION (in inches)

TEMPERATURE (in degrees Fahrenheit)

each station name: M.A.P. = mean annual precipitation (inches); M.A.P.D. = mean annual number of days with measurable precipitation; M.A.T. = mean annual temperature (°F); M.A.T.R. = mean annual temperature range (°F).

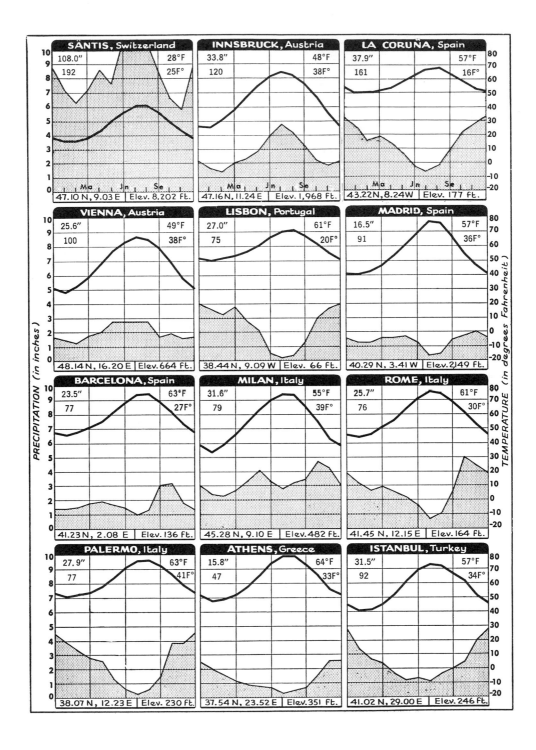

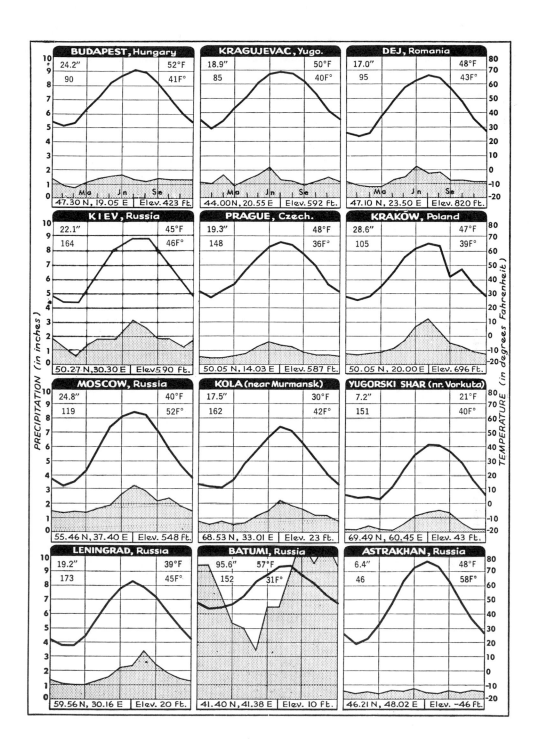

III. Statistical Tables

The statistical tables on pages 642–656 have been compiled from various sources. The reader should be warned about the difficulty of making international comparisons, especially if the statistics are prepared by different agencies, and he is reminded that the reliability of the data varies greatly. Even for those countries where reasonably reliable statistics are available, the figures obtained by different collecting agencies vary in quality.

An effort has been made to present data in the most comparable form. This has meant that frequently one unit of measurement had to be converted into another (e.g., kilometers into miles) and that many of the figures have been rounded off. The listing of comparative measures and weights given below will be found useful.

Precise definitions of commodities, areas, and other classifications vary from country to country and from source to source. For details the reader should consult the basic statistical sources below and the sources cited in each table; more recent data will be found in later issues of the sources given. In many cases data are available only for a limited number of countries. Statistics for the U.S.S.R. generally include both the Asiatic and the European parts, and separate figures for the European part are not always available. A series of special tables has been compiled which gives the reader an up-to-date picture of the growth of the Soviet economy.

It should also be explained that the figures in this statistical summary are not necessarily always the same as those in the text. Because a certain comparability was desired in the Appendix, compilations here are based on a select and small number of sources. The text, on the other hand, contains figures based on national statistics, official announcements, and special reports published by the United Nations. These are usually the latest available data.

Basic sources for the statistical compilations of European countries (other than the U.S.S.R.) are:

United Nations:

Statistical Yearbook, 1960, 1961, 1967
Demographic Yearbook, 1955, 1956, 1962, 1964, 1966
Yearbook of International Trade Statistics, 1958, 1960, 1961, 1966
Yearbook of National Accounts Statistics, 1966
World Energy Supplies, 1963–1966, Statistical Papers, Series J, No. 11, 1968
Economic Commission for Europe, *Annual Bulletin of Electric Energy Statistics for Europe,* vol. V, 1959 (1960); vol. XII, 1966 (1967)
Food and Agricultural Organization, *Production Yearbook,* 1958, 1966.

Population Reference Bureau, Washington, D.C., *World Population Data Sheet,* March 1968.

For additional sources, see compilations for individual countries.

COMPARATIVE MEASURES AND WEIGHTS

UNITS OF LENGTH

1 millimeter (mm) = 0.0394 inch	1 inch = 2.540 centimeters
1 centimeter (cm) = 0.3937 inch	
1 meter (m) = 3.2808 feet	1 foot = 0.3048 meter
	1 yard = 0.9144 meter
1 kilometer (km) = 0.62137 mile	1 statute mile = 1.609 kilometers = 5,280 feet
	1 nautical mile = 1.853 kilometers = 6,080 feet

UNITS OF AREA

1 square meter = 10.7639 square feet	1 square yard = 0.8361 square meter
1 hectare (ha) = 2.471 acres	1 acre = 0.4047 hectare
1 square kilometer = 0.3861 square mile	1 square mile = 2.590 square kilometers

UNITS OF WEIGHT

1 metric ton = 1.1023 short tons = 0.9842 long ton	1 short ton = 2,000 pounds = 0.9072 metric ton
	1 long ton = 2,240 pounds = 1.0160 metric tons
1 quintal = 220 pounds	1 U.S. hundredweight (cwt) = 100 pounds
	1 U.K. hundredweight (cwt) = 112 pounds
	1 gross registered ton = 100 cubic feet

UNITS OF DRY MEASURE

1 liter = 0.9081 quart	1 quart = 1.1012 liters
= 0.02837 bushel	1 bushel = 35.2383 liters

UNITS OF LIQUID MEASURE

1 liter = 1.0567 quarts	1 quart = 0.9463 liter
= 0.264 gallon	1 gallon (U.S.) = 3.785 liters
	1 gallon (imperial) = 1.2 gallons (U.S.)
1 metric ton (petroleum) = 264.4175 U.S. barrels	

MISCELLANEOUS

1 board foot (fbm) = 144 cubic inches
1 barrel (42 gallons) crude petroleum = 306.6 pounds = 139.07 kilograms = 158.984 liters

NOTE: In the Statistical Tables a dash (−) indicates "none" or "negligible amount"; blank spaces indicate no data available.

Table 1. Statistical Comparison: Europe and the World, 1966

	World	Europe	Percentage of World
Population (million)	3,353	449 [a]	13
Rate of increase, 1963–1966	1.9	0.9	
Density (per sq. km.)	25	91	
Agricultural products: [b]			
Barley	115	39.8	35
Maize	238	32.9	14
Oats	48	16.3	34
Rye	31	15.5	50
Wheat	309	62.7	20
Potatoes	294	137	47
Rice	254	1.5	0.6
Fish	57	11.5	20
Meat	73	18.4 [c]	25
Coal [b]	2,097	557.5	27
Lignite [b]	748	550	74
Petroleum [b]	1,641	36.6 [d]	2
Iron ore (Fe content) [b]	319	53.1	17
Bauxite [b]	37	5.0 [d]	14
Paper excl. newsprint [b]	85	25.4	30
Newsprint [b]	18	5.2	29
Cement [b]	463	180.4	39
Steel [b]	459	156.4	34
Aluminum [b]	5.6	1.5 [d]	27
Motor vehicles (millions)	24.5	9.5	39
Electricity (thousand million kwh)	3,602	1,060.3	29
Energy coal equivalent [b]	5,621	918.9	16
Consumption: [b]			
Cotton	11	2.1	19
Steel	469	147.7	31
Energy	5,505	1,462.9	27
Newsprint	18	4.9	27
Trade ($ million):			
Imports	215,800	98,480	46
Exports	203,800	107,260	53

[a] Excluding European U.S.S.R., with estimated population of 159 million.
[b] Million tons.
[c] 1965.

[d] Excluding the U.S.S.R.

SOURCE: United Nations, *Statistical Yearbook for 1967* (New York, 1968).

Table 2. The British Isles, 1956–1957 and 1966

| | Eire | | United Kingdom | |
	1956	1966	1957	1966
Area (sq. mi.)	27,558		94,214 [a]	
Population (000's)	2,898	2,881	51,430	55,068
Density (per sq. mi. of agricultural land)	158	158	1,061	1,149
In towns of 2,000 or more inhabitants (per cent of total)	43	44 [b]	78.6 [c,d]	77.1 [d]
Annual rate of increase (per 1,000)	9.3	9.5	4.3 [c]	6.1
Proportion of active population:				
In manufacturing, mining, and construction	23.0	26.8	48	43
In agriculture, forestry, and fishing	38.5	31.9	4	2
In trade, services, and other activities	38.5	41.3	52	55
Cultivated land (per cent of total)	20.2	17.9	29.1	30.7
Fertilizer used (kg per hectare of arable land) [e]	82	172	151	206
Length of railway lines (miles per sq. mi. of territory)	0.07	0.05	0.21	0.15
Estimated per capita income	$467 [f]	$783 [g]	$1,005 [f]	$1,451 [g]
Energy consumption in coal equivalent (metric tons per capita)	1.8 [h]	2.5	4.8	5.1
Energy sources (000's of metric tons, coal equivalent):				
Exports:				
Coal	32 [h]	95	7,167	2,813
Lignite	—	—	—	—
Crude oil	—	—	—	169
Natural gas	—	1.3	—	—
Electricity	—	—	—	4
Imports:				
Coal	1,275 [h]	1,008	2,897	—
Lignite	—	—	—	—
Crude oil	—	2,041	37,437	92,937
Natural gas	—	—	—	813
Electricity	—	—	—	48
Major trading patterns (per cent of total):				
Exports:				
EEC	9.9	11.2	13.8	19.0
EFTA	83.1 [i]	70.9	11.3	14.7
Other Europe	1.3	0.9	8.0	12.4
United States	3.0	6.9	7.3	12.3
Rest of world [j]	2.7	10.1	59.6	41.6
Imports:				
EEC	10.9	13.5	12.1	18.5
EFTA	60.5 [i]	55.2	11.5	14.1
Other Europe	3.7	3.8	8.1	11.1
United States	7.5	9.4	11.8	12.1
Rest of world	17.4	18.1	56.5	44.2

[a] Great Britain = 88,762 sq. mi.; Northern Ireland = 5,452 sq. mi.

[b] 1961.

[c] 1956.

[d] Urban population based on official designation of "urban districts" in England, Wales, and Northern Ireland and of "cities and burghs" in Scotland; no population limits defined. Within the United Kingdom there is considerable variation in the percentage of urban population: England and Wales, 80.3%, 78.9%; Scotland, 70.0%, 71.7%; Northern Ireland, 53.4%, 53.2%. (Percentages are for 1956 and 1966 respectively.)

[e] Agricultural years 1956–1957 and 1965–1966.

[f] 1958.

[g] 1965.

[h] 1957.

[i] Most of Ireland's trade is with the United Kingdom. Percentages of exports for 1956 and 1966, respectively, were 82.5% and 69.7%; imports for the same years were 56.9% and 51.8%.

[j] Includes re-exports.

ADDITIONAL SOURCES: OECD, *Commodity Trade Statistics*, 1957, 1967; United Nations, *Commodity Trade Statistics*, 1967; FAO, *Fertilizers, An Annual Review of World Production, Consumption and Trade*, 1966; national statistics and other miscellaneous official statistics.

Table 3. Northern Europe,

	Denmark		Finland	
	1957	1966	1957	1966
Area (sq. mi.)	16,625		130,085	
Population (000's)	4,488	4,797	4,324	4,639
Density (per sq. mi. of agricultural land)	384	411	372	399
In towns of 200 or more inhabitants (per cent of total) [a]	69.0 [b,c]	71.2	32.3 [d,e]	55.9 [f]
Annual rate of increase (per 1,000)	7	8	11	8
Proportion of active population:				
In manufacturing, mining, and construction	32.3	36.5	27.2	31.5
In agriculture, forestry, and fishing	22.9	17.5	46.0	35.5
In commerce, transportation, and other services	41.8	44.3	24.9	32.7
Cultivated land (per cent of total)	64.2	62.7	7.7	8.5
Fertilizer used (kg. per hectare of arable land)	123	187	63	116
Length of railway lines (miles per sq. mi. of territory)	0.17	0.15	0.02	0.03
Estimated per capita income	$888 [h]	$1,639 [i]	$736 [h]	$1,476
Energy consumption in coal equivalent (metric tons per capita)	2.4 [j]	4.5	1.4 [j]	2.8
Energy sources (000's of metric tons, coal equivalent):				
Coal exports	—	—	—	—
Coal imports	4,608	4,657	3,085	2,774
Crude oil imports	—	6,073	—	4,849
Natural gas imports	75	92	—	—
Electricity exports	17	130	—	32
Electricity imports	64	207	—	21
Major trading patterns (per cent of total):				
Exports:				
EEC	30	27	23	28
EFTA	43	47	27	33
Eastern Europe	—	4	—	21
USA, Canada	9	8	5	6
Other	—	14	—	12
Imports:				
EEC	36	36	25	31
EFTA	41	36	25	34
Eastern Europe	—	4	—	18
USA, Canada	10	9	6	7
Other	—	15	—	10

[a] In general, the governments of Northern Europe use a population of 200 inhabitants to distinguish urban agglomerations from rural areas.

[b] 250 or more inhabitants.

[c] 1955 census.

[d] Places legally established as towns or boroughs; no population limits indicated.

[e] 1950 census.

1957 and 1966

	Iceland		Norway		Sweden	
	1957	*1966*	*1957*	*1966*	*1957*	*1966*
	39,758		125,148		173,620	
	165	195	3,492	3,753	7,364	7,808
	18	21	898	965	514	545
	72.8 [e,g]	80.9	52.0	57.2	72.8 [f]	77.4
	22	18	10	8	5	7
	29.3	36.3	35.6	36.5	37.9	45.1
	40.0	22.6	25.9	19.5	20.4	13.8
	30.7	35.8	37.1	43.6	38.1	40.8
	0.001	0.008	2.6	2.6	8.2	7.1
	100	224	150	200	72	126
	0.0	0.0	0.02	0.02	0.06	0.05
	$964 [h]	$1,870	$871 [h]	$1,556	$1,342 [h]	$2,395
	4.0 [j]	4.1	2.5 [j]	4.0	3.0 [j]	5.1
	—	—	—	180	—	—
	35	6	1,134	1,116	5,139	3,147
	—	—	150	3,814	2,592	4,831
	—	—	—	—	—	—
	—	—	—	124	64	323
	—	—	—	79	15	186
	15	20	28	25	33	31
	27	42	39	45	38	43
	—	11	—	4	—	4
	9	17	7	10	5	7
	—	10	—	16	—	15
	15	22	31	29	39	38
	30	37	39	42	26	32
	—	16	—	3	—	4
	14	17	13	11	13	10
	—	8	—	15	—	16

[f] 1960 census.

[g] 300 or more inhabitants.

[h] 1958.

[i] 1965.

[j] 1959.

ADDITIONAL SOURCES: *Yearbook of Nordic Statistics, 1966; Statistical Yearbook of Sweden, 1967.*

Table 4.   Western Europe,

	Belgium	
	1957	1966
Area (sq. mi.)	11,776	11,781
Population (000's)	8,989	9,700 [a]
Density (per sq. mi. of agricultural land)	1,355	1,478 [b]
In towns of 2,000 or more inhabitants (per cent of total)	82.3 [c]	84.9 [d,e]
Annual rate of increase (per 1,000)	5.0	3.8
Proportion of active population: [j]		
In manufacturing, mining, and construction	46.0	45.3
In agriculture and forestry	10.0	5.1
In services	44.0	48.7
Cultivated land (per cent of total)	32.4	30.7 [b]
Fertilizer used (kg. per hectare of arable land) [k]	348	475
Length of railway lines (miles per sq. mi. of territory)	0.25	0.24
Estimated per capita income	$936 [j]	$1,406 [b]
Energy consumption in coal equivalent (metric tons per capita)	4.2	4.6
Energy sources (000's of metric tons, coal equivalent):		
Exports:		
Coal	3,962	1,191
Lignite		
Crude oil	—	208
Natural gas	—	—
Electricity	50	69
Imports:		
Coal	5,102	6,156
Lignite		
Crude oil	7,222 [l]	21,567
Natural gas	—	120
Electricity	37	58
Major trading patterns (per cent of total):		
Exports:		
EEC	46.1	62.8
EFTA	16.2	11.7
Other European nations	4.9	4.8
United States	8.2	8.7
Rest of world	24.6	12.0
Imports:		
EEC	43.5	55.9
EFTA	15.4	12.5
Other European nations	3.8	3.9
United States	12.4	7.9
Rest of world	24.9	19.8

[*] The percentages for France have been calculated from the United Nations *Yearbook of International Trade Statistics*, 1958 and 1966, rather than from national statistics.

[a] Mid-1968 estimate.

[b] 1965.

[c] 1947.

[d] 1961.

[e] On December 31, 1966, Belgium had 82.6 per cent of its population in settlements of more than 2,500.

[f] 1954.

1957 and 1966

Luxembourg		France *		Netherlands	
1957	1966	1957	1966	1957	1966
999		212,766	212,919	12,529	12,895
318	335	44,311	50,400 [a]	11,021	12,700 [a]
585	645 [b]	271	478 [b]	1,238	1,412 [b]
65.4 [c]	70.3 [h]	58.6 [f]	63.4 [g]	88.4 [h,i]	90.4 [i]
3.7	3.4	6.4	6.8	13.7	11.1
[c]		[j]		[c]	
38.9	45.9	40.6	39.9	31.3	42.8
26.0	12.9	29.0	17.6	19.3	8.5
35.1	41.2	30.4	42.6	49.4	48.7
30.1	26.7 [b]	38.7	38.0 [b]	32.4	28.8 [b]
172	288	82	149	435	581
0.20	0.20	0.12	0.11	0.16	0.16
$1,077 [j]	$1,498 [b]	$1,003 [j]	$1,436 [b]	$695 [j]	$1,265 [b]
Incl. with Belgium		2.5	3.0	2.5	3.5
—	—	6,107	906	882	1,850
—	—	—	—	—	—
—	—	—	—	—	186
11	113	85	235	46	61
312	80	18,130	11,504	8,813	6,735
Incl. with Belgium		31,281 [l]	84,019	18,209 [l]	38,532
Incl. with Belgium		—	506	—	—
7	235	118	618	26	23
Incl. with Belgium					
		24.9	42.3	41.6	55.5
		15.6	14.7	24.3	18.2
		5.2	9.0	5.3	5.5
		4.8	6.1	5.0	4.5
		49.5	27.9	23.8	16.3
		21.2	41.0	41.1	54.0
		10.1	10.7	15.3	12.6
		4.2	5.8	3.7	4.2
		13.2	10.1	13.1	11.4
		51.3	32.4	26.8	17.8

[g] 1962.

[h] 1960.

[i] Settlements of more than 5,000 population.

[j] 1958.

[k] Agricultural years 1956–1957 and 1965–1966.

[l] Imports from *third* countries (outside the EEC).

ADDITIONAL SOURCES: Office Statistique des Communautés Européennes: *Statistiques Sociales,* Supplément 1967, Emploi 1965–1966, and *Statistiques de l'Énergie,* 1955–1966; *Statesman's Yearbook,* 1968–1969; national statistics and other miscellaneous statistics.

Table 5. Central Europe, 1957 and 1966

	Austria 1957	Austria 1966	E. Germany 1957	E. Germany 1966	W. Germany 1957	W. Germany 1966	Switzerland 1957	Switzerland 1966	Liechtenstein 1957	Liechtenstein 1966
Area (sq. mi.)	32,376		41,648		95,923	95,962	15,941		67	
Population (000's)	6,998	7,400[a]	17,411	17,100[a]	53,994	60,300[a]	5,160	6,200[a]	14.8[b]	19.9
Density (per sq. mi. of agricultural land)	444	492	697	688	972	1,110	615	742	426	677
In towns of 2,000 or more inhabitants (per cent of total)	65.5[c]	68.2[d]	71.4	72.9	75.2	79.6	68.2[e]	72.9[f]	38.3[g]	63.1[h]
Annual rate of increase (per 1,000)	4.2	5.1	3.3	3.0	5.1	6.2	7.7	9.0	14.0	12.4[i]
Proportion of active population:	e	d			e	d	e	f	e	
In manufacturing, mining, and construction	35.0	46.5	47.2	46.7	41.6	47.7	45.4	49.6	50.0	59.6
In agriculture, forestry, and fishing	32.1	22.8	20.4	15.9	22.3	13.4	16.5	11.1	21.8	7.4
In trade, services, and other activities	32.9	30.7	32.4	37.4	36.1	38.9	38.1	39.3	28.2	33.0
Cultivated land (per cent of total)	21.1	20.6[l]	48.0	46.2[j]	36.1	33.4[l]	38.1	39.3		
Cultivated land (per cent of total)	21.1	20.6[l]	48.0	46.2[j]	35.1	33.4[l]	10.8[k]	10.2[j]	12.5[l]	25.4
Fertilizer used (kg. per hectare of arable land) [m]	103	203	168[n]	255	246	349	170	317		
Length of railway lines (miles per sq. mi. of territory)	0.11	0.10	0.22	0.22	0.23[k]	0.22[l]	0.14	0.14[l]		
Estimated per capita income	$588[g]	$970[l]		$1,240[l]	$838[g]	$1,447[l]	$1,195[g]	$1,928[l]		
Energy consumption in coal equivalent (metric tons per capita)	1.9[g]	2.7	4.3[g]	5.5	3.4[g]	4.3	1.7[g]	2.7		
Energy sources (000's of metric tons, coal equivalent): Exports:										
Coal	—	—	3,185	3,521	13,168	16,015	—	—		
Lignite	—	—	—	—	—	740	—	—		
Crude oil	—	—	—	—	—	182	—	—		
Natural gas	—	—	—	27	—	402	—	—		
Electricity	238	698	45	93	381	506	236	920	3	1.4

648

Imports:									
Coal	4,599	3,424	5,753	9,168	22,395	7,073	27,495	888	28.0
Lignite	472	271	1,245	1,520	—	325	o	55	56.1[p,q]
Crude oil	—	1,508	1,296	8,372	10,736	87,993	—	3,055	} 15.9
Natural gas	—	—	—	85	—	67	—	—	
Electricity	83	100	4	89	460	1,444	197	330	1.9
Major trading patterns (per cent of total):									
Exports:									
EEC	50.0	44.7	13.7	12.8	29.2	36.3	39.1	38.0	
EFTA	13.5	19.3	3.4	3.3	27.3	25.2	16.3	19.6	
Other European nations	19.3	21.5	5.6	3.9	8.2	10.3	7.8	8.3	
United States	4.2	4.6	0.3	0.3	6.9	8.9	9.9	10.8	
Rest of world	13.0	9.9	4.9	8.0	28.4	19.3	26.9	23.3	
			68.1[r]	68.7[r]					
			4.0[s]	3.0[s]					
Imports:									
EEC	54.0	58.8	19.6	15.0	23.4	38.2	58.1	60.4	
EFTA	16.4	15.7	4.8	4.4	19.0	16.5	11.1	15.6	
Other European nations	13.6	12.9	3.0	3.1	8.3	7.9	5.2	4.2	
United States	12.3	4.3	0.2	0.8	17.7	12.6	11.4	9.0	
Rest of world	3.7	8.3	2.9	7.0	31.6	24.8	14.2	10.8	
			65.6[r]	67.4[r]					
			3.9[s]	2.3[s]					

a Mid-1968 estimate.
b 1955 census.
c 1951 census.
d 1961 census.
e 1950 census.
f 1960 census.
g 1958.
h 1963.
i 1965.
j 1964.
k 1956.

l 1953.
m Agricultural years 1957–1958 and 1965–1966.
n Agricultural years 1956–1957 and 1964–1965.
o Included with coal.
p 40.5 per cent of all exports went to Switzerland.
q Includes Finland.
r COMECON.
s Non-European socialist countries.

ADDITIONAL SOURCES: National statistics and other miscellaneous official statistics.

Table 6. Southern Europe,

	Cyprus		Greece		Italy	
	1957	1966	1957	1966	1957	1966
Area (sq. mi.)	3,572		50,547		116,303	
Population (000's)	560[a]	600[b]	8,100	8,800[b]	48,400	52,800[b]
Density (per sq. mi. of agricultural land)	275	310	241	245[c]	600	647[d]
In towns of 2,000 or more inhabitants (per cent of total)	26[f]	36[a]	53[g]	56[h]		48[h]
Annual rate of increase (per 1,000)	19.6 [a]	18.8	11.7 [h]	10.2	8.1 [g]	9.4 [j]
Proportion of active population:						
In manufacturing, mining, and construction	25	24	19	23	32	41
In agriculture, forestry, and fishing	41	39	54	47	43	24
In trade, services, and other activities	34	37	27	30	25	35
Cultivated land (per cent of total)	46[l]	46[d]	27[m]	30[e]	52	51[d]
Fertilizer used (kg. per hectare of arable land)	22[o]	27[p]	33[o]	65[q]	46[o]	69[q]
Length of railway lines (miles per sq. mi. of territory)	No rwys.		0.03[m]	0.03[d]	0.12	0.11[d]
Estimated per capita income	$457[l]	$700[j]	$326[l]	$600[j]	$478[l]	$960[j]
Energy consumption in coal equivalent (metric tons per capita)	0.95	1.0	0.4	0.8	0.9	2.0
Energy sources (000's of metric tons, coal equivalent):						
Exports:						
Coal	—	—	—	—	—	157
Lignite	—	—	—	—	—	—
Crude oil	—	—	—	—	—	—
Natural gas	—	—	—	—	—	—
Electricity	—	—	—	2	5	64
Imports:						
Coal	—	—	259	398	11,549	11,363
Lignite	—	—	—	—	—	—
Crude oil	—	—	—	4,048	24,779	102,687
Natural gas	—	—	7	5	—	—
Electricity	—	—	—	3	63	1,355
Major trading patterns (per cent of total):						
Exports:						[j]
EEC	50	32	44	35	25	39
EFTA	31	35	15	10	22	16
Other European nations	5	22	18	30	13	13
United States	8	1	13	11	9	10
Rest of world[t]	6	10	10	14	31	22
Imports:						[j]
EEC	27	28	41	41	21	35
EFTA	53	36	20	19	17	12
Other European nations	6	12	10	12	6	12
United States	3	5	16	11	19	11
Rest of world	11	19	13	12	37	30

[a] 1960.
[b] Mid-1968 estimate.
[c] 1964.
[d] 1965.
[e] 1963.
[f] 1947.
[g] 1951.
[h] 1961.
[i] 1950.
[j] 1967.

[k] 1954.
[l] 1958.
[m] 1956.
[n] 1962.
[o] Agricultural year 1957–1958.
[p] Agricultural year 1964–1965.
[q] Agricultural year 1965–1966.
[r] Agricultural year 1955–1956.
[s] Nearly 80 per cent is broad gauge.
[t] Includes ships' stores and bunkers.

1957 and 1966

| Malta | | Portugal | | Spain | | Andorra | | Vatican City | |
1957	1966	1957	1966	1957	1966	1957	1966	1957	1966
122		35,340		194,345		191		0.2	
319	319[b]	8,900	9,500[b]	29,400	32,400[b]	6	14	0.9	1
3,934	5,228[d]	558	492[e]	348	237[d]				
51	52[d]	31[i]	23[a]	60[i]	56[a]				100
18.3	7.8[c]	12.7[i]	11.4[j]	11.9[i]	12.3[j]	8.4[k]	12.1[a]		
37	32	25	33	24	31				
10	9	49	40	49	36				
53	59	26	27	27	33				
53[n]	50[d]	52	49[e]	41	41[d]				
10[r]	25[q]	34[o]	38[q]	28[o]	36[q]				
No rwys.		0.06[m]	0.06	0.06[m]	0.05[s]	No rwys.		No rwys.	
$357[l]	$500[j]	$216[l]	$407[j]	$299[l]	$580[j]				
0.6	0.5	0.3	0.5	0.8	1.1				
—	—	—	—	160	13				
—	—	—	—	—	—				
—	—	—	—	—	—				
—	—	—	—	—	—				
—	—	—	2	9	311				
—	—	558	760	628	1,526				
—	—	—	—	—	—				
—	—	1,441	2,197	7,145	21,208				
—	3	—	105	—	—				
—	—	—	—	11	23				
					[j]				
15	15	22	20	30	32				
16	32	20	27	28	20				
3	10	3	7	3	8				
—	10	9	11	10	15				
66	33	46	35	29	25				
					[j]				
26	27	37	28	21	37				
47	42	21	22	17	16				
4	7	2	6	3	3				
3	4	11	6	26	17				
20	20	29	38	33	27				

ADDITIONAL SOURCES: United Nations, *Annual Bulletin of Transport Statistics for Europe,* 1967; United Nations, *ILO, Yearbook of Labor Statistics,* 1967; IBRD-FAO, *The Development of Agriculture in Greece,* December 1966; Banco de Bilbao: *Informo Economico,* 1967, p. 243, and *The Spanish Economy in Figures,* January 1968; Commercial Office of the Italian Embassy, Washington, D.C., *Italy, An Economic Profile, 1962* (1963), p. 22, and *1967* (1968), p. 30; Chemical Bank New York Trust, *International Economic Survey: Portugal,* January 1968; *Europa Yearbook,* vol. 1, 1968; *Statesman's Yearbook,* 1959; New York *Times,* January 15, 1968, p. 60 ff.; Chase Manhattan Bank, *World Business,* September 1967, p. 19; FAO, *Production Yearbook,* 1961, 1963; and national statistics.

Table 7. Eastern Europe,

	Albania 1957	Albania 1965	Bulgaria 1957	Bulgaria 1966	Czechoslovakia 1957	Czechoslovakia 1966
Area (sq. mi.)	11,100		42,796	42,822	49,354	49,370
Population (000's)	1,462	2,000[a]	7,667	8,400[a]	13,353	14,400[a]
Density (per sq. mi. of agricultural land)	305[b]	421	353	375	472	522
In towns of 2,000 or more inhabitants (per cent of total)	28.8	33.2	33.6[c,d]	46.5[d,e]	47.6[f]	59.0
Annual rate of increase (per 1,000)	27.3	25.4	10.1[c]	6.6	8.9	5.8
Proportion of active population:	[i]		[c]	[e]	[i]	
In manufacturing, mining, and construction	15	46	18.6	33.3	39.4	46.7
In agriculture, forestry, and fishing	75	18	64.2	44.9	34.0	20.6
In trade, services, and other activities	20	36	17.2	21.8	26.6	32.7
Cultivated land (per cent of total)	16.0[b]	17.8	40.9	41.1	42.2	42.0
Fertilizer used (kg. per hectare of arable land)	0.6[m]	7	16[m]	79	78[m]	158
Length of standard gauge railway lines (miles per sq. mi. of territory)	0.007[b]	0.009[p]	0.05	0.06	0.17	0.17
Estimated per capita income[e]		$315		$407		$804
Energy consumption in coal equivalent (metric tons per capita)	0.3[b]	0.3	1.0[b]	2.7	4.7[b]	5.6
Energy sources (000's of metric tons, coal equivalent):						
Exports:						
Coal	—	—	270	—	776	2,077
Lignite	—	—	q	—	924	686
Crude oil	284	369	263	26	—	—
Natural gas	—	—	—	—	—	—
Electricity	—	—	—	1	35	123
Imports:						
Coal	—	—	142	3,150	2,292	4,030
Lignite	—	—	—	—	—	—
Crude oil	—	—	—	3,385	1,587	8,466
Natural gas	—	—	—	—	—	—
Electricity	—	—	2	1	6	372
Major trading patterns (per cent of total):						
Exports:		[p]				
EEC	2.0	5.8	6.2	9.8	8.3	7.9
EFTA	0.3	1.0	2.8	5.0	7.3	7.1
COMECON	93.4	46.9	82.5	70.6	56.1	63.6
Other European nations	1.5	2.3	3.0	4.6	5.3	4.7
Non-European socialist countries	2.3	43.3	1.1	3.2	7.2	3.2
United States	—	0.2	—	0.2	0.5	1.0
Rest of world	0.5	0.5	4.4	6.6	15.3	12.5
Imports:		[p]				
EEC	3.5	4.5	8.3	16.3	8.3	8.2
EFTA	0.3	1.4	4.1	6.5	8.2	8.9
COMECON	83.4	28.0	79.8	66.2	64.3	64.1
Other European nations	0.8	1.1	2.4	3.4	2.9	3.8
Non-European socialist countries	11.1	64.7	1.4	1.7	4.9	3.5
United States	—	—	—	0.1	0.1	1.6
Rest of world	0.9	0.3	4.0	5.8	11.3	9.9

[a] Mid-1968 estimate.   [b] 1958.   [c] 1956.

[d] Official administrative designation as urban areas; no specified population limits.   [e] 1965.   [f] 1961 census.

[g] 1960.   [h] Towns of 5,000 or more inhabitants.   [i] 1955.

[j] 1949 census.

[k] Computed on the basis of FAO estimate of agricultural workers plus official statistics for the socialized sector of the other branches of the economy.

[l] 1953 census.

1957 and 1966

	Hungary		Poland		Romania		Yugoslavia	
	1957	1966	1957	1966	1957	1966	1957	1966
	35,919		120,359		91,671	91,699	98,740	98,766
	9,815	10,200[a]	28,300	32,300[a]	17,829	19,400[a]	18,005	20,200[a]
	354	415	359	419	317	339	312	354
	39.7[g]	39.8[e]	48.1[g]	46.3[h]	31.3[c,d]	38.2[d]	28.3[f]	40.0
	6.4	3.5	18.0	9.4	12.7	6.1	13.1	12.2
	[j]	[g]	[g]	[e,k]	[g]		[l]	[f]
	23.2	33.7	29.0	32.8	10	17	15.4	22.0
	52.9	38.4	47.7	42.4	83	74	66.8	57.3
	23.9	27.9	23.3	24.8	7	9	17.8	20.7
	61.9	60.4	52.0	50.3	42.6	44.3	32.4	32.7
	25[n]	62	23[m]	71	6[o]	29	20	56
	0.15	0.24	0.12[b]	0.14	0.07[b]	0.07	0.06	0.06
		$701		$710		$353		$406
	2.1[b]	2.8	2.8[b]	3.6	1.2[b]	2.1	0.7[b]	1.2
	—	74	13,357	22,407	—	—	135	114
	31	—	1,235	1,518	—	—	—	—
	—	—	—	—	—	—	—	421
	—	—	—	—	—	166	—	—
	—	19	11	132	2	152	18	12
	2,427	2,380	345	1,141	151	723	1,729	1,836
	[q]	[q]	62	144	—	—	—	—
	1,343	3,785	819	4,351	—	—	844	2,863
	—	166	—	932	—	—	—	—
	38	218	43	116	—	58	—	28
			[b]					
	12.2	13.0	11.3	9.2	11.9	18.4	32.0	27.8
	9.4	9.6	13.9	12.4	4.5	8.1	15.7	10.5
	56.1	64.1	52.0	55.7	68.8	55.9	26.5	36.5
	7.6	4.2	7.0	5.9	2.8	3.8	3.9	3.5
	6.0	1.2	5.1	2.5	6.3	4.2	1.0	0.6
	0.2	0.3	2.7	3.5	0.2	0.4	8.5	6.1
	8.5	7.6	8.0	10.8	5.5	9.2	12.4	15.0
	12.1	13.2	10.8	9.6	10.6	23.2	27.1	26.0
	9.1	10.1	13.3	12.7	3.9	9.2	12.9	10.6
	66.0	61.3	57.1	60.0	74.8	52.8	21.5	31.3
	3.9	4.4	4.3	4.6	2.2	3.2	1.7	2.8
	4.6	0.6	3.4	1.9	3.7	3.0	1.6	0.6
	0.4	1.0	4.5	1.8	0.2	2.2	26.3	13.5
	3.9	9.4	6.6	9.4	4.6	6.4	8.9	15.2

[m] Agricultural year 1957–1958.
[n] Agricultural year 1958–1959.
[o] 1959.
[p] 1964.
[q] Included with coal.

ADDITIONAL SOURCES: National statistics and other miscellaneous official statistics.

Table 8a. Population of the Soviet Republics, 1940, 1951, and 1968 *

| | (In Thousands) | | |
	1940	1951	1968
Russian SFSR	110,098	102,945	127,911
Western republics:			
Ukrainian SSR	41,340	37,223	46,381
Belorussian SSR	9,046	7,781	8,820
Moldavian SSR	2,468	2,392	3,484
Lithuanian SSR	2,925	2,561	3,064
Latvian SSR	1,886	1,954	2,298
Estonian SSR	1,054	1,104	1,304
Transcaucasia:			
Georgian SSR	3,612	3,560	4,659
Azerbaidzhan SSR	3,274	2,933	4,917
Armenian SSR	1,320	1,360	2,306
Central Asia:			
Kazakh SSR	6,054	6,733	12,678
Uzbek SSR	6,645	6,514	11,266
Kirghiz SSR	1,528	1,764	2,836
Tadzhik SSR	1,525	1,554	2,736
Turkmen SSR	1,302	1,225	2,029
USSR total	194,077	181,603	236,689

* As of January 1 of each year.

Source: *SSSR v tsifrakh v 1967 godu [USSR in Figures in 1967].* Moscow: Statistika, 1968, p. 7.

Table 8b. Population of the Thirty Largest Soviet Cities, 1939 and 1968 *

| | (In Thousands) | |
	1939	1968
Moscow	4,137	6,567
Leningrad	3,385	3,755
Kiev	847	1,457
Tashkent	556	1,295
Baku	775	1,218
Kharkov	833	1,148
Gorky	644	1,140
Novosibirsk	404	1,080
Kuibyshev	390	1,016
Sverdlovsk	423	981
Tbilisi	519	861
Donetsk	466	855
Chelyabinsk	273	851
Kazan	398	838
Dnepropetrovsk	527	837
Perm	306	811
Minsk	237	805
Omsk	289	801
Odessa	602	797
Rostov-on-Don	510	774
Volgograd	445	757
Saratov	372	738
Ufa	258	724
Riga	348	691
Yerevan	204	687
Alma-Ata	222	668
Voronezh	344	626
Zaporozhe	282	616
Krasnoyarsk	190	592
Lvov	340	524

* As of January 1 of each year.

Source: *SSSR v tsifrakh v 1967 godu [USSR in Figures in 1967].* Moscow: Statistika, 1968, p. 9.

Table 8c. Soviet Grain Production, 1950 to 1967

Year	Million Metric Tons	Year	Million Metric Tons
1950	82	1959	120
1951	79	1960	126
1952	92	1961	131
1953	82	1962	140
1954	86	1963	108
1955	104	1964	152
1956	125	1965	121
1957	103	1966	171
1958	135	1967	148

Source: *SSSR v tsifrakh v 1967 godu [USSR in Figures in 1967].* Moscow: Statistika, 1968, p. 66.

Table 8d. Regional Distribution of Soviet Fuels and Power, 1940, 1960, and 1966

	1940	1960	1966
Electric power capacity (million kilowatts):			
European USSR	8.6	41.5	71.7
Urals	1.3	9.9	16.8
Asian USSR	1.3	15.3	34.5
Total	11.2	66.7	123.0
Electric power output (billion kilowatt-hours):			
European USSR	37.6	174.8	321.7
Urals	6.2	54.3	89.0
Asian USSR	4.5	63.2	133.9
Total	48.3	292.3	544.6
Petroleum production (million metric tons):			
European USSR	27.5	108.4	185.5
Urals	1.6	28.9	58.3
Asian USSR	2.0	10.6	21.3
Total	31.1	147.9	265.1
Natural gas production (billion cubic meters):			
European USSR	3.2	42.4	113.2
Urals	0.01	1.8	4.5
Asian USSR	0.02	1.1	25.3
Total	3.2	45.3	143.0
Coal production (million metric tons):			
European USSR	106.4	268.2	290.7
Urals	11.9	58.5	57.8
Asian USSR	47.6	182.9	237.1
Total	165.9	509.6	585.6

SOURCE: *Strana Sovetov za 50 let [The Country of Soviets During 50 Years]*. Moscow: Statistika, 1967, p. 58.

Table 8e. Regional Distribution of the Soviet Iron and Steel Industry, 1940, 1960, and 1966

	(In Million Metric Tons)		
	1940	1960	1966
Iron ore:			
European USSR	21.3	66.9	107.1
Urals	8.1	27.3	27.3
Asian USSR	0.5	11.7	25.9
Total	29.9	105.9	160.3
Pig iron:			
European USSR	10.6	28.1	43.8
Urals	2.8	15.1	19.9
Asian USSR	1.5	3.6	6.6
Total	14.9	46.8	70.3
Steel ingots:			
European USSR	12.4	37.3	57.8
Urals	4.0	21.9	30.8
Asian USSR	1.9	6.1	8.3
Total	18.3	65.3	96.9

SOURCE: *Strana Sovetov za 50 let [Country of the Soviets during 50 Years]*. Moscow: Statistika, 1967, pp. 58–59.

Table 8f. Soviet Trade, by Commodities and Countries, 1938, 1950, and 1966

Commodity Category	1938 Imports (%)	1938 Exports (%)	1966 Imports (%)	1966 Exports (%)
Machinery	34.5	5.0	32.4	20.8
Metals	25.4	1.6	} 8.7	20.1
Ores	2.7	2.2		
Fuels	1.2	8.8	2.4	16.4
Wood products	0.8	20.3	1.9	7.0
Textile fibers	9.7	4.2	4.8	5.2
Furs	—	9.4	—	0.8
Grain exports and food imports	12.7	21.3	19.6	9.2
Consumer goods	1.0	7.9	16.4	2.4
Others	12.0	19.3	12.8	18.1

Country	1950 (Per Cent of Total)		1966 (Per Cent of Total)	
Communist bloc	80.8		66.5	
China		17.7		1.9
Poland		13.9		9.2
Czechoslovakia		13.0		10.8
East Germany		10.6		15.8
Romania		7.8		4.7
Hungary		6.5		6.1
Bulgaria		5.1		8.1
Others		6.2		9.9
Non-Communist	19.2		33.5	
Britain		4.4		3.0
Finland		1.7		2.8
United States		1.7		0.6
Egypt		1.5		2.1
India		0.2		2.3
France		0.2		1.7
West Germany		—		1.9
Others		9.5		19.1

Note: Among commodities, contrast between 1938 and 1966 is most meaningful. Among trade partners, however, prewar and postwar countries cannot be compared, because of political shifts. Therefore, 1950 and 1966 have been selected for the country table. Because there is no significant difference between exports and imports in the country breakdown, they have been combined.

Source: *Vneshnyaya torgovlya SSSR, 1918–1966 [Foreign Trade of the USSR, 1918–1966].* Moscow: Mezhdunarodnye Otnosheniya, 1967, pp. 15, 73.

Index

657